To Stuart Rabinowitz,

with respect and
appreciation for your
executive leadership,
especially your commitment
to presidency studies.

Meena Bose

November 2008

THE NEW YORK TIMES ON THE
PRESIDENCY, 1853–2008

MEENA BOSE

CQ PRESS

A Division of SAGE
Washington D.C.

CQ Press

2300 N Street, NW, Suite 800

Washington, DC 20037

Phone: 202-729-1900; toll-free, 1-866-4CQ-PRESS (1-866-427-7737)

Web: www.cqpress.com

Cover and interior design: Matthew Simmons, www.myselfincluded.com

Compositor: Circle

♾ The paper used in this publication exceeds the requirements of the American National
Standard for Information Sciences—Permanence of Paper for Printed Library Materials,
ANSI Z39.48-1992.

Printed and bound in the United States of America

12 11 10 09 08   1 2 3 4 5

LIBRARY OF CONGRESS CATALOGING-IN-PUBLICATION DATA

The New York Times on the presidency / Meenekshi Bose.

   p. cm.

  Includes index.

  ISBN 978-0-87289-763-2 (cloth : alk. paper) 1. Presidents—Press coverage—United
States—History. 2. New York times. 3. Government and the press—United States—
History. 4. United States—Politics and government. I. Bose, Meenekshi

  JK554.N49 2009

  973.09'9—dc22

                      2008038076

OTHER TITLES FROM
TIMESREFERENCE FROM CQPRESS

2008

The New York Times on the Supreme Court, 1857–2008

2009

The New York Times on Critical Elections, 1860–2008

The New York Times on Emerging Democracies, 1980–2009

2010

The New York Times on Booms and Busts, 1851–2010

CONTENTS

ABOUT THE EDITORIAL CARTOONS IN
THE NEW YORK TIMES
ON THE PRESIDENCY

Franklin Pierce: Whig presidential candidate Gen. Winfield Scott pulls the "Presidential Chair" out from under Democrat Franklin Pierce in this Currier cartoon, exclaiming "Sorry to disappoint you Pierce, but the people wish me, to take this chair." Although Franklin Pierce won only a slim majority of the popular vote, he won decisively in the Electoral College (see p. 7).

James Buchanan: The only president never to be married, James Buchanan is shown in this 1856 Currier cartoon repairing his coat, which references his lack of family, his 1828 conversion from a Federalist to a Democrat, and U.S. designs on annexing Cuba in the 1850s (see p. 19).

Abraham Lincoln: After losing to Stephen A. Douglas in a race for the U.S. Senate in 1858, Abraham Lincoln faced him in the 1860 presidential election. In this 1860 cartoon, Douglas and Lincoln are shown sparring in front of the White House (see p. 32).

Andrew Johnson: A bedraggled Andrew Johnson holds a leaking teapot representing the post–Civil War South in this 1866 cartoon. Columbia, cradling a baby representing the yet-to-be ratified 14th Amendment, encourages haste in Johnson's Reconstruction policies (see p. 60).

Ulysses S. Grant: Cartoonist Joseph Keppler presents Ulysses S. Grant clutching a "Whiskey Ring" and a "Navy Ring" (references to scandals during his presidency) while supporting members of his administration associated with corruption (see p. 77).

Rutherford B. Hayes: Contrasting the aggressive Reconstruction policies of Grant with those of Rutherford B. Hayes, James Wales shows Hayes plowing under a carpetbag and bayonets while agricultural commerce thrives in the background. Hayes ended military rule in the South, thereby bringing an end to Reconstruction. [The original cartoon appeared juxtaposed with a view of Grant riding a carpetbag filled with bayonets and other weapons.] (See p. 94.)

James A. Garfield: Frederick Opper shows former president Hayes (dressed as a woman fleeing around the corner) leaving a screaming baby labeled "Civil Service Reform" on President James A. Garfield's doorstep in this 1881 cartoon. Civil service reform was a major priority for Hayes and remained so for Garfield (see p. 109).

Chester A. Arthur: Joseph Keppler depicts Chester A. Arthur as a showman attempting to satisfy all of the divergent factions of his Republican Party, shortly after assuming the presidency in 1881. Despite implications of patronage, Arthur continued his predecessors' fight for civil service reform (see p. 114).

Grover Cleveland: In Frank Beard's 1884 cartoon, Glover Cleveland holds his ears as he runs by a child who cries, "I want my Pa." Cleveland came under fire during the election for having fathered a child out of wedlock (see p. 127).

Benjamin Harrison: In this 1890 parody of Poe's "The Raven," Joseph Keppler depicts Benjamin Harrison dwarfed by an enormous hat, with a burst of sunshine illuminating the classical bust of his grandfather, President William Henry Harrison. His secretary of state, James Blaine, perches atop the bust as the raven (see p. 150).

William McKinley: In this 1899 cartoon, Grant Hamilton shows William McKinley swatting at a mosquito representing General Emilio Aguinaldo, who led Filipino forces against the United States following the Spanish-American War (see p. 163).

Theodore Roosevelt: Depicted here by cartoonist Louis Dalrymple as a globe-dominating policeman swinging his big stick of "New Diplomacy," Theodore Roosevelt became known for acting first and sorting out the details later (see p. 182).

William Howard Taft: As Theodore Roosevelt left the White House in the hands of his successor, it was expected that William Howard Taft would continue Roosevelt's bold and progressive agenda.. In this 1909 cartoon by S.D. Ehrhart, Roosevelt leaves Taft with his policy baby—who bears a strong resemblance to Roosevelt—at the White House steps (see p. 204).

Woodrow Wilson: Although in the end staunch Republican opposition prevented U.S. ratification of a "general association of nations," Woodrow Wilson is shown here roosting on the League of Nations, an organization for which he campaigned tirelessly (see p. 219).

Warren G. Harding: Following the international turmoil of World War I, Warren G. Harding promised a "return to normalcy." Here, Rollin Kirby references Harding's "America First" speech, in which he spoke of "patriotic devotion" and the need to focus on U.S. interests. The sign refers to Sen. Boies Penrose, R-Pa., whose support helped Harding win the 1920 nomination (see p. 242).

Calvin Coolidge: Rollin Kirby highlights Calvin Coolidge's involvement in Latin American affairs in this 1928 cartoon. Coolidge not only attended the Pan-American Conference in Havana, but also continued U.S. military involvement in Nicaragua to quell violence and allow for national elections (see p. 258).

Herbert Hoover: Otto Soglow depicts Herbert Hoover looking on as World War I veterans march through Washington. Hoover was strongly criticized for his handling of the 1932 "Bonus March," during which veterans who demanded early payment of their bonuses were teargassed and forcibly removed from makeshift quarters by the army (see p. 275).

Franklin D. Roosevelt: In 1937 Franklin D. Roosevelt attempted to increase the number of Supreme Court justices to as many as fifteen in hopes of establishing a more administration-friendly bench. The proposal faced staunch public disapproval and congressional opposition, as evidenced in this cartoon (see p. 297).

Harry S. Truman: This Clifford Berryman cartoon reflects the prevailing notion that Thomas Dewey would beat Harry S. Truman in the 1948 election (see p. 334).

Dwight D. Eisenhower: Dwight D. Eisenhower is simply looking on as the "Civil Rights Crisis" burns, in this 1956 Herb Block cartoon. Although he was not an active proponent of civil rights reform, Eisenhower dispatched the National Guard to enforce school desegregation in Little Rock, Arkansas, in 1957 and signed the Civil Rights Act of 1957 (see p. 358).

John F. Kennedy: Soviet premier Nikita Khrushchev is shown soaring over John F. Kennedy and a missile-supported "Space Race" hurdle in this Bill Mauldin cartoon, published in 1961, a few months after the Soviet Union sent a man into space for the first time (see p. 382).

Lyndon B. Johnson: Despite an ambitious domestic policy agenda, Lyndon B. Johnson's second term was dominated by the Vietnam War. Bill Mauldin illustrates the policy difficulties faced by Johnson in this April 1965 cartoon (see p. 404).

Richard Nixon: John Pierotti depicts Richard Nixon lamenting the growing Watergate investigation. In 1973 Nixon's counsel, John Dean, agreed to testify before the Senate Watergate Committee (see p. 427).

Gerald Ford: Bill Sanders depicts Gerald Ford encountering a bruised and broken Uncle Sam and pledging to piece him back together. Ford pardoned Richard Nixon in an attempt to heal the wounds of Watergate (see p. 462).

Jimmy Carter: Parodying artist Grant Wood's painting "American Gothic," Mike Peters presents Jimmy Carter and his wife Rosalynn in place of the farmer and his wife—with the White House as the backdrop (see p. 478).

Ronald Reagan: Bill Sanders spoofs the Reagan administration's tax policy immediately following Ronald Reagan's 1984 reelection. Reagan, depicted as Peter Pan, encourages a child to trust his campaign tax promise before leaping out of a window (see p. 499).

George H.W. Bush: The savings and loan crisis of the late 1980s resulted in a substantial federal bailout of failing financial institutions. In this 1990 Herb Block cartoon, George H.W. Bush is depicted as providing an insufficient solution to the crisis (see p. 529).

Bill Clinton: Bill Clinton, who famously played his saxophone on the *Arsenio Hall Show* during his presidential campaign, is rousing the Democratic donkey and Republican elephant from bed. Pat Oliphant implies that Clinton would invigorate American politics and bring youthful energy to the White House (see p. 550).

George W. Bush: Cartoonist Gary Markstein shows George W. Bush as a (lame) duck flying from the White House (see p. 577).

ABOUT

TIMESREFERENCE FROM CQ PRESS

The books in the TimesReference from CQ Press series present unique documentary histories on a range of topics. The lens through which the histories are viewed is the original reporting of *The New York Times* and its many generations of legendary reporters.

Each book consists of documents selected from *The New York Times* newspaper accompanied by original narrative written by a scholar or content expert that provides context and analysis. The documents are primarily news articles, but also include editorials, op ed essays, letters to the editor, columns, and news analyses. Some are presented with full text; others, because of length, have been excerpted. Ellipses indicate omitted text. Using the headline and date as search criteria, readers can find the full text of all articles in *The Times'* online Archive at nytimes.com, which includes all of *The Times'* articles since the newspaper began publication in 1851.

The Internet age has revolutionized the way news is delivered, which means that there is no longer only one version of a story. Today, breaking news articles that appear on *The Times'* Web site are written to provide up-to-the-minute coverage of an event and therefore may differ from the article that is published in the print edition. Content may also differ between early and late editions of the day's printed paper. As such, some discrepancies between these versions may be present in these volumes.

The books are illustrated with photographs and other types of images. While most of these appeared in the print and/or online edition of the paper, not all were created by *The Times*, which, like many newspapers, relies on wire services for photographs. There are also editorial features in these books that did not appear in *The Times*—they were created or selected by CQ Press to enhance the documentary history being told. For example, in *The New York Times on the Presidency*, we chose an editorial cartoon and a created a quick fact box for each president.

Readers will note that many articles are introduced by several levels of headlines—especially in pieces from the paper's early years. This was done to emphasize the importance of the article. For very important stories, banner headlines stretch across the front page's many columns; every attempt has been made to include these with the relevant articles. Over the years, *The Times* added datelines and bylines at the beginning of articles.

Typographical and punctuation errors are the bane of every publisher's existence. Because all of the documents included in this book were re-typeset, CQ Press approached these problems in several different ways. Archaic spellings from the paper's early days appear just as they did in the original documents (for example, "employe" rather than "employee"). CQ Press corrected minor typographical errors that appeared in the original articles to assist readers' comprehension. In some cases, factual or other errors have been marked [sic]; where the meaning would be distorted, corrections have been made in brackets where possible. In addition, for clarity, CQ Press has italicized the names of ships, airplanes, publications, and the like, even though that is not "newspaper" style.

INTRODUCTION

For more than 150 years, *The New York Times* has covered American politics and the American presidency. Since 1851, when the paper was called the *New-York Daily Times,* it has reported on the activities of presidential campaigns, recorded significant details of historic events such as presidential inaugurations, and followed the frequently tumultuous tussle among presidents, their advisers, Congress, interest groups, and others over policymaking. Both in the early days and more recently, the coverage has sparked controversy over issues ranging from the abolition of slavery to the Vietnam War to government surveillance of suspected terrorists since the devastating attacks of September 11, 2001. Despite sometimes heated criticism from government officials and other sources, *The Times* is indisputably recognized today as the essential locus of information on presidential politics.

The purpose of this volume is to trace the evolution of the American presidency through the lens of *The Times'* coverage. The book examines every presidential administration that the paper has followed from start to finish, beginning with the successful candidacy of Franklin Pierce in 1852 and continuing through the influence of the George W. Bush presidency on the 2008 presidential election. In so doing, it illustrates the rise of the president as the central figure in American politics as well as the expansion of the institution of the presidency.

As U.S. responsibilities have developed both domestically and internationally, so, too, has presidential authority expanded to encompass those expectations. The growth of presidential power is not strictly linear. After the strong leadership asserted by President Abraham Lincoln during the Civil War, executive initiative was less evident for the rest of the nineteenth century. But the vast and enduring expansion of presidential responsibilities in the twentieth century, beginning with the administration of Franklin D. Roosevelt, which is widely recognized as the advent of the "modern presidency," is unmistakable.

Tracking *The Times'* coverage of the American presidency requires some understanding of the history of the paper itself. *The Times* was founded in 1851 by a banker, George Jones, and a reporter, Henry J. Raymond, who was its first publisher. Raymond helped to create the

Republican Party in the 1850s; he also served in the New York State Assembly, as lieutenant governor of New York, and in Congress. He was a strong supporter of President Abraham Lincoln during the Civil War. After Raymond's death, Jones became publisher, and during his tenure *The Times* gained prominence for its exposure of corruption in the New York City political machine known as Tammany Hall.

In 1896 Adolph Ochs purchased the paper, and this event began the evolution of *The Times* as the leading chronicler in American journalism. Ochs added the famous motto "All the News That's Fit to Print," which still graces the front page of the paper today. Ochs's descendants, whether by marriage or birth, have continued to manage *The Times,* and the current publisher is his great-grandson, Arthur Ochs Sulzberger Jr.

The Times' reporting on American chief executives reveals some important transitions in the presidency that coincided with critical periods in American politics. The first period starts with the paper's founding before the Civil War and continues to the 1896 presidential campaign. The second begins with the successful candidacy of President William McKinley, who presided over the rise of the United States as a global power, and goes through the depths of despair during the Great Depression in the Herbert Hoover administration. The third follows the unprecedented four presidential terms of Franklin D. Roosevelt and continues into the divisive debates over the Vietnam War in the Lyndon B. Johnson and Richard M. Nixon administrations. The fourth period commences with the conclusion of Vietnam War and the Watergate scandal during the Nixon presidency and continues through the current controversies over the George W. Bush administration's actions in combating terrorism and waging the Iraq War.

THE EARLY YEARS

From the outset, *The Times* combined factual reporting with keen observation and analysis, particularly for momentous events in the American presidency. Before Franklin Pierce's inauguration in 1853, for example, the president-elect and his wife experienced a horrific tragedy in which their young son died in a railway accident. The *Times* reporter conveyed the news poignantly, noting that the boy "was a fine little fellow." He also wrote in the first person, "I glean this information . . ."—even though bylines typically were not included at the time. We do find exceptions to the byline rule, such as the vivid portrayal of the Battle of Gettysburg in 1863 titled "Our Special Army Correspondence" and prepared by Mr. Lorenzo L. Crounse, one of *The Times'* chief correspondents in the Civil War. His first-person account traced the three days of the battle, recounting "the ferocity and desperation with which it was fought by both armies."

Many of the documents selected from this period are editorials. They stand out because of their incisive summary of events combined with crisply strong, sometimes passionate, commentary. The editorial about Lincoln's second inaugural address, for example, which was published after his assassination, describes the speech as "earnest, humane, truly but not technically religious, filled with forgiveness and good will." In some cases, documents are identified as articles in *The Times'* database, but appear to be editorials, such as the March 6, 1869, selection titled "President Grant's Cabinet," which declares, "The Cabinet is eminently and evidently one of the President's own selection."

Letters to the editor vary in length and often reveal as much about the writer as they do about the subject. An 1860 letter from a minister presents seven reasons why he endorses Lincoln for president, including his view that the candidate "is a fair man in ability, up to the average of our Presidents hitherto." Fifteen years later, a letter writer strongly opposes a third term for President Ulysses S. Grant: "Twice I voted for Gen. Grant. That's enough! I wouldn't give a third term to George Washington himself."

In its early years *The Times* was considered a Republican paper, which was not surprising given that the first publisher helped to create the Republican Party. But in 1884 *The Times* for the first time endorsed a Democratic presidential candidate, Gov. Grover Cleveland of New York. Cleveland won the election—and indeed became the only U.S. president to date who served two nonconsecutive terms—but the paper paid a price for its choice. It lost advertising revenue from Republican sources, and its financial situation became so precarious that its viability seemed uncertain. The paper's future changed when Ochs bought it.

TRANSITIONING INTO THE TWENTIETH CENTURY

The Times' reputation for independent and authoritative journalism dates back to Ochs's era. The slogan "All the News That's Fit to Print" has received its share of criticism over the years, but Ochs set a standard that his staff and their successors have endeavored to achieve. He also recognized the need to separate the business and news divisions of the paper to maintain impartiality in news coverage as much as possible.

The growth of professionalization of the news was evident early into Ochs's tenure. A June 22, 1900, article on the Republican Party's nomination of President William McKinley for a second term reported that "the nomination was made with enthusiasm," but also said, "The demonstrations were not as prolonged, however, as they have been in conventions where nomination has been preceded by conflict." The article went on to identify vice-presidential candidate Theodore Roosevelt as "the idol of the convention," and further noted, "The tumult over him was manifestly spontaneous, universal, and sincere."

When Roosevelt became president after McKinley's assassination in September 1901, *The Times* described him as "one of the most unique and picturesque figures in American public life." Roosevelt's energetic disposition augured well for active presidential leadership, and *The Times* diligently covered his efforts to enact domestic legislation and promote American interests abroad. The public responded to Roosevelt's energy as well; as *The Times* reported in 1908, three hundred to four hundred letters were arriving weekly at the White House urging the president to seek a third term.

Roosevelt did just that in 1912, after a four-year hiatus in which he became increasingly critical of the leadership of President William Howard Taft, who had served in the Roosevelt administration as secretary of war. Even though *The Times* endorsed Woodrow Wilson for president, it opposed Roosevelt's decision to divide the Republican Party by running on a third-party ticket. An editorial published on the day of the election declared, "Mr. Taft should lead Mr. Roosevelt in the Electoral and the popular vote" because "it is to the interest of the Nation that the Republican Party should be preserved as an organized, coherent opposition." Wilson won, and Roosevelt came in ahead of Taft, but the Republican Party persevered.

The Times was highly critical of the Republicans' nomination of Sen. Warren G. Harding for president in 1920. An editorial stated that his nomination "will be received with astonishment and dismay," and it compared the candidate to nineteenth-century president Franklin Pierce, "if we would seek a President who measures down to his political stature." The paper criticized "the cowardice and imbecility of the Senatorial cabal" that decided on Harding's nomination. But *The Times* also published a laudatory article on Harding's "front-porch campaign" by Frank Parker Stockbridge, who also had witnessed McKinley's similar campaign twenty-four years earlier, and the paper included a byline for the piece.

THE RISE OF THE MODERN PRESIDENCY

By the 1930s bylines had become more common in *The Times,* and several reporters covered the White House regularly. Washington bureau chief and four-time Pulitzer Prize winner Arthur Krock covered Franklin D. Roosevelt's acceptance speech at the 1932 Democratic

National Convention, in which the candidate declared that his decision to break with tradition and address the convention in person signified "the task of [the Democratic] party to break foolish traditions."

Reporter James C. Hagerty, who became President Dwight D. Eisenhower's press secretary, wrote that FDR's famous first inaugural address was presented "with earnestness and directness and with no attempt at oratorical embellishments." Given the gravity of the national economic situation at the time, Hagerty's focus on the new president's political agenda was logical for a news article, but the speech is remembered in history as much for its rhetorical flourishes—the most famous of which surely is "the only thing we have to fear is fear itself"—as for its policy prescriptions.

Naturally, *The Times* reported on FDR's controversies as well as his accomplishments. Turner Catledge, who covered the Supreme Court and the White House, and later became managing editor and a company vice chairman, wrote about the president's push to increase the size of the Supreme Court in 1937. Describing FDR's appeal to the American people for support, Catledge wrote that the president "sought to assure millions of Americans gathered around their radios that in this new project he was seeking only to protect them from the usurpations of a Supreme Court which had left its place at the scales of justice to set itself up as a 'super-legislature.' " But the "court-packing plan" was highly unpopular and marked a major political failure for FDR.

In 1940 *The Times* decided not to endorse FDR for a third term. As it explained in a lengthy editorial, its support for Republican Wendell Willkie was based on the Wall Street entrepreneur's qualifications as well as respect for the two-term precedent set by George Washington and followed by every other president until FDR's third victory. The paper did, however, endorse FDR in 1944 for a fourth term.

During the cold war, *The Times* faced a perennial challenge for the media in covering the presidency: balancing the public's right to know what the White House is doing with the government's need to protect national security interests. This dilemma became evident during the Bay of Pigs invasion in April 1961, in which John F. Kennedy's administration provided assistance to Cuban rebels seeking to overthrow Fidel Castro's Communist regime. After the invasion failed, some people in *The Times'* newsroom questioned whether the paper should have investigated the administration's plans more aggressively before the attack.

Even President Kennedy later said he wished the media had reported more beforehand, as that might have revealed flaws in the plan, which had been conceived in the Eisenhower administration. But writing after the event, *Times* columnist James Reston, winner of two Pulitzer Prizes, pointed out that "how [Kennedy] reacts to [the defeat] may very well be more important than how he got into it. For this will be a critical test of the character and perspective of the new President." Kennedy appeared to pass that "test" the following year through his skillful leadership during the Cuban missile crisis.

Despite disagreements over coverage at times, Kennedy got along well with the media, as did many of his other communications-savvy predecessors, such as FDR. But journalists became more wary of presidents and their advisers in the aftermath of serious conflicts in the early 1970s. In June 1971 *The Times* and the *Washington Post* began publishing the Pentagon Papers, a classified study prepared by the Department of Defense on the origins of the Vietnam War. President Richard M. Nixon tried to prevent publication of the documents, but the Supreme Court ruled in favor of the newspapers.

One year later, a burglary of Democratic National Committee headquarters at the Watergate office complex in Washington, D.C., sparked investigations that led to the first resignation of a president who otherwise likely would have faced impeachment. After Nixon's resignation, even his supporters, such as *Times* columnist William Safire, who had been one of the president's speech writers, accepted the need for this outcome. The Vietnam War and Watergate undercut public and journalists' trust in government and contributed to what is subsequently viewed by many as the "adversarial media."

FROM THE POST–VIETNAM WAR/WATERGATE ERA TO THE POST–9/11 WORLD

News coverage of presidential governance has evolved in significant ways since Vietnam and Watergate. The rise of more personal reporting about the White House raises questions about the appropriate balance between news and analysis. This tension is well illustrated by the writings of *Times* reporter and columnist Maureen Dowd, who won a Pulitzer Prize in 1999 for her columns on the Monica Lewinsky scandal in Bill Clinton's administration. In 1994 Dowd wrote a front-page story on President Clinton's trip to Oxford University, which began, "President Clinton returned today for a sentimental journey to the university where he didn't inhale, didn't get drafted and didn't get a degree." The statement was factually correct, but was viewed by some critics as more appropriate for an opinion piece than for front-page news.

The Times has published editorials and letters to the editors since its earliest days, but its daily full page devoted to opinion pieces and columns (now two or more pages on Sundays) is a relatively recent innovation. The introduction of an Op-Ed page in fall 1970 marked a major development for the paper. The page was created to provide more space for external perspectives on pressing issues.

The wide array of contributors includes presidential advisers, and a famous example is the essay by James A. Baker III in August 2002. Baker had served as secretary of state in the George H. W. Bush administration, and his article was widely seen as a cautionary note from the former president to his son, President George W. Bush. Baker endorsed the need for military intervention to achieve "regime change" in Iraq, but he favored seeking a UN Security Council resolution to authorize such action, so the United States would have an international coalition to share responsibilities, particularly the costs, and thus maintain public support.

Although the Iraq War is the most controversial of the Bush administration's post–9/11 foreign policy decisions, many other actions taken by the president have sparked heated debate, including assertions of unilateral executive power. *The Times* became a part of those debates when reporter James Risen wrote about a covert surveillance program that the president had approved for spying on suspected terrorists without seeking proper authorization. Risen also revealed a program to track people who financed terrorism, and he won the Pulitzer Prize for his investigative journalism. Critics claimed *The Times* was hindering the government's efforts to capture terrorists, while others were troubled by the administration's willingness to act without political, or perhaps even legal, support to achieve its goals.

Despite a sometimes adversarial, even acrimonious, relationship between the paper and the presidency, they are linked closely. Presidential administrations provide a wide-ranging basis for reporting by *The Times,* and the newspaper is the premier source for people to read to understand national and international events. In the twenty-first century, *The New York Times* continues to inform the presidency as much as the presidency informs *The Times*.

Through its depiction of the evolution of the presidency, this book identifies a fundamental development in American politics: The institution of the chief executive has expanded vastly in the past seventy-five years—far more than even the most ardent proponents of presidential power among those who designed the U.S. government likely envisioned. Understanding the sources as well as the consequences of that authority is essential to understanding how policy making operates in the United States. *The New York Times* provides an indispensable lens for the public to learn about the American presidency and American politics.

THE PRESIDENCY OF FRANKLIN PIERCE

MARCH 4, 1853 – MARCH 4, 1857

The administration of Franklin Pierce witnessed the United States moving slowly but steadily toward civil war. In particular the growing division between northern and southern states as to whether new territories should be permitted to have slaves made clear that peaceful resolution of this issue was becoming unlikely. Even though Pierce was a native of New Hampshire, his views hewed closer to those of his southern colleagues in Congress, making both party and presidential leadership difficult. Pierce's limited ambitions for the position further constrained his actions.

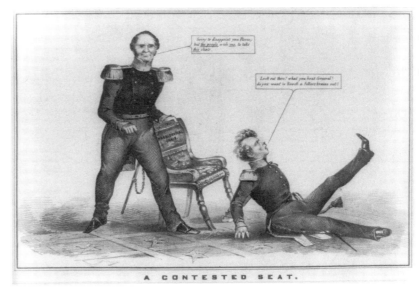

A CONTESTED SEAT.

Pierce observed politics at work firsthand through his father, Revolutionary War hero Benjamin Pierce, who served as governor of New Hampshire. Pierce graduated from Bowdoin College in 1824, where he befriended Nathaniel Hawthorne, who would one day write a campaign biography on Pierce's behalf. After studying law Pierce entered politics, first serving in the New Hampshire legislature and then winning election to Congress, where he served four years in the House and six years in the Senate. A lifelong Democrat, Pierce identified more closely with his southern partisans than with northern Whigs on the issue of slavery. During congressional debates in the 1830s over the "gag rule," which prohibited debates on antislavery legislation, Pierce supported the Democratic Party in favoring such rules. Pierce returned to New Hampshire in the early 1840s to practice law, and he served as brigadier general in the Mexican-American War. Festering divisions within the Democratic Party over slavery would prompt his return to national politics.

THE 1852 CAMPAIGN

In 1852 northern Democrats who supported the abolition of slavery were popularly known as Free-Soil Democrats or Barnburners, and they could not reach agreement with southern Democrats on a presidential candidate. On the thirty-fifth ballot at the Democratic convention, Pierce was nominated largely because he was found palatable to both wings of the party, and he won the nomination on the forty-ninth ballot. Calling him "Young Hickory of the Granite Hills," the Democrats simultaneously invoked the spirit of Andrew Jackson and recognized Pierce's New Hampshire background.

The Whig Party faced similar turmoil, finally nominating Gen. Winfield Scott on the fifty-third ballot. Although Scott's military record was far more distinguished than Pierce's— whose service was mocked due to an unfortunate accident in which he fell from his horse and fainted during the Mexican-American War—Pierce's support for slavery, especially the

QUICK FACTS ON FRANKLIN PIERCE

BIRTH	November 23, 1804, Hillsboro, N.H.
EDUCATION	Bowdoin College Law Studies
FAMILY	Wife: Jane Means Appleton Pierce Children: Franklin Pierce, Franklin Robert Pierce, Benjamin Pierce
WHITE HOUSE PETS	None
PARTY	Democratic
PRE-PRESIDENTIAL CAREER (SELECTED)	New Hampshire legislature, 1829–1833 U.S. House of Representatives, 1833–1837 U.S. Senate, 1836–1842
PRESIDENTIAL TERM	March 4, 1853–March 4, 1857
VICE PRESIDENT	William Rufus De Vane King
KEY EVENTS (SELECTED)	Kansas-Nebraska Act (1854) Gadsden Treaty (1854) Ostend Manifesto (1854)
POST-PRESIDENCY	Travel, retirement
DEATH	October 8, 1869, Concord, N.H.

Compromise of 1850, proved decisive. Pierce won all but four states in the Electoral College. He received a slim popular-vote majority over Scott (approximately 1.6 million or 51 percent of the vote, to Scott's 1.4 million or 44 percent of the vote). The election was significant more for the impending decline of the Whig Party than for Pierce's victory.

THE PIERCE ADMINISTRATION

Pierce's presidency was overshadowed by personal tragedy from the outset, when his young son, Benjamin, died in a train accident two months before Pierce's inauguration. Jane Pierce subsequently took little interest in the presidency (not even attending her husband's inauguration), apparently viewing her son's death as divine intervention to free her husband from domestic concerns so he could concentrate completely on fulfilling his professional duties. The broken-hearted president refused to use the Bible at his inauguration, and he affirmed rather than swore his loyalty to the Constitution in taking the oath of office.

Pierce's cabinet was notable primarily for its constancy, as all seven members stayed in office through the comple-

tion of his term. Pierce took care to extend appointments to the various factions within the Democratic Party. He selected southern leader Jefferson Davis to serve as secretary of war and Massachusetts politician Caleb Cushing (who, like Pierce, did not support the abolition of slavery) to serve as attorney general. He also invited a "Barnburner," New Yorker John A. Dix, to serve as assistant secretary of the treasury.

Vice President William Rufus De Vane King died just weeks after Pierce's inauguration, and his position remained empty for the rest of the administration. With the special permission of Congress, King took the oath of office in Havana, Cuba, where he had traveled for health reasons. Perhaps the most distinguishing feature of King's short tenure is that he is the only one of all U.S. presidents and vice presidents to take the oath of office in a foreign country.

MAJOR ISSUES

The most significant events in the Pierce presidency were the expansion of the United States and the growing divide between northern and southern states over slavery. Through the Gadsden

Treaty of 1854, Pierce paid $10 million to extend the U.S. border approximately 45,000 square miles into Mexico. The president hoped to expand the United States even further through buying Cuba, and the Ostend Manifesto of 1854 pursued this goal. But northern opposition, particularly to the declaration that the United States would forcibly wrest Cuba from Spain if necessary, ultimately blocked Pierce's plan.

The expansion of U.S. territory raised the question of whether slavery would be permitted in the acquired land, and this issue came to define the Pierce presidency through the Kansas-Nebraska Act of 1854. This law effectively repealed the Missouri Compromise of 1820, which had declared much of the northern land from the Louisiana Purchase to be free territory. Some thirty years later, however, slaveholding states fought to overturn this legislation, calling instead for popular sovereignty in the territories to settle the question. Pierce supported the Kansas-Nebraska bill and subsequently saw his party lose seats in almost all of the Free-Soil states in the 1854 midterm elections.

In addition to the electoral losses incurred by the Democratic Party, the Kansas-Nebraska Act prompted the early battles that would lead to the Civil War. Settlers in Kansas organized two governments, one proslavery and one in favor of abolition, and the two sides were irreconcilable. By May 1856 they had turned to bloodshed, leading to cries of "Bleeding Kansas." Pierce's efforts to appease the opposing wings of his party through compromise had clearly failed.

Although Pierce cannot be held solely accountable for the turmoil caused by "Bleeding Kansas," neither can his inability to bridge the chasm within the Democratic Party over slavery be ignored. Pierce's southern sympathies made him impatient with northern abolitionists and prevented him from leading either his party or the nation effectively. In 1856 Pierce lost his spot on the Democratic ticket—the only sitting president ever to seek his party's nomination again and be denied. But the battles over slavery ignited in his administration would only continue to grow.

· ·

"The Democratic Nomination," June 7, 1852

The Democratic Party's sharply divergent views on slavery made selecting a presidential candidate in 1852 extremely difficult. With southerners who supported slavery, northerners who supported their southern counterparts, and northerners who advocated abolition, the Democrats faced tremendous obstacles to find a presidential candidate who could garner the two-thirds vote required to win the nomination. Franklin Pierce, former senator from New Hampshire, was introduced as a candidate after more than thirty ballots, and he secured the party's nomination on the forty-ninth. *The New York Times* aptly noted that Pierce was selected from "utter obscurity," and that "the fact that he was unknown to the country, is the great fact which controlled the action of the Convention."

June 7, 1852
The Democratic Nomination.

The Democratic Convention has ended its arduous labors. Four days' session, and forty-nine ballots, were spent in the effort to select from the half dozen leading Democrats of the Union, a Presidential candidate. The task was too much for them. The attempt was finally abandoned, and every candidate named during the first three days, or voted for during the first thirty-five ballots, was thrown aside. The Democracy took refuge from their embarrassments in utter obscurity. They have selected a candidate whose name not one in a thousand of the American people ever heard before, and who has neither high character nor

eminent service to show as his warrant for so high a trust. The fact that he was unknown to the country, is the great fact which controlled the action of the Convention.

Yet it must by no means be supposed that the nomination is necessarily a weak one. We do not so consider it. It is true that the course of the party now is an exaggerated imitation of that pursued in 1844; and that Mr. Polk was far more widely known, and had shown far greater abilities in the public service, than Mr. Pierce. He had been Chairman of the Committee of Ways and Means, and thus leader, and afterwards Speaker of the House of Representatives, and in both positions had displayed very decided talent and a marked aptitude for public business. He had, moreover, shown very great popularity at home, and as Governor of Tennessee had shown administrative faculties of no common order. To no similar proofs of talent on behalf of Mr. Pierce, can his supporters point. He has been a member of both Houses of Congress,—yet in neither did he raise himself for an hour into public notice. He did nothing and said nothing which any human being can now remember:—and but for the friendly services of his partizan biographers, the very fact of his ever having held a seat in the public Councils would have faded from the public recollection. In the War with Mexico, he received from President Polk,—more of course as a party favor than from any military pretensions on his part,—an appointment as Brigadier General, and in that capacity served under General Scott during part of his great campaign, resigning his commission before the war was over and coming home. We believe that in this position he showed good conduct,—but we find neither in the official reports or elsewhere, mention of any special act of valor or activity. He deserves, however, marked credit for having kept himself aloof from the conspiracy which was formed by political foes against

General Scott, after he had conquered Mexico, and for having vindicated that great commander from the malignant persecution of his enemies, on returning home.

But the Whigs must not suppose that this lack of conspicuous merit on the part of the Democratic candidate is to make the contest easy or victory secure. The mistake they made in the case of Mr. Polk should warn them against such an error. There is much in the position of Mr. Pierce to make him, under the circumstances, the most formidable candidate who could have been selected.

In the first place, the Democratic party, North and South, is *united* in his support. Not a whisper will be heard against him from any quarter of the Democratic ranks. He will receive their united, harmonious and energetic support. This fact alone is quite enough to show the Whigs that they have no easy game to play—no holiday fight, to be waged simply for their own amusement. They will find it essential to select their strongest candidate, put him in the strongest possible position, and secure for him the largest possible vote. And they may learn something from the *special object* which the nomination of Pierce is expected to accomplish.

It is very clear that *he is relied upon to carry the Free-Soil vote of the Northern States*.

- -

"Acceptance of the Democratic Nominees," June 25, 1852

Apart from having no expectation of becoming the Democratic nominee for president in 1852, Franklin Pierce also was simply following nineteenth-century tradition in formally accepting the nomination by letter several days later. Not until Franklin D. Roosevelt's nomination in 1932 did presidential candidates accept their position in person at the party convention. In their acceptance letters, both Pierce and his running mate, Sen. William Rufus De Vane King of Alabama, expressed their appreciation for the nomination without engaging any of the issues festering within the party and the country. Pierce's reference to "the overthrow of sectional jealousies" would prove to be far more optimistic than the political reality.

JUNE 25, 1852
ACCEPTANCE OF THE DEMOCRATIC NOMINEES.
FROM THE WASHINGTON UNION, JUNE 24.

We have received for publication the following correspondence from the Committee delegated by the National Democratic Convention to communicate its nominations for the Presidency and the Vice-Presidency to the distinguished gentlemen upon whom they were conferred; and we have great pleasure in now laying before the Democ-

racy of the country the patriotic and eloquent letters in which its chosen leaders signify their acceptance of the elevated positions to which they have been called:

Concord, (N. H.) June 17, 1852.

Gentlemen: I have the honor to acknowledge your personal kindness in presenting to me this day your letter officially informing me of my nomination, by the Democratic National Convention, as a candidate for the Presidency of the United States.

The surprise with which I received the intelligence of the nomination was not unmingled with painful solicitude, and yet it is proper for me to say that the manner in which it was conferred was peculiarly gratifying. The delegation from New-Hampshire, with all the glow of State pride and all the warmth of personal regard, would not have submitted my name to the Convention, nor would they have cast a vote for me, under circumstances other than those which occurred.

I shall always cherish with pride and gratitude the recollection of the fact that the voice which first pronounced for me—and pronounced alone—came from the mother of States—a pride and gratitude rising far above any consequences that can betide me personally.

May I not regard it as a fact pointing to the overthrow of sectional jealousies, and looking to the perennial life and vigor of a Union cemented by the blood of those who have passed to their reward—a Union wonderful in its formation, boundless in its hopes, amazing in its destiny! I accept the nomination, relying upon an abiding devotion to the interests, the honor and the glory of our whole country, but, beyond and above all, upon a power superior to all human might—a power which, from the first gun of the revolution, in every crisis through which we have passed, in every hour of our acknowledged peril, when the dark clouds have shut down around us, has interposed as if to baffle human wisdom, out march human forecast, and bring out of darkness the rainbow of promise. Weak myself, faith and hope repose there in security. I accept the nomination upon the Platform adopted by the Convention, not because this is expected of me as a candidate, but because the principles it embraces command the approbation of my judgment; and with them I believe I can safely say there has been no word nor act of my life in conflict.

I have only to tender my grateful acknowledgments to you, gentlemen, to the Convention of which you were members, and to the people of our common country.

Franklin Pierce was sworn into office on March 4, 1853, just two months after the death of his son in a railway accident.

Source: The Granger Collection, New York

I am, with the highest respect, your most obedient servant,

FRANK Pierce.

To Hon. J. S. Barbour, J. Thompson, Alpheus Felch, Pierre Soule.

From Hon. William R. King.

Senate Chamber, June 22, 1852.

Gentlemen:—I have the honor to acknowledge the receipt of your letter, notifying me that I have been nominated by the Democratic Convention as Vice-President of the United States.

This distinguished manifestation of the respect and confidence of my Democratic brethren commands my most grateful acknowledgments, and I cheerfully accept the nomination with which I have been honored.

Throughout a long public life I am not conscious that I have ever swerved from those principles which have been cherished and sustained by the Democratic party; and in whatever situation I may be placed, my countrymen may rest assured that I shall adhere to them faithfully and zealously—perfectly satisfied that the prosperity of our common country and the permanency of our free institutions can be promoted and preserved only by administering the government in strict accordance with them.

The Platform, as laid down by the Convention, meets with my cordial approbation. It is national in all its parts; and I am content not only to stand upon it, but on all occasions to defend it.

For the very flattering terms in which you have been pleased, gentlemen, to characterize my public services, I feel that I am indebted to the personal regard which I am proud to know you individually entertain for me, and that you greatly overrate them. The only merit I can lay claim to is an honest discharge of the duties of the various positions with which I have been honored. This I claim—nothing more.

With the highest respect and esteem, I am, gentlemen, your fellow-citizen,

WILLIAM R. KING.

To Messrs. J. S. Barbour, J. Thompson, Alpheus Felch, and P. Soule.

- -

"SAD RAILROAD ACCIDENT; SON OF GEN. PIERCE KILLED," JANUARY 7, 1853

The Pierce family faced personal tragedy on January 6, 1853, when President-elect Pierce's eleven-year-old son, Benjamin, was killed in a train accident. Pierce and his wife, Jane, were traveling with Benjamin from Boston to Concord, New Hampshire, when their train went off the track. Having experienced the deaths of two other children—a son who died in infancy and another who died at age four—the Pierces were overcome by sorrow. Jane. Pierce never recovered from the "melancholy fatality" described by *The Times* in reporting the disaster.

JANUARY 7, 1853
LATEST INTELLIGENCE
BY TELEGRAPH TO THE NEW-YORK DAILY TIMES.
SAD RAILROAD ACCIDENT.
SON OF GEN. PIERCE KILLED.
Narrow Escape of the President Elect.

CONCORD, Thursday, Jan. 6.

News has just been received here of a terrible accident on the Boston and Maine Railroad, one mile north of Andover. Several persons were severely injured, and the only child of Gen. Pierce was killed.

The train left Boston at 12¼ o'clock.

Gen. Pierce, wife and child were on the cars—the latter having been killed. The General is said to have been considerably injured, but his wife is unhurt. They had been visiting friends at Andover. The boy was eleven years old, and was a fine little fellow.

Gen. Pierce appeared composed, but Mrs. Pierce was taken away in a very high state of mental anguish. Her screams were agonizing. The little boy was their only child, an elder brother having died some ten years ago.

The New-Hampshire Legislature adjourned immediately. The name of Gen. Pierce's son was Benjamin. He is said to be the only one killed. The passenger-car ran off the track and fell among the rocks, down a precipice twenty feet, and was turned so as to change ends.

Four persons were badly injured. I glean this information from Mr. Peaslee, a passenger, who has just arrived, with his head cut severely. One man's legs were broken twice. There is great sensation here. . . .

FOURTH DISPATCH.

Concord, Thursday, Jan. 6.

Considerable apprehension is felt here lest this melancholy fatality may prove serious in its consequences to Mrs. Pierce. She has been for several years in delicate health, caused partly by the loss of her first child. The boy killed to-day was almost idolized by his mother and father.

The announcement of the accident, at 4 o'clock, caused great excitement in the House. A member came in and stated that General Pierce himself was dead. The floor and galleries were crowded—the charge of bribery against Judge Butler being under consideration.

The Governor, Council, and most of the Senators were present. Instantly every member was on his feet, and exclamations of regret were heard from every quarter.

The veteran Ichabod Bartlett, of Portsmouth, the oldest member—a political opponent, but strong personal friend of General Pierce—was observed to weep like a child. Others were much affected.

The House adjourned instantly, and the members rushed to the hotel and telegraph offices, and the most intense anxiety to obtain particulars has prevailed ever since.

The evening train has just arrived. The corpse of young Pierce was taken to the Andover Almshouse, near which the accident happened.

General and Mrs. Pierce went back to Mr. Aiken's. It is thought that neither he nor his lady are seriously injured, although both were somewhat bruised. . . .

General Pierce, lady and son, were seated four or five seats from the forward end of the car.

The boy was struck on the forehead by a fragment of the frame-work.

The car is said to have broken near the middle. The baggage car in front was not thrown off. A brakeman stood on the end of it, and witnessed the accident unharmed.

"THE GADSDEN TREATY RATIFIED," APRIL 26, 1854

Although he sought to achieve greater territorial expansion, Pierce nevertheless was pleased with the U.S. acquisition of land through the Gadsden Treaty of 1854. Named after its negotiator, James Gadsden, the treaty purchased territory from Mexico for $10 million. Some critics declared that the United States should have received more territory, while others decried the expansion. The treaty marked one of the signature achievements of the Pierce administration.

APRIL 26, 1854
THE GADSDEN TREATY RATIFIED.

We learn from Washington that the Gadsden Treaty was *ratified* by the Senate yesterday, after sundry modifications. It has been amended so that the extent of territory acquired is only about *half* as much as the original document ceded to the United States:—the portion ceded includes a Southern route for the Pacific Railroad. The sum to be paid to Mexico is fixed at *ten millions* of dollars, and the eleventh article of the Treaty of Guadalupe, by which the United States agrees to protect Mexico against incursions of the Indians, is abrogated. The treaty also contains a recognition of the Sloo grant for a route across the Isthmus of Tehuantepec, which will answer the purposes of

the holders of that grant. The treaty makes no provision for the settlement of American claims against Mexico.

These, we have reason to believe, are the leading provisions of the treaty as it has been modified by the Senate,—though as the injunction of secrecy has not yet been removed from the Senate's proceedings, it is not easy to speak with as much exactness on these points as would be desirable. The treaty must now be submitted to Santa Anna, and if the changes made receive his assent, it will become binding. The opinion is generally entertained at Washington that his need of money will induce him to accede to the Senate's amendment.

"THE NEBRASKA BILL—PROSPECTS AND RESULTS OF ITS PASSAGE," MAY 12, 1854

Perhaps the most significant event of the Pierce administration was the Kansas-Nebraska Act of 1854. Previously, the 1820 Missouri Compromise had dictated which parts of the United States would be permitted to have slaves and which would remain free. But the 1854 legislation gave local populations in new territories the power to decide. *The Times* took a clear stand on this issue: "The political equilibrium between Slavery and Freedom is to be destroyed." While intended as a compromise, the Kansas-Nebraska Act ultimately moved the United States closer to civil war.

> The Missouri Compromise, which gave peace to the country thirty years ago, and has preserved it ever since, will be repealed.

MAY 12, 1854
THE NEBRASKA BILL—PROSPECTS AND RESULTS OF ITS PASSAGE.

It is pretty clear that the Nebraska bill is to pass. The decree has been registered, and the scenes of yesterday show conclusively that the conspirators have the power and the will to carry it into effect. No slave-driver was ever half so absolute on his own plantation, as was the President's Vice-gerent, Mr. Richardson, in the House of the People's Representatives yesterday. The same insolent, domineering dictation which has proved potent hitherto, will carry the scheme to its full completion. The bill will be passed. The Missouri Compromise, which gave peace to the country thirty years ago, and has preserved it ever since, will be repealed. An area of country ten times as large as all New-England, which, thirty years ago, the South solemnly covenanted, for value received, should be free forever, is to be seized for Slavery. The political equilibrium between Slavery and Freedom is to be destroyed, and the slave-holding interest is to dominate in the public councils with perpetual and relentless sway. These are the results aimed at by the Nebraska movement. If they are averted, it will be simply because the conspirators overshoot their mark;—because the People take alarm at this amazing and defiant stride of the Slave Power, towards complete domination over the Union, and turn back the tide upon those by whom it has been raised to such a gigantic swell.

We have no doubt the minority in Congress will resort to all the means in their power to defeat the bill. In ordinary cases, on questions which had entered into the elections, and where the will of the people had thus been consulted, it would be the duty of the minority to submit to such legislation as the majority in Congress might see fit to pass. But this is not such a case. When the present members of Congress were elected, no human being in the Union *dreamed* that they would be required to vote for, or against, the repeal of the Missouri Compromise. The project has been sprung on the country suddenly and treacherously. From one end of the Union to the other, it has been received with an outburst of popular indignation. From every part of the Free States, at which it is especially aimed, the most intense and unanimous denunciation has been visited upon it. Not a solitary petition has been presented in its favor. Not a single meeting beyond the shadow of a Custom-House has urged its passage. Under such circumstances, the slightest respect for the popular will should induce Congress to defer action upon it, until the people could be consulted.

On the contrary, we see the whole power of the Government,—all the patronage put by the Constitution in the hands of the President,—Executive menaces and Executive bribery,—the power of party discipline, every weapon which ingenuity can invent and audacity suggest, are unscrupulously used to *dragoon* Congress into an insolent disregard of the public will, and a high-handed assumption of power which they have no right to exercise.

Under these circumstances the minority will render to the country the highest service, by resorting to every means which Parliamentary law puts in their hands, to defeat the bill. If their *secession, from the House,* or their *resignation* and appeal to the people, would prevent or delay action upon it, until the people can be consulted and their will ascertained, they would be cordially and triumphantly sustained. We trust they will resort to every means in their power *to secure an appeal to the People* on this most important subject. Whether successful or not, they will have done their duty, and will have cleared their skirts of all responsibility for whatever action the majority in Congress may see fit to take.

Still we cannot shut our eyes to the fact, that, in spite of all their exertions, the bill will probably pass. The present Congress was elected under the full pressure of the great Union movement of 1850,—when the desire to harmonize public sentiment throughout the Union, and full confidence in the good faith of the Slaveholding interest, prevailed over all other considerations, and stifled as dangerous and useless every thought connected with the preservation of our national soil from Slavery. Many of the members elected from Free States, therefore, are pliable and purchaseable on that subject. The representatives of the Slaveholding States have come forward almost in a solid body, with a degree of faithlessness for which even their worst enemies were not prepared, to the support of the bill. And the whole power of the National Government, with a shameless defiance of justice and of the limitations of the Constitution, has been put forward in its support. Under these circumstances the chances are, as they always have been, that the bill will pass.

"Cuba—War and Slavery," April 11, 1855

This letter to the editor about Cuba addresses one of the most contentious foreign policy issues in the Pierce administration. President Pierce supported U.S. annexation of Cuba, and James Buchanan, the U.S. ambassador to Great Britain (and future president), pursued the matter through private diplomacy. But the 1854 Ostend Manifesto (named after a conference of foreign ministers in Ostend, Belgium) upended the negotiations because of aggressive language inserted by Pierre Soule, the U.S. ambassador to Spain, about potentially seizing Cuba from Spain. Because Cuba had slaves, annexation was injected into the growing conflict between northern and southern states. Public outcry—as demonstrated by the letter writer's concern "that every possible means are taken to throw the country into a war with Spain"—blocked further discussion.

APRIL 11, 1855
LETTER TO THE EDITOR
CUBA—WAR AND SLAVERY.

To the Editor of the New-York Daily Times:

I perceive by the latest news from Washington, that every possible means are taken to throw the country into a war with Spain, seemingly for the acquisition of the Island of Cuba. The President is abused, the Secretary of the State is ridiculed in every shape and manner, that those who are so over zealous for the annexation may be gratified. It is strange, that if the annexation of Cuba is of such vital importance to this country, that there would not be more of the popular will displayed upon the subject. We only hear of the noise made by a small number concerning the annexations; the major portion of the country apparently view with much indifference the question.

I am rather inclined to be fearful that we will compromise the true honor of the country, in proving to the enlightened portion of the world that the well intending majority is incapable of restraining the minority in enterprises of adventure where gain may possibly hold a flattering prospect. Our reputation, as a nation, may suffer immensely, and perhaps irretrievably, in the estimation of those who hitherto have been foremost in the loudest praise of our Republicanism. I would now ask, shall the good name, which has been so dearly bought, be quickly lost or sacrificed for the sake of a few Spanish ambitious aspirants, who have come among us, and with their bright gold won discontented geniuses to espouse their imagined grievances, even to purchase the Press, beset the heads of the Government, and provoke in every possible form an open rupture with a weak, though friendly Government? If we should use the say, namely, "Look on this picture, then on this," we would candidly discover that we are more sinning than sinned against.

We have had more than one expedition to leave our shores to overthrow the Government of the Island of Cuba, and while the rumor is that another is about to sail, and every precaution is adopted to defeat the piratical undertaking, we find our Government urged upon to pick at every trifle to fan discontent into a war. Where this will end is not to be answered, should war be the result. It is threatening in several shapes, and probably in the dissolution of the States, as it is sufficiently evident that the non-slaveholding States will never permit Cuba to annex herself with more than a half a million of slaves; if she does, it will be under the "Southern Confederacy." Can such things be, and not awaken the attention of those who justly prize the value of the Union of the States? I sincerely trust that the disinterested and Republican admirers of our country will awake in time to expose and avert the threatened danger which awaits the peace and unity of these States, which must as a natural consequence, should the Island of Cuba be annexed in any shape.

AN AMERICAN.

- -

"Startling News from Kansas," May 26, 1856

The Kansas-Nebraska Act of 1854 set the stage for a showdown over slavery in the western territories. Supporters of slavery from Missouri entered the neighboring Kansas territory and helped proslavery settlers there to establish a sympathetic legislature. But antislavery settlers, also supported by outsiders, created their own government in Topeka. In May 1856 opponents turned to bloodshed, with the destruction of Lawrence, a Free-Soil town, and the murder of five proslavery settlers in Pottawatomie Creek, led by abolitionist John Brown. More than two hundred people died in "Bleeding Kansas," and President Pierce would face the consequences in his failed quest for renomination.

MAY 26, 1856
STARTLING NEWS FROM KANSAS.

The news from Kansas which we publish this morning is of the most startling character. The war between the Free-State men and their enemies has commenced in very earnest. Lawrence has been attacked; its citizens have been slaughtered or driven from their homes, and the town has been destroyed. Such is the substance of a telegraphic dispatch received from St. Louis. It may or may not be true; but from the events that have lately taken place in the Territory, we have not been without forewarnings of this disastrous intelligence. Nevertheless, in the report that has reached us there are particulars which bear upon their face the stamp of unmitigated falsehood. We are told that two Pro-Slavery men, while traveling from Lecompton to Franklin, were hailed by a party of Free State men who demanded their names and destination. This question was answered, whereupon the Free-State men immediately fired on the two. One was wounded, but the other, so the story goes, shot the leader of the party, *and the remainder fled.* The tale is too absurd to be credited for a moment. In the first place the source (the St. Louis *Republican*) is suspicious. That journal, throughout the whole of the Kansas difficulties, has taken a violent party side, and its correspondents have never scrupled at misstating facts. But there is other and more positive evidence that the account is incorrect; and we venture to assert that when the truth is known—if there be any foundation for the story at all—the parties to the transaction will be reversed. Our own advices from Kansas, as well as those published in other Northern journals, have established the fact that armed Pro-Slavery parties, during the last six weeks, have been prowling round Lawrence, exercising a surveillance over its citizens, questioning those who go out and come in, arresting those whom they saw fit, in defiance of all law, and in other ways displaying unchecked and odious villainy. It is in keeping with their antecedents that a party of Missouri ruffians should murder or attempt to murder two citizens on their way from Lecompton to Franklin, but in times when they were most sorely pressed and most severely tried, the Free-State men have never even been accused of committing a similar outrage. We therefore cast from us this part of the story as altogether too improbable for belief.

The intelligence in relation to the attack on Lawrence is of the briefest description. One dispatch to the St. Louis *Democrat* states that a battle had been fought at Lawrence, and that a number of persons had been killed on both sides. Another dispatch from Boonville to the *Republican* says simply, "Lawrence was destroyed on Wednesday." The two accounts, so far, corroborate each other, and a telegraphic dispatch received in Washington from Louisville, Ky., is to the same effect. We greatly fear that the news is true, or, at least, partially so. Wednesday was the day previously fixed upon by the ruffians for their attack, and though the citizens of Lawrence have declared over and over again that they would offer no resistance to the Federal authorities,

the determined and vindictive hatred of their invaders is too well known for us to expect that this would deter them from their purpose. Their numbers were so greatly superior to those of the Free-State party, that the latter scarcely had a chance, as though they were fighting with savages instead of men of their own blood and country, their only hope was in flight, or if that was impossible, in selling their lives as dearly as they could.

The particulars of this event will be looked for with an interest rarely if ever felt by the people of the Free States. We know not yet who have fallen—who, for the first time since the Revolutionary struggle, are to be recorded in our country's history as martyrs to freedom. The first battle in Kansas has been fought; but let not the invaders, the abettors, or the instruments of this great wrong, fancy, in the insolence of power, that the free men of Kansas are to be subdued. The end has yet to come.

"Poor Pierce," June 9, 1856

The uproar and bloodshed that marked "Bleeding Kansas" overshadowed the 1856 presidential election. Although President Pierce had not initiated the legislation that sparked the battles, his sympathy for the southern states ensured that he would not win the Democratic nomination again. In an attempt to steer clear of the domestic divide engulfing the country, the Democrats instead chose James Buchanan, who had served the United States abroad in the Pierce administration.

If Pierce should ever feel like amusing himself with the pen after retiring . . . what a book he might write on the ingratitude of parties!

JUNE 9, 1856
POOR PIERCE.

Just four years ago Franklin Pierce was a rising man; he was the nominee of the Baltimore Democratic Convention for the Presidency, and all eyes were turned towards him as the sun and hope of his party; a hundred pens were busy in writing his biography, cannon were fired in all parts of the country in demonstrations of joy at his nomination, and thousands of politicians were hurrying to his home in Concord to congratulate him on his felicity, and to receive a gracious smile from his countenance. He was the man of the hour. But now? After being three years in office he is deserted by his party, he is hung in effigy in his native town, he is fast sinking into the obscurity from which

he was accidentally dragged, and his former rival is now the cynosure of Democratic eyes. If Pierce should ever feel like amusing himself with the pen after retiring to the deep shades of domestic life in New-Hampshire, what a book he might write on the ingratitude of parties! What a sinking of the heart, what a terrible revulsion of feeling such a man must experience as he looks back upon his official career and reflects that all his subserviency and debasement, the sacrifice of principle, and the laceration of conscience, which he has suffered, to conciliate the political Mokanna in whose hands he placed his destiny, have failed to gain him the respect or confidence of that insatiable power.

The Slaveocracy aim at power, and no considerations can induce them to sacrifice the chance of success to a generous impulse. Four years ago Buchanan was shoved aside because he was unavailable; and now, having, fortunately for himself, been placed where he could not be identified with the movement which has crushed all his former rivals, he is the only available candidate they could light upon. Three years spent at the Court of St. James, in making pleasant speeches at Lord Mayors' feasts, in writing diplomatic notes, and paying visits of ceremony in courtly circles, have made Mr. Buchanan available for the Presidency. It was a remarkable course of training for such a piece of good fortune. But poor Pierce, with all the resources of the Government at his command, has been unable to secure for himself the empty honor of a renomination. He was taken up, in the first place, because he was unknown, and now he is spurned because he is known. The feelings of this Belshazzar of the White House, as he read the *mene, mene,* of the telegraph, without the aid of an interpreter, on Friday, could hardly find a compensation in the remembrance of his three years of Presidential glory. He is doomed to see a lurking smile of contempt in the faces of all who visit him between now and the close of his official career in March, and to be conscious of retiring to private life poorer in reputation, and in all that makes life happy, than when he emerged from it to accept the perilous honors bestowed upon him.

In addressing the crowd that rushed to the White House, on Saturday, to serenade the rejected candidate, he made a speech which must have sadly contrasted with his secret feelings. His rejection by the Cincinnati Convention was neither more nor less than an open proclamation to the whole world that his conduct in the Presidency has been such that his party did not dare to renominate him, either because they feared defeat by the people with him for their candidate, or because they did not consider him competent to discharge the duties of the office. Else, why should they reject him? Virginia, who had been the first to give him her vote in 1852, would not now pay him the empty compliment of a ballot. His position before the country is a more humiliating one than any occupant of the White House has yet filled. But, he has had his day, and though he has a little longer official existence to linger out, he is already among the things that were. He is as dead, politically, as any of his predecessors in the exalted office, which, unhappily for the peace of the country, in an evil hour he was elected to fill. But why should not Mr. Pierce have been renominated, since the policy of his administration is to be continued by Mr. Buchanan if he should be elected? It is rather remarkable that in all the speeches that have been made by his friends applauding the nomination of his successor, not a single apology has been offered, nor a reason given for rejecting Pierce.

THE PRESIDENCY OF JAMES BUCHANAN

MARCH 4, 1857 – MARCH 4, 1861

The presidency of James Buchanan was marked foremost by the increasingly certain path to civil war. Although Buchanan was a northern Democrat, he had strong prosouthern sympathies about slavery and opposed its abolition. Consequently, Buchanan strived to protect states that permitted slavery and to unite his party around this position. He failed in both areas, and by the time he departed office in 1861, the secession of southern states from the Union had begun. As a result, the Buchanan presidency is noted for leading the nation toward civil war, not for the president's campaign goal of easing sectional conflict. Economic challenges and foreign affairs, although important aspects of the Buchanan administration, are overshadowed by what followed his term in office.

A Pennsylvania native, Buchanan graduated from Dickinson College in 1809 and became a lawyer, but spent most of his prepresidential career in state and national politics. He served in the Pennsylvania legislature before going to Congress, where he represented his state in both the House of Representatives and the Senate. Buchanan also served as secretary of state from 1845 to 1849 under James Polk and as ambassador to Great Britain from 1853 to 1856 under his predecessor, Franklin Pierce. With strong party loyalties, Buchanan sought primarily to maintain harmony among Democratic factions divided over slavery. His quiet leadership style was one of accommodation rather than initiative, which ultimately proved to be insufficient to address the challenges at hand.

THE 1856 CAMPAIGN

Because he was serving abroad during the Pierce administration, Buchanan avoided the acrimonious battles over whether slavery should be permitted in new U.S. territories. He won the Democratic nomination in 1856 largely because he had not taken a public position on the controversial Kansas-Nebraska Act of 1854, which permitted new territories to vote on whether to permit slavery. The law had led to civil unrest

Source: Library of Congress

A SERVICEABLE GARMENT —
OR REVERIE OF A BACHELOR.

and bloodshed in what became known as "Bleeding Kansas," costing the incumbent president, Franklin Pierce, his party's nomination for a second term. Buchanan was selected on the seventeenth ballot, and John C. Breckinridge of Kentucky was chosen as his vice-presidential running mate.

Buchanan's main competition for the presidency was from the newly created Republican Party, which nominated John C. Fremont of California for president. The Republican Party had replaced the Whig Party, and it was dominated by its antislavery wing. Also in the race was former president Millard Fillmore of New York, who was nominated by

QUICK FACTS ON JAMES BUCHANAN

BIRTH	April 23, 1791, Cove Gap, Pa.
EDUCATION	Dickinson College Law studies
FAMILY	Bachelor
WHITE HOUSE PETS	Herd of elephants (present from King of Siam); pair of bald eagles; Newfoundland ("Lara")
PARTY	Democratic
PREPRESIDENTIAL CAREER (SELECTED)	U.S. House of Representatives, 1821–1831 U.S. minister to Russia, 1832–1833 U.S. Senate, 1834–1845 Secretary of state, 1845–1849 U.S. ambassador to Great Britain, 1853–1856
PRESIDENTIAL TERM	March 4, 1857–March 4, 1861
VICE PRESIDENT	John C. Breckinridge
SELECTED EVENTS	Supreme Court's *Dred Scott* decision (1857) Defeat of proslavery Lecompton Constitution in Kansas (1858) John Brown's raid of federal arsenal, Harper's Ferry, Virginia (1859) Secession of southern states (1860–1861) Formation of Confederate States of America (1861)
POSTPRESIDENCY	Retirement
DEATH	June 1, 1868, Lancaster, Pa.

the American, or "Know-Nothing," Party. In this three-way race, Buchanan won about 45 percent of the popular vote and only four of fourteen northern states in the Electoral College. Most telling, many northern Democrats voted for Fremont to demonstrate their frustration with their proslavery partisans.

THE BUCHANAN ADMINISTRATION

Buchanan did not ease the fears of northern Democrats with his cabinet appointments, which included slaveholding southerners for prominent positions, such as Howell Cobb of Georgia for secretary of treasury and John B. Floyd of Virginia for secretary of war. Although Buchanan appointed northerners as well, he chose men who shared his prosouthern stance. His choice for secretary of state was Lewis Cass

of Michigan, who was not active in office due to ill health, and Attorney General Jeremiah Black of Pennsylvania, who had strong southern sympathies. Many Democrats endorsed Illinois senator Stephen A. Douglas's view that new states should vote on whether to permit slavery within their borders, but Douglas's supporters were not part of Buchanan's inner circle of advisers.

The only president to remain a bachelor throughout his term, Buchanan invited his niece, Harriet Lane, to serve as his official hostess. He socialized frequently with his cabinet officers, inviting them and their wives to dine with him on a regular basis. Buchanan's close association with advisers who shared his views on slavery served to insulate him from the growing dissension within the country and to strengthen his desire to maintain stability in the slaveholding states.

Major Issues

President Buchanan was forced to confront the slavery debate from the outset of his term because the Supreme Court issued its most significant ruling on the issue just two days after his inauguration. The Court held in *Dred Scott v. Sandford* that the Constitution defined slaves as property, and therefore slavery could not be banned in any U.S. territories. By ruling the Missouri Compromise of 1820 unconstitutional, the *Dred Scott* case mounted a direct assault on the abolitionist movement, paving the way for the Civil War. Buchanan had stated in his inaugural address that he would accept the Court's decision, and in this case, it matched his own views.

The president's reaction to other slavery disputes further illustrated his opposition to abolition. When Kansas settlers in 1858 approved a proslavery constitution, known as the Lecompton Constitution (after the town where it was drafted), Buchanan advocated the admission of Kansas to the Union as a slave state, even though only a minority of settlers had voted. The Lecompton Constitution ultimately failed in a second vote, despite Buchanan's intervention. In 1859 abolitionist John Brown led an armed rebellion in Harpers Ferry, Virginia, which was intended to spark a slave revolt. The assault was quickly halted, but Buchanan feared further such violence and sought to ensure that the Democratic Party would endorse congressional candidates who would support stability and protect the interests of southern states.

Buchanan's party leadership illustrated his continuing desire to protect proslavery interests. Just as his cabinet appointments favored southern interests, so, too, did his campaigns for fellow Democrats. In the 1858 midterm elections, for example, Buchanan opposed Senator Douglas's reelection because Douglas had criticized the Lecompton Constitution in Kansas and called for popular sovereignty to determine the permissibility of slavery there. Douglas kept his seat, but he would face Buchanan's opposition again in the 1860 presidential election.

The 1860 Election

Buchanan had pledged to serve only one term, and his party did not encourage him to do otherwise, but it could not agree on a successor. A fractured Democratic Party ultimately nominated three presidential candidates in 1860, and the splintered vote fostered the election of the first Republican president, Abraham Lincoln. After fifty-seven ballots at its first convention in Charleston, South Carolina, the Democrats held a second convention in Baltimore, where Senator Douglas won the nomination. But southern Democrats held a separate convention and endorsed Vice President Breckinridge of Kentucky for president, with Buchanan's support. A third group of Democrats, who called themselves the Constitutional Union Party (formerly the American Party that had nominated Millard Fillmore in 1852) nominated John Bell of Tennessee for president. The dispute over slavery had shattered the party of Andrew Jackson.

The divisions displayed with the Democratic Party's multiple presidential nominations carried through to the general election. Douglas fared best with more than 1.3 million votes, while Breckinridge garnered nearly 850,000, and Bell won almost 600,000. But Lincoln won the election, to Buchanan's dismay.

Buchanan opposed secession, but he did not mount a strong defense of the Union, and on December 20, 1860, South Carolina seceded, followed soon after by Mississippi, Florida, Alabama, Georgia, Louisiana, and Texas. By the time Buchanan left office, federal troops were guarding Fort Sumter in South Carolina, with conflict on the verge of eruption.

Although no single person at the time likely could have prevented the Civil War, James Buchanan contributed to the growing conflict with his support for the southern wing of his party at the expense of the north. Furthermore, he failed to keep southern states from seceding after Lincoln was elected. The pressure of the office took its toll on Buchanan, and he was eager to pass on the burden to his successor. Any opportunities for compromise among the states had passed, and the next president would govern in wartime.

"Decision of the Supreme Court in the Dred Scott Case," March 7, 1857, and "The Dred Scott Decision," July 15, 1857

The momentous *Dred Scott* decision by the Supreme Court in March 1857 narrowly interpreted the Constitution to hold that slaves were not U.S. citizens and that Congress lacked the power to prohibit slavery in U.S. territories, as it had done in the Missouri Compromise of 1820. Scott was a slave from Missouri who had lived for many years in so-called "free" territory and maintained that doing so established his freedom. But Chief Justice Roger Taney declared that Scott could not file suit because he was not a citizen, and furthermore, that Congress should not have declared some U.S. territory to be off-limits to slavery.

The New York Times' opinion on the Court's ruling came four months later, a delay that would be unthinkable today. *The Times* did not view the ruling as revolutionary, declaring that it "did not decide adversely to the abstract rights of any class or race of men to citizenship in the United States." *The Times* further insisted that the ruling did not make the Missouri Compromise unconstitutional. *The Times'* position was consistent with the Court's narrow reading of the Constitution, but this interpretation is not accepted today.

MARCH 7, 1857
LATEST INTELLIGENCE.
BY TELEGRAPH TO THE NEW-YORK DAILY TIMES.

Magnetic Telegraph Co.'s Offices—5 Hanover-st., and 181 Broadway.

IMPORTANT FROM WASHINGTON.
Decision of the Supreme Court in the Dred Scott Case.
The Ordinance of 1787 and the Missouri Compromise Declared Unconstitutional.
MR. BUCHANAN'S CABINET.

Washington, Friday, March 6.

The opinion of the Supreme Court in the Dred Scott case was delivered by Chief Justice Taney. It was a full and elaborate statement of the views of the Court. They have decided the following important points:

First—Negroes, whether slaves or free, that is, men of the African race, are not citizens of the United States by the Constitution.

Second—The Ordinance of 1787 had no independent constitutional force or legal effect subsequently to the adoption of the Constitution, and could not operate of itself to confer freedom or citizenship within the Northwest Territory on negroes not citizens by the Constitution.

Third—The provisions of the Act of 1820, commonly called the Missouri Compromise, in so far as it undertook to exclude negro slavery from, and communicate freedom and citizenship to, negroes in the northern part of the Louisiana cession, was a Legislative act exceeding the powers of Congress, and void, and of no legal effect to that end.

In deciding these main points, the Supreme Court determined the following incidental points:

First—The expression "territory and other property" of the Union, in the Constitution, applies "in terms" only to such territory as the Union possessed at the time of the adoption of the Constitution.

Second—The rights of citizens of the United States emigrating into any Federal territory, and the power of the Federal Government there depend on the general provisions of the Constitution, which defines in this, as in all other respects, the powers of Congress.

Third—As Congress does not possess power itself to make enactments relative to the persons or property of citizens of the United States, in a Federal Territory, other than such as the Constitution confers, so it cannot constitutionally delegate any such powers to a Territorial Government, organized by it under the Constitution.

Fourth—The legal condition of a slave in the State of Missouri is not affected by the temporary sojourn of such slave in any other State, but on his return his condition still depends on the laws of Missouri.

As the plaintiff was not a citizen of Missouri, he, therefore, could not sue in the Courts of the United States. The suit must be dismissed for want of jurisdiction.

JULY 15, 1857
THE DRED SCOTT DECISION.

When the country was convulsed by the tidings that the Supreme Court, at Washington, in deciding upon the claims of a negro man, named Dred Scott, to the possession of his own person, had laid down the doctrine that, under the Constitution of the United States, no person of the African race could be a citizen of this Union, we declined pronouncing upon the merits of the case, for the good and sufficient reason that the news of this extraordinary result could not be accepted as authentic before its verification by the accurate publication of the Decision itself. . . .

And it now appears that the Supreme Court, in deciding the case of Dred Scott, did not decide adversely to the abstract rights of any class or race of men to citizenship in the United States. Three of the Judges, it appears, went out of the record of the case to express an opinion of this sort—which is worth just as much as any other *obiter dictum*, and no more—while of the rest of the bench, one, Judge Curtis, took occasion to express a directly contrary opinion; two, Judges McLean and Catron, are known to have expressed a directly contrary opinion in former cases, and three expressed no opinion at all on the subject.

The delivery of this opinion occupied about three hours, and was listened to with profound attention by a crowded Court-room. Among the auditors were gentlemen of eminent legal ability, and a due proportion of ladies.

In the bitterness of our dissent, therefore, from the doctrines volunteered by the Chief Justice and his two associates, we must be very careful not to stigmatize the Supreme Court as an enemy to freedom—for the Supreme Court has done nothing whatever to invite such a stigma. The *obiter dicta* of the Pro-Slavery Justices have a political value of which we must not lose sight, and illustrate in a very striking way the tendencies of opinion in certain sections of this country. But they have absolutely no other value, and illustrate nothing else.

Equally unfounded is the impression, that in the Dred Scott case, the Supreme Court pronounced the Missouri Compromise unconstitutional. This subject, also, was not within the purview of the Judges in the case before them; and here again applies the principle recognized by the Supreme Court, that nothing shall be held to be a decision of that Court, which is not a decision of a subject actually before it. An able article in the current number of the *Law Reporter*, discusses the whole case with singular clearness and ability, and those who would estimate more fully for themselves the value of the decision, cannot do better than to read that paper, which is attributed, we may add, to two gentlemen of the Suffolk Bar, Mr. Horace Gray, Jr., and Mr. John Lovell.

"The Lecompton Constitution," February 1, 1858, and "A Lecompton Trap," March 26, 1858

In the continuing battle over whether slavery should be permitted in Kansas, *The Times* criticized the Lecompton Constitution as well as President Buchanan's support of it. *The Times* declared that Buchanan sought to move Kansas out of the public eye by accepting the Lecompton Constitution, which permitted slavery, but that such a step would, in fact, achieve the opposite. Because only a minority of Kansas settlers had voted in favor of the document, its approval by Congress would never be viewed as legitimate. *The Times* called for popular sovereignty to decide the issue, optimistically stating that this approach would bring "peace to the Territory and satisfaction to the country at large." A letter to the editor further criticizes the Lecompton Constitution, warning that if enacted, the groundswell of opposition would be so great that it would lead to civil war. The charter was not approved, but the letter writer's fears nevertheless would prove prophetic.

> The South and the North demand of him opposite and hostile action in regard to it [Kansas]. He cannot satisfy both.

FEBRUARY 1, 1858
THE LECOMPTON CONSTITUTION.

The attempt of the Administration to secure the admission of Kansas under the Lecompton Constitution, is not without a very strong and a very plausible motive. The President desires to end the Kansas controversy. The affairs of this Territory have occupied too large a share of the public attention, and he seizes, with the eagerness of disgust, upon the earliest opportunity to remove the Kansas question from the field of national politics, by drawing around it the high walls of a State organization. When Kansas once enters the Union, her interests and her political contests, her rights and her wrongs, her Constitution and her laws, cease to be national affairs and become matters of purely local concern. Congress and the Executive cease to be responsible for Kansas. Her wounds no longer afflict the body politic, and claim no surgery from the Federal head.

Mr. Buchanan has strong personal reasons for eagerly desiring such a consummation. His official and political prosperity depends upon it. Kansas was the rock on which his predecessor split, and it lies full and high in his own political channel. The South and the North demand of him opposite and hostile action in regard to it. He cannot satisfy both: and so long as the subject remains open and requires action at his hands, so long is he certain to offend one section or the other. It is perfectly natural, therefore, that he should desire to banish it from the political field,—and

that he should seize upon the first opportunity that chance may offer, to place Kansas in the condition of a Sovereign State and thus get it off his hands altogether.

But beyond this personal and party motive, the condition and necessities of the country second this earnest wish of the President. The people at large sympathize with it. The great mass of the people, in all sections, would gladly see the Kansas question disappear from the field of national politics. They are sick of the whole subject. They are disgusted with the long series of wrong, of violence, of perfidy, of fanaticism and reckless folly, which constitutes its history for the last three years. They have seen it used so long for party ends, that they have come to look upon the whole trouble as the result of party schemes, as the deliberate work of designing men, and have ceased to feel any special interest in its incidents or any marked concern in its issue. The extreme factions are alone interested in prolonging the contest. The fanatical Abolitionists and the fanatical Disunionists both hope that strife may grow out of it, which will involve the Territory and the whole country in civil war, and thus bring about their common object, the dissolution of the Federal Union. Active leaders of the Republican Party see also, in the prolongation of the issues to which this question has given rise, the means of securing for the North in 1860 an absolute ascendancy in the Federal Government. But the mass of the people do not sympathize with these motives. They would gladly see the whole thing end and would indorse and approve any measure, not absolutely inconsistent with justice and the principles of republican democracy, which would banish the Kansas question forever from the halls of Congress.

Mr. Buchanan relies upon this popular sentiment to sustain him in forcing upon Congress the adoption of the Lecompton Constitution. He thinks that when the deed is done,—when Kansas has once become *a State,* no matter under what circumstances or with what Constitution, the whole contest will be ended,—the question will disappear from Congress and the people will gladly turn their attention to other topics. If these expectations seemed to us to be well-founded, we should be strongly inclined to urge the policy upon which they rest. If Kansas alone were concerned in the issue, and if her admission under the Lecompton Constitution would restore peace to the Territory and give to her people the quiet and undisturbed control of their own affairs, we could at least find excuses for a course of action which promised such results. But there are circumstances connected with this case which should cause the President and Congress to pause before taking such a step.

In the first place, if Kansas is admitted under the Lecompton Constitution, it will be against the expressed will of a large majority of her inhabitants. Congress is empowered to "*admit*"—but not thus to *force*—new States into the Union. And if a new State may thus be added, under a Constitution passed by a packed Convention, upon the application of a minority, and regardless of the will of the great majority of her inhabitants, why may we not hereafter see State after State brought in as the will or the convenience of a reckless dominant party may require? The admission of Kansas now would create a precedent for Arizona, New-Mexico, and new States in Texas, which would certainly be followed whenever the special interests of the party in power may require.

Besides this, Mr. Buchanan must see that the course he is pursuing is absolutely certain to throw Kansas into the hands of the ultra Free-State leaders, and to make it one of the most aggressive Abolition States in the Union. Gov. Walker forewarned him of this result long ago, with the sagacity, and with something of the unscrupulous partisanship of long political experience. Gov. Walker assured the President, in his official letters, that the only way to make Kansas a Democratic State was for the Democratic Party to take the lead of the unquestionable and irresistible Free-Soil sentiment of the State. They could not *defeat* it, but they might *guide* and control it. If Mr. Buchanan had followed this advice, he could not have made Kansas a Slave State, but he might have made it a Democratic State.

As things now stand, if he forces the Lecompton Constitution upon them, he drives into the Republican ranks the great mass of the Free State Democrats:—he exasperates the public feeling of the whole State: he gives prodigious strength to the ultra Free-Soil agitators:—he secures two Free-Soil Senators, and two or three Free-Soil members in Congress: and he plants upon the borders of the Slaveholding section, by the side of Missouri, and at the gateway of the great West, a State as thoroughly and as fiercely Abolition in its sentiments and its efforts as Vermont or Massachusetts. We find it quite impossible to perceive how his Administration is to be strengthened, or the peace and welfare of the country promoted by such a result.

These consequences are likely to follow the adoption of the Lecompton Constitution, even if the people of Kansas should assent to that measure. But there is abundant reason to apprehend that they would not assent to it, or permit it to go into operation. After the clear and unmistakable evidence afforded by the late elections that a large majority of the people are opposed to that instrument, it is scarcely to be expected that they should permit it to be forced upon them. If the Free State officers are elected, it is possible that they might use the power of the Constitution to secure its overthrow. But if the opposite party receive certificates of election, unless the most trustworthy sources of information mislead us, they will never be permitted to exercise the functions of their office. They will be driven from the Territory, and nothing but the direct intervention of the federal troops can protect them for a single day in the performance of their official duties.

We believe that the most direct escape from the difficulties of the case will be found in *the acceptance of the recent elections as decisive of the popular will, and in yielding to the vote of the majority.* Let Congress assume that the people of Kansas have the right to decide upon their own Constitution;—that the 13,000 who voted *against* the Lecompton document are entitled to outweigh the 6,700 who voted in its favor;—and that the minority application,—which is actually no application at all, for admission, shall be rejected,—and the way would at once be smoothed for a satisfactory adjustment of the whole difficulty. The Territorial Legislature, with Governor Denver, would remain in possession of full authority: and they would summon a new Convention to frame a new Constitution, which could be submitted to the people, and, if approved, sent to Congress before the expiration of its present session. No party and no section could object to such a proceeding: it would be strictly in accordance with justice, with precedent and with popular rights; and it would end the controversy in the only way which promises peace to the Territory and satisfaction to the country at large.

MARCH 26, 1858
LETTER TO THE EDITOR
A LECOMPTON TRAP.

To the Editor of the New-York Times:

Will you allow a plain man, one who is not a politician, to call your attention to a phase of this *Kansas affair,* which he has not seen noticed before.

The American public must be well satisfied by this time that the Lecompton Party will not, as it has not heretofore, stop at any fraud that will give them power.

It is declared in the act of admission, "that nothing in this act shall be construed to abridge or infringe any right of the people, asserted in the Constitution of Kansas, at all times, to alter, reform, or abolish this form of government, &c.," and then Congress goes on to disavow any power to interfere with the said Constitution. Now strike out the words "asserted in the Constitution of Kansas," and it will be all right. But with them in, how are they to alter their form of government, but as that instrument dictates?

Again, if Mr. Calhoun, by leaving the Territory, has lost his right, (as Senator Douglas says he has,) to issue the certificates of election to the Republican members, what shall prevent, in his absence from the Territory, the President *pro tem.* of the Convention from issuing these certificates to the Lecomptonites as soon as Kansas shall be declared a State. If he does so, and I have no doubt that he will, what power short of a revolution by the people themselves, shall prevent such a legislature from re-enacting all those test oaths, and other infernal laws of the first fraudulent legislature, and thereby disfranchising all Republicans in their future attempts to modify their laws.

If the ideas I have given above are at all plausible, would it not be well for Northern members of Congress to pause and consider their actions before bringing upon the country so great an evil as a civil war.

Yours, W. W. J.

"SENATORIAL CONTEST IN ILLINOIS—SPEECH OF MR. LINCOLN," JULY 16, 1858, AND "ADMINISTRATION WAR ON DOUGLAS," OCTOBER 2, 1858

President Buchanan played a role in the Illinois Senate race of 1858 by opposing incumbent senator Stephen A. Douglas, even though they were both Democrats. Angered by Douglas's rejection of the Lecompton Constitution in Kansas, Buchanan opposed the senator's reelection and pressured others in Illinois to do the same. Douglas ultimately defeated his Republican opponent, Abraham Lincoln, without presidential support, but Lincoln's campaign would serve him well in the 1860 presidential race.

The seven Lincoln-Douglas debates are hallmarks of American campaign rhetoric and continue to be widely studied and referenced today. When the senatorial campaign formally began about a month before the first debate, *The Times* noted that Lincoln would be a formidable opponent, given his supporters in the Republican Party leadership as well as in the former Whig Party. *The Times* also aptly described President Buchanan's "personal animosity" toward Douglas, which hurt the senator in his quest for the presidency two years later.

JULY 16, 1858
SENATORIAL CONTEST IN ILLINOIS—SPEECH OF MR. LINCOLN.

The Republican candidate for United States Senator, the Hon. Abraham Lincoln, was present, on Saturday evening, when Mr. Douglas made his address, published in Tuesday's Times, to the crowd assembled in honor of his arrival at Chicago. On Monday evening Mr. Lincoln replied to his distinguished competitor; and we give his speech in full this morning. He, too, received an enthusiastic welcome, and the war between the two champions was fitly inaugurated in the chief city of Illinois. Both the speeches were able, and marked, we are glad to say, by respectful courtesy no less than by unsparing political antagonism.

It will be seen that Mr. Lincoln places himself upon the strictest party grounds. In assuming this position he disappoints the expectations of a portion of his political friends at the East, who had hoped to see Mr. Douglas rewarded for his Anti-Lecompton services by the support of the Illinois Republicans. But this was scarcely practicable, and Mr. Douglas himself, who has ever been a partisan of the straitest sect, could hardly have expected his life-long opponents to sustain him. Indeed, he evinces no wish to conciliate them, but goes into the fight with all his accustomed gallantry, and with more than his usual *prestige,* waging unsparing war, as well upon the Republican forces as upon the supporters of the Buchanan Administration.

We judge from the manifestations at Chicago, that all the old Whig feeling is aroused in favor of Mr. Lincoln, and that the leaders, if not the masses, of the Republican Party will feel a peculiar gratification in the defeat of Mr. Douglas. He has been so long the invincible leader of the Democracy in Illinois, and has triumphed so often over the routed forces of the old Whig Party, that something like a personal interest is felt by every Republican politician in his overthrow.

Until November, therefore, the contest will go on with unceasing vigor. Mr. Douglas has an undertaking on hand which will task his utmost powers, and he is not the man to flinch from a contest because the odds are against him.

President James Buchanan, seated at the end of the table, meeting with his cabinet in 1858. He would soon face discontent and a number of resignations.

Source: Collection of the New-York Historical Society

OCTOBER 2, 1858

Administration War on Douglas.—The conflict between President Buchanan and Senator Douglas is daily assuming more and more the character of embittered personal hate. Especially is this the case on the side of the Administration. Our special Washington dispatch this morning announces the approaching removal of Mr. Faran, the Cincinnati Postmaster, for the crime of defending Douglas. It is but a short time since Mr. Buchanan appointed Faran, whom he is now about to sacrifice.

The President is not able to control his party in this war, a considerable portion of which, at the South as well as at the North, openly sympathizes with the Illinois Chieftain in his audacious revolt. But the office-holders can be reached; and it has been given out that every one of these who ventures to say a word in favor of Douglas shall suffer speedy decapitation. Mr. Buchanan must long ago have seen the futility of attempting to make the Lecompton Bill a party test. When even the Slave States refuse to stand by him on that issue the case is manifestly hopeless. Personal animosity must therefore be the motive in the war waged upon Douglas' friends.

"THE VIRGINIA INSURRECTION," OCTOBER 19, 1859

The short-lived seizure of a federal arsenal in Harpers Ferry, Virginia, in October 1859 and the subsequent execution of rebel leader John Brown heightened national concerns over antislavery insurrection. Brown, who had previously led an attack on proslavery settlers in Kansas, hoped to spark a slave revolt with the Harpers Ferry raid, but the rebellion did not materialize. Though injured in the fight, Brown managed to stand trial, where he grandly and fervently promoted the case against slavery. He was convicted of treason and executed, becoming a martyr for the abolitionist movement. As *The Times* concluded, "He will probably pay the penalty of his rash insanity with his life, and leave, we trust, no inheritors of his passion or his fate." Events soon proved otherwise, despite the efforts of the Buchanan administration.

OCTOBER 19, 1859
THE VIRGINIA INSURRECTION.

The insurrection at Harper's Ferry, which startled the public yesterday morning, though sufficiently alarming at the outset, proves to have been but a short-lived affair. It was very speedily crushed by the formidable military forces brought against it from Washington, Baltimore and Virginia,—but, unhappily, not without serious loss of life. The parties actively engaged in it seem never to have numbered over fifty or sixty, though ten times that number were before the close of the affair induced or coerced into an apparent support of the movement. So far as appears, it was not the result of any combination among the slaves themselves, but was merely the explosion of a clumsy plot concocted by a single man, John Brown, of Kansas notoriety, with the aid of his two sons and one or two other accomplices.

Brown, it will be remembered, suffered severely, in the loss of his property and in the death of one of his sons, during the reign of ruffianism in Kansas. He was a fearless, fanatical, energetic old man to begin with, and the death of his son made him nearly frantic. Having sworn vengeance against the authors of his calamities, he made himself very conspicuous, and universally dreaded by the ruffians, during the subsequent troubles in Kansas. He was the leader of the fight at Ossawatomie, where he was said to have killed several of the invading borderers with his own hand. After the troubles in Kansas had been quieted, Brown's uneasy spirit extended its resentment to the Missourians, and especially to the slaveholders whom he regarded as the authors of his wrongs. He entered into plots for promoting the escape of their slaves, and succeeded in getting twenty or thirty of them away, and in so alarming the slaveholders throughout that section of the State, that they forthwith commenced sending their slaves to the Southern States. He himself escaped unharmed, and came, it now appears, over a year ago to the neighborhood of Harper's Ferry, and commenced preparations to renew his operations in Virginia. It was the very general belief of those who knew him in Kansas that Brown, after the death of his son, became insane upon this subject; and his proceedings in this affair certainly give countenance to the belief. A wilder and more hopeless project than that in which he embarked cannot well be imagined.

There seems to be no reason for believing that the plot had any extensive ramifications, or that any further danger is to be apprehended. Yet the affair can scarcely fail to startle the public mind in Virginia, and it may have the same effect as Brown's movements had in Missouri, and increase, largely and rapidly, the transfer of slaves from Virginia to the more Southern States. Every such outbreak, from whatever causes it may spring, quickens the public sense of the insecurity of slave property on the borders of the slaveholding States, and so tends to the removal southward of that frontier.

As a matter of course, the violent partisan prints will seek to make the most of the affair. But we see no reason for supposing that it had any connection whatever with any political movement, or that any party can with justice be held responsible for it. It seems to have been the work of a single man,—smarting under a sense of personal wrong, and insanely seeking to avenge them upon a whole community. He will probably pay the penalty of his rash insanity with his life, and leave, we trust, no inheritors of his passion or his fate.

• •

"What Mr. Buchanan Means," December 22, 1860, and "The President's Message," January 11, 1861

Led by South Carolina, southern states began to secede from the Union following Lincoln's election to the presidency in 1860. As a lame-duck president with four months left in office, Buchanan was unable to please either unionists or secessionists, declaring that secession was unconstitutional but also expressing sympathy for southern grievances against the Union. *The Times* initially was skeptical of Buchanan's leadership, criticizing what it called the president's "complete disloyalty to the country and the Constitution." But after Buchanan took steps to protect Fort Sumter, South Carolina, from rebel attack, *The Times* viewed his leadership more favorably, even applauding "the old Jacksonian ring" in the president's words.

DECEMBER 22, 1860
EDITORIAL
WHAT MR. BUCHANAN MEANS.

In his Message Mr. Buchanan urges the necessity of making certain specified amendments to the Constitution. He believes them necessary to secure the rights of the Southern States. He does not believe that Congress or the country is prepared to concede them now,—or that they would have any chance of success if presented and urged in the ordinary way, and on the ordinary motives which govern public action. But he *does* believe that if the Southern States, or any considerable number of them, were to withdraw from the Union,—organize themselves into a new Confederacy *for the purpose of negotiation,* and then offer to come back on condition that these amendments should be made,—the North would assent at once, and thus secure the end desired.

This, therefore, is the plan on which he is managing this secession business. He is playing a political game on behalf of the Southern States. He is favoring the secession movement,—not with a deliberate purpose of permanently dissolving the Union, but with a view to give the slaveholding States new guarantees in the Constitution. He has done everything in his power thus far to aid secession. He has argued its rightfulness in his Message,—he has kept its leaders and promoters in his counsels and his Cabinet, he has withdrawn every obstacle from its path, and he will go to the utmost limit, compatible with safety, in making the General Government subservient to its objects and its plans. When it has been accomplished, then will come the time for negotiation. And it will be for those then in power to say, whether they will restore the Union on the new basis proposed,—or permit it to fall to pieces and drift into the condition of the Republics of Mexico and South America.

This, we have reason to believe, is the programme of Mr. Buchanan. It is marked by his characteristic reliance upon intrigue, and his constitutional crookedness of purpose and policy. It lacks, a good many elements essential to success,—common sense and a knowledge of the temper of the people being among them. As President of the United States he has the power to try the experiment. He can make secession successful,—that is, he can bring about the withdrawal of five or six of the Gulf States, and enable them to put themselves in a position to open negotiations on this subject, without any difficulty. He will find the task easy. It involves nothing but *quasi* perjury and complete disloyalty to the country and the Constitution. These are small sacrifices for him to make, for the gratification of political resentments and the prospect of a partisan triumph. He has already entered into negotiations and engagements with the Secessionists, by which he hopes to escape the necessity of enforcing the law, and defending the forts;—but if he should be deceived in his expectations, he will surrender both.

The new Administration must expect, therefore, to find these complications on its hands when it comes into power. It will find several States nominally out of the Union,—and ready to negotiate for a return.

> " Mr. Buchanan seems finally to have shaken off the political nightmare which has oppressed him for so many years. "

JANUARY 11, 1861
EDITORIAL
THE PRESIDENT'S MESSAGE.

In the Message transmitted by the President to the Senate of the United States on last Wednesday, we find in a single phrase the key unlocking many secrets of Mr. Buchanan's later policy—the partial explanation and apology for nearly all his former short-comings with reference to the question of secession. "Time," writes the President, "is a great conservative power"—an axiom one of the clearest in itself, in certain limited aspects, but capable of infinite mischief when perverted by designing advisers into the plea and excuse for passivity, while the treason in which they were participants was being extended and organized. "Do nothing," said Cobb. "Let the evil cure itself. Time is a great conservative power." And the same plea, we may well imagine, was urged by Floyd as an excuse for not sending the necessary reinforcements to Fort Moultrie. "Time is a great conservative power," whispered the President to himself; and, with a conscientious desire to avoid bloodshed, the dulcet sophistry of this phrase was accepted for much more than it is worth.

But now that James Buchanan has been released from the bondage and blindness inflicted on his Administration by corrupt and traitorous advisers; now that he is surrounded, in at least the most important posts of his Cabinet, by honest and patriotic officers, who have the perpetuity of the Union at heart, and who report to him faithfully the actual condition of affairs, as brought to their knowledge from the most authentic sources, we find the President entering boldly on a new and energetic career of duty, rendering it not only quite possible, but quite probable, that he may yet redeem to a great extent all the errors of the past, and survive in history as "one who meant well for his country." An old man at the time of his election, and thoroughly imbued with the routine discipline of the party which had elevated him to power, it is not perhaps so much to be wondered at that he should have surrendered the active control of his Government to the intriguing and daring politicians thrust into his Cabinet by the clamors and importunities of the extreme South, as that he should eventually have found the will and the firmness to free himself from their ruinous and deceitful yoke.

Many of the declarations in his last Message savor strongly and warmly of a patriotic devotion worthy of the best days of the Republic. In the phrase, "Time is a great conservative power," we find the sedative argument so long and successfully used by those Cabinet recreants who were exerting all the powers of their official positions to break up the Government of which they were the perjured and unworthy servants. But the day of awakening has at last arrived, and Mr. Buchanan seems finally to have shaken off the political nightmare which has oppressed him for so many years. He begins to realize that time is not a conservative power, but the very reverse, when the house in which one lives has caught fire; or when a cancer is gnawing away the flesh; or when treason to the Constitution is organizing for armed collision with the supporters of that instrument. Time is the destroyer of things, not the preserver, and it is no less dangerous to temporize with rebellion than to allow a fire to gain headway within the walls of a powder magazine.

Coming late to the President as this knowledge has come, we feel none the less grateful for the frank and firm disposition which he now manifests to retrace his deviations from the path of national duty, and to redeem the unwitting errors of policy into which he was led by false and interested advisers, in whose counsels he so long reposed implicit

faith. His declaration of the "clear and undeniable right" and duty of the National Government "to use military force defensively against those who resist the Federal officers in the execution of their legal functions, and against those who assail the property of the United States," cannot fail to have a most wholesome effect upon such of the Southern States as still remain amenable to reason. It has much of the old Jacksonian ring in its nervous utterance, and has been welcomed by loyal citizens of all sections, with but little distinction of party. Let Mr. Buchanan persist in this policy for but a few weeks longer, and the services of his closing days of office may yet entitle him to a high pedestal amongst the patriots whom our posterity will delight to honor.

THE PRESIDENCY OF ABRAHAM LINCOLN

MARCH 4, 1861 – APRIL 15, 1865

The presidency of Abraham Lincoln in many ways marked the second founding of the United States. The Framers of the Constitution had argued over whether slaves should be permitted in the new country, and the compromises of 1787, such as the constitutional provision that a slave would count as three-fifths of a person for determining a state's population and number of seats in the House of Representatives, would no longer suffice. Over the course of Lincoln's presidency, the country would come to the brink of collapse in the Civil War and then renew itself as a new nation that disavowed the morally abhorrent doctrine of slavery.

Lincoln's background did not suggest that he would rise to become

THE UNDECIDED POLITICAL PRIZE FIGHT.

Source: The Granger Collection, New York

one of the finest presidents of the United States—indeed, the one most often ranked as "great" in presidential ratings surveys. Lincoln worked on a farm at an early age and had little formal schooling, never attending college. His family moved from Kentucky to Indiana, where his mother died in 1818, when he was nine. His father remarried in 1819, and his father and stepmother later moved the family from Indiana to Illinois. As a young adult, Lincoln volunteered for the army, but he never saw action on the battlefield. He married Mary Todd in 1842, and they had four sons, two of whom died in childhood. Only one son, the eldest, lived to old age.

Despite his limited education, Lincoln read extensively on his own, and he practiced law before entering politics. He served in the Illinois state legislature and then went on to complete one term in the U.S. House of Representatives, as a member of the Whig Party. As that party declined, Lincoln joined the movement to create the new Republican Party. He ran unsuccessfully for the Senate twice and competed for the party's first vice-presidential nomination in 1856.

On the most significant issue of the day, Lincoln was a firm opponent of slavery, although he did not advocate equality between blacks and whites. At the Illinois Republican Party's first convention in 1856, Lincoln spoke out against slavery, and his audience was so engaged that the reporters did not take notes. He declared in accepting the senatorial nomination in 1858 that "A house divided against itself cannot stand," and he made several stirring statements about the morality of abolishing slavery in the well-known debates with his opponent, Democratic senator Stephen A. Douglas. Douglas won the race, but Lincoln rose to national prominence during the campaign, which would assist him greatly in seeking the presidency two years later.

THE 1860 ELECTION

The 1860 election illustrated the nation's divisions over slavery. The Democratic Party had three candidates, representing northern states, southern states, and as some remnants

QUICK FACTS ON ABRAHAM LINCOLN

BIRTH	February 12, 1809, Hodgenville, Ky.
EDUCATION	Little formal schooling; independent law studies
FAMILY	Wife: Mary Todd Lincoln Children: Robert Todd Lincoln, Edward Baker Lincoln, William Wallace Lincoln, Thomas "Tad" Lincoln
WHITE HOUSE PETS	Cats, dogs ("Jip" was president's dog), goats ("Nanny," "Nanko"), pig, ponies, rabbit, turkey ("Jack")
PARTY	Republican
PREPRESIDENTIAL CAREER (SELECTED)	U.S. Army volunteer, 1832 Postmaster, New Salem, Ill., 1833–1835 Illinois legislature, 1835–1841 U.S. House of Representatives, 1847–1849 Candidate for Republican vice-presidential nomination, 1856 Lincoln-Douglas debates in U.S. Senate race, 1858
PRESIDENTIAL TERMS	March 4, 1861–March 4, 1865 March 4, 1865–April 15, 1865
VICE PRESIDENTS	Hannibal Hamlin; Andrew Johnson
SELECTED EVENTS	Start of Civil War (1861) Battle of Antietam (1862) Emancipation Proclamation (1862, 1863) Battle of Gettysburg; Gettysburg Address (1863) Reelection (1864) End of Civil War (1865) Assassinated by John Wilkes Booth (1865)
DEATH	April 15, 1865, Washington, D.C.

of the Whig Party. Of all the Democrats, Senator Douglas received the most votes, but he carried only one state (Missouri) in the Electoral College (plus three votes from New Jersey). The Republican convention had nominated Lincoln on the third ballot and selected Hannibal Hamlin of Maine for the vice-presidential spot. In the general election, Lincoln won eighteen states and nearly 60 percent of the Electoral College vote, but he received less than 40 percent of the popular vote, as the southern states all voted for the southern Democratic candidate, John C. Breckinridge of Kentucky.

Within weeks of Lincoln's election, the southern states seceded from the Union, starting with South Carolina and followed soon after by Alabama, Florida, Georgia, Louisiana, Mississippi, and Texas. These seven states formed the Confederate States of America, and they elected Jefferson Davis of Kentucky as their president in February 1861. Two weeks later, Lincoln was inaugurated.

THE LINCOLN ADMINISTRATION

Lincoln's cabinet consisted of the secretaries of state, treasury, war, navy, and interior as well as the attorney general and postmaster general. Only the State Department was headed by the same person, William H. Seward of New York, throughout Lincoln's presidency. Seward had competed for the Republican presidential nomination, as had several others that Lincoln appointed to his cabinet: Salmon P. Chase of Ohio, who became treasury secretary; Simon Cameron of Pennsylvania, who became secretary of war; and Edward Bates of Missouri, who became attorney general. Historian Doris Kearns Goodwin has aptly described Lincoln's cabinet as a "team of rivals."

First Lady Mary Todd Lincoln, born in Kentucky like her husband, did not play an active role in her husband's presidency. She had family members who served in the Confederate Army, which sparked controversy about her own loyalties. Of the Lincolns' four children, one died before turning four, and another died at age eleven in the White House in 1862. This tragedy overshadowed the rest of Lincoln's presidency.

Major Issues (First Term)

Lincoln's presidency quickly became a wartime administration, as the president called for troops to protect Fort Sumter, South Carolina, from rebel forces in April 1861. Exercising unprecedented executive power, Lincoln imposed an economic blockade on southern states, doubled U.S. troops, and suspended the writ of habeas corpus (the right of prisoners to have a court hearing to determine if the state has legal grounds to detain them). Lincoln took all of these actions without calling Congress into special session, even though Article II of the Constitution specifically authorizes the president to do so.

With his Civil War leadership, Lincoln employed what historians have since termed "prerogative power," or authority that is assumed without explicit constitutional provision. Lincoln defended his actions, declaring that "measures *otherwise unconstitutional* might become lawful by becoming indispensable to the preservation of the nation" (emphasis added). In other words, actions that would be considered unconstitutional in normal times would be justified by the exigencies of war. When Chief Justice Roger B. Taney wrote in *Ex parte Merryman* (1861) that the president could not constitutionally suspend the writ of habeas corpus, Lincoln ignored the decision.

Congress and the Supreme Court largely upheld Lincoln's actions, although the Court did rule in *Ex parte Milligan* (1866) that the government could not try civilians in military courts in areas where the civilian court system was operating. But coming a year after the war ended, the decision circumscribed presidential power retroactively, that is, in theory, not practice. Support from the other branches of government combined

with retrospective public approval justified Lincoln's actions, despite the lack of constitutional grounding.

At the beginning, the war went badly for the Union. Confederate forces prevailed in the First Battle of Bull Run in 1861, and repeated their victory one year later. Lincoln went through several generals in the war's early years, one of whom, Gen. George B. McClellan, won a Union victory at the Battle of Antietam in September 1862. To celebrate the victory, Lincoln issued a preliminary Emancipation Proclamation, declaring that slaves in rebel states would be freed unless the war ended and those states returned to the Union. On January 1, 1863, Lincoln issued the Final Emancipation Proclamation, freeing the slaves in the rebellious states.

One of the costliest battles of the Civil War took place in Gettysburg, Pennsylvania, where Union forces under the command of Gen. George G. Meade prevailed over Confederate troops in July 1863. Visiting the battlefield later that fall to dedicate the soldiers' cemetery, Lincoln gave perhaps the most famous speech of his presidency. Harking back to the Declaration of Independence, Lincoln reminded listeners that from its creation, the nation had been "dedicated to the proposition that all men are created equal." And consistent with the Constitution, the nation would have "a new birth of freedom," in which "government of the people, by the people, for the people, shall not perish from the earth."

In addition to planning for the postwar reintegration of the South into the Union, Lincoln had to contend with domestic protests about the war. He sent troops to New York City in 1863 to control riots that formed in opposition to conscription. A few months later, Lincoln presented a plan for postwar reconstruction, in which a state would form a civilian government when one-tenth of its voting population from 1860 had declared loyalty to the Union. But some of the president's own party members, who would become known as Radical Republicans, opposed the so-called "10 Percent Plan," because it did not guarantee voting rights for black citizens and the 10 percent threshold was too low. Two Republicans, Rep. Henry W. Davis of Maryland and Sen. Benjamin F. Wade of Ohio, introduced a different plan—the Wade-Davis bill—that would require 50 percent of a state's population to swear allegiance to the Union, but Lincoln pocket-vetoed the bill.

The 1864 Campaign

In opposing Wade-Davis, Lincoln may have sought to present himself as a moderate voice in his party that would facilitate the reentry of rebel states into the Union, particularly given the upcoming presidential election. With the nation at war, another president might well have decided that holding an election would be too burdensome, but Lincoln insisted that the country uphold this fundamental democratic tradition. Although some Republicans, including Treasury Secretary Chase, initially contested Lincoln's nomination, the president was nominated on the party's first ballot. To attract more supporters, the Republican Party renamed itself the Union Party for the election, and it selected Sen. Andrew Johnson of Tennessee, a southerner who supported the Union, as Lincoln's running mate. Lincoln soundly defeated the Democratic candidate, General McClellan, winning 2.2 million votes to McClellan's 1.8 million, and more than 90 percent of the Electoral College vote.

A Brief Second Term

For his second term, Lincoln hoped to recreate the Union both by bringing back the southern states and by guarantee-

ing political rights and economic opportunities for the newly freed black population. The Confederacy began to fall with the capture of Atlanta in September 1864, and Gen. Robert E. Lee surrendered at Appomattox on April 9, 1865, just over a month after Lincoln's second term began. In his second inaugural address, Lincoln emphasized forgiveness and reconciliation, concluding: "With malice toward none, with charity for all, with firmness in the right as God gives us to see the right, let us strive on to finish the work we are in, to bind up the nation's wounds."

Lincoln did not live long enough to enact the vision that he laid out so eloquently for his second term. On April 14, 1865, John Wilkes Booth shot the president as he and Mary Lincoln watched a play at Ford's Theater in Washington, D.C. Lincoln died hours later. His body lay in state at the White House and the Capitol rotunda for five days, after which a twelve-day funeral procession brought him to Springfield, Illinois, for burial. Lincoln's legacy was the preservation of the Union that he had fought so hard to keep; reconstituting the nation would be the responsibility of his successors.

- -

"Reasons for Voting the Republican Ticket," November 2, 1860

This letter to the editor shows that popular support for Lincoln in 1860 stemmed foremost from his commitment to protecting the Union. The author emphasizes that the Constitution is what is most important to the nation, *not the president*. Slavery underlay the divisions between North and South, and this letter illustrates the view that the country might resolve the dispute over abolition while remaining intact—a hope that soon would diminish with secession and war.

NOVEMBER 2, 1860
REASONS FOR VOTING THE REPUBLICAN TICKET.

To the Editor of the New-York Times:

Will you permit a man who has not one penny to gain or to lose by the success or failure of any of the candidates for the Presidency now before the public, to state his reasons for the vote he expects so soon to give. And before stating these reasons, I wish to say a few things in reference to myself.

1. I am no politician; and for *mere* politicians I have a great disregard. They are not to be trusted by fair men.

2. I am no Abolitionist; in public and private I have opposed abolitionism as insane philanthropy, as tending to aggravate the evil it would remove, yet I am no Pro-Slavery man.

3. I am a minister who believes the Old School Presbyterian Church to be *the* Church of this land, as to its catholic and conservative spirit, and as to the intelligence of its ministry and membership. And with its deliverances on the Slavery subject I cordially coincide. This much you will permit me to say for myself, in order that my reasons may be free from the imputation of improper motives.

I have made up my mind to vote for Lincoln;—not because he is the best man that could have been selected from his party; not because he is a more able man than his competitors; not because I expect from him a more patriotic administration than from Douglas, Breckinridge or Bell; but,

1. Because I wish it to be definitely settled that the majority of the people of this land have the right to say who shall be their President.

2. Because I am sick, to the highest point of disgust, with the cry of disunion from the South. I wish the cry to be stopped; and nothing will stop it sooner, or better, than the election of Lincoln.

3. I wish to satisfy the South that they are as safe under the rule of a Republican as of a Democratic President. And the only way fully to satisfy them is to put the question to a fair trial, by the election of Lincoln.

4. I wish to have it settled that the Constitution of the United States is the safeguard and bulwark of all our interests, North and South, and not the President, from whatever party he may be selected. When the Constitution is violated, then is the time to resist, or to secede, if the violator cannot be brought to justice according to law.

5. The question as to whether a citizen with Republican views may be safely elected as President, has to be settled sooner or later; now is the best time to settle it.

6. I believe that Lincoln is a fair man in ability, up to the average of our Presidents hitherto; of fair moral character, and that with patriotic integrity, he will administer the Government, as to every part, and every interest, of the country.

7. I like a *straight-out* man of whatever party. If not honest in his convictions, he is in his actions. I have a strong disrelish for *fusion* movements and men. It is seeking to do, by unfair means, what they cannot do by fair.

These are my reasons for the vote which I expect to give for Abraham Lincoln in a few days. And I invite all those who consider these reasons to be good ones, to vote with me. The election of Lincoln I shall esteem a political blessing to the whole country.

John Witherspoon.

"The Republicans now have it in their power to lay the basis for the most useful, popular and permanent administration the country has seen for a long time. But they must not conceal from themselves the obstacles which they will be compelled to encounter.

"The Election—Lincoln Triumphant," November 7, 1860

Writing the day after the presidential election, *The New York Times* recognizes the significance of Lincoln's victory, declaring that it will keep slavery from further expanding throughout the country. Yet *The Times* understates the difficulty of this task, only referring obliquely to "obstacles" that the Republican Party will face in controlling the slave-holding states.

NOVEMBER 7, 1860
EDITORIAL
THE ELECTION—LINCOLN TRIUMPHANT.

It is too early to speak confidently of detailed results of yesterday's election. But there can be no reasonable doubt that the Republicans have elected their President. It has been universally conceded that the issue lay with New-York,—and New-York casts her vote for Lincoln. What the majority will be cannot yet be known. We believe, however, that it will fall very little, if any at all, below our estimate of 40,000. Pennsylvania has very largely increased her majority of October, and there is no reason to doubt that the New England States and the West are largely Republican.

We have no disposition to exult over this victory, signal and important as it is. The contest, on the part of the Republicans, has been throughout one of principle;—on the part of their opponents it has been waged almost exclusively on the basis of fear. There has been no union of principle among them,—nor have they been able to concentrate their strength upon a single candidate. The result is what might have been expected,—disorganization, demoralization and defeat.

This election will inaugurate a marked and most important change in the administration of the Government. The policy of extending Slavery, and increasing its political power, will now be checked. The Slave interest will no longer impose its claims and its law upon the Federal Government. The Constitution will no longer be regarded as a mere instrument for fortifying and increasing Slavery. The African Slave-trade will not be reopened, and more vigorous and effective measures will be taken for its suppression.

But above all, we shall have established at Washington a rule of honesty and patriotism, in place of the corruption, imbecility and intrigue which have controlled our public councils for the last few years. It is quite time we had a change in these respects. The Republicans now have it in their power to lay the basis for the most useful, popular and permanent administration the country has seen for a long time. But they must not conceal from themselves the obstacles which they will be compelled to encounter.

• •

"THE NEW ADMINISTRATION," MARCH 5, 1861

With its multiple headlines emphasizing the importance of the event, *The Times* presented extensive, in-depth coverage of Lincoln's inauguration, which occurred on March 4, 1861. It was a solemn affair, coming as it did just weeks after the Confederate states recognized Jefferson Davis as their president. Lincoln spoke of the fundamental need to uphold the Constitution, and he prophetically warned, "In *your* hands, my dissatisfied fellow-countrymen, and not in *mine,* is the momentous issue of civil war." Yet the new president himself soon would have to take action to protect U.S. property from the southern rebels, and thus began the Civil War.

MARCH 5, 1861
THE NEW ADMINISTRATION.

Abraham Lincoln President of the United States.

THE INAUGURATION CEREMONIES.

A Tremendous Crowd and No Accidents.

THE INAUGURAL ADDRESS.

How it was Delivered and How it was Received.

AN IMPRESSIVE SCENE AT THE CAPITOL.

Mr. Lincoln's First Audience at the White House.

Visit of the New-York Delegation to Senator Seward.

MR. SEWARD MAKES A SPEECH.

What was Done at the Grand Inauguration Ball.

MISCELLANEOUS INCIDENTS OF THE OCCASION.

OUR WASHINGTON DISPATCHES.

Washington, Monday, March 4.

THE DAWNING OF THE DAY.

The day to which all have looked with so much anxiety and interest has come and passed. Abraham Lincoln has been inaugurated, and "all's well."

At daylight the clouds were dark and heavy with rain, threatening to dampen the enthusiasm of the occasion with unwelcome showers. A few drops fell occasionally before 8 o'clock, but not enough to lay the dust, which, under the impulse of a strong northwest wind, swept down upon the avenue from the cross streets quite unpleasantly. The weather was cool and bracing, and, on the whole, favorable to the ceremonies of the day. . . .

RECEPTION OF THE INAUGURAL.

The opening sentence, "Fellow-citizens of the United States," was the signal for prolonged applause, the good Union sentiment thereof striking a tender chord in the popular breast. Again, when, after defining certain actions to be his duty, he said, "And I shall perform it," there was a spontaneous, and uproarious manifestation of approval, which continued for some moments. Every sentence which indicated firmness in the Presidential chair, and every statement of a conciliatory nature, was cheered to the echo; while his appeal to his "dissatisfied fellow-countrymen," desiring them to reflect calmly, and not hurry into false steps, was welcomed by one and all, most heartily and cordially. The closing sentence "upset the watering pot" of many of his hearers, and at this point alone did the melodious voice of the President elect falter.

Judge Taney did not remove his eyes from Mr. Lincoln during the entire delivery, while Mr. Buchanan, who was probably sleepy and tired, sat looking as straight as he could at the toe of his right boot. Mr. Douglas, who stood by the right of the railing, was apparently satisfied, as he exclaimed, *sotto voce,* "Good," "That's so," "No coercion," and "Good again."

THE OATH OF OFFICE.

After the delivery of the address Judge Taney stood up, and all removed their hats, while he administered the oath to Mr. Lincoln. Speaking in a low tone the form of the oath, he signified to Mr. Lincoln, that he should repeat the words, and in a firm but modest voice, the President took the oath as prescribed by the law, while the people, who waited until they saw the final bow, tossed their hats, wiped their eyes, cheered at the top of their voices, hurrahed themselves hoarse, and had the crowd not been so very dense, they would have demonstrated in more lively ways, their joy, satisfaction and delight.

SHAKING HANDS.

Judge Taney was the first person who shook hands with Mr. Lincoln, and was followed by Mr. Buchanan, Chase, Douglas, and a host of minor great men. A Southern gentleman, whose name I did not catch, seized him by the hand, and said, "God bless you, my dear Sir; you will save us." To which Mr. Lincoln replied, "I am very glad that what I have said causes pleasure to Southerners, because I then know they are pleased with what is right."

"About Fort Sumpter," March 18, 1861

President Lincoln's determination to protect a federal fort in South Carolina from rebel attack provides an early illustration of his views on executive power. *The Times* asks whether the president has the power to raise troops independently to protect the garrison, then known as Fort Sumpter, suggesting that the executive should have that power, but also noting that the previous Congress did not specifically grant such authority. Lincoln, however, did not wait for congressional approval to take action.

MARCH 18, 1861
EDITORIAL
ABOUT FORT SUMPTER.

There is probably not a particle of truth in the report so widely circulated that orders have been issued to Major Anderson to surrender Fort Sumpter. Indeed, we have good reason, if not authority, for saying that, in spite of all that has been said on the subject, the proposition to surrender that fort has not been considered, *nor even made,* in the councils of the President at Washington.

In the Inaugural Mr. Lincoln proclaimed his purpose to use the force at his command to hold, occupy and possess the forts and other property belonging to the United States. The only question which has been discussed in the Cabinet, so far as Fort Sumpter is concerned, is how this pledge can be fulfilled. Instead of proposing its surrender, the President has called upon the proper Departments for information as to the means of reinforcing it. He desires and intends to retain it, and will use all the means at his command, and resort to every measure which the law and the public good will sustain him in employing, for the accomplishment of that end. He desires to reinforce Fort Sumpter with both men and provisions; and has taken the first step towards executing that design, by calling upon the proper military authorities for information as to the force required for that purpose.

It is understood that Major Anderson regards it as nearly impossible for any vessel to reach the gates of Fort Sumpter, in face of the batteries erected to guard the entrance of the harbor. No matter what armament she might carry, nor what destruction she might cause, she would inevitably be sunk before reaching the Fort. If this opinion, however, should prove to be incorrect, and one or more vessels should reach the gates, the fires of three heavy batteries could be concentrated upon that point and render their disembarkation impossible without fearful loss, if not the entire destruction of the force. It will be remembered that while firing blank cartridges for practice at Morris Island, not long since, one of the guns proved to have been shotted, and the ball struck the threshold of the gate of Fort Sumpter. A prompt apology was made on the pretext that the shot was accidental;—but it is not easy to load a cannon with ball accidentally; and it is much more likely that it was deemed important to test the range and aim of guns, trained upon a particular point for a specific purpose. Whether accidental or not, the shot proved the feasibility of destroying any force that might land at the gates of the Fort.

It becomes indispensable, therefore, to *take these hostile batteries* as the first step towards reinforcing the Fort. Upon this point, we believe, the President and his Cabinet are agreed. Every military and naval officer who has been consulted concurs in the opinion that a force must be landed sufficient to take these batteries,—and that a reinforcing vessel can only enter the harbor after this has been accomplished. The next point, therefore, is, what force is required for this purpose? Major Anderson, we believe, thinks it could not be done with less than 20,000 men,—while Gen. Scott believes it may be attempted, with a fair probability of success, with 12,000. It is not probable that the President will act against the advice, or disregard the opinion, of the Commanding General; he will, therefore, not attempt to reinforce the Fort with less than this force, properly supported by vessels of war.

The next question to be decided, therefore, is whether he has authority, under the law, to raise such a force; and this, we presume, is the point on which his action will turn. If he has such authority, he will probably exercise it and reinforce the Fort. If not, we presume he will scarcely be expected to make the attempt. The last Congress, it is well known, failed to pass any law enlarging his powers with reference to the present emergency.

Whether laws already in existence give him that authority, is a point on which the opinion of his Attorney-General will be required. If that is favorable, we shall look for immediate and vigorous measures for the reinforcement of Fort Sumpter. If it is unfavorable, and Major Anderson is compelled, either with or without an engagement, to surrender the Fort, it will only show with what success the last Administration pursued its policy of disarming the Government, and placing it at the absolute mercy of the Southern traitors.

• •

"THE HABEAS CORPUS, AND THE MERRIMAN CASE," JUNE 2, 1861

When the Civil War began, President Lincoln suspended the writ of habeas corpus, saying that wartime prohibited the normal functioning of civilian courts. The Constitution says habeas corpus may be suspended only "when in Cases of Rebellion or Invasion the public Safety may require it," but it does not grant this power to the chief executive; indeed, this statement appears in Article I, which discusses Congress. Yet when secessionist John Merryman—the court misspelled his name—of Maryland was arrested in 1861, the military would not surrender him in response to a writ from Chief Justice Roger Taney. When Taney asked Lincoln to comply, the president refused. *The Times* noted that technically, habeas corpus had not been suspended because Taney was free to issue his writ; at the same time, the U.S. Army was justified in its noncompliance because "The country was at war." This conflict between the executive and judicial branches of government illustrated the difficulty of imposing boundaries on presidential power in wartime.

JUNE 2, 1861
EDITORIAL
THE HABEAS CORPUS, AND THE MERRIMAN CASE.

There is a vast deal of patriotic indignation among the Southern sympathizers just now, over what they are pleased to term the unconstitutional suspension of the *habeas corpus* by Gen. Cadwallader. They affect to see infinite danger to constitutional freedom in his refusal to surrender a military prisoner in his custody, and in the further refusal to give up his command, and yield himself a prisoner upon the attachment issued for his arrest. If these cavilers would take time to consider the nature and office of the writ of *habeas corpus*, and the facts of the case which they criticise so severely, we think that, unless their sympathies are permitted to control their deliberate judgment, their convictions on this subject would be changed.

We concede fully the value and importance of the writ of *habeas corpus*. We regard it as one of the most essential instrumentalities for the preservation of liberty, but it should be remembered also that it may be used to shield villainy and protect guilt against merited punishment. We will concede, too, for the sake of the argument, that the power to suspend this writ exists only in Congress, though, as a practical fact, we hold that exigencies may arise when the President or a commanding officer of a military district may lawfully suspend it for the time being. Whether we are right or wrong in this opinion is immaterial now, for the reason that there has been no suspension of the *habeas corpus,* by Gen. Cadwallader or any one else. It is one thing to prohibit or suspend the right of issuing the writ at all, and another and very different thing to deny its authority in a particular instance. A sheriff making an illegal arrest, may rightfully be required to produce his prisoner before the magistrate issuing the writ, while a general having fought a battle and captured a regiment of the enemy, would be entirely justified in refusing to obey the mandate of a judge requiring him to parade his captives in Court. It is a great fallacy to suppose that the civil authority is at all times, and under all circumstances, superior to that of the military. In the presence of an enemy, when there is actual danger of collision, when the strong arm of physical force is necessary to save the country from imminent peril, the civil power must give way, for the time, to the military. It needs no constitutional provision, no legislative enactment, to legalize its authority. It is inherent in the nature of things, existing from necessity, growing out of, and is a part of the great law of instinct and self-preservation, which is higher than Constitutions, older and stronger than the statute book.

In the case under consideration there was no "suspension" of the writ of *habeas corpus*. Judge Taney was at perfect liberty to issue his writ and enforce obedience to its mandates in all cases within its legitimate province. In every case of civil arrest under the forms of civil process or by color of the civil authority, there was no impediment in his way. But the difficulty is that this was not such a case. The country was at war. Call it a rebellion if you please, a revolt, or by any other name, still it was an organized war, with armies confronting each other with weapons and array prepared for battle. The danger of collision was imminent. The Government itself was in peril. Under such circumstances, Gen. Cadwallader, the commander of the Government forces and of a military district, found within his jurisdiction a man holding a commission in the ranks of the enemy, aiding them by enlisting men for their service, by inciting an armed mob to attack and kill the Government troops, by burning bridges and destroying railroads to cut off communication between the Government forces, and he made him a prisoner. . . . In our judgment, he acted wisely, and in accordance with legal and constitutional right. Any other course would have furnished at once the pretext and the precedent for the release of every prisoner taken by the army so long as Judge Taney retained the physical ability to issue his writ.

• •

"Increase of the Regular Army," July 9, 1861

To fight southern secession and protect U.S. interests, such as Fort Sumter, Lincoln increased the armed forces without seeking congressional approval. Congress, as *The Times* noted, likely would (and did) support such measures, but Lincoln's decision to take action without calling Congress into emergency session raised questions about the expansion of executive power in wartime. *The Times* supported Lincoln's action, even suggesting that a larger increase would be needed, and that the country now required a standing army for its own security.

July 9, 1861
Editorial
INCREASE OF THE REGULAR ARMY.

The expediency of an increase of the regular army of the United States is generally admitted, and the steps taken by President Lincoln to augment that branch of the service by the addition of 25,000 men will, no doubt, meet the ready approval of Congress. The entire number of the regular army will then be 42,000 men; and so far from attracting attention as a large force, we are sure it will generally be regarded as quite too small; considering the proportions the rebellion has attained, and the probability of extensive and lingering conflicts ahead.

In his suggestions on the subject of the proposed increase of the regular army, Secretary Cameron rightfully enough remarks that, in accordance with precedent, it may be reduced at the close of the war, if then found too large. And he adds that, in making such reduction, "a just regard to the public interests would imperatively require that a force amply sufficient to protect all the public property, wherever it may be found, should be retained." With only such increase as the Secretary contemplates, it is not at all likely that at the close of the war any reduction of the regular army would be found compatible with the National security. At the beginning of the present rebellion, the regular army bore no proportions to the territory they should have been able to protect, nor to the forces that on a sudden were marshaled against them. In many cases property of the United States Government, costing millions of dollars, had not a dozen bayonets to guard it; and at no time in the incipiency of the rebellion was it possible for the Government to have concentrated, at any point of threatened attack by rebel force, so insignificant a force as 5,000 men, within six weeks from the date when their presence became necessary. If such was the weakness of the Government with an authorized regular army of about 20,000 men, will the mere doubling of that force be adequate to the necessities of the Nation in this time of actual war? . . .

There has been a deep popular prejudice in this country against so-called "standing armies." This prejudice springs from two causes; first, the expense of maintaining an army; and, secondly, the apprehension of danger to the liberties of the people. With regard to the expense of a regular army, we think it is already clear that it would have been economy of life, treasure and liberty, to have had a regular army of 50,000 men on the 4th of March last; and that it will be true economy and prudence to keep at least 75,000 regulars in service for several years to come. With regard to the danger to the liberties of the people, there is no reason to fear, in a country of such vast extent of territory as this, where the nature of the service would keep the force we have indicated so much dispersed. It is only when large bodies of soldiers are kept together, and allowed to become a distinct and ruling element in a city or State, that their solidarity and selfishness become dangerous elements to a free society. And this danger, supposed to attach exclusively to a "standing army," will be found an inherent evil of any large bodies of soldiers, even of volunteers, if kept for years in the service, as the vicissitudes of the Government may in future require.

One very strong reason in favor of relying, to a much greater extent than we have heretofore done, on the services of an adequate regular army for the public defence, is the extremely demoralizing influence of a camp life upon the volunteers. The citizen soldier who goes to war as an honest man and peaceful farmer or mechanic, is in much danger of leaving camp a much worse man in heart and habits. It is a chance if he returns to his plough or his workshop at all, or if he does, with the same health of body and purity of morals that he carried away with him. Who can estimate the fearful evils of disease and debauch that the present war will inflict on the 400,000 men that, on our side, will take part in it?

Another very strong reason in favor of the employment of a regular force, though minor to the above, is the vast and unequal expense of a volunteer soldiery as compared with regulars. We have not at hand the comparisons made by competent authorities, but we believe the cost is nearly as five to one. In volunteer movements everything is extemporized—everything is got up for the special occasion—and consequently everything is charged for at enormous prices. No just conception can be had of the stupendous frauds, impositions, peculations and villainies attending the raising and bringing of volunteer regiments into the field. If all that has been done in this way during the past sixty days could be exposed to the American people—as we hope it may be—it would blow to atoms one of the popular delusions in which we have long been living.

Finally, the act of certain States in the recent peril of the Republic, in refusing to furnish volunteers to the Government when called for according to the Constitution and laws, shows that the Congress and President, who are the exponents of the nation's war power, should have something more instantaneous and reliable for the public defence. There is nothing adequate to the purposes of Government, as experience shows, but a regular army, fitly proportioned to the population and territory to be defended.

"The President's Proclamation," September 28, 1862, and "Emancipation: President Lincoln's Proclamation," January 3, 1863

In the aftermath of the Union's narrow victory on the battlefield of Antietam in 1862, President Lincoln made a historic proclamation: slaves in the unconquered rebel states would be free as of January 1863. *The Times'* 1862 editorial considers the Emancipation Proclamation, and its effects on the country, including slaves. The 1863 article consists of the full text of the Emancipation Proclamation. The president's statement did not go nearly as far as the Radical Republicans wanted, as it did not abolish slavery, and its rationale for freeing some slaves was based on practical and military, not moral, grounds—namely, that the labor disruptions in the affected states would hinder their ability to continue fighting. Nevertheless, the Emancipation Proclamation set the stage for ending slavery, as the newly freed population could not be expected realistically to return to slavery at war's end. Lincoln later would seek to embed abolition in the Constitution through the Thirteenth Amendment, rather than impose it by executive fiat. As *The Times* explained, issuing the proclamation was not an action justified by the Constitution, but a military necessity.

> It is a war measure, overriding State laws and personal rights, striking right at the heart and strength of this atrocious rebellion. . . . It finds its technical and legal justification in "military necessity." Its moral justification will be found in the approval of mankind and the increasing voice of admiration through all future history.

SEPTEMBER 28, 1862
EDITORIAL
THE PRESIDENT'S PROCLAMATION.

The Proclamation of Emancipation by President Lincoln, looking at its possible economical and moral results in the future, is undoubtedly one of the great events of the century. Still, it should be remembered that it has been given out, especially as a military measure, with the authority indeed of Congress, but by the Commander-in-Chief of the armies and navy of the United States, for the purpose of putting down the rebellion.

It is not pretended to be justified by the Constitution, except as a means of self-preservation, even as war itself on the part of the General Government is justified.

It is a war measure, overriding State laws and personal rights, striking right at the heart and strength of this atrocious rebellion. It belongs to the same category with the orders of the Government to bombard rebellious cities or to take the lives of rebellious citizens, or with the measures establishing military governments over States

in armed resistance to the National authority. It finds its technical and legal justification in "military necessity." Its moral justification will be found in the approval of mankind and the increasing voice of admiration through all future history. But what, regarding it as a military measure, will be its peculiar effects?

This war has corrected several wide-spread errors in regard to the race this proclamation is designed especially to affect. We discover that the slaves are by no means so inclined for insurrections or bloody acts of violence as was formerly supposed. They are evidently a remarkably good-natured, mild, forgiving folk, who would far rather run away than attempt any doubtful or perilous venture of insurrection or warfare. We find, too, that, despite all Southern ideal pictures, they are most earnestly desirous of liberty, and have very little attachment for their masters. It is evident, also, that there is much more understanding among them of the questions at issue in this war, and a far more rapid and secret diffusing of intelligence and news through the plantations than was ever dreamed of at the North.

On the 1st of January next, in the States then in rebellion, the slaves will probably generally understand that if they can escape from rebel jurisdiction anywhere within our lines they are free. Should we hold at that time—as we may reasonably expect—Savannah, Mobile, and Charleston, an immense population of this ignorant peasantry will have abandoned their masters' estates and have placed themselves within reach of our protection.

The agriculture of the South will have been almost disorganized; a general sense of insecurity will pervade the rural districts; men who would have enlisted, will prefer to remain for the protection of their homes from dangers, which are all the more terrible from being imaginary; regiments will be obliged to return to guard against this insurrectionary population. Soon, it is probable that the Southern masters, finding themselves losing their property, will resort to cruel preventive measures, which may call out the very outbreaks they were designed to discourage.

A natural result of these large gatherings of able-bodied men within our lines—our own numbers becoming diminished from sickness and battle—will be the arming of them for their own protection and for use, as a kind of *Sepoys* in our armies. This result will be postponed as long as possible, both from dislike of the negro and from dread thus of throwing away the scabbard against the South. But the logic of events, if the rebellion continue, must force it upon us. The burden of the draft, the devilish spirit of the insurrection, the necessity of protecting these refugees in our lines, and the military duty of weakening the enemy, will all compel it. Then all the devil in the fierce passions of the South will be aroused, and in reprisal they will endeavor to make the war a death-struggle, without mercy or any consideration of humanity.

The punishment for this will be terrible and awful, and will involve nothing less than the utter extermination of the slaveholding aristocracy of the Cotton States, and an entire reorganization of society.

How much wiser, how much healthier for the vast future, would be a rational return by the Cotton States to their allegiance, and an acceptance of the wise proposition of the President, affirmed by Congress, organizing a gradual emancipation. They stand now on the verge of an abyss whose depth and horrors no human eye can measure.

With them is the choice, whether to return, or to take the fatal leap.

JANUARY 3, 1863
EMANCIPATION.

President Lincoln's Proclamation.

The Slaves in Arkansas, Texas, Mississippi, Alabama, Florida, Georgia, South Carolina and North Carolina Declared to be Free.

Parts of Louisiana and Virginia Excepted.

The Negroes to be Received into the Armed Service of the United States.

Washington, Thursday, Jan. 1, 1863.

By the President of the United States of America—a Proclamation:

Whereas, on the twenty-second day of September, in the year of our Lord one thousand eight hundred and sixty-two, a Proclamation was issued by the President of the United States containing among other things the following, to wit:

That on the first day of January, in the year of our Lord, one thousand eight hundred and sixty-three, all persons held as slaves within any State or designated part of a State, the people whereof shall there be in rebellion against the United States, shall be then, thenceforth, and *forever free;* and the Executive Government of the United States, including the Military and Naval authority thereof will recognize and maintain the freedom of such persons, and will do no act or acts to repress such persons or any of them in any effort they may make for their actual freedom. That the Executive will, on the first day of January aforesaid, by Proclamation, designate the States and parts of States, if any, in which the people therein, respectively, shall then be in rebellion against the United States, and the fact that any State or the people thereof, shall on that day be in good faith represented in the Congress of the United States by Members chosen thereto at elections wherein a majority of the qualified voters of such States shall have participated, shall in the absence of strong countervailing testimony, be deemed conclusive evidence that such State and the people thereof, are not then in rebellion against the United States."

Now, therefore, I, Abraham Lincoln, President of the United States, by virtue of the power in me vested, as Commander-in-Chief of the Army and Navy of the United States, in time of actual armed rebellion against the authority and Government of the United States, and as a fit and necessary war measure for suppressing said rebellion, do, on this first day of January, in the year of our Lord one thousand eight hundred and sixty-three and in accordance with my purpose so to do, publicly proclaimed for the full period of one hundred days from the day of the first above-mentioned, order, and designate as the States and parts of States wherein the people thereof respectively, are this day in rebellion against the United States, the following, to wit:

ARKANSAS, TEXAS, LOUISIANA—except the Parishes of St. Bernard, Plaquemines, Jefferson, St. John, St. Charles, St. James, Ascension, Assumption, Terrebone, Lafourche, St. Mary, St. Martin, and Orleans including the City of New-Orleans—MISSISSIPPI, ALABAMA, FLORIDA, GEORGIA, SOUTH CAROLINA, NORTH CAROLINA and VIRGINIA—except the forty-eight counties designated as West Virginia, and also the counties of Berkley, Accomac, Northampton, Elizabeth City, York, Princess Ann, and Norfolk, including the cities of Norfolk and Portsmouth, and which excepted parts, are for the present, left precisely as if this proclamation were not issued.

And, by virtue of the power, and for the purpose aforesaid, I do aver and declare that all persons held as slaves within said designated States and parts of States are, and henceforward, shall be free, and that the Executive Government of the United States, including the military and naval authorities thereof, will recognize and maintain the freedom of said persons.

And I hereby enjoin upon the people so declared to be free, to abstain from all violence unless in necessary self-defence, and I recommend to them that in all cases, when allowed, they labor faithfully for reasonable wages.

And I further declare and make known that such persons of suitable condition, will be received into the armed service of the United States, to garrison forts, positions, stations, and other places, and to man vessels of all sorts in said service.

And, upon this—sincerely believed to be an act of justice, warranted by the Constitution—upon military necessity—I invoke the considerate judgment of mankind and the gracious favor of Almighty God.

In witness whereof I have hereunto set my hand and caused the seal of the United States to be affixed.

Done at the City of Washington, this first day of January, in the year of Our Lord one thousand eight hundred and sixty-three, and of the Independence of the United States of America the eighty-seven[th].

(Signed) ABRAHAM LINCOLN.

By the President, Wm. H. Seward, Secretary of State.

"OUR SPECIAL ARMY CORRESPONDENCE," JULY 8, 1863, AND "THE HEROES OF JULY," NOVEMBER 20, 1863

The Battle of Gettysburg marked a turning point in the Civil War, with three days of harsh and bitter fighting resulting in a decisive Union victory. *The Times'* article is written by its special correspondent, L. L. Crounse, who provided readers with a vivid first-hand account of the bloody combat. Four months later, on November 20, President Lincoln traveled to Gettysburg to dedicate the National Cemetery. His short speech—less than three hundred words and given in under three minutes—is among the most memorable in presidential rhetoric and, indeed, in American history.

> " History will never chronicle a tenth part of the gallant deeds performed during these bloody days; but the satisfaction of having nobly performed his duty shall be the sweet recompense of every patriot's heart. "

JULY 8, 1863
OUR SPECIAL ARMY CORRESPONDENCE.
FURTHER DETAILS OF THE GREAT BATTLES OF FRIDAY.

Gettysburgh, Penn., Sunday, July 5.

As the details, the incidents and the general history of the great victory are brought to light, it is clearly defined as the most hotly contested and destructive engagement of the great rebellion. The peculiar feature of the battle is the ferocity and desperation with which it was fought by both armies, and the glorious issue places the lustre of the National arms, and the valor of the Army of the Potomac in the imperishable annals of brilliant history.

The battle occupied three days. Six hours fighting on Wednesday, four hours on Thursday, and including the artillery firing on Friday, thirteen hours that day, making a total of twenty-three hours, during which the battle raged with extreme fury.

The momentous and decisive part of the battle was that on Friday. It began really at daylight, and continued until 10 o'clock, the principal part of the musketry fighting being on the right, with Slocum's corps. A lull of three hours followed, during which the enemy massed his artillery on our centre, held by Hancock with the Second, and Newton with the First corps. At 1 o'clock one hundred and twenty guns opened on that position, and rained shot and shell in a perfect deluge for one hour and forty minutes. A graphic description of this awful period has already been furnished to the Times by an abler pen than mine, for that writer and one of the Times' messengers had the exciting felicity of enduring that storm of iron during the whole time. Mr. Wilkeson is today engaged in the mournful duty of obtaining the remains and effects of his eldest son, the gallant young Bayard, who was mortally wounded on Wednesday, left on the field, and dying finally, after ten hours suffering, without a friend or a word to soothe the dying agonies of his soul. Lieut. Wilkeson was but nineteen years old, yet had command of Battery G, Fourth regular artillery. His death adds another noble soul to the holocaust of this terrible war.

I rode this morning over the entire length of the battle-field, and it is not too much to say, for I have seen nearly every other battle-field in Maryland and Virginia, that the slaughter was perfectly unparalleled. Our details were busily engaged in collecting and burying the dead, and the ghastly, terrible sights were enough to shock a heart of adamant.

The vast number of dead lying in front of Slocum's line, on the right, and of Hancock's and Newton's on the centre, attracted much comment. They had been literally mown down by whole ranks at a single discharge. Slocum accomplished a bloody repulse of Ewell's corps on Friday morning, sustaining but small loss himself, his position being very formidable, against which the enemy insanely charged.

But the field, full of the greatest incidents and the scene of the most desperate fighting, was on the centre, in front of Hancock and Newton, against whom Longstreet's corps was precipitated. The enemy's front was that of one division in line of battle; there were two such lines, and a very heavy line of skirmishers, almost equal to another line of battle. Out of their concealment in the woods they came across the open fields and up the gentle crest, on the top of which was our line—a weak line of men behind a line of defences hastily thrown up and composed partly of stone walls, partly of rifle-pits, and partly of natural projections of soil and rock. The first charge was repulsed; the line broke and fell back before it had reached a point two-thirds the way over. A second line was formed; the officers came to the front, and with the onset of fierce and brutal hearts they rushed. Our men looked with astonishment, while fighting with great vigor; their line was dangerously weak; the defences were not formidable. A few men temporarily gave way; our advance, in some instances, slightly faltered. The artillery engaged was small in force, having been seriously weakened during the early part of the fight. The rebels came on so close that their expressions of fierce rage were plainly distinguished; some of them actually gained the inside of the first wall—but they never returned. Our immortal men, nerved to a degree of desperation never before equaled, poured forth such a devastating fire, and the artillery joining with its terrible canister, that the two long lines of the foe literally sank into the earth. Of the divisions of Pickett and Heth, who made that charge, composed of eight brigades, positively not two brigades returned uninjured across the field. *The color-bearers of thirty-five rebel regiments,* who were in that charge, were shot down, the colors fell on the field, and were gathered by the victorious veterans of the Second corps. Being repulsed, large numbers of the enemy started back on the retreat, but our fire was so destructive that they fell flat on their faces, or again rushed about and implored mercy at our hands as prisoners of war. . . .

History will never chronicle a tenth part of the gallant deeds performed during these bloody days; but the satisfaction of having nobly performed his duty shall be the sweet recompense of every patriot's heart.

The enemy, by a partially secret and ignominious retreat, has awarded to this gallant army the acknowledgment of victory. His forces are now on their way back to Virginia, beaten, weakened and demoralized by a terrible defeat; he is hotly pursued, a victorious army on his rear, a strong local force on his flank, and a swollen river in his front, are the obstacles to his successful retreat.

L. L. CROUNSE.

President Abraham Lincoln's speech at Gettysburg remains one of the most enduring of all presidential addresses.
Source: Brown Brothers, Sterling, PA.

NOVEMBER 20, 1863
THE HEROES OF JULY.

A Solemn and Imposing Event.
Dedication of the National Cemetery at Gettysburgh.
IMMENSE NUMBERS OF VISITORS.
Oration by Hon. Edward Everett—Speeches of President Lincoln,
Mr. Seward and Governor Seymour.
THE PROGRAMME SUCCESSFULLY CARRIED OUT.

The ceremonies attending the dedication of the National Cemetery commenced this morning by a grand military and civic display, under command of Maj.-Gen. Couch. The line of march was taken up at 10 o'clock, and the procession marched through the principal streets to the Cemetery, where the military formed in line and saluted the President. At 11¼ the head of the procession arrived at the main stand. The President and members of the Cabinet, together with the chief military and civic dignitaries, took position on the stand. The President seated himself between Mr. Seward and Mr. Everett after a reception marked with the respect and perfect silence due to the solemnity of the occasion, every man in the immense gathering uncovering on his appearance.

The military were formed in line extending around the stand, the area between the stand and military being occupied by civilians, comprising about 15,000 people and including men, women and children. The attendance of ladies was quite large. The military escort comprised one squadron of cavalry, two batteries of artillery and a regiment of infantry, which constitutes the regular funeral escort of honor for the highest officer in the service.

After the performance of a funeral dirge, by Birgfield, by the band, an eloquent prayer was delivered by Rev. Mr. Stockton. . . .

PRESIDENT LINCOLN'S ADDRESS.

The President then delivered the following dedicatory speech:

> Fourscore and seven years ago our Fathers brought forth upon this Continent a new nation, conceived in liberty and dedicated to the proposition that all men are created equal. [Applause.] Now we are engaged in a great civil war, testing whether that nation, or any nation so conceived and so dedicated, can long endure. We are met on a great battle-field of that war. We are met to dedicate a portion of it as the final resting-place of those who here gave their lives that that nation might live. It is altogether fitting and proper that we should do this. But in a larger sense we cannot dedicate. We cannot consecrate, we cannot hallow this ground. The brave men, living and dead, who struggled here have consecrated it far above our power to add or detract. [Applause.] The world will little note nor long remember, what we say here, but it can never forget what they did here. [Applause.] It is for us, the living, rather to be dedicated here to the refinished work that they have thus so far nobly carried on. [Applause.] It is rather for us to be here dedicated to the great task remaining before us, that from these honored dead we take increased devotion to that cause for which they here gave the last full measure of devotion; that we here highly resolve that the dead shall not have died in vain; [applause] that the Nation shall under God have a new birth of freedom, and that Governments of the people, by the people and for the people, shall not perish from the earth, [Long continued applause.]

Three cheers were then given for the President and the Governors of the States.

"The Reign of the Rabble," July 15, 1863

The multiple headlines in this article demonstrate how unstable the Union had become. Shortly after the Battle of Gettysburg, President Lincoln was forced to send troops to New York City to control the massive rioting that broke out in opposition to the draft. Rioters murdered black Americans and committed arson and other damage before troops restored order.

JULY 15, 1863
THE REIGN OF THE RABBLE.

Continuation of the Riot—The Mob Increased in Numbers.

DEMONSTRATIONS IN THE UPPER WARDS

Encounters Between the Mob, the Metropolitans and the Military.

Large Numbers of the Rioters Killed.

COLONEL O'BRIEN MURDERED AND HUNG.

Streets Barricaded, Buildings Burned, Stores Sacked, and Private Dwellings Plundered.

Gov. Seymour in the City—He Addresses the Mob and Issues a Proclamation.

Increased Preparations on the Part of the Authorities.

The Mercantile Community Aroused—Citizens Volunteering en Masse.

REPORTED SUSPENSION OF THE DRAFT.

The reign of the mob which was inaugurated on Monday morning has not yet ceased, although today will probably witness the end of its infamous usurpation. All Monday night the rioters, unchecked, prosecuted their depredations, and yesterday morning found the lawless spirit not a whit abated. On the contrary, the malignant originators of the disturbance grew bolder at the impunity with which they were necessarily permitted to indulge in their first day's career, and at one time more serious consequences than any which have yet occurred were threatened. Happily, however, the military and police authorities early in the day recovered from the partial paralysis into which the sudden demonstrations of the mob had thrown them, and in sufficient force were able to contend with the truly formidable organization of lawless men. A few wholesome but severe lessons were administered to the rioters during the day wherever they showed themselves most turbulent, and toward evening there seemed to be unmistakable indications that the supremacy of law would soon be acknowledged even by the most rabid of the offenders. Perhaps, however, the mere fact that a score or more of the rioters were killed in the various conflicts with the military and the police was not solely the cause of this abatement of the spirit of violence. The proclamation of Gov. Horatio Seymour, and the announcement, made early in the afternoon, that President Lincoln had ordered the draft in this City to be suspended, may also have had something to do with restoring the malcontents to reason. At any rate, after nightfall the streets were comparatively quiet.

There is no question that the rioting yesterday was engaged in by vastly larger numbers than on Monday, and the spectators of the disorderly scenes were increased also by many thousands. This may be accounted for by the fact that all the large manufacturing establishments were closed, labor on the docks and at the ship-yards was suspended, and every branch of business was arrested, leaving thousands of persons at liberty to participate in the excesses, either passively as spectators, or in an active manner.

In the movements of the mob yesterday, moreover, there was no mistaking the fact that pillage was the prime incentive of the majority. "Resistance to the draft" was the flimsiest of veils to cover the wholesale plundering which characterized the operations of the day.

"The President's Message," December 10, 1863

The Civil War continued after the Battle of Gettysburg, but President Lincoln was already considering how southern states would be permitted to reenter the Union after the war ended. In late 1863 he proposed a plan for amnesty and postwar reconstruction, which became known popularly as the "10 Percent Plan." Lincoln's proposal would allow southern states to establish civilian governments once 10 percent of a state's voting population from 1860 had declared allegiance to the United States. *The Times* described Lincoln's plan as "simple and yet perfectly effective," noting that it would permit reconstruction to progress efficiently while demanding that southern states affirm their loyalty to the Union. Radical Republicans, however, opposed Lincoln's plan for its minimal requirements and demanded that rebel states meet stricter standards for demonstrating their patriotism before rejoining the Union.

DECEMBER 10, 1863
EDITORIAL
THE PRESIDENT'S MESSAGE.

President Lincoln delivers himself, in this document, with all his characteristic clearness and simplicity. The rhetorical flourishes and sentimental generalities, with which the later Presidents were accustomed to stuff out their State papers of this class, have no place here. It is the shortest Message we have had for a generation; and yet, this year has been the most eventful since the Government began. There never has been one thousandth part so much to spend words upon, and yet there has never been so little indulgence in words. Abraham Lincoln is one of the few men who believe that words stand for things; he economizes them accordingly. . . .

The most striking feature of the Message is that part which relates to the revival of State Governments, as the Southern territory is redeemed from rebel power. The President here, for the first time, commits himself to a definite policy and method in respect to this most important matter. He gives no countenance to the project, which has been so vehemently advocated, of reducing the redeemed States to a territorial condition, that they may continue to be directly governable by Federal authority. Yet he recognizes the necessity of securing State Governments that shall be loyal to the Union. This he declares to be not only a necessity, but a constitutional obligation, inasmuch as the Constitution imposes upon the General Government the duty of securing to every State a Republican form of government, which it would fail to do if it allowed a State to remain in the hands of its enemies. To establish this loyalty, he sets forth a comprehensive and stringent oath of allegiance, the taking of which shall be a condition precedent to the grant of amnesty and pardon for having participated in the rebellion. To make the loyalty thus secured available at the earliest day, he provides that whenever one-tenth part of the number of the voters in the States in 1860, take this oath, and desire to put the State Government again in action, they shall be authorized and aided to do so; with the single restriction that no action shall be taken by the revived State Government against the Emancipation Proclamation, which, as a war measure, is an accomplished irrevocable fact in his judgment, and which he will feel it his duty to maintain, in its full breadth, unless it shall be adjudicated by the Supreme Court of the United States to have been repugnant to the Constitution, and therefore null and void.

The process of reconstruction, as the President puts it, is simple and yet perfectly effective. The *motive* to reassume loyal obligations is secured by making it the only means of escaping confiscation of property and all the other penalties of treason. The *act* is secured with the very highest sanction possible, by making it rest on a most emphatic and solemn oath. The *effect* is secured by enabling those who thus comply to revive and carry on the State Government, just so soon as they comprise a certain definite proportion of the whole number of the voting population before the rebellion. Those who are for the Emancipation Proclamation are satisfied by the President's declared determination to maintain it until pronounced null by the highest judicial authority of the land; while those who have opposed it as an unconstitutional assumption of power cannot complain, for they have it in their power to test the unconstitutionality by an appeal at any time to that Court for a decision. Certain categories of traitors of peculiar dye are exempted from the benefit of the oath, which, of course, will meet the approbation of every loyal man. Other minor provisions are made, to complete the equity and efficiency of the plan. We believe that the closer it is examined, the more it will be discovered to be completely adapted to the great end desired. The public mind, after due reflection, we have not a doubt, will accept it as another signal illustration of the practical wisdom of the President.

• •

"THE UNION NATIONAL CONVENTION—NO POSTPONEMENT," APRIL 27, 1864, AND "THE BALTIMORE NOMINATION," JUNE 10, 1864

Holding a presidential election in the midst of civil war created much concern in 1864, as many thought that an election campaign could hinder the war and further fracture the already divided nation. Some suggested that the country would be better served by delaying the election cycle until there was greater unanimity on presidential nominees and the war had concluded. *The Times* opposed any delay, pointing out that no presidential nominee except George Washington ever had received unanimous support and that Lincoln's actions as commander in chief would not change because of the election. Indeed, *The Times* noted that if Gen. Ulysses S. Grant was not successful in waging the Union cause, "it would be preposterous to refuse to renominate President Lincoln because of Gen. Grant's failure." Lincoln himself, in accepting the nomination, famously remarked that he was "reminded, in this connection, of a story of an old Dutch farmer, who remarked to a companion once that 'it was not best to swap horses when crossing streams.' "

APRIL 27, 1864
EDITORIAL
THE UNION NATIONAL CONVENTION—NO POSTPONEMENT.

Certain members of our State Senate, with a few other gentlemen, have taken it upon themselves to address the National Executive Committee of the Union and Republican parties, by a joint letter, requesting a postponement of the National Convention. The letter is dated a month ago. It is a little singular that the *Tribune,* and other presses which favor the movement, should now, for the first time, bring the document to light. It is now hardly better than waste paper. Since its date, the sentiment of loyal men generally has been manifested so decidedly against the postponement that the committee have in fact hardly been able to consider it an open question. As representatives of the loyal cause, they are not the men to override popular opinion.

The motives of these gentlemen are excellent, we don't doubt, but their reasons are not. They say that "it is very important that all parties friendly to the Government shall be united in support of a single candidate," and they declare it to be their opinion that "such unanimity cannot be reached before the time now designated for the convention." What does this mean? Do these gentlemen intend to say that a convention ought not to take place until there is a perfect identity of feeling in respect to the selection of a candidate? There never has been such a national convention of any party. Invariably a diversity of opinion has prevailed in respect to the proper nomination to be made. Different States, different parts of the country, have different favorites. . . .

The other reason urged for the postponement is that "upon the result of the measures adopted by the Administration to finish the war during the present Spring and Summer will depend the wish of the people to continue in power their present leaders, or to change them for those from whom they may expect other and more satisfactory results." If the war is not brought to a substantial end this Summer, it will not be the fault of the President. He has remitted the entire conduct of the war to the military skill of Lieut.-Gen. Grant, and that, too, with the almost unanimous approval of the people. Gen. Grant may fail, though we trust not; but if he does, it will be his failure, and not that of President Lincoln. It would be preposterous to refuse to renominate President Lincoln because of Gen. Grant's failure. The case might be different if Gen. Grant had been put in command of the armies contrary to the judgment and wishes of the people. But as it is, the people will no more think of turning against the President if disappointed in Gen. Grant, than of stultifying themselves. They know that the President has acted for the best, and in accordance too with their own judgment. Thus assured, they will sustain him in September as staunchly as they now do, even though Gen. Grant may not accomplish what all now anticipate.

The two reasons we have mentioned are the only ones given for the postponement. No others can be given; and neither of these has any real weight. The convention will be held in June, with general approval; its nominee, whoever he may be, will surely receive the support of all the true men of the Union party, and will be elected with hardly a dissentient electoral vote.

JUNE 10, 1864
THE BALTIMORE NOMINATION.

Mr. Lincoln's Acceptance—Address of Gov. Dennison—The Platform—Its Indorsement by the President—Address of the National Union League—The President's Reply.

Washington, Thursday, June 9.

At 2:30 o'clock to-day the committee appointed yesterday by the National Union Convention at Baltimore to inform President Lincoln of his nomination by that convention, reached the White House, when they were invited into the East Room, where the President was conversing with members of the delegation who had previously called upon him. . . .

[President Lincoln addresses the delegation:]

Mr. Chairman and Gentlemen of the Committee: I will neither conceal my gratification, nor restrain the expression of my gratitude, that the Union people, through their convention, in the continued effort to save and advance the nation, have deemed me not unworthy to remain in my present position. I know no reason to doubt that I shall accept the nomination tendered; and yet, perhaps, I should not declare definitely before reading and considering what is called the platform. I will say now, however, that I approve the declaration in favor of so amending the Constitution as to prohibit Slavery throughout the nation. When the people in revolt, with the hundred days' explicit notice that they could within those days resume their allegiance without the overthrow of their institutions, and that they could not resume it afterward, elected to stand out, such an amendment of the Constitution as is now proposed became a fitting and necessary conclusion to the final success of the Union cause. Such alone can meet and cover all cavils. I now perceive its importance and embrace it. In the joint names of Liberty and Union let us labor to give it legal form and practical effect.

At the conclusion of the President's speech, all of the committee shook him cordially by the hand and offered their personal congratulations.

The members of the National Union League adjourned yesterday from Baltimore to this city and called upon the President this afternoon, by whom they were cordially received in the east room of the White House. The Chairman of the deputation spoke to the President as follows:

Mr. President: I have the honor of introducing to you the representatives of the Union Leagues of the loyal States, to congratulate you upon your renomination, and to assure you that we will not fail at the polls to give you the support that your services in the past so highly deserve. We feel honored in doing this, for we are assured that we are aiding in reelecting to the proud position of President of the United States one so highly worthy of it, one among not the least of whose claims is that he was the emancipator of four millions of bondmen.

The President replied as follows:

Gentlemen: I can only say, in response to the remarks of your Chairman, that I am very grateful for the renewed confidence which has been accorded to me, both by the convention and by the National League. I am not insensible at all to the personal compliment there is in this, yet I do not allow myself to believe that any but a small portion of it is to be appropriated as a personal compliment. The convention and the nation, I am assured, are alike animated by a higher view of the interests of the country for the present and the great future, and that part I am entitled to appropriate as a compliment is only that part which I may lay hold of as being the opinion of the convention and of the League, that I am not unworthy to be intrusted with the place I have occupied for the last three years. I have not permitted myself, gentlemen, to conclude that I am the best man in the country; but I am reminded, in this connection, of a story of an old Dutch farmer, who remarked to a companion once that "it was not best to swap horses when crossing streams."

The prolonged laughter which followed this characteristic remark should have been heard. It was tumultuous.

"The President's Proclamation on Reconstruction," July 11, 1864

The question of how to bring the southern states back into the Union vexed the president and Congress well before the Civil War ended. The so-called Radical Republicans in Congress viewed Lincoln's "10 percent plan" as too generous to the Confederacy and demanded more rights for black Americans as well as more punitive measures for southern states. The Wade-Davis bill of 1864, drafted by Sen. Benjamin F. Wade of Ohio and Rep. Henry W. Davis of Maryland, stated that 50 percent of a state's white male population would have to declare their loyalty to the United States for the state to return to the Union. The bill additionally would grant voting rights to former slaves. But Lincoln pocket-vetoed the bill—that is, he chose not to sign it while Congress was in recess, thus killing the measure—perhaps to show that his policies would not be defined by the Radical Republicans. Nevertheless, Lincoln recognized his party's agenda and may well have been more sympathetic to it following the 1864 elections. *The Times* reports that Lincoln did not sign the Wade-Davis bill simply because "it was passed at so late an hour that he had no time to examine it."

JULY 11, 1864
EDITORIAL
THE PRESIDENT'S PROCLAMATION ON RECONSTRUCTION.

The failure of the President to sign the bill providing for the reorganization of civil government in the reclaimed States, has been attributed to a disapproval of its features. Had it, indeed, been true that there was a serious variance between the executive and legislative branches of the Government on this subject, it would have been very unfortunate. To hasten a general reconciliation, it is important that the reclaimed States should be relieved of military rule, and returned to their old positions in the Union, just as soon as they can be trusted. But neither the President nor Congress singly can do the work necessary to such restoration. The President, as Commander-in-Chief, has the power to appoint and maintain Military Governors, during the war, as long as in his judgment the military situation requires it. Congress, under the clause of the Constitution which gives the two bodies the exclusive right to determine the qualifications of their members, has the sole power to decide when the States shall be reinstated in the national councils. To make the restoration a substantial thing, there must be conjoint action between the President and Congress. The want of it would produce mischievous, if not disastrous confusion.

The Proclamation of the President dispels all fears of any such variance. He did not sign the Congressional bill, primarily because it was passed at so late an hour that he had no time to examine it. Now that the president has examined it, he announces that he "is fully satisfied with the system of restoration contained in the bill, as one very proper for the loyal people of any State choosing to adopt it," and that he will give to any such people the Executive aid and assistance. So far, therefore, as the positive action of the bill is concerned, it will have for every State that seeks the benefit of it, the same effect as if it had become a law. The Executive will aid their efforts to re-establish the civil government, and Congress will admit the Senators and Representatives elected under that government.

But though the method of the bill in itself, so far as realizable, is excellent, it is quite possible that there may be circumstances which will justify and even require a deviation from it, and on that account we think it fortunate that it did not receive the President's signature. It indeed would be somewhat singular, if exactly the same process of reconstruction could be offered to all of the reclaimed States. Nothing like this was realized in the admission of the twenty-two States which have been added to the original Union. Texas was transferred into the Union from the condition of an independent government; California from military rule; Western Virginia from a provisional civil government; Vermont from no definable *status.* Even the States which grew from territorial organizations had no uniform mode of securing a place in the Union. Some were admitted with a previous enabling bill of Congress, others without; some with a quarter part of the population that was demanded of others; some with conditions and provisos, others unconditionally. No part of our Congressional legislation, in past time, has been less squared by rule and more shaped by circumstances, than that erecting new States. It would be singular if something like the same necessity did not assert itself in the work of re-erecting old States. The circumstances of this work, in respect to the different States, will widely vary. Some already, to a greater or less extent, have resumed civil government with the sanction and aid of the National authorities. . . .

It is well, as the President says, that there should be no inflexible rule established in respect to reconstruction. A general line of policy can consistently be marked out, but room should be left for any deviation which peculiar circumstances may urge. We have no doubt that Congress itself will recognize the wisdom of this when it again takes action upon the subject. It cannot be said that the President's disinclination to bind himself to square his action exactly with the requirements of this elaborate measure, proceeds from any desire to retain power over the conquered territory. The bill gives him the power to appoint Provisional Governors, and in interposing new difficulties for the reestablishment of civil government, it directly tends to prolong this power. His anxiety from the first has been to terminate the military power at the earliest day possible. It was that wish solely that impelled him to the plan of giving to a tenth of the population of a reclaimed State, who had taken the necessary oath, the privilege of initiating a civil government. Congress, in insisting upon an absolute majority, might prevent his divesting himself of this Governor-appointing power, for months and even years.

· ·

"WHAT MAKES THE TRIUMPH COMPLETE," NOVEMBER 21, 1864

Lincoln's reelection in November 1864 signified popular support for both the president and the Union. Defeating Gen. George McClellan, the Democratic candidate, by more than 400,000 votes, Lincoln demonstrated his appeal throughout the North with his widespread victory in twenty-two states. Only three states, Delaware, Kentucky, and New Jersey, cast their Electoral College votes for McClellan. (The eleven states in the Confederacy did not participate in the election.) *The Times* noted that Lincoln's supporters were both civilian and military, revealing a "unanimity of conviction and of feeling between the military and civilian elements engaged in the cause, that supplies the last consummate pledge of success." Victory for the Union seemed imminent.

NOVEMBER 21, 1864
WHAT MAKES THE TRIUMPH COMPLETE.

Men call the re-election of President Lincoln a triumph of the Union cause. This don't tell the story. The re-election might have occurred, and have exposed the Union cause to greater danger than ever. A bare electoral majority would have surely had that effect. It would have encouraged the opposition to the Government to make its organization yet more complete, and keep itself ready for the first new opportunity to seize power. The second term of Mr. Lincoln would have seen all the faction and sedition of the first, with ten-fold greater activity. In all earthly probability we should have had flagrant insubordination here in the North long before that second term had expired.

But if the mere re-election of President Lincoln does not express the triumph, neither does the fact that it was effected by the immense majority of at least four hundred thousand. That is grand. Such a preponderance of intelligent judgments and strong wills in favor of the war vastly confirms its strength both materially and morally. Yet it does not of itself constitute a full triumph. It falls short of establishing an absolute security. If this four hundred thousand majority had been given by one or two only of the geographical divisions of the North, it might have proved a new source of jealousy, discord and weakness. But all parts of the North (using the term in its widest sense) contribute to this majority—New-England, some 150,000 toward it; the Middle States, (including Maryland,) 40,000; the West, 180,000; and the Pacific slope, 30,000. What is peculiarly gratifying is, that the West, the section upon which the rebellion, from the beginning, has counted most for sympathy and cöoperation, is the very portion of the North which has sustained the Union cause with the greatest number of votes. Suppose the majorities given by the West for President Lincoln had been given the other way, would not every loyal man have felt it to be portentous? Would any majorities in the other portions, however great, have saved the Government from the danger of a new rebellion? Possibly before this year were out, we should see the treasonable associations of the Northwest lighting up the whole section with the flames of revolt, and in open connection with the Southern Confederacy. The spirit of the Western opposition leaders for the last twelve months, in open speech and secret conspiracy, fully warrants the assumption that they would have carried their section to any extremity of treason, had any considerable majority of the Western people sustained them at the polls. But the loyal will of the Western people has been declared with an emphasis that forever silences faction. Nobody will be mad enough hereafter to dream of alienating the West from the Government. Even that district of the West which was formerly accounted the least attached to the Union cause—the so-called Egypt of Illinois—has given President Lincoln a large popular majority, and sent no less than three Congressmen to sustain him in Congress. Loyalty is shown to be the predominant spirit everywhere from Ohio to the base of the Rocky Mountains,

and thus the last hope of those who looked for sectional diversions in the North disappear. The triumph of the Union cause is as satisfactory in its geographical aspects as in its numerical results.

But one thing more was necessary to give this triumph completeness. Whatever the numerical majority among the people in favor of Mr. Lincoln, however well distributed that majority was from the Atlantic to the Pacific, yet had our gallant soldiers in the field shown themselves at variance with it, there would have been room for serious misgiving. Of course, it cannot be imagined that our heroic armies would have abandoned their flag, however much they might have disagreed with the popular will in this election; yet they would have been more than men had not such a fact chilled their ardor, and generated a certain estrangement between them and the people. What gives this election its crowning security and glory is, that it meets the will of our soldiers in the field just as decidedly as of our people at home. The voters who are under orders pass the same judgment upon President Lincoln as those who still remain in civil life. There is a unanimity of conviction and of feeling between the military and civil elements engaged in the cause, that supplies the last consummate pledge of success. No popular declaration for the Baltimore Platform would have given a perfect confidence, if the military declaration had been adverse to it. The drilled and trained veterans of the field are the most necessary of all instrumentalities to the overthrow of the rebellion. Had they sided with the Chicago Platform, and announced by their votes that in their estimation the war was a "failure," and that the time had come for a "cessation of hostilities," what a hollow mockery would have been all these rejoicings over the decision of the people that the war must and shall go on. Were such the manifested *morale* of this army, we might well turn a deaf ear to all these shouts of civic victory, and set the cause down as doomed. But nothing of that kind appears. In spite of all their hardships undergone, and all their blood spilled, the soldiers are even more staunch for the war than when they went fresh from their homes. All their suffering for the flag has but strengthened their resolution to stand by it to the last. They vied with the people in pledging themselves to this at the recent election. It is this which gives the late election result its full triumphant rounding—its last finishing guarantee.

"PRESIDENT LINCOLN SHOT BY AN ASSASSIN," APRIL 15, 1865, AND "THE MURDER OF PRESIDENT LINCOLN," APRIL 16, 1865

Although President Lincoln had made plans for post–Civil War reconstruction, he did not live to enact them. The president was shot on April 14, 1865, just one month after his second-term inauguration, and he died the following morning. Assassin John Wilkes Booth, an actor who had supported the Confederacy in the Civil War, was captured and killed several days later. Lincoln was the first president to be assassinated and the third to die in office (William Henry Harrison died on April 4, 1841, and Zachary Taylor on July 9, 1850). The first article is a report from Secretary of War Edwin M. Stanton describing the horrific event. The second selection is an editorial, in which *The Times* writes that "the stability of our government and the welfare of our country do not depend upon the life of any individual," but that Lincoln's death was especially shocking because of the public's high "personal regard" for the president. Lincoln's legacy would forever be grounded in public respect and appreciation for his leadership of the nation in its most trying time. *The Times* also recognized Andrew Johnson as the new president, describing him as the people's "agent" for the next four years.

APRIL 15, 1865
PRESIDENT LINCOLN SHOT BY AN ASSASSIN.

The Deed Done at Ford's Theatre Last Night.

THE ACT OF A DESPERATE REBEL

The President Still Alive at Last Accounts.

No Hopes Entertained of His Recovery.

Attempted Assassination of Secretary Seward.

DETAILS OF THE DREADFUL TRAGEDY.

[OFFICIAL.]

War Department,
Washington, April 15—1:30 A.M.

Maj.-Gen. Dix:

This evening at about 9:30 P.M., at Ford's Theatre, the President, while sitting in his private box with Mrs. Lincoln, Mrs. Harris, and Major Rathburn, was shot by an assassin, who suddenly entered the box and approached behind the President.

The assassin then leaped upon the stage, brandishing a large dagger or knife, and made his escape in the rear of the theatre.

The pistol ball entered the back of the President's head and penetrated nearly through the head. The wound is mortal. The President has been insensible ever since it was inflicted, and is now dying.

About the same hour an assassin, whether the same or not, entered Mr. Seward's apartments, and under the pretence of having a prescription, was shown to the Secretary's sick chamber. The assassin immediately rushed to the bed, and inflicted two or three stabs on the throat and two on the face. It is hoped the wounds may not be mortal. My apprehension is that they will prove fatal.

The nurse alarmed Mr. Frederick Seward, who was in an adjoining room, and hastened to the door of his father's room, when he met the assassin, who inflicted upon him one or more dangerous wounds. The recovery of Frederick Seward is doubtful.

It is not probable that the President will live throughout the night.

Gen. Grant and wife were advertised to be at the theatre this evening, but he started to Burlington at 6 o'clock this evening.

At a Cabinet meeting at which Gen. Grant was present, the subject of the state of the country and the prospect of a speedy peace was discussed. The President was very cheerful and hopeful, and spoke very kindly of Gen. Lee and others of the Confederacy, and of the establishment of government in Virginia.

All the members of the Cabinet except Mr. Seward, are now in attendance upon the President.

I have seen Mr. Seward, but he and Frederick were both unconscious.

EDWIN M. STANTON,
Secretary of War.

> "In this hour of mourning and of gloom, while the shadow of an awful and unparalleled calamity hangs over the land, it is well to remember that the stability of our government and the welfare of our country do not depend upon the life of any individual."

APRIL 16, 1865
EDITORIAL
THE MURDER OF PRESIDENT LINCOLN.

The heart of this nation was stirred yesterday as it has never been stirred before. The news of the assassination of Abraham Lincoln carried with it a sensation of horror and of agony which no other event in our history has ever excited. In this city the demonstrations of grief and consternation were without a parallel. Business was suspended. Crowds of people thronged the streets—great gatherings sprung up spontaneously everywhere seeking to give expression, by speeches, resolutions, &c., &c. to the universal sense of dismay and indignation which pervaded the public mind.

Perhaps the paramount element in this public feeling was evoked by personal regard for Abraham Lincoln. That a man so gentle, so kind, so free from every particle of malice or unkindness, every act of whose life has been so marked by benevolence and goodwill, should become the victim of a cold-blooded assassination, shocked the public heart beyond expression. That the very moment, too, when he was closing the rebellion which had drenched our land in blood and tears—by acts of magnanimity so signal as even to excite the reluctant distrust and apprehensions of his own friends—should be chosen for his murder, adds a new element of horror to the dreadful tragedy.

But a powerful element of the general feeling which the news aroused was a profound concern for the public welfare. The whole nation had come to lean on Abraham Lincoln in this dread crisis of its fate with a degree of confidence never accorded to any President since George Washington. His love of his country ardent and all-pervading,—swaying every act and prompting every word,—his unsuspected uprightness

and personal integrity,—his plain, simple common sense, conspicuous in everything he did or said, commending itself irresistibly to the judgment and approval of the great body of the people, had won for him a solid and immovable hold upon the regard and confidence even of his political opponents. The whole people mourn his death with profound and sincere appreciation of his character and his worth.

Andrew Johnson, of Tennessee, is now the President of the United States. We have no doubts and no misgivings in regard to the manner in which he will discharge the duties which devolve so suddenly upon him. This country has no more patriotic citizen than he—no one among all her public men who will bring to her service a higher sense of his responsibilities, a sounder judgment in regard to her interests, or a firmer purpose in the maintenance of her honor and the promotion of her welfare. He has suffered, in his person, his property and his family relations, terribly from the wicked rebellion which has desolated the land; but he is not the man to allow a sense of personal wrong to sway his judgment or control his action in a great national emergency. Traitors and rebels have nothing to expect at his hands, but strict justice, tempered with such mercy only as the welfare of the nation may require.

In this hour of mourning and of gloom, while the shadow of an awful and unparalleled calamity hangs over the land, it is well to remember that the stability of our government and the welfare of our country do not depend upon the life of any individual, and that the great current of affairs is not to be changed or checked by the loss of any man however high or however honored. In nations where all power is vested in single hands, an assassin's knife may overthrow governments and wrap a continent in the flames of war. But here the People rule, and events inevitably follow the course which *they* pre- scribe. Abraham Lincoln has been their agent and instrument for the four years past; Andrew Johnson is to be their agent for the four years that are now to come. If the people have faith, courage and wisdom, the result will be the same.

· ·

"THE LAST ADDRESS OF THE PRESIDENT TO THE COUNTRY," APRIL 17, 1865

Lincoln's second inaugural address, which he had delivered on March 4, 1865, took on special resonance after the president's untimely death. In an editorial just days after the president's assassination, *The Times* recognized the modesty and generosity of one of Lincoln's last speeches. In particular, *The Times* pointed out the "tone of perfect kindness and good-will to all, whether enemies or political opponents," that captured so well the spirit of reconciliation that would be needed to move the nation beyond its devastating civil war. *The Times* described the speech in glowing terms: "earnest, humane, truly but not technically religious, filled with forgiveness and goodwill." Lincoln's words would set the standard for subsequent generations to follow in bringing the promises of Reconstruction to fruition.

APRIL 17, 1865
EDITORIAL
THE LAST ADDRESS OF THE PRESIDENT TO THE COUNTRY.

Probably all men in all quarters of the world, who read President Lincoln's last Inaugural Address, were impressed by the evident tone of solemnity in it, and the want of any expression of personal exultation. There he stood, after four years of such trial, and exposed to such hate and obloquy as no other great leader in modern history has experienced, successful, rëelected, his policy approved by the people and by the greater test of events, the terrible rebellion evidently coming to its end, and he himself now certain of his grand position in the eyes of history—and yet not a word escaped him of triumph, or personal glory, or even of much hopefulness. We all expected more confidence—words promising the close of the war and speaking of the end of our difficulties. Many hoped for some definite line of policy to be laid out in this address. But instead, we heard a voice as if from some prophet, looking with solemn gaze down over the centuries, seeing that both sides in the great con- test had their errors and sins, that no speedy victory could be looked for, and yet that the great Judge of the world would certainly give success to right and justice. The feeling for the bondmen and the sense of the great wrong done to them, with its inevitable punishment, seemed to rest with such solemn earnestness on his soul, that to the surprise of all and the derision of the flippant, an official speech became clothed in the language of the Bible. The English and French critics all observed this peculiar reli- gious tone of the Inaugural, and nearly all sensible persons felt it not unsuited to the grandeur and momentous char- acter of the events accompanying it. Many pronounced it a Cromwellian speech; but it had one peculiarity, which Cromwell's speeches never possessed—a tone of perfect kindness and good-will to all, whether enemies or political opponents.

"With charity to all and malice for none," President Lincoln made his last speech to the world. Men will repe- ruse that solemn address with ever increasing interest and emotion, as if the shadow of his own tragic fate and the near and unseen dangers to the country, rested un- consciously on its words. It will seem natural that no ex- pression of exultation or personal triumph escaped the great leader of this revolution, but that his mind was filled with the impressive religious lessons of the times. It will be thought characteristic of his sense of justice and his sincere humanity, that his last public address to the country was most of all occupied by the wrongs done to the helpless race, whose friend and emancipator he had been. And it will seem but a part of his wonderful spirit of good-will to all, that not a syllable of bitterness toward the enemies of his country, to the traitors at home, or his personal revilers, passed his lips.

It is such a speech to the world as a Christian statesman would gladly have his last—earnest, humane, truly but not technically religious, filled with forgiveness and good will.

When generations have passed away, and the unhappy wounds of this war are healed, and the whole nation is united on a basis of universal liberty, our posterity will read the dying words of the great Emancipator and leader of the people with new sympathy and reverence, thanking God that so honest and so pure a man, so true a friend of the oppressed, and so genuine a patriot, guided the nation in the time of its trial, and prepared the final triumph which he was never allowed to see.

THE PRESIDENCY OF ANDREW JOHNSON

APRIL 15, 1865 – MARCH 4, 1869

The presidency of Andrew Johnson began the post–Civil War reconstruction of the Union. President Johnson sought to enact policies that would not impose harsh demands upon southern states before they were eligible to reenter the Union, but he was opposed by the so-called Radical Republicans in Congress. Conflict between the president and Congress culminated in Johnson's impeachment in 1868. The president was acquitted in the Senate by just one vote. Because of his weakened position, Johnson was forced to let Congress take the lead in setting Reconstruction policies.

The hardships of Johnson's early years illustrate the overwhelming obstacles he overcame to enter politics and eventually the White House. Born to parents who could neither read nor write, Johnson never attended school. He became an apprentice to a tailor at age thirteen. He learned to read at work, but writing and basic math came later, when he met Eliza McCardle, whom he married at age eighteen.

Johnson gave up his trade for politics, moving steadily forward in local and state Tennessee government. He joined the U.S. House of Representatives in 1843, serving for four terms before returning to Tennessee to win the governorship twice. He entered the U.S. Senate in 1857, and distinguished himself (in northern eyes, at least) by being the only southern senator to stay in office after his state's secession. President Abraham Lincoln appointed Johnson military governor of Tennessee in 1862 after Union forces took the

MENDING THE FAMILY KETTLE.

COLUMBIA—" *Now, Andy, I wish you and your boys would hurry up that job, because I want to use that kettle right away. You are all talking too much about it.*"

state, and Tennessee was the only seceding state to outlaw slavery before Lincoln issued his Emancipation Proclamation in 1863.

THE 1864 CAMPAIGN

Johnson was an ideal vice-presidential candidate for the Republican Party in 1864, which had renamed itself the National Union Party to include Unionist Democrats such as him. Nominating a southern Democrat for vice president would broaden the ticket's appeal and strengthen support

QUICK FACTS ON ANDREW JOHNSON

BIRTH	December 29, 1808, Raleigh, N.C.
EDUCATION	No formal education
FAMILY	Wife: Eliza Johnson Children: Martha Johnson; Charles Johnson; Mary Johnson; Robert Johnson; Andrew Johnson
WHITE HOUSE PETS	Mice
PARTY	Democratic (National Union Party in 1864 election)
PREPRESIDENTIAL CAREER (SELECTED)	Mayor, Greenville, Tenn., 1830–1833 Tennessee state politics, 1835–1843 U.S. House of Representatives, 1843–1853 Governor of Tennessee, 1853–1857 U.S. Senate, 1857–1862 Military governor of Tennessee, 1862–1865 Vice president, 1865
PRESIDENTIAL TERM	April 15, 1865–March 4, 1869
VICE PRESIDENT	None
SELECTED EVENTS	Ratification of Thirteenth Amendment (1865) Military Reconstruction Act passed over his veto (1867) Tenure of Office Act passed over his veto (1867) U.S. acquisition of Alaska (1867) Impeachment and acquittal (1868) Ratification of Fourteenth Amendment (1868)
POSTPRESIDENCY	U.S. Senate, March 4–July 31, 1875
DEATH	July 31, 1875, Carter's Station, Tenn.

for President Lincoln's policies. Lincoln and Johnson won an overwhelming victory over the Democrats, Gen. George B. McClellan and George H. Pendleton, with more than 90 percent of the Electoral College vote and 2.2 million popular votes to 1.8 million for the Democratic ticket.

Johnson's vice presidency did not start favorably. Recovering from typhoid fever, Johnson drank heavily before his inauguration on March 4, 1865, and gave a rambling and embarrassing speech before taking the oath of office. Yet because Johnson was not known to drink regularly, the incident did not harm his relationship with President Lincoln. The two had little chance to discuss policy, as Lincoln was assassinated just six weeks after the start of his second term. Andrew Johnson was now president.

THE JOHNSON ADMINISTRATION

Because of the circumstances in which he took office, Johnson made no immediate changes in the cabinet. Secretary of State William H. Seward served through Johnson's term, as did Treasury Secretary Hugh McCulloch and Navy Secretary Gideon Welles. Johnson eventually appointed Henry Stanberry as attorney general and James Harlan as secretary of the interior. Johnson's most controversial move by far was his decision to replace Secretary of War Edwin M. Stanton. Congress opposed the president's decision and the resulting showdown led to Johnson's impeachment.

Because Johnson's wife, Eliza, was an invalid, their two daughters Martha Johnson Patterson and Mary Johnson

Stover served as White House hostesses for their mother. The Johnsons also had three sons, one of whom died before his father became president.

MAJOR ISSUES

Within weeks of taking office, Johnson declared his approach to Reconstruction. His Amnesty Proclamation of May 1865 pardoned rebels and returned their property (but not slaves), provided that they declared their loyalty to the Union. Senior Confederate leaders and people with substantial property holdings were not included; they would have to receive special approval from the president to regain the right to vote and hold office. Johnson also established a model for rebel states to reenter the Union, beginning with North Carolina. A state would have a presidentially appointed governor who would call a convention to draft a new state constitution. Only eligible voters from 1861 who had declared national loyalty would be permitted to vote on the constitution, a rule that excluded rebels who required presidential pardons and the freedmen. The state would rejoin the Union upon approval of its new constitution. Johnson also supported the Thirteenth Amendment, which outlawed slavery; it was ratified in 1865.

Although Congress largely supported Johnson's policies, Radical Republicans had some concerns about his failure to support suffrage for blacks. This concern heightened in 1866 when Johnson vetoed a bill that would have made permanent the Freedmen's Bureau, an organization that was established late in the Civil War to provide assistance to former slaves. Johnson then vetoed the Civil Rights Act of 1866, which made blacks U.S. citizens and guaranteed them legal protections. In response, Congress used its constitutional power to overturn a presidential veto with a two-thirds vote for the first time. Johnson also opposed the Fourteenth Amendment, which promised due process and equal protection of the laws for all citizens. (The amendment won the required approval from three-quarters of the states by 1868.) In the congressional midterm elections of 1866, the Republican Party increased its representation in Congress, despite Johnson's active and vitriolic campaign in opposition to its candidates. The executive and legislative branches clearly were on a collision course.

The showdown began in early 1867 when Congress passed the Military Reconstruction Act and the Tenure of Office Act,

again over Johnson's vetoes. The Reconstruction Act set reentry conditions for the remaining states outside the Union, placing them under military rule and requiring that they ratify the Fourteenth Amendment. The Tenure of Office Act expanded the Senate's power in executive appointments to include approval of presidential dismissals. When Secretary of War Stanton began to implement the military reconstruction program, Johnson ordered him to leave office and asked Civil War hero Ulysses S. Grant to replace him. Grant complied reluctantly, but the Senate rejected Stanton's dismissal. Grant returned the office key, and Stanton locked himself in his office. Johnson then tried to appoint Maj. Gen. Lorenzo Thomas as secretary of war, and again Stanton refused to leave his office. Congress, angered that Johnson had refused to accept its decision not to dismiss Stanton, passed eleven articles of impeachment against the president in 1868.

This vote was the first time the House of Representatives had exercised its impeachment power against a president. Its charges of "high crimes and misdemeanors" (the constitutional grounds for impeachment, along with bribery and treason) consisted primarily of violations of the Tenure of Office Act and ridicule of Congress in the 1866 midterm election campaigns. Despite Republican control of the Senate, Johnson was acquitted when the vote fell one short of the two-thirds required for conviction. The president completed his term, although effective political power rested with Congress following his impeachment trial.

One of the Johnson administration's most significant accomplishments was the acquisition of Alaska in 1867. Secretary of State Seward successfully negotiated its purchase from Russia for $7.2 million. Johnson also oversaw the construction of the transcontinental railroad, which was almost completed at the end of his term. One of the administration's more controversial legacies was its efforts to move Indians in the West onto reservations. All of these policies, however, were overshadowed by Johnson's battles with Congress over Reconstruction and his subsequent impeachment.

Although Johnson sought a second term in 1868, the Democratic Party denied him the nomination, instead selecting Horatio Seymour, former governor of New York, from forty-seven candidates in twenty-two ballots. Johnson returned to Tennessee, where he ran unsuccessfully for House and Senate seats in Congress until winning election to the Senate in 1874. He served for less than five months before suffering a fatal stroke.

"THE AMNESTY PROCLAMATION," MAY 31, 1865, AND "THE FORM OF A PARDON," AUGUST 21, 1865

President Johnson's decision to issue an Amnesty Proclamation for many, but not all, rebels marked a moderate path between opponents of any type of forgiveness for treason and advocates of a blanket pardon, regardless of the person's actions in the Civil War. In granting amnesty, Johnson established two requirements. The first was that participants declare their loyalty to the Union, an obvious condition of forgiveness for treason. The second was that participants not have served the Confederacy in senior leadership positions. Taken together, the excluded groups comprised what *The New York Times* described as "nearly every political leader in the secession movement." Johnson also did not grant amnesty to senior military officers in the Confederacy, whom *The Times* described as having "heart[s] thoroughly steeped in the rebel spirit." Even these individuals, however, could apply to the president for an individual pardon.

MAY 31, 1865
EDITORIAL
THE AMNESTY PROCLAMATION.

President Johnson has well done a very difficult piece of work. An amnesty of some sort was a necessity. Statutory punishment of all who have committed treason, would bring to death nearly every man and woman in the South, for nearly all have either "levied war" against the United States, or given those who did so, "aid and comfort." A universal amnesty, on the other hand, would have been a full absolution of the greatest crime of the age, and the greatest of all injuries to the authority and majesty of law. The amnesty must needs be only partial. Its limits had to be fixed with reference to two objects: First, security for the future; second, equity.

To shape the amnesty so as to realise the security was not difficult. It was simply necessary to make the taking and the keeping of a strict oath of allegiance and obedience a condition of all participation in the amnesty. The oath prescribed in this proclamation will effectually accomplish that purpose. It bars out, at the very outset, all who are still determined on disloyalty, and leaves the government still free to proceed against them, as it may choose. To constrain the keeping of the oath by those who take it, the proclamation declares that its violation shall entail the forfeiture of all benefits of the amnesty.

It was the other point that was the hard one—how to frame the amnesty with a proper observance of equity, so that the punishment which did fall, should fall only on the guiltiest. To make inquisition into the particular degree of the guilt of every Southern rebel was a pure impossibility.

The only practicable method was to discriminate by classes. But it was perplexing to fix these classes specifically, as strict justice would require. Again, even when this classification was made, it would at best cause a great deal of inequality. A very guilty rebel might be so circumstanced as to be included within the amnesty, while a comparatively innocent one would be excluded.

President Johnson has met these difficulties in the best manner possible. To insure the exclusion of as many as possible, who are guilty in the first degree, he makes no less than fourteen excepted classes. Then he reserves to himself the privilege of extending hereafter the amnesty to each individual within these classes who may apply for pardon, and whom he may think fit subjects for it.

The fourteen categories of exceptions embrace most of the special guilt connected with the Confederacy. The original planners of the rebellion were almost all members, either of the Senate or of the House of Representatives in the Federal Congress, or else Governors of States. The exclusion of all Congressmen who left their seats "to aid the rebellion," and of all Governors of States in insurrection, of itself exposes to the law the "very head and front of the offending." When to these are joined the civil and diplomatic officers, and domestic and foreign agents of the Confederate Government nearly every political leader in the secession movement is included. Jeff. Davis gave his official patronage almost entirely to original Secessionists. That was one of the standing complaints of his political opponents. The bare fact of having held office from his hand is *prima facie* evidence of the rankest kind of treason. This fact applies as well to his military appointments. He had the nomination of all these; and we may very well take for granted that every man of the rebel officers, above the rank of Colonel, excluded by President Johnson from the amnesty, has a heart thoroughly steeped in the rebel spirit.

AUGUST 21, 1865
THE FORM OF A PARDON.

The following is the form of the pardons granted by the President:

ANDREW JOHNSON, PRESIDENT OF THE UNITED STATES OF AMERICA.

To all whom these presents may come, greeting:

Whereas, —— ——, of Richmond, Va., by taking part in the late rebellion against the Government of the United States, has made himself liable to heavy pains and penalties:

And whereas, the circumstances of his case render him a proper object of executive clemency:

Now, therefore, be it known, that I, Andrew Johnson, President of the United States of America, in consideration of the premises, divers good and sufficient reasons me thereunto moving, do hereby grant to the said —— —— a full pardon and amnesty for all offences by him committed, arising from participation, direct or implied, in the said rebellion, conditioned as follows, namely: This pardon to begin and take effect from the day on which the said —— —— shall take the oath prescribed in the proclamation of the President, dated May 29, 1865, and to be void and of no effect if the said —— —— shall hereafter, at any time, acquire any property whatever in slaves, or make use of slave labor; and that he first pay all costs which may have accrued in any proceedings hitherto instituted against his person or property:

And upon the further condition, That the said —— —— shall notify the Secretary of State, in writing, that he has received and accepted the foregoing pardon.

In testimony whereof, I have hereunto signed my name and caused the seal of the United States to be affixed. Done at the City of Washington, this 12th day of August, A.D., 1865, and of the Independence of the United States the ninetieth.

ANDREW JOHNSON.

By the President:

William H. Seward, Secretary of State.

"THE CIVIL RIGHTS BILL AND THE PRESIDENT'S VETO," MARCH 28, 1866

Johnson's veto of the 1866 civil rights bill met with praise from *The Times,* based largely on questions of federalism, or national versus state powers. Congress had passed this legislation in response to the passage of "black codes" in the southern states, which were laws that effectively denied voting and other rights to blacks, through literacy, income, and other requirements instead of race. *The Times* expressed concern about the powers that the bill granted to the federal government to override state judges in enforcing civil rights for blacks, noting that giving the federal government wide latitude to implement the law would "undermin[e] the independence of the judiciary." Congress overrode this veto, but the law did not achieve its intended results. Indeed, the battle would resume a century later, when it became clear that the federal government would have to be aggressive in implementing the promise of civil rights for black Americans.

MARCH 28, 1866
THE CIVIL RIGHTS BILL AND THE PRESIDENT'S VETO.

The Message of the President announcing his veto of the Civil Rights Bill, which we publish in full in other columns, may not command universal assent. But we venture to think that few state papers have ever been given to the world that will so thoroughly compel the attention of thinking men of whatever creed, or kindred, or party.

The President deals almost exclusively with the details of the bill as it passed through Congress, reserving his comments upon its policy to a few sentences at the close of the message. The analysis of the details, however, is of so keen and searching a character, the logic is so irresistible, that we should hope even the strongest advocates of the measure will see how vastly important it is that the constitutional power of the veto should exist, and how important also, in a higher sense, it is that such a constitutional power should be intrusted to a President endowed with judgment, discretion and most uncommon courage.

The point in the President's argument which stands out in boldest relief, is that which portrays with almost startling vividness the danger—not only possible, but certain—of undermining the independence of the judiciary. If Federal District-Attorneys, Marshals, Deputy Marshals, Agents of the Freedmen's Bureau, and other officials are to be intrusted with the power of arraigning any State Judge who may interpret a State law in a way which a claimant of justice may disapprove, of what possible use can be State laws, and of what conceivable use can be State Judges? Better abolish both at once. But not only are these petty Federal officials empowered, under this Civil Rights Bill, to appear as accusers of the State Judiciary; they have a premium held out to them to prefer charges. For every case of alleged injustice to freedmen, they get a fee. The accused may be innocent; if so, the fee comes out of the United States Treasury. If the accused is guilty, he has to pay his share of the perquisites accruing to the Federal official.

The strictly legal interpretation which the President applies to particular sections of the act is so overwhelmingly strong, that the members "learned in the law," who voted for it, can hardly help blushing to find themselves so entirely at fault, under the sharp logic of a layman. So far as we can learn the sentiment of the more discreet portion of the majority that voted for the bill, they are ready to confess that the President's reasons are too strong for them,

and they are fain to fall back on what they call his political *animus* to excuse their non-acceptance of his arguments. Those who have throughout doubted the expediency of multiplying discriminating laws in favor of a class which has achieved an enfranchisement and social elevation unexampled in its suddenness and completeness in the history of the human race, must necessarily be pleased that the President goes even further in his veto than to interpret the mere technicalities of the law. To moderate and rational reformers the few simple but pregnant words which Mr. Johnson utters on the policy of enforcing the laws of *political economy* through the agency of a countless army of stipendiaries, have a value far beyond the mere enforcement of the immediate argument. They are words which have a scope and a bearing aside from the provisions of this or any other negro protection bill. And they show how far above the majority which desires to control his action, are the views of the Executive in all that appertains to the maintenance of constitutional freedom.

We may here note that the vote on the bill, as it originally passed the Senate, showed 33 in favor to 12 against it; five members being absent. Of the yeas all were "Unionists;" of the nays three were Unionists and nine "Democrats." Three "Unionists" and two "Democrats" were absent. In the House the yeas numbered 111 and the nays 38. There were 34 members absent from the vote. Six "Unionists" voted with the minority: and of the absentees twenty-six were Unionists and eight Democrats.

These facts may not furnish any clear index of the disposition with which members will approach the question of passing the bill over the Veto. But they indicate what was the apparent sentiment of both Houses before the President threw additional light upon the subject. It may be hoped that arguments so cogent as those employed in the message will not be thrown away. It is not every day that members have an opportunity of listening to reason and common sense. They may find this appeal a seasonable and acceptable change. Be that as it may, the President's message will be read and studied outside of Congress, and everywhere throughout the civilized world; and wherever it is read and studied the American name and character will be elevated, in so far as Andrew Johnson is held to represent the American people.

"The Contest and Its Results," November 8, 1866

The 1866 midterm elections in Congress strengthened the position of the Republican Party in opposition to the president. The Republican victory was especially significant because for the first time, the incumbent president had participated aggressively in congressional campaigns. Johnson sought to build popular support for his Reconstruction policies, but his strong denunciations of the Republican agenda, as well as his heated, sometimes vulgar, exchanges with hecklers, hindered his cause. The election results clearly showed, as *The Times* noted, that the nation "explicitly declare[d] the Democratic Party unworthy of its confidence."

NOVEMBER 8, 1866
THE CONTEST AND ITS RESULTS.

We are curious to see how the Democratic oracles will treat the result of Tuesday's work. When Pennsylvania and Ohio and Indiana rendered their verdict for Congress and against the President, the Democrats invented stories of marked though indecisive gains to lessen the mortification of defeat. "We have not won," they said, "but we have nearly done so; wait till next time." The pretence was as hollow as their previous boasting, but as it seemed to afford consolation in the midst of disaster, it had been unkind to raise a controversy on the subject.

What will the Democrats say now? The time for retrieving the losses of October has come and gone, and where are the predicted successes? The struggle on which they staked everything is over, and in what direction shall we look for the signs of growth of which we were forewarned? In what quarter of the extended field of battle may we discover traces of the strength which pledged itself to victory, or of the combinations which were to overcome all adversaries? . . .

But though the net result be thus favorable to the Republicans—though it assures us of a two-thirds majority in the next Congress, with a round dozen of members to spare—the circumstances which have almost everywhere attended the contest, are yet more conclusive as to the convictions predominant in the loyal States. For strike out of the reckoning this City and Brooklyn, and the rebel sympathizers of Maryland, and what State, North or West, affords consolation to the Democrats? In not one can they truthfully claim evidence of numerical progress. Everywhere the returns exhibit large Republican additions. Where formerly we battled against overwhelming odds, we now show growing power, as in tiny Delaware, whose radical Democratic majorities indicate a time not distant when even there Democratic domination shall be numbered with the things of the past. New-Jersey has planted herself squarely on the Republican platform. Michigan has, for the first time, made a clean sweep. Minnesota has rejected gallant soldiers solely because they allied themselves with the Democracy, and has re-elected her Republicans. Missouri has declared that there shall be no step backward. Kansas remains true to the traditions of her struggle for freedom. Illinois, Wisconsin and Massachusetts have rolled up Republican majorities larger than were ever known in their history. And the Empire State has more than overcome the unprecedented vote of this City. . . .

It cannot be honestly alleged that in this extended and decisive conflict the Democrats have not had fair opportunities of developing their strength. The contrary is the case. They have had the advantage of fighting in the President's name, under the shelter of his policy, and aided with all the resources at his command. But for this circumstance their defeat had been more signal that it is. And the fact that despite these advantages they have been—not merely defeated, but—routed, scattered, and rendered practically powerless, is evidence of the deep-seated determination of the people. They will endure nothing that may contribute to the frustration of the work in which Congress is engaged. They will tolerate no interference by the Executive in matters controlled by themselves. Above all, they will repose no confidence, and vest no authority in the Democracy, which is gibbeted in their memories as the party which labored constantly, though happily ineffectually, throughout the war, to embarrass the operations of the Government, and so to aid the plans of its enemies.

From the verdict of Tuesday there is no appeal. The judgment rendered by four States a month ago was held up as one likely to be reversed. The argument has been heard, and nine States have disposed of the points in issue, finally, and with no chance of reversal. There is no further room for doubt or equivocation. The country indorses the action of Congress, upholds the Constitutional Amendment as the basis of compromise, and explicitly declares the Democratic Party unworthy of its confidence.

- -

"THE TENURE OF OFFICE BILL," MARCH 4, 1867

One of Congress's most controversial actions during the Johnson administration was the passage of the Tenure of Office Act in 1867. The Constitution granted the president the power to appoint executive officials "with the Advice and Consent of the Senate," but how these officials would be removed from office was not established explicitly. The First Congress had tried to grant the Senate authority in the removal process, and Vice President John Adams had to cast a tie-breaking vote in favor of giving the president sole removal power. The post–Civil War Congress again tried to circumscribe presidential power by preventing the chief executive from removing an executive official without Senate approval. Although the political rationale of preventing Johnson from removing Republican appointees may have been desirable, the approach was problematic. *The Times* generally supported the concept of protecting civil service officials from political battles. It made an exception for the cabinet, finding that an insistence on shared removal power for such senior appointees had "the appearance of being aimed at Mr. Johnson."

MARCH 4, 1867
THE TENURE OF OFFICE BILL.

The bill regulating the tenure of civil officers appointed with the consent of the Senate, has become law over the President's veto.

By this measure the appointing power of the Executive is greatly circumscribed. It deprives him of the power of removing civil officers whose appointments come before the Senate for confirmation; or rather limits the exercise of the power to cases in which the Senate concur. And in this provision the Cabinet advisers of the President are included.

It has been supposed that the veto would hinge upon this particular application of the principle, as an infraction of a privilege always accorded to the Executive by reason of the confidential relations in which the Cabinet officers stand. But the message takes exception to the whole scope of the bill, as an invasion of the power of removal which by the usage of the Government has been vested exclusively in the President. It is admitted, however, that though this usage has been sustained by Story and Kent and other eminent interpreters of the Constitution, its validity has always virtually rested upon the decision of Congress, speaking through majorities, and has as constantly been disputed by statesmen of admitted weight. A Constitution which one majority affirmed may, then, be reversed by another majority without wrong; and this is what the expiring Congress has done.

So far as it imparts a certain permanence to qualified occupants of civil offices, the bill effects a desirable reform. A more satisfactory measure would be that of Mr. Jenckes, which would leave the entire civil service of the country out of the slough of politics, and secure an amount of efficiency at present unattainable. But the step now taken is an advance, excepting only in its bearing upon the Cabinet; and in that respect it has the appearance of being aimed at Mr. Johnson. His Message would have been stronger in argument, though perhaps not more effective in Congress, had it applied solely to this point, instead of ranging over a wide ground, where, on his own showing, Congress has a right to legislate untrammelled by precedent or the dicta of commentators.

"OUR NEW POSSESSIONS ON THE PACIFIC COAST—PEACEABLE ANNEXATION," SEPTEMBER 22, 1867

The U.S. acquisition of Alaska from Russia marked one of the signature accomplishments of the Johnson administration and was recognized as such in *The Times*. The paper found that the purchase cost and expenses for protection were quite reasonable. As for charges of colonization, *The Times* explained that "it is colonization which has so little in it of political or territorial aggrandizement, that the only jealousy it has ever awakened is a jealousy growing out of our own sectional divisions at home." The national divisions over postwar Reconstruction policy would be far more intense than debate over the acquisition of Alaska.

SEPTEMBER 22, 1867
OUR NEW POSSESSIONS ON THE PACIFIC COAST—PEACEABLE ANNEXATION.

Our new territorial acquisitions in the North Pacific will be known—pending the organization of a civil government therein—as the Military District of Alaska.

The district is to be attached to the Department of California—a fact significant in an international as well as in an economic sense. Contrary to the predictions of those who, from party motives, opposed the purchase of the Russian possessions in America, there is no formidable outlay contemplated in the assumption of authority over the newly-ceded territory; and there has not, thus far, been the first symptom of complications with any foreign Power on the question of the extended political influence, or the territorial expansion which the purchase may be said to involve. . . .

The original purchase-money—even if the bargain had contemplated nothing beyond the procurement of a Station for our whalers and other merchantmen generally in the North Pacific—could hardly be regarded as a lavish and inconsiderate outlay. And the maintenance of a garrison two hundred strong for the furtherance of that special object, would hardly challenge criticism on any broader grounds than those of partisan opposition. The enterprise, it is true, is one of colonization, outside of what have been considered our settled boundaries. But it is colonization which has so little in it of political or territorial aggrandizement, that the only jealousy it has ever awakened is a jealousy growing out of our own sectional divisions at home. It was urged against the Secretary of State that in seeking to divert attention from the failure of the Government policy of reconstruction, he was ready to involve the country in any outside schemes, however expensive, which might seem for the moment to gratify the national pride. It was argued that he was indifferent to the consideration, whether his policy of territorial expansion, involved a difficulty with foreign Powers or not. The argument against him, founded—but never sincerely founded—upon theories of financial economy is practically overthrown in this military order of Gen. Halleck. The post at Sitka is as easy of access from San Francisco, as the post at Galveston is from New-York. In the latter case the stores may be sent in quarterly or monthly instalments. In the first case they have to be sent in the shape of yearly supplies. There is no valid plea of economy that can be urged in the one case, which may not be held to apply equally well in the other.

The appeal to international relationships time has shown to have no stronger or broader foundation. The only power whose political and territorial influence could in any measure be affected by the cession of the Russian possessions in America to the United States is Great Britain. But the Colonial policy of England, of late years, has, as every one knows, been a policy looking to the contraction rather than the expansion of her authority. However much the British American colonists may plume themselves on the value in which they are held as dependencies of the Mother country, the secret aim and desire of English statesmen has been, of recent years—and is now—to give both the Atlantic and the Pacific Provinces the chance of cutting loose from their leading strings. Confederation, to the judgment of some persons, may not present itself in this aspect; but no one who has carefully watched the progress of that measure can avoid the conclusion that all the special Imperial subsidies, whether for railroads or for the building and repair of forts, and all the

Concessions to the Colonial Governments in the way of regulating their own tariffs and establishing postal and commercial treaties with foreign States on their own account, are but parts of a scheme preparatory to their assumption of complete independence, or the formation, on their own responsibility, of such new relationships as they may hold to be conducive to their material and political interests.

"THE PRESIDENT AND MR. STANTON," DECEMBER 17, 1867

President Johnson's conflict with Congress over the Tenure of Office Act came to a head with his efforts to dismiss Secretary of War Edwin M. Stanton in 1867. Angered by Stanton's support for congressional Republicans and opposition to the White House agenda, Johnson requested Stanton's resignation. The president cited Stanton's failure to halt a violent race riot in New Orleans as a reason to remove him. When Stanton refused to resign, citing the Tenure of Office Act, Johnson suspended him and appointed Ulysses S. Grant in his stead, even though Grant was not keen to take the position. *The Times* agreed with Johnson that the president should have the full dismissal power independent of Congress, given "the propriety of not saddling the President with a constitutional adviser against his will." Congress vehemently disagreed, and two months later voted to impeach the president for his actions.

DECEMBER 17, 1867
THE PRESIDENT AND MR. STANTON.

We publish this morning the President's communication to the Senate giving his reasons, in accordance with the "Tenure of Office" bill, for suspending Mr. Stanton from office. It is a document of decided acuteness and force. In it the President does not confine himself to the technical requirements of the law, in obedience to which the Message itself is sent;—he gives a general statement of his reasons for not wanting Mr. Stanton in his Cabinet any longer, and avails himself of the opportunity also to transfer to him some of the responsibility which he thinks has rested upon himself long enough.

1. The first point he makes is that Mr. Stanton declined to resign his place after he had become fully aware of the President's wish that he should do so, and that his final refusal to resign, when requested, was couched in terms and based upon considerations which made it an insult and defiance to his superior officer. The act of Congress creating the War Department distinctly recognizes the Secretary as the subordinate of the President—saying that he shall perform such duties as the President may prescribe, and that he may be removed at the President's discretion. It is the Tenure of Office Law, passed by the last Congress, under which Mr. Stanton feels called upon to retain his office in spite of the President's request that he should resign; and the President says that when that law was before him in the shape of a bill awaiting his signature, he was officially advised by Mr. Stanton that it was unconstitutional, and that it was his "duty to defend the power of the President from usurpation, and veto the bill." "After all this," says the President, "I was not prepared to find him assuming the vindication of a law which he had advised me was unconstitutional."

2. The President says that there is no part of his administration for which he has been more denounced than for the plan on which he thought reconstruction should proceed. Yet, he says, he did not originate it;—he found it awaiting his action when he succeeded to the Presidency,—and took it as part of the unfinished business of his predecessor. It was prepared for Mr. Lincoln by Mr. Stanton, who has since testified that he had no doubt of the President's right and power to carry it out. Yet, in spite of this, Mr. Stanton alone, of all the members of his Cabinet, differed from him in regard to it, and yet refused to withdraw, after that difference was found to be irreconcilable. This, he thinks, was an unjustifiable departure from a rule which has always obtained in

the administration of the Government, and upon which three members of his own Cabinet had acted under similar circumstances.

3. Coming to more specific charges of dereliction of duty, the President cites the New-Orleans riot, for which, he says, he has been widely held responsible. On the 28th of August he was advised by telegraph that the Convention was to assemble, and that civil process would be issued against the members of it by the civil courts which were then in full operation; and he was asked whether the military should interfere to *prevent* execution of the process. He answered that the military was expected to "sustain, not interfere with, the proceedings of the courts." On the same day Gen. Baird sent a dispatch to Mr. Stanton asking for orders. Mr. Stanton received it on Sunday, the 29th, but neither replied to it nor informed the President of it,—and on the 30th (Monday) the riot occurred. Gen. Baird afterward complained that he received no instructions;—and for this delinquency, which is alleged to have caused the riot, the President

has been held responsible, and Mr. Stanton has allowed this impression to prevail without any attempt to correct it. "There may be those," says the President, "ready to say that I would have given no instructions even if the dispatch had reached me in time; but all must admit that I ought to have had the opportunity."

The President closes by urging some general considerations, which show the propriety of not saddling the President with a constitutional adviser against his will; and by assuring the Senate that the public interests have not suffered from Mr. Stanton's suspension, inasmuch as "salutary reforms have been introduced and great reductions of expense have been effected" by his successor.

The document will probably not satisfy the Senate that the President had valid reasons for removing Mr. Stanton,—but it will do something toward relieving the President, in the public mind, from responsibilities hitherto saddled upon him, but which he has not fairly incurred. We take it for granted that in any case Mr. Stanton will not resume his seat in Mr. Johnson's Cabinet.

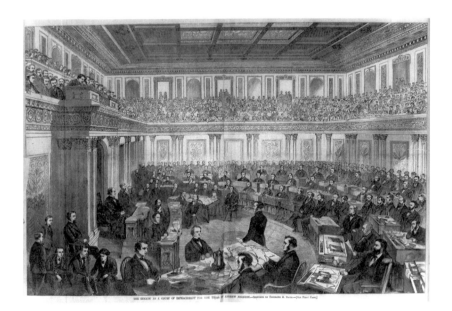

In May 1868 the Senate conducted the first impeachment trial of a chief executive and acquitted President Andrew Johnson by a narrow margin.

Source: Library of Congress

"The Effects of Acquittal," May 16,1868, and "Impeachment Ended," May 27, 1868

Johnson's impeachment nearly marked the end of his presidency, as the Senate voted 35 to 19 to convict him, just one vote short of the two-thirds constitutionally required. Seven Republican senators joined with the Democrats to support acquittal. *The Times* focused on the political ramifications of impeachment, suggesting that Johnson would do well to consider Congress's views on his executive appointees if he were permitted to stay in office. And Johnson did just that following his acquittal, appointing a new candidate for secretary of war endorsed by the Senate—Maj. Gen. John M. Schofield. Johnson also permitted the Military Reconstruction Act to be implemented as Congress wanted, despite his own opposition. In so doing, he succeeded, as *The Times* wrote, in "reciprocat[ing] the Senate's regard for law by cooperating with Congress during the remainder of his term."

MAY 16, 1868
THE EFFECTS OF ACQUITTAL.

A dispatch from Washington informs us that Gen. Grant thinks "the President ought to be removed, because the Government cannot go on safely in its present demoralized condition." Gen. Grant has a perfect right to hold and to express that opinion,—though we do not understand upon what it rests. We believe, as we have more than once said, that the practical working of the machinery of the Government must be very imperfect and unsatisfactory, so long as the President and Congress are at loggerheads. But what there is to imperil its *safety,* in the acquittal of the President, neither Gen. Grant nor Gen. Schenck has at all shown us.

But Gen. Grant's opinion is one thing and the action of a Senator is quite another. He may very properly believe and say that the welfare of the country would be promoted by the President's removal; and every member of the Senate may concur in that opinion, and yet not feel at liberty to vote for his conviction upon the impeachment which has just been tried. Senators act in this matter under special obligations which do not rest on Gen. Grant. They have taken very solemn oaths to decide certain definite and distinctly specified points,—to declare whether, in their judgments, and upon the testimony submitted to them, the President has or has not done certain *acts,* and also whether those acts constitute such "crimes and misdemeanors" as render him liable to impeachment and removal from office. If they believe both these allegations to be true, they are bound to vote to convict him; and if they do not believe

them both to be true, they cannot vote to convict him,—no matter what their opinion of the wisdom of his removal may be, without perjuring themselves. Mr. Fessenden, in his very cogent judgment on this case which we published yesterday, stated this necessity which rests upon each individual Senator, in language which must command the assent and respect of every man who holds the obligations of duty and of conscience higher than the dictates of political passion or the interests of political parties. "I should consider myself," he said, "undeserving of the confidence that just and intelligent people have imposed upon me in this great responsibility, and unworthy a place among honorable men, if, for any fear of public reprobation, and for the sake of securing popular favor, I should disregard the conviction of my judgment and my conscience. The consequences which may follow, either from conviction or acquittal, are not for me, with my convictions, to consider."

The results of acquittal would depend upon circumstances, mainly upon the President's manner of taking it. If he should consider it a personal triumph—a verdict in his favor as against Congress, on the political action which both have taken hitherto, a distinct sanction of the policy he has pursued, the temper he has shown, and the objects he has sought to accomplish, he could undoubtedly keep the political affairs of the country in a good deal of confusion for some months to come. But we do not see how he could very seriously affect or interfere with any of the leading objects of legislation, or with any of the great interests of the country. He can neither retard nor expedite reconstruction. He can neither keep States out nor bring them in. He can neither secure the admission or the exclusion of their members from either House of Congress. Nor is his control over the patronage of the Government such as to make it at all formidable to the country or the Republican Party.

But we receive from Washington intimations that the President has agreed to change his Cabinet, and thus to bring the general course and policy of his administration more closely into harmony with the sentiments and the will of Congress. This is the first symptom of practical good sense we have seen on his part. It shows that even Mr. Johnson is not utterly and hopelessly one of the proverbial Bourbons,—that even he can and does learn something from experience. If he had turned his face in this direction one or two years ago, he could have avoided all the disasters he has since encountered, and secured for himself a useful and successful administration, as well as for the country that peaceful resumption of its normal activity and prosperity which it so much needs. But it is a great deal better late than never. If Mr. Johnson has at last discovered that the Government does not exist for him, nor even for his high office, alone,—that it is a complicated machine, and that the cooperation of its several agencies,—the harmonious working of all its parts,—is essential to its stability and success,—and that it is quite

as much, (to say the least,) his duty to consult the sentiments and convictions of Congress, as it is the duty of Congress to consult and respect his; and if he is prepared to act, wisely and in good faith, upon this discovery, he can very easily deliver the Government from the deadlock into which his obstinate and perverse consistency has brought it.

Such a course, we do not hesitate to say, would be infinitely wiser and better for all the interests of the country than either his acquittal or conviction, on the naked merits of the case, and without any stipulation for the future conduct of affairs. His unqualified acquittal, without any assurances or precautions as to his future course, even if Senators should feel bound by their oaths to declare it, would leave the country in a state of anxiety and distrust. His conviction and removal, under the extraordinary pressure that has been brought to bear upon the Senate, would not receive the sanction of public sentiment, and would put the whole control of the Republican Party, and of public affairs, into the hands of the most ultra and least judicious and responsible of its leaders. Either of these results would involve more or less of disaster to the public interests. A medium course, which would secure a wise and harmonious administration of the Government, for the residue of Mr. Johnson's term, would conduce to the public peace, and to the promotion of all the great interests involved in the contest.

MAY 27, 1868
IMPEACHMENT ENDED.

Impeachment is out of the way at last. It was not without an effort, however, that the High Court approached its work yesterday. There were two motions for adjournment—one to Sept. 1, the other to June 23; and the rejection of the latter was effected by the casting vote of the Chief Justice.

After much fencing, a vote was taken on the second article, which alleged a violation of the Constitution and of the Tenure of Office act by the appointment of Lorenzo Thomas as Secretary of War *ad interim,* without the advice and consent of the Senate, at the time in session. The vote stood 35 to 19, and, therefore, again fell short of the requisite two-thirds. The seven Republican Senators who pronounced the President not guilty on the eleventh article, renewed their verdict yesterday. The third article, which was a variation of the same charge, was also submitted to a vote, with the same result. And the Court then adjourned *sine die.*

The formalities might have been better observed, perhaps. All the articles should have been voted upon or withdrawn, in order that the *debris* of the case might be cleared away, and the end reached with regularity, if not with dignity. But we will not be critical. It is satisfactory to have the trial ended, and some allowance may be made for the neglect of ceremony on an occasion into which feeling evidently entered rather largely.

The course being once more clear for business, let us hope that Congress will waste no further time in quarrels about the President, or in listening to suggestions for his removal. The impeachers have had the amplest opportunities of making out a case, with all the aid that party machinery could afford them. Having failed, let them take consolation in the glorious uncertainty of trial by jury, and address themselves to the urgent matters which await their attention. Active effort is prescribed by holy men as the best antidote to scepticism; and the majority who would have rejoiced over the President's removal, may find compensation for their disappointment in the energetic prosecution of work which the country will appreciate. There are services to be rendered in the next couple of months which Mr. Johnson's continuance in office can neither retard nor prostrate.

As for Mr. Johnson, it is not too much to expect that the impartiality which marked the proceedings of the Court, and the conscientiousness which led political opponents to vote for his acquittal, will in some measure influence his future action toward Congress. The case against him derived not a little of its strength from the presumption that acquittal would be misconstrued into indorsement. It is for the President to falsify this anticipation, and by the moderation of his conduct to avert further collision. He may not succeed in pleasing those who arraigned him, but at least he may reciprocate the Senate's regard for law by cooperating with Congress during the remainder of his term. The public remembrance of impeachment will be somewhat affected by the use he makes of his acquittal.

· ·

"Johnson as the Democratic Candidate," June 24, 1868

After Johnson's acquittal, his prospects for staying in office after his term ended were bleak. But Johnson, one of nearly fifty candidates, pursued the Democratic presidential nomination, and he won almost a third of the votes required to get the spot. *The Times* noted that Johnson had not been part of the Democratic Party since it seceded from the Union in the Civil War, but that his policies more closely reflected Democratic than Republican doctrine. Johnson's political record and his name recognition, *The Times* concluded, could serve the Democrats well in the election. But the party disagreed and nominated former New York governor Horatio Seymour for president.

JUNE 24, 1868
JOHNSON AS THE DEMOCRATIC CANDIDATE.

The Washington correspondent of the Baltimore *Gazette says:*

> "Friends of the President here claim that he will receive the largest vote on the first ballot in the New-York Convention, and anticipate on the part of the President, within the next three or four days, *some official demonstrations which will secure him the nomination.* They claim that Mr. Johnson's gallant stand for the Constitution entitles him to the gratitude and favor of the Conservative Party, and that some bold stroke of policy is all that is needed to secure it. Hence they say that important events are near at hand."

To claim the nomination as an acknowledgment of Mr. Johnson's "gallant stand for the Constitution," is one thing—and to make "official demonstrations" for the purpose of securing it, is quite another. If the Democratic Party were at all influenced by the considerations they speak of—if their regard for the Constitution and for the President's views of it, were as sincere as it is voluble, they would make Mr. Johnson their candidate at once. He has sustained their views of public policy for the last two years with a degree of ability and vigor for which they can find no parallel among the members of their own party. Setting aside entirely the correctness of his opinions, and the motives upon which he has acted, it is certainly due to Mr. Johnson to confess, that he has maintained his position and defended the Democratic faith with wonderful power and tenacity of purpose. Not one of the three last Democratic Presidents can compare with him for a moment in these respects.

Mr. Johnson, speaking in a party sense, has no claim on the Democrats for a nomination. He left the party—or rather the party left him—when he took ground against secession in the Senate: and although he has fallen back and acted upon very many Democratic doctrines and political opinions since that time, he has never re-enlisted in the party service. He has never surrendered the patronage of his office to the control of the party. He has never made its leaders his special advisers or allowed them to dictate either his policy or his action. He has been in the main independent of all outside dictation and advice; probably we have never had in this country before, a President who deferred to the opinions of others so little, and who had such unconquerable faith in his own, as Mr. Johnson. But without intending it as a party service, he has done more, by far, to keep alive the Democratic faith, and to present the Democratic doctrines strongly and clearly to the people, than any statesman of the Democratic Party, or than all of them put together. In the whole record of Congressional reports and speeches for the last three years, there is not a single speech or document that will compare, in intellectual force or in vigor and effectiveness of argument, with any of his principal veto messages.

But Presidents are not nominated for such services by the Democratic Party. What the party wants is *office; and what they need to get office is* votes. Mr. Johnson has not given them office to the extent of their desires, while he has had the power; nor have they faith that his name would give them the votes necessary to get office now. Hence they are not at all likely to put him in nomination. But upon all the grounds which used to be recognized as constituting a valid title, Mr. Johnson's claim on the Democratic Party is stronger than that of any other man who has been named in connection with the office. And we think it not at all unlikely that his name would be stronger with the people than three-fourths of those that are most loudly talked about.

> [D]oes any clear-headed man for a moment suppose that Mississippi, or Louisiana, or South Carolina would exclude the negroes from the suffrage, when by so doing they would sacrifice nearly one-half of their power in the United States Congress? The ratification of the Fourteenth Amendment furnishes, therefore, the strongest motive to the Southern States to support the reconstruction measures.

"The Fourteenth Amendment," July 31, 1868

One of the most significant actions in the Reconstruction era was the ratification of the Fourteenth Amendment to the Constitution in 1868. The amendment guarantees to all citizens of the United States "due process of law" and "equal protection of the laws," clauses that would be interpreted broadly by the Supreme Court in the twentieth century to expand civil liberties and civil rights. But in the nineteenth century the amendment was not enforced for black citizens. *The Times* idealistically wrote that ratification presented "the strongest motive to the Southern States to support the reconstruction measures." Although President Johnson opposed the measure, he did not have the power to stop it, as the Constitution includes only Congress, the states, and the people in the amendment process.

JULY 31, 1868
THE FOURTEENTH AMENDMENT.

The Secretary of State has promulgated the ratification of the Fourteenth Amendment. This official act sets at rest all questions hitherto raised upon the legitimacy or otherwise of the ratification. That is a great point gained. But what is settled by the Fourteenth Amendment? That is the important question.

I. No State can abridge the privileges or immunities of citizens of the United States, *i.e.*, of "persons born or naturalized in the United States, and subject to the jurisdiction thereof." The equal protection of the laws is guaranteed to all, without any exception.

II. The basis of representation is altered. If the negroes of the South are excluded from the franchise, then the Southern States lose the representation based upon the number of colored population.

III. No person who has violated his oath to support the Constitution of the United States can become a Senator or Representative, or a Presidential Elector, or hold any civil or military office under either the State or the Federal Government. But this disability can be annulled by a two-thirds vote of each House of Congress.

IV. The validity of the public debt—including debts incurred for the payment of soldiers' pensions and bounties—is placed beyond question. And all obligations incurred in the aid of rebellion are pronounced illegal and void.

That is the accomplished result. And it must be observed, in regard to political disabilities and the invalidity of the rebel debt, that the provisions of the amendment are general—they are not confined in their operation to the special case of the late rebellion.

Thus stands the Constitution to-day. Even the election of Seymour for President cannot alter the matter. The nullification of reconstruction cannot repeal this constitutional amendment.

And what will be the effect of this amendment in its operation in the South? It takes all its strength from the Democratic platform. That platform nullifies reconstruction, but does any clear-headed man for a moment suppose that Mississippi, or Louisiana, or South Carolina would exclude the negroes from the suffrage, when by so doing they would sacrifice nearly one-half of their power in the United States Congress? The ratification of the Fourteenth Amendment furnishes, therefore, the strongest motive to the Southern States to support the reconstruction measures.

- -

"Ex-President Johnson," February 4, 1875

Despite the failures of his presidency, Johnson eked out one last political victory in 1875, when the Tennessee legislature elected him to the U.S. Senate. (Senators were not popularly elected until the ratification of the Seventeenth Amendment in 1913.) Johnson therefore has the distinction of being the only former president elected to the Senate. He served for just a few months before succumbing to a fatal stroke.

FEBRUARY 4, 1875
EX-PRESIDENT JOHNSON.
HOW HIS ELECTION TO THE SENATE WAS BROUGHT ABOUT.

After describing Mr. Johnson's uncompromising war upon the ex-Confederate Democratic leaders in Tennessee in the political campaign of 1872 and 1874, the Knoxville *Chronicle* explains the method by which his election to the United States Senate has just been achieved. It says:

"The Legislature, in round numbers, was composed of seventy-eight ex-Confederates and twenty-two Union men. Politically, it was divided, ninety-two Democrats, seven Republicans and one Independent Republican. Johnson went to Nashville with the 'rebel military ring' bitterly opposed to him. His supporters were in a large minority in the Legislature, and it will hardly be controverted, even now, that his chances for election were considered very poor. The people recognized the issue. In the Legislature the lines were drawn between the Union and ex-rebel element. The exceptions were, when some of the ex-Confederates represented constituents who pledged them before election to vote for Johnson. Among the people, especially in East Tennessee, the lines were not so closely drawn, for many of his supporters here were ex-Confederates. But we fairly state the case, leaving out these exceptions, when we say the issue was between those who wore the gray and those who wore the blue. Gen. Brown, Gen. Bate, Gen. Quarles, Mr. Stephens, Mr. Ewing, and Mr. Henry, were all ex-rebels, and bitterly hostile personally to Johnson. In and about Johnson's head-quarters at Nashville, the fight was always claimed to be against the 'rebel Generals.' With this issue clearly defined, the eight Republicans voted naturally with Mr. Johnson. The Union Democrats stood by them, and among them the issue was well understood. As the fight progressed and the issue became too plain to be mistaken, the liberal element of the ex-Confederate wing of the Democracy saw the danger that would follow Johnson's defeat, and they aided the Union element to break down the 'military ring.' Gen. Gordon telegraphs to Nashville to know the number of Confederates who voted for Johnson. He is answered that of the fifty-two votes he received, thirty were ex-Confederates. But he was not told that of these thirty, at least fourteen voted for him under 'instructions,' and against their own personal inclinations. These instructions came largely from Conservative Union constituents. Without the Republican vote Johnson could never have been elected. Without the Union Conservative vote, he would have been dropped in the balloting the first day. If left to the mercy of his Confederate ex-Democratic associates, instead of being a Senator to-day he would be loaded with all the disgrace and mortification an overwhelming defeat could administer, in what he and his friends said was the 'old man's last fight.' These are facts, and upon these let the verdict of the country be rendered."

THE PRESIDENCY OF ULYSSES S. GRANT

MARCH 4, 1869 – MARCH 4, 1877

Ulysses S. Grant's presidency is remembered more for its problems than for its accomplishments. The architect of Union victory in the Civil War, Grant won election to the presidency in 1868 primarily because of his distinguished military record. His military success did not translate into political acumen. During his two terms in the White House, Grant oversaw Reconstruction of the southern states, but his efforts were overshadowed by financial scandals involving some of his top advisers. Although Grant was not personally involved in the scandals, his reputation and legacy were nevertheless tarnished by them.

An Ohio native, Grant was named Hiram Ulysses Grant at birth, but he switched his first and middle names when he entered the United States Military Academy at West Point. The school registered his name as Ulysses S. Grant, and Grant never corrected it. He was not keen on attending the military academy, but his father secured an appointment for him, and Grant accepted. This reluctance may have contributed to his mediocre performance, as he ranked twenty-first out of thirty-nine in his graduating class of 1843. Grant entered the army and served with distinction in the Mexican War of 1846–1848. But the postwar army brought less promising assignments that separated Grant from his family, and in 1854 he resigned from the military.

This period marked perhaps the most difficult time in Grant's prepresidential years. He tried his hand at farming and real estate in Missouri and failed. In 1860 he accepted a position in the family hardware and leather store in Galena, Illinois. Working for his younger brother in his father's business was not satisfying, but Grant would endure it for less than a year before events intervened.

With the onset of the Civil War, Grant reentered the army and earned quick recognition for his superb performance. Promoted to brigadier general in 1861, Grant oversaw the first major Union victory with the capture of Fort Donelson in Tennessee. As major general—with the nickname "Uncondi-

Source: Library of Congress

tional Surrender" for his insistence that Confederate forces do just that—in 1862 Grant successfully defeated Confederate forces in Shiloh, Tennessee, and was elevated to the command of all Union forces. Following the Union victory in Vicksburg, Mississippi, in 1863, Grant was promoted to lieutenant general and general in chief of the army in 1864. One year later, Gen. Robert E. Lee, the Confederate commander, surrendered to Grant in Appomattox, Virginia.

With the end of the war, Grant was promoted in 1866 to general of the armies of the United States, the first person to be awarded four stars. His national fame brought

QUICK FACTS ON ULYSSES S. GRANT

BIRTH	April 27, 1822, Point Pleasant, Ohio
EDUCATION	United States Military Academy, West Point, N.Y.
FAMILY	Wife: Julia Grant Children: Frederick Dent Grant; Ulysses Simpson Grant; Ellen Wrenshall Grant; Jesse Root Grant
WHITE HOUSE PETS	Horses, ponies, parrot, dog
PARTY	Republican
PREPRESIDENTIAL CAREER (SELECTED)	Served in Mexican War, 1846–1848 Resigned from army, 1854 Clerk in father's hardware/leather store, Galena, Ill., 1860–1861 Brigadier general, 1861 Major general, 1862 Lieutenant general, 1864 Lee surrenders to Grant at Appomattox, Va., 1865 General of the Army, 1866, the first person to be awarded four stars by Congress
PRESIDENTIAL TERMS	March 4, 1869–March 4, 1873 March 4, 1873–March 4, 1877
VICE PRESIDENTS	Schuyler Colfax (first term) Henry Wilson (second term)
SELECTED EVENTS	Public Credit Act (1869) Ratification of Fifteenth Amendment (1870) Creation of Department of Justice (1870) Ku Klux Klan Act (1871) Treaty of Washington (1871) Crédit Mobilier scandal (1872) Invention of telephone by Alexander Graham Bell (1876) Defeat of Gen. George A. Custer by Sitting Bull at Little Big Horn River, Mont. (1876)
POSTPRESIDENCY	World tour, 1877–1879 Unsuccessful candidate for Republican presidential nomination, 1880 Financial failure, 1884 Completion of memoirs, four days before death, 1885
DEATH	July 23, 1885, Mount McGregor, N.Y.

gifts such as a house in Galena, Illinois, and another in Philadelphia. With his army command, Grant and his family settled in Washington, D.C. Despite Grant's reluctance, President Andrew Johnson appointed him secretary of war, after dismissing the incumbent, Edwin M. Stanton. When Congress declared that the president had violated the Tenure of Office Act by not seeking its approval for dismissing Stanton, Grant resigned, much to Johnson's dismay, as the president had hoped to wage battle with Congress over the law with Grant's help.

THE 1868 CAMPAIGN

Given Grant's national popularity by the end of the Civil War, he was a natural choice for the Republican presidential nomination in 1868. Indeed, both the Republican and Democratic Parties had considered nominating Grant in 1864, and President Abraham Lincoln confirmed that Grant would not accept such an offer before promoting him to lieutenant general. But by 1868, particularly after his refusal to support Johnson's efforts against the Tenure of Office Act, Grant was open to a presidential run. He received a unanimous nomination at the Republican Party convention, and the party selected Rep. Schuyler Colfax of Indiana as his running mate.

The Democratic Party was in such disarray that Grant was able to wage a comfortable election campaign with the simple slogan, "Let us have peace." After more than twenty ballots, the Democrats nominated former New York governor Horatio Seymour for president and Francis P. Blair Jr. of Missouri as his running mate. Grant won 214 Electoral College votes (26 states) and more than 3 million popular votes to Seymour's 80 Electoral College votes (8 states) and 2.7 million popular votes. Three former Confederate states—Mississippi, Texas, and Virginia—did not participate.

THE GRANT ADMINISTRATION (FIRST TERM)

Upon entering office, Grant appointed a cabinet composed primarily of Republicans loyal to him and moderately conservative in their views on Reconstruction. Former New York governor Hamilton Fish became secretary of state. (He was preceded for just a few days in the new administration by Elihu H. Washburne of Illinois, a friend of the president who became minister to France with the distinction of saying he had served in Grant's cabinet.) Secretary of War John A. Rawlins also was a good friend of Grant's, but he served for less than six months; Gen. William T. Sherman of Ohio held the position for a few weeks, and then William W. Belknap of Iowa served for the remainder of Grant's first term and into his second.

Treasury Secretary George S. Boutwell of Massachusetts came from Congress and was one of the few Radical Republicans selected by Grant. For attorney general, Grant chose E. Rockwood Hoar of Massachusetts (followed by Amos T. Akerman of Georgia and George H. Williams of Oregon). He chose Jacob D. Cox of Ohio to be secretary of the interior. Rounding out the cabinet were Postmaster General John A. J. Creswell of Maryland and Secretary of the Navy Adolph E. Borie of Pennsylvania, who was soon replaced by George M. Robeson of New Jersey.

First Lady Julia D. Grant was a popular White House hostess who took an interest in politics and advised her husband on matters of state. She befriended women's rights activist Susan B. Anthony, who supported President Grant's second term, even though a woman presidential candidate, Victoria C. Woodhull, also ran for the first time (with distinguished antislavery activist and first black vice-presidential candidate Frederick Douglass) in 1872. The Grants had four children. Ulysses Jr. became presidential secretary for his father, and daughter Ellen ("Nellie") was married at the White House in 1874.

MAJOR ISSUES (FIRST TERM)

Perhaps the most pressing issue for President Grant was Reconstruction of the South, and he could report some progress in this area by the end of his first term. The Fifteenth Amendment guaranteeing that the right to vote would not be denied "on account of race, color, or previous condition of servitude" was proposed in Congress just before Grant's first inauguration, and it was ratified in 1870 with the president's support. By 1871 all southern states had seated members of Congress and agreed to comply with the Fifteenth Amendment.

Grant also asked Congress to pass legislation that would permit him to impose martial law in places where local officials were not enforcing black citizens' rights, and Congress did so with the Ku Klux Klan Act of 1871. The president additionally spurred Congress to extend amnesty to almost all Confederate soldiers in 1872. But recognizing the stiff obstacles presented by southern states, neither the administration nor Congress enforced Reconstruction aggressively. Not until the civil rights movement nearly one hundred years later would Reconstruction legislation be fully implemented to grant political rights to black Americans.

In other areas, the Grant administration had similarly mixed success. The Public Credit Act of 1869 helped to reduce the national debt and avoid inflation through the use of gold rather than the issuance of additional paper money. Wealthy businessmen close to Grant sparked a financial panic on September 24, 1869, that became known as "Black Friday," and prompted a congressional investigation. Although Grant was not involved in the scandal, his contact with those responsible proved embarrassing.

The Grant administration successfully negotiated the Treaty of Washington with Great Britain in 1871 to receive compensation for British support of the Confederacy in the Civil War. But Grant failed in his effort to annex Santo Domingo, with senators from both parties opposing the treaty. The administration also was tainted by the Crédit Mobilier scheme in 1872, which involved profits associated with the creation of the transcontinental railroad and would taint both of Grant's vice presidents.

THE 1872 REELECTION CAMPAIGN

The 1872 presidential election presented no difficulties for Grant. His party unanimously nominated him for a second term on the first convention ballot and chose Henry Wilson of Massachusetts as his running mate. Liberal Republicans, disappointed with Grant's leadership on Reconstruction, economic policy, and civil service reform, joined with Democrats to nominate newspaper editor Horace Greeley of New York for president and Benjamin G. Brown of Missouri for vice president. Grant won overwhelmingly, with nearly 3.6 million votes to Greeley's 2.8 million—the largest percentage of the popular vote since Andrew Jackson's victory in 1828. In the Electoral College, Grant won 286 of 352 votes, representing 29 states. Because Greeley died just three weeks after the election, the Electoral College votes in the six states that he carried were cast for others. Two states, Arkansas and Louisiana, did not participate.

THE GRANT ADMINISTRATION (SECOND TERM)

Angered by criticism from his own party's Liberal Republicans, Grant became even more attentive to personal loyalty from his appointees in his second term. Hamilton Fish continued as secretary of state, but Grant had to make several new appointments in the other cabinet departments. Over two terms, he nominated twenty-five men for seven cabinet positions, including five new appointments during his final year in office. Grant's focus on loyalty hindered his selection of top advisers, resulting in numerous scandals that reflected poorly on the administration, even though the president was not personally responsible.

Grant's second-term appointments led to investigations, trials, and impeachment of corrupt officials. Treasury Secretary Benjamin F. Bristow discovered that some federal agents responsible for collecting liquor taxes were taking bribes instead, a scandal that became known as the "Whiskey Ring." Grant's private secretary, Orville E. Babcock, was involved, but the president refused to believe the charges and demanded that Bristow resign. Secretary of War Belknap also was discovered to be accepting bribes, and, although he resigned, the House of Representatives still impeached him. Despite these crises, Grant had support for a third term, but he disavowed the possibility with a public letter. The Republicans won the presidency again in 1876, but the administration of Grant's successor, Gov. Rutherford B. Hayes of Ohio, would be overshadowed by Hayes's failure to win the popular vote.

After leaving office, Grant and his wife took a worldwide tour. He sought the Republican presidential nomination again in 1880 and won more than three-quarters of the required votes, but ultimately lost to James A. Garfield. When financial scandal hurt Grant's reputation and income late in life, he agreed to write his memoirs to support his family. Suffering from cancer, Grant completed his manuscript just days before his death. The book became a financial success, due in no small part to the efforts of Mark Twain (Samuel Clemens), a close friend of Grant's who encouraged publication. In many respects, Grant's prepresidential and postpresidential years illustrated his leadership and talents more than his time in the White House.

• •

"GRANT'S GREAT TRIUMPH," NOVEMBER 4, 1868

General Grant's national popularity following the Civil War carried him into the White House in 1868. As *The New York Times* noted, Grant won three-quarters of the states in the Union and by larger majorities than expected. *The Times* captured national sentiment in its description of Grant: "He represented the supremacy of the Union and the Constitution, the supremacy of liberty and loyalty, the supremacy of law, order and peace." Grant sought to achieve the same goals as president, but his military leadership style did not serve him as well in the political realm.

NOVEMBER 4, 1868
GRANT'S GREAT TRIUMPH.

It is now seen that the assurance which the Republicans have always expressed in Grant's election was amply justified.

He has carried three-fourths of all the States of the Union; and he has carried them by larger majorities than were expected even by sanguine calculators.

It is fortunate for the country that the vote for him has been so large as to leave no possibility of dispute, no ground for questioning the validity of the eletion [sic] in any respect, and no necessity for close calculations or close shaving to prove a success.

All the frauds of the Democracy in the North,—all the coercion and intimidation of colored voters in the South,—have failed to give victory to the Democratic Party. They might carry New-York by a reign of fraud, and Louisiana by a reign of terror;—they might carry Kentucky and Maryland by the votes of men who were lately arrayed in battle against the American flag;—they might have voted in Texas, Mississippi and Virginia, as they threatened to do, and might have carried these States;—and yet the Republicans would have given them greater odds and still won a decisive success.

The country may well be congratulated on this result.

It has now been shown that the assurance of the Republicans before the election was not mere empty boasting. Their confidence was perfectly intelligible and natural. It was based on the fact that Grant stood as the representative of the principles that are acknowledged to be of the highest importance to the American people, and for the maintenance of which a million of American citizens were but lately in arms. He represented the supremacy of the Union and the Constitution, the supremacy of liberty and loyalty, the supremacy of law, order and peace. For the past, he represented the triumphant ideas of the war; and for the future, he represented the ideas that constitute the foundation of national well-being. Whatever merits may have been claimed for Mr. Seymour, it has not been claimed that he stood as the representative of these principles and ideas. In his late speeches he has constantly and vehemently protested that he loved his country; and we do not dispute the statement. But the people demanded different evidences of patriotism from those which he was able to furnish. They demanded the proof of patriotic services rendered in the times that tried men's souls. And it is sufficient to account for his defeat when we say that Mr. Seymour was not able to furnish such proofs of the magnitude of his patriotic services, and the fervor of his loyal devotion, as were offered by Gen. Grant. Had his record, on this single point, been better than the record of Gen. Grant, we have not a doubt that he would yesterday have been elected President of the United States.

It was upon the profound appreciation of this matter by the American people that we based our confidence in Grant's election. Not during this generation, nor during the next, will the people of this country lose sight of the great war, or forget the part played in it by those who have been leaders, or who may aspire to be leaders. To have been false to the Republic in that tremendous crisis, or to have been lukewarm in its service, will be a brand of political ruin for many a year to come. It will be useless during this century for any political party to nominate a Presidential candidate, who cannot show that he battled for the Union with hand and heart when rebelion [sic] had the sword at its throat. And in this determination the American people are perfectly justified—even from the highest grounds of conciliation, fraternity and peace.

. . . .

"GEN. GRANT'S INAUGURAL," MARCH 5, 1869

President Grant's first inaugural address laid out simple themes of governance. The new president promised to further Reconstruction, repay the nation's war debt, support the Fifteenth Amendment, and promote a foreign policy that would respect other nations as they respected the United States. The straightforward agenda illustrated Grant's moderate approach to governance; as *The Times* wrote, "All that the office requires of Gen. Grant he will strive to perform."

MARCH 5, 1869
GEN. GRANT'S INAUGURAL.

The characteristics which distinguish Gen. Grant, and command the confidence which marks his entrance upon the duties of the Executive, are conspicuous in his inaugural address. It is brief, clear, emphatic and to the purpose. It touches great wants, indicates great duties, and propounds a great policy with a distinctness that leaves nothing in doubt, and the force of true-born earnestness. Gen. Grant had something to say, and he has said it strongly and well.

All that the office requires of Gen. Grant he will strive to perform. He assumes the Presidential office with a full sense of its responsibilities, but without misunderstanding or fear. The laws will have in him no feeble administrator. His opinions in reference to their merits will not interfere with their enforcement. He will have a "policy to recommend," but "none to enforce against the will of the people."

The necessity of perfecting the restoration of the Union and healing the wounds of war is positively affirmed. "Calmly, without prejudice, hate or sectional pride," he invokes the consideration of whatever may be needed to secure these ends. The security of person and property, and the freedom of "religious and political opinion in every part of our common country, without regard to local prejudice," he will uphold under existing laws.

The sacredness of the war debt, and the duty of discharging every dollar in gold where currency is not specifically prescribed, are points in which the address is very emphatic. The repudiator Gen. Grant stigmatizes as unworthy of trust in any public position. The honor and interests of the country alike require the amplest consideration for the public creditor. The debt ceases to be formidable when compared with the resources of the Republic; and neither principal nor interest will under proper management fall heavily upon the debtor class.

Firmness and good faith upon this subject will, in Gen. Grant's judgment, enable us soon to replace outstanding bonds with others bearing a lower rate of interest. Still further to promote this object and lessen the burdens of the people, he urges more attention to the collection of the revenue: "A strict accountability to the Treasury for every dollar collected, and the greatest possible retrenchment in expenditure in every department of Government."

The payment of the public debt, to the last dollar, and the resumption of specie payments, are objects which Gen. Grant would have the country keep constantly in view. To the empiricism which would construct short roads to either object he affords no encouragement. Nothing will be gained by hurry. Legislation "may not be necessary now nor even advisable, but it will be when the civil law is more fully restored in all parts of the country, and trade resumes its wonted channels."

The Fifteenth Amendment he commends for ratification, as a desirable settlement of the question of suffrage.

In regard to foreign policy the language of the address is guarded and general. The prophets who foretold hard words on the *Alabama* question are signally belied. Gen. Grant lays down the Golden Rule as that by which he proposes to be guided in intercourse with foreign Governments. He will respect their rights and demand equal respect for our own. If they fail in their duty, "we may be compelled to follow their precedent." Beyond these declarations, we have no clue to his policy toward other nations, and none else is now required.

Naturalized citizens are associated with native citizens in the pledge of protection at home or abroad.

Gen. Grant, in conclusion, invokes patient forbearance in regard to his own purposes and plans, and cordial coöperation on the part of all in a determined effort to restore national unity and happiness.

We shall be mistaken if this revelation of his spirit, and this brief exposition of his policy be not heartily approved by the American people.

"President Grant's Cabinet," March 6, 1869

Despite concerns that the new president would be beholden to others with his cabinet choices, Grant's appointees demonstrated the political skill necessary to hold high office in the executive branch. Their common traits were prior public service and loyalty to the president. As *The Times* wrote, Grant "has appointed the men who compose [the cabinet], because they suited *him,*—not because they suited someone else." But some of Grant's advisers ultimately would prove to be more interested in private profit than the public good.

MARCH 6, 1869
PRESIDENT GRANT'S CABINET.

The Cabinet appointed by Gen. Grant yesterday took everybody by surprise. Nothing can illustrate more clearly how perfectly Grant has succeeded in keeping his own counsel than the fact that not one of the names most commonly mentioned for any Cabinet position proved to be the one selected. The Cabinet is eminently and evidently one of the President's own selection. He has appointed the men who compose it, because they suited *him,*—not because they suited somebody else. They are not taken from the class of prominent politicians of *any* school or of any party. They are all Republicans of pronounced views, and both active and effective in political affairs; but it is not *as* politicians that they have made their mark or evinced the qualities that caused their appointment to high office. Yet political experience is by no means

wanting in the Cabinet. Several of its members have seen already a good deal of public life, and have vindicated their claim to public confidence by the ability and fidelity with which they have met its responsibilities and performed its duties. . . .

The Cabinet as a whole will not commend itself to the favor of politicians, because it has not been taken from their ranks; nor are the men who compose it sufficiently well known to the public at large to command in advance the full confidence of the community. But in the very freshness of its character, in the fact that its members are business men rather than politicians, and are likely to make the practical interests of the country their first care, we see ground for believing that the Cabinet will, by its practical working, vindicate the wisdom of its selection.

"The Public Credit Bill," March 15, 1869

The Public Credit Act of 1869 was passed to establish a program for repaying the debt incurred by the United States in the Civil War. To prevent inflation, the act, strongly supported by both President Grant and Congress, declared that payment would be made in gold rather than paper money, to prevent inflation.

MARCH 15, 1869
THE PUBLIC CREDIT BILL.

The "act to strengthen the public credit of the United States," which was quietly pocketed by Mr. Johnson, will now reach General Grant curtailed in one important particular. Both the Senate and House having stricken out the section relating to gold contracts, the measure

is now precisely what its title indicates—an explicit declaration of the light in which the United States regards its obligations to the public creditor, and its purpose to discharge them in coin. We are glad to see retained the provision forbidding the payment of any portion of the gold-interest debt before it matures, unless meanwhile resumption of specie payments be effected. The language of the bill upon this point will bear repeating:

> "None of said interest-bearing obligations not already due shall be redeemed or paid before maturity, unless at such time United States notes shall be convertible into coin at the option of the holder, or unless at such time bonds of the United States bearing a lower rate of interest than the bonds to be redeemed can be sold at par in coin; and the United States shall also solemnly pledge its faith to make a provision at the earliest practicable period for the redemption of United States notes in coin."

We accept this provision as a rebuke to the schemes of those who, in utter disregard of the condition of trade and the onerous taxation borne by the people, would cultivate a surplus for the discharge of liabilities not yet due. By this bill Congress protests—as the President protested in his Inaugural—against the financial policy which ignores the interests of the debtor class; and there are reasons for believing that the course it foreshadows will be followed by the Administration. There is no better method of strengthening the public credit than that which aims at reducing the burdens and promoting the prosperity of the country, for thus will specie payments be most quickly reached.

The ground upon which the gold contract clause has been expunged does not appear unreasonable. The Supreme Court has decided that gold contracts are already legal, and, as Mr. Sumner asks, What more is required? It might be desirable so to fence about the rights of debtors that an usurious creditor should be unable to take unfair advantage of their necessities; but so far as the mere legalization of gold bargains is concerned, the recent decision has affirmed all that has been wanted. Questions may hereafter come up requiring some more specific enactment than is now in force, but for all the immediate purposes of business the decision of the Supreme Court is sufficient. So at least, Congress has intimated by its amendment of Mr. Schenck's bill.

"THE RECONSTRUCTION POLICY OF THE SOUTH," MARCH 2, 1870

As Reconstruction continued in the Grant administration, the challenge of reuniting North and South in spirit as well as law became clear. Writing one year into Grant's term, *The Times* pointed out that both sides needed to work toward their common goal, the North by accepting amnesty for Confederate soldiers and the South by tempering its sectional rhetoric. The paper also noted "many recent expressions of a reviving spirit of bitterness in the Southern Press."

 Our people must become homogeneous in political thought and action, as well as in interest. The political sentiment of all sections must be nationalized, before we can harvest the full fruits of our grand struggle.

MARCH 2, 1870
THE RECONSTRUCTION POLICY OF THE SOUTH.

Reconstruction is now so nearly perfected, and its adjustment so definitely assured, that the probable resulting effects are a matter of legitimate and profitable inquiry. The grand problem to be solved very naturally divides itself into two substantive points. The North must insist, most uncompromisingly, upon a permanent recognition and settlement of the political principles which constituted the issue upon which the war of the rebellion was fought; we must turn our backs, forever, upon the ancient political heresies of the old Calhoun school, and move forward to the realization of the perfected nationality which lies before us. So far as mere legislation can do this, it has been done, and it only remains for us, as a people, to adjust the minor details of social and sectional reconciliation. The chief of these forms the second of the substantive points we have mentioned. It is to obliterate the asperities which have been engendered by the war, and especially to heal the older animosities and prejudices of sectionalism which have been strengthened by half a century of antagonism between the North and the South.

Our people must become homogeneous in political thought and action, as well as in interest. The political sentiment of all sections must be nationalized, before we can harvest the full fruits of our grand struggle. The problem is hardly less difficult of solution than it was ten years ago—it certainly is not less a matter of patriotic solicitude than it was in 1796, when Washington solemnly warned his countrymen to frown upon "every attempt to alienate any portion of our country from the rest, or to enfeeble the sacred ties which now link together the various parts." It is to this work of pacification that present political action must tend, if we would hope fully to realize the American Rennaissance.

To that end an equal obligation rests upon all sections. We recently pointed out the duty as well as the policy of conciliation and amnesty upon the part of the North; we desire now to counsel a reciprocal action, based upon a corresponding obligation which rests upon the South. We have been moved to do so by encountering many recent expressions of a reviving spirit of bitterness in the Southern Press, and by a feeling that, if not guarded against, the ancient fire of sectionalism will again break out, and complicate and retard, if it does not thwart, that true reconstruction which can only come from sectional harmony.

Southern demagogues are as numerous and as mischievous as Northern ones, and both must be discountenanced. We are sure that a little reflection upon the part of intelligent political observers of both sections would cause them to rebuke the mischief-makers. Already we encounter outcroppings of the old Southern arrogance and defiance which was so common before and during the war. Especially has this been the case within the last few weeks. We might cite many illustrations, but a few specimens will suffice. The Montgomery (Ala.) *Mail* recently said: "Congress have reached the length of their tether, and will not *dare* to interfere further in the affairs of a State." The Mobile *Tribune,* of Friday last, denounces Northern emigration, and especially that from New-England, and said:

> "The influx of people not homogeneous, and the consequent spreading of populations through the vast northwestern territory, all greatly tinctured

with the fanatically self-righteous and malignantly envious spirit of New-England, contributed greatly towards giving a preponderating influence to the section rendered encroaching and anarchical by the very natures of its people and their institutions. This spirit, culminating in triumph in 1860, forced the South, as its last and only resort, to take shelter behind its reserved rights of sovereignty, and to withdraw from the constitutional compact of union."

It declares that "recuperation or extinction is the alternative set before us by the implacable New-England demoniacs," and significantly asks:

> "Shall we submit to be mongrelized to gratify and satiate Northern hate, or shall we snatch up some little of the spirit of our hero-dead, and scout the abhorrent thought?"

The Augusta (Ga.) *Chronicle* recently said:

> "Those who direct the Government of the United States, acted and still act towards the people of the South not as assured of power of the Government nor of its continued existence, but as winners of a doubtful game from an antagonist still too powerful to be trusted."

These are but average specimens of a very general expression of feeling upon the part of the Southern Press. We submit that they are faint echoes of the old gasconade which was rung in our ears before the war, and from which we have won immunity. We remember how, in the past, similar utterances gathered strength by iteration, and finally seduced the South into the fatal mistake—to them—of rebellion. That error will never be repeated; but if the South shall persist in its sectionalism, the result will be a new "irrepressible conflict" which will paralyze its future material progress, and possibly postpone indefinitely the realization of a perfected nationality.

There should be no further serious impediment in the path of our future adjustments. The nation has passed the most serious stumbling blocks and overcome its organic inheritances of evil. A grand future confronts it, and if the North and the South would but realize their mutual obligations, and temper their political and social intercourse with moderation and a realizing sense of a common destiny, all would be well.

"THE FIFTEENTH AMENDMENT," APRIL 2, 1870

The Fifteenth Amendment to the Constitution was ratified in 1870 and guaranteed that the right to vote would not be denied based on "race, color, or previous condition of servitude." Although the president has no part in the amendment process—the Constitution gives that power to Congress, the states, and special conventions of the people—President Grant supported the amendment and encouraged its ratification.

APRIL 2, 1870
THE FIFTEENTH AMENDMENT.

A Demonstration in Washington—Remarks by the President, the Vice-President, and Senator Sumner.

WASHINGTON, April 1.—A Committee appointed at a meeting of the First Ward Republican Club, last night, waited on President Grant today, and tendered him their thanks on behalf of the colored people for making the ratification of the Fifteenth Amendment the subject of a message to Congress, and for the interest he had manifested in promoting their political and social interests. The Committee tendered him a serenade, for which the President thanked them and said it would afford him pleasure to receive them to-night. Accordingly, at 8½ o'clock this evening, a large crowd gathered before the Executive Mansion, when the band played "Hail to the Chief," and the President, accompanied by Col. J. W. Forney, representing the Republican Association, appeared at the door of the Executive mansion. After repeated applause at the appearance of the President and the introduction to him of the Committee, Col. Forney, on behalf of the Republican citizens, announced to the President that they called upon him to express their profound gratification for the proclamation which seals the great work of their emancipation. Col. Forney also briefly described the beneficial results which would ensue to the race by the adoption of the Fifteenth Amendment.

To this the President responded:

I can assure those present that no consummation since the close of the war affords me so much pleasure as the ratification of the Fifteenth Amendment to the Constitution by three-fourths of the States of the Union. I have felt the greatest anxiety ever since I was called to this House to know that this was to be secured. It looked like the realization of the Declaration of Independence. [Applause.] I cannot say near so much on this subject as I would like to, not being accustomed to speaking, but I thank you for your presence this evening.

When the applause, which greeted the President's remarks, had subsided, Vice-President Colfax, who was present, was called upon. He made a short address, assuring those present that his heart was with them in gratitude for the proclamation which has declared to the people of this Republic and to the people of the world the ratification of the Fifteenth Amendment.

"ORDER IN THE SOUTH," MAY 27, 1871

The Ku Klux Klan Act of 1871 aimed to enforce national laws protecting black citizens in the South. Passed shortly after the ratification of the Fifteenth Amendment, the new law granted broad powers to the federal government to ensure the rights of black Americans.

MAY 27, 1871
ORDER IN THE SOUTH

When a Democratic journal is about to show what a monstrous act of tyranny the Kuklux bill is, it usually begins by assuring us that the South is really more tranquil and orderly than any other section of the country. To be sure, appearances are a little against this agreeable theory, and malevolent Republicans and evil-disposed negroes have a vexatious way of getting themselves shot and beaten every now and then, which is a trifle embarrassing. But when we learn that they do this out of pure malignity, in order to blast the character of Southern society, and bring upon it the minions of a military despotism, our doubts are relieved. If negro preachers will bellow, and Republicans will hold offices which rightfully belong to their Democratic neighbors, of course they must expect to be shot, or whipped to death. And the high-toned and chivalric gentlemen who do the shooting and whipping ought not to be blamed for what is at best a sad necessity forced on them by the designing persons aforesaid.

Accepting this view of the situation, and conceding that those midnight diversions of the Kuklux, which seem to our prejudiced eyes wanton and cowardly murders, are in reality only Republican devices to bring odium on a magnanimous people, it is, perhaps, true that there is no more crime and bloodshed on the average in the South than in the North. But when we come to examine the character of the criminal classes in the two sections, we find a very remarkable and ominous difference. With us there are people who murder, and people who are murdered, and they constitute in the main two distinct portions of the population. Besides, except in certain places like New-York, where Democratic rule has fostered a certain tropical liberality of sentiment in such matters, promiscuous homicide is here regarded with disfavor. Punishment, too, is for the most part to all alike. The learned philologist is hung as speedily as the ignorant tramp. Of course in the North, too, there are family feuds which sometimes lead to murder. Only last Wednesday, from such a cause, Mr. William L. Parmlee, President of the First National Bank of Yongerstown, in Ohio, came to be shot and wounded by Mr. James R. Tyne, his wife's cousin. But to show how differently we are impressed as regards the social condition of the two sections, we shall expect to hear that Mr. Tyne has been, at least, arrested. But when a bank President in the South is even killed by his wife's cousin, we only expect to hear that the latter is in turn assassinated by some kinsman of his victim. And so the dead-roll grows. . . .

With pastimes like this in vogue, with almost nightly raids of Kuklux marauders in almost every State, with men and women here and there shot down in broad daylight, and above all with a public sentiment singularly callous to the sinfulness of bloodshed, is it not hard to believe that the South is altogether so tranquil and orderly as Democratic optimists would have us believe? And would it not be well for Southern men, who have at heart the welfare of their people and of the whole country, to consider if no means can be found to create a more wholesome feeling on so important a matter?

"British 'Humiliation' in the Treaty of Washington,"
June 29, 1871

The Treaty of Washington marked a significant foreign policy success for the Grant administration. Secretary of State Hamilton Fish negotiated the agreement, which penalized Great Britain for failing to observe neutrality in the Civil War. The United States would receive monetary compensation from Great Britain for the war damage caused by British-built ships for the Confederacy, such as the *Alabama*.

JUNE 29, 1871
BRITISH "HUMILIATION" IN THE TREATY OF WASHINGTON.

Official announcement has been made of the exchange of ratifications of the Treaty of Washington, and, so far as the two Governments are concerned, the agreement on its terms is complete. The sentiment current among Englishmen, in regard to its provisions, is expressed somewhat as follows: "We are glad this ugly business is settled, but we don't see why we should be made to pay damages on principles of law which did not exist in our code." In the British Press we find frequent reference to "the abject submission" of the English Commissioners, in allowing the question to be determined "by principles of law which did not exist when the offense was committed, but which are to exist hereafter." In the recent debate in the House of Lords, Earl Russell and other opponents of the treaty took continually the same ground. One noble orator likened the advantages of the United States Government in the international dispute to those of "a member of a family who has a notoriously bad temper." Everybody yields to him beforehand because it is known he is so unreasonable.

The "average Englishman," who, on such topics, is a model of stupidity, will evidently think himself wronged by this treaty, and, if the decision of the arbitrator be against Great Britain, will feel that he has to pay damages on unreasonable rules of law, got up after the offense by his adversary. Now this whole idea and popular statement is perfect nonsense. And those who desire a reasonable settlement of the international difficulties on grounds which "the average man" everywhere will understand, should make this evident to the British popular mind.

In the first place, the British and American municipal law are almost precisely the same as bearing on the questions at issue. The British "Foreign Enlistment act" is almost exactly modeled after our Neutrality acts of 1794 and 1818. The only difference between them is that the tenth and eleventh sections of our act are omitted in the British, and these only require the owners or consignors of armed vessels about to sail from our ports, to give security that they shall not be employed for hostile purposes against a Power at peace with the United States, and authorize revenue officers to detain vessels built for warlike purposes, and whose cargo shall consist chiefly of munitions of war, when warlike *intent* is probable. Both laws forbid making the ports of their countries the base of warlike expeditions, and constitute it a criminal act to fit out, arm, or equip a vessel, with intent to employ it in the service of a foreign State against a Power at peace with the country passing the law. The only difference between the two acts is, that our own makes it the duty of municipal officers to be more strict in arresting vessels for probable warlike intent than does the British act. Both forbid the same things, and both have apparently the same humane and reasonable object: To prevent a belligerent from making use of the resources and ports of a neutral to injure his opponent. As it happens, the British authorities had interposed the law selfishly, and continued to do so during our civil war. Our Government has been consistent, public spirited and honest in its execution of the Neutrality laws from the beginning. We urged neutral rights, when a weak Power, even at the cannon's mouth, against a superior one. We stood by our own principles toward inferior Powers, when our interest was in stretching belligerent rights. There is no duplicity or false dealing in this matter through our history. We again urged these principles on the British Government when rebellion had split the nation in two, and was apparently draining its life-blood. And even then, in our life-and-death struggle, we would have gone to war with Great Britain had these principles been utterly and openly trampled on by the British authorities. We are still foremost, in this treaty, advocating the same "rules" or "principles" when they have ceased to be of advantage to us, and are of immense importance to Great Britain.

The new "rules" adopted by both parties in the settlement of the *Alabama* claims, are simply the principles at the basis of both their municipal laws; that "due diligence" shall be used to prevent the equipping of a vessel intended to cruise against a Power at peace with Great Britain, and to prevent her departure, if she has been prepared for warlike purposes within British jurisdiction. Also that no belligerent shall use neutral ports as a base of operations, and that each Power shall exercise "due diligence" to prevent any violation of these rules. These certainly are not very oppressive or unreasonable "rules." They do not look much like "hectoring" or "bullying." If they were not international law, they ought to be. And they are above all in the interest of Great Britain, as the great commercial Power. It is not our fault that they convey a rebuke; that they intimate that "due diligence" had not been used by British authorities heretofore in executing even their own municipal laws. There is nothing in them inconsistent with the British legislation. And if British or American readers will ever review the British legal decisions on the escape of the rebel privateers, though they will find some most disgraceful and pettifogging ruling by the Chief Baron as to the interpretation of the law, they will also discover that no law was settled in the British Courts as to the questions involved between the two nations. The American interpretation is certainly quite as probable and reasonable as that which the Chief Baron and his associates expressed.

"A Fragment of History," March 30, 1872

Perhaps Grant's greatest disappointment in foreign policy was the U.S. failure to annex Santo Domingo in the Caribbean. Grant's personal secretary, Orville Babcock, visited the small country twice to discuss U.S. interest and drafted a treaty, but it failed in the Senate. Although Charles Sumner, chairman of the Senate Foreign Relations Committee, indicated support for U.S. annexation, as suggested in *The Times* article, he opposed the treaty and encouraged rejection.

MARCH 30, 1872
A FRAGMENT OF HISTORY.

Mr. Sumner, in his recent speech in the Senate on San Domingo affairs, holds up the conduct of Spain, in her attempt to repossess herself of her ancient colony in 1861, as a bright and shining example. He states that "in the act of reannexation the Dominicans were spontaneous, free, and unanimous—that no Spanish emissaries were in the territory to influence its people; nor was there a Spanish bottom in its waters or a Spanish soldier on its land."

A statement so glaringly inaccurate could only be uttered by one who had never properly looked into the facts of the question. Every one who knows anything of the history of San Domingo for the past ten years, knows that its so-called annexation to Spain was nothing more nor less than a military occupation of its territory by Spain. Indeed, it is notorious that this act of annexation was sprung upon the Dominican people by Santana on the 18th of March, 1861, and the first intimation that even the greater part of the Government officials had of the projected scheme, was in a circular letter addressed to them by "Pedro Santana, Liberator of the Country, General-in-Chief of the Army and President of the Republic," and dated "Santo Domingo, March 2, 1861"—in which, after informing them that annexation to Spain had been agreed upon, he adds: "That this may be carried into effect with all possible order, and that the free expression of the will of the Dominican people may be unfettered, *necessary orders have been given for the timely arrival of land and sea forces to protect their spontaneous declarations.*" Ships of war were on the coast of San Domingo before the act of annexation was proclaimed at the capital; and within two weeks from the date of the proclamation, or before the 1st of April, 1861, three war vessels of the first class appeared off San Domingo City, and several regiments of Spanish troops were landed.

At Samana, when the Spanish flag was hoisted, three thousand troops were landed to protect it. "How unlike old Spain!" exclaims Mr. Sumner, has been the conduct of the United States. How unlike old Spain, indeed! Not a soldier of the United States has been landed upon Dominican soil—nor has such an act been at any time contemplated. When the star-spangled banner was displayed at Samana—under the rights granted us in the lease—two citizens of Samana were hired to look after it, and this *force* used by the United States in San Domingo is the sum total of all the force on which Mr. Sumner rings so many changes. This force of two colored men at Samana, with the prestige of our flag, has brought to the island a condition of peace, industry, and progress such as three-quarters of a century had not before witnessed. It would be idle to pursue the comparison between the results of the Spanish occupation of San Domingo, and what may reasonably be expected from its annexation to the United States. There is a difference between freedom and despotism, between the life-giving vigor of our young Republic, and the benumbing influences of the effete old Monarchy of Spain. As Mr. Sumner has cited the conduct of Spain in her occupation of San Domingo as an exemplary example, it is as well that he should be set right on the facts of the case.

"THE TWO CANDIDATES," NOVEMBER 1, 1872

The Times fully endorsed Grant in the 1872 presidential election over Democratic challenger Horace Greeley, who was the editor of the *New York Tribune*. In six numbered points on each candidate, *The Times* explained its support for Grant, discussing his economic policies, his enforcement of Reconstruction, and his leadership in foreign affairs.

NOVEMBER 1, 1872
EDITORIAL
THE TWO CANDIDATES.

The time for argument is nearly passed; but if there are any who yet hesitate as to their duty and interest on Tuesday, let them ask themselves the following questions, and give them a candid answer:

1. Would not the election of Mr. Greeley make the future of business uncertain? Would it be possible to tell what he would do with the Treasury Department, or what influence his course would have on the credit of the country?

2. Would not Mr. Greeley's election tend to make every extreme secessionist feel that a party favorable to his views of Government, and sympathizing with his passions and prejudices, was in power?

3. Would not Mr. Greeley's election give good ground to those affected by the Fourteenth and Fifteenth Amendments—both to those restrained and to those protected thereby—to think that those amendments would not be enforced firmly or thoroughly? And would not such a feeling tend to a disastrous state of affairs in the Southern States?

4. Would not the election of Mr. Greeley, with his known peculiarities of temperament, and his avowed views with reference to several questions in our foreign affairs, involve considerable danger of foreign complications, plunged into without deliberation, and managed without dignity or wisdom?

5. Would not the election of Mr. Greeley be likely to be fatal to the progress of real civil service reform, on account of the impossibility of applying its principles to the redistribution of a vast number of offices, and also on account of the notorious hostility of the leaders of the Democratic Party to any such reform?

6. Finally, would not Mr. Greeley's election be substantially the installation of the Democratic Party, with nearly all the objections unremoved which have kept the people from trusting that party for the past twelve years?

On the other hand:

1. Would not the election of Gen. Grant give all reasonable assurance of a prosperous business future—and certainly of the steady maintenance of the line of conduct by the Treasury, now so well known and approved by the country? Would it not be certain that nothing would be done to impair the credit of the Government, or to give any sudden shock to the business interests of the country?

2. Would not Gen. Grant's election make every earnest, honest Union man feel that the Government was in the hands of a party heartily in sympathy with his own sentiments, and bound to see, under all circumstances, that the integrity of the country should never be even questioned?

3. Would not the election of President Grant insure the temperate but impartial enforcement of the recent amendments to the National Constitution, and put an end to all fear or hope that they could be violated with impunity—and would not this one fact do more than anything else could do to insure lasting reconciliation at the South?

4. Would not Gen. Grant's election be the strongest possible guarantee that our foreign affairs would be conducted with honor, with prudence, and with the aid of the very best minds of the country?

5. Would not the election of Gen. Grant give us grounds to expect a greater progress than has even now been made in the direction of civil service reform; and is it not true that the President has already *done* for this reform more than Mr. Greeley dares to *promise* to do?

6. Finally, would not the election of Gen. Grant over the desperate coalition formed against him, be likely to result in the disintegration of the Democratic Party, in the practical withdrawal of all opposition to the results of the war, and in greater attention from politicians generally to the material wants of the country?

These are questions which every intelligent man can answer for himself, and it is the duty of such men to do so. There never was a canvass where the right way for men who are not extreme partisans, but are careful citizens, who seek the real interests of the country, was so plain.

· ·

"President Grant on the Third-Term Question," May 31, 1875, and "No Third Term," November 5, 1875

Some Grant supporters in the Republican Party advocated an unprecedented third term for the president. Grant finally rejected this possibility in a public letter. Public concerns about a third term are illustrated in the letter to the editor, which bluntly states, "Twice I voted for Gen. Grant. That's enough! I wouldn't give a third term to George Washington himself."

MAY 31, 1875
WASHINGTON.
PRESIDENT GRANT ON THE THIRD-TERM QUESTION.
A LETTER TO THE CHAIRMAN OF THE REPUBLICAN STATE CONVENTION OF PENNSYLVANIA— A BLOW TO THE HOPES OF "THIRD-TERM" POLITICIANS AND EDITORS.

Special Dispatch to the New-York Times.

WASHINGTON, May 30.—The President's letter to Gen. Harry White, Chairman of the Pennsylvania Republican Convention, has settled for the future all controversy and doubts about the third term. For months many of the most earnest Republicans and truest friends of the President have wished he would write a strong letter on the third term, and his silence has been felt on all hands to be, considering the form which the discussion had assumed, exceedingly injurious to the prospects of the Republican Party. In the meantime, some sycophantic politicians and newspaper editors, who supposed they were engaged in commendable service, zealously advocated a third term. One prominent Senator from the North has not concealed, in private conversations, his advocacy of the third term, and Southern Republicans have been wholly committed to it. Sometimes patronage has been unblushingly arranged on the basis of support of a third term, in such a way that parties to the arrangement were led to believe that it had authority. Propositions concerning patronage and a third term have been made to some of the purest men in Congress. It turns out now, as ought to have been known then, that such propositions were the devices of unscrupulous politicians to serve their own selfish ends. But harm was done which only the President himself could undo. He has now taken the action which becomes necessary, and which he would have taken before the elections of last year, if he had not regarded the proposal as a harmless opposition slogan invented for the canvass and if he had not believed voters would not be influenced by the false accusation. It has been plain for a long time that the President was by no means shaping his course for the purpose of securing a renomination, and his appointment to his Cabinet of Judge Pierrepont, well known to be opposed to a third term, was almost as decisive as the letter to Gen. White. But the President's own letter was necessary, and that has not been delayed long enough to embarrass in any way the activity of the canvasses in Pennsylvania, Ohio, and other important States.

NOVEMBER 5, 1875
LETTER TO THE EDITOR
NO THIRD TERM.

To the Editor of the New-York Times:

The victory, which is due to your efforts more than to any other single agency, is one to be proud of. It will inspire confidence at home and abroad. It will prove to the world that we are not repudiationists. It presages a greater victory next year for the party that has done so much for the true honor, preservation, and freedom of our country. Business will revive. "Now shall our farmers gather in their crops, and busy tradesmen mind their crowded shops."

Your paper is a power, and I hope you will never throw away your vast influence as did the *Tribune* by its gross inconsistency.

Be true to your pledge as to the "third term," and you'll find that politicians will think twice ere they oppose "the Thunderer."

Twice I voted for Gen. Grant. That's enough! I wouldn't give a third term to George Washington himself. Yours respectfully,

JOHN W. SEYMOUR,
Tremont, N.Y., Wednesday, Nov. 3, 1875

The cabinet of President Ulysses S. Grant in session in 1869. Grant is seated at the far end of the table.

Source: The Granger Collection, New York

"Impeachability after Resignation of Office," March 8, 1876

The scandals that engulfed the second term of the Grant administration resulted in investigations, the resignation of Grant's personal secretary, and even the impeachment of Grant's secretary of war, William W. Belknap on charges that he had received bribes. Belknap resigned just before the House prepared to impeach him. Grant was widely criticized for accepting the resignation given the pending proceedings, but *The Times* defended the president, pointing out that "compulsory holding of civil office is not allowed by our law." *The Times* also declared that the impeachment should move forward, and it did, resulting in Belknap's narrow acquittal.

MARCH 8, 1876
EDITORIAL
IMPEACHABILITY AFTER RESIGNATION OF OFFICE.

The crime of Secretary Belknap is a stain upon the public life of the country, but our justice may be vindicated by the prompt infliction of the full measure of constitutional punishment. The power to impeach him has been doubted, because of the resignation of his office. If there is any doubt as to the power of impeachment, no more suitable opportunity can occur to solve it and settle the proper construction of the Constitution. Judge Story has been cited as denying the power. He did not deny it, but said "it might be argued with some force that it would be a vain exercise of authority to try a delinquent for an impeachable offense when the most important object for which the remedy was given was no longer necessary or attainable. And although a judgment of disqualification might still be pronounced, the language of the Constitution may create some doubt whether it can be pronounced without being coupled with a removal from office." Having cautiously suggested a doubt, he with equal caution suggests the counter view. "There is also much force in the remark that an impeachment is a proceeding purely of a political nature. It is not so much designed to punish an offender as to secure the State against gross official misdemeanors. It touches neither his person nor his property, but simply divests him of his political capacity." Of course his political incapacity can be produced only by a judgment disqualifying him to hold office, which is really

"the most important object for which the remedy is given." We think that the suggested doubt will vanish when the precedents and the underlying reasons of the Constitution are duly considered. . . .

It seems to us entirely clear, upon the text of the Constitution, upon policy and reason, and upon the unbroken chain of authorities, that the resignation of his office has not affected the power of the House to impeach nor of the Senate to try Secretary Belknap, and that those who have affirmed the contrary have merely begged the question.

The President has been harshly censured for accepting Mr. Belknap's resignation. Surely it was not desirable to continue him in office after his delinquency became known. It would have been the plain duty of the President to remove him if he had not resigned. The President accepted his resignation without reference to the question of impeachment, and the President was right. It was no more in the President's power to prevent his resignation of the office than it was in his power to compel his acceptance of an appointment to it. Compulsory holding of civil office is not allowed by our law, and it is nonsense to talk of forcing a man to continue in office that he may be punished by turning him out of it. But for the offenses committed by him while in office the punishment should be prompt, certain, and to the utmost limit of the power of the Government.

THE PRESIDENCY OF **RUTHERFORD B. HAYES**

MARCH 4, 1877 — MARCH 4, 1881

The presidency of Rutherford Birchard Hayes was marred from the outset by a highly controversial election. Hayes lost the popular vote but ultimately prevailed in the Electoral College by one vote. The votes of three states were disputed and awarded to Hayes by a special commission. This narrow and contentious victory overshadowed Hayes's administration and hindered his ability to govern. Hayes's decision to end Reconstruction in the South, which was widely seen as a deal made by Republicans to gain the support of Democrats on the election commission, and his efforts to promote civil service reform became his legacy.

Hayes was the second president born in Ohio (Grant, his predecessor, was also from there). Hayes graduated from Kenyon College, where he was valedictorian, and then earned his law degree at Harvard. He returned to Ohio to practice law and entered local politics in Cincinnati. When the Civil War began, Hayes joined the army and served with distinction. He was promoted to brigadier general and breveted major general for leadership in battle. He ran for the U.S. House of Representatives in 1864 but refused to leave the military to campaign. He won the election, but did not take office until the war ended. Hayes served in the House for four years and then turned to state politics in Ohio, where he served as

Source: The Granger Collection, New York

THE "WEAK" GOVERNMENT 1877–1881.

governor for four years. After retiring briefly from politics, Hayes was drafted to enter the gubernatorial race again in 1875 and won.

QUICK FACTS ON RUTHERFORD B. HAYES

BIRTH	October 4, 1822, Delaware, Ohio
EDUCATION	Kenyon College Graduated from Harvard Law School, 1845
FAMILY	Wife: Lucy Ware Webb Hayes Children: Birchard A. Hayes; James W. C. Hayes; Rutherford P. Hayes; Joseph T. Hayes; George C. Hayes; Fanny Hayes; Scott R. Hayes; Manning F. Hayes
WHITE HOUSE PETS	Canaries, cows, dogs, goat, kittens, horses
PARTY	Republican
PREPRESIDENTIAL CAREER (SELECTED)	City solicitor of Cincinnati, Ohio, 1857–1861 Commissioned major in Ohio Volunteer Infantry, 1861 Promoted to brigadier general, 1862 Breveted major general, 1865 U.S. House of Representatives, 1865–1868 Governor of Ohio, 1868–1872; 1876–1877
PRESIDENTIAL TERM	March 4, 1877–March 4, 1881
VICE PRESIDENT	William A. Wheeler
SELECTED EVENTS	Withdrawal of federal troops from New Orleans; end of Reconstruction (1877) Federal troops sent to Pennsylvania to halt violence from railroad strike (1877) Bland-Allison Act authorizing silver coinage passes over presidential veto (1878) First woman, Belva Ann Lockwood, admitted to U.S. Supreme Court bar (1879) New York City, not including Brooklyn, becomes first city with population of 1 million (1879)
POSTPRESIDENCY	Philanthropy
DEATH	January 17, 1893, Fremont, Ohio

THE 1876 CAMPAIGN

As a sitting governor in 1876, Hayes did not actively seek the Republican presidential nomination. The favorite candidate was Rep. James G. Blaine of Maine, a former Speaker of the House. Blaine failed to receive the votes required for nomination, and the convention turned to other candidates. Hayes was nominated on the seventh ballot, largely because no one objected to his candidacy. The convention selected William A. Wheeler of New York as his running mate.

The 1876 presidential election marked the second time in American politics that the victor lost the popular vote (the first was in 1824). Further complicating the election was a dispute over the Electoral College results, which finally was resolved just three days before inauguration day. Hayes's opponent, Democratic governor Samuel J. Tilden of New York, won the popular vote, but he fell just one vote short of the number required to prevail in the Electoral College. Because three states—Florida, Louisiana, and South Carolina—submitted Electoral College votes for both parties, Congress created a special commission to certify the contested votes.

The commission was supposed to be bipartisan, with seven Republicans, seven Democrats, and one independent. But when the independent member stepped down, a Republican was appointed as his replacement. Voting took a full month, and commission members stayed true to their political party, with all eight Republicans voting for Hayes and all seven Democrats doing the same for Tilden. Hayes was awarded the twenty disputed Electoral College ballots, which allowed him to prevail in the election by one vote. Historians generally agree that the Democrats accepted the commission's decision with the understanding that the Republican Party would agree to end military rule in the South, which also ended Reconstruction.

Because inauguration day, March 4, fell on a Sunday, Hayes became the first president to take the oath of office privately in the White House, on Saturday, March 3, 1877. The formal inauguration ceremony took place the following Monday, followed by a reception, but no parade or celebration ball.

The Hayes Administration

Upon taking office, Hayes made clear that his narrow victory would not inhibit his leadership, as his cabinet appointments illustrated. Rather than strictly following the party line, Hayes appointed both Republicans and Democrats, much to the dismay of Republican leaders in Congress. Republican William M. Evarts of New York, who had defended President Andrew Johnson in his impeachment trial, became secretary of state. Alexander Ramsey of Minnesota was appointed secretary of war, and John Sherman of Ohio was chosen to head the Treasury Department. Republican Carl Schurz of Missouri became secretary of the interior, and Southern Democrat David M. Key was chosen for postmaster general. Rounding out the cabinet were Charles Daven of Massachusetts as attorney general and Richard W. Thompson of Indiana as secretary of the navy.

First Lady Lucy Hayes brought a new approach to White House social life. Because she and President Hayes did not drink alcohol, she would not serve it at White House functions, and she became popularly known as "Lemonade Lucy." She also had the distinction of being the first president's wife who had graduated from college. Of the eight Hayes children (seven sons and one daughter), three sons died before age two.

Major Issues

Perhaps the most significant event in the Hayes administration was the decision to end military rule in the South, which brought Reconstruction to a close. The Republican Party was concerned about the power of the Democratic Party in the South and whether the newly reconstituted southern states would protect black citizens. The two Republican-governed states in the region, Louisiana and South Carolina, were dependent on federal troops to protect their authority. In deciding to withdraw those troops, Hayes hoped that southern Democrats would protect black citizens and enforce the Reconstruction agenda instituted by law and constitutional amendment. But the Democrats did not live up to Hayes's expectations, and the end of Reconstruction also marked the end of post–Civil War Republican governance in the South.

Hayes tried to enact civil service reform, even at his own party's expense. He authorized an investigation of the New York Customhouse, an organization that was under the political control of the state's Republican senator Roscoe Conkling. The findings included bribery and coercion, and they castigated several officials, such as collector Chester A. Arthur, one of Conkling's close allies. Hayes's response to these findings, however, was modest. He declared that employees should not be forced to contribute to the Republican Party, but voluntary donations would be permitted, which made little difference in practice. Still, by calling for an investigation, Hayes publicly questioned the power of political bosses and set the stage for future reform. He also removed Arthur and other Conkling officials, although he required Democratic support in the Senate to overcome Conkling's resistance to these changes.

Hayes had mixed results in other battles with Congress on domestic and foreign issues alike. Governing in a time of economic depression, Hayes opposed using silver to expand the currency, but the Bland-Allison Act of 1878, passed over his veto, allowed some silver coinage. As the economy regained strength, the exchange of paper currency grew more popular as well. Hayes did succeed in halting a national railroad strike in 1877, sending federal troops to restore order when strikers attacked railroad property. In foreign affairs, the Hayes administration initially opposed a new government in Mexico, but later recognized it. Hayes also vetoed a bill that would have limited Chinese immigration to the United States, but his administration still imposed such restrictions through negotiations with China.

Having pledged to serve only one term of office, Hayes did not run for reelection in 1880. He was pleased to see fellow Ohio Republican James A. Garfield successfully win the race, and to have both chambers of Congress return to Republican control. (Hayes had faced a Democratic House upon taking office and a Democratic majority in both chambers for his last two years.) After his term ended, Hayes returned to Ohio, where he remained active in public affairs until he died of a heart attack in 1893.

"Presidential Election: Results Still Uncertain," November 8, 1876, and "Election Excitement: The Public Still Anxious About the Result," November 11, 1876

The uncertainty surrounding the 1876 presidential election was faithfully recorded in *The New York Times*. Writing the day after the election, *The Times* declared that the election results were "still in doubt," with Democratic candidate Samuel J. Tilden having 184 of the 185 votes required to prevail in the Electoral College. Days later, the election was still undecided, as both parties claimed the Electoral College votes of Florida, Louisiana, and South Carolina. Public interest in the electoral dispute was high, with "surging mobs of eager citizens clustered in front of the various bulletin-boards in Printing-house square" to learn the latest news. The crowds were largely calm, accepting, *The Times* wrote, President Ulysses S. Grant's "assurances of a fair count with confidence." Grant directed General Sherman to provide army protection to the authorities counting the vote in the disputed southern states.

NOVEMBER 8, 1876
PRESIDENTIAL ELECTION.

RESULTS STILL UNCERTAIN.
SOLID SOUTH EXCEPT LOUISIANA, FLORIDA AND SOUTH CAROLINA FOR THE DEMOCRACY—TILDEN CARRIES HIS OWN STATE, CONNECTICUT, AND INDIANA— THE NORTH DIVIDED.

At the hour of sending *The Times* to press this morning, the result of the Presidential election, held yesterday, is still in doubt. Conceding to the Democrats New-York, New-Jersey, Connecticut, Indiana, [indecipherable] and all the Southern States except Louisiana and South Carolina, Tilden will have 184 electoral votes. Necessary to elect, 185. The Republicans have carried the following States: Colorado, California, Illinois, Iowa, Kansas, Maine, Massachusetts, Michigan, Minnesota, Nevada, Nebraska, New-Hampshire, Oregon, Ohio, Pennsylvania, Rhode Island, Vermont, Wisconsin, Louisiana, and South Carolina. These States will give Hayes 181 electoral votes.

Elections were held yesterday for full lists of State officers in Connecticut, Illinois, Kansas, Louisiana, Massachusetts, Michigan, Missouri, Nebraska, New-York, North Carolina, South Carolina, and Tennessee. A Governor and Lieutenant-Governor were chosen in Florida, and a Secretary of State and other State officers in Iowa, it is safe to assume that in such case the results on the National and State Tickets are identical.

The returns for New-York from 256 towns and cities, outside of Kings and New-York Counties, give Tilden a net gain of 6,427, as compared with the vote of 1872. This indicates that the Democrats will carry the State by a small majority.

NOVEMBER 11, 1876
ELECTION EXCITEMENT.

THE PUBLIC STILL ANXIOUS ABOUT THE RESULT.
LARGE CROWDS AROUND THE VARIOUS BULLETIN-BOARDS—THE SITUATION EAGERLY DISCUSSED—CONFIDENCE IN A REPUBLICAN TRIUMPH— PRESIDENT GRANT'S ORDER RECEIVED IN A MOST FAVORABLE MANNER.

Notwithstanding the dampening effect of the rain yesterday, the popular interest in the election showed few signs of decrease. The same surging mobs of eager citizens clustered in front of the various bulletin-boards in Printing-house square, and conned the results displayed thereon with as much avidity as ever. There was less cheering than on Thursday, but the public uncertainty was in nowise abated. Around the *Times* bulletin was a crowd numbering several hundreds, the major portion of them evidently business men, who watched the appearance of each fresh announcement with the utmost patience and good humor. Hayes was evidently their favorite, and as successive dispatches from the disputed States came in the popular satisfaction broke out into cheers. . . . Late in the afternoon a new direction was given to the popular interest by the appearance of the President's letter to Gen. Sherman, directing him to instruct the Army officers in the Southern States to afford all needed protection to the legal authorities in counting of the vote, and to expose any attempt at cheating by either party. The order was displayed prominently on the bulletins of *The Times* and other newspapers, and at once became the topic of eager discussion. By the Republicans of all classes the order was approved as a courageous and praiseworthy endeavor on the part of the President to secure an honest canvass and count at the South, regardless of party interests. Among the better class of Democrats the order was generally pronounced a fair one, and even

among the lowest and roughest elements in the crowd, it was difficult to get up any excitement. A group of the latter, in front of the *Tribune* office, muttered a few oaths, and predicted "trouble" if the order was carried out, but their bluster was short-lived and elicited little attention.

A tall Irishman in front of the *Express* bulletin, attracted some notice by swearing that "Hayes would be assassinated if he ever passed through Baltimore on his way to the White-House," and a few other threats of a similar nature were uttered by others of the same nationality, but only with the effect of raising a smile on the faces of passers by. In fact there was considerably less excitement than had been manifested the day previous over conflicting election returns. Toward evening calcium lights were mounted in front of *The Times* and other offices, and the latest returns displayed for the benefit of the throngs of business men on their way homeward. Among this class there was little difference of opinion over the President's order, both parties accepting his assurances of a fair count with confidence.

- -

"Closing Acts of the Count," March 3, 1877

Four months after the 1876 presidential election took place, the results were finally decided on March 2, 1877. In the early dawn, a very sleepy Congress convened to hear the official announcement of the special election commission's decision—that the disputed Electoral College votes would go to Rutherford B. Hayes, giving him a one-ballot victory margin of 185 votes to Tilden's 184. Some House Democrats protested by refusing to stand when the Senate entered their chamber, but otherwise the most contentious presidential race in decades concluded without incident.

MARCH 3, 1877
CLOSING ACTS OF THE COUNT.
THE NIGHT SESSION OF BOTH HOUSES—DECLARATION OF THE RESULT
OF THE NOVEMBER ELECTION—THE BLACK EAGLE'S QUILL.
Special Dispatch to the New-York Times.

WASHINGTON, March 2.—At 4:05 o'clock this morning, amid an almost breathless silence, which was in marked contrast to the noise and confusion that had prevailed during the day, Mr. Speaker Randall announced that the House was ready to meet the Senate, for the purpose of completing the Presidential count. When the Clerk of the House reached the Senate Chamber to make the announcement, he found it almost deserted. Mr. Ferry, the Presiding Officer, sat in the chair calm, cool, and vigilant as ever, but most of the Senators were either asleep in their seats or dozing in the cloak

rooms. Mr. Patterson sat near Mr. Bogy smoking, while Senator Sherman and one or two others wrote letters. After it was announced that the House was ready to go into joint session, the clerks and pages of the Senate were for nearly 10 minutes occupied in waking Senators and getting them in condition to proceed to the other chamber. Then the procession was formed, and five minutes afterward the Sergeant at Arms of the Senate, together with President Ferry, appeared at the entrance to the hall of Representatives. As they did so the Speaker, in conformity with the usages of Congress, rapped once with his gavel and announced the Senate of the United States. Upon this all the respectable members of the House rose and stood in their places. A large number of Democrats, however, with neither respect for themselves nor their associates, left their seats in accordance with a previous agreement and stood outside the bar of the House to protest by their action, as they said, against the consummation of the fraud committed by the Electoral Commission, a tribunal, it will be remembered, which they themselves created. The Senators did not seem to be at all annoyed by this little show of childish spite, and they took their seats with as much apparent satisfaction as if they had been received with the utmost respect by all parties.

Mr. Ferry then took his place beside the Speaker, and in a firm, clear voice, announced that the last joint session of the two houses to complete the Electoral count was then in order. The further proceedings were as brief as they were impressive. The Presiding Officer called upon the tellers to announce the vote of Wisconsin. This duty was performed by Senator Allison, who declared that the 10 votes of the State named should be counted for the Republican candidates. Then the Electoral vote was enumerated by the same Senator, who declared that 185 votes had been cast for Rutherford B. Hayes, of Ohio, and William A. Wheeler, of New-York, and that 184 votes had been cast for Tilden and Hendricks. In accordance with the declaration, Mr. Ferry, in slow and distinct tones, announced that Rutherford B. Hayes and William A. Wheeler, having received a majority of all the Electoral votes cast, were duly elected President and Vice President of the United States. Then, with a trembling hand, which demonstrated plainly the high state of excitement under which he was laboring, he took the black eagle's quill which was sent to him for the purpose, and signed the declaration of the result. Then the houses separated and shortly after adjourned, and the flag was hauled down from the Capitol after flying for 29 days. The declaration is dated Feb. 1, that legislative day under the Electoral bill being constructively continued until 4:30 this morning.

The electoral commission meeting by candlelight on March 2, 1877, to determine the results of the 1876 presidential election.

Source: Library of Congress

[No Headline] March 6, 1877

Not surprisingly, given the disputed election, President Hayes's inauguration was a simple affair. In its coverage, *The Times* reflected the American tradition of viewing the inauguration as a time to move beyond election disputes to focus on national unity. *The Times* described the event as "a legitimate triumph of the right," and expressed its confidence in President Hayes, praising him as "exceptionally well fitted to fulfill the exacting requirements of the task imposed on him."

MARCH 6, 1877

The topic which to-day overshadows all others is the inauguration of President Hayes. It was peaceful, of course, and it has been hailed with greater cordiality and good feeling than the circumstances immediately preceding it could have led us to expect. Even those who did not unreservedly accept it for what it is—a legitimate triumph of the right—helped to swell the chorus of welcome amid which the new President entered upon his duties. Save by a gloomy and vindictive circle of malcontents throughout the country, President Hayes will be fairly and appreciatively judged, and his accession will be regarded as the best possible guarantee for the obliteration of sectional feeling, the purification of the Government, and the elimination of all the disturbing elements of political uncertainty by which enterprise has been paralyzed and the healthy development of business retarded. No man has assumed the responsibilities of power who had a better opportunity of becoming a source of blessing to all ranks of his fellow-citizens, and we think it may be confidently predicted that President Hayes will show himself exceptionally well fitted to fulfill the exacting requirements of the task imposed on him.

. . . .

"THE NORTHERN DEMOCRATS AND MR. HAYES," APRIL 2, 1877

From the start of his administration, President Hayes faced criticism from northern Democrats who thought his victory was a fraud, granted by the special commission in return for a promise to end southern Reconstruction. The historical consensus is that the two political parties did reach an agreement, but Hayes was not personally engaged in the deal. Nevertheless, Democratic criticism shadowed Hayes throughout his presidency. In this article, *The Times* defended Hayes against charges by northern Democrats, and pointed out that a decision to withdraw federal troops from Louisiana and South Carolina could be justified without any discussion of a political deal. President Hayes soon would implement such a decision and bring Reconstruction to a close.

APRIL 2, 1877
EDITORIAL
THE NORTHERN DEMOCRATS AND MR. HAYES.

Whatever may be the practical effect of Mr. Hayes' Southern policy upon the welfare of the section with which it is immediately concerned, it is plain that there is nothing in the recent conduct of the Democrats of the North to lead to the conclusion that they will profit by it. In fact, if they had started out with the intention of cutting themselves off from taking advantage of any changes which Mr. Hayes' plan might temporarily bring about, they could hardly have acted differently. They have from the first placed themselves in an attitude of blind opposition. They would not concede that anything good, or even tolerable, could come from the President. He was to be under the guidance of the men who, they said, shaped Gen. Grant's policy. His inaugural was a mere parade of glittering generalities. He might think he could change matters, but he would soon find out his mistake. He never could withstand the pressure that would be brought to bear upon him. The leaders who, they declared, had planned and profited by the rule of the "carpet-baggers" in the South, held the key of the situation, and as soon as Mr. Hayes began to send in his nominations, he would discover their real strength and his essential weakness. No President could conduct the Government without the aid of the party managers, and the party managers, they assumed, were not in sympathy with Mr. Hayes' policy. Thus they did everything they could to make their Southern allies believe that nothing would come from the new Administration which would help the South, or which the South could accept without stultification and danger of betrayal. It is plain that this line of argument on the part of the Northern Democrats would place them in an embarrassing position if Mr. Hayes should carry out the indications of his policy afforded by his inaugural, and especially if he should do so in the particular form desired by the Southern leaders.

Not content, however, with generalization regarding the President's intentions, the Northern Democratic organs, during a great part of the last fortnight, have been making a tremendous uproar over what they are pleased to style his "broken pledges." They first gave all possible prominence to the reports that Mr. Hayes' friends had made an agreement to withdraw the troops from New-Orleans and Columbia, to which agreement Mr. Hayes was a consenting party, in consideration of support given by Southern Democrats to the decisions of the Electoral Commission. They declared that this agreement was distinct and explicit; that it was made with the intention of deceiving the South; that it was a part of a general scheme of fraud, of which the proceedings of the Commission were another part; that the agreement was being deliberately broken, and that the South would find, when it was too late, that its representatives had fastened upon their section an Administration which would be far worse than that of Gen. Grant. The folly and short-sightedness of a portion of these accusations have already been demonstrated. It has been shown that there was no such agreement as was described; that some of the Southern members of Congress who were said to have taken part in it deny that their course depended on any promises whatever; that others acted against the count, instead of facilitating it; that the papers which were alleged to contain the agreement contained nothing about the withdrawal of the troops, and that,

finally, the President was not in any sense a party to the transaction, such as it was. The Democratic organs, therefore, which have had so much to say about "broken pledges," find themselves exposed as the discoverers or inventors of a ridiculous mare's nest. That is their position already. What it will be if it is found that, after all, the President, without any preliminary bargain, and acting solely on considerations of his duty and the welfare of the country, concludes to withdraw the troops from the capitals of Louisiana and South Carolina, can be readily imagined.

There are many indications that the Southern leaders are sick of being made the cat's-paw of the Northern managers, and of playing the part of martyrs to furnish the latter with political capital. Observers in the South report that this feeling is very freely expressed, not only by prominent politicians, organizers and leaders in the "White League," but by active and influential men in all classes of Southern society. The conclusion is general that the Northern Democratic managers would rather that the South should not be relieved of the difficulties with which it has contended than that relief should come from Mr. Hayes; that these managers would prefer bad government for the South if it could be attributed to Republicans, to good government if the Republicans were to receive any of the credit for the latter. It cannot be denied that this conclusion is sustained by the course of the Northern Democrats. It is not easy, therefore, to see, should the Administration be able to bring about an adjustment in South Carolina and Louisiana substantially in accord with the wishes of the Southern leaders, what sort of an active opposition the Democratic Party will present to the Administration at the called session of Congress in June.

· ·

> " [T]he conclusion was reached that should the State Governments be unable to cope with the mob the President should at his discretion issue a proclamation declaring martial law in the districts where lawlessness prevails. "

"The Situation at Washington," July 23, 1877

A nationwide railroad strike caused by wage disputes between the railroad companies and workers in 1877 sparked violence that would require federal intervention to restore order. Not since the Civil War had the country seen such turmoil, which disintegrated into riots that attacked railroad property. In a clear assertion of executive power, President Hayes sent federal troops to Pittsburgh and other cities to reestablish control.

JULY 23, 1877
THE SITUATION AT WASHINGTON.
PRESIDENT HAYES AND HIS CABINET IN CONSULTATION—THE POWERS AND
DUTIES OF THE EXECUTIVE—MARTIAL LAW MAY BE DECLARED—WORKING MEN
IN SYMPATHY WITH THE STRIKERS—GUARDING THE UNITED STATES TREASURY—
THE MAILS.

Special Dispatch to the New-York Times.

WASHINGTON, July 22.—The railroad riots have monopolized attention here to-day. While the President and his Cabinet were consulting over the grave situation and graver possibilities of the strike the laboring man was discussing it at the corner with his neighbor. The sympathy of the working classes, of whom there are now in Washington an unusual number unemployed, is strongly with the rioters, and although there has been no marked demonstration, indications have shown plainly that it required but the slightest agitation to precipitate trouble. Crowds of working men of both colors have been at the depots all day watching the departure of every train, and it being Sunday, with nothing else to occupy their attention, they have gathered in larger numbers than yesterday. No demonstrations were made except an occasional cheer when intelligence was announced from Baltimore, Pittsburg, or other places favorable to the strikers. . . .

The President and Mrs. Hayes attended church as usual this morning. After church the President was driven to the White House where he remained in the Executive Chamber until late in the afternoon. Mr. Evarts was waiting for him when he arrived, and Secretary Thompson, Secretary McCrary, and Secretary Devens called at once. Postmaster-General Key drove in from Edgewood, the old Chase mansion, where he is living, and reached the White House about 1 o'clock. Mr. Schurz was the only member of the Cabinet who was absent, having gone to spend the Sabbath with his family, who are in New-Jersey. An informal meeting of the Cabinet was then held. The powers and duties of the Executive, should the emergency arise requiring action on the part of the Federal authorities, was discussed, and the conclusion was reached that should the State Governments be unable to cope with the mob the President should at his discretion issue a proclamation declaring martial law in the districts where lawlessness prevails. This action would be preliminary to the occupation of the districts in which the insurrection exists by the military forces of the United States. The great difficulty which will be experienced by the Government in its efforts to suppress the disorders will arise from the absence of any appropriation for the Army, and, should the troubles increase, and the State authorities be unable to suppress them, it may become necessary for the President to immediately call Congress to assemble, in order that the necessary funds may be provided for transporting the Army and meeting the extraordinary expenses which would follow its movements in the emergency. The propriety of calling upon the military of States was also considered, and the general opinion expressed seemed to be against such a course. It is believed that to bring the Militia of one State to operate against the people in a neighboring State would have a very bad effect, and would aggravate existing troubles, and create a feeling of antagonism between the States which would take years to overcome. The opinion of all the members of the Cabinet is that if the Government be called upon to act it will be better to exhaust every effort to restore peace by the use of the national forces before any movement is made to call upon the Militia of States in which no insurrection exists. The members of the Cabinet concur in the opinion that the President has authority to declare martial law in insurrectionary districts, and advised that this course be pursued should it become necessary. This is the only point upon which any conclusion was reached, and the hope is indulged that the State authorities will be able to successfully quell the disturbances, and render any action on the part of the Government unnecessary. Some members of the Cabinet express themselves in favor of immediately calling Congress to assemble, in order that provisions may be made to enable the President to restore and preserve the peace. Everything will be done in the way of precaution to prevent the troubles from extending, so far as the President has the authority and means to act.

"What of Civil Service Reform?" September 9, 1877

In seeking to enact civil service reform, President Hayes faced the overwhelming challenge of reining in the political machines that viewed positions of government service largely as opportunities for party patronage. This challenge would span several administrations and become one of the primary goals of the Progressive movement in the late nineteenth and early twentieth centuries. In an editorial, *The Times* described Hayes as an ideal choice to promote reform because he came to the White House without an extensive background in politics and without ties to a political machine. *The Times* urged Hayes to act on his campaign promise to support reform with "a clear position" that would be upheld "in a consistent and intelligent manner."

SEPTEMBER 9, 1877
EDITORIAL
WHAT OF CIVIL SERVICE REFORM?

Our readers are well aware that we have long regarded the question of civil service reform as one of the most important with which this country has to deal. It is important to the Republican Party, which, possessing the upper house of Congress and the Executive, is solely responsible for the character of the civil service, for the principles on which it [is] conducted, and for any serious defects which may exist in it. But the question is not a partisan one. It concerns every citizen of the Republic, and it is not too much to say that if it cannot be intelligently and effectively solved within a reasonable period the experiment of representative Government based on universal suffrage, which the American people is trying, will be exposed to very great danger and possibly to disastrous and humiliating failure. This is a question, therefore, which is likely to outlast all others. There are forces at work, which, sooner or later, with the passage of time, will settle what we call the Southern question. The institution of slavery is done with now, and, as that was the chief barrier which shut out the influences prevailing in the free States and tending toward order and progress, we may expect the South to get on, on the whole, as well as the rest of the country. Its development will be slower, but it is practically assured. The financial question is in a fair way toward adjustment, and, however the end may be delayed, the course demanded by the general and permanent interests of the mass of the people of all classes and occupations is so plain that the end is a question of time, and probably of no very long time.

But with the question of civil service reform it is different. That is a matter which involves the essence of our institutions. We have allowed a complex and deeply-rooted system to come up and strengthen itself, which not only produces a certain amount of incapacity and corruption in the Government, but which perverts the suffrage itself and defeats the representative principle in the nation. Theoretically, the Government is the choice of the people, as nearly as a majority vote can express it, and is supposed to reflect popular views and desires. Practically, the Government is in great part the choice of a body of professional politicians, who obtain power not by their fitness to embody in action the purposes of the majority, but by the skillful use of elaborate political machinery, the mainspring of which is patronage. Theoretically, the Government is made up of men selected because of known views or special ability. Really, it is largely composed of men without convictions, without even the information necessary to form convictions, with whom professions of opinion are mere checks and counters in a game of politics in which the prize is office. It would not be just to say that this is true of all the officers of the Government—representative and executive— but no one who has examined the facts carefully will be likely to deny that it is true of the major part of the most active men and the men of most influence in public life. The evil is not, of course, confined to any one party, as the system which produces it is not. Both parties suffer from it; both are degraded and enfeebled by it; both have heretofore treated it with nearly equal insincerity, cowardice, and cynicism. But the Republican Party, which is not responsible for the origin of the system, *is* responsible for its maintenance, because it has the power to abolish it if it chose to do so.

" The people cannot rally about a President who does not take a clear position and maintain it in a consistent and intelligent manner. "

There was much reason to anticipate that Mr. Hayes' Administration would take up this all-important task earnestly and efficiently. It had peculiar advantages in any effort to do so. Mr. Hayes was to an unusual extent free from the "entangling alliances" of a long political career. He owed his nomination to no powerful politician who had any claim for special consideration. He showed, by his choice of a Cabinet, that he understood his independence, and the people showed by their reception of that first act of his Administration that they appreciated his independence and would sustain him in all proper ways. In his inaugural address the President repeated and emphasized a statement of principles regarding the reform of the civil service which he had already made in his letter of acceptance to the Republican Convention, and which was succinct, logical, and practically complete. Soon after the inaugural it was announced that these principles were about to be embodied in a series of rules, which would be uniformly and firmly applied to the civil service. The announcement was made on the authority of members of the Administration, and no doubt reflected the then intention of the President. It was received with general and hearty satisfaction, for every one interested in the subject believed, as the President had emphatically declared, that no reform was possible through hap-hazard and disconnected efforts, but only by the adoption and steady enforcement of an intelligible and uniform system.

Since then we have seen or heard nothing of the promised system. We do not say that nothing has been done. Some things have been done, and very good things in their way. There have been some good appointments and some good removals, and the order to office-holders—just in principle and wise in purpose—has been issued. But, on the other hand, there have been things done on the old, bad method, involving "trade and dicker" to "harmonize the party," to "conciliate" this element and that, and for other motives not intelligible to the public, until a good many politicians are sneering at the President's reform as a "humbug," and those who do not believe it to be so are far from being able to prove that it is not. Under these circumstances the bad things offset the good, and we make no appreciable progress. What is needed to awaken and concentrate a practical popular movement in support of a reform of the civil service is an actual, comprehensive, consistent reform to support. It is idle to try to stimulate such a movement in the face of ridiculous inconsistencies, such as occurred in connection with the Baltimore Custom-house, such indecision and trifling as has been shown in New-York, and such feebleness as was displayed in the recent appointment in Chicago. The people cannot rally about a President who does not take a clear position and maintain it in a consistent and intelligent manner. That is what is now wanted of Mr. Hayes.

"THE PRESIDENT'S POSITION," MARCH 2, 1878

One of President Hayes's most devastating political defeats was the passage, over his veto, of the Bland-Allison Act authorizing limited silver coinage to combat the country's economic depression. Hayes maintained that silver currency would spark inflation and that the United States should increase its gold reserves. But Congress sharply disagreed, overriding the president's veto within hours. *The Times* was mildly critical of Congress for acting so quickly but focused on Hayes's "isolation" in government. In particular, *The Times'* editorial rebuked the president for "never pausing to seek counsel and never condescending to profit by it," with the result that he was "unable or unwilling to comply with the terms essential to success." Economic recovery soon followed, but the battle with Congress illustrated the president's difficulty in enacting his agenda.

MARCH 2, 1878
EDITORIAL
THE PRESIDENT'S POSITION.

One of the Washington dispatches states that the friends of the President are chagrined at the want of respect shown toward his veto Message by the Senate. The House, it seems, is accustomed to do rude things, and its contemptuous indifference therefore excites no surprise. But the more dignified Senate was expected to act differently. It has usually treated a veto with at least a pretense of consideration, always discussing it respectfully, and deferring that proceeding until the document has been printed. In the present instance the Senators were as ill-mannered as the demagogues of the House, and the courtiers who flutter in the sunshine of the Executive Mansion are grieved in consequence. They protest that the President has been cruelly used by the opponents of the bill, and particularly by sympathizers with his Administration. The complainants forget, apparently, that those who are supposed to occupy the latter relation in an especial degree in either chamber happen to be strenuous supporters of the new law, and are themselves aggrieved by the President's disregard for their wishes.

Personally mortifying as the incident must be, it will not be without compensating advantages if it lead the President and that small and select circle who constitute his friends to reflect upon the helplessness of the Administration as regards both the course of legislation and the outside currents of public opinion. There have been Presidents and Cabinets who toward the close of the four years' term have found themselves deserted by the party that created them, and despised by the party that had profited by their policy. Such a state of things before the expiration of the first year is, however, unprecedented, and that must be marvelous self-complacency which ignores its existence or its lesson. The jolly miller of the Dee might be happy while boasting that he cared for nobody and that no one cared for him, but the President cannot afford thus to confound isolation with independence. The old song describes his position, nevertheless. He chooses his own path and follows it, never pausing to seek counsel and never condescending to profit by it, and the result is that with three years of service still before him, he stands all but alone, with scarcely a soul who cares enough about him to ask whither he is going or what he proposes to do. When he does speak, as in his remonstrance against the Silver bill, his words are unheeded. Having decided upon an attempt to conduct the business of the Presidency with proud indifference to party, and with a sublime unconsciousness of

the value of friends, he is left to realize the embarrassment and humiliation which he has brought upon himself.

To what extent this position is attributable to want of familiarity with practical statesmanship or to actual inability to discriminate between partisan subserviency and the proper conditions of party allegiance, others may determine. The truth is, that the President, though entering office with a just sense of its responsibilities, has from the first been unable or unwilling to comply with the terms essential to success. He began as a zealous reformer and a model conciliator, and he has persisted in trying to play both parts in spite of accumulating proofs that, "solitary and alone," he could not be effective in either. Now and then a man appears upon the public stage whose genius or force redeems such an effort from ridicule. President Hayes was not cast in this mold. The misfortune is that he is unable to comprehend deficiencies which to others are plain enough. Needing help, he refuses to accept it when tendered disinterestedly. He seems to suspect those whose party record should place them above suspicion, and to reserve his confidences for persons notoriously unfitted to receive them. At every step, consequently, he has blundered. Enemies have multiplied while friends have disappeared. The only accomplished fact in the policy he marked out—the withdrawal of military authority from the South—has in its attendant circumstances been so woefully mismanaged that it has brought him neither strength nor glory. His civil service reform has been so belied in practice that it has become contemptible. The reform element in the Republican Party turns from the method pursued and from its results in disgust, and the devotees of the old system laugh at pretensions whose fruits are as bad as the worst of those for which apologies have been considered necessary. And now comes the financial question, with the President playing fast and loose with important principles, and speaking with so little authority in regard even to the nation's honor that not a Senator utters a syllable in his behalf or pauses to think of the objections he has urged.

What does the President propose to do about it? How do the unseen friends whose indignation the telegraph is flashing over the land propose to improve the situation? We apprehend that the Mohammed who prophesies at one end of Pennsylvania-avenue will call in vain to the marble pile at the other end. Will he, then, discover his powerlessness as against Congress in time to render the discovery useful to himself or the people? There are persons who imagine that the country could get on very well without a President, and who, meanwhile, would reduce that official to the grade of a departmental chief. Mr. Hayes soared so high in his inaugural flight that he is not likely to accept this modest estimate of his vocation. What influence, however, can a President have in Congress, who has cut adrift from party and has not a corporal's guard to help him when vital questions are under consideration in that body? True, his function is to execute the laws, not to make them.

But the head of an Administration, being also as he ought to be, the head of a great party, should wield an influence that would be felt in the party's councils and in legislation. He cannot otherwise contribute to the settlement of grave questions as they arise or to the formation of the national policy of which he should be the acknowledged exponent. This standard of duty President Hayes cannot attain so long as he cherishes the isolation which reduces him to a nobody, and so perverts the idea of independence as to render friends and enemies indistinguishable.

· ·

"THE PRESIDENT AND THE CUSTOM-HOUSE," JULY 12, 1878, AND "THE CUSTOM-HOUSE CHANGES," JULY 15, 1878

One year after its call for civil service reform, *The Times* published an editorial sharply criticizing President Hayes's efforts to enact such changes in the New York Customhouse. The Customhouse was under the control of New York senator Roscoe Conkling, and Hayes decided to take on the Conkling machine by dismissing several top officials, including collector (and future president) Chester A. Arthur. Arthur was certainly loyal to Conkling, but *The Times* fairly noted that "the most searching investigation has failed to discover that he sacrificed official probity, fairness, or industry to the interests of the men to whom he owed his position." Still, Congress ultimately supported the president's decisions. As Treasury Secretary John Sherman told *The Times,* "What had been done was purely in the interest of the public service."

JULY 12, 1878
EDITORIAL
THE PRESIDENT AND THE CUSTOM-HOUSE.

The latest manifestation of what, by perversion of terms, is called the civil service policy is, on the whole, the most ridiculous. The Administration that has given us Comly and Le Duc, Fitzsimmons and William Henry Smith, which put Dennis in the Supervising Architect's office, and sent Diechman as Minister to the United State of Colombia, cannot be said to have any very clear conception of the meaning of civil service reform. The Presidential candidate who said that every public officer should be secure in his tenure as long as his personal character remained untarnished and the performance of his duties satisfactory, finds it possible as President to suspend Collector Arthur without being able to produce a single charge against his character or his competency. If that is but one illustration the more of the folly of expecting either consistency or conscientiousness from the present Administration, it is also one reason the less for anticipating the triumph in the near future of any intelligible system of civil service reform. For this latest exercise of Executive power

has been applauded in advance by one of the chief apostles of the divorce of politics from the responsibilities of public office; the "reorganization" of the New-York Custom-house has been foreshadowed in the columns of *Harper's Weekly.*

The facts in regard to the Collectorship are briefly these: Gen. Arthur was appointed at a time when political service was demanded as one of the requisites of the position. That he doubtless gave to the best of his ability, but the most searching investigation has failed to discover that he sacrificed official probity, fairness, or industry to the interests of the men to whom he owed his position. Successive committees have been baffled in the attempt to cast a slur upon his energy or his honesty, and the reforms which have been recently recommended in Custom-House administration have been found, by a reference to the files of the Treasury Department, to have been in nearly every case urged long before by the Collector. In pursuance of what has been called its "policy," the present Administration sought, during the session of the Senate, to remove Gen. Arthur. No charges were preferred against him, and no reasons were assigned save the exceedingly vague one of mutual incompatibility. That is to say, the Collector scrupulously obeyed the new civil service rules while affecting neither enthusiasm for, nor belief in, them; the Administration treated its own rules with contempt, but demanded an ostentatious profession of faith in the people who formulated them. Unregenerate as he was, according to the tests of White House reformers, Gen. Arthur had never appointed a subordinate officer who had not graduated from the lower ranks of the service; consistent converts as the President and Secretary of the Treasury ought to have been, they pestered him with applications to put new men in positions requiring experience, and they used their power to force into such positions over the heads of old employes persons who had no qualifications save those of political and personal influence.

Admirable as was the character of the gentleman whom the President selected as Gen. Arthur's successor, the Senate found reason enough in the President's own principles to refuse to consider the office vacant. It is quite possible to have the very lowest estimate of the motives which induced Senator Conkling to work for the retention of Collector Arthur, and yet to conclude that he and those who voted with him had the best of the argument. It is totally impossible to have the slightest respect for the motives, the methods, or the manliness of an Administration which, being fairly baffled in its attempt to remove an officer against whom it could allege no sufficient grounds of removal, now seizes the opportunity of suspending him for a few months in order to make up a better case for his removal when the Senate reassembles. The upper house may have recently shown a waning self-respect; it has certainly enough left to resent an insult like this. The people may have lost the power of being either scandalized or astonished by the performances of the Administration; the wayfaring man, though a fool, can hardly fail to perceive the mingled imbecility and meanness of this latest effort in the direction of "reform."

And the officer whom public sentiment declared worthy to keep his place, even against Theodore Roosevelt, has been temporarily replaced by E. A. Merritt! Instead of being taken out of politics, the Custom-house has been plunged into a very quagmire of political intrigue. It is merely a "Conkling machine," says *Harper's Weekly,* and it ought to be "dislocated." What is it now? A Fenton-Sherman-Hayes machine, working for ends about which only this much is certain, that they are not the ends desired by the public. If the Administration had proofs that the Custom-house was being used to assist in re-electing Mr. Conkling, it was entirely within its power to block its wheels and arrest its motion. If the President seriously objected to its being a political machine in anybody's interest, why does he select as its overseer a man who has had no profession save that of a politician, who has earned no money save as a lobbyist or office-holder, and who, trained under one of the most wily and least scrupulous politicians in this State, has learned to be all things to all men, that by all means he should put something in his own pocket? We should like to see every Conkling machine "dislocated," here and elsewhere, but we do not believe in opposing the re-election of Senator Conkling by means more despicable than those to which he has ever stooped. We believe in keeping the public service "out of politics," but we regard as among the very worst foes of such a movement an Administration which considers all allegiance "political" except the political service paid to and by its own adherents, and which holds no instruments too mean to be used for its own selfish ends. If the President had tried to furnish political capital for Senator Conkling, he could not have done it more effectually than by his latest move on the New-York Custom-house; if he had sought to give Collector ARTHUR a lasting claim on the sympathy of the public and the support of the Republican Party, he could not have taken a more direct way to such an end. All the humiliation there is in the case rests with the Administration; all the honor and self-respect remain with the man whose incumbency of the office of Collector has been temporarily interrupted.

JULY 15, 1878
THE CUSTOM-HOUSE CHANGES.
SECRETARY SHERMAN'S EXCUSES FOR THE RECENT REMOVALS—BUT HE DOES NOT DARE ATTACK GEN. ARTHUR'S INTEGRITY.
Special Dispatch to the New-York Times.

WASHINGTON, July 14.—Secretary Sherman was visited by *The Times'* correspondent this evening, and, in response to inquiries relative to the changes in the New-York Custom-house, he said that he did not feel at liberty to state the reasons that prompted the President's action in the premises, but they were amply sufficient to justify the course that had been pursued. Collector Arthur's management of the New-York Custom-house, Mr. Sherman declared, had been for some time past far from satisfactory. The affairs of that institution had been loosely and carelessly administered, and had resulted in a large loss of revenue to the Government. The Secretary wished to have it understood, however, that no one questioned the integrity of Gen. Arthur, which he regarded as unimpeachable. The Secretary had no doubt that when the cause for the removal of Gen. Arthur and Mr. Cornell was made known, it would be generally acknowledged that the President acted properly in making the changes. Upon this point he did not entertain the slightest doubt. What had been done was purely in the interest of the public service. The Secretary further stated that the appointment of Messrs. Merritt and Burt was determined upon without the knowledge of those gentlemen, and without any solicitation on their behalf. In reply to a question whether the official bonds of the new appointees had been approved by him, Mr. Sherman said that they had not, and that it would require a few days to examine them with proper care. In this connection the Secretary added that Gen. Merritt's bond was for a very large sum, and that he had been required to furnish it upon very short notice. Touching the appointment of Gen. Merritt's successor in the Surveyorship, Mr. Sherman said that the vacancy would be filled very soon, but declined to state the name of the person selected. In conclusion the Secretary expressed the belief that the wisdom of the changes that had been made would become manifest within a short time after the new officials assumed control of the Custom-house.

THE PRESIDENCY OF JAMES A. GARFIELD

MARCH 4, 1881 – SEPTEMBER 19, 1881

The presidency of James Abram Garfield ended just months after it started. Garfield was shot by a disgruntled party member in July 1881 and died three months later. His goals of fighting corruption and pursuing civil service reform would fall to succeeding administrations.

An Ohio native and Civil War veteran, Garfield came to the presidency from humble beginnings. He was born in a log cabin and lost his father in infancy. Garfield attended school in the winter and worked on the family farm in the summer to help his mother. As he grew older, he earned money by working on the Ohio and Erie Canal, doing carpentry, and teaching. He put himself through school at Williams College, graduating with honors in 1856. Garfield studied law while serving in the Ohio state senate and as president of the Western Reserve Eclectic Institute (now Hiram College); he was admitted to the bar in 1860. He led Union troops to success on the battlefield in the Civil War and was promoted to major general before resigning his commission to serve in the U.S. House of Representatives, where he became minority leader. In 1880 Garfield was elected to represent Ohio in the U.S. Senate, but the presidential nomination altered his path.

Source: Library of Congress

THE 1880 CAMPAIGN

The Republican Party in 1880 was divided into several groups: Radical Republicans, or "Stalwarts"; less-radical Republicans, known as "Half-Breeds"; and liberal Republicans, described as "Reformers" or "Independents." Because none of these groups could gain enough support to select a presidential nominee, the convention chose Garfield, who had served as campaign manager for one of the candidates, on the thirty-sixth ballot. Chester A. Arthur, who was closely tied to the Stalwart wing, was selected as his running mate. Garfield defeated the Democratic candidate, Civil War hero Winfield Scott Hancock, by a sound margin in the Electoral College, but by just ten thousand popular votes.

THE GARFIELD ADMINISTRATION

Garfield's political appointments reflected the factions in the Republican Party. His cabinet included Sen. James G. Blaine of Maine, who had been the Half-Breed candidate for the presidency, as secretary of state, and Robert Todd Lincoln of Illinois,

QUICK FACTS ON JAMES A. GARFIELD

BIRTH	November 19, 1831, Orange Township, Ohio
EDUCATION	Williams College
FAMILY	Wife: Lucretia R. Garfield Children: Eliza A. Garfield, Harry A. Garfield, James R. Garfield, Mary "Molly" Garfield, Irvin M. Garfield, Abram Garfield, Edward Garfield
WHITE HOUSE PETS	Horse; dog ("Veto")
PARTY	Republican
PREPRESIDENTIAL CAREER (SELECTED)	Worker on Ohio canals, 1848 Teacher, 1849 President, Western Reserve Eclectic Institute, 1857–1861 Ohio state senate, 1859 Civil War service, 1861–1863 U.S. House of Representatives, 1863–1880 Election to U.S. Senate, 1880 Presidential nomination, 1880
PRESIDENTIAL TERM	March 4, 1881–September 19, 1881
VICE PRESIDENT	Chester A. Arthur
SELECTED EVENTS	Dispute with New York senators over federal appointments (1881) Shot by Charles J. Guiteau, July 2, 1881
DEATH	September 19, 1881, Elberon, N.J.

son of President Abraham Lincoln, as secretary of war. Garfield also appointed members of the Stalwart wing, led by New York senator Roscoe Conkling, but angered this group when he selected one of Conkling's political opponents for a New York position. These intraparty divisions led to Garfield's assassination.

First Lady Lucretia R. Garfield also was an Ohio native who met her husband while attending school, where he served for a time as her tutor. The Garfields had seven children, five sons and two daughters. One boy and one girl died in infancy. A son, James R. Garfield, became secretary of the interior under President Theodore Roosevelt.

On July 2, 1881, Charles J. Guiteau shot the president at the train station in Washington, D.C. Angry that he had not received a diplomatic appointment in the new administration, Guiteau shouted, "I am a Stalwart . . . now Arthur is president!" as he attacked. Guiteau's lawyers argued for acquittal on grounds of insanity but were unsuccessful. Guiteau was hanged on June 30, 1882. Doctors spent two months trying to remove a bullet from the president's back, which caused infection, leading to blood poisoning. President Garfield was taken to the Jersey Shore to recuperate, but he died there on September 19, 1881.

"THE NEW-YORK NOMINEES," APRIL 2, 1881

In nominating William H. Robertson to become collector of the Port of New York, President Garfield refused to bow to the demands of Sen. Roscoe Conkling, who was also the New York Republican Party boss. *The New York Times* noted that the president wanted to keep this position free of "partisan purpose," but the article did not discuss how Secretary of State James G. Blaine, who headed an opposing wing in the party, had pressed for Robertson's nomination. President Garfield persuaded Republican senators to support the appointment, thus scoring a political victory over Conkling, who opposed it. Conkling resigned from the Senate in protest. (Conkling thought the New York state legislature would reelect him, but he was mistaken.)

Charles Guiteau, angry at not receiving a patronage position, shot President James A. Garfield in the left shoulder and back. Wounded on July 2, 1881, the president died ten days later.

Source: AP Photo/New York Public Library

APRIL 2, 1881
THE NEW-YORK NOMINEES

WHY JUDGE ROBERTSON WAS SELECTED FOR COLLECTOR.
THE OFFICE REGARDED BY THE PRESIDENT AS ONE OF A NATIONAL CHARACTER—HE DISCLAIMS ANY INTENTION OF SLIGHTING THE NEW-YORK SENATORS—A STATEMENT BY MR. BLAINE.

WASHINGTON, April 1.—The interest in the recent Federal appointments for New-York has not abated, although there is now comparatively little discussion of the subject outside of the persons immediately interested in the result of the anticipated contest in the Senate over confirmation. There has been considerable controversy over the methods and motives of the President in nominating Judge Robertson to succeed Collector Merritt, the charge being made on the one hand and denied on the other, that the nomination was sent to the Senate in violation of an understanding, expressed or implied, with the New-York Senators, and with a deliberate purpose on the part of the President to incite a contest with Senators Conkling and Platt.

Without expressing any opinion touching these controverted points, there is good ground for stating that the President holds that in nominating Judge Robertson he was guided solely by a desire to subserve the public interest and promote harmony in the Republican Party in New-York. The President, it is credibly reported, did discuss with Mr. Conkling, in a general way, the Federal appointments for New-York, but did not say anything to that Senator in reference to the appointment of Judge Robertson as Collector of Customs. Previous to nominating Judge Robertson, he had nominated several New-York gentlemen for offices who were known to be friends of Mr. Conkling, among them being Postmaster-General James and Minister Morton. Before leaving Mentor for Washington, he determined to nominate Judge Robertson for Collector of Customs, because he regarded him as a competent man for that office and because he desired to recognize that element of the Republican Party in New-York of which Judge Robertson is a prominent representative. The President admits that this element is largely in the minority in New-York, but as the local officers nominated by him had been selected from among Mr. Conkling's friends, he thought it advisable to name Judge Robertson for an office that he regards as national in character. The nomination was not made with a view of placing an opponent of Mr. Conkling in charge of the Custom-house, and with a view of using its vast patronage for or against any individual or faction. On the contrary, the President is determined that the Custom-house shall not be used for any partisan purpose, and should Judge Robertson be confirmed the President has expressed a determination to instruct him that any attempt to use his office for the promotion of the political interests of any man or faction will result in his speedy removal. Regarding, as he does, the Collector of Customs at New-York as a national, and not a local, officer, the President does not believe that he was required by any rule of courtesy or practice relating to the selection of Federal officers to consult the New-York Senators in reference to that particular appointment.

The President, it is further reported, claims that Judge Robertson's nomination was his individual act, free from suggestion, and without consultation with any of his constitutional advisers.

There is good ground also for stating that Secretary Blaine disclaims any responsibility for Judge Robertson's appointment. He has no special interest in the question as to who shall occupy the position of Collector of Customs at New-York, for the reason that he is determined never again to be a candidate for the Presidency, and therefore does not, as has been alleged, entertain a desire to have any particular person appointed to that office because of services rendered in the past or from any expectation for services in the future calculated to promote his political interests.

The above is credibly reported to be the substance of conversations held recently with the President and Secretary Blaine, and are given merely as a contribution to the history of Judge Robertson's appointment, the causes that led to, and the results expected to be accomplished by, it.

"In a certain sense the act of Guiteau was an accident, for it was entirely out of the range of any ordinary motives, but it is not inexplicable; it is clearly of those accidents which bring more vividly to the mind the forces that create them."

"THE ASSASSINATION," JULY 3, 1881

The day after Garfield was shot, *The Times* criticized the partisan fervor that underlay the act. Political patronage had sparked "passionate animosity" between party factions, and the attack on the president was a "patriotic humiliation." The tragedy of President Garfield's death would prompt legislation to limit patronage in executive appointments through civil service requirements.

JULY 3, 1881
EDITORIAL
THE ASSASSINATION.

In the crime which was committed at Washington yesterday there is the very irony of fate. Considering his origin and the circumstances of his youth, no man has passed a career more remarkable or attained a dignity more striking than that of President Garfield. Beginning life the son of an almost penniless widow, forced to struggle as few men must for the bare maintenance of an equality with his fellow-men, he has risen step by step to one of the most honorable positions offered by the Government of any nation. It was his fortune to fall upon a time when great opportunities awaited great qualities, and to all occasions he presented qualities not unworthy of them. He entered manhood as the political contest with slavery approached its crisis, and he threw all the energies of a strong nature on the side of freedom. From the field of discussion and the ballot the conflict with slavery was taken to the field of war, and without hesitation, with absolute devotion, with a courage which knew no fear, he entered on this new and terrible task. In all the tests of fitness for the citizenship of a free Republic to which he was subjected he won high distinction, until at last his country called him to the greatest office within its gift. And this President, to whom Americans had pointed proudly and justly as a splendid example of what our country and its cherished principles were able to do for manhood—simple manhood, unfavored of fortune and unaided by any inheritance of title or precedence—is shot down without a moment's warning by an assassin whose hatred was directed not to the man but to the President.

The whole country is bowed with deep grief and indignation at this event. It is inevitable that it should be. There are few men who enjoy, and none who deserve to enjoy, the name of American citizen to whom this crime does not bring a sense of personal sorrow and a profound feeling of patriotic humiliation. Whatever may have been the criticisms which they have passed upon the President, all American citizens must feel the "deep damnation" of this attempted "taking off." He was an obscure son of the Republic who had brought to its most distinguished post gifts of mind and character which conferred credit on the office, and almost at the outset of his term his life is assailed by a wretch who represents as distinctly the evil in our system as President Garfield represents the good. For, though the murderer was obviously of disordered mind, it is impossible to ignore the causes which led immediately to this act—which directed his ill-regulated will to its final aim. He was a disappointed office-seeker, and he linked the bitterness of his personal disappointment with the passionate animosity of a faction. His resentment was inflamed and intensified by the assaults upon the President which have been common in too many circles for the past few months. Certainly, we are far from holding any party or any section of a party responsible for this murderous act, but we believe it our duty to point out that the act was an exaggerated expression of a sentiment of narrow and bitter hatred which has been only too freely indulged. It is not too much to say, in the first place, that if Mr. Garfield had not been the chief of a service in which offices are held out as prizes to men of much the same merit and much the same career as this murderer he would not have been exposed to this attack. And while this is beyond dispute, it is also probable that the murderer's mad spite would not have been "screwed to the sticking point" if it had not been stirred by the license that has prevailed in certain quarters with reference to the President. The event, therefore, is one which may and ought to convey a lesson, which should teach us the folly and the wrong of the insane pursuit of office which our methods of public employment invite, which should show us the danger and disgrace of the unbridled political passion aroused by these methods. In a certain sense the act of Guiteau was an accident, for it was entirely out of the range of any ordinary motives, but it is not inexplicable; it is clearly of those accidents which bring more vividly to the mind the forces that create them.

THE PRESIDENCY OF CHESTER A. ARTHUR

SEPTEMBER 20, 1881 – MARCH 4, 1885

Source: Library of Congress

A PRESIDENTIAL CONJUROR.
WHAT MR. ARTHUR MUST BE TO SATISFY ALL THE POLITICIANS.

Chester Alan Arthur's presidency was both unexpected and uneventful. Arthur was elevated to the office from the vice presidency following the assassination of President James A. Garfield in 1881. The vice presidency was Arthur's first elective office, and he had been nominated as a compromise candidate to appease New York Republican Party leaders. Arthur had few ambitions for his new position, but he surprised supporters by accepting his predecessor's plans for civil service reform, even though he owed his own advancement to political patronage.

Arthur was born and raised in Vermont. He attended Union College in Schenectady, New York, and then pursued legal studies. He was admitted to the bar in 1854 and began practicing in New York. An early and active supporter of the Republican Party, Arthur was appointed quartermaster general of the New York militia during the Civil War, with the rank of brigadier general. He excelled in this administrative position and moved up steadily in the state Republican hierarchy. With New York senator Roscoe Conkling's strong recommendation, Arthur became collector of the Port of New York, serving for seven years in this senior post. He was dismissed in 1878 as part of President Rutherford B. Hayes's effort to rein in political patronage. Ironically, although Arthur was appointed to the position because of his political connections, he was largely recognized for his fair performance in collecting tariff revenues. This recognition helped him gain the Republican vice-presidential nomination two years later.

QUICK FACTS ON CHESTER A. ARTHUR

BIRTH	October 5, 1829, Fairfield, Vt.
EDUCATION	Union College Law studies
FAMILY	Wife: Ellen L. H. Arthur Children: William L. H. Arthur, Chester A. Arthur, Ellen H. Arthur
WHITE HOUSE PETS	None known
PARTY	Republican
PREPRESIDENTIAL CAREER (SELECTED)	New York state militia, 1861 Quartermaster general, with rank of brigadier general, 1862 Collector of Port of New York, 1871–1878 Vice president, March 4–September 19, 1881
PRESIDENTIAL TERM	September 20, 1881–March 4, 1885
VICE PRESIDENT	None
SELECTED EVENTS	Chinese Exclusion Act (1882) Pendleton Civil Service Reform Act (1883) Negotiated treaty with Nicaragua to build canal (1884) Dedication of Washington Monument, Washington, D.C. (1885)
DEATH	November 18, 1886, New York, N.Y.

The 1880 Campaign

The sharply divided Republican Party had great difficulty selecting its presidential ticket in 1880. Radical Republicans—labeled such for their advocacy of harsh Reconstruction measures in the post–Civil War South and also known as "Stalwarts"—supported former president Ulysses S. Grant for a third term. Their opponents, known as "Half-Breeds" because they were perceived as less radical, favored Sen. James G. Blaine of Maine, who was also a former U.S. House Speaker. Another faction in the party sought to end political patronage, and its members were known as "Reformers" or "Independents." None of these groups could muster sufficient support on its own for a presidential candidate. On the thirty-sixth ballot, they united behind Senator-elect James A. Garfield of Ohio, primarily because he had little opposition. The Stalwarts, headed by Conkling, succeeded in having a top Conkling associate, Chester A. Arthur, selected for the vice-presidential spot.

The Garfield-Arthur ticket won narrowly in 1880, with a victory margin of approximately seven thousand popular votes. In the Electoral College, Garfield won 214 votes, and the Democratic contender, Gen. Winfield Scott Hancock, won 155. New York's 35 electoral votes were decisive, a testament to Conkling's influence. Just four months after taking office, President Garfield was shot by a disgruntled party member, Charles J. Guiteau, who had expected an appointment in the new administration. When he did not receive one, he blamed the president. The doctors' attempts to remove the bullets resulted in blood poisoning, to which Garfield succumbed on September 19, 1881. Early the following morning, at 2:15 a.m., Arthur was sworn in as president in his Manhattan residence.

The Arthur Administration

Perhaps the biggest surprise of Arthur's presidency was his determination not to use the office to please the Stalwarts, despite his close affiliation with political boss Conkling.

Conkling was not invited to join the cabinet, and he declined a seat on the Supreme Court. The Stalwarts that Arthur appointed had independent qualifications for their posts. For example, he chose Sen. Frederick T. Frelinghuysen of New Jersey as his secretary of state. Arthur also included Senator Blaine's Half-Breed faction in his cabinet by appointing William E. Chandler as navy secretary. Significantly, the president did not dismiss the collector of the New York Customhouse—the position that Arthur lost when President Hayes removed him to rein in Conkling's political machine. Arthur refused to fire people simply to make room for patronage appointments.

President Arthur served without a first lady, as his wife, Ellen, had died before the 1880 presidential election. His sister, Mary McElroy, assisted as White House hostess, and the president gave lavish state dinners during his administration. He lived in the White House with his ten-year-old daughter and seventeen-year-old son (the Arthurs' first son had died in early childhood). The president did not welcome inquiries about his family, choosing to keep his personal life private.

Major Issues

Unlike his predecessor, Arthur was not a strong proponent of civil service reform; nevertheless, he set the foundation for a professional work force in the federal government. In addition to his cabinet appointments, Arthur demonstrated his willingness to move away from the "spoils" system of patronage appointments by signing the Pendleton Civil Service Reform Act in 1883. This law established the Civil Service Commission, whose mission was to make federal appointments based on merit, as evaluated through special examinations. Although the legislation covered just over 10 percent of federal positions, it marked the beginning of a professional civil service, which Progressive reformers had long advocated.

President Arthur also exercised leadership on immigration, vetoing a bill that banned Chinese immigration for twenty years. His veto spurred Congress to pass a new bill that limited the ban to ten years, a change that mattered little in fact, as Congress renewed the legislation several times. The president's action showed that he would not simply follow Congress's lead in policymaking.

The most significant initiative in the Arthur administration was the modernization of the U.S. Navy. Arthur supported this cause throughout his term, endorsing the construction of new cruisers, which became known as the ABCD ships. Only one was completed by the end of his term, but the plans foreshadowed the naval revolution of the next decade.

In other areas, President Arthur was less successful. His secretary of state negotiated a treaty with Nicaragua to build a canal, but the Senate refused to ratify it. When the Supreme Court narrowly interpreted civil rights law to provide few protections for black citizens, Arthur did not endorse new legislation. Not surprisingly, the Republican Party decided against nominating him for president in 1884, even though he was willing to seek a full term. Instead, Arthur returned to New York City, where he died of kidney disease less than two years later. His administration would be remembered not only for the tragic circumstances in which it began, but also for the president's ability to accept changes to the "spoils" system that had served him so well.

"The Oath Administered," September 20, 1881, and "President Arthur," September 21, 1881

The circumstances that brought Vice President Arthur to the White House cast a somber shadow over his ascension. Upon learning of President Garfield's death, Arthur took the oath of office at his home in New York City in the early morning of September 20, 1881. He received a generous endorsement from *The New York Times,* which praised his sensitivity in refraining from assuming his predecessor's responsibilities while Garfield was still alive.

In an editorial, *The Times* cautioned the new president to be careful of the counsel he kept, noting that Arthur's loyalty to political allies could hinder his leadership. In presenting comparisons to Presidents Ulysses S. Grant and Rutherford B. Hayes, *The Times* warned of the problems that might arise from letting personal ties override professional decisions—and of the need to respect the presidency "not as a personal perquisite, but solely as a public trust."

On September 20, 1881, New York Supreme Court judge Brady administers the oath of office to Chester A. Arthur in New York City, after the death of President Garfield.

Source: Library of Congress

SEPTEMBER 20, 1881
THE OATH ADMINISTERED

GEN. ARTHUR MADE PRESIDENT OF THE UNITED STATES.

WITHIN THREE HOURS OF THE CABINET'S NOTIFICATION OF PRESIDENT GARFIELD'S DEATH—JUDGE JOHN R. BRADY OF THE SUPREME COURT, ADMINISTERS THE OATH.

Gen. Arthur spent the day and evening in his house, No. 123 Lexington-avenue, where he received his first intelligence of the President's death. The news was brought by a messenger boy and was confirmed by a number of telegraphic messages which poured in from Elberon within the next half-hour. With Gen. Arthur at the time were Commissioner of Police Stephen B. French, District Attorney Daniel G. Rollins, Elihu Root, and John C. Reed, his private secretary. The colored doorkeeper was asked if the General would give the press any information as to his probable movements.

"I daren't ask him," was the reply; "he is sitting alone in his room sobbing like a child, with his head on his desk and his face buried in his hands. I dare not disturb him." The General's son, who had heard the news came driving furiously up to the house in a coupé about midnight, and shortly afterward Barney Biglin and P. C. Van Wyck walked up the avenue. Mr. Biglin stood on the sidewalk and awaited the reappearance of his companion, who had been admitted to the house. Half a dozen uniformed messengers sped up the street within the next half-hour and disappeared for a moment within the arthue vestibule door. At 12:25 came the formal notification of the President's death, dated Elberon, and signed by the members of the Cabinet.

Although declining to see members of the press, Gen. Arthur was not altogether oblivious of the anxiety which they manifested in his movements. He authorized the statement that he had received a number of dispatches in relation to the death of President Garfield, all of which, however, he considered confidential save the formal message from the Cabinet. A few minutes before 1 o'clock Gen. Arthur's friends retired, and soon after Commissioner French disappeared around the corner of Twenty-eighth-street, and a roundsman, accompanied by a patrolman, appeared and stationed themselves in front of No. 123.

Ten minutes before 2 o'clock District Attorney Rollins and Mr. Root returned accompanied by Judge John R. Brady, of the Supreme Court, and 20 minutes afterward Commissioner French appeared with Judge Donohue, also of the Supreme Court. The light which had been burning in the library on the second floor was suddenly turned low, and the gas in the front parlor was as suddenly lighted. The whole party repaired to this room and were joined by Gen. Arthur's oldest son. At 2:15 o'clock Judge Brady administered the oath which is prescribed in the Constitution.

It was stated by Secretary Reed that requests to be present for the purpose of administering the oath had been sent to both Judge Brady and Judge Donohue; that Judge Brady, arriving first, was requested to perform this act, and that out of courtesy to Judge Donohue the party waited for him to appear. Both Judges Brady and Donohue are Democrats.

No. 123 Lexington-avenue, which becomes historic, is one of a row of plain brick dwellings, three stories in height, with a veneering of brown stone for its front. Save the presence of half a dozen carriages and a group of reporters, there was nothing unusual in the street outside that would indicate that an event of historical importance was occurring behind the closed green blind of the Arthur residence.

Secretary Reed said, at the conclusion of the ceremony, that it was not probable the President Arthur would leave his house before this morning. A dispatch was received at the house during the evening from one of the Washington hotel-keepers saying that apartments would be reserved for him until such time as he chooses to occupy them.

SEPTEMBER 21, 1881
EDITORIAL
PRESIDENT ARTHUR.

On the 3d of July *The Times* found occasion to say that "the man to whom the crime of Guiteau ought to bring the gravest reflections is the man who has apparently most to gain from its fatal issue." No phrase or statement of the article of which that sentence was a part requires modification at our hands to-day. We said then that Gen. Arthur was able to profit from such a demonstration of public feeling toward him as the crime of the assassin had elicited, and there is every evidence that he has done so. His conduct during the trying period of President Garfield's struggle with death has been such as to command the respect of those most disposed to find fault with him. He has effaced himself after a fashion as manly as it was statesmanlike. The extra-constitutional action recommended to him by volunteer jurists and superserviceable journalists he never showed the slightest disposition to take. He has never visibly lost sight of the fact that he was merely the Vice-President of the United States, watching like the rest of his fellow-citizens over a life which he and they were alike sincerely anxious should be spared.

The only feature of Gen. Arthur's conduct which has been unfavorably criticised during the long period of sus-

pense over the slow martyrdom of the late President has been the character of the men who were apparently admitted to his private confidence. These are probably better men than the general verdict of the public has adjudged them to be; but better or worse, Gen. Arthur regards them as his friends, and that is probably all the explanation he thinks necessary to justify their frequent access to him. It may be admitted that one secret of the political influence and personal popularity which have made Gen. Arthur what he is has been his undeviating and ungrudging fidelity to those whom he regarded as his friends. Admirable as such a quality may be in ordinary life, potent as it is to command respect and support for an aspiring politician, it is one which the President of the United States must keep under wholesome restraint. In his broad and resolute way, President Grant carried it to excess, and made it fruitful of blunders equally disastrous to himself and his party. In a narrower, and, though outwardly more respectable, in an essentially less defensible, fashion, President Hayes succeeded in making his attachment to his friends ridiculous. The one conspicuous blunder of President Garfield's Administration arose out of his desire to reward a political adherent with an office which was not vacant, and for which the appointee had no especial fitness. President Arthur may or may not be warned by the failure of his immediate predecessors to administer the Presidency not as a personal perquisite, but solely as a public trust; the observance of such a distinction is, nevertheless, one on which his own future and that of the party which he represents absolutely depends.

It may be a matter of pride for Chester A. Arthur to be able to say that no new honors can transform him into other than the warm-hearted, impulsive man which he has always been, and so far as his individual character goes, he can make that statement with entire truth. But a faithful observance of the oath which he has taken requires him to make the good of his country his supreme and only law. If he is to prove equal to the great position he occupies he must know principles rather than individuals, he must subordinate personal preference as well as acquired prejudice to the accomplishment of certain well-defined public ends. The moment he selects an administrative officer because the nominee is his friend and not at all because he possesses the qualities which render him obviously fit to perform certain designated public duties, that moment his Administration will be discredited, and the party, which must abide by its record, will be placed on the defensive. No man ever assumed the Presidency of the United States under more trying circumstances; no President has needed more the generous appreciation, the indulgent forbearance of his fellow-citizens. He will be credited with carrying with him into the highest position in the country the rancor of factional strife, and with

being capable not so much of excessive partisanship as of the blunder of assuming that a clique of a fraction of the party contains the representative Republicans of the United States. That mistake has been made before and has been to some extent condoned, but it cannot be made with impunity by President Arthur. It would be seized on by his enemies as the one thing which he might be expected to do, and it would close the mouths of his friends, who would see in it the one thing he ought to have avoided.

Standing at the dividing of the ways, President Arthur has the gravest need of wise counsel, the most imperative necessity for a passionless, impartial, and judicial habit of mind. He is a much better and broader man than the majority of those with whom his recent political career has been identified. It is for him to show that his nature has not been subdued to what it works in, and that his culture, his insight, his executive ability, are fitted to the responsibilities of the great career which opens before him. There are few newspapers of his own party which would not be ready to embrace the opportunity of commending him for judicious action; the leading organs of the opposite party have shown every disposition to deal with him fairly and generously. He can disarm the public distrust which his elevation excites by leaving undone anything that is obviously superfluous, and by walking steadily in the path of reform which was marked out for his predecessor. He can earn for himself everlasting odium and for his party disunion and defeat by repeating as President blunders which he has already made in a lower sphere.

- -

[No Headline] May 9, 1882

In signing the Chinese Exclusion Act of 1882, President Arthur demonstrated his ability to influence legislation. Congress initially had approved a twenty-year ban on Chinese immigration, but changed the ban to ten years after the president vetoed the first bill and indicated he would support a shorter suspension.

May 9, 1882
Editorial

The President has signed the new bill to suspend the immigration of Chinese laborers for a period of ten years. It is to be hoped that this will settle the much-vexed Chinese question for a time at least. The bill was

drawn with special reference to the objections raised by the President in his Message disapproving the first bill passed by Congress. As it now stands, the law suspends the immigration of Chinese laborers, whether skilled or unskilled or employed in mining. It provides for a system of certificates, to be issued on the identification of Chinese persons now living in this country or who may hereafter arrive here under provisions of the law authorizing them to come. The naturalization of all Chinese is expressly forbidden. Various fines and penalties are imposed upon the masters of vessels who shall bring unauthorized Chinese persons into this country, and upon any person who shall forge, alter, or make fraudulent use of the certificates to be issued to Chinese who are allowed residence in the United States. The bill as it has become a law does not infringe upon any of the rights of China as defined in existing treaties. The people of California will probably be satisfied with all its features, unless they may object to the shortness of the term during which immigration is to be suspended.

- -

"REFORM AGAIN TRIUMPHS," JANUARY 5, 1883, AND "THE REFORM COMMISSIONERS," FEBRUARY 11, 1883

The enactment of civil service reform in 1883 marked a significant victory for the Progressive movement. The Pendleton Act did not abolish political patronage, but it introduced the concept of government service that was not contingent upon party loyalty. To achieve this goal, the law created the Civil Service Commission to develop a merit system for hiring federal employees. Just weeks after President Arthur signed the Pendleton Act, *The Times* chided him for "making haste with the greatest possible slowness" in appointing commission members. In fact, the president did appoint officials who would work vigorously to implement the law.

JANUARY 5, 1883
REFORM AGAIN TRIUMPHS
THE PENDLETON BILL PASSED BY THE HOUSE.
THE MEASURE RUSHED THROUGH WITHOUT DEBATE OR AMENDMENT BY A VOTE OF MORE THAN THREE TO ONE.

WASHINGTON, Jan. 4—By a vote of more than 3 to 1 and after only 30 minutes' debate the Pendleton Civil Service Reform bill was this afternoon passed by the House precisely as it came from the Senate, and now it needs nothing but the approval of the President to make it a law of the land. While the majority in favor of the bill was very large, and the Democrats contributed a share of the affirmative votes on its final passage, they seized the only opportunity offered to them to cause delay by voting for a motion to recommit for amendment, a motion that would, if successful, have been fatal to the bill by delaying it beyond the possibility of passage during the present session. On the direct proposition to accept or reject the bill about half of the Democrats who had voted to send it back to the committee were constrained to change to the affirmative, a decent regard for public opinion, no doubt, preventing them from putting their names on record against a measure with the object of which they do not sympathize.

To most of the members of the House the expeditious passage of the bill was a surprise. To many Democrats who had hoped to be able to talk the reform to death its passage within two hours and a half after it was reported was a painful disappointment. To a few earnest friends of the measure the course pursued was only the performance of a programme arranged last night, and carried out to the very letter. Mr. Hiscock, whose services in behalf of the bill must cause his name to be remembered gratefully by the friends of civil service reform, last night held a consultation with several friends of the Pendleton bill, at which it was decided that as soon as the Army Appropriation bill was disposed of the Pendleton bill should be brought in by Mr. Kasson, and that it should be pressed to its passage before an adjournment. The scheme was entirely successful.

" President Arthur is making haste with the greatest possible slowness in setting to work the system required by the Civil Service Reform law. "

FEBRUARY 11, 1883
EDITORIAL
THE REFORM COMMISSIONERS.

President Arthur is making haste with the greatest possible slowness in setting to work the system required by the Civil Service Reform law. That measure was signed on the 16th of January—late in the afternoon. It has, therefore, been a part of the law of the land for twenty-six days. The bill contemplated the complete inauguration of the machinery provided in it within sixty days at the latest. At the expiration of that period the offices in the Treasury and Post Office Departments which are brought within the scope of the bill must be classified for the purposes of the bill; that is to say, in order that examinations may be held. It is obvious that it would be very desirable, if not necessary, that this classification should proceed with the general knowledge and proper assistance of the members of the commission. Though they have, of course, no authority over it, they would be able to get on with their work better if they were intimately acquainted with the first steps in it. After the expiration of these sixty days, four months are allowed for perfecting the rules, selecting the Chief Examiner and the Boards of Examiners in the various departments or bureaus, instructing them in their general duties, devising the various questions which must be adapted to the practical needs of the service in each case, and making arrangements for the holding of examinations. The time is certainly not too long.

Nearly one-half of the first period named has gone by, and no names of Commissioners have been sent to the Senate. Necessarily the choice of these officers is not an easy one. It is attended with some peculiar difficulties, possibly, for President Arthur, because a large number of gentlemen who have been somewhat intimately associated with him in the past, and who still claim, for purposes of their own, to have a great deal of influence with him, at heart, would like to see the Commissioners so chosen as to make the law a failure. It is not to be presumed that they have the President's ear, or that he is at all inclined to invite gratuitous contempt by yielding to their wishes or advice, but they have it in their power to influence public opinion in an embarrassing manner, and are doing so. They are sedulously spreading the impression that Mr. Arthur intends to thwart the purposes of the reform by appointing Commissioners not in sympathy with the law, and it is possible that in the atmosphere of Washington, where this class of men have an influence upon public opinion out of all proportion to their real merits or strength, they may throw some obstacles in the way of the President's prompt and direct and proper discharge of this delicate and important duty.

But if this be the case, there is no road out of the difficulty so short and so straight as to make nominations of the right kind, and to make them very soon. It is one of the peculiarities of this reform that the lions in its way, of which the politicians have made a great parade, have disappeared the moment that they were resolutely faced. Ten years ago, when President Grant began his attempt at reform, we were told, at the outset, that it was a visionary proceeding, that it would throw the service into the greatest confusion, and that within a year the departments would be in such a tangle that it would have to be abandoned. But at the end of a year the commission, in spite of the novelty of their task and the extreme opposition which they were compelled to overcome, were enabled to present a body of testimony from the various branches of the service to the substantial benefits produced by the system such as would have made its abandonment by any responsible Government absolutely impossible. And this is only an instance in many of the utter discomfiture of the prophets of evil in connection with the reform. No doubt the gentlemen who are preaching on the street corners and in the hotel lobbies at Washington that the Republican Party will be ruined if the President does not fill the commission with political hacks, who will emasculate the reform law, will do their best to make their predictions come true. But they are of no consequence. The President must know as well as any one what a poor lot they are, how little they represent the great party of which he is the head, how little the people care for them or listen to them, and how entirely unsafe it would be for him to pay any attention to them.

We do not, for that matter, imagine that this motley crew have any influence with the President, or have been directly or indirectly the cause of his long delay in selecting the Commissioners. But they make such persistent claims in this regard, they are so noisy and pretentious, that it is not surprising that some people are inclined to credit their blatant assertions, particularly as it is not very easy to find any reasons at once sound and plausible for the Presi- dent's procrastination. It is, therefore, extremely desirable from every point of view that Mr. Arthur should proceed as promptly as possible to the work of fairly establishing the reform system, the first step to which is necessarily the choice of proper Commissioners.

- -

"Civil Rights Cases Decided," October 16, 1883, and "Colored Men Disappointed," October 17, 1883

The United States tried with limited success to enact civil rights protections for black citizens following the Civil War. The Supreme Court ruled in 1883 that Congress had exceeded its authority with the Civil Rights Act of 1875, which had broadly interpreted the Fourteenth Amendment's guarantee of "equal protection of the laws" for all citizens. The ruling was highly disappointing for black Americans; as *The Times* reported, presenting the views of noted civil rights activist Frederick A. Douglass, who said the ruling moved "colored people again outside of the law and place[d] them [in any public setting] . . . at the mercy of any white ruffian who may choose to insult them."

In an editorial, *The Times* endorsed the Court's decision, noting that the legislation had tried to authorize "social privileges" by granting equal access to transportation, hotels, and restaurants, but that the law had never been enforced. In calling for states to provide these protections, *The Times* echoed the prevailing sentiment of the day. Some eighty years later, the federal government would revisit these efforts with more promising results.

OCTOBER 16, 1883
EDITORIAL
CIVIL RIGHTS CASES DECIDED.

The Supreme Court of the United States has finally de- cided against the constitutionality of the Civil Rights act of March 1, 1875, in a number of cases from various parts of the country submitted to the court a year ago on written arguments. The act provided that all persons within the jurisdiction of the United States should be entitled to equal accommodations and privileges in inns, public conveyanc- es on land and water, and in theatres and other places of public amusement, subject only to conditions established by law and applicable alike to persons of every race and color. Penalties were provided for violations of the rights defined, and provisions were made for their enforcement in the Federal courts. The act was intended to enforce equal civil rights in respect to the matters referred to in behalf of the colored citizens of the United States, and was based on the power of Congress to enforce the provisions of the fourteenth amendment of the Federal Constitution by "appropriate legislation."

The fourteenth amendment declares that "no State shall make or enforce any law which shall abridge the privileges or immunities of citizens of the United States; nor shall any State deprive any person of life, liberty, or property without due process of law, nor deny to any person within its jurisdiction the equal protection of the laws." Efforts have been made from time to time to give great elasticity to this amendment. It was assumed by Congress in 1875 that it gave to that body the power by direct legislation to secure to colored persons the right to first-class accommodations, or any accommodations they might demand which were accorded to others, on railroad trains and steam-boats, in hotels and restau- rants, and in theatres and other places of amusement, and certain Judges have held that it operated to restrict the power of States in matters of taxation. Its full scope and effect have not yet been authoritatively defined, but the Supreme Court is rapidly drawing the lines which are to limit its force.

In the temper which the people have now reached in dealing with questions that formerly had a sectional significance and that pertain to the relations of the races in this country it seems as though nothing were necessary but a careful reading of the amendment to show that it did not authorize such legislation as the Civil Rights act, and yet Judge Harlan is to file a dissenting opinion which may present considerations that do not occur to the ordinary mind. The prohibition of the amendment is specifically directed against the making and enforcing of laws by the States which shall abridge the privileges and immunities of citizens. Assuming that these include the right to equal accommodations in public conveyances and places of entertainment, it does not appear in any of these cases that any State has in its legislation or the enforcement of its laws made the discriminations complained of. The amendment does not give to Congress the power itself to legislate in regard to these rights except so far as it may be necessary to counteract the prohibited legislation of the States.

This is the exact ground taken by the Supreme Court in the decision just rendered.

The decision is not likely to have any considerable practical effect, for the reason that the act of 1875 has never been enforced. Spasmodic efforts have been made to give it effect, and occasional contests have been made in the courts, but the general practice of railroads, hotels, and theatres has remained unchanged and has depended mainly on the prevailing sentiment of the communities in which they are located. The question of absolute right is not affected by the constitutional amendment or the decision of the Supreme Court. There is a good deal of unjust prejudice against negroes, and they should be treated on their merits as individuals precisely as other citizens are treated in like circumstances. But it is doubtful if social privileges can be successfully dealt with by legislation of any kind. At any rate, it is now certain that they are beyond the jurisdiction of the Federal Congress. If anything can be done for their benefit it must be through State legislation. They are guaranteed against adverse and discriminating action by the States, and favorable action can only be secured through State authority. This remands the whole matter to the field in which it rightly belongs and in which alone it can be effectually dealt with.

OCTOBER 17, 1883
COLORED MEN DISAPPOINTED.
THE CIVIL RIGHTS DECISION REGARDED AS A STEP BACKWARD.

WASHINGTON, Oct. 16.—The decision of the Supreme Court declaring the Civil Rights act unconstitutional has been the subject of much comment here to-day, Several of the most prominent colored men of the District have given their opinions as to the moral effect of the decision. Naturally the majority of them express regret that the Supreme Court has rendered such a decision, and are inclined to regard it as an obstacle to the progress of the colored race. Mr. Bruce, Register: of the Treasury, declares it a most unfortunate decision, and one that "will carry the country backward fifteen years at least:" also, that it does not reflect the sentiment of the people, and is a revival of the theory of States' rights. Fred Douglass say the decision puts the colored people again outside of the law

and places them, when on a steam-boat or railroad train, or in a theatre, restaurant, or other public place, at the mercy of any white ruffian who may choose to insult them. Prof. Greener says that, in view of this decision, every colored man with any self-respect, must continue to demand the fullest protection of the law, both as a man and as an American citizen, and that he does not think the civilization of the age can be turned back even by the Supreme Court of the United States.

At a conference of colored people of the District to-day It was decided to hold a meeting on Monday night to express the sentiment of the colored race with respect to the decision, and to consider what course to pursue in view of that decision.

"Rebuilding the Navy," December 8, 1883

The Times endorsed the Arthur administration's proposals for modernizing the navy, praising the investment as money well spent to keep the United States on par with other nations. In fact, *The Times* urged the administration to develop a more ambitious program, suggesting that the United States should seek to "build a great navy that shall be equal in power, speed, and endurance to any in the world."

DECEMBER 8, 1883
EDITORIAL
REBUILDING THE NAVY.

The report of the Secretary of the Navy is unexpectedly conservative in tone. The Secretary has no radical suggestions to make, but contents himself with references to the work of augmenting the navy already authorized by Congress, with a few hints as to what should be authorized hereafter. The three new steel war vessels, of which the *Chicago,* carrying 14 guns, is the largest, will represent three main types of unarmored vessels. The *Chicago,* it is affirmed, will have no superior in the world for speed, endurance, and armament. In the other two, the *Atlanta* and the *Boston,* speed and endurance, rather than armament, have precedence. These will carry 8 guns each and will make 14 knots an hour. The *Chicago* will make 16 knots an hour. If the promise of these vessels does not exceed their performance, as is usually the case with vessels built and planned under the supervision of the Navy Department, we shall have made a satisfactory, though very small, beginning of a new navy. The *Dolphin,* a 1,500-ton dispatch boat, carrying one gun, is expected to make 15 knots an hour, and of her the Secretary complacently remarks that she will be a model commerce destroyer of a high rate of speed.

But, turning from these vessels, which are to cost $2,440,000 altogether, we are met with the proposition that a thorough reconstruction of our navy requires, at the very least, the building of seven additional unarmored steel cruisers. It is proposed that three of these should conform to the types represented in the vessels just now mentioned, and that the other four should be heavily armed cruising gun-boats, of about 1,500 tons displacement. The total cost of these additions to the war fleet of the Republic, it is estimated by the Naval Advisory Board, would be about $4,283,000. This estimate, it must be admitted, is moderate. If the vessels could be trusted to make, say, 13 knots, and to carry an armament that would be sufficiently formidable to secure actual fighting qualities with an average rate of speed,

the estimated cost would not be deemed excessive. The Secretary deprecates the building of any war vessel which shall attempt to rival in speed any of the well-known transatlantic steamers. He says that, in order to match these vessels, it would be necessary to build vessels of at least 11,000 tons displacement. How can a "commerce destroyer" hope to overtake a merchant steamer that has the the [*sic*] speed of the *Alaska,* for example? And why does the Secretary believe that in case of war all of these fast transatlantic steamers "would be withdrawn from their ordinary pursuits?"

If, as the Secretary says, later on in his report, we can never hope to have a navy which can cope on equal terms with the foremost European naval armaments, most people (agreeing with the Secretary) will ask why we should spend millions in the reinforcement of a navy which, after all, will only serve as a training school. It is not pretended that the proposed additions to the navy will make the force formidable. They will serve as means to keep alive the knowledge of war, while our main reliance will be that the country shall be defended by the intelligence, skill, and peaceful intent of our people. The proposition is somewhat inconsistent. The Secretary asks that the large sum of $7,449,581 shall be appropriated for an increase of the navy, although this increase is demanded only, as we may say, for the purpose of keeping alive a knowledge of the art of naval warfare. We are, therefore, brought face to face with this problem: Shall we continue to spend money to maintain a naval training school; or shall we build a great navy that shall be equal in power, speed, and endurance to any in the world; or shall we allow our navy to decay utterly and rely upon our peculiar political position as a defense against the attacks of all nations? Compared with this, the Secretary's scheme of absorbing the Revenue Marine Service, and other projects for inflating the importance of the Navy Department, are of small moment.

"Arthur's Weakness in New-York," April 8, 1884

President Arthur's bleak prospects for reelection in 1884 were illustrated by his weak support in New York, the state where he had made his political career. *The Times* attributed the president's low popularity to his continued engagement in machine politics, criticizing as insincere his efforts at civil service reform. Indeed, the Republican Party would pass over Arthur at its nominating convention, selecting instead his political opponent, James G. Blaine of Maine.

APRIL 8, 1884
EDITORIAL
ARTHUR'S WEAKNESS IN NEW-YORK.

It is one of the conceded points in the Presidential canvass of the present year that it will not be safe for the Republican Convention to nominate a candidate who is not reasonably sure of carrying the State of New-York. President Arthur's hope of receiving the nomination, to say nothing of his chance of election, depends absolutely on his strength in this State. In the face of this fact it becomes more and more clear every day that Mr. Arthur is decidedly weak in the State where he has most need of strength, and where, in the view of the country at large, he ought to be strong if anywhere. It is here that he is best known. It is here that his political and official record was made before he became Vice-President of the United States. Even his nomination for that office was a concession to the New-York men who worked so hard for the nomination of Gen. Grant for the head of the ticket in 1880.

The causes of his weakness here may not be fully understood in other States. It is admitted that his course in the Executive chair has been in most respects conservative, prudent, and judicious, and that he has made a better President than the country had reason to expect. And yet it is not necessary to go back to his career prior to 1880 to find the sources of his weakness in his own State. That merely furnishes light for the interpretation of some of his actions since he became President. He is known here as a machine politician of the most advanced type, a believer in organization which uses the rewards and punishments of official power and patronage to promote party ends. In his present high position he has known better than to use the methods of the politician too openly, but he has not lost faith in their efficacy, for they are still the methods which he uses, so far as prudence permits.

The sentimental objection to Mr. Arthur that he profited by the shooting of Garfield, and was politically in sympathy with those who harassed his brief Presidential career, would have little weight if it were an isolated incident in his political life. But the people do not forget that when he was Vice-President he came to the capital of this State and did all in his power to induce the Legislature to re-elect as Senators the two men whom the people of this State desired to keep in retirement. Then he sacrificed much of the respect which he might have retained, and lost strength which he can never recover. In placing the patronage of the Government at the command of Gen. Mahone in Virginia he gave evidence of the insincerity of his professions regarding the principles of civil service reform which is not easily forgotten. One of the chief sources of the distrust with which he is regarded by independent voters is the fact that, while he has not failed to commend those principles in his public utterances, he has on many occasions disregarded them when he has had an object to gain in making appointments. In fact, whenever there has been a political object to gain he has made his appointments with a view to that object rather than the good of the service. Civil service reformers do not trust Mr. Arthur.

Moreover, the disaster which overtook the Republican Party in this State in 1882 is very largely attributed to the President. It was with his countenance and encouragement that the political machine which looked to him for its inspiration forced upon the party a candidate who was not so much objectionable personally as the method of his nomination was utterly distasteful and revolting. And now the very tactics that were used to secure a State Convention favorable to the nomination of Mr. Folger are resorted to throughout the State to secure delegates to Chicago favorable to Mr. Arthur. They have served to increase the opposition to him among the people, and are to be added to other causes of his weakness.

That as a candidate for re-election Mr. Arthur is weak in this State is undeniable. That he could not secure the Electoral vote of the State is as certain as anything political in the future can be. The conviction that he could not be elected is with many Republicans who make no profession of independence of mere partisan considerations a sufficient reason why he should not be nominated and why the party in his own State should not try to secure his nomination. The President's strength lies almost wholly in that machinery of politics which derives its motive power from public office and public patronage.

Where that controls party action he is strong, but in this State it can no longer direct the action of caucuses and conventions, save at certain points where its force is concentrated. The party vote it can nowhere carry with it in its entirety. The independent vote it actually repels, and the candidate to carry New-York must have the independent vote.

- -

"THE NICARAGUA TREATY," JANUARY 17, 1885

In negotiating a canal treaty with Nicaragua, the Arthur administration foreshadowed the creation of the Panama Canal, which would revolutionize U.S. trade routes and markets. Although this treaty had many shortcomings, as *The Times* identified, and would fail to win Senate ratification, it laid the groundwork for future negotiations.

JANUARY 17, 1885
EDITORIAL
THE NICARAGUA TREATY.

Certain persons who urge that the Nicaragua Canal treaty should be ratified without delay assert that its provisions are all that this Nation could desire and declare that the agreement has been carefully drawn. Assuming that the Panama Canal will be completed and that the privileges that can be granted by Nicaragua will not, for that reason, be regarded as of great value by any European nation, it seems to us that the United States can secure more favorable terms than those set forth in the pending treaty. A canal in Nicaragua would cost at least $100,000,000, and it might cost $200,000,000, or even $250,000,000. If there should be in successful operation at Panama a competing canal at the sea level it might be difficult, if not impossible, to get a fair interest upon the money invested by this Government

in Nicaragua. Undue weight should not be given, it is true, to this matter of a return in dollars and cents, but it should not be disregarded. A consideration of all phases of the question proves that our Government, that proposes to do all the work and pay all of the expenses, should receive more than two-thirds of the net revenues. The completion and use of a canal in its territory would be of great benefit to Nicaragua, even if that republic should receive no share of the net revenue.

The treaty has not been carefully drawn, and if its provisions are not to be changed its form should be amended. Abundant evidence of hasty and careless work can be found in those paragraphs that relate to the use and acquisition of land.

THE PRESIDENCY OF GROVER CLEVELAND

MARCH 4, 1885 – MARCH 4, 1889, MARCH 4, 1893 – MARCH 4, 1897

Grover Cleveland was the only president in American history to serve two nonconsecutive terms. Cleveland won the popular vote three times—in 1884, 1888, and 1892, but in 1888 he lost the Electoral College vote to Benjamin Harrison. President Cleveland has the distinction of completing one term in office, returning to private life, and then returning to the White House four years later, after defeating Harrison. Despite his unique tenure as president, Cleveland was not shy about exercising executive power, using the veto and the full extent of his authority to promote economic reforms as well as law and order.

Cleveland was born in New Jersey and grew up in New York State. His given name was Stephen Grover, but he soon stopped using his first name. His father died when Cleveland was sixteen, and young Grover began working to help support his family. Although he did not attend college, Cleveland served an apprenticeship in a law firm and was admitted to the New York bar in 1859. He became active in New York Democratic politics, serving as assistant district attorney and sheriff in Erie County, then winning elections as mayor of Buffalo and governor of New York. By the time he entered the presidential race in 1884, Cleveland was well-steeped in executive experience at the local and state levels.

Another voice for Cleveland.

THE 1884 CAMPAIGN

The Democratic Party nominated Cleveland for president in 1884 largely because of his reform record as mayor and governor. Although he had not made significant policy achievements

in either position, he had fought corruption and denied patronage to New York City's Democratic political machine, known as Tammany Hall. Consequently, he was respected as an honest politician who did not let politics influence his decisions. The Democratic National Convention nominated Cleveland on the second ballot and selected Thomas A. Hendricks of Indiana as his running mate.

Cleveland came under attack in the campaign for two personal matters. During the Civil War, he had hired a substitute to take his place in the Union Army so he could continue to support his family. The law permitted him to do so, and Cleveland was by no means the only one to take advantage of this opportunity, but it sparked much criticism during the

127

QUICK FACTS ON GROVER CLEVELAND

BIRTH	March 18, 1837, Caldwell, N.J.
EDUCATION	Studied law privately
FAMILY	Wife: Frances Folsom Cleveland Children: Ruth Cleveland, Esther Cleveland, Marion Cleveland, Richard Folsom Cleveland, Francis Grover Cleveland
WHITE HOUSE PETS	Canaries, mockingbird, Japanese poodle
PARTY	Democratic
PREPRESIDENTIAL CAREER (SELECTED)	Assistant district attorney, Erie County, N.Y., 1863–1865 Sheriff, Erie County, 1871–1873 Mayor, Buffalo, N.Y., 1882 Governor of New York, 1883–1885
PRESIDENTIAL TERMS	March 4, 1885–March 4, 1889 March 4, 1893–March 4, 1897
VICE PRESIDENTS	Thomas A. Hendricks (first term; died November 25, 1885.) Adlai E. Stevenson (second term)
SELECTED EVENTS	Presidential Succession Act (1886) Appointment of first Interstate Commerce Commission (1886) Dedication of Statue of Liberty (1886) Interstate Commerce Act (1887) Creation of Department of Agriculture (1889) Repeal of Sherman Silver Purchase Act (1893) Wilson-Gorman Tariff Act (1894) Federal troops halt strike by Pullman Company workers (1894) Hawaii becomes a republic (1894)
POSTPRESIDENCY	Law practice in New York City (after first term) Trustee of Princeton University (after second term) Elected president, Association of Presidents of Life Insurance Companies, 1907
DEATH	June 24, 1908, Princeton, N.J.

presidential campaign, particularly because many northerners proudly touted their military service in support of the Union. Further complicating Cleveland's candidacy was the news that he had fathered a child out of wedlock. Cleveland did not deny this—in fact, he had provided financial support for the child—but it nevertheless presented another opportunity for his opponents to assail his character.

Cleveland ultimately prevailed in the race because the Republican candidate, James G. Blaine of Maine, failed to address a last-minute uproar created by one of his own partisans. Blaine had a long career in national politics that included Speaker of the U.S. House, senator, and secretary of state. Yet he failed to appreciate the political consequences of a statement made by one of his supporters just days before the election that the Democratic Party stood for "rum, Romanism, and rebellion." Blaine did not immediately reject the anti-Catholic sentiment and lost many votes in New York, which cost the Republicans a state they expected to carry. Cleveland won in the general election with a small margin in the popular vote and 219 Electoral College votes to Blaine's 182.

The Cleveland Administration (First Term)

The first Democratic president to take office after the Civil War, Cleveland took care to include southerners in his cabinet and appoint them to other federal positions as well. He selected Lucius Q. C. Lamar of Mississippi (a future Supreme Court justice) for secretary of the interior and Augustus H. Garland of Arkansas as attorney general. Cleveland's other appointments included Thomas F. Bayard of Delaware as secretary of state, Daniel Manning of New York as treasury secretary, William C. Endicott of Massachusetts as secretary of war, William C. Whitney of New York as navy secretary, and William F. Vilas of Wisconsin as postmaster general. The Department of Agriculture became a cabinet post just weeks before the end of Cleveland's first term, and the president appointed Norman J. Colman of Missouri to be its first secretary.

Cleveland entered the presidency as a bachelor, but he married Frances Folsom in a quiet White House ceremony on June 2, 1886. The bride was his former law partner's daughter and had been Cleveland's ward since her father's death. When they married, Folsom was twenty-one—the youngest first lady in American history—and the president was forty-nine. The couple had five children, three girls and two boys. Two of the children were born during Cleveland's second term.

Major Issues (First Term)

The significant legislation passed during President Cleveland's first term had little to do with executive influence. Cleveland supported the Interstate Commerce Act of 1887, which aimed to regulate the railroad industry. He approved the Dawes Severalty Act of 1887, which allocated small plots of land for individual Native Americans rather than their tribes and permitted settlers to purchase the perceived "excess" territory. Cleveland favored making the Agriculture Department a cabinet-level agency, and this status was conferred in 1889. Although Cleveland had promised in his campaign to implement and expand civil service reform, he did not pursue the matter vigorously once in office.

In many ways, Cleveland's use of executive power in his first term concentrated more on denying legislation through the presidential veto rather than seeking to enact a policy agenda. He was committed to controlling government spending and did not hesitate to reject what he considered "pork-barrel" legislation intended primarily to benefit specific congressional interests. He also vetoed many private pension bills to aid individual soldiers who fought in the Civil War. In 1887 Cleveland vetoed the Dependent Pension Bill, which would have given pensions to the parents of soldiers who died in the line of duty.

One of Cleveland's main concerns was tariff reduction. Seeking to use a federal budget surplus to help farmers and other workers, Cleveland urged Congress to expand the money supply by ending or reducing tariffs on items such as wool, lumber, and steel. Indeed, the president's annual message to Congress in December 1887 concentrated entirely on the need for lower tariffs. But once Congress began to consider the bill, Cleveland did not pursue its passage, and the bill failed in the Senate. Tariffs became a primary source of contention when the president stood for reelection.

Cleveland did not campaign in 1888, deciding it would be inappropriate for an incumbent president to be so openly engaged in politicking. The Democratic convention nominated him for president on its first ballot and selected Allen G. Thurman of Ohio as his running mate. The Republican Party, in contrast, waged an aggressive campaign that focused primarily on the importance of maintaining high tariffs to protect American interests. The Republican National Convention nominated Sen. Benjamin Harrison of Indiana for president and Levi P. Morton of New York for vice president on the eighth ballot. Harrison prevailed narrowly in both Indiana and Cleveland's home state of New York, which enabled him to defeat the president in the Electoral College, 233 to 168. Had Cleveland carried New York, he would have won the election. Of small consolation to the president was his victory in the popular vote, with about 5.5 million ballots to Harrison's 5.4 million.

The 1892 Campaign

The 1892 presidential campaign replayed the 1888 contest, but this time with a uniform victory for Cleveland. Despite his historic loss four years earlier, Cleveland won the Democratic Party's nomination again on the first ballot in 1892, with Adlai E. Stevenson of Illinois selected as his running mate. The Republicans nominated President Harrison on the first ballot as well and chose Whitelaw Reid of New York as his running mate. The newly formed Populist Party also nominated a presidential ticket, James B. Weaver of Iowa for president and James G. Field of Virginia for vice president, and the third party garnered more than 1 million votes. Nevertheless, Cleveland soundly defeated Harrison, winning 5.5 million popular votes to Harrison's 5.1 million, and 277 Electoral College ballots to Harrison's 145. The Democratic Party also took control of both chambers of Congress, which gave Cleveland a unified government at the start of his second term.

The Cleveland Administration (Second Term)

Cleveland's second-term cabinet reflected the geographic diversity of the United States. From the Northeast came Secretary of War Daniel S. Lamont and Postmaster General Wilson S. Bissell of New York, as well as Attorney General Richard Olney of Massachusetts. From the South came Treasury Secretary John G. Carlisle of Kentucky and Navy Secretary Hilary A. Herbert of Alabama. Rounding out the cabinet were Secretary of State Walter Q. Gresham of Illinois, Secretary of the Interior John M. Reynolds of Pennsylvania, and Secretary of Agriculture Julius S. Morton of Nebraska.

Major Issues (Second Term)

Upon taking office in 1893, President Cleveland confronted a severe economic depression, with rising unemployment and several bank failures. Convinced that silver money was contributing to inflation, Cleveland sought to restore confidence in the economy by persuading Congress to repeal the Silver Purchase Act of 1890, despite strong resistance within his own party. He was less successful in pursuing tariff reform, a significant issue from his first term. The Wilson-Gorman Tariff Act, which included an income tax provision, passed in 1894 without his signature.

In addition to the nation's economic woes, President Cleveland also faced a challenge to law and order when the Pullman rail company's workers went on strike in 1894. Ignoring the strong opposition of Illinois governor John P. Altgeld, the president sent army units to Chicago after violence erupted there. The business community endorsed Cleveland's action, while the labor movement opposed it.

In foreign affairs, President Cleveland successfully pressured Great Britain to arbitrate a boundary dispute between Venezuela and British Guiana. He withdrew from Senate consideration a treaty drafted in the Harrison administration that would have annexed Hawaii. Cleveland opposed the treaty because it lacked popular support in Hawaii. He refused to initiate war with Spain over its suppression of a rebellion in Cuba, despite popular support for such an endeavor.

By the end of his second term, President Cleveland's differences with Democrats over economic policy, particularly tariff reform and silver coinage, were so great that he actually favored Republican candidate William McKinley over William Jennings Bryan, his party's nominee. Cleveland's preference was not surprising, as he had exercised little party leadership after the Republican Party took control of Congress in the 1894 midterm elections.

After leaving office, President Cleveland retired to Princeton, New Jersey, where he became a trustee of Princeton University. He died eleven years later of a heart attack. The legacy of the Cleveland presidency would be defined foremost by the nonconsecutive terms as well as the president's stubborn adherence to his policies, regardless of party or congressional opposition.

* * *

"The Charges Swept Away," August 12, 1884, and [No Headline], October 27, 1884

The 1884 presidential campaign is memorable more for its alleged scandals than for substance. Democratic candidate Grover Cleveland made headlines with reports that he had fathered a child out of wedlock years earlier and that he had paid a substitute to fight in his place during the Civil War.

In the first excerpt, a group of independent Republicans reported as false the allegations of "drunkenness and gross immorality" against Cleveland. They included a statement from a minister who acknowledged Cleveland's "illicit connection," but also pointed out that Cleveland had accepted responsibility for the child he fathered. Foreshadowing the twentieth-century debate over how much a presidential candidate's personal life should matter in a political campaign, the minister concluded, "For my part I can forgive it, when it has not been denied, and its bitter fruit has been accepted, and all the duties which grew out of it generously discharged." Even after Cleveland admitted his actions, opponents continued to mock him with the refrain, "Ma, Ma, where's my Pa? Gone to the White House, ha ha ha." The Civil War controversy was defused with the news that Cleveland had paid for his substitute, in accordance with the law at the time.

" The general charges of drunkenness and gross immorality which are made against Gov. Cleveland are absolutely false. "

AUGUST 12, 1884
THE CHARGES SWEPT AWAY

A POLITICAL SCANDAL SPEEDILY SETTLED.
REPORT OF A COMMITTEE OF INDEPENDENT REPUBLICANS, DWELLING
IN BUFFALO, CONCERNING ACCUSATIONS AGAINST GOV. CLEVELAND.

Slanders upon the private life of Gov. Cleveland which have gained circulation have been investigated by independent Republicans of Buffalo, and the following report, the result of the inquiry, is now officially given to the public:

To the Independent Republicans of the Nation:

As Republicans and independents residing in Buffalo, and having peculiar means of knowledge, we have been called upon by private letter and otherwise for information in regard to the scandals which have been put in circulation respecting Gov. Cleveland's private life. We have felt it to be a duty imposed on us by circumstances to examine these stories in detail and to make a formal statement of the results. No such examination would have been necessary to satisfy ourselves; but it was due to those who have read the charges against Gov. Cleveland without knowing personally his general character and reputation in this community, and without knowing either the position or the means of information of those who have made the charges, that we should not put forth a mere general statement without a previous investigation.

We have therefore, through a committee appointed from our number for that purpose, carefully and deliberately made an investigation, and we have taken every available means to ascertain the precise facts in each case.

The general charges of drunkenness and gross immorality which are made against Gov. Cleveland are absolutely false. His reputation for morality has always been good. There is no foundation for any statement to the contrary. He was sought out and nominated for the Mayoralty against his will, and was supported for that position by the larger portion of the educated, intelligent, and moral citizens of Buffalo without regard to politics, and on purely

personal grounds. After he had gone through this contest he was again put forward as one of the most distinguished citizens of Buffalo as a candidate for the Governorship, and again received the support of the same class of his fellow-citizens. In this community, where he had lived for 29 years, and where his life was known and his character well understood, this support would not have been given to him had he been either a drunkard or a libertine. We are able to speak from personal knowledge as his acquaintances of long standing, and to say that his general private life has been that of a quiet, orderly, self-respecting, and always highly respected citizen.

Since he assumed his present office his visits to Buffalo have been few and of short duration. It is susceptible of absolute proof, and has been proved to us that upon no one of these visits has anything occurred to justify the statements which have been made by his detractors. The charge that he has recently taken part in a drunken and licentious debauch in Buffalo on the occasion of such a visit is entirely false.

We have been particularly careful and thorough in our investigations of the alleged betrayal, abduction, and inhuman treatment of a woman of this city as detailed in a local newspaper. The circumstances out of which this story was fabricated occurred eight years ago. The woman in question was at that time a widow, between 30 and 40 years of age, with two children, the younger of whom was 10 years old. The facts of the case show that she was not betrayed, and that the allegations respecting her abduction and ill-treatment are wholly false. We deem these the only features of the charge in connection with this matter which constitute a public question requiring any declaration on our part.

Our examination of the other charges which have been made against Gov. Cleveland's private character shows that they are wholly untrue. In every instance in which the reports and insinuations have been tangible enough to furnish a clue to guide us in our investigation they have been positively proved to be false.

The attack upon Gov. Cleveland's character is thoroughly discredited when we consider the sources from which it comes. It was first publicly made in Buffalo by a newspaper of no standing whatever. We have twice called upon the editor of this paper and asked him to produce his proofs—the names, dates, and other particulars—which he had publicly stated he was at liberty to show. He declines to do so or to facilitate investigation into the truth of either his own charges or those contained in the anonymous letter which he published. He admitted that he had no evidence to support any accusation against Gov. Cleveland, except in the one instance to which we have particularly referred. He rested his case on that story, and as to that story he is contradicted by the witnesses having personal knowledge.

The two clergymen whose profession has been invoked to give weight to these charges have no personal knowledge of the facts, and under the circumstances could not possibly have such knowledge. They have ventured to state as facts known to themselves stories which rest upon the merest hearsay, and which, when traced to their alleged sources, are in every case denied by the persons to whom they are ascribed.

We have designed to make a candid and judicial statement of the results of our investigation of this matter without partisan coloring. We have not thought it necessary or proper to repeat the charges against Gov. Cleveland in detail, nor to present in full the evidence by which they have been disproved.

JOHN H. COWING,	JOSIAH C. MUNRO,
ANSLEY WILCOX,	L. D. RUMSEY,
WILLIAM F. KIP,	G. BARRETT RICH,
THOMAS CARY,	CHAS. P. NORTON,
GEORGE P. SAWYER,	JOHN B. OLMSTEAD,
RALPH STONE,	J. TALLMAN DAVIS,
JOHN E. RANSOM,	HENRY ALTMAN,
HENRY W. SPRAGUE,	J. N. LAARNED.

BUFFALO, N.Y., Aug. 9, 1884.

A CLERGYMAN'S TESTIMONY.

In the issue of the *Independent* for the the [*sic*] current week the Rev. Dr. Kinsley Twining makes the following statement:

Letters having been received at the office of the *Independent* from two reputable clergymen in Buffalo, N.Y., charging Mr. Cleveland, the candidate of the independent Republicans, with habits of gross immorality, which, if true, would render it impossible for any Christian man or decent journal to support him, it was thought best, on consultation, that I should go to Buffalo and make personal and thorough investigation of the facts.

Accordingly, I went to Buffalo, and spent two full days in the most thorough investigation. One day I spent with the gentlemen, journalists, clergymen, and others who are responsible for the dissemination of the stories, and following up lines of investigation suggested by them, and another in visiting the leading citizens of Buffalo, Republicans and Democrats, who best know Gov. Cleveland, and who know all about the stories, and in getting their judgment as to his character. This investigation I made absolutely thorough. I depended on no reports of the newspapers, or of local clergymen, or others, but only on my own personal investigation of the case. I am satisfied that I know the case from fuller information than do any of those who have given it private or public currency.

Now, it is not my purpose here to repeat the particulars of the reported scandal in its grosser or its corrected version. Those who want it can get it from the publisher of the Buffalo *Telegraph,* who will be glad to sell copies. If necessary, I am ready with the full facts; but it is not necessary here.

The kernel of truth in the various charges against Mr. Cleveland is this, that when he was younger than he is now he was guilty of an illicit connection; but the charge, as brought against him, lacks the elements of truth in these substantial points. There was no seduction, no adultery, no breach of promise, no obligation of marriage; but there was at that time a culpable irregularity of life, living as he was a bachelor, for which it was proper and is proper that he should suffer. After the primary offence, which is not to be palliated in the circle for which I write, his conduct was singularly honorable, showing no attempt to evade responsibility, and doing all he could to meet the duties involved, of which marriage was certainly not one. Everything here was eminently to his credit under circumstances which would have seemed to many men of the world to justify him in other conduct than that which he accepted as his duty. There was no abduction, only proper legal action under circumstances which demanded it. . . .

It is now proper that I should indicate my own view of the effect the truth in reference to these unexpected charges should have upon independents who were ready to give their support to Mr. Cleveland. There is nothing in it that would naturally placate them toward Mr. Blaine, or mitigate their opposition to him. That rests upon grounds of public political morality. It does not require them to withdraw their support from Mr. Cleveland. That rests on the same grounds as their opposition to Mr. Blaine. But it does send them into the canvass with a fact in the history of their candidate which they cannot forget, and which they will have to carry as a burden.

For there is no interest, public and political, higher than that of the family. If Mr. Cleveland is a rebel against the law of the family, he is a public enemy; and when he is shown to be so I will abandon him. But such he is not, even though the lapse of which he was guilty, and whose punishment he was man enough to accept, is not to be palliated. Whether such an offense can, in the course of years, be forgiven, will depend on one's eagerness to cast the first stone. For my part I can forgive it, when it has not been denied, and its bitter fruit has been accepted, and all the duties which grew out of it generously discharged.

Serious, therefore, as this matter is, I cannot, amid the great responsibilities and pressing necessities of the political situation, see that it authorizes us to set aside the conclusions which the whole independent party has drawn from the tried, trusty, and admirable public career of Gov. Cleveland, nor permit us to forget that above any other American citizen now living and known to the country he possesses in himself the administrative ability which is the great and primary requirement of the Presidential office.

OCTOBER 27, 1884
EDITORIAL

The latest lie, up to date, about Gov. Cleveland, told in a circular of the Veteran Logan Legion of Erie County, is that he got a substitute, when drafted, from the penitentiary, free of cost to himself. The fact, as he has stated in response to an inquiry, is that he sent as a substitute a sailor on the lakes, and paid him. "If he is alive yet," says the Governor, "I don't think either of the noble veterans who signed this circular would care to meet him after he had read it." The Blaine managers ought to realize by this time that these inventions do their candidate more harm than good.

● ●

" 'FOR PRESIDENT, GROVER CLEVELAND!' WHY?" OCTOBER 4, 1884

The New York Times endorsed a Democratic presidential candidate for the first time in 1884, when it supported Grover Cleveland's candidacy. An editorial published one month before the election listed may reasons for the endorsement, the foremost being Cleveland's respect for the principle "that public office is a public trust."

OCTOBER 4, 1884
EDITORIAL
"FOR PRESIDENT, GROVER CLEVELAND!" WHY?

Because he represents above all the principle which now most needs to be emphasized in this country—that public office is a public trust.

Because in his hands civil service reform would be safe. It was by his help that the New-York laws were passed and made effective. He has been one of the surest friends of the reform. He is one of the few Democrats who can resist the pressure of "a hungry and thirsty party," and civil service reform is not fully assured until it has stood through the crisis of a change of party. Now is the time and here is the man to make that change with safety.

Because he stands for the best of the Democratic Party and Blaine represents the worst of the Republican Party. Many of the best Republicans are against Blaine, to his discredit; many of the worst Democrats are against Cleveland, to his credit. And we are not willing to believer that the worst Republican is better than the best Democrat; that one-half of the American people are all that is bad, or that manly Republicans can permit themselves to adopt the partisan war cry of "Vote for the Evil One if he is the party candidate."

Because the principles of the Republican Party are above the party itself. In the election of James G. Blaine Republican principles would go down. The party can outlive his defeat, but it could not survive his election. The highest loyalty to the party compels resistance to the corruptionist candidate.

Because no personal interest or private weakness or political fear has ever affected one of his public acts. He is the best friend of the workingman because he dared to veto bills that were only sham appeals to popular favor, like the Mechanics' Lien bill, which only played into the hands of sharks, and the Car Drivers' bill, which would have cut down wages as well as hours and have done no good. His veto of the elevated railroad fare bill, whether mistaken or not, was a brave stand for what he believed constitutional safeguards, directly against his political preferment. The country needs a man who does not know how to truckle.

Because in every new place and upon every new issue he has shown capacity equal to the task. The sound common sense that gave Abraham Lincoln power and the sturdy political morality that goes with it make him always master of the situation.

Because as Executive he will execute the people's will, without fear, favor, or personal bias, as represented by Congress, in matters, such as those of revenue, specially committed to its hands. He will be the people's President.

Because his foreign policy will be, not bluster and back-down, like Blaine's, but dignified and firm. "We do not claim," said Grover Cleveland, Mayor of Buffalo, "to make laws for other countries, but we do insist that, whatever those laws may be, they shall, in the interest of human freedom and the rights of mankind, so far as they involve the liberty of our citizens, be speedily administered." This would be the spirit of the Administration of Grover Cleveland, President of the United States.

Because his election would be the rebuke of the most threatening vice of our time and country—the spirit of reckless speculation in business and of shameless jobbery in politics. The two are one evil. The election of James G. Blaine would be a direct appeal to every young man to adopt dishonesty and effrontery as the methods of success.

These are some of the reasons which justify Republicans in supporting a candidate not of their party. The American people must elect as President James G. Blaine, corruptionist, or Grover Cleveland, reformer. For which, reader, will you cast your vote?

• •

"THE VICTORY OF HONESTY," NOVEMBER 9, 1884

Despite the many attacks on his character, Cleveland prevailed in the 1884 presidential election. Effectively dismissing the campaign scandals in light of Cleveland's frank response, *The Times'* front-page article heralded Cleveland's election as "The Victory of Honesty."

NOVEMBER 9, 1884
THE VICTORY OF HONESTY
CELEBRATING THE ELECTION OF GOV. CLEVELAND.
NO CHANGES IN THE GENERAL RESULT, BUT ONLY CONFIRMATION OF A VICTORY
FOR THE REFORM GOVERNOR.

The reports received from the various States yesterday do not change the general result of the Presidential election, but only confirm the choice of Gov. Cleveland. In New-York State a few changes, caused by recounts in three counties, reduce the Democratic plurality to 1,280. The Electoral College, therefore, remains as given yesterday morning, 219 for Cleveland and 182 for Blaine. From other States more full details are given of the result, especially in the election of Congressmen. The feature of the day yesterday was the widespread celebration by Democrats and independent Republicans of their success in electing Cleveland and Hendricks.

"THE INDIANS' SURPLUS LAND," APRIL 5, 1886

One of the most hotly contested subjects in American history is the treatment of the American Indians, or Native Americans. During Cleveland's first term, Congress passed legislation that would grant nominal sections of territory to individual Native Americans, but reserve the vast majority of the land for settlement. *The Times* supported this plan, noting that "the great unoccupied reservations must be opened to settlement under the pressure of advancing civilization." The consequences, however, would not be uniformly beneficial.

APRIL 5, 1886
EDITORIAL
THE INDIANS' SURPLUS LAND.

The Dawes bill relating to the Sioux Reservation in Dakota, whose provisions we explained a few days ago, has been reported in the House without material amendment. It has already been passed by the Senate. Its passage by the House will probably mark the beginning of a movement for the opening of large Indian reservations in an equitable way.

This reservation is almost as large as the State of Indiana, and it is occupied by only 28,000 Indians. A great part of the land is arable, for the reservation lies in the Dakota wheat belt. The tract is almost surrounded by settlers. Railroads are ready to traverse it. The Indians cannot use these millions of acres. The game has disappeared, and they are not farmers. But they hold all this land under a treaty which binds the Government to deprive them of no part of it without the consent of three-fourths of all the men in the tribe. Plainly it is for the interest of the Government to get possession of the part which the Indians cannot use, for it is needed for the use of settlers. Plainly

it is for the interest of the Indians to dispose of their surplus land if they can get a fair price for it, for the money will make them rich, and a refusal to sell the acres which they do not need and cannot use will encourage those who have no respect for Indian treaties, and may work to their great disadvantage. Their best friends support the bill. They admit that the great unoccupied reservations must be opened to settlement under the pressure of advancing civilization. Shall they be opened legally and fairly or unjustly and in violation of solemn agreements? That is the question, and the Dawes bill is satisfactory to them because while it gives to the settler the land which ought to be improved, it also recognizes the treaty and pays the Indian a fair price for the land which he surrenders.

If three-fourths of the men of the tribe shall consent the Government will take 11,000,000 acres and sell this land to settlers for 50 cents an acre, setting aside the proceeds as a fund for the Indians' benefit. The Sioux will then have 11,000,000 or 12,000,000 acres left, and hereafter they will probably sell the greater part of this remainder. All persons interested will be benefited by the settlement proposed in the bill. The farmer will get his land at a very low price, ($80 for a farm of 160 acres), the Indians will receive a large income from the sale of lands which are now of no value to them, and the Government will not be forced to pay for the Indians' support so much as it is paying now.

The surplus lands of other Indians must ere long be opened for settlement and cultivation. There are millions of acres held under treaties which should not remain unoccupied and unused while for miles around the country is dotted with farmhouses and villages. It is folly for the Government to pay hundreds of thousands of dollars every year for the support of these Indians in idleness while they possess property sufficiently valuable to support them. If the Government shall succeed in obtaining the surplus

lands of the Sioux it will not be difficult to get possession of the surplus lands of other tribes in the same way. The Indians have common sense, and if they shall be approached by honest men they will not refuse to sell for a fair price the land which they do not need and cannot use.

Statutes under which such transfers of land are made should contain provisions for the protection of the money which the Indians receive. The Government can save the Indian's money by taking charge of it and allowing him the income, and can insure him an abiding place by protecting for a score of years his title to a farm taken under the severalty laws.

It is very plain that the Indians' surplus and unused lands cannot be withheld from settlement much longer. All friends of the Indian and supporters of the treaties should welcome the opportunity to advocate such legislation as is proposed in the Dawes bill.

* *

"THE WHITE HOUSE BRIDE," MAY 29, 1886, AND "THE PRESIDENT'S WEDDING," JUNE 2, 1886

President Cleveland's wedding to Frances Folsom on June 2, 1886, aroused a great deal of public interest, and *The Times* provided full details on the ceremony plans. Comparing the wedding to a royal marriage, *The Times* justified the public curiosity about such minutiae by noting that the first lady was "an official personage," and as a result, "every American man and woman wishes to know something about her."

MAY 29, 1886
THE WHITE HOUSE BRIDE
THE WEDDING ANNOUNCED FOR NEXT WEDNESDAY EVENING.
A SIMPLE SERVICE TO BE PERFORMED IN THE BLUE ROOM.
ONLY MEMBERS OF THE CABINET AND INTIMATE FRIENDS OF PRESIDENT
CLEVELAND AND MISS FOLSOM TO ATTEND—NO WEDDING TRIP PROJECTED.

WASHINGTON, May 28.—The President authorizes the announcement to-night that he will be married next Wednesday evening at the White House to Miss Frances Folsom. This announcement relieves and gratifies everybody, and the President is glad to be able to do what a great many inconsiderate and impatient persons have been criticising him for not having done several weeks ago. The wedding was not to have taken place until about the 19th, although the date had not been positively fixed. The death of Col. Folsom made it uncertain whether it could take place in June, and it was not until after Miss Folsom's arrival in New-York last night that it was decided that the date should be advanced

instead of being postponed. The wedding would have taken place in the White House whether it was celebrated in June or later, but if the death of Col. Folsom had not occurred it would probably have been a more ceremonious affair than that contemplated for next week.

The ceremony is to take place at 7 o'clock on Wednesday evening in the pretty Blue Room, where the President receives the diplomatic representatives, and where he has stood so often in the midst of the brilliant reception parties to shake hands with throngs of guests. The main corridor behind the elaborate screen separating the vestibule from the Red, Blue, and Green Parlors will be decorated with

President Grover Cleveland and his wife, Frances Folsom, returned to the White House when Cleveland was elected to a second nonconsecutive term. Cleveland was the only President to be married in the White House.

Source: Library of Congress

potted plants, the greenhouse will furnish an abundance of cut flowers and plants for the East Room, and the interior of the building will be a glow of light. In the vestibule the Marine Band will furnish orchestral music. The Rev. Byron Sunderland, the Pastor of the First Presbyterian Church, in which the President has a pew, and of which he is a regular attendant, will perform the marriage service.

The wedding party will be a small one. Of the President's family there will be present probably only Mrs. Hoyt and Miss Cleveland. Of the bride's family there are to be present Mrs. Folsom, her mother, and Mr. Benjamin Folsom, who has been traveling with Mrs. and Miss Folsom in Europe. Mr. Folsom will give the bride away. Besides these relatives and friends and Col. and Mrs. Lamont, who stand next in the order of intimacy, those who will be in the Blue Room during the ceremony will be Secretary Bayard, Secretary and Mrs. Manning, Secretary and Mrs. Whitney, Postmaster-

General Vilas and Mrs. Vilas, Secretary and Mrs. Endicott, Secretary Lamar, and possibly Attorney-General Garland and his mother. The Attorney-General has been invited, but it is not certain that he will break his rule against appearing in society, and set aside his prejudice against a dress coat long enough to appear in a proper garb at the President's wedding.

After the wedding ceremony there will be a collation, set in the state dining room, which is to be made cheerful with tropical plants and a wealth of art flowers. The arrangements described are possible within the resources of the White House. There will be no attempt at ostentation. It will be a plain wedding, without parade for the public, and without any exhibition of elaborate costumes or gifts. The newly wedded pair will remain at the White House. The President cannot leave Washington now for a wedding trip of even short duration, and will postpone that pleasure until later in the year, after Congress has adjourned. He has no intention of taking his bride to "Pretty Prospect," or "Rosedale," the variously named property which he has just acquired in the suburbs. He expects to use that as a refuge from visitors when he has business on hand that requires uninterrupted attention.

There have been no changes in the interior arrangements of the White House in anticipation of the bride's coming. There has been such a Spring cleaning as the establishment would have received if there had been no wedding in contemplation. After such a cleaning it is not such a mean house, with all that has been said of it, and the President has said that the house which the people think good enough for the President to live in must surely be regarded as good enough for the President's wife.

Miss Rose Cleveland, the President's sister, arrived at the White House to-night. There will be no happier person in the circle that will assemble in the Blue Room on Wednesday evening, excepting, of course, the bride and the groom, than this sister of the President. She has known for several years of the probability of the marriage of Miss Folsom and her brother, and she has shared with all the members of the family a sincere gratification in contemplating it. An exceedingly cruel and false story of the relations existing between the President and his sister, which appeared a day or two ago, and which was a baseless fabrication, furnishes an excuse for referring to this subject. No brother and sister were ever more cordially affectionate or considerate of each other. While Miss Cleveland was the lady of the White House she was treated with the kindliest consideration by the President, and her friends were frequent and unrestricted visitors. The President knew of her intention to publish her book, and neither opposed it nor pretended to any indignation that he did not feel. On the contrary, he appreciated and shared in the cordial reception accorded to the work, with which he was fully acquainted before it appeared in print.

" The social success of an Administration with this official body counts for a great deal in its political success, and this social success depends much more upon the President's wife than upon the President. "

JUNE 2, 1886
EDITORIAL
THE PRESIDENT'S WEDDING.

The interest taken by the people of the United States in the wedding of the President is without doubt widespread and sincere. Crude as some of the expressions of it have been, it is neither snobbish nor intrusive, but respectful and cordial. The annoyances to which the President has been subjected from inquisitive persons were simply the maladroit expressions of an unformulated belief that the people "had a right" to know something about the matrimonial intentions of the Chief Magistrate.

We need not go so far as this in order to maintain that the public interest in the marriage that is to be solemnized this evening is an entirely legitimate feeling. Royal marriages excite an interest far beyond the circle of those who are likely to be brought into association with the wedded pair, and this interest is gratified by public and official announcements, and except where there are special reasons to the contrary by public weddings. The wife of the President of the United States, it may be said, is an official personage. Every American man and woman wishes to think well of her; every American man and woman wishes to know something about her. In a democratic republic the official society of the capital is as far as possible from constituting a Court, and the aping of the manners of Courts can be nothing but a ridiculous burlesque. But this very fact makes the character of the mistress of the White House a subject of more general importance than it would otherwise be. The President's wife has not in the full sense the liberty to choose her own society which belongs to every American lady who is not the wife of an official. Everybody may look forward to being presented to her, and it is consequently the concern of everybody to know what manner of woman she is.

It would be a great mistake to suppose that because our politics are not Court politics the influence of women goes for little in them. Everybody can recall instances of American public men who have been weighted and handicapped by uneducated or tactless wives, and of other American public men who owe their prominence to the cleverness with which their talents have been made the most of and their failings dissembled by clever wives. The official society of Washington, take it altogether, is a very important body, the influence of which is felt to the remotest parts of the country. The social success of an Administration with this official body counts for a great deal in its political success, and this social success depends much more upon the President's wife than upon the President. When Andrew Jackson conducted an Administration upon the issue of forcing the "social recognition" of one woman, and made the politics of the country revolve around and depend upon the social intrigues of Washington, he furnished an extreme instance of the extent to which social questions may determine political questions, and he also showed what an abyss of blundering a headstrong man may fall into for want of a wife possessed of social culture and social tact. There are other instances less glaring, indeed, but not less pertinent of the interaction of national politics and Washington society.

So long as our politics have any social element, and until the President and the officers of the Cabinet have "desk room" in public buildings and go home when their office hours are over, to choose their own society, or to abstain from any society whatever, if they choose, like other people, the President's wife, or the mistress of the White House, if there be no President's wife, will continue to be a personage. In this point of view it is a public misfortune that the President should be a bachelor, although the last bachelor before Mr. Cleveland who was elected President had the great good fortune to have the social side of the Administration so well cared for that his bachelorhood was scarcely a misfortune. All those who wish well to Mr. Cleveland's Administration, and we are persuaded they are a very great majority of the people of the country, will rejoice that this peril is to be removed from it by his choice of a bride of whom all men and all women who know her speak in praise.

"Railroad Regulation," January 16, 1887

The Interstate Commerce Act of 1887 sparked debate over whether it would impose undue regulations on the railroad industry. Congress was the driving force behind the legislation; President Cleveland played little role in its ratification beyond signing the bill into law.

January 16, 1887
Railroad Regulation.
WALL-STREET'S VIEW OF THE INTERSTATE COMMERCE BILL.

Railroad men talked yesterday a good deal about the Inter-State Commerce bill, which passed the Senate Friday. The subject was discussed also among brokers. In general the effect of the passage of the bill was depressing. It seemed to be assumed that the House also would pass it. Yet it was a dangerous day to gamble on the effect of the bill even should it become law. Bull points that were given out on roads not to be affected by the bill might as well have been kept quiet, for they did not stir the market to any important extent. Their failure to do so strengthened the hopeful and relieved the despondent. Many concluded, before evening, that perhaps matters would adjust themselver [*sic*] properly under the bill, and then the danger line was passed.

Speaking of the bill, President James D. Smith, of the Stock Exchange, said: "It is one of the most impracticable measures, in my opinion, that ever came before Congress for serious attention. It gives practically the control of the railroads of the United States to five Commissioners, who cannot be interested in the securities of those roads. It gives these five Commissioners more to do than any five men ever did before, or than any five men can do if they perform the duties imposed upon them by the bill. It was expected that the prospect of the bill's passage would have a depressing influence on the stock market, if the measure seemed likely to become a law; but on account of the general impression that it would be inoperative the prospect had no depressing effect at all. It is a significant fact that many of the Senators who voted for the bill felt themselves called upon to apologize for casting their votes in its favor, and alleged as their excuse for voting for it that their constituents demanded it."

President Smith's opinion was widely held down town. On the other hand, many were disposed—the number increasing as the day went on—to agree with Commissioner Blanchard that the bill would hardly touch roads east of Chicago, the rates being now as well graduated as they could be by law.

- -

"The Pension Veto," February 12, 1887

President Cleveland did not hesitate to use his constitutional power to veto legislation, as illustrated by his rejection of the Dependent Pension Bill of 1887. In so doing, the president aimed to limit government spending. *The Times* supported the veto, praising the president for "having courageously and firmly followed the dictates of his own conscientious judgment."

February 12, 1887
EDITORIAL
The Pension Veto.

The President's message returning to Congress for its reconsideration the Dependent Pension bill is a clear, logical, and forcible document for which, we should say, a good many members of Congress ought to be profoundly thankful. Those of them who voted for the bill without sufficient study of its character or an adequate conception of its effect, but in good faith, certainly will be so, since it gives them an opportunity to review their action and ample information by which to be guided. It is probable that there are enough members of Congress of this class to prevent the bill from receiving the two-thirds vote necessary to pass it notwithstanding the objections of the President. But whether this shall be the case or not, there is no room for doubt that the course of the President will be approved by intelligent public opinion. It is plain that he has been influenced by a sense of duty, and that he has disregarded some political considerations which, with a weaker man, or one less loyal to his convictions, might have had much weight. Mr. Cleveland cannot, of course, be ignorant of the use that will be made of this veto by unscrupulous partisan opponents, or of the extent and nature of the prejudices to which they will appeal. He can judge as to this by the recent past, by the partisan attacks based on his numerous well considered vetoes of private pension bills. But he can very well afford to ignore this prospect; first, because he can trust the fairness and common sense of the American people, and, second, because no partisan abuse can deprive him of the supreme satisfaction of having courageously and firmly followed the dictates of his own conscientious judgment.

- -

"THE PRESIDENT'S MESSAGE," DECEMBER 7, 1887

In pursuing tariff reform, President Cleveland went against the wishes of a significant wing of the Democratic Party. *The Times* wrote, "Judged by any ordinary standard of political expediency, the President's act is inexpedient," particularly because he was raising the issue "on the eve of a national contest." Tariffs would become the hot-button issue in the 1888 presidential election. The protectionist Republican candidate, Benjamin Harrison, won a lopsided victory over Cleveland by prevailing in the Electoral College, even though he lost the popular vote.

DECEMBER 7, 1887
EDITORIAL
THE PRESIDENT'S MESSAGE.

Mr. Cleveland has done an act of statesmanship in the best sense. Recognizing a great duty, he has performed it with courage, with firmness, and at the right time. And he has performed it so that every honest man must see that it is an honest act, disinterested, faithful to the requirements of conscience, without hope or purpose of personal or party advantage except such as comes from the public recognition of public service. Judged by any ordinary standard of political expediency, the President's act is inexpedient. He has forced upon his party an issue as to which the party is divided, and so divided that unless the minority yield, it can defeat the will of the majority. He has done this on the eve of a national contest in which a considerable number of men of influence in the party have been urging him to avoid this issue, and threatening him and the party with disaster if he did not avoid it. On the other hand, there is nothing in this issue, thus presented, by which Mr. Cleveland could hope to draw from the Republican Party any votes to compensate those he is in danger of losing and which he has been warned over and again by leaders of his own party that he would lose. Nor this alone, for if the protectionist faction in the Democratic Party carry out their own desires, or do what they have continually declared that they would do, Mr. Cleveland has done the one thing by which he could imperil the prospect of his own renomination. From the point of view of the politician, he has shown a courage that is temerity in the pursuit of an end of no value to himself.

But it is not by this standard that statesmen are guided, and it is by ignoring it that Mr. Cleveland shows that he is a statesman. His view is fixed on the needs of the country. He states them succinctly and clearly, and he points out what he believes to be the sound way to meet them. If he endangers his immediate interest, he deserves, and will, we believe, receive the support of the great body of the people to whose interests he is loyal. If he defies the dictates of party expediency, he gives to his party a policy worthy of a national organization and invites them to a task to which they can rally intelligent men. In this policy the Democratic Party may find a sound and valid reason for existence, an end of real importance and enduring interest, an object above the plane on which all parties have so long been dragging their weary way, and, beyond all, substantial principles wholly disconnected with the old and worn-out questions that are absolutely and forever settled, and on which it was their misfortune, while they were still pending, to be generally on the wrong side. This is good politics. It places Mr. Cleveland far above any of the leaders to whom the Republican Party has of late lent a hearing, and above most of the leaders of his own party.

The elevation of American politics is not a slight service at this time for a President to engage in. Mr. Cleveland has done his part in it before, and his contributions have been solid and valuable. This latest is the best of all. The manner in which he has made it is characteristic of the man. It is marked by his simplicity, directness, boldness, and candor. It is unprecedented for any President to summon a Congress at the threshold of a session to consider one subject only, to emphasize his purpose by setting aside all other matters, and to call on the representatives of the people to look straight at one controlling question. A weaker man, one more subject to the influence of precedent, less capable of complete conviction, less profoundly devoted to what his own mind declares to be right, would have surrounded this appeal to Congress with the usual volume of statements and recommendations, or would have reserved it for a special communication. But not Mr. Cleveland. This,

he says to Congress, is the "state of the Union." It is "shown in the present condition of the Treasury, and our general fiscal situation, upon which every element of our safety and prosperity depends." He asks them to study it; he points out the treatment it requires. There is no room for doubt or misunderstanding.

It will be observed that the President practically recommends the reduction of tariff duties only. He refers to the internal revenue taxes but to say that "there appears to be no just complaint of this taxation by the consumers of those articles" that are taxed. But "our present tariff laws, the vicious, inequitable, and illogical source of unnecessary taxation, ought to be at once revised and amended." It is to these we owe the "indefensible extortion and culpable betrayal of American fairness and justice" involved in the present condition of the Treasury. It is to these that Congress should address itself with moderation and with candor, not "dwelling upon theories," but looking at facts. "It is a condition which confronts us—not a theory." "The simple and plain duty which we owe the people is to reduce taxation to the necessary expenses of an economical operation of the Government, and to restore to the business of the country the money which we hold in the Treasury through the perversion of governmental powers." It remains to be seen how Congress will regard the appeal made by the President. It is a wise appeal, based on facts that no one can deny, and pointing to a policy that must be adopted sooner or later. If it be not adopted now, then, in the words of the message, "the responsibility must rest where it belongs."

"Mr. Cleveland's Popular Plurality," December 6, 1888

The results of the 1888 presidential election made it one of the most newsworthy races in American history. Only on two other occasions in the nineteenth century—1824 and 1876—did the winner of the popular vote not become president. After the election, *The Times* questioned the merits of the Electoral College, expressing concern about having a president "whom a large plurality of the voters of the country have declared to be less acceptable to them than his opponent."

DECEMBER 6, 1888
EDITORIAL
MR. CLEVELAND'S POPULAR PLURALITY.

Commenting upon the fact that President Cleveland received at the recent election a plurality of the popular vote, which it puts at 80,000, but which is probably not much short of 100,000, the Philadelphia *Times* declares that "this is the first time in the history of the Government that the popular vote has been overruled by the Electoral College" since it was the House of Representatives, voting by States, that gave John Quincy Adams his election over Jackson in 1824, when the latter had a majority of 50,000, and the Electoral Commission, not the Electoral College, which seated Hayes in 1876, when Tilden had a popular plurality of 250,000 votes. Though he will be a minority President, Mr. Harrison will not for that reason be any the less the President of the party which gave him and bought for him a majority in the Electoral College. That party will expect him to make the "sweep" just as clean, to reward the active partisan and favor the faithful worker just as generously as though the popular plurality had been on his side; and the beneficiaries of tariff trusts will not be less forward to press upon him their personal views concerning duties on imports.

About the only comfort Democrats can get out of Mr. Cleveland's popular plurality, unprecedented as it is for a defeated candidate, is the lawful privilege of affirming that the country is with the President and not against him, and that it favors tariff reform. These assertions cannot be gainsaid, but since the constitutional machinery for registering the will of the people in choosing Presidents takes account only of the Electors chosen in the various States, and ignores the popular vote of the country as a unit, the exercise of this privilege will not be likely to convince the least resolute Republican that the popular figures possess any significance which he is bound to respect.

As confirming the well-grounded charge that Mr. Harrison's election was procured through bribery and corrupt bargaining, a charge which finds new supporting evidence and wider belief every day, these figures will receive, however, the attention of students of our electoral method. The increase in Mr. Cleveland's popular vote as compared with 1884 is much greater than the increase of Harrison's vote over Blaine, and the plurality of Mr. Cleveland now is 98,000, against 62,000 four years ago. It is evident from this that the popular drift is toward the Democratic Party, not away from it. This tendency Mr. Quay and Mr. Dudley and Mr. Wanamaker could not have triumphed over had the election been determined by the vote of the people at large. Profuse as were the contributions of the protected manufacturers and trusts, they were swallowed up in the purchase of a plurality of 14,000 in New-York and one of 2,000 in Indiana, with some further outlay, of course, in other States like West Virginia and New-Jersey and what moralists and politicians would agree in calling the "legitimate" expenses of the campaign. To have overcome the plurality of nearly 100,000 still remaining to Mr. Cleveland would have been impossible without frying out of the protected millionaires the last vestige of their accumulated "fat"—a process to which they would never have submitted.

Without the interposition of the cumbrous electoral machinery Mr. Cleveland would have been President four years more. But it is objected that the device of an Electoral College enables us to determine the result within a few hours of the closing of the polls, and so averts doubts and disputes. That is true. It is not certain, however, that celerity in gaining the knowledge is worth providing for at the expense of seating in the Executive chair a man whom a large plurality of the voters of the country have declared to be less acceptable to them than his opponent.

"A NEW CABINET OFFICER," FEBRUARY 1, 1889

The creation of the Department of Agriculture gave President Cleveland an opportunity to appoint a new member of his cabinet just weeks before the end of his term. The department had existed since the Civil War, but cabinet status was not conferred until 1889.

FEBRUARY 1, 1889
A NEW CABINET OFFICER

HIS TITLE WILL BE SECRETARY OF AGRICULTURE.
IT IS AGREED UPON IN CONFERENCE WITH SOME MODIFICATIONS—
THE SEED-DISTRIBUTING FRAUD.

WASHINGTON, Jan. 31.—The long contest in conference between the Senate and House on the bill establishing a new Department of Agriculture, the chief officer of which shall be Secretary of Agriculture, was ended late this afternoon by the House conferrees agreeing to recede from all the amendments made to the Senate bill by the House. The conference has been unusually prolonged. It began early in December and has been sitting intermittently ever since. The original House amendment added the Signal Service to the new department. It was rejected by the Senate, and some time ago the House conferrees decided to recede. Then an effort was made by the House conferrees to add the Geological Survey and the Fish Commission to the new department. This change was advocated by the heads of both those bureaus, but the Senate conferrees held out for the Senate bill, and the House conferrees at last surrendered.

All meetings of the conference committee have been presided over by Senator Palmer, Chairman of the Senate Committee on Agriculture. Mr. Palmer has labored with a great deal of patience to bring about the result that has been reached, and the agreement is very largely due to his efforts. The House will now agree to the Senate bill and it will go to the President for signature, and it is generally believed that he will sign it.

As soon as it becomes a law he will have the appointment of a Secretary of Agriculture for the term of about three weeks. It is thought probable that he will name either Commissioner Norman J. Colman, W. H. Hatch of Missouri, or John E. Russell of Massachusetts for the office. The passage of the law will also add one more name to the Cabinet of President Harrison. Senator Palmer's name is prominently mentioned for the place, but he has long ago declared that he would not accept it. The creation of the new department may, however, have a serious effect upon the political ambitions of Gen. Alger, for Jonathan J. Woodman of Paw Paw, Mich., has been a prospective candidate for the place for many months, and has an armful of petitions and recommendations ready to file with the President-elect at an instant's notice.

Cleveland and Stevenson have been chosen to the highest offices in the gift of the American people by a majority in the Electoral College so large that the meaning is unmistakable.

"MR. CLEVELAND IS ELECTED," NOVEMBER 9, 1892

President Cleveland's reelection in 1892, four years after leaving the White House, marked an historic victory for the president and the Democratic Party. The Democrats also took control of both the House and Senate, returning unified government to Washington.

NOVEMBER 9, 1892
MR. CLEVELAND IS ELECTED

A GREAT TRIUMPH FOR DEMOCRACY AND TARIFF REFORM.
NEW-YORK HEADS THE LIST OF STATES.
NEW-JERSEY, CONNECTICUT, AND INDIANA FOLLOW.
SOME SURPRISES IN THE WEST.
ILLINOIS AND WISCONSIN OUT OF THE REPUBLICAN LINE.
TWO HUNDRED AND EIGHTY-ONE VOTES IN THE ELECTORAL COLLEGE FOR
THE DEMOCRATIC CANDIDATES—TWO DEMOCRATIC SENATORS FROM NEW-YORK
WILL HELP TO SWELL THE DEMOCRATIC MAJORITY IN THE UPPER HOUSE
OF CONGRESS WHEN MR. CLEVELAND TAKES HIS SEAT—WEAVER BREAKS
INTO THE REPUBLICAN COLUMN.

The people's trust in Grover Cleveland, the moral revolt from the Republican Party, and the hearty union of the Democracy upon the great issue of tariff reform produced a Democratic landslide in the election of yesterday. Cleveland and Stevenson have been chosen to the highest offices in the gift of the American people by a majority in the Electoral College so large that the meaning is unmistakable.

The Times of Monday showed that Mr. Cleveland would have 232 Electoral votes and that his election would be assured. In the election yesterday the doubtful States were found in the Cleveland line. New-York gives him 40,000, New-Jersey 10,000, Connecticut 1,500 to 2,000. Indiana's new ballot law makes the count in that State slow, but at midnight there was little reason to question that it is safely Democratic. The same is true concerning West Virginia. Ex-Gov. Gray has telegraphed the National Democratic Committee that Indiana will give Cleveland 10,000 to 12,000 majority. . . .

The House of Representatives in the Fifty-third Congress will be controlled by the Democrats, but not by so large a majority of Democrats as in the Fifty-second Congress. According to the latest reports there will be of the 356 members 224 Democrats, 117 Republicans, and 15 members of the People's Party, a Democratic majority of 92 and a Democratic lead over the Republicans of 107.

There is also abundant reason for believing that the Democrats have carried the State Legislatures in a sufficient number of States to give them a majority in the United States Senate on March 4, 1893, so that, for the first time in many years, the entire Government will be in the hands of the Democratic Party.

• •

"THE PRESIDENT'S MESSAGE," AUGUST 8, 1893

President Cleveland's second-term policies were consistent with his first-term agenda, particularly with respect to economic affairs. The president opposed silver coinage, and he urged Congress to repeal the Silver Purchase Act of 1890, which it soon did.

AUGUST 8, 1893
THE PRESIDENT'S MESSAGE.

BELIEF THAT MR. CLEVELAND WILL SIMPLY ADVISE SILVER-PURCHASE REPEAL.

WASHINGTON, Aug. 7.—The House was not prepared to-day to ask the President to send in his message, but to-morrow the Committee of Notification, appointed by the Speaker this afternoon, will go to the White House, to announce the readiness of the House to hear from him, and it is probable that early in the day the message will be read in the Senate and the House of Representatives.

All manner of conjecture has been indulged in as to the contents of the message, but nothing definite is known that can be said to come from the President by authority. There is reason to believe that the President will not recommend anything affirmatively as to silver coinage, unless perhaps it may be for an extension of subsidiary coinage, the present time, with silver at the lowest price known in years, being one unfavorable for the consideration of propositions for free coinage or for establishing a new ratio. From what he has permitted his friends to recommend and work for, it is assumed that the President will be content with advising the simple repeal of the silver-purchase clause of the Sherman act at this time and that silver legislation be maturely considered before any bill is enacted for coinage or for the establishment of a new ratio.

Some inquiries, made by newspaper men who desire to know what space they are to allow for the message, lead to the conclusion that it will be short—not more than a column and a half or two columns of a newspaper of the average size. From this information, it is assumed that the discussion of the money question will not be elaborate, and that the references to other questions must be merely tentative.

If the tariff is referred to, it is believed that it will be treated as a matter not to be taken up until something be done with the money question that will encourage business men to believe that, whatever comes, the coin and paper of the Government will retain stability and inspire the fullest confidence in those who use them.

The feeling among members is hopeful and reasonable. The impression made upon other members by the earnest talk of the New-York men is deepening, and the determination to do rash things to gratify sectional preferences is not perceptible. At no time since the silver question began to be a matter of heated discussion has the prospect for conservative action been so good as it is now. There is no one here who desires to see the country go to everlasting smash. There is a universal desire among Democrats to see the President at the head of his party leading the way out of depressed conditions, and it seems probable that the President will get from the Congress pretty nearly all that he asks, and it is believed that he will ask nothing that is not good for the whole people.

"BACK TO BUZZARD'S BAY," AUGUST 12, 1893

Unbeknownst to the American public, President Cleveland underwent surgery for a cancer in his mouth in July 1893. The surgery took place aboard a friend's yacht, and the president's recovery was smooth but slow. After returning to Washington briefly in August, the president soon departed again, issuing a public statement that obliquely attributed his need for rest from the challenges of executive leadership.

AUGUST 12, 1893
BACK TO BUZZARD'S BAY.

The President Quietly Left Washington Yesterday—Statement of His Reasons.

WASHINGTON, Aug. 11.—Not until this afternoon did the members of Congress learn that the President had left the city early this morning, instead of deferring his departure until this afternoon, as had been announced in the papers of yesterday and to-day.

Many members of Congress who had hoped to be able to see him for a moment before he left, were, of course, disappointed, and some of them were more than disappointed to-night, when they learned that no nominations are to be taken up while the President is away. They at once reached the conclusion that the business of nominating will not be attended to while the proposition to repeal the Sherman law is pending.

The facts about the President's health were stated in *The New-York Times* this morning. If he had simply announced that he was ill and in need of rest and then had gone away, his friends are of the opinion that he would have made all the announcement to the people that might be considered requisite. The statement given to the press was left at the White House when the President and Secretary Lamont left at 6:30 this morning. It was not supplied to the press until this afternoon, after the afternoon papers were published. In that way the chance of calling together the reporters in New-York to meet him was avoided. The President was in New-York before it was known in Washington that he had gone away.

The members of the Cabinet, excepting Secretaries Morton, Smith, and Herbert, are all out of the city to-night, and Mr. Herbert will leave to-morrow for Philadelphia to see the launching of the *Minneapolis*. Congress will be left to itself next week. There will be no excuse for visits to the White House or the departments, for there will be no one in either of those places to attend to members who have constituents anxious to be put in office. There will be an uninterrupted opportunity to listen to reasoning on the silver question.

The President's statement is as follows:

"My absence from the capital at this time may excite some surprise, in view of my intense interest in the subject now awaiting the determination of Congress. Though my views and recommendations have already been officially submitted to that body, and though I am by no means certain I could further aid in bringing about the result which seems so necessary, it would be a great satisfaction to me if I could remain at the scene of action. But whether I am here or elsewhere, I shall look with hope and confidence to the action of those upon whom the responsibility now rests for relieving our people from their present dangers and difficulties.

"I am going back to my Summer home at the seashore because I am not sufficiently rested from the strain to which I have been subjected since the 4th of March to fit me again to assume the duties and labors which await me here. I have been counseled by those whose advice I cannot disregard that the further rest I contemplate is absolutely necessary to my health and strength. I shall remain away during the month of August, and shall devote myself to rest and outdoor recreation.

"My day's doings will be devoid of interest to the public, and I shall be exceedingly pleased if I can be free from the attentions of newspaper correspondents."

"SECOND PROCLAMATION MADE," JULY 10, 1894

When the Pullman railroad company's workers went on strike in 1894, violence soon erupted. President Cleveland issued a proclamation demanding a return of law and order. The rioters did not comply, and the president sent troops to Chicago to restore stability.

JULY 10, 1894
SECOND PROCLAMATION MADE
PRESIDENT CLEVELAND GIVES A GENERAL WARNING.
RIOTERS IN ALL STATES MUST DISPERSE.
After Three o'Clock To-day All Such Law Violators Will Be Public Enemies.
NAVY DEPARTMENT CALLED UPON.
Forces upon the Pacific Coast Will Co-operate with Land Forces in Opening Traffic on the Central Pacific Railroad—Fear Entertained that State Militia Is Not Loyal—Monitor *Monterey and War Ship* Thetis May Be Called into Action—Senator Sherman Introduced a Petition Asking for the Passing of a Law to Punish Labor Organizations for Violating Laws—Bill Introduced in the House Providing for an Increase in the National Army.

WASHINGTON, July 9.—The President this evening added to his proclamation of last night another of the same tenor, but more general in its application.

As Chief Executive of the United States, Mr. Cleveland commands all persons engaged in, or in any way connected with, the unlawful obstruction of railroads, combinations, or assemblages in any of the States where disorders and rioting prevail, to disperse and retire peaceably to their homes before 3 o'clock in the afternoon of July 10.

After that hour and time all law violators referred to will be regarded as public enemies.

The decision to issue such a proclamation was made this morning, and part of the day was devoted to arranging its terms. To-night Secretary Lamont, Attorney General Olney, Postmaster General Bissell, and Major Gen. Schofield met the President at the White House and expressed satisfaction with the scope of the manifesto, in which they had a share in perfecting.

The conference to-night was devoted largely to a discussion of the new phase of the situation consequent on the failure of the arbitration negotiations and the decision of the trades unions to join the American Railway Union in its strike.

The conference ended shortly after 10 o'clock. Gen. Miles telegraphed that everything was quiet, and that he was going to retire for the night, and the President and his advisers concluded to do likewise. Gen. Miles also advised that the mass meeting of trades unionists was off for to-night.

Secretary Lamont and Major Gen. Schofield remained with the President for some time after Secretary Gresham, Attorney General Olney, and Postmaster General Bissell had left. When Gen. Schofield left the White House at 11 o'clock he said that matters looked better to-night than they had at any time since the strike began.

The General said that no State troops in any State had been ordered to hold themselves in readiness for service, although the President had specific constitutional authority to call them out. He also said that no additional regular troops had been sent to Chicago or elsewhere. . . .

By the President of the United States of America: A PROCLAMATION.

Whereas, By reason of unlawful obstructions, combinations, and assemblages of persons, it has become impracticable, in the judgment of the President, to enforce, by the ordinary course of judicial proceedings, the laws of the United States at certain points and places within the States of North Dakota, Montana, Idaho, Washington, Wyoming, Colorado, and California, and the Territories of Utah and New-Mexico, and especially along the lines of such railways traversing said States and Territories as are military roads and post routes and are engaged in inter-State commerce and in carrying United States mails;

And, Whereas, For the purpose of enforcing the faithful execution of the laws of the United States, and protecting property belonging to the United States or under its protection, and of preventing obstructions of the United States mails and of commerce between the States and Territories, and of securing to the United States the right guaranteed by law to the use of such roads for postal, military, naval, and other Government service, the President has employed a part of the military forces of the United States:

Now, therefore, I, Grover Cleveland, President of the United States, do hereby command all persons engaged in or in any way connected with such unlawful obstructions, combinations, and assemblages, to disperse and retire peaceably to their respective abodes on or before 3 o'clock in the afternoon on the tenth day of July, instant.

In witness whereof I have hereunto set my hand and caused the seal of the United States to be hereto affixed.

Done at the City of Washington this ninth day of July in the year of our Lord one thousand eight hundred and ninety-four and of the independence of the United States the one hundred and nineteenth.

By the President:
GROVER CLEVELAND.
W. Q. GRESHAM,
Secretary of State.

"The New Tariff in Operation," August 28, 1894

Despite President Cleveland's efforts to enact tariff reform, his own party members in Congress were strong supporters of protectionist policies, and they succeeded in enacting a tariff bill in 1894. The president opposed the bill, which became law without his signature.

AUGUST 28, 1894
THE NEW TARIFF IN OPERATION.

The Bill Became a Law Without the President's Signature.

WASHINGTON, Aug. 27.—The Tariff bill of 1894 will be the law of the land from to-morrow. The bill that reached the President Aug. 15, and which had been in his possession ten full days at noon to-day, becomes a law without his signature, and with only his qualified approval, expressed in a strong private letter to Representative Catchings of Mississippi. As intimated in that letter, the President was disposed to let the bill become the law without any comment whatever from him. The Speaker, Mr. Catchings, Mr. Clark of Alabama, and other tariff reformers of the House urged the President to sign, in the belief that his approval, even if it were qualified by a memorandum setting forth his views of the bill's imperfections, would have a salutary effect in modifying prejudice against it, and in stimulating the Democrats of the country to renewed efforts to advance the work begun by the present session of Congress.

The letter to Mr. Catchings was the outcome of the conversations the President has had with the men of the House who had advocated the Wilson bill. The letter pleases the House Democrats, who are still sensitive about the shabby treachery that induced them to take the Senate bill under the impression, created by what appeared to be honest promises, evidently sanctioned by high official indorsement, that the free raw material bills, or at least the free sugar bill, would be passed by the Senate if the Senate bill were accepted. The President makes some references to "treachery and half-heartedness in the camp." Everybody who has read the newspapers and who reads this letter will be at liberty to construe the meaning of these words as broadly as they please. They are full of suggestions, and the suggestions are not likely to be lost. In the House there is intimate acquaintance with the latest instances of treachery in the Democratic camp, instances that are explicable only by the assumption of the grossest corruption. The difficulty of proving Senatorial corruption by investigation conducted by Senators has been demonstrated. The suspicions that existed before that committee began its work and rendered its Scotch verdict remain indelibly impressed upon the American people. They will never be removed until the perfect work is accomplished to which the President points the way for the Democratic Party.

"THE COUNTRY IS AROUSED," DECEMBER 20, 1895

In calling for Great Britain to resolve the boundary dispute between Venezuela and British Guiana, President Cleveland asked Congress to create a commission to examine the issue. Great Britain had resisted submitting the dispute to arbitration, but in the face of the president's determination, it agreed to do so. The rise of the United States as a presence in global affairs had begun.

DECEMBER 20, 1895
THE COUNTRY IS AROUSED

It Stands Firmly by the President in the Venezuela Matter.
CONGRESS WILL DO ITS FULL DUTY
The Senate as Determined as the House to Maintain the Nation's Honor.
DISPOSED TO PROCEED CAREFULLY
Probable that the Bill Providing for a Commission Will Become a Law This Week.

WASHINGTON, Dec. 19.—The delay caused in the Senate in the passage of the Hitt bill, to authorize the President to appoint a commission to investigate the Venezuela boundary question for the information of the Administration and the Congress, should not be taken as an indication of flagging interest in the dispute between the United States and Great Britain. But the first flush of excitement had passed, the parties had had some chance to cultivate rivalries, and reasons not altogether free from partisanship helped to make it easier to let the bill go to the Committee on Foreign Relations than to force it through by a vote not altogether unanimous. The Senate Committees are to be changed soon.

Willing to Trust the President.

Mr. Morgan, who is Chairman to-day, in a few days may be succeeded by Mr. Sherman, and it is evident that, while the Republicans are not unwilling to co-operate with the President, they are not indifferent to securing such commendation for their party as may be obtained by prompt and patriotic action in which they may lead.

There are more plans for amending the bill in the newspapers and in the corridors of the Senate than can be traced to any sponsors. One hears that a proposition will be made to make the commission one of six or nine members, the members to be named by the President, the House, and the Senate, each naming a third of them.

Mr. Morgan was more than usually friendly and trustful to-day when he declared that, for his part, he was willing to leave the investigation entirely to the President; and as the Hitt bill imposed no limitations upon the President, according him freedom as to the number and character of the commission, and Mr. Morgan was frank in declaring that he would not amend it, it may be the bill will come back from the committee unchanged in that respect.

Against Making a Time Limit.

There is little acceptation of the proposition of Mr. Lodge to prescribe the time in which the commission must report. If the President shall be permitted to control the commission, and he shall discharge his duty with as much acceptability as he so far has shown in this matter, it is assumed he will not permit any time to be wasted.

One purpose in the minds of some of the Senators is the amendment of the Hitt bill to reassert the Monroe doctrine as a part of the expression of the will of the Congress in giving the President the power to investigate, in order to be guided in future recommendations. The fact that the doctrine never has been expressed in a law is urged as the best reason for this amendment of this bill. This suggestion may meet with better acceptation than any which shall propose a limitation upon the President.

There is a patriotic desire to give the impression, in anything that may be done, that the President is acting for the Nation, and not for a party or parts of all parties. No better way of conveying the National feeling can be devised than that of throwing upon the President the opportunity and the responsibility of securing in his own way the report that is desired.

No One Questions His Patriotism.

There admittedly is no doubt of his patriotism. It is conceded cordially by all men here that he has met fully every expectation that American citizens have formed of what the President should be in such an emergency. It will be hurtful to the United States and its cause if at this time any indiscreet or embarrassing limitations, conceived in a mere party spirit, be imposed upon President Cleveland. The United States should be heard through the law the Senate is about to pass, and no mistake should be made in having the will of the people expressed in such a way that the impression made in England shall be doubtful or carry an intimation of reluctance on our part to trust fully the Chief Magistrate.

THE PRESIDENCY OF **BENJAMIN HARRISON**

MARCH 4, 1889 – MARCH 4, 1893

The presidency of Benjamin Harrison is significant in American history because Harrison won election without winning the popular vote. His opponent, incumbent president Grover Cleveland, defeated him by nearly 100,000 votes, but Harrison prevailed in the Electoral College by winning Cleveland's home state of New York. Four years later, the two men competed for the office again, and this time Harrison lost to challenger Cleveland, making Harrison the only president in American politics to be preceded and followed by the same person. Harrison's legacy includes significant legislation in economic and commercial policy, but the controversial election results in 1888 are perhaps the most memorable aspect of his presidency.

The Harrison family's involvement in politics dated back to the Revolutionary period, when Harrison's great-grandfather, Gov. Benjamin Harrison of Virginia, signed the Declaration of Independence. Harrison's grandfather, William Henry Harrison, was elected president in 1840, but served for only one month before dying in office. Benjamin Harrison was born in Ohio on his grandfather's farm in 1833. He completed his college education and legal studies in his home state and was admitted to the Ohio bar in 1853. In 1854 he moved to Indianapolis, where he opened a law practice and joined the Republican Party. He served with distinction in the Civil War and was promoted to brigadier general in 1865. In 1876 Harrison lost the gubernatorial race in Indiana, but he remained involved in Republican politics and won election to the U.S. Senate a few years later. Harrison served in the Senate for one term, losing his reelection bid when Democrats took control of the Indiana state legislature and opposed his candidacy. (State legislatures elected senators until passage of the Seventeenth Amendment in 1913.)

THE 1888 ELECTION

Without a clear-cut choice for the presidential nomination in 1888, the Republican Party considered several choices before nominating Harrison on the eighth ballot. Levi P. Morton of

PUCK.

THE RAVEN.

New York was chosen as the vice-presidential nominee. The political parties were sharply divided on tariffs, with Democratic president Cleveland supporting their reduction to promote free trade and Republican candidate Harrison advocating higher tariffs to protect American business. Cleveland refused to campaign, considering it inappropriate for a sitting president to engage so openly in politics, while Harrison employed a "front-porch" strategy in which he hosted many campaign events at his home. With narrow wins in large states such as New York, Pennsylvania, Indiana, and Ohio, Harrison defeated Cleveland

QUICK FACTS ON BENJAMIN HARRISON

BIRTH	August 20, 1833, North Bend, Ohio
EDUCATION	Farmer's College (Cincinnati, Ohio) Miami University (Oxford, Ohio)
FAMILY	First wife: Caroline L. S. Harrison (died October 25, 1892) Children: Russell B. Harrison, Mary S. Harrison Second wife: Mary Harrison (married April 6, 1896) Children: Elizabeth Harrison
WHITE HOUSE PETS	Dogs, billy goat ("His Whiskers")
PARTY	Republican
PREPRESIDENTIAL CAREER (SELECTED)	Starts law practice in Indiana, 1854 Elected Indianapolis city attorney, 1857 Elected reporter of Indiana Supreme Court, 1860 Civil War service, 1862–1865; breveted brigadier general, 1865 Loses gubernatorial race in Indiana, 1876 U.S. senator from Indiana, 1881–1887
PRESIDENTIAL TERM	March 4, 1889–March 4, 1893
VICE PRESIDENT	Levi Parsons Morton
SELECTED EVENTS	Inter-American Conference (1889, 1890) Sherman Antitrust Act (1890) Sherman Silver Purchase Act (1890) McKinley Tariff Act (1890) Dependent and Disability Pension Act (1890) Treaty of annexation for Hawaii (1893; not ratified)
POSTPRESIDENCY	Represents Venezuela in boundary dispute with Great Britain, 1897–1899
DEATH	March 13, 1901, Indianapolis, Ind.

in the Electoral College, even though Cleveland had enough support in the southern states to win the popular vote.

THE HARRISON ADMINISTRATION

In selecting his cabinet, Harrison appointed some personal and political allies, but he did not support patronage as actively as Republican Party loyalists wanted. Former Republican presidential candidate and House Speaker James G. Blaine of Maine became secretary of state, and Harrison's law partner, William Henry Harrison Miller of Indiana, was chosen for attorney general. Harrison selected Benjamin

Franklin Tracy of New York to be secretary of the navy, bypassing senior Republican leaders in New York who wanted to join the cabinet. For postmaster general, Harrison chose John Wanamaker of Pennsylvania, who had been important in Harrison's campaign. Completing the cabinet were William Windom of Minnesota as treasury secretary, Redfield Proctor of Vermont as secretary of war, John W. Noble of Missouri as secretary of the interior, and Jeremiah M. Rusk of Wisconsin as agriculture secretary.

First Lady Caroline Lavinia Scott Harrison also was an Ohio native. The Harrisons had two children, both of whom were adults when their father was elected to the White House.

Caroline Harrison became ill during her husband's term, and she died of tuberculosis in October 1892. In her final two years, her widowed niece, Mary Scott Lord Dimmick, lived at the White House and oversaw social functions on the first lady's behalf. President Harrison married Mary Dimmick in 1896, after leaving the White House. They had one daughter.

Major Issues

As president, Harrison signed a number of important and controversial economic acts. In summer 1890 he approved both the Sherman Antitrust Act, which forbade businesses from forming cartels to restrict trade, and the Sherman Silver Purchase Act, which expanded silver coinage. President Harrison also signed the McKinley Tariff Act of 1890 to protect agricultural products and other goods, albeit with high prices. In addition, he supported increased pension funds for veterans. Government spending expanded sharply in the Harrison administration, with Congress appropriating $1 billion in funds for the first time by the end of the president's term. Public dismay at high prices and federal expenditures led to sharp Republican losses in the 1890 midterm elections; the president's party lost nearly half its seats in the House and control of the chamber, and kept control of the Senate by just eight seats.

In foreign policy, the Harrison administration hosted the Inter-American Conference (which became the Pan-American Union and later the Organization of American States). The conference established a forum for the United States and Latin American nations to discuss cooperation on trade and related issues. President Harrison also succeeded in receiving an official apology and compensation from Chile after U.S. sailors were killed and injured by rioters while on shore leave in Valparaiso. In the Pacific, Secretary of State Blaine negotiated a tripartite agreement with Great Britain and Germany to maintain a protectorate over the Samoa Islands. But the administration failed in its effort to annex Hawaii—the Senate refused to ratify an annexation treaty before Harrison left office, and President Cleveland subsequently withdrew it from consideration.

The Republican Party considered nominating other candidates for president in 1892, but ultimately chose Harrison on the first ballot at the national convention. For the first time in American history, both the Republican and Democratic presidential nominees already had held the office. After losing to Cleveland, Harrison returned to practicing law in Indiana. He was encouraged to seek the presidency again in 1896, but he declined. Harrison successfully represented Venezuela before an international tribunal in a boundary dispute with Great Britain. He died of pneumonia in 1901.

- -

"Tariff Reform Deferred," November 8, 1888

In reporting the results of the 1888 presidential election, *The New York Times* focused on Harrison's victory in the Electoral College, particularly in highly contested states such as New York. *The Times* attributed Harrison's election to widespread support for his protectionist agenda in trade policy. The attention to the Electoral College vote suggests that the contradiction between those results and the popular vote was not immediately evident.

NOVEMBER 8, 1888
TARIFF REFORM DEFERRED
THE REPUBLICAN NATIONAL TICKET VICTORIOUS.
CONGRESS DEMOCRATIC BY A SMALL MAJORITY—RE-ELECTION OF GOV. HILL—
THE STATE LEGISLATURE REPUBLICAN.

Harrison and Morton have been elected President and Vice-President of the United States. The majority for the Republican candidates in the Electoral College will be fourteen more than that cast in 1884 for Cleveland and Hen-

dricks. Harrison has carried New-York, Indiana, California, Michigan, and Colorado, all of which had been regarded as debatable States. The majority in this State for Harrison will not be far from 11,000. In Indiana it will be very small,

INAUGURAL BALL MARCH 4ᵀᴴ 1889. WASHINGTON.D.C.

Inaugural Ball program for Benjamin Harrison's inauguration, March 4, 1889.

Source: The New York Times

but in Minnesota, Iowa, and Michigan, where the interest manifested in the tariff question was relied upon to effect a considerable change in the vote, the Republicans have developed their full strength, and obtained pluralities for the national ticket much larger than those cast for Blaine in 1884.

Connecticut gives a small majority for Cleveland, and shows marked Democratic gains in the manufacturing towns, where the question of tariff taxation was constantly and thoroughly discussed during the long campaign. New-Jersey, a State greatly interested in manufacturing, not only more than doubled its Democratic majority of 1884, but chose a Legislature that will elect a Democratic United States Senator to succeed McPherson.

The returns from the Western States are still very imperfect, but it is apparent that Merriam (Rep.) has been elected Governor of Minnesota, Hoard (Rep.) in Wisconsin, and Luce (Rep.) in Michigan, and that the legislative contests in those States have resulted to the advantage of the Republicans.

The Congressional elections have been hotly contested, and the outcome of the battles in many districts is surprising. By the latest reports it appears that the Fifty-first Congress will be controlled by the Democrats by an extremely small majority, which may be wiped out altogether by the corrected returns from Virginia, Arkansas, North Carolina, and Michigan, in all of which States there are disputed results. The Democrats secure a solid delegation from West Virginia, including Mr. William L. Wilson, a member of the Ways and Means Committee, who was re-elected by an increased lead. The defeat of Mr. Clifton R. Breckinridge, another member of the Ways and Means Committee, in the Second Arkansas District, is claimed by the allied Wheelers and Republicans, but is not admitted by the Democrats.

Gov. Hill has been re-elected in his State by a majority of about 19,000, and there seems to be no doubt that Lieut.-Gov. Jones has also been re-elected, and that Justice Gray has been retained as a member of the Court of Appeals.

The Republicans will have 79 members of the next Assembly and the Democrats 49. Full returns show that there are only a few changes to be made in the tables printed in *The Times* of yesterday. They are as follows: Peter Schaaf, (Dem.,) in place of John Reitz, Seventh Kings; James P. Graham, (Dem.,) in place of D. W. Tallmadge, Twelfth Kings; Moses Dinkelspiel, (Dem.,) in place of Sol D. Rosenthal, Twelfth New-York; William Murray, (Dem.,) in place of T. Irving Burns, First Westchester; Bradford Rhodes, (Rep.,) re-elected, Second Westchester.

A revision of the vote in this city gives Cleveland a plurality of 57,213 and to Hill, for Governor, a plurality of 58,353. The vote cast for Governor was also larger by several thousands than that cast for President, which is unusual. Warner Miller, the Republican candidate for Governor, received 3,198 more votes than Harrison, and Hill 4,238 more than Cleveland.

"THE FINAL PREPARATIONS," DECEMBER 15, 1889

The United States aimed to improve trade relations with Latin America by hosting the first Inter-American conference in 1889 and 1890. The Harrison administration carefully organized arrangements for the seventeen participating nations, even organizing a tour of the country for delegates. Although the conference did not achieve the far-reaching goals that President Harrison desired in promoting international trade, it did create the Pan-American Union (now the Organization of American States) to foster future discussions.

DECEMBER 15, 1889
THE FINAL PREPARATIONS.
HOW THE PAN-AMERICAN DELEGATES WILL BE RECEIVED.

The Pan-American delegates will come to town to-morrow, and the committee that proposes to make their stay a pleasant and profitable one had its final meeting in the Governor's Room at the City Hall yesterday. There was a large attendance of the members, over whom Cornelius N. Bliss presided. The silver buttonhole badges which will serve to designate the members of the committee were given out. They are about the size of a half dollar. The inscription, "International American Congress, City of New-York, Hon. Hugh J. Grant, Mayor, 1889," appears around the coat of arms of the city. The back of the catch on the button bears the words "solid silver," and there can be no mistake about the quality of this particular button.

A neat programme, tied with strings of red, white, and blue, has been issued. According to it the delegates and their friends will leave Washington at 9:30 A.M., and reach Cortlandt-street, this city, where they will be met by an escort of mounted police and members of the committee, at 3:30 P.M. Then will follow the reception by the Mayor in the Governor's room, and the programme already printed in *The Times* will be followed out with no material changes. The names of the members of the different committees and the names of the Pan-American delegates are printed with the programme.

Chairman Bliss urged all the members of the committee to meet the delegates at the station in Jersey City, and from there start with them on their jaunts about town. A mounted police escort, comprising one Sergeant, one Roundsman, and ten patrolmen, will lead the way on all the trips of the visitors.

While Secretary T. C. T. Crain was reading the minutes of the last meeting he read off the name of Ambrose Monell as having been added to the committee to represent the maritime interest. The members of the committee looked astonished and puzzled. Mr. Bliss asked Mr. Crain to read again, and this time he read the name of Ambrose Snow. Then the puzzled look on the faces of the members vanished, and Mr. Crain went on with his reading.

"A NEW ANTI-TRUST BILL," MARCH 19, 1890

The Sherman Antitrust Act, named for Sen. John Sherman of Ohio, was designed to regulate businesses with prohibitions against collusion to limit competition in trade. President Harrison supported the measure, but his administration did not implement it aggressively. Subsequent administrations would make better use of the law, particularly beginning with the presidency of Theodore Roosevelt.

MARCH 19, 1890
A NEW ANTI-TRUST BILL.
A MEASURE WHICH SENATOR SHERMAN THINKS CANNOT BE EVADED.

WASHINGTON, March 18.—Mr. Sherman, from the Senate Committee on Finance, reported to-day a substitute for his Anti-Trust bill. In the shape presented to-day Mr. Sherman thinks he has met and overcome all objections to the measure on the ground of unconstitutionality. The members of the committee reserve the right to express their opinion of the bill when it comes up for consideration.

The substitute provides that all arrangements, contracts, agreements, trusts, or combinations between two or more citizens or corporations, or both, of different States, or between two or more citizens or corporations, or both, of the United States and foreign States, or citizens or corporations thereof, made with a view or which tend to prevent full and free competition in the importation, transportation, or sale of articles imported into the United States, or with a view or which tend to prevent full and free competition in articles of growth, production, or manufacture of any State or Territory of the United States, with similar articles of the growth, production, or manufacture of any other State or Territory or in the transportation or sale of like articles the production of any State or Territory of the United States into or within any other State or Territory of the United States, and all arrangements, trusts, or combinations between such citizens or corporations, made with a view or which tend to advance the cost to the consumer of any such articles, are hereby declared to be against public policy, unlawful, and void.

The Circuit Court of the United States shall have original jurisdiction of all suits of a civil nature at common law or in equity arising under this section, and to issue all remedial process, orders, or writs proper and necessary to enforce its provisions. And the Attorney General and the several District Attorneys are hereby directed, in the name of the United States, to commence and prosecute all cases to final adjournment and execution.

Any person or corporation injured or damnified by such arrangement, contract, agreement, trust, or combination, defined above, may sue for and recover in any court of the United States of competent jurisdiction, without respect to the amount involved, of any person or corporation a party to a combination described in the first section of the act, twice the amount of damages sustained and the costs of the suit, together with a reasonable attorney's fee.

· ·

"BID FOR SOLDIERS' VOTES," APRIL 1, 1890

In contrast to President Cleveland, who vetoed a dependent pension bill for soldiers in an effort to control government spending, President Harrison approved an expansion of veterans' pensions. The Dependent and Disability Pension Act authorized pensions for the dependents of veterans—including parents, children, and widows—as well as disability payments for injured soldiers. Harrison and Congress both faced criticism for their willingness to expand the federal budget.

APRIL 1, 1890
BID FOR SOLDIERS' VOTES
THE DEPENDENT PENSION BILL PASSED.
MR. PLUMB'S AMENDMENT, ADDING $500,000,000 OR MORE TO THE EXPENDITURE, REJECTED.

WASHINGTON, March 31.—The Dependent Pension bill, which President Cleveland vetoed three years ago, was passed by the Senate to-day after a long debate and by a decisive majority. Unsuccessful attempts were made by Mr. Plumb to add to the measure a repeal of the limitation of arrears of pensions and a provision for a service pension pure and simple. Both attempts were defeated by large majorities, but many Republican Senators, who objected to these measures as amendments to the Dependent Pension bill, assert their readiness to support them in independent bills.

The most modest estimate of the addition the Dependent Pension bill will make to the expenditures for pensions is $36,000,000 a year. There is every reason to believe that it will be very much more, and one member of the Senate Pension Committee, who voted for the bill, says it will take twice $36,000,000 out of the Treasury every year....

Finally the vote on the passage of the bill was reached, and it went through by a vote of 42 to 12. All the negative votes were cast by these Democrats: Messrs. Bate, Berry, Blackburn, Cockrell, Colquitt, Daniel, Harris, Jones of Arkansas, Pugh, Reagan, Vest, and Wilson of Maryland.

"Don't Like the Bill," June 8, 1890

The Times was highly critical of the Republican Party's decision to increase tariffs in 1890. The McKinley Tariff Act, named after Rep. William McKinley of Ohio (a future president), raised tariffs on many products, resulting in higher prices. President Harrison had expressed strong support for tariff protection in the 1888 election, and he endorsed this legislation. *The Times* prophetically warned that the bill likely would diminish the Republican Party's prospects in the next presidential election. As the paper bluntly stated: "If [the tariff] will not help the Republican Party it is 'no good.' "

> No considerable interests demand it, no large number of the people anywhere have expressed any desire for it, and it does not respond to any pledges made and approved in the national campaign.

JUNE 8, 1890
EDITORIAL
"DON'T LIKE THE BILL."

We suppose that no one regards the McKinley Tariff bill as other than a partisan measure, concocted for partisan purposes. If it will not help the Republican Party it is "no good." No considerable interests demand it, no large number of the people anywhere have expressed any desire for it, and it does not respond to any pledges made and approved in the national campaign. Would it not be, then, the part of common sense for the leaders in the Senate, with whom the fate of the bill now rests, to pay a little more attention than those in the House have thought necessary to the evidence that is accessible to any one who wishes it as to the opinion of Republicans regarding this measure? They cannot do so without finding that if the tariff is to be two years hence, as it was two years since, the controlling issue in the Presidential canvass, and if their party takes upon itself the burden of this bill or one anything like it, it will surely be beaten. Senator Plumb the other day told his friends in the Senate that when they went before the country they would be asked why they had increased duties when it was expected that they would reduce them. That is the simple, exact truth as to the tariff issue. Mr. Plumb, at least, has heard aright the voice of the people. It will be the part of prudence for the Finance Committee of the Senate to try to look at the facts as they are. The bill is now before the country. Its main provisions, as it passed the House, are pretty well known. The views of the Republicans of the country are being everywhere made public, and there is no excuse for mistake regarding them.

[No Headline], October 28, 1890

The Times found much to dislike in the Sherman Antitrust Act. In particular, the paper questioned a declaration by Sen. John Sherman of Ohio, who had sponsored the legislation, that the law was successfully preventing the formation of corporate trusts. Harshly criticizing the senator's words, *The Times* questioned whether the law had demonstrated "any effect whatever except to exhibit more plainly the insincerity of its projector and of many other Senators who voted for it?"

OCTOBER 28, 1890
EDITORIAL

In that speech at Wilmington, Ohio, Mr. John Sherman boasted of the enactment of the so called anti-trust law and said: "Senators from Eastern States, where these combinations mainly exist, shared in the opposition and succeeded in carrying amendments that would have defeated the objects of the bill. Nevertheless the bill became a law, somewhat shorn of its most effective provisions, *and has already had a beneficial effect.*" In what way? Has it prevented ex-Gov. Charles Foster of your State, Mr. Sherman, from entering the new Window-Glass Trust, that has been formed in your State since the bill was passed, or did it restrain your friend McKinley from inserting in the new tariff during the conference a proviso concerning the size of boxes that was suggested by the members of this Trust then holding a meeting in Chicago? Has it had any effect whatever except to exhibit more plainly the insincerity of its projector and of many other Senators who voted for it?

"Comfort for Harrison," November 6, 1890

The economic agenda of tariffs and increased spending cost the Republican Party dearly in the 1890 midterm elections. It lost control of the House by a huge margin and lacked firm party support in its reduced Senate majority. *The Times* noted that the Democratic Party attributed its success in part to the McKinley Tariff bill; the attempt to pass the "Force bill," which would have provided federal oversight of congressional elections to ensure that black citizens would not be denied their right to vote; and "the reckless extravagance of the Republican Congress." But *The Times* did see one possible benefit for President Harrison in the aftermath of his party's "Waterloo": Other Republicans would not be likely to seek their party's presidential nomination in 1892, which greatly improved the president's chances of running for reelection.

NOVEMBER 6, 1890
COMFORT FOR HARRISON
ONE RESULT OF THE WATERLOO OF TUESDAY LAST.
THE PRESIDENT'S RIVALS FOR THE NOMINATION OF 1892 DECREASING—
THE DEATH BLOW OF "REEDISM" AND THE FORCE BILL.

WASHINGTON, Nov. 5.—The astonishment with which the Republicans here heard the election returns last night has been added to so persistently and steadily all day that to-night they are fairly dazed. They can only throw up their hands and exclaim, "What next?" As district after district, and State after State heretofore thought to be Republican under any circumstances is shown to have gone Democratic yesterday, most of them are too dumfounded to try to make excuses. The plea that local issues decided the day against the Administration has been dropped, for it does not stand to reason that local issues have had the same effect the same day in every State and every Congressional district in the Union. The excuse that Democratic "boodle" is responsible is also too unreasonable for use, for money enough has never been coined to buy up the whole Nation. The familiar twaddle about an "off year" might account for the Republican loss here and there, but those who are making this excuse realize that it is not good enough to account for such an overwhelming defeat as the Republicans have suffered.

Most of the defeated politicians, therefore, are trying to dodge all persons who might ask them to tell why they were beaten. A few, however, frankly admit that the Tariff bill and the Force bill—the enactment of the one and the attempt to pass the other—are the principal causes of yesterday's Waterloo. The Democrats have no trouble to explain their victory. They find the causes in the McKinley Tariff bill, the Force bill, the reckless extravagance of the Republican Congress, Reedism in the House of Repre-

put such an infamous partisan measure upon the statute books. So plainly does this appear that Republicans cannot afford to call an extra session to consider the Force bill. It is believed that yesterday settled the fate of the Force bill in the regular session. Republicans say the rebuke the party leaders have received is great enough to convince the Senators that they cannot safely force the measure through.

Yesterday's victory will also make it very much harder for the Republicans to pass this Winter the Reapportionment bill. Indorsed as they have been by the whole people, the Democrats will feel more than ever bound to go to the utmost lengths to compel the Republicans to make the reapportionment on a basis fair and just to both parties. Speaker Reed will find it more difficult than in the last session to force an unfair partisan measure through the House, for there as well as in the Senate, the Democratic minority will find its backbone wonderfully stiffened by the election yesterday.

By a good many persons the Republican defeat is known to mean that the burdens imposed upon the people

> "[T]he President may yet come to look upon yesterday as another evidence that Providence has its kindly eye upon him."

sentatives, Quayism in the Republican councils, a general disgust with the hypocrisy of the Administration, and the inability of the protected monopolists and great corporations to dictate what votes their employes shall cast, through the adoption of the Australian ballot system in so many States. The Democrats counted upon all these things to help them, but they are almost as much surprised at the result as the Republicans. They were ready to congratulate themselves and the country if they obtained twenty majority in the next House. Few were sanguine enough to predict a majority of fifty. To-night the returns gave them more than a hundred, with more yet in sight. "Jubilant" is a very mild term to indicate their feelings.

The first effect of the great victory here has been suddenly to put a stop to the talk about an extra session of Congress for this month. It is quite certain that President Harrison had decided to call an extra session provided the Democratic majority had been so small that it could have been attributed to local disaffection in a few districts, and not as an expression of the popular will. But such a wholesale victory cannot be treated in that way. It is an unmistakable declaration that the people disapprove of the Force bill, and will not support any party that proposes to

by the McKinley bill must be removed within three years. A very prominent Republican who has been influential in the party councils said to-day that he knew from personal conversations with Republican Senators that not less than six of them had determined to be guided by the result of the Congressional elections this year in their future action upon tariff legislation. This meant, he said, that enough Republicans would heed the handwriting on the wall to bring about a new Tariff bill on exactly opposite lines from the McKinley bill, but this, he added, would not be done until the people had elected a Democratic House for the Fifty-third Congress, two years hence. The emphatic indorsement received by Messrs. Plumb, Paddock, and Pettigrew for voting against the McKinley bill would, he declared, simply confirm the determination of other Western and Northwestern Senators that they could not afford to vote any longer for high prices and high taxes. It is at any rate evident that the Republicans' boast that the tariff question was settled for the next ten years is not well founded.

President Harrison is one of the Republicans who have nothing to say to-night about the elections. He declines to be interviewed by newspaper men, declaring that things are still in too chaotic a condition for one to form any opinion concerning them. About the only ray of comfort that fell upon the White House to-day was when the New-York newspapers arrived, and the President learned from the *Tribune* that the Republicans would have a majority of two in the next House of Representatives. But the ray was a trifle dim, and it was soon lost in the chaotic condition of things which prevails just now in the White House. If, however, talk among the Republicans here is any indication of the general feeling in the party, the President may yet come to look

upon yesterday as another evidence that Providence has its kindly eye upon him. These Republicans declare that Harrison's chances for a renomination are 100 per cent. better than they were twenty-four hours ago, for since yesterday morning numerous would-be rivals of the President have concluded that a contest for the Presidency on the Republican ticket in 1892 is not wholly and unqualifiedly desirable. Mr. Harrison will have fewer competitors for the chief place in that contest than he might have expected one day ago.

"WISE AND SENSIBLE CHILE!" JANUARY 26, 1892

In many respects, President Harrison was more successful in his foreign policy agenda than in his domestic economic programs. He reacted strongly when rioters in Valparaiso, Chile, attacked U.S. sailors on shore leave, killing two and injuring many others. Harrison demanded an investigation and threatened retaliation if Chile's response was unsatisfactory. Ultimately, Chile apologized and offered reparations, thus averting a war with the United States. *The Times* supported the U.S. position, but its explanation would hardly be acceptable today—that these demands "should be the conviction of every person who is capable of reasoning as a man and not as a woman, as a citizen and not as a partisan, as an American and not as an immigrant."

JANUARY 26, 1892
EDITORIAL
WISE AND SENSIBLE CHILE!

Our just complaints against Chile, as set forth in the President's message and the published correspondence, are based upon two specific grounds—the vindictive attack upon the *Baltimore's* men and Minister Matta's offensive note of Dec. 11. The first of these acts complained of is an injury, since two United States seamen were killed and many others wounded; it is also a national affront, since the resentment so violently exhibited by the Chileans was directed, not against the individuals assaulted, but against their uniform and their American nationality. Minister Matta's note is an insult simply, unmixed with material injury.

For both the insult and the injury Chile very wisely, sensibly, and honorably offers full reparation. The insulting note she withdraws and disavows. The affair of Oct. 16 she offers to leave to the arbitration of a neutral nation, or to the decision of the Supreme Court. That offer is equivalent to an acknowledgment that the Chilean position in respect to the matter was unsound and could not be sustained, and on the determined facts either form

of settlement almost of necessity must involve a decree of indemnity and reparation for the injury, as Chile, no doubt, is well aware in making the offer.

In the matter of the offensive note, we did all that the case calls for in threatening to recall our Minister to Chile. That is all that self-respect demanded or modern customs impose. In the graver matter of the *Baltimore's* men, self-protection, as well as self-respect, bade us so to bear ourselves that no more United States sailors would be wantonly murdered in Valparaiso or in any other port.

That we were bound so to bear ourselves, or else abandon all pretense of protecting our own flesh and blood on foreign soil, should be the conviction of every person who is capable of reasoning as a man and not as a woman, as a citizen and not as a partisan, as an American and not as an immigrant. It is always timely to picture forth the horrors of war. No humane person is ever unmoved by such delineations. But the shooting and stabbing of our sailors was horrible and bloody, a cruel, cowardly assault on unarmed men by a furious mob of citizens, soldiers, and police. Before we could quite make up our minds that a few sailors more or less were not worth the cost and risk and the possible horrors of an armed demonstration, we had to consider somewhat the actual horrors of Oct. 16, and not merely that, but the repetition of such horrors in all the ports of the civilized world whenever it should become known that the United States of America allowed the murdering of its sailors to go unnoticed and unpunished, and whenever a feeling of hostility against our Government might move a street mob to acts of violence against our citizens. The fact that we did consider these things and gave evidence of it, undoubtedly influenced Chile in her conclusion. . . .

The statements of the President's message and the evidence of the correspondence leave no reasonable doubt that the assault upon the *Baltimore's* sailors was, as our

Government has claimed in Mr. Blaine's note of Jan. 21, "an attack upon the uniform of the United States Navy, having its origin and motive in a feeling of hostility to this Government, and not in any act of the sailors or of any of them." To allow such an incident to pass without reparation or the attempt to exact reparation would be tantamount to withdrawing the national protection from United States citizens sojourning on foreign soil. Our provocation must be held to be just and well grounded unless we are disposed to believe that the officers and seamen of our navy have lied about the cause and progress of the affray of Oct. 16, and that the Chileans alone have told the truth. But we cannot doubt the evidence before us on that point. We can hardly arbitrate as to the fact that the assault on our sailors was wanton and injurious. We may under Chile's offer propose to arbitrate the terms of settlement, and such a proposition we ought to make.

- -

"END OF THE HOMESTEAD STRIKE," NOVEMBER 21, 1892

In 1892 workers at Carnegie Steel Company's Homestead division went on strike. After five months, a conflict between strikers and detectives hired by the company turned violent, resulting in many deaths. The Harrison administration sent armed forces to protect nonunion employees brought in to replace the strikers, which damaged the president's reputation with labor interests.

NOVEMBER 21, 1892
END OF THE HOMESTEAD STRIKE.
IT IS FORMALLY DECLARED OFF BY THE AMALGAMATED ASSOCIATION.

PITTSBURG, Nov. 20.—The great strike at Carnegie's Homestead Steel Works has been declared off. After a five-months' struggle which for bitterness has never been equaled in this country, the strikers finally decided to-day to give up the fight.

This action was taken at a meeting of the lodges of the Amalgamated Association at Homestead this afternoon, the vote standing 101 in favor of declaring the strike off, and 91 against it. Among those present at the meeting were Vice President Carney, Secretary Killgallon, Treasurer Madden and David Lynch of the Advisory Board. The officials addressed the members, and in plain words told them the strike was lost, and advised them to take steps to better their condition. The remarks met with considerable opposition, but when the vote was taken it showed a majority of ten in favor of declaring the strike off.

Those who were in favor of calling the strike off were jubilant, while those who were against it were badly put out. Most of the latter were men who were obstinate, and many of them were men who had either applied for positions in the mill and had been refused or felt sure that their names were on the company's black list and they could not get positions. A member of the Advisory Board said to-day that he had been trying to get the strike declared off for some weeks, as he knew it was lost, and it would have been better for the men, as a great many of them could have got their places back. Those who cannot get back are in a bad fix, as the relief funds will be stopped, and many hundreds of them have nothing to live on.

The people in Homestead, especially the business men, are highly elated over the declaration to call the strike off, for if it had continued much longer it would have ruined the town. Many business houses have fallen into the hands of the Sheriff since the strike has been on. Business is expected to resume its normal condition soon.

The Homestead strike has proved one of the most disastrous in the history of the country. It originated from a reduction in wages in the departments in which members of the Amalgamated Association of Iron and Steel Workers were employed. The hitch was on what is known as the sliding scale. It is a scale which regulates the wages by the market price of steel billets. Nearly every mill in this vicinity signed the scale, including other mills of the Carnegie Company. On the refusal to sign the scale at the Homestead mills a lock-out occurred, and the strikers were joined by the mechanics' laborers, who struck out of sympathy only, their wages not being reduced. The strikers were determined to keep non-union men out of the mills, and adopted military discipline.

The story of the arrival of and fight with the Pinkertons on July 6, the subsequent riotous proceedings, and the calling out of the National Guard and its departure after three months' duty, is too well known to repeat. For six weeks the mill has been running almost as well as before the strike, but until within the last week the strikers have steadfastly refused to admit defeat.

The news of to-day's action was received with dismay by the strikers in the two Lawrenceville mills of the Carnegie Company. These men were sympathy strikers, and went out at the time the men at Beaver Falls and Duquesne struck. The Duquesne men gave up the fight in three weeks and the Beaver Falls men decided to go back yesterday. The Lawrenceville men, however, were steadfast and had no intention of giving in. They are now in the position of striking for no cause. They are very angry at the Homestead men, and will probably declare the strike off to-morrow.

The strike at one time involved nearly 10,000 men, and the loss in wages will reach, it is said, in the neighborhood of $2,000,000. Then there is the immense loss to the firm, which cannot be estimated, but which conservative people put at least double the amount lost by the men in wages. To this can be added nearly $500,000 paid to the State troops and the costs to the County of Allegheny for the riot, treason, and other cases growing out of the strike.

- -

"OPPOSED TO THE TREATY," FEBRUARY 18, 1893

One of President Harrison's final goals in office was to annex Hawaii to the United States, and he sent a treaty to the Senate for ratification just weeks before his term ended. Many senators opposed the treaty, and *The Times* warned that its advocates faced "a more difficult task than they at first supposed was before them." Democratic opposition prevented ratification and spurred Harrison's successor, Grover Cleveland, to withdraw the treaty upon taking office.

FEBRUARY 18, 1893
OPPOSED TO THE TREATY
AGAINST THE PROPOSED METHOD OF ACQUIRING HAWAII.
INDICATIONS OF A WARM CONTEST IN THE SENATE—MANY WHO OBJECT TO THE DOCUMENT, ALTHOUGH NOT TO SECURING THE ISLANDS—WHAT THE SENATORS SAY.

WASHINGTON, Feb. 17.—After waiting until the public had been afforded the opportunity to read the convention entered into between the United States and the Commissioners representing the provisional Government of Hawaii and the correspondence relating to it, the Senate to-day solemnly removed the seal of secrecy it placed upon it two days ago, and ordered it to be published. This action was taken in a short executive session, in which the Committee on Foreign Relations reported favorably the treaty, which had been referred to it. No further action was taken regarding the matter.

There are indications to-night that the convention will not be ratified by the Senate without a warm contest. In the last twenty-four hours the opposition to the annexation of the Hawaiian Islands, which was thought to be confined to a comparatively few Senators, seems to have grown, and now the opinion is openly expressed by some that ratification of the treaty is not possible—at least, not in the present session. While the friends of annexation in the Senate still profess to be confident of success, it is plain that they realize that they have a more difficult task than they at first supposed was before them.

There have been rumors to-day of a Democratic combination to defeat favorable action. One Democratic Senator, who did not care to have his name mentioned, said to the correspondent of *The New-York Times* that Hawaii would not become a possession of the United States through any action of the present Senate.

"I am confident," he said, "that those who favor annexation have not the strength to make the treaty operative. Up to the present time they have been aided by the Administration and have had practically no opposition. There is a movement on foot now, however, to block their game, and I am confident it will succeed. Personally I am not against the acquisition of Hawaii, but the methods adopted do not meet my approbation, and I am sure that there are many senators who feel precisely as I do."

THE PRESIDENCY OF WILLIAM MCKINLEY

MARCH 4, 1897 – SEPTEMBER 14, 1901

During William McKinley's presidency the United States became a global power. After the Spanish-American War of 1898, the United States acquired territories in the Atlantic and Pacific Oceans and engaged more consistently in international affairs. President McKinley did not initiate this change, but neither did he oppose it, and his steady leadership moved the nation peacefully into the twentieth century. But McKinley had little opportunity to experience the growing importance of the United States in the world, as he was killed by an anarchist assassin in 1901, less than a year after winning election to a second term.

A native of Ohio, McKinley was the fifth president born in that state. (All five of these presidents served within a span of thirty-two years, beginning with Ulysses S. Grant in 1869 and continuing through the administrations of Rutherford B. Hayes, James A. Garfield, and Benjamin Harrison, and concluding with McKinley's death in 1901.) McKinley was the seventh of nine children. His father managed an iron production business, and the family placed great stock in education, moving when McKinley was nine so he could attend a private school. McKinley attended Allegheny College in Pennsylvania for one year, but he dropped out because of illness and because he lacked sufficient funds to pay for his schooling.

Returning to his hometown, McKinley taught school and worked in the post office to support himself. The last president to serve in the Civil War, McKinley enlisted as a private when the war broke out, and he served in the same unit as Major

HIT HIM **HARD!**

PRESIDENT McKINLEY—"Mosquitoes seem to be worse here in the Philippines than they were in Cuba."

(and future president) Hayes. By war's end, McKinley had been promoted to brevet major and recognized for his courageous service. He completed a term at Albany Law School in New York, was admitted to the Ohio bar in 1867, and began his practice in Ohio. McKinley won election to the U.S. House of Representatives in 1876 (the same year that Hayes became president) and served for seven terms. A strong supporter of high tariffs, McKinley sponsored the 1890 law that bore his name, but the resulting higher prices cost him his seat in the midterm elections that same year. Returning to Ohio, McKinley

QUICK FACTS ON WILLIAM MCKINLEY

BIRTH	January 29, 1843, Niles, Ohio
EDUCATION	Allegheny College (did not complete degree) Law studies, 1865–1867
FAMILY	Wife: Ida Saxton McKinley Children: Katherine McKinley, Ida McKinley
WHITE HOUSE PETS	Mexican double-yellow-headed parrot
PARTY	Republican
PREPRESIDENTIAL CAREER (SELECTED)	Teacher, 1859 Civil War service, 1861–1865; attained rank of brevet major Prosecutor, Stark County, Ohio, 1869–1871 U.S. House of Representatives, 1877–1883, 1885–1891 Governor of Ohio, 1892–1896
PRESIDENTIAL TERMS	March 4, 1897–March 4, 1901 March 4, 1901–September 14, 1901
VICE PRESIDENTS	Garret Augustus Hobart (first term; died November 21, 1899) Theodore Roosevelt (second term)
SELECTED EVENTS	Dingley Tariff Act (1897) Explosion of USS *Maine* (1898) U.S. annexation of Hawaii (1898) Spanish-American War (1898) Gold Standard Act (1900) Shot by Leon Czolgosz at Pan-American Exposition, Buffalo, N.Y. (September 6, 1901)
DEATH	September 14, 1901, Buffalo, N.Y.

ran successfully for governor, and he was widely viewed as a likely presidential candidate. He chaired the 1892 Republican National Convention and received many votes for the nomination, but the party chose the incumbent president, Benjamin Harrison, on the first ballot.

THE 1896 ELECTION

By 1896 the Republican Party's choice of McKinley for president was all but assured, thanks in large part to the influence of Ohio industrialist and political boss Mark Hanna. Advocating a platform of high tariffs and protection of the gold standard, the Republican Party nominated McKinley on the first ballot and selected Garret Augustus Hobart of New Jersey

as his running mate. McKinley actually had supported silver coinage in Congress, but he renounced his past position in the presidential race.

The Democratic Party, in contrast, endorsed silver coinage to put more money in circulation and help farmers. Inspired by former U.S. representative William Jennings Bryan's impassioned declaration "You shall not crucify mankind upon a cross of gold," the Democrats nominated Bryan for president and Arthur Sewall of Maine for vice president. Bryan also won the nomination of the Populist Party. He waged an aggressive campaign, actively courting votes through travel and speeches, while McKinley campaigned largely from his front porch and won the support of the financial community, which feared that silver coinage would cause inflation. McKinley prevailed in the general election, winning more than 7 million popular votes to Bryan's 6.5 million, and 271 Electoral College votes to Bryan's 176.

The McKinley Administration

Upon taking office, President McKinley rewarded Hanna by making Ohio senator John Sherman secretary of state, which cleared the way for Hanna's election to the Senate. This decision sparked criticism, especially because Sherman, at seventy-three, would not be an active proponent of U.S. diplomacy. President McKinley's closest advisers included Treasury Secretary Lyman J. Gage of Illinois and Agriculture Secretary James Wilson of Iowa. McKinley chose Russell A. Alger of Michigan as secretary of war, Joseph McKenna of California (a future Supreme Court justice) as attorney general, John Davis Long of Massachusetts to be secretary of the navy, Cornelius N. Bliss of New York as secretary of the interior, and James A. Gary of Maryland as postmaster general.

First Lady Ida McKinley suffered from epilepsy and other health problems and was unable to walk without a cane. She nevertheless managed to serve as hostess for most White House events. Contributing to Mrs. McKinley's poor health were the untimely deaths of her two children. The McKinleys had two daughters soon after they married in 1871, but one died in infancy and the other at age four.

Major Issues (First Term)

Consistent with his past positions, McKinley continued to support tariff protection as president, though he also became receptive to international trading opportunities. To combat the nation's economic depression, he endorsed the Dingley Tariff Act of 1897. The legislation raised tariff rates, but it also raised the possibility of reciprocal trade agreements with other nations, recognizing the growing engagement of the United States in world affairs. By the end of his presidency, McKinley's speeches on economic policy acknowledged the benefits of lowering tariffs to promote international trade. And, as the nation's economic outlook improved, demands for silver coinage decreased.

Despite McKinley's long-standing involvement in economic policy, his presidency was defined by foreign affairs. Most significant was the Spanish-American War of 1898, which catapulted the United States onto the world stage. The conflict started in Cuba, where Spain's brutal treatment of rebels galvanized media coverage, and consequently American public opinion, in opposition to the colonial power. Seek-ing to avoid war, President McKinley unsuccessfully tried to intervene diplomatically between Cuba and Spain. He sent the battleship USS *Maine* to Cuba to demonstrate U.S. strength, but the move backfired when the ship exploded and 266 people died. Two months later, Congress declared war at President McKinley's request.

American naval superiority over Spain ensured a speedy victory. Commodore George Dewey led U.S. forces to victory over Spain in the Pacific, and U.S. troops took control of Cuba and Puerto Rico in the Caribbean. Fighting ended in August, and Spain signed a peace treaty in December that turned over Puerto Rico, Guam, and the Philippines to the United States, and called for Cuba's independence. But the U.S. empire would come at great cost: Filipino rebels opposed American control just as they had despised Spanish domination, and defeating the insurrection cost more American lives and money than the Spanish-American War. In Cuba, the United States retained the right of intervention, which meant that it would continue to be entangled in the small island's politics for the foreseeable future.

The McKinley administration expanded American control through diplomatic channels as well. Unlike his predecessor, Grover Cleveland, President McKinley supported the annexation of Hawaii, and Congress approved such a resolution in July 1898, during the Spanish-American War. Secretary of State John Hay, who took office in September 1898, negotiated with other great powers to maintain an "open-door" policy toward China with respect to each other's trade and commercial rights. (When Chinese nationalists rebelled against external domination in the Boxer Rebellion, the United States sent troops as part of an international force to assist captured diplomats.) The United States negotiated the partition of the Samoan Islands with Germany as well.

The 1900 Election

President McKinley's steady leadership resulted in a unanimous nomination on the first ballot for a second term at the Republican convention in 1900. Vice President Hobart had died in 1899, and party members endorsed Theodore Roosevelt to be McKinley's running mate. Roosevelt had served as assistant secretary of the navy under McKinley until he resigned in 1898 to lead the Rough Riders to victory in Cuba during the Spanish-American War. The Democrats again nominated William Jennings Bryan for president, and he campaigned on an anti-imperialist platform. Bryan and his running mate, Adlai E. Stevenson of Illinois, lost the race with 6.3 million popular votes to McKinley's 7.2 million, and 155 Electoral College votes to McKinley's 292.

A BRIEF SECOND TERM

Half a year into his second term, President McKinley spoke at the Pan-American Exposition in Buffalo, New York, to endorse interstate cooperation in the Western Hemisphere. Shaking hands in a public reception, he came face-to-face with Leon Czolgosz, an anarchist who shot the president twice, hitting him in the face and stomach. McKinley lingered for a week and died of gangrene on September 14, 1901. During McKinley's campaign for a second term, Hanna had told him he had a duty to live for four more years, so Theodore Roosevelt, whom Hanna derided as a "cowboy," would not become president. But McKinley's assassination put Vice President Roosevelt in the White House.

- -

"MCKINLEY AND HOBART OF NEW-JERSEY," JUNE 19, 1896

William McKinley's nomination on the Republican ticket for president in 1896 was no surprise. Ohio political boss Mark Hanna had carefully engineered this outcome; as *The New York Times* noted, "The ticket is Hanna's. The platform is the work of the convention." Perhaps the most contentious issue in the platform was its endorsement of the gold standard. When advocates of bimetallism, or silver coinage, were unsuccessful in changing this plank, they walked out of the convention. Sen. Henry M. Teller of Colorado led the revolt, and the so-called "Silver Republicans" urged him to run for president. After briefly seeking the Democratic presidential nomination, Teller endorsed the Democratic ticket and permanently switched his political affiliation to the Democratic Party.

JUNE 19, 1896
MCKINLEY AND HOBART OF NEW-JERSEY

Nominated at St. Louis by the Republican Party for President and Vice President.

VOTE FOR THE GOLD PLATFORM 812 ½ TO 110 ½

Twenty-one Silver Men Bolt the Convention, Led by Teller, Who Weeps Copiously as He Leaves the Hall.

FOUR SENATORS AND TWO REPRESENTATIVES WALK OUT

They Are Going to Chicago to Make an Attempt to Capture the Democratic Nomination for Teller—Chairman Carter Decides to Stick to His Party—Convention Adjourns Sine Die and Delegates Start for Home.

ST. LOUIS, June 18.—William McKinley of Ohio was nominated this afternoon as the candidate of the Republican Party for President, and Garret A. Hobart of New-Jersey was named for Vice President.

This outcome, secured in one prolonged session of the convention, the fourth sitting since it was called to order on Tuesday, was more than half expected last night. Gov. Morton's chances were then very doubtful, partly owing to his reiterated disinclination to accept the nomination for Vice President "under any circumstances," and partly because of the bitter opposition to Gov. Morton in his own State—an opposition that was cultivated with complete disregard of the tarnish that it was putting upon the State and its Chief Executive, and which provoked the contempt of Gov. Morton's opponents in other States.

Hanna came to St. Louis, as has been repeatedly stated in these dispatches, determined to make Hobart the candidate with McKinley. He resented the fight made to put "gold" in the financial plank, and he was alarmed when he found that his resentment was not only futile to keep "gold" out, but that the men who were for the use of the word "gold" were disposed to express their thanks to Mr. Platt and the

" To the people the ticket is not likely to be as interesting as the platform. "

gold people of New-York by voting for Morton for Vice President if he would present him. Morton's dispatch of declination to Mr. Depew helped Hanna. It assisted the protesting anti-Platt men to fix the impression that Morton could not get the unanimous indorsement of his own State.

Battered though his influence was after the fight for a straddle, Hanna was still influential, and his power was fully restored when Mr. Morton to-day telegraphed Mr. Depew that he could only take the Vice Presidency if nominated unanimously. Hanna, Warner Miller, and Bliss had made that impossible.

The ticket is Hanna's. The platform is the work of the convention. At Hanna's request the declaration on the tariff was allowed to come first. Mr. Lodge had promised that, and Foraker was not enough concerned about the order of the paragraphs to assert his contempt for Hanna by insisting that the most important policy should be asserted in the first paragraph of the platform.

To the people the ticket is not likely to be as interesting as the platform. If the Republicans shall be successful in November it will be the money plank, not the tariff plank nor the names of McKinley and Hobart, that will win the victory.

The thoughtful and well-informed Republicans here know that in the bolt of Teller and his following of silver men to-day lies the menace of a serious breaking of party lines. To such Republicans it is known that the silver fever is higher than generally supposed, and that it is prostrating victims heretofore regarded as sound with the suddenness and completeness with which grip overcomes the subjects of its attacks. The wide distribution of the silver bacilli, as suggested by Teller's elaborate farewell, was ominous and threatening.

The platform makers were alive to the condition of the country and to the general indifference to talk about McKinley duties; otherwise it would not have been pos-

sible to secure from a Republican convention a practical denunciation of McKinleyism on the same day that McKinley, for making his unpopular bill, was honored with the nomination for the highest office in the land. It was a tub to a whale, a bait to catch those Republicans who are not so zealous for protection as they were in 1890.

Teller's desertion of his party may make him the candidate of the silver party and the Populists, and if the Chicago Convention, affected to conservative action by the gold stand of the Republicans, shall take the middle course indicated by Hanna, as the one to be followed by the Republicans and shall name a doubtful man, rejecting Bland and Boies, it would not be at all astonishing to see another St. Louis ticket, with Teller and Bland, or Teller and some silver Democrat at its head.

This will not help the Republicans. It will make the selection of McKinley depend very largely upon the nomination of a gold Democrat of character and capacity, the division of the Democratic vote in several States in which the Republican vote is large, but not a majority, and the prevention of a silver success by a reference of the contest to the House of Representatives.

The convention presented no incident so thrilling as that of the bolt of Teller and his silver associates. The noisy demonstrations for candidates were evidently contrived with the properties and music prepared in advance by a political theatrical manager. It was a disorderly convention, badly officered with perhaps the least efficient Sergeant at Arms and the most utterly useless corps of assistants ever collected for a similar purpose. The presiding officer, Senator John M. Thurston, really presided, commanding the noisy body well, speaking briefly when occasion required, and inspiring confidence in the audience by his own composure and by an easy assumption of the authority conferred upon him.

"Bryan's Bid for First Place," July 10, 1896

The currency issue caused high drama in both the Republican and Democratic National Conventions of 1896. Legendary orator William Jennings Bryan roused the Democrats with his fiery speech condemning the gold standard. *The Times* painstakingly depicted the convention's frenzy after Bryan's speech, saying, "The silver delegates fell over each other in their efforts to reach him." The next day, Bryan won the Democratic presidential nomination on the fifth ballot.

JULY 10, 1896
BRYAN'S BID FOR FIRST PLACE.
The Silver Men Swept Away by a Flood of Prairie Oratory.

CHICAGO, July 9.—The silverites had their inning when Russell had finished and Bryan, "the boy orator" and general demagogue of Nebraska, took the platform. They yelled and raved, waved flags, threw hats into the air, and acted like wild men for five minutes.

Bryan wore trousers which bagged at the knees, a black alpaca coat, and a low-cut vest. A black stud broke the white expanse of his shirt bosom. His low, white collar was partially hidden by a white lawn tie. Bryan began fishing yesterday for the Presidential nomination. If there was any doubt of his ambition in the minds of the friends of other candidates, that doubt was dispelled to-day by his speech and the events that followed. He dwelt upon the necessity of another Andrew Jackson to rise up and crush the National banks and other agents of the "money kings" and indulged in many like utterances calculated to attract the attention of the silver fanatics to himself. The applause with which his remarks were punctuated attested to the audience's relish for his revolutionary expressions.

Bryan's chief qualification as an orator is his splendid voice. His views on public affairs are those of a wild theorist filled with a desire of personal advancement. No better evidence of the diseased condition of the minds of the silver delegates could be desired than that furnished to-day by their indorsement of Bryan's utterances.

The demonstration at the close of Bryan's speech struck terror to the hearts of the Bland and Boies and McLean and Stevenson boomers. The declaration by him that the people must not be crucified on the cross of gold was the signal for an avalanche of cheers which speedily developed into a measureless outburst. As he started for his seat one policeman stood ready to clear the way and another to prevent the crowd closing in upon him. Their efforts were unavailing.

Demonstration with a Purpose.

The silver delegates fell over each other in their efforts to reach him. The aisles became congested. Bryan found himself in the midst of a shouting, pushing mob, every man anxious to grasp his hand. He was not at all averse to the proceedings. Already the prospect of a unanimous nomination began to dance before his eyes. The storm grew intensely as he neared his seat. The Tennessee and Texas delegations gave a hint to the other fanatics by carrying their banners to the Nebraska reservation and ranging themselves about Bryan. Immediately there was a movement toward that point by the bearers of the banners of the other silver States. While the deafening din was maintained, the banners waved about the conspicuous form of Bryan, who had been lifted on the shoulders of several sturdy admirers, so that the people might look upon this new defender of the people. Bryan is heavy, and the men holding him grew tired; so he stepped upon a chair and beamed upon the assemblage. His reappearance above the sea of heads intensified the noise. Thousands in the Coliseum were shouting.

While the excitement was at its height, the man carrying the Kentucky banner, a ponderous individual, who previously had given the impression that nothing could shake his fealty to Blackburn, organized a new feature of the entertainment. Holding his banner aloft, he marched up the main aisle. Behind him came men carrying the blue banners of Alabama, Nebraska, Louisiana, Colorado, Kansas, Ohio, Indiana, Michigan, Tennessee, California, North Carolina, Texas, West Virginia, Florida, North Dakota, Georgia, Oklahoma, Nevada, Iowa, Idaho, Missouri, Montana, Indian Territory, Arkansas, Utah, Wyoming, Virginia, New-Mexico, and Washington.

The only banners not seen in the combination were those of Delaware, Connecticut, Alaska, New-Hampshire, Maine, Maryland, Minnesota, Massachusetts, New-York, New-Jersey, Rhode Island, Pennsylvania, South Dakota, Vermont, and Wisconsin.

To the accompaniment of the ear-splitting yells of the silverites, this procession moved around the confines of the delegates' reservation, the banner bearers adding to the confusion as best they could. There was no cessation of the noise for fourteen minutes. The Chairman made no effort at first to quell it, being willing to see the Hill demonstration overshadowed.

The first sign of willingness on the part of the silver yawpers to subside was met by the men in the Bryan delegation with an appeal for a fresh outburst. This was successful, and the walls again resounded to a perfect Niagara of sound, which continued five minutes. It was twenty-five minutes after the demonstration began before the business of the convention could be proceeded with.

A tribute more conclusive of the regard of the fanatics and repudiators for Bryan could not be given. As may be readily imagined, the talk of Bryan as the possible nominee of the convention took a tremendous jump as the result of this ovation. The Georgia delegation, which already had declared for Bland, decided, while confusion yet reigned, to throw its votes to Bryan. Other delegations were said to be contemplating similar action. The Bryan men were overjoyed. Their leader was quick to see the possibilities contained in the events of the last half hour and to set his lieutenants to working among the different delegations.

The constant running of delegates to him and the consultations being held had a most dispiriting effect upon the managers of the other booms.

"Prices and the Tariff," May 20, 1897

President McKinley's support for the Dingley Tariff Act of 1897 raised concerns about higher prices. In an editorial, *The Times* warned, "Whatever the advance in price may be, it is paid by the consumer." Despite his long history of supporting high tariffs, as president, McKinley became more open to the concept of trade reciprocity. Although he did not purse the topic vigorously, he made reference in speeches to how international trade agreements would benefit the United States.

MAY 20, 1897
EDITORIAL
PRICES AND THE TARIFF.

There is, of course, the keenest interest as to whether retail prices will advance in consequence of the higher duties proposed in the Tariff bill now before the Senate. Whatever changes are made in this bill before its passage, the rates are sure to be much higher than at present and higher even than under the McKinley act of 1890.

The general effect of such legislation is succinctly stated by Mr. Hugh O'Neill in an interview published in *The Times* on the 18th. He said:

"If the retailers have money enough, you may be sure they will lay in a big stock at low-tariff prices. That is good business, and it is the logic of the situation. It is perfectly natural that they should do this. . . .

"As to the advance in prices, this will be sure to follow. I do not think it will come before the tariff goes into effect, as it would be too apparently an effort to do business in 'futures.' Even after the tariff goes into effect, competition, which is perhaps keener in our business than in any other, will tend to keep prices from advancing to the full extent of the tariff increase."

This has been the substantially uniform experience. Prices advance in consequence of greater cost, and in anticipation imports increase. If times are dull and competition eager, the accumulated stock is sold somewhat under the advance in the cost of goods purchased after the tariff goes into effect. Whatever the advance in price may be, it is paid by the consumer.

The average advance in prices, as calculated by Mr. Isidor Straus of R. H. Macy & Co., will be "from 25 per cent. to 33 per cent. on woolens and worsteds, 15 per cent. to 50 per cent. on pottery, 35 per cent. to 100 per cent. on linens." In all cases the advance is heaviest on the cheaper goods needed and used by persons of moderate means.

It does not take a long memory to recall what happened when the McKinley rates went into force. The increased taxes now proposed are from a lower range than prevailed before the McKinley law was passed to a range decidedly higher than that of the McKinley law. The net change will be approximately twice as great as that which took place in 1890.

"The *Maine* Blown Up," February 16, 1898

The explosion of the battleship *Maine* in Havana Harbor shocked the United States. Given American opposition to Spain's harsh treatment of Cuban rebels, it was not surprising that Spain was blamed for the explosion. Spain denied the charges, saying the explosion must have been an accident. Subsequent investigations have not reached a uniform verdict, with the primary question being whether the ship sank from an internal or external explosion. Although the sinking of the *Maine* did not cause the Spanish-American War, the resulting public outcry put strong pressure on President McKinley to request a declaration of war from Congress, which he did two months later.

FEBRUARY 16, 1898
THE *MAINE* BLOWN UP.

Terrible Explosion on Board the United States Battleship in Havana Harbor.
MANY PERSONS KILLED AND WOUNDED.
All the Boats of the Spanish Cruiser *Alfonso XII.* Assisting in the Work of Relief.
None of the Wounded Men Able to Give Any Explanation of the Cause of the Disaster.

HAVANA, Feb. 15.—At 9:45 o'clock this evening a terrible explosion took place on board the United States battleship *Maine* in Havana Harbor.

Many persons were killed or wounded. All the boats of the Spanish cruiser *Alfonso XII.* are assisting.

As yet the cause of the explosion is not apparent. The wounded sailors of the *Maine* are unable to explain it. It is believed that the battleship is totally destroyed.

The explosion shook the whole city. The windows were broken in nearly all the houses.

The correspondent of the Associated Press says he has conversed with several of the wounded sailors and understands from them that the explosion took place while they were asleep, so that they can give no particulars as to the cause.

WHAT SENOR DE LOME SAYS.

He Declares That No Spaniard Would Be Guilty of Causing Such a Disaster.

Señor de Lome, the departing ex-Minister of Spain to this country, who arrived in this city last night, and went to the Hotel St. Marc, at Fifth Avenue and Thirty-ninth Street, was awakened on the receipt of the news from Havana.

He refused to believe the report at first. When he had been assured of the truth of the story he said that there was no possibility that the Spaniards had anything to do with the destruction of the *Maine.*

No Spaniard, he said, would be guilty of such an act. If the report was true, he said, the explosion must have been caused by some accident on board the warship.

THE *MAINE'S* VISIT TO HAVANA.

First American Warship to Visit Cuba Since the Struggle Began.

The *Maine* was ordered to Havana on Jan. 24 last, and was the first American warship to visit that port since the outbreak of the Cuban rebellion. . . .

The vessel is designed to carry a crew of 800 men. She has accommodations for a flag officer and staff.

"Hawaii Is Now American," July 8, 1898

The U.S. annexation of Hawaii in July 1898 marked the culmination of negotiations that had begun two presidential administrations earlier. President Benjamin Harrison sent an annexation treaty to the Senate just before leaving office in 1893, but his successor, President Grover Cleveland withdrew it from consideration. Although sugar plantation owners had endorsed annexation for economic reasons, not all Hawaiians supported such ties to the United States. Queen Liliuokalani had tried to increase her powers a few years earlier, but opponents, with the assistance of U.S. Marines, overturned her regime. Hawaii became a U.S. territory in 1900 and a state, along with Alaska, in 1959.

JULY 8, 1898
HAWAII IS NOW AMERICAN
President McKinley Signs the Annexation Resolution Completing the Work.
ADMIRAL MILLER TO SAIL OUT
The *Philadelphia* Will Carry the Flag to the Islands—A Commission to be Appointed
Before Congress Adjourns.

WASHINGTON, July 7.—The President signed the Hawaiian annexation resolution at 7 o'clock this evening.

Secretary Long to-day gave orders for the departure of the *Philadelphia* from Mare Island for Hawaii. She will carry the flag of the United States to those islands and include them with the Union. Admiral Miller, commanding the Pacific station, who is now at Mare Island, will be charged with the function of hoisting the flag that was hauled down by Commissioner Blount. The ship will be ready for sea in a very few days under the Secretary's orders, and should make the trip in a week.

Meanwhile the President will appoint a commission immediately to frame the laws necessary for the changed condition of affairs in Hawaii. This must be done before the adjournment of Congress, as the Commissioners are subject to confirmation.

Senators and Representatives who conferred with the President to-day gained the impression that for the present the government of the Hawaiian Islands would be left largely in the hands of President Dole. Under the joint resolution annexing the islands the government, until otherwise provided by Congress, is vested in such person or persons as the President of the United States may determine. Besides President Dole some other person, in Hawaii and one or more citizens of the United States may be selected to act with him. It has been pointed out that citizens of the United States familiar with the laws of this country ought to be members of the provisional Govern-

ment, as the laws of the United States are extended over the islands.

Minister Hatch Sees Judge Day.

Minister Hatch of Hawaii arrived at the State Department at 11 o'clock, and held an extended conference with Secretary Day on the consummation of the annexation of Hawaii to the United States. The Hawaiian authorities had taken steps to convey the good news at the earliest possible moment to Hawaii. Mr. Hatch sent extended official dispatches to the Hawaiian agent in San Francisco to be forwarded by the steamer sailing to-day. The Minister will leave here to-morrow to catch the steamer *Alameda*, sailing for Hawaii on July 13.

Lorin M. Thurston, Hawaiian Commissioner, goes with Mr. Hatch, but will wait till July 16, to take the steamer *Rio de Janeiro* to Hawaii. It is understood also that Mrs. Dominis, formerly Queen Liliuokalani, and her party, who have been in Washington for many months, contemplate taking an early steamer for Hawaii.

Minister Hatch and Mr. Thurston expressed the deepest satisfaction at the favorable outcome of this long struggle. As they entered the State Department to-day they received congratulations on every hand. Mr. Thurston remarked that it felt good to be an American. It is the view of the Hawaiian authorities that Hawaii becomes a part of the United States at the moment that the President attaches his signature to the resolution of Congress. The annexation is said to be complete without any further action, here or in Hawaii. At the same time it is possible that the Hawaiian Legislature may pass a resolution similar to the one passed by our Congress. While it was said that this was not necessary, yet it will be a formality accomplished, and remove every possible chance for quibble over the regularity of the procedure.

"An American Protectorate," July 8, 1898

As the United States gained overseas territories in the Spanish-American War, its responsibilities in these areas were widely debated. This letter to the editor proposed creating "an American Protectorate" to ensure that the United States would "foster the independent development of the peoples of these several countries until they shall be able to assume wise self-control."

> To 'take possession of the islands and keep them for our own use and profit' would be worse than 'Quixotic'; it would be Spanish.

JULY 8, 1898
LETTER TO THE EDITOR
AN AMERICAN PROTECTORATE.

To the Editor of The New York Times:

Do we not find in Aguinaldo's proclamation a helpful hint toward the solution of the problem "What to do with the Philippines?" "The great North American Nation," he says, "the repository of true liberty, and therefore the friend of freedom for our nation, has come to afford its inhabitants a protection as decisive as it is doubtless disinterested." As a suggestion in addition to the four possible solutions already ably discussed in your columns, may there not be established, not only over the Philippines, but also over Cuba, the Ladrone, and the Caroline Islands, an American protectorate, the purpose and aim of which shall be to foster the independent development of the peoples of these several countries until they shall be able to assume wise self-control? That this would not be a "Quixotic business" is demonstrated by the civilization of Hawaii by Americans, and without any such protectorate, and by the progress already made in the Caroline Islands before that progress was arbitrarily interrupted by Spain in 1885.

It would be humiliating indeed to suppose that the American Nation is not sufficiently disinterested and virtuous to accept the unconscious challenge of Aguinaldo.

To "take possession of the islands and keep them for our own use and profit" would be worse than "Quixotic"; it would be Spanish. We are bound both by our honor and by the disclaimer of Congress respecting Cuba to pursue a magnanimous policy toward all the dependencies of Spain which may come under our control. Is it not possible to devise such a protectorate as shall secure popular education, religious freedom, and industrial development, a suitable revenue from the islands providing for cost of administration, and the surplus to accrue to the benefit of the islands themselves?

Such a policy might require half a century for the accomplishment of its purpose, but the financial outlay, beyond the cost of the present war, might easily be provided for as I have suggested, and the present commerce of Hawaii with the United States and its desire for annexation are but a suggestion of the advantages which would flow back spontaneously from peoples whom we had so assisted to a prosperous independence.

A. C. Sewall,
Schenectady, N.Y., July 7, 1898.

"War Suspended, Peace Assured," August 13, 1898

The Spanish-American War concluded just four months after it began in April 1898. Both countries formally agreed to begin peace negotiations, and President McKinley announced the good news with a proclamation declaring the "suspension of hostilities."

AUGUST 13, 1898
WAR SUSPENDED, PEACE ASSURED

President Proclaims a Cessation of Hostilities.

PROTOCOL IS NOW IN FORCE

Cambon and Day Formally Complete Preliminary Agreement.

CONCESSIONS MADE BY SPAIN

Yields Cuba and Puerto Rico and Occupation of Manila.

WORK ON THE TREATY

Not More Than Five Commissioners on Each Side, to Meet in Paris by Oct. 1.

WASHINGTON, Aug. 12.—The plenipotentiaries of the United States and Spain having this afternoon at 4:23 o'clock signed the protocol defining the terms on which peace negotiations are to be carried on between the two countries, President McKinley has issued the following proclamation:

By the President of the United States of America.
A PROCLAMATION.

Whereas, By a protocol concluded and signed Aug. 12, 1898, by William R. Day, Secretary of State of the United States, and his Excellency Jules Cambon, Ambassador Extraordinary and Plenipotentiary of the Republic of France at Washington, respectively representing, for this purpose, the Government of the United States and the Government of Spain, the Governments of the United States and Spain have formally agreed upon the terms on which negotiations for the establishment of peace between the two countries shall be undertaken; and,

Whereas, It is in said protocol agreed that upon its conclusion and signature hostilities between the two countries shall be suspended, and that notice to that effect shall be given as soon as possible by each Government to the commanders of its military and naval forces:

Now, therefore, I, William McKinley, President of the United States, do, in accordance with the stipulations of the protocol, declare and proclaim on the part of the United States a suspension of hostilities, and do hereby command that orders be immediately given through the proper channels to the commanders of the military and naval forces of the United States to abstain from all acts inconsistent with this proclamation.

In witness whereof I have hereunto set my hand and caused the seal of the United States to be affixed.

Done at the City of Washington, this 12th day of August, in the year of our Lord one thousand eight hundred and ninety-eight, and of the independence of the United States the one hundred and twenty-third.

William McKinley.

By the President,
William R. Day,
Secretary of State.

A copy of this proclamation has been cabled to our army and navy commanders. Spain will cable her commanders like instructions.

"OUTLINE OF THE TREATY," DECEMBER 14, 1898, AND "SENATE RATIFIES THE PEACE TREATY," FEBRUARY 7, 1899

The peace treaty following the Spanish-American War turned the United States into a global power. The treaty, which the Senate ratified by only one vote more than the necessary two-thirds, granted the United States control over Cuba, Guam, the Philippines, and Puerto Rico. Implementation of U.S. control over these territories would prove to be a formidable task.

DECEMBER 14, 1898
OUTLINE OF THE TREATY

Probable Contents of the Document Signed in Paris.
SOME CONCESSIONS TO SPAIN
Agreements as to Trade, Shipping, and Copyrights—
Our Commissioners' Farewell to France.

LONDON, Dec. 14—The Paris correspondent of *The Times* gives the following as the text of the Hispano-American treaty, omitting diplomatic circumlocutions:

"Spain relinquishes all claims of sovereignty over and title to Cuba, and, as the Island is, upon its evacuation by Spain, to be occupied by the United States, the latter will, so long as such occupation shall last, assume and discharge the obligations in respect to protection of life and property which may, under international law, result from the fact of its occupation.

"Spain cedes to the United States the Island of Puerto Rico and the other islands now under Spanish sovereignty in the West Indies, with Guam in the Mariana, or Ladrone, Islands. Spain cedes to the United States the archipelago known as the Philippine Islands.

"The United States will, for a term of ten years from the date and exchange of ratifications of the present treaty admit Spanish ships and merchandise to the ports of the Philippine Islands on the same terms as the ships and merchandise of the United States.

"The United States will, upon the signature of the present treaty, send back to Spain at its own cost the Spanish soldiers taken as prisoners of war on the capture of Manila by the American forces. The arms of the soldiers in question shall be restored to them. Spain will, upon the signature of the present treaty, release all prisoners of war and all persons detained or imprisoned for political offenses in connection with the insurrections in Cuba and the Philippines and the war with the United States.

"On their part the United States will release all persons made prisoners of war by the American forces, and will undertake to obtain the release of all Spanish prisoners in the hands of the insurgents in Cuba and the Philippines.

"The United States will at their own cost return to Spain, and the Government of Spain will, at its own cost, return to the United States, Cuba, Puerto Rico, or the Philippines, according to the situation of their respective homes, the prisoners released or caused to be released by them, respectively, under this provision.

"The United States and Spain mutually relinquished all claim for indemnity, National and individual, of every kind, of either Government, or of its citizens or subjects, against the other Government that may have arisen since the beginning of the late insurrection in Cuba and prior to the exchange of ratifications of the present treaty, including all claims for indemnity for the cost of the war. The United States will adjudicate and settle the claims of its citizens against Spain, relinquished under this stipulation.

"Spanish subjects, natives of the Peninsula, residing in the territory over which Spain by the present treaty relinquishes or cedes her sovereignty, may remain in such territory or may remove therefrom, retaining in either event all their rights of property, including the right to sell or dispose of such property or proceeds; and they shall also have the right to carry on their industry, commerce, and profession, being subject in respect thereof to such laws as are applicable to other foreigners. In the event of their remaining in the territory, they may preserve their allegiance to the Crown of Spain by making, before a court of record, within a year from the date of the exchange of ratifications of the treaty, a declaration of their decision to preserve such allegiance, in default of which declaration they shall be held to have renounced it and to have adopted the nationality of the territory in which they may reside.

"The civil rights and political status of the native inhabitants of the territory hereby ceded to the United States shall be determined by Congress. The inhabitants of the territory over which Spain relinquishes or cedes her sovereignty shall be secured in the free exercise of their religion.

"Spaniards residing in the territories over which Spain by this treaty cedes or relinquishes her sovereignty, shall be subject, in matters civil as well as criminal, to the jurisdiction of the courts of the country in which they reside, pursuant to the ordinary laws governing the same, and they shall have the right to appear before such court and to pursue the same course as citizens of the country to which the courts belong.

"The right of property secured by copyrights and patents acquired by the Spaniards in the Island of Cuba and in Puerto Rico and the Philippines and the other ceded territories at the time of the exchange of the ratifications of the treaty shall continue and be respected. Spanish scientific, literary, and artistic works, not subversive of public order in the territories in question, shall continue to be admitted free of duty into such territories for a period of ten years, to be reckoned from the date of the exchange of the ratifications of the treaty.

"Spain shall have the right to establish Consular officers in the ports and other places of the territories, sovereignty over which has been either relinquished or ceded by the present treaty. The Government of each country will, for a term of ten years from the exchange of ratifications, accord to the merchant vessels of the other country the same treatment in respect of all port charges, including entrance and clearance dues, light dues, and tonnage duties, as it accords to its own merchant vessels not engaged in coastwise trade. This provision may at any time be terminated on six months' notice given by either Government to the other.

"It is understood that any obligation assumed in this treaty by the United States with respect to Cuba is limited to the time of the occupation by the United States of that island; but the United States Government will, upon the termination of such occupation, advise any Government established in the island to assume the same obligations."

FEBRUARY 7, 1899
SENATE RATIFIES THE PEACE TREATY
Fifty-seven For the Convention to Twenty-seven Against.
ONE VOTE MORE THAN NEEDED
Supporters Feared Defeat Until the Last Moment.
Senators McEnery and McLaurin Save the Day for the Friends of the Administration.

WASHINGTON, Feb. 6.—At 3:25 o'clock this afternoon—twenty-five minutes after the first bell rang through the Senate halls and committee rooms to announce the first roll call on the Paris treaty of peace—a shout rang along the halls and reached to the doors of the galleries that the treaty had been ratified. The battle of the Administration was over, and the efforts of the Senators who had opposed the convention with Spain were thwarted. The treaty had been approved by a vote of 57 to 27.

It had been a greater victory for the friends of the treaty than some of the advocates of ratification were willing to believe possible last night, and to others it has been a disappointment because of the narrow margin of excess in the vote. To Mr. Gorman the success of the Administration is a double defeat. He has been beaten at the same time by the Republicans and by his own party associates. Up to the very moment of taking the vote he was sure, as he had told intimate friends before the meeting of the Senate, that the treaty would lack one vote of the number necessary to ratify it. His reliance upon his power of leadership has again been shaken.

It was a great throng that filled the galleries this morning. Notwithstanding the knowledge which everybody possessed that the treaty would be considered in closed session, and in spite of a pitiless snowstorm, the second in two days, there was not a seat to be had when Senator Allen began an interesting speech, in which he gave currency through *The Congressional Record* to reports about Mr. Gorman's political ambition that had been only matters of newspaper report up to that moment. . . .

It is impossible to trace to any authority the intimations of some Democrats in the Senate that the number of votes necessary to ratify was obtained by promises made by the Administration to the Senators who broke the Democratic

line and made ratification possible when the friends of the treaty were trembling lest it fail by just one vote. That they were really fearful of defeat there is now no doubt. They were misled by the remarks of men who had been claimed by the Gorman party, but who still talked about being in doubt.

The danger of defeat that the treaty was exposed to is apparent to any one who will just rearrange the vote so that it shall look as it did to Senator Lodge at 2 o'clock. Counting McEnery and McLaurin as voting against ratification, there would have been twenty-nine votes in opposition and fifty-five for the treaty. That would have given the opposition just one more than enough to reject. If only one of the Democrats had joined the Administration party, and Jones of Nevada had voted as he declared to Senator Stewart he would vote, the same result would have been reached. With the vote only of one of the Democrats secured at the last moment, and Jones of Nevada voting "aye," the treaty would have received a tie vote and Vice President Hobart would have been called upon to decide the contest.

· ·

"THE OPEN DOOR IN CHINA," DECEMBER 31, 1899

After the Spanish-American War, the McKinley administration continued to expand U.S. influence overseas with its attention to China. Secretary of State John Hay successfully negotiated an open-door policy toward China with Great Britain, France, Germany, Japan, and Russia. This agreement meant that each nation would not seek to block the commercial interests of the others in China.

DECEMBER 31, 1899
THE OPEN DOOR IN CHINA
European Powers and Japan Favor This Country's Policy.
BRITISH ANSWER THE FIRST
Germany, France, and Russia in Line and a Favorable Reply Now Assured from Italy.

WASHINGTON, Dec. 30.—The negotiations opened by Secretary Hay with the great powers of Europe and with Japan toward obtaining a common understanding for a continued open-door policy throughout China have met with success. The State Department is unwilling at present to make public the nature of the replies received, as this information will be embodied in a special message to Congress. But in other quarters thoroughly reliable and in a position to have trustworthy and accurate information it is learned that favorable responses have been made by Great Britain, Germany, France, Japan, and Russia, the Russian

communication having been received yesterday. There is no doubt, it is thought here, that Italy, the remaining country addressed, will make a favorable answer. The position of Italy is felt to be assured by the course adopted by the other four great powers of Europe.

The importance of this unanimous verdict by all the first-class powers of the world—Great Britain, Russia, Germany, France, Italy, and Japan, in conjunction with the United States—can hardly be overestimated, so far as it relates to the future of China and the commerce of the world in that empire. The State Department is loath to discuss the far-reaching results to be obtained when the agreement advances to the stage of formal consummation. Each favorable response is conditioned on the favorable action of all the other parties, so that in each case the negotiations may be regarded as short of absolute finality. But while the department is silent, the details come from sources believed to be fully conversant with what has occurred.

"M'KINLEY AND ROOSEVELT," JUNE 22, 1900

The Republican Party did not hesitate to nominate President McKinley for a second term in 1900, and the incumbent deferred to the convention in the selection of a vice-presidential nominee. (Vice President Garret Augustus Hobart had died in 1899.) The convention endorsed New York governor Theodore Roosevelt, whose bravery in the Spanish-American War had made him highly popular. As *The Times* wrote, "Gov. Roosevelt was the idol of the convention."

JUNE 22, 1900
M'KINLEY AND ROOSEVELT

Ticket Nominated by the Republican Convention.

TUMULT OVER THE GOVERNOR

Great Enthusiasm in the Republican Convention.

The President's Renomination Unanimous—Gov. Roosevelt Received Full Vote of the Convention, Minus His Own.

Special to The New York Times

PHILADELPHIA, June 21.—The twelfth Republican National Convention to-day completed its work by the nomination of William McKinley for President and Theodore Roosevelt for Vice President.

President McKinley's nomination was made with enthusiasm, the customary tumult of shouts, the frantic fluttering of banners, hats, handkerchiefs, plumes, and flags.

The demonstrations were not as prolonged, however, as they have been in conventions where nomination has been preceded by conflict.

Gov. Roosevelt was the idol of the convention, but the idolatry was not frenzied. His speech was a model of directness and conciseness, his bearing was soldierly, dignified, and satisfactory to his most anxious friend.

The tumult over him was manifestly spontaneous, universal, and sincere. It was not overdone. His conduct plainly strengthened him in the estimation of the convention.

The work of the convention was closed up in a session less than five hours long. This was made possible by the abandonment by Senator Quay of his amendment to the rules proposing to fix future representation.

McKinley and Roosevelt were nominated upon a call of the roll, as provided by the rules. McKinley received every vote in the convention. Roosevelt received 929, one delegate not voting. The delegate who did not vote was Theodore Roosevelt.

The temper of the convention was admirable. Its balance was maintained, although the hall was overcrowded, and many incapable speakers tried the forbearance of the vast, sweltering audience as well as the nerves of Senator Lodge, the presiding officer.

All the States except New York are cordially glad of the nomination of Roosevelt with McKinley. The West is sure that Roosevelt will help the party. A few Republicans are anxious about the State of New York, but they are not many.

Senator Hanna accepted the outcome not only with cheerfulness, but with enthusiasm. He waved a triple plume to spur on the cheers, and afterward consented to be re-elected Chairman of the National Committee.

"The Republicans' Sweeping Victory," November 8, 1900

The presidential election of 1900 reprised the 1896 race but with an even greater victory for William McKinley. The Democrats nominated William Jennings Bryan for a second time (and would do so once again in 1908), but his campaign lacked the energy and fervor of the previous one. *The Times* noted in its front-page story that Bryan lost even his home state of Nebraska in the general election.

NOVEMBER 8, 1900
THE REPUBLICANS' SWEEPING VICTORY

Bryan Loses His Own State, Which Elects Opposition Legislature.
MCKINLEY HAS 292 VOTES
Kentucky Gives Bryan Its Votes and Elects Beckham, Democrat, as Governor—
Idaho Is Democratic.

Chief of the day's developments as to the election is the transferring of Nebraska from the list of doubtful States to the long list of those States whose voters pronounced in favor of McKinley and Roosevelt. Advices up to the hour of going to press indicate that the Republicans have control of the Legislature by three or four votes on joint ballot. This insures two Republican Senators in place of John M. Thurston, whose term expires in March, and of William V. Allen, Populist, who was appointed to occupy the seat of Monroe L. Hayward, who died before taking the oath of office. It also puts an end to the hopes of the friends of William Jennings Bryan, who had planned to elect him Senator in case he failed to secure the higher office to which he aspired.

Idaho has probably chosen Bryan Electors by a small plurality.

A feature of the later returns is the large pluralities given for the Republican Electoral ticket in the States of the far West, where "imperialism" has no terrors, but some attractions. California is reported to have given 40,000 plurality for the McKinley Electors, Oregon 14,000, North Dakota 12,000, South Dakota 7,500, Washington 5,000, and Wyoming 4,000.

Kentucky has unquestionably given its Electoral vote to Bryan, and Beckham, the Democratic candidate, has probably beaten Yerkes in the race for Governor.

A striking feature of the result in Virginia is that Mr. Bryan carries the State by a plurality of several thousand less than the aggregate pluralities of the Democratic Congressmen.

New York State gives McKinley a plurality of 145,243 and Odell 111,399.

The Fifty-seventh Congress will have a Republican majority of 22 in the Senate and 43 in the House.

Corrected police returns covering all the boroughs in the City of New York show a plurality for Bryan in the greater city of 27,621, the same territory giving Mr. Stanchfield a plurality of 44,968 over Odell. In the Borough of Manhattan and the Bronx, Bryan's plurality over McKinley was 27,805 and Stanchfield's over Odell 38,770. In Kings, McKinley's plurality was 3,044 and Stanchfield carried the county by 2,386.

"Boston Witness's Story," September 8, 1901, and "Mr. M'Kinley Dies after a Brave Fight," September 14, 1901

Less than a year into his second term, President McKinley became the third chief executive in American history to be assassinated. Shaking hands at the Pan-American Exposition in Buffalo, New York, the president attempted to greet a man whose hand was hidden in a handkerchief. The handkerchief concealed a revolver, which Leon Czolgosz used to shoot the president twice. President McKinley died in Buffalo on September 14, 1901. Czolgosz was quickly convicted in court and electrocuted six weeks later.

SEPTEMBER 8, 1901
BOSTON WITNESS'S STORY.

Says President Prayed that Assassin Might Be Forgiven.

Special to The New York Times.

BOSTON, Mass., Sept. 7.—"I was within five feet of President McKinley when he was shot yesterday afternoon," said Charles J. P. Lucas of Cambridge this afternoon. "The scene that followed the shooting was one of pandemonium, and the horror of the attempt to murder the Nation's Chief was something I do not care to go through again."

Mr. Lucas is a prominent athlete of Cambridge and was in Buffalo competing in the international events at the Exposition grounds. He went to the Temple of Music to meet the President and was only four persons behind Czolgosz, the assassin, in the line. Mr. Lucas reached home at noon to-day.

"The Secret Service men," he continued, "seemed to have their eyes on a certain man in the line, several feet ahead of Czolgosz. He was a rather hard looking individual, a foreigner in appearance, with unkempt hair and beard, and a hard look on his face. Secret Service man Foster moved very close to the man, and followed him along, holding his arm in such a manner as would lead one to believe that he was going to grab the man. Nothing happened, however, and after a hearty handshake on the part of the President, the man passed on.

President William McKinley, in a receiving line at the Pan American Exposition in Buffalo, on September 6, 1901, is shot by anarchist Leon F. Czolgosz. McKinley died eight days later.

Source: Brown Brothers, Sterling, PA

"Next came a woman holding a little girl by the hand. President McKinley shook hands with the woman, but his eyes were riveted upon the light-haired child, who seemed to have caught his eye. He stooped over in a kindly manner, and, grasping the hand of the little miss, asked her name, but her answer was inaudible.

"All this time a man with his hand tied up in a handkerchief, resembling a bandage that appeared to be the work of a surgeon, followed. When he came within one person of the President one of the Secret Service men looked him over and also glanced at the man's right hand, which was held near the region of the diaphragm. No ends were open in the bandage, the hand being done up in a manner that would lead one to think that it was attached to a splint.

"President McKinley slowly raised his hand, as if tired, to grasp that of the would-be assassin. As he took the hand of the foreigner he raised it to the ordinary height in handshaking, and as he did so the man, pressing his elbow close to his side, turned the muzzle of the gun toward the President's breast, and, without the slightest sign of anything unusual, fired two shots in quick succession.

"So rapidly was the deed committed that the police, detectives, soldiers, and every one stood still without moving a muscle.

"The crowd did not have the opportunity of venting its feelings, however, as the marines and cavalrymen surrounded the man.

"As the President sank into a chair, to which he was half carried, he was heard to say by those within several feet of him, "May God forgive him." After the shooting I stood near the President for several minutes. He bore his sufferings with fortitude.

SEPTEMBER 14, 1901
MR. M'KINLEY DIES AFTER A BRAVE FIGHT
End Comes at 2:15 o'Clock This Morning.

MR. ROOSEVELT SUMMONED

President's Touching Farewell to Stricken Wife.

"God's Will Be Done" Were His Last Words—A Remarkable Display of Vitality Marks the Final Hours of Suffering.

Special to The New York Times

BUFFALO, Sept. 14.—President McKinley died at 2:15 o'clock this morning. He had been unconscious since 7:50 o'clock last night. His last conscious hour on earth was spent with the wife to whom he devoted a lifetime of care. He died unattended by a minister of the Gospel, but his last words were a humble submission to the will of the God in whom he believed. He was reconciled to the cruel fate to which an assassin's bullet had condemned him, and faced death in the same spirit of calmness and poise which had marked his long and honorable career.

For three hours before his death the President apparently suffered no pain. He uttered no connected sentences. Those at his bedside say that the words of the hymn "Nearer, My God, to Thee" were running in his mind, and that occasionally he would murmur a few of the words.

Senator Hanna left the house with Harry Hamlin at 2:25 o'clock. As he walked to the corner his head was bowed and shoulders stooped. When he entered the runabout tears were streaming from his eyes. He bowed his head upon the head of his cane, sobs that were audible shook his frame, he had not a word to say. Abner McKinley and his wife left five minutes after Senator Hanna.

His last conscious words reduced to writing by Dr. Mann, who stood at his bedside, when they were uttered, were as follows:

"GOD'S WILL BE DONE."

"Good bye. All good bye. It is God's way. His will be done, not ours."

The announcement to the members of the Cabinet of the President's death was made by Webb Hayes, who said: "It is all over."

Mrs. McKinley last saw her husband between 11 and 12. At that time she sat by the bedside holding the hand of her dying husband. The members of the Cabinet were admitted to the sickroom singly at that time.

Death probably occurred about 2 o'clock, it being understood that Dr. Rixey delayed the announcement until 2:15 to assure himself.

THE DEATH SCENE.

From authoritative officials the following details of the final scenes in and about the death chamber were secured:

The President had continued in an unconscious state since 8:30 P.M. Dr. Rixey remained with him at all times, and until death came. The other doctors were in the room at times, and then repaired to the front room where their consultations had been held.

About 2 o'clock Dr. Rixey noted the unmistakable signs of dissolution; and the immediate members of the family were summoned to the bedside. Mrs. McKinley was asleep, and it was deemed desirable not to awaken her for the last moments of anguish.

Silently and sadly the members of the family entered the room. They stood about the foot and sides of the bed where the great man's life was ebbing away.

Five minutes passed, then six, seven, eight—

Now Dr. Rixey bent forward, and then one of his hands was raised as if in warning. The fluttering heart was just going to rest. A moment more and Dr. Rixey straightened up, and, with choking voice, said: "The President is dead."

The announcement of the news to those waiting below was postponed until the members of the family had withdrawn. Through Secretary Cortelyou the waiting newspaper men received the notification. There was the keenest excitement on the broad avenue, but there was no semblance of disorder.

THE PRESIDENCY OF **THEODORE ROOSEVELT**

SEPTEMBER 14, 1901 – MARCH 4, 1909

Source: The Granger Collection, New York

THE WORLD'S CONSTABLE.

Theodore Roosevelt's presidency energized the office of chief executive as much as it strengthened the United States nationally and internationally. Vice President Roosevelt ascended to the presidency when President William McKinley died on September 14, 1901. At age forty-two, Roosevelt would be the youngest person ever to become president. (At forty-three, John F. Kennedy in 1961 would become the youngest elected president.) Showing no hesitation about asserting his authority, Roosevelt sought out challenges. He oversaw the building of the Panama Canal and negotiated an end to the Russo-Japanese War, a diplomatic triumph that earned him the Nobel Peace Prize. Domestically, Roosevelt was an ardent proponent of conservation of public land as well as federal regulation of industry. His

enormous enthusiasm for politics and governance set a precedent for executive leadership that his successors have strived to emulate.

Born to a wealthy New York family in 1858, Roosevelt demonstrated from an early age his determination to overcome challenges through sheer willpower. As a child, he suffered from asthma and nearsightedness, and was often quite ill. When his father, whom he idolized, said he should become stronger, Roosevelt immersed himself in physical exercise, from lifting weights to boxing to wrestling, and his health improved. He was academically talented, graduating from Harvard College in 1880 as a member of the Phi Beta Kappa honor society. Roosevelt studied law at Columbia University, but left the program without completing his degree.

QUICK FACTS ON THEODORE ROOSEVELT

BIRTH	October 27, 1858, New York, N.Y.
EDUCATION	Harvard College Columbia University Law School (one year)
FAMILY	First wife: Alice Hathaway Lee Roosevelt; died February 14, 1884 Children: Alice Lee Second wife: Edith Kermit Carow Roosevelt Children: Theodore Roosevelt, Kermit Roosevelt, Ethel Carow Roosevelt, Archibald Bulloch Roosevelt, Quentin Roosevelt
WHITE HOUSE PETS	Badger, cats, dogs, guinea pigs, horses, macaw, snakes
PARTY	Republican
PREPRESIDENTIAL CAREER (SELECTED)	Member, New York State Assembly, 1882–1884 Appointee, U.S. Civil Service Commission, 1889–1895 President, New York City Board of Police Commissioners, 1895 Assistant secretary of Navy (1897–1898) Leaves navy position to fight in Spanish-American War, 1898 Governor of New York, 1899–1901 Vice president, 1901
PRESIDENTIAL TERMS	September 14, 1901–March 4, 1905 March 4, 1905–March 4, 1909
VICE PRESIDENT	Charles W. Fairbanks (second term)
SELECTED EVENTS	Coal strike in Pennsylvania (1902) Newlands Reclamation Act (1902) Elkins Act (1903) Immigration Act (1903) Creation of Department of Commerce and Labor (1903) Panama agrees to U.S. control of Canal Zone (1903) Airplane flight by Wright brothers (1903) Supreme Court upholds Sherman Antitrust Act (1904) Roosevelt Corollary to Monroe Doctrine (1904) Russo-Japanese Peace Treaty (1905) Awarded Nobel Peace Prize (1906) Hepburn Act (1906) San Francisco earthquake (1906) Pure Food and Drug Act (1906) Great White Fleet's world cruise (1907–1909)
POSTPRESIDENCY	Hunting and scientific expedition in Africa, 1909 Presidential candidate, Progressive ("Bull Moose") Party, 1912 Survives assassination attempt, 1912 Travel to South America, 1913–1914 Refuses Progressive Party's presidential nomination, 1916
DEATH	January 6, 1919, Oyster Bay, N.Y.

Winning election to the New York State Assembly in 1881, Roosevelt served three one-year terms and began to build a reputation as a reformer who opposed government corruption. His world turned upside down in 1884, however, when his young wife, Alice, died on February 14, just two days after giving birth to their daughter, Alice Lee. Compounding this tragedy, Roosevelt's mother, Martha, died the same day. Devastated, Roosevelt moved west for two years, managing a cattle ranch and briefly serving as a deputy sheriff in the Dakota Territory. He returned to New York in 1886, ran unsuccessfully for mayor, and then married a childhood friend, Edith Kermit Carow. The couple had five children, one daughter and four sons, one of whom would die in combat in World War I. The family settled in a home known as Sagamore Hill in Oyster Bay, Long Island, and Roosevelt began writing books on history and the American West.

Roosevelt's return to politics came in 1889, when President Benjamin Harrison appointed him to the U.S. Civil Service Commission. In his six years on the commission, Roosevelt continued to support a Progressive agenda of reform, opposing political patronage and supporting the expansion of a merit-based civil service. He became president of the New York City Board of Police Commissioners in 1895, and took his anticorruption agenda there. President William McKinley appointed Roosevelt assistant secretary of the navy in 1897, but Roosevelt resigned one year later to fight in the Spanish-American War. He organized a volunteer cavalry regiment, the Rough Riders, and led his troops to victory in a fierce battle in the San Juan Hills of Cuba. Roosevelt's fearlessness in battle helped him to win the New York gubernatorial race in 1898.

Two years later, Republican political bosses in New York, frustrated by Roosevelt's opposition to patronage, advocated his nomination as vice president on the party's ticket. President McKinley did not oppose Roosevelt's nomination, and the two candidates easily defeated the Democratic ticket in 1900, winning just over 65 percent of the Electoral College vote and nearly 1 million more popular votes than their opponents. Inaugurated on March 4, 1901, Vice President Roosevelt did little beyond preside over the Senate for a few days during his six months in office. Then, on September 6, 1901, President McKinley was shot at the Pan-American Exposition in Buffalo, New York, and died a week later. Roosevelt was now president.

Major Issues (First Term)

Although elected president only once, in 1904, Roosevelt in effect served two terms in office, completing nearly all of what would have been McKinley's second term. He established his mark in the office from the outset. In 1902 he supported the passage of the Newlands Reclamation Act, which funded irrigation projects in the West. A staunch supporter of conservation, Roosevelt used executive orders to protect public lands from private development, doubling the number of national parks and increasing national forests by more than 100 million acres. He ended a coal miners' strike in Pennsylvania by getting mine owners to agree to arbitration, which came through a presidential commission that gave workers a raise. In response to McKinley's assassination by anarchist Leon Czolgosz, Roosevelt signed the Immigration Act of 1903, which authorized deportation of anarchists.

Roosevelt's most significant domestic accomplishment in his first term was government regulation of industry. To enforce the Sherman Antitrust Act of 1890, the Roosevelt administration filed suit against Northern Securities Company, a newly created railroad conglomerate. In 1904 the Supreme Court upheld the antitrust law and consequently the break-up of the cartel. This victory brought Roosevelt national acclaim as a trustbuster, even though in fact Roosevelt was not unsympathetic to corporate interests in economic cooperation. But the perceived arrogance of the nation's leading financiers prompted Roosevelt's aggressive approach to their monopolies, in pursuit of what he would term a "square deal" for the American people.

In foreign affairs, Roosevelt oversaw what would become one of the most contentious issues in Latin American politics in the twentieth century—the creation of the Panama Canal. When Colombia, which controlled Panama, refused to give the United States building rights for a canal, Roosevelt supported a revolution in Panama in 1903 to overthrow the colonial power. The United States then quickly negotiated a canal treaty, despite opposition within the newly independent nation. Through skillful manipulation, the administration achieved its goal, and President Roosevelt traveled to Panama in 1906 to oversee construction of the canal.

The 1904 Election

In 1904 the Republican Party nominated President Roosevelt unanimously on the first convention ballot and selected Charles W. Fairbanks of Indiana as his running mate. The Democrats nominated Judge Alton B. Parker of New York for president and Henry G. Davis of West Virginia for vice president. The Socialist Party also endorsed a presidential candidate for the first time, nominating Eugene V. Debs of Indiana for president and Benjamin Hanford of New York as his running mate. Debs won more than 400,000 popular votes but none in the Electoral College. Roosevelt lost the southern states, but triumphed in the North and West, winning 7.6 million popular votes to Parker's 5 million, and just over 70 percent of the Electoral College votes. For the first time in U.S. history, a president who had succeeded to the office upon the death of his predecessor was elected to a full term of his own.

THE ROOSEVELT ADMINISTRATION

Upon taking office in 1901, Roosevelt kept McKinley's cabinet largely intact; even when he made changes, he frequently rotated people from one position to another. Several people in the nine-member cabinet, including Secretary of the Interior Ethan A. Hitchcock of Missouri, Secretary of War William Howard Taft of Ohio (a future president and chief justice of the United States), and Agriculture Secretary James Wilson of Iowa—not only completed Roosevelt's first term but also continued into his second term, and Wilson served through Roosevelt's entire presidency. After Secretary of State John Hay's death in 1905, Elihu Root of New York was appointed to the position. Root had served as secretary of war under McKinley, and he continued in that position until 1904, when Taft replaced him. Taft served through most of Roosevelt's second term before successfully running for president in 1908. Hitchcock headed the Interior Department until 1907, when James R. Garfield of Ohio, son of the late president, James A. Garfield, took the position.

Roosevelt appointed Lyman J. Gage of Illinois to head the Treasury Department. Gage served until 1907 and was replaced by George B. Cortelyou of New York. Roosevelt had three attorneys general—Philander C. Knox of Pennsylvania, who served until 1904; William H. Moody of Massachusetts, who served until 1906, when Roosevelt named him to the Supreme Court; and Charles J. Bonaparte of Maryland. Moody had become navy secretary in 1902 and was succeeded by several others. Three men served as postmaster general in Roosevelt's first term; in the second term, Cortelyou held the position until 1907; when he moved to the Treasury Department, George von Lengerke Meyer of Massachusetts was appointed. Roosevelt was the first president to appoint a secretary for the newly created Department of Labor and Commerce in 1903. He selected Cortelyou, who was succeeded by Victor H. Metcalf of California (1904–1906) and finally by Oscar S. Straus of New York.

First Lady Edith Roosevelt devoted her energies primarily to raising the Roosevelt children, four of whom were not yet teenagers when their father became president. President Roosevelt's daughter from his first marriage, Alice, married U.S. representative and future House Speaker Nicholas Long-

worth IV at the White House in 1906. The youngest Roosevelt child, Quentin, died in combat in France during World War I. The eldest son, Theodore Jr., served in both World War I and World War II and died in France just weeks after the Allied D-Day invasion in 1944. He also held the public offices of assistant secretary of the navy, governor of Puerto Rico, and governor-general of the Philippines.

MAJOR ISSUES (SECOND TERM)

In his second term, Roosevelt continued to champion his Progressive reform agenda with great success. In 1906 he approved significant legislation to regulate industry, namely, the Pure Food and Drug Act, and the Meat Inspection Act, which gave federal agencies authority to oversee the production, sale, and transportation of certain goods. Roosevelt also endorsed the Hepburn Act of 1906, which increased the powers of the Interstate Commerce Commission to set price controls. These laws further promoted Roosevelt's "Square Deal" by seeking to ensure that corporations did not profit unduly at the expense of the people who served them and bought their products.

Roosevelt's foreign policy agenda was perhaps even more ambitious and consequential than his domestic policy achievements. Upon winning election in 1904, Roosevelt announced that he would not hesitate to send U.S. forces to intervene in nations in the Western hemisphere to address problems of "chronic wrongdoing." His statement became known as the Roosevelt Corollary to the Monroe Doctrine, adding an activist component to the nineteenth-century statement that had warned European powers to stay out of the Americas. Consistent with the corollary, Roosevelt took control of the Dominican Republic's customhouse in 1905 to ensure that civil disorder did not interfere with the country's foreign debt payments. He excelled in personal diplomacy as well, serving as mediator for the peace talks following the Russo-Japanese War of 1904–1905. Roosevelt was awarded the Nobel Prize for Peace in 1906 for his efforts; he was the first American and the first president to be so recognized. President Roosevelt also was not shy about advertising U.S. military power. To showcase the U.S. Navy, he sent the Great White Fleet on an international cruise from 1907 to 1909, launching the voyage before Congress had approved funding for it.

Roosevelt's penchant for acting first and sorting out details later was indicative of a governing style that favored energetic leadership at all times. In his memoirs, Roosevelt refers to the president as the "steward of the people," responsible for doing all that the constitutional powers of the office permitted. He famously called the presidency a "bully pulpit"—an excellent platform for promoting a political agenda. Roosevelt enjoyed talking with reporters, and he sometimes presented ideas to them as "trial balloons" to see how the public would respond before deciding how to proceed. He added the West Wing to the White House to provide sufficient space for the executive office's growing staff and operations.

Roosevelt's love for the presidency made stepping aside in 1908 especially difficult. He had promised in 1904 that he would not seek a third term, and he kept that promise, endorsing Secretary of War Taft, who won the Republican nomination and the presidency. At age fifty, Roosevelt left the White House and returned to private life—for a short time.

POSTPRESIDENCY

After the presidency, Roosevelt traveled the globe, visiting Africa with his son, Kermit, and Europe with his wife. But he missed politics, and he repeatedly found fault with his successor for not aggressively pursuing the reform agenda that he had promoted. In 1912 Roosevelt reentered presidential politics, first campaigning against President Taft for the Republican nomination and then breaking away from the party to mount an independent run as a Progressive or "Bull Moose" Party candidate. Roosevelt campaigned fiercely and relentlessly, even surviving an assassination attempt at a campaign rally and

famously refusing to depart for the hospital before he completed his speech. (A copy of the speech in Roosevelt's vest pocket deflected the bullet, which nevertheless wounded him.)

Ultimately, Roosevelt's third-party challenge to President Taft split the Republican Party, resulting in a victory for Democratic candidate Woodrow Wilson with just 42 percent of the popular vote. Roosevelt came in second, with 4 million votes, and Taft placed third with nearly 3.5 million votes. Together, Taft and Roosevelt won more votes than Wilson, who garnered almost 6.3 million popular votes, but Wilson had a clear victory in the Electoral College with more than 80 percent of the vote. Some Republicans blamed Taft for not upholding his predecessor's legacy, and others criticized Roosevelt for dividing the party.

After losing in 1912, Roosevelt declined an invitation to run again for president on the Progressive ticket four years later. But he remained an active voice in American politics, heartily endorsing U.S. involvement in World War I and chastising opponents of the war as unpatriotic. Roosevelt even volunteered to command troops, but President Wilson declined his offer. Shortly after the war's end, in January 1919, Roosevelt died from a blood clot. Despite the tumult of his postpresidential years, Theodore Roosevelt's presidency redefined the role of the national government in American politics and the place of the United States in the world.

· ·

"MR. THEODORE ROOSEVELT," SEPTEMBER 14, 1901

Well before the unexpected start of his presidency in September 1901, Theodore Roosevelt was a source of fascination for the American public. His distinguished family background was enhanced by his own achievements: physical skill, literary success, military prowess, and political acclaim. As *The New York Times* noted, for two decades, Roosevelt had been "one of the most unique and picturesque figures in American public life."

SEPTEMBER 14, 1901
MR. THEODORE ROOSEVELT
Varied Career of the Next President of the United States.
His Achievements in Politics, War, and Literary Pursuits Have Been Notable.

Theodore Roosevelt, who has become President of the United States through the death of Mr. McKinley, for two decades past has been one of the most unique and picturesque figures in American public life. His diversified and vigorous activities have not only brought him recognition and advancement in political life, but have won him

renown upon the field of battle, in the Bad Lands of the West, as ranchman, hunter, and cowboy, and also in the more peaceful pursuit of honors in the literary world.

Mr. Roosevelt the man is the exact physical antithesis of Theodore Roosevelt the boy, though the mental characteristics exhibited in early youth by the President are conceded to be the same as those which have now made him famous.

From a romantic and novelistic point of view, Theodore Roosevelt started life with two of the greatest handicaps an ambitious youth could have—wealth and ill-health. In further contravention of well-established tradition concerning National heroes, the President was born in a great city. His birthplace was 28 East Twentieth Street, this city; the date, October 27, 1858, which makes him the youngest of all the Presidents. His father, Theodore, was a wealthy descendant of an old Knickerbocker family, and was well known throughout the city as a philanthropist and patriot. His mother was a descendant of Archibald Bullock, first President of Georgia during the Revolution.

Eight generations of President Roosevelt's family have lived in New York, and from the middle of the Seventeenth Century the name has been common in the annals of the city,

ident during his progress from legislator, Police Commissioner, and cavalry Colonel to President the exponent of that vigorous and forceful public life which is popularly termed "strenuous."

Young Roosevelt was sent to private schools during his early school years and preparation for Harvard University to avoid the rough treatment of boys in the public schools. He entered Harvard with the determination to make a man of himself, mentally and physically. By obedience to the laws of health and careful exercise the puny, sickly boy grew to robust manhood. At Harvard the tastes of young Roosevelt, already exhibited, for natural history and hunting were plainly manifested. His rifle with which he had roamed the woods in Summer near his Oyster Bay home, with the trophies of his chase, were the most conspicuous objects in his room. Live turtles, other animals, and insects were kept frequently in his room. His stubborn defense of his own

'Politics and war are the two biggest games that are played.'

having been almost equally prominent in political, business, and social affairs. The founder of the family in America was Klass Marenson Roosevelt, who came from Holland in 1641 and settled in New York. His son, Nicholas Roosevelt, come to be an Alderman of the city when that was a much greater distinction than it is now, and took up the cause of the colonists against England, despite considerable wealth.

Another of President Roosevelt's ancestors, James J. Roosevelt, was Captain in the New York State troops and served for seven years. James Henry Roosevelt, founder of the Roosevelt Hospital, which he endowed with the bulk of his estate, was also a relative of the President.

The young Theodore is described in early youth as a "weak-eyed, pig-chested boy, too frail to take part in the sports of lads of his age."

Though frail, however, young Theodore, or "Teddy," as he was familiarly called by his playmates—a name which clung to him in later years—was not at all lacking in ambition nor in courage. In the veins of his ancestors there flowed Dutch, Irish, Scotch, and French Huguenot blood.

"He obtained his name," writes one of his biographers, "from the Dutch; from the Scotch his obstinacy; from the French his impetuosity, and from the Irish his 'blarney,' or gift of tongue."

These constituent parts of his mental make-up, coupled with that grim determination and perseverance which overcame his physical disadvantages, have made the Pres-

convictions, even against the opinion of his instructors, are still remembered by his classmates with vividness.

Athletics at Harvard received from him due consideration. He soon became the champion light-weight boxer in the gymnasium. Not long since Mr. Roosevelt said about this boxing: "When I was in Harvard and sparred for the championship I suffered a heavier punishment than any man there did, and I have been knocked out at polo twice. I thoroughly believe in boxing and football, and other rough and manly games." Young Roosevelt was also a fair catch-as-catch-can wrestler, a good runner, and a lively polo player. For a time he was Captain of the college polo club. Under his Captaincy the team never won a championship.

Photographs of young Roosevelt taken while at college show him to have been a handsome youth, with no trace of his present mustache, nor eyeglasses, nor prominent teeth, which in later years have been so mercilessly played upon by cartoonists in political campaigns.

Young Roosevelt was graduated from Harvard in 1880, and though a close student, with no impairment of health. After extended travel in Europe, he returned to this country, studied law for a few months, and then plunged at once into the maelstrom of municipal politics. He was elected in 1881 an Assemblyman from the Twenty-first Assembly District. At Albany he was promptly dubbed a "silk stocking" and a "freak" of a popular election. Mr. Roosevelt, then but twenty-three years old, soon succeeded in making himself a storm centre.

In his opinion, "Politics and war are the two biggest games that are played." In one year Mr. Roosevelt was known all over the country as a new power in the Albany halls of legislation. His best known work in the Legislature at this time was in connection with the passage of the acts abolishing the fee system in county offices and in depriving the Board of Aldermen of their veto power of the Mayor's appointments. This was a relic of the Tweed régime.

He also headed the legislative investigating committee which bore his name, and which made an investigation into New York's municipal administration.

In 1884 Mr. Roosevelt went to Chicago as Chairman of the New York delegation to the Republican National Convention. He opposed the nomination of Blaine, but when Mr. Blaine became the Republican choice, Mr. Roosevelt fell into line and worked for the party candidate's success.

The next two years of the President's life bore unexpected and unforeseen fruit. They made him an author, paved his way for appointment as Assistant Secretary of the Navy, and undoubtedly suggested to him the formation of the famous Regiment of Rough Riders. After retirement from the Legislature Mr. Roosevelt went each Summer to the ranch he had purchased in the Bad Lands of North Dakota. He became there an expert rider of the vicious horse, and gained a reputation as a courageous man, an indefatigable hunter of big game, and a sportsman of ability. There he became intimately acquainted with the ranchmen, rustlers, and cow punchers, who subsequently formed the nucleus of the regiment of Rough Riders.

In 1886 Roosevelt was again in the turmoil of New York City politics. Henry George was a candidate for Mayor. Abram S. Hewitt was the nominee of the Democrats. Mr. Roosevelt was put in the field by the Republicans. Mr. Hewitt won. Roosevelt next attracted notice as a hunter of big game. He delighted in hunting the grizzly bears and other fierce wild animals of the West.

President Harrison in 1889 appointed Mr. Roosevelt United States Civil Service Commissioner. He was a firm believer in the competitive merit system, and put his ideas in force at once. President Cleveland retained him in office, although Mr. Roosevelt resigned in 1895 to become President of the New York Board of Police Commissioners.

The Police Department had just been exposed as corrupt to such an extent that many felt that only a reorganization would work any radical improvement. The Roosevelt police régime is remembered yet in the Police Department as one of the ablest the department ever knew. Under Mr. Roosevelt the morale of the force became higher than it has ever been since, and the efficiency of the men advanced in proportion. Mr. Roosevelt began by saying what he meant.

He told the police to be honest, and that if they were not they would suffer for it, and that if they were, they would not be persecuted therefor by any individual or political party.

Within a month after taking office Roosevelt was at once the best-hated and the best-liked man in New York. He determined that the law requiring Sunday closing of saloons must be enforced. He enforced it. This act aroused much criticism from press and people, but it effectually stopped the police blackmail of saloon keepers.

President McKinley nominated Mr. Roosevelt on April 6, 1897, to be Assistant Secretary of the Navy. From the very first he foresaw the possibility of a conflict with Spain and he set about preparing his department for it. He left nothing undone that could secure the highest efficiency in the service when the time for action came. When actual hostilities began Mr. Roosevelt resigned his post in the Navy Department, returned to the Bad Lands, and organized a regiment of rough riders.

Mr. Roosevelt was a member of the National Guard from 1884 to 1888, being a member of the Eighth Regiment, and though for a time he was a Captain he did not think his experience was sufficient to qualify him to command a regiment, and so when the Rough Riders were organized he declined to become Colonel. He became the second in command. Dr. Leonard Wood of the regular army was made Colonel.

The history of Roosevelt and his Rough Riders during the Santiago campaign is too well known to be repeated. After Guasimas and San Juan Hill, Col. Wood was made a Brigadier General and Lieut. Col. Roosevelt the regiment's Colonel. After the campaign was over, Col. Roosevelt returned to the United States the idol of the country. He found himself already talked of for the Gubernatorial nomination of this State. Not until he was a private citizen again, on Sept. 15, would he talk politics. He then entered into the campaign with his customary vigor and impetuosity, and was, after nomination at Saratoga by the Republican Convention, on Sept. 27, 1898, elected Governor of the State of New York over Augustus Van Wyck, the Democratic candidate, by 17,786 votes.

From the Governor's chair to the Vice Presidency was but a step, although an unwilling one, for Mr. Roosevelt. He was nominated at Philadelphia June 21, 1900, for the second highest office in the gift of the people of the United States. Mr. Roosevelt was unwilling to have his name presented to the convention, declaring that he did not desire the nomination. The popular demand for his nomination was so great that he finally was forced to yield to the delegates' desire and accept the nomination as President McKinley's running mate.

The wife of President Roosevelt was Miss Edith Kermit Carow. She is said to have been a great spur to her husband in his distinguished career and to have been, perhaps, more ambitious for him than he was for himself. Personally, she shrinks from publicity.

The President has six children. The eldest, Miss Alice, is now seventeen years old. Theodore Roosevelt, Jr., now thirteen, bears a striking resemblance to his father and is like him in many ways. Kermit, aged eleven years, is named for his mother's family. Next comes Ethel, nine years old; then Archibald, six, and Quentin, three. The youngest was named for an old Huguenot ancestor.

The President has been twice married, the first union ending in a tragedy. Miss Alice Lee of Boston was his first choice. She died in 1884, leaving the infant daughter who bears her name. Miss Carow was her intimate friend.

One of the most astonishing things in the President's life is the great amount of literary work he has accomplished, despite his manifold other concerns. He began to write before he left Harvard, and in the year after he was graduated he produced his "Naval War of 1812." He wrote a "Life of Thomas H. Benton," and also a biography of Gouverneur Morris, which was followed in 1888 by his "Ranch Life and Hunting Trail," which proved a very popular book. "The Winning of the West," however, he considers his greatest literary work.

Other productions of his pen are "Historic Towns," "History of New York City," "Essays on Practical Politics," and "The Wilderness Hunter." He also wrote "American Political Ideals," and in collaboration with Henry Cabot Lodge produced a volume entitled "Hero Tales from American History." All his writings are remarkable for their vigor of style and clearness of expression.

* *

"President Roosevelt Worries Senators," September 29, 1901

The responsibilities that fell to him after President McKinley's untimely death clearly affected Roosevelt. Two weeks after he became president, *The Times* wrote that Roosevelt had "acquired a degree of gravity that he did not before have." Given the circumstances in which he took office, Roosevelt not surprisingly declared at the outset that he would continue his predecessor's policies. This statement raised concern among some senators with respect to the McKinley administration's efforts to negotiate reciprocity in free trade agreements between the United States and other nations.

SEPTEMBER 29, 1901
PRESIDENT ROOSEVELT WORRIES SENATORS
They Wonder What His Reciprocity Views Are.
The President's First Full Week—Takes Abundant Exercise—His Family—
Other Washington Topics.
Special to The New York Times

WASHINGTON, Sept. 28.—President Roosevelt has not yet been an occupant of the White House a week, but has been there long enough to enable him to give assurances to many visitors that he has taken up the responsibilities imposed upon him in the spirit of his predecessor. If he has begun his career as President a little more vigorously than some of those who have preceded him, it is because Mr. Roosevelt is about the most active man as well as the youngest who ever reached the chair of President.

A man who has learned to love the open air, the woods and the fields, and the freest of exercise cannot, if he would,

at once give up all healthful exercise and devote himself to meeting statesmen and politicians and give up his time and appetite in order that the wants of these persons can be attended to. The President took possession of his office to find it equipped with the force employed in part when Mr. Cleveland was President, later by Mr. McKinley, and there was not one employe who had any fear that he would suffer loss of place for the coming of Roosevelt unless he were incompetent.

Horseback riding with Gen. Leonard Wood, with Assistant Secretary of War Sanger, or with some other companion who could talk while riding, now and then a walk, and always a cheerful greeting for visitors have shown the new President to be unchanged in manner, though perhaps those who know him best are right in fancying he has acquired a degree of gravity that he did not before have. Visitors upon him have scarcely been interrupted on their way from the door of the White House to the reception room of the President.

There do not appear to have been any confidential communications by the President to callers, for all talks have been heard by all who happened to be in the reception room while the President was conversing with any particular man or group of men. As a matter of course, the visitors were not principally of the Congressional class, only a few Senators and Representatives having come here at this time, but were mostly of the office-holding and managing sort, the men who desire to know early, by personal contact, just the man they have to look to for party guidance for a few years. Later on, just prior to the assembling of Congress, the members of the two houses will make themselves known with their requests and demands.

The President seems to have learned from some source, since the funeral of Mr. McKinley, that there were some members of the Senate who were strangely jealous of the President and his Cabinet almost from the moment Mr. Roosevelt announced, at Buffalo, that he would be guided in his Administration by the policies of President McKinley. There is no doubt that some sort of dissatisfaction was felt and talked about here, while the funeral procession was on its way from the capital to Canton, by Senators who have had long experience and who now occupy most influential positions in the party councils.

The burden of the complaints uttered by these Senators was that to declare adhesion to the McKinley policies at a time when people were applauding the interpretation of McKinley's words as much as the very words spoken, was injudicious. Before declaring a policy or policies, the President, according to these Senators, should have consulted with Senatorial leaders to ascertain whether it would not be necessary to offer some modification of the policy of McKinley, say, as to reciprocity.

That comes pretty near to explaining all reasons for dissatisfaction, for the Senators who were most influential in shelving the reciprocity treaties negotiated by Secretary Hay are among those who now believe that modification of reciprocity plans is important if pledges to protected manufacturers are to be kept. Possibly the President may

regard his responsibility to the people as not to be qualified by personal pledges made by Senators, but Senators will have opportunity to find that out for themselves.

Every Senator will have a chance to tell the President what he thinks about reciprocity and why he thinks as he does. They will learn from the President that he will lean upon them for assistance and not undertake to usurp their functions nor abdicate his own. When he declared his intention to stand by the promises made by McKinley, it was not so convenient to ascertain the advice of Senators as it was to take the advice of the members of the President's official family.

A President at the age of forty-three is a novelty, and so young a President with so large a family of young children has never before occupied the White House since John Adams entered it a short time before the close of his term of office, when the building was scarcely fit for habitation. Adams became President at the very mature age of sixty-two, and he had a small family. Jefferson was a widower for twenty years when he reached the Presidency, and his daughter, Mrs. Randolph, had a family of something like a dozen children, of whom it is related that they attended a school kept for their improvement in one of the second-floor rooms of the building.

William Henry Harrison would have brought a family of six sons and four daughters to the White House, but he died before the family had arranged their affairs at home sufficiently to permit them to join him in this city. Mr. Cleveland, after Mr. Roosevelt, was the youngest President, reaching the office at the age of forty-five. When the new President has assembled his two daughters and four sons under the historic roof it will be the most numerous Presidential family gathered there since 1801.

It is not likely, however, that all of Mr. Roosevelt's children will be here often at the same time. Already it is known here, where everything about the White House arrangements and accommodations has been familiar knowledge for these many years, that there is scant space in the living rooms of the house for a family of eight that has been accustomed to liberal living space. Then there are servants to be thought of and now and then a guest, but President Roosevelt will not be able to invite many guests at one time, unless the family puts itself to inconvenience in order that visitors may be comfortable. Of course the oft-repeated suggestion for an enlarged house, or for a new residence apart from the White House, will be made and will again be dropped, as being of no political importance.

"The Irrigation Bill," June 16, 1902

The Newlands Reclamation Act, named after Rep. (and later senator) Francis G. Newlands of Nevada, provided funding for irrigation projects in sixteen Western states. As a former frontiersman, President Roosevelt was a staunch supporter of this legislation. In an editorial, *The Times* recognized the president's "vigorous support" of the bill, pointing out that this issue had captured his interest most in domestic affairs to date.

JUNE 16, 1902
EDITORIAL
THE IRRIGATION BILL.

The country is to be congratulated that the Senate Irrigation bill goes to the President substantially unchanged. It is to be credited largely to the vigorous support given by the President, who has been more closely interested in this measure than in almost any relating to internal policy.

The objections to the bill were not very serious. Some of them were amusing. Some of the opponents thought that the money should be taken directly from the Treasury instead of from the sale of lands which in part are devoted to the agricultural colleges. As any deficit in the payment to the colleges is to be made up from the Treasury, this objection had little weight, and its good faith was questioned. There is no doubt, however, of the entire good faith of the gentleman from Indiana who protested that the farmers of the Middle West, after getting their lands in condition to cultivate at their own expense, were now asked to pay for irrigating lands the products of which would come into competition with their own. That is the old cry of the timid and the short-sighted, and its genuineness cannot be ques-

tioned. It was first raised long years ago before the Federal Constitution had been adopted, against a "more perfect union," which would bring the products of New York into closer competition with those of Connecticut, and prevent that State from protecting its interests by proper legislation. It is the cry of the sugar beet men against Cuban reciprocity. It is the cry of Mr. Nixon against free trade in ships. It is the cry of all who are afraid of a fair field and of progress.

But it is belated in this matter of irrigation. When the United States Government paid the first installment toward opening up the territory, then a wilderness, from which the Indiana Representative is now elected, it made free competition throughout the entire continent inevitable. And it is precisely that freedom that has made the country the most powerful and wealthy of the world. The irrigation plan is but adding to the general resources of the Nation in furtherance of the impulse which has carried our vigorous race from the little fringe along the Atlantic to the shores of the Pacific and far into Asian waters.

"President Roosevelt Talks on Coal Strike," September 6, 1902

Just one year into his presidency, Roosevelt showed how the power of the office could be used to resolve crises even without direct presidential involvement. When coal miners went on strike in 1902, negotiations between mine owners and the workers' union made no progress at first. The president expressed his dismay at the stalemate, declaring, as *The Times* reported, that he was "grieved beyond measure." Although he denied that the government could intervene in the dispute, he did suggest that "the Republican principles, which are framed alike for high and low, will level the problem to an equity." Perhaps sensing that the president could complicate matters, the two sides ultimately agreed to arbitration.

SEPTEMBER 6, 1902
PRESIDENT ROOSEVELT TALKS ON COAL STRIKE

Reported as Declaring There Is a Remedy.

Quoted as Saying He Thinks Republican Leaders in Pennsylvania Can Settle the Matter Amicably.

PHILADELPHIA, Sept. 5.—*The Record* to-morrow will print an interview on the coal strike with President Roosevelt, who passed through this city to-day on his way to Washington. The President is quoted as follows:

"I am grieved beyond measure at the difficulty in Pennsylvania and other coal-producing States over the wage and kindred questions."

"What remedy is at hand?" he was asked.

"There is a remedy," said the President.

"Do you mean that the Government of the United States can interfere other than as a law-preserving body?"

"No," replied the President, emphatically.

"What can be done?" was then asked.

"I would refer you to the men at the head of the Republican Party, who are in control of affairs in the State of Pennsylvania. I am sure that their conservative opinion of the difficulties rampant will ultimately result in an amicable settlement of this great question. Of course, politics do not enter into the mining problem, yet I sincerely hope that the Republican principles, which are framed alike for high and low, will level the problem to an equity."

• •

"CHECKS ON IMMIGRATION," MARCH 4, 1903

The assassination of President McKinley by a self-proclaimed anarchist prompted calls for restricting individuals and groups who opposed the government. The Immigration Act of 1903 addressed these concerns by prohibiting several groups of people, including anarchists, from entering the United States. As defined in *The Times,* the term *anarchist* meant "persons who believe in or advocate the overthrow by force or violence of all government or the assassination of public officials." Although the law was not meant to punish people for "purely political" acts, that distinction would prove difficult to apply in practice.

MARCH 4, 1903
CHECKS ON IMMIGRATION.

Act Passed by Congress More Strict in Its Provisions.

Special to The New York Times

WASHINGTON, March 3.—The Immigration act which has passed both houses of Congress and will be laid before the President for approval is substantially in the form it was passed by the Senate.

It provides that a tax of $2 shall be collected for every alien immigrant who enters the United States, the tax to be paid at the port of entry by the master or owner of the vessel on which the immigrant arrives. The money thus collected shall constitute a permanent appropriation to be called the "Immigrant Fund," and used to defray the expenses of administering the immigrant law. The tax is not to be levied upon aliens in transit

through the United States nor upon those who have once paid it.

The classes excluded from admission are idiots, insane persons, epileptics and persons who have been insane within five years previous, paupers, persons likely to become a public charge, persons afflicted with a loathesome, dangerous, or contagious disease; persons who have been convicted of crime or misdemeanor involving mortal turpitude, polygamists, Anarchists, or persons who believe in or advocate the overthrow by force or violence of all government or the assassination of public officials, women of bad repute and persons who attempt to bring in such women, and persons whose tickets or passage is paid for with the money of another or who are assisted by others to come.

These exclusions are not to apply to prevent persons living in the United States from sending for relatives or friends not of the excluded classes, nor is the act to be construed to exclude persons convicted of offenses purely political, nor to exclude professional actors, artists, lecturers, singers, ministers, college professors, or persons belonging to any learned profession, or persons strictly employed as personal or domestic servants. Violation of these provisions of the act is punishable by a fine of $1,000 for every offense.

"PRESIDENT TO MAKE TREATY," NOVEMBER 14, 1903

One of President Roosevelt's most significant assertions of executive power was his negotiation of the Panama Canal pact without prior congressional approval. The United States had long sought canal rights and actually had come close to securing a treaty with Colombia, when it controlled Panama. When Colombia rejected the treaty, the United States worked behind the scenes to aid Panamanian rebels in their quest for independence. Instead of negotiating the canal treaty with the new leaders of Panama, however, the Roosevelt administration worked with French engineer Philippe Bunau-Varilla, who had long promoted development of a canal and who gave away far more control than the Panamanian government would have allowed. The administration made the case that Congress had approved funding for a canal in the 1902 Spooner Act and that no further legislative authorization was needed.

NOVEMBER 14, 1903
PRESIDENT TO MAKE TREATY.

Administration Holds It Has Full Power to Act in Panama Matter.
Special to The New York Times

WASHINGTON, Nov. 13.—As a result of the many conferences that have been going on in Administration circles during the week, and after a thorough discussion of the whole matter in the Cabinet to-day, it has been decided that it shall be the policy of the Administration to hold that the President has full powers under existing law to negotiate a treaty with the Republic of Panama.

It is held that no legislation by Congress is necessary to that end, and that the President may conclude an agreement with the Panama Canal Company, and, when the treaty with the Republic of Panama has been ratified by the Senate he may, without further legislation by Congress, and acting under existing law, pay whatever sum is agreed upon as the price of the Panama franchise, and may pay the canal company for its property.

This decision has been reached with great care. It is said it rests on the opinions of the Attorney General, the leading members of the Cabinet, and those Senators and Representatives whose part in the history of canal legislation renders their advice of the highest value.

The legal construction that has been put on the Spooner act holds that Congress has appropriated the money to pay the canal company and to pay Colombia or the Republic of Panama for the franchise, and that no further legislation is required for the execution of that part of the canal project.

It was stated to-day by one of the highest authorities near the President that the alternative presented by the Spooner act is that he may go on and construct the Nicaraguan canal without going to Congress for any authorization except the ratification by the Senate of a treaty for the right of way from Nicaragua and Costa Rica, or he may go on and negotiate for the Panama property and the Panama franchise with the necessity of asking only the ratification by the Senate of the treaty with the Republic of Panama. In other words, it is held that so far as the payments for either project are concerned, he has full powers under the act.

The indications are that there will be little delay in framing a treaty between the United States and the Panama Republic. The initiative will be taken by Mr. Hay, who has

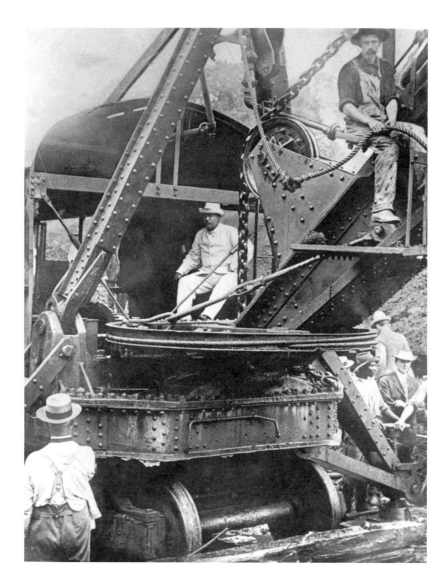

Theodore Roosevelt sits on a steam shovel during his visit to a Panama Canal construction site in 1906. This trip made him the first president to travel overseas.

Source: The Mariners' Museum/CORBIS

already shaped into tentative form the general scope and intent of the proposed convention.

Minister Varilla said to-night that he was prepared to enter on the negotiations, and was awaiting the pleasure of the State Department. He would not undertake to outline the extent of the treaty, but intimated that as he was armed with the fullest powers the convention would embrace not only the agreements desired in regard to the canal franchise but also all other necessary matters to be understood in a treaty between one Government and another.

M. Varilla would not permit himself to go into details as to the articles pertaining to the canal, but said that the agreement would be sufficient and fair.

"I am free to say," he said, "that my people desire first of all to be fair in their negotiations with the United States. I understand it will be for Mr. Hay to make the propositions covering what is desired shall be set forth in the treaty. It will be for me as the representative of my country to accept or to decline.

"I should say that in the main the best features of the Hay-Herran treaty will be employed, and I can also say that those parts of it which were objectionable will be omitted. These negotiations will not find my country in the attitude of haggling or grasping.

"The difficulties which were encountered when the negotiations were taken up with Mr. Concha for Colombia will be absent. I cannot say what amount will be considered as the payment for the canal franchise, nor is it possible for me to say whether it will be more or less than the ten millions which were to be paid to Colombia. That is a matter about which I have had no instructions.

". . . I can only speak of the terms of the treaty when they come before me. Everything about this treaty will be first of all fair, and I shall confidently expect it to meet with popular approval in this country and my own."

· ·

"Supreme Court Wrecks Merger," March 15, 1904

The Supreme Court's 1904 decision to uphold the government's authority to break up corporate trusts marked a significant victory for federal regulation of business. By a 5–4 vote, the Court upheld the Sherman Antitrust Act of 1890, under which the Roosevelt administration had sued to break up Northern Securities Company, which consolidated the railroad industry. As *The Times* reported, the Court ruled that the company had been created "to prevent competition between its constituent companies," a purpose that clearly violated the antitrust law. Dissenting justices, however, protested that the decision "interfered with the exercise of powers incidental to the ownership of property."

MARCH 15, 1904
SUPREME COURT WRECKS MERGER
Northern Securities Company an Unlawful Combination.
DECISION BY CLOSE MARGIN
Minority of Four Declare the Doctrine Enunciated Might Lead to Interference
With State and Personal Freedom.
Special to The New York Times

WASHINGTON, March 14.—The United States Supreme Court to-day handed down an opinion in the merger case of the United States versus the Northern Securities Company sustaining the contention of the Government that the railroad merger was illegal, and affirming the judgment of the United States Circuit Court of Appeals.

The decision was reached only by the narrowest possible margin, the alignment of the Justices being five to four. Justices Harlan, Brewer, Brown, McKenna, and Day formed the majority, while Chief Justice Fuller and Justices Holmes, White, and Peckham dissented. The narrowness of the Government's victory is accentuated by the fact that though Justice Brewer assents to the judgment of the majority, he reaches his conclusion by a different course of argument and writes a separate opinion to explain his views.

The Prevailing Opinion.

The prevailing opinion was written by Justice Harlan and proceeded on the theory that Congress has a right under the Constitution to control inter-State commerce, no matter how conducted.

Justice Harlan holds that the evidence shows the Northern Securities Company to constitute such restraint of inter-State commerce as violates the Anti-Trust act and that the original purpose of the merger was to prevent competition between its constituent companies.

"The mere existence of such a combination," says Justice Harlan, "constitutes a menace" to the freedom of commerce which the public is entitled to have protected.

Justice Harlan goes on to hold that the Anti-Trust act is not limited to application in unreasonable restraints on trade and commerce, but applies to all such restraints, reasonable or unreasonable, and declares that an act of Congress, constitutionally passed, "is binding upon all as much as if it were included in terms in the Constitution itself."

It is held that the court, having found an unlawful combination, has the power to end its existence.

Justice Brewer in his separate opinion expresses the view that recent anti-trust decisions have gone too far, and holds that the anti-trust act should not be interpreted as applying to reasonable restraints on commerce, but only to unreasonable ones. He is, however, persuaded that the formation of the Northern Securities Company constitutes such an unreasonable restraint.

Views of Dissenters.

Justice Holmes, in behalf of the minority, protested against the decision on the ground that it interfered with the exercise of powers incidental to the ownership of property. He declared that such a doctrine might be extended so that "the advice or mere existence of one man might be a crime."

Justice White declared that mere ownership of stock in a State corporation could in no sense be held to be an interference with traffic between States. Such a doctrine, he asserted, would give power to Congress to control the organization of all railroads doing an inter-State business, and to abrogate every charter and every consolidation of such lines. Such power might even extend to the prevention of organization of labor associations.

"Indeed," he said, "the doctrine must in reason lead to a concession of the right in Congress to regulate concerning the aptitude, the character, and capacity of persons."

The decree of the Circuit Court which was affirmed "enjoined the Securities Company, its officers and stockholders:

"From acquiring or attempting to acquire any more of such stock.

"From exercising or attempting to exercise any control, direction, supervision, or influence on the acts of either railway company by virtue of its holding of stock therein.

"From paying any dividends on such stock to the Securities Company.

"From permitting the Securities Company or its officers, &c., to exercise any control over the corporate acts of such railway companies."

An Expectant Audience.

An effort was made by the court to prevent knowledge of the fact that the opinion was to be rendered to-day from getting to the public, but when the members of the court filed into the chamber at noon they were awaited by an expectant crowd which filled every seat.

Attorney General Knox and Secretary Taft and an unusual number of Senators and members of the House of Representatives were present when Justice Harlan began the delivery of the opinion. The Justice read his opinion from a printed copy, which consumed about an hour and a quarter in its delivery.

All told, the court consumed two hours and three-quarters in disposing of the case. The fact was noted by several persons that the argument in the case was begun Dec. 14, just three months previous to the decision. For so important a case, this is considered a very brief interim between the arguments and the decision.

The case decided was originally brought by the United States against the Northern Securities Company, a corporation of New Jersey; the Great Northern Railway Company, a corporation of Minnesota; the Northern Pacific Railway Company, a corporation of Wisconsin; James J. Hill, a citizen of Minnesota, and William P. Clough, D. Willis James, John S. Kennedy, J. Pierpont Morgan, Robert Bacon, George F. Baker, and Daniel Lamont, citizens of New York.

- -

"ROOSEVELT: SWEEPS NORTH AND WEST AND IS ELECTED PRESIDENT," NOVEMBER 9, 1904

Roosevelt's widespread popularity translated into an easy victory in the 1904 presidential election. He prevailed in the Electoral College with 336 votes to 140 for the Democratic nominee, Judge Alton B. Parker. (*The Times'* initial report said Roosevelt won 325 votes, but he ultimately lost seven of Maryland's eight electoral votes and won all of Missouri's eighteen.) Triumphant in winning the executive office in his own right, Roosevelt issued a statement that he would come to regret. Recognizing that he already had served almost an entire term since McKinley's assassination, Roosevelt promised to respect the customary two-term limit on the presidency that all of his predecessors had observed. "Under no circumstances will I be a candidate for or accept another nomination," he declared. Roosevelt kept his word in 1908, but his perspective would change four years later.

NOVEMBER 9, 1904
ROOSEVELT: SWEEPS NORTH AND WEST AND IS ELECTED PRESIDENT.

SAYS HE WILL NOT RUN AGAIN

Will Have 325 Electoral Votes—Republican Gains in Congress—Folk, La Follette
and Douglas Win Governorship Fights.

Theodore Roosevelt was yesterday elected President of
the United States for four years more, overwhelming majorities having been given to the Republican Electoral tickets in all
of the States which had been classed as doubtful. The returns
received up to midnight indicate that Roosevelt will have 325
votes in the Electoral College to 151 for his opponent, Alton
B. Parker. The total number of votes in the Electoral College
is 476, of which 239 are necessary to a choice. Mr. Roosevelt,
therefore, will have a majority in the Electoral College of 174.
The only State about whose Electoral vote there was any
doubt at a late hour was Maryland. The returns indicated that
it had gone Republican by several thousand, but the Democratic State Committee had not abandoned hope.

As soon as it became certain that he had carried the
country Mr. Roosevelt issued the following statement at
the White House, in Washington:

"Washington, Nov. 8, 1904.

"I am deeply sensible of the honor done me
by the American people in thus expressing their
confidence in what I have done and have tried to
do. I appreciate to the full the solemn responsibility this confidence imposes upon me, and I shall
do all that in my power lies not to forfeit it. On
the Fourth of March next I shall have served three
and one-half years, and this three and one-half
years constitutes my first term. The wise custom
which limits the President to two terms regards
the substance and not the form. Under no circumstances will I be a candidate for or accept another
nomination."

President Roosevelt . . . used all the influence which is his and every plea at his command in an effort to turn the tide and pave the way toward peace between Russia
and Japan.

"PRESIDENT'S ACT MAY BRING PEACE," AUGUST 20, 1905

Roosevelt's leadership style as president incorporated both decisiveness and diplomacy. In summer
1905 he organized a peace conference in Portsmouth, New Hampshire, for Russia and Japan to negotiate a treaty to end their war, which had begun the previous year. Roosevelt also invited delegates from
both countries to separate meetings at Sagamore Hill, his home in Oyster Bay, Long Island. Describing
the president's role in negotiations, *The Times* wrote that he "used all the influence which is his and
every plea at his command." The two sides reached agreement, and President Roosevelt was awarded
the Nobel Peace Prize the following year for his actions. He accepted the award after leaving office and
gave the prize money to charity.

AUGUST 20, 1905
PRESIDENT'S ACT MAY BRING PEACE

Rosen Cheerful After Seeing Mr. Roosevelt.

PROPOSITION TO RUSSIA

Belief That It Will End Portsmouth Deadlock.

SATO SURE OF SUCCESS

Would Wager 5 to 1 That a Treaty Will Be Made—European Capitals Are Hopeful.

Special to The New York Times

OYSTER BAY, Aug. 19.—For an hour to-day the centre of activity in the negotiations to end the war in the Far East shifted from Portsmouth to Sagamore Hill.

For that space of time this evening President Roosevelt, in conference with Baron Rosen, the Russian Ambassador at Washington and junior Russian peace envoy, used all the influence which is his and every plea at his command in an effort to turn the tide and pave the way toward peace between Russia and Japan.

No word has come from Sagamore Hill to-night that even by innuendo could be utilized as a basis for a forecast as to what the outcome of to-day's meeting is likely to be, but the President's determination to step into the breach between the two warring nations can lead to only one inference—Mr. Roosevelt does not despair of a peaceful outcome of the negotiations which were begun under his auspices.

It is known, moreover, that the President did not trust to his persuasive powers alone in urging the Russian envoys through Baron Rosen to do all in their power to bring about peace. Mr. Roosevelt, when he asked Baron Rosen to come to Sagamore Hill for a conference, did not do so merely for the purpose of discussing the desirability from Russia's point of view of an early peace, even though it might prove bitter to Russia to pay the price.

The President was enabled to place before the Russian envoy certain inducements, substantial enough to be worthy of Russia's consideration, which may end the differences which have arisen between the envoys of Russia and Japan.

Followed a Visit by Kaneko.

In connection with this, it is significant that the visit of Baron Rosen followed closely upon the one paid at Sagamore Hill last night by Baron Kaneko, who, while he apparently holds no official position, is believed to be a personal representative of the Mikado in this country.

Until the present time President Roosevelt has refrained from any action, even by indirection, that might be construed as interference in the work of the plenipotentiaries. He announced at the beginning of the negotiations that, neither by word nor act, would he participate in the proceedings of the conference, although he made it perfectly clear to the envoys of both Russia and Japan that he would be ready, at any time, to assist them in a proper way in the great work which they had been designated by their respective Emperors to undertake.

In anticipation, however, of the failure of the envoys to agree upon certain of the articles and in the expectation that he might be appealed to by one side or the other before the conclusion of the conference, the President has been in communication with the great neutral powers. His purpose was to enlist their support in a final effort to secure an honorable peace. He communicated with King Edward, because Great Britain is the ally of Japan, and with President Loubet, because France is the ally of Russia. Germany, too, was appealed to, and Emperor William, as well as King Edward and M. Loubet, is exerting his influence for peace. Tremendous and worldwide pressure is being brought to bear upon the Governments at St. Petersburg and Tokio not to permit the conference to fail. It can be said that there is ground for the hope that it will not fail.

"Meat Bill Is Passed After Brief Debate," June 20, 1906

Investigative journalists, known as muckrakers in the Roosevelt era, spurred the federal government to regulate the food industry. For example, Upton Sinclair's 1906 novel *The Jungle,* although fiction, described the horrific conditions in meat processing plants and sparked a public outcry for reform. In response to such exposés, Congress passed the Meat Inspection Act of 1906, which gave the Department of Agriculture the authority to inspect factories and ensure the quality of their products. President Roosevelt strongly supported this Progressive legislation.

JUNE 20, 1906
MEAT BILL IS PASSED AFTER BRIEF DEBATE
Senate Is Expected Now to Accept the Amended Measure.
DE ARMOND SOLE OBJECTOR
Williams Eulogizes Wadsworth—Criticism Directed Only Against Placing Cost
of Inspection.
Special to The New York Times

WASHINGTON, June 19.—With only one dissenting vote—that of De Armond of Missouri—the House passed to-day the re-revised Meat Inspection bill agreed on yesterday by the President and Speaker Cannon.

In the brief debate that was allowed there was some slight criticism of the bill, three Democrats and one Republican voicing it, but it was all directed at one paragraph—that providing the method of paying for the new inspection service.

The bill was put through under suspension of the rules, which allowed but forty minutes for debate, half of which was controlled by Chairman Wadsworth of the Committee on Agriculture and the other half by Mr. Lamb, the senior Democrat of the committee. But in that short time the measure received a hearty approbation, and Chairman Wadsworth was made the object of an unequivocal indorsement by John Sharp Williams, the minority leader. Wadsworth himself, referring to the court review amendment, which had been eliminated, declared that he had just as high an opinion of a Federal Judge in Chicago as of one in Omaha or anywhere else, and believed them all to be upright. This was by way of retort to the expression of the President in his first letter to the committee Chairman.

Wadsworth's Explanation.

As soon as the reading of the bill was ended Mr. Wadsworth made an explanation of the bill. He began with a reference to the action of the House yesterday in recommitting the bill at the request of the committee, and said that all the amendments which it had been desired to incorporate had been inserted in the copy which had just been read to the House.

"Most of them, with two exceptions, are mere verbiage," he said. "These two exceptions are the clause eliminating the civil service provision and what might be called the appeal or court review clause."

Then Judge Olmsted, referring to the exemption of the farmer and retail butcher, contended that the section of the bill preventing carriers from transporting meat or meat food products, which did not bear inspection labels, would also prevent them from handling the products of these small concerns.

Mr. Wadsworth replied that the clause referred to did not apply as Mr. Olmsted thought, and argued that the exemption provision was sufficiently explicit.

Further on, explaining the changes in verbiage, Mr. Wadsworth referred to the addition of the word "unclean," saying:

"Generally speaking, in regard to all these small changes and verbiage, if, like soothing syrup, they soothe, pacify, and quiet, let them all go in. No one objects to them." [Laughter.]

"Guard Purity of Food by Strict Regulations," October 21, 1906

The Pure Food and Drug Act of 1906 further expanded the federal government's regulatory reach. This law placed restrictions on the production and sale of food and medicine. A special commission developed specific regulations under the law to ensure basic safety standards. As *The Times* wrote, "Under these regulations not only must products be labeled, but the label must give the ingredients of the package, so that no one buying it may be left in any doubt about what he is getting." The responsibility for setting standards and enforcing them eventually went to a new federal agency, the Food and Drug Administration.

OCTOBER 21, 1906
GUARD PURITY OF FOOD BY STRICT REGULATIONS

Commission Agrees on Rules to Enforce the New Law.
SOME MODIFICATIONS MADE
American Wines May Be Champagnes, but Must Not Be Sold as Foreign Products.
Special to The New York Times

WASHINGTON, Oct. 20.—The regulations under the pure food law were promulgated to-day by Secretary Wilson after having received the approval of himself and Secretaries Shaw and Metcalf. They were drafted by a commission consisting of Dr. H. W. Wiley of the Department of Agriculture, Dr. S. N. D. North of the Commerce Department, and James L. Gerry of the Treasury Department.

Under these regulations not only must products be labeled, but the label must give the ingredients of the package, so that no one buying it may be left in any doubt about what he is getting.

Candy manufacturers will be the persons chiefly affected by the provision that in coloring no ingredient injurious to human health shall be used. The use of mineral substances of all kinds is forbidden, whether they be injurious or not.

The regulations prohibit adulteration, but standard drugs, if branded so as to show their actual strength or purity, will not be considered adulterated.

Preservatives of a deleterious or poisonous character are to be used externally only and so that they will not permeate to the interior of the product. These preservatives must be of such character that until removed the product cannot be eaten.

To prevent misbranding the regulations require that the label on each product must bear the name of the product and the name of the manufacturer, and must show whether the article is a compound, mixture, or blend. There is a prohibition against the use of any false or misleading statement, design, or device on the label. Drug labels must show the proportion of alcohol or deleterious drugs used.

The commission recommended the regulations unanimously, but before reaching its conclusions there were some disagreements. At first the commission intended to prohibit the use of well-known generic names, such as champagne, for American articles, on the ground that such names were deceptive. Ultimately the commission changed its view on this subject, and manufacturers of the so-called champagne can use the name if their product is so labeled as to show that the wine was made in America. The reason for this modification is that the commission became convinced that in such cases the purchaser would know what he was getting and would not be made the victim of any deception.

The label on any product must be attached to an original, unbroken package. Samples of original packages shall be collected only by authorized agents of the Agricultural Department, or by State, Territorial, or district officials authorized by the Secretary of Agriculture. The analysis of these samples is provided for carefully, and the publication of the results of the analysis may be made under certain conditions. The factories where proprietary foods are manufactured must be open to inspection by properly designated officers.

No dealer in food or drug products is to be liable to prosecution if he can establish that the goods were sold under a guarantee by the wholesaler, manufacturer, or jobber, or other party residing in the United States from whom purchased.

The Secretary of Agriculture is to determine the wholesomeness of colors, preservatives, and other substances which are added to foods, and he shall, when necessary, examine the raw materials used in the manufacture of food and drug products.

"Battleship Fleet to Circle World," September 5, 1907

President Roosevelt's decision to send U.S. battleships around the world heralded U.S. naval strength and illustrated that the United States was indeed a global power. In the aftermath of Japan's victory in the Russo-Japanese War, Roosevelt was determined to show that the United States had the ability to protect its interests in the Pacific and the Atlantic. He was so keen to promote the fleet that he dispatched the cruise despite congressional resistance and then challenged Congress to cut off funding if it disapproved, which he knew it would not do. The sixteen battleships would come to be known as "The Great White Fleet," and they were greeted with much fanfare throughout their worldwide tour.

SEPTEMBER 5, 1907
BATTLESHIP FLEET TO CIRCLE WORLD

From Pacific Coast It Will Go to Hawaii and Philippines and Back by Way of Suez.

NEW FLEET ON GUARD HERE

Six Powerful Battleships and Three Cruisers Will Be in Commission Early Next Year.

From a high authority *The Times* received yesterday two important pieces of information bearing on the sending of Admiral Evans's battleship fleet to the Pacific.

In the first place, it is not the present intention of the Government to confine the armada's movements to our Pacific Coast. The President's plan, according to *The Times's* informant, is to send the ships, after their visit to California ports, on to Hawaii and the Philippines. When orders are given for their return the route designated will be by way of the Suez Canal, completing the world tour.

In the meantime the Atlantic Coast will not be left unprotected. At the instance of President Roosevelt the Navy Department has already begun to formulate plans for the establishment of another Atlantic fleet, one that will replace the armada under Admiral Evans.

Although the dispatch of these sixteen battleships removes from Atlantic waters the chief naval reliance of this country, it is now known that the Government has no intention of keeping the Atlantic seaboard denuded of naval defense. Its plans, which are now being hurried to completion, contemplate the establishment of another powerful fleet of armorclads, whose base will be in Atlantic waters. This disposes of all the idle talk that President Roosevelt had entered into an understanding with the German Emperor by which German fleets were to guard these shores after the departure of Admiral Evans and his sixteen battleships.

The flagship of the new fleet is to be the *New Hampshire,* a 16,000-ton battleship, which is to be ready for commission early in January. Soon after her pennant is broken

out she will be joined by the *Mississippi* and *Idaho,* two first-class battleships which the Cramps are building and which are now more than 90 per cent. completed.

The *New Hampshire* is similar to the *Connecticut,* the present flagship of Rear Admiral Evans. The main battery consists of four 12-inch rifles, eight 8-inch and twelve 7-inch guns. In the secondary battery will be twenty 3-inch, twelve 3-pounder semi-automatic, two 1-pounder semi-automatic, and a full score of machine guns of smaller calibre. The hull is protected by a complete belt of armor with a uniform thickness of nine inches.

The *Idaho* and the *Mississippi* are of a different type—are in fact of a type peculiar to themselves. Although of only 13,000 tons, as against the 16,000 tons of the *New Hampshire,* and vessels of her class, the *Mississippi* and *Idaho* carry in their main batteries guns almost identical in calibre and number to those mounted on the larger vessels. The only difference is that whereas the *New Hampshire* carries twelve 7-inch the *Mississippi* mounts but ten of this calibre. Owing to the reduction in length from 450 feet to 375 feet, the secondary battery is somewhat smaller than that carried by the *Connecticut.* Part of this reduction is also due to the fact that in order to secure the heavy main battery and corresponding armor protection essential to a battleship of the first class, it was found necessary to reduce the freeboard aft, as in the *Maine type,* and to omit the after military mast.

These three ships are alone as powerful as was the Atlantic battleship fleet at the time of the war with Spain. They are to have as consorts three of the veterans of that war, the *Iowa, Indiana,* and *Massachusetts.* All three of these are now being modernized and when completed will be far more powerful and efficient than they were during the Santiago campaign.

Thus there are six powerful battleships which will soon be gathered into another Atlantic fleet. This fleet will have as its auxiliaries the three new scout cruisers which are now almost ready for service, these being the *Chester, Birmingham,* and *Salem*. These vessels are of 3,750 tons each, and are expected to attain the extraordinary speed of twenty-five knots an hour.

It is these nine vessels which the Navy Department means to form into a newer Atlantic fleet. The fleet will subsequently be increased by the addition of the two 16,000-ton battleships *South Carolina* and *Michigan*, and those two fast armored cruisers, *North Carolina* and *Montana*, vessels of 14,500 tons, and an improvement on any that are now in service.

- -

"MANY URGE THIRD TERM," MAY 1, 1908

Just as Roosevelt loved being president, so too did the American public enjoy his ebullient leadership. As the presidential election of 1908 drew near, Roosevelt received numerous requests to run for another term. *The Times* reported in May that people were sending between three hundred and four hundred letters a day to the White House urging the president to reconsider his vow four years earlier to respect the two-term limit established by George Washington and followed throughout the nineteenth century. Roosevelt kept his word in 1908, but changed his mind in 1912.

MAY 1, 1908
MANY URGE THIRD TERM.
Roosevelt Gets 300 or 400 Such Letters a Day.

WASHINGTON, April 30.—It is asserted on good authority that between three and four hundred letters are received daily at the White House urging President Roosevelt to run again. These come from all parts of the country, it is said, from members of all political parties, and in them various arguments are used by the writers to induce Mr. Roosevelt to again accept a nomination.

They have increased in volume in the last few weeks. The writers argue that the President is in the thick of his campaign for the establishment of complete Government control over inter-State commerce and other reforms; that it is impossible to transfer this work successfully to another, since Mr. Roosevelt's personality is a powerful factor in achieving this success; that the Republican Party cannot afford to nominate any man who is not sure of election, and that the President is the only Republican who would be certain to defeat any other candidate.

In all of his replies to such letters the President simply reminds his correspondents of his former declarations on the subject and reiterates that his position is unchanged.

- -

"200 ROOSEVELT MEN BOLT," JUNE 30, 1912

Theodore Roosevelt's decision to run for president again in 1912 galvanized Progressive Republicans to create their own political party. Although Roosevelt had prevailed in the Republican primaries, party leaders ensured that incumbent president Taft received the party nomination. Consequently, Progressives broke away and nominated Roosevelt as an independent candidate. In so doing, they split the party vote between Taft and Roosevelt, clearing the way for Democratic candidate Woodrow Wilson's White House victory.

JUNE 30, 1912
200 ROOSEVELT MEN BOLT.

And Form Progressive Party in Bay State—Chicago Delegates Stay Regular.

Special to The New York Times

BOSTON, June 29.—Two hundred Republicans who were active in the Roosevelt campaign bolted the Republican Party at a meeting in Fordham this afternoon and formed "The Progressive Party in Massachusetts."

The new party takes over the offices and campaign machinery of Matthew Hale. The resolutions adopted make the usual allegations of thievery and fraud at Chicago and indorse Theodore Roosevelt's "splendid courage, integrity, ability, high sense of public and private honor, magnetic force, rugged personality," &c. and call upon the plain people to rally about him as their champion.

A dinner followed in Kingsley Hall in honor of the Roosevelt delegates to Chicago, from which two-thirds of the eighteen significantly absented themselves.

"It doesn't matter whether we lose two or three leaders or not," said Mr. Hale at the dinner. "The movement will go on just the same."

This telegram was sent to the Colonel at Oyster Bay:

"By unanimous vote we send you greetings. The Progressive Party of Massachusetts is born with unbounded enthusiasm and a powerful organization. We have indorsed you unanimously as our candidate for President."

A picture of Col. Roosevelt was brought in, and raising it aloft, Mr. Hale led in a march around the hall, while the orchestra played "Everybody's Doing It."

While these progressives were shedding their party affiliations, another group, headed by Charles S. Baxter, who led the Roosevelt delegates at Chicago, was preparing to organize a progressive movement within the Republican Party for the purpose of gaining control of the State machine and nominating progressives for all the offices. Mr. Baxter says he and his fellow-delegates will support Col. Roosevelt if he is nominated, but will work for the Republican State ticket. The delegates he represents issued a statement to this effect to-night after Mr. Baxter had failed to come to an agreement with Mr. Hale as to first consulting Col. Roosevelt regarding the proper course to pursue. The statement reads:

"We believe in the principles advocated by Theodore Roosevelt. We believe that Theodore Roosevelt was rightfully entitled to the Republican nomination for President, and that a majority of the Republicans of the country who voted in the recent primaries favored him as their candidate. If Mr. Roosevelt becomes a candidate for the Presidency, we shall support him as the legitimate candidate of the Republican Party.

"Some Progressives in Massachusetts believe that the wrong done at Chicago can only be righted by the formation of a new party. We do not agree with them.

"We believe in remaining in the party and continuing our fight for progressive principles. We shall, during the campaign, use all our efforts to see that only Progressives are nominated and elected by the Republicans for the various State and National offices. We propose also to see that the State Committee is controlled by those who favor the progressive principles as set forth by Theodore Roosevelt. An organization is under way and we shall have headquarters and push the fight from now on."

THE PRESIDENCY OF WILLIAM HOWARD TAFT

MARCH 4, 1909 – MARCH 4, 1913

As president, William Howard Taft exercised power cautiously, making modest efforts to maintain the national government's growing role in policymaking. Although the Republican Party nominated Taft for president with the expectation that he would continue the Progressive, or nationalist, agenda of his predecessor, Theodore Roosevelt, Taft in fact was a more conservative Republican. Roosevelt had aggressively expanded the boundaries of executive power; Taft adopted a more restrictive approach, seeking to ensure that his office did not exceed its constitutional authority. Taft's restrained personality was better suited to judicial than executive leadership, as demonstrated by his successful postpresidential appointment as the nation's chief justice.

A native of Cincinnati, Ohio, Taft came from a well-to-do family that appreciated the virtue of public service. His father, Alphonso Taft, was a successful lawyer who served as secretary of war and attorney general under President Ulysses S. Grant, and later became U.S. ambassador to Austria-Hungary and Russia. William Taft was a talented scholar and athlete who graduated second in his class at Yale University and then attended Cincinnati Law School, which later became part of the University of Cincinnati. Taft became active in local politics, serving as assistant prosecuting attorney and assistant city solicitor in Cincinnati, and then winning election to a judgeship on the Superior Court of Cincinnati.

Taft entered national politics in 1890, when President Benjamin Harrison appointed him solicitor general. Two years later, Taft became a federal circuit court judge, a position that he held for eight years, during which he also was dean of the University of Cincinnati Law School. In 1900 President William McKinley chose Taft to head the U.S. Philippines Commission,

which was responsible for setting up that country's civil government; Taft subsequently became governor-general of the Philippines. Although he initially had not wanted to leave the circuit court, Taft became active in establishing the Philippine government and even twice refused a Supreme Court appointment because of his pressing responsibilities in the Philippines. In 1904 President Theodore Roosevelt selected Taft to become secretary of war, and the two developed close ties that later led Taft to the presidency.

QUICK FACTS ON WILLIAM HOWARD TAFT

BIRTH	September 15, 1857, Cincinnati, Ohio
EDUCATION	Yale College Cincinnati Law School
FAMILY	Wife: Helen Herron Taft Children: Robert A. Taft, Helen H. Taft, Charles P. Taft
WHITE HOUSE PETS	Cow (Pauline Wayne)
PARTY	Republican
PREPRESIDENTIAL CAREER (SELECTED)	Assistant prosecuting attorney, Cincinnati, 1881–1882 Judge, Superior Court of Cincinnati, 1887–1890 U.S. solicitor general, 1890–1892 Judge, U.S. federal circuit court, 1892–1900 Dean, University of Cincinnati Law School, 1896–1900 President of Philippines Commission, 1900–1902 Governor-general of Philippines, 1901–1903 Secretary of war, 1904–1908
PRESIDENTIAL TERM	March 4, 1909–March 4, 1913
VICE PRESIDENT	James Schoolcraft Sherman (died October 30, 1912)
SELECTED EVENTS	Payne-Aldrich Tariff Act (1909) Throws first ball to open the baseball season in American League (1910) Mann-Elkins Act (1910) U.S. intervention in Honduras (1911) U.S. intervention in Nicaragua (1910, 1912) New Mexico and Arizona admitted to the Union (1912) Ratification of Sixteenth Amendment authorizing federal income tax (1913) Department of Commerce and Labor reorganized as two departments (1913)
POSTPRESIDENCY	Professor of law, Yale University, 1913–1921 Chief justice of the United States, 1921–1930
DEATH	March 8, 1930, Washington, D.C.

THE 1908 ELECTION

Taft ran for president in 1908 primarily because President Roosevelt had promised not to seek what would have been his third term. He supported Taft's nomination, and the Republican Party chose Taft on its first convention ballot and selected James Schoolcraft of New York as his running mate. Opposing Taft was three-time Democratic presidential candidate William Jennings Bryan and vice-presidential nominee John W. Kern of Indiana. Taft defeated Bryan, winning 7.6 million popular votes to Bryan's 6.4 million, and 321 votes in the Electoral College to Bryan's 162.

THE TAFT ADMINISTRATION

Given their close ties, Roosevelt expected that Taft would largely keep the same people and policies in place, but President Taft decided otherwise. He replaced almost all of Roosevelt's cabinet, keeping only Secretary of Agriculture James Wilson of Iowa. Philander Chase Knox of Pennsylvania, who had served as attorney general in Roosevelt's first term, became secretary of state, and Roosevelt's postmaster general, George von Lengerke Meyer of Massachusetts, became Taft's navy secretary. Taft's other appointees included Franklin MacVeagh of Illinois as treasury secretary, Jacob McGavock Dickinson of Tennessee as secretary of war (succeeded by Henry Lewis Stimson of New York in 1911), George W. Wickersham of New York as attorney general, Frank H. Hitchcock of Massachusetts as postmaster general, Richard A. Ballinger of Washington as interior secretary (succeeded by Walter L. Fisher of Illinois in 1911), and Charles Nagel of Missouri as secretary of commerce and labor. A majority of the cabinet came from the corporate legal sector, and none were Progressive Republicans, in clear contrast to Roosevelt's cabinet.

First Lady Helen Herron Taft was an active part of her husband's presidency. She established a new tradition by riding with the president from Capitol Hill to the White House following his inauguration in 1909. She was keenly interested in politics, particularly in women's suffrage. Mrs. Taft had a stroke in 1909 and underwent a lengthy recovery, but by 1911, she was well enough for the Tafts to celebrate their silver wedding anniversary in the White House. The Tafts had two sons, Robert Alphonso and Charles Phelps, and one daughter, Helen Herron. President Taft was over six feet tall and weighed more than 300 pounds, making him the heaviest person ever to occupy the Oval Office.

Major Issues

President Taft marked his departure from the Progressive agenda at the outset by approving the 1909 Payne-Aldrich Tariff, which barely reduced tariff rates. He furthered angered Roosevelt Progressives by not promoting conservation policies as aggressively as his predecessor; this issue sparked a public outcry (and congressional hearings) and led to the dismissal of Forestry Service head Gifford Pinchot, a Roosevelt appointee. Taft did succeed in passing the 1910 Mann-Elkins Act, which increased federal regulation of railroads and expanded the powers of the Interstate Commerce Commission. He continued Roosevelt's antitrust battles, and his administration ultimately filed about twice as many suits as the previous administration. But Taft's failure to maintain Republican unity severely hurt the party in the 1910 congressional midterm

elections, when the Democrats took control of the House and gained a dozen seats in the Senate.

In foreign affairs, the Taft administration pursued stability abroad, particularly in Latin America, through financial investments, a policy that became known as "dollar diplomacy." He tried, for example, to offer compensation to Colombia for its loss of Panama in the Roosevelt administration. President Taft also sent U.S. forces to Honduras and Nicaragua to establish order in response to revolutionary uprisings. In international trade, Taft negotiated a reciprocity treaty with Canada, which won Senate ratification but ultimately lost Canadian support. He also drafted a treaty to permit arbitration with Great Britain and France over international disputes, but the effort failed when the Senate refused to approve the agreement without amendments that in effect would have negated its purpose.

By 1912 Republican Progressives were so dissatisfied with Taft's policies that they bolted from the party and created their own National Progressive, or "Bull Moose" Party, which nominated Theodore Roosevelt for president. Roosevelt accepted the nomination and campaigned vigorously against Taft. With the Republican Party split, Democratic governor Woodrow Wilson of New Jersey won the election with an overwhelming majority in the Electoral College (forty states) but just 42 percent of the popular vote (nearly 6.3 million votes). Roosevelt came in second with 4.1 million popular votes and six states, and Taft placed third with nearly 3.5 million popular votes and two states.

Postpresidency

Departing the White House was not difficult for President Taft, who returned to his first love, the law, by becoming a law professor at Yale University. In 1916 he published a book about the presidency, *Our Chief Magistrate and His Powers*. The title revealed Taft's perspective that the nation's chief executive should focus foremost on constitutional rather than political responsibilities. Five years later, President Warren Harding appointed Taft chief justice of the United States, and Taft spent the rest of his life on the Supreme Court, retiring just a few weeks before his death in 1930. He was the first president to be buried in Arlington Cemetery.

The only person to serve in the White House and on the Supreme Court, Taft is one of the few presidents whose legacy is defined primarily by his postpresidential years.

"Tariff Bill Ready for House To-day," March 17, 1909

Within two weeks of taking office, President Taft called Congress into special session to consider tariff reform. But the Payne-Aldrich Tariff Act of 1909 fell far short of the president's original goals and alienated Progressive Republicans who had expected Taft to promote the same policies as his predecessor and mentor, Theodore Roosevelt.

MARCH 17, 1909
TARIFF BILL READY FOR HOUSE TO-DAY

Final Changes Made to Suit Cushman, New Member of Ways and Means Committee.
SHORT MESSAGE FROM TAFT
Only 333 Words In It and Both Houses Are Highly Pleased by Contrast
with Roosevelt.
Special to The New York Times

WASHINGTON, March 16.—Tariff making by Congress will begin to-morrow. President Taft sent his message on the subject to-day and the Payne bill, as finally drafted by the Republican members of the Ways and Means Committee, is ready to be placed before the House. It was to have been introduced to-day, but the appointment of Mr. Cushman of Washington to the Republican vacancy on the committee led to a recasting of schedules in which he was interested.

President Taft's message, which had been awaited with great interest, was presented to Congress soon after it convened to-day. It was as follows:

Text of President's Message.

To the Senate and House of Representatives:

I have convened the Congress in this extra session in order to enable it to give immediate consideration to the revision of the Dingley Tariff act. Conditions affecting production, manufacture, and business generally have so changed in the last twelve years as to require a readjustment and revision of the import duties imposed by that act. More than this, the present Tariff act, with the other sources of Government revenue, does not furnish income enough to pay the authorized expenditures. By July 1 next, the excess of expenses over receipts for the current fiscal year will equal $100,000,000.

The successful party in the late election is pledged to a revision of the tariff. The country, and the business community especially, expect it. The prospect of a change in the rates of import duties always cause a suspension or halt in business because of the uncertainty as to the changes to be made and their effect. It is therefore of the highest importance that the new bill should be agreed upon and passed with as much speed as possible consistent with its due and thorough consideration.

Justifies a Special Session.

For these reasons I have deemed the present to be an extraordinary occasion, within the meaning of the Constitution, justifying and requiring the calling of an extra session.

In my inaugural address I stated in a summary way the principles upon which, in my judgment, the revision of the tariff should proceed, and indicated at least one new source of revenue that might be properly resorted to in order to avoid a future deficit. It is not necessary for me to repeat what I then said.

I venture to suggest that the vital business interests of the country require that the attention of the Congress in this session be chiefly devoted to the consideration of the new tariff bill, and that the less time given to other subjects of legislation in this session the better for the country.

WILLIAM H. TAFT.

"PINCHOT OUSTED; PARTY WAR ON," JANUARY 8, 1910, AND "LA FOLLETTE ATTACKS TAFT," JANUARY 15, 1910

President Taft's dismissal of U.S. Forest Service chief Gifford Pinchot, a Roosevelt appointee, further divided the Republican Party. Pinchot had battled with Interior Secretary Richard A. Ballinger, and Progressive Republicans viewed the president's decision to support Ballinger as a betrayal of Roosevelt's conservation legacy. Congressional hearings found no evidence of wrongdoing, but revealed that the Taft administration was more sympathetic to business interests in natural resources than the Roosevelt administration, illustrating Taft's conservative Republican philosophy.

[T]he fight between the Roosevelt radicals and the conservative wing of the Republican Party is on in deadly earnest.

JANUARY 8, 1910
PINCHOT OUSTED; PARTY WAR ON

President Dismisses Forester, Censuring Him in Letter—
Two Others in Bureau Dropped.
REPUBLICANS BADLY SPLIT
Fight Between the Roosevelt Radicals and the Conservatives May Make
Serious Breach.
INSURGENTS DEFEAT CANNON.
Combine with Democrats and Take from Speaker Power to Appoint
Ballinger Investigators.
Special to The New York Times

WASHINGTON, Jan. 7.—President Taft has dismissed Gifford Pinchot, Chief of the Forestry Bureau, and the fight between the Roosevelt radicals and the conservative wing of the Republican Party is on in deadly earnest. The President's action came after a Cabinet session that lasted practically all day. When it broke up, just before dinner time this evening, there was issued at the White House a copy of a letter sent by the President to Mr. Pinchot. In this letter, after summing up the acts of the forester that led him to take such action, Mr. Taft said:

"By your conduct you have destroyed your usefulness as a helpful subordinate of the Government, and it therefore becomes my duty to direct the Secretary of Agriculture to remove you from your office as the Forester."

Secretary Wilson was swift in carrying out the decision of the President. He addressed to Mr. Pinchot, to Overton W. Price, Associate Forester, and Albert C. Shaw, assistant law officer of the Forestry Bureau, letters substantially identical. That to Mr. Pinchot reads:

Sir: By direction of the President you are hereby removed from your office as Forester. You will deliver possession of your office affairs belonging to the Government to Mr. Albert F. Potter, Assistant Forester.

Respectfully,
JAMES WILSON,
Secretary of Agriculture.

Mr. Price and Mr. Shaw were charged with being especially active in the anti-Ballinger propaganda.

Even before the President's letter was given out the fight began. It was in the House, and the conservatives met defeat at the hands of the radicals, aided by the Democrats. Speaker Cannon for once was helpless. The allies took away from him the power to appoint the House members of the joint committee to investigate the Ballinger-Pinchot affair, and placed it in the hands of the whole House. Their resolution to that effect was adopted by a vote of 149 to 146.

JANUARY 15, 1910
LA FOLLETTE ATTACKS TAFT.

Says Pinchot in Writing Letters Followed the Example of Ballinger.

MADISON, Wis., Jan. 14.—"The Ballinger letter called forth and was responsible for the Pinchot letter. The Ballinger letter received no rebuke from the President. The Pinchot letter is made the basis of an executive order removing from office a man of the highest character whose public service is an enduring monument to his name."

In this language Senator La Follette to-day, in the leading editorial of his magazine, characterizes the dismissal of Chief Forester Pinchot. In contrast he holds up the fact that Secretary of the Interior Ballinger sent a letter to Senator Jones of Washington which was read on the floor of the Senate in the same manner as Chief Forester Pinchot's letter to Dolliver was read.

"Search the records for a case to match it," says Senator La Follette, referring to the Ballinger letter. "Behold a member of the Cabinet, whose department has been charged with corrupt or improper practices relative to coal lands in Alaska, angered at other officials of the Executive Department because, as he says, they are the source and inspiration of the charges. Behold him ignore his superior, the President, and come by letter upon the floor of the Senate to file charges against his official colleagues of the Forestry Service, members of the executive family. He does not complain that they have violated any statute or betrayed any public trust, but that they have criticised and inspired criticism and charges against other officials of the same administrative household and urges that they be investigated by Congress. He ignores the fact that under the Constitution the Executive and the legislative are separate, independent, and co-ordinate branches of the Government; that Congress has no authority over these executive officials; that the President alone can deal with them, acquit or condemn, approve or punish."

"TAFT IS NOT PLEASED BY ROOSEVELT PLAN," SEPTEMBER 3, 1910

Dissatisfied with Taft's leadership, former president Roosevelt by 1910 had become a spokesman for the Progressive wing of the Republican Party. Roosevelt advocated a "New Nationalism" that would expand the federal government's oversight of business practices and labor conditions. As *The New York Times* reported, President Taft was critical of this agenda, which he viewed as extending the government's reach beyond its constitutional authority.

SEPTEMBER 3, 1910
TAFT IS NOT PLEASED BY ROOSEVELT PLAN

Tells Friend That Constitution Must Be Changed to Carry Out Some Ideas.
PRESIDENT NOT TO STUMP
Takes Up Public Business—Civil Service for Assistant Postmasters—
No Extra Session of the Senate.
Special to The New York Times

BEVERLY, Mass., Sept. 2.—President Taft to-day had a pointed comment for the "new nationalism" that his predecessor has been launching in the West. He told a friend who saw him at the cottage that it would be necessary to revise the Constitution before the Roosevelt doctrine could be put into operation. The President is not eager to write a new Constitution.

Only a few sentences were spoken on the subject. The President, however, left no doubt whatever about his attitude. He mentioned two items in the Roosevelt platform. One was the enactment of a child labor law, the other "comprehensive workmen's compensation acts." The President spoke of the first as unconstitutional and of the second in like vein, adding that it trenched upon the authority of the States.

His comments applied specifically to plank thirteen of Col. Roosevelt's platform as announced at Osawatomie last Wednesday. That plank calls for the regulation of the terms and conditions of labor by means of comprehensive working-men's compensation acts, and "State and National laws to regulate child labor and the work of women." The Senate a few Winters ago engaged in a long and profound legal debate upon the constitutionality of a child labor law, and the opinion of sound lawyers then was that Congress could not enact such a law that would stand in the courts. Finally a provision was enacted authorizing an investigation by Federal officials.

The President, in speaking of the difficulty of enacting the Roosevelt programme, alluded to troubles the country was experiencing in getting the income tax amendment to the Constitution ratified. He mentioned no other planks in the Roosevelt platform, some of which are in accord with his own activities as President, and the conversation passed to other topics.

"Democrats Sweep Country; Win Congress, Many States," November 9, 1910

Intraparty rivalry cost the Republican Party dearly in the 1910 congressional midterm elections, when Democrats took control of the House and increased their seats in the Senate. President Taft faced divided government for the rest of his term, which further complicated his efforts to enact his policy agenda.

NOVEMBER 9, 1910
DEMOCRATS SWEEP COUNTRY; WIN CONGRESS, MANY STATES

New York, New Jersey, Ohio, Massachusetts, Indiana and Connecticut Carried.
HOUSE DEMOCRATIC BY 40 VOTES
Foss Wins Massachusetts by 22,000—Beveridge Beaten for Senator in Indiana—
Baldwin Elected in Connecticut.

The Democratic Party carried the Union yesterday. The landslide put the historic Folger year, 1882, in the background and eclipsed the avalanche years of 1890 and 1892. In the language of Col. Theodore Roosevelt, the Democrats whipped the Republicans "to a frazzle" and put them "over the ropes."

Such traditionally Republican States as Massachusetts followed in Maine's lead by tremendous majorities. New Hampshire was long in doubt and finally elected Senator Bass, the Republican candidate for Governor, by a majority of only about 6,000.

New York took her place at the head of the procession, with a Democratic majority for John A. Dix of 64,074 and elected a Democratic Legislature. A Democratic Senator will succeed Chauncey M. Depew.

President Taft has got to face the one danger he most dreaded and which he besought the Republican voters to prevent—a hostile House of Representatives to nullify what remains of his legislative programme. The next House will be Democratic by a majority of 40. Whatever is to be done in the way of tariff reform will have to be done by mutual forbearance and agreement on the part of a Republican Senate and a Democratic House—unless, indeed, later returns should indicate the election of a Democratic Senate.

In the United States Senate the Democrats gain four seats certainly and probably seven.

The two great leaders of the Republican Party, Taft and Roosevelt, have received body blows. Their own States have voted for the opposition party. Harmon defeated Harding in Ohio by a great plurality, probably 40,000.

President William Howard Taft throws the first ball of the 1911 baseball season—a tradition he started the year before.

Source: AP Photo

"Reapportionment Passes," August 4, 1911

In 1911 Congress increased the size of the U.S. House of Representatives to 433 members, and ultimately to 435 when Arizona and New Mexico were admitted to the Union. The number of seats has remained unchanged since then, raising questions about whether the ratio of constituents to elected officials has become too great to achieve genuine representative democracy.

AUGUST 4, 1911
REAPPORTIONMENT PASSES.

Senate Adopts Amendments Affecting Election of New House Members.

Special to The New York Times

WASHINGTON, Aug. 3.—After safely voting down all amendments aimed at holding down the size of the House of Representatives, the Senate this afternoon passed the House Reapportionment bill without a roll call. Two minor amendments, both proposed by Mr. Burton of Ohio, were adopted. One amendment permits the initiative and referendum to be applied to the State redistricting statutes in States where that system prevails. The other provides that members at large in States where the new districts are not marked off before the next election shall be nominated in the same way that the candidates for Governor in the particular State are named.

The bill as passed increases the membership of the House from 391 to 433, with a provision that when Arizona and New Mexico are admitted they shall each have one seat. The Burton amendment allowing for the application of the initiative and referendum by declaring that the redistricting shall be done "in the manner provided by the laws" of the State instead of simply by the Legislature, as the House bill read, was adopted by an almost strictly party vote of 39 to 28—Mr. Clarke of Arkansas alone voting with the Republicans.

This amendment was aimed especially to meet conditions in Ohio and Missouri. The effort of Mr. Reed of Missouri, where the Democrats are particularly afraid of the action of the Republican Governor, to kill the effect of this amendment by a substitute failed by a vote of 29 to 38. Each party voted solidly, except that Mr. Bourne of Oregon bolted the majority and voted with the Democrats.

Senator Root, who yesterday spoke warmly against increasing the already unwieldy House, then offered his amendment keeping the present membership, but redistributing allotments. Republicans from States that lost under the Root proposal joined the Democrats, and the amendment went out by a vote of 23 to 46. Mr. McCumber then tried to fix the number at 405, but a vote of 22 to 47 declared against him.

That put the bill on its passage and a roll call was not demanded. The bill will reach the House to-morrow and will then probably be sent to conference on the amendments, though no delay is expected to result from the disagreement of the two Houses.

• •

"An Untrammeled Judiciary," August 16, 1911

In 1911 Congress approved statehood for Arizona and New Mexico, but President Taft vetoed the legislation because of a provision in Arizona's state constitution that permitted recall votes to remove judges from office. *The Times* agreed with the president's rationale and praised his "masterly analysis of the real nature of popular government." President Taft approved the admission of both states in 1912, making them the forty-seventh and forty-eighth states to enter the Union.

AUGUST 16, 1911
EDITORIAL
AN UNTRAMMELED JUDICIARY.

One of the best American State papers that we can recall was sent to the House of Representatives yesterday by President Taft giving his reasons for disapproving the admission of Arizona and New Mexico as States. These reasons relate wholly to the provision in the Constitution of Arizona for the recall of Judges by popular vote. Since Arizona and New Mexico were coupled in the same resolution, Mr. Taft was required to deal with both at once, though the Constitution of the latter is not objectionable.

The President brushes aside all narrow considerations and bases his action on the broad ground of the Executive responsibility in the enactment of laws as to which "my discretion," he remarks, "is equal to that of Congress."

We cannot without injustice to the document summarize the argument of the President. His message is one that every citizen should read, ponder, and inwardly digest. It is very comprehensive, soberly stated, clear, simple, and practical. It includes, of course, the President's view of the functions of the judiciary, the utility of those functions, the conditions in which they should be performed, and the effect of their performance on the general welfare. His large experience on the bench, his eminence as a lawyer and a Judge, give to this part of the message a value and authority that it would be hard to match in the country. Still more valuable, however, is his masterly analysis of the real nature of popular government as it is provided for by constitutional law in the various States of the Union. Here in relatively few words, but with real amplitude, he defines the purposes of government, the principles underlying our method of government, and the actual rights and duties of the citizen in a democratic community.

Take this passage:

In a popular government the laws are made by the people—not by all the people, but by those supposed and declared to be competent for the purpose, as males over 21 years of age, and not by all of these, but by a majority of them only. Now, as the Government is for all the people, and is not solely for a majority of them, the majority in exercising control either directly or through its agents is bound to exercise power for the benefit of the minority as well as the majority. . . . A popular government is not a government of a majority, by a majority, for a majority of the people. It is a government of the whole people, by a majority of the whole people under such rules and checks as will secure a wise, just, and beneficent government for all the people. It is said you can always trust the people to do justice. If that means all the people, and they all agree, you can. But ordinarily they do not all agree, and the maxim is interpreted to mean that you can always trust a majority of the people. This is not invariably true; and every limitation imposed by the people upon the power of the majority in their Constitutions is an admission that it is not always true. No honest, clear-headed man, however great a lover of popular government, can deny that the unbridled expression of the majority of a community converted hastily into law or action would sometimes make a government tyrannical and cruel. Constitutions are checks upon the hasty action of the majority. They are the self-imposed restraints of a whole people upon a majority of them to secure sober action and a respect for the rights of the minority, and of the individual in his relation to other individuals, and in his relation to the whole people in their character as a State or Government.

No more pregnant statement of the nature of a popular government, and of the essential provisions for securing the union of liberty and justice under popular government, is known to us. The application of these principles to the case in hand, the description of the actual system of recall for Judges included in the Arizona Constitution, and of the specific ways in which this system is sure to operate, are as admirable as the general statement. We print the message in full, and we earnestly urge our readers to study it candidly and carefully, especially those who may have found in the notion of recall a manifestation of the spirit of liberty. They can hardly fail to find in it, on the contrary, provision for the worst form of denial of just liberty.

- -

"Taft Urges Treaty to Help Honduras," October 14, 1911

President Taft's foreign policy toward Central America focused primarily on using American investments to promote stability in nations such as Honduras and Nicaragua. The president objected to the description of his agenda as "dollar diplomacy," saying it "invoke[d] the condemnation of the muckraking journals." The term gained popularity, however, and is still used today to describe Taft's efforts to achieve political advances in these nations through financial strategies.

OCTOBER 14, 1911
TAFT URGES TREATY TO HELP HONDURAS
He Says Central American Trade Will Be Valuable if Countries Are Aided Financially.
PLAN OF NEW YORK BANKERS
President Makes First Important Speech in California at Sacramento—
Now in San Francisco.

SACRAMENTO, Cal., Oct. 13.—President Taft's first important speech in California was delivered here to-day from the steps of the State Capitol Building. The President spoke in behalf of proposed treaties with Nicaragua and Honduras and vigorously defended the policy of the Administration, which he said "muckraking journals" have labeled "dollar diplomacy."

Broadly speaking, Mr. Taft said, the proposed treaties with these countries would secure for them a financial agent in the United States which would settle their existing debts on a just basis and which would point the road to peace and prosperity to two republics rich in natural resources but torn by strife and revolution.

Mr. Taft pointed out the efficacy of a similar arrangement with Santo Domingo, where this Government collects the customs and sees that foreign debts are paid, exercising a beneficent supervision that Mr. Taft said has accrued to the up-building of Santo Domingo.

Objection to the treaties in the United States Senate, the President said, was based largely on the proposition that they would make entangling alliances with republics in this hemisphere for the promotion of a banking contract since the money for the payment of the debts of the two republics would be furnished by American interests.

Another objection discussed by the President was that the Monroe Doctrine was sufficient bond between the United States and the Latin-American republics.

"It is objected that this is 'dollar diplomacy,' " said Mr. Taft, "and that we ought to have none of it. Give a dog a bad name and you know what follows. To call a piece of State craft 'dollar diplomacy' is to invoke the condemnation of the muckraking journals whose chief capital is the use of phrases of a lurid character."

The President said further:

"We have heard a great deal during the past six months in favor of general arbitration treaties for the promotion of the peace of the world. I believe there has been of late more genuine expression of sentiment among all the people of the earth for peace than ever before in the world's history. The craving for some effective means of promoting peace grows not so much out of actual war as out of the desperation with which the great nations are increasing the stupendous burden of armies and armament, making Europe an armed camp, with the growing menace of bankruptcy.

"In Honduras there have been seven revolutions in fifteen years. Its territory reaches from ocean to ocean, and its neutrality is rarely preserved when its neighbors are at war. These conditions necessitate the keeping up, at great expense, of its army. General arbitration treaties can have little influence over countries subject to these conditions. The shifting of Government from one group to another would weaken greatly the practical binding force of such treaties, and the unsettled condition of the population makes it necessary that a more effective method to secure tranquillity and quiet must be found, and thereby the forces among these peoples making for civilization and progress must be given full opportunity to achieve their beneficent ends.

Importance of Custom Houses.

"Our experience with Santo Domingo, once a volcano of revolution constantly in eruption, suggests a possible and practicable method of meeting the same difficulties that are presented to these Central American republics. A study of the revolutions shows that their first object is the seizure of custom houses through which import taxes are collected. The custom houses are the only sources of revenue at such times, and provide the sinews of war for the professional revolutionist. With these as a basis of operation he moves into the country and ultimately and for the time being secures control of the whole republic."

"An American Force Lands in Nicaragua," August 6, 1912

President Taft was forced to augment his financial foreign policy program with military force when rebels in Central America threatened U.S. business interests in the region. In 1910 and 1912 the United States sent U.S. troops to Nicaragua to protect American lives and property there, illustrating the limits of "dollar diplomacy."

AUGUST 6, 1912
AN AMERICAN FORCE LANDS IN NICARAGUA

One Hundred Bluejackets and Marines from the *Annapolis* Sent to Managua.

ORDER RESTORED BY THEM

Nicaraguan Government's Inability to Protect American-Owned Property

Was Confessed.

Special to The New York Times

WASHINGTON, Aug. 5.—At the request of the Diaz Government in Nicaragua the United States "intervened" yesterday afternoon, landing 100 bluejackets and marines from the gunboat *Annapolis* for the protection of American property.

For the time being Minister Weitzel and Americans on the spot say the situation seems improved. But it is not unlikely that within the next few days a much larger force will be required, and in that case marines will be sent from Guantanamo.

The outbreak comes as an apparent setback to Secretary Knox's "dollar diplomacy" policy. It is pointed out, however, that should the situation in the little republic call for more serious intervention, in the end the Senate may be forced, for the protection of American interests in Nicaragua, to ratify the treaty now sleeping on the Senate executive calendar and guarantee a loan of $10,000,000. That loan, first offered by the Morgan syndicate, is now sponsored by the Whitney Central Bank of New Orleans, representing many individuals.

Should the ratification of the treaty, as the only means of insuring order in Nicaragua, result from the present demand for American marines in the republic, it would really prove a step forward for the Knox policy. That seems to look in general toward preserving stability in the smaller republics by putting them under bond to keep the peace. That would be insured by loans guaranteed by this Government, which would hold the National finances under strict control.

The immediate trouble yesterday arose from the seizure by Gen. Mena's rebel forces of vessels on Lake Nicaragua, belonging to the American syndicate operating the railroad and steamship line from the coast at Corinto into the interior. These vessels were used by the rebels in an effort to bombard the unfortified town of San Jorge.

When Minister Weitzel learned the facts and heard the protest of the Americans against this seizure of their property he took the matter up at once with the Diaz Government. The Nicaraguan Foreign Office gave him the answer that the Government was using every power at its command to maintain order and protect all foreign property, but could give no assurance of being able to do so. The Foreign Minister said he regretted that the entire force of the Government was required to put down disorders in various parts of the country, and he would not be able for the present to comply with the request of the American Minister. This answer came to Mr. Weitzel in a formal note, which closed with the request that the forces of the United States be employed to protect American citizens in Nicaragua.

The fact is that the Nicaraguan Government, with a depleted treasury and a condition of starvation among portions of the population, is confronted with an impossible situation. The long delay in the American loan, which depends upon the ratification of the Nicaraguan treaty, has thrown the Nicaraguan Government into financial despair.

Minister Weitzel yesterday, after receiving the request that this country protect American property in Nicaragua, demanded of Gen. Mena that the property that had been seized be returned, and at once asked Commander Terhune of the *Annapolis* at Corinto to land a force to protect American property. Within a few minutes a hundred bluejackets were landed. At 3:30 o'clock yesterday afternoon they reached Managua, and quiet was restored there for the time being.

The *Tacoma* is on the way from Guantanamo to Bluefields, and will probably reach there to-morrow. The collier *Justin* arrived at Corinto to-day, but she has only a merchant crew, and would be of use simply to give protection to the cable station.

To-day's advices regarding the Nicaraguan revolution report that the Government forces have been defeated at Tipatapa, near Managua. Leon will probably be declared in a state of siege because of the release of a large number of political prisoners. The Government expects to protect the San Juan del Sur cable station.

"WILSON FIRST, TAFT SECOND," NOVEMBER 5, 1912, AND "WILSON WINS," NOVEMBER 6, 1912

The Times endorsed Woodrow Wilson's election in the 1912 presidential race, but it also supported President Taft over his erstwhile mentor and independent candidate Roosevelt. The paper held that a second-place finish by Roosevelt would signal the collapse of the Republican Party and "the rise of discordant factions in place of a compact organization." But the paper was wrong on both counts: Roosevelt came in second and well ahead of Taft, but the Republican Party rebounded from the internal dissension and elected a president again in 1920.

> [T]he Democratic Party has wandered in strange places, has committed itself to unsafe doctrines under distrusted leaders. That has been cured. The Democracy has returned from its wanderings.

NOVEMBER 5, 1912
EDITORIAL
WILSON FIRST, TAFT SECOND.

The first and vital object to be accomplished to-day is the election of Woodrow Wilson. It is next in importance that Mr. Taft should lead Mr. Roosevelt in the Electoral and the popular vote. It has for many years been desirable that political power in the Nation should be transferred from the Republicans to the Democrats. The desired transfer has been postponed because the Democratic Party has wandered in strange places, has committed itself to unsafe doctrines under distrusted leaders. That has been cured. The Democracy has returned from its wanderings, it is again a united party, and its candidate, passing in triumph all the tests and challenges of the campaign, stands before the country as a man of high equipment for the office, worthy of the full confidence of the people. Without misgiving, with entire safety, and to the advantage of the Nation, the Democrats may now be returned to power. The country has made up its mind upon that point. Mr. Wilson will be elected to-day.

It is to the interest of the Nation that the Republican Party should be preserved as an organized, coherent opposition. The public welfare is not served by the collapse of a great party, by the rise of discordant factions in place of a compact organization. It is of great moment, it is of urgent need, that the Republican candidate should come out second in the poll, second, not third, in the Electoral College and in the popular vote. The party will then be in a position to rebuild, to free itself from the influences that have diminished its estate, to hold again the place in the politics and in the affairs of the Nation to which it is entitled by its historic achievements.

More urgent yet is the need that the Progressive Party and its candidates should be put in third place. It would be of ill omen, it would be a disquieting indication of unsound popular judgement, of unsteadiness, and of want of sense and responsibility in the electorate, if so large a part of the people should yield to the appeals of Mr. Roosevelt as to put him second in the polling. The essential part of his programme is the crippling and overthrow of institutions of which we are with good reason most proud, of established parts of our Governmental system which we cannot without the gravest danger permit to be effaced. That Mr. Roosevelt is unsafe in counsel and in policy is proved again by the authoritative review of his Madison Square Garden speech in which Elihu Root, John G. Milburn, Louis Marshall, and William D. Guthrie show that in his attack upon the courts of this State Mr. Roosevelt totally misapprehended the law and absolutely misstated the facts of the cases, very important cases, upon which he based his arguments. His misstatements were not of negligible detail, but of the very substance of the litigations. Sober-minded men do not need to be warned that a man who blunders in this way with respect to decisions of courts of record, whose appeals for votes rest upon the grossest misapprehension of law and fact, cannot with safety be vested with the highest powers under our Government of laws. We are accustomed to feel and to believe that the American people are enlightened, that their collective judgment is sound. It would be a cause not merely for chagrin but for apprehension if the larger part of the great party that has so long held power should now yield to the persuasions of a man whom in their wisdom and their calmness they should reject.

NOVEMBER 6, 1912
WILSON WINS

He Gets 409 Electoral Votes; Roosevelt, 107, and Taft, 15.
206,000 OVER TAFT IN NEW YORK
Illinois and Pennsylvania for Roosevelt, but Close—House Democratic By 157—
May be Senate, Too—Cannon Beaten

Woodrow Wilson was elected President yesterday and Thomas R. Marshall Vice President by an Electoral majority which challenged comparison with the year in which Horace Greeley was defeated by Grant. Until now that year has always been the standard of comparison for disastrous defeats, but the downfall of the Republican Party this year runs it a close second.

The apparent results at 4 o'clock this morning gave Wilson 409 Electoral votes, Roosevelt 107, and Taft 15.

Wilson carried 38 States, Roosevelt 6, and Taft 4.

The Republican Party is wiped off the map. Nearly everywhere Taft ran third, with Roosevelt capturing a large majority of the old Republican vote, and in many States Taft's vote was almost negligible.

New York gave Wilson a plurality over Taft of about 206,000. Wilson's vote in the State was 698,000, Taft's 493,000, and Roosevelt's 419,000.

The Democratic plurality in the House of Representatives will not be less than 157, and the United States Senate will probably be Democratic also.

• •

"INCOME TAX RATIFIED BY DELAWARE'S VOTE," FEBRUARY 4, 1913

The Sixteenth Amendment was ratified in 1913 and authorized the levying of a federal income tax. Although the president does not formally play a role in amending the Constitution, President Taft had recommended an income tax amendment during the debate over the Payne-Aldrich Tariff in 1909.

FEBRUARY 4, 1913
INCOME TAX RATIFIED BY DELAWARE'S VOTE

Similar Action by Wyoming and New Mexico Gives Two Over the Majority Needed.
CONGRESS NOW FREE TO ACT
President Will Issue Proclamation Adding New Amendment to Constitution—
Result of Four Years' Effort.
Special to The New York Times

WASHINGTON, Feb. 3.—The first change in the Federal Constitution in forty-three years was made certain to-day through the ratification of the income tax amendment by the Legislatures of Delaware, Wyoming, and New Mexico. This will be known as the Sixteenth Amendment. Its text reads:

Article 16. The Congress shall have power to lay and collect taxes on incomes, from whatever source derived, without apportionment among the several States, and without regard to any census or enumeration.

The assent of three-fourths of the States was necessary to the adoption of the amendment. Up to to-day thirty-five States, or one less than the required three-fourths, had ratified the proposed Constitutional change. With Delaware, Wyoming, and New Mexico recorded in the affirmative, the ratification has been accomplished with two votes to spare, and it is expected that New Jersey will fall into line before the amendment is proclaimed. When the Secretary of State of the United States has been notified by the governments of Delaware or Wyoming, or both, the President will issue a proclamation, setting forth that the Sixteenth Amendment has been added to the Federal Constitution.

The last previous amendment, the Fifteenth, which prohibited restriction of the voting franchise on account of race, color or previous condition of servitude, was proposed to the States by Congress on Feb. 27, 1869. It was proclaimed a part of the Federal Constitution on March 30, 1870, having been ratified by twenty-nine of the thirty-seven States.

- -

"What Taft Plans at Yale," February 26, 1913

After completing his term, President Taft returned to his undergraduate alma mater, Yale University, to become a law professor. He declared his great interest in making sure that students "appreciate" the Constitution. Taft stayed at Yale until his appointment as chief justice of the United States in 1921.

FEBRUARY 26, 1913
WHAT TAFT PLANS AT YALE.
Need of Respect for Constitution and Danger of Political Nostrums.

NEW HAVEN, Conn., Feb. 25.—President Taft, in a letter to *The Yale News* to-day, discusses the work which he is soon to take up at Yale as Kent Professor of Law in the college. In part he says:

"It is with no great claim to erudition that I come back to Yale, but it is with the earnest hope that from a somewhat extensive and varied experience I may have gleaned something which may be of use to the young men with whom I shall come in almost daily contact. There is need that our young men should appreciate the Constitution of the United States, under which we have enjoyed so many blessings and under which we must work out our political and economic salvation. And this need is especially keen in a day when that instrument is regarded so lightly by a class of fanatical enthusiasts seeking short cuts to economic perfection, on the one hand, and by unscrupulous demagogues who, to promote their own interests, do not hesitate to inculcate disrespect and even contempt for the Constitution and the laws enacted under it, on the other.

"If I can help the men of Yale to know the value of our institutions and to appreciate the danger of accepting every nostrum that is offered and of abandoning those foundations without which our Government could not have been, I will be thrice content."

THE PRESIDENCY OF **WOODROW WILSON**

MARCH 4, 1913 – MARCH 4, 1921

The presidency of Woodrow Wilson brought the United States into war and established a vision of an international community that would work together to prevent future interstate conflicts. After World War I ended, President Wilson was influential in drafting the Treaty of Versailles and particularly in designing the League of Nations, the precursor to the United Nations. Although Wilson failed in his effort to convince the Senate that the United States should join the league, he is credited with being one of the original architects of a global system of states that would emphasize collaboration over conflict. He also has the distinction of being the only American president with a doctoral degree, and in a discipline most relevant to the executive office, namely, government.

Born Thomas Woodrow Wilson in Virginia in 1856, he was raised in the South, in both Georgia and South Carolina. His father, a Presbyterian minister, was a pastor and later a seminary teacher. Wilson attended Davidson College in North Carolina for a year, but dropped out due to illness. He then enrolled at Princeton University, where he studied government and was active in debate. Wilson studied law at the University of Virginia, but he dropped out again because of ill health and later completed his law studies independently. After practicing law for a few years in Atlanta, Wilson commenced graduate studies in history and government at Johns Hopkins University, earning his doctorate in 1886.

Wilson taught history and political science at Bryn Mawr College, Wesleyan University, and Princeton, and he also coached the football team at Wesleyan. In 1885 he published *Congressional Government*, in which he advocated a parliamentary system of government and paid little attention to the institution of the presidency. After teaching at Princeton for more than a decade, Wilson was chosen unanimously by the trustees to become president of the university. He served in that position until 1910, when he was elected governor of New Jersey. Two years later, Wilson, who had not held political office before becoming governor, became the Democratic Party's successful presidential candidate.

THE 1912 ELECTION

Wilson's presidential victory in 1912 was due at least in part to a split within the Republican Party. Former president Theodore Roosevelt had contested his successor, incumbent president William Howard Taft, for the Republican nomination. When Taft won, Roosevelt's supporters bolted from the party and formed an independent Progressive Party, known as the Bull Moose Party, to mount Roosevelt's candidacy. In the general election, Roosevelt won just over 4 million popular votes, Taft won almost 3.5 million, and Wilson nearly 6.3 million. The Socialist Party presidential candidate, Eugene V. Debs of Indiana, who had run for president three times previously, won just over 900,000 popular votes.

Wilson, who had been nominated on the forty-sixth ballot at the Democratic National Convention, with Thomas R. Marshall of Indiana selected as his running mate, did win an overwhelming majority in the Electoral College, with 435 votes to Roosevelt's 88 and Taft's 8. Despite his strong showing in the Electoral College, Wilson prevailed in the race with less than 50 percent of the popular vote.

QUICK FACTS ON WOODROW WILSON

BIRTH	December 29,1856, Staunton, Va.
EDUCATION	Davidson College College of New Jersey (now Princeton University), 1879 University of Virginia Law School Independent law studies Johns Hopkins University, Ph.D., political science, 1886
FAMILY	First Wife: Ellen Louise Axson Wilson (died August 6, 1914) Children: Margaret Woodrow Wilson, Jessie Woodrow Wilson, Eleanor Randolph Wilson Second Wife: Edith Bolling Galt Wilson
WHITE HOUSE PETS	Tobacco-chewing ram ("Old Ike"); sheep (to cut lawn costs)
PARTY	Democratic
PREPRESIDENTIAL CAREER (SELECTED)	Law practice, Atlanta, Ga., 1882–1883 Teaches history and political science, Bryn Mawr College, 1885 Publishes *Congressional Government*, 1885 Professor, Wesleyan University, 1888–1890 Professor of jurisprudence and social economy, Princeton, 1890–1902 President of Princeton University, 1902–1910 Governor of New Jersey, 1911–1913
PRESIDENTIAL TERMS	March 4, 1913–March 4, 1917 March 4, 1917–March 4, 1921
VICE PRESIDENT	Thomas Riley Marshall
SELECTED EVENTS	Ratification of Seventeenth Amendment (1913) Underwood-Simmons Tariff Act (1913) Federal Reserve Act (1913) World War I begins (1914) Creation of Federal Trade Commission (1914) Clayton Anti-Trust Act (1914) Sinking of *Lusitania* by German submarine (1915) U.S. signs treaty making Haiti a protectorate (1916) U.S. troops sent to Mexico to search for rebel Francisco "Pancho" Villa (1916) Federal Farm Loan Act (1916) Keating-Owen Child Labor Act (1916) Adamson Act (1916) German submarines sink three U.S. merchant vessels (1917) United States enters World War I (1917) Espionage Act (1917) Sedition Act (1918) Wilson presents "Fourteen Points" to Congress (1918) Ratification of Eighteenth Amendment (1919) Treaty of Versailles signed; rejected by Senate (1919) Ratification of Nineteenth Amendment (1920) Awarded Nobel Peace Prize (1920)
DEATH	February 3, 1924, Washington, D.C.

The Wilson Administration (First Term)

The cabinet in the Wilson administration was composed of ten executive departments. To head the departments, President Wilson selected people who reflected the geographic and political diversity of the Democratic Party. Secretary of State William Jennings Bryan of Nebraska, for example, had thrice run for president on the Democratic ticket and spoke for agricultural interests in the party. Navy Secretary Josephus Daniels of North Carolina represented the South. Secretary of the Interior Franklin K. Lane hailed from California, Agriculture Secretary David F. Houston came from Missouri, and Postmaster General Albert S. Burleson was from Texas. From the Northeast, Judge Lindley M. Garrison of New Jersey became secretary of war, and William B. Wilson of Pennsylvania the secretary of labor. Three cabinet appointees came from New York: Attorney General James C. McReynolds (a future Supreme Court justice and born and raised in the South), Treasury Secretary William G. McAdoo, and Commerce Secretary William C. Redfield.

President Wilson's first wife, Ellen, died in 1914, and the oldest of the Wilson's daughters, Margaret, served as White House hostess. In 1915 the president married Edith B. Galt, who took over the first lady duties. Social events halted in the White House when the president suffered a stroke that paralyzed him in the left arm and leg in 1919. Edith Wilson controlled the president's schedule after his stroke and through the remainder of his presidency, deciding who would see him and which materials he would review.

Major Issues (First Term)

One of Wilson's most significant contributions to the presidency was his use of rhetoric to promote his policy agenda. Breaking with more than a hundred years of tradition, Wilson spoke directly to Congress in presenting his first State of the Union address in 1913. Not since John Adams had a president treated this constitutionally required message as an opportunity for public ceremony and discourse. The primary subject of the address, tariff reform, was less significant than the president's public address.

At the same time, trade and economic policy formed an important part of Wilson's first-term agenda. He lowered tariffs with the Underwood-Simmons Tariff Act of 1913, which dropped rates to their lowest level in more than fifty years. The law also implemented the Sixteenth Amendment by levying an income tax. The Federal Reserve Act of 1913 created federal banks to oversee monetary policy. The Clayton Anti-Trust Act of 1914 increased the government's power to regulate corporate trusts, and the creation of the Federal Trade Commission that same year established government oversight of business. The Adamson Act of 1916 authorized an eight-hour day for railroad workers.

In foreign policy, the Wilson administration negotiated a treaty with Colombia to provide compensation for its loss of Panama, but it failed in the Senate. In response to civil warfare in Haiti and the Dominican Republic, President Wilson sent troops to restore order, action that began a twenty-year U.S. occupation of Haiti and a ten-year occupation of the Dominican Republic. U.S. troops also intervened in the Mexican civil war and ultimately recognized the new government it had initially opposed.

Perhaps the most significant event in world affairs during Wilson's first term was the outbreak of World War I in August 1914. The United States pledged neutrality in the conflict, but this policy was sorely tested in 1915, when a German submarine sank the British ship *Lusitania,* killing more than one hundred Americans. The Wilson administration demanded that Germany halt unrestricted submarine warfare, but the president, reflecting both congressional and public interest, still hoped to avoid war.

The 1916 Election

Wilson's successful diplomacy in 1916 enabled him to campaign for reelection with the slogan "He kept us out of war." The Democratic Party nominated Wilson and Vice President Marshall for a second term by acclamation on the first convention ballot. The Republican Party nominated former New York governor Charles Evan Hughes, who had resigned from the U.S. Supreme Court to run for president, and selected Charles W. Fairbanks of Indiana as his running mate. The Progressive Party tried to nominate Theodore Roosevelt again, but he declined to run.

The election results were so close that President Wilson went to sleep on November 7, 1916, thinking he had lost to Hughes. (Several newspapers actually reported the next morning that Wilson had lost, based on early returns that indicated—erroneously—that Hughes would prevail in California.) Wilson was even prepared to make a victorious Hughes secretary of state and then enable him to ascend to the presidency immediately—rather than wait through a four-month transition—by having Vice President Marshall resign and then doing the same himself. But in fact, Wilson narrowly prevailed in the Electoral College, with 277 votes to Hughes's 254, and more than 9 million popular votes to Hughes's 8.5 million. Due to votes cast for other candidates, including more than half a million votes for the Socialist Party nominee, Wilson won election for a second time with less than 50 percent of the popular vote.

THE WILSON ADMINISTRATION (SECOND TERM)

All of Wilson's cabinet continued well into his second term, and three cabinet appointees—the secretaries of the Navy and Labor Departments and the postmaster general—served through Wilson's entire presidency. Robert Lansing of New York had replaced William Jennings Bryan as secretary of state in 1915, and he served until the last year of the Wilson administration. Secretary of War Newton D. Baker of Ohio took office in 1916, and he served through Wilson's second term. Carter Glass of Virginia became treasury secretary in 1918, and Alexander M. Palmer of Pennsylvania was appointed attorney general in 1919. In addition to making changes at the State and Treasury Departments in his last year in office, President Wilson also appointed new secretaries of the interior, agriculture, and commerce toward the end of his second term. He appointed a woman, Annette A. Adams, to be assistant attorney general in 1920.

MAJOR ISSUES (SECOND TERM)

Within a month of Wilson's second inauguration, his campaign slogan of keeping the United States out of the war in Europe had become outdated. On April 2, 1917, in response to Germany's continued submarine warfare, the president, saying U.S. intervention was necessary to make the world "safe for democracy," asked Congress for a declaration of war. Four days later, the United States formally entered World War I. In support of the war, Congress approved emergency powers for President Wilson to manage the economy—including oversight of food and fuel, as well as the provision of materials for war-related industries—and to control the nation's railroad system. Congress approved the Selective Service Act to increase the army's size in wartime. The president and Congress approved two controversial laws, the Espionage Act in 1917 and the Sedition Act in 1918, to squelch opposition to the war, seeing it as detrimental to public morale.

American participation in World War I proved decisive, and on November 11, 1918, Germany signed an armistice agreement. President Wilson now had the opportunity to enact his famous "Fourteen Points," which he had outlined in an address to Congress in January 1918. The president called for far-reaching postwar goals such as ending secret agreements, ensuring freedom of the seas and free trade, and creating an international organization to prevent future conflicts. Wilson traveled to France in December 1918 to partici-

pate in the peace conference, and he played a significant role in drafting the Treaty of Versailles, which endorsed the creation of the League of Nations and the rest of the Fourteen Points. In return, Wilson agreed to severe punitive measures for Germany, such as significant reparations and loss of territory.

The Treaty of Versailles would become both Wilson's shining legacy and his great failure. The president won the Nobel Peace Prize in 1920 for his leadership in drafting the treaty, and he is credited for establishing the foundation for the post–World War II United Nations. Yet Wilson could not persuade the Senate to ratify the treaty, despite a strenuous and unprecedented presidential speaking tour to rally public support.

Senate Republicans, led by Henry Cabot Lodge of Massachusetts, chairman of the Foreign Relations Committee, opposed the League of Nations because of concerns that it would infringe upon U.S. sovereignty. Lodge was willing to accept the treaty with certain reservations to protect American independence, but Wilson adamantly refused to compromise. Had the president included Republican leaders in the delegation to draft the treaty, he might have anticipated and addressed some of these concerns beforehand, but he refused to do so, even after Republicans won control of both chambers of Congress in the 1918 midterm elections. President Wilson's intransigence stiffened Republican opposition to his agenda.

Instead of negotiating with his Lodge, Wilson embarked on a national speaking tour in September 1919, giving more than two dozen speeches in three weeks. The tour ended when Wilson became ill, and soon after returning to Washington, D.C., he suffered a paralyzing stroke. Unable to govern, Wilson was in no shape to negotiate with the Senate, which rejected the treaty twice in four months. Although a majority of senators supported it, the treaty did not have the necessary two-thirds vote without the inclusion of reservations, which Wilson would not endorse. The Treaty of Versailles and the League of Nations were enacted without the United States.

Wilson's final year in office did not bring the same leadership that the country had seen before the president's illness. First Lady Edith Wilson zealously guarded access to her husband after his stroke, and he had little energy for governance. President Wilson declared that the 1920 presidential election would be a referendum on the League of Nations, but this challenge failed when the Republican nominee, Ohio senator Warren G. Harding, won a resounding victory over Democrat James M. Cox, the governor of Ohio. Three years after leaving office, Wilson died of another stroke. His visionary legacy in foreign affairs would continue to shape American politics long after his presidency.

"Congress Cheers Greet Wilson," April 9, 1913, and "The President's Innovation," April 9, 1913

President Wilson's decision to deliver his first message to Congress in person generated great excitement on Capitol Hill. His opening remarks suggested humility—Wilson said he was giving the speech to show that "the President of the United States is a person and not a mere department of the Government." In reviewing the speech, *The New York Times* concurred with this modest assessment, noting that Wilson "has usurped no new power, and has not in the least magnified the authority of the office he fills." But the importance of a personal address by the president rather than a written message sent to Congress soon would become evident.

Wilson's personal delivery of his State of the Union message before Congress set a precedent that all of his successors have followed. By making a direct case to Congress for passing their policy agenda, presidents increase their visibility and build popular support that can, in turn, influence Congress. Wilson's strategy marks one of the foundations of what scholars subsequently have identified as the "rhetorical presidency," in which presidents use speeches to build political support for their programs.

APRIL 9, 1913
CONGRESS CHEERS GREET WILSON

House Floor and Galleries Are Packed to Hear President's Oral Message.

EVENT FREE FROM POMP

Nine-Minute Speech Urging Immediate Change in Tariff Wins Vigorous Applause.

ALSO ADMONISHES CAUTION

Explains He Wishes to be Known as Person Rather Than Mere Arm of the Government.

Special to The New York Times

WASHINGTON, April 8.—For the first time within the life of any person now alive, unless it be true that there are people living who are more than 112 years old, a President of the United States to-day appeared before the two houses of Congress, assembled in joint session, and in person gave them "information of the state of the Union," and recommended to their consideration "such measures as he shall judge necessary and expedient," as required by the Federal Constitution.

In other words, President Wilson delivered as an oral address the message he had prepared for the guidance of Congress in the extra session which convened yesterday. Thus he revived the practice born of the British "address from the throne," established in this country by the first President, continued by the second, and abandoned by the third, and, as he said in the opening sentence of his address, verifying for himself "the impression that the President of the United States is a person and not a mere department of the Government."

The announcement that the President of the United States would appear in the hall of the House of Representatives to communicate with Congress in spoken words instead of in writing, drew a big crowd to the Capitol building. The galleries for spectators were jammed and the corridors outside of them were filled with people who vainly sought to obtain admission. The floor of the House was crowded, too, for the entire membership of the Senate had seats there along with the Representatives. The ceremony itself was very brief and exceedingly simple. President Wilson was present in the House not quite ten minutes, and the preliminaries covered only a period measured in seconds.

Ceremony Free from Display.

To rob the affair of as much formality as possible and make it wholly free from ostentatious display, the President went to the Capitol unaccompanied by any one save James Sloan, his faithful Secret Service guard. His secretary, Joseph P. Tumulty, went from the White House to the big building on Capitol Hill in his own motor car. Such members of the Cabinet as attended the session made their way to the Capitol as they pleased. The scene on the floor of the House was in striking contrast to that in the Senate Chamber on March 4, when Woodrow Wilson witnessed the inauguration of Thomas R. Marshall as Vice President of the United States, preliminary to his own installation in the office of President on the open-air stand at the east front of the building. The inaugural ceremonials brought together in the Senate Chamber the members of the Diplomatic Corps, nearly all of whom were in gay uniforms; the Chief Justice and the Associate Justices of the Supreme Court of the United States, in their sombre robes of office;

high ranking officers of the army and navy, in full-dress uniform, and a host of distinguished persons.

To-day in the House the ceremonial, if it may properly be called that, was of the plainest character. There were no uniforms worn by those who sat on the floor, and the whole proceedings had about them an air of democratic simplicity. There was plenty of color, however, in the galleries, where the dresses of the women spectators, mostly the wives and daughters of Senators and Representatives, made a riot of color, with blue in all its shades predominating.

APRIL 9, 1913
EDITORIAL
THE PRESIDENT'S INNOVATION.

President Wilson's overturning of a century-old precedent in appearing personally at the joint session of both houses of Congress to deliver his first message has been variously judged. Naturally the older Senators and Representatives regard it as a revolutionary proceeding, but these are not the days in which the views of the maturer minds prevail. Undoubtedly the custom was abandoned 112 years ago for good reasons. We have no idea that Mr. Wilson intends to be revolutionary in reviving it. He must have reasons, though they may not be satisfying to Congress. There may often be some advantage alike to the Executive and the legislators in having a message of counsel and appeal spoken effectively, with the emphasis

was an innovation, it might lead to unfortunate results, and any reasonable objections to it, clearly uttered, are worth heeding. Mr. Wilson's declaration that "the President of the United States is a person, not a mere department of the Government hailing Congress from some isolated island of jealous power" probably sounded better than it reads. The strong personal force of Presidents like Jackson, Lincoln, and Cleveland was never questioned. The Chief Magistrate's office has never been regarded as an "isolated island," and why should his "power" be "jealous"? The danger, therefore, is obvious that the messages, under the new order, may contain too many oratorical phrases of that sort which will not well bear inspection in print.

> "[H]e has laid himself open to the charge of airing his vanity."

properly placed, and not droned in a perfunctory manner by the clerk at the desk. The message was listened to yesterday. President Wilson probably has no equal in this country as an effective speaker.

The greatest advantage to Congress and the Nation in this manner of presenting the Chief Magistrate's view of public policy is that the spoken message must always be reasonably short. No President would attempt to speak a 20,000-word message to Congress. If the day of long messages has passed the country is to be congratulated. Mr. Wilson spoke just ten minutes yesterday, he was well received, and there seems no room for doubt that a majority of his hearers found the innovation agreeable. But it

There is another point of view from which the direct delivery of the message deserves consideration. The President's address was applauded yesterday. Perhaps the audible expression of approval was grateful to him. But if approval in Congress of a President's message, delivered orally by him, is to be expressed in applause, may disapproval also be expressed? Surely a President courting and receiving applause may also run the risk of being hissed. It might be said that no Senator or Representative would so lower himself as to hiss the President, but one can easily imagine a condition of public feeling which might cause a rude manifestation of opposition to the President's remarks. That would certainly be deplorable.

Mr. Wilson acquitted himself admirably in his first attempt, but we do not believe that, however favorably his personality impressed Congress, his message will impress the Nation more deeply than it would if it had been sent by messenger and read by a clerk. Meanwhile he has laid himself open to the charge of airing his vanity, which is the worst that can be made in the circumstances. He has usurped no new power, and has not in the least magnified the authority of the office he fills. If he prefers to speak to Congress hereafter, instead of writing to it, Congress will probably submit with good grace. The wonder is that in seven years Theodore Roosevelt never thought of this way of stamping his personality upon his age.

• •

"Popular Election of Senate in Force," June 1, 1913

The Seventeenth Amendment to the Constitution represented a significant victory for democracy in the United States. This amendment transferred the power to elect U.S. senators from state legislatures to the people. In so doing, it extended popular sovereignty to both chambers of Congress, thus rejecting the perspective of many framers of the Constitution that the public at large lacked the interest or knowledge to select its representatives in government. Illustrating the high barriers that must be overcome to amend the Constitution, *The Times* noted that support for popular election of senators dated back to the early nineteenth century.

JUNE 1, 1913
POPULAR ELECTION OF SENATE IN FORCE
Bryan Promulgates the Addition of the 17th Amendment to the Constitution.
END OF 87 YEARS' FIGHT
Secretary Uses Four Silver Pens to Sign Enacting Document—Pioneers of
Reform Present.
Special to The New York Times

WASHINGTON, May 31.—The seventeenth amendment to the Constitution, providing for the election of United States Senators by the direct vote of the people, became effective to-day when Secretary Bryan formally announced its adoption by the Legislatures of thirty-six States, that number being the required two-thirds necessary to attach the amendment to the Constitution.

The signing of the document promulgating the amendment was made the occasion of considerable ceremony. Mr. Bryan entered into the spirit of the occasion with a rejoicing sense of its importance historically.

One of those invited to be present was ex-Congressman Harry St. George Tucker of Virginia, who was the ranking member of the majority side of the House Committee on the Election of President and Vice President in the Fifty-second Congress, when the resolution providing for the submission of the amendment to the Legislatures was first favorably reported to the House and adopted by that

body. Mr. Tucker is the sole survivor of the prominent Democrats on the committee who were active in supporting the resolution.

Mr. Bryan also invited Representative William W. Rucker of Mississippi, Chairman of the Committee on Election of President and Vice President in the Sixty-second Congress, when the resolution was again passed by the House, and Senator William E. Borah of Idaho, of the Senate Committee on Judiciary, on whom fell the duty of championing the measure in the Senate, and to whom credit was given for its success in that body, where it had often met defeat in previous Congresses.

Four silver pens had been provided for Mr. Bryan's use in signing his name. One was tied with a red ribbon, another with a white ribbon, the third with a blue ribbon, and the fourth with two white ribbons. Mrs. Bryan and Miss Mary Sharp, sister-in-law of Mr. Tucker, and a large number of department officials also witnessed the signing of the amendment.

Mr. Bryan took the pen with the red ribbon and signed his first name, immediately handing the pen to Mr. Tucker. Then he took the white ribboned pen and signed "Jennings," and this pen he handed to Judge Rucker. With the blue-ribboned pen he signed "Bryan." This pen the Secretary gave to Mrs. Bryan. With the double white-ribboned pen he wrote in "thirty-first," the day in May on which the new amendment was to go into effect, and gave this pen to Senator Borah.

The tri-partite signature occupied the Secretary just three minutes, the last word being blotted at 11:16 o'clock. Edward Savoy, the veteran chief messenger to Secretaries of State, whose first departmental service was under Secretary Hamilton Fish in 1869, got the blotter used by Mr. Bryan. A certificate that the blotter had been used on this occasion was written on it by Mr. Bryan in lead pencil.

"That marks the end of a long fight," said Mr. Bryan as he arose from his chair. "The struggle for election of Senators by the people began twenty-one years ago in Congress, and eighty-seven years ago among the people."

"Yes," said Senator Borah, "it began in 1826."

Secretary Bryan expressed his gratification that the making of this official announcement of the ratification of the amendment had fallen to him as one of his official duties. He mentioned that he was elected to Congress in 1890 upon a platform containing such a plank.

Mr. Bryan voted in both the Fifty-second and Fifty-third Congresses for the resolution submitting the amendment, and assisted in the writing of four National platforms which indorsed it. Mr. Bryan said that he regarded it as the most important reform made in a century affecting the Federal Government.

- -

"Tariff Bill Passed; May Sign It To-day," October 3, 1913

The subject of President Wilson's first address to Congress was tariff reform, and the president signed this legislation just months later. The Underwood-Simmons Tariff Act of 1913, named after the primary sponsors in Congress, lowered tariff rates significantly and established a federal income tax. The Sixteenth Amendment, ratified in 1913, had granted Congress the power to levy an income tax.

OCTOBER 3, 1913
TARIFF BILL PASSED; MAY SIGN IT TO-DAY
Vote in the Senate 36 to 17 on the Adoption of the Conference Report.
Special to The New York Times

WASHINGTON, Oct. 2.—The signatures of Speaker Clark, Vice President Marshall and President Wilson are all that is lacking to put the Underwood Tariff bill on the statute books, and will be affixed early to-morrow afternoon. To-night, with many Republicans absent and unpaired, the Senate adopted the conference report by a vote of 36 to 17—more than two to one. Then, in accordance with an understanding to save Senators from embarrassment, the Senate voted without a roll call to disagree to the House compromise on the tax on cotton futures, then receded from its original amendment levying the tax, and the whole subject was stricken from the bill.

This action by the Senate will leave no loophole for further attempts in the House to insist on the tax in any form. But it is understood that some of the extreme radicals, like Representative Wingo of Arkansas, are studying

the rules in an effort to force another vote. To prevent any mishap Majority Leader Underwood has sent out instructions for every Democrat to be in his place tomorrow, when both houses will convene at noon.

The bill, with notice of the Senate's action, will be sent promptly to the House, where the Speaker will order it enrolled and then sign it. As fast as messengers can rush it the bill will then be sent back to the Senate for the Vice President's signature. As soon as possible thereafter President Wilson will make it a law. Most of the bill's provisions will then be in full force after midnight to-morrow.

There was talk to-night that as to-morrow is Friday the President might be asked by superstitious Democrats to delay signing the bill until Saturday. An argument in support of this delay that had no vestige of superstition in it was that as the act would become effective on the day following its passage, the customs officials would be overwhelmed on Saturday, a "short day," by hundreds of tons of goods held in bonded warehouses until the lower duties of the Underwood law went into operation. The customs officials want the act to go into effect on Monday instead of Saturday.

Wilson Ready for Bill.

It is not likely that President Wilson will be influenced by these considerations, superstitious or practical. He said to-day that he would sign the act the minute it was laid before him.

"WILSON APOLOGY TO COLOMBIA?" APRIL 9, 1914

President Wilson's effort to apologize to Colombia for the U.S. acquisition of Panama sparked some controversy. Supporters of former president Theodore Roosevelt, who had quickly won U.S. control of Panama immediately following the nation's short-lived independence from Colombia, blocked the Wilson administration's treaty, which would have awarded $25 million to Colombia. The United States eventually approved this compensation under Wilson's successor, President Warren G. Harding.

APRIL 9, 1914
WILSON APOLOGY TO COLOMBIA?

'Friendly Expression of Regret' for Panama Revolution Said to Go with New Treaty.
ROOSEVELT MADE DENIAL
Disclaimed Indignantly in Message to Congress Complicity of United States in Rising.
INDEMNITY OF $25,000,000
Right to Ship Coal and Petroleum Toll Free Through Canal—Strip of Land Restored.
Special to The New York Times

WASHINGTON, April 8.—What was described as "a friendly expression of regret" on the part of the United States over the manner in which the secession of the present Republic of Panama from Colombia was brought about through the alleged connivance of the United States Government is said to be contained in or to accompany the treaty signed yesterday at Bogota by representatives of Colombia and the United States, which also provides for the payment of an indemnity of $25,000,000 for the loss suffered by Panama.

When Robert Lansing, Counselor of the State Department, who is Acting Secretary of State during the illness of Secretary Bryan, was asked late tonight whether the new treaty carried such an expression, he answered, after some hesitation, "That is something I cannot talk about."

From another source it was learned that the matter of accompanying the treaty with a statement from this Government, containing a "friendly expression of regret," had been discussed by the negotiators at Bogota. The informant of *The New York Times* said that from his knowledge of the situation he felt certain that some such expression had been put into the treaty.

"TRADE BOARD BILL PASSES THE SENATE," AUGUST 6, 1914

The creation of the Federal Trade Commission in 1914 marked a significant victory for the Wilson administration. The commission was empowered to investigate large corporations and ensure their compliance with antitrust legislation. Creating the commission was part of the president's Progressive agenda for government regulation of business.

AUGUST 6, 1914
TRADE BOARD BILL PASSES THE SENATE
First of Three Anti-Trust Measures of the President Is Adopted by 53 Votes to 16.

MAJORITY IS BIPARTISAN

Four of Regular Republicans Support It—Stock and Bond Bill Comes Up Next.

Special to The New York Times

WASHINGTON, Aug. 5.—President Wilson won what was perhaps his greatest legislative triumph this afternoon when the Senate, by the overwhelming bipartisan vote of 53 to 16, passed the Trade Commission bill.

Twelve Republican Senators voted for it, and only two more than that voted against it, while the Democratic ranks were practically unbroken, as only two Democrats were against the measure. They were Mr. Thomas of Colorado, a supporter of Mr. Bryan, who has shown erratic tendencies that have put him out of harmony with his colleagues, and Mr. West of Georgia, a new member.

The Trade Commission bill is the first of the three anti-trust measures to receive consideration in the Senate.

It would provide for a trade commission of five members to succeed to the duties, now performed by the Commissioner of Corporations, with greatly extended authority. Its powers would be in two classes, one the investigation into the business, the financial condition, conduct, and management of corporations engaged in interstate commerce, and the other the issue of orders against "unfair competition" by corporations.

No sooner was the vote announced this afternoon, than on motion of Mr. Kern of Indiana, the majority leader, the Clayton bill, supplementing the Sherman law, was made the unfinished business. That will be taken up in earnest tomorrow, and may be disposed of without much more than a week's debate.

- -

"LUSITANIA SUNK BY A SUBMARINE, PROBABLY 1,000 DEAD," MAY 8, 1915, AND "WILSON PROCLAIMS NEUTRALITY AGAIN," MAY 26, 1915

The sinking of the British liner *Lusitania* shocked Americans and raised questions about whether the United States could maintain neutrality in World War I. The Wilson administration demanded that Germany halt its submarine attacks on unarmed passenger ships. Yet just a few weeks after the *Lusitania* crisis, in response to Italy's entry into the war, the United States again affirmed its neutrality in the European conflict. As *The Times* reported, the proclamation declared that American citizens must follow "the duty of impartial neutrality during the existence of the contest [of war]."

MAY 8, 1915
LUSITANIA SUNK BY A SUBMARINE, PROBABLY 1,000 DEAD;

Shocks the President: Washington Deeply Stirred by Disaster and Fears a Crisis.

BULLETINS AT WHITE HOUSE

Wilson Reads Them Closely, but Is Silent on the Nation's Course.

RUMOR OF CONGRESS CALL

Loss of *Lusitania* Recalls Firm Tone of Our First Warning to Germany.

CAPITAL FULL OF RUMORS

Reports That Liner Was to be Sunk Were Heard Before Actual News Came.

Special to The New York Times

WASHINGTON, May 7.—Never since that April day, three years ago, when word came that the *Titanic* had gone down, has Washington been so stirred as it is tonight over the sinking of the *Lusitania*. The early reports told that there had been no loss of life, but the relief that these advices caused gave way to the greatest concern late this evening when it became known that there had been many deaths. Although they are profoundly reticent, officials realize that this tragedy, probably involving the loss of American citizens, is likely to bring about a crisis in the international relations of the United States.

It is pointed out that the sinking of the *Lusitania* is the outcome of a series of incidents that have been the cause of concern to this Government in its endeavor to maintain a strictly neutral position in the great European war.

It is impossible to say tonight what effect the loss of American lives on the *Lusitania* will have on the Government. Judged from the little that can be learned it is a safe prediction that President Wilson will endeavor to ascertain all the facts, including evidence as to whether a German submarine was responsible for the sinking of the vessel, before proceeding to determine the course to be pursued. The news that many lives had been sacrificed, probably as many as a thousand, was given to him at the White House about 1 o'clock this evening, but no word came from him as to what effect this intelligence had on him.

The State Department tonight sent instructions to the American Embassy in London to send the names of any Americans who might have been killed or injured in the disaster. A bulletin from *The Times,* saying probably 1,000 lives had been lost, was sent to the White House as soon as received and laid before President Wilson. The news that two torpedoes had been fired into the *Lusitania* by a submarine and that the *Lusitania* sank fifteen minutes afterward was also sent to the White House, but reached there after the President had gone to bed. The President retired about 11 o'clock.

Rumors of Congress Session.

There were reports this evening that Congress would be called in extra session, but these were not justified and the most that can be said is that while the Government is greatly concerned over the situation, it has shown no inclination toward excitement or taking hasty action.

This afternoon and early this evening officials were relieved over the reports that no lives had been lost. But in spite of the calmness in the upper official circle during this period, there was little effort elsewhere to conceal the view that even if no Americans went down with the liner this Government might find itself face to face with a grave situation.

The statement from London that the *Lusitania* was torpedoed without warning was regarded as showing the delicacy of the situation, for this Government, in the warning it delivered to Germany concerning the proposed submarine warfare on merchant ships, laid down the principle that the obligation to visit and search a merchant ship before sinking or taking her captive was imposed on the German Government.

But it is too soon to say, or even to attempt to predict, what course the United States Government will adopt. It is clear that the first move of the Government will be to ascertain all the facts obtainable and that the inquiry will be pursued, as far as possible, by officers of the United States. Until such an investigation has been completed and President Wilson and his advisers have determined what attitude the facts warrant the Government in adopting, no formal diplomatic action may be expected. For the present the higher officials content themselves with a refusal to answer questions as to the position likely to be taken and with expressions of the hope that the early reports that no lives were lost in the *Lusitania* are true. That was Secretary Bryan's way of treating the matter before the alarming bulletins began to arrive.

MAY 26, 1915
WILSON PROCLAIMS NEUTRALITY AGAIN
New Statement Made Necessary by Italy's Entrance Into the War.

WASHINGTON, May 25.—A neutrality proclamation by the United States covering the entry of Italy in the European war was published today by the State Department under date of May 24.

The proclamation cautions American citizens that "the laws and treaties of the United States, without interfering with the free expression of opinion and sympathy, or with the commercial manufacture or sale of arms or munitions of war, nevertheless impose upon all persons who may be within their territory and jurisdiction the duty of impartial neutrality during the existence of the contest."

As was the case in the other neutrality proclamations, issued during the present war, the laws of the United States forbidding recruiting for the belligerents in this country or the fitting out of war vessels are recited and also the laws governing belligerent warships entering American ports. The protection of the United States, it is declared, will be denied to such American citizens as "may misconduct themselves in the premises."

The language of the proclamation is identical with the others.

The State Department issued this statement:

"The American Consul at Venice has telegraphed the Department that on May 23 German and Austrian aeroplanes made a scouting attack on Venice at dawn. Several bombs were thrown and several persons were wounded—one bomb falling near the arsenal and another at San Nicoletto di Lodi, in the water. One aeroplane flew directly over the consulate amid a hail of machine gun, shrapnel, and shell fire. The Consul reports that there was no sign of panic among the citizens who watched the flight through glasses."

The Italian Post Office Department today notified the United States of the suspension of parcel post between the two countries. Packages now in the mails will be returned to the senders.

The American military observers are likely to be sent with the Italian Army, and any naval observations that are made will be conducted by the American Naval Attaché at Rome. None of the observers sent to the other Allies has had such opportunity for observation, and for that reason War Department officials think it useless to send more.

"MORE MARINES LANDED IN SANTO DOMINGO," MAY 16, 1916

To protect American financial interests in the Caribbean, the Wilson administration sent U.S. troops to Haiti in 1915 and the Dominican Republic in 1916. The troops intervened to halt revolution in each nation and reestablish order. These interventions were the beginning of a long-term and controversial U.S. presence in the region.

MAY 16, 1916
MORE MARINES LANDED IN SANTO DOMINGO
Caperton's Forces Take Possession of Dominican Capital After Rebels Evacuate the City.

SANTO DOMINGO, May 15.—American marines who had been landed on Dominican soil entered Santo Domingo to-day and took possession of the centre of the city. The rebel leaders had withdrawn with their forces Saturday night after being warned by the American Minister, W. W. Russell, that the city would be taken by force unless the rebels evacuated it by Sunday morning. The entry of the American forces was unopposed.

The public was advised today through officers of the Municipal Government that Minister Russell had made it known that the object of the American occupation was to guarantee the free election by Congress of a Provisional President to succeed General Juan I. Jiminez, who resigned.

Order is being maintained.

"Wilson The Victor, M'Cormick Insists," November 8, 1916

President Wilson narrowly won reelection in 1916, and his supporters followed the election-night results with tense anticipation. Despite some significant victories by Republican candidate Charles Evan Hughes, who took his home state of New York as well as other states rich in Electoral College votes, President Wilson ultimately prevailed. California was not the most populous state at the time, but it nevertheless proved decisive in ensuring Wilson's victory.

Intensive peace and prosperity campaigning helped Woodrow Wilson win the 1916 election.

Source: The New York Times

NOVEMBER 8, 1916
WILSON THE VICTOR, M'CORMICK INSISTS

Late News, He Says, Makes His Claim of Electoral Majority a Certainty.

REASSURED BY LATE NEWS

At Tammany Hall Interest Appears to Centre Only in Vote for Dowling and McIntyre.

At Democratic National Headquarters the atmosphere changed several times last evening. As early as 5 o'clock in the evening the party managers felt sure President Wilson was re-elected. Their optimism was based on the first returns from Kansas and Massachusetts. It appeared then that it was all over but the shouting. By 8 o'clock, however, an entirely different face was put upon the situation. By that time the big Republican pluralities began to show themselves, and when the indications piled up that New York State had gone to Hughes by between 100,000 and 150,000, gloom settled down upon the crowd assembled at National Headquarters to hear the returns.

At 3 o'clock this morning Chairman McCormick issued the following statement.

"We've got 'em. Wilson's vote is rolling up every minute. Wilson will have close to 300 votes in the Electoral College."

The following telegram was received early this morning by Mr. McCormick from United States Senator H. F. Hollis of New Hampshire:

"Returns from country districts give Hughes 24,114 and Wilson 24,218—more than half of the State figures. Strong Democratic cities to be heard from. Predict you will carry New Hampshire by 2,000."

It was announced at Democratic Headquarters that Democratic leaders all over the country had been notified to "sit tight"—that the fight had been won for Wilson, according to the best information received at headquarters.

It was announced early this morning at Headquarters that Wilson would receive 291 electoral votes and Hughes 240. This statement, it was said, was based on figures sent to the Democratic Committee from all parts of the country.

At 2:45 o'clock this morning Democratic National Headquarters became suddenly enthusiastic over a bulletin from San Francisco that President Wilson had carried California. A crowd of about 100, including Chairman McCormick, was on hand and the greatest rejoicing ensued. Every one shouted and threw hats into the air. Chairman McCormick wore a broad smile and simply said that he had stood by his prediction all night that the latest returns would show that the President was re-elected.

Democratic State Chairman Finley of Ohio telephoned Chairman McCormick at headquarters at 2:40 o'clock this morning that the Democrats would carry Ohio by 50,000 plurality.

State Chairman Kolbly of Indiana telegraphed: "Wilson ahead and holding lead. Expect to have figures within one hour."

- -

"Government Acts Swiftly," April 7, 1917

President Wilson's second term in office was defined primarily by U.S. entry into the war raging in Europe. Congress passed a resolution declaring war on Germany on April 6, 1917, and the president signed the resolution the same day. The era of U.S. neutrality in European affairs had ended, at least for this conflict.

" War came to the United States at 1:18 o'clock this afternoon. "

APRIL 7, 1917
GOVERNMENT ACTS SWIFTLY
War Tidings Fly to Navy and Army When Wilson Signs Resolution.
CABINET IN LONG SESSION
Co-operation with Entente a Leading Theme—Other Big Problems Under Discussion.
WORLD TOLD OF ACTION
Proclamation by the President Fixes Aliens' Bounds and Summons Citizens to Aid.
Special to The New York Times

WASHINGTON, April 6.—War came to the United States at 1:18 o'clock this afternoon—war by the Government and people of this nation against the Imperial German Government. At that exact moment President Wilson signed the Congressional resolution declaring that "the state of war . . . which has thus been thrust upon the United States, is hereby formally declared."

Within a few minutes thereafter formal notice was being flashed to every American war vessel and naval station, every fort and army post in this country and the possessions of the United States, and to American diplomatic and consular representatives abroad.

Three minutes later orders were sent by the Navy Department to mobilize the naval forces of the United States. This meant that not only the fleet in commission but all reserve warships, all vessels and men of the Naval Militia, all vessels and men of the Coast Guard and the Lighthouse Service were placed on a war footing, and those vessels not in commission or under other departments of the Government were brought into active service under the Secretary of the Navy.

The President was at luncheon when the war resolution reached the Executive Offices from the Capitol. It had been adopted by the House of Representatives at 3:12 o'clock this morning, attested immediately by Speaker Clark, and then held in the custody of the Clerk of the House until the Senate, which adopted it Wednesday night, met at noon. When the Senate assembled the resolution was presented, and at 12:14 o'clock it was signed without ceremony by Vice President Marshall, who preserved the pen that he used. The document was then dispatched to the White House.

With the President at luncheon when the resolution arrived were Mrs. Wilson and his cousin, Miss Helen Woodrow Bones. They went at once to the ushers' room off the lobby of the mansion, in which Rudolph Forster, execu-

tive clerk to the President, was waiting with the official parchment draft of the resolution.

Mrs. Wilson had obtained a pen for use by the President and she handed it to him as he sat down at the table in the little room and attached his signature to the document that took the American nation into the greatest war in history. Mrs. Wilson, Miss Bones, Mr. Forster, and Isaac Hoover, head usher of the White House, surrounded him as he did so. Mr. Forster then hurried over to the Executive offices and announced the fact to the waiting newspaper men.

⸱ ⸱

"APPEALS TO GERMAN PEOPLE," JANUARY 9, 1918, AND "THE PRESIDENT'S TRIUMPH," JANUARY 11, 1918

Even while the United States was fighting in World War I, President Wilson was developing a vision for the postwar world. In his now-famous "Fourteen Points" address to Congress on January 8, 1918, the president presented his recommendations for ensuring global peace, which included freedom of the seas, reducing the number of armaments in the world, and creating an association of nations to facilitate cooperation. In praising Wilson's historic speech, *The Times'* editorial noted that it "has been described as the greatest product of Mr. Wilson's mind and statesmanship, as the most remarkable State paper of the war."

JANUARY 9, 1918
APPEALS TO GERMAN PEOPLE
Wilson Declares We Must Know for Whom Their Rulers Speak.
READY TO FIGHT TO END
Insists That Principle of Justice to All Nations Is Only Basis for Peace.
DEMANDS FREEDOM OF SEAS
Congress Cheers Utterance as Momentous Declaration of Entente War Aims.
Special to The New York Times

WASHINGTON, Jan. 8.—The terms upon which Germany may obtain peace were given to the American Congress for the benefit of the whole world by President Wilson today. With scant notice of his coming, notice barely sufficient to enable the Senate and the House to make the necessary arrangements for a joint session, the President appeared at the Capitol, and in an address, brief by comparison to the momentous issues discussed, enumerated the conditions for a cessation of hostilities, the rejection of which will place upon Germany the responsibility for the further bloodshed that must precede the final victory of the allied nations.

President Wilson's address bore a striking resemblance to the speech made last Saturday by Mr. Lloyd George, the British Prime Minister, before the Trade Union Conference on Man Power, in which he specified the war aims and peace conditions of the British Government. The diversions in the President's address from statements of the Prime Minister were for the most part more in the form than in the substance.

But in the opinion of many of those who compared Mr. Wilson's address with the utterances of Mr. Lloyd George the President was more definite in declaring that the wrong done to France through the annexation of Alsace-Lorraine must be righted and he differed from Mr. Lloyd George with regard to the Russian situation in that he held out to the Russian people an offer of assistance from America, and tendered sympathy for the aims that those now in control of the affairs of that perturbed country are seeking to achieve.

Leaves No Doubt of Unity.

By the President's official utterances he has pledged this Government to the achievement of ends that affect Europe more intimately and deeply than the United States. No doubt was left in the minds of those who listened to the President's words that this Government has entered heart and soul into the cause of the Entente Allies, to fight for the objects for which they are fighting, to free Europe from the menace of Prussianism, to take Alsace-Lorraine from German domination, to prevent Russia from becoming part of the German Empire, to see that Italy has restored to her those portions of the Austro-Hungarian Empire that are inhabited by a people who are Italian in heart and blood, to bring all the Polish peoples into a common Government, to restore Belgium, Serbia, and the small nations that have been devastated by Teuton hordes, to their own, to give the separate nationalities of Austria-Hungary, Turkey and the Balkan States the right to govern themselves as separate entities, to have Northern France restored to French control.

And, in addition to these aims, the allied nations, in order to find a peace acceptable to them, must be assured of freedom of the seas, the establishment of an equality of trade conditions among the nations of the world, the reduction of armaments, and an association of nations in a league to enforce peace. There must also be no secret agreements among nations that would threaten again the peace of the world.

Immediately following the delivery of the President's address, there was a disposition manifest to refer to his outline of the conditions which Germany must accept before the war could end as a definition of peace terms. But in the official quarters best qualified to interpret the meaning of the President, it was declared that his statement must be taken as a definition of war aims. The President left no doubt that, unless Germany consented to enter into peace exchanges on the basis of the conditions set forth in his address, the United States and the Allies would fight on until the Central Powers realised that there could be no peace in any other way. "It was an outline of war aims, not a peace address," declared one official.

JANUARY 11, 1918
EDITORIAL
THE PRESIDENT'S TRIUMPH.

President Wilson has done what he set out to do. No appeal to "the opinions of mankind" upon matters of great moment ever called forth a more prompt and assenting response than has been given to his statement, addressed to Congress but also to the whole world, of the purpose for which war is being waged against Germany. No one who has read the countless newspaper columns which in the last few days have set forth the judgments of representative men of all classes of society in the allied countries upon the President's address can have failed to see that it has swept away doubt, hesitation, suspicion, and has united the peoples of the allied countries in the determination to sanction and support the prosecution of the war and to bear with fortitude its costs and sacrifices until a just and lasting peace has been made sure by the destruction of Germany's military power and lust of conquest. The address has been described as the greatest product of Mr. Wilson's mind and statesmanship, as the most remarkable State paper of the war. We may leave it to history to assign its deserved place and rank among the utterances of statesmen and the proclamations of Governments since the war began, but inasmuch as Mr. Wilson spoke with the intent to unite allied public opinion, and since he has so wonderfully accomplished that very thing, it would be hard to take exception to any form of eulogy, however enthusiastic, which the contemporary judgment of mankind may bestow upon the address and upon its author.

"Republicans Win Senate and House," November 6, 1918

Wilson's success in foreign affairs in 1918 did not spill over into domestic politics, as the Democrats lost control of both chambers of Congress in the 1918 midterm elections. Despite Republican victories, the president refused to negotiate with Senate leaders about the terms of victory following the end of World War I. In particular, Wilson's indifference to Republican concerns about U.S. sovereignty in an association of nations would prove to be an insurmountable obstacle in achieving his postwar agenda.

NOVEMBER 6, 1918
REPUBLICANS WIN SENATE AND HOUSE

Control of Both Legislative Branches Apparently Lost by the President.
FORD AND LEWIS BEATEN
Champ Clark Defeated—Senate Probably 50 to 46—Republican Majority in House About 19.

On the face of the latest returns of the contest for the election of Senators and Representatives in Congress, the Democrats appear to have lost control of the legislative branches of the Government.

The Senate, in which the Democrats have now a majority of eight, seems to be Republican by a majority of four. These estimates are based on returns received up to 3 o'clock this morning.

In the present Senate there are 52 Democrats and 44 Republicans. The next Senate, the term of which will begin on March 4, 1919, probably will be composed of 50 Republicans and 46 Democrats.

In the present House there are 214 Democrats, 207 Republicans, and 7 independents, leaving the Democrats a plurality of 7 over the Republicans, but no majority over Republicans and independents combined.

Although later returns probably will change the total slightly, figures received up to 3 o'clock this morning indicate that the next House, which has been elected to serve from March 4, 1919, to March 4, 1921, will be composed of 227 Republicans, 207 Democrats, and 1 Socialist, giving the Republicans a clear majority of 19.

"War Ends at 6 O'clock This Morning," November 11, 1918

World War I officially ended on November 11, 1918, when Germany signed an armistice agreement with the United States and its European allies. Peace negotiations, in which President Wilson would play a primary role, began soon after.

NOVEMBER 11, 1918
WAR ENDS AT 6 O'CLOCK THIS MORNING

The State Department in Washington Made the Announcement at 2:45 o'Clock.

ARMISTICE WAS SIGNED IN FRANCE AT MIDNIGHT

Terms Include Withdrawal from Alsace-Lorraine, Disarming and Demobilization
of Army and Navy, and Occupation of Strategic Naval and Military Points.

By The Associated Press.

WASHINGTON, Monday, Nov. 11, 2:48 A.M.—The armistice between Germany, on the one hand, and the allied Governments and the United States, on the other, has been signed.

The State Department announced at 2:45 o'clock this morning that Germany had signed.

The department's announcement simply said: "The armistice has been signed."

The world war will end this morning at 6 o'clock, Washington time, 11 o'clock Paris time.

The armistice was signed by the German representatives at midnight.

This announcement was made by the State Department at 2:50 o'clock this morning.

The announcement was made verbally by an official of the State Department in this form:

"The armistice has been signed. It was signed at 5 o'clock A.M., Paris time, [midnight, New York time,] and hostilities will cease at 11 o'clock this morning, Paris time, [6 o'clock, New York time.]

The terms of the armistice, it was announced, will not be made public until later. Military men here, however, regard it as certain that they include:

Immediate retirement of the German military forces from France, Belgium, and Alsace-Lorraine.

Disarming and demobilization of the German armies.

Occupation by the allied and American forces of such strategic points in Germany as will make impossible a renewal of hostilities.

Delivery of part of the German High Seas Fleet and a certain number of submarines to the allied and American naval forces.

Disarmament of all other German warships under supervision of the allied and American Navies, which will guard them.

Occupation of the principal German naval bases by sea forces of the victorious nations.

Release of allied and American soldiers, sailors, and civilians held prisoners in Germany without such reciprocal action by the associated Governments.

⸱ ⸱

"OVATION TO THE PRESIDENT," JULY 11, 1919

President Wilson's commitment to enacting the Treaty of Versailles was evident in his decision to deliver the treaty personally to the Senate in July 1919. His speech was well received by his fellow Democrats, but Republicans were subdued, a sign of the conflicts over ratification that soon followed.

JULY 11, 1919
OVATION TO THE PRESIDENT

But Most Republican Senators Fail to Join in Applause.

MESSAGE HEARD IN SILENCE

Finale Is Dramatic, with Wilson Laying Aside Manuscript for Peroration.

ADDRESS AIMS AT PEOPLE

President at His Best in Depicting Necessity of World-Wide League.

Special to The New York Times

WASHINGTON, July 10.—President Wilson personally delivered the Peace Treaty with Germany to the Senate in open session this afternoon. It was the first time that a treaty had been submitted by a President in such a manner.

The President spoke before an audience such as is seldom seen in the Senate Chamber and received a most enthusiastic greeting except by the Republicans of the Senate. Both when he entered under escort of the committee, headed by Senator Lodge, and when he concluded his address, 37 minutes later, he was the recipient of stirring ovations from the galleries, the Democrats of the Senate, the Cabinet officers, seated in a semicircle in front of the Vice President, and members from the House who had crowded into the circular space behind the Senators. There were cheers mingled with the rebel yell.

But most of the Republicans took no part in the demonstration. When the President entered the Chamber the Republicans arose in unison with all on the floor and the galleries, but few joined in the applause. Senator Nelson applauded while the President was being escorted to the rostrum. Senator Warren also applauded a little when the President appeared. After the President's speech Senator McCumber was the only Republican seen to applaud.

The President's address was heard with the keenest interest by his splendid audience, but it was heard in silence. He was not at his best in the delivery of his speech, but this may have been due to a purpose on his part not to try for effect. Several times during the first half of his address he dropped a word in reading the typewritten copy, on small cardboards, which he held in his hand, and then reread these sentences. His reading improved when he reached the portions dealing with the League of Nations, and it was there that he placed greater emphasis upon his sentences.

The President attempted only a general characterization of the scope and purpose of the treaty, discussed the role the American Peace Commissioners played at Paris, and declared that a League of Nations was "a practical necessity" for the maintenance of the new order of affairs, and was recognized as "the hope of the world." He added that the only question now was whether we could reject the confidence of the nations of the world.

· ·

"CROWDS BESIEGE PRESIDENT'S TRAIN, NOW SPEEDING EAST," SEPTEMBER 23, 1919

President Wilson undertook an unprecedented speaking tour in September 1919, hoping that public support would encourage senators to approve the Treaty of Versailles. Great throngs of people converged to greet the president at every stop, which pleased him greatly. As The Times reported, Wilson told his audience in Sacramento that it made his heart strong "that you should have given me so extraordinary and delightful a welcome as this." The public accolades did not, however, overcome Republican senators' concerns about the treaty.

SEPTEMBER 23, 1919
CROWDS BESIEGE PRESIDENT'S TRAIN, NOW SPEEDING EAST

Great Throng Welcomes Him at Sacramento, Senator Johnson's Home City.

RENO'S GREETING WARM

He Declares That the United States Cannot and Will Not Go Back Now.

LEAVES CALIFORNIA HAPPY

Senator's Friends Admit His Home Prestige Has Been Hurt by President's Campaign.

Special to The New York Times

RENO, Nev., Sept. 22.—President Wilson's train passed today through the Sierra Mountain ranges on his way eastward and there were crowds out at many stations along the route. At one point in the mountains the train was stopped on the edge of a great gorge so that the President and his party might view the magnificent scenery.

A stop was made at noon at Sacramento, Senator Johnson's home city. The greeting here was most cordial. Almost everybody in the city and its suburbs turned out to greet Mr. Wilson.

People lined the tracks for more than two miles from the outskirts of the city and formed a great sea of faces about the station, where the train stopped for twenty minutes. Here they fought to obtain vantage points near the rear platform of his car where they could hear and see the President and pay their respects to Mrs. Wilson.

The train arrived at 8 o'clock tonight in this city where his only set speech of the day was scheduled. Crowds filled the streets and cheered continuously as he passed to the Auditorium.

The meeting here was opened by the audience giving three cheers for the President and Mrs. Wilson and for the League of Nations.

Governor Boyle spoke first and introduced as Chairman Charles Chandler, a Republican. Mr. Chandler said that he was glad to hear the enthusiasm as "it speaks well for the success of the League of Nations."

"I deny the right," Chandler continued," of any group of Republicans to commit the Republican Party to opposition to the League of Nations. It contains many Republican principles."

"This treaty was not written essentially at Paris," the President said in his speech here. "It was written at Château-Thierry, Belleau Wood, and the Argonne." The soldiers had fought to free the world, he went on, and the work would be carried through.

The President said that America, which had herself thrown off the yoke of another Government, would never attempt to interfere in the internal struggles of any peoples, and that the League did not bind this country to any such thing.

The Senators who wanted to get out, said the President, would find that they were getting out by themselves. "We are not going to get out," he added, and the audience applauded.

The rest of the world, the President asserted, depended on the United States to make good the guarantees under the League and that without the participation of the United States the League would fail.

The President spoke of the disordered conditions in Europe, and said that the infection had spread here until some groups were even going to the extreme of agitating the overthrow of the Government. Such movements could never get control here, he said, but it was of the greatest importance to restore the balance of the world.

In the brief address which he made at Sacramento (the President was permitted to speak but a few minutes because it was an outdoor meeting) he said: "I cannot let the occasion go by without telling you how strong it makes my heart that you should have given me so extraordinary and delightful a welcome as this."

"Wilson's Illness Disturbs Senate," September 27, 1919

President Wilson's speaking tour took a significant toll on his health. He returned to Washington, D.C., ahead of schedule, in late September and then suffered a debilitating stroke. The president's slow recovery prevented him from participating directly in critical negotiations on the Treaty of Versailles, which mattered so much to him. First Lady Edith Wilson closely guarded access to the president during his illness, prompting much speculation about her influence on policymaking.

SEPTEMBER 27, 1919
WILSON'S ILLNESS DISTURBS SENATE
Speculation as to Effect It May Have on Fight Against Peace Treaty.
REPUBLICANS ARE UNEASY
Fear Opposition May Prove Boomerang—Johnson's Prominence Displeases Some.
Special to The New York Times

WASHINGTON, Sept. 26.—The effect of President Wilson's unexpected return to Washington on the situation in the Senate growing out of the opposition to the Versailles Peace Treaty cannot be determined until after the President's arrival. His physical condition will have, of course, a bearing on the matter to the degree that he will or will not be able to participate in the effort of his senatorial supporters to have the treaty and the League of Nations covenant ratified without amendment or even interpretative reservations.

For the present there cannot be said to be any change in the situation due to the indisposition of the President. It had been indicated that upon his return to the capital he would assume personal charge of the pro-treaty contest and there was expectation that he would make an extensive campaign to bring critics of the covenant to accept his view that necessity existed for the acceptance of the treaty and the covenant without amendment or other modification, direct or indirect. Whether he will be able, on account of his state of health, to exert any influence in favor of unqualified ratification is something that Senators are anxious to know.

Tour Shortened Only Two Days.

The curtailment of the President's transcontinental tour is not as serious from the viewpoint of covenant supporters as may appear on its face. The itinerary called for his arrival in Washington on Tuesday morning, so the tour has been shortened only two days.

The speeches which he will not make on account of the change in plans were to have been delivered in Kansas, Oklahoma, Arkansas, and Tennessee. Kansas has two Republican Senators, and each of the other States named has two of the Democratic faith. The attitude of Senator Shields of Tennessee, Democrat, has been uncertain, while Senator Gore of Oklahoma is one of the three Democratic Senators who have been counted on by the Republican leadership in the Senate to vote for important modifications of the covenant.

As matters stand, however, the President will find the situation in the Senate better from his standpoint than when he left Washington on Sept. 3 for his country-wide campaign in favor of the treaty and the covenant. There are indications of dissension in the ranks of those opposed to the covenant as it stands, and this all works to the President's advantage.

"Wilson Has a Ride; First in Five Months," March 4, 1920

Five months after his stroke, President Wilson left the White House for the first time. *The Times* reported on his short drive around Washington and noted a "marked improvement in the President's condition."

MARCH 4, 1920
WILSON HAS A RIDE; FIRST IN 5 MONTHS

Motors for an Hour, Accompanied by Mrs. Wilson and Admiral Grayson.

BENEFITED BY HIS OUTING

Trip Supposed to be Preliminary to His Leaving Washington for Convalescence.

Special to The New York Times

WASHINGTON, March 3.—President Wilson went motor riding today for the first time in five months. It was his first appearance outside the White House grounds since a few days after his return to Washington, a sick man, at the end of September. He took a few motor rides in the week following his breakdown, but was obliged to take to his bed in the early days of October.

The Springlike weather, coincident with the marked improvement in the President's condition, aroused in him a desire to get out of doors. Yesterday, when the air had a balmy softness, he expressed a desire to take a motor ride, and while it was intended at first to grant his wish the plan was abandoned for some unexplained reason when his motor car was at the rear door of the White House awaiting him. Today he renewed the request and Mrs. Wilson and Rear Admiral Grayson acquiesced.

- -

"AMERICA ISOLATED WITHOUT TREATY," MARCH 20, 1920

The Senate's rejection of the Treaty of Versailles was a disappointment for its supporters and U.S. allies in Europe. The Senate voted twice on the treaty, in November 1919 and March 1920, and it failed both times. A majority of forty-nine senators voted for it the second time, but with thirty-five of their colleagues opposed, the treaty still fell seven votes short of the two-thirds required for ratification. After the second vote, *The Times* reported, "America's isolation is now a reality." Although other countries signed the covenant and enacted its provisions, the League of Nations would have little effect without U.S. participation.

MARCH 20, 1920
AMERICA ISOLATED WITHOUT TREATY

Its Defeat, Washington Feels, Will Add to Our Unpopularity Abroad.

STILL TECHNICALLY AT WAR

Hope Expressed That Wilson Will Take Steps to Re-establish Relations.

Special to The New York Times

WASHINGTON, March 19.—In its international aspects the rejection of the Versailles Treaty by the Senate leaves the United States in an awkward position. America's isolation is now a reality. Not only is this Government not a member of the world league, designed to prevent future conflicts between nations, but it is also still at war with Germany.

A secondary effect of the Senate's action will be the withdrawal of the United States Government from participation in the arrangements now being discussed at Paris for the disposition of the Turkish Empire.

And this is not all. The feeling that has grown up in Europe on account of Senate opposition to the League of Nations is bound to be emphasized by today's action. President Wilson, who fought to have the League covenant accepted, is now in disfavor in France and Italy and is being criticised.

Recent expression in the European press has indicated that America itself was in disfavor. It might be going too far to say that the United States has lost the friendship of the world, but to say that the world's friendship has declined would not be far wrong.

Apparently nobody knows what course President Wilson will take now that the treaty has been rejected. If the Senate, as seems likely, follows its action of today by adopting Senator Knox's resolution declaring that a state of peace exists between the United States and Germany, the President is practically certain to ignore it. He holds that this is an act constitutionally vested in the Executive and that no action by Congress can compel him to follow any other course than that which he chooses.

"PRESIDENT HAILS SUFFRAGE VICTORY," AUGUST 20, 1920

The ratification of the Nineteenth Amendment guaranteeing women the right to vote took place in the final months of the Wilson administration. Congress had sent the amendment to the states for ratification in 1919, and just over a year later, it won the required approval of three-fourths of the states for enactment. After Tennessee put the amendment over the threshold with its favorable vote in August 1920, President Wilson hailed the victory for women's rights.

AUGUST 20, 1920
PRESIDENT HAILS SUFFRAGE VICTORY

He Sends a Telegram to Gov. Roberts Expressing Satisfaction at Tennessee's Action.
WAR ON SENATORS TO START
Women Expect to Fight Wadsworth, Moses and Brandegee—Lady Astor Sends Congratulations.
Special to The New York Times.

WASHINGTON, Aug. 19.—President Wilson sent a telegram to Governor Roberts of Tennessee today expressing his satisfaction over the ratification of the suffrage amendment by the Tennessee Legislature. The text of the message was not made public at the White House, where it was said that the President preferred that Governor Roberts should make known its contents.

Miss Alice Paul and other leaders of the National Woman's Party, while elated over the result in Tennessee, are instructing their representatives in Nashville to be on the alert to prevent any defections in the ranks of the legislators who voted for the suffrage amendment in the Tennessee House of Representatives yesterday when the House tomorrow reconsiders the vote.

Miss Paul has also communicated with Mrs. Abby Scott Baker of Washington, the Woman's Party representative at Marion and Dayton, urging her to obtain renewed assurances from Senator Harding and Governor Cox that they would use additional efforts to keep members of their respective parties in the Tennessee Legislature in line for suffrage.

Mrs. Baker reported that she had seen Governor Cox and had been assured that he would leave nothing undone to hold Democratic votes for the amendment. She said that she would motor to Marion to interview Senator Harding.

With the Federal amendment apparently ratified by the requisite number of States, Miss Paul has communicated with members of the party's Executive Committee to ascertain what is the earliest date that a meeting of the committee can be held in Washington to determine plans for the party's national convention. Tentative plans were made today to have a four days' session of the convention in Washington within the next two months. . . .

Lady Astor, first woman member of the British Parliament, sent this message:

"Women's quality of moral courage is essential in public life, to help the growth of better social and international relations."

THE PRESIDENCY OF WARREN G. HARDING

MARCH 4, 1921 – AUGUST 2, 1923

Warren Gamaliel Harding's presidency was limited in both ambition and accomplishments. Governing after the tumultuous war years, Harding won election on a platform promising a "return to normalcy," and he upheld that slogan in the White House. Harding did preside over some important developments in the American presidency, most notably the creation of the Bureau of the Budget, which in time would assume responsibility for preparing the federal government's annual budget proposal. But the Harding legacy was tarnished by political scandals involving some of the president's close advisers. Although Harding himself was not directly implicated in these scandals, his failure to control corruption in his administration reflected poorly on his leadership. The pressures of the office took their toll on his health, and he died on August 2, 1923, having served for only two-and-a-half years in the White House.

Source: The Granger Collection, New York

THE CANNED CANDIDATE IN ACTION

The first sitting U.S. senator to be elected president, Harding came to the Oval Office directly from Congress, but his formative career experiences were in state politics. Born in Ohio just months after the Civil War ended, Harding was the oldest of eight children and he was raised in modest comfort. After graduating from Ohio Central College, where he edited the student newspaper, he taught school for a year, then sold insurance, and entered journalism by purchasing a newspaper with two partners. The *Marion Star* became a successful and well-regarded Ohio paper, and Harding's work as editor made him a visible presence in the community.

In 1899 Harding won election to the Ohio Senate, where he served for four years, followed by a two-year term as the state's lieutenant-governor. A few years later, Harding ran for governor of Ohio and lost. He won election to the U.S. Senate in 1914, and was one of the first senators to be elected by popular vote, after adoption of the Seventeenth Amendment, which called for the people, rather than state legislatures, to elect senators. But he was not an active legislator, preferring instead to socialize with his colleagues over drinks and poker games. He voted for Prohibition and for women's suffrage, but he opposed the post–World War I Treaty of Versailles.

QUICK FACTS ON WARREN G. HARDING

BIRTH	November 2, 1865, Corsica (Blooming Grove), Ohio
EDUCATION	Ohio Central College
FAMILY	Wife: Florence Kling De Wolfe Harding
WHITE HOUSE PETS	Dogs ("Laddie Boy" and "Old Boy"), canaries
PARTY	Republican
PREPRESIDENTIAL CAREER (SELECTED)	Schoolteacher, 1882 Insurance business, 1883 Purchase of Ohio newspaper, 1884 County auditor, Marion, Ohio, 1895 Ohio Senate, 1899–1903 Lieutenant-governor of Ohio, 1904–1905 U.S. Senate, 1915–1921
PRESIDENTIAL TERM	March 4, 1921–August 2, 1923
VICE PRESIDENT	Calvin Coolidge
SELECTED EVENTS	Immigration Restriction Act (1921) Budget and Accounting Act (1921) Washington Disarmament Conference (1921) Five-Power Limitation on Naval Armaments Treaty (1922) Fordney-McCumber Tariff Act (1922) First presidential visit to Alaska (1923)
DEATH	August 2, 1923, San Francisco, Calif.

THE ELECTION OF 1920

Harding's political career did not suggest a route to the presidency. Indeed, his election was due primarily to public dissatisfaction with eight years of Democratic leadership in the White House and the Republican Party's inability to find another acceptable candidate. Harding became known in the Republican Party after giving the nomination speech for President William Howard Taft at the 1912 Republican National Convention. Eight years later, the Republicans could not rally around a candidate, and, when party leaders huddled together to discuss possibilities, they settled on Senator Harding. His good looks, affability, and support for the party agenda carried him to the nomination on the tenth ballot. The convention selected Calvin Coolidge of Massachusetts as his running mate.

Following the model of former Republican presidents James A. Garfield, Benjamin Harrison, and William McKinley

(all of whom also were from Ohio), Harding ran a "front-porch" campaign in which he gave speeches to groups of people who visited him in Marion. The strategy was resoundingly successful: In the general election, Harding and Coolidge overwhelmingly defeated the Democratic presidential candidate, Gov. James M. Cox of Ohio, who shared the ticket with vice-presidential candidate, Franklin D. Roosevelt of New York, the assistant secretary of the navy. The Republican ticket won more than 16 million popular votes to 9 million for the Democrats, and Harding prevailed in the Electoral College with 404 votes to Cox's 127.

THE HARDING ADMINISTRATION

In selecting his ten-member cabinet, President Harding appointed Republicans representing different groups within the party. Charles Evans Hughes of New York, who had resigned from the U.S. Supreme Court in 1916 to run for president, became secretary of state, a surprising choice given his support for the League of Nations and Harding's opposition. (Hughes returned to the Court as chief justice in 1930.) The president appeased opponents of the league by selecting John Weeks of Massachusetts for secretary of war. Weeks was the choice of Sen. Henry Cabot Lodge, who had led the fight against the Treaty of Versailles. For treasury secretary, Harding appointed financier Andrew W. Mellon of Pennsylvania. Future president Herbert C. Hoover of California was selected for commerce secretary.

Harding also appointed some close friends to his cabinet: Sen. Albert Fall of New Mexico became interior secretary, and Harding's campaign manager and longtime political sponsor, Harry M. Daugherty of Ohio, became attorney general. Both appointments later caused trouble for the Harding administration, as did the selection of Edwin Denby of Michigan for secretary of the navy.

First Lady Florence Kling De Wolfe Harding, nicknamed "The Duchess," was a native of Marion and instrumental in the success of the *Marion Star* newspaper. She was five years older than her husband and had a child from a previous marriage, but the Hardings had no children together. Warren Harding had a longtime affair with a woman named Nan Britton, whom he knew from Ohio, and she claimed after his death that he was the father of her daughter.

Major Issues

Upon taking office in 1921, President Harding called Congress into special session to address various economic concerns. After much debate, Congress reduced taxes and raised tariffs. The most significant legislation from this period was the Budget and Accounting Act of 1921, which established the Bureau of the Budget and became the basis for executive initiative in preparing the annual federal budget proposal. Restrictions on immigration also were imposed with the Immigration Restriction Act of 1921. The following year, the president signed legislation to regulate and assist farmers and a bill (Fordney-McCumber Tariff Act) to raise tariffs further. In foreign affairs, the Harding administration sponsored a multilateral naval disarmament conference in Washington, D.C., which produced a five-power agreement in 1922 to reduce the navies of the participating nations.

The Harding administration is, however, remembered more for its problems than its policies. The close friends that President Harding appointed to high office took advantage of their positions to profit from selling government resources, and the president was blamed for their corruption. Charles Forbes, director of the Veterans Bureau, sold government supplies and awarded contracts dishonestly. Forbes resigned when the president learned of his actions, and a Senate investigation ultimately resulted in his conviction and imprisonment. Interior Secretary Fall accepted bribes to lease oil reserves to businessmen, and he too faced conviction and jail time. Navy Secretary Denby also was implicated in this matter—dubbed the "Teapot Dome" scandal after an oil reserve in Wyoming. Perhaps most disastrous for Harding's legacy was the downfall of his political mentor, Attorney General Daugherty. A 1924 Senate investigation of the Justice Department implicated Daugherty in illegal activities, but he was not convicted at trial.

Although the bulk of these scandals came to light after Harding's unexpected death, charges of corruption and misbehavior in his administration were raised during his presidency, to his great sorrow. A pleasant and amiable man, who met regularly with the press, Harding preferred poker and golf to politics. As a senator, he had supported the Eighteenth Amendment authorizing Prohibition, but Harding drank and smoked heavily. These habits along with growing criticism of his presidency had a negative effect on Harding's health and mental state.

In summer 1923 Harding became the first president to visit Alaska. He was to inspect the territory and get some much-needed rest. But he became ill on the return trip and died suddenly in San Francisco on August 2, either from a blood clot in the brain or heart failure. Just as Harding's candidacy for the White House had been unexpected three years earlier, so too was his death a shocking end to his presidency.

"Arranged During Recess," June 13, 1920, and "The Nomination of Harding," June 13, 1920

With no clear choice for its presidential candidate in 1920, the Republican Party selected Sen. Warren G. Harding of Ohio on the tenth ballot at its national convention in Chicago. (Democrats were similarly undecided, selecting their candidate on the forty-fourth ballot.) The deal brokered by party bosses evoked the "smoke-filled rooms" that defined nominating conventions in the nineteenth and early twentieth centuries. Harding's success was due largely to the efforts of his close political ally, Harry M. Daugherty, an Ohio lobbyist and political operative. In a scathing editorial, *The New York Times* described Harding's limited ambitions and surprising nomination for the presidency. The editorial calls him "a very respectable Ohio politician of the second class. He has never been a leader of men or a director of policies."

JUNE 13, 1920
ARRANGED DURING RECESS

Deal for Harding Goes Through When Lowden Frees Delegates.

BIG GAIN ON NINTH BALLOT

When the New York Delegates Swing to Him the Shouting Begins.

URGED AT NIGHT COUNCILS

But Leaders in the Race Refused to Yield at That Time—Later the Break Came.

Special to The New York Times

CHICAGO, June 12.—Senator Warren G. Harding of Marion, Ohio, was nominated for President of the United States by the Republican Party represented by its delegates assembled in national convention at the Coliseum this evening. Calvin Coolidge, Governor of Massachusetts, was nominated for Vice President.

The nomination of the Presidential candidate came on the tenth ballot. In the ninth ballot the whole trend of the convention sentiment was toward Harding. When New York, with its heavy representation, went to him on the tenth, everything was over except the shouting—and the shouting began immediately.

Senator Harding's nomination was the outcome of a complex situation that did not begin to clear until last evening. After four ineffective ballots yesterday the convention had adjourned until this morning. Four additional ballots in the forenoon and early afternoon of today had developed Harding strength, but General Leonard Wood

and Governor Frank O. Lowden had remained in the lead. A recess was taken for two hours, and during that short period combinations were formed that made Harding's nomination certain.

The real stampede of delegates to Harding began when Governor Lowden, abandoning his intention to address the convention, issued instead a formal announcement that his delegates were released from their pledges to him.

Interesting, and even thrilling, as the open proceedings in the convention were, moves behind the scenes, of which most of the convention knew nothing, had their dramatic side. The nomination of the candidate for President was arranged in conferences in hotel rooms. The prediction made in Washington weeks ago that the convention would get into a deadlock over candidates that would necessitate a combination arranged by a comparatively few of the party's dominating spirits was fulfilled to the letter.

> Warren G. Harding is a very respectable Ohio politician of the second class.

JUNE 13, 1920
EDITORIAL
THE NOMINATION OF HARDING.

Upon a platform that has produced general dissatisfaction, the Chicago convention presents a candidate whose nomination will be received with astonishment and dismay by the party whose suffrages he invites. Warren G. Harding is a very respectable Ohio politician of the second class. He has never been a leader of men or a director of policies. For years a protégé of Foraker, he rose to a subordinate office by favor of "Boss" Cox of Cincinnati. Beaten by Judson Harmon in the contest for the Governorship in 1910, he has never shown independent strength in his own State save when he was named for Senator in 1914, having a majority of a little more than 100,000 over his Democratic competitor; and outside of Ohio he has only such strength as he now derives from his place at the head of the Republican ticket. Senator Harding's record at Washington has been faint and colorless. He was an undistinguished and indistinguishable unit in the ruck of Republican Senators who obediently followed Mr. Lodge in the twistings and turnings of that statesman's foray upon the Treaty and the Covenant.

The nomination of Harding, for whose counterpart we must go back to Franklin Pierce if we would seek a President who measures down to his political stature, is the fine and perfect flower of the cowardice and imbecility of the Senatorial cabal that charged itself with the management of the Republican Convention, against whose control Governor Beeckman so vehemently protested. Rejecting Leonard Wood, probably the strongest candidate with the people the party could have chosen, because they knew he would never be dictated to by them, they favored Governor Lowden until Borah served upon them his notice of a veto of that nomination. Borah was commanding and truculent because he knew that he had to deal with a group of white-livered and incompetent politicians. If Republican leadership had not fallen into the hands of pigmies the chief men at Chicago would have told Borah to bolt and be hanged, just as upon the issue of the League they would have defied Johnson to do his worst. But they ran like a frightened flock, surrendered everything, Mr. Lodge finally throwing off all disguises and standing out as the open foe of the Covenant of the League of Nations, even with his own reservations.

What has befallen the Republican Party of the early days, the party of sixty years ago, when it was possessed of moral purposes, or of forty and thirty years ago, when it could still profess to have them and find believers?

. . . .

"THAT IDEAL CAMPAIGN FRONT PORCH," JUNE 20, 1920

Consistent with his slogan calling for a "return to normalcy," Republican candidate Warren Harding maintained a relaxed schedule during the 1920 presidential campaign, frequently giving speeches to people from his front porch in Marion, Ohio. President William McKinley of Ohio had employed this strategy to great success in 1896, and a *Times* writer who had viewed McKinley's campaign compared Harding's approach favorably.

Campaigning for president in 1920, Warren Harding makes a front porch speech from his home in Marion, Ohio.

Source: The New York Times

JUNE 20, 1920
THAT IDEAL CAMPAIGN FRONT PORCH

Candidate to Follow Example of McKinley, One of His Political Heroes—
Mrs. Harding, "The Duchess," as a Waffle-Maker
By FRANK PARKER STOCKBRIDGE.

Senator Warren Gamaliel Harding announces that he is going to make a front-porch campaign. It is twenty-four years since his distinguished fellow-Ohioan, William McKinley, conducted his famous front-porch campaign at Canton. Mr. Bryan set the fashion of rear-platform campaigning in 1896, and since then every candidate for the Presidency but one has done most of his campaigning by train. The one was Alton B. Parker, who didn't travel much—nor far.

I spent a considerable part of the Summer of 1896 on Major McKinley's front porch, and watched the lawn disintegrate into a mudhole under the feet of visiting "delegations" from every part of the United States. They used to say that Major McKinley got so tired of hearing "brass bands" play "Hail to the Chief" that he asked General Horace Porter, who was marshal of the inaugural parade of 1897, to keep them from playing it on that occasion; likewise that the General's appointment as Ambassador to France was partly by way of reward for his success in that matter.

Be that as it may, Senator Harding may not yet get so tired of band music as Major McKinley did. The Major never played in a brass band himself, but the Senator did. Of that, more anon; I was about to speak of front porches.

An Ideal Campaign Porch.

Roomy and ample as was the McKinley porch at Canton, the Harding porch at Marion is ampler and roomier. Moreover, it has a circular bulge or rostrum at one end that makes the finest sort of a platform from which to make speeches to the assembled multitude. There is room for a considerable multitude, too, on the Harding lawn, the next-door neighbor's lawn and the sidewalk and street in front of the house. It would not be difficult, I should say, to dispose some 10,000 persons so they would all be within hearing of the candidate's voice as he spoke from the circular end of the porch. He has a strong voice, pitched to carry well either up or down wind.

It is the best porch in Marion on which to eat hot waffles. Indeed, and I say this with full knowledge of the waffle-bearing capacity of Ohio front porches, it is the best porch in Ohio on which to eat hot waffles. We sat on the porch one day—Mr. Harding and the writer—and ate hot waffles as fast as Mrs. Harding could cook them.

"Mr. Harding's Attorney General," February 22, 1921

President Harding's decision to reward campaign manager Harry Daugherty by appointing him attorney general sparked much controversy, particularly given Daugherty's limited legal expertise. In an editorial sharply criticizing the appointment, *The Times* aptly described it as "a reward for political services rendered. . . . Mr. Harding has been content merely to choose a best friend."

FEBRUARY 22, 1921
EDITORIAL
MR. HARDING'S ATTORNEY GENERAL.

From Hughes to Daugherty is a pretty long step. If the appointment of the first was intended to make that of the second more palatable, we fear that Mr. Harding will be disappointed. The suggestion that Mr. Daugherty might be made Attorney General has been before the public ever since the November election, and if it has anywhere been received with favor it has escaped our notice. On the contrary, it has provoked strong protests even from Republicans.

The reasons are perfectly understood. Mr. Daugherty has long been known as a politician. He appears never to have been known as a lawyer whom even his friends would think of as fit to be Attorney General of the United States. His most important practice would seem to have been politico-legal. If the impartial opinion of the Ohio bar had been sought, it would surely have been that Mr. Daugherty was not qualified, by either knowledge or experience, to be Attorney General.

Mr. Harding unquestionably feels deeply in Mr. Daugherty's debt, politically. The appointment is admittedly a reward for political services rendered. But the feeling of the country will be that some other office should have been selected as the visible proof of Mr. Harding's gratitude. If a best mind is needed anywhere, it is in the Department of Justice. Instead, Mr. Harding has been content to choose merely a best friend.

• •

"Taft Selected as Chief Justice of the Supreme Court," March 29, 1921

One of President Harding's more successful appointments was his selection of former Republican president William Howard Taft to become chief justice of the United States. In colorful writing, *The Times* reported that this position fit the former president's interests, expertise, and personality perfectly, in contrast to his term in the White House.

MARCH 29, 1921
TAFT SELECTED AS CHIEF JUSTICE OF SUPREME COURT
Harding Decides to Name ex-President to Place Which Friends Desire for Him.
WHITE EXPECTED TO RESIGN
Believed That He Wishes to Make Way for the Man Who Appointed Him in 1910.
WANTS HIM AS SUCCESSOR
Present Chief Justice Has Held On, It Is Said, to Await Choice of Taft.
Special to The New York Times

WASHINGTON, March 28.—One evening in January, 1908, President Roosevelt entertained at dinner in the White House a company which included Secretary of War William H. Taft and Mrs. Taft. When the gentlemen had joined the ladies in the library after dinner, President Roosevelt, reclining in an easy chair, whimsically closed his eyes and said:

"I am the seventh son of a seventh daughter, I have clairvoyant powers. I see standing before me a man weighing about 350 pounds, and there is something hanging over his head. I cannot quite make out what it is. It is hanging by a slender thread. At one time it looks as if it was the Presidency, and then, again, it looks like the Chief Justiceship."

"Make it the Presidency!" exclaimed Mrs. Taft.

"Make it the Chief Justiceship!" cried Mr. Taft.

Mrs. Taft had her wish. When the whirling plummet of President Roosevelt's vision came to rest over Mr. Taft's head it presented the "Presidency" side to the world.

President Harding has now seen the same plummet whirl and come to rest above Mr. Taft's head. This time the face it presents is labelled "Chief Justiceship." Appar-

ently the ambitions of both Mr. and Mrs. Taft are to be realized.

The New York Times correspondent has information, of a character sufficiently definite to furnish good ground for credence, that William H. Taft has been selected by President Harding for appointment as Chief Justice of the United States in the event of the expected resignation of the present Chief Justice, Edward Douglass White. This information was not obtained as a consequence of Mr. Taft's visit to Washington last week when he saw President Harding and Attorney General Daugherty, and probably will come as a surprise to Mr. Taft's friends, who had been somewhat blue over what they believed was the prospect that he would not be appointed Chief Justice.

"IMMIGRATION BILL PASSED BY SENATE," MAY 4, 1921

The Immigration Restriction Act of 1921 sharply decreased immigration to the United States by imposing quotas for the first time. Only 3 percent of a foreign nation's immigrant population in the United States, based on the 1910 census, would be permitted to enter the country. The law reduced immigration to less than 360,000 people annually, with a majority of those individuals coming from northern and western Europe, and the rest from southern and eastern Europe.

MAY 4, 1921
IMMIGRATION BILL PASSED BY SENATE
Reed Alone Votes Against the Measure Limiting Admission of Aliens.
JOHNSON AMENDMENT LOST
Senators Reject Proposal to Let in Victims of Religious or Political Persecution.
Special to The New York Times

WASHINGTON, May 3.—The Dillingham Immigration bill, which limits annual immigration to 3 per cent. of the persons of various nationalities in the United States in 1910, was passed by the Senate this afternoon by a vote of 78 to 1, the only Senator voting against the measure being Reed, Democrat, of Missouri.

The Senate rejected, by a vote of 60 to 15, the Johnson amendment, which would have permitted the immigration of persons who could prove to the American authorities that they were the victims of political or

religious persecution. Rejection of the Johnson amendment automatically rejected the House amendment, which permitted the victims of religious persecution to enter.

The bill now goes to conference, and its supporters assert that it will go to the President in practically the same form and language as it passed the Senate this afternoon. The general opinion is that the House will accept the Senate bill. The conferees who will represent the Senate are Senators Dillingham, Colt and King.

"Senate Agrees to New Budget Bill," May 27, 1921

The Budget and Accounting Act of 1921 formally established executive initiative in preparing the annual federal budget. A new agency, the Bureau of the Budget, was created to assist the executive branch in this responsibility.

MAY 27, 1921
SENATE AGREES TO NEW BUDGET BILL

Adopts Conference Report on Measure Establishing General Government Accounting System.

HOUSE WILL ACCEPT TODAY

President to Appoint Director and Assistant Director—

Controller General to Serve 15 Years.

Special to The New York Times

WASHINGTON, May 26.—With the adoption today by the Senate of the conference report on the bill providing for a national budget system and independent audit of Government accounts, and its prospective approval by the House tomorrow, there is every likelihood that the budget bill will be sent to the White House not later than Saturday and may become law next week.

Immediately after its approval the President will begin consideration of the personnel of the new budget organization, and name the director and controller general provided for by the measure. The new general accounting system is to go into effect on July 1, 1921, the opening of the fiscal year 1922, and the budget system becomes effective upon the signing of the bill.

As agreed to in conference the bill is practically the same as passed by the House and Senate, with the exception of two important features.

The Senate bill provides that the Bureau of the Budget shall be in the Treasury Department. The House agrees to this location of the bureau with the modification that the bureau shall prepare the budget for the President under such rules and regulations as he may prescribe, and that the director of the bureau shall perform the administrative duties personal to the bureau under such rules and regulations as the President may prescribe.

The Senate bill provides that the director of the budget and the assistant director shall be appointed by the President, with the advice and consent of the Senate. The House bill provides that they shall be appointed by the President, and this was agreed to by the conferees.

The Senate bill provides that the Controller General and the Assistant Controller General shall hold office for seven years, but may be removed at any time for the causes named in the bill by joint resolution. The House bill provides that the Controller General and his assistant shall hold office during good behavior, but may be removed at any time by concurrent resolution of Congress for the causes named in the bill. The bill as agreed upon in conference fixes the terms of office of the Controller General and the Assistant Controller General at fifteen years, provides for their removal at any time by joint resolution of Congress for the causes named in the bill, and further provides that no Controller General shall serve more than one term.

The provision in the Senate bill making applicable to employes of the Bureau of the Budget the additional compensation to civilian employes of the Government during the fiscal years 1921 and 1922 is incorporated in the bill as agreed upon. The House provision for the creation of a bureau of accounts in the Post Office Department to take over the duties of the administrative examination of accounts and vouchers of the postal service is incorporated in the bill. The provision in the Senate bill requesting the General Accounting Office to furnish the Bureau of the Budget such information relating to expenditures and accounts as may be required from time to time is also incorporated.

"Ratify Colombia Payment," October 15, 1921

In 1921 the United States ratified a treaty authorizing a $25 million payment to Colombia for its loss of Panama nearly two decades earlier. Theodore Roosevelt's administration had encouraged Panamanians to revolt against Colombia in 1903, after which the administration swiftly negotiated a treaty to guarantee U.S. development of what became the Panama canal. Roosevelt supporters in the Senate had previously rejected this implicit apology to Colombia.

OCTOBER 15, 1921
RATIFY COLOMBIA PAYMENT.

$25,000,000 From United States Accepted by Bogota Senate.

BOGOTA, Colombia, Oct. 13 (Associated Press).—The Colombian Senate, after three sessions during which there was much discussion, today ratified the treaty with the United States by which Colombia is to receive $25,000,000.

The treaty, which was ratified by the United States Senate last April, is an outgrowth of difficulties between the United States and Colombia in connection with the acquisition of the Panama Canal route.

- -

"Conference to Open With Aim to Speed Arms Cut Decision," November 11, 1921

One of the Harding administration's few initiatives in foreign affairs was hosting a five-nation conference in Washington, D.C., to discuss naval disarmament. The United States, France, Great Britain, Italy, and Japan negotiated a treaty to reduce the size of their navies.

NOVEMBER 11, 1921
CONFERENCE TO OPEN WITH AIM TO SPEED ARMS CUT DECISION

Program for Tomorrow Announces Speeches by Harding and Presiding Officer Only.
HUGHES TO BE CHAIRMAN
Adjournment Will Be Taken Until Tuesday—Americans to Sit at Head of Table.
HOPE TO END BY CHRISTMAS
Two Main Committees Will Consider Armament and Far Eastern Problems.
Special to The New York Times

WASHINGTON, Nov. 10.—The formal program for the first session of the Conference on the Limitation of Armament, to be held at 10:30 o'clock Saturday morning, was sent today by the State Department to the members of the various delegations.

There will be two addresses, one by President Harding and the other by the delegate who is chosen to the conference as its presiding officer. It is accepted that this post will go to Secretary of State Hughes, head of the American delegation.

It was announced that, in accordance with the desire which has been expressed on behalf of the missions, no responses will be made to President Harding's address.

A Secretary General will be selected, and this office, it is understood, will be given to John W. Garrett, former Minister of the United States to Argentina. Committees on program and procedure will then be named and the conference will adjourn to meet again on Tuesday, Nov. 15. . . .

Two Main Committees.

There will be two committees on program and procedure, one to deal with the limitation of armaments and the other with Pacific and Far Eastern questions. The former committee will be composed of the heads of the five principal delegations, those of Great Britain, France, Japan, Italy and the United States. The latter committee will include, in addition to the five named, the heads of the four other delegations invited to participate in discussions of Pacific and Far Eastern questions—China, The Netherlands, Portugal and Belgium.

"President Is Expected to Pardon Debs When Freeing Other War Offenders Friday," December 21, 1921

President Harding used his constitutional pardoning power to free many people who had been jailed for antiwar activity (often speeches) during World War I. Perhaps the most famous was Socialist Party leader Eugene V. Debs, a five-time presidential candidate, who actually had run from prison against Harding in 1920. The president released Debs on Christmas Day 1921. The pardon was not to apply to members of the Industrial Workers of the World (IWW) union, which Debs had helped to found.

DECEMBER 21, 1921
PRESIDENT IS EXPECTED TO PARDON DEBS WHEN FREEING OTHER WAR OFFENDERS FRIDAY
Special to The New York Times

WASHINGTON, Dec. 20.—Announcement will be made at the White House Friday of the release of a certain number of so-called political prisoners whose cases have been outlined by Attorney General Daugherty to President Harding. An official statement to this effect was made today after a meeting of the Cabinet.

The President will not issue a proclamation of general amnesty to prisoners who have been convicted under wartime legislation, according to the White House statement, and in arriving at decisions to release the prisoners he has considered each case separately on its merits. Mr. Harding has intimated that he will not extend executive clemency to I. W. W.'s, on the ground that he does not consider these cases as lying within the political category.

The Department of Justice completed last week a summary of the offenses, trials and sentences against 206 Federal prisoners, including Eugene V. Debs, who were convicted under the Espionage act and other war-time laws. This was forwarded to the White House early this week, and the President has spent several evenings in studying the cases.

It is the general impression in Administration circles that, while the President may parole some prisoners or commute their sentences, he will give an out-and-out pardon to Debs, who, as Socialist candidate for President, was Mr. Harding's opponent in the 1920 election. The President has let it be known that he considers the fact that Debs was his opponent puts his case in a class by itself.

As for the other prisoners who may be permitted to return to their homes in time for Christmas, it is thought that President Harding will adopt three methods of accomplishing their release. Having indicated that he desires to consider each case separately, paying particular attention to the offenses for which the prisoners were sentenced, it appears likely that the President will regard some as deserving of full pardon and consequent restoration of citizenship, while others will have their sentences commuted so that they will come under the requirements demanded for paroles.

"WASHINGTON DAZED BY BIG REVERSAL," NOVEMBER 9, 1922

Public dissatisfaction with the Harding administration, particularly the president's opposition to a bonus bill for soldiers, led to severe losses for the Republican Party in the 1922 congressional midterm elections. Although Republicans narrowly maintained control of the House and Senate, the large popular vote majority that President Harding won in 1920 all but disappeared.

NOVEMBER 9, 1922
WASHINGTON DAZED BY BIG REVERSAL

Republican Reorganization Is Talked Of—Vote Gives Power to the Progressive Wing.
ADMINISTRATION CRIPPLED
Tariff, Labor Troubles, Bonus and Other Causes of Discontent Are Cited.
Special to The New York Times

WASHINGTON, Nov. 8.—Republican defeat in yesterday's election far exceeds the gloomiest apprehensions of the Republican leaders on the eve of the voting, and exceeds just as greatly the wildest hopes of the Democrats.

The verdict at the polls portends a reorganization of the Republican Party and gives great encouragement to the Democratic Party as to 1924, besides developing several outstanding Presidential contenders. In the next Senate the balance of power will be held by the progressive-radical group led by Senator La Follette.

Control of Congress in the sense that a majority will exist sufficiently cohesive to operate in conjunction with the Administration to put through either a party or an Administration program will not obtain after the fourth of next March. Measures which can command the support of Congress majorities will have to be progressive ones with special privileges and sectional features eliminated.

That such a result could follow so soon after the Republican tidal wave of 1920 no one seemed to expect. The more than seven million majority given to President Harding has been wiped out. The demonstration of disapproval of the Administration was unmistakable.

· ·

"DAUGHERTY CHARGES ARE HELD NOT TRUE," JANUARY 10, 1923

The problems with President Harding's appointment of close allies to high office became evident in 1923 with an impeachment effort against Attorney General Daugherty for corruption in the Justice Department. These charges were dismissed, but subsequent investigations proved far more damaging.

JANUARY 10, 1923
DAUGHERTY CHARGES ARE HELD NOT TRUE

Judiciary Committee, 12 to 2, Recommends Dismissal of Impeachment Case.
ADVERSE REPORT ON KELLER
Committee, 11 to 2, Says House Has Power to Punish Him by Imprisonment
or Otherwise.

WASHINGTON, Jan. 9.—Dismissal of impeachment charges brought against Attorney General Daugherty by Representative Keller, Republican of Minnesota, is recommended to the House in a resolution adopted today, 12 to 2, by the Judiciary Committee, which held public hearings on the charges last month.

At the same time the committee approved, 11 to 2, a formal report to the House holding that that body had the power to punish Mr. Keller by imprisonment or otherwise for his refusal to obey a subpoena issued for him immediately after his dramatic withdrawal from the case on the third day of the hearings.

Both the resolution and the report will be submitted to the House tomorrow by Chairman Volstead, but whether there will be formal action on them appears now to be a moot question. Some Committeemen are of the opinion that House action is unnecessary, but others think the resolution and the report with regard to Mr. Keller should receive formal consideration.

The resolution proposing dismissal of the charges, which was opposed by Representatives Sumners of Texas and Thomas of Kentucky, Democrats, is as follows:

"Resolved, that your committee has made an examination touching the matters charged to ascertain if there is any probable ground to believe that any part of the charges are true; and on consideration of the charges and the evidence obtained it does not appear that there is any ground to believe that Harry M. Daugherty, Attorney General, has been guilty of any high crime or misdemeanor requiring the interposition of the impeachment powers of the House.

"Resolved, that the Committee on Judiciary be discharged from further consideration of the charges and proposed impeachment of Harry M. Daugherty, Attorney General of the United States, and that House Resolution 425 (the Keller impeachment resolution) be laid upon the table."

"HARDING WORN OUT, COOLIDGE HOLDS," AUGUST 1, 1923

Charges of corruption in his administration hurt the president deeply, and he left Washington to embark on a speaking tour in the summer of 1923. The trip, including the first presidential visit to Alaska, ended unexpectedly and disastrously.

AUGUST 1, 1923
HARDING WORN OUT, COOLIDGE HOLDS
Has Never Spared Himself in Service of Country, Declares Vice President.
PAINSTAKING IN HIS DUTIES
News of Illness Delayed by Isolation of Coolidge Family's Vermont Retreat.
Special to The New York Times

PLYMOUTH, Vt., July 31.—Vice President Calvin Coolidge expressed confidence today that President Harding would recover from his illness. He said he had received a telegram from his secretary at Washington that the condition of the President had improved considerably.

"In common with all Americans," Mr. Coolidge said, "I am distressed at the illness of the President, and besides that I am grieved at the sufferings of a man with whom I have been so intimately associated on terms of more than ordinary friendship. Recent reports indicate to me that he will recover to resume the important service which he is rendering to his country."

Earlier in the day Mr. Coolidge said:

"It is evident that President Harding has worn himself down, very much as Mrs. Harding did, in the service of the American people. It is my opinion that he is the truest friend that our country has. It is no wonder that every one was distressed to learn of his illness and is rejoicing at the prospect of his recovery.

"He has never spared himself, but has been constant in the most earnest efforts to perform the duties of his office, even to the minutest detail. It is this painstaking effort that is apparently the main cause of his illness."

"Death Stroke Came Without Warning," August 3, 1923

President Harding became ill toward the end of his speaking tour and died in San Francisco on August 2. First Lady Florence Harding would not permit an autopsy, so the cause of death was not identified definitively, but it likely was either heart failure or a blood clot in the brain. Thousands mourned the departed president as his funeral procession returned slowly to Washington, D.C.

AUGUST 3, 1923
DEATH STROKE CAME WITHOUT WARNING

Mrs. Harding Was Reading to Her Husband When First Sign Appeared—
She Ran for Doctor
BUT NOTHING COULD BE DONE TO REVIVE PATIENT
News of Tragic End Shocks Everybody, Coming After Day Said to Have Been the
Best Since His Illness Began a Week Ago.
Special to The New York Times

SAN FRANCISCO, Aug. 2.—President Harding died at 7:30 o'clock tonight [11:30 o'clock New York time] of a stroke of apoplexy.

The end came suddenly while Mrs. Harding was reading to him from the evening newspaper, and after what had been called the best day he had had since the beginning of his illness exactly one week ago.

A shudder ran through the President's frame and he collapsed.

Mrs. Harding and the two nurses in the sick room knew the end had come, and Mrs. Harding rushed out of the room and asked for Dr. Boone and the others to "come quick."

Dr. Boone and Brig. Gen. Sawyer reached the President before he passed away, but were not able to avert the inevitable.

This formal announcement following soon after told the story of the tragic end:

"The President died at 7:30 P.M. Mrs. Harding and the two nurses, Miss Ruth Powderly and Miss Sue Drusser, were in the room at the time. Mrs. Harding was reading to the President, when, utterly without warning, a slight shudder passed through his frame; he collapsed, and all recognized that the end had come. A stroke of apoplexy was the cause of his death.

"Within a few moments all of the President's official party had been summoned."

Shocking in Its Suddenness.

Nothing could have been a more shocking surprise. Shortly before the President's sudden collapse General Sawyer had been telling newspaper men that Mr. Harding had had the best day since he became seriously ill. He said that the President had definitely entered upon the stage of convalescence and that everything went to show that Mr. Harding was on the road to ultimate recovery.

The members of the official party had no warning that the President was in danger. They, like the newspaper men, had been assured that a fatal termination of the President's illness was a thing not likely and with good care he would be able to recover health and strength. Most of the members of the official party were at dinner when the news came. George B. Christian Jr., secretary to the President and his devoted friend, was in Los Angeles with Mrs. Christian. He had gone there at the President's solicitation to read at a gathering of the Knights Templar tonight an address which the President had prepared in the expectation that he would deliver it in person. Mr. Christian had declined to leave San Francisco until he was positively assured by the President's physicians that there was no likelihood of any set-back in the President's condition.

The newspaper men had an engagement with General Sawyer for 8 o'clock. He was to tell them of how the President was progressing toward recovery. In view of what he had said on prior occasions during the day and statements in two official bulletins, the newspaper men had every expectation that they would be able to record that Mr. Harding was one step nearer the goal of recovery.

"There will be a bulletin," said one of the White House messengers gathered in the corridor of the Presidential suite. In a few minutes copies of the bulletin on thin white paper were handed to the waiting reporters. Instead of informing them that the President's condition continued to improve, it gave them the astounding information that he was dead.

"Government Opens Teapot Dome Suit; Secrecy Admitted," March 10, 1925

Corruption investigations against President Harding's advisers continued after his death, culminating in exposure of the infamous "Teapot Dome" scandal. Interior Secretary Albert Fall and others were convicted of accepting bribes from businessmen for leasing government oil reserves, including the Teapot Dome reserve in Wyoming.

> [O]ne of the greatest frauds ever practiced on the Government.

MARCH 10, 1925
GOVERNMENT OPENS TEAPOT DOME SUIT; SECRECY ADMITTED
Pomerene Declares Sinclair and Fall Perpetrated Big Fraud Under Cover.
TESTIMONY BACKS CHARGE
Finney Testifies Fall Ordered Silence—Navy Oil Chief Says He Was Kept in Dark.
COL. STEWART NOW AT SEA
Witness to Canadian Deal Goes to Latin America—
Two Others in France Won't Return.
Special to The New York Times

CHEYENNE, Wyo., March 9.—The Government's suit for the cancellation of the Teapot Dome naval oil reserve lease to the Sinclair oil interests was called in the Federal Court at 10 o'clock this morning.

That the battle is to be a fight to the finish was indicated before the first session was an hour old. The Government bluntly charged that Harry F. Sinclair, head of the oil interests bearing his name, and former Secretary of the Interior Albert B. Fall were conspirators in one of the greatest frauds ever practiced on the Government, and that the Teapot Dome reserve was secretly and fraudulently transferred to Sinclair's control, the consideration being Liberty bonds exceeding $233,000 in value.

Coincident with the beginning of the trial it was admitted by representatives of the Standard Oil Company of Indiana that Colonel Robert W. Stewart, the Chairman of the board of that company, is now outside the jurisdiction of the American courts, somewhere on the Atlantic, bound either for Mexico or for South America.

The admission that Colonel Stewart is safely outside the process-serving zone was made by John D. Clark, Vice President of the Standard Oil Company of Indiana and assistant to the Chairman of the Board. Mr. Clark admitted that he gave the information with reluctance, explaining that Colonel Stewart is "southbound" on a business deal so important that the company desired to keep his movements secret.

"Daugherty Indicted as Conspirator in Alien Metals Sale," May 8, 1926

Former attorney general Harry Daugherty was tried on corruption charges a few years after the impeachment effort against him failed. He was charged with defrauding the government by accepting bribes, but he was not convicted at trial.

MAY 8, 1926
DAUGHERTY INDICTED AS CONSPIRATOR IN ALIEN METALS SALE

Ex-Attorney General Accused With Miller and King in the Transfer of $7,000,000.
$441,000 FEE IS ALLEGED
Agent of Swiss Concern Said to Have Rewarded Officials—His Case to Be Dropped.
INNOCENT, DAUGHERTY SAYS
Never Heard of Case Till It Was Disposed Of, He Declares—Senate Circles Stirred.

Harry M. Daugherty, Attorney General in President Harding's Cabinet; Colonel Thomas W. Miller, Alien Property Custodian in that Administration, and John T. King, formerly Republican National Committeeman from Connecticut, were indicted yesterday on a charge of conspiracy to "defraud the United States of its governmental functions and rights, and of the honest, impartial and unprejudiced services and judgment" of Mr. Daugherty and Colonel Miller in their official capacities.

The indictment was returned by the special Federal Grand Jury which has been investigating for the last five months the transfer of $7,000,000 of the funds of the American Metal Company, Ltd., from the custody of the Government, which had seized the money during the war, to a Swiss corporation. The true bill does not allege that the defendants actually defrauded the Government of that amount of money, but that in accepting $441,000 in commissions from the foreign claimants the Government officials defrauded their Government of their honest and unbiased judgment.

THE PRESIDENCY OF CALVIN COOLIDGE

AUGUST 3, 1923 – MARCH 4, 1929

The presidency of Calvin Coolidge emphasized economic investment and some international diplomacy. Vice President Coolidge became president on August 3, 1923, when President Warren G. Harding died unexpectedly in San Francisco. Although Coolidge had not sought the presidency actively (his name was entered for consideration at the 1920 Republican National Convention, but he did not secure significant support), he assumed the responsibilities of the office seriously. He would face criticism later for failing to regulate the financial industry, but during his presidency, his limited and efficient governance was well-received.

Named John Calvin at birth, Coolidge was raised on a family farm in Vermont. He graduated from Amherst College, studied law, and was admitted to the Massachusetts bar in 1897. He opened a law practice in Northampton, and began a steady progression in local and state politics.

Source: The Granger Collection, New York

"DO I HEAR FIRING?"

Coolidge served on the city council, as city solicitor, and as chairman of the county Republican committee. Coolidge only lost one election in his life, when he ran for the Northampton school board in 1905. He was elected to the Massachusetts House of Representatives, and after two terms there, returned to Northampton and became its mayor in 1910.

Coolidge next won election to the Massachusetts Senate, becoming its president in 1914. He was elected lieutenant governor of Massachusetts in 1915, and he won the state's top office three years later. Governor Coolidge received national attention for his management of the Boston police strike in 1919. He sent in the state militia to restore order, and when the labor movement criticized him, Coolidge responded: "There is no right to strike against the public safety by anybody, anywhere, any time." He handily won reelection the following year.

The selection of Coolidge as the Republican vice-presidential candidate in 1920 was a surprise. His name had been entered in contention for the presidency at the national convention, but he was not expected to prevail. After Sen. Warren Harding of Ohio won the presidential nomination on the tenth ballot, the convention chose Coolidge as his running mate. The two easily defeated Democratic presidential candidate James M. Cox of Ohio and his running mate, Franklin D. Roosevelt of New York, winning more than 16 million votes to just over 9 million for the Democratic ticket, and the Electoral College vote, 404–127.

QUICK FACTS ON CALVIN COOLIDGE

BIRTH	July 4, 1872, Plymouth, Vt.
EDUCATION	Amherst College
FAMILY	Wife: Grace Anna Goodhue Coolidge Children: John Coolidge, Calvin Coolidge
WHITE HOUSE PETS	Dogs, canaries, goose, mockingbird, cats, donkey ("Ebenezer"), raccoons, lion cubs, wallaby, pigmy hippo, bear
PARTY	Republican
PREPRESIDENTIAL CAREER (SELECTED)	City Council, Northampton, Mass., 1899 City solicitor, Northampton, Mass., 1900–1901 Massachusetts House of Representatives, 1907–1908 Mayor, Northampton, Mass., 1910–1911 Massachusetts Senate, 1912–1915; Senate president, 1914–1915 Lieutenant governor of Massachusetts, 1916–1918 Governor of Massachusetts, 1919–1920 U.S. vice president, 1921–1923
PRESIDENTIAL TERMS	August 3, 1923–March 4, 1925 March 4, 1925–March 4, 1929
VICE PRESIDENT	Charles Gates Dawes (second term)
SELECTED EVENTS	Senate investigations of scandals in Harding administration (1923–1924) Immigration Act (1924) Rogers Act creating U.S. Foreign Service (1924) Revenue Act (1926) Tacna-Arica Conference between Chile and Peru in Washington, D.C. (1926) Transatlantic solo flight by Charles Lindbergh (1927) Ratification of Kellogg-Briand Pact (1929)
POSTPRESIDENCY	President of American Antiquarian Society, 1930–1932 Syndicated newspaper column, 1930
DEATH	January 5, 1933, Northampton, Mass.

Coolidge was not active in the Harding administration, and he was vacationing in Vermont when the news came just after midnight on August 3, 1923, that Harding had died in San Francisco. Coolidge's father was a notary public, and he immediately swore his son into office. President Coolidge returned to Washington, D.C., on August 4.

Coolidge's unexpected rise to the presidency did not preclude him from firm governance. Harding's administration had been rife with corruption, and Senate investigations soon implicated former interior secretary Albert B. Fall in the

"Teapot Dome" scandal. Fall was accused of accepting bribes in exchange for leasing government oil fields. Attorney General Harry M. Daugherty, a close Harding ally, was charged with illegal activity as well. Coolidge demanded Daugherty's resignation and appointed a special counsel to investigate the Teapot Dome scandal. President Coolidge also expanded upon the restrictive immigration legislation passed under his predecessor, approving a 1924 law that limited immigrants from a country to 2 percent of the people already in the United States from that place, based on the 1890 census.

THE 1924 PRESIDENTIAL ELECTION

Coolidge ran for president in 1924 and won decisively. The Republican Party National Convention selected him on the first ballot and Charles G. Dawes of Illinois, the first director of the Bureau of the Budget, as his running mate. The Democratic National Convention, in contrast, held a historic 103 ballots to decide on its nominees, John W. Davis of West Virginia for president and Charles W. Bryan of Nebraska for vice president. Coolidge won with 15.7 million popular votes to almost 8.4 million for Davis, and 382 Electoral College votes to 136 for Davis.

THE COOLIDGE ADMINISTRATION

Upon taking office in 1923, Coolidge had kept President Harding's cabinet largely intact through 1924. In response to corruption charges, he replaced Attorney General Daugherty with Harlan Fiske Stone of New York. Navy Secretary Edwin Denby of Michigan was implicated in the Teapot Dome scandal, and Coolidge replaced him with Curtis D. Wilbur of California. After winning election in 1924, Coolidge made some changes in his ten-member cabinet, such as appointing Franklin B. Kellogg of Minnesota secretary of state and Dwight F. David of Missouri secretary of war. Treasury Secretary Andrew W. Mellon of Pennsylvania had the distinction of serving through both the Harding and Coolidge administrations, as did Labor Secretary James J. Davis of Pennsylvania.

First Lady Grace Coolidge was a former teacher for the deaf who balanced the president's reticence with her friendly demeanor. The Coolidges suffered an unspeakable tragedy when their sixteen-year-old son, Calvin Jr., died suddenly in July 1924 from blood poisoning. President Coolidge continued to govern, and even won election to a full term of office a few months later, but he and his wife never recovered from their horrific loss. Their other son, John, would become the oldest living child of an American president, dying in June 2000 at age ninety-three.

MAJOR ISSUES

President Coolidge's primary agenda as president was to promote financial prosperity by limiting federal spending and letting the economy grow unfettered by government restraints. With Treasury Secretary Mellon, he endorsed a major tax reduction program in 1926 that benefited wealthy as well as lower-income Americans and reduced other levies such as the estate tax. The Coolidge administration also worked vigorously to control the federal budget and succeeded in reducing the national debt. President Coolidge was credited for the nation's financial success at the time, but his support for limited government intervention in the economy would be viewed less favorably with the economic collapse that resulted in the Great Depression.

In foreign affairs, President Coolidge made some modest achievements. He supported the Kellogg-Briand Pact, ratified by the Senate in 1929. The pact declared war illegal—an ideal rather than a policy, which became outdated with the start of World War II. Coolidge reestablished U.S. ties with Mexico and endorsed diplomatic efforts to halt civil war in Nicaragua. The president tried unsuccessfully to persuade Congress not to prohibit Japanese immigration in its 1924 legislation.

In late 1927 President Coolidge announced that he would not run for reelection. He returned to Northampton, where he wrote a syndicated newspaper column as well as his memoirs. He also joined the board of directors of New York Life Insurance Company. He died in January 1933 of a heart attack.

· ·

"COOLIDGE TAKES THE OATH OF OFFICE," AUGUST 3, 1923, AND "COOLIDGE SWORN IN AT FARM HOMESTEAD," AUGUST 4, 1923

The death of President Warren G. Harding shocked the nation. Upon learning of the news in the early hours of August 3, 1923, Vice President Coolidge released a statement praising Harding as "a great and good man." He also announced that his father, a notary public whom Coolidge was visiting in Vermont, would administer the oath of office. *The New York Times* reported that Coolidge was sworn in "directly across the road from the house in which he was born."

AUGUST 3, 1923
COOLIDGE TAKES THE OATH OF OFFICE

His Father, Who Is a Notary Public, Administers It After Form Is Found
By Him in His Library.
ANNOUNCES HE WILL FOLLOW THE HARDING POLICIES
Wants All Who Aided Harding to Remain in Office—Roused After Midnight to Be
Told the News of the President's Death.
Statement by President Coolidge
Special to The New York Times

PLYMOUTH, Vt., Aug. 3.—President Calvin Coolidge issued the following statement early this morning:

Reports have reached me, which I fear are correct, that President Harding is gone. The world has lost a great and good man. I mourn his loss. He was my chief and my friend.

It will be my purpose to carry out the policies which he has begun for the service of the American people and for meeting their responsibilities wherever they may arise.

For this purpose I shall seek the co-operation of all those who have been associated with the President during his term of office.

Those who have given their efforts to assist him I wish to remain in office that they may assist me. I have faith that God will direct the destinies of our nation.

It is my intention to remain here until I can secure the correct form for the oath of office, which will be administered to me by my father, who is a notary public, if that will meet the necessary requirement. I expect to leave for Washington during the day.

CALVIN COOLIDGE.

AUGUST 4, 1923
COOLIDGE SWORN IN AT FARM HOMESTEAD

Oath Wired From Washington Is Administered by His Father at 2:43 o'Clock
in Morning.
OIL LAMP LIGHTS THE SCENE
President Was Aroused From Bed at Midnight to Be Informed of Mr. Harding's Death.
Special to The York Times

PLYMOUTH, Vt., Aug. 3.—Facing his father and with his wife at his side, Calvin Coolidge was sworn in as the thirtieth President of the United States at 2:43 this morning, standard time, in the parlor of the Coolidge homestead, directly across the road from the house in which he was born.

The President's father, John Calvin Coolidge, 78 years old, administered the oath of office. It was the first time in the history of the Republic that a father installed his son as the Chief Executive of the nation.

The ceremony took place in a typical New England parlor or sitting room, a comfortably furnished, livable room in the father's farm house at Plymouth Notch, in the southern part of the Green Mountains, nearly 2,000 feet above the level of the sea.

The faint light of an old-fashioned kerosene lamp, with a fluted top chimney and etched sides, was sufficient to throw the faces of the President and his father into bold relief. The rest of the small group that witnessed the simple ceremony were in a half light, almost a shadow. Back of the President was a large framed portrait of himself, which occupies the position of honor in his father's home.

The President's father, sturdy and active despite his years, stood at the south side of a small centre table that held the lamp, the family bible and a number of other books.

The President stood at the other side of the table, facing his father. Mrs. Coolidge, her face saddened by the gravity of the occasion and sympathy for Mrs. Harding, expressed a few minutes earlier, stood in the space formed by a bay window, less than a yard from her husband.

"COOLIDGE MEETS 150 CORRESPONDENTS," AUGUST 15, 1923

President Coolidge was famous for his sparing use of words, but he appreciated the importance of political communication, holding press conferences twice a week. These conferences were off the record, but they nevertheless enabled the president to convey his agenda to the press, and to address their questions as well. As *The Times* noted after Coolidge's first press conference, "The President is not silent when he does not want to be."

AUGUST 15, 1923
COOLIDGE MEETS 150 CORRESPONDENTS
Calls for Keeping of Traditional Confidence, Then Proves He Can Talk in Reply to Questions.
Special to The New York Times

WASHINGTON, Aug. 14.—President Coolidge held his first White House conference with the newspaper correspondents this afternoon. The President talked as if he had known the 150 newspaper men who were present all their lives. He explained that he expects these conferences to be intimate and confidential, adding that he knew his confidence would never be violated.

The rules against quoting the President, directly or indirectly, will be continued while Mr. Coolidge is President. Like Mr. Harding, he will see the correspondents twice a week. Questions are to be submitted in writing in advance of the conferences.

Those who attended today's conference came away with the knowledge that the President is not silent when he does not want to be. The conference today lasted nearly an hour, and the President did practically all of the talking.

He answered today's long list of questions in ample detail, and when he had finished he said, with a smile:

"Well, I guess I have given you a stickful."

Likewise he showed a keen sense of humor. And with it all he was frankly spoken, affable and courteous.

After the conference today the President posed with the newspaper men, first for the still cameras and then for the movies. When one of the moving picture operators called for three cheers the President smiled, adding, "This also includes the opposition," whereupon the Democrats, it seemed, yelled louder than did the Republicans.

"A FOREIGN SERVICE AT LAST," MAY 22, 1924,
AND "FOREIGN SERVICE UNIFIED," MAY 25, 1924

The Rogers Act of 1924 established the U.S. Foreign Service. It unified the diplomatic and consular services and was designed to make a diplomatic career more financially feasible for people who lacked an independent private income. In an editorial, *The Times* praised the measure for improving morale in the foreign service and for creating a more professional system for advancement.

MAY 22, 1924
EDITORIAL
A FOREIGN SERVICE AT LAST.

The Rogers bill for the reorganization and consolidation of the consular and diplomatic services has finally passed both House and Senate. It will doubtless receive the President's signature. It provides for the amalgamation of the two services on an interchangeable basis, making it possible to transfer men from the consular to the diplomatic service and vice versa, thus facilitating the more thorough training of men in both branches. It creates a uniform salary scale better adjusted than heretofore to the needs of the men in different ranks and posts. Furthermore, it provides a representation allowance, in order to lessen the demands on the private means of Ambassadors and Ministers, thus making it possible to appoint men to important positions, even if they are not wealthy. Finally, it establishes a retirement system based on the principles of the Civil Service Retirement and Disability act.

This means a great strengthening of the entire foreign service. The consolidation in itself offers a wider range of work and a larger number of men to draw from for the highest positions. Under the old system, in which the consular and diplomatic services were separate, the young men in either had a more limited horizon. Those in the diplomatic service, in particular, missed the training in practical affairs to be had in the consular service. By the new plan of interchangeability, this they may now obtain. Also, the pay of the men in the different classes will be sufficient to make the service much more attractive. It is no longer imperative to have a private income in order to take up foreign work. Salaries range from $3,000 to $9,000. Finally, the so-called "representation allowance" is sufficiently elastic to permit the Secretary of State to furnish added compensation for expenses in capitals where living costs are unusually high.

Two important objects are thus accomplished. The morale of the foreign service is greatly strengthened and it can now offer to young men of talent but no wealth a career worth striving for. To be sure, no definite arrangements are yet made for appointments from the service to the posts of Ambassador and Minister. But the bill provides that a list shall be compiled each year of those showing special merit, with the idea that in so far as it is practicable vacancies in the higher posts will be filled from the ranks of the foreign service. This is as it should be and will further encourage men of the best type to enter the service of their country abroad.

The passage of this bill is of greatest significance in the development of our foreign relations. It is proof that the country is at last awake to the importance of diplomatic and consular work, and that it appreciates the fact that our world position today demands that we strengthen our foreign service in every way possible. To Congressman Rogers of Massachusetts, and to others who have so long fought for this measure, much credit is due. They have rendered their country a real service.

MAY 25, 1924
FOREIGN SERVICE UNIFIED.
Coolidge Signs Act Combining Diplomatic and Consular Branches.
Special to The New York Times

WASHINGTON, May 24.—The bill fathered by Representative Rogers of Massachusetts, which provides for unification and a new classification of the diplomatic and consular services, was approved by President Coolidge today. Hereafter the combined organizations will be known as the United States Foreign Service.

In the future members of the diplomatic service may be shifted to consular positions and vice versa. The training for the combined service will be unified so that new members will be required to perform both diplomatic and consular functions.

"PRESIDENT'S SON, CALVIN JR., 16, DIES AS PARENTS WATCH," JULY 8, 1924, AND "10,000 SENT SYMPATHY TO COOLIDGES BY WIRE; PRESIDENT'S FATHER WITH HIM IN WHITE HOUSE," JULY 12, 1924

Tragedy struck the Coolidge family in the summer of 1924 with the unexpected death of the president's younger son, Calvin Jr., from blood poisoning. The nation mourned with the president and his family, sending more than 10,000 telegrams expressing condolences. The Coolidges buried their son in Vermont and then returned to the White House.

JULY 8, 1924
PRESIDENT'S SON, CALVIN JR., 16, DIES AS PARENTS WATCH

End Comes at 10:30 P.M. in Walter Reed Hospital After Gallant Struggle.

OXYGEN AS LAST RESORT

Hope Finally Abandoned at 8 P.M., When the Boy Began to Sink Rapidly.

MESSAGES OF SYMPATHY

Mr. and Mrs. Coolidge Worn Out by Long Vigil—

Funeral May Be in Northampton, Mass.

Special to The New York Times

WASHINGTON, July 7.—Calvin Coolidge Jr., the bright and lovable sixteen-year-old son of the President and Mrs. Coolidge, died at the Walter Reed Army General Hospital at 10:30 o'clock tonight from septicaemia, or blood poisoning.

All that loving hands and skill of modern science could do in a brave battle failed to save the life of the boy.

President and Mrs. Coolidge were at the bedside of their son in the main administration building of the big hospital when death came. John Coolidge, the boy's brother, remained at the White House during the evening. The only persons present at the death bed were the President and his wife and the physicians.

Word of the death of the President's youngest son reached the White House executive force at 10:32 o'clock, but the people of Washington—like those of most of the nation—received the news first by radio from Madison Square Garden, when it was announced that the National Convention would adjourn immediately through respect to the President.

President and Mrs. Coolidge returned almost immediately to the White House from the hospital, which is four miles north of the Executive mansion, reaching there a few minutes before 11 o'clock. They came alone in a White House automobile, which was followed by others carrying Frank W. Stearns of Boston, the President's devoted friend, and C. Bascom Slemp, secretary to the President.

Prepared for the End.

Secretary Slemp said that young Calvin died without recovering consciousness. It had been evident since 8 o'clock this evening that he could not survive. At 7 o'clock the boy had a serious sinking spell, and his physicians thought then that he would live only a short time. However, he rallied, only to fall into another spell an hour later, from which he never recovered. In fact, at 7:55 o'clock tonight Edward T. Clark, personal secretary to the President, announced at the hospital that the boy was dying.

The tenacity of the boy in clinging to life was truly remarkable and amazed even his physicians, used as they were to cases of this kind. It was not until two hours and a half after it was announced he was dying, that the end came. His well-ordered life and disciplined habits counted as strong factors in the tremendous battle he made, even though his physique was frail, most of his energy having been absorbed by his rapid growth.

This is the first time that a President in office has faced the tragedy of the loss of a young son since the Lincoln regime.

President Lincoln's son, William Wallace Lincoln, died in the White House in 1862. While President Coolidge's boy did not die in the White House, Walter Reed Hospital, where he expired tonight, is almost within a stone's throw of historic Fort Stevens, the only point where Lincoln was under fire of battle during the Civil War.

When the President and Mrs. Coolidge arrived at the White House late tonight, pathetic efforts had been made to try to lighten their burden. Lights were burning downstairs in the White House kitchen and the cooks had hurriedly prepared coffee and warm food. Isaac Hoover, chief usher at the White House, was waiting on the portico and offered his arm to Mrs. Coolidge as the President helped his wife out of the automobile.

> " If a personal letter is written to each person who sent a telegram of sympathy, it will necessitate an addition of 35 or 40 employes over a period of several weeks. "

JULY 12, 1924
10,000 SENT SYMPATHY TO COOLIDGES BY WIRE; PRESIDENT'S FATHER WITH HIM IN WHITE HOUSE
Special to The New York Times

WASHINGTON, July 11.—More than 10,000 telegrams of condolence had been received tonight by President and Mrs. Coolidge on the death of their son, Calvin Jr. Letters and resolutions were just beginning to arrive and the White House staff expected that these would outnumber the telegrams.

It is a policy of President Coolidge that each communication to the White House should be given individual attention and this policy already has greatly increased the size of the stenographic staff.

If a personal letter is written to each person who sent a telegram of sympathy, it will necessitate an addition of 35 or 40 employes over a period of several weeks, a White House employe estimated today. To acknowledge the letters and resolutions will require, of course, an even larger force.

Returning this morning on their special train from Vermont, where their younger son was buried yesterday, President and Mrs. Coolidge spent the greater part of the day in seclusion at the White House. No callers were received and the President attended to only the most pressing executive business. Both the President and his wife were very tired from their journey and worn by grief.

In the early afternoon the President accompanied his father, Colonel John C. Coolidge, who came to Washington

with the Presidential party, to the naval dispensary, where the father had his eyes examined. Later the President went for a quiet drive in Potomac Park.

Mrs. Coolidge was said to be somewhat rested this afternoon, but in spite of her splendid courage it was feared that she might suffer a reaction, and those about her, including her devoted friends, Mr. and Mrs. Frank W. Stearns, were doing everything they could to help her.

Colonel Coolidge, who saw his son yesterday for the first time since he swore him in as President of the United States in August last year, and who had not been to Washington since his son was inaugurated as Vice President, will remain here for an indefinite period.

Shortly after breakfast President Coolidge went to his desk in the Executive Offices, where he remained occupied until lunch time. He saw no one today except the members of his Cabinet now here—Secretaries Hughes, Wallace and Davis and Attorney General Stone—in a half hour's meeting, during which nothing of great importance was brought up for discussion, it was later said. Secretary Hughes, who leaves tomorrow for London, had two conferences alone with the President, one in the forenoon, the other about 3:30 P.M.

"Mellon Tells Chief of Hopes in Europe," September 5, 1924

The Dawes Plan of 1924 established a plan for Germany to pay the reparations imposed after World War I. Named after Charles G. Dawes, who was elected U.S. vice president the same year, the program instituted loans to Germany and established taxes to provide money for reparations. Treasury Secretary Andrew W. Mellon praised the Dawes Plan, which did improve the German economy, though it would not provide sufficient funds for Germany's reparations obligations over the long term.

SEPTEMBER 5, 1924
MELLON TELLS CHIEF OF HOPES IN EUROPE
Reports Dawes Plan Will Save Germany and Revive Whole Continent.
PROPOSED LOAN EXTOLLED
America Will Have More Influence Abroad if Not a Member of League, He Tells Press.
Special to The New York Times

WASHINGTON, Sept. 4.—Secretary Mellon reported to President Coolidge today that acceptance of the Dawes plan by the European nations meant not only the salvation of Germany but the restoration of the economic life of the Continent. Later the Secretary reiterated these views in an interview with the press in which he expressed confidence that from now on European conditions would become steadily better as the result of the agreement.

Outstanding in the impressions which the Secretary received during his European survey was the willingness of the foreign nations to come together on the Dawes plan as a solution of their difficulties.

"It should be gratifying to this country," he said, "that the European nations give the United States credit for playing an important part in solving their difficulties because Secretary Hughes many months ago suggested the appointment of a committee of experts and because American representatives participated so prominently in the negotiations."

The change in Europe during the last year has been "wonderful," Mr. Mellon declared, there being a decided improvement in trade and a new confidence displayed by business men in general. He did not fear any harmful competition from Germany, he said, for the reason that she would now have to go into the market to buy large quantities of raw material, and these great purchases would counteract any attempt on her part to flood the rest of the world with goods made with her cheap labor.

Any competition by Germany in the industrial field would be far outweighed by the benefit to the world of the increased buying power of European nations brought about by the Dawes plan, the Secretary of the Treasury declared. He appeared in no way alarmed by speculation in some of the British and French papers that Germany might immediately become a strong competitor in the world markets.

Credits by American bankers are even now being extended to Germany, he stated, and also said that the amount of credit granted in this fashion, as an aid to trade, would be very much greater than the amount available through an international loan. Reports from Germany brought the news to Mr. Mellon that conditions had greatly improved there and that German industrialists were now negotiating for the purchase of raw materials in the United States.

Dealing with the theory that European nations might begin to arm themselves heavily for fear that Germany might regain her commercial and military strength, Secretary Mellon told correspondents there seemed no general disposition of this kind and thought, on the other hand, the foreign powers appeared anxious to do everything possible to prevent future trouble.

"The fact of an economic basis for the rehabilitation of Europe and the evacuation of the Ruhr is the greatest move toward world peace in Europe," said Mr. Mellon. "The Dawes plan is the basis upon which the foreign nations can cooperate to enable Germany to meet her obligations and to establish economic stability. That's the one thing we have been waiting for right along."

"Coolidge Dictated Campaign Policies," November 9, 1924

President Coolidge's overwhelming election victory in 1924 was credited largely to his own campaign strategy. *The Times* reported that the president's "Silent Cal" image served him well in the race, demonstrating his responsibility and work ethic. Coolidge's preference for few words burnished his public reputation and, ironically for his opponents, became an effective means of political communication.

NOVEMBER 9, 1924
COOLIDGE DICTATED CAMPAIGN POLICIES

Public Was Never Aware of Advisory Publicity Board Which He Directed.
ALL SPEECHES CENSORED
President Himself Sponsored Portrayal of His Characteristics to the Voter.

Republican campaign workers who know "the inside story" of the campaign strategy which elected President Coolidge by such a decisive vote are hailing the President as one of the master political strategists of American history. They say that he has emerged from the campaign as a much bigger figure in the public eye than before he had won the Presidency in his own name. Moreover, they predict that henceforth little will be heard of the comment about "Silent Cal," or the charges that he said nothing because he had nothing to say, made by some of his opponents in the campaign.

The main thing these workers said was that the presentation of President Coolidge to the country as a silent, reserved man, an exponent of common sense and a faithful performer of his daily task, rather than a heroic or spectacular figure, was no accident or makeshift, but was a deliberate, well-calculated policy, for which the President himself was responsible.

President Coolidge, knowing his own strength and believing that he understood the psychology of the voters, undertook to capitalize his strength by presenting himself to the country in the light in which he wished to be viewed. To that end he called to his service all the weapons of modern publicity, which he utilized with a skill for which his subordinates in the campaign give him the highest credit.

The President began his publicity campaign by appointing an Advisory Publicity Board to direct and supervise all speeches, radio talks and newspaper statements made by Republican orators and spokesmen. Although this board was appointed long before election, no public announcement was ever made of its existence or its functions. It remained in the background as far as the public was concerned, but it worked silently and efficiently under the President's direct authority.

"Coolidge to Accept Estate Tax Repeal," January 23, 1926

President Coolidge and Treasury Secretary Mellon achieved much of their economic agenda with the Revenue Act of 1926. This legislation reduced taxes significantly, consistent with the president's view that business and investment should flourish with few government restrictions.

JANUARY 23, 1926
COOLIDGE TO ACCEPT ESTATE TAX REPEAL

Will Support Bill if Treasury Experts Find Public Debt Can Be Paid Without It.

MELLON ALSO A SUPPORTER

Secretary Believes Reduced Tax Rates Will Spur Business and Increase Revenue.

Special to The New York Times

WASHINGTON, Jan. 22.—President Coolidge is expected to support taxation revision which repeals estate taxes, provided the Treasury experts find that the repeal can be made without breaking down the Administration's present policy of adding an annual amount to the sinking fund sufficient to permit the retirement of the war debt in twenty-five years.

It was explained today in official circles that President Coolidge has not in the least changed his views relative to the Federal Government withdrawing from the inheritance tax field. He has urged that the Government should retire from this field when this can be done with the assurance of sufficient revenue to take care of the war debt and the heavy current expenses.

Investigation is now being made by the Treasury experts to determine whether the Senate bill reducing the taxes below the limit set in the House bill and repealing the estate taxes will yield enough revenue and at the same time assure the maintenance of the 2½ per cent. payment to the sinking fund.

The inquiry is expected to show that the present policy of the Administration can be continued respecting the sinking funds and that the surplus due to continued prosperity will be greater than was estimated when the House tax bill was framed.

Mellon Won't Oppose Repeal.

Although the Senate bill would reduce taxes $26,000,000 more than the reduction that was thought possible by the Treasury experts, who estimated that the condition of the Treasury would not permit of a reduction of more than $326,000,000, it is understood that Secretary Mellon will not oppose the Senate bill. He feels that reduced tax rates will stimulate business and that the surplus will be great enough to permit of the Senate reduction, including elimination of the estate taxes.

President Coolidge feels that the Federal Government should retire from the estate tax field just as soon as it can be done. When the original estimate of the surplus had been made he thought that this tax could not be given up entirely at this time, but he is now inclining to the view that it may be made effective in the present bill.

While Mr. Coolidge is not definitely committed to repeal at this time, every indication is that the reports of the experts will convince him it can be safely done now. He does not intend to take any position in the fight between the Senate and House in reference to estate taxes, but, it is believed, would approve of a tax bill without estate taxes if it comes to him in that shape.

President Coolidge always has opposed the Federal inheritance taxes, but has thought that perhaps sufficient revenues could not be raised to pay the war debt without holding on to them for some time in some reduced form. He made his views evident before the National Tax Association conference here on Feb. 19, 1925, when he said the Federal Government had levied inheritance taxes only as a war emergency and should leave this tax to the States.

- -

"COOLIDGE FACING A HOSTILE SENATE," NOVEMBER 4, 1926

Despite President Coolidge's policy successes, the Republican Party lost seats in the 1926 midterm elections. With the Senate almost evenly divided between the parties, Coolidge faced numerous political challenges in his remaining two years in office.

NOVEMBER 4, 1926
COOLIDGE FACING A HOSTILE SENATE

Democrats Now Have 47 Seats and With Insurgents Can Upset Legislation.

CONTROL OF HOUSE IS SAFE

But There Also the Radicals May Endanger Republicans by Joining Opposition.

By RICHARD V. OULAHAN.

For the balance of the term he is now serving as President, Calvin Coolidge will have a hostile Senate to face in seeking legislation.

As a result of Tuesday's elections the Republicans will lose their majority in that body. Through the Democrats gaining seven seats now held by Republicans and the expected election of a Republican Senator in a special election in Maine on Nov. 29, the Republicans will have exactly half the membership of the upper house in the next Congress, whose term will extend from March 4, 1927, to March 4, 1929.

In oher words, the next Senate will be a tie between forty-eight Republicans and a combined opposition of forty-seven Democrats and one Farmer-Laborite. The House in the next Congress will have a continuation of a Republican majority. Although the exact number of Republicans in excess of the combined opposition of Democrats and minor party members cannot be determined until complete returns have been received from several close districts, the indications are that the Republican control for the two years ending with President Coolidge's term will be an actual and not merely a nominal control.

Granting that the Democrats will capture all the districts in which contests are still in doubt, the figures compiled by *The New York Times* show that the Republicans will still have a majority of thirty-two over the combined opposition of Democrats and minor party representatives. Included in this majority of thirty-two are those of the insur-

gent contingent, but their number is not sufficient to provide a coalition with the Democrats and minor party men to overcome the Republican regulars, although through such a coalition the regular Republican majority may be reduced to three or four and in some cases may be even lower. However, the Republican regulars seem to be assured of a complete majority over any opposition combination that may be formed.

Rebuke to Republicans.

Judged by the outcome of the Senatorial elections, the Republican Party and the Coolidge Administration appear to have received a severe rebuke from the country. While many of the contests for Senate seats were fought on issues almost purely local, the very general trend of sentiment against Republican candidates will be construed by many political observers as proving the Democratic contention that President Coolidge has "slipped" amazingly in popular estimation since his overwhelming victory at the polls only two years ago.

The President's own State of Massachusetts has rejected his close friend and political adviser, Senator William M. Butler, in the face of a virtual appeal by Mr. Coolidge to the Massachusetts electors to send Mr. Butler back to the Senate. The defeat of Mr. Butler as the President's favorite candidate was further emphasized by the fact that the Massachusetts voters triumphantly re-elected Alvin T. Fuller, Mr. Butler's Republican running mate.

"TEXT OF PRESIDENT COOLIDGE'S STATEMENT OF RENUNCIATION, MADE BY HIM YESTERDAY," DECEMBER 7, 1927

More than a year before the 1928 presidential election, Coolidge ruled out the possibility of running again. He had declared on August 2, 1927, that he would not seek the presidency in 1928, and he reaffirmed that statement at the end of the year.

President Calvin Coolidge addresses ten thousand members of the Sioux tribe at the Pine Ridge Reservation in South Dakota in 1927.

Source: The New York Times

DECEMBER 7, 1927
TEXT OF PRESIDENT COOLIDGE'S STATEMENT OF RENUNCIATION, MADE BY HIM YESTERDAY

Special to The New York Times

WASHINGTON, Dec. 6.—Here, textually, are the ninety-five words which President Coolidge added today to the twelve in which on Aug. 2 he said: "I do not choose to run for President in nineteen-twenty-eight."

This is naturally the time to be planning for the future. The party will soon place in nomination its candidate to succeed me. To give time for mature deliberation I stated to the country on Aug. 2 that I did not choose to run for President in 1928.

My statement stands. No one should be led to suppose that I have modified it. My decision will be respected.

After I had been eliminated the party began, and should vigorously continue, the serious task of selecting another candidate from among the numbers of distinguished men available.

"REGULARS QUIT COOLIDGE," MAY 25, 1928

President Coolidge battled with Congress over domestic legislation in his final year of office, vetoing bills that called for farm relief and other measures. Congress successfully overrode some of the president's vetoes with the required two-thirds vote in both chambers.

MAY 25, 1928
REGULARS QUIT COOLIDGE

Join With the Insurgents and the Democrats in Showing Resentment.

THREE BILLS ARE NOW LAW

Postal Measures Already Passed by House Which Adopts Disabled Officers' Pay Bill.

CONFER ON FARM BILL TEST

Supporters of Measure Inclined to Try to Obtain Its Passage Over Veto.

Special to The New York Times

WASHINGTON, May 24.—Roused to rebellion, the Senate today expressed its resentment at the chastisement administered to it yesterday by President Coolidge in his veto message on the McNary-Haugen Farm Relief bill and by overwhelming votes overrode his vetoes of four measures.

Three of these vetoed measures became laws, for the House had already passed two of them over the veto, and took similar action on a third this afternoon. The expectation is that the House will concur in overriding the veto of the fourth.

The three measures thus enacted are:

A 10 per cent. wage bonus for night postal employes.

Increasing the allowance of fourth-class postmasters for light and heat.

Giving to disabled emergency officers of the World War retirement pay equal to that of regular army officers.

The Senate Vetoes.

By a vote of 70 to 9 the Senate over-rode the veto on the bonus for night postal employes. The House voted 319 to 14 on Tuesday.

By a vote of 63 to 17 the Senate rejected the veto on higher allowances for fourth-class postmasters. The House voted 318 to 46 on Tuesday.

By a vote of 66 to 14 the Senate overrode the veto on the pay bill for disabled emergency officers. The House this afternoon sustained the Senate action by a vote of 245 to 101.

By a vote of 57 to 22 the Senate overrode the veto on a bill to authorize three annual appropriations of $3,500,000 for roads in certain States. The House has not acted on this veto.

While the four measures are relatively unimportant as compared with the McNary-Haugen bill, the Senate's action served to illustrate the pitch to which the feelings of its members had risen. It has been many a day since a President has faced such a swift and sudden rebellion within a few hours.

"COOLIDGE PLEASED BY HIS ROLE ABROAD," NOVEMBER 7, 1928

In assessing his foreign policy record before leaving office, President Coolidge highlighted his administration's successful diplomacy in Latin America and China. Of particular importance were recent elections in formerly war-torn Nicaragua and the mediation of a territorial dispute over the border provinces of Tacna and Arica between Chile and Peru.

NOVEMBER 7, 1928
COOLIDGE PLEASED BY HIS ROLE ABROAD

He Believes Nicaraguan Poll and Events in China and Mexico Show His
Policy's Success.

READY TO RETIRE MARINES

President, Returning to Washington, Reviews Entire Foreign Situation and Sees No
Difficulties Looming.

From a Staff Correspondent of The New York Times.

ON BOARD THE PRESIDENT'S TRAIN, RETURNING FROM NORTHAMPTON TO WASHINGTON, Nov. 6.— President Coolidge, commenting today upon this Government's policies in Latin America and the Far East, showed that he considers that the American attitude adopted toward Nicaragua, Mexico and China has been successful, as evidenced recently in the peaceful election in the former country and the trends of events in Mexico and China.

The disputes in Nicaragua and China have been calmed, sufficiently so that in his opinion most of the marines can be safely withdrawn from those countries with the assurance that American lives and property there will be safeguarded.

As he nears the end of his Administration the President believes that all of the controversial disputes with foreign countries are on the way toward settlement or will have been composed in the next two months, so that he will complete his administration of seven and a half years with the United States enjoying good relations with the world and domestic tranquillity and prosperity.

Returning to Washington after he and Mrs. Coolidge had cast their ballots in Northampton, Mass., where he began his long public career, the President reviewed developments in Nicaragua and China as his train traveled through the Connecticut valley. He seemed happy that he had performed his civic duties.

Pleased by Nicaraguan Poll.

In his opinion, the outcome of the election in Nicaragua has been particularly successful and especially agreeable to the United States. He believes that the election has demonstrated that this country has pursued the right course. He recalls that the marines were in that country for many years. He was anxious to withdraw them and they were nearly all withdrawn, but at the solicitation of the Nicaraguan Government they were returned before they had been away thirty days.

The marines were sent to Nicaragua, the President observed, to protect American property and lives while a terrible warfare was in progress. Colonel Stimson was then sent to Nicaragua and plans were made which were successfully carried out in the election Sunday.

Nicaragua, the President feels, held an orderly and peaceful election which apparently is an expression of the will of that country. The American policy in Nicaragua, it was asserted, had been very similar to its policy in Mexico and China, of trying peacefully to compose our differences.

In the President's opinion the United States is succeeding admirably in Mexico and China.

In China, where there was a real crisis in 1926 and 1927, the differences have been composed; so much so that this Government has under consideration the raising of its legation there to an embassy.

Hopes for Tacna-Arica Accord.

President Coolidge let it be known that he was also hopeful of getting a final settlement in the Tacna-Arica controversy. It seems quite apparent to him that there is now a new spirit in Chile and Peru. They have resumed diplomatic relations and, as neighbors, have large commercial interests. Developments gave assurance that their dispute of forty years would soon be settled.

The President opposed those who besought him to make a strong military move against China, letting it be known today that he had always opposed such suggestions, which emanated here and abroad, thinking such a course would prevent the Chinese people from settling their own differences and intensify the conditions of revolt and disorder that have existed for the past few years in that republic. Instead, this Government refused to interfere in their domestic disputes and did nothing more than protect the interests of the American people in China.

The policy dictated by President Coolidge in relation to all these different countries, it was explained, has been one of peace, conciliation, good will, patience and cooperation.

Believes Prosperity Will Continue.

While the President feels that the interests of the United States have suffered some from uncertainties and confusion, the results seem to demonstrate that the best course has been taken for the protection of American property and lives and for the maintenance of friendly relations with all these different countries that have had long-existing disputes with the United States and also troubles at home.

While the President cannot say that all foreign questions have been settled, yet they are being closed slowly and with no indications on the horizon of developments that will impair the present good relations and spirit of cooperation existing between the United States and the rest of the world.

In the domestic field, Mr. Coolidge finds that prosperity has continued during the Presidential campaign and

that business is better today than in the same period last year. The President sees no indication of unfavorable developments and looks ahead to a continuance of the progress that has come to be known to some as the "Coolidge prosperity."

He returns to Washington tonight after visiting the scenes of his first political victories in Massachusetts feeling that he will turn over to his successor on March 4 a United States at peace with the world, prosperous and on the threshold of its greatest industrial progress and the upbuilding of an interior waterway system exceeding the cost of the Panama Canal.

> He returns to Washington tonight . . . feeling that he will turn over to his successor on March 4 a United States at peace with the world, prosperous and on the threshold of its greatest industrial progress.

"COOLIDGE PUTS NAME TO OUR ACCEPTANCE OF ANTI-WAR TREATY," JANUARY 18, 1929

The Kellogg-Briand Pact was perhaps President Coolidge's signature achievement in international affairs. With this treaty, the United States and France agreed to outlaw war, and, although this promise would not be fulfilled, it nevertheless presented an ideal to which nations would aspire.

JANUARY 18, 1929
COOLIDGE PUTS NAME TO OUR ACCEPTANCE OF ANTI-WAR TREATY
Kellogg Signs After President in an Impressive Ceremony at White House.
HAPPY MOMENT FOR BOTH
Cabinet Members and Many Senators Are Grouped Around Them in the East Room.
PEN FROM FRANCE IS USED
Capital Recalls Long Fight Made by Secretary to Have Pact Signed While in Office.
Special to The New York Times

WASHINGTON, Jan. 17.—America's final approval was given to the Kellogg-Briand anti-war pact today when, with a ceremony appropriate to what he considers one of the main achievements of his administration, President Coolidge affixed his signature to the "instrument of ratification" proclaiming this country's complete acceptance of the treaty. The Cabinet and many Senators were present at the impressive ceremony in the East Room of the White House.

Using a gold pen presented to Secretary Kellogg by the

city of Havre, France, President Coolidge signed two copies of the instrument of ratification. Each then was signed by Secretary Kellogg, who sat beside the President at the old desk which served as a Cabinet table from the time of John Adams to the administration of Theodore Roosevelt.

One copy of the instrument was sent to the State Department to be filed. The other was deposited with the treaty.

Both the President and Secretary smiled as they attached their signatures and appeared most happy over the conclusion of the long and successful fight to place the United States in the position among the world powers as favoring the renunciation of war. . . .

Kellogg's Fight for Treaty.

The 72-year-old Secretary of State will now retire to private life on March 4 with his important work as Secretary accomplished. Mr. Kellogg has worried over and worked and fought for the treaty from the day he first made his counter-proposal to Aristide Briand of France a year ago. Bringing it home from Paris in a brand-new yellow suitcase, he kept it in the personal safe in his own office most of the time, there to show it to recalcitrant Senators in the fight to get it ratified.

Mr. Kellogg began his association with the pact by being rather shy of it. After spending six months trying to make up his mind what to do about M. Briand's proposal that the United States and France renounce war, he proposed that the entire world renounce war, and then devoted six months' intensive work to the effort to get his proposal accepted.

During that period Mr. Kellogg "ran his secretaries ragged." He took his diplomatic correspondence home with him. He got his legal experts out of bed at all hours of the night and kept the telegraph office of the State Department on the alert with queries as to when M. Briand's notes were arriving. He practically ate, slept and lived with the treaty.

Mr. Kellogg's enthusiasm was contagious. It won over the diplomatic representatives of two of the most hesitant countries: Sir Esme Howard, Ambassador of Great Britain, and Paul Claudel, Ambassador of France. They became his most enthusiastic supporters with their Foreign Offices.

When the treaty was concluded Mr. Kellogg went to Paris to sign it. He refused to take any credit for the pact, but during the ceremony of signing appeared flushed and happy.

THE PRESIDENCY OF **HERBERT HOOVER**

MARCH 4, 1929 – MARCH 4, 1933

The presidency of Herbert Clark Hoover is remembered fore-most for the economic disaster that befell the nation. By the time President Hoover left office in March 1933, the Great Depression was affecting every sector of the U.S. economy: One quarter of the nation was unemployed, banks had closed in thirty-eight states, and the New York Stock Exchange had halted securities trading. President Hoover had not created these problems, but his failure to take aggressive action to address the nation's growing economic troubles would forever tarnish his legacy. The United States entered the Depression in the first year of the Hoover administration, and the president was voted out of office in the next presidential election because he had not demonstrated that the federal government would improve the situation.

Born in 1874 in West Branch, Iowa, Hoover was the first president from west of the Mississippi River. He lost both of his parents to illness when he was young and moved to Oregon, where he was raised by relatives who shared his parents' Quaker faith. (Hoover was the first Quaker president of the United States.) After attending business school, Hoover won admission to Stanford University, a new engineering school in California. He graduated in 1895 and became a mining engineer, working for an international company that sent him to manage mines in North America, Europe, Africa, Asia, and Australia. Highly successful in his profession, Hoover was a millionaire before age forty.

After seventeen years as a mining engineer, Hoover be-came active in politics. During World War I, he chaired a committee that assisted Americans stranded in Europe to return home safely. He also chaired a commission that raised funds to aid people in Belgium, which was ravaged by the war. When the United States entered the World War I in 1917, President Woodrow Wilson appointed Hoover as U.S. food administrator. In this position, he promoted food production as well as its distribution and conservation. Hoover attended the postwar peace conference in Versailles as an economic adviser to President Wilson.

The Bonus Marchers—1932.

Source: The Granger Collection, New York

Despite his work for the Wilson administration, Hoover was a Republican, and when fellow Republican Warren G. Harding became president in 1921, he appointed Hoover secretary of commerce. In this position, Hoover promoted an eight-hour workday and worked to end child labor. He had the distinction of serving for nearly two full presidential terms as commerce secretary, stepping down in the last year of the Coolidge administration in 1928 to run for president.

THE 1928 ELECTION

The Republican Party nominated Hoover for president on the first ballot at its national convention in 1928 and selected Charles Curtis of Kansas as his running mate. Heading the

QUICK FACTS ON HERBERT HOOVER

BIRTH	August 10, 1874, West Branch, Iowa
EDUCATION	Stanford University
FAMILY	Wife: Lou Henry Hoover
	Children: Herbert Clark Hoover Jr., Allan Henry Hoover
WHITE HOUSE PETS	Dogs
PARTY	Republican
PREPRESIDENTIAL CAREER (SELECTED)	Mining engineer consultant, 1895–1913
	Chairman of American Relief Committee, London, 1914–1915
	Chairman of Commission for Relief, Belgium, 1915–1918
	U.S. food administrator, 1917–1919
	Chairman of European Relief Council, 1920
	Secretary of commerce, 1921–1928
PRESIDENTIAL TERM	March 4, 1929–March 4, 1933
VICE PRESIDENT	Charles Curtis
SELECTED EVENTS	Agricultural Marketing Act (1929)
	Stock market crash (October 24, 1929)
	Smoot-Hawley Tariff Act (1930)
	Creation of Veterans Administration (1930)
	Economic Stabilization Act (1931)
	"Star Spangled Banner" becomes national anthem (1931)
	Creation of Reconstruction Finance Corporation (1932)
	Veterans launch "Bonus Army" march on Washington, D.C. (1932)
POSTPRESIDENCY	Coordinator of European food program, 1946
	Chairman of Commission on Organization of the Executive Branch of the Government, 1947–1949, 1953–1955
DEATH	January 20, 1964, New York, N.Y.

Democratic ticket was Gov. Alfred E. Smith of New York, the first major party Catholic nominee for the presidency. His running mate was Sen. Joseph T. Robinson of Arkansas. Hoover soundly defeated Smith in the general election, winning more than 21 million popular votes to Smith's 15 million, and 444 Electoral College votes to Smith's 87.

THE HOOVER ADMINISTRATION

Several of President Hoover's ten cabinet members served throughout his administration. Among these advisers were Henry L. Stimson of New York as secretary of state, William De Witt Mitchell of Minnesota as attorney general, Ray L. Wilbur of California as interior secretary, and Arthur M. Hyde of Missouri as agriculture secretary. Secretary of War James W. Good of Illinois served for less than a year before he was replaced by Patrick J. Hurley of Oklahoma, who served for the rest of Hoover's term. Treasury Secretary Andrew W. Mellon of Pennsylvania took office under president Warren G. Harding in 1921, and he stayed in office until the last year of the Hoover administration, the only treasury secretary to serve three presidents. When Mellon became U.S. ambassador to Great Britain in 1932, Ogden L. Mills of New York, who had been his undersecretary, replaced him.

First Lady Lou H. Hoover was also an Iowa native, who met her husband when they were students at Stanford University. Because the Hoovers already had lived in Washington, D.C., for several years while he served as commerce secretary, they had a well-established circle of friends when they moved to the White House in 1929. The Hoovers had two sons, both of whom were adults when their father became president. The elder son, Herbert Hoover Jr., would later serve as undersecretary of state in the Eisenhower administration.

Major Issues

The collapse of the national economy under Hoover defined his administration, even though the president himself did not bear responsibility for the disaster. Years of stock speculation and loose credit functioning free of virtually any government regulation had made a financial downturn almost unavoidable. On October 24, 1929—a day now known as "Black Thursday"—the stock market crashed, ultimately resulting in unemployment for nearly a quarter of the workforce.

President Hoover's philosophy was that the federal government should play a limited role in economic matters and permit the country to regain its financial footing as the stock market regained strength. But this philosophy provided little comfort to Americans desperate for food, clothing, and shelter, and they blamed the president for their woes. In 1931 Hoover approved legislation to initiate public works programs, but it fell far short of the demand for jobs. The Hoover administration created the Reconstruction Finance Corporation in 1932 to assist the agricultural and financial sectors, and it established a committee on unemployment to promote relief, but this group was ill-equipped to deal with the waves of people who required assistance.

The federal government's limited efforts to help people improve their situation sparked anger, blame, and resentment in the American public, and these feelings were directed primarily at President Hoover. People who lost their homes and were forced to live in small shacks began to refer to them as "Hoovervilles." Others began hunger marches. In spring 1932 approximately fifteen thousand World War I veterans arrived in Washington, D.C., to demand early payment of a soldiers' bonus. The protestors marched peacefully before Capitol Hill and the White House, and then many of them stayed on,

setting up makeshift camps. In July President Hoover ordered the army to intervene, sending Gen. Douglas MacArthur to remove the veterans. MacArthur's troops used tear gas to force the protestors out of their camp, sparking severe recriminations in the court of public opinion and magnifying the Hoover administration's image as harsh and uncaring.

America's economic problems also affected its foreign policy and blocked the possibility of any major initiatives. President Hoover signed the Smoot-Hawley Tariff Act in 1930, which raised prices on foreign imports and resulted in a trade war that hurt the United States as much as it did its trading partners. In response to the Japanese invasion of Manchuria in 1931, the United States declared its support for China and hoped that its ally would ultimately prevail. Hoover also tried to build upon the naval disarmament program begun in the Harding administration, sponsoring a London conference on disarmament in 1930, but it did not make significant progress.

Despite his rapidly declining popularity, Hoover won the Republican Party's nomination for a second term. But the dire state of the nation demanded change, and Hoover was overwhelmingly defeated by his Democratic opponent, New York governor Franklin D. Roosevelt, who promised a "new deal" for the American people. FDR won nearly 23 million popular votes, 7 million more than Hoover, and carried 42 states and 531 Electoral College votes to just 6 states and 59 Electoral College votes for Hoover. The election also produced a party realignment, in which significant blocs of voters cast their lot with the Democratic Party, and would stay there for decades to come.

Hoover returned to California, where he became a vocal critic of the New Deal. After World War II, President Harry S. Truman made Hoover chairman of the Famine Emergency Commission, which worked to bring food to the legions of starving people in postwar Europe. Hoover also became chairman of the Commission on Organization of the Executive Branch of the Government, popularly known as the "Hoover Commission," which recommended significant organizational changes in the executive branch. President Dwight D. Eisenhower asked Hoover to chair a similar commission in the 1950s. Herbert Hoover died in 1964 at age ninety, living longer than any president up to that time except John Adams, who had survived four months longer.

"Hoover Signs the Farm Relief Bill," June 16, 1929

Upon taking office in 1929, President Hoover quickly signed the Agricultural Marketing Act, a farm relief measure to purchase surplus goods and try to keep the prices of those goods at a sustainable level for farmers. In a statement released after he signed the bill, the president described the legislation as "the most important measure ever passed by Congress in aid of a single industry." Within a few months, however, the stock market crash would obliterate the modest gains made by this legislation.

JUNE 16, 1929
HOOVER SIGNS THE FARM RELIEF BILL; WILL ASK $150,000,000 TO START WORK; PROMISES TO PICK 'FARM-MINDED' BOARD

PRESIDENT HAILS EVENT

'Most Important Measure Passed in Aid of a Single Industry.'

WILL NAME BOARD SOON

He States Selection of Experienced Body Will Require 2 or 3 Weeks.

CAMERAS SNAP THE SIGNING

Farm Leaders and Congress Conferee on Bill in Attendance at Ceremony.

Special to The New York Times

WASHINGTON, June 15.—President Hoover signed the farm relief bill today and announced that he was asking Congress at once for a preliminary appropriation of $150,000,000 from the $500,000,000 fund created by the bill for use in starting the work of aiding agriculture.

After affixing his signature to the measure the President issued this statement:

"After many years of contention we have at last made a constructive start at agricultural relief with the most important measure ever passed by Congress in aid of a single industry.

"It would have introduced many cross currents to have initiated any movement toward the selection of the farm board until after the legislation was completed and no steps have been taken in this direction beyond the receipt of several hundred recommendations. It will require two or three weeks to make these selections. The choice of the board is not easy, for its members must in a measure be distributed regionally over the country. It must at the same time be chosen so as to represent, so far as possible, each major branch of agriculture.

"Moreover, the board must be made up of men of actual farm experience, and inasmuch as its work lies largely in marketing in conjunction with farm cooperatives, its membership should be comprised of men who have been actually engaged in directing farmers' marketing organizations.

"It is desirable that the board should have in its constitution at least one man experienced in general business and one with special experience in finance.

"I am asking for a preliminary appropriation of $150,000,000 at once out of the $500,000,000 that has been authorized, and as Congress will be in session except for short periods, the board will be able to present its further requirements at almost any time."

It is expected that the President will ask Congress for the $150,000,000 appropriation on Monday.

"Prices of Stocks Crash in Heavy Liquidation, Total Drop of Billions," October 24, 1929, and "Financial Markets," October 25, 1929

The stock market crash on October 24, 1929, which would become known as "Black Thursday," shocked the nation. An initial burst of sales set off a panic in which stockholders frantically began unloading their shares, and by day's end, as *The New York Times* reported, "the full force of the storm was felt." The causes for the panic were not immediately evident, but the consequences were severe and enduring.

 [T]housands of stockholders dumped their shares on the market . . . in such an avalanche of selling as to bring about one of the widest declines in history.

OCTOBER 24, 1929
PRICES OF STOCKS CRASH IN HEAVY LIQUIDATION, TOTAL DROP OF BILLIONS
PAPER LOSS $4,000,000,000

2,600,000 Shares Sold in the Final Hour in Record Decline.

MANY ACCOUNTS WIPED OUT

But No Brokerage House Is in Difficulties, as Margins Have Been Kept High.

ORGANIZED BACKING ABSENT

Bankers Confer on Steps to Support Market—Highest Break Is 96 Points.

Frightened by the decline in stock prices during the last month and a half, thousands of stockholders dumped their shares on the market yesterday afternoon in such an avalanche of selling as to bring about one of the widest declines in history. Even the best of seasoned, dividend-paying, shares were sold regardless of the prices they would bring, and the result was a tremendous smash in which stocks lost from a few points to as much as ninety-six.

Loss in Market Values.

The absolute average decline of active and so-called inactive issues yesterday was 2,995, or roughly three points. Using this figure as a base and taking the percentage of shares listed on the Exchange in relation to the percentage of issues traded in, the loss in value of listed securities amounted to $2,210,675,184. This, however, does not measure up to the full value of the loss, for the reason that many lesser-known issues of small capitalization did not figure in the sharp declines. It might be conservatively estimated that the actual loss in market value on the New York Stock Exchange ran to about $4,000,000,000.

Since there are 1,048,359,363 shares listed on the Exchange, a decline of one point a share would mean more than $1,000,000,000. Obviously all issues were not traded in, but those which were not declined in bid and asked representation, so that while no sales were actually recorded the market position of most issues was lowered.

In addition to the situation on the big board there was also the decline on the Curb market, where values were ruthlessly cut, and to this must be added declines in securities in other markets affected sympathetically by the New York Stock Exchange fluctuations and declines in the over-the-counter market. The wiping out of open-market values throughout the country therefore probably ranged as high as $6,000,000,000. The $4,000,000,000 decline on the New York Stock Exchange represented a loss of about one twenty-second in the value of all listed securities, which on Oct. 1 was rated at $87,073,630,423.

Crash in Final Hour.

The collapse of the market in the final hour of trading seemed the more violent because of its suddenness, the mystery which surrounded it, particularly as to the identity of the sellers, and the tremendous volume of the trading, which reached a total of 2,600,000 shares in the hour between 2 and 3 o'clock.

Statistically the market made a sorry showing. The railroad shares, as measured by *The New York Times* average of twenty-five representative stocks, were down 5.52 and the industrial shares 30.97. The total combined average of fifty representative issues was down 18.24, marking the largest decline since the start of the compilation of these records in 1911. Sales on the Exchange were 6,374,960 shares, marking the eleventh time the sales on the Exchange have exceeded the 6,000,000-share figure. On the Curb they were 1,793,415 shares.

Stocks Opened Strong.

The day had opened calmly enough. Many prices were higher. Trading was quiet in mid-morning, but featured by a sudden and unexplained wave of liquidation in the motor accessory issues. When this burst of selling had spent its force the market wavered and began to slip, slowly at first and then faster. By 1 o'clock the decline had reached large proportions, but it was not until the last hour that the full force of the storm was felt.

OCTOBER 25, 1929
FINANCIAL MARKETS
Panicky Liquidation on Stock Exchange Partly Checked; Sales Largest on Record.

In what was possibly the culmination of this week's crash, yesterday's stock market passed for a time almost into a state of panic. The market's condition was, indeed, deemed sufficiently critical to call for a conference of important bankers, not ostensibly to provide relief through concentrated buying orders but to examine into the underlying situation. Their statement was reassuring in that it found no credit embarrassments impending; which is undoubtedly a result of the high "margin requirements" that commission brokers exacted from the speculating public of some months ago, even when describing in their daily bulletins the prospect for a still greater rise in prices. These 50 per cent margins, as compared with the 25 per cent of no very long time ago, were evidence that, however far experienced Wall Street may have been swept from its mental moorings by the market's seemingly boundless capacity to rise, their business instinct warned them of what the end would be.

Yesterday's sweeping decline of prices—running in many active stocks to 25 points or more, with total transac-tions of 12,894,000 shares, the largest by 4,600,000 in the history of the Stock Exchange—was clearly the result of frightened liquidation. "Bear selling" almost certainly cut a minor figure; it is in such markets as yesterday's that large speculators for the fall are most apt to cover their commitments. The selling, where it had not become compulsory through exhausted margins, resulted unquestionably from the alarm created by the sight of values crumbling in a manner such as Wall Street had predicted would never again be seen.

At the climax of such a movement, the speculative imagination runs as wild as it does on the crest of an excited rise. Whereas it pictured impossible achievement in prosperity and dividends last August and last February, it now looks for equally impossible immediate disasters. In the nature of things, the movement of prices under such hysteria is sure to be overdone, whichever direction it may take. Yet it will have to be admitted that the speculative community had itself, with absolute persistence, prepared the way and provided the material for just such a reckoning as yesterday's.

"President Names Hughes Chief Justice as Taft Resigns Because of Ill Health When Trip to Asheville Fails to Aid Him," February 4, 1930, "Hoover Names O. J. Roberts for the Supreme Court; Drys Bring Up Old Speech," May 10, 1930, and "Cardozo is Named to Supreme Court; Nomination Hailed," February 16, 1932.

Although the national economic catastrophe would forever mark President Hoover's record, his legacy includes three significant appointments to the Supreme Court. In 1930 Hoover selected Charles Evan Hughes of New York to replace Chief Justice William Howard Taft. Hughes previously had served on the Court, resigning in 1916 to run unsuccessfully for president against incumbent Woodrow Wilson. Just a few months later, Hoover nominated Owen J. Roberts of Pennsylvania for the Supreme Court, after his previous nominee failed to win Senate approval. And two years later, in 1932, Hoover nominated Benjamin N. Cardozo of New York, chief judge of the New York State Court of Appeals, and a highly popular choice in the Senate, to the nation's highest court.

FEBRUARY 4, 1930
PRESIDENT NAMES HUGHES CHIEF JUSTICE AS TAFT RESIGNS BECAUSE OF ILL HEALTH WHEN TRIP TO ASHEVILLE FAILS TO AID HIM
SENATE GETS NOMINATION

Speedy Confirmation Is Forecast for New Head of Supreme Court.

OLD OPPOSITION PASSES

Mr. Hoover Acts Quickly as Rumors of Other Choices Circulate at Capital.

TAFT RETIRES ON FULL PAY

Successor's Son, C. E. Hughes Jr., Will Immediately Resign as Solicitor General.

By RICHARD V. OULAHAN.

Special to The New York Times

WASHINGTON, Feb. 3.—Charles Evans Hughes of New York, who resigned as associate justice of the United States Supreme Court in 1916 to be the Republican candidate for President, was nominated this afternoon by President Hoover to be chief justice of the United States to succeed William Howard Taft of Ohio, whose resignation was tendered and accepted by the President a few hours earlier. Chief Justice Taft was 72 years old on Sept. 15. Mr. Hughes will be 68 on April 11.

Chief Justice Taft, who will continue to draw full pay of $20,500 a year while on the retired list, is on his way to Washington from Asheville, N.C., where he recently went for the benefit of his health. There is reason to believe that the retiring chief justice is seriously ill. His impaired physical condition was the sole reason for his resignation.

Retirement Law Has Changed.

A change made in the judiciary retirement law last March provided that the ten years' service on the Federal bench required to qualify a judge under the retirement rules need not be continuous, as heretofore, and this enabled Chief Justice Taft to go on the retired list. His service on the Supreme bench began in 1921, but he had served as a United States Circuit judge prior to holding certain political offices, including that of President, and this gave him more than the ten years of service which the law stipulated.

Shortly after Mr. Hughes's nomination was sent to the Senate it was announced by the Department of Justice that his son, Charles Evans Hughes Jr., would resign from the office of Solicitor General of the United States, a position which requires frequent appearances before the Supreme Court.

There is no indication of any opposition to the confirmation of Mr. Hughes's nomination. This is surprising to some, who had been aware of a critical attitude toward Mr. Hughes among Senators when there was talk at various times in the past that he might be asked to return to the Supreme bench.

It was contended that a man who left the Supreme Court to run for political office, as Mr. Hughes did in 1916 when he was nominated for President, had impaired his eligibility for further service in the highest court.

An expression used by those who maintained that critical view was that "the Supreme Court should not be used as a stepping stone to political office," and this was reversed to uphold the contention that after a justice of the high court had left it to seek an elective position of a political character, he should not be permitted to return to the court.

MAY 10, 1930
HOOVER NAMES O. J. ROBERTS FOR THE SUPREME COURT; DRYS BRING UP OLD SPEECH

CRITICIZED AMENDMENT

But Reed Hears From Roberts That Address Was Legal View Only.

SHEPPARD HAS DOUBTS

But Confirmation for Vacancy to Which Parker Was Named Is Held Likely.

HIS RECORD IS PRAISED

Southern Senators Wanted Another Southerner Nominated for the Position.

Special to The New York Times

WASHINGTON, May 9.—Owen J. Roberts of Philadelphia, special counsel for the government in the naval oil lease cases, and one of America's celebrated lawyers, was nominated today by President Hoover to succeed the late Edward T. Sanford, as an Associate Justice of the Supreme Court of the United States.

Mr. Roberts was chosen by the President in the place of Judge John J. Parker of North Carolina, whose nomination was rejected by the Senate last Wednesday by a vote of 41 to 39.

When Mr. Roberts's nomination reached the Senate, it was hailed as a victory by those who voted against Judge Parker, but a short time later dissatisfaction was evidenced when it was reported that Mr. Roberts had made a speech critical of the prohibition laws, and that he was affiliated with corporations, both personally and in a legal way.

These things seemed for a time to point to another fight against one of President Hoover's Supreme Court nominees, but Mr. Roberts's friends asserted tonight that the situation had been cleared up, and that he would be confirmed with little or no opposition.

FEBRUARY 16, 1932
CARDOZO IS NAMED TO SUPREME COURT; NOMINATION HAILED

Hoover Sends Appointment to Senate and Confirmation at Once Is Expected.

"GEOGRAPHY" IS IGNORED

President Selects a Third New Yorker for the Bench After Conference With Borah.

REGARDED AS A "LIBERAL"

Nation-Wide Support Was Based on Belief That the Judge's Views Resembled Those of Holmes.

Special to The New York Times

WASHINGTON, Feb. 15.—Benjamin Nathan Cardozo, Chief Judge of the New York State Court of Appeals, was nominated by President Hoover today to be an Associate Justice of the Supreme Court of the United States to fill the vacancy caused by the retirement of Justice Oliver Wendell Holmes.

Seldom, if ever, in the history of the court has an appointment been so universally commended as that of Judge Cardozo. Senators, by whom he must be confirmed, were unanimous in praising his selection, and Republicans, Democrats and Progressives vied with each other in commendation of the President's action.

The nomination reached the Senate this afternoon and was immediately referred to the Committee on Judiciary, of which Senator Norris is the chairman. It is expected that the nomination will be reported favorably to the Senate tomorrow afternoon and there is no question of immediate and favorable action on the motion to confirm.

Senator Norris has favored Judge Cardozo for the vacancy from the day Justice Holmes retired and was one of the first to express his approval of the appointment.

Endorsements Nation-Wide.

No announcement beyond the simple fact that the President had sent Judge Cardozo's name to the Senate was made at the White House. Neither was there much surprise when the decision was announced, since from every part of the country the President has been importuned to name him as the man best qualified to fill the seat left vacant by Justice Holmes.

From the moment the retirement of Justice Holmes was announced the demand has been general and nonpartisan that the man appointed should be a man of the mental stature of Justice Holmes, one of the same "liberal" views, and one of comparable learning in the law. In the opinion of many who urged the appointment, Judge Cardozo possessed these qualifications.

Scores of names were suggested for the Holmes vacancy, but only in the case of Judge Cardozo were the endorsements nation-wide in origin.

"The Tariff Bill Has Set Records," March 16, 1930

The contentious battle over the Smoot-Hawley Tariff Act of 1930 reflected the long-standing debate over the merits of raising tariffs on foreign goods to promote domestic products. Free trade advocates declared that tariffs ultimately hurt the U.S. economy and economic interests abroad; tariff proponents insisted that the measure was necessary to protect farmers from unfair foreign competition and to provide some price protection for U.S. goods. Although the tariff had strong support at the time, leading to its passage, it would have dire consequences for an already weakened U.S. economy.

MARCH 16, 1930
THE TARIFF BILL HAS SET RECORDS
Long Struggle Over Hawley-Smoot Measure Nears Its Final Stage—
Some of the Steps in the Bitter Controversy
By R. L. DUFFUS.

The Hawley-Smoot tariff bill, which, unless something unforeseen happens, is near its final stage in the Senate, stands out even among tariff bills in the amount of time consumed, the controversies stirred up and the number of scandals in the offing. It has furnished both houses of Congress with surprises and done a good deal to make or break several promising careers.

Officially speaking, the present bill may be said to have had its inception when the Republican Party at Kansas City on June 14, 1928, pledged itself to "an examination and where necessary a revision" of the tariff of 1922. Chairman Hawley of the House Ways and Means Committee amplified this statement, just before work was begun on the new measure, by saying: "Our aim will be to provide the rates that will adjust the difference in the cost of production at home and abroad so as to give the American manufacturer, farmer and laborer at least an equal opportunity in the American market."

The Fordney-McCumber act, passed in 1922, had taken a year and a half to be put through. When the Ways and

Means Committee began hearings on Jan. 7, 1929, Chairman Hawley predicted that the new act would be ready to go to a special session of the new Congress in April; that it could be sent to the Senate in June; and that it might go into effect before Fall.

Demands for Protection.

Into the House committee rooms came a stream of witnesses and petitioners—most of them demanding higher rates. The chief exceptions to this rule were in cases of manufacturers who wished low rates or free trade on their imported raw materials and high protection on their finished product. Farmers asked protection against foreign vegetable oils, while soap makers wanted reduced rates; stained-glass window makers and bottle-blowers asked protection against the Czechoslovak factories. Paper manufacturers asked a low rate on casein, dairymen a high rate; demands were made for increases in the sugar tariff; the farm group asked an average increase of 100 per cent on agricultural products.

The results of these hearings were bequeathed to the Seventy-first Congress by the expiring Seventieth. Three days after his inauguration, President Hoover called a special session to consider agricultural relief and "limited changes in the tariff." In his message to the new Congress on April 16 Mr. Hoover suggested a reorganization of the Tariff Commission and again repeated his phrase about "the necessity for some limited changes in the schedule."

· ·

"HOOVER GROUP PLANS WIDESPREAD EFFORT TO AID UNEMPLOYED," OCTOBER 19, 1930, AND "EMPLOYMENT PROBLEMS," OCTOBER 24, 1930

As the economy worsened after the stock market crash of October 1929, President Hoover appointed a committee to assist the unemployed. Composed of six cabinet members and a member of the Federal Reserve Board, the committee was to promote public works programs. *The Times* noted that "this will be spurred as an incentive to the public utilities to push forward their works," but the committee would face far more demand than it could possibly accommodate. *The Times* warned of this problem in an editorial about the Emergency Employment Committee, prophetically declaring, "It is unhappily inevitable that there will be a large amount of destitution which even temporary employment cannot of itself relieve."

OCTOBER 19, 1930
HOOVER GROUP PLANS WIDESPREAD EFFORT TO AID UNEMPLOYED
Present Organization Will Be Broadened if Needed to Meet National Situation.
LAMONT WILL BE CHAIRMAN
Burden of Finding Jobs Will Be Put on Government, State and Big Utilities.
DROUGHT MONEY TO GO OUT
States Affected Will Receive Road Allotments—Ripley Calls on President.
Special to The New York Times

WASHINGTON, Oct. 18.—President Hoover's committee of six Cabinet members and Governor Meyer of the Federal Reserve Board, named yesterday to formulate plans for strengthening Federal activities in relieving unemployment during the Winter, is expected to organize next week with Secretary Lamont as chairman.

It was stated today that this committee, composed of Secretaries Lamont, Davis, Wilbur, Hurley, Hyde, Mellon and Mr. Meyer, would be merely a starting committee if the unemployment situation did not improve, and it was confirmed that the country would be organized on a basis similar to that of 1921 if a turn in trade did not soon bring relief.

President Hoover was chairman of the unemployment conference called by President Harding to plan the organization to tide the country over the lean Winter of 1921–22. The idea was accepted as fundamental then that only a positive organization would work in the absence of a trade revival, and, warned by the happenings of the past year, the administration is laying the ground work for that organization now.

A trade revival came along late in the 1921–22 season and started things on the upgrade. The new life in business at that time was said to have been caused by the revival of construction, brought about largely through the work of the unemployment committees with Mayors of cities and municipalities.

There was a shortage in housing at that time and a need for private buildings of most every description.

Situation Now Contrasted.

The situation today presents a different aspect, according to administration officials, which puts the burden largely on the Federal and State Governments, and the public utilities who have surpluses and are willing to use them in pushing up their building programs and getting work started at an early date. Private building now, in many places, is considered overdone.

Public building, however, particularly in roads and post-offices, is still behind, and this will be spurred as an incentive to the public utilities to push forward their works.

OCTOBER 24, 1930
EDITORIAL
EMPLOYMENT PROBLEMS.

It should not be inferred from the announcement of the Emergency Employment Committee that the funds collected by it and placed in the hands of two private charitable organizations—the Charity Organization Society and the Association for Improving the Condition of the Poor [AICP]—in order to provide work for the unemployed heads of families, will meet the urgent need. The aid of every private society and association will be needed in addition to what the public authorities can do. And all their activities looking in this direction should be mobilized and coordinated under one all-embracing supervision. The Jewish and Catholic agencies which are already federated would thus be working in cooperation with those named by the committee. It is essential, too, that all the boroughs should be included in one comprehensive scheme of investigation and assistance.

To find or create opportunities for employment is the best sort of aid that can be given. Under the A. I. C. P. plan, which was adopted in 1914–15 and again during the depression of 1921–22, men who were unable to obtain employment and whose families were in distress were given a daily wage of $3. Through an arrangement with the Park Department, work was found for them outside of that provided for in the city budget. This plan will again be followed in principle. It will, however, doubtless be necessary to extend the work to other departments, where those being paid "relief wages" will not be in competition with other workmen, but may perform labor of public benefit not paid for out of taxes.

It is unhappily inevitable that there will be a large amount of destitution which even temporary employment cannot of itself relieve. This will mean an additional heavy demand upon the resources of all the charitable societies for this Winter. To meet this situation will require such general response in kind and in spirit as was made in providing the war loans or in gathering funds for the destitute abroad during and following the war. This is a community condition and requires prompt and continuing community action. That means the "mobilizing" both of opportunities for work and of funds for relief.

"Wagner Act Signed by the President," February 11, 1931, and "The Wagner Bill," February 15, 1931

President Hoover continued his efforts to promote employment with the Economic Stabilization Act of 1931. Also known as the Wagner-Graham Act, after its cosponsors, Democratic senator Robert F. Wagner of New York and Republican representative George S. Graham of Pennsylvania, the legislation authorized the construction of public works programs. In signing the bill, the president said, "It is not a cure for business depression, but will afford better organization for relief in future depressions." *The Times* cautioned that the new law would require strong leadership for effective implementation, noting in an editorial, "It will take more courage than most public officials can muster to warn of impending difficulties."

FEBRUARY 11, 1931
WAGNER ACT SIGNED BY THE PRESIDENT

Measure for Advance Planning of Public Works to Curb Unemployment
Is Termed Admirable.
NOT A CURE FOR SLUMPS
But Better Organization for Relief in the Future Is Provided, Says the Executive.
Special to The New York Times

WASHINGTON, Feb. 10.—President Hoover today signed the Wagner bill which provides for preparations for a reserve of public construction in order that prompt measures may be taken to counteract unemployment in business depressions. The President, in announcing his approval of the bill, declared it to be an admirable piece of legislation which, while not a cure, "will afford better organization for relief in future depressions."

"I have had great pleasure today in approving the act providing for advance planning of construction and Federal public works in preparation for future unemployment relief," the President said. "Senator Wagner and Representative Graham have worked out an admirable measure in which they adopted the constructive suggestions of the various government departments.

"The act gives wider authority and specific organization for the methods which have been pursued by the administration during the past fourteen months in respect to the planning and acceleration of Federal construction work for purposes of relief to unemployment in times of depression. It is not a cure for business depression, but will afford better organization for relief in future depressions.

"I feel it is just that I should take this occasion to make known two men who have had a large part in development of these ideas and their ultimate consummation—Mr. Edward Eyre Hunt of the Department of Commerce and Mr. Otto Mallory of Harrisburg, Pa.

"Proposals of such an organization for advanced planning were first advocated at the Unemployment Conference in 1921 by these men. The subject was exhaustively investigated by committees in which these two gentlemen participated in 1923 and 1928. The principles of this act were suggested to Congress at various times during the past five years, but it was not until we experienced this depression that their usefulness was recognized. I shall place the organization set up under the act under the Secretary of Commerce."

The new law creates the Federal Employment Stabilization Board, composed of four Cabinet officers. It will be a permanent instrumentality of government whose function it will be to adjust and time the huge quantity of Federal construction in order to provide employment and purchasing power on a large scale when private industry is slack.

The law calls for advance planning, including preparation of detailed construction plans, of public works by the construction agencies and the board.

Every department engaged in any construction is called upon to prepare and always keep in readiness construction plans covering six years in the future.

The board is to watch the volume of private and public construction, the index of employment and other statistics. Whenever, in its judgment, a depression is imminent, it will suggest to the President that public works must be expanded.

"Similar legislation is a fundamental necessity in every State and municipal government," Senator Wagner said this afternoon. "The intelligent administration of this act and of similar acts in the several States will contribute mightily to the stabilization of business and the steadiness of employment."

FEBRUARY 15, 1931
EDITORIAL
THE WAGNER BILL.

Senator Wagner has been one of the Administration's severest critics, particularly on the score of unemployment relief legislation. In signing the Senator's stabilization bill, President Hoover heaped coals of fire on his head. "Senator Wagner and Representative Graham have worked out an admirable measure," he remarked, "in which they adopted the constructive suggestions of the various government departments." He added that the control of public works made possible by the bill, following the recommendations of the "Committee on Recent Economic Changes," while not to be regarded as a cure for business ills, would at least afford "better organization for relief in future emergencies." It is indeed an interesting experiment in political economics, significant both for the Federal policy it enunciates and the example it may set to the States and municipalities.

The "Employment Stabilization Act of 1931" bears little resemblance to the fantastic scheme for a $3,000,000,000 national "prosperity reserve" put out by Governor Brewster of Maine some years ago, which was mistakenly assumed at the time to have the President's endorsement. No funds are set aside. There is no provision for concerted action with local authorities, although they may well follow where the Federal Government leads. The program is ambitious enough without those features. An "Employment Stabilization Board" is established, to consist of four Cabinet officers, whose duty it will be to keep the President advised as to business trends and especially to warn him of the "approach of periods of business depression and unemployment."

The board must evidently be prepared to put on the mantle of a prophet. To aid it in that difficult task, it is to have the advice of a permanent staff, which will serve as a clearing house for all information bearing on business conditions now collected by the various bureaus at Washington. Construction contracts are expected to be its chief reliance, although it may also take into consideration the index of employment prepared by the Department of Labor and any other information, official or unofficial, that comes its way. Whenever, upon the recommendation of the board, the President finds that there exists, "or that within six months there is likely to exist," a period of business depression, he is courteously invited to transmit to Congress whatever supplementary estimates for emergency appropriations he deems advisable, to be expended on authorized construction—highways, rivers and harbors, flood control, public buildings, and so on.

On its part Congress undertakes, from this time forth, "to arrange the construction of public works so far as practicable in such a manner as will assist in the stabilization of industry and employment." That means advance planning—a somewhat radical departure for a body given to making up its mind at the last minute. All the bureaus charged with construction must accordingly prepare their plans six years in advance, for submission to the Stabilization Board and the Budget Bureau. Here is the nucleus of a "capital outlay budget" such as that which cities and States have often been urged to adopt. Bureau chiefs and Congress will need prodding if they are to live up to this pledge. The President, too, has assumed no mean responsibility. It will take more courage than most public officials can muster to warn of impending difficulties.

"Congress Returns to Big Tasks Today," January 4, 1932

By 1932 the U.S. economic situation was so dire that President Hoover and Congress were working desperately to provide national assistance. The government took several measures, most significantly the creation of the Reconstruction Finance Corporation to provide loans to banks and businesses. But this organization would fall far short of the administration's goals in combating the financial turmoil.

JANUARY 4, 1932
CONGRESS RETURNS TO BIG TASKS TODAY

Leaders Promise Quick Action on Hoover Credit Measures and Aid to Business.
HOME FOLKS INSISTENT
Democratic Policy Committee Will Shape the Party's Tariff Plans
as First Consideration.
Special to The New York Times

WASHINGTON, Jan. 3.—Congress will reconvene tomorrow with the leaders of both parties determined to speed action upon President Hoover's emergency recommendations. Returning to the capital today members reported that the home districts insist on quick disposition of measures aimed to correct credit conditions and afford assistance to the railroads.

Senator Watson, Republican, of Indiana, said he found his constituents very insistent on action in regard to matters that affect business.

"I believe that business would go ahead very rapidly if Congress would very early this year dispose of the remedial legislation, taxes and railroad consolidation plans," he said.

Early action will be taken in the House on tariff changes. Democrats were reported tonight to favor the passage of a resolution requesting the President to call an international conference to work out reciprocal duties.

After the tariff resolution is passed the House leaders plan to get action before the end of the week, if possible, on the Reconstruction Finance Corporation bill and to begin hearings on a tax revision bill.

Before entering upon its fourteen-day Christmas holiday both Houses had passed the international debt moratorium resolution and the House had disposed of the bill increasing the capitalization of the farm land banks by $100,000,000, the first of the Administration's relief measures. Hearings also were begun by the Banking and Currency Committees of both Houses on the $500,000,000 Reconstruction Finance Corporation proposal, with indications that this far-reaching measure will be reported to the Senate this week without essential change.

The terms of the Democratic tariff bill will be decided upon by the party's Joint Policy Committee, which will meet tomorrow in Speaker Garner's office. The party's position on taxation and the administration's economic program will be discussed, with the likelihood that a legislative program will be laid down.

The calling of an international conference on tariff matters has been recommended by John J. Raskob, chairman of the Democratic National Committee, who has also urged that the flexible provision of the tariff law be amended to require the Tariff Commission to report to Congress instead of to the President.

Indications today were that the policy committee will oppose retroactive income taxes and an increase in the rate on small incomes. Generally speaking, the Democrats are reported favorable to a program embracing higher surtaxes, increased inheritance taxes and the restoration of the gift taxes.

The policy committee, it was said tonight, would pledge the party not to obstruct reconstruction measures recommended by the President. Senator Robinson, the Senate floor leader, said that such legislation would receive the party's support, although the Democrats would offer amendments to perfect the administration bills, and may go so far as to largely to rewrite some of them.

Baruch Talks to Leaders.

Informal conferences of Democratic leaders were held today on pending legislation and party policies. Bernard M. Baruch of New York had long conferences with Senator Robinson and with Representative Rainey, House floor leader, on the Reconstruction Finance Corporation bill which he is reported to favor, with some changes which would place a limitation on the bonds and other securities which it is proposed to make eligible for rediscount by the Federal Reserve banks.

Mr. Baruch has been mentioned as a probable member of the Reconstruction Finance Corporation if it is set up.

The view was expressed by Democratic members that the Policy Committee would go on record in such a way as to impress upon the country that the party would act conservatively and pave the way to avoid controversy and delay which would further disturb business.

A bill guaranteeing deposits in all national banks and member banks of the Federal Reserve System will be introduced in the House tomorrow by Representative La Guardia of New York. The guarantee fund under his bill would be created in each Federal Reserve district by contributions by Federal Reserve System banks. Supervision of the fund would be by the Federal Reserve Board. Banks would be assessed in instalments of one-quarter of 1 per cent of the average daily deposits for a period of two years. From that point on, the semi-annual assessment would be one-twentieth of 1 per cent.

* *

"Note Is Sent to Far East," January 8, 1932

In response to Japan's invasion of Manchuria in 1931, the Hoover administration sent a diplomatic note to both the Japanese and Chinese governments affirming the U.S. open-door policy toward China. In so doing, the administration sought to recognize China's integrity and deter Japan from further aggression.

JANUARY 8, 1932
NOTE IS SENT TO FAR EAST

Warns Japan and China We Will Not Tolerate Violation of Open Door.

HOPEFUL OF LEAGUE MOVE

Washington Action, Secretary Says, Is Result of Elimination of Chinese Authority.

EXPECTS AID FROM OTHERS

Washington Accepts Apology for Attack on Consul, but Demands Punishment of Japanese.

Special to The New York Times

WASHINGTON, Jan. 7.—The United States Government today sent an identic note to the Japanese and Chinese Governments invoking its own rights and those of its citizens in Manchuria under the Nine-Power China treaty of 1922 and the Kellogg-Briand anti-war pact.

This action was taken because of the ending of Chinese administrative authority in Manchuria with the advance of the Japanese Army to Chinchow and beyond in pursuance of the military operations begun on Sept. 18, 1931.

The note was forceful in tone yet restrained in language and was officially described as a declaration, not a protest. It does not necessarily mean that any action will be required in support of the note. Rather it is construed as a strong assertion of American rights that must be reckoned with when a permanent solution of the Sino-Japanese

controversy is achieved. The Nine-Power pact calls only for communication among the signatories and adherents when an emergency arises.

Warning Against Coercion.

The administration believes the action taken today will clarify the situation in the Far East and at the same time protect the historic policy of the open door in China. The assertion in support of the Kellogg-Briand anti-war treaty amounts to a warning to Japan that she must not expect to wring undue concessions from China by military force. That this treaty is no empty expression was reiterated today on high authority.

Secretary Stimson's message dealt first with the Nine-Power treaty, although not by name, and with the open-door policy of the late John Hay, included in that pact, and in its concluding sentence reasserted the Pact of Paris, commonly known as the Kellogg-Briand anti-war treaty, which was first invoked last Fall jointly by the world powers, including the United States, by invitation of the Council of the League of Nations.

So far as the reiteration of the United States government's stand in support of the integrity of China and the open door was concerned, the note is in line with the one sent by President Wilson and Secretary of State Bryan on May 13, 1915, to Japan and China in protest against the twenty-one demands made by the Tokyo Government on China. In that communication the Wilson Administration served notice that the rights of the United States must be observed. . . .

Nine-Power Treaty Terms.

The basis for Secretary Stimson's note is found in Articles I and VII of the Nine-Power Treaty, which read as follows:

ARTICLE I.

The contracting powers, other than China, agree:

1. To respect the sovereignty, the independence and the territorial and administrative integrity of China.

2. To provide the fullest and most unembarrassed opportunity to China to develop and maintain for herself an effective and stable government.

3. To use their influence for the purpose of effectually establishing and maintaining the principle of equal opportunity for the commerce and industry of all nations throughout the territory of China.

4. To refrain from taking advantage of conditions in China in order to seek special rights or privileges which would abridge the rights of subjects or citizens of friendly States, and from countenancing action inimical to the security of such States.

ARTICLE VII.

The contracting powers agree that whenever a situation arises which in the opinion of any one of them involves the application of the stipulations of the present treaty, and renders desirable discussion of such application, there shall be full and frank communication between the contracting powers concerned.

Hoover Stresses Peace Hope.

The intention of Secretary Stimson to assert American rights in Manchuria, regardless of what other governments may do, was supported by President Hoover this afternoon when Dr. W. W. Yen presented his credentials as the new Chinese Minister. Dr. Yen has been here several days and it was considered significant that he was received by the President on the day the declaration of American rights was made to the Far East.

"My government," said Dr. Yen, "has considered it a matter of moment that in view of the very critical international situation in the Far East and of the earnest efforts which are being made to arrive at a just, equitable and peaceable settlement, I should enter into the duties of my office, in order to render any assistance that may be needed to restore conditions to peace and normalcy—a consummation highly to be desired."

"Hoover Orders Eviction," July 29, 1932

President Hoover was widely criticized for his harsh treatment of U.S. veterans petitioning the government to distribute a promised bonus ahead of schedule. On July 28, 1932, the president sent federal troops to disperse the veterans from the temporary housing they had erected in Washington, D.C. The use of tear gas against the veterans sparked much public opposition, as did the president's statement that the protestors included Communists and criminals.

JULY 29, 1932
HOOVER ORDERS EVICTION

Blaming Reds, He Asserts Bonus Camps Included Many Criminals.

QUICK ACTION BY SOLDIERS

Eject Squatters After Police Fail and Then Burn Camps in and Near Capital.

BONUS ARMY SCATTERED

Demoralized by Soldiers' Gas Attack, Remnants Are Left Leaderless and Helpless.

Special to The New York Times

WASHINGTON, July 28.—Amidst scenes reminiscent of the mopping-up of a town in the World War, Federal troops late today drove the army of bonus seekers from the shanty village near Pennsylvania Avenue in which the veterans had been entrenched for months. Earlier in the day the police had fought and lost a battle there which resulted in the death of one veteran, possibly fatal injuries to a policeman and a long list of other casualties, many of them serious.

Ordered to the scene by President Hoover after the District of Columbia authorities confessed defeat, detachments of infantry, cavalry, machine-gun and tank crews laid down an effective tear-gas barrage which disorganized the bonus-seekers, and then set fire to the shacks and tents left behind by the veterans on the government land near Third and Pennsylvania Avenues, scene of the earlier clash with the police.

Begin to Clear Anacostia.

After the disputed area near the Capitol had been cleared, the troops moved late in the evening on Camp Marks, on the Anacostia River, the bonus army's principal encampment. At 10 o'clock this evening infantrymen with drawn bayonets advanced into the camp, driving the crowd before them with tear gas bombs. Then they applied the torch to the shacks in which the veterans lived.

Troops shortly afterward halted at the main bonus camp in response to what General Perry L. Miles, commanding the soldiers, said was a Presidential order. Theodore G. Joslin, the President's secretary, later denied positively that the President had issued any such order, and word came from the camp that the troops would resume operations within an hour.

At 11:15 P.M. the first troop of cavalry had moved into the disordered camp, now a mass of flames as the bonus-seeking veterans set fire to their own miserable shacks. At midnight practically all the veterans had left the place.

Warned that the soldiers would use tear gas the veterans had arranged to evacuate the 600 women and children earlier.

The normal population of Camp Marks was augmented by more than 2,000 veterans who had been evicted from other camps, bringing the total male population to 7,000.

Troops Avoid Bloodshed.

Soon after the khaki-clad regulars descended on the various camps along Pennsylvania Avenue this afternoon the bonus seekers were straggling sullenly away from the ominous blue mist of the tear gas, leaderless and apparently demoralized, seeking shelter in other open places scattered afar through the city. A few of them were sore from minor bruises, but on the whole the Federal troops had conducted their offensive without bloodshed. The veteran who was killed in the earlier clash with the police was identified tonight as William Hashka of Chicago.

The day's disturbances were blamed on the radical element among the bonus-seekers. Walter W. Waters, the young veteran from Oregon who led the unsuccessful bonus march to Washington, disclaimed responsibility for his followers' part in resisting the first eviction order of the police. Waters announced tonight that he was "through."

"The men got out of control. There was nothing and there is nothing that I can do to control them," he said.

With the bonus army in the city proper dispersed into straggling and woebegone remnants, the hovels and tents which had been their homes were the scene of another kind of fight tonight—when numerous fire crews were called out to control the flames started by the torches of the victorious army troops. The bonus men will be unable to "dig in" to their old camp sites in the city because the land is now being prepared for the Federal building operations which government authorities have decided should not be delayed any longer.

The clash with the police earlier in the day was short and furious. The advancing police, met by a hail of brickbats, first used their nightsticks and then began to shoot, after one of the bluecoats, George Scott, was felled by a brick that fractured his skull. His condition tonight was serious, and so was that of one of the wounded veterans.

In ordering out the troops to take the situation in hand after the police had failed, President Hoover explained that many of the bonus seekers who had stayed on after Congress had adjourned, were not veterans. The President said that many were "Communists and persons with criminal records."

The necessity of proclaiming martial law was avoided by War Department officials through an order to the army officers to turn over all prisoners to the civil authorities.

The order issued by Secretary of War Hurley to General Douglas MacArthur, chief of staff, which quickly brought the troops from near-by forts and camps in Virginia, read as follows:

"The President has just informed me that the civil government of the District of Columbia has reported to him that it is unable to maintain law and order in the District.

"You will have United States troops proceed immediately to the scene of the disorder. Cooperate fully with the District of Columbia police force, which is now in charge. Surround the affected area and clear it without delay.

"Turn over all prisoners to the civil authorities.

"In your orders, insist that any women and children who may be in the affected area be accorded every consideration and kindness. Use all humanity consistent with the due execution of this order."

Soon afterward the troops, with steel helmets and fixed bayonets, were marching down Pennsylvania Avenue past a throng of citizens, some of whom jeered them and cheered the veterans. Cavalry, tanks, machine gunners, engineers and infantrymen went to work immediately. Meanwhile huge army trucks waited in readiness to carry off those who refused to move. Ambulances were mobilized to care for possible casualties.

On side streets army tanks and machine gunners waited to reduce to rubble and smoking ruin the shanty towns which the veterans had stubbornly refused to vacate, even in the face of a sweeping eviction order that was issued by Attorney General Mitchell after the first fight with the police.

Throughout the afternoon most of the citizenry here had gone about their business as usual, but when the military began their offensive this evening the crowds of spectators grew by leaps and bounds. A mile away from the scene of the offensive he had ordered, President Hoover worked at his desk in the White House.

A bugle call at 4:20 P.M. was the signal for the troops to fall in. One minute later the mopping-up began, the cavalrymen leading the way, followed by the tanks, machine gunners and the infantry. Generals MacArthur and Miles accompanied the infantry, accompanied by General George Van Horn Moseley, Deputy Chief of Staff.

Reaching the first of the series of veterans' shanty towns, the infantry and cavalry donned gas masks and moved systematically in a contracting circle, hurling tear gas bombs before them and giving the veterans an unwilling taste of old times, when they used similar methods on German strongholds in the World War.

"He was held responsible for the sins of others."

"The Hoover Tragedy," November 9, 1932, and "Hoover Gets Six States," November 10, 1932

The sweeping victory of Franklin D. Roosevelt over President Hoover in the 1932 presidential race reflected public frustration with the government's limited efforts to move the nation out of the Great Depression. The election represented a repudiation of the Republican Party platform as well: Not only did the Democratic presidential candidate win after twelve years of Republican rule, but also the Democrats won by large margins in both chambers of Congress. In an editorial about Hoover's loss, The Times was sympathetic to the departing president, describing him as "a man exerting all of his strength against formidable and insurmountable obstacles. It was a clear case of an individual made to suffer unjustly for the mistakes and crimes of others." The headline in the news article refers to Socialist Party candidate Norman Thomas of New York, who won more than 880,000 popular votes.

NOVEMBER 9, 1932
EDITORIAL
THE HOOVER TRAGEDY.

For the President personally in his defeat there will be a feeling of kindness touched by the pathos of the political misfortunes against which he has struggled in vain. The strong god circumstance was too powerful for him. He was held responsible for the sins of others. Upon his individual head was wreaked the spirit of resentment and of vengeance for events which neither he nor any other man in public office could control. It is true that he partly exposed himself to such attack by identifying himself with the wrong policies and foolish promises of his party four years ago; but to single him out as if he were the sole man accountable, the only one to bear the burden, the fitting target for the slings and arrows of outrageous fortune, was no doubt inevitable, as human nature goes—especially as the nature of the political animal goes—but distinctly and grossly unfair. Mr. Hoover was deserted by his friends as well as assaulted by his enemies. The campaign was going against him almost by default, until he stepped forward to assume the whole load of it. To the end he presented the pathetic spectacle of a man exerting all of his strength against formidable and insurmountable obstacles. It was a clear case of an individual made to suffer unjustly for the mistakes and crimes of others.

Herbert Hoover ought to be remembered for his abilities, his successes as well as his failures. Through all the great crisis he certainly displayed great qualities. No President ever worked harder in the hope of helping the people to escape from their troubles. Mr. Hoover also worked with rare intelligence. His grasp of facts was phenomenal. His adherence to what he believed sound principles was heroic. For fully three years he was compelled to pass through the furnace of political affliction, and came out of it, to be sure, with certain defects and flaws revealed, yet with a large amount of the pure gold of statesmanlike talent, along with an undoubted and unsparing devotion to the public good.

Into his coming retirement the American people will follow him with respect. They will regret that he fell upon evil days wherein his unusual powers could not be rightly appreciated or made completely effective. There is a tragic element, as of a stroke of fate, in this closing of a political career, in the presence of which people of delicate sensibilities can only, as Judge Holmes said, "stand in awe."

President Herbert Hoover, right, hands his ballot to an election offical in his home district, Palo Alto, California.

Source: The New York Times

NOVEMBER 10, 1932
HOOVER GETS SIX STATES

Roosevelt's Plurality Is Put at 6,801,000 in Late Estimates.

CONGRESS SWEEP GROWS

Tally Now Gives Democrats 161 Majority in the House and 22 in the Senate.

CABINET SPECULATION RIFE

Record Vote of More Than a Million Expected for Thomas in Final Count.

By ARTHUR KROCK.

Millions of American citizens, numbering probably one-third of the total population, went about their normal tasks as usual yesterday after the voting out of the Republican party on Tuesday with a majority at least as great as it received four years ago. But in the political community, these matters being not merely an affair of one day every four years, there was intense activity.

President-elect Franklin D. Roosevelt, having received the delayed message of congratulation which President Herbert Hoover dispatched to him from Palo Alto, Cal., about 9:15 o'clock on election night, sent an equally gracious response in which he suggested that the "immediate future" of the country, as well as that which will follow March 4, 1933, was of proper concern to both of the recent rival candidates. This aroused speculation as to whether, and when, he and Mr. Hoover will meet to go over the state of the Union with a view to agreement on plans to meet emergencies.

The President, after a day of indecision as to his personal movements, decided to entrain for the Capital in time to reach there next Wednesday night. There was some speculation, not based on any word or clue from Mr. Hoover, as to whether he will move to turn over the government to the Democrats at once, as Abraham Lincoln and Woodrow Wilson are both supposed to have planned to do in crises to which the President has in his speeches likened the existing economic situation.

Roosevelt on State Job.

This could be accomplished simply by the appointment of Mr. Roosevelt as Secretary of State, the subse-

quent resignations of Messrs. Hoover and Curtis and the automatic succession of the President-elect. But even if Mr. Hoover has any such plan in mind, with the good of the country as his motive, there is no evidence that Mr. Roosevelt agrees to the necessity or would be a party to the arrangement. So the speculation must go down as the kind of gossip which follows the repudiation by the voters of emergency arguments such as the President made for his own re-election.

Certainly there was nothing in Mr. Roosevelt's words or actions which supports the rumor. He arose late, made a brief radio address to the country and returned to Albany to plunge into the budget of the State of New York, of which he will be Governor until Jan. 1. The isolation which is the fate of those elected as President had already begun to enclose him. Otherwise it would seem that he would have heard from all over the country a buzzing sound which was discussion of when he will announce his Cabinet and who its members are to be.

As fuller returns came in during the day it was demonstrated that the indications of election night were accurate. Mr. Roosevelt carried all but six States, which gave Mr. Hoover a modern record low of fifty-nine electoral votes. These, Maine, Vermont, New Hampshire, Connecticut, Pennsylvania and Delaware, are all on or contiguous to the Eastern seaboard. Every other State, with a total of 472 votes, went to the Democrats.

The estimate of Governor Roosevelt's plurality, based on the latest returns, is 6,801,000.

"Meet at the White House," November 23, 1932

President-elect Roosevelt visited the White House to meet with President Hoover to discuss the nation's economic and political conditions. But Roosevelt refrained from committing himself to any joint efforts with the president, preferring to wait until the start of his administration four months later. The difficulties posed by such a long interregnum were apparent, and, indeed, 1933 would be the last time that a U.S. president would be inaugurated in March. The Twentieth Amendment, ratified just before FDR took office, moved inauguration day up to January 20.

NOVEMBER 23, 1932
MEET AT THE WHITE HOUSE

'Progress' Reported in a Statement Issued for the President.
AGREE ON NO SUSPENSION
But Roosevelt Acts Chiefly in Role of Listener to the President's Views.
HOOVER FOR FUNDING BOARD
Will Urge Congress to Re-create Commission for New Action on War Loans.
Special to The New York Times

WASHINGTON, Nov. 22.—President Hoover will not recommend suspension of the December payments on the European debts to this country, but will urge Congress to re-create the war debts funding commission with a view to possible revision, *The New York Times* learned on good authority tonight.

Governor Roosevelt came to Washington today at President Hoover's invitation to discuss the debt question. After the conference the President-elect at a meeting at the Mayflower Hotel late tonight took Democratic leaders in Congress into his confidence and related to them in some detail what took place at the White House.

Governor Roosevelt, it was learned, participated very little in the discussions with the President, but made no effort to oppose the course mapped out by Mr. Hoover; neither did he make any commitments. It was understood that the two agreed that there should be no request for suspension of the December payments, as has been forecast, due to the short time intervening between the opening of Congress and Dec. 15, when the payments are due.

It was the opinion of participants in tonight's conference at the Mayflower Hotel that the White House would issue a statement along this line within the next twenty-four hours.

No Commitment on Revision.

With regard to the President's proposal again to recommend to Congress re-creation of the debt funding commission to study the entire structure of foreign obligations, Mr. Roosevelt made no commitments whatsoever at the White House conference.

It has been frequently stated that Governor Roosevelt tended toward the position that war debts should not be considered as a separate problem, but should be looked into in a broad manner along with other world economic problems, such as tariff and disarmament.

In one high administration quarter tonight considerable optimism was expressed at the result of the White House conference, and the view was taken that there really had been progress, as a statement issued by the White House insisted. This view, it was believed, was predicated upon Governor Roosevelt's attitude toward world economic problems as a whole, leading to the belief that while he might be unwilling to take responsibility for any far-reaching action on war debts alone before he enters the White House, he would not be opposed to a consideration of war debts in conjunction with other problems.

Leading Democrats have favored a world economic conference covering these matters, and it was considered possible that they might be brought within the agenda of the coming conference negotiated by the Hoover administration, but which will not take place until after Mr. Roosevelt becomes President.

While Democratic Senators, as well as many Republicans, are almost unanimous in opposing revision of the war debts as such, some of them, including Senator Hull, one of the leading Democratic authorities on world economy, have left the door open to possible revision provided other problems which they consider linked with war debts in retarding prosperity are considered simultaneously.

The war debt complication and correlated international problems were considered for more than two hours by President Hoover and President-elect Roosevelt.

Afterward, the White House issued a forty-word statement, but Governor Roosevelt made no statement.

"It is felt that progress has been made," said the White House announcement.

The President-elect after the conclusion of his conference with President Hoover arranged to confer not only late tonight, but again tomorrow morning with Democratic leaders before departing early in the afternoon for Warm Springs, Ga.

Nevertheless, it was made plain that Governor Roosevelt will not attempt to dictate to the present Congress, and will maintain the attitude previously expressed—that the immediate question raised by the European debtors, in the last analysis, "creates a responsibility which rests upon those now vested with executive and legislative authority."

THE PRESIDENCY OF **FRANKLIN D. ROOSEVELT**

MARCH 4, 1933 – APRIL 12, 1945

The presidency of Franklin Delano Roosevelt redefined American politics and the American presidency. When FDR took office in 1933, the nation was mired in the Great Depression, with high unemployment, failing banks, and limited financial or industrial activity. Two years earlier, nearly 100,000 Americans had sought employment in the Soviet Union. Public confidence in government and the economy had fallen so low that some questioned whether the United States would endure this crisis.

With the stirring words of his first inaugural address—"The only thing we have to fear is fear itself"—FDR made clear that indeed the nation would endure and see prosperous times again. Through a vast expansion of the federal government's role in society, with programs ranging from federally insured bank deposits to Social Security, FDR slowly reinvigorated the economy and rebuilt public confidence in the United

Source: The Granger Collection, New York

States. When World War II began, the United States did not intervene immediately, but FDR insisted on aiding the Allied powers, and the horrific attack on Pearl Harbor prompted U.S. entry into the war. Just as he had led the nation in the dark days of the Depression, FDR directed the war clearly, decisively, and spiritedly. His leadership in both domestic and foreign affairs leaves a legacy that continues to shape American politics today.

Born to a wealthy New York family, FDR was the only child of James and Sara Roosevelt. FDR attended Groton, the prestigious preparatory school in Massachusetts, and then matriculated at Harvard University. He served as editor of the campus newspaper and graduated in three years. He

spent a fourth year at Harvard doing graduate work in history and economics, and then joined the law program at Columbia University. After passing the bar exam in 1907, he left the law school without completing his degree.

FDR began his professional career as a lawyer but soon moved into the field that interested him most, politics. He was elected to the New York Senate in 1910 and reelected two years later, but he stepped down to join the administration of Woodrow Wilson as assistant secretary of the navy, a position once held by FDR's distant cousin, Theodore Roosevelt, in the McKinley administration. FDR requested transfer to active duty during World War I, but President Wilson asked him to keep his

QUICK FACTS ON FRANKLIN D. ROOSEVELT

BIRTH	January 30, 1882, Hyde Park, N.Y.
EDUCATION	Harvard College, B.A., 1903 Columbia Law School, 1904–1907
FAMILY	Wife: Anna Eleanor Roosevelt Roosevelt Children: Anna Eleanor Roosevelt, James Roosevelt, Franklin Roosevelt, Elliott Roosevelt, Franklin Delano Roosevelt Jr., John Aspinwall Roosevelt
WHITE HOUSE PETS	Dogs; best known was Scottish terrier Fala
PARTY	Democratic
PREPRESIDENTIAL CAREER (SELECTED)	Law practice, 1907–1910 New York State Senate, 1911–1913 Assistant secretary of navy, 1913–1920 Unsuccessful Democratic vice-presidential candidate, 1920 Vice president, Fidelity and Deposit Company, 1920–1928 Governor of New York, 1929–1933
PRESIDENTIAL TERMS	March 4, 1933–January 20, 1937 January 20, 1937–January 20, 1941 January 20, 1941–January 20, 1945 January 20, 1945–April 12, 1945
VICE PRESIDENTS	John Nance Garner (first and second terms) Henry A. Wallace (third term) Harry S. Truman (January 20, 1945–April 12, 1945)

SELECTED EVENTS	Announcement of Good Neighbor policy toward Latin America (1933)
	Bank Holiday (March 5–13, 1933)
	"Hundred Days" special session of Congress (March 9–June 16, 1933):
	    Agricultural Adjustment Act, creation of Civilian Conservation Corps
	    and Federal Deposit Insurance Corporation, and other legislation
	U.S. recognition of Soviet Union (1933)

post. He served until 1920, when he resigned to run for vice president with James M. Cox of Ohio. The Republican ticket headed by Warren G. Harding soundly defeated the Democrats, and Roosevelt returned to private life. He joined a New York law firm and became vice president of a bond firm.

FDR experienced a life-altering crisis in 1921, when he became ill with polio. Although he recovered, he lost the use of his legs and needed to use a wheelchair for the rest of his life. Through sheer personal perseverance, he worked to build his upper body strength, and he even managed to walk for brief periods with leg braces and canes. In fact, FDR became so skillful at this feat that during his presidency, most Ameri-

cans were not aware of his disability. The White House press corps observed an unwritten agreement not to photograph the president being helped into or out of his wheelchair.

In many respects, the battle to regain his health may have helped FDR prepare for reentering the tumultuous world of politics. In 1924 he gave the nomination speech for New York governor Alfred E. Smith at the Democratic National Convention in New York City. Although Smith did not win the nomination, FDR's speech, delivered on crutches at Madison Square Garden, made him a highly visible person in the Democratic Party. Four years later, Smith won the Democratic presidential nomination, and he urged FDR to enter the New

Ratification of Twenty-first Amendment repealing Prohibition (1933)
Philippine Independence Act (1934)
Creation of Securities and Exchange Commission (1934)
Creation of Federal Communications Commission (1934)
Establishment of Works Progress Administration (1935)
Wagner Labor Relations Act (1935)
Neutrality Act (1935)
Social Security Act (1935)
"Court-packing" plan controversy (1937)
Wagner-Steagall Housing Act (1937)
Recession (1937)
Fair Labor Standards Act (1938)
Administrative Reorganization Act (1939)
Hatch Act (1939)
World War II begins (1939)
Destroyers for Bases agreement with Great Britain (1940)
Alien Registration ("Smith") Act (1940)
Selective Training and Service Act (1940)
"Four Freedoms" speech (1941)
Lend-Lease Act (1941)
MacArthur becomes commander of U.S. forces in Philippines (1941)
Atlantic Charter issued by United States and Great Britain (1941)
Japan attacks Pearl Harbor, Hawaii, and Guam and Philippines
   (December 7, 1941)
United States enters World War II (December 8, 1941)
MacArthur commands Allied forces in Australia and southwest Pacific (1942)
Allies invade North Africa (1942)
U.S. naval victory at Guadalcanal (1942)
Invasion of Italy (1943)
Tehran Conference (1943)
D-Day invasion (June 6, 1944)
Servicemen's Readjustment Act (G.I. Bill of Rights) (1944)
United Nations Monetary and Financial Conference, Bretton Woods, N.H. (1944)
Dumbarton Oaks Conference on United Nations (1944)
Yalta Conference (1945)

DEATH   April 12, 1945, Warm Springs, Ga.

York gubernatorial race in his place. Roosevelt won the election and then was reelected in 1930 for a second two-year term. In response to the growing economic crisis from the Great Depression, Roosevelt established a government agency to provide jobs for unemployed New Yorkers.

THE 1932 ELECTION

In 1932 FDR entered the presidential race. Lacking the necessary two-thirds of delegates to win the Democratic nomination, he promised to support House Speaker John Nance Garner for the vice-presidential spot if Garner would drop out of the presidential race. Garner agreed, and FDR won the Democratic nomination on the fourth convention ballot, with Garner selected afterward as his running mate. FDR traveled to Chicago to deliver his acceptance speech to the convention in person, the first presidential candidate to do so. The Republican Party nominated President Herbert Hoover and Vice President Charles Curtis for a second term on the first ballot, but the worsening economic conditions in the country proved to be an insurmountable obstacle for the incumbent administration. Roosevelt won nearly 23 million popular votes to Hoover's almost 16 million, and he prevailed in the Electoral College, with 472 votes from 42 states to just 59 votes from 6 states for Hoover.

The Roosevelt Administration (First Term)

FDR's ten-member cabinet in his first term included a diverse group of Democrats. Senior statesman Cordell Hull of Tennessee became secretary of state. Hull served in this post for twelve years, the longest tenure of any occupant of the office. George H. Dern of Utah was appointed secretary of war and he served until his death in 1936, when Assistant Secretary Harry H. Woodring of Kansas took over. William H. Woodin of New York served briefly as treasury secretary but resigned within a year due to poor health; he was replaced by Henry Morgenthau Jr. of New York. Homer S. Cummings of New York was named attorney general. One of FDR's most significant cabinet appointments was the selection of fellow New Yorker and close political ally Frances Perkins as labor secretary. Perkins was the first woman to hold a cabinet office, and she served throughout FDR's presidency, stepping down shortly after Harry S. Truman became president in 1945.

FDR's wife, Eleanor, was Theodore Roosevelt's niece and a distant relation to her husband. Eleanor's parents died when she was a small child, and her uncle walked her down the aisle at her wedding in 1905. The Roosevelts had six children, one girl and five boys, one of whom died in infancy. The Roosevelt marriage suffered a devastating blow during FDR's tenure in the Wilson administration when Eleanor learned that her husband was having an affair with her personal secretary, Lucy Mercer. Although their personal life was forever changed (and FDR would continue to see Lucy Mercer secretly until his death in 1945), their political alliance continued. When FDR became president, Eleanor Roosevelt became the most politically active first lady the United States had seen up to that time.

Major Issues (First Term)

FDR took office on March 4, 1933, making him the last president to be inaugurated in March. The Twentieth Amendment shortened the transition period, and the next presidential term would begin on January 20, 1937. The 1933 inauguration also was important because the president-elect had narrowly escaped an assassin's bullet in Miami just weeks earlier. Had the assassin met his target, the new president would have been John Nance Garner, who allegedly once remarked that the vice presidency was not worth "a pitcher of warm spit" (or something less tasteful). With FDR's inauguration, a new era commenced in American politics.

Roosevelt's first inaugural address ranks as one of the finest speeches in American history. He declared that "the only thing we have to fear is fear itself—nameless, unreasoning, unjustified terror which paralyzes needed efforts to convert retreat into advance." He made clear that his administration would not retreat from the task at hand: to reinvigorate the national economy and help people suffering the effects of the Depression. The new president promised to work with Congress to achieve these goals, but he also warned that if Congress did not take action, he would not hesitate to request from it "broad executive power to wage a war against the emergency as great as the power that would be given me if we were in fact invaded by a foreign foe." Just as Lincoln had asserted broad presidential power in the Civil War, so too did FDR claim a similar right to battle the national economic catastrophe.

His first task was to reopen the nation's banks. To prevent a run on bank deposits, he had declared a four-day bank holiday and convened Congress in a special session to consider an emergency banking bill. It passed in less than eight hours. Recognizing the momentum for action, FDR recommended a number of other measures, all of which quickly became law. Continuing until the special session of Congress ended in mid-June 1933, this period became known as the "Hundred Days." Legislation passed in this period included the Agricultural Adjustment Act, the Tennessee Valley Authority Act, the Homeowners' Loan Act, the Emergency Farm Mortgage Act, and the Farm Credit Act. The Civilian Conservation Corps was created to create jobs for unemployed people through special federal projects. The Glass-Steagall Banking Act established the Federal Deposit Insurance Corporation, which provided federal insurance for bank deposits. FDR explained the new programs to the American people through radio addresses that became known as "fireside chats."

The hundred days of legislation marked just the beginning of the New Deal. The Securities and Exchange Commission was created in 1934 to regulate the financial industry. The National Industrial Recovery Act established federal codes to strengthen industries, but the Supreme Court ruled it unconstitutional in 1935. The Wagner Labor Relations Act of 1935 provided protection for workers in the private sector to join labor unions, strike, and engage in collective bargaining. Perhaps the most significant legislation in this period was the Social Security Act of 1935, which provided income for the elderly as well as welfare for the poor. In foreign affairs, the United States promoted a "good neighbor" policy with Latin America, recognized the Soviet Union, withdrew troops from Haiti, and agreed that the Philippines would become an independent nation in 1946.

The 1936 Presidential Election

The president easily won his party's nomination by acclamation, and Vice President Garner was endorsed for a second term. The Republicans nominated Kansas governor Alfred M. Landon for president and Frank Knox of Illinois for vice president. FDR swept the election, carrying 46 of 48 states in the Electoral College, and nearly 27.5 million popular votes. Landon won only two states, Maine and Vermont, and just over 16.5 million popular votes. A New York periodical, the *Literary Digest,* had predicted the opposite result—that Landon would win overwhelmingly—based on a poll it had conducted. Their mistake? Their sample included people who owned telephones or automobiles, a small and wealthy group of people in 1936 who did vote for Landon, but were by no means representative of the entire voting population.

THE ROOSEVELT ADMINISTRATION (SECOND TERM)

Nearly half of FDR's cabinet continued into his second term, including Secretary of State Hull, Treasury Secretary Morgenthau, Interior Secretary Harold Ickes of Illinois, and Labor Secretary Perkins. War Secretary Woodring served until the summer of 1940, when he was replaced by Henry L. Stimson of New York. Attorney General Cummings served until 1939, when Frank Murphy of Michigan assumed the position; he served for one year and was replaced by Robert H. Jackson of New York.

MAJOR ISSUES (SECOND TERM)

Flush with victory, Roosevelt decided early in his second term to take on the institution that was frustrating his political agenda: the Supreme Court. In his first term, the Court had struck down several of his New Deal programs as unconstitutional exercises of federal power. The president did not have the opportunity to appoint a single justice in his first term, and he was determined to remedy that situation to create a Supreme Court more favorable to his policies. He proposed that the size of the Court be increased from nine (its size since the post–Civil War era) to a maximum of fifteen, with the president permitted to appoint a new justice for every sitting justice over the age of seventy. The plan would allow him to appoint six new justices.

FDR claimed that the plan was necessary to assist the Court with its enormous workload, but his motive was political: to create a Court that would endorse his policies. The "court-packing" plan, as it became known, sparked a backlash of criticism of the president for seeking to encroach upon judicial power. Congress and the public strongly opposed the plan, and it went nowhere. FDR had suffered the first real political defeat of his presidential career. Although the court-packing plan was a colossal political mistake, FDR still achieved his goal. One justice who previously had voted against New Deal legislation suddenly began to approve it, and this became known as "the switch in time that saved nine." In the course of his presidency,

FDR also made eight Supreme Court appointments, including two people who had served him as attorney general, Murphy and Jackson, as well as one chief justice appointment.

As his political opponents realized that FDR was not immune to defeat, they became more critical of his policies. Conservative Democrats in particular began to vote together against New Deal legislation. FDR vowed that these Democrats would lose their seats in the 1938 congressional midterm elections, but he failed in his effort to "purge" them from the party. Republicans gained seats in Congress for the first time in a decade, presenting another obstacle to his program.

Despite these setbacks, Roosevelt remained a strong president, especially as foreign affairs began to crowd out domestic matters. The growing conflict between Germany and other nations in the 1930s sparked concern that the United States would become enmeshed in another European war. Congress tried to prevent that possibility by passing neutrality legislation in 1935, 1936, 1937, and 1939. Still, when World War II began in 1939, FDR was determined to provide aid to U.S. allies. Despite the opposition of isolationists in Congress, FDR negotiated the Destroyers for Bases agreement in 1940. The United States would give Great Britain naval destroyers in exchange for leases on military bases in the Caribbean and Newfoundland. American loyalty in the worldwide conflict was evident.

THE 1940 PRESIDENTIAL ELECTION

With war raging in Europe and Asia, FDR made the unprecedented decision in 1940 to seek a third presidential term. Despite U.S. support for the Allied powers, FDR pledged that the United States would not become involved in the war. The Democratic Party nominated him for a third term on its first convention ballot and selected Henry A. Wallace of Iowa as his running mate. The Republican Party nominated New York entrepreneur Wendell L. Willkie, a former Democrat who had not previously run for public office, and Charles L. McNary of Oregon as his running mate. FDR was victorious in the election, winning 27 million popular votes to Willkie's 22 million, and 449 Electoral College votes to Willkie's 82. Still, the president's margin of victory was narrower than it had been in his previous two races, suggesting that some people had concerns about his decision to breach the traditional two-term limit.

THE ROOSEVELT ADMINISTRATION (THIRD TERM)

More than half of FDR's second-term cabinet members continued through his third term, including Treasury Secretary Morgenthau, Secretary of War Stimson, Interior Secretary Ickes,

Labor Secretary Perkins, Commerce Secretary Jesse H. Jones of Texas, and Agriculture Secretary Claude R. Wickard of Indiana. Secretary of State Hull served until late 1944, when he was replaced by Edward R. Stettinius of Virginia. Francis Biddle of Pennsylvania became attorney general in 1941 and served for the rest of FDR's presidency.

Major Issues (Third Term)

Despite FDR's campaign promise that the United States would not fight in World War II, the country was slowly inching closer to war. In December 1940 the president gave a fireside chat in which he declared that the United States must become the "great arsenal of democracy," providing ships, planes, and other military resources for its allies. Less than a week later, he said that the United States was dedicated to protecting four universal freedoms: freedom of speech, freedom of religion, freedom from want, and freedom from fear. In March 1941 Congress passed the Lend-Lease Act, which authorized aid to Great Britain and later to the Soviet Union. In calling for this legislation, FDR had compared the assistance to lending a water hose to a neighbor whose house was on fire. After taking care of the emergency, the neighbor would return the hose. Yet despite these measures, the country still resisted war; in September 1941 the U.S. House of Representatives approved legislation to extend the military draft by just one vote.

On December 7, 1941, Japan attacked U.S. naval forces in Pearl Harbor, Hawaii, killing more than 2,500 people. The next day, FDR requested a declaration of war on Japan from Congress, which passed unanimously in the Senate and with only one dissenting vote in the House. (The sole opponent was Rep. Jeanette Rankin of Montana.) In response to declarations of war on the United States by Germany and Italy, Congress authorized war against those countries a few days later.

The United States fought the war on multiple fronts. U.S. forces prevailed in the Battle of Midway in the Pacific in 1942, but they suffered severe losses in the Battle of the Philippines that year. (The United States regained control of the Philippines in 1944–1945.) In late 1942 Gen. Dwight D. Eisenhower led military forces in a successful invasion of North Africa, and FDR decided to make Eisenhower supreme allied commander in Europe. On June 6, 1944, Eisenhower led Allied troops in the historic D-Day landings in Normandy, France, which paved the way for freeing Western Europe from German control.

At the same time he was waging war, FDR was planning for the postwar world. In late 1943 he met with British prime minister Winston Churchill and Soviet leader Joseph Stalin to discuss continued cooperation after the war ended. The United States convened a multilateral conference in Bretton Woods, New Hampshire, in July 1944 to establish institutions for international economic assistance. The conference resulted in the creation of the International Monetary Fund and the World Bank. Later that year delegations from around the world met at Dumbarton Oaks in Washington, D.C., to establish the foundations of a new international organization that would work to prevent future world wars, the United Nations.

The 1944 Presidential Election

With the nation at war, FDR decided to run for a fourth presidential term. He argued that he was no longer "Dr. New Deal," but "Dr. Win the War," and that the United States needed consistent leadership in wartime. The Democrats nominated him and chose Sen. Harry S. Truman of Missouri as his running mate. The Republicans nominated Thomas E. Dewey of New York, with John W. Bricker of Ohio as his running mate. FDR was victorious again, albeit by the smallest margin in his four presidential races: He won just over 25 million popular votes to 22 million for Dewey, and he prevailed in the Electoral College with 432 votes in 36 states to Dewey's 99 votes in 12 states.

A Brief Fourth Term

FDR's final term in office lasted less than three months. In February 1945 he met Churchill and Stalin at Yalta to negotiate the postwar international system. He won Stalin's agreement to have the Soviet Union fight against Japan after Germany's defeat, but he also agreed that Eastern Europe would fall under Soviet control, a decision that sparked much subsequent criticism.

Upon returning from the grueling conference in the Crimea, the president traveled to Warm Springs, Georgia, to regain his strength. He was preparing for another major international meeting, the conference to create the United Nations, which would begin soon in San Francisco. But FDR did not make this trip. On April 12 he suffered a cerebral hemorrhage and died the same day. The nation and the world mourned FDR, who was buried at his home in Hyde Park, New York. He had brought the nation out of the Great Depression and into World War II; he had reinvigorated the American spirit and set the foundation for a postwar order in which the United States would play a central role. Now it was up to his successor, Harry Truman, to put those plans into practice.

"Roosevelt Puts Economic Recovery First in His Acceptance Speech at Convention; Garner for Vice President by Acclamation," July 3, 1932

In 1932 Franklin D. Roosevelt established a new tradition for presidential candidates by traveling to the Democratic National Convention in Chicago to accept his party's nomination in person. In his acceptance speech, he famously promised a "new deal for the American people," a phrase that would come to define his domestic agenda as president.

JULY 3, 1932
ROOSEVELT PUTS ECONOMIC RECOVERY FIRST IN HIS ACCEPTANCE SPEECH AT CONVENTION; GARNER FOR VICE PRESIDENT BY ACCLAMATION

FAMILY FLIES TO CHICAGO

Thundering Cheers Greet the Governor at Airport and in Stadium.

'100%' FOR THE PLATFORM

"Eighteenth Amendment Is Doomed From This Day," He Declares in Speech.

PLEDGES SELF TO 'NEW DEAL'

He Calls for Enlightened International Outlook and Shorter Work Day and Week.

By ARTHUR KROCK.

Special to The New York Times

CHICAGO, July 2.—Before it adjourned tonight, after unanimously nominating Speaker John N. Garner of Texas for Vice President, the Democratic National Convention saw and heard its Presidential choice of yesterday, Governor Franklin D. Roosevelt of New York.

Mr. Roosevelt confessed that in coming here he was breaking a tradition.

"Let it be from now on," he said, "the task of our party to break foolish traditions. We will break foolish traditions and leave it to the Republican leadership … to break promises."

Pledges Aid to "Forgotten Man."

His speech was aggressive. He pledged his aid, "not only to the forgotten man, but to the forgotten woman, to help them realize their hope for a return to the old standards of living and thought in the United States." He would, he said, "Restore America to its own people."

Mr. Roosevelt began with a tribute to Woodrow Wilson. He then described the economic situation from his own viewpoint, saying that swollen surpluses went into the building of "unnecessary plants and Wall Street call money." The government should be "made solvent" again, said Mr. Roosevelt.

The galleries warmed to him when he firmly endorsed the platform plank advocating repeal of the Eighteenth Amendment and modification of the Volstead act, and the Southern delegations noted his pledge to protect the dry States in their wish to keep out intoxicating liquors and to prevent the return of the saloon.

Work and Security the Need.

He suggested as one means of decreasing unemployment, putting men at work on reforesting waste areas. As to agriculture, he would aid that by production planning, by the adoption of a tariff equalizing world prices and by lowering interest rates of farm loans. He expressed it as his firm conviction that the popular welfare depends on the granting of what the great mass of the people want and need.

Their demand is for work and reasonable security, he declared, and he pledged his efforts to effect them.

In concluding, he told his hearers that he intended to make a number of short visits during the campaign to various parts of the country.

Jefferson, the father of the Democratic party, rode to his inaugural on horseback, but the nominee of 1932 flew to the scene of his triumph by airplane from Albany and covered the ninefold greater distance in less time. The convention rose enthusiastically to the voyager of the skies, and accepted his method of travel and the fact that he endured its rigors so well as a proof of his venturesome spirit and fine physical equipment for the office of President of the United States.

• •

"SWEEP IS NATIONAL," NOVEMBER 9, 1932

The results of the 1932 presidential election starkly illustrated the American public's earnest desire for a change in political leadership to combat the Great Depression. FDR won forty-two of the forty-eight states in the Electoral College as well as 7 million more popular votes than incumbent president Herbert Hoover. This election marked a significant political realignment in which several groups of voters coalesced to form what would become an enduring allegiance to the Democratic Party, including urban areas, labor unions, religious supporters (especially Catholic and Jewish voters), and more.

NOVEMBER 9, 1932
SWEEP IS NATIONAL
Democrats Carry 40 States, Electoral Votes 448.

SIX STATES FOR HOOVER

He Loses New York, New Jersey, Bay State, Indiana and Ohio.

DEMOCRATS WIN SENATE

Necessary Majority for Repeal of the Volstead Act in Prospect.

RECORD NATIONAL VOTE

Hoover Felicitates Rival and Promises Every Helpful Effort for Common Purpose.

Roosevelt Statement.

President-elect Roosevelt gave the following statement to *The New York Times* early this morning:

"While I am grateful with all my heart for this expression of the confidence of my fellow-Americans, I realize keenly the responsibility I shall assume and I mean to serve with my utmost capacity the interest of the nation.

"The people could not have arrived at this result if they had not been informed properly of my views by an independent press, and I value particularly the high service of *The New York Times* in its reporting of my speeches and in its enlightened comment."

By ARTHUR KROCK.

A political cataclysm, unprecedented in the nation's history and produced by three years of depression, thrust President Herbert Hoover and the Republican power from control of the government yesterday, elected Governor Franklin Delano Roosevelt President of the United States, provided the Democrats with a large majority in Congress and gave them administration of the affairs of many States of the Union.

Fifteen minutes after midnight, Eastern Standard Time, The Associated Press flashed from Palo Alto this line: "Hoover concedes defeat."

It was then fifteen minutes after nine in California, and the President had been in his residence on the Leland Stanford campus only a few hours, arriving with expressed confidence of victory.

A few minutes after the flash from Palo Alto the text of Mr. Hoover's message of congratulation to his successful opponent was received by *The New York Times,* though it was delayed in direct transmission to the President-elect. After offering his felicitations to Governor Roosevelt on his "opportunity to be of service to the country," and extending wishes for success, the President "dedicated" himself to "every possible helpful effort . . . in the common purpose of us all."

This language strengthened the belief of those who expect that the relations between the victor and the vanquished, in view of the exigent condition of the country, will be more than perfunctory, and that they may soon confer in an effort to arrive at a mutual program of stabilization during the period between now and March 4, when Mr. Roosevelt will take office.

The President-elect left his headquarters shortly before 2 A.M. without having received Mr. Hoover's message.

As returns from the Mountain States and the Pacific Coast supplemented the early reports from the Middle West and the eastern seaboard, the President was shown to have surely carried only five States with a total of 51 elec-

toral votes. It is probable that Mr. Roosevelt has captured forty-two States and 472 electoral votes. With two States in doubt he has taken forty States and 448 votes. Only 266 are required for the election of a President. It also appeared certain that the Congress elected by the people yesterday will be wet enough not only to modify the Volstead act, as pledged in the Democratic platform, but to submit flat repeal of national prohibition.

· ·

"Roosevelt Address Stirs Great Crowd," March 5, 1933

FDR's first inaugural address was a call to action for the government to alleviate the immense suffering caused by the Great Depression. He inspired Americans with his strong and confident rhetoric and spurred Congress to pass legislation that would become the foundation of the New Deal.

MARCH 5, 1933
ROOSEVELT ADDRESS STIRS GREAT CROWD

Declarations for 'Direct Action,' War Powers and Bank Supervision Cheered.

EARNEST AND UNSMILING

With Unemployed Primary Problem, He Looks to 'Recruiting'

for Government Work.

SOME SEE INFLATION HINT

Criticism of Lending as Depression Remedy Is Held to Forecast Check on R.F.C.

By JAMES A. HAGERTY.

Special to The New York Times

WASHINGTON, March 4.—Immediate action through a special session of Congress to remedy the paralysis of the nation's banking system was pledged today by President Roosevelt in his inaugural address.

In the event that the remedies provided by Congress should prove insufficient or should the national emergency continue critical, the new President declared that he would ask Congress for broad executive power to wage a war against the emergency, as great a power, he added, as would be given to him if the United States were invaded by a foreign foe.

This was construed by some Congress leaders as implying that Mr. Roosevelt, should the situation not show speedy improvement, would seek to create in this emergency what would amount to a dictatorship, and there seemed to be a general opinion that Congress would grant him this power if it should become necessary.

The immediate reaction to the address among leaders in Congress, even among the Republicans, was gen-

erally favorable. This was particularly true of the views on the President's declaration for the need of immediate action and his assertion that he would call Congress to meet in special session to act on a definite program for relief.

Declaring that the only thing the American people had to fear was fear itself, "nameless, unreasoning, unjustified terror," the new President asserted that there must be a strict supervision of all banking credits and investments, and an end to speculation with other people's money and provision for "an adequate but sound currency."

Declarations Cheered.

Applause and cheers greeted his declaration for an adequate but sound currency, which was interpreted in some Congressional circles as indicating that he would favor a certain measure of inflation to meet the present situation, provided this inflation were kept under control. The new President also was applauded by the crowd of more than a hundred thousand for the expression of his willingness to assume broader powers than ever before were exercised by an American President in peace time.

With direct reference to the banking situation, Mr. Roosevelt charged the financial leaders of the nation with stubbornness and incompetence.

"Practices of the unscrupulous money changers stand indicted in the court of public opinion, rejected by the hearts and minds of men," he said.

He brought applause when he said a moment later:

"The money changers have fled from their high seats in the temple of our civilization. We may now restore that temple to the ancient truths."

Both President Roosevelt and the members of the huge throng that gathered on the Capitol grounds to hear his address sensed the seriousness of the occasion. Faced with a situation more critical on the day of his inauguration than any other President since Lincoln, Mr. Roosevelt delivered his speech with earnestness and directness and with no attempt at oratorical embellishments.

"Spirit of Congress Grim in Bank Task," March 10, 1933, and "Banking Normal Again," March 14, 1933

Encouraged by the president, Congress passed his proposed banking reform legislation within hours, before many members even knew the details. The momentum for action was clear, and one representative echoed the faith many placed in the new president: "We rely on leadership whose face is lifted to the skies." *The New York Times* praised FDR's innovation of "fireside chats" to explain the new policies to Americans. As the paper wrote in an editorial, the radio address was "a fresh demonstration of the wonderful power of appeal to the people which science has placed in his hands." FDR used the fireside chats sparingly—only two and a half dozen over the course of his presidency—but they were a significant component of his leadership.

MARCH 10, 1933
SPIRIT OF CONGRESS GRIM IN BANK TASK

Prayerfully Takes Up Bill of Which It Knew but Little, Relying on President.
GALLERIES ARE SERIOUS
Large, Intent Crowds Fill the Capital—Mrs. Roosevelt Knits in House Gallery.
Special to The New York Times

WASHINGTON, March 9.—It was a grim Congress which met today, the most momentous gathering of the country's legislators since war was declared in 1917.

It is trite to say that they declared war, but it is nevertheless true that they hurled against the enemy of depression and despondency a weapon which they hoped would penetrate the subtle armor of an allegorical or Bunyan-like antagonist.

Congress hardly knew what was in the bill it passed today. In the House there were no copies of the measure, and it was read and explained on the floor by Representative Steagall. There was no time to study the implications and ramifications.

In the Senate copies had been printed by the time consideration began, and members followed the clerk's reading with an attention seldom devoted to a measure offered for their action.

In both chambers, with slight differences, the members gave the impression of men, who, like poker players, throw in some of their last chips in the belief that they will win.

They were glad to place the responsibility for action in the hands of one man, happy that a man had offered to assume that burden, and showed in their demeanor their hope that the revolutionary means they were adopting would bring to the country some surcease from growing economic casualties.

Representative Steagall voiced this feeling when, with arms widespread and voice ringing through the large chamber of the House, he said:

President Franklin D. Roosevelt delivers a "fireside chat" from the White House in 1938.

Source: Franklin D. Roosevelt Presidential Library and Museum

"We rely on leadership whose face is lifted to the skies."

It was a declaration of faith, almost a prayer, and in it there was an unmistakable note of optimism. Whatever the outcome of today's action may be, it was taken with the belief that by that way, and no other, could confidence and economic peace return, even though slowly, to the people of the United States.

This deeply emotional feeling permeated the entire day's proceedings. When the two branches met at noon their members, both new and old, took their seats with a seriousness which is seldom seen, particularly in the volatile lower house.

The galleries were filled, and in the corridors outside long lines of people waited in the vain hope that they might some time enter.

In the House gallery Mrs. Roosevelt sat in a front row, dressed in white. The informality of the new occupants of the White House was never more forcefully evident. Not only did she wear no hat, but she knitted almost constantly, occasionally looking up at the proceedings, sometimes acknowledging with a smile the bow of a member below her. With her were her son, James; Miss Helvina Thompson, her secretary; Mrs. Henry Morgenthau Jr. and Mrs. Nancy Cook.

MARCH 14, 1933
EDITORIAL
BANKING NORMAL AGAIN.

Banks opened quietly in New York yesterday, and in the other Federal Reserve cities. Certain restrictions are still in force, but there is every evidence of restored confidence. It is the old story over again—when people know that they can draw money from their bank, they don't want it. The fear and panic which led to the banking moratorium appear to have almost entirely passed. This happy result must be due in part to the calm and reassuring radio address which President Roosevelt made on Sunday evening. His simple and lucid explanation of the true function of a commercial bank; his account of what had happened, why it had happened, and the steps taken to correct the mischief were admirably fitted to cause the hysteria which had raged for several weeks before the banks were closed to abate if not entirely to subside.

Incidentally, the President's use of the radio for this purpose is a fresh demonstration of the wonderful power of appeal to the people which science has placed in his hands. When millions of listeners can hear the President speak to them, as it were, directly in their own homes, we get a new meaning for the old phrase about a public man "going to the country." When President Wilson undertook to do it in 1919, it meant wearisome travel and many speeches to different audiences. Now President Roosevelt can sit at ease in his own study and be sure of a multitude of hearers beyond the dreams of the old-style campaigner. His use of this new instrument of political discussion is a plain hint to Congress of a recourse which the President may employ if it proves necessary to rally support for legislation which he asks and which the lawmakers might be reluctant to give him.

"Ending Comes Suddenly," June 16, 1933

Banking reform marked the start of the famous "Hundred Days" of legislation in 1933. Upon taking office, FDR called Congress into special session, and with the enthusiastic response to his banking proposals, he seized the opportunity to initiate a series of federal programs to energize the economy. When the special session ended in June, a new era for the federal government in policy making had begun.

JUNE 16, 1933
ENDING COMES SUDDENLY

Senate Yielding Paves Way for Final Action at 1:20 A.M.

GREAT RECORD LEFT BEHIND

Amount and Importance of Legislation Unsurpassed for Peace-Time Session

FINAL ROOSEVELT TRIUMPH

Senate Yields on Veterans Compromise after Debating Until After Midnight

Special to The New York Times

WASHINGTON, Friday, June 16.—The first session of the Seventy-third Congress adjourned sine die at 1:20 o'clock this morning.

The end of the session came suddenly after the Senate, following long hours of oratory, had yielded on the long-contested veteran's compromise in the Independent Offices Appropriation Bill.

The Senate passed the adjournment resolution at 1:15 A.M. and the house acted five minutes later.

The Congress went out from the Capitol leaving a record for peacetime legislation. Called first to deal with a pressing emergency, it broadened its scope under the leadership of the president and gave legislative form to a program planned to restore prosperity to the country.

Just before the adjournment the Senate heard read from the desk a note from President Roosevelt giving thanks for its cooperation during the strenuous session. The note was sent to Vice President Garner on Saturday.

In the final day complete victories for the President were won in both houses on the troublesome veterans' issue. His control was only one whit less absolute at the end than when he called the special session here March 9 to deal with the banking crisis.

This slight diminution in his mastery of Congress resulted from the contest over the veteran's compensation to the end that he finally had to yield about $100,000,000 in his completed economy program.

"Lame Duck Sessions Officially Abolished," October 15, 1933

The Twentieth Amendment to the Constitution recognized the expanding role of the federal government and the need for more time to meet its increasing responsibilities. The amendment changed the presidential inauguration day from March 4 to January 20, shortening the transition period between administrations. It also moved the starting date for each session of Congress to January 3, thereby ensuring that the two branches of government would function with virtually the same calendar. The Twentieth Amendment was ratified in 1933 and implemented for the first time in 1937 with FDR's second term. The Twenty-first Amendment repealing Prohibition also was ratified in 1933.

OCTOBER 15, 1933
LAME DUCK SESSIONS OFFICIALLY ABOLISHED
Twentieth Amendment, Becoming Effective Today, Set Two New Records.

WASHINGTON, Oct. 14 (AP).—The Twentieth Amendment to the Constitution, abolishing the so-called lame-duck session of Congress, becomes effective tomorrow with two unique records in American history.

Besides changing the dates for the inauguration of the President and the beginning of Congressional sessions, the amendment established a record for being the only change in the Constitution which had the unanimous approval of the forty-eight States. The speed of the ratification set another mark.

- -

"Roosevelt Signs Exchange Curb Bill," June 7, 1934

The Securities and Exchange Act of 1934 created the Securities Exchange Commission, which would be responsible for regulating the stock market. The legislation was drafted with the goal of preventing a recurrence of the freewheeling financial practices of the 1920s.

JUNE 7, 1934
ROOSEVELT SIGNS EXCHANGE CURB BILL
President Will Name Control Commission by July 1, When Law Is Effective.
SEVEN SPONSORS GET PENS
Pecora Predicts Act Will Improve Business, Both 'Ethically and Otherwise.'
Special to The New York Times

WASHINGTON, June 6.—The Securities and Exchange Act of 1934 was signed by President Roosevelt at noon today while many of those instrumental in putting through this legislation stood near his desk.

The act provides for a control commission, to become operative on July 1, the effective date of the bill.

This commission will regulate Stock Exchange operations and in addition will take over from the Federal Trade Commission sixty days from today the administration of the Federal Securities Act, supervising the issuance of new securities.

Those present at the signing, each of whom received as a souvenir one of the pens used by President Roosevelt, were Senator Fletcher and Representative Rayburn, chairmen of the Senate Banking and Currency and the House Interstate and Foreign Commerce Committees; Ferdinand Pecora, Senate counsel in the stock market investigation; Representatives Lea of California and Mapes of Michigan;

Benjamin V. Cohen, assistant counsel of the Public Works Administration, and Thomas V. Corcoran, assistant counsel of the Reconstruction Finance Corporation. Messrs. Cohen and Corcoran helped draft the bill.

To Delay Appointments.

President Roosevelt said at a press conference prior to signing the measure that he had not given any consideration to appointees to the commission. He has received fifty to 100 names, he said, all of which had been filed for consideration.

He said he did not expect to take up this task until after Congress's adjournment.

Mr. Pecora was particularly happy over the signing of the bill, which to a large extent grew out of disclosures developed under his direction at hearings before the Banking and Currency Committee.

Holding up his souvenir pen as he left the President's office, Mr. Pecora said:

"I shall treasure this pen as the pen that made effective one of the most constructive pieces of legislation ever enacted. And I really mean that."

"Will it affect the business of the Stock Exchange?" Mr. Pecora was asked.

"I think it will improve business there both ethically and otherwise," he replied.

"How about volume of trading?"

"Well, in so far as pool operations are concerned, these will disappear," Mr. Pecora said.

When Mr. Pecora was asked if he would become a member of the Control Commission, he replied that he could not discuss a position that had not been offered to him.

"Democrats Gain 10 Senate Seats," November 7, 1934

FDR's New Deal programs received an overwhelming endorsement in the midterm elections of 1934. For the first time in decades, the president's political party gained seats in both chambers of Congress, marking a clear victory for the Democratic Party's political agenda.

NOVEMBER 7, 1934
DEMOCRATS GAIN 10 SENATE SEATS
They Defeat the Republicans in Twenty-six of the Thirty-five Contests.
238 SURE IN THE HOUSE
Midnight Returns Show Majority Party Has Five More Members There.

A certain gain by the Democrats of ten seats in the Senate and possible increase in their already overwhelming majority in the House were among the results shown by election returns from all sections of the country last night.

Of the thirty-five Senate seats involved in yesterday's contests, twenty-six were captured by Democrats, according to returns available at 3 A.M. today. Three were won by New Deal Republicans, only two by old line Republicans and one by the incumbent Farmer-Laborite, Shipstead of Minnesota.

Three seats still remained in doubt, those held by Senators Vandenberg of Michigan and Townsend of Delaware, Republicans, and O'Mahoney of Wyoming, a Democrat. The

O'Mahoney seat was the only one which the Republicans stood to win from a Democrat.

The returns thus had given the Democrats an outright Senate majority of forty-two, even should they lose the three doubtful seats.

Instead of the loss of twenty to forty seats, as expected by the Democratic leaders, the New Deal forces had registered a net gain of five in the early morning hours. Former Republican strongholds yet to be heard from indicated possible further Democratic gains in this second of the Roosevelt landslides.

Of the 435 House seats to be voted upon, returns indicated that the Democrats had won 238, the Republicans 95, the Farmer-Laborites 3 and the Progressives 3, with 96 left in doubt.

"Social Security Bill Is Signed; Gives Pensions to Aged, Jobless," August 15, 1935

One of FDR's greatest political legacies is Social Security. In August 1935, just eight months after legislation was introduced in Congress, FDR signed into law the program of economic assistance for the elderly. The program was designed to benefit all Americans, who contribute to it through payroll taxes in their working years and then receive a monthly pension upon retirement. The law also created unemployment insurance, survivors' benefits, and welfare assistance for the poor.

AUGUST 15, 1935
SOCIAL SECURITY BILL IS SIGNED; GIVES PENSIONS TO AGED, JOBLESS

Roosevelt Approves Measure Intended to Benefit 30,000,000 Persons When States Adopt Cooperating Laws—He Calls the Measure 'Cornerstone' of His Economic Program.
Special to The New York Times

WASHINGTON, Aug. 14.—The Social Security Bill, providing a broad program of unemployment insurance and old-age pensions, and counted upon to benefit some 30,000,000 persons, became law today when it was signed by President Roosevelt in the presence of those chiefly responsible for putting it through Congress.

Mr. Roosevelt called the measure "the cornerstone in a structure which is being built but is by no means complete." He was referring to his program for economic rehabilitation.

He added that the present session of Congress would have become historic had it done nothing beyond completion of this law. The text of the measure as originally introduced was published in *The New York Times* Jan. 18.

The President said he hoped that three members of a board provided by the law to supervise the social projects could be named before the Congress session ended.

He gave no indication of the persons he had in mind for these posts, but it was reported that among possible appointees are Arthur J. Altmyer, Assistant Secretary of Labor, and Murray Latimer, chairman of the Railroad Pensions Board, an organization now in abeyance because the Supreme Court declared unconstitutional the law establishing the board. The third member will be a political appointee.

The signing took place in the Cabinet Room of the White House offices, where motion picture and still photographers had been invited to record the event as a result of the President's desire to obtain the widest possible publicity for the measure, which he said had not received due publicity because of the press of other news.

Among about thirty persons who stood grouped around the President as he read a statement and then signed the act were Secretary Perkins, Senator Wagner, who was one of the first advocates in Congress of legislation of this character; Representative Lewis of Maryland, co-author with Senator Wagner of the bill; members of the Senate Finance Committee, headed by Chairman Harrison, and of the Ways and Means Committee, of which Representative Doughton is chairman.

The scene was recorded in film, both as to sound and action, but no newspaper men were invited to the ceremonies. According to the photographers, the President sat at a desk for about ten minutes while lights were being adjusted and then began reading the statement.

The President's statement, passed among reporters after the ceremonies, read as follows:

"Today a hope of many years' standing is in large part fulfilled. The civilization of the past hundred years, with its startling industrial changes, has tended more and more to make life insecure. Young people have come to wonder what would be their lot when they came to old age. The man with a job has wondered how long the job would last.

"This Social Security measure gives at least some protection to 30,000,000 of our citizens who will reap direct benefits through unemployment compensation, through old-age pensions and through increased services for the protection of children and the prevention of ill health.

"We can never insure 100 per cent of the population against 100 per cent of the hazards and vicissitudes of life, but we have tried to frame a law which will give some measure of protection to the average citizen and to his family against the loss of a job and against poverty-ridden old age.

"This law, too, represents a cornerstone in a structure which is being built but is by no means complete, a structure intended to lessen the force of possible future depressions, to act as a protection to future administrations of the government against the necessity of going deeply into debt to furnish relief to the needy, a law to flatten out the peaks and valleys of deflation and of inflation—in other words, a law that will take care of human needs and at the same time provide for the United States an economic structure of vastly greater soundness.

"I congratulate all of you ladies and gentlemen, all of you in the Congress, in the executive departments and all of you who come from private life, and I thank you for your splendid efforts in behalf of this sound, needed and patriotic legislation.

"If the Senate and the House of Representatives in their long and arduous session had done nothing more than pass this bill, the session would be regarded as historic for all time."

Several Pens Used.

Mr. Roosevelt apparently used more than one pen for the writing of each letter of his name, for Stephen T. Early, assistant secretary to the President, said the President gave a pen used in signing the bill to each of the officials who attended the ceremonies.

The first went to Secretary Perkins, it was learned, and the second to Senator Wagner. Another was given to Senator Guffey for transmittal to Frank E. Hering of South Bend, Ind., secretary of the National Order of Eagles, an organization credited by Senator Guffey with many years of work in behalf of legislation such as that which became law today.

- -

"Roosevelt, Speaking to Victory Procession at Hyde Park, Predicted Record Sweep," November 4, 1936

Popular support for FDR propelled him to success in the 1936 presidential election. He surpassed his 1932 victory of forty-two states, this time carrying all but two states in the Electoral College. Speaking of the victory to supporters in his hometown of Hyde Park, New York, FDR recognized the historic moment, saying, "It looks as though we are going to have one of the largest sweeps ever heard of in the United States."

NOVEMBER 4, 1936
ROOSEVELT, SPEAKING TO VICTORY PROCESSION AT HYDE PARK, PREDICTED RECORD SWEEP
By CHARLES W. HURD
Special to The New York Times

HYDE PARK, Nov. 3.—With wire returns indicating a landslide for President Roosevelt far in excess of the majority necessary to re-elect him, President Roosevelt said tonight that he thought the "sweep" might carry every section of the United States.

Speaking to several hundred loyal followers who staged a victory procession through rain from Hyde Park to Mr. Roosevelt's home, Hyde Park House, at 10:30 P.M., he said:

"The returns are not all in yet, so I can't say anything official or final, but it looks as though we are going to have one of the largest sweeps ever heard of in the United States."

"As a matter of fact, from the returns now, it looks as though this sweep has carried every single section of the country," he exclaimed.

The President, laughing and happy, spoke while standing on the open porch of his house, looking out over a crowd whose faces were illuminated by red-fire torches and the calcium flares used for light for motion pictures.

He waved aside sound microphones, saying: "This is just a home party."

The crowd cheered the President, Mrs. Roosevelt, and his mother, Mrs. Sara Delano Roosevelt.

The assemblage cheered loudly when Mr. Roosevelt said one of his happiest moments came with the word that he had carried the village of Hyde Park, although he lost the township.

The crowd remained for half an hour, with some enthusiastic persons shouting "How about 1940?"

Mr. Roosevelt leaned on the arm of his son, Franklin Jr. Beside him were his wife and mother. Grouped behind him was a small party including his daughter, Mrs. Anna Boettiger, and Mr. Boettiger, Mrs. James Roosevelt, his daughter-in-law, and other relatives.

Others in the party included Secretary and Mrs. Morgenthau, Judge and Mrs. Sam Rosenman, Frederick A. Delano and members of the White House staff and newspaper correspondents.

"Time Is Held Vital," March 10, 1937

Despite his overwhelming reelection in 1936, FDR faced some surprising political defeats in his second term. In 1937 he unsuccessfully proposed that the size of the Supreme Court be increased from nine to fifteen justices. In a fireside chat, the president tried to persuade Americans that this change was necessary to keep the Court from overpowering the other branches of government, but he failed to win popular support for his proposal.

He simply proposed to return the court to its 'rightful and historic place,' and save the Constitution from 'hardening of the judicial arteries.'

MARCH 10, 1937
TIME IS HELD VITAL
He Declares Bench Has Set Itself Up Today as 'Super-Legislature'
CALLS FOR MODERN MINDS
Constitution to Be Saved From Justices, He Says—Will Not Pick 'Spineless Puppets'
SENATE STILL HAS ITS SAY
Real Purpose Is to Stop Usurpation of Power, He Asserts in His 'Fireside Chat'
BY TURNER CATLEDGE
Special to The New York Times

WASHINGTON, March 9.—In a second appeal within six days for popular support for his plan to reorganize the Federal judiciary, President Roosevelt tonight sought to assure millions of Americans gathered around their radios that in this new project he was seeking only to protect them from the usurpations of a Supreme Court which had left its place at the scales of justice to set itself up as a "super-legislature."

Seated in the diplomatic reception room at the White House and speaking into the microphones of the three national broadcasting chains, the President asked most of all that the country trust him to do the right thing by American democracy.

He had no intention, he said, of packing the bench with "spineless puppets." He simply proposed to return the court to its "rightful and historic place," and save the Constitution from "hardening of the judicial arteries."

Again he shoved aside as impractical or too slow proposals for amending the Constitution to bring about the results he desired. He put forward the proposed legislation as the best method, first, because he believed it could be passed at this session of Congress, and second, "because it would provide a reinvigorated, liberal-minded judiciary necessary to furnish quicker and cheaper justice from bottom to top."

SPEAKS ON EVE OF HEARINGS

The President's broadcast came on the eve of public hearings on his Supreme Court enlargement bill, which will open before the Senate Judiciary Committee tomorrow with Attorney General Cummings as the first witness.

Senate opponents of his plan were preparing tonight to put the Attorney General through a cross-examination and one of their number, Senator Wheeler of Montana, was on his way to Chicago to deliver their official answer to the President's Victory Dinner speech last Thursday and tonight's "fireside chat." Senator Wheeler will appear in a joint discussion of the subject with James M. Landis, chairman of the Securities and Exchange Commission, before a congress of Midwest women.

"NEUTRALITY RESOLUTIONS," MARCH 20, 1937

After World War I the United States strongly resisted continued involvement in European affairs. Even as nations moved toward war in the 1930s, the United States passed several neutrality resolutions to remain apart from the conflict. Assistance to allies such as Great Britain would take the form of "cash-and-carry" policies to limit U.S. involvement. In evaluating the neutrality policy, *The Times* editorial prophetically pointed out that "because a large majority of the American people now favors a policy of isolation, it does not follow that this attitude will not change."

MARCH 20, 1937
EDITORIAL
NEUTRALITY RESOLUTIONS

At most points there is little to choose between the two resolutions which the House and the Senate have now adopted as the new basis of American foreign policy. Both resolutions are aimed at achieving a "neutrality" which is more legalistic than real. Both rely on a "cash-and-carry" plan which would fortuitously favor maritime Powers and Powers heavily armed, at the expense of other Powers. Both base their hope of keeping the United States at peace on a policy of extreme isolation in time of war rather than on a policy of concerted action to prevent the outbreak of war itself. Both fail to make any distinction, in the embargoes and restrictions they propose to place upon American commerce, between nations which have deliberately attacked a neighbor and nations which are victims of aggression. If there is any substantial difference between the House and Senate versions of the plan, any point of distinction which is well worth saving when the two measures go to conference, it is that provision in the House resolution which places a two-year limitation on the life of the "cash-and-carry" system.

For the practical effect of this provision, if it is enacted into law, should be to confront Congress two years hence with the necessity of reconsidering the whole question of American foreign policy, and there is a distinct advantage in this course. "Cash-and-carry" is not the last word in American diplomacy, or the final contribution of the Amer-

ican people to the cause of international peace. Rather, it seems probable that the state of mind responsible for the present legislation is no more than an extremist attitude from which a natural reaction may set in.

Various influences, easily identified, have helped over a span of twenty years to shape this attitude, and to persuade the American people to put their present trust in a policy of uncompromising isolation. The existing machinery of international consultation and enforcement has not worked well in practice. Wars have been fought on several continents in the last dozen years. Treaties have been destroyed. Efforts to limit armaments have broken down. War debts have been defaulted. The depression everywhere deepened distrust of "the foreigner," and encouraged nations to raise almost impossible barriers to trade. All this has played increasingly into the hands of a policy of American withdrawal from the world's affairs.

But because a large majority of the American people now favors a policy of isolation, it does not follow that this attitude will not change. We live, after all, in a world which steadily grows smaller as modern means of communication and transportation annihilate both time and distance. We have an inescapable interest in the fortune of other nations. We are certain to be affected by the decisions they may make between democracy and dictatorship, between peace and war. We have a rich stake in their markets, in their science, in their culture. And in the long run it seems probable that we shall recognize the necessary limitations of a policy of isolation and come to accept, however gradually, the share of responsibility which falls naturally to a great world Power.

It is possible, in fact, that historians of the future will find in the "neutrality resolutions" of 1937 the full flow that precedes the turning of the tide. Meantime we shall think more clearly if we regard these resolutions as the accurate reflections of a mood rather than as the settled convictions of a nation.

"ROOSEVELT LIMITS 'PURGE' CAMPAIGNS TO 3 STILL ON LIST," SEPTEMBER 9, 1938

Facing challenges from conservatives within his political party, FDR campaigned to remove these opposition Democrats from office in the 1938 congressional midterm elections. His attempted "purge" of party members was unsuccessful, indicating the voters' concerns about the president's New Deal agenda.

SEPTEMBER 9, 1938
ROOSEVELT LIMITS 'PURGE' CAMPAIGNS TO 3 STILL ON LIST
No Further Step in Primaries Besides Fight on Tydings, George and O'Connor
CUMMINGS AT HYDE PARK
Lonergan Will Not Be Opposed by New Deal at Connecticut Convention Next Week
BY FELIX BELAIR Jr.
Special to The New York Times

HYDE PARK, N.Y., Sept. 8.—President Roosevelt's "purge" of the party conservative and anti-New Deal Democrats will be limited for the present to the few candidates he has already marked for opposition in the primaries, it was indicated today after a conference between the Chief Executive and Attorney General Cummings.

Mr. Cummings stopped at Hyde Park House on his way to Connecticut where, next week, he will be a delegate to the State convention. It was understood after the conference that there would be no attempt by the Roosevelt forces to displace Senator Lonergan at the convention, despite his record of opposition to New Deal measures. It was reported that the President saw eye to eye with the Cabinet member on this issue.

Mr. Cummings was reluctant to discuss details of his talk with the President, but volunteered the information that he had reported on the general political situation throughout the country and had described New Deal prospects as "very good indeed."

While no further steps will be taken by the Washington leaders of the party in the Congressional primaries, it seemed apparent that the President has no intention of dropping his drive for election of liberals in November, even if this means open support of Republican candidates in isolated instances.

Although Mr. Roosevelt hinted that he had concrete instances of liberal Republican candidates in mind when he expressed his preference for them as against conservative members of his own party, he has yet to disclose the names of the candidates to whom he indirectly referred.

"REPUBLICANS IN ELECTION HELD ALL CONGRESS SEATS," NOVEMBER 12, 1938

Many historians consider the 1938 congressional midterm elections to mark the end of the New Deal era. Economic recession and rising unemployment prevented Democrats from replicating their historic midterm victories of 1934. Although they maintained control of both chambers of Congress, the Democrats lost a significant number of seats in each. As the president's agenda in domestic policy became more constrained and war in Europe loomed, he turned his attention to foreign affairs.

NOVEMBER 12, 1938
REPUBLICANS IN ELECTION HELD ALL CONGRESS SEATS
By The Associated Press.

WASHINGTON, Nov. 11.—Republican forces in Congress came through Tuesday's election without the loss of a seat. Veteran officials here said today, that as far as they were able to determine, the record was unique for a major party.

Republicans took eight seats from Democrats in the Senate. In the House they won seventy-two from Democrats, five from Progressives, and four from Farmer-Laborites.

Of twenty-five former Representatives and Senators who tried comebacks, fourteen succeeded. Former Senator W. Warren Barbour, Republican of New Jersey, was the only one returned to the Upper House.

• •

"BRITAIN AND FRANCE IN WAR AT 6 A.M.; HITLER WON'T HALT ATTACK ON POLES; CHAMBERLAIN CALLS EMPIRE TO FIGHT," SEPTEMBER 3, 1939

Germany invaded Poland on September 1, 1939, and two days later, Great Britain and France declared war on Germany. The United States did not enter the war for another two years, but FDR found ways to provide assistance to America's allies in the global battle.

SEPTEMBER 3, 1939
BRITAIN AND FRANCE IN WAR AT 6 A.M.; HITLER WON'T HALT ATTACK ON POLES; CHAMBERLAIN CALLS EMPIRE TO FIGHT
TO END OPPRESSION
Premier Calls It 'Bitter Blow' That Efforts for Peace Have Failed
WARNING UNHEEDED
Demand on Reich to Withdraw Army From Poland Ignored

Prime Minister Neville Chamberlain announced to the world at 6:10 o'clock this morning that Great Britain and France were at war with Germany. He made the announcement over the radio, with short waves carrying the measured tones of his voice throughout all continents, from 10 Downing Street in London.

Mr. Chamberlain disclosed that Great Britain and France had taken concurrent action, announcing that "we and France are, today, in fulfillment of our obligations, going to the aid of Poland."

France, however, had not made any announcement beyond stating that the French Ambassador to Berlin would make a final call upon Foreign Minister Joachim von Ribbentrop at 6 o'clock this morning, and it was assumed the French had proclaimed the existence of the state of war.

Speaks With Solemnity

With the greatest solemnity Mr. Chamberlain began his declaration by reporting that the British Ambassador to Berlin had handed in Great Britain's final ultimatum and that it had not been accepted. Without hesitation he announced Britain's decision and, after touching briefly on the background of the crisis, he expressed the highest confidence that "injustice, oppression and persecution" would be vanquished and that his cause would triumph.

Mr. Chamberlain appealed to his people, schooled during the last year as the crisis deepened in measures of defense and offense, to carry on with their jobs and begged a blessing upon them, warning that "we shall be fighting against brute force."

The declaration came after Great Britain had given Chancellor Adolf Hitler of Germany extended time in which to answer the British Government's final ultimatum of Friday. In the final ultimatum Herr Hitler had been told that unless German aggression in Poland ceased, Britain was prepared to fulfill her obligations to Poland.

Warning Was Sharp

Britain's last warning at 4 o'clock this morning, New York time, left no doubt of her stand, for the phrase, "fulfillment of Britain's obligations to Poland," was replaced by a flat statement that a state of war would exist between the two countries as of the hour of the deadline.

After Mr. Chamberlain had finished his statement, which had been introduced as "an announcement of national importance," the announcer warned the British people not to gather together, broadcast an order that all meeting places for entertainment be closed, and gave precautions to prepare the people against air bombings and poison gas attacks.

· ·

"The Choice of a Candidate," September 19, 1940, and "Big Electoral Vote," November 6, 1940

With World War II under way, in 1940 FDR believed the United States should not have a change in leadership in a time of international conflict. Breaking with the tradition established by George Washington, Roosevelt ran for a third term and won a clear victory, though by a narrower margin than in his previous two elections. For the first (and only) time, *The Times* endorsed FDR's opponent, deciding that Wendell Willkie was "better equipped" to address national needs and seeking to preserve the unofficial two-term limit on the presidency. FDR campaigned on a platform of keeping the United States out of war, but events nullified this pledge the following year.

SEPTEMBER 19, 1940
EDITORIAL
"THE CHOICE OF A CANDIDATE"

The New York Times supported Franklin D. Roosevelt for the Presidency in 1932 and again in 1936. In 1940 it will support Wendell Willkie.

It has made its choice, as all Americans must make their choice, in one of the great crises of this nation's history. The liberties of the American people are in danger. A hostile Power, openly proclaiming its hatred of the democratic way of life, has swept across Europe and is now

battering at the gates of England, seeking to grasp the eastern approaches to that Atlantic world in which our own democracy has lived and prospered.

Both Mr. Roosevelt and Mr. Willkie understand the critical nature of this threat to the United States. Both are citizens of the world. Both know that it is impossible to isolate ourselves from the consequences of a world revolution. Both know that we must take sides morally or count for nothing. Both are opposed to actual intervention in the war, but short of war both favor every possible aid that can be given to the one democracy in Europe that still stands in Hitler's path.

This agreement between the two Presidential candidates on the fundamentals of a foreign policy is a deeply fortunate fact for the American people. Without it we might now be involved in a bitter controversy which would wreck our unity. As matters stand, the choice before us has been narrowed to this question: In whose hands, Mr. Roosevelt's or Mr. Willkie's, is the safety of the American people likely to be more secure during the critical test that lies ahead?

We give our own support to Mr. Willkie primarily for these reasons: Because we believe that he is better equipped than Mr. Roosevelt to provide this country with an adequate national defense; because we believe he is a practical liberal who understands the need of increased production; because we believe that the fiscal policies of Mr. Roosevelt have failed disastrously; because we believe that at a time when the traditional safeguards of democracy are falling everywhere it is particularly important to honor and preserve the American tradition against vesting the enormous powers of the Presidency in the hands of any man for three consecutive terms of office.

NOVEMBER 6, 1940
BIG ELECTORAL VOTE

Large Pivotal States Swing to Democrats in East and West
POPULAR VOTE CUT
First Time in History That Third Term Is Granted President
By ARTHUR KROCK

Over an apparently huge popular minority, which under the electoral college system was not able to register its proportion of the total vote in terms of electors, President Roosevelt was chosen yesterday for a third term, the first American in history to break the tradition which began with the Republic. He carried to victory with him Henry A. Wallace to be Vice President, and continued control of the House of Representatives by the Democrats was also indicated in the returns.

But in many of the larger States so many precincts were still missing early this morning, and the contest in these States was so close, that Wendell L. Willkie, the Republican opponent, whose name Mr. Roosevelt never mentioned throughout the campaign, refused to concede defeat. He said it was a "horse race," and that the result would not be known until today. He went to bed in that frame of mind.

As the returns mounted there seemed little, however, to sustain Mr. Willkie's hope. New York, Massachusetts, Connecticut, Rhode Island, Pennsylvania, Ohio and Illinois, of the greater States, all appeared to have been carried safely by the President. The Solid South had resisted all appeals to revolt against Mr. Roosevelt's quest for a third

term. The Pacific and Mountain States were following the national trend. . . .

The Electoral Vote

Listing as doubtful nine States, including several like California, Ohio and Indiana, which seem certain to join the Democratic column, there were at 3 A.M. only 51 electoral votes in possible dispute. The President had an apparently certain total of 429, while with more or less security in Mr. Willkie's column were only 51 votes.

No shift or series of shifts could affect the electoral result and the indications were that the President's total would reach. . . . to 470.

Either figure would be much less than the nearly clean sweeps he had in 1932, when he carried forty-two States, and in 1936, when only Maine and Vermont went Republican. And unless the Far West and the Mountain States shall be shown to have given incredible majorities and late returns from the Eastern States pile up the President's votes higher than indications seem to make possible, Mr. Roosevelt's popular majority will be far less than he had against Herbert Hoover and Alf M. Landon.

"ROOSEVELT CALLS FOR GREATER AID TO BRITAIN," DECEMBER 30, 1940, AND "FINAL STEP SWIFT," MARCH 12, 1941

Shortly after winning his third presidential race, FDR gave a fireside chat on American foreign policy. He declared that the United States would become "the great arsenal of democracy," meaning that it would provide military resources to its allies without engaging directly in war itself. Just a few months later, the president approved the Lend-Lease Act to help Great Britain, and later the Soviet Union, to fight the war.

DECEMBER 30, 1940
ROOSEVELT CALLS FOR GREATER AID TO BRITAIN AS BEST WAY TO HALT DICTATORS AND AVERT WAR; NAZIS SET BIG LONDON FIRES; SEA RAIDER ROUTED

'AXIS WILL NOT WIN'
President Bars Peace Move While Nazis Seek 'to Conquer World'
'ARSENAL' OUR ROLE
Asking Mighty Effort, He Rules Out Strikes and Lockouts
By TURNER CATLEDGE
Special to The New York Times

WASHINGTON, Dec. 29—In a radio "fireside chat" directed primarily to the American people but broadcast throughout the world, President Roosevelt tonight proclaimed for the United States what might be called a policy of "dynamic non-belligerence" which he said he believed, but frankly could not guarantee, would keep the country out of war.

Expressing a belief, "based on the latest and best information," that the Axis powers "are not going to win this war," the President ruled out all suggestions that this government lend its influences toward negotiating peace, at least until the "unholy alliance" of Germany, Italy and Japan had abandoned its effort to conquer the world.

He declared the United States' determination to send more and more munitions and supplies to the British, the Greeks and others in the front lines of democracy's battle, and said that no dictator or "combination of dictators" would weaken that determination by threats of how they might construe it.

Would Bar Strikes and Lockouts

He summoned the American people for their mightiest effort yet to increase production so this country might live up to the obligation, which he assumed for it tonight, of being the "arsenal of democracy." And to this end he called upon labor and management to reconcile all differences between them without sacrificing any of the gains or dignity of either.

"The nation expects our defense industries to continue operation without interruption by strikes or lockouts," the President declared. "It expects and insists that management and workers will reconcile their differences by voluntary or legal means, to continue to produce the supplies that are so sorely needed."

The President solemnly called the roll of nations that have already fallen because they thought they could live in peace or deal safely with the Nazi hordes, and the United States would not be the only other one in danger if Britain fell, he said. Every South American nation would come immediately under the threat, he asserted, and added:

"Could Ireland hold out? Would Irish freedom be permitted as an amazing, pet exception in an unfree world?"

Activity Expected at Capital

The President's speech was considered in Washington, and apparently by himself, as his most important since the dark days at the beginning of his first administration, when the banking emergency was troubling the people. Delivered in the Diplomatic Reception Room of the White House, where representatives of the warring nations have gathered time and again, the address was regarded as a pattern of action which would set diplomatic circles, Congress and the Administration buzzing, with activity, maybe within a matter of hours.

Specifications of what the United States will do next were lacking in the speech, but these are expected to be filled in either by separate announcements or by the President's annual message to Congress, now slated for Jan. 6.

The capital gathered from one or more of his remarks tonight, however, that the Administration is giving sympathetic consideration to the proposal of commandeering several hundred foreign ships laid up in American harbors as a result of the war, and either turning them over directly or transferring a comparable amount of tonnage to the British to help them meet the strains of submarine and aerial warfare.

MARCH 12, 1941
FINAL STEP SWIFT

White House Is Waiting When the House Votes Bill, 317 to 71

MATERIALS MOVED AT ONCE

Kind of Assistance Sent First Is Not Revealed—Greece Is Sharing and China May

By TURNER CATLEDGE

Special to The New York Times

WASHINGTON, March 11—President Roosevelt signed the history-making lease-lend bill at 3:50 P.M. today immediately after receiving it from the Capitol, where the House completed action by accepting the Senate amendments by a vote of 317 to 71.

Five minutes after the bill was signed the President approved a list of undisclosed quantities of war materials to be transferred at once from the American Army and Navy to the British and the Greeks, to bolster these powers in their life-and-death struggle with the Axis. Most of these first materials, the nature of which the President guarded, will go to Great Britain.

Having thus promptly set the machinery in motion toward making the United States "the arsenal of democracy," Mr. Roosevelt began work on a request to be sent to Congress tomorrow for an immediate appropriation of $7,000,000,000 with which to press the lease-lend effort to the fullest possible extent under the new law. This, he intimated, would be likely to include help to China as well as to Great Britain and Greece, and to all other nations which later may find themselves under threat of the Berlin-Rome-Tokyo alliance.

The President apparently paid no attention to threats of "isolation" Senators to continue their opposition in an appeal to the country. Proposals for a campaign "to keep the United States out of war" were reported to have been discussed at a meeting of opponents of the lease-lend bill at the Capitol today.

* *

"MEN UNDER ARMS," AUGUST 13, 1941, AND "ROOSEVELT SIGNS DRAFT EXTENSION," AUGUST 19, 1941

Although war was raging in Europe, the United States remained largely removed from the conflict in summer 1941. Consequently, legislation to extend the peacetime draft sparked much controversy, and the bill passed by just one vote in the U.S. House of Representatives. In endorsing the legislation, *The Times* wrote in an editorial that Americans needed to "make this sacrifice now to forestall a worse sacrifice later on."

AUGUST 13, 1941
EDITORIAL
MEN UNDER ARMS

When the House of Representatives voted yesterday on the proposal to extend the present period of military training under the Selective Service Act it had before it the advice of the two public officials above all others whose expert opinion on this question was entitled to respect. The Chief of Staff of the Army had warned the House that the result of failure to approve this plan would be "virtual disbandment or immobilization of two-thirds of our trained enlisted strength," and that this in turn "might well involve a national tragedy." The Secretary of State had warned the House that defeat of the proposal would have "an exceedingly bad effect" on this country's position in international affairs. There cannot be the slightest doubt of the accuracy of this diagnosis. Rejection of the plan would have dismayed our friends abroad, in Europe, in Asia and perhaps, above all, in South America, and given our enemies a legitimate chance to rejoice over the apparent half-heartedness of our defense effort.

It is deeply regrettable that a single vote should have determined the margin by which the House chose yesterday to heed the clear warnings sounded by General Marshall and Secretary Hull. But at least it is now certain that the new American Army will be kept intact. And before our enemies abroad attempt to draw large conclusions from the strength of the opposition in the House they will do well to note—what any American could tell them—that considerations of domestic politics had an important part in the result. Unfortunately, Republicans in Congress are still playing the old-fashioned American game of politics and still trying to manoeuvre themselves into a position in which they can profit, some day, from a hoped-for popular "reaction" against the President's leadership.

As a consequence of the decision which Congress has now made, a great many young Americans who will soon have contributed a full year of their lives to the service of their country will be called upon to make a further sacrifice. But they make this sacrifice now to forestall a worse sacrifice later on. They give their time in order that an unprepared American Army may not be butchered in a war brought on by its own weakness, or an unprepared country be exposed to the whims of a dictator. The price is high. But in this uncertain world of 1941 it is a good bargain.

AUGUST 19, 1941
ROOSEVELT SIGNS DRAFT EXTENSION

Measure Providing 2½ Years of Service for Selectees Is Legally Approved

DEFERMENT ALSO A LAW

Men of 28 Now Exempted Under Act as Passed—New Air Bases Authorized

Special to The New York Times

WASHINGTON, Aug. 18—President Roosevelt today signed legislation authorizing retention in Federal service for eighteen months beyond their regular terms of service of selectees, National Guardsmen, reservists and enlisted men of the Regular Army.

Coincidently it was revealed that on Saturday the President put his signature upon another bill deferring from compulsory military service all men who were 28 years of age or over on July 1, 1941.

The resolution extending the time of service for members of the Federal military forces—the subject of long controversy in Congress—declared the national interest to be imperiled and for this reason authorized the retention of selectees in service beyond the one-year limit originally set.

The measure authorizes the Army to keep selectees, Guardsmen and Reservists in service for a total of two and a half years and regulars for four and a half years. All will receive a bonus of $10 a month, in addition to their regular salary, after their first year in the Army.

One provision of the measure requires the Army to release selectees and Guardsmen who can prove that their retention in the Army beyond their initial term of service would work "undue hardship" upon their dependents. Such discharges would take place when not in conflict with the national interest.

The service-extension provisions of the law are not mandatory. High ranking Army officers have expressed the opinion that relatively few men will be retained for the full additional eighteen months.

The new law also provides for the Secretary of War to dismiss from service selectees who reached 28 on or before July 1, 1941. The selectees must apply for such discharge and the Secretary is required to dismiss them "as soon as practicable and when not in conflict with the interests of national defense."

President Roosevelt also signed a bill authorizing acquisition of bases for lighter-than-air craft at Norfolk, Va.; Cape Hatteras, N.C., and Boston at a cost of $6,500,000 each and miscellaneous facilities costing a total of $3,000,000.

The measure also transfers jurisdiction of the former air station at Sunnyvale, Calif., from the War to the Navy Department, and its employment for lighter-than-air purposes.

"Japan Wars on U.S. and Britain; Makes Sudden Attack on Hawaii; Heavy Fighting at Sea Reported," December 8, 1941, and "Unity in Congress," December 9, 1941

Japan's surprise attack on Pearl Harbor, Hawaii, and U.S. possessions in the Pacific shocked the world and galvanized the nation to enter World War II. In a speech to Congress the following day, FDR famously declared that December 7, 1941, was "a date which will live in infamy," and he requested a declaration of war. With just one dissenting vote, Congress complied.

DECEMBER 8, 1941
JAPAN WARS ON U.S. AND BRITAIN; MAKES SUDDEN ATTACK ON HAWAII; HEAVY FIGHTING AT SEA REPORTED

GUAM BOMBED; ARMY SHIP IS SUNK

U.S. Fliers Head North From Manila—Battleship *Oklahoma* Set Afire by Torpedo Planes at Honolulu

104 SOLDIERS KILLED AT FIELD IN HAWAII

President Fears 'Very Heavy Losses' on Oahu—Churchill Notifies Japan That a State of War Exists

By FRANK L. KLUCKHOHN

Special to The New York Times

WASHINGTON, Monday, Dec. 8—Sudden and unexpected attacks on Pearl Harbor, Honolulu, and other United States possessions in the Pacific early yesterday by the Japanese air force and navy plunged the United States and Japan into active war.

The initial attack in Hawaii, apparently launched by torpedo-carrying bombers and submarines, caused widespread damage and death. It was quickly followed by others. There were unconfirmed reports that German raiders participated in the attacks.

Guam also was assaulted from the air, as were Davao, on the island of Mindanao, and Camp John Hay, in Northern Luzon, both in the Philippines. Lieut. Gen. Douglas MacArthur, commanding the United States Army of the Far East, reported there was little damage, however.

[Japanese parachute troops had been landed in the Philippines and native Japanese had seized some communities, Royal Arch Gunnison said in a broadcast from Manila today to WOR-Mutual. He reported without detail that "in the naval war the ABCD fleets under American command appeared to be successful" against Japanese invasions.]

Japanese submarines, ranging out over the Pacific, sank an American transport carrying lumber 1,300 miles from San Francisco, and distress signals were heard from a freighter 700 miles from that city.

The War Department reported that 104 soldiers died and 300 were wounded as a result of the attack on Hickam Field, Hawaii. The National Broadcasting Company reported from Honolulu that the battleship *Oklahoma* was afire. [Domai, Japanese news agency, reported the *Oklahoma* sunk.]

Nation Placed on Full War Basis

The news of these surprise attacks fell like a bombshell on Washington. President Roosevelt immediately ordered the country and the Army and Navy onto a full war footing. He arranged at a White House conference last night to address a joint session of Congress at noon today, presumably to ask for declaration of a formal state of war.

This was disclosed after a long special Cabinet meeting, which was joined later by Congressional leaders. These leaders predicted "action" within a day.

After leaving the White House conference Attorney General Francis Biddle said that "a resolution" would be introduced in Congress tomorrow. He would not amplify or affirm that it would be for a declaration of war.

Congress probably will "act" within the day, and he will call the Senate Foreign Relations Committee for this purpose, Chairman Tom Connally announced.

[A United Press dispatch from London this morning said that Prime Minister Churchill had notified Japan that a state of war existed.]

As the reports of heavy fighting flashed into the White House, London reported semi-officially that the British Empire would carry out Prime Minister Winston Churchill's pledge to give the United States full support in case of hostilities with Japan. The President and Mr. Churchill talked by transatlantic telephone.

This was followed by a statement in London from the Netherland Government in Exile that it considered a state of war to exist between the Netherlands and Japan. Canada, Australia and Costa Rica took similar action.

"Americans 'will remember the character of the onslaught against us,' a day, he remarked, which will live in infamy."

DECEMBER 9, 1941
UNITY IN CONGRESS
Only One Negative Vote as President Calls to War and Victory
ROUNDS OF CHEERS
Miss Rankin's Is Sole 'No' as Both Houses Act in Quick Time
By FRANK L. KLUCKHOHN
Special to The New York Times

WASHINGTON, Dec. 8—The United States today formally declared war on Japan. Congress, with only one dissenting vote, approved the resolution in the record time of 33 minutes after President Roosevelt denounced Japanese aggression in ringing tones. He personally delivered his message to a joint session of the Senate and House. At 4:10 P.M. he affixed his signature to the resolution.

There was no debate like that between April 2, 1917, when President Wilson requested war against Germany, and April 6, when a declaration of war was approved by Congress.

President Roosevelt spoke only 6 minutes and 30 seconds today compared with Woodrow Wilson's 29 minutes and 34 seconds.

The vote today against Japan was 82 to 0 in the Senate and 388 to 1 in the House. The lone vote against the resolution in the House was that of Miss Jeanette Rankin, Republican, of Montana. Her "No" was greeted with boos and hisses. In 1917 she voted against the resolution for war against Germany.

The President did not mention either Germany or Italy in his request. Early this evening a statement was issued at the White House, however, accusing Germany of doing everything possible to push Japan into the war. The objective, the official statement proclaimed, was to cut off American lend-lease aid to Germany's European enemies, and a pledge was made that this aid would continue "100 per cent."

A Sudden and Deliberate Attack

President Roosevelt's brief and decisive words were addressed to the assembled representatives of the basic organizations of American democracy—the Senate, the House, the Cabinet and the Supreme Court.

"America was suddenly and deliberately attacked by naval and air forces of the Empire of Japan," he said. "We will gain the inevitable triumph, so help us God."

Thunderous cheers greeted the Chief Executive and Commander in Chief throughout the address. This was particularly pronounced when he declared that Americans "will remember the character of the onslaught against us," a day, he remarked, which will live in infamy.

"This form of treachery shall never endanger us again," he declared amid cheers. "The American people in their righteous might will win through to absolute victory."

Then, to the accompaniment of a great roar of cheering, he asked for war against Japan.

"Roosevelt Thanks Go to Eisenhower," November 15, 1942

Under the leadership of Gen. Dwight D. Eisenhower, the Allies prevailed over German forces in North Africa in late 1942. FDR took note of Eisenhower's decisive leadership and would soon select him to lead the Allied attack in 1944 on German troops in Western Europe.

NOVEMBER 15, 1942
ROOSEVELT THANKS GO TO EISENHOWER

Message of Congratulation on African Coup Stresses Dash and Skill of Operation
NATION HELD REASSURED
President Emphasizes Invasion Reaction Here—Admiral Cunningham Is Praised
Special to The New York Times

WASHINGTON, Nov. 14—Speaking both for himself and on behalf of the entire American nation, President Roosevelt today sent a message of congratulation to Lieut Gen. Dwight D. Eisenhower, Commander in Chief of the expeditionary forces in North Africa, for the "successful accomplishment" of his forces in seizing a large part of North Africa. The congratulations were directed not only to the commander but every member of his command.

The text of the President's message follows:

Eisenhower:

Both personally and on behalf of the American people I send sincere congratulations to you and every member of your command on the highly successful accomplishment of a most difficult task.

Our occupation of North Africa has caused a wave of reassurance throughout the nation not only because of the skill and dash with which the first phase of an extremely difficult operation has been executed, but even more because of the evident perfection of the cooperation between the British and American forces.

Give my personal thanks to Admiral Cunningham [Admiral Sir Andrew Browne Cunningham] and the other British leaders for their vital and skillful assistance without which the operation could not have been undertaken.

FRANKLIN D. ROOSEVELT.

"Washington Hails Unity at Teheran," December 7, 1943

As World War II continued, FDR and the other Allied leaders began to prepare for changes in the international balance of power after the war's end. In late 1943 U.S., British, and Soviet leaders met in Tehran to discuss prospects for the postwar order. Although they did not make definitive plans, the conference achieved "a meeting of minds," as *The Times* put it, for defeating the Axis powers of Germany, Italy, and Japan.

DECEMBER 7, 1943
WASHINGTON HAILS UNITY AT TEHERAN

Hull Stresses 'Concerting' of Plans to Crush Axis Forces—Congress Leaders Pleased

By BERTRAM D. HULEN

Special to The New York Times

WASHINGTON, Dec. 6—Opinion in the executive branch of the Government concerning both the Teheran and the Cairo conferences was set forth by Secretary of State Cordell Hull today in a statement declaring that the concerted plans adopted "will undoubtedly result in making effective to the fullest extent the fighting strength of all of the United Nations."

Opinion in general in the capital was that the communiqué issued on the Teheran conference showed that the three Chiefs of Government, President Roosevelt, Prime Minister Churchill and Premier Stalin, had had a meeting of minds and had reached detailed decisions for destroying the German Army, even though the declaration, perhaps significantly, did not use the phrase "unconditional surrender."

All in all, the announcement gave grounds for encouragement at a time when America is entering the third year of the war.

Way Open for Small Nations

It was of first importance that the three leaders had met, it was felt. And in meeting they had agreed to cooperate in the war and in the peace, and to invite the collaboration of small nations.

There were conjectures as to whether this collaboration might include the German people, if they sought it as a chastened people free of nazism and militarism.

Military details, obviously, could not be revealed, it was realized, but the announcement seemed to point to the opening of a "second front" and even a "third front" in western Europe and possibly in the Balkans.

In his statement Secretary Hull said:

"The conferences of the Chiefs of Government at Cairo and Teheran have naturally attracted keen and universal attention because of the widespread importance and significance of the discussions and decisions.

"At both of these conferences military plans were concerted for the destruction of Axis forces on all fronts.

"It should be welcome news to all the United Nations that in the European theatre complete agreement has been reached 'as to the scope and timing of the operations to be undertaken from the east, west and south.' These concerted plans will undoubtedly result in making effective to the fullest extent the fighting strength of all of the United Nations.

"The meetings of the Chiefs of State have further cemented the friendship and cooperation between our respective countries and assure their fullest possible collaboration."

Rayburn Halts House for News

Opinion in Congress was for the most part marked by approval. The Senate was not in session, but in the House Speaker Sam Rayburn brought his gavel down promptly at 1 P.M., when the Teheran communiqué was released for publication, and had the clerk read the announcement. It was received with applause.

While members of Congress were pleased that Messrs. Roosevelt and Churchill had at last met with Premier Stalin, some were disappointed that the Teheran communiqué was not more specific about the political future of Europe. There were others who had hoped for an ultimatum to the German people to surrender.

Speaker Rayburn said he was pleased that the three chiefs of government were "so much in accord" and said he was now looking forward "to a better world for all people."

Representative Joseph W. Martin Jr. of Massachusetts, the House Republican leader, said that, while he had hoped for more details, "we all devoutly hope the meeting will hasten the day of the decisive victory for the Allies."

"Eisenhower Acts," June 6, 1944, and "Landing Puts End to 4-Year Hiatus," June 7, 1944

On June 6, 1944, Allied forces landed in Normandy, France, to battle German troops and retake Western Europe. Led by General Eisenhower, this invasion marked a turning point in the war.

JUNE 6, 1944
EISENHOWER ACTS

U.S., British, Canadian Troops Backed by Sea, Air Forces
MONTGOMERY LEADS
Nazis Say Their Shock Units Are Battling Our Parachutists
Communique No. 1 On Allied Invasion
By Broadcast to The New York Times.

LONDON, Tuesday, June 6—The Supreme Headquarters of the Allied Expeditionary Force issued this communiqué this morning:

"Under the command of General Eisenhower, Allied naval forces, supported by strong air forces, began landing Allied armies this morning on the northern coast of France."

By RAYMOND DANIELL
By Cable to The New York Times.

SUPREME HEADQUARTERS ALLIED EXPEDITIONARY FORCES, Tuesday, June 6—The invasion of Europe from the west has begun.

In the gray light of a summer dawn Gen. Dwight D. Eisenhower threw his great Anglo-American force into action today for the liberation of the Continent. The spearhead of attack was an Army group commanded by Gen. Sir Bernard L. Montgomery and comprising troops of the United States, Britain and Canada.

General Eisenhower's first communiqué was terse and calculated to give little information to the enemy. It said merely that "Allied naval forces supported by strong air forces began landing Allied armies this morning on the northern coast of France."

After the first communiqué was released it was announced that the Allied landing was in Normandy.

 This was D-day and it has gone well.

JUNE 7, 1944
LANDING PUTS END TO 4-YEAR HIATUS

Fiery Renewal of Battle for France—Britain Recalls Grimness of Dunkerque
By RAYMOND DANIELL
By Cable to The New York Times.

LONDON, June 6—This was D-day and it has gone well.

At daybreak Anglo-American forces dropped from the skies in Normandy, swarmed up on the beaches from thousands of landing craft and renewed the battle for France and for Europe, broken off four years ago at Dunkerque.

And when darkness fell, on the word of no less than Winston Churchill, the King's First Minister, who is still

this country's best reporter, they had toeholds on a broad front and were fighting as far back from the coast as Caen, which is eight and a half miles behind the Channel beaches and 149 miles from Paris.

At the time he spoke the Prime Minister said that the battle which was just beginning was progressing in "a thoroughly satisfactory manner." But even he, like most people in this island, had his fingers crossed.

The Germans' resistance until now has been surprisingly, perhaps ominously, slight. Several obstacles to any amphibious operation have been surmounted. The concentration of ships has escaped serious bombardment from the air and the huge armada has crossed the Channel without encountering real enemy naval opposition. Submarine obstacles and shore batteries, which had been pounded relentlessly by the Allied air forces, were less lethal than had been expected.

Weather Not Favorable

The weather was uncertain but possibly a decisive factor. It was not favorable to the attacking forces. It was revealed at the Supreme Headquarters of the Allied Expeditionary Force that the great blow had been postponed one day because the barometer had started to fall—not an unusual occurrence in this land of fickle weather.

On the basis of reports from his meteorologists, General Eisenhower postponed the launching of his attack twenty-four hours. Then the weather men assured him that an improvement was coming and he was faced with the problem of gambling on their science or postponing the attack another month. His was a grim decision, for it was learned at Supreme Headquarters that had the meteorologists been wrong the whole expedition might have met with disaster.

As it was, the weather was not good, but it improved. At the start clouds obscured air targets and winds swept the Channel into one of its hellish moods, so a large part of the invading force must have been seasick when they landed to do battle with the enemy.

- -

"Roosevelt Signs 'G.I. Bill of Rights,'" June 23, 1944

Even before World War II ended, the United States gave thanks to its soldiers for their dedication and service with the passage of the G.I. Bill of Rights. Signed by FDR in June 1944, the legislation provided funding for veterans to attend college, purchase homes, and start businesses. It also authorized the creation of veterans' hospitals as well as services to help veterans find employment after the war.

JULY 23, 1944
ROOSEVELT SIGNS G.I. BILL OF RIGHTS
And Asks That Broad Benefits Given Armed Forces Be Extended to Merchant Marine
Special to The New York Times

WASHINGTON, June 22—President Roosevelt signed today, in a semi-public ceremony, the "G.I. Bill of Rights," which authorizes a broad program of benefits for veterans of this war.

Coincident with the signing, he read a statement in which he expressed the hope that the Congress would soon provide comparable benefits for the members of the merchant marine, and then press on to consider legislation assuring the smooth transition of workers from war jobs to peacetime ones.

"A sound post-war economy is a major present responsibility," Mr. Roosevelt said.

The bill signed today by Mr. Roosevelt represented, he said, the considered conclusions of Congress based on recommendations he made in a series of messages in 1943.

The Principal Provisions

The principal provisions in the bill are as follows:

1. It authorizes for veterans up to 52 weeks of unemployment compensation at the rate of $20 a week, with adjusted compensation for self-employed veterans restoring themselves in business rather than seeking jobs from others.

2. It guarantees 50 per cent of loans up to $2,000 to veterans, at interest of not more than 4 per cent, for the purpose of establishing homes or businesses.

3. It appropriates $500,000,000 for construction of additional veterans' facilities, including hospitals, and strengthens provisions to assist veterans in finding employment through the United States Employment Service.

4. It authorizes allowances for four years of individual grants of $500 a year for training and education, plus

monthly subsistence pay of $50 a month for single and $75 a month for married veterans.

The President signed the bill, seated at his desk in his oval-shaped office, while ranged behind him stood Senate and House leaders principally responsible for the legislation, and representatives of the Veterans of Foreign Wars and American Legion, the older veterans' groups, who advised on preparation of the legislation.

The bill will become in the future the basic authorization-in-law for appropriations necessary to finance the great task of reinstating more than 10,000,000 members of the armed forces in normal civilian life.

Mr. Roosevelt remarked that the bill gave "emphatic notice to the men and women in our armed forces that the American people do not intend to let them down."

Mr. Roosevelt used ten pens to sign his name to the bill in order to distribute as many as possible among his guests. The first pen was given to Mrs. Edith Nourse Rogers, of Massachusetts.

"Roosevelt Appeal for Unity Starts Monetary Parley," July 2, 1944

The United States convened representatives from forty-four countries in Bretton Woods, New Hampshire, in 1944 to plan for the postwar international economic order. The conference led to creation of the International Monetary Fund to provide financial assistance to countries in need and the World Bank to provide development aid.

JULY 2, 1944
ROOSEVELT APPEAL FOR UNITY STARTS MONETARY PARLEY

Word to Men of 44 Countries at Bretton Woods Asks Cooperation in Peace as in War

MORGENTHAU TELLS PLANS

Champions Stabilization Fund and International Bank as Vital Post-War Needs

By RUSSELL PORTER

Special to The New York Times

BRETTON WOODS, N.H., July 1—With delegates from forty-four countries participating, the United Nations Monetary and Financial Conference opened here this afternoon on a solemn but hopeful keynote struck in a message from President Roosevelt.

The Chief Executive warned that the meeting would test the Allies' capacity "to cooperate in peace as we have in war," but expressed confidence that the conferees would be able to adjust "possible differences" and work together for "an enduring program of future economic cooperation and peaceful progress."

Mr. Roosevelt revealed that the present conference marked the beginning of a broad program of international cooperation to establish "a dynamic and soundly expanding" post-war world economy with rising standards of living in general. Previously, United Nations' conferences, he pointed out, had dealt either with military and production problems for the war or with immediate post-war emergencies, such as the food conference at Virginia Hot Springs last spring and the Relief and Rehabilitation Conference in Atlantic City last fall.

Check on Rivalries Sought

Later conferences are expected to deal with foreign trade, shipping, aviation and other matters in an effort to stimulate world trade, production and employment, to minimize international rivalries, and thus to lay the economic foundation for lasting world peace and prosperity.

The President's message was read by Dr. Warren Kelchner of the State Department, secretary-general of the conference, at the inaugural plenary session at which Henry J. Morgenthau Jr., Secretary of the Treasury and chairman of the United States delegation, was elected permanent president of the conference.

In an address following his election, Secretary Morgenthau stated that the first proposal on the agenda was "the formulation of a definite proposal for a stabilization fund of the United and Associated Nations" and that the second was a plan for "an international bank for post-war reconstruction."

As hitherto reported, the plan for the stabilization fund calls for total subscriptions of eight billions of dol-

lars from the United and Associated Nations, of which the United States quota would be from two to two and three-quarters billions. If the whole world should be included eventually, the total would increase to ten billions and our share possibly to as much as three billions.

"WORLD BODY ASKED TO MAINTAIN PEACE BY ITS JOINT FORCE," OCTOBER 10, 1944

Learning from Woodrow Wilson's failed efforts to have the United States join the League of Nations after World War I, President Roosevelt was determined not to repeat history after World War II. The United States, Great Britain, the Soviet Union, and China met in Washington, D.C., in fall 1944 to establish the framework for an international organization that would promote cooperation among states. Dubbed the Dumbarton Oaks Conference after the Georgetown mansion where the meeting took place, the session paved the way for the creation of the United Nations the following year.

OCTOBER 10, 1944
WORLD BODY ASKED TO MAINTAIN PEACE BY ITS JOINT FORCE
United Nations, as New League, Charted at Washington With Power to Avert War
AIR, SEA, LAND ACTION SET
Roosevelt, Hull and Stettinius Commend Proposals Drafted at Dumbarton Oaks
By JAMES B. RESTON
Special to The New York Times

WASHINGTON, Oct. 9—The United States, Great Britain, Soviet Russia and China today announced the decision of the Dumbarton Oaks Conference to recommend the creation of an international security organization, to be called "The United Nations" and to be empowered "to take such action by air, naval or land forces as may be necessary to maintain or restore international peace and security."

In a 5,000-word statement of "tentative proposals" which would give to the United States, Britain, Russia, China and France special responsibility and authority for enforcing peace, the conferees made clear their intention to attack potential aggressors of the future before rather than after they had made war.

In a statement praising the work of the conferees during the past seven weeks, President Roosevelt said:

"This time we have been determined first to defeat the enemy, assure that he shall never again be in position to plunge the world into war, and then to so organize the peace-loving nations that they may through unity of desire, unity of will, and unity of strength be in position

to assure that no other would-be aggressor or conqueror shall ever get started."

Details of Organization

To assure prompt operation of this principle, which is the core of the proposals, the conferees recommended a simple, flexible organization with almost all power put in the hands of an eleven-nation Security Council dominated by five "permanent members," the United States, Britain, Russia, China and France, the latter to become a permanent member "in due course."

In addition to this Security Council, the agreement proposed creation of a General Assembly of all nations, whose powers would be mainly advisory, an international court of justice which may adopt the protocol of the present World Court at The Hague, a Secretariat, an Economic and Social Council and a Military Staff Committee to work with the Security Council in directing the force necessary to maintain peace.

Officials explaining the document today emphasized that nothing was binding in the decisions taken at

Dumbarton Oaks, the conferees having put forward a series of incomplete "tentative proposals," which must be filled out in a meeting of chiefs of state, reviewed by the United Nations in a conference and then accepted by each Government "in accordance with their constitutional processes."

"DEWEY CONCEDES," NOVEMBER 8, 1944

Despite his weakening health, FDR shattered precedent once more in 1944 by winning election to a fourth presidential term. Although his margin of victory had narrowed again, he prevailed with 25 million popular votes and Electoral College victories in thirty-six states. His last term of office, however, was a brief eleven weeks.

NOVEMBER 8, 1944
DEWEY CONCEDES

His Action Comes as Roosevelt Leads in 33 States
BIG ELECTORAL VOTE
Late Returns in Seesaw Battles May Push Total Beyond 400
By ARTHUR KROCK

Franklin Delano Roosevelt, who broke more than a century-old tradition in 1940 when he was elected to a third term as President, made another political record yesterday when he was chosen for a fourth term by a heavy electoral but much narrower popular majority over Thomas E. Dewey, Governor of New York.

At 3:15 A.M. Governor Dewey conceded Mr. Roosevelt's re-election, sending his best wishes by radio, to which the President quickly responded with an appreciative telegram.

Early this morning Mr. Roosevelt was leading in mounting returns in thirty-three States with a total of 391 electoral votes and in half a dozen more a trend was developing that could increase this figure to more than 400. Governor Dewey was ahead in fifteen States with 140 electoral votes, but some were see-sawing away from him and back again. Typical of these were Wisconsin, where he overtook the President's lead about 2 A.M.; Nevada, where Mr. Roosevelt passed him at about the same time, and Missouri.

In the contests for seats in Congress, the Democrats had shown gains of 11 to 20 in the House of Representatives, assuring that party's continued control of this branch. In the Senate the net of losses and gains appeared to be an addition of one Republican to the Senate, which would give that party twenty-eight members—far short of the forty-nine necessary to a majority. A surprise was the indicated defeat of the veteran Pennsylvania Republican, Senator James J. Davis.

"YALTA PARLEY ENDS," FEBRUARY 13, 1945

Shortly after his fourth inauguration, FDR traveled to Yalta in the Crimea to meet with his British and Soviet counterparts to continue discussions on the postwar international order. The president was later criticized for appearing to acquiesce to Soviet domination in Eastern Europe, but others argued that such control was unavoidable, and that FDR had correctly prioritized U.S. interests in winning Soviet support to fight Japan if necessary after victory in Europe.

FEBRUARY 13, 1945
YALTA PARLEY ENDS

Unified Blows at Reich, Policing Spheres and Reparations Shaped

FRANCE TO GET ROLE

Broader Polish, Yugoslav Regimes Guaranteed—Curzon Line Adopted

By LANSING WARREN

Special to The New York Times

WASHINGTON, Feb. 12—Allied decisions sealing the doom of Nazi Germany and German militarism, coordinating military plans for Germany's occupation and control and maintaining order and establishing popular Governments in liberated countries were signed yesterday by President Roosevelt, Marshal Stalin and Prime Minister Churchill near Yalta in the Crimea, the White House announced today.

The conference, held in the summer palace of former Czar Nicholas II on the Black Sea shore, also called for a United Nations security conference in San Francisco on April 25.

The parleys, hitherto shrouded in secrecy except for a brief outline of the agenda issued Feb. 7, were held day and night from Feb. 4 until the final signatures were affixed. The announcement did not refer to President Roosevelt's future movements except that he had left the Crimea.

Main Points of Accord

Major decisions of the conference include:

(1) Plans for new blows at the heart of Germany from the east, west, north and south.

(2) Agreement for occupation by the three Allies, each of a separate zone, as Germany is invaded, and an invitation to France to take over a zone and participate as a fourth member of the Control Commission.

(3) Reparations in kind to be paid by Germany for damages, to be set by an Allied commission. The repara-

tions commission, which will establish the type and amount of payments by Germany, will have its headquarters in Moscow. [Secretary of State Stettinius and Ambassador Harriman arrived in Moscow Monday.]

(4) Settlement of questions left undecided at the conference at Dumbarton Oaks and decision to call a United Nations conference at San Francisco April 25 to prepare the charter for a general international organization to maintain peace and security.

(5) Specific agreements to widen the scope of the present Governments in Poland and Yugoslavia and an understanding to keep order and establish Governments in liberated countries conforming to the popular will and the principles of the Atlantic Charter.

(6) A general declaration of determination to maintain Allied unity for peace.

German People Apart

The statement announced common policies for enforcing unconditional surrender and imposing Nazi Germany's doom. The document draws a distinction between the Nazi system, laws and institutions, the German General Staff and its militarism, which will be relentlessly wiped out, and the German people.

"It is not our purpose," it declared, "to destroy the people of Germany, but only when nazism and militarism have been extirpated will there be hope for a decent life for Germans, and a place for them in the comity of nations."

• •

"END COMES SUDDENLY AT WARM SPRINGS," APRIL 13, 1945, AND "FRANKLIN D. ROOSEVELT," APRIL 13, 1945

Twelve years after taking the presidential oath of office for the first time, President Franklin Delano Roosevelt died in Warm Springs, Georgia, on April 12, 1945. Vice President Harry S. Truman was sworn in as president at the White House that evening. FDR had led the United States through the Great Depression and World War II, but he did not live to see the fruits of his labors. *The Times* editorial noted the sad timing of FDR's death, writing that "a great and gallant wartime leader has died almost in the very hour of the victory to which he led the way."

APRIL 13, 1945
END COMES SUDDENLY AT WARM SPRINGS

Even His Family Unaware of Condition as Cerebral Stroke Brings Death to Nation's
Leader at 63

ALL CABINET MEMBERS TO KEEP POSTS

Funeral to Be at White House Tomorrow, With Burial at Hyde Park Home—

Impact of News Tremendous

By ARTHUR KROCK

Special to The New York Times

WASHINGTON, April 12—Franklin Delano Roosevelt, War President of the United States and the only Chief Executive in history who was chosen for more than two terms, died suddenly and unexpectedly at 4:35 P.M. today at Warm Springs, Ga., and the White House announced his death at 5:48 o'clock. He was 63.

The President, stricken by a cerebral hemorrhage, passed from unconsciousness to death on the eighty-third day of his fourth term and in an hour of high triumph. The armies and fleets under his direction as Commander in Chief were at the gates of Berlin and the shores of Japan's home islands as Mr. Roosevelt died, and the cause he represented and led was nearing the conclusive phase of success.

Less than two hours after the official announcement, Harry S. Truman of Missouri, the Vice President, took the oath as the thirty-second President. The oath was administered by the Chief Justice of the United States, Harlan F. Stone, in a one-minute ceremony at the White House. Mr. Truman immediately let it be known that Mr. Roosevelt's Cabinet is remaining in office at his request, and that he had authorized Secretary of State Edward R. Stettinius Jr. to proceed with plans for the United Nations Conference on international organization at San Francisco, scheduled to begin April 25. A report was circulated that he leans somewhat to the idea of a coalition Cabinet, but this is unsubstantiated.

Funeral Tomorrow Afternoon

It was disclosed by the White House that funeral services for Mr. Roosevelt would take place at 4 P.M. (E.W.T.) Saturday in the East Room of the Executive Mansion. The Rev. Angus Dun, Episcopal Bishop of Washington; the Rev. Howard S. Wilkinson of St. Thomas's Church in Washington and the Rev. John G. McGee of St. John's in Washington will conduct the services.

The body will be interred at Hyde Park, N.Y., Sunday, with the Rev. George W. Anthony of St. James Church officiating. The time has not yet been fixed.

Jonathan Daniels, White House secretary, said Mr. Roosevelt's body would not lie in state. He added that, in view of the limited size of the East Room, which holds only about 200 persons, the list of those attending the funeral services would be limited to high Government officials, representatives of the membership of both houses of Congress, heads of foreign missions, and friends of the family.

President Truman, in his first official pronouncement, pledged prosecution of the war to a successful conclusion. His statement, issued for him at the White House by press secretary Jonathan Daniels, said:

"The world may be sure that we will prosecute the war on both fronts, East and West, with all the vigor we possess to a successful conclusion."

News of Death Stuns Capital

The impact of the news of the President's death on the capital was tremendous. Although rumor and a marked change in Mr. Roosevelt's appearance and manner had brought anxiety to many regarding his health, and there had been increasing speculation as to the effects his death would have on the national and world situation, the fact stunned the Government and the citizens of the capital.

It was not long, however, before the wheels of Government began once more to turn. Mr. Stettinius, the first of the late President's Ministers to arrive at the White House, summoned the Cabinet to meet at once. Mr. Truman, his face gray and drawn, responded to the first summons given to any outside Mr. Roosevelt's family and official intimates by rushing from the Capitol.

Mrs. Roosevelt had immediately given voice to the spirit that animated the entire Government, once the first shock of the news had passed. She cabled to her four sons, all on active service:

"He did his job to the end as he would want you to do. Bless you all and all our love. Mother."

Those who have served with the late President in peace and in war accepted that as their obligation. The

> " No President of the United States has died in circumstances so triumphant and yet so grave. "

comment of members of Congress unanimously reflected this spirit. Those who supported or opposed Mr. Roosevelt during his long and controversial years as President did not deviate in this. And all hailed him as the greatest leader of his time.

No President of the United States has died in circumstances so triumphant and yet so grave. The War of the States had been won by the Union when Abraham Lincoln was assassinated, and though the shadow of post-war problems hung heavy and dark the nation's troubles were internal. World War II, which the United States entered in Mr. Roosevelt's third term, still was being waged at the time of his death, and in the Far East the enemy's resistance was still formidable. The United States and its chief allies as victory nears, were struggling to resolve differences of international policy on political and economic issues that have arisen and will arise. And the late President's great objective—a league of nations that will be formed and be able to keep the peace—was meeting obstacles on its way to attainment.

Mr. Roosevelt died also in a position unique insofar as the history of American statesmen reveals. He was regarded by millions as indispensable to winning the war and making a just and lasting peace. On the basis of this opinion, they elected him to a fourth term in 1944. He was regarded by those same millions as the one American qualified to deal successfully and effectively with the leaders of other nations—particularly Prime Minister Winston Churchill and Marshal Joseph Stalin—and this was another reason for his re-election.

APRIL 13, 1945
EDITORIAL
FRANKLIN D. ROOSEVELT

A great and gallant wartime leader has died almost in the very hour of the victory to which he led the way. It is a cruel and bitter irony that Franklin D. Roosevelt should not have lived to see the Allied armies march into Berlin. It is a hard and stunning blow to lose the genius and the inspiration of his leadership in this decisive moment of the war. The people of the United States, our comrades in the Allied Nations, the cause of democracy throughout the whole free world, have suffered a heartbreaking loss.

THE PRESIDENCY OF HARRY S. TRUMAN

APRIL 12, 1945 – JANUARY 20, 1953

Harry S. Truman's presidency laid the foundation for America's role in the world today. Truman did not have presidential aspirations, but when Franklin D. Roosevelt (FDR) died on April 12, 1945, Vice President Truman did not hesitate to assume the responsibilities that had fallen upon him. And those responsibilities were immense indeed, especially in foreign policy. With the end of World War II, the United States returned to peacetime governance, but it did not recede from global affairs as it had following World War I. Instead, the United States became embroiled in a prolonged conflict with its wartime ally, the Soviet Union, in what became known as the cold war. Although Truman's advisers were the architects of the U.S. containment policy to deal with the Soviet Union, the president provided steady and decisive leadership in guiding the United States in this new era.

Source: U.S. Senate Collection, Center for Legislative Archives

John and Martha Truman named their first child Harry S. Truman, but the middle initial actually was not an abbreviation for anything, as Truman's parents were unable to decide which of his grandfathers to honor, Andersen Shippe Truman or Solomon Young. Truman grew up in Independence, Missouri. He was a studious child, in part because his poor eyesight hindered his ability to play outdoors. He was unable to afford college and instead took on a series of jobs, including bank teller and mailroom clerk. He then took over his family's farm, working there until he joined the army just before U.S. entry into World War I. He served with distinction as a field artillery officer, earning the rank of major before his discharge in 1919.

Truman returned to Missouri and briefly entered the business world, opening a haberdashery store in Kansas City. But the store failed, and Truman turned to politics. He successfully ran for an administrative judge position in Jackson County with the support of the local Democratic machine headed by political boss Tom Pendergast. Truman lost his first bid for reelection, but with Pendergast's support, in 1926 he was elected presiding judge of the county court, where he served until 1934. As an administrative judge, Truman oversaw patronage positions as well as public works projects, and, although he remained close to the political machine that had put him in office, he also was recognized for his honesty. In 1934, again with Pendergast's endorsement, Truman successfully ran for the U.S. Senate.

Senator Truman's ties to Pendergast were well known, but his reputation for honesty continued as well, and he was

QUICK FACTS ON HARRY S. TRUMAN

BIRTH	May 10, 1884, Lamar, Mo.
EDUCATION	High school degree Law studies, Kansas City Law School, 1923–1925
FAMILY	Wife: Elizabeth "Bess" Virginia Wallace Truman Children: Mary Margaret Truman
WHITE HOUSE PETS	Dogs
PARTY	Democratic
PREPRESIDENTIAL CAREER (SELECTED)	Bank official, 1903–1905 Worked on family farm, 1906–1917 Field artillery officer in World War I, 1917–1919 Haberdashery business, Kansas City, Mo., 1919–1921 County court judge, Jackson County, Mo., 1922–1924 County court presiding judge, Jackson County, Mo., 1926–1934 U.S. Senate, 1935–1945 Chairman of Special Senate Committee investigating national defense, 1941–1944 Vice president, January 20, 1945–April 12, 1945
PRESIDENTIAL TERMS	April 12, 1945–January 20, 1949 January 20, 1949–January 20, 1953
VICE PRESIDENT	Alben W. Barkley (second term)
SELECTED EVENTS	Germany surrenders in World War II (May 7, 1945) Signing of United Nations Charter in San Francisco (June 1945) Potsdam Conference (July 1945) Atom bomb dropped on Hiroshima, Japan (August 6, 1945) Atom bomb dropped on Nagasaki, Japan (August 9, 1945) Japan surrenders in World War II (August 14, 1945) Philippines wins independence (1946) Creation of Atomic Energy Commission (1946) Truman Doctrine (1947) National Security Act (1947) Taft-Hartley Labor-Management Relations Act (1947) Presidential Succession Act (1947) Berlin airlift (1948–1949) Marshall Plan (1948) Creation of North Atlantic Treaty Organization (1949) American Housing Act (1949) Korean War (1950–1953) Survives assassination attempt (1950) Ratification of Twenty-second Amendment (1951) Dismissal of General MacArthur (1951) Seizure of steel mills (1952) Puerto Rico becomes U.S. commonwealth (1952) United States explodes hydrogen bomb (1952)
POSTPRESIDENCY	Publication of memoirs, 1955, 1956
DEATH	December 26, 1972, Independence, Mo.

reelected to the Senate in 1940, even though Pendergast was convicted of tax evasion. He supported President Roosevelt's New Deal program as well as the president's assistance to U.S. allies in the early years of World War II. Truman gained most recognition in the Senate for chairing a special oversight committee on national defense, which sought to impose fiscal responsibility upon defense contractors.

In 1944 FDR decided to select a new running mate, as many Democrats thought Vice President Henry Wallace was too liberal. The president accepted a party leader's endorsement of Senator Truman, who won the vice-presidential nomination on the second ballot at the Democratic National Convention. The Democratic ticket was victorious, but Truman would serve as vice president for less than three months. He was sworn in as president at the White House on April 12, 1945, just hours after FDR died suddenly from a cerebral hemorrhage in Warm Springs, Georgia.

The Truman Administration (First Term)

Truman kept FDR's cabinet intact for his first few months in office, but he soon began to bring in a new advisory team. James F. Byrnes of North Carolina became secretary of state in the summer of 1945, serving for just over eighteen months before Gen. George C. Marshall of Pennsylvania took the post. Truman selected two new secretaries of war between 1945 and 1947, Robert P. Patterson of New York and Kenneth C. Royall of North Carolina. When that position became secretary of defense, James V. Forrestal of New York was the first to hold it. Attorney General Thomas C. Clark of Texas was appointed in the summer of 1945, as was Treasury Secretary Frederick M. Vinson of Kentucky, who was replaced by John W. Snyder of Missouri in 1946. Truman selected Vinson to head the Supreme Court that year, and he later appointed Clark to the Court as well.

First Lady Elizabeth "Bess" Truman was the president's childhood love, whom he married when he returned from the war in 1919. Bess Truman preferred to remain out of the spotlight. The Trumans had one child, Margaret, who was twenty-one when her father became president. Margaret Truman resided at the White House with her parents while she completed her undergraduate degree in history at George Washington University. She gained public recognition as a concert singer and through television appearances and later became a well-known mystery writer.

Major Issues (First Term)

President Truman took office just as World War II was coming to a close in Europe. On May 7, 1945, Germany surren-

dered unconditionally. But the war in Asia continued, and Truman soon faced perhaps the most momentous decision of his presidency: whether to use the newest and potentially deadliest weapon ever created, the atom bomb. Hoping that the bomb would save American soldiers' lives by making a U.S. invasion of Japan unnecessary, Truman approved its use, and on August 6, 1945, the United States dropped an atomic bomb on Hiroshima, Japan. Three days later, it dropped a second atomic bomb on Nagasaki, Japan. The bombs destroyed the two cities, killing more than 200,000 people and injuring many more. On August 14 Japan agreed to surrender, and did so officially on September 2 on board the USS *Missouri*. President Truman never second-guessed his decision, but historians have debated whether using the atomic bomb was necessary to end the war.

With the war won, Truman turned his attention to domestic policy. He proposed a housing program, fair-employment legislation, and other initiatives, but Congress resisted these measures. Congress endorsed the creation of the Council of Economic Advisers to assist the president in policymaking, but it continued to battle with him over the need for postwar price controls to combat inflation. The president's approval ratings declined, and his party lost control of both chambers of Congress in the 1946 midterm elections, resulting in a Republican-led Congress for the first time in more than a decade. In 1947 Congress passed the Taft-Hartley Act, which narrowed the power of labor unions, over Truman's veto.

Truman had greater success in foreign affairs than in domestic policy. He had met British prime minister Winston Churchill and Soviet premier Joseph Stalin in Potsdam, Germany, in July 1945 to discuss their nations' postwar interests. The three states agreed to partition Germany into separate occupation zones, foreshadowing the regional divisions that would develop with the cold war. In 1947 President Truman declared that the United States would help combat the spread of communism in Greece and Turkey. The following year, the Truman administration created an ambitious foreign-aid program, known as the Marshall Plan, to rebuild Western Europe. The purpose of these programs was to limit Soviet influence in Europe, and they were cornerstones of the "containment" policy that would guide the United States for the next forty years.

The 1948 Election

Although Truman won the Democratic presidential nomination in 1948, with Sen. Alben W. Barkley of Kentucky chosen as his running mate, he faced a bitterly divided party. Liberal Democrats nominated Henry Wallace of Iowa, on the Progressive Party ticket, and southern Democrats who opposed Truman's support for civil rights nominated South Carolina governor James "Strom" Thurmond on the Dixiecrat Party ticket. The Republicans nominated New York governor Thomas E. Dewey and California governor Earl Warren as his running mate. Public opinion polls incorrectly indicated that Dewey would prevail; in fact, Truman won 303 Electoral College votes to Dewey's 189, and nearly 3 million more popular votes than Dewey.

THE TRUMAN ADMINISTRATION (SECOND TERM)

After winning election to his own full term, Truman made some important changes to his nine-member cabinet. He appointed Dean G. Acheson of Connecticut as secretary of state and James H. McGrath of Rhode Island as attorney general; both served for the rest of Truman's presidency. For defense secretary, Truman first selected Louis A. Johnson of West Virginia, then turned to George Marshall, who was followed by Robert A. Lovett of New York. Several first-term cabinet appointees remained in office, including Treasury Secretary Snyder, Commerce Secretary Charles Sawyer of Ohio, and Agriculture Secretary Charles F. Brannan of Colorado.

Because the White House was in serious need of renovation, President Truman and his family resided at Blair House, across from the White House, for much of his second term. The president faced a near-fatal threat there in 1950, when two Puerto Rican nationalists tried to break into Blair House to assassinate him. Truman escaped injury, but a Secret Service agent was killed in the attack, as was one of the assassins.

MAJOR ISSUES (SECOND TERM)

President Truman promoted an ambitious domestic policy agenda in his second term, but it did not translate into policy achievements. Building on FDR's New Deal program, Truman promised a "fair deal" that would include civil rights legislation, affordable housing, a higher minimum wage, and a national health care program. The Democratic Party would embrace these proposals in the coming years, but they did not become law under Truman.

The United States also faced internal conflict in Truman's second term over the possibility of Communist infiltration, and these fears became more pronounced after the fall of China to communism in late 1949. Republican senator Joseph R. McCarthy of Wisconsin accused the Truman administration of harboring Communists in the State Department, and his charges marked the start of a prolonged investigation of Americans purported to have Communist ties, allegations that turned out to be largely unsubstantiated.

As in his first term, Truman accomplished more in foreign policy than he did in domestic affairs. In 1949 the United States joined a collective security alliance, the North Atlantic Treaty Organization (NATO), with Canada and several European states. Shortly thereafter, the United States forced the Soviet Union to lift its nearly yearlong blockade of West Berlin through the success of the famous Berlin airlift, in which food and supplies were regularly dropped into the city.

The foreign policy conflict that dominated Truman's second term was the Korean War. After North Korea invaded South Korea in June 1950, the United States immediately sent troops to combat the incursion, with the support of a United Nations resolution authorizing military action. Once U.S. forces successfully pushed North Korean troops back to the thirty-eighth parallel that previously had divided the two sides, the war entered a stalemate that would not be resolved in the Truman administration. Truman faced further criticism for his decision to relieve the U.S. commander in Korea, Gen. Douglas MacArthur, in 1951 after the general's disagreements with the president's war leadership became public.

With declining approval ratings and a war that had been waged for nearly two years with no end in sight, Truman decided not to run for reelection in 1952. He campaigned vigorously against the Republican candidate, World War II hero Gen. Dwight D. Eisenhower, but Eisenhower prevailed over the Democratic candidate, Illinois governor Adlai E. Stevenson II. Truman's opposition was especially surprising because he had selected Eisenhower to be his first NATO commander just a few years earlier, and the two shared similar views on U.S. containment policy in the cold war. But the 1952 campaign destroyed any friendship between the two, and their transition on inauguration day was coldly formal. Truman returned to Independence, Missouri, where he gave lectures, published his memoirs, and oversaw the creation of his presidential library. He died nearly twenty years later in 1972.

"Truman Is Sworn in the White House," April 13, 1945, and "President Truman," April 14, 1945

President Roosevelt's health had been in decline for some time, but his death on April 12, 1945, shocked the nation and the world. Upon learning the news, Vice President Harry S. Truman rushed to the White House, where he asked First Lady Eleanor Roosevelt how he could help. She replied, "Tell us what we can do. Is there any way we can help you?" Truman was sworn in as president that evening, and *The New York Times* noted that although the "farmer's son from the Missouri Valley" was not well known, his background and record indicated that he would meet his responsibilities well.

APRIL 13, 1945
TRUMAN IS SWORN IN THE WHITE HOUSE
Members of Cabinet on Hand as Chief Justice Stone Administers the Oath
By C. P. TRUSSELL
Special to The New York Times

WASHINGTON, April 12—Vice President Harry S. Truman of Missouri, standing erect, with his sharp features taut and looking straight ahead through his large, round glasses, became the thirty-second President of the United States in a ceremony lasting not more than a minute in the Cabinet Room of the White House at 7:09 o'clock tonight.

The oath was administered by Chief Justice Harlan F. Stone two hours and thirty-four minutes after the sudden death of President Roosevelt at Warm Springs. Mr. Truman had picked up a Bible from the end of the big Cabinet conference table, held it with his left hand and placed his right hand upon the upper cover. After repeating the oath, he bowed his head, lifted the Bible to his lips and kissed it.

Even before he had taken the oath Mr. Truman had asked President Roosevelt's Cabinet to continue in service. He also authorized Edward R. Stettinius Jr., Secretary of State, to announce that the United Nations Conference for International Organization would go on as scheduled.

To the newsmen at the White House he sent this word, through Stephen Early, press secretary:

"For the time being I prefer not to hold a press conference. It will be my effort to carry on as I believe the President would have done, and to that end I have asked the Cabinet to stay on with me."

Soon after he became President, Mr. Truman left the White House for the five-room Connecticut Avenue apartment where he has resided with Mrs. Truman and their 20-year-old daughter, Mary Margaret, for four years. He said he was "going home, to bed."

It was shortly after he had finished presiding over the Senate debate on the United States-Mexican Water Treaty late this afternoon that Mr. Truman received word from the White House of President Roosevelt's death. This was at about 5:15 P.M., a half hour before the news was made public. Reaching for his hat, he dashed out of the office, calling back to his staff that he was going to the White House.

Arriving at the White House, the Vice President was taken to Mrs. Roosevelt. The President, she told him, had passed away.

"What can I do?" Mr. Truman asked.

"Tell us what we can do," Mrs. Roosevelt said. "Is there any way we can help you?"

APRIL 14, 1945
EDITORIAL
PRESIDENT TRUMAN

In one of the great moments of American history there steps into the office of the Presidency of the United States, and into a position of worldwide influence and authority such as no other living American has ever held, a man who is less well known to the people of this country than many other public figures and almost totally unknown abroad. This man is a farmer's son from the Missouri Valley, a veteran of the last war, a self-styled "practical politician," a two-term member of the Senate, a compromise candidate for the comparatively obscure office from which fate, with dramatic suddenness, has now catapulted him to power. We look at this record, and we look behind the record at the man himself, and we find much in both that is reassuring to the people of the United States and to our comrades in arms throughout the world.

That he was admittedly a compromise candidate for the office of the Vice Presidency—"the second Missouri compromise," we called him—seems to us the first and far from the least important item in the record. "Compromise," in the sense in which it was accurately applied to Mr. Truman's nomination—compromise in the sense of

finding an acceptable middle ground between more extreme positions on either side—is not a bad recommendation for a man whose enormous responsibility it will be to find an acceptable middle road for the American people in the difficult post-war years, and to help put together the pieces of a broken world. When a great war ends, and when there is a sudden lifting of the pressure which has held men to a common effort, there comes a swift and inevitable tendency of groups within nations, and of nations themselves, to fly apart. We have the soundest of reasons for believing that we shall find it valuable, in such a period of shock and readjustment, to have in a position of authority a man who is President today primarily because of the very fact that his candidacy was acceptable to every group and could unite rather than divide, hold together rather than splinter, the factions which compose the dominant political party of the United States. It is part of the record that, once nominated, he received the genuinely sincere support of Left and Right, of North and South, of Democratic trade unionist and Democratic manufacturer.

· ·

"THE WAR IN EUROPE IS ENDED! SURRENDER IS UNCONDITIONAL; V-E WILL BE PROCLAIMED TODAY; OUR TROOPS IN OKINAWA GAIN" MAY 8, 1945

The Allied powers' victory over Germany in May 1945 sparked widespread celebration in the United States, Great Britain, and the Soviet Union. But the recent death of America's beloved President Roosevelt cast a shadow over the occasion, as did the continued fighting in the Pacific.

MAY 8, 1945
THE WAR IN EUROPE IS ENDED! SURRENDER IS UNCONDITIONAL; V-E WILL BE PROCLAIMED TODAY; OUR TROOPS IN OKINAWA GAIN
Wild Crowds Greet News In City While Others Pray
By FRANK S. ADAMS

New York City's millions reacted in two sharply contrasting ways yesterday to the news of the unconditional surrender of the German armies. A large and noisy minority greeted it with the turbulent enthusiasm of New Year's

Eve and Election Night rolled into one. However, the great bulk of the city's population responded with quiet thanksgiving that the war in Europe was won, tempered by the realization that a grim and bitter struggle still was ahead in the Pacific and the fact that the nation is still in mourning for its fallen President and Commander in Chief.

Times Square, the financial section and the garment district were thronged from mid-morning on with wildly jubilant celebrators who tooted horns, staged impromptu parades and filled the canyons between the skyscrapers with fluttering scraps of paper. Elsewhere in the metropolitan area, however, war plants continued to hum, schools, offices and factories carried on their normal activities, and residential areas were calmly joyful.

One factor that helped to dampen the celebration was the bewilderment of large segments of the population at the absence of an official proclamation to back up the news contained in flaring headlines and radio bulletins. With the premature rumor of ten days ago fresh in everyone's mind, and millions still mindful of the false armistice of 1918, there was widespread skepticism over the authenticity of the news.

By mid-afternoon loudspeakers were blaring into the ears of the exulting thousands in the amusement district the news that President Truman's proclamation was being held up by the necessity of coordinating it with the announcements from London and Moscow, and that the formal celebration of the long-awaited V-E Day would be delayed until today.

This sobering note gradually calmed the wild demonstration that had started in the heart of the city within a few minutes after The Associated Press flash at 9:35 A.M. had given the world its first news of the surrender. For six hours Times Square was closed to all vehicular traffic by a crowd that the police placed at 500,000 between noon and 1 P.M., but by 4:30 P.M. the police had cleared the streets sufficiently for street cars and buses to operate.

Jubilation in the other areas in which crowds gathered, such as the district centering about Wall and Broad Streets, the Borough Hall section of Brooklyn, Union, Madison and Herald Squares, and the garment manufacturing center in the West Thirties, followed an almost identical pattern. Along Fifth Avenue, on the other hand, the excitement never attained the crescendo that it did elsewhere.

- -

"2D FORMAL PARLEY," JULY 19, 1945

To prepare for the postwar era, President Truman met with his British and Soviet counterparts in summer 1945 in what became known as the Potsdam Conference. The U.S. alliance with Great Britain was strong, but prospects for continued cooperation with the Soviets were less clear. After the meeting, Truman was optimistic about working with Soviet leader Joseph Stalin. The rise of the cold war soon erased any such possibility.

JULY 19, 1945
2D FORMAL PARLEY
Truman Lunches First With Churchill and Then With Stalin
BYRNES VISITS EDEN
Molotoff Among Guests at Conference With Russian Leader
By THE ASSOCIATED PRESS.

POTSDAM, July 18—President Truman, Premier Stalin and Prime Minister Churchill conferred again late today.

This second formal meeting of the Big Three was as heavily blanketed by security as yesterday's, but the trend of thought among the American and British delegations seemed to make it certain that the ways and means for Japan's defeat would be fully aired before Premier Stalin. Earlier in the day, Mr. Truman conferred separately with Mr. Churchill and Premier Stalin.

The day's events indicated that the leaders had agreed on reaching as promptly as possible full agreement on the issues facing them—issues on which a speedier end of the war with Japan and the future peace of Europe may depend. Mr. Truman, the presiding officer of the sessions, seeks as his chief goals a quicker triumph over Japan and the bulwarking of peace through the solution of longstanding disputes.

He lunched at 1 P.M. with Mr. Churchill, and then later with Premier Stalin. He was accompanied at the second luncheon by Secretary of State James F. Byrnes, his close friend and an experienced negotiator.

The President walked from his residence to the local equivalent of 10 Downing Street and was greeted at the gate by Mr. Churchill and his soldier-daughter, Mary, an announcement from the British delegation said. Fifty men of the Second Battalion of Scots Guards formed an honor guard on the tree-shaded lawn and a Royal Marine band struck up "The Star-Spangled Banner."

Messrs. Truman and Churchill talked cordially on the terrace while photographs were taken and then they lunched inside at a table set for two. When Mr. Truman was leaving, Mr. Byrnes emerged from Foreign Secretary Anthony Eden's house next door, where he had lunched, and met the President at the entrance. The British delegation did not say how long Messrs. Churchill and Truman had conferred, nor was there any hint of their topics.

Molotoff Among Guests

Premier Stalin was host to the President at 3 P.M. at a comparatively brief luncheon, but there were evidences that it was cordial. Caviar, fish and meat apparently were on the menu. Mr. Byrnes, Foreign Commissar Vyacheslaff M. Molotoff, the President's military and naval aides, Brig. Gen. Harry H. Vaughan and Capt. James K. Vardaman Jr. and Charles E. Bohlen, the State Department's Russian expert, were also guests of Premier Stalin.

Mr. Truman's calls today returned the visits paid to him by Mr. Churchill on Monday and by Premier Stalin on Tuesday. The President is understood to be planning a dinner soon at which both will be honor guests.

First Talk Under Formal Chairman

This is the first Big Three conference that has had a formal chairman. It was reported unofficially from Teheran in 1943 that President Roosevelt then was informal chairman most of the time. At the Yalta meeting Premier Stalin was understood to have filled that office in fact, although some Americans said that Mr. Roosevelt had presided.

During the afternoon, Gen. George C. Marshall, Field Marshal Sir Alan Francis Brooke and other high American, British and Russian officers reviewed the veteran Second Armored (Hell on Wheels) Division, drawn up in a two-and-a-half-mile column of men, tanks and vehicles along the Avus Autobahn. General Marshall declared after the forty-minute review that "it is a splendid looking outfit. It was most impressive."

⸱ ⸱

"New Age Ushered," August 7, 1945

The United States brought World War II to a close in summer 1945 by dropping two atomic bombs on Japan. Never before had the world seen such devastation inflicted so suddenly. The fierce and destructive power of nuclear weapons would make them a significant strategic resource in the cold war.

AUGUST 7, 1945
NEW AGE USHERED
Day of Atomic Energy Hailed by President, Revealing Weapon
HIROSHIMA IS TARGET
'Impenetrable' Cloud of Dust Hides City After Single Bomb Strikes
By SIDNEY SHALETT
Special to The New York Times

WASHINGTON, Aug. 6—The White House and War Department announced today that an atomic bomb, possessing more power than 20,000 tons of TNT, a destructive force equal to the load of 2,000 B-29's and more than 2,000 times the blast power of what previously was the world's most devastating bomb, had been dropped on Japan.

The announcement, first given to the world in utmost solemnity by President Truman, made it plain that one of the scientific landmarks of the century had been passed, and that the "age of atomic energy," which can be a tremendous force for the advancement of civilization as well as for destruction, was at hand.

At 10:45 o'clock this morning, a statement by the President was issued at the White House that sixteen hours earlier—about the time that citizens on the Eastern seaboard were sitting down to their Sunday suppers—an

What is this terrible new weapon, which the War Department also calls the 'Cosmic Bomb'?

American plane had dropped the single atomic bomb on the Japanese city of Hiroshima, an important army center.

Japanese Solemnly Warned

What happened at Hiroshima is not yet known. The War Department said it "as yet was unable to make an accurate report" because "an impenetrable cloud of dust and smoke" masked the target area from reconnaissance planes. The Secretary of War will release the story "as soon as accurate details of the results of the bombing become available."

But in a statement vividly describing the results of the first test of the atomic bomb in New Mexico, the War Department told how an immense steel tower had been "vaporized" by the tremendous explosion, how a 40,000-foot cloud rushed into the sky, and two observers were knocked down at a point 10,000 yards away. And President Truman solemnly warned:

"It was to spare the Japanese people from utter destruction that the ultimatum of July 26 was issued at Potsdam. Their leaders promptly rejected that ultimatum. If they do not now accept our terms, they may expect a rain of ruin from the air the like of which has never been seen on this earth."

Most Closely Guarded Secret

The President referred to the joint statement issued by the heads of the American, British and Chinese Governments, in which terms of surrender were outlined to the Japanese and warning given that rejection would mean complete destruction of Japan's power to make war.

[The atomic bomb weighs about 400 pounds and is capable of utterly destroying a town, a representative of the British Ministry of Aircraft Production said in London, the United Press reported.]

What is this terrible new weapon, which the War Department also calls the "Cosmic Bomb"? It is the harnessing of the energy of the atom, which is the basic power of the universe. As President Truman said, "The force from which the sun draws its power has been loosed against those who brought war to the Far East."

"Atomic fission"—in other words, the scientists' long-held dream of splitting the atom—is the secret of the atomic bomb. Uranium, a rare, heavy metallic element, which is radioactive and akin to radium, is the source essential to its production. Secretary of War Henry L. Stimson, in a statement closely following that of the President, promised that "steps have been taken, and continue to be taken, to assure us of adequate supplies of this mineral."

The imagination-sweeping experiment in harnessing the power of the atom has been the most closely guarded secret of the war. America to date has spent nearly $2,000,000,000 in advancing its research. Since 1939, American, British and Canadian scientists have worked on it. The experiments have been conducted in the United States, both for reasons of achieving concentrated efficiency and for security; the consequences of having the material fall into the hands of the enemy, in case Great Britain should have been successfully invaded, were too awful for the Allies to risk.

All along, it has been a race with the enemy. Ironically enough, Germany started the experiments, but we finished them. Germany made the mistake of expelling, because she was a "non-Aryan," a woman scientist who held one of the keys to the mystery, and she made her knowledge available to those who brought it to the United States. Germany never quite mastered the riddle, and the United States, Secretary Stimson declared, is "convinced that Japan will not be in a position to use an atomic bomb in this war."

"Change Accepted by Party Leaders," November 7, 1946

The Democratic Party faced sobering losses in the 1946 congressional midterm elections. The Republicans took control of the U.S. House of Representatives for the first time since 1930 and of the U.S. Senate for the first time since 1932. The election results not only reflected national concern about the Democrats' ability to govern in the postwar era but also registered the public's dissatisfaction with President Truman's leadership.

NOVEMBER 7, 1946
CHANGE ACCEPTED BY PARTY LEADERS
Hannegan Reminds Victors of Responsibility Now and Reece Takes Challenge
WALLACE, PEPPER SHARP
Ex-Secretary Says Party Must Go Progressive or Die and Senator Sees 'Hard Days'
By JOHN D. MORRIS
Special to The New York Times

WASHINGTON, Nov. 6—Resignation, tinged in some instances with despair, pervaded the high command of the Democratic party today, while the jubilation of Republican leaders was noticeably modified by the realization of heavy responsibilities to come.

President Truman, returning to the White House after casting his vote in Missouri, was silent, but Robert Hannegan, Democratic national chairman, issued a statement after discussing the election results with the Chief Executive.

Reminding the Republicans of the "great responsibility" facing them as the majority party in the next Congress, Mr. Hannegan called for bipartisan efforts toward one basic objective, which was "the strength and well-being of the nation."

Carroll Reece, Republican national chairman, accepted the challenge of responsibility and in turn called on the Democratic Administration to acquiesce to the leadership of the Republican party.

Liberals Urged to Fight On

While Democrats here generally accepted defeat without recriminations, Senator Claude Pepper of Florida, a leader of left-of-center forces, predicted "hard days ahead for people here and abroad."

He and Henry A. Wallace, former Secretary of Commerce, pleaded for "liberals" to continue their fight despite the setback at the polls.

The first post-election promise of specific Congressional action when Republicans take control in January came from Representative Harold Knutson of Minnesota. He is slated to be in charge of tax bills as chairman of the Ways and Means Committee. Mr. Knutson reasserted his intention of cutting income taxes 20 per cent and further pledged reduction in excise taxes.

Mr. Knutson said that the unofficial house Republican tax study committee headed by Representative Reed of New York would meet in Washington later this month to begin drawing the legislation.

In the first tax slicing bill in sixteen years, Congress cut the Federal burdens by $6,000,000,000 for 1946, sweeping 12,000,000 low income persons off the tax rolls and killing the war-imposed 95 per cent excess profits tax on corporations.

The Republican proposal for a 20 per cent further cut would trim another $3,000,000,000 from individual burdens plus large savings on excise levies.

Mr. Hannegan spent most of the day at his desk in the Postoffice Department, while officials at Democratic headquarters showed increased gloom as one message of defeat after another arrived from late-reporting districts.

"TRUMAN'S SPEECH LIKENED TO 1823 AND 1941 WARNINGS," MARCH 13, 1947

The Truman Doctrine of 1947 represented the administration's first public declaration of its containment strategy in the cold war. To prevent Communist rebels from taking control of Greece and Turkey, President Truman pledged that the United States would provide $400 million in economic and military aid to combat the insurgents. A few months later, Congress and the president established the institutional apparatus for waging the cold war through the National Security Act of 1947, which created the Central Intelligence Agency, the National Security Council, the Department of Defense, and the Joint Chiefs of Staff.

MARCH 13, 1947
TRUMAN'S SPEECH LIKENED TO 1823 AND 1941 WARNINGS
Capital Puts It on Par With Monroe Doctrine and Inception
of Lend-Lease
By JAMES RESTON
Special to The New York Times

WASHINGTON, March 12—The tentative conclusions of responsible observers on the significance of President Truman's address today may be summarized as follows:

(1) His statement was comparable in importance to the late President Roosevelt's announcement of the lend-lease program and President Monroe's warning to the European autocrats in 1823. Like the lend-lease program, it proposed defending America by aiding those who are working for a free and non-Communist world. Like the Monroe Doctrine, it warned that the United States would resist efforts to impose a political system or foreign domination on areas vital to our security.

(2) It brought the relations between Russia and the west to the most critical point since the British and French, seven years ago this week, gathered an expeditionary force of 100,000 men to send against the Soviet Union during the Russian-Finnish War (this force was not dispatched because that war ended while London and Paris were trying to arrange passage for the troops across Norway and Sweden).

Major Issue for Congress

(3) It placed squarely before Congress the most serious foreign-policy issue that a Republican majority has been asked to face since the late President Wilson asked a guarantee for France against German aggression at the end of the first World War.

It also, significantly, produced what appeared to be a fundamental division between the two most powerful members of the Republican Senate majority Arthur H. Vandenberg of Michigan and Robert A. Taft of Ohio.

Mr. Vandenberg, while asserting that Congress must explore the methods by which the loans should be made to Greece and Turkey, said emphatically that "the President's hands must be upheld" and "the independence of Greece and Turkey must be preserved." Mr. Taft, however, although approving relief loans, saw in the President's proposal to send technical military missions there an attempt to "secure a special domination over the affairs" of these countries. He suggested that such action was similar to Russia's demands for domination in her sphere of influence.

Gave Impetus to U.N. Drive

(4) The President's statement advertised the United Nations' weakness but by so doing gave impetus to the movement to get military forces behind the organization. At the same time, it advertised the weakness of the Council of Foreign Ministers, now meeting in Moscow, but, as in the United Nations' case, highlighted the fact that the United States and Russia could not make peace for others until they made peace with themselves.

Though there was some loose talk on Capitol Hill to the effect that the speech was a "declaration of war," the general feeling among responsible experts in this field is that the danger of war lies in a display not of American strength but of American weakness. What worries these observers is not that the clarification of the east-west conflict might produce war, but that concealing and not facing the conflict might result in the nations' drifting into war.

• •

"Senate Votes $5,300,000,000 for European Recovery; All Amendments Defeated," March 14, 1948

President Truman's initial containment strategy emphasized the importance of economic assistance to combat the spread of communism. In a commencement address at Harvard University on June 5, 1947, Secretary of State George C. Marshall presented American plans for rebuilding Europe. Because the Soviet Union would not allow its satellite states to participate, the program ultimately focused on U.S. allies in Western Europe. The legislation passed by Congress in 1948 was formally titled the European Recovery Program, but it was popularly known as the Marshall Plan. (Given his low popularity at the time, Truman decided that the program would more likely win bipartisan support in Congress with Marshall's name associated with it.) Over the years, the United States sent nearly $13 billion in economic assistance to Western Europe.

MARCH 14, 1948
SENATE VOTES $5,300,000,000 FOR EUROPEAN RECOVERY; ALL AMENDMENTS DEFEATED
BALLOT IS 69 TO 17
Adoption Is Bipartisan in Sitting Which Goes Beyond Midnight
BASIC FORM IS UNCHANGED
Vandenberg Holds Control at All Times and 'Revisionists' Meet Repeated Defeat
By FELIX BELAIR Jr.
Special to The New York Times

WASHINGTON, Sunday, March 14—The Senate approved at 12:05 A.M. today the Economic Cooperation Act of 1948 embodying the European Recovery Program and authorizing $5,300,000,000 for loans and grants in the first twelve months of the four-year undertaking.

The vote was 69 to 17. Thirty-eight Democrats joined with thirty-one Republicans in favor, while four Democrats sided with thirteen Republicans in opposition.

Intended to put the sixteen nations of western Europe back on their feet economically and politically by 1952 and forestall the march of communism to the Atlantic, the measure now goes to the House of Representatives, where a stormier passage was in prospect.

Toward the close of debate the ranks of the "revisionists" thinned and at 9 o'clock last night all was in readiness for a vote. At that hour the third reading of the bill had been completed, cutting off all further amendments, but the Senators talked on.

A few minutes before reaching the third reading the Senate voted, 68 to 22, to kill a substitute proposal for a $5,000,000,000 international Reconstruction Finance Corporation.

Vandenberg in Full Control

Senator Arthur H. Vandenberg, chairman of the foreign relations committee, was in complete control of the legislative situation and unwanted amendments were quickly disposed of throughout the afternoon and evening. The result was that the measure emerged basically unchanged from the form in which he introduced it two weeks ago.

As the legislation went into the stretch Senator Vandenberg signaled his approval and brought adoption of a proposal by Senator Joseph R. McCarthy, Republican, of Wisconsin, calling for the repatriation by the end of the year of all prisoners of war seeking a return to their homelands.

As approved by the Senate, the bill did not have the moral commitment to a $17,000,000,000 continuing authorization originally asked by the Administration. The continuing authorization remained, but the amount was to be filled in by succeeding sessions of Congress.

A provision was added, however, whereby $3,000,000,000 of the first year's authorization would be appropriated from the current fiscal year's Federal budget surplus. Another added provision would enable the recovery program to begin upon enactment by the President.

"ZIONISTS PROCLAIM NEW STATE OF ISRAEL; TRUMAN RECOGNIZES IT AND HOPES FOR PEACE; TEL AVIV IS BOMBED; EGYPT ORDERS INVASION," MAY 15, 1948

The state of Israel came into existence on May 14, 1948, and President Truman immediately recognized the new nation. From the outset, the United States made explicit its steadfast support for this democratic ally in the Middle East.

MAY 15, 1948
ZIONISTS PROCLAIM NEW STATE OF ISRAEL; TRUMAN RECOGNIZES IT AND HOPES FOR PEACE; TEL AVIV IS BOMBED; EGYPT ORDERS INVASION
U.S. MOVES QUICKLY
President Acknowledges de Facto Authority of Israel Immediately
TRUCE AIM STRESSED
Soviet Gesture to New Nation Anticipated—Others Due to Act
By BERTRAM D. HULEN
Special to The New York Times

WASHINGTON, May 14—President Truman announced early tonight recognition by the United States of the new Jewish State of Israel. The President acted instantly upon being informed that the new nation had been proclaimed.

"This Government," he announced, "has been informed that a Jewish state has been proclaimed in Palestine and recognition has been requested by the provisional government thereof.

"The United States recognizes the provisional government as the de facto authority of the new State of Israel."

These two paragraphs constituted the text of the President's statement.

Coupled with the announcement was an expression of hope for peace in Palestine. This was made known through a separate White House statement issued by Charles G. Ross, Presidential press secretary.

"The desire of the United States to obtain a truce in Palestine," this said, "will in no way be lessened by the proclamation of a Jewish state.

"We hope that the new Jewish state will join with the Security Council Truce Commission in redoubled efforts to bring an end to the fighting—which has been throughout the United Nations' consideration of Palestine a principal objective of this Government."

[Pending stabilization of the Palestine situation and indications that the State of Israel was in control of its borders, Britain, it was reported, plans to withhold recognition of the Jewish sovereignty. At Flushing Meadow, Andrei A. Gromyko indicated that the Soviet Government would recognize the new state.]

By acting promptly, President Truman anticipated recognition by other countries, including Russia.

"PRESSES FOR RIGHTS," JULY 27, 1948

President Truman's decision to decree the racial integration of the armed forces and nondiscrimination in federal hiring practices by executive orders in 1948 was a milestone in civil rights in the United States. Although he did not achieve congressional legislation to promote civil rights, Truman showed inspirational leadership in his determination to recognize fundamental rights of black Americans. (The "FEPC" mentioned in the headline is the Fair Employment Practices Commission established under FDR.)

JULY 27, 1948
PRESSES FOR RIGHTS

President Acts Despite Split in His Party Over the Chief Issue

LITTLE 'FEPC' IS CREATED

'Merit, Fitness' Set as U.S. Employment Guides—Military Equality Is Demanded

By ANTHONY LEVIERO

Special to The New York Times

WASHINGTON, July 26—President Truman ordered today the end of discrimination in the armed forces "as rapidly as possible" and instituted a fair employment practices policy throughout the civil branch of the Federal Government.

On the eve of his appearance before Congress, the President issued two executive orders to carry out his sweeping aims. He said that men in uniform should have "equality of treatment and opportunity" without regard to race, color, religion or national origin.

Similarly, he decreed that "merit and fitness" should be the only application for a Government job, and that the head of each department "shall be personally responsible for an effective program to insure that fair employment policies are fully observed in all personnel actions within his department."

The two orders were expected to have a thunderbolt effect on the already highly charged political situation in the Deep South, a situation which is expected to be aggravated further tomorrow when Mr. Truman makes his omnibus call on Congress for action. The message, in one of its eleven major elements, is expected to go down the line for his ten-point civil rights program, which last February started the deep fissures in the Democratic party.

Enforcement Machinery Set Up

The Presidential orders, which require no Congressional sanction, specified in detail the machinery that would be employed to monitor both anti-discrimination programs.

In the National Military Establishment, Mr. Truman created an advisory panel, called the President's Committee on Equality of Treatment and Opportunity in the Armed Services. It will consist of seven members, none of whom was named today.

It was said, however, that one man who probably would be recommended for membership is Dr. Frank Graham, president of the University of North Carolina. It was believed he would be acceptable to North and South, Negro and white.

The civilian employe order directed that a Fair Employment Board be formed from among members and employes of the Civil Service Commission. This, too, is to be a seven-member board, as yet unnamed.

The committee of the armed forces received the mission of determining how present practices might be altered to carry out the Presidential order. In stipulating rapid application of the policy, Mr. Truman said that it should be done with due regard to "the time required to effectuate any necessary changes without impairing efficiency or morale."

"ELECTION PROPHETS PONDER IN DISMAY," NOVEMBER 4, 1948

The 1948 presidential election surprised pollsters and the public, but not the president. Despite numerous preelection polls indicating he would lose, President Truman campaigned vigorously, even undertaking an energetic cross-country tour in which enthusiastic supporters routinely shouted, "Give 'em hell, Harry." And so he did. Perhaps the most famous image of the election is Truman gleefully holding a copy of the *Chicago Daily Tribune,* which was so confident of the results that its front page the day after the election boldly—and incorrectly—declared "DEWEY DEFEATS TRUMAN."

President Harry S. Truman holds up an election day edition of the *Chicago Daily Tribune* which mistakenly announced "Dewey Defeats Truman" on November 4, 1948.

Source: AP Photo/Byron Rollins

NOVEMBER 4, 1948
ELECTION PROPHETS PONDER IN DISMAY
Polltakers and Others Who Put Dewey in White House Try to Analyze Their Errors
By KENNETH CAMPBELL

Officials of the country's three nation-wide public opinion polls, all of which forecast a Dewey victory, were studying election returns yesterday to find out why President Truman was right when he said their faces would be red after Election Day. Nearly all the nation's newspaper publishers and political experts were engaged in similar research.

Dr. George Gallup, director of the Institute of Public Opinion, said he was seeking answers to the following questions:

"Which voters stayed home? Only 47,000,000 voters went to the polls Tuesday. Another 47,000,000 stayed home. Was it the Republicans, or the independent voters who failed to show up at the polls?

"Did the Wallace strength early in the campaign return to Truman? Unquestionably the sharp decline in the Wallace vote was a great help in many pivotal states. Wallace insured the Dewey victory in New York State. On the other hand, the absence of the Wallace ticket on the ballot in Illinois undoubtedly made the difference between a Dewey victory and defeat."

Elmo Roper Is Puzzled

Elmo Roper, public opinion specialist who directs the Roper poll, said:

"On Sept. 9 I predicted that Mr. Dewey would win by a wide margin and that it was all over but the shouting. Since then, I have had plenty of chance to hedge on that prediction. I did not do so.

"I could not have been more wrong. The thing that bothers me most at this moment is that I don't know why I was wrong. I have, of course, always known that it was in the field of finding out why people vote as they do or why and

how firmly they hold certain opinions that we researchers had made the least progress."

Mr. Roper explored various possibilities for gross error—the aroused labor vote brought quietly to the polls; President Truman's ability to dramatize what he believed to be the shortcomings of the Eightieth Congress—but in each instance he said he did not know the answer.

"In this acknowledgement of all the things that we do not yet know about public opinion, it may not be out of place for me to say that there is one thing that I do know," he continued. "That is, President Harry S. Truman proved to be a far better election predicter on Nov. 3, 1948, than the professional pollsters, politicians and pundits."

"12 Nations to Sign Atlantic Alliance at Capital Today," April 4, 1949

The military component of the Truman administration's containment strategy became evident with the creation of the North Atlantic Treaty Organization (NATO) in 1949. Through the NATO treaty, the United States, Canada, and their West European allies pledged to assist one another in the event of a military attack. Originally designed to provide a bulwark against Soviet aggression, NATO survived the cold war and now has more than two dozen members, including several East European states previously under Soviet domination.

APRIL 4, 1949
12 NATIONS TO SIGN ATLANTIC ALLIANCE AT CAPITAL TODAY
President Will Be at Ceremony to Hail Policy of Mutual Aid for Western Countries
WORLD BROADCASTS SET
Secretary of State Acheson to Open Historic Assembly of Ministers at 3 P.M.
By JAMES RESTON
Special to *The New York Times*.

WASHINGTON, April 3—The North Atlantic treaty, ending the military isolation of the United States as the United Nations and the European Recovery Program ended its political and economic isolation, will be signed at the State Department auditorium on Constitution Avenue here tomorrow afternoon.

Secretary of State Acheson, who as an Assistant Secretary and later as Under-Secretary of State helped devise the United Nations, the ERP, and the Truman Doctrine policies, will open the ceremonies at 3 P.M. and sign for the United States.

President Truman will make a short speech at the close of the ceremony, welcoming the policy of mutual assistance among the members of the North Atlantic community.

The Foreign Secretaries and nations signing the treaty, in the order of signature, will be as follows: Paul-Henri Spaak, Belgium; Lester B. Pearson, Canada; Gustav Rasmussen, Denmark; Robert Schuman, France; Bjarni Benediktsson, Iceland; Count Carlo Sforza, Italy; Joseph Bech, Luxembourg; Dr. Dirk U. Stikker, the Netherlands; Halvard M. Lange, Norway; José Caeiro da Matta, Portugal; Ernest Bevin, United Kingdom; and Dean G. Acheson, United States.

> [T]he treaty . . . will commit its signatories to consider an armed attack on one of them as an armed attack on all.

Seven Ratifications Required

The ceremonies, including the speeches of the President and the Foreign Ministers, will be broadcast beginning at 2:45 P.M., EST to the nation by all radio and television networks and to the world in forty-three languages in the largest arrangement of shortwave facilities ever assembled.

The terms of the pact will be presented to the United States Senate as a treaty soon after it is signed by the various Governments. It will not be ratified by the President until two-thirds of those present and voting in the Senate approve its terms, and it will not come into force until ratifications have been deposited here by seven nations, the United States, Britain, Canada, France, the Netherlands, Belgium and Luxembourg.

For Canada, Denmark, Norway, and Iceland, this will be the first multilateral mutual assistance treaty in peacetime. The United States made a brief treaty of alliance with France late in the eighteenth century, a commitment to defend Panama early in this century, and, in 1947, a mutual assistance engagement with the other nations of the Western Hemisphere.

But even for Britain, France, and the other members of the Brussels alliance, this intercontinental treaty is unprecedented in scope.

Though no immediate commitment will be involved by tomorrow's signature, the treaty, when properly ratified, will commit its signatories to consider an armed attack on one of them as an armed attack on all. And in consequence of this commitment, each signatory will agree, under its own constitutional processes, to take forthwith "such action as it deems necessary, including the use of armed force, to restore and maintain the security of the North Atlantic area."

There has been not the slightest tendency on the part of any of the nations that will sign the pact tomorrow to hesitate as a result of the opposition of the Soviet Union to the pact.

"House Passes Housing Bill; Low Rent Section Retained; A Major Fair Deal Victory," June 30, 1949

Although much of President Truman's "Fair Deal" domestic agenda did not become law, the American Housing Act of 1949 was a signature accomplishment. This legislation providing funding for urban renewal and public housing, and it set the foundation for more extensive federal housing programs in the future.

JUNE 30, 1949
HOUSE PASSES HOUSING BILL; LOW-RENT SECTION RETAINED, A MAJOR FAIR DEAL VICTORY

VOTE IS 228 TO 185

Follows 8-Hour Battle Seeing Heart of Plan Cut Out for a Time

LIKE SENATE'S MEASURE

Adopted Without a Crippling Amendment, Bill Calling for Billions Faces Conference

By CLAYTON KNOWLES

Special to *The New York Times*.

WASHINGTON, June 29—President Truman's Fair Deal scored its first major triumph tonight as the House voted final approval of the National Housing Bill.

The final vote was 228 to 185, a seemingly safe margin, but it followed a gripping see-saw battle during eight long hours of furious legislating in which the low-rent public housing section, the very heart of the program, was knocked out by 3 votes, then restored on a record vote by 5.

The onslaught against the bill was led by Representatives Joseph W. Martin Jr., Charles A. Halleck, Jesse P. Wolcott and others of the Republican leadership.

But on the key roll call, twenty-four liberal Republicans gave Administration forces the votes they needed to put the public housing section back into the bill. Sixty-four Democrats, all but two from the South or border states, joined the hard core of the Republican opposition in trying to vitiate the bill.

- -

"U.S. 'Not at War,' President Asserts," June 30, 1950

President Truman's decision to send U.S. troops to combat North Korean aggression marked a significant expansion of presidential power. Truman did not seek a declaration of war from Congress, claiming that a UN Security Council resolution authorizing military action was sufficient. In a press conference, Truman described the conflict as a "police action" rather than a war. But as U.S. involvement continued for three years, critics have questioned whether Truman overstepped his authority.

JUNE 30, 1950
U.S. 'NOT AT WAR,' PRESIDENT ASSERTS

Truman Allows Quotation—Calls Operation Police Action for U.N. on 'Bandits'

By ANTHONY LEVIERO

Special to The New York Times

WASHINGTON, June 29—President Truman declared today the United States was "not at war." He characterized United States combat operations in Korea as police action for the United Nations against an unlawful bandit attack on the South Korean Republic.

He expressed confidence that the Korean Republic would survive as a result of United States intervention.

The United States air and naval intervention against North Korean Communist forces was a move in favor of

peace, and moreover it had the support of most members of the United Nations, Mr. Truman said.

In his weekly news conference the Chief Executive faced the correspondents for the first time since he made the momentous decisions to fight against North Korea, place a protective naval cordon around Formosa and strengthen the Philippines and anti-Communist Indo-China.

He sharply refused to answer any question that touched on strategic plans that might be in the making. Specifically he declined to comment on questions relating to the use of United States ground troops in the conflict and to the atomic bomb.

Points to Public Support

Among the indications of the upsurge of public opinion were the more than 1,200 telegrams and letters the President has received, endorsing his position at least ten to one.

Late in the afternoon, the Chief Executive presided at an hour-long meeting of the National Security Council in which the nation's military and civil leaders studied developments in the Korean conflict and in all other sensitive areas of the world where its repercussions might be felt. None of those who attended would say a word about the course of events.

With an emphatic manner, Mr. Truman gave permission at his news conference to quote him directly on some of his observations on the war and in defense of the role in the crisis played by Secretary of State Dean Acheson. The President denied all suggestions that Mr. Acheson had been in conflict with other members of the Cabinet and had been reversed. In the circumstances he demonstrated his typical loyalty to members of his official family.

"Mr. President, everybody is asking in this country, are we or are we not at war," a reporter said.

The President replied that we were not at war. Under White House rules, the President's statements in news conferences may not be quoted without specific permission. Several other questions intervened and then Mr. Truman was asked if the phrase might be quoted.

The Chief Executive responded that he would allow the news men to use in quotes: "We are not at war."

"Since issuing your statement [on the Korea situation, Tuesday] can you give us any indication as to the effect it might have on peace?" was another question.

Actions Aimed at Peace

His idea in issuing the statement and the orders preliminary to its issuance was that they amounted to a move in favor of peace. If he had not thought so, he would not have taken these steps, the President said.

"Have you had any indications whether it is being universally accepted as that?"

Only the fact that most members of the United Nations were in full accord, replied the President. He also said he was very happy that India had decided to support the United Nations, adding he had been sure India would do that.

"Would you elaborate a little more on the reasons for this move and the peace angle on it?"

Mr. Truman recalled that the Republic of Korea was set up with the United Nations' help. It was the Government recognized by the members of the United Nations, and it was unlawfully attacked by a bunch of bandits, who were neighbors in North Korea.

The United Nations Security Council had held a meeting and passed on the situation, asking the members to go to the relief of the Korean Republic. The members of the United Nations were doing that—going to the relief of the Korean Republic to suppress a bandit raid on the Korean Republic. Mr. Truman later gave permission to quote him on the word "bandits."

"Would it be correct to call this a police action under the United Nations?"

Yes, replied Mr. Truman, that was exactly what it amounted to.

Asked whether he believed South Korea would survive as an independent republic, in view of the apparent military reverses, Mr. Truman replied that he was sure it would survive. That was what his program was for.

"U.S. SAID TO IGNORE UNION FALSE OATHS," SEPTEMBER 29, 1950

Although the cold war was primarily a foreign policy conflict, a domestic component was waged in the United States as well. The "Red Scare" of the 1950s referred to the fear that Communists had infiltrated the government and American industries, and Sen. Joseph R. McCarthy fueled these emotions with widely publicized hearings sponsored by the Senate Permanent Subcommittee on Investigations. Before the Senate censured McCarthy for misusing his power, his investigations forced many Americans to defend their patriotism and demonstrate that they did not have Communist ties.

SEPTEMBER 29, 1950
U.S. SAID TO IGNORE UNION FALSE OATHS

McCarthy Asserts F.B.I. Found Fraud in U.E. Non-Red Writs, but Evidence Is Buried

By WILLIAM S. WHITE

Special to The New York Times

WASHINGTON, Sept. 28—The Truman Administration was accused today by Senator Joseph R. McCarthy, Republican of Wisconsin, of ignoring evidence that officers of the United Electrical, Radio and Machine Workers of America had filed affidavits falsely disclaiming Communist affiliation.

"The Federal Bureau of investigation," he asserted in a statement appearing in this morning's appendix to *The Congressional Record,* "has furnished the complete and detailed evidence to the Justice Department.

"But Mr. Peyton Ford, the assistant to the Attorney General, who received all this proof, has under Administration direction turned a deaf ear and buried the information in the files."

Mr. Ford's office said that he was out of the city. The Department of Justice declined comment on these fresh accusations of Mr. McCarthy, whose charges of Communist penetration of the State Department were denounced by a Democratically controlled Senate investigation committee as knowingly fraudulent.

Schoeppel Hits Chapman Anew

While Mr. McCarthy was returning to the attack on the Administration, Senator Andrew F. Schoeppel, Republican of Kansas, renewed his demands for further investigation of his charges that Oscar Chapman, Secretary of the Interior, once had "a personal alliance" with the Soviet cause.

Using the same forum as that of Mr. McCarthy, *The Congressional Record,* in which members of Congress have immunity from any suit for libel, Senator Schoeppel asserted that "many of the questions" he had raised against Mr. Chapman were "still unanswered."

At the time of the original accusations, the Secretary had vainly challenged the Senator to repeat them outside Congress and thus outside his immunity from legal action.

Told of Senator Schoeppel's new attack on Mr. Chapman, Senator Joseph C. O'Mahoney, Democrat of Wyoming, whose Senate Interior Committee after investigation had declared the Schoeppel accusations to be "exploded," told reporters there would be no further inquiry.

At the time the Secretary was on the stand in public hearing, Senator O'Mahoney recalled Senator Schoeppel had been invited to cross-examine the Cabinet officer, but had offered only "a deafening silence."

Senator McCarthy based his assault on the fact that the Taft-Hartley Act denies the services of the National Labor Relations Board to any union, the heads of which do not swear that they are not Communists.

"NEVADA, UTAH VOTE," FEBRUARY 27, 1951

The ratification of the Twenty-second Amendment in 1951 established a two-term limit for U.S. presidents. Drafted in reaction to the unprecedented four elections won by FDR, the amendment did not apply to President Truman. Nevertheless, he decided not to run for reelection in 1952.

FEBRUARY 27, 1951
NEVADA, UTAH VOTE

Proposal Becomes Law Automatically as Two Legislatures Approve

POLITICAL EFFECTS WIDE

President After 2d Election Would Have Less Control—'Changing Horses' Possible

By ROBERT F. WHITNEY

Special to *The New York Times.*

WASHINGTON, Feb. 26—The Constitution of the United States was amended tonight to forbid any President from being elected for more than two terms or from being elected more than once if he had served in excess of two years of his predecessor's term.

The amendment will not apply to President Truman. He may run again for his second elected term in the Presidential election of 1932 or in future campaigns, should his party wish to nominate him.

It was the Twenty-second Amendment to the Constitution and its ratification became complete with the approval of the Legislature of the State of Nevada providing the needed thirty-six states, or three-quarters' approval. Earlier in the day Utah's lawmakers had backed it as the thirty-fifth state.

It was eighteen years since the Constitution had been changed. Then the ratification was that of the Twenty-first Amendment repealing National Prohibition Dec. 5, 1933. The dry law repeal was initiated by President Roosevelt and completed in the first year of his first term.

Inspired by Roosevelt

It was President Roosevelt who "inspired" the Twenty-second Amendment by his election four times to the Presidency. The Eightieth Congress, in which the Republicans gained control for the first time since President Hoover's term, started the action on the opening day, the third of January, 1947.

- -

"REPUBLICANS CALL FOR FULL INQUIRY ON TRUMAN POLICY," APRIL 17, 1951

As the Korean War continued in the winter of 1951, Allied Commander Gen. Douglas MacArthur urged an attack upon China, which had entered the war to assist North Korea. This recommendation conflicted with the Truman administration's policy, and when MacArthur pressed his own views (including in a letter to the House minority leader, Republican Joseph Martin of Massachusetts, who released it for public distribution), the president relieved MacArthur of his command. Truman faced much public criticism for his action, and Republicans in Congress held hearings to review the decision as well as Truman's Korean War policies. But MacArthur had violated the fundamental constitutional principle of civilian control of the military, and history has vindicated Truman's decision.

APRIL 17, 1951
REPUBLICANS CALL FOR FULL INQUIRY ON TRUMAN POLICY
Senators Seek to Investigate Foreign and Military Phases in Clash Over MacArthur

TWO DEMOCRATS CONCUR

Welcome Move for Review—House Affirms Plan to Hear General on Thursday

By WILLIAM S. WHITE

Special to The New York Times

WASHINGTON, April 16—Senate Republicans demanded today an investigation of all the Truman Administration's foreign and military policies as a consequence of President Truman's dismissal of General of the Army Douglas MacArthur from his Far East commands.

The House of Representatives unanimously agreed to meet jointly with the Senate next Thursday to hear an address by the General. In this he will be free to speak over the head of the Commander in Chief, Mr. Truman, who broke him for rejecting the highest Administration policy in Asia.

General MacArthur will talk from a dais in the House chamber ordinarily reserved for the most important messages to Congress of the President himself.

The action of the House was moved by the Democratic floor leader, Representative John W. McCormack of Massachusetts, and carried without objection. It would make unnecessary the adoption of pending formal Republican resolutions asking General MacArthur to come before Congress.

The Senate was in recess, however, and it was possible that it might go through the motion tomorrow of approving the accomplished fact of the House's invitation. The Senate, in any case, is bound to participate.

Move for Inquiry

While the Democratic leaders were acting to bring General MacArthur to the Congressional rostrum without further controversy, the Senate Republicans were moving for the most important Congressional inquiry since that of 1945 into the Pearl Harbor disaster.

Meeting in the organization of all Senate Republicans that is called the Conference, they also raised new suggestions of a possible attempt later to oust President Truman by the process of impeachment, or indictment, by a simple majority vote of the House and a trial in the Senate. There a conviction would require a two-thirds majority of all Senators voting.

No observer considered any impeachment action to be more than remotely possible. The renewal of the suggestion simply reflected the great partisan bitterness still sweeping Congress.

A full-scale Congressional investigation of the foreign and military policies of the Administration, however, seemed entirely possible, and some sort of inquiry was certain.

"HE BARS ANY DRAFT," MARCH 30, 1952

President Truman announced that he would not seek reelection at the Democrats' 1952 Jefferson-Jackson Day dinner. The president's approval ratings were low, in large part because of the stalemated Korean War, and Truman actually lost the New Hampshire primary to Tennessee senator Estes Kefauver. Although primaries were not decisive in candidate selection at the time, the results were disappointing for Truman.

MARCH 30, 1952
HE BARS ANY DRAFT

President Also Maps the Party's Strategy, Says It Can Win Again

ASSAILS G.O.P. DRIVE

Lashes 'Dinosaurs' and 'Loud Talkers' Among the Republicans

By W. H. LAWRENCE

Special to The New York Times

WASHINGTON, March 29—President Truman dramatically announced tonight that he would not be a candidate for re-election and would not accept the nomination if he were drafted by the Democratic convention.

He made the announcement in almost dead-pan fashion toward the end of his speech before the 5,300 Democrats attending the party's traditional $100-a-plate Jefferson-Jackson Day dinner in the National Guard Armory here.

Following is the text of the statement interpolated into his prepared speech:

"I shall not be a candidate for re-election. I have served my country long and I think efficiently and honestly. I shall not accept a renomination. I do not feel that it is my duty to spend another four years in the White House."

The audience was taken completely by surprise by the announcement since there had been no indication anywhere in the earlier part of his speech nor in the advance word given to highest officials on his staff that he intended at this point to bow out of the 1952 political campaign.

"Oh no, oh no," shouted a few people on the floor.

Statement Total Surprise

But there was less demonstration than might have been expected because the huge crowd was taken totally by surprise.

Many of those in the audience appeared not to have heard or understood the import of Mr. Truman's statement. Others simply were stunned.

As soon as he had made his matter-of-fact disclaimer of any intentions to run again, Mr. Truman hurried on to finish the rest of the speech. The crowd applauded, not more vigorously than might have been expected, and the President hurriedly left the hall.

One man sitting near him said that the President's announcement, in long hand, rested on the speaker's rostrum alongside the typescript of his prepared speech.

The President inserted his statement just after he had declared that the record his administration had made would be the one on which the Democratic nominee would have to run "whoever the Democratic nominee . . . may be this year."

As the President left the armory he was stopped by reporters who asked, "Is this decision subject to any change at all?"

Any Change Ruled Out

"None whatsoever," Mr. Truman replied.

Mrs. Truman, who was with him, was asked whether she agreed with the decision.

"Of course," she said, "anything he says goes."

"SUPREME COURT VOIDS STEEL SEIZURE, 6 TO 3; HOLDS TRUMAN USURPED POWERS OF CONGRESS; WORKERS AGAIN STRIKE AS MILLS ARE RETURNED," JUNE 3, 1952

When U.S. steel workers threatened to go on strike in spring 1952, President Truman ordered his commerce secretary to seize control of the steel mills, declaring that the demands of the Korean War authorized the chief executive to prevent a labor stoppage. But the Supreme Court disagreed, ruling 6–3 in *Youngstown Sheet and Tube Co. v. Sawyer* that Congress had explicitly prohibited such presidential action.

JUNE 3, 1952
SUPREME COURT VOIDS STEEL SEIZURE, 6 TO 3; HOLDS TRUMAN USURPED POWERS OF CONGRESS; WORKERS AGAIN STRIKE AS MILLS ARE RETURNED

BLACK GIVES RULING

President Cannot Make Law in Good or Bad Times, Majority Says

VINSON IS DISSENTER

Rejects Idea Executive Is 'Messenger Boy' in Crisis—Steel Curbed

By JOSEPH A. LOFTUS

Special to The New York Times

WASHINGTON, June 2—The Supreme Court of the United States ruled, 6 to 3, today that President Truman's seizure of the steel industry to avert a strike violated the Constitution by usurping the legislative powers reserved to Congress.

The President bowed promptly by directing Secretary of Commerce Charles Sawyer to release the properties to their private owners, and the United Steelworkers of America, C.I.O., went on strike.

As a result of the walkout the Government ordered a halt in deliveries of steel from retail warehouses to consumer goods producers in an effort to conserve steel for defense needs.

Authorities said the action was directed at preventing a drain on warehouses by buyers who usually got their steel at the mills. Manufacturers who ordinarily receive steel from warehouses will continue to do so, they added. No order was issued against steel exports.

The Supreme Court justices who voted to uphold District Judge David A. Pine's order dispossessing the Government were: Hugo L. Black, Felix Frankfurter, William O. Douglas, Robert H. Jackson, Harold H. Burton and Tom C. Clark.

Dissenting were: Chief Justice Fred M. Vinson and Justices Stanley F. Reed and Sherman Minton.

Founding Fathers' Action Cited

The court ruled in effect that when the President seized the steel mills he seized the lawmaking power, because only Congress could authorize the taking of private property for public use.

"The Constitution did not subject this law-making power of Congress to Presidential or military supervision or control," said the opinion of the court, written by Justice Black.

"The founders of this nation entrusted the lawmaking power to the Congress alone in both good and bad times," it added. "It would do no good to recall the historical events, the fears of power and the hopes for freedom that lay behind their choice. Such a review would but confirm our holding that this seizure order cannot stand."

Chief Justice Vinson, writing a vigorous dissent, declared that the President's action to keep steel flowing was warranted by the world emergency.

"History bears out the genius of the founding fathers, who created a Government subject to law but not left subject to inertia when vigor and initiative are required," the Chief Justice wrote.

THE PRESIDENCY OF **DWIGHT D. EISENHOWER**

JANUARY 20, 1953 – JANUARY 20, 1961

Dwight David Eisenhower's presidency expanded the containment strategy of the Truman administration and aimed to maintain U.S. strength in the cold war without drastically increasing defense expenditures. A World War II military hero, Eisenhower was an overwhelmingly popular president who was well known in the United States and abroad when he took office. Eisenhower maintained his popularity during his eight years as president by publicly evincing little interest in political matters while privately working carefully behind the scenes, particularly in foreign affairs, to promote his policies. Despite his military background, Eisenhower keenly appreciated the importance of conserving resources for domestic programs while also protecting U.S. national security interests.

The third of seven sons, Eisenhower grew up in Abilene, Kansas. His parents, David and Ida, had lived there previously, but then moved briefly to Texas, where Eisenhower was born. Eisenhower's birth name was David Dwight, but the order was switched to Dwight David when he enrolled at West Point. He always was known popularly as "Ike."

Given his family's modest means, Eisenhower could not afford college. He successfully applied for a congressional nomination to the U.S. Military Academy at West Point, which provided full tuition and expenses for students in return for military service. Eisenhower played football at West Point and was known more for his demerits than for academic performance, despite his keen intellectual abilities. He graduated sixty-fifth in a class of 164 in 1915.

Eisenhower did not see combat during World War I, as the army made him a training instructor within the United States. After the war, Eisenhower served in the Panama Canal Zone, where he learned about military strategy under the tutelage of Gen. Fox Conner. With Conner's endorsement, Eisenhower was selected to attend the army's advanced strategy program, the Command and General Staff College at Fort Leavenworth, Kansas, and he graduated first in his class in 1926. In the 1930s Eisenhower became an aide to Gen. Douglas MacArthur, the army chief of staff. Major Eisenhower accompanied MacArthur to the Philippines in 1935 and was promoted to lieutenant colonel.

"Tsk Tsk — Somebody Should Do Something About That"

Source: The Herb Block Foundation

Eisenhower's superior skills as a military leader propelled his meteoric rise to the highest levels of the army during World War II. He led the War Plans Division, which was responsible for strategic planning, in the War Department in 1942. He was appointed commanding general of the European Theater of Operations, and he led the Allied invasion of North Africa in late 1942. In 1943 he became a full general and directed Allied invasions of Sicily and Italy. Impressed with Eisenhower's performance, President Franklin D. Roosevelt made him supreme commander of all Allied forces in Europe. Eisenhower commanded the historic D-Day invasion of Normandy, France, on June 6, 1944, and he accepted Germany's surrender in May 1945.

After the war, Eisenhower commanded the U.S. occupation zone in Germany and then served as army chief of staff. He retired from the service in 1948 and became president of Columbia University. But he returned to active duty a few years later when President Harry S. Truman asked him to become the first supreme commander of North Atlantic Treaty Organization (NATO) forces in Europe. Eisenhower served in this position until mid-1952, when he stepped down to run for president.

THE 1952 PRESIDENTIAL ELECTION

After his triumphant return from World War II, Eisenhower was widely viewed as a presidential contender, and Republicans and Democrats alike courted him in 1948. Eisenhower would not consider a presidential run then, but changed his mind four years later. The stalemated Korean War and skyrocketing defense budget undoubtedly influenced his decision. Eisenhower declared his Republican affiliation in January 1952, resigned his NATO command a few months later, and won his party's nomination on the first convention ballot, with Sen. Richard M. Nixon of California selected as his running mate.

President Truman had decided not to seek another term, and the Democratic Party nominated Illinois governor Adlai E. Stevenson II on the third convention ballot and chose Sen. John J. Sparkman of Alabama to complete the ticket. Both parties waged vigorous campaigns, but Eisenhower's popularity combined with a pledge shortly before the election to go to Korea if elected to evaluate the war situation himself brought a Republican victory. Eisenhower won with nearly 34 million popular votes to Stevenson's 27 million,

and 442 Electoral College votes in 39 states to 89 votes in 9 states for Stevenson.

THE EISENHOWER ADMINISTRATION (FIRST TERM)

Eisenhower's ten-member cabinet reflected the business and political interests of the Republican Party. Foreign policy elder John Foster Dulles of Washington, D.C., was appointed secretary of state, and General Motors president Charles E. Wilson of Michigan was selected as secretary of defense. Steel executive George M. Humphrey of Ohio became treasury secretary, and New York attorney Herbert Brownell Jr. was chosen for attorney general. Eisenhower selected one Democrat for his cabinet, Labor Secretary Martin P. Durkin of Illinois (who served for less than one year), and one woman, Oveta C. Hobby of Texas, who headed the newly created Department of Health, Education, and Welfare.

The president and First Lady Mamie Eisenhower had been married for more than forty-five years when they came to the White House. They had two sons, one of whom died as a young child. Their younger son, John, an Army officer, served in the White House during his father's presidency. John Eisenhower's son, David, would later marry Julie Nixon, daughter of Eisenhower's vice president (and future president) Richard Nixon.

President Dwight D. Eisenhower practicing his golf game on the White House lawn in 1955. He did this almost every day except Wednesday—when he played a full round at a Maryland Country Club.

Source: The New York Times

QUICK FACTS ON DWIGHT D. EISENHOWER

BIRTH	October 14, 1890, Denison, Texas
EDUCATION	United States Military Academy, West Point, New York
FAMILY	Wife: Marie "Mamie" Geneva Doud Eisenhower Children: Dwight Doud Eisenhower, John Sheldon Doud Eisenhower
WHITE HOUSE PET	Dog
PARTY	Republican
PREPRESIDENTIAL CAREER (SELECTED)	Service in Panama Canal Zone, 1922–1924 Graduation from Command and General Staff College, Fort Leavenworth, Kansas, 1926 Army War College, 1928 Executive officer to assistant secretary of war, 1929–1933 Assistant to Gen. Douglas MacArthur; in Philippines, 1933–1939 Chief, War Plans Division, Department of War General Staff, 1942 Commanding general, European Theater of Operations, 1942 Commander in chief of Allied forces in North Africa, 1942 Promotion to full general, 1943 Directs invasions of Sicily and Italy, 1943 Supreme commander, Allied Expeditionary Force, 1943 Directs D-Day invasion of Normandy, France, 1944 Promotion to General of the Army 1944 Accepts surrender of German Army, 1945 Commander of U.S. occupation forces in Europe, 1945 U.S. Army chief of staff, 1945–1948 Retirement from active duty army, 1948 President of Columbia University, 1948–1950 First commander of NATO forces in Europe, 1950–1952 Resignation from army, 1952

MAJOR ISSUES (FIRST TERM)

Perhaps the most significant aspect of President Eisenhower's leadership was its understated style. Eisenhower firmly believed that he had a responsibility to build public confidence and avoid divisive policy debates. His carefully cultivated public image suggested that he was more interested in golf and fishing than politics, but behind the scenes, Eisenhower was an activist president, at least in foreign policy. When Republican senator Joseph R. McCarthy of Wisconsin alleged that Communist spies had infiltrated the government and the army, Eisenhower succeeded in diminishing McCarthy's influence without attacking him publicly. Eisenhower also adapted his military system of operations to White House governance, creating a chief of staff and special assistant for national security affairs (today's national security adviser), and holding weekly National Security Council and cabinet meetings to assist his policymaking.

In foreign policy, Eisenhower modified the containment strategy of the Truman administration to rely on nuclear deterrence to prevent Soviet aggression, which enabled him to control defense spending through lower expenditures for conventional weapons. Critics claimed that this "massive retaliation" strategy would lead the United States into nuclear war, but Eisenhower was confident that his skillful leadership would avoid such an outcome. And his foreign policy record was impressive: He successfully negotiated an armistice agreement to end the Korean War in 1953; he

PRESIDENTIAL TERMS	January 20, 1953–January 20, 1957
	January 20, 1957–January 20, 1961
VICE PRESIDENT	Richard M. Nixon
SELECTED EVENTS	Execution of spies Julius and Ethel Rosenberg (1953)
	End of Korean War (1953)
	Sen. Joseph R. McCarthy's hearings investigating U.S. Army (1954)
	U.S. Supreme Court ruling for racial desegregation of schools (1954)
	Geneva agreement to end war in Indochina (1954)
	Creation of Southeast Asia Treaty Organization (1954)
	Senate censure of Senator McCarthy (1954)
	United States guarantees defense of Formosa (Taiwan) against aggression from Communist China (1955)
	Suffers heart attack (1955)
	Federal-Aid Highway Act (1956)
	Suez Canal crisis (1956)
	Eisenhower Doctrine (1957)
	Civil Rights Act (1957)
	Sends federal troops to desegregate high school in Little Rock, Arkansas (1957)
	Launching of Soviet satellite Sputnik (1957)
	Suffers stroke (1957)
	Economic recession (1957–1958)
	U.S. intervention in Lebanon (1958)
	Creation of National Aeronautics and Space Administration (1958)
	National Defense Education Act (1958)
	Alaska and Hawaii admitted to the Union (1959)
	U-2 spy plane shot down over Soviet Union (1960)
	Collapse of Paris peace summit (1960)
	United States ends diplomatic ties with Cuba (1961)
POSTPRESIDENCY	Published two-volume history of presidential years in 1963 and 1965
	Published memoir, 1967
DEATH	March 28, 1969, Washington, D.C.

kept the United States out of war in Indochina in 1954; and he opposed the 1956 intervention by Great Britain, France, and Israel in response to Egypt's seizure of the Suez Canal.

In domestic policy, Eisenhower exercised more cautious leadership. He was primarily interested in controlling spending, particularly for defense, and he achieved a budget surplus three times during his presidency. He nominated California governor Earl Warren to become chief justice of the United States, and in 1954 Warren led the Court to declare racially segregated schools unconstitutional. Eisenhower was not a proponent of civil rights initiatives, but he recognized the Court's authority and implemented its decision when a challenge arose in his second term. Eisenhower was constrained in domestic policy partly by an opposition Congress, as the Democrats won control of both chambers in 1954.

The 1956 Presidential Election

The 1956 presidential race expanded upon the victories of 1952. Eisenhower easily won his party's nomination, and Vice President Nixon remained on the ticket, even though Eisenhower initially had some interest in replacing him. They again faced Governor Stevenson, who ran this time with Sen. Estes Kefauver of Tennessee. Eisenhower won with more than 35.5 million popular votes and 457 Electoral College votes in 41 states to nearly 26 million popular votes and 73 Electoral College votes in 7 states for Stevenson.

THE EISENHOWER ADMINISTRATION (SECOND TERM)

Eisenhower's second-term cabinet included several new members, particularly in the top positions. Robert B. Anderson of Texas became treasury secretary in 1957, and William P. Rogers of New York was appointed attorney general in 1958. Neil H. McElroy became defense secretary in 1957 and served for two years, after which Thomas S. Gates Jr. of Pennsylvania was appointed to the position. Secretary of State Dulles continued through much of Eisenhower's second term, but resigned due to ill health in 1959 and died shortly thereafter. Eisenhower then chose Christian A. Herter of Massachusetts for the post. Agriculture Secretary Ezra T. Benson of Utah had the distinction of serving throughout Eisenhower's eight years in office, and Labor Secretary James P. Mitchell of New Jersey served nearly as long.

MAJOR ISSUES (SECOND TERM)

The most contentious issue in Eisenhower's second term was defense policy. After the Soviet Union sent an artificial satellite into space in late 1957, many Americans questioned whether the Soviets would soon develop intercontinental missile capabilities, leading to fears of an imminent "missile gap" in the cold war. In fact, the United States was well ahead in missile production and capability—as Eisenhower knew due to secret reconnaissance flights over the Soviet Union—but he did not engage in public debate about U.S. military strength. Consequently, criticism of Eisenhower's efforts to control defense spending increased, particularly as his term came to a close.

In domestic policy, Eisenhower signed the Civil Rights Act of 1957, which established the Civil Rights Division in the Justice Department to investigate race-based obstacles to voting. The law also created the Civil Rights Commission to examine discrimination in voting. That same year, Eisenhower deployed federal troops to enforce the desegregation of Central High School in Little Rock, Arkansas.

In foreign policy, Eisenhower used nuclear deterrence to keep Communist China from seizing small islands under the control of Chinese Nationalists, and this strategy brought the United States close to war in 1955 and 1958. In summer 1958 Eisenhower sent U.S. troops to Lebanon to assist the government in battling insurgents. Perhaps Eisenhower's greatest disappointment as president was his failure to improve U.S.-Soviet relations. Eisenhower and his counterparts in Great Britain, France, and the Soviet Union had met in Geneva, Switzerland, in 1955 to discuss common interests, and the president had hosted Soviet leader Nikita S. Khrushchev at the presidential retreat Camp David (named for Eisenhower's grandson) in 1959. But in May 1960, just weeks before the two leaders were scheduled to meet in Paris, a U.S. spy plane was shot down over the Soviet Union, and Khrushchev consequently refused to pursue further discussions.

The first president to be limited to two terms by the Twenty-second Amendment, Eisenhower endorsed Nixon's candidacy. Nixon faced heavy criticism for the Eisenhower administration's defense policies, which Democrats considered insufficient to contain Soviet aggression. He lost the race to Democratic senator John F. Kennedy of Massachusetts. President Eisenhower retired to his Gettysburg, Pennsylvania, farm, where he raised cattle and wrote several books. In the early 1960s Eisenhower also provided advice to President Kennedy during foreign policy crises upon request. After suffering several heart attacks in the late 1960s, Eisenhower died in March 1969, just two months after Richard Nixon was inaugurated as president.

"EISENHOWER NOMINATED ON THE FIRST BALLOT," JULY 12, 1952

Although both the Democratic and Republican Parties had courted Gen. Dwight D. Eisenhower as a potential presidential candidate, he still faced obstacles to his nomination when he entered the race for the Republican nomination. Sen. Robert A. Taft of Ohio, a three-time presidential candidate (and son of former president William Howard Taft), mounted a stiff challenge to Eisenhower's candidacy. Eisenhower narrowly won the nomination on the first convention ballot, and he recognized that unifying the party would be his first responsibility, seeking—and receiving—Senator Taft's support.

JULY 12, 1952

EISENHOWER NOMINATED ON THE FIRST BALLOT; SENATOR NIXON CHOSEN AS HIS RUNNING MATE; GENERAL PLEDGES 'TOTAL VICTORY' CRUSADE

REVISED VOTE 845

Minnesota Leads Switch to Eisenhower and Others Join Rush

BUT SOME HOLD OUT

First Call of the States Gave General 595 to 500 for Taft

By W. H. LAWRENCE

Special to The New York Times

CONVENTION BUILDING in Chicago, July 11—General of the Army Dwight D. Eisenhower won a hard-fought first-ballot nomination today as the Republican candidate for President and Senator Richard M. Nixon of California was chosen by acclamation as his running mate for the Vice Presidency.

The former Supreme Allied Commander in Europe went before the 1,206 Republican delegates tonight to accept the nomination and pledge that he would lead "a great crusade" for "total victory" against a Democratic Administration he described as wasteful, arrogant and corrupt and too long in power. He said he would keep "nothing in reserve" in his drive to put a Republican in the White House for the first time since March 4, 1933.

The Republican convention adjourned finally at 8:21 P.M., Central daylight time (9:21, New York time) after it had heard Senator Nixon accept the Vice-Presidential nomination. He pledged a "fighting campaign" to insure election not only of a Republican President, but also a House and Senate controlled by his party.

Bitterly Divided Convention

General Eisenhower won in a bitterly divided Republican convention. In the last week the general had taken leadership in the contest from Senator Robert A. Taft of Ohio, the chief party spokesman in Congress, who was making his third unsuccessful bid for nomination to the office once held by his father, William Howard Taft.

Victory came for General Eisenhower on the first ballot. The official results were 845 for General Eisenhower, 280 for Senator Taft, 77 for Gov. Earl Warren of California, and 4 for General of the Army Douglas MacArthur.

But that figure did not represent truly the voting sentiments of these delegates as they faced the crucial and final showdown between General Eisenhower and Senator Taft.

When the first roll-call of the states was completed, General Eisenhower had 595 votes—nine short of the required majority of 604—and Senator Taft had 500. The balance of power rested with favorite-son candidates, such as Governor Warren, who had 81 votes, and Harold E. Stassen, former Minnesota Governor, with 20. General MacArthur had received only 10 votes.

Others Then Changed

And while Governor Warren's California delegation held firm for him in the hope of a deadlock, Mr. Stassen's Minnesota delegates, no longer bound because he had received less than 10 per cent of the vote, broke away and cast nineteen votes for General Eisenhower before a first ballot result could be announced.

The nineteen, added to the General's previous total, gave him 614, or ten more than a majority. Then other states began to change their votes in order to be recorded on the side of the winner.

Thus, while General Eisenhower's nomination later was made unanimous on the motion of principal backers of Senator Taft and Governor Warren, who pledged the support for their principals to the nominee, it was made clear that General Eisenhower was the choice of a divided convention, and that one of his first tasks would be to restore party unity and heal the deep wounds inflicted during the fierce competition for the nomination.

To that end, General Eisenhower's first act, after he knew he had won, was to call on Senator Taft to ask—and receive—from him assurances that the Ohioan would campaign actively for the Eisenhower-Nixon ticket.

The Republicans who picked the 61-year-old commander of the Allied invasion of Europe and the 39-year-old California Senator believed this to be their best chance of victory over the Democrats in twenty years, and their only fear was that continued bitterness over the outcome would make it possible for the Democrats to run to six their consecutive string of victories in national elections.

"RACE IS CONCEDED," NOVEMBER 5, 1952, AND "OUTLOOK FOR THE REPUBLICAN PARTY," NOVEMBER 9, 1952

The 1952 general election was much less contentious than the Republican nomination. Eisenhower easily defeated Democrat Adlai E. Stevenson II, becoming the first victorious Republican presidential candidate in twenty-four years. *The New York Times* compared Eisenhower's "landslide victory" to the historic election of Democrat Franklin D. Roosevelt in 1932.

NOVEMBER 5, 1952
RACE IS CONCEDED

Virginia and Florida Go to the General as Do Illinois and Ohio
SWEEP IS NATION-WIDE
Victor Calls for Unity and Thanks Governor for Pledging Support
By ARTHUR KROCK

Gen. Dwight D. Eisenhower was elected President of the United States yesterday in an electoral vote landslide and with an emphatic popular majority that probably will give his party a small margin of control in the House of Representatives but may leave the Senate as it is—forty-nine Democrats, forty-seven Republicans and one independent.

Senator Richard M. Nixon of California was elected Vice President.

The Democratic Presidential candidate, Gov. Adlai E. Stevenson of Illinois, shortly after midnight conceded his defeat by a record turnout of American voters.

At 4 A.M. today the Republican candidate had carried states with a total of 431 electors, or 165 more than the 266 required for the selection of a President. The Democratic candidate seemed sure of 69, with 31 doubtful in Kentucky, Louisiana and Tennessee.

General Eisenhower's landslide victory, both in electoral and popular votes, was nation-wide in its pattern, extending from New England—where Massachusetts and Rhode Island broke their Democratic voting habits of many years—down the Eastern seaboard to Maryland, Virginia and Florida and westward to almost every state between the coasts, including California.

General Wins Illinois

The Republican candidate took Illinois, Governor Stevenson's home state. In South Carolina, though he lost its electors on a technicality, he won a majority of the voters. And, completing the first successful Republi-

can invasion of the States of the former Confederacy, the General carried Texas and broke the one-party system in the South.

The personal popularity that enabled him to defeat Senator Robert A. Taft of Ohio in the Republican primaries in Texas, and present him with the issue on which he defeated the Senator for the Republican nomination, crushed the regular Democratic organization of Texas that was led by Speaker Sam Rayburn of the House of Representatives and had the blessing of former Vice President John N. Garner.

The tide that bore General Eisenhower to the White House, though it did not give him a comfortable working majority in either the national House or the Senate (the Democrats may still nominally control the machinery of that branch), probably increased the number of Republican governors beyond the present twenty-five.

"My fellow citizens have made their choice and I gladly accept it," said Governor Stevenson at 1:46 A.M., Eastern standard time, and he asked all citizens to unite behind the President-elect. The defeated candidate said he had sent a telegram of congratulation to General Eisenhower.

At 2:05 A.M., from the Grand Ballroom of the Commodore Hotel, General Eisenhower said he recognized the weight of his new responsibilities and that he would not give "short weight" in their execution. He also urged "unity" and announced he had sent a telegram of thanks to the Democratic candidate for his promise of support.

NOVEMBER 9, 1952
EDITORIAL
OUTLOOK FOR THE REPUBLICAN PARTY
By W. H. LAWRENCE
Special to The New York Times

WASHINGTON, Nov. 8—For President-elect Eisenhower, one of the more gratifying results of Tuesday's landslide victory was that it applied the final binding of cement to the structure of Republican party unity for which Candidate Eisenhower had labored so hard, often under discouraging and difficult circumstances.

The party is now united after an election for the first time in twenty years. Victory always is conducive to unity behind the winner, just as defeat quite naturally spawns division and criticism of the man who led the losing cause.

Whatever may have been the post-convention and pre-election differences between General Eisenhower and his closest associates and the other elements of the Republican party, these are now, for a time at any rate, submerged by the flood of ballots from across the continent that testified that the people had given a strong vote of confidence to him personally, and not necessarily to the party he led.

The situation is, in many ways, comparable to that which existed in 1932 after the then President-elect Franklin D. Roosevelt had led a divided Democratic party to a decisive triumph at the polls.

· ·

"EISENHOWER, HERE, CONFIDENT OF SPEEDING KOREA SOLUTION; CALLS HIS TRIP A 'BEGINNING,'" DECEMBER 15, 1952

President-elect Eisenhower made good on a campaign promise to visit Korea to make a first-hand assessment of the stalemated war. Several cabinet appointees accompanied him, which provided the opportunity for Eisenhower to discuss his policy agenda with his new advisers while en route from Guam to Hawaii on the cruiser *Helena*. In early January 1953 Eisenhower also held a pre-inaugural cabinet meeting, which again permitted him to promote his policy initiatives and build a cohesive advisory team.

DECEMBER 15, 1952
EISENHOWER, HERE, CONFIDENT OF SPEEDING KOREA SOLUTION; CALLS HIS TRIP A 'BEGINNING'
GENERAL HOPEFUL
He Hints at Measures to 'Induce' Reds to Want Peace Also
PLANS 'POSITIVE' PROGRAM
Stresses Training of the R.O.K. and 'Problems of Supply'—Praises Allied Armies
By LEO EGAN

Gen. Dwight D. Eisenhower returned to New York yesterday from his 22,000-mile visit to war-ravaged Korea and voiced confidence that a satisfactory solution of the struggle there could be speeded by taking measures that would "induce" Communist aggressors to want peace also.

Looking fit and rested after his sixteen-day journey, the President-elect stepped from the Military Air Transport

Service Constellation that flew him back from Hawaii at the Marine Air Terminal of La Guardia Airport at 2:03 P.M.

He distributed a brief prepared statement on his trip to reporters who met the plane and supplemented it with a short extemporaneous talk for the benefit of those witnessing the scene on television or listening on radios.

Afterward he was driven directly to his home at 60 Morningside Drive. He is scheduled to return to his desk in his headquarters at the Hotel Commodore today.

Praises Troops in Korea

In the prepared statement distributed at La Guardia Airport, General Eisenhower warned that there was no simple formula for achieving a "swift victorious end" to the Korean war. He added that his first-hand look at the situation there, and the conferences held aboard the cruiser *Helena,* which took him from Guam to Hawaii, would prove very helpful in establishing a positive program to deal with the global struggle between communism and free governments.

"This journey marks not the end but the beginning of a new effort to conclude honorably this phase of the global struggle," the statement continued.

"This is not the moment to state more than that resolve. For we face an enemy whom we cannot hope to impress by words, however eloquent, but only by deeds—executed under circumstances of our own choosing."

The statement reported that the American Army in Korea was "as fine a fighting force of its size as our nation has ever assembled." It is well equipped for the Korean climate and possessed of high morale, his statement continued. Moreover, "the spirit of unification among the branches of our armed forces is superlative," he declared.

· ·

" 'INTERNATIONALIST' INAUGURAL ACCLAIMED IN BOTH PARTIES," JANUARY 21, 1953

Eisenhower's first inaugural address focused on foreign policy and reflected his agreement with much of his Democratic predecessor's containment strategy. Unlike Republicans who favored a more isolationist approach, Eisenhower firmly committed the United States to an internationalist policy. He endorsed collective security and the importance of foreign alliances, which was not surprising, given his role as commander of NATO military forces in the Truman administration. But Eisenhower's differences with Truman's foreign policy leadership soon would become evident.

JANUARY 21, 1953
'INTERNATIONALIST' INAUGURAL ACCLAIMED IN BOTH PARTIES
By WILLIAM S. WHITE
Special to The New York Times

WASHINGTON, Jan. 20—Congress responded with general warmth and in many cases with profound bipartisan approval today to President Eisenhower's Inaugural Address. There was an all but visible gathering behind him of great blocs of members of both houses, Democrat and Republican alike, in his strong, somber pledge to carry this nation forward in full unity with the free world.

His speech, though lacking specifications, was interpreted by many as one of the most internationalist ever delivered to the country—not excluding the addresses of Franklin D. Roosevelt and Harry S. Truman.

President Eisenhower thus was heard with what almost amounted to joy by all those in both parties who for years had fought for foreign aid and foreign association and foreign alliance.

Some of the Democrats privately and jubilantly twitted some in the isolationist or near-isolationist wing of the Republican party to show where in world affairs General Eisenhower differed in any great principle from Mr. Truman and Mr. Roosevelt.

The Senate Democratic Leader, Senator Lyndon B. Johnson of Texas, carried this theme into a public statement. Senator Johnson first had commented only that the Inaugural Address was "a dignified statement of the dreams and aspirations that motivate millions of people."

But, on encountering a small group of reporters in the Senate dining room, he added:

"It was a statement, and a very good statement, of Democratic programs of the last twenty years."

Senator Robert A. Taft of Ohio, the Republican Senate leader, declared formally:

"It was a great and inspiring beginning, a great and inspiring speech."

"President Revises Strategy Council," March 24, 1953

Upon taking office, Eisenhower made significant institutional changes in the office of the American presidency. He made greater use of the National Security Council (NSC) than Truman had, holding weekly meetings and establishing special staffs to prepare meeting agendas and implement decisions. He also created the position of special assistant for national security affairs to manage NSC decision making, a role that has evolved into the national security adviser, the president's top White House aide in foreign affairs.

MARCH 24, 1953
PRESIDENT REVISES STRATEGY COUNCIL
Sets Up New Planning Board Under Cutler and Enlarges National Security Panel
Special to The New York Times

WASHINGTON, March 23—President Eisenhower reorganized the staff and procedures of the National Security Council today to strengthen it for the mission of advising him on vital security issues during the world crisis.

The changes he made were these:

• Robert Cutler, former Boston lawyer and banker, now an administrative assistant to the President, was designated a special assistant to the President for National Security Affairs. He will be the principal executive officer of the council and chairman of its planning board.

• The former Senior Staff of the council was renamed the Planning Board, and it will meet three times weekly, instead of twice weekly.

• The Director of Defense Mobilization, when he is appointed, will attend all meetings of the council.

• The Secretary of the Treasury also will attend the weekly meetings of the council.

Procedure Under Truman

The attendance of the Secretary of the Treasury is not an innovation, however. President Truman had his Secretary of the Treasury, John W. Snyder, attend the meetings. The present Secretary is George M. Humphrey.

The statutory members of the council are the President, the Vice President, the Secretary of State, the Secre-

tary of Defense, the Director for Mutual Security and the chairman of the National Security Resources Board.

Thus the only real change in the composition of the council itself is in the requirement that the Director of Defense Mobilization shall attend, when he is appointed. He would substitute for the chairman of the National Security Resources Board, an office vacant for several months.

James C. Hagerty, the White House press secretary, said that there would be an announcement about the Resources Board later this week. It has been forecast, however, that the President will send to Congress a reorganization plan that will propose putting the board in the Office of Defense Mobilization, whose acting director is Arthur S. Flemming.

Other Leaders to Attend

Today's announcement said that others who would attend the Wednesday morning meetings of the council were General of the Army Omar N. Bradley, Chairman of the Joint Chiefs of Staff; Allan Dulles, Director of the Central Intelligence Agency, and C. D. Jackson, the President's special assistant for "cold war" planning (psychological warfare).

General Bradley and Gen. W. Bedell Smith, then the Director of the C.I.A., also attended the meetings during the Truman Administration. General Smith now is Under Secretary of State.

"Dulles Sets Goal of Instant Rebuff to Stop Aggressor," January 13, 1954

Perhaps the most significant change in national security strategy during the Eisenhower administration was the increased reliance on nuclear deterrence to prevent Communist aggression. Although the president was determined not to employ nuclear weapons, he was comfortable with using the threat of action to halt potential conflicts. Secretary of State John Foster Dulles described the strategy in a 1954 speech as the ability to show "a great capacity to retaliate, instantly, by means and at places of our own choosing," a doctrine popularly known as "massive retaliation."

JANUARY 13, 1954
DULLES SETS GOAL OF INSTANT REBUFF TO STOP AGGRESSOR
Aims at Prompt Retaliation at Sites of 'Own Choosing,' Not Local Defense
DEALS WITH REDS BARRED
Secretary, Honored at Dinner Here, Explains Adaptation of Military, Foreign Policy

John Foster Dulles, Secretary of State, said last night that the nation's military and foreign policy was being adapted to a basic decision: To confront any aggressor with "a great capacity to retaliate, instantly, by means and at places of our own choosing." The decision was made by the National Security Council, he said.

President Eisenhower's program seeks more effective and less costly security in cooperation with the allies of the United States "by placing more reliance on community deterrent power, and less dependence on local defensive power," Mr. Dulles said.

Speaking at a dinner given in his honor by the Council on Foreign Relations at the Hotel Pierre, Secretary Dulles promised continued efforts at negotiations with the Soviet Union on such issues as atomic energy, Germany, Austria and Korea.

But with the Berlin conference of the Big Four foreign ministers less than two weeks off, Secretary Dulles pledged there would be "no plan for a partnership division of world power with those who suppress freedom."

Dulles Hopeful on Peace

Mr. Dulles foresaw hope of peace because "there are limits to the power of any rulers indefinitely to suppress the human spirit." He reported signs that Soviet leaders were bending to their people's desire for more food, more household goods and more economic freedom.

The Secretary's speech, entitled "The Evolution of Foreign Policy," had been heralded by the State Department as a major statement. The address, which pulled together a review of the Eisenhower course, was broadcast nationally over the Du Mont television network, and rebroadcast later by the Mutual and National Broadcasting Company radio systems.

Many pre-Eisenhower foreign policies were "good," Mr. Dulles said. He cited aid to Greece and Turkey, the European Recovery Program, the Berlin airlift, United Nations resistance to attack in Korea and the building up of American and Western European armed strength.

But these were emergency actions, imposed on us by our enemies, Mr. Dulles said, and they were costly. He pictured new planning by President Eisenhower and his National Security Council, recognizing that there was no local defense that alone would contain the mighty land power of the Communist world.

"A potential aggressor must know that he cannot always prescribe battle conditions that suit him," Mr. Dulles said. "The way to deter aggression is for the free community to be willing and able to respond vigorously at places and with means of its own choosing."

"Conflict in Indo-China Is Vital to Free World," March 28, 1954

The United States came close to conflict in Vietnam in spring 1954. Vietnamese nationalists were fighting to overthrow colonial rule by France, which sought military support from its American ally. President Eisenhower did not send troops to assist the French in Dien Bien Phu, and the Vietnamese succeeded in gaining control of their country, though its partition would spark a new conflict.

> " Indo-China is a strategic, military and political keystone in Western efforts to contain communism in Asia. "

MARCH 28, 1954
CONFLICT IN INDO-CHINA IS VITAL TO FREE WORLD
France, U.S. Especially Are Playing For High Stakes in the War
By HANSON W. BALDWIN

The future of Indo-China, and perhaps of Southeast Asia, was hanging in the balance last week.

The continuing battle at Dienbienphu, now in its fifteenth day; American-French consultations in Washington; new evidences of war-weariness in Saigon and Paris, and the shadow of next month's Geneva conference on Far Eastern affairs—all emphasized the importance of Indo-China to current history.

Indo-China is a strategic, military and political keystone in Western efforts to contain communism in Asia and it is also a major factor in the politics and future complexion of Europe.

The approaches to Indo-China from China offer the best land gateways through the mountain ramparts of Southern China to Southeast Asia. Indo-China's seacoast helps to dominate the South China Sea.

Indo-China, along with Burma and Thailand—adjoining countries—are the three major rice-exporting nations of the Orient; if Communist China dominated them she would not only solve her own food problems, but would have an economic stranglehold upon Japan and other Asiatic nations.

Indo-China is contiguous to rich-but-weak Thailand and divided Burma, and via the Kra Isthmus to rubber-rich British Malaya, already torn by a protracted struggle against Communist guerrillas. And just across the Strait of Malacca from Singapore lies the oil and rubber of the Indonesian Republic, a new nation with an unstable and weak Government.

Symbol of Prestige

Indo-China is thus a political, an economic and a military keystone in an area of political and military weakness. But it has also become a symbol of the prestige and power of both France and the United States. The basic importance of Indo-China to France is, from the French view, neither economic in the form of profits nor political in the form of an anti-Communist bastion, but psychological. For French defeat in Indo-China, Paris fears, would have incalculable but dangerous effects upon French possessions and interests in Africa and throughout the world.

Though the United States has no such colonial interests, United States power and prestige in the Orient are almost equally involved. For the United States is now scheduled in the next fiscal year to pay some 78 per cent of the costs of the Indo-China war, and all the Orient knows that American war materials and technical assistance have been pitted against Russian and Communist Chinese aid to Ho Chi Minh. It is the Asian rampart in our policy of containment of communism; the breaching of this rampart would represent a prestige and strategic victory for the Chinese Communists and a defeat for the United States.

"1896 Ruling Upset," May 18, 1954, and "All God's Chillun," May 18, 1954

In 1954 the Supreme Court issued a landmark decision, *Brown v. Board of Education of Topeka,* which overturned racial segregation in U.S. schools. The unanimous decision decreed that "separate educational facilities are inherently unequal." Endorsing the decision, *The Times* evoked the Declaration of Independence, writing, "If men are equal, children are equal, too." The effect of the Court's decision would be muted for the near future, however, by its 1955 follow-up ruling, known as *Brown II.* The Court declared that school desegregation should take place "with all deliberate speed," a provision that states used to delay implementation.

MAY 18, 1954
1896 RULING UPSET

'Separate but Equal' Doctrine Held Out of Place in Education
By LUTHER A. HUSTON
Special to The New York Times

WASHINGTON, May 17—The Supreme Court unanimously outlawed today racial segregation in public schools.

Chief Justice Earl Warren read two opinions that put the stamp of unconstitutionality on school systems in twenty-one states and the District of Columbia where segregation is permissive or mandatory.

The court, taking cognizance of the problems involved in the integration of the school systems concerned, put over until the next term, beginning in October, the formulation of decrees to effectuate its 9-to-0 decision.

The opinions set aside the "separate but equal" doctrine laid down by the Supreme Court in 1896.

"In the field of public education," Chief Justice Warren said, "the doctrine of 'separate but equal' has no place. Separate educational facilities are inherently unequal."

He stated the question and supplied the answer as follows:

"We come then to the question presented: Does segregation of children in public schools solely on the basis of race, even though physical facilities and other 'tangible' factors may be equal, deprive the children of the minority group of equal educational opportunities? We believe that it does."

States Stressed Rights

The court's opinion does not apply to private schools. It is directed entirely at public schools. It does not affect the "separate but equal doctrine" as applied on railroads and other public carriers entirely within states that have such restrictions.

The principal ruling of the court was in four cases involving state laws. The states' right to operate separated schools had been argued before the court on two occasions by representatives of South Carolina, Virginia, Kansas and Delaware.

In these cases, consolidated in one opinion, the high court held that school segregation deprived Negroes of "the equal protection of the laws guaranteed by the Fourteenth Amendment."

MAY 18, 1954
EDITORIAL
"ALL GOD'S CHILLUN"

The Supreme Court took a long and careful time to arrive at the unanimous decision read yesterday by Chief Justice Warren that "segregation of children in the public schools solely on the basis of race, even though the physical facilities and other 'tangible' factors may be equal, deprives the children of the minority group of equal educational opportunities." But the decision reached was inevitable in the year 1954 regardless of what may have been the case in 1868, when the Fourteenth Amendment was adopted, or in 1896, when the "separate but equal" doctrine was laid down in the case of *Plessy v. Ferguson*.

In the cases under consideration the facilities offered to Negro children appeared to be equal, or were to be made equal, "with respect to buildings, curricula, qualifications and salaries of teachers and other 'tangible' factors," to those available to white children. The question, therefore, was more fundamental than in any previous case. It was whether Negro children segregated solely on the basis of race, even though offered equal facilities, were thereby deprived of equal educational opportunities. The court holds that such segregation does have "a detrimental effect upon the colored children," that it had "a tendency to retard [their] educational and mental development . . . and to deprive them of some of the benefits they would receive in a racially integrated school system."

The court, speaking through Chief Justice Warren, therefore concludes that "separate educational facilities are inherently unequal," that the plaintiffs and others similarly situated "are by reason of the segregation complained of deprived of the equal protection of the laws guaranteed by the Fourteenth Amendment." The due process clause is not involved. It is not needed.

What the court is saying, in its formal but not complicated style, is a part of what Eugene O'Neill said in a play called "All God's Chillun Got Wings." It is true, of course, that the court is not talking of that sort of "equality" which produces inter-racial marriages. It is not talking of a social system at all. It is talking of a system of human rights which is foreshadowed in the second paragraph of the Declaration of Independence, which stated "that all men are created equal." Mr. Jefferson and the others who were responsible for the Declaration did not intend to say that all men are equally intelligent, equally good or equal in height or weight. They meant to say that men were, and ought to be, equal before the law. If men are equal, children are equal, too. There is an even greater necessity in the case of children, whose opportunities to advance themselves and to be useful to the community may be lost if they do not have the right to be educated.

"Democrats Offer Harmony in Rule of 84th Congress," November 5, 1954

The Republican Party had won control of both the White House and Congress in 1952, but it did not maintain unified government for long. Democrats won majorities in both chambers of Congress in the 1954 midterm elections, and Eisenhower faced divided government for the rest of his presidency.

November 5, 1954
DEMOCRATS OFFER HARMONY IN RULE OF 84TH CONGRESS
Capture House by Margin of 29 Seats and Senate Probably by One Vote
By WILLIAM S. WHITE
Special to The New York Times

WASHINGTON, Nov. 4—A coalition Government, with the Democrats in narrow command of its legislative arm, is in prospect from Tuesday's bitterly contested Congressional elections.

The Democrats captured the House of Representatives by a margin of twenty-nine seats in a total of 435, results showed today.

They took the Senate as well—though by a single vote—barring some overturn in Oregon of Richard L. Neuberger's thin apparent victory over Senator Guy Cordon, the Republican incumbent, which would send to the Senate the first Democrat from Oregon in forty years.

Assuming that Mr. Neuberger's success survives a re-count, and the apparent victory in New Jersey of the liberal Republican, Clifford P. Case, does likewise, the Senate in the Eighty-fourth Congress meeting in January will be thus divided:

Democrats 48

Republicans 47

Independent, 1, Senator Wayne Morse of Oregon.

Senator Morse has said he would vote with the Democrats on organization of the Senate.

The old division had been:

Republicans 49

Democrats 46

Independent 1

Line-Up in the House

The new House stands:

Democrats 232

Republicans 203

The old House had stood on election morning:

Republicans, 218, one Republican vacancy; Democrats, 212, three Democratic vacancies; one Independent.

- -

"VOTE ON MCCARTHY," DECEMBER 5, 1954

Republican senator Joseph McCarthy's anti-Communist crusade came to a halt after the Senate censured him in 1954. The action marked a victory for Eisenhower, who privately opposed McCarthy's tactics, but used what has been described as a "hidden-hand" strategy to diminish the senator's influence.

DECEMBER 5, 1954
VOTE ON MCCARTHY
67 to 22 for Censure

The controversial career of Joseph R. McCarthy began on the night of Feb. 9, 1950, in Wheeling, W.Va., when he declared he had the names of 205 (later reduced to 57) Communists in the State Department.

A climax of his career came last Wednesday afternoon in the Senate of the United States when Vice President Nixon brought down his gavel and said: "The yeas and nays have been ordered and the clerk will call the roll." The roll-call, the first of several, was on the question of whether Senator McCarthy should be censured for bringing the Senate into disrepute.

The climactic week came after a year in which the Senate had been more occupied with Senator McCarthy's conduct than any other matter. There had been thirty-six days of hearings last spring on his row with the Army; three days of debate on the original motion of censure offered by Sena-

tor Ralph E. Flanders in August; nine days of hearings by the Select censure committee, headed by Arthur V. Watkins of Utah; nine days of initial debate on the censure recommendations by the Watkins committee, followed by a 10-day recess for treatment of Senator McCarthy's sore elbow.

Through four turbulent days last week, the anti-censure and pro-censure blocs fought it out along the lines that the debate has followed since its outset. The McCarthy forces took the floor again and again to reiterate the charge that Senator McCarthy was being punished for his strong campaign against communism and that the censure move was the outcome of pro-Communist efforts to halt his investigations. The pro-censure forces argued as tenaciously that the question of dealing with internal communism has nothing to do with the censure issue; that McCarthy was "on trial" for his behavior toward the Senate and its instruments.

- -

"PRESIDENT SIGNS FORMOSA MEASURE; SEES PEACE GUARD," JANUARY 30, 1955

An important test of Eisenhower's "massive retaliation" strategy came in response to a dispute between Communist China and Chinese Nationalists in Formosa (Taiwan) over small islands near China's coast. In 1955 and 1958 China indicated through shelling the offshore islands that it might seize the territories. Eisenhower never explicitly stated whether he would use nuclear weapons to assist the Nationalists, but the threat may have deterred China, which did not take further aggressive action.

JANUARY 30, 1955
PRESIDENT SIGNS FORMOSA MEASURE; SEES PEACE GUARD
Hails Congress' Move Backing Authority to Take Defense Steps at Risk of War
STRESSES NATION'S UNITY
Support of U.N. Cease-Fire Efforts Pledged—Capital Settles Back to Wait
By ELIE ABEL
Special to The New York Times

WASHINGTON, Jan. 29—President Eisenhower today signed the Congressional resolution endorsing his authority to defend Formosa at the risk of war.

The President's signature, at 8:42 A.M., gave the force of law to the joint measure passed last night, 85 to 3, by the Senate at his request. The House of Representatives had approved it on Tuesday, 409 to 3.

General Eisenhower hailed Congress' action as a step to preserve peace in the Formosa Strait by making it clear that the United States would fight, if need be, to help the Chinese Nationalists resist invasion from the Communist mainland.

"We are ready to support a United Nations effort to end the present hostilities in the area," he said, "but we also are united in our determination to defend an area vital to the security of the United States and the free world."

The President's emergency powers are to be invoked with orders to the Seventh Fleet to raise an air umbrella over the evacuation of Nationalist garrison troops from the Tachen Islands, 210 miles north of Formosa.

Islands Not Named

The Congressional resolution endorses the President's authority to secure and protect not only Formosa and the Pescadores Islands, which have been guarded by the Seventh Fleet since 1950, but also "such related positions and territories" as the Quemoy and Matsu Islands, off the Communist-held mainland.

These islands are not named in the resolution. They were omitted deliberately to leave the United States a measure of flexibility in any cease-fire talks, and to avoid entangling the United Nations Security Council in a jurisdictional squabble.

Although the Administration has never said so publicly, it recognizes that Quemoy and Matsu are unquestionably Chinese territory, unlike Formosa and the Pescadores, which belonged to Japan until the end of World War II.

⸱ ⸱

"EISENHOWER IS IN HOSPITAL WITH 'MILD' HEART ATTACK," SEPTEMBER 25, 1955

The second-oldest president to occupy the White House (after William Henry Harrison) up to that time, Eisenhower was sixty-two when he took office, and his health was a source of concern during his administration. He suffered a heart attack in 1955 and had an operation the following year for an intestinal problem. In late 1957 Eisenhower had a small stroke. In each case, he recovered from his illness, though he required some time for recuperation.

SEPTEMBER 25, 1955
EISENHOWER IS IN HOSPITAL WITH 'MILD' HEART ATTACK;
STRICKEN IN SLEEP
President Is Placed in an Oxygen Tent but Only as Precaution
By RUSSELL BAKER
Special to The New York Times

DENVER, Sunday, Sept. 25—President Eisenhower suffered a heart attack early yesterday morning and has entered Fitzsimons Army Hospital near Denver.

At 10:20 last night (1:20 A.M. Sunday, New York time) the White House reported that the President had been under an oxygen tent since being admitted to the hospital at 2:30 P.M.

James C. Hagerty, the White House press secretary, said at 1:30 A.M. today that three physicians who had examined the President had given an optimistic report on his condition.

Their bulletin, Mr. Hagerty said, stated that "from the original onset, at 2:45 A.M. Saturday, the President has withstood the attack well. At this time there are no complications. His blood pressure and pulse have remained stable. The President has been resting comfortably."

Mr. Hagerty added that there was no special significance to the President's being in an oxygen tent. The three physicians, he reported, said "that was routine—to permit the President to secure complete rest."

"41 STATES TO GO TO G.O.P.," NOVEMBER 7, 1956

The 1956 presidential election resembled the previous one in many ways. Eisenhower and Stevenson competed against each other again, and Eisenhower was victorious a second time, with more popular and Electoral College votes than he received in 1952. As *The Times* noted, for the first time in more than fifty years, a Republican president had won reelection. (Incumbent Theodore Roosevelt won the 1904 race, but he had not been elected to his first term; he became president after William McKinley was assassinated in 1901.)

NOVEMBER 7, 1956
41 STATES TO G.O.P.
President Sweeps All the North and West, Scores in South
By JAMES RESTON

Dwight David Eisenhower won yesterday the most spectacular Presidential election victory since Franklin D. Roosevelt submerged Alfred M. Landon in 1936.

The smiling 66-year-old hero of the Normandy invasion, who was in a Denver hospital recuperating from a heart attack just a year ago today, thus became the first Republican in this century to win two successive Presidential elections. William McKinley did it in 1896 and 1900.

Adlai E. Stevenson of Illinois, who lost to Mr. Eisenhower four years ago, thirty-nine states to nine, conceded defeat at 1:25 this morning.

At 4:45 A.M. President Eisenhower had won forty-one states to seven for Mr. Stevenson. His electoral lead at that time was 457 to 74 for Stevenson, and his popular vote was 25,071,331 to 18,337,434—up 2 per cent over 1952. Two hundred and sixty-six electoral votes are needed for election.

Victory in All Areas

This was a national victory in every conceivable way. It started in Connecticut. It swept every state in New England. It took New York by a plurality of more than 1,500,000. It carried all the Middle Atlantic states, all the Midwest, all the Rocky Mountain states and everything beyond the Rockies.

More than that, the Republican tide swept along the border states and to the South, carried all the states won by the G.O.P. there in 1952—Virginia, Texas, Tennessee and Florida—and even took Louisiana for the first time since the Hayes-Tilden election of 1876.

For the President and his 43-year old Vice Presidential running mate, Richard M. Nixon of California, who carried much of the Republican campaign, it was a more impressive victory than for the Republican party.

· ·

"Senate Votes Rights Bill and Sends It to President; Thurmond Talks 24 Hours," August 30, 1957

The Civil Rights Act of 1957 took initial steps to protect the voting rights of black Americans. Although the legislation did not overturn the systematic discrimination that dated back to the Civil War's end, it did represent incremental change that would pave the way for the civil rights revolution of the 1960s. The legislation passed despite the efforts of Democratic (later Republican) senator Strom Thurmond of South Carolina to derail it with a twenty-four hour filibuster.

AUGUST 30, 1957
SENATE VOTES RIGHTS BILL AND SENDS IT TO PRESIDENT; THURMOND TALKS 24 HOURS
MARGIN IS 60-15

Adjournment at Hand as South Carolinian Abandons Fight

By WILLIAM S. WHITE

Special to The New York Times

WASHINGTON, Friday, Aug. 30—The Senate passed last night the first major civil rights legislation in the eight decades since the Reconstruction Era following the Civil War. The vote was 60 to 15.

The final action on the most significant achievement of the Democratic Eighty-fifth Congress was a bill to protect the voting right with Federal injunctions.

The Senate then passed conference-approved compromises on the remaining major issues before Congress. These were the $3,435,810,000 foreign aid appropriation, and bills to restrict defendants' access to Government files in criminal trials and to correct hardships arising from present immigration laws.

Thus, the first session of the Eighty-fifth Congress will be able to adjourn today after the House approves these three compromises.

The Senate recessed at 12:50 A.M. today until 9 A.M.

Thurmond Ends Talk

The Senate's action sending the civil rights measure to the White House was made possible at 9:12 P.M., when Senator Strom Thurmond, a right-wing South Carolina Democrat, surrendered the floor after holding it for twenty-four hours and eighteen minutes against the bill.

The civil rights bill was a basically Democratic revision of a far more sweeping version that had been proposed by President Eisenhower. Administration spokesmen have said that the President will approve it.

The measure would:

• Create a Federal civil rights commission with subpoena powers.

• Establish a special civil rights division within the Department of Justice.

• Empower federal prosecutors, acting with or without the consent of the victim, to obtain Federal court injunctions against actual or threatened interference with the right to vote.

Jury Not Required

Persons refusing to obey these injunctions—say Southern election officials denying the ballot to qualified Negroes—could be imprisoned for civil contempt by a Federal judge, sitting without a jury, and held indefinitely, or until they consented to comply.

In cases of criminal contempt, where the purpose of the judge is simply to punish, there will be a qualified right to a jury trial.

The Administration had originally wanted no jury trial in any case.

· ·

"Eisenhower Address on Little Rock Crisis," September 25, 1957

The obstacles to implementing the 1954 Supreme Court decision outlawing racial discrimination in schools became painfully evident in Little Rock, Arkansas, in 1957. When state officials and local residents tried to block integration of the local high school, President Eisenhower issued an executive order authorizing federal troops to ensure the safety of black students in the school.

SEPTEMBER 25, 1957
EISENHOWER ADDRESS ON LITTLE ROCK CRISIS

Following is the text of President Eisenhower's radio-television talk from Washington last night to the country on his moves in the Little Rock school integration problem as recorded by The New York Times:

Good evening, my fellow citizens.

For a few minutes this evening, I should like to speak to you about the serious situation that has arisen in Little Rock. To make this talk I have come to the President's Office in the White House.

I could have spoken from Rhode Island where I have been staying recently. But I felt that, in speaking from the house of Lincoln, of Jackson and of Wilson, my words would better convey both the sadness I feel in the action I was compelled today to make, and the firmness with which I intend to pursue this course until the orders of the Federal Court at Little Rock can be executed without unlawful interference.

In that city, under the leadership of demagogic extremists, disorderly mobs have deliberately prevented the carrying-out of proper orders from a Federal Court. Local authorities have not eliminated that violent opposition. And under the law I yesterday issued a proclamation calling upon the mob to disperse.

This morning the mob again gathered in front of the Central High School of Little Rock, obviously for the purpose of again preventing the carrying-out of the court's order relating to the admission of Negro children to that school.

Inescapable Duty

Whenever normal agencies prove inadequate to the task and it becomes necessary for the Executive Branch of the Federal Government to use its powers and authority to uphold Federal Courts, the President's responsibility is inescapable.

In accordance with that responsibility I have today issued an Executive Order directing the use of troops under Federal authority to aid in the execution of Federal law at Little Rock, Ark. This became necessary when my proclamation of yesterday was not observed and the obstruction of justice still continues.

It is important that the reasons for my action be understood by all our citizens. As you know the Supreme Court of the United States has decided that separate public educational facilities for the races are inherently unequal and therefore compulsory school segregation laws are unconstitutional.

Our personal opinions about the decision have no bearing on the matter of enforcement; the responsibility and authority of the Supreme Court to interpret the Constitution are very clear. Local Federal courts were instructed by the Supreme Court to issue such orders and decrees as might be necessary to achieve admission to public schools without regard to race—and with all deliberate speed.

· ·

"U.S. Missile Experts Shaken by Sputnik," October 13, 1957

Soviet success in deploying the Sputnik satellite into space in October 1957 sparked fears that the United States was falling behind its adversary in military strength. These fears proved to be unfounded a few years later, but criticisms of Eisenhower's defense policies continued for the rest of his presidency.

OCTOBER 13, 1957
U.S. MISSILE EXPERTS SHAKEN BY SPUTNIK
Weight of Satellite Called Evidence of Soviet Superiority in Rocketry
By JOHN W. FINNEY
Special to The New York Times

WASHINGTON, Oct. 12—Defense officials listened anxiously this week to the mysterious beeping from the sputnik and to the strident Soviet boasts about intercontinental ballistic missiles. What they heard disturbed them—so much so that tentative signals went up for a speed-up in the United States program to develop ocean-spanning ballistic missiles.

The defense officials were not disturbed so much by the piece of Soviet hardware flying overhead or the fact that the Soviet Union had bested the United States to place the first earth satellite in space. They were more concerned over the 184-pound weight of the satellite and the fact that Soviet rocket engines had been able to hurl such a hefty sphere about 560 miles upward into an earth-circling orbit.

To United States missile experts the Soviet rocketry accomplishment contained one significant and sobering piece of evidence—namely that the Soviet Union apparently had a more powerful rocket booster [indecipherable] than any yet developed by the United States.

Forced Reappraisal
The evidence fitted into a growing picture of Soviet progress in missile development. While still incomplete, the picture was detailed enough to force a reappraisal of the intense United States-Soviet race to develop missiles that speed to the edge of space and hit targets thousands of miles away.

President Eisenhower for the first time publicly expressed some guarded concern over Moscow's proved ability to hurl a rocket for a long distance. Neil H. McElroy, only four hours after taking over as Secretary of Defense, told reporters that in view of the Soviet missile accomplishments the Defense Department was seriously considering speeding up the United States missile program by removing some of the "bottlenecks."

These official reactions were in marked contrast to those following the Soviet Union's announcement of Aug. 27 that it had test fired an intercontinental ballistic missile "a huge distance." Then, from President Eisenhower on down, the official reaction had been that the test firing signified little, that it was a long way from one test firing to an arsenal of ballistic missiles capable of hitting a target.

"Senate Vote Hits G.O.P. Right Wing," November 8, 1958

Although the Republican Party controlled the White House for most of the 1950s, it shared governance with the Democratic Party, which increased its representation in Congress in the 1958 midterm elections. Moderate Republicans whose policy views were close to President Eisenhower's won more seats than conservative Republicans, but the party as a whole kept its minority status in both chambers.

NOVEMBER 8, 1958
SENATE VOTE HITS G.O.P. RIGHT WING

Democrats Show a Net Gain of 12 Seats—Majority Now Up to 62-34

By RUSSELL BAKER

The Democrats staggered the right-wing of the Republican party in Tuesday's election and swept control of the Senate by nearly a two-thirds majority.

With a net gain of twelve seats in the Tuesday balloting, and a thirteenth won earlier in Maine, the Democrats rolled up a 62 to 34 majority and looked forward to additional gains in the voting for Alaska's two new seats Nov. 25.

Not since the palmiest days of the "New Deal" had they made such a complete sweep of the field. Their last comparable triumph was in 1940 when they counted sixty-six Senators. Their gains, in fact, were so extensive that the Republicans were left virtually no chance of recapturing the Senate even in 1960.

The Republicans salvaged only eight of the twenty-one seats put before the voters this year.

· ·

"INTELLIGENCE ACTS ADMITTED BY U.S.," MAY 8, 1960, AND "HARSH EXCHANGE," MAY 17, 1960

President Eisenhower's foreign policy agenda halted in spring 1960 with the news that Soviets had captured an American spy plane flying over their territory. The United States initially denied that the U-2 plane was on a reconnaissance mission, which in fact it was. After this news was revealed, Soviet leader Nikita S. Khrushchev rescinded an invitation for Eisenhower to visit the Soviet Union and refused to pursue high-level discussions between the two nations.

MAY 8, 1960
INTELLIGENCE ACTS ADMITTED BY U.S.

Both Soviet and American Efforts in Field Cited in Statement on Plane

By JACK RAYMOND

Special to The New York Times

WASHINGTON, May 7—The United States statement today on the plane downed in the Soviet Union contained the first official Government disclosure that this country was engaged in aerial intelligence efforts.

Heretofore such activities have been only hinted at through announcements of Soviet activities and military strength.

For example, it was the United States that first announced Soviet atomic and hydrogen bomb explosions. The United States has consistently made public, officially or indirectly, statistical estimates of Soviet military strength, including missiles.

The State Department's announcement called attention to both the United States' own intelligence-gathering efforts and those of the Soviet Union, saying that these are "certainly no secret."

Planes Active in Turkey

It has been known for many years that in Turkey the United States has sent aircraft high into the skies, equipped with radar and various electronic instruments, to seek to learn secrets of the Soviet nuclear explosions, missile-launching bases and other military materials.

The United States has constructed giant radar antennas in Turkey, which it has used to study Soviet missile launchings with considerable accuracy. So acute have the United States "ears" become that the State Department was able in 1958 to release a tape recording of Soviet pilots talking to each other over their intercommunication systems as they prepared for an attack on a United States Air Force transport plane.

Officials today would not amend the story they issued at that time that the Air Force C-130, which was downed by the Russians, had accidentally flown over the Soviet border. President Eisenhower hinted then that the Soviet Union might have lured the Air Force craft over Soviet territory with a false radio signal.

Similar efforts by airborne reconnaissance efforts off the Soviet Union's Pacific coast and off the shores of Communist China also have been assumed, in view of the types of patrols that have been announced.

The intelligence activities, as the State Department noted, have not been one-sided by any means. Not only have Soviet spies been caught, tried and convicted in this country, but the Russians also have engaged in a "cat-and-mouse game" of attempted detection of secrets by skirting the boundaries of the United States.

MAY 17, 1960
HARSH EXCHANGE

Russian Asks Parley Be Postponed for 6 to 8 Months
By DREW MIDDLETON
Special to The New York Times

PARIS, May 16—The summit conference suffered an apparently mortal blow at its opening session today when Premier Khrushchev and President Eisenhower exchanged charges that blighted hopes for an early relaxation of tension between East and West.

The Soviet Premier bluntly told the United States President that he would not be welcome if he went to the Soviet Union on his proposed visit next month.

The Soviet Government is convinced, Mr. Khrushchev continued, that the next United States Administration, or even the one after that, will understand that there is no other course but peaceful coexistence with the Soviet Union.

'No Better Way Out'

There is "no better way out" of the dispute arising from United States intelligence flights over Soviet territory, the Premier said, than to postpone the conference for six to eight months.

At the close of his blistering speech, the system of high-level consultation and negotiation seemed wrecked. The Big Four adjourned their closed sessions without setting a date for another meeting in Paris.

Mr. Khrushchev demanded that President Eisenhower fulfill three conditions if there were to be summit talks. His demands followed a tirade against the United States for having sent U-2 photo-reconnaissance planes over the Soviet Union. One such plane was shot down in the Urals May 1.

President Eisenhower met one demand only. He announced that the flights had been suspended after the recent incident "and are not to be resumed."

Move at U.N. Planned

The President also said he planned, in the event an accord with the Soviet Union on the subject proved impossible, to submit to the United Nations a proposal for "aerial surveillance to detect preparations for attack."

These moves failed to satisfy Mr. Khrushchev, who had demanded, first, condemnation of "inadmissible provocative actions" on the part of the United States Air Force; second, a ban on flights now and in the future and, finally, United States punishment of those "directly guilty" of "deliberate violation of the Soviet Union."

• •

"PRESIDENT DESCRIBES NIXON ROLE IN ADMINISTRATION'S DECISIONS,"
AUGUST 25, 1960

Vice President Nixon faced many questions in the 1960 presidential campaign about his role in the Eisenhower administration, and those queries increased when President Eisenhower said at a press conference that he would need a week to think of an example of Nixon's influence. The statement later was cast as a light-hearted joke, but it fueled Democratic charges that the vice president had little expertise in executive decision making.

AUGUST 25, 1960
PRESIDENT DESCRIBES NIXON ROLE IN ADMINISTRATION'S DECISIONS
By W. H. LAWRENCE
Special to The New York Times

WASHINGTON, Aug. 24—President Eisenhower gave his own version today of Vice President Nixon's participation in Administration policy decisions.

The President told his news conference that he, and he alone, made the key Executive decisions after consultation with his Cabinet, major aides and the Vice President. . . .

Asked to give an example of a "major idea" put forth by Mr. Nixon that the President had subsequently adopted as a final governmental decision, President Eisenhower responded:

"If you give me a week, I might think of one. I don't remember." . . .

The Republican party's platform gave the Vice President equal billing with the President in describing such things as the "Eisenhower-Nixon" atoms-for-peace policy, national highway program, and a firmness-for-peace stance based on military power second to none.

"VIGILANCE URGED," JANUARY 18, 1961

Three days before he left office, President Eisenhower gave a farewell address to the nation in which he warned of the need to prevent the "military-industrial complex" from accruing too much power in policymaking. For a president whose entire career outside of the White House had been in the military, the statement illustrated Eisenhower's keen understanding that the nation's defense needs were a means to an end, and that the country should not lose sight of its fundamental goals in pursuing its national security interests.

" He warned Americans that they faced a long struggle in the 'cold war.' "

JANUARY 18, 1961
VIGILANCE URGED
Talk Bids Godspeed to Kennedy—Voices Hopes for Peace
By FELIX BELAIR Jr.
Special to The New York Times

WASHINGTON, Jan. 17—President Eisenhower cautioned the nation in a farewell address from the White House tonight to be vigilant against dangers to its liberties implicit in a vast military establishment and a permanent armaments industry unparalleled in peacetime.

In his speech, which brought down the curtain on fifty years of public service, the President also warned of a second threat— "the prospect of domination of the nation's scholars by Federal employment, project allocations and the power of money." He said this danger was "ever present and is gravely to be regarded."

The President concluded his televised speech with a prayer for the well-being of "all the peoples of the world."

Sees a 'Long Struggle'

He warned Americans that they faced a long struggle in the "cold war." He also cautioned the nation against being tempted by any "miraculous solution" to world problems.

President Eisenhower also spoke as an old soldier preparing to turn over the burdens of the Presidency to his much younger successor, President-elect John F. Kennedy. The two men will hold their second and final discussion of problems confronting the nation Thursday morning.

Foremost among these problems, the President listed the continuing Communist threat to the West and the need to combat it while striving for universal disarmament. It was "with a definite sense of disappointment" that he contemplated the failure to make greater progress toward a lasting peace.

Wishes Kennedy Well

He said that, with all Americans, "I wish the new President and all who will labor with him Godspeed" in working for solutions.

The President stressed the need to guard against "the acquisition of unwarranted influence, whether sought or unsought by the military-industrial complex."

This warning against the political potential of the huge military-arms production apparatus by the President came as a surprise to many in the capital. A more sentimental leave taking had been expected from the old soldier.

He noted that the conjunction of an immense military establishment and a large arms industry—both essential to national and free world security—was something new in American experience.

"The total influence—economic, political, even spiritual—is felt in every city, every state house, every office of the Federal Government," the President said.

Stressing the need for constant vigilance against undue influence in the hands of the newly combined military and industrial sector, the President went on to say "The potential for the disastrous rise of misplaced power exists and will persist."

Closely related to this new development in the American system, President Eisenhower said, is the increasing centralization of research under Federal control or direction. This necessary evil has been part of the technological revolution of recent decades and its increasingly complex and costly nature, he continued.

"Partly because of the huge costs involved, the Government contract becomes virtually a substitute for intellectual curiosity," the President reflected. "For every old blackboard there are now hundreds of new electronic computers."

THE PRESIDENCY OF JOHN F. KENNEDY

JANUARY 20, 1961 – NOVEMBER 22, 1963

John Fitzgerald Kennedy's presidency lasted less than three years, but made a significant imprint on American politics. President Kennedy faced a difficult first year in foreign affairs with the disastrous Bay of Pigs invasion in Cuba, a contentious meeting with Soviet premier Nikita S. Khrushchev in Vienna, and the building of the Berlin Wall. But Kennedy went on to successfully defuse the Cuban missile crisis—an event that brought the United States closest to direct conflict with the Soviet Union in the cold war—and sign the first arms control treaty with the Soviet Union, which prohibited nuclear weapons testing in the atmosphere. In domestic policy, the Kennedy administration endorsed civil rights actions, and the president called for congressional legislation to enforce civil rights more uniformly and vigorously. Kennedy did not, however, live to see the enactment of his political agenda; he was assassinated in Dallas, Texas, on November 22, 1963.

The second son of Joseph P. Kennedy, a wealthy financier, and Rose Elizabeth Fitzgerald Kennedy, daughter of a highly popular former Boston mayor, John—or "Jack" as he often was known—grew up in a family steeped in American politics. His father served as U.S. ambassador to Great Britain in the late 1930s. One of nine children, John Kennedy attended the prestigious preparatory school Choate in Connecticut, and then enrolled at Princeton University, but he withdrew after one semester due to poor health. He entered Harvard College in 1936, where he wrote an insightful senior thesis on British reluctance to confront Nazism in the 1930s that later was published as a book, *Why England Slept*. Kennedy graduated with honors from Harvard in 1940.

After college, Kennedy joined the U.S. Navy, and he was commissioned as an ensign in 1941. He commanded a patrol torpedo (PT) boat in the South Pacific in 1943. His boat, PT-109, was attacked and sunk by a Japanese destroyer in August. Kennedy led the eleven surviving members of his crew in a four-hour swim to reach land, and Kennedy himself towed an injured man to safety, injuring his already frail back in the process. Upon returning to the United States, Kennedy

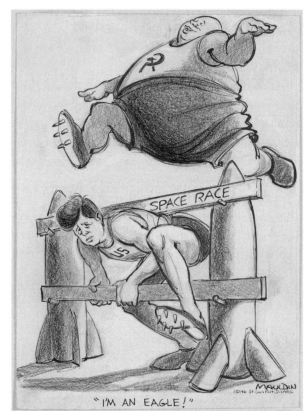

"I'M AN EAGLE!"

Source: Copyright 1961 by Bill Mauldin. Reprinted courtesy of the William Mauldin Estate.

fell ill with malaria, and he also had surgery on his back. He was discharged with honors in 1945.

In spring 1945 Kennedy, reporting for the Hearst International News Service, covered the San Francisco Conference that drafted the United Nations charter. He ran successfully for Congress on the Democratic ticket in Massachusetts in 1946 and served three terms in the House before winning election to the Senate in 1952. During his Senate tenure, Kennedy's back problems flared up again, and he underwent two more operations in 1954 and 1955. While recovering, he wrote a study of senators who had made tough decisions in the face of strong opposition. In 1957 he won the Pulitzer Prize for Biography for *Profiles in Courage*. He competed unsuccessfully for the vice-presidential spot on the Democratic

QUICK FACTS ON JOHN F. KENNEDY

BIRTH	May 29, 1917, Brookline, Mass.
EDUCATION	Princeton University for one term, 1935 Harvard College
FAMILY	Wife: Jacqueline Lee Bouvier Kennedy Children: Caroline Bouvier Kennedy, John Fitzgerald Kennedy Jr., Patrick Bouvier Kennedy (died in infancy)
WHITE HOUSE PETS	Dogs, cat, canary, parakeets, ponies, hamsters, rabbit, horse
PARTY	Democratic

PREPRESIDENTIAL CAREER (SELECTED)	Publication of senior thesis, *Why England Slept*, about British reaction
	   to Nazi aggression in 1930s, 1940
	U.S. Navy, 1941–1945
	Leads crew members to safety after their PT-109 torpedo boat is hit
	   by Japanese destroyer, 1943
	Awarded Navy and Marine Corps Medal, and Purple Heart, 1945
	Newspaper correspondent, 1945
	U.S. House of Representatives, 1947–1953
	U.S. Senate, 1953–1961
	Spinal surgeries, 1954, 1955
	Unsuccessful attempt to win Democratic vice-presidential nomination, 1956
	Wins Pulitzer Prize for Biography for *Profiles in Courage*, 1957

PRESIDENTIAL TERM	January 20, 1961–November 22, 1963
VICE PRESIDENT	Lyndon B. Johnson
SELECTED EVENTS	First live televised press conference (1961) Creation of Peace Corps (1961) Ratification of Twenty-third Amendment (1961) Bay of Pigs invasion (1961) "Freedom rides" challenge segregation on interstate buses (1961) Meeting with Soviet premier Nikita S. Khrushchev in Vienna (1961) Soviets build Berlin Wall (1961) Creation of Agency for International Development (1961) John H. Glenn Jr. becomes first U.S. astronaut to orbit the earth (1962) Violence erupts in response to desegregation at University of Mississippi (1962) Cuban missile crisis (1962) Confrontation with Gov. George C. Wallace Jr. over desegregation of University of Alabama (1963) Supports civil rights legislation (1963) Civil rights march on Washington, D.C. (1963) Limited Nuclear Test Ban Treaty (1963)
DEATH	November 22, 1963, Dallas, Texas

ticket in 1956, but his efforts paved the way for a nomination to head the ticket four years later.

THE 1960 PRESIDENTIAL ELECTION

Although Kennedy faced several competitors for the 1960 Democratic presidential nomination, he ultimately won on the first convention ballot. Senate Majority Leader Lyndon B. Johnson of Texas came in second, and Kennedy asked Johnson to be his running mate. Opposing them were Vice President Richard M. Nixon, who headed the Republican ticket, and his running mate, Henry Cabot Lodge of Massachusetts.

Kennedy and Nixon held the first televised presidential election debates, four in all, in American history. The debates highlighted Kennedy's impressive communication skills and image, and he prevailed in the election, winning 303 Electoral College votes to Nixon's 219, but only about 120,000 more popular votes than his opponent. The 1960 presidential election was historic for many reasons: Not only was Kennedy, at age forty-three, the country's youngest elected president (Theodore Roosevelt became president at age forty-two, but he succeeded to the office after William McKinley's assassination) but also Kennedy was the nation's first Catholic president.

THE KENNEDY ADMINISTRATION

Kennedy's ten-member cabinet was noteworthy in several ways. Most significant was his selection of his younger brother, Robert F. Kennedy, to be attorney general. Throughout Kennedy's presidency, his brother was an indispensable source of counsel. For treasury secretary, Kennedy crossed party lines to select Republican C. Douglas Dillon of New Jersey, who had served in the Eisenhower administration. Defense Secretary Robert S. McNamara of Michigan was a successful business executive with Ford Motor Company and the company's first president who was not a member of the Ford family. Secretary of State Dean Rusk of New York had served in the State Department in the Truman administration.

Like her husband, First Lady Jacqueline Lee Bouvier Kennedy came from a wealthy background. The two married in 1953, and they had three children, the last of whom, a premature son, lived only two days. Daughter Caroline and son John Jr. were exuberant youngsters, and the president's attractive family was the subject of much media coverage. (Not since the administration of Theodore Roosevelt had such young children lived in the White House.) Jacqueline Kennedy undertook an extensive restoration of the mansion, which resulted in a nationally televised tour in which she displayed the historic American art and artifacts she had acquired. She was a continual source of fascination for the public and the media, and she regularly set fashion trends with her couture selections.

MAJOR ISSUES

In his first year in office, President Kennedy faced numerous challenges in foreign affairs. In spring 1961 Kennedy executed an operation planned in the Eisenhower administration to assist Cuban rebels seeking to overthrow Communist leader Fidel Castro. The Bay of Pigs invasion, as it was known, failed, resulting in the capture of twelve hundred Cuban exiles and a major public humiliation for the United States. A few months later, Kennedy had a contentious meeting in Vienna, Austria, with Soviet leader Nikita S. Khrushchev, who showed little interest in seeking to defuse tensions between the two superpowers. In fact, the cold war conflict heightened that summer in Germany and resulted in the building of the Berlin Wall.

But Kennedy also demonstrated an ability to learn from his mistakes. He achieved a peaceful resolution to the Cuban missile crisis in October 1962, perhaps the most confrontational cold war event between the United States and the Soviet Union. The Soviet Union was building offensive missile bases in Cuba, and when the United States discovered them through aerial reconnaissance photography, it demanded that construction be halted. President Kennedy imposed a naval blockade around Cuba to prevent Soviet shipments, and the two superpowers teetered precariously close to war. Khrushchev agreed to withdraw Soviet missiles in return for a secret agreement that the United States would remove its Jupiter missiles from Turkey. The two countries would work together well for the remainder of Kennedy's term, even signing an arms control treaty banning some nuclear testing in 1963. Kennedy also increased the number of American military advisers in Vietnam, gradually escalating U.S. involvement there.

In domestic policy, Kennedy is perhaps best remembered for progress in civil rights, even though he did not live to see the legislation he proposed in 1963 enacted. He deployed federal troops to establish law and order in the South during several conflicts over civil rights, including the integration of the University of Mississippi and the University of Alabama. Kennedy created the Peace Corps, an organization that sent American volunteers overseas to work in developing nations, and he established the Alliance for Progress aid program for Latin America. In economic affairs, Kennedy successfully reversed steel price increases in 1962. He endorsed tax cuts to promote economic growth, which Congress failed to enact during his presidency.

A Shocking Tragedy

On November 22, 1963, President Kennedy and his wife traveled to Dallas, Texas, for a political visit. While riding in an open car, Kennedy was shot twice, and he died soon afterward. Police quickly captured the assassin, Lee Harvey Oswald, a former marine who had renounced his U.S. citizenship, and who was shot himself in full view of television cameras three days later. Vice President Johnson was sworn in as president aboard *Air Force One* in Dallas. Johnson appointed a panel headed by Chief Justice Earl Warren to investigate the assassination. The Warren Com-

mission concluded that Oswald acted independently, but ever since then questions have surrounded the assassination, and many theories about who did it and why have been proposed.

President Kennedy was buried in Arlington National Cemetery, next to his infant son Patrick. In 1968 Jacqueline Bouvier Kennedy married Aristotle Onassis, a wealthy Greek shipping magnate, and she, too, was buried next to President Kennedy upon her death in 1994. Tragedy struck this family again in 1999, when John F. Kennedy Jr. piloted a plane that crashed into the Atlantic near the Massachusetts coast, killing him, his wife, and her sister.

● ●

"Beyond the Victory," July 14, 1960

The Democratic Party's nomination of Sen. John F. Kennedy of Massachusetts for president in 1960 signaled a generational change in the party. The first Democratic presidential candidate to enter politics after World War II and the first born in the twentieth century, Kennedy campaigned for president on a platform of change. He called for a "New Frontier" in his nomination acceptance speech, and he used the simple campaign slogan, "Let's get the country moving again." *The New York Times* reporter James Reston aptly noted that in winning the nomination, Kennedy "won the right, not only to represent his party as its youngest nominee, but to represent his generation, and to represent himself."

JULY 14, 1960
BEYOND THE VICTORY
Kennedy Has Won Right to Represent His Party, His Generation and Himself
By JAMES RESTON
Special to The New York Times
News Analysis

LOS ANGELES, July 13—John F. Kennedy won more than the Presidential nomination tonight. For he won the right, not only to represent his party as its youngest nominee, but to represent his generation, and to represent himself. This last, ironically, is important to Kennedy. For he is free at last to be judged for what he is. The focus will now be on him as a human being, not on his father, or his money, or his attractive young wife, but on his personal qualities of mind and character.

These outside considerations have been important to him and he would be the first to admit it. Without them, he would probably not be his party's Presidential nominee tonight. He has benefited greatly by his family, his money, his church and his wife, but he reached a point about halfway through this campaign where these assets overwhelmed

everything else and turned the individual candidate into a tribe and even, according to his political opponents, into a kind of conspiracy.

This was, and still is, a major problem for Kennedy. He has reached a pinnacle of success unknown to any man of his age in this party, but he is also the victim of the political and public relations attributes that have helped him succeed. For the popular assets that helped him get where he is tonight fit so neatly into the shorthand of modern journalism and television that they have obscured his own personal qualifications for the high office he seeks.

Campaign to Give Answer

It is early yet to pass judgment on these deeper qualities of character and ability—the campaign will soon provide an adequate test—but the primaries and the convention have already indicated what these qualities are.

It is obvious that aside from all the help he has had, he is a remarkably gifted young man: experienced well beyond the normal expectation of his years, at home in both the intellectual and political institutions of the nation, articulate particularly in the give and take of modern television discussion and debate, industrious, energetic, and above all courageous.

Four times in the last few months he has been confronted suddenly by challenges from his opponent and every time he has come through under circumstances where he was on his own.

The first of these was last November when the Roman Catholic bishops of his own church took a position against the dissemination of birth control information by the nation to other nations. He took an independent line on this at once and declared that he would not only decide the point on whatever was best for the nation, but that he would put his constitutional oath of office above every other obligation spiritual or temporal. Reflective men are still debating this point.

The second test came in the West Virginia primary election, when he was up against charges that he had won the Wisconsin primary with the aid of a "Roman Catholic vote," and when he was faced with agitation among the predominantly Protestant West Virginia voters to retaliate by taking a position against him.

"EXCHANGE IS CALM," SEPTEMBER 27, 1960

The Kennedy-Nixon presidential election debates in the fall of 1960 made history in many ways. The live performances attracted large television audiences, particularly for the first debate, in which Nixon looked pale and uncomfortable, while Kennedy appeared robust and calm. Although there is little empirical evidence to sustain the popular view that radio listeners preferred Nixon and television viewers favored Kennedy, certainly the debates played to Kennedy's strengths. In a close election, they may have helped to tilt the balance in his favor.

SEPTEMBER 27, 1960
EXCHANGE IS CALM

Sharp Retorts Are Few as Candidates Meet Face to Face
By RUSSELL BAKER
Special to The New York Times

CHICAGO, Sept. 26—Vice President Nixon and Senator John F. Kennedy argued genteelly tonight in history's first nationally televised debate between Presidential candidates.

The two men, confronting each other in a Chicago television studio, centered their argument on which candidate and which party offered the nation the best means for spurring United States growth in an era of international peril.

The candidates, without ever generating any real heat in their exchanges, clashed on the following points:

• Mr. Nixon's farm program, which Senator Kennedy said was merely another version of policies that had been tried and had failed under Ezra Taft Benson, Secretary of Agriculture.

• The Republican and Democratic performance records on efforts to increase the minimum wage of $1 an hour and broaden its coverage, school construction legislation and medical care for the aged. Mr. Kennedy charged that the Republican record on these measures showed the party gave only "lip service" to them.

• The comparative records of the Truman and Eisenhower Administrations on fiscal security. Mr. Nixon asserted that in school and hospital construction the Republican years had seen an improvement over the previous seven Democratic years. Moreover, he said, wages had risen "five times as much" in the Eisenhower Administration as during the Truman Administration, while the rise in prices has been only one-fifth of that in the Truman years.

"Results Delayed," November 10, 1960

Kennedy won the 1960 presidential election by a margin of less than 1 percent in the popular vote. On election night, the results were so close that Kennedy allegedly went to sleep not knowing if he had won the race. Vice President Nixon conceded the election to Kennedy the following day. In addition to the historic firsts of Kennedy's victory (youngest elected president, first Catholic president), the results also marked an end to divided government, with Democratic control of both the White House and Congress for the first time since the Truman administration.

NOVEMBER 10, 1960
RESULTS DELAYED
Popular Vote Almost Even—300–185 Is Electoral Tally
By JAMES RESTON

Senator John F. Kennedy of Massachusetts finally won the 1960 Presidential election from Vice President Nixon by the astonishing margin of less than two votes per voting precinct.

Senator Kennedy's electoral vote total stood yesterday at 300, just thirty-one more than the 269 needed for election. The Vice President's total was 185. Fifty-two additional electoral votes, including California's thirty-two, were still in doubt last night.

But the popular vote was a different story. The two candidates ran virtually even. Senator Kennedy's lead last night was little more than 300,000 in a total tabulated vote of about 66,000,000 cast in 165,826 precincts.

That was a plurality for the Senator of less than one-half of 1 per cent of the total vote—the smallest percentage difference between the popular vote of two Presidential candidates since 1880, when James A. Garfield outran Gen. Winfield Scott Hancock by 7,000 votes in a total of almost 9,000,000.

End Divided Government

Nevertheless, yesterday's voting radically altered the political balance of power in America in favor of the Democrats and put them in a commanding position in the Federal and state capitals unknown since the heyday of Franklin D. Roosevelt.

They regained control of the White House for the first time since 1952 and thus ended divided government in Washington. They retained control of the Senate and the House of Representatives, although with slightly reduced margins. And they increased their hold on the state governorships by one, bringing the Democratic margin to 34-16.

The President-elect is the first Roman Catholic ever to win the nation's highest office. The only other member of his church nominated for President was Alfred E. Smith, who was defeated by Herbert Hoover in 1928.

"Inaugural Contrast," January 22, 1961

President Kennedy's inaugural address stands out as one of the most famous speeches in American history. On a bitterly cold day, Kennedy inspired millions with his famous charge, "Ask not what your country can do for you—ask what you can do for your country." The speech was replete with other singular lines as well, and The Times reporter Arthur Krock captures the importance of the address well in his discussion of the contrasts it made with the previous administration.

President John F. Kennedy delivers his inaugural address. Seated nearby are Jacqueline Kennedy and former President Eisenhower.

Source: UPI Telephoto

JANUARY 22, 1961
INAUGURAL CONTRAST

Kennedy Dramatizes the Change but the Basic Aspirations Remain

By ARTHUR KROCK

WASHINGTON, Jan. 21—The millions who, by direct or indirect medium, saw the ceremonies by which John F. Kennedy legally became the President of the United States, and listened to his inaugural address, were also afforded a study in contrasts which were extraordinary, even on these occasions. For the first time a man born in the twentieth century, though it is now ten years beyond its half way mark, was assuming the highest and most powerful office in the land and the potential leadership of the non-Communist world, replacing the last of his predecessors who were born in the nineteenth. And for the first time those of the new President's generation who came to maturity after the First World War were tak-

ing over the responsibility, not only of the Presidency, but also of nearly all the high executive offices of an entire administration.

This unusual contrast between the old and new, not provided at any inaugural since Theodore Roosevelt succeeded seven Chief Executives who were of military age at the beginning of the War Between the States, was repeatedly reflected in President Kennedy's inaugural address. He called on "friend and foe alike" throughout the world to witness "that the torch has been passed to a new generation of Americans—born in this century. . . ." And he noted that Americans of the age group he embodies were among the "few . . . who have been granted the role of defending freedom in its hour of maximum danger," and who "would not exchange places with any other . . . generation."

Then there was the striking physical contrast between the retiring and incoming President. Although General Eisenhower showed vigor and a glow of health which belie his seventy years, Mr. Kennedy has a much more youthful look than is normally associated with a man of forty-three.

And finally there was the contrast between the tone and style of General Eisenhower's farewell and President Kennedy's hail to the nation. There were many similarities in the statements of goals and ideals, naturally to have been expected from two Americans of high purpose who, though at different levels, had fought to maintain the freedom they cherish for human beings and nations. But, quite as naturally, General Eisenhower dwelt mainly on the past and on forebodings of the future; while President Kennedy dwelt on the past not at all. He also employed only brief references to the present, chiefly to emphasize his vision of the future which he has been called upon to shape according to this vision and his capability. . . .

May Differ

The methods and measures of Mr. Kennedy, his concept of national and world leadership, may prove to be as different from General Eisenhower's as forecast by the new President's personality, age, campaign speeches, and—with due allowances for its irresponsible pledges to attract the votes of special interest groups—the 1960 platform of his party.

But friends and foes of this people, and those Americans who accentuate our internal divisions on partisan or personal animations, would save themselves from the errors of false expectations if they will note the similarities of ideals and purposes in the most recent public addresses of the outgoing and incoming President.

Not in their delivery and rhetoric, because Mr. Kennedy's recalled Woodrow Wilson's first inaugural address to this reporter, who viewed and heard both. But General Eisenhower warned the people that failure in the noblest or programs can be the consequence of "arrogance, or our lack of comprehension, or readiness to sacrifice." President Kennedy said to the people: "Ask not what your country can do for you, but what you can do for your country."

- -

"PRESS CONFERENCE ON LIVE TV," JANUARY 27, 1961

Kennedy's decision to hold live, televised press conferences provided a superb public relations opportunity for the new president, given his talents as a public speaker. He did not face particularly difficult questions, as the mindset of the "adversarial media" had not taken hold at this time. Nevertheless, the sessions still required the president to think quickly and frame his remarks without the benefit of after-the-fact editing. And he excelled in this setting, offering deft, thoughtful, and sometimes humorous commentary that was well-received by press and viewers alike.

JANUARY 27, 1961
EDITORIAL
PRESS CONFERENCE ON LIVE TV

Mr. Kennedy's experiment in holding a live television Presidential press conference was a success. He surmounted with apparent ease and equanimity the perils of saying too much or not enough, of saying the wrong things in the wrong way with inevitably instantaneous effect and potentially dangerous results. Skilled television performer that he is, President Kennedy runs less risk in committing such errors before the cameras and the microphones than would many other men in public life;

but the hazard remains and must be weighed against the benefits of bringing the White House press conference into the nation's living room.

On the basis of Mr. Kennedy's first performance, we believe that the benefits are likely to be greater than the risks. The greatest benefit is public education in the field of government; for although Presidential press conferences have been broadcast previously (at least in part) from film or tape, the sense of immediacy gained from live broadcasting of the entire conference—and at the early evening hour—will surely induce vast numbers of people to tune in who would never have bothered to do so before. They will see and hear some of the most vital questions of the day discussed by the Chief Executive himself; and they will be brought face to face with problems of public policy in more intimate and direct a manner than they could hope to realize by any other means. As Mr. Kennedy said, "this is a very difficult time in the life of our country"; and it is of profound importance in this democracy that the people understand the problems facing the President and the Congress. The nationally televised press conference can be of tremendous service in bringing the Government a little closer to the people.

The possibility that this powerful medium might be used for mere theatrics is of course always present; but it is doubtful that demagogues could stand up for long under television's bright lights without exposure, especially under hammering of expert newsmen.

At any rate, Mr. Kennedy acquitted himself well. His remarks were brief and to the point when he wished them to be; he neatly refused to answer when he felt that was the better policy. Removal of the requirement that reporters announce their names will have a healthy effect in expediting the questions and in silencing publicity seekers. But we think another change would add to the dignity of the conference, whether televised or not: its closing should be entirely under the President's control, not that of anyone in the audience.

"KENNEDY DEFENSE STUDY FINDS NO EVIDENCE OF A 'MISSILE GAP,'" FEBRUARY 7, 1961

President Kennedy faced an embarrassing situation in February 1961, when reports surfaced that his administration had determined that allegations of a "missile gap" favoring the Soviet Union were incorrect. These charges had dogged the Eisenhower administration since the Soviets sent the Sputnik satellite into space in 1957. Kennedy had strongly criticized his predecessor's defense policies, arguing that the United States needed to strengthen its military posture, and the news that there was no missile gap blunted his critique. Nevertheless, President Kennedy continued with his arms programs, increasing conventional and strategic forces.

FEBRUARY 7, 1961
KENNEDY DEFENSE STUDY FINDS NO EVIDENCE OF A 'MISSILE GAP'
By JACK RAYMOND
Special to The New York Times

WASHINGTON, Feb. 6—Studies made by the Kennedy Administration since Inauguration Day show tentatively that no "missile gap" exists in favor of the Soviet Union.

The conclusion appeared to back the views of former President Dwight D. Eisenhower, who told Congress last month that the missile gap "shows every sign" of being a fiction.

The term "missile gap" was used by Democrats two years ago, when it was disclosed that the Eisenhower Administration planned to build fewer intercontinental missiles than the Soviet Union was capable of producing.

Published reports then were that by 1960 the Soviet Union would have thirty-five 5,000-mile missiles with nuclear

warheads, against eighteen for the United States. These reports asserted that the relationship in 1961 would be 140 to 200 Russian missiles, against fifty-four in the United States.

The United States now has at least nine operational Atlas missiles, along with two missile-armed Polaris submarines, each bearing sixteen medium range ballistic missiles.

The Kennedy Administration, in studying the country's defense posture, also is understood to have come to the conclusion that the Soviets did not engage in a "crash program" to build intercontinental ballistic missiles.

It appeared from early conclusions that the Soviet Union did not produce as many such missiles as it could have.

At the same time, it is reported that early studies have reinforced the view of the new Administration that strategic planning in the past has had many shortcomings.

· ·

"U.S. Avoiding Questions on Cuba Bombing Details," April 17, 1961, and "Kennedy's First Defeat: How Will He React?" April 23, 1961

The failed Bay of Pigs invasion in April 1961 raised many questions about the Kennedy administration's foreign policy agenda. Although he had inherited the invasion plans from his predecessor, Kennedy was responsible for its botched execution. After the invasion, he faced criticism both from opponents of assistance to Cuban rebels as well as rebel supporters who thought he had not provided sufficient military assistance for the invasion to succeed. Kennedy took responsibility for the failure and vowed that his administration would not make the same organizational mistakes again in crisis decision making.

APRIL 17, 1961
U.S. AVOIDING QUESTIONS ON CUBA BOMBING DETAILS
By E. W. KENWORTHY
Special to The New York Times

WASHINGTON, April 16—Government officials were avoiding probing questions today on the point of origin of the B-26 planes that bombed three Cuban military air bases yesterday. The questions were prompted by some puzzling circumstances attending the attack and the statement made by one of the pilots, who landed his damaged bomber at Miami International Airport.

One of the unanswered questions was how the president of the Cuban Revolutionary Council in New York, Dr. José Miró Cardona, could have had advance knowledge of the mission if the pilots were all members of the Cuban Air Force and if the decision to make the attacks was made suddenly only last Thursday, as the B-26 flier said in Miami.

Another question that got no satisfactory answer here is why immigration authorities withheld the name of the pilot who landed in Miami even though pictures were taken and published that clearly showed his features and the number of the plane.

In his statement, the pilot said he was a pilot of Premier Fidel Castro's air force and had been based at San Antonio de los Baños, which is about twenty-five miles from Havana. Two of his fellow pilots who participated in the defection flights and bombings, he said, were based at Camp Libertad on the outskirts of Havana.

At a military funeral today for seven persons killed in the bomb-and-rocket attack on the airfields, Premier Castro said that no Cuban Air Force bombers had been stationed at Camp Libertad and that the pilots were not defectors from the air force but foreign mercenaries who had flown from foreign bases.

The Cuban Premier challenged President Kennedy to present the pilots to the United Nations to prove that they had carried out their raids while defecting from the Cuban Air Force.

Mr. Kennedy was at his Glen Ora home in Middleburg, Va., today. There was no reaction from official sources here to the Castro challenge.

At the United Nations yesterday, Adlai E. Stevenson, the United States representative, said "these pilots and certain other crew members have apparently defected from Castro's tyranny."

"These two planes," said Mr. Stevenson, "to the best of our knowledge, were Castro's own air force planes and, according to the pilots, they took off from Castro's own air force fields."

APRIL 23, 1961
EDITORIAL
KENNEDY'S FIRST DEFEAT: HOW WILL HE REACT?

By JAMES RESTON

WASHINGTON, April 22—For the first time in his life, John F. Kennedy has taken a public licking. He has faced illness and even death in his 43 years, but defeat is something new to him, and Cuba was a clumsy and humiliating one, which makes it worse.

How he reacts to it may very well be more important than how he got into it. For this will be a critical test of the character and perspective of the new President, and of the brilliant young men he has brought to the pinnacle of American political power.

The temptation to lash back and "get even" in Cuba is very great. The politician's natural reaction to a dramatic defeat is to try for a dramatic victory as soon as possible. He has the power to do so. No doubt the proud spirit of the country would support his landing the Marines in Cuba.

Moreover, former President Eisenhower, who knows the agony of choosing between desperate courses of action, would undoubtedly support him. Former Vice President Nixon is quoted as saying publicly that he would go along even if this meant putting United States forces on the beaches in Cuba. And some of the President's closest advisers, deeply involved in the defeat, are eager to recoup the losses of the last few days.

Sudden Diplomacy?

Nevertheless, this is no time for sudden action, but for a little more careful reflection and staff work than went into the original decision to allow the Cuban refugees to engage the prestige of the United States.

is more of a menace to the other states of the Caribbean and the rest of Latin America than it is to the United States, but if Castro tries to use his military power against any other state in the Caribbean or the hemisphere, then the issue will be clear. At that point, the United States can wipe him out, with the requisite sanction of law on its side.

After all, the mere presence of military force in a weak country is not necessarily a threat to a strong country. Turkey, for example, has been getting from the United States far more power than Castro ever dreamed of getting from the Russians. This United States power, including even rockets with nuclear warheads, has been situated in Turkey for a long time, but the Russians, while annoyed by this fact, have not felt obliged to use their power to invade Turkey.

Kennedy's Approach

It all depends on how President Kennedy looks at all this. He can look at it in personal and political terms and concentrate on redressing the blunders of the last few weeks by landing two or three divisions in Cuba. In other words, he can put the immediate situation ahead of all the other world-wide social and economic programs he has been working so hard to emphasize ever since he came to power.

On the other hand, he can look at the wider world picture, now greatly darkened by the events in Laos and the sudden insurrection of the French Army that has broken out in Algeria.

> Kennedy . . . is now facing not only Castro and Khrushchev but the history and meaning of the American story.

Cuba is not a present danger to the United States. Even if and when it gets the 150 Communist MIG fighter planes and the Cuban pilots now being trained in Czechoslovakia—the fear of which played such an important part in the decision to launch this week's adventure—this is no serious menace to the security of the Republic.

As the President said in his press conference yesterday, the threat of the rising power and ideology of Cuba

He can try to deal with social and economic problems in Cuba by military means, and risk the whole inter-American and United Nations systems in the process.

But it does come back to his personal decision. He has the authority to act in historic and world terms or in terms of the limited immediate problems of the Cuban crisis.

Either way the decision will involve risks. This is a gloomy and impatient city this week-end. It is acting as if this were the last half of the ninth inning and Cuba were vital to the security of the United States, whereas the facts are that this is merely the first half of the first inning and Cuba can be dealt with at whatever time the President likes.

Kennedy, in short, is now facing not only Castro and Khrushchev but the history and meaning of the American story, and how he reacts to it will tell a lot about the kind of leadership he has in mind to offer for the United States and the free world.

- -

"Congress to Hear President Today," May 25, 1961

President Kennedy's decision to give a second State of the Union message in May 1961 indicated the urgency of his political priorities. In the previous few months, the United States had faced a series of disappointments, from the Bay of Pigs invasion failure to Soviet astronaut Yuri Gagarin's historic successful orbit of the Earth. Kennedy made a number of proposals to Congress, of which the most famous almost certainly was his call for the United States to put a man on the moon by the end of the decade.

MAY 25, 1961
CONGRESS TO HEAR PRESIDENT TODAY

Message on National Needs to Be Given in Person
By W. H. LAWRENCE
Special to The New York Times

WASHINGTON, May 24—President Kennedy will deliver in person tomorrow a message on "urgent national needs" to a joint session of Congress.

It will be carried to the nation by all television and radio networks beginning at 12:30 P.M. Eastern daylight time.

The President's decision to deliver the message in person marked a change in White House thinking in the last twenty-four hours. The decision is regarded as evidence of the increasing importance Mr. Kennedy attaches to the proposals he will place before the lawmakers.

Mr. Kennedy's main emphasis will be on a greatly accelerated and expanded space research program, including

an attempt to put a man on the moon and do it first if possible.

He will tell the Congress that swifter, deeper space probes are urgent to national survival even though the ultimate cost will be heavy and impose considerable sacrifices on the American people.

Civil Defense Proposal

The Presidential message will also deal with civil defense, foreign aid and the armed forces' capability for conventional warfare.

- -

"Kennedy Vows All Means to Find Solution on Berlin," August 11, 1961

In summer 1961 the United States moved closer to conflict with the Soviet Union in Berlin, Germany. The crisis did not result in war, but it did spur the physical division of East and West Berlin with the Berlin Wall, which became one of the dominant symbols of the cold war.

AUGUST 11, 1961
KENNEDY VOWS ALL MEANS TO FIND SOLUTION ON BERLIN
Special to The New York Times

WASHINGTON, Aug. 10—President Kennedy said today that he had found nothing new in Premier Khrushchev's latest discussion of the Berlin crisis. But the President promised to use "every device available" to find a peaceful solution.

The President pledged that all diplomatic techniques would be employed to get a more precise definition of the phrases, words and thoughts of the Soviet leaders on Berlin, Germany and Central Europe. But he gave no timetable for negotiations and no hint of what concessions the United States might consider.

On the contrary, Mr. Kennedy indicated that Soviet pressure on Berlin would be countered with diplomatic and propaganda offensives designed to prove that Moscow was disrupting the peace in Europe, blocking a nuclear test ban and flaunting its nuclear might before the world.

Silent About Fighting

The President refused to entertain questions on the kind of fighting that might result if the Berlin crisis was not resolved at the conference table. He clearly looked ahead to new discussions with the Soviet Union, though not with Premier Khrushchev personally.

"AFTERMATH IN MISSISSIPPI," OCTOBER 14, 1962

The Kennedy administration enforced the integration of the University of Mississippi in October 1962 by sending federal troops to the campus to protect James H. Meredith, the first black student to enroll there. Mississippi governor Ross Barnett's strong opposition to Meredith's admission sparked violent protests, and President Kennedy sent federal troops to restore order.

OCTOBER 14, 1962
AFTERMATH IN MISSISSIPPI
State Faces a Long Struggle Over Integration Issue But There Are Some
Signs of Progress
By CLAUDE SITTON
Special to *The New York Times*

ATLANTA, Oct. 13—The University of Mississippi has drifted through its second week of desegregation without major incident. But there is little evidence in the state of a willingness to adjust to the change.

Neither the shock of a riot nor the desire to be rid of Federal troops stationed on the campus at Oxford has brought significant support for those who advocate obedience to the courts.

Thus, the Kennedy Administration faces the task of shepherding James H. Meredith through the eighteen months of instruction he must have to become the first Negro graduate of Ole Miss.

Mississippians confront a potentially long and bitter struggle over the necessity of bowing to Federal authority, a struggle that may have unfortunate consequences for the state's social, economic and political life.

Best Hope

Some residents have shown an awareness of these consequences. In the opinion of observers, this development offers the best hope, however dim, that the state will reject the continued resistance being urged upon it by Gov. Ross R. Barnett and the Citizens' Council.

More than 125 business and professional leaders have spoken out against the lawless outburst that greeted Mr. Meredith's arrival on the campus Sept. 30 and left two dead and hundreds injured. The group has agreed to meet again in its effort to prevent a recurrence.

There are other signs of progress. Governor Barnett has made no move to close the university. He implied before Mr. Meredith's admission that he might take this step as a last resort.

Observers in Jackson, the state capital, contend that the militantly racist Citizens' Councils no longer command the unquestioning support they once enjoyed.

Perhaps the most promising sign is the concern heard throughout the state that the desegregation dispute may damage not only the university but also Mississippi's campaign for new industry.

However, these positive developments still seem to be outweighed by the negative aspects of the situation.

Only a few persons, mostly educators and clergymen, have called on officials and others to support compliance with the desegregation rulings of the courts. Without this compliance, there can be no return to normalcy.

⋅ ⋅

"President Grave," October 23, 1962

The Cuban missile crisis marked a turning point in the cold war. Instead of escalating their conflict with nuclear weapons, the United States and the Soviet Union narrowly averted a showdown due to painstaking diplomacy between President Kennedy and Premier Khrushchev. On October 22, 1962, Kennedy revealed on national television that the Soviet Union had placed missiles in Cuba, just ninety miles from the coast of Florida. As *The Times* reported, the president "made it clear that this country would not stop short of military action" to force the Soviet Union to withdraw its missiles. At no other point in the cold war did the two nations come so close to nuclear war. But war was averted when Khrushchev agreed to remove the missiles, ending the thirteen-day crisis.

OCTOBER 23, 1962
PRESIDENT GRAVE

Asserts Russians Lied and Put Hemisphere in Great Danger
By ANTHONY LEWIS
Special to *The New York Times*

WASHINGTON, Oct. 22—President Kennedy imposed a naval and air "quarantine" tonight on the shipment of offensive military equipment to Cuba.

In a speech of extraordinary gravity, he told the American people that the Soviet Union, contrary to promises, was building offensive missile and bomber bases in Cuba. He said the bases could handle missiles carrying nuclear warheads up to 2,000 miles.

Thus a critical moment in the cold war was at hand tonight. The President had decided on a direct confrontation with—and challenge to—the power of the Soviet Union.

Direct Thrust at Soviet

Two aspects of the speech were notable. One was its direct thrust at the Soviet Union as the party responsible for

the crisis. Mr. Kennedy treated Cuba and the Government of Premier Fidel Castro as a mere pawn in Moscow's hands and drew the issue as one with the Soviet Government.

The President, in language of unusual bluntness, accused the Soviet leaders of deliberately "false statements about their intentions in Cuba."

The other aspect of the speech particularly noted by observers here was its flat commitment by the United States to act alone against the missile threat in Cuba.

Nation Ready to Act

The President made it clear that this country would not stop short of military action to end what he called a "clandestine, reckless and provocative threat to world peace."

Mr. Kennedy said the United States was asking for an emergency meeting of the United Nations Security Council to consider a resolution for "dismantling and withdrawal of all offensive weapons in Cuba."

He said the launching of a nuclear missile from Cuba against any nation in the Western Hemisphere would be regarded as an attack by the Soviet Union against the United States. It would be met, he said, by retaliation against the Soviet Union.

"DEMOCRATS GAIN 4 SENATE SEATS TO UPSET A MIDTERM TRADITION," NOVEMBER 8, 1962

Just weeks after the Cuban missile crisis, President Kennedy scored another victory when his party gained Senate seats in the 1962 midterm elections. The president's party typically loses seats at midterm, which made the Democratic victories even more significant.

NOVEMBER 8, 1962
DEMOCRATS GAIN 4 SENATE SEATS TO UPSET A MIDTERM TRADITION
By JOHN D. MORRIS

Democrats upset political tradition in Tuesday's Congressional elections by gaining strength in the Senate and holding their House losses to a minimum.

Final unofficial Senate returns showed that the new Senate would have the following division:

Democrats—68.

Republicans—32.

The Senate division in the expiring 87th Congress was 64 Democrats and 36 Republicans.

In the 39 Senate races Tuesday, the Democrats captured six seats now held by Republicans and lost two of their own, for a net gain of four. . . .

The Democrats thus upset the historical pattern of midterm elections—those in which the Presidency is not at stake. With rare exceptions, the party in power loses strength in both the Senate and House. And the House losses ordinarily are far greater than the number the Democrats incurred this year.

"NEGROES' ADMISSION DUE TODAY—U.S. SHOW OF FORCE MAY BE NEEDED," JUNE 11, 1963

In June 1963 President Kennedy enforced the integration of the University of Alabama despite the opposition of Gov. George C. Wallace, who physically blocked the door to keep two black students from enrolling. Kennedy called National Guard troops into federal service to carry out a court order to admit the students. When the two students arrived with Deputy U.S. Attorney General Nicholas Katzenbach and federal marshals, Wallace yielded and permitted them to enroll.

JUNE 11, 1963
NEGROES' ADMISSION DUE TODAY—U.S. SHOW OF FORCE MAY BE NEEDED

By CLAUDE SITTON

Special to *The New York Times*

TUSCALOOSA, Ala., June 10—Gov. George C. Wallace arrived here today to oppose the court-ordered admission of two Negroes to the University of Alabama tomorrow.

He gave no indication whether he would press his defiance of Federal authority to the point at which President Kennedy would be forced to send troops to carry out the court order.

Sources close to Governor Wallace said he believed that some show of military force was necessary before he could retreat from a pledge to prevent desegregation in Alabama. This is the only state that maintains complete segregation throughout its public educational system.

The Governor asserted repeatedly after his arrival that no violence would mark what may be the last Federal-state showdown on a grand scale over the desegregation issue. One of his first acts was to inspect the 500 national guardsmen he had called up to assist 850 state law enforcement officers in preserving the peace.

The confrontation on the tree-shaded campus by the Black Warrior River is scheduled to take place at 12:30 P.M., New York time, at the entrance of Foster Auditorium.

The Negro applicants, Jimmy A. Hood and Vivian Malone, both 20 years old, will arrive then, accompanied by Nicholas deB. Katzenbach, Deputy United States Attorney General, other Federal officials and a small group of Federal marshals.

Governor Wallace has said he will meet the applicants at the auditorium's entrance, "the school house door" of his campaign pledge last year. He will then formally deny them admission to the university.

Neither Mr. Wallace nor his aides have disclosed whether state troopers under Col. Albert J. Lingo, Commissioner of Public Safety, will join him in blocking the Negroes. Colonel Lingo declined to say this afternoon what he would do if Federal officials sought to force their way into the auditorium, where registration began today.

Edwin O. Guthman, special assistant for public information to Attorney General Robert F. Kennedy, said here that every effort would be made to enroll the two students.

If these attempts fail, the Federal officials are expected to withdraw from the campus. President Kennedy is then likely to sign a proclamation federalizing units of the Alabama National Guard that are now in summer training at Fort McClellan, near Anniston, Ala.

The troops, members of the 31st (Dixie) Division, would then take over the campus and assure admission of the Negroes.

• •

"PRESIDENT IN PLEA," JUNE 12, 1963, AND "CONGRESS TO OPEN CIVIL RIGHTS FIGHT WITH 2 HEARINGS," JUNE 24, 1963

The same day that the University of Alabama was desegregated, President Kennedy endorsed congressional legislation to ensure civil rights for black Americans. In a nationally televised address on June 11, 1963, Kennedy declared that every American should be treated "without regard to his race or color." He subsequently sent Congress a civil rights bill, which became the landmark Civil Rights Act of 1964.

JUNE 12, 1963
PRESIDENT IN PLEA

Asks Help of Citizens to Assure Equality of Rights to All

By TOM WICKER

Special to *The New York Times*

WASHINGTON, June 11—President Kennedy told the nation tonight that it faced a "moral crisis" as a result of the rising tide of Negro discontent.

"This is a problem which faces us all in every city of the North as well as the South," Mr. Kennedy said in a brief address televised by all three national networks.

It is a time to act, the President said. He promised to send to Congress next week sweeping legislation to speed school desegregation and open public facilities to every American, regardless of color.

Problem 'Must Be Solved'

Above all, Mr. Kennedy solemnly told the millions of citizens watching him speak from the White House, the problem of the Negro's place in American life "must be solved in the homes of every American across the country."

The objective of every citizen, the President said, must be "for every American to enjoy the privilege of being American without regard to his race or color"—to be treated "as one would wish his children to be treated."

This is, he said, "a matter which concerns this country and what it stands for, and in meeting it I ask the support of all our citizens."

He asked it, the President said, because "this nation for all its hopes and all its boasts will not be fully free until its citizens are free."

Makes Broad Appeal

Mr. Kennedy's address, arranged late today, was made in part as the result of the successful desegregation of the University of Alabama. But the President seized the occasion to make a broad appeal that Negroes and liberals of both parties had been urging upon him for weeks.

The Administration had laid plans well in advance for meeting the Alabama crisis. An executive order federalizing the Alabama National Guard was ready for Mr. Kennedy's signature when the White House received word of Gov. George C. Wallace's defiance of court orders not to interfere with desegregation of the university.

Mr. Kennedy's address was one of the most emotional speeches yet delivered by a President who has often been criticized as being too "cool" and intellectual. Near the end of his talk, Mr. Kennedy appeared to be speaking without a text, and there was a fervor in his voice when he talked of the plight of some Americans.

Education Is Cited

"Today there are Negroes unemployed—two or three times as many compared to whites," he said. "Inadequate education, moving into the large cities, unable to find work, young people particularly out of work, without hope, denied equal rights, denied the opportunity to eat at a restaurant or a lunch counter, or go to a movie theater, denied the right to a decent education, denied—almost today—the right to attend a state university even though qualified.". . .

"The Negro baby born in America today . . . has about one-half as much chance of completing high school as a white baby, born in the same place on the same day; one-third as much chance of completing college; one-third as much chance of becoming a professional man; twice as much chance of becoming unemployed; about one-seventh as much chance of earning $10,000 a year; a life expectancy which is seven years shorter and the prospects of earning only half as much."

To white Americans, Mr. Kennedy addressed these questions:

"Who among us would be content with the counsels of patience and delay?"

Who among us would be content to have the color of his skin changed and stand in his place?"

The Nergo's plight is not entirely a sectional situation, Mr. Kennedy emphasized repeatedly.

"The fires of frustration and discontent are burning in every city, North and South, where legal remedies are not at hand," he said.

"Difficulties over segregation and discrimination exist in every city, in every state of the Union, producing in many citizens a rising tide of discontent that threatens the public safety."

JUNE 24, 1963
CONGRESS TO OPEN CIVIL RIGHTS FIGHT WITH 2 HEARINGS
Robert Kennedy to Testify on Proposals This Week in House and Senate
TOTAL PROGRAM PUSHED
Attorney General Declares Desegregation Essential in Places Serving Public
By E. W. KENWORTHY
Special to *The New York Times*

WASHINGTON, June 23—President Kennedy's civil rights bill starts up the long, tough legislative trail this week.

On Tuesday Senator Warren G. Magnuson, Democrat of Washington, who is chairman of the Senate Commerce Committee, expects to open hearings on Title II. This is the controversial section of the bill that would prohibit discrimination in privately owned public accommodations.

The first witness will be Attorney General Robert F. Kennedy.

On Wednesday Representative Emanuel Celler, Democrat of Brooklyn, who heads the House Judiciary Committee, will start hearings on the Administration's omnibus bill. Again the Attorney General will lead off.

Attorney General Firm

Attorney General Kennedy took a firm position tonight on the section of the proposed legislation prohibiting segregation in hotels, restaurants and other places of public accommodation. He called it "essential."

This is the part of the Administration bill that has aroused the most controversy. Some Republicans, whose votes will be needed, have been critical of it.

But Mr. Kennedy said the ban on segregation at lunch counters and such places was urgently needed to remove the cause of Negro demonstrations.

"Negroes are insulted daily" by being turned away from business establishments open to the general public, he said. He spoke on the National Broadcasting Company radio-television show, "Meet the Press."

The Attorney General said it was "possible" that the Administration might accept some limitation so that the provision would not apply to the smallest establishments. But he said it was premature to discuss that now.

"President Hailed by Over a Million in Visit to Berlin, June 27, 1963

President Kennedy received a warm welcome when he visited Berlin in the summer of 1963. In a rousing speech, he famously declared his pride that "Ich bin ein Berliner," or "I am a Berliner." In another address, he referred to a commencement speech he had delivered at American University on June 10, in which he called for world peace with an inspirational reminder: "In the final analysis, our most basic common link is that we all inhabit this small planet. We all breathe the same air. We all cherish our children's future. And we are all mortal."

JUNE 27, 1963
PRESIDENT HAILED BY OVER A MILLION IN VISIT TO BERLIN

He Salutes the Divided City as Front Line in World's Struggle for Freedom

LOOKS OVER THE WALL

Says Berliners' Experience Shows Hazard in Trying to Work With Communists

By ARTHUR J. OLSEN

Special to The New York Times

BERLIN, June 26—President Kennedy, inspired by a tumultuous welcome from more than a million of the inhabitants of this isolated and divided city, declared today he was proud to be "a Berliner."

He said his claim to being a Berliner was based on the fact that "all free men, wherever they may live, are citizens of Berlin."

In a rousing speech to 150,000 West Berliners crowded before the City Hall, the President said anyone who thought "we can work with the Communists" should come to Berlin.

However, three hours later, in a less emotional setting, he reaffirmed his belief that the great powers must work together "to preserve the human race."

Warning on Communism

His earlier rejection of dealing with the Communists was a warning against trying to "ride the tiger" of popular fronts that unite democratic and Communist forces, Mr. Kennedy explained in an interpolation in a prepared speech.

The President's City Hall speech was the emotional high point of a spectacular welcome accorded the President by West Berlin. He saluted the city as the front line and shining example of humanity's struggle for freedom.

Those who profess not to understand the great issues between the free world and the Communist world or who think Communism is the wave of the future should come to Berlin, he said.

In his later speech, at the Free University of Berlin, President Kennedy returned firmly to the theme of his address at American University in Washington June 10 in which he called for an attempt to end the cold war.

Wounds to Heal

"When the possibilities of reconciliation appear, we in the West will make it clear that we are not hostile to any people or system, provided that they choose their own destiny without interfering with the free choice of others," he said.

"There will be wounds to heal and suspicions to be eased on both sides," he added. "The difference in living standards will have to be reduced—by leveling up, not down. Fair and effective agreements to end the arms race must be reached."

The changes might not come tomorrow, but "our efforts for a real settlement must continue," he said.

• •

"SENATE REJECTS ALL RESTRICTIONS ON TEST BAN PACT," SEPTEMBER 24, 1963

In fall 1963 the United States and Soviet Union signed their first arms control agreement. The treaty banned nuclear testing in the atmosphere, outer space, and under water.

SEPTEMBER 24, 1963
SENATE REJECTS ALL RESTRICTIONS ON TEST BAN PACT
Clears Way for Ratification of Nuclear Treaty Today—80 'Yes' Votes Expected
GOLDWATER PLAN LOSES
But Closest Fight Arises on Move to Spell Out Right to Use A-Bomb in War
By ANTHONY LEWIS
Special to The New York Times

WASHINGTON, Sept. 23—The Senate decisively rejected today all proposed reservations to the nuclear test ban treaty.

A grueling day of cut-and-thrust debate and roll-calls cleared the way for the final vote on ratification. That will come at 10:30 tomorrow morning, with approximately 80 of the 100 Senators expected to favor the treaty.

The biggest fight today came as an apparent surprise to the leaders. It was over a proposed "understanding" to make clear that the treaty does not affect the right of the United States to use nuclear weapons in war.

Leaders Oppose Move

A number of treaty supporters swung behind this amendment to the resolution of ratification before the leaders stepped in with some strong speeches against it. The proposal was then tabled, or killed, by a vote of 61 to 33.

The "understanding" was sponsored by Senators John G. Tower, Republican of Texas, and Russell B. Long, Democrat of Louisiana.

Earlier, a vote of 75 to 17 rejected a reservation proposed by Senator Barry Goldwater, Republican of Arizona.

The Goldwater proposal would have made the test-ban treaty effective only after the Soviet Union had withdrawn all its forces from Cuba. Major political attention had centered on it because of the Senator's leading position now as a contender for the 1964 Republican Presidential nomination.

* *

"KENNEDY IS KILLED BY SNIPER AS HE RIDES IN CAR IN DALLAS; JOHNSON SWORN IN ON PLANE," NOVEMBER 23, 1963, AND "JOHN FITZGERALD KENNEDY," NOVEMBER 23, 1963

The news of President Kennedy's assassination on November 22, 1963, stunned the nation and the world. In a poignant editorial, *The Times* described the slain president as "a man of intellect as well as action" and depicted his enduring commitment to human rights around the globe.

NOVEMBER 23, 1963
KENNEDY IS KILLED BY SNIPER AS HE RIDES IN CAR IN DALLAS; JOHNSON SWORN IN ON PLANE
Gov. Connally Shot; Mrs. Kennedy Safe
President Is Struck Down by a Rifle Shot from Building on Motorcade Route—
Johnson, Riding Behind, Is Unhurt
By TOM WICKER
Special to The New York Times

DALLAS, Nov. 22—President John Fitzgerald Kennedy was shot and killed by an assassin today.

He died of a wound in the brain caused by a rifle bullet that was fired at him as he was riding through downtown Dallas in a motorcade.

Vice President Lyndon Baines Johnson, who was riding in the third car behind Mr. Kennedy's, was sworn in as the 36th President of the United States 99 minutes after Mr. Kennedy's death.

Mr. Johnson is 55 years old; Mr. Kennedy was 46.

Shortly after the assassination, Lee H. Oswald, who once defected to the Soviet Union and who has been active in the Fair Play for Cuba Committee, was arrested by the Dallas police. Tonight he was accused of the killing.

Suspect Captured After Scuffle

Oswald, 24 years old, was also accused of slaying a policeman who had approached him in the street. Oswald was subdued after a scuffle with a second policeman in a nearby theater.

President Kennedy was shot at 12:30 P.M., Central standard time (1:30 P.M., New York time). He was pronounced dead at 1 P.M. and Mr. Johnson was sworn in at 2:39 P.M.

Mr. Johnson, who was uninjured in the shooting, took his oath in the Presidential jet plane as it stood on the runway at Love Field. The body of Mr. Kennedy was aboard. Immediately after the oath-taking, the plane took off for Washington.

Standing beside the new President as Mr. Johnson took the oath of office was Mrs. John F. Kennedy. Her stockings were spattered with her husband's blood.

Gov. John B. Connally Jr. of Texas, who was riding in the same car with Mr. Kennedy, was severely wounded in the chest, ribs and arm. His condition was serious, but not critical.

The killer fired the rifle from a building just off the motorcade route. Mr. Kennedy, Governor Connally and Mr. Johnson had just received an enthusiastic welcome from a large crowd in downtown Dallas.

Mr. Kennedy apparently was hit by the first of what witnesses believed were three shots. He was driven at high speed to Dallas's Parkland Hospital. There, in an emergency operating room, with only physicians and nurses in attendance, he died without regaining consciousness.

Mrs. Kennedy, Mrs. Connally and a Secret Service agent were in the car with Mr. Kennedy and Governor Connally. Two Secret Service agents flanked the car. Other than Mr. Connally, none of this group was injured in the shooting. Mrs. Kennedy cried, "Oh no!" immediately after her husband was struck.

Mrs. Kennedy was in the hospital near her husband when he died, but not in the operating room. When the body was taken from the hospital in a bronze coffin about 2 P.M., Mrs. Kennedy walked beside it.

Her face was sorrowful. She looked steadily at the floor. She still wore the raspberry-colored suit in which she had greeted welcoming crowds in Fort Worth and Dallas.

But she had taken off the matching pillbox hat she wore earlier in the day, and her dark hair was windblown and tangled. Her hand rested lightly on her husband's coffin as it was taken to a waiting hearse.

Mrs. Kennedy climbed in beside the coffin. Then the ambulance drove to Love Field, and Mr. Kennedy's body was placed aboard the Presidential jet. Mrs. Kennedy then attended the swearing-in ceremony for Mr. Johnson.

As Mr. Kennedy's body left Parkland Hospital, a few stunned persons stood outside. Nurses and doctors, whispering among themselves, looked from the window. A larger crowd that had gathered earlier, before it was known that the President was dead, had been dispersed by Secret Service men and policemen.

Priests Administer Last Rites

Two priests administered last rites to Mr. Kennedy, a Roman Catholic. They were the Very Rev. Oscar Huber, the pastor of Holy Trinity Church in Dallas, and the Rev. James Thompson.

Mr. Johnson was sworn in as President by Federal Judge Sarah T. Hughes of the Northern District of Texas. She was appointed to the judgeship by Mr. Kennedy in October, 1961.

The ceremony, delayed about five minutes for Mrs. Kennedy's arrival, took place in the private Presidential cabin in the rear of the plane.

About 25 to 30 persons—members of the late President's staff, members of Congress who had been accompanying the President on a two-day tour of Texas cities and a few reporters—crowded into the little room.

No accurate listing of those present could be obtained. Mrs. Kennedy stood at the left of Mr. Johnson, her eyes and face showing the signs of weeping that had apparently shaken her since she left the hospital not long before.

Mrs. Johnson, wearing a beige dress, stood at her husband's right.

As Judge Hughes read the brief oath of office, her eyes, too, were red from weeping. Mr. Johnson's hands rested on a black, leather-bound Bible as Judge Hughes read and he repeated:

"I do solemnly swear that I will perform the duties of the President of the United States to the best of my ability and defend, protect and preserve the Constitution of the United States."

Those 34 words made Lyndon Baines Johnson, one-time farmboy and schoolteacher of Johnson City, the President.

> The personal loss is deep and crushing; the loss to the nation and the world is historic and overpowering.

NOVEMBER 23, 1963
EDITORIAL
JOHN FITZGERALD KENNEDY

The incredible, devastating news that engulfed all America and the world yesterday afternoon is still difficult of comprehension. Hours after the event it remains almost inconceivable that John Fitzgerald Kennedy, President of the United States, whose every word and action typified life and youth and strength, now lies dead of an assassin's bullet.

All of us—from the country's highest leaders to the humblest citizen—all of us are still in a state of shock from this stunning blow, that even now seems unreal in its grotesque horror. And hundreds of millions of people beyond our borders—throughout the hemisphere and across the seas—mourn, too, the loss of a President who gave worldwide reality to the American ideals of peace and freedom.

One's first thought turns in human sympathy to the President's family, to his wife who was by his side when he was struck down, to his little children, to his parents, to his brothers and sisters. The acutely personal loss they have suffered is intensified by the unusual closeness of their relationships within this tight-knit family.

The personal loss is deep and crushing; the loss to the nation and the world is historic and overpowering. John F. Kennedy was a man of intellect as well as action. He represented the vitality and the energy, the intelligence and the enthusiasm, the courage and the hope of these United States in the middle of this 20th century. On that day less than three years ago when he took the oath of his great office, he said:

"Let the word go forth from this time and place, to friend and foe alike, that the torch has been passed to a new generation of Americans—born in this century, tempered by war, disciplined by a hard and bitter peace, proud of our ancient heritage—and unwilling to witness or permit the slow undoing of those human rights to which this nation has always been committed, and to which we are committed today at home and around the world."

John F. Kennedy died in and for this belief, the belief in those human rights to which this nation has always been committed, and to which in his day it recommitted itself—rights which we hope to see exercised around the world, but which we are determined to see exercised within our borders.

No madman's bullet can stop this inexorable march of human rights; no murder, however tragic, can make it falter. In death as in life, the words and spirit of this our most newly martyred President will lead the nation ever closer toward fulfillment of the ideals of domestic brotherhood and international peace by which his Administration has been guided from the start.

Among the last words John F. Kennedy wrote were these: "In a world full of frustrations and irritations, America's leadership must be guided by the lights of learning and reason."

The light of reason was momentarily extinguished with the crack of a rifle shot in Dallas yesterday. But that light is, in reality, inextinguishable; and, with God's help, it will show the way to our country and our country's leaders as we mourn for John F. Kennedy in the darkening days ahead.

THE PRESIDENCY OF LYNDON B. JOHNSON

NOVEMBER 22, 1963 – JANUARY 20, 1969

Lyndon Baines Johnson's presidency left a split legacy of high achievement in domestic policy and enormous conflict and disarray in foreign affairs. The horrific event that brought Johnson into office—the assassination of President John F. Kennedy—overshadowed his five years in office. Johnson successfully enacted some components of Kennedy's agenda, particularly in civil rights, and made his own mark in other areas such as housing and health care for the elderly and poor. But the nation's growing entanglement in the Vietnam War under Johnson tarnished his record and raised continuing questions about his executive leadership abilities.

A Texas native, Johnson was the eldest of five children and grew up in a family of limited financial means but strong involvement in local politics. Johnson's father and both grandfathers served in the Texas state legislature, and the town of Johnson City, close to where Johnson lived as a boy, was named in recognition of his paternal grandfather. Johnson graduated from Southwest Texas State Teachers College (now Texas State University–San Marcos) in 1927 and briefly taught high school public speaking and debate. During his college years, he also taught in a school in the Mexican-American community.

The lure of politics was strong for Johnson, and in 1931 he moved to Washington, D.C., to become an aide to Richard Kleberg, a newly elected Democratic representative from Texas. Johnson worked for Kleberg for four years, and he became a strong supporter of President Franklin D. Roosevelt's New Deal program. In 1935 FDR appointed Johnson to be Texas director of the National Youth Administration, an organization that helped young people complete their studies and find work.

In 1937 Johnson won a special election for an open Texas seat in the U.S. House of Representatives, and his victory marked the start of a congressional career that would span more than two decades. He served in the House for twelve years, taking a brief leave of absence during World War II to enter active duty in the U.S. Navy, where he became a lieutenant commander. After an unsuccessful Senate run (again in a special election for an open seat) in 1941,

"FROM THIS NETTLE, DANGER, WE PLUCK THIS FLOWER, SAFETY." (Shakespeare, Henry IV)

Source: Copyright 1965 by Bill Mauldin. Reprinted courtesy of the William Mauldin Estate.

Johnson narrowly prevailed in a 1948 Senate race in Texas, winning by just eighty-seven votes. The victory earned him the nickname "Landslide Lyndon." After just four years in the Senate, Johnson became minority leader, and when Democrats won control of the chamber in 1954, he became majority leader. He honed his legislative skills well in this position, gaining fame for his ability to work out political compromises to enact laws.

Johnson entered the presidential race in 1960, but lost the Democratic nomination to John F. Kennedy. Given Johnson's popularity in the South, especially in Texas, Kennedy invited him to become the vice-presidential nominee, and Johnson accepted. The Democratic ticket narrowly prevailed over Republican nominee, Vice President Richard M. Nixon, who ran with former senator Henry Cabot Lodge of Massachusetts, and Johnson's ability to bring in supporters from states rich in Electoral College votes likely made the difference. Vice President Johnson was not an insider in the Kennedy administration, however; his role largely was limited to diplomatic missions abroad. But President Kennedy did seek Johnson's political advice, and Johnson accompanied Kennedy on his trip to Dallas, Texas, in November 1963. After the news that Kennedy had not survived the assassination attack on November 22, Johnson boarded *Air Force One,* where he took the oath of office and became the nation's thirty-sixth president.

The Johnson Administration (First Term)

Given the circumstances in which he took office, Johnson made no immediate changes to Kennedy's cabinet. Nearly all of Kennedy's ten-member cabinet, in fact, served through Johnson's election victory in 1964, including Secretary of State Dean Rusk of New York, Defense Secretary Robert S. McNamara of Michigan, and Treasury Secretary C. Douglas Dillon of New Jersey. The cabinet member who faced the most difficulty in serving a new president undoubtedly was Attorney General Robert F. Kennedy. Shocked by his brother's death, Robert Kennedy was unable to work closely with President Johnson, and in summer 1964, he decided to run for a U.S. Senate seat from New York, which he won.

Johnson's first lady was fellow Texan Claudia Alta Taylor, whom he married in San Antonio, Texas, in 1934. Her childhood nickname "Lady Bird" stayed with her through her lifetime, and she was well known for seeking to temper her husband's abrasive, even bullying, personality. As first lady, she actively promoted projects for highway beautification across the nation. The Johnsons had two daughters, Lynda and Luci, both of whom were married during their father's presidency. Lynda Johnson's wedding to Charles S. Robb, a future governor of and U.S. senator from Virginia, took place at the White House in 1967.

Major Issues (First Term)

In his first address to Congress just days after becoming president, Johnson promised to enact Kennedy's legislative agenda. Congress complied in establishing the political legacy of the slain president, passing a tax cut bill in 1964 that provided an important stimulus to the economy. The most significant legislation was the landmark Civil Rights Act of 1964, which prohibited discrimination based on race or sex by employers and in public accommodations. The legislation also created the Equal Employment Opportunity Commission to investigate allegations of discrimination. Kennedy had proposed this legislation in 1963, and Johnson championed it in 1964. His virtually unparalleled expertise in building legislative coalitions in Congress enabled the successful passage of the bill.

Although foreign policy was not Johnson's area of interest, events in Southeast Asia intruded upon his presidency and came to dominate it by the end of his term. President Kennedy had steadily increased the number of U.S. military advisers in South Vietnam during his administration, and by 1964 the United States was facing increasing pressure to assist its ally in combating the Communist regime in North Vietnam. In August 1964 the North Vietnamese allegedly attacked two U.S. naval destroyers. (At least one allegation was later found to be incorrect.) In response, President Johnson approved retaliatory air strikes and, more significantly, requested a congressional resolution to authorize continued military action against North Vietnam. On August 7, with just two dissenting votes in the Senate and unanimous support in the House, Congress passed the Gulf of Tonkin Resolution, which approved the use of military force to assist allies in Southeast Asia in their national defense. This resolution was the only legislative authorization for U.S. involvement in the Vietnam War.

The 1964 Presidential Election

Less than a year after he became president, Johnson won election to the office in his own right. The Democratic Party nominated him unanimously on the first convention ballot and selected Sen. Hubert H. Humphrey of Minnesota as his running mate. The Republican Party nominated Sen. Barry M. Goldwater of Arizona for president and Rep. William E. Miller of New York for vice president.

In his nomination acceptance speech, Goldwater declared that "extremism in the defense of liberty is no vice," and he maintained this hard-line approach to politics throughout his campaign. Goldwater's professed willingness to use nuclear weapons to protect U.S. and allied interests sparked fears that he would launch a global conflict. The Johnson campaign played upon this fear with the famous "Daisy" commercial, in which a nuclear weapon explodes as a young girl counts the petals she is pulling off a daisy. (The ad sparked such an outcry that it aired only once.) Johnson easily defeated Goldwater, winning nearly 43 million popular votes to Goldwater's 27 million, and a landslide victory in the Electoral College of 486 votes

QUICK FACTS ON LYNDON B. JOHNSON

BIRTH	August 27, 1908, Stonewall, Texas
EDUCATION	Southwest Texas State College
FAMILY	Wife: Claudia Alta "Lady Bird" Taylor Johnson Children: Lynda Bird Johnson, Luci Baines Johnson
WHITE HOUSE PETS	Dogs, including beagles "Him" and "Her"; hamsters; lovebirds
PARTY	Democratic
PREPRESIDENTIAL CAREER (SELECTED)	Teaches grade school in Texas, 1928–1929 Teaches high school debate and public speaking, 1930–1931 Secretary to U.S. Rep. Richard M. Kleberg, 1932–1935 State director, National Youth Administration for Texas, 1935–1937 U.S. House of Representatives, 1937–1948; wins first time in a special election U.S. Naval Reserve, 1940 Loses special election for U.S. Senate, 1941 Leave of absence from House to enter active duty in navy, December 1941; awarded Silver Star in 1942 U.S. Senate, 1949–1961 Senate Democratic whip, 1951–1953 Senate Democratic leader, 1953–1961 Suffers heart attack, 1955 Unsuccessful bid for presidential nomination, 1960 Vice president, 1961–1963
PRESIDENTIAL TERMS	November 22, 1963–January 20, 1965 January 20, 1965–January 20, 1969

to 52. The Democratic Party picked up seats in both chambers of Congress as well.

The Johnson Administration (Second Term)

Johnson's second-term cabinet included leaders of two new agencies, the Department of Housing and Urban Development (HUD) and the Department of Transportation (DOT). The first HUD secretary, Robert C. Weaver of New York, took office in 1966, and the first DOT secretary, Alan S. Boyd of Florida, began his term in 1967. Secretary of State Rusk stayed in office, and would have the distinction of being one of a few cabinet members to serve through both the Kennedy and Johnson administrations. Defense Secretary McNamara stepped down in February 1968 and was replaced by Clark M. Clifford of

Maryland. After Robert Kennedy resigned as attorney general, Johnson first appointed Nicholas deB. Katzenbach of Washington, D.C., and then William R. Clark of Texas for the post. Johnson selected Henry H. Fowler of Virginia to lead the Treasury Department in his second term, followed briefly by Joseph W. Barr of Indiana.

Major Issues (Second Term)

With a popular mandate and a cooperative Congress, Johnson moved quickly in his second term to implement an ambitious domestic agenda that he described as the "Great Society" and the "War on Poverty." The Social Security Act of 1965 established Medicare, a health care program for the elderly, and Medicaid, a health care program for the poor. Johnson endorsed legislation that promoted education, housing, urban renewal, and highway safety. In civil rights, he enacted the

VICE PRESIDENT	Hubert H. Humphrey (second term)
SELECTED EVENTS	Appointment of Warren Commission to investigate President John F. Kennedy's assassination (1963)
	Ratification of Twenty-fourth Amendment banning poll taxes in federal elections (1964)
	Civil Rights Act (1964)
	Gulf of Tonkin Resolution (1964)
	United States sends combat troops to Vietnam (1965)
	Selma-Montgomery Freedom March (1965)
	U.S. Marines enter Dominican Republic (1965)
	First American, Maj. Edward H. White, walks in space (1965)
	Medicare and Medicaid approved (1965)
	Voting Rights Act (1965)
	Creation of Department of Housing and Urban Affairs (1965)
	France withdraws from defense system in NATO (1966)
	Creation of Department of Transportation (1966)
	Ratification of Twenty-fifth Amendment addressing presidential disability (1967)
	United States promises neutrality in Arab-Israeli War (1967)
	Race riots in Newark and Detroit (1967)
	Seizure of USS *Pueblo* by North Korea (1968)
	Announces he will not seek another term (1968)
	Assassination of Rev. Martin Luther King Jr. (1968)
	Fair Housing Act (1968)
	Assassination of Sen. Robert F. Kennedy (1968)
	Violent protests at Democratic National Convention, Chicago (1968)
	Johnson halts bombing of North Vietnam (1968)
DEATH	January 22, 1973, Johnson City, Texas

Voting Rights Act of 1965, which expanded voter registration for black citizens and outlawed obstacles such as literacy tests.

Despite Johnson's keen desire to focus on domestic policy, the Vietnam War dominated his political agenda in his second term. After the partition of Vietnam in 1954, the United States had provided economic and military assistance to its South Vietnamese ally to repel advances from the Communist regime in North Vietnam. As the conflict between the two sides continued, President Johnson decided in 1965 to send U.S. combat troops to Vietnam, which he gradually increased to more than half a million.

The underlying problems with Johnson's Vietnam policy were the absence of clearly defined goals for the United States and the failure to develop a comprehensive analysis of the resources required to pursue U.S. interests in Southeast Asia. Although the American public initially supported the president, opposition developed as the gradual escalation of U.S. troops continued. Student protesters on college campuses, many of whom were eligible for the draft, questioned

why the United States was fighting in Vietnam and wanted the war to end. They denounced the president's failure to attain a decisive military victory that would lead to peace negotiations. Members of Congress also began to criticize the war, which drew resources away from Johnson's domestic agenda. At the same time, racial tensions erupted into riots in major cities across the United States, reflecting frustration with the nation's treatment of black Americans as well as with the Vietnam War. By late 1967 public support for the war had dropped below 50 percent, and public confidence in Johnson's war leadership had fallen to the low twenties.

Johnson's foreign-policy problems continued into 1968. In January North Korean troops seized the USS *Pueblo*, which had been on patrol near its border, and imprisoned its crew. After eleven months of tortuous negotiations, North Korea freed the crew members. Just a week after the *Pueblo* crisis began, the North Vietnamese launched an enormous assault in South Vietnam during the Tet celebrations for the lunar new year. Although U.S. and South Vietnamese forces ultimately prevailed in the Tet Offensive, the surprisingly fierce battle dominated public perceptions and raised concerns about how long the United States would be entangled in the region. When Gen. William C. Westmoreland, the commander of U.S. military forces in Vietnam, requested 200,000 more troops, President Johnson recognized that he faced a turning point in the war and his career.

On March 31, 1968, Johnson announced in an address to the nation that he would not run for reelection and that he would devote the remainder of his presidency to pursuing a settlement in the Vietnam War. Despite his incumbency, Johnson would have faced competition for his party's nomination. In the New Hampshire primary just weeks earlier, Sen. Eugene J. McCarthy of Minnesota, a strong opponent of the war, had won more than 40 percent of the vote. A few days later, Sen. Robert Kennedy of New York, who also opposed the war, entered the race for the Democratic presidential nomination. Johnson's surprise announcement stunned the nation but reflected its political realities.

Tragedy and conflict defined the remaining months of Johnson's presidency. On April 4, 1968, civil rights leader Martin Luther King Jr. was assassinated in Memphis, Tennessee. Two months later, Robert Kennedy was fatally shot in Los Angeles, just hours after winning the California presidential primary. President Johnson chose not to attend the Democratic convention in Chicago. Vice President Humphrey became the party's nominee at a convention marred by violence in the streets outside the hall, as police fought with antiwar demonstrators. That same week, Soviet troops invaded Czechoslovakia to halt a revolutionary movement, effectively ending any prospects for an arms treaty in Johnson's term. His political capital was largely spent, as demonstrated by the Senate's rejection in October of his nomination of Justice Abe Fortas to head the Supreme Court. Johnson's negotiating team was unable to produce an agreement with North Vietnam, and Vice President Humphrey faced the results of this failure, losing the presidential election to the Republican candidate, former vice president Richard M. Nixon.

After leaving office, Johnson returned to Texas, where he wrote his memoirs. The presidency had taken a severe physical toll on him, and he died of a heart attack in 1973. He is buried at his ranch near Johnson City, Texas.

"PRESIDENT JOHNSON," NOVEMBER 23, 1963

The assassination of President Kennedy thrust the newly elevated president into the national spotlight. Shocked by the circumstances that had propelled him into the Oval Office, Johnson promised to make Kennedy's political agenda his own in honor of the fallen president. Although Johnson succeeded in enacting much of that agenda, most notably in domestic policy and civil rights, he never escaped the resentment from some, particularly Kennedy's closest aides, that he had intruded upon the presidency. As The New York Times wrote, "The burden of responsibility that now falls upon the shoulders of Lyndon Johnson is heavy," and so it would remain throughout his time in office.

NOVEMBER 23, 1963
EDITORIAL
PRESIDENT JOHNSON

Mourning a lost leader, let us close ranks behind his successor and demonstrate before the world that we are a united and a dedicated people.

The burden of responsibility that now falls upon the shoulders of Lyndon Johnson is heavy. He must rally the country from the profound shock into which it has been plunged. He must establish as swiftly as possible a confident relationship between the coordinate branches of the Government. He must convince the country that this bitter tragedy will not divert us from our proclaimed purposes or check our forward movement. He must demonstrate to our friends and allies overseas that our goals remain unchanged and that our strength is undiminished.

To these tasks Lyndon Johnson brings experience and qualities of character that should stand him in good stead. He is thoroughly at home in the Congress, which must now share with him the responsibility of steadying the country through the crisis which confronts it. He is well known in all parts of the country, but no one can really know his qualities as leader until he has had a chance to demonstrate them in an assignment more difficult than any other on earth. He is a man of moderate views, with a talent for bringing concord out of disagreement.

A man of the South, he has aligned himself unmistakably with President Kennedy's civil rights program. In another equally important field of action he has played an increasingly constructive role in the expression of this nation's foreign policy. Particularly in recent years he has traveled much abroad, looked closely into problems with which he will have to deal, made contacts which will be

of value to him and been accepted as a trustworthy representative of the American people and an authoritative spokesman of their ideals.

These are assets he will bring to the Presidency in this sad hour. On his side he can count upon the great fund of goodwill which will flow to him spontaneously. He can be sure that every move he makes to steady the country and to lead it forward will meet with a ready response. He can be confident that in a time of crisis the traditional resourcefulness and determination of the American people will help to sustain him. The challenges are great; the country will support greatness in its new President.

• •

"President Urges New Federalism to 'Enrich' Life," May 23, 1964

President Johnson presented his vision for a "Great Society" domestic agenda in a commencement speech at the University of Michigan in 1964. He called for making the United States a place where people would enrich themselves to the greatest possible extent through education and other opportunities, regardless of their race. To accomplish this goal, Johnson declared that a "creative federalism" would be necessary in which the federal government worked with the states to promote development and fight poverty. In the course of his five years as president, Johnson made great progress toward these goals, and the "Great Society" became a hallmark of his political legacy.

MAY 23, 1964
PRESIDENT URGES NEW FEDERALISM TO 'ENRICH' LIFE
In Talk to Michigan Class He Bids U.S., Localities Join in Rebuilding Country
CITES CITIES' PROBLEMS
Johnson Exhorts Students to Beautify Nation and to Raise School Standards
By TOM WICKER
Special to The New York Times

ANN ARBOR, Mich., May 22—President Johnson called today for a "creative federalism" of local and national authorities to rebuild American cities, preserve the American countryside and develop an educational system that "grows in excellence as it grows in size."

As a first step, he promised the 4,862-member graduating class of the University of Michigan, he will "establish working groups to prepare a series of White House conferences and meetings—on the cities, on natural beauty, on the quality of education, and on other emerging challenges."

In an appeal directed primarily to the nation's youth, Mr. Johnson said that the "challenge of the next half-century" was to use American resources "to enrich and

elevate our national life and to advance the quality of American civilization."

Challenge of the Cities

Nowhere is the challenge more pressing than in the cities, the President told about 85,000 persons sitting in the sun in the world's largest college-owned stadium.

"In the next 40 years," Mr. Johnson said, "we must rebuild the entire urban United States."

Outside the cities, he said, "we must act to prevent an ugly America"—turning back the threats of polluted air, water and food, disappearing fields and forests, and overcrowded recreational areas.

In the classroom, Mr. Johnson continued, "we must give every child a place to sit and a teacher to learn from."

"Poverty must not be a bar to learning and learning must offer an escape from poverty," he declared.

Interrupted by Applause

Even more important, the President said, is that the nation's educational system should "find new ways to stimulate the love of learning and the capacity for creation."

Mr. Johnson was interrupted frequently for applause, particularly when he urged better teacher salaries and spoke of civil rights.

• •

"PRESIDENT SIGNS CIVIL RIGHTS BILL; BIDS ALL BACK IT," JULY 3, 1964

The Civil Rights Act of 1964 marked the most significant advance in U.S. race relations since the post–Civil War Reconstruction agenda nearly one hundred years earlier. The Fourteenth and Fifteenth Amendments to the Constitution, ratified in 1868 and 1870, respectively, had promised "due process" and "equal protection of the laws" for all Americans, as well as the prohibition of race-based restrictions on voting. The federal government, however, had not taken the initiative in enforcing these guarantees, and states found many ways to work around the letter of the law and maintain racial segregation. The 1964 law explicitly banned discrimination based on race or sex in employment and public life, and it authorized federal oversight of school desegregation. President Johnson personally campaigned for the law, using all of his political leverage in Congress to end a Senate filibuster and broker a majority political coalition.

JULY 3, 1964
PRESIDENT SIGNS CIVIL RIGHTS BILL; BIDS ALL BACK IT
Approves Sweeping Measure 5 Hours After Passage in House by 289–126 Vote
ASKS END OF INJUSTICE
Johnson Urges Closing of 'Springs of Racial Poison'—Maps Enforcement
By E. W. KENWORTHY
Special to The New York Times

WASHINGTON, July 2—President Johnson signed the Civil Rights Act of 1964 tonight.

It is the most far-reaching civil rights law since Reconstruction days. The President announced steps to implement it and called on all Americans to help "eliminate the last vestiges of injustice in America."

"Let us close the springs of racial poison," he said in a short television address.

The President signed the bill in the East Room of the White House before television cameras shortly before 7 o'clock. That was about five hours after the House of Representatives had completed Congressional action on the sweeping bill.

Among other things, it prohibits discrimination in places of public accommodation, publicly owned facilities, employment and union membership and Federally aided programs.

Adopts Senate's Changes

The House approved, by a vote of 289 to 126, the changes that the Senate had made. All provisions of the measure became effective with President Johnson's signature except the one prohibiting discrimination in employment and union membership. This one goes into effect a year from now.

In announcing his implementation program, the President said he was, as had been previously indicated by White House sources, appointing former Gov. LeRoy Collins of Florida as director of the new Community Relations Service. Mr. Collins is now president of the National Association of Broadcasters.

Among other implementation steps, the President said he would name an advisory commission to help Mr. Collins resolve disputes arising under the bill. He will also ask

President Lyndon B. Johnson shakes hands with Rev. Dr. Martin Luther King Jr. while signing the Civil Rights bill into law at a White House ceremony, July 2, 1964.

Source: UPI Telephoto

Congress, Mr. Johnson said, for a supplemental appropriation to finance initial operations under the new law.

Surrounded by the leaders of both parties in both houses, who had labored to frame and pass the bill, President Johnson began his address to the nation by recalling that 188 years ago this week, "a small band of valiant men began a struggle for freedom" with the writing of the Declaration of Independence.

That struggle, he said, was a "turning point in history," and the ideals proclaimed in the Declaration of Independence still shape the struggles "of men who hunger for freedom."

Nevertheless, he declared, though Americans believe all men are created equal and have inalienable rights, many in America are denied equal treatment and do not enjoy those rights, or the blessings of liberty, "not because of their own failures, but because of the color of their skins."

The reasons, the President said, can be understood "without rancor or hatred" because they are deeply embedded in history, tradition and the nature of man.

"But it cannot continue," the President said with great earnestness.

Treatment Forbidden

The Constitution, the principles of freedom and morality all forbid such unequal treatment, he declared.

"And the law I will sign tonight forbids it," he said.

The President then sought to set fears at rest and to correct misapprehensions by stating that the new law would not restrict anyone's freedom "so long as he respects the rights of others," and would not give special treatment to any citizen.

"It does say that those who are equal before God shall now be equal in the polling booths, in the classrooms, in the factories, and in hotels, restaurants, movie theaters, and other places that provide service to the public."

Turning to the future, the President besought the cooperation of state and local officials, religious leaders, businessmen, and "every working man and housewife" in bringing "justice and hope to all our people—and peace to our land."

"My fellow citizens," he closed in solemn adjuration, "we have come to a time of testing. We must not fail.

"Let us close the springs of racial poison. Let us pray for wise and understanding hearts. Let us lay aside irrelevant differences and make our nation whole. Let us hasten that day when our unmeasured strength and our unbounded spirit will be free to do the great works ordained for this nation by the just and wise God who is the father of us all."

Discrimination Banned

The new law—the most sweeping civil rights legislation ever enacted in this country—goes beyond the proscribing of various forms of discrimination.

It gives the Attorney General authority to initiate suits to end discrimination in jobs and public accommodations when he finds such discrimination is part of a practice or pattern. It also gives him new powers to speed school desegregation and enforce the Negro's right to vote.

While the bill provides for the final enforcement of its sanctions by Federal court orders, it also gives state and local agencies primary jurisdiction to deal with complaints for a limited time.

· ·

"RESOLUTION WINS," AUGUST 8, 1964

Just weeks after passage of the Civil Rights Act, President Johnson secured a congressional resolution that authorized him to use military force in Southeast Asia. The Gulf of Tonkin Resolution was later criticized as giving the president a "blank check" to wage war. Congress never declared war against North Vietnam, and many critics, including some members of Congress who originally had voted for the 1964 resolution, later declared that Johnson had overextended his authority in bringing the United States into war without explicit congressional approval.

AUGUST 8, 1964
RESOLUTION WINS
Senate Vote Is 88 to 2 After House Adopts Measure, 416–0
By E. W. KENWORTHY
Special to The New York Times

WASHINGTON, Aug. 7—The House of Representatives and the Senate approved today the resolution requested by President Johnson to strengthen his hand in dealing with Communist aggression in Southeast Asia.

After a 40-minute debate, the House passed the resolution, 416 to 0. Shortly afterward the Senate approved it, 88 to 2. Senate debate, which began yesterday afternoon, lasted nine hours.

The resolution gives prior Congressional approval of "all necessary measures" that the President may take "to repel any armed attack" against United States forces and "to prevent further aggression."

The resolution, the text of which was printed in *The New York Times* Thursday, also gives advance sanction for "all necessary steps" taken by the President to help any nation covered by the Southeast Asia collective defense treaty that requests assistance "in defense of its freedom."

Johnson Hails Action

President Johnson said the Congressional action was "a demonstration to all the world of the unity of all Americans."

"The votes prove our determination to defend our forces, to prevent aggression and to work firmly and steadily for peace and security in the area," he said.

"I am sure the American people join me in expressing the deepest appreciation to the leaders and members of both parties in both houses of Congress for their patriotic, resolute and rapid action."

The debates in both houses, but particularly in the Senate, made clear, however, that the near-unanimous vote did not reflect a unanimity of opinion on the necessity or advisability of the resolution.

Except for Senators Wayne L. Morse, Democrat of Oregon, and Ernest Gruening, Democrat of Alaska, who cast the votes against the resolution, members in both houses uniformly praised the President for the retaliatory action he had ordered against North Vietnamese torpedo boats and their bases after the second torpedo boat attack on United States destroyers in the Gulf of Tonkin.

There was also general agreement that Congress could not reject the President's requested resolution without giving an impression of disunity and nonsupport that did not, in fact, exist.

There was no support for the thesis on which Senators Morse and Gruening based their opposition—that the resolution was "unconstitutional" because it was "a predated declaration of war power" reserved to Congress.

Nevertheless, many members said the President did not need the resolution because he had the power as Commander in Chief to order United States forces to repel attacks.

Several members thought the language of the resolution was unnecessarily broad and they were apprehensive that it would be interpreted as giving Congressional support for direct participation by United States troops in the war in South Vietnam.

"JOHNSON'S PLURALITY SETS RECORD; MANY DEMOCRATS GAIN BY SWEEP," NOVEMBER 5, 1964

President Johnson's landslide election in 1964 was one of the record presidential victories in the twentieth century. He won more than 60 percent of the popular vote and an astounding 90 percent of the Electoral College vote. Only Franklin D. Roosevelt in 1936 and Richard M. Nixon in 1972 achieved similarly impressive results. Emboldened by his electoral success, Johnson set out to enact an ambitious policy agenda, and the first two years of his term produced many enduring and significant accomplishments in domestic affairs.

NOVEMBER 5, 1964
JOHNSON'S PLURALITY SETS RECORD; MANY DEMOCRATS GAIN BY SWEEP
By TOM WICKER

The Republican party, divided by Barry Goldwater and smashed by Lyndon B. Johnson, surveyed yesterday the wreckage of one of the worst election defeats in American history.

From the Pacific Coast through the so-called Republican heartland in the Middle West to the New England hills, the Democratic party stood triumphant—and by some of the most remarkable margins ever recorded.

With only 2 per cent of the nation's voting districts not yet reported, the President's plurality stood at 15,529,886, a record.

Only in a belt of five states across the Deep South could Mr. Goldwater claim victory for his brand of conservatism. In those states his victory margins were rolled up in predominantly rural, segregationist areas.

Even though the Senator's home state, Arizona, was finally counted into his column, the plain fact still was that the only base a Goldwater-style Republican party could command was in the most segregationist area of the South.

As for the Democrats, not since 1936 and the 46-state landslide of Franklin D. Roosevelt had they so nearly commanded all they surveyed. Even Mr. Roosevelt's great victory, in some ways, was not so impressive as that of the Texas Democrat who once was thought to be too conservative for a major party nomination.

Mr. Johnson compiled the greatest plurality in the nation's history, eclipsing the totals of such vote-getters as F. D. R. and Dwight D. Eisenhower, even in a year when the total voter turnout fell off from the last Presidential election by about two million.

With 98 per cent of all voting units reporting, the President's total stood at 41,727,846 to 26,197,960 for Mr. Goldwater.

Mr. Johnson carried 44 states and the District of Columbia. Included in his column were such brass-collar Republican states as Indiana, Vermont (which had never gone Democratic in a Presidential election), Nebraska and Kansas. He carried conservative, Republican-oriented Colorado by the largest majority in its history—and also rolled up record majorities in the Democratic strongholds of New York, New Jersey and Rhode Island.

"2,500 Men Fly In," April 30, 1965

In spring 1965 President Johnson sent U.S. Marines to the Dominican Republic to restore order following a popular rebellion against the government. Johnson declared that U.S. troops were needed to protect American lives and to keep Communist forces from taking control of the nation. The marines attained a cease-fire between the warring factions, and a peacekeeping force assembled by the Organization of American States deployed to the Dominican Republic the following month.

April 30, 1965
2,500 MEN FLY IN
Two Battalions to Aid 1,700 Marines in Anti-Red Move
By TAD SZULC
Special to The New York Times

SANTO DOMINGO, Friday, April 30—United States airborne troops began landing here early today as a further step under President Johnson's policy of using American forces to protect American lives and restore order in the Dominican Republic.

The Army airborne troops landed at 12:30 A.M., Eastern daylight time, at San Isidro Air Force Base, where the two-day-old Dominican military junta has its headquarters.

[The State Department announced Friday that two battalions of the United States 82d Airborne Division—about 2,500 men—were landing at San Isidro to reinforce 1,700 marines already in the Dominican Republic, The Associated Press reported.]

Quick Action Expected

It was expected that both the marines, which are based in the southern section of the city, and the airborne troops, which were arriving on the eastern bank of the Ozamo River, would enter into action later today. They would support the forces of the Dominican military junta in their attempts to smash a Communist-infiltrated revolt that had already brought heavy casualties.

The hard-pressed military junta was reported last night to have requested direct intervention by the United States to restore law and order to this embattled capital.

A quickly deteriorating civil war situation added to the pressures for intervention.

The marines were ordered here Wednesday to protect the evacuation of Americans and other nationals. More than 500 landed that day, and other landings began yesterday.

Marines were drawn into action already yesterday to repulse a series of rebel sniping raids on the American Embassy. The marines killed six of the snipers.

[Similar sniping attacks were reported by the embassies of El Salvador, Peru, Mexico and Ecuador, The Associated Press reported.]

1,000 Dead Reported

Fighting raged throughout this war-torn city most of the day, and an official estimate said that as many as 1,000 persons may have been killed since the outbreak of the revolution last Saturday.

At that time, rebel forces favoring the return to power of the exiled former President, Juan Bosch, deposed the civilian junta that had succeeded him in 1963.

The current three-man military junta, backed by the counter-revolutionary forces of Brig. Gen. Elias Wessin y Wessin, was named Wednesday.

A high-ranking United States Navy officer declared that the function of the marines was not only to protect the continuing evacuation but also "to see that no Communist government is established in the Dominican Republic."

Last night, American sources here described the situation as nearing anarchy. It was in view of this that it appeared that active participation by American troops was required to bolster the junta's efforts to control the rebellion.

"U.S. to Increase Military Forces by 330,000 Men," July 30, 1965

President Johnson's decision to authorize a major increase in U.S. troops was announced with little fanfare in summer 1965. The president declared that the active-duty military would expand by approximately 330,000 troops, in large part to wage the Vietnam War. The United States would raise the number of troops in Vietnam from 75,000 to 125,000. This increase was the beginning of the open-ended U.S. commitment to Vietnam that would result in the deployment of more than 540,000 troops there by the end of Johnson's presidency.

JULY 30, 1965
U.S. TO INCREASE MILITARY FORCES BY 330,000 MEN
Rise in Draft and Enlisting to Push Total to 3 Million for First Time in 10 Years
By JACK RAYMOND
Special to The New York Times

WASHINGTON, July 29—The Administration plans to increase its active-duty military forces by about 330,000 men, official sources said today.

This would bring the total to about three million men for the first time in 10 years.

The armed forces totaled 2,653,861 on July 1, and 2,935,000 in 1955. The last time the total was more than three million was in 1954. Then it was 3,302,000.

The build-up in military manpower, planned to support the war in South Vietnam, will be accomplished through increased draft calls and intensified recruitment of volunteers, officials said.

President Johnson announced yesterday that military conscription quotas now running at 17,000 men a month would be gradually doubled to 35,000 a month.

Commitment Growing

The President also announced that 50,000 more men were being ordered to South Vietnam, increasing the United States' military manpower commitment there to 125,000.

However, officials at the Pentagon called attention today to the President's statement yesterday that still more

troops would be sent to South Vietnam when they were requested by military authorities.

Such requests are regarded as inevitable, if not already filed. The increments ordered by President Johnson were considered to be part of an early phase in a broader program of military requirements set forth during Secretary of Defense Robert S. McNamara's meetings in Saigon earlier this month.

Increase Held Mandatory

Qualified sources said that a slow-paced build-up in American forces to assist the South Vietnamese war against Communist insurgency was made mandatory by the logistical supplies and support facilities available in South Vietnam.

New docking facilities, airports, encampment areas and depots are in an early building stage in South Vietnam, it was pointed out. At the same time officials cautioned against acceptance as valid some reports that United States military officials in Saigon had recommended full-scale war mobilization and a commitment of Korean war proportions.

"President Signs Medicare Bill; Praises Truman," July 31, 1965

The creation of Medicare and Medicaid in 1965 marked a policy triumph whose origins dated back to the Truman administration. After World War II, President Harry S. Truman had proposed the creation of a national health insurance program, and twenty years later, the United States enacted federally funded medical care for the elderly and the poor. Labeled the Social Security Act because it expanded upon the Social Security program created in 1935, this legislation provided a guarantee of basic health care services for people over sixty-five as well as for the poor and disabled.

JULY 31, 1965
PRESIDENT SIGNS MEDICARE BILL; PRAISES TRUMAN
He Flies to Independence, Mo., to Hold Ceremonies at Presidential Library
20-YEAR CAMPAIGN ENDS
Social Security Is Expanded to Provide Medical Care for Americans Over 65
By JOHN D. MORRIS
Special to The New York Times

INDEPENDENCE, Mo., July 30—President Johnson flew to Independence today and signed the medicare-Social Security bill in a moving tribute to former President Harry S. Truman.

Mr. Truman, beaming, sat beside Mr. Johnson on the stage of the Harry S. Truman Library auditorium. More than 200 persons, including Vice President Humphrey, Congressional leaders and Administration officials, witnessed the ceremony.

President Johnson chose Independence for the signing because Mr. Truman was the first President who proposed a Federal program of health insurance under Social Security.

It was in a special message Nov. 19, 1945, that Mr. Truman asked Congress to enact such legislation.

'A Reality for Millions'

"The people of the United States love and voted for Harry Truman," the President said, "not because he gave them hell but because he gave them hope.

"I believe today that all America shares my joy that he is present now when the hope he offered becomes a reality for millions of our fellow citizens."

The 81-year-old former President, opening the ceremonies with a brief talk, found himself uncharacteristically at a loss for words at one point.

"I am glad to have lived this long and to witness today the signing of the medicare bill," he said.

Then, welcoming those who came to Independence, he groped briefly for a phrase to express his feelings. . . .

"I thank you all most highly for coming here," he said. "It's an honor that I haven't had done to me—well, in quite a while, I'll say that to you."

In his address at the signing ceremonies, Mr. Johnson said:

"No longer will older Americans be denied the healing miracle of modern medicine. No longer will illness crush and destroy the savings that they have so carefully put away over a lifetime so that they might enjoy dignity in their later years."

The Senate completed Congressional action on the bill Wednesday, capping a 20-year effort to steer such legislation to final passage.

The bill expands the 30-year-old Social Security insurance program to provide hospital care, nursing home care, home nursing services and out-patient diagnostic service for all Americans over 65 years old.

It also sets up a supplementary program of Federal insurance covering most of the doctors' bills and some other health costs of persons over 65. The supplementary insurance will be available on a voluntary basis with participants paying $3 a month in premiums.

Other provisions include a 7 per cent increase in cash benefits under the present old age, survivors and disability insurance program.

To finance the basic hospital and nursing care insurance and the new cash benefits, Social Security taxes will be increased in steps over the next 22 years starting next Jan. 1.

"U.S. ACTS QUICKLY TO ENFORCE LAW ON VOTING RIGHTS," AUGUST 8, 1965

The Voting Rights Act of 1965 was enacted to ensure that black Americans would be able to exercise their constitutional right to vote, which had been granted nearly one hundred years earlier with the ratification of the Fifteenth Amendment. The amendment states: "The right of citizens of the United States to vote shall not be denied or abridged by the United States or by any State on account of race, color, or previous condition of servitude." But states had found numerous ways to keep blacks from voting by enacting measures that did not focus explicitly on race. Some states passed laws requiring literacy tests or the payment of poll taxes for voting. For poor white citizens who could not read, states would enact a "grandfather clause," which permitted the descendents of people who were allowed to vote before the Civil War to vote. The 1965 law overturned many of these restrictions on voting and authorized the Justice Department to oversee voter registration of black citizens in areas where they had been systematically denied this right.

AUGUST 8, 1965
U.S. ACTS QUICKLY TO ENFORCE LAW ON VOTING RIGHTS
Literacy Testing Suspended Throughout 7 States and in Parts of 2 Others
EXAMINERS STANDING BY
Federal Steps Taken a Day After the New Legislation Is Signed by President
By JOHN HERBERS
Special to The New York Times

WASHINGTON, Aug. 7—The Government began today to enforce the Voting Rights Act of 1965, which was signed into law by President Johnson yesterday. Enforcement began in two phases.

First, literacy tests as a prerequisite to voting were suspended in seven states—Alabama, Alaska, Georgia, Louisiana, Mississippi, South Carolina and Virginia—and in 26 counties of North Carolina and one county in Arizona.

Second, the Justice Department filed suit in the United States District Court in Jackson, Miss., to abolish the Mississippi poll tax as a requirement for voting in state and local elections. The department will file similar suits Tuesday in the other poll tax states—Texas, Alabama and Virginia.

About 45 Federal voting examiners, all employes of the Civil Service Commission, were standing by in the Deep South, waiting to move into 15 to 20 counties that have a history of resistance to Negro voting. These counties are to be designated Monday by the Justice Department, and the examiners will begin registering eligible Negroes on Tuesday.

Landmark Law

The new act, a landmark in civil rights legislation, is expected to result in the addition of several hundred thousand Negroes to the voter registration rolls of the Deep South in the next year or so.

In signing the bill yesterday in a ceremony at the Capitol, President Johnson said: "Congress acted swiftly in passing this act. I intend to act with equal dispatch in order to enforce it."

"G.O.P. Finds '68 Outlook Brighter as It Counts Election Successes," November 10, 1966

The 1966 congressional midterm elections reversed some of the gains that the Democratic Party had made two years earlier. Although Democrats retained control of Congress, they lost seats in both the House and the Senate. Additionally, Republicans won several gubernatorial races, of which perhaps the most significant was Ronald Reagan's victory in California. His entry into electoral politics established the foundation for his successful presidential run fourteen years later.

NOVEMBER 10, 1966
G.O.P. FINDS '68 OUTLOOK BRIGHTER AS IT COUNTS ELECTION SUCCESSES: GAIN OF 47 IN HOUSE, 8 GOVERNORS

PARTY IS SPURRED

Victories Bring 4 Men to Front in Picture for Presidency

By WARREN WEAVER Jr.

After two painful years of looking back at 1964, the Republicans were suddenly looking forward to 1968 yesterday with a heady new optimism born of impressive election victories.

Tuesday's balloting, which brought the resurgent Republicans a net gain of three Senators, 47 House seats and eight Governors, also presented the party with three or perhaps four Presidential candidates for 1968. They were:

• Gov. George Romney of Michigan, who won an impressive 500,000-vote re-election majority and carried with him Senator Robert P. Griffin and five new Republican House members, in a major display of drawing power.

• Former Vice President Richard M. Nixon, who campaigned relentlessly for many of the Republican winners and gained further favor in the party by predicting more accurately than any other leader the campaign victories.

• Ronald Reagan, the film star turned politician, who won the governorship of California going away to become, without a day in public office, the favorite Presidential candidate of Republican conservatives.

• Charles H. Percy, the 47-year-old Illinois industrialist who decisively defeated Senator Paul H. Douglas and won himself immediate consideration as a national candidate with liberal support.

'New Solutions' Urged

At the same time, the election results weakened, perhaps critically, President Johnson's influence in the Congress over the next two important years and did not add luster to his reputation as a party leader and candidate for re-election.

The net effect, politicians of both persuasions agreed, was to reconstitute the two-party system on the national level after the withering Goldwater defeat of 1964 had reduced the Republican party to a disorderly, ineffective minority.

Mr. Nixon was quick to emphasize the Republican advance. He called the size of the Democratic loss in the House "the sharpest rebuff of a President in a generation" and a "rebuke to the President's lack of credibility and lack of direction abroad."

The size of the Republican advances, the former Vice President declared, has given President Johnson "a mandate to open his mind to new solutions, to accept constructive criticism and to reinstitute the tradition of a bipartisan foreign policy."

In Texas, the President had no direct comment on the election results. His acting press secretary, George Christian, told reporters that Mr. Johnson "obviously wishes every man that he wanted elected were elected."

The press aide said that the Senate elections left the Democrats "a pretty good majority" and that the party's House margin would be in the neighborhood of 65 seats.

"25TH AMENDMENT, PRESIDENCY PLAN, HAS BEEN RATIFIED," FEBRUARY 11, 1967

After President Johnson took office in 1963, the office of vice president remained vacant until the inauguration of Hubert Humphrey, who was elected on the Democratic ticket with Johnson in 1964. The Twenty-fifth Amendment was enacted to ensure a succession plan for such vacancies before the next election. It provided for the president to nominate a vice president, with confirmation by a majority vote in both chambers of Congress. The amendment also established a provision for presidential disability—that is, for the vice president to assume the powers of the presidency if the president were incapacitated or otherwise unable to govern.

FEBRUARY 11, 1967
25TH AMENDMENT, PRESIDENCY PLAN, HAS BEEN RATIFIED
Change in U.S. Constitution Designed for Continuity in Case of Disability
NOMINATION POWER SET
President Is Enabled to Name Someone to Fill Vacant No. 2 Office
By JOHN HERBERS
Special to The New York Times

WASHINGTON, Feb. 10—The 25th Amendment, designed to assure clear lines of Presidential succession and continuity of power in case of disability, became part of the Constitution today when it was ratified by the 38th state.

It enables the Vice President to act as President when the President is physically or mentally unable to carry out the duties of his office, and it authorizes the President to nominate a Vice President should the No. 2 office become vacant.

Under previous law the office remained vacant until the next regular Presidential election.

The amendment automatically became law when it was ratified by three-fourths of the 50 states.

Peril Found Averted
Senator Birch Bayh of Indiana, the chief author of the amendment, said a peril that had existed in the executive branch for almost 200 years had been alleviated. That danger was that the nation's highest office might be occupied by an incapacitated man.

It was not clear which state put the amendment over. North Dakota, Minnesota and Nevada all were vying for the honor.

"MARSHALL NAMED FOR HIGH COURT, ITS FIRST NEGRO," JUNE 14, 1967

In addition to his steadfast pursuit of civil rights legislation, President Johnson demonstrated his personal commitment to promoting opportunities for black Americans by nominating the first black person, Solicitor General Thurgood Marshall, to the Supreme Court. Marshall's distinguished legal career had focused on fighting racial discrimination. He had argued the historic *Brown v. Board of Education* (1954) case before the Supreme Court. Accepting Marshall's arguments, the justices outlawed racial segregation in public schools. In announcing his nomination, President Johnson emphasized that Marshall was the "best qualified by training and by very valuable service to the country. I believe it is the right thing to do, the right time to do it, the right man and the right place."

> 'I believe it is the right thing to do, the right time to do it, the right man and the right place.'

JUNE 14, 1967
MARSHALL NAMED FOR HIGH COURT, ITS FIRST NEGRO

Johnson Calls Nominee 'Best Qualified,' and Rights Leaders Are Jubilant—Southerners Silent on Confirmation

By ROY REED

Special to The New York Times

WASHINGTON, June 12—President Johnson named Solicitor General Thurgood Marshall to the Supreme Court today.

Mr. Marshall, the great-grandson of a slave, will be the first Negro to serve on the Court if the Senate confirms him.

He is the best-known Negro lawyer of the century because of his battles against segregation. Southerners in the Senate once delayed his appointment to the Federal judiciary for several months. But judging from initial reaction in the Senate today, his confirmation to the Court seems likely.

Non-Southern Senators applauded the appointment, and southerners accepted it, at least for the moment, in silence.

Hailed by Negro Leaders

Negro leaders were jubilant. Floyd B. McKissick, the militant chairman of the Congress of Racial Equality, said the appointment had stirred "pride in the breast of every black American."

Mr. Marshall, 58 years old, is to succeed Associate Justice Tom C. Clark, who retired yesterday.

It had been expected for years that Mr. Marshall would eventually become the first Negro justice, but recent speculation had given him no special edge over other prospective nominees at this time.

The President, as is his custom, gave no advance hint of his selection. Reporters were unexpectedly called into the White House Rose Garden outside his office shortly before noon.

Blinking in the sun, Mr. Johnson stepped in front of the microphones and matter-of-factly announced what may be the most dramatic appointment of his Presidency.

'A Place in History'

Mr. Marshall stood by with his hands in his pockets, his usually mobile face solemn, as the President told of his nomination.

"I believe he has already earned his place in history," Mr. Johnson said. "But I think it will be greatly enhanced by his service on the Court."

Mr. Johnson declared that Mr. Marshall had earned the appointment by his "distinguished record" in the law. He added:

"He is best qualified by training and by very valuable service to the country. I believe it is the right thing to do, the right time to do it, the right man and the right place."

Mr. Marshall's official selection was chiefly the work of two Texans—Lyndon Johnson and his Attorney General, Ramsey Clark, the son of the retiring Justice.

Attorney General Clark recommended Mr. Marshall, who as solicitor general has been the Number 3 man in the Justice Department, with enthusiasm matching the President's.

"Thurgood Marshall will bring to the Supreme Court a wealth of legal experience rarely equalled in the history of the Court," Mr. Clark said in a statement today.

"It was my strong recommendation to the President that Thurgood Marshall be appointed to the Supreme Court," he said. "I have no doubt that his future contributions will add even more prominence to his already well-established place in American history."

Mr. Marshall, reportedly acting on White House instructions, said he would have little to say about his nomination until the Senate acts. He described his appointment as "not something you'd expect but something you hope for."

Mr. Marshall was the towering figure of the legal phase of the Negro's fight for equality in this century. He tried and won dozens of lawsuits striking down discriminatory laws, including the suit that led to the Supreme Court's 1954 decision outlawing school segregation.

That case and other school suits—he was involved in such notable battles as the desegregation of the schools of Little Rock and New Orleans—once cast considerable doubt on his chances of sitting on the Supreme Court. Powerful Southerners in the Senate saw him as one of the nation's baleful influences.

But in recent years he has become identified with a more moderate element of Negro leadership, in large part because younger men have emerged as more militant. And he has now proved his acceptability to the Senate twice, winning its confirmation first as a Federal judge and then as Solicitor General.

- -

"U.S. Troops Sent Into Detroit," July 25, 1967

Tensions over race relations in the United States sparked severe riots in the 1960s. The Watts section of Los Angeles experienced devastating violence in summer 1965, and similar upheaval and destruction occurred in Cleveland the following year, as well as in Newark in 1967, and in Washington, D.C., after the assassination of Martin Luther King Jr. in 1968. The 1967 riot in Detroit broke out when police raided a black after-hours drinking club at 3 a.m. on a Sunday and a crowd gathered to protest. President Johnson was forced to send in army paratroopers to restore order.

JULY 25, 1967
U.S. TROOPS SENT INTO DETROIT; 19 DEAD; JOHNSON DECRIES RIOTS; NEW OUTBREAK IN EAST HARLEM

TANKS IN DETROIT

800 Are Injured and 2,000 Arrested—Business at Halt

By GENE ROBERTS

Special to The New York Times

DETROIT, Tuesday, July 25—President Johnson rushed 4,700 Army paratroopers into Detroit at midnight last night as Negro snipers besieged two police stations in rioting that brought near-paralysis to the nation's fifth largest city.

The death toll stood at 19, and damage from fire and looting—estimated by police at $150 million—was worse than in any riot in the country's history.

Tanks rumbled into the city's East Side to rescue more than 100 policemen and National Guardsmen who were trapped inside the precinct houses. Negro snipers fired into windows and doors, and policemen and Guardsmen fought back with machineguns, shotguns and high-velocity rifles.

"It looks like Berlin in 1945," said Mayor Jerome P. Cavanagh, who along with Gov. George Romney had met with resistance from the White House in trying to have the Federal troops put into action here immediately.

He and Gov. George Romney had pleaded with Cyrus H. Vance, the President's personal representative here, until just before midnight when a reluctant White House finally agreed to send the paratroopers into action.

Vance Held Back

Although the President had ordered the air lifting of the troops to nearby Selfridge Air Force Base from Fort Campbell, Ky., and Fort Bragg, N.C., Mr. Vance declined for hours to commit the men in the hope that the city and state could bring the situation under control.

Federal troops have been used in recent years to enforce Federal desegregation laws, but have not been used in a riot situation since Detroit's racial riot in 1943.

Before the President announced on nationwide television his decision to use the soldiers, Mayor Cavanagh, a Democrat, had taken strong exception to the hesitancy shown by the White House, but he said that he "understood the traditional Federal desire not to get involved in this type of dispute."

"With more and more cities getting involved in riots," he said, "the Government is asking: 'How involved can we get?'"

Hundreds of new fires were reported, bringing the total in two days of violence to more than 731. Large areas of the city were blanketed in smoke.

Thousands of workers stayed away from their jobs, scores of downtown restaurants and businesses shut down and two airlines—Tag and Commuter—canceled their night flights for fear of sniper fire.

The Detroit Tigers canceled a three-game baseball series with the Baltimore Orioles that had been scheduled for the Stadium here. Two games will be played in Baltimore, tomorrow and Thursday nights. The third will be played in Detroit on Aug. 11.

Meanwhile, the arrest total climbed to nearly 2,000. More than 800 were injured, including 20 policemen and 15 firemen.

Late at night, the police and National Guardsmen were battling with snipers entrenched in apartment buildings. The looters are also spreading to the south.

Looting swept, too, through such suburbs as River Rouge, home of the Ford Motor Company's largest plant, and Hamtramck, which once had the largest Polish population outside of Warsaw and is now heavily populated by Negroes.

Firebombers and looters struck in commercial districts in almost every area of the city—north, east and west.

· ·

"Johnson Says He Won't Run," April 1, 1968

With college campuses in uproar over the lingering Vietnam War and the military's request for more U.S. troops, the president would have faced a difficult election in 1968. Johnson's personal dismay with the war was revealed by a comment he reportedly made when CBS news anchor Walter Cronkite reported after the Tet Offensive in early 1968 that the war could not be won: "If I've lost Cronkite, I've lost America." Just weeks later, Johnson withdrew from consideration for the presidential race.

"
'I shall not seek and I will not accept the nomination of my party as your President.'
"

APRIL 1, 1968
JOHNSON SAYS HE WON'T RUN;
SURPRISE DECISION
President Steps Aside in Unity Bid—Says 'House' Is Divided
By TOM WICKER
Special to The New York Times

WASHINGTON, March 31—Lyndon Baines Johnson announced tonight: "I shall not seek and I will not accept the nomination of my party as your President."

Later, at a White House news conference, he said his decision was "completely irrevocable."

The President told his nationwide television audience:

"What we have won when all our people were united must not be lost in partisanship. I have concluded that I should not permit the Presidency to become involved in partisan decisions."

Mr. Johnson, acknowledging that there was "division in the American house," withdrew in the name of national unity, which he said was "the ultimate strength of our country."

"With American sons in the field far away," he said, "with the American future under challenge right here at home, with our hopes and the world's hopes for peace in the balance every day, I do not believe that I should devote an hour or a day of my time to any personal partisan causes or to any duties other than the awesome duties of this office, the Presidency of your country."

Humphrey Race Possible

Mr. Johnson left Senator Robert F. Kennedy of New York and Senator Eugene J. McCarthy of Minnesota as the only two declared candidates for the Democratic Presidential nomination.

Vice President Humphrey, however, will be widely expected to seek the nomination now that his friend and political benefactor, Mr. Johnson, is out of the field. Mr. Humphrey indicated that he would have a statement on his plans tomorrow.

"Martin Luther King Is Slain in Memphis," April 5, 1968

Rev. Dr. Martin Luther King Jr.'s courageous battle for civil rights came to an untimely end on April 4, 1968. The Nobel Peace Prize winner was assassinated at age thirty-nine in Memphis, Tennessee. Escaped convict James Earl Ray pleaded guilty to the murder, but later claimed he had not shot King. President Johnson declared a national day of mourning in honor of King's heroic efforts to promote civil rights.

APRIL 5, 1968
MARTIN LUTHER KING IS SLAIN IN MEMPHIS
A WHITE IS SUSPECTED
JOHNSON URGES CALM
GUARD CALLED OUT
Curfew Is Ordered in Memphis, but Fires and Looting Erupt
By EARL CALDWELL
Special to The New York Times

MEMPHIS, Friday, April 5—The Rev. Dr. Martin Luther King Jr., who preached nonviolence and racial brotherhood, was fatally shot here last night by a distant gunman who then raced away and escaped.

Four thousand National Guard troops were ordered into Memphis by Gov. Buford Ellington after the 39-year-old Nobel Prize-winning civil rights leader died.

A curfew was imposed on the shocked city of 550,000 inhabitants, 40 per cent of whom are Negro.

But the police said the tragedy had been followed by incidents that included sporadic shooting, fires, bricks and bottles thrown at policemen, and looting that started in Negro districts and then spread over the city.

White Car Sought

Police Director Frank Holloman said the assassin might have been a white man who was "50 to 100 yards away in a flophouse."

Chief of Detectives W. P. Huston said a late model white Mustang was believed to have been the killer's getaway car. Its occupant was described as a bareheaded white man in his 30's, wearing a black suit and black tie.

The detective chief said the police had chased two cars near the motel where Dr. King was shot and had halted one that had two out-of-town men as occupants. The men were questioned but seemed to have nothing to do with the killing, he said.

Rifle Found Nearby

A high-powered 30.06-caliber rifle was found about a block from the scene of the shooting, on South Main Street. "We think it's the gun," Chief Huston said, reporting it would be turned over to the Federal Bureau of Investigation.

Dr. King was shot while he leaned over a second-floor railing outside his room at the Lorraine Motel. He was chatting with two friends just before starting for dinner.

"KENNEDY IS DEAD, VICTIM OF ASSASSIN; SURGERY IN VAIN," JUNE 6, 1968

Just two months after Martin Luther King Jr. was shot dead by a sniper, the nation experienced further trauma with the assassination of Robert Kennedy on June 5, 1968. After winning the California primary and greeting supporters in Los Angeles, Kennedy and five others were shot in the early morning in a Los Angeles hotel kitchen. Kennedy had just spoken to supporters cheering his victory. He died the following day. Palestinian nationalist Sirhan Sirhan was convicted of his murder. In response to the horrific news, President Johnson declared a national day of mourning for Kennedy.

JUNE 6, 1968
KENNEDY IS DEAD, VICTIM OF ASSASSIN; SURGERY IN VAIN
President Calls Death Tragedy, Proclaims a Day of Mourning
By GLADWIN HILL
Special to The New York Times

LOS ANGELES, Thursday, June 6—Senator Robert F. Kennedy, the brother of a murdered President, died at 1:44 A.M. today of an assassin's shots.

The New York Senator was wounded more than 20 hours earlier, moments after he had made his victory statement in the California primary.

At his side when he died today in Good Samaritan Hospital were his wife, Ethel; his sisters, Mrs. Stephen Smith and Mrs. Patricia Lawford; his brother-in-law, Stephen Smith; and his sister-in-law, Mrs. John F. Kennedy, whose husband was assassinated 4½ years ago in Dallas.

In Washington, President Johnson issued a statement calling the death a tragedy. He proclaimed next Sunday a national day of mourning.

The Final Report

Hopes had risen slightly when more than eight hours went by without a new medical bulletin on the stricken Senator, but the grimness of the final announcement was signaled when Frank Mankiewicz, Mr. Kennedy's press secretary, walked slowly down the street in front of the hospital toward the littered gymnasium that served as press headquarters.

Mr. Mankiewicz bit his lip. His shoulders slumped.

He stepped to a lectern in front of a green-tinted chalkboard and bowed his head for a moment while the television lights snapped on.

Then, at one minute before 2 A.M., he told of the death of Mr. Kennedy.

Following is the text of the statement from Mr. Mankiewicz:

"I have a short announcement to read which I will read at this time. Senator Robert Francis Kennedy died at 1:44 A.M. today, June 6, 1968. With Senator Kennedy at the time of his death was his wife, Ethel; his sisters, Mrs. Patricia Lawford and Mrs. Stephen Smith; his brother-in-law, Stephen Smith, and his sister-in-law, Mrs. John F. Kennedy.

"He was 42 years old."

Senator Kennedy's body will be taken to New York this morning and then to Washington.

The man accused of shooting Mr. Kennedy early yesterday in a pantry of the Ambassador Hotel was identified as Sirhan Bishara Sirhan, 24 years old, who was born in Palestinian Jerusalem of Arab parentage and had lived in the Los Angeles area since 1957. Sirhan had been a clerk.

"Humphrey Nominated on the First Ballot After His Plank on Vietnam Is Approved," August 29, 1968

The violence surrounding the Democratic National Convention in August 1968 overshadowed the nomination of Vice President Hubert Humphrey for president. Police officers used tear gas against antiwar protestors outside the convention hall. Inside, some delegates called for the session to be adjourned because of the uproar. Still, Humphrey won the party nomination on the first ballot, with antiwar candidate Sen. Eugene McCarthy placing a distant second. After the tumultuous convention, the Democratic Party rewrote its rules for nominating presidential candidates to rely primarily on the popular vote in primaries and caucuses, rather than on the preferences of party delegates.

AUGUST 29, 1968
HUMPHREY NOMINATED ON THE FIRST BALLOT AFTER HIS PLANK ON VIETNAM IS APPROVED;
VICTOR GETS 1,761

Vote Taken Amid Boos For Chicago Police Tactics in Street

By TOM WICKER

Special to The New York Times

CHICAGO, Thursday Aug. 29—While a pitched battle between the police and thousands of young antiwar demonstrators raged in the streets of Chicago, the Democratic National Convention nominated Hubert H. Humphrey for President last night, on a platform reflecting his and President Johnson's views on the war in Vietnam.

Mr. Humphrey, after a day of bandwagon shifts to his candidacy, and a night of turmoil in the convention hall, won nomination on the first ballot over challenges by Senator Eugene J. McCarthy of Minnesota and George S. McGovern of South Dakota.

The count at the end of the first ballot was:

Humphrey 1,761¾

McCarthy 601

McGovern 146½

Phillips 67½

Others 32¾

Violence Draws Attention

There was never a moment's suspense in the balloting, and throughout a turbulent evening, the delegates and spectators paid less attention to the proceedings than to television and radio reports of widespread violence in the streets of Chicago, and to stringent security measures within the International Amphitheatre.

Repeated denunciations of Mayor Richard J. Daley from convention speakers and repeated efforts to get an adjournment or recess were ignored by convention officials and Mr. Daley.

He sat through it all, usually grinning and always guarded by plainclothes security men, until just before the roll call. Then he left the hall. A few miles away, the young demonstrators were being clubbed, kicked and gassed by the Chicago police, who turned back a march on the convention hall.

Watched From Hotels

Most of the violence took place across Michigan Avenue from the convention headquarters hotel, the Conrad Hilton, in full view of delegates' wives and others watching from its windows.

From the convention rostrum, Senator Abraham A. Ribicoff of Connecticut, denounced "Gestapo tactics in the streets of Chicago."

Julian Bond, the Negro insurgent leader from Georgia, in announcing his delegation's votes, spoke of "atrocities" in the city.

Wire services reported that Mr. Humphrey had chosen Senator Edmund S. Muskie of Maine for Vice President. Mr. Humphrey's staff denied that a decision had been made, although they would not rule out Mr. Muskie, 54 years old, a Roman Catholic of Polish extraction.

Even the roll-call of the states that nominated Mr. Humphrey could begin only over the protests of New Hampshire, Wisconsin and Mr. Conyers, all of whom moved for a recess or adjournment because of the surrounding violence and the pandemonium in the hall.

Vote Begins Amid Boos

Representative Carl Albert of Oklahoma, the chairman, ignored all the motions and ordered the roll-call to begin amid a huge chorus of boos.

When Illinois's turn came to vote, the huge old amphitheater rocked with the sounds of boos and jeers, and the recording secretary had to ask for a restatement of its vote—112 votes for Mr. Humphrey.

Early in the evening, even Mr. Humphrey got a whiff of tear gas when it was wafted through his window at the Hilton, from the street fighting below.

Mr. McCarthy saw some of the violence from his window and called it "very bad." Later, it was reported at the convention hall, he visited a hospital where some of his young supporters, wounded in the streets, were being treated.

At one point, the police broke into the McCarthy suite at the Hilton, searching for someone throwing objects out of the hotel windows.

Mr. McGovern described the fighting as a "blood bath" that "made me sick to my stomach." He said he had "seen nothing like it since the films of Nazi Germany."

"ELECTOR VOTE 287," NOVEMBER 7, 1968

Vice President Humphrey won the Democratic nomination, but he lost the general election. Although his popular vote tally was close to the victorious Richard Nixon's—30.9 million to 31.7 million—Humphrey received just 35.5 percent of the Electoral College vote (191 votes in 13 states plus Washington, D.C.) to Nixon's nearly 56 percent (301 votes in 32 states). Third-party candidate George Wallace won nearly 9.5 million popular votes and 8.5 percent of the Electoral College vote (46 votes in 5 states).

NOVEMBER 7, 1968
ELECTOR VOTE 287

Lead in Popular Tally May Be Smaller Than Kennedy's in '60
By MAX FRANKEL

Richard Milhous Nixon emerged the victor yesterday in one of the closest and most tumultuous Presidential campaigns in history and set himself the task of reuniting the nation.

Elected over Hubert H. Humphrey by the barest of margins—only four one-hundredths of a percentage point in the popular vote—and confronted by a Congress in control of the Democrats, the President-elect said it "will be the great objective of this Administration at the outset to bring the American people together."

He pledged, as the 37th President, to form "an open Administration, open to new ideas, open to men and women of both parties, open to critics as well as those who support us" so as to bridge the gap between the generations and the races.

Details Left for Later

But after an exhausting and tense night of awaiting the verdict at the Waldorf-Astoria Hotel here, Mr. Nixon and his

closest aides were not yet prepared to suggest how they intended to organize themselves and to approach these objectives. The Republican victor expressed admiration for his opponent's challenge and reiterated his desire to help President Johnson achieve peace in Vietnam between now and Inauguration Day on Jan. 20.

The verdict of an electorate that appeared to number 73 million could not be discerned until mid-morning because Mr. Nixon and Mr. Humphrey finished in a virtual tie in the popular vote, just as Mr. Nixon and John F. Kennedy did in 1960.

With 94 per cent of the nation's election precincts reporting, Mr. Nixon's total stood last evening at 29,726,409 votes to Mr. Humphrey's 29,677,152. The margin of 49,257 was even smaller than Mr. Kennedy's margin of 112,803.

THE PRESIDENCY OF RICHARD NIXON

JANUARY 20, 1969 – AUGUST 9, 1974

The presidency of Richard Milhous Nixon started with high ambitions and ended with the first presidential resignation in American history. Nixon was a visionary in some aspects of foreign affairs: He opened U.S. ties to China in the cold war and signed a major arms control agreement with the Soviet Union. The Vietnam War ended during his presidency, though Nixon's strategy for this achievement, particularly his authorization of U.S. incursions into Cambodia, was highly controversial. He signed major domestic policy legislation, particularly to combat crime, promote environmental protection, and regulate occupational safety. But the Nixon presidency was undone by the Watergate burglary and cover-up, a scandal that reached all the way to the Oval Office and forced the president's resignation in the face of likely impeachment. Consequently, the Nixon years are remembered for both high achievements and devastating disappointments.

A California native, Nixon was the second of five sons. His father made a modest living as manager of a gas station and store, and Nixon attended the local undergraduate institution, Whittier College. He was student president, a football player, and a debater, and he also excelled academically, graduating second in his class with a history degree. He won a scholarship to Duke University Law School and graduated third in his class in 1937. Nixon returned to California to practice law and became partner in a firm. He served as a naval officer in World War II, deploying to the Pacific and rising to the rank of lieutenant commander.

After the war, Nixon began his career in politics. He won election to the U.S. House of Representatives in 1946, campaigning vigorously against an incumbent Democratic by depicting him as a Socialist. He served two terms in the House and built his reputation as a staunchly anti-Communist leader through chairing a subcommittee of the House Committee on Un-American Activities. Nixon aggressively investigated alleged Communists in the government, most famously former State Department official Alger Hiss, who later was convicted of perjury. In 1950 Nixon won election to the Senate, accusing his opponent, Rep. Helen Gahagan Douglas, of having

'YOU CAN'T TRUST ANYBODY'

Source: The Granger Collection, New York

Communist ties and being "pink." Nixon's critics, in turn, referred to him as "Tricky Dick."

In 1952 Nixon won the Republican Party's vice-presidential nomination, but his candidacy was nearly derailed by charges that he had used political funds for personal expenses. Nixon saved his career by going on national television and giving the famous "Checkers" speech, in which he denied the allegations and said his family was of modest means. He did admit that he had accepted the gift of a dog, which his daughters had named "Checkers," and that they would keep their beloved pet. Public support for Nixon skyrocketed after the speech, and presidential candidate Dwight D. Eisenhower promised to keep him on the ticket. They won election in 1952.

As vice president, Nixon chaired policy committees and was a visible representative of the administration. Nixon was

QUICK FACTS ON RICHARD NIXON

BIRTH	January 9, 1913, Yorba Linda, Calif.
EDUCATION	Whittier College, B.A., 1934 Duke University Law School, J.D., 1937
FAMILY	Wife: Thelma Catherine "Patricia" Ryan Nixon Children: Patricia "Tricia" Nixon, Julie Nixon
WHITE HOUSE PETS	Dogs ("Checkers" during vice presidency; others as president)
PARTY	Republican
PREPRESIDENTIAL CAREER (SELECTED)	Naval officer, World War II, 1943–1945 U.S. House of Representatives, 1947–1951 U.S. Senate, 1951–1953 Vice president, 1953–1961 Presidential candidate, 1960 Gubernatorial candidate, 1962 *Six Crises* memoir published, 1962
PRESIDENTIAL TERM	January 20, 1969–January 20, 1973 January 20, 1973–August 9, 1974
VICE PRESIDENTS	Spiro T. Agnew (January 20, 1969–October 10, 1973) Gerald R. Ford (December 6, 1973–August 9, 1974)
SELECTED EVENTS	First astronauts, Neil A. Armstrong and Edwin E. "Buzz" Aldrin, 　land on moon (1969) Senate rejects two Nixon Supreme Court nominees (1969 and 1970) Senate Foreign Relations Committee repeals 1964 Gulf of Tonkin 　Resolution (1970) Nixon sends U.S. troops to Cambodia (1970) Four students fatally shot by National Guard during anti–Vietnam War 　protests, Kent State University (1970) Organized Crime Control Act (1970)

not in the inner circle of Eisenhower advisers, however, and the president considered dropping him from the ticket in 1956. But Nixon ultimately prevailed, and they easily won reelection. In his second vice-presidential term, Nixon represented the United States abroad. He traveled to Latin America in 1958, where he was heckled by protesters, and he visited the Soviet Union in 1959, where he had an unplanned but highly publicized informal debate with Soviet leader Nikita S. Khrushchev about capitalism versus communism.

Nixon ran for president in 1960 against Democratic senator John F. Kennedy, and the two candidates waged a vigorous and closely fought campaign. They held the first televised presiden-

tial debates in American history, but the sessions did not play to Nixon's advantage, as he looked uncomfortable and ill during the first debate, while Kennedy appeared cool and confident. Nixon lost the race by less than 120,000 popular votes, but Kennedy beat him soundly in the Electoral College, 303–219. After losing the presidential race, Nixon resumed his legal career in California. He ran for governor in 1962 but lost that election to Edmund G. Brown. Angered by his second major electoral loss, Nixon blamed what he viewed as excessively critical media coverage compared to that of his competitors. After the election, he held a press conference and told reporters that he would no longer participate in politics, so they would not "have Richard

Comprehensive Drug Abuse Prevention and Control Act (1970)

Creation of Occupational Safety and Health Administration (1970)

Supreme Court ruling permits busing for school desegregation (1971)

Pentagon Papers published; Supreme Court later upholds right
    of publication (1971)

Ratification of Twenty-sixth Amendment, lowering voting age
    from 21 to 18 (1971)

Nixon visits China (1972)

Nixon visits Soviet Union (1972)

United States and Soviet Union sign Strategic Arms Limitation Treaty (1972)

United States and Soviet Union sign Anti-Ballistic Missile Defense
    Treaty (1972)

Burglary of Democratic National Committee headquarters,
    Watergate Hotel (1972)

Supreme Court ruling *Roe v. Wade* on abortion (1973)

Vietnam cease-fire agreement (1973)

Senate establishes special committee to investigate Watergate scandal (1973)

Three White House advisers resign in connection with Watergate (1973)

Assignment of special Watergate prosecutor (1973)

Presidential aide reveals Nixon's secret system of taping conversations (1973)

Vice President Agnew resigns (1973)

Dismissal of special prosecutor ("Saturday Night Massacre") (1973)

Appointment of new special Watergate prosecutor (1973)

Passage of War Powers Resolution over presidential veto (1973)

Congress confirms Vice President Ford (1973)

Seven former presidential aides indicted in Watergate scandal; Nixon named
    as unindicted co-conspirator (1974)

Supreme Court rules against president on release of White House tapes (1974)

House Judiciary Committee approves three articles of impeachment (1974)

Nixon resigns (1974)

POSTPRESIDENCY   Pardoned by President Ford, September 8, 1974

Disbarred in New York, 1976

Published numerous books, 1978–1994

DEATH   April 22, 1994, New York, N.Y.

Nixon to kick around anymore." He then moved to New York City to practice law, but would soon enter politics again.

THE 1968 ELECTION

With the United States torn apart by the Vietnam War and civil rights struggles in 1968, Nixon decided that he would give the presidential race another try. The Republican National Convention nominated him on the first ballot and selected Gov. Spiro T. Agnew of Maryland as his running mate. The Democratic Party was highly divided over the war, and in a convention marred by battles between police and protesters,

nominated Vice President Hubert H. Humphrey of Minnesota for president and Sen. Edmund S. Muskie of Maine for vice president. Segregationist Alabama governor George C. Wallace mounted a third-party presidential campaign with Gen. Curtis E. LeMay of Ohio as his running mate. They won forty-six Electoral College votes in five states on their American Independent Party ballot. Nixon prevailed in the race with 31.7 million popular votes and 301 Electoral College votes to nearly 31 million popular votes and 191 Electoral College votes for Humphrey. Because Wallace won nearly 9.5 million popular votes, Nixon became president with a plurality of about 43 percent, but not a majority, of the popular vote.

THE NIXON ADMINISTRATION (FIRST TERM)

Nixon's twelve-department cabinet included William P. Rogers of Maryland as secretary of state and Melvin R. Laird of Wisconsin as defense secretary. For attorney general, Nixon first picked John N. Mitchell of New York, who was followed by Richard G. Kleindienst of Arizona in 1972. Nixon had three treasury secretaries in his first term: David M. Kennedy of Illinois, John B. Connally Jr. of Texas in 1971, and George P. Shultz of Illinois in 1972. Perhaps even more significant than his cabinet members were the men he chose as his White House aides. His closest advisers included Chief of Staff Harry R. "H. R." Haldeman of California and domestic policy adviser John D. Ehrlichman of Washington, both of whom had worked for Nixon's earlier political campaigns. In foreign affairs, Nixon selected Harvard professor and international affairs strategist Henry A. Kissinger as national security adviser.

First Lady "Pat" Nixon was a high school teacher who met her future husband in a theater group in Whittier, California. They married in 1940 and had two daughters, Patricia and Julie. Julie Nixon married Dwight David Eisenhower II, the grandson of President Eisenhower, in New York City in 1968, just one month before her father became president. Tricia Nixon married Edward Cox in a White House Rose Garden ceremony in 1971.

MAJOR ISSUES (FIRST TERM)

Nixon had promised in the 1968 presidential campaign that he would produce "peace with honor" in the Vietnam War, and upon taking office, he immediately focused on this agenda. He endorsed a policy of "Vietnamization," in which the United States would shift responsibility for waging war to its South Vietnamese ally, but continue to provide training and weapons while slowly withdrawing American troops. This process stretched to four years, during which antiwar demonstrators staged many protests. Particularly controversial was Nixon's decision to invade Cambodia in 1970 to cut off assistance to North Vietnam. This incursion sparked a domestic uproar, and it resulted in a devastating event at Kent State University in Ohio, when the National Guard killed four student protesters. A few days later, Nixon impulsively decided to attend an antiwar demonstration at the Lincoln Memorial to meet with protesters, but he kept the conversation light, talking about college life rather than the war.

Despite the protests, Nixon retained public support for his Vietnam policy. His decision to escalate the air war against North Vietnam while withdrawing U.S. combat forces did not advance the peace talks, but Nixon's approval ratings remained strong. Congress, however, was critical of executive usurpation of its war power (which dated back to the start of the war in the Johnson administration) and in 1970 repealed the 1964 Gulf of Tonkin resolution that had granted the president the authority to protect U.S. interests in Southeast Asia.

The hallmark of Nixon's foreign policy was his rapprochement with both China and the Soviet Union. Nixon and Kissinger pursued a strategy of engagement with China in hopes that these ties would cause friction between the two leading Communist powers, China and the U.S.S.R. In February 1972 Nixon visited China, and the two nations approved the Shanghai Communiqué, marking a new era in U.S.-China relations. A few months later, Nixon visited the Soviet Union, where he and Soviet leader Leonid Brezhnev signed two arms control treaties. The Nixon-Kissinger diplomacy set the foundation for U.S. policy toward China and the Soviet Union for the rest of the cold war.

In economic affairs, Nixon's primary concern was to control the growth of inflation. In 1971 he instituted wage and price controls, which, combined with greater spending, temporarily halted price increases and lowered unemployment. But when the president removed the controls toward the end of his administration, inflation rose again, abetted partly by high oil prices due to an Arab oil embargo. The United States would combat the twin problems of high inflation and high unemployment throughout the 1970s.

Although domestic policy was not Nixon's primary area of interest, he was responsible for several important initiatives. He dismantled some of President Lyndon B. Johnson's War on Poverty programs and instead promoted a "New Federalism," in which the federal government disbursed funds to the states with flexible guidelines for their use. Nixon endorsed strict standards for pollution control and approved the creation of the Environmental Protection Agency in 1970. That same year he approved the establishment of the Occupational Safety and Health Administration to regulate workplace safety. The Nixon administration endorsed aggressive efforts, such as wiretapping, to combat crime, but civil liberties advocates criticized such moves. Nixon opposed busing students to promote racial desegregation in schools, but his administration instituted affirmative action programs to provide opportunities for black American in federal building projects.

Inside the Nixon White House, the president's top aides were pursuing a top-secret agenda at Nixon's behest to battle political opponents. Nixon authorized the Federal Bureau of Investigation (FBI) to employ wiretaps without judicial warrants, and for some time, he had the Internal Revenue Service (IRS) conduct audits of groups that opposed his programs.

Nixon's aides created a group known as the "Plumbers" specifically to ferret out information about perceived enemies of the president. When *The New York Times* and the *Washington Post* began publishing a classified history of the Vietnam War known as the Pentagon Papers, Nixon's aides secretly looked for damaging information on Daniel Ellsberg, the former government official and military analyst who had leaked the information. Shortly after the Pentagon Papers controversy, Nixon installed a secret taping system to record his conversations in the Oval Office and a few other locations. This record of his administration's undercover operations would prove fatal to his presidency in the Watergate scandal.

In June 1972 an attempted break-in at Democratic Party headquarters at the Watergate office complex in Washington, D.C., was discovered. The Committee to Re-elect the President (CREEP) had authorized this burglary for the purposes of obtaining information and placing listening devices. Top Nixon administration officials, including Attorney General Mitchell and White House counsel John Dean, had known of these plans. Nixon was informed about the connection to the White House, and in a fateful conversation on June 23, 1972, he told Haldeman that the FBI's investigation should be obstructed on national security grounds. This evidence of the president's role in the cover-up was not released for two years, but Nixon's close involvement in the plans dominated the remainder of his administration.

THE 1972 ELECTION

Although the Watergate burglary was under investigation in 1972, it did not affect the presidential election. President Nixon easily won his party's nomination for a second term on the first convention ballot, and Vice President Agnew also was renominated. The Democratic Party nominated Sen. George S. McGovern of South Dakota for president and Sen. Thomas F. Eagleton of Missouri for vice president. Just a few weeks after the convention, Eagleton resigned from the campaign when it was revealed he had been hospitalized in the past for exhaustion and had received electric shock treatments. Instead, R. Sargent Shriver of Maryland, a brother-in-law of former president John F. Kennedy, was chosen to be the Democratic vice-presidential candidate.

The 1972 presidential election had one of the widest margins of victory in the twentieth century. Nixon won more than 60 percent of the popular vote, 46.7 million ballots to 28.9 million for McGovern. Furthermore, Nixon won every state in the Electoral College except Massachusetts and Washington, D.C. The overwhelming popular support for the president suggested bright prospects for his second term, but the Watergate cover-up would soon derail his mandate.

THE NIXON ADMINISTRATION (SECOND TERM)

Nixon's second-term cabinet had one less member than his first, as the office of postmaster general became part of the United States Postal Service in 1971 and lost cabinet rank. The president's most significant cabinet appointment was the selection in 1973 of National Security Adviser Kissinger to take charge of the State Department as well. Kissinger would be the only person ever to hold both offices at the same time. Nixon replaced other cabinet members in his second term, but the more consequential change in his advisory team was the removal of top aides Haldeman and Ehrlichman in 1973, in response to the growing controversy over the Watergate scandal. The president also had to nominate a new vice president in late 1973, when news that Agnew was guilty of accepting bribes and evading taxes forced his resignation. Nixon nominated House Minority Leader Gerald R. Ford to succeed Agnew. Ford's approval by Congress marked the first implementation of the succession section of the Twenty-fifth Amendment.

MAJOR ISSUES (SECOND TERM)

In January 1973, at the beginning of Nixon's second term, the Vietnam War finally came to a close when the parties signed a cease-fire agreement in Paris. Kissinger was awarded the Nobel Peace Prize for his negotiations, but the peace in Vietnam did not endure. In 1975 the Communist regime seized control of South Vietnam. Other significant events also took place in 1973: the end of the military draft in the United States and the legalization of abortion with the landmark Supreme Court decision *Roe v. Wade*. But the overriding issue of importance in the second term was the Watergate scandal, and Nixon fought for more than a year and a half to protect his presidency before resigning on August 9, 1974.

In early 1973, seven people arrested in connection with the Watergate burglary either pleaded guilty or were convicted at trial. Soon after, Dean told Justice Department prosecutors about the White House's role in the cover-up, which led to the forced resignations of Haldeman and Ehrlichman. The Justice Department appointed a special prosecutor, Harvard law professor Archibald Cox, to lead the Watergate investigation. The Senate held hearings on Watergate in summer 1973. The most startling moment came when White House aide Alexander Butterfield revealed that Nixon had tape-recorded his Oval Office conversations. This explosive news resulted in a yearlong battle between Congress and the president over access to those tapes, and it would require Supreme Court intervention for resolution.

Nixon refused to turn over the White House tapes to the Senate investigating committee, insisting that they were private conversations protected under the concept of executive privilege. Special prosecutor Cox also requested the tapes, and when he rejected a compromise proposal of a summary transcript, Nixon demanded his dismissal. Attorney General Elliot L. Richardson refused to fire Cox and resigned; Nixon then fired Deputy Attorney General William Ruckelshaus when he, too, refused to dismiss Cox. Solicitor General Robert H. Bork carried out Nixon's order, but the chain of events, which became known as the "Saturday Night Massacre," reflected unfavorably on Nixon and led to calls for an impeachment inquiry. Another special prosecutor, Leon Jaworski, replaced Cox, and Nixon acquiesced to an agreement with congressional leaders that he would not dismiss this special prosecutor without their endorsement.

By spring 1974 several of Nixon's former advisers, including Haldeman, Ehrlichman, Dean, and Mitchell, had been charged with conspiracy and obstruction of justice. Nixon was identified as an unindicted co-conspirator, although this information was not made public immediately. The House Judiciary Committee began its impeachment inquiry soon after and issued subpoenas for the Nixon tapes, as did Jaworski. In response, Nixon released transcripts of some conversations, but when he refused to release all of the tapes, Jaworski appealed his case to the Supreme Court. In July in an 8–0 decision (Justice William H. Rehnquist recused himself because he had served in the Justice Department in Nixon's first term), the Court ruled that the president did not possess

an absolute power of executive privilege and that Nixon must turn over the tapes.

The tapes revealed the "smoking gun" of Nixon's role in the Watergate cover-up with the June 23, 1972, conversation in which the president had told his chief of staff to have the CIA derail the FBI's investigation. The House Judiciary Committee already had approved three articles of impeachment against Nixon for violation of his constitutional responsibilities, abuse of power, and contempt of Congress. With the release of this conversation, an impeachment vote by the House was almost certain. Rather than face impeachment and a Senate trial, Nixon decided to resign. He announced his decision to the nation on August 8, 1974, and resigned the following day. Gerald Ford became the first U.S. president who was not elected either to that office or the vice presidency.

One month after he left the White House, Nixon received an unconditional pardon from Ford for any federal offenses he might have committed in office. The pardon removed the possibility that Nixon would face further investigation and criminal charges for Watergate. But the pardon would not erase his involvement in the cover-up conspiracy, nor would it erase the tapes' revelation of Nixon as a crude, vengeful, and bitter person. For the next two decades, Nixon sought to become a senior statesman in U.S. foreign affairs, writing several books and traveling abroad extensively. He also continued the fight over access to his White House tapes and presidential papers, waging numerous court battles to keep these materials private, efforts that were ultimately unsuccessful. In April 1994 Nixon died in New York City after suffering a massive stroke. Despite his policy accomplishments and controversies, Watergate would remain the center of his complicated legacy.

"Nixon Wins by a Thin Margin," November 7, 1968

Nixon's 1968 presidential election victory marked a stunning turnaround for a politician who just six years earlier had declared after losing the California gubernatorial race that he would no longer participate in politics. Public frustration with the Vietnam War contributed to Nixon's election, as did the candidacy of segregationist Alabama governor George C. Wallace, who won five southern states that might otherwise have voted Democratic. Nixon had campaigned on a platform of having a secret plan to end the Vietnam War, but once in office, he found this goal difficult to achieve.

NOVEMBER 7, 1968
NIXON WINS BY A THIN MARGIN,

PLEADS FOR REUNITED NATION

ELECTOR VOTE 287

Lead in Popular Tally May Be Smaller Than Kennedy's in '60

By MAX FRANKEL

Richard Milhous Nixon emerged the victor yesterday in one of the closest and most tumultuous Presidential campaigns in history and set himself the task of reuniting the nation.

Elected over Hubert H. Humphrey by the barest of margins—only four one-hundredths of a percentage point in the popular vote—and confronted by a Congress in control of the Democrats, the President-elect said it "will be the great objective of this Administration at the outset to bring the American people together."

He pledged, as the 37th President, to form "an open Administration, open to new ideas, open to men and women of both parties, open to critics as well as those who support us" so as to bridge the gap between the generations and the races.

Details Left for Later

But after an exhausting and tense night of awaiting the verdict at the Waldorf-Astoria Hotel here, Mr. Nixon and his closest aides were not yet prepared to suggest how they intended to organize themselves and to approach these objectives. The Republican victor expressed admiration for his opponent's challenge and reiterated his desire to help President Johnson achieve peace in Vietnam between now and Inauguration Day on Jan. 20.

The verdict of an electorate that appeared to number 73 million could not be discerned until mid-morning because Mr. Nixon and Mr. Humphrey finished in a virtual tie in the popular vote, just as Mr. Nixon and John F. Kennedy did in 1960.

With 94 per cent of the nation's election precincts reporting, Mr. Nixon's total stood last evening at 29,726,409 votes to Mr. Humphrey's 29,677,152. The margin of 49,257 was even smaller than Mr. Kennedy's margin of 112,803.

Meaning Hard to Find

When translated into the determining electoral votes of the states, these returns proved even more difficult to read, and the result in two states—Alaska and Missouri—was still not final last night. But the unofficial returns from elsewhere gave Mr. Nixon a minimum of 287 electoral votes, 17 more than the 270 required for election. Mr. Humphrey won 191.

Because of the tightness of the race, the third-party challenger, George C. Wallace, came close to realizing his minimum objective of denying victory to the major-party candidates and then somehow forcing a bargain for his support on one of them. Although he did not do nearly as well as he had hoped and as others had feared, he received 9,291,807 votes or 13.3 per cent of the total, and the 45 electoral votes of Alabama, Georgia, Louisiana, Mississippi and Arkansas.

Mr. Wallace's support ranged from 1 per cent in Hawaii to 65 per cent in his home state of Alabama, and his presence on the ballot in all 50 states unquestionably influenced the outcome in many of them. But there was no certain way of determining whether Mr. Nixon or Mr. Humphrey was the beneficiary of the third-party split-offs.

Mr. Humphrey's narrow victory in states such as Texas was probably due to Mr. Wallace's strong showing there. Conversely, Mr. Wallace's drain-off in traditional Democratic strongholds, such as New Jersey, probably helped Mr. Nixon.

"250,000 WAR PROTESTERS STAGE PEACEFUL RALLY IN WASHINGTON," NOVEMBER 16, 1969

Nixon's strategy of escalating the air war in Vietnam while gradually withdrawing U.S. troops did not satisfy antiwar protestors, who continued to demonstrate against the administration. A November 1969 march on Washington, D.C., had a turnout of more than a quarter million people. But even before this demonstration, Nixon had declared that the protestors did not represent the American public, which he famously described as the "great silent majority," whose support he would seek.

NOVEMBER 16, 1969
250,000 WAR PROTESTERS STAGE PEACEFUL RALLY IN WASHINGTON; A RECORD THRONG

Young Marchers Ask Rapid Withdrawal From Vietnam
By JOHN HERBERS
Special to The New York Times

WASHINGTON, Nov. 15—A vast throng of Americans, predominantly youthful and constituting the largest mass march in the nation's capital, demonstrated peacefully in the heart of the city today, demanding a rapid withdrawal of United States troops from Vietnam.

The District of Columbia Police Chief, Jerry Wilson, said a "moderate" estimate was that 250,000 had paraded on Pennsylvania Avenue and had attended an antiwar rally at the Washington Monument. Other city officials said aerial photographs would later show that the crowd had exceeded 300,000.

Until today, the largest outpouring of demonstrators was the gentle civil rights march of 1963, which attracted 200,000. Observers of both marches said the throng that appeared today was clearly greater than the outpouring of 1963.

At dusk, after the mass demonstration had ended, a small segment of the crowd, members of radical splinter groups, moved across Constitution Avenue to the Labor and Justice Department buildings, where they burned United States flags, threw paint bombs and other missiles and were repelled by tear gas released by the police.

There were a number of arrests and minor injuries, mostly the result of the tear gas.

• •

"NIXON SENDS COMBAT FORCES TO CAMBODIA TO DRIVE COMMUNISTS FROM STAGING ZONE," MAY 1, 1970, AND "4 KENT STATE STUDENTS KILLED BY TROOPS," MAY 5, 1970

Opposition to the Nixon administration's Vietnam policy boiled over with the news that the president had ordered U.S. combat troops to invade Cambodia. Nixon argued that the invasion was necessary to cut off supplies to Communist insurgents in Vietnam. *The New York Times* described the president's rhetoric in announcing the invasion on national television as "tough—probably the toughest of his tenure in office." College students across the nation staged protests against the invasion, and at Kent State University, Ohio, four students were shot dead by members of the National Guard. The shootings shocked the nation and showed the fear, anger, and distrust that had developed between protestors and forces of law and order.

MAY 1, 1970
NIXON SENDS COMBAT FORCES TO CAMBODIA TO DRIVE COMMUNISTS FROM STAGING ZONE

'NOT AN INVASION'
President Calls Step an Extension of War to Save G.I. Lives
By ROBERT B. SEMPLE Jr.
Special to The New York Times

WASHINGTON, April 30—In a sharp departure from the previous conduct of war in Southeast Asia, President Nixon announced tonight that he was sending United States combat troops into Cambodia for the first time.

Even as the President was addressing the nation on television, several thousand American soldiers were moving across the border from South Vietnam to Cambodia to attack what Mr. Nixon described as "the headquarters for the entire Communist military operation in South Vietnam."

The area was described by sources here as the Fishhook area of Cambodia, some 50 miles northwest of Saigon.

White House sources said they expected tonight's operation to be concluded in six to eight weeks. They said its primary objective was not to kill enemy soldiers but to destroy their supplies and drive them from their sanctuaries.

Aimed at Staging Areas

"Our purpose is not to occupy the areas," the President declared. "Once enemy forces are driven out of these sanctuaries and their military supplies destroyed, we will withdraw."

The President described the action as "not an invasion of Cambodia" but a necessary extension of the Vietnam war designed to eliminate a major Communist staging and communications area. Thus it is intended to protect the lives of American troops and shorten the war, he asserted.

The President further described the action as "indispensable" for the continued success of his program of Vietnamization—under which he has been withdrawing American ground combat troops as the burden of fighting is gradually shifted to the South Vietnamese.

The President's rhetoric was tough—probably the toughest of his tenure in office—and was reminiscent of some of the speeches of Lyndon B. Johnson during the last years of his term as President.

Nixon Appears Grim

The President appeared grim as he delivered his address while sitting at his desk in the Oval Office of the White House. Occasionally he used a nearby map to point out the Communist-held sanctuaries, which were shaded in red. But no gesture could match the solemnity of his words.

He portrayed his decision as a difficult one taken without regard to his political future, which he said was "nothing compared to the lives" of American soldiers.

Discussing this future, Mr. Nixon said: "I would rather be a one-term President and do what I believe is right than to be a two-term President at the cost of seeing America become a second-rate power and to see this nation accept the first defeat in its proud 190-year history."

He added that he regarded the recent actions of the North Vietnamese as a test of American credibility requiring firm response.

"This action puts the leaders of North Vietnam on notice," he said, "that we will be patient in working for peace, we will be conciliatory at the conference table, but, we will not be humiliated. We will not be defeated. We will not allow American men by the thousands to be killed by an enemy from privileged sanctuaries."

"We live in an age of anarchy, both abroad and at home," the President declared. "We see mindless attacks on all the great institutions which have been created by free civilizations in the last 500 years. Here in the United States, great universities have been systematically destroyed. Small nations all over the world find themselves under attack."

'We live in an age of anarchy, both abroad and at home,' the President declared.

MAY 5, 1970
4 KENT STATE STUDENTS KILLED BY TROOPS
8 Hurt as Shooting Follows Reported Sniping at Rally
By JOHN KIFNER
Special to The New York Times

KENT, Ohio, May 4—Four students at Kent State University, two of them women, were shot to death this afternoon by a volley of National Guard gunfire. At least 8 other students were wounded.

The burst of gunfire came about 20 minutes after the guardsmen broke up a noon rally on the Commons, a grassy campus gathering spot, by lobbing tear gas at a crowd of about 1,000 young people.

In Washington, President Nixon deplored the deaths of the four students in the following statement:

"This should remind us all once again that when dissent turns to violence it invites tragedy. It is my hope that this tragic and unfortunate incident will strengthen the determination of all the nation's campuses, administrators, faculty and students alike to stand firmly for the right which exists in this country of peaceful dissent and just as strongly against the resort to violence as a means of such expression."

In Columbus, Sylvester Del Corso, Adjutant General of the Ohio National Guard, said in a statement that the guardsmen had been forced to shoot after a sniper opened fire against the troops from a nearby rooftop and the crowd began to move to encircle the guardsmen.

Frederick P. Wenger, the Assistant Adjutant General, said the troops had opened fire after they were shot at by a sniper.

"They were under standing orders to take cover and return any fire," he said.

This reporter, who was with the group of students, did not see any indication of sniper fire, nor was the sound of any gunfire audible before the Guard volley. Students, conceding that rocks had been thrown, heatedly denied that there was any sniper.

Gov. James A. Rhodes called on J. Edgar Hoover, director of the Federal Bureau of Investigation, to aid in looking into the campus violence. A Justice Department spokesman said no decision had been made to investigate.

At 2:10 this afternoon, after the shootings, the university president, Robert I. White, ordered the university closed for an indefinite time, and officials were making plans to evacuate the dormitories and bus out-of-state students to nearby cities.

Robinson Memorial Hospital identified the dead students as Allison Krause, 19 years old, of Pittsburgh; Sandra Lee Scheuer, 20, of Youngstown, Ohio, both coeds; Jeffrey Glenn Miller, 20, of 22 Diamond Drive, Plainview, I.L., and William K. Schroeder, 19, of Lorain, Ohio.

"PRESIDENT ASKS FOR FUNDS FOR SCHOOL DESEGREGATION," MAY 22, 1970

President Nixon supported racial desegregation of American public schools, but he did not endorse court rulings that ordered school busing to enforce integration. Instead, Nixon called for using federal funds to assist school districts in implementing desegregation. Congress did not support such legislation, however, and the Supreme Court ruled in *Swann v. Charlotte-Mecklenberg Board of Education* (1971) that busing was an acceptable means of ensuring the racial integration of public schools.

MAY 22, 1970
PRESIDENT ASKS FOR FUNDS FOR SCHOOL DESEGREGATION
Seeks $150-Million on 'Emergency Basis'—Some of $1.5-Billion in 2-Year Plan Urged for Racially Isolated Pupils
By ROBERT B. SEMPLE Jr.
Special to The New York Times

WASHINGTON, May 21—President Nixon formally asked Congress today for $1.5-billion over the next two years to be used primarily to help finance the desegregation of Southern schools and to provide incentives for Northern school districts to integrate.

According to White House sources who briefed newsmen this morning, the President's express wish is to earmark the bulk of the money for desegregation and only a relatively small amount for so-called compensatory funds for schools that remain largely segregated.

The emphasis placed on desegregation drew immediate praise from liberal educators and represented a triumph for a band of moderates in the Nixon Administration led by Secretary of Labor George P. Shultz.

The message asked Congress for $150-million immediately on an "emergency basis"; it asked for $350-million more in the 1971 fiscal year and $1-billion in 1972.

All the money would be "new" money, according to the Budget Bureau sources, meaning that it would not be diverted from existing programs. The first $150-million would come from previous Congressional authorizations for which the money has not yet been appropriated; the rest would be appropriated under a bill submitted today called the Emergency School Aid Act of 1970.

• •

"NIXON SIGNS VOTE-AT-18 BILL BUT ASKS FOR COURT TEST," JUNE 23, 1970

To further promote racial integration, in 1970 President Nixon endorsed the extension of the 1965 Voting Rights Act. The 1970 legislation was especially significant because it also lowered the voting age to eighteen from twenty-one. Upon signing the bill, Nixon questioned its constitutionality, and in *Oregon v. Mitchell* (1970) the Supreme Court agreed with him, ruling that the federal government could not set the voting age for state elections. The issue was resolved with the ratification in 1971 of the Twenty-sixth Amendment, which changed the minimum age for voting to eighteen in all U.S. elections. The amendment was ratified within months after it was introduced in Congress, in large part because many people agreed that individuals who were old enough to be drafted and sent to fight in Vietnam were old enough to vote.

JUNE 23, 1970
NIXON SIGNS VOTE-AT-18 BILL BUT ASKS FOR COURT TEST;
VOTES HOSPITAL GRANTS
'65 ACT EXTENDED
11 Million More Would Be Allowed to Ballot in All Elections
By JACK ROSENTHAL
Special to The New York Times

WASHINGTON, June 22—President Nixon resolved a political dilemma today by signing into law a historic measure lowering the voting age from 21 to 18—and then immediately calling for a court challenge to decide if it is constitutional.

The measure was a rider on a bill that extends for five more years the protection of the Voting Rights Act of 1965 against racial discrimination. Since its passage, nearly a million Negro residents of Southern states have registered to vote.

The measure lowering the voting age, if it survives a challenge, would make 11 million more young people eligible to vote in the next Presidential election. It goes into effect on Jan. 1 and applies to all elections, Federal, state, and local.

Approves Despite Doubts

President Nixon emphasized, in a statement, that the voting rights extension was of such great importance that he was giving his approval to the entire measure, despite his serious constitutional doubts about the 18-year-old vote provisions.

Mr. Nixon's action was promptly hailed by Roy Wilkins, executive director of the National Association for the Advancement of Colored People. Mr. Wilkins said the association noted "with satisfaction that President Nixon regards the safeguarding of the Negro's right to vote as a prime consideration in his signing of the measure."

'Act of Statesmanship'

Clarence Mitchell, director of the N.A.A.C.P.'s Washington bureau, said the signing was "an act of statesmanship undergirded by faith in the rule of just law."

Mr. Nixon took pains in his statement to reiterate his support of the 18-year-old vote and his belief that it was the method of achieving it, not the result, that he questioned.

The Constitution leaves the establishment of voting qualifications to the states. Mr. Nixon said he believed, "along with most of the nation's leading constitutional scholars," that lowering the voting age thus required a constitutional amendment, not simply an act of Congress. The dilemma for the President, White House sources said, lay between the constitutional argument and the feelings of youth and Negroes, neither of whom are likely to be attentive to constitutional subtleties.

"NIXON PROPOSES 2 NEW AGENCIES ON ENVIRONMENT," JULY 10, 1970

To promote tough environmental standards, especially for clean air and water, President Nixon supported the creation of two agencies. The Environmental Protection Agency would be responsible for setting standards for pollution control, and the National Oceanic and Atmospheric Administration would conduct research in support of environmental policies. Previously, Nixon had endorsed the creation of the Council on Environmental Quality in 1969. Nixon also supported the Clean Air Act of 1970, but he opposed the Clean Water Act of 1972 because of its cost, and the law ultimately passed over his veto.

JULY 10, 1970
NIXON PROPOSES 2 NEW AGENCIES ON ENVIRONMENT
Major Reshuffling Scheduled Unless Senate or House Objects in 60 Days
INITIAL REACTION WARM
Muskie Praises Message—Some in Cabinet Oppose Losing Men and Funds
By JAMES M. NAUGHTON
Special to The New York Times

WASHINGTON, July 9—President Nixon called today for a major reshuffling of Government agencies to coordinate efforts to understand, protect and enhance the nation's environment.

In separate reorganization plans he sent to Congress, Mr. Nixon proposed transferring most pollution control activities to an independent Environmental Protection Agency and combining air and sea research under a new National Oceanic and Atmospheric Administration. The latter would be in the Department of Commerce.

Both plans will take effect automatically unless either branch of Congress objects within 60 days.

'Concerted Action'

There were no new functions or powers suggested in the message today, but the President said that consolidation of activities now spread throughout the Government would permit a more effective assault on despoilers of the environment.

"Our national Government today is not structured to make a coordinated attack on the pollutants which debase the air we breathe, the water we drink, and the land that grows our food," Mr. Nixon said. "Indeed, the present governmental structure for dealing with environmental pollution often defies effective and concerted action."

Under the reorganization, the Environmental Protection Agency—reporting directly to the President—would take over responsibility for clean air and water programs, pesticide research and standard-setting, and radiation monitoring.

"Curbs on Crime and Drug Abuse Gain in Congress," October 8, 1970

To combat crime and drug abuse, President Nixon endorsed "law and order" legislation in 1970. The Organized Crime Control Act gave the federal government increased authority to investigate organized crime and impose stricter penalties for such activity. The Comprehensive Drug Abuse Prevention and Control Act gave the Justice Department increased power to combat illegal drug trafficking. Critics questioned whether such expansion of federal law enforcement power would infringe upon individual civil liberties.

OCTOBER 8, 1970
CURBS ON CRIME AND DRUG ABUSE GAIN IN CONGRESS
The House and Senate Move Quickly to Vote Measures Requested by President
By MARJORIE HUNTER
Special to The New York Times

WASHINGTON, Oct. 7—Congress moved swiftly today to give President Nixon legislation he has sought to control organized crime, campus bombings and narcotics use and traffic.

Action on the President's "law and order" proposals came first in the House, which passed, 341 to 26, a bill to combat organized crime and permit Federal agents to investigate campus bombings.

Several hours later, the Senate approved, 54 to 9, a bill designed to crack down on narcotics traffic and abuse but reducing penalties for lesser drug violations.

Objections Brushed Aside

Final Congressional clearance of the two bills, however, rests on the ability of Senate and House conferees to resolve differences in the versions passed by the two bodies.

In the House, a small band of Democratic liberals protested to the end that many provisions of the anticrime bill were unconstitutional.

But their objections were brushed aside as the Democratic-controlled House moved to erase charges by the Nixon Administration that the Democrats are "soft on crime."

Somewhat similar legislation cleared the Senate last January, but the House added a number of new provisions, including the death penalty for those convicted of fatal bombings and permission for Federal agents to investigate campus bombings and arson.

"Nixon Signs Job Safety Bill, Ending Long Struggle," December 30, 1970

The creation of the Occupational Safety and Health Administration in 1970 was a bipartisan effort to establish federal standards for American workers. It resulted from extensive negotiations between business and labor interests, as well as between Capitol Hill and the White House, over the establishment and enforcement of workplace safety standards.

DECEMBER 30, 1970
NIXON SIGNS JOB SAFETY BILL, ENDING LONG STRUGGLE
By ROBERT B. SEMPLE Jr.
Special to The New York Times

WASHINGTON, Dec. 29—President Nixon signed today an occupational health and safety bill giving the Secretary of Labor authority to set safety standards for factories, farms and construction sites and creating a three-member panel to enforce the standards.

The bill is viewed by its bipartisan sponsors and by the White House as an important piece of social legislation. It will eventually require the creation of a separate monitoring agency within the Department of Labor employing at least 2,000 persons and budgeted at more than $25-million annually.

Mr. Nixon signed the bill this morning in an atmosphere of festive bipartisanship at the Department of Labor, thus ending a long struggle between management and labor and between Capitol Hill and the executive branch over the substance of the bill.

'Goal We All Wanted'

Despite the differences among its many proponents, Mr. Nixon said today, the bill "in substance attains the goal we all wanted to achieve." He defined this goal as improving not only the safety but also the "total environment" of 55 million American workers.

The measure is essentially an accommodation between the original House bill, supported by the Nixon Administration and the business community, and an early Senate version backed by organized labor.

The key dispute involved who should set safety standards and enforce them.

Organized labor and liberal Democrats argued that both functions should reside with the Secretary of Labor, whereas the business community and the Administration proposed that two separate Presidentially appointed boards set standards and enforce them.

Labor objected to the Administration's plan on two grounds. First, it felt that Presidentially appointed panels tended to become captives of the industries they were supposed to represent. Second, labor believed that its influence with the Secretary of Labor was likely to remain strong no matter which party occupies the White House.

"Court Move Hailed at Washington Post; More Articles Due," July 1, 1971, and "The Court's Decision," July 4, 1971

The release of the Pentagon Papers in June 1971 sparked a heated battle between the Nixon administration and two nationally renowned newspapers, *The New York Times* and the *Washington Post,* over freedom of the press. The Pentagon Papers, commissioned in the Lyndon B. Johnson administration, were a top-secret Defense Department history of U.S. involvement in Vietnam. President Nixon sought a federal injunction prohibiting publication of the documents, but in a landmark ruling, the Supreme Court declared that such action represented an unconstitutional prior restraint on the press, a violation of the First Amendment. In applauding the decision, *The Times* editorial said the ruling was "a striking confirmation of the vitality of the American democratic form of government."

JULY 1, 1971
COURT MOVE HAILED AT WASHINGTON POST; MORE ARTICLES DUE
Special to The New York Times

WASHINGTON, June 30—Executives of *The Washington Post* applauded the Supreme Court's decision today and published in their Thursday issue, three articles based on their partial collection of the Pentagon papers.

Katharine Graham, publisher of *The Post*, said:

"We are terribly gratified by the result in this historic case, not just for the sake of the press but for the sake of the public and the good of the country."

"It's beautiful," said Benjamin Bradlee, the executive editor, shortly after the Court's verdict was announced. "It's by far the most important thing I've ever been involved in."

Mr. Bradlee said that *The Post* had 4,415 pages from the more than 7,000-page study of American involvement in the Vietnam war. He also said that fresh material from the official study was still coming in from the office of Senator Mike Gravel, Democrat of Alaska.

The Post had printed two long articles on the secret Pentagon study on June 18 and 19 before being restrained by a three-judge panel of the United States Court of Appeals for the District of Columbia.

> "[T]he American people have a presumptive right to be informed of the political decisions of their Government and that when the Government has been devious with the people, it will find no constitutional sanction for its efforts to enforce concealment by censorship."

JULY 4, 1971
EDITORIAL
THE COURT'S DECISION

The decision of the Supreme Court allowing *The Times* and other newspapers to continue to publish hitherto secret Pentagon documents on the Vietnam war is in our view less important as a victory for the press than as a striking confirmation of the vitality of the American democratic form of government.

Despite the potentially far-reaching significance of doubts and reservations expressed in the confusing welter of individual opinions—each of the nine Justices wrote his own—the outcome of this case is a landmark for the press in its centuries-old battle against the efforts of Governmental authority to impose prior restraints. But we believe its real meaning goes deeper than that, in the context of the present time and place. We believe that its more profound significance lies in the implicit but inescapable conclusion that the American people have a presumptive right to be informed of the political decisions of their Government and that when the Government has been devious with the people, it will find no constitutional sanction for its efforts to enforce concealment by censorship.

For this is the essential justification of *The Times'* grave decision to take on itself the responsibility of publishing the Pentagon papers. It was a decision not taken lightly; but *The Times* felt that the documents, all dating from 1968 or earlier, belonged to the American people, were now part of history, could in no sense damage current military operations or threaten a single life, and formed an essential element in an understanding by the American people of the event that has affected them more deeply than any other in this generation, the Vietnam war.

The decision had to be made whether or not the embarrassment to individuals, or even to governments, outweighed the value to the American public of knowing something about the decision-making process that led into the war and its subsequent escalation. Furthermore, it was evident that Governmental documents have been so generally overclassified and misclassified for so many years that the mere fact of labeling bore no necessary relationship to the national security. An intensive review of classification procedures is sure to be one beneficial result of this affair.

But there will be other results. We hope that the great lesson to have been learned from publication of the Pentagon papers is that the American Government must play square with the electorate. We hope that this Administration and those to come will realize that the major decisions have to be discussed frankly and openly and courageously; and that the essence of good government as of practical politics is, in Adlai Stevenson's phrase, to "talk sense to the American people."

The Pentagon papers demonstrate the failure of successive Administrations to carry out this policy in respect to Vietnam. We do not think it is a question of personal morality, but rather of private attitudes. We do not think that the respective officials involved made recommendations or took decisions that they did not conscientiously believe to be in the public interest. As an early opponent of the escalation of American military force in Vietnam, this newspaper has never attacked the motives of those leaders, but we have criticized and we continue to criticize their wisdom, their sense of values and their failure fully to apprise the people and Congress of the implications of decisions taken in secret.

Even if these decisions, now being revealed in the Pentagon papers, had been generally understood by the public at the time, we are not at all sure that in the climate of those days, the results would have been any different. Given the fear of Communist penetration and aggression throughout the '50's and most of the '60's, it is quite likely that the American public would have supported the basic rationale on escalation even if the respective Administrations had been as forthcoming as democratic procedures demanded.

The fact remains that out of the publication of this material, the American people emerge the gainers. They have gained in knowledge of the past, which should serve them well in the future. They have gained in an understanding of their rights under the Constitution. And they have gained in the perennial effort of free men to control their government rather than vice versa.

"Nixon Orders 90-Day Wage-Price Freeze," August 16, 1971

The post–World War II international monetary system known as Bretton Woods (after the New Hampshire resort where it was created in 1944) ended in 1971 with President Nixon's decision to take the U.S. dollar off the gold standard. No longer would the dollar be pegged to an exact value in gold; instead its value would "float" based upon foreign market conditions. Ending the gold standard devalued the dollar, but it promoted U.S. exports.

AUGUST 16, 1971
NIXON ORDERS 90-DAY WAGE-PRICE FREEZE, ASKS TAX CUTS, NEW JOBS IN BROAD PLAN: *SEVERS LINK BETWEEN DOLLAR AND GOLD*
A WORLD EFFECT
Unilateral U.S. Move Means Others Face Parity Decisions
By EDWIN L. DALE Jr.
Special to The New York Times

WASHINGTON, Aug. 15—President Nixon announced tonight that henceforth the United States would cease to convert foreign-held dollars into gold—unilaterally changing the 25-year-old international monetary system.

How many pounds, marks, yen and francs the dollar will buy tomorrow will depend on decisions of other countries. In some countries, the value of the dollar may "float," moving up and down in day-to-day exchanges. A period of turmoil in the foreign-exchange markets is all but certain, which means uncertainty for American tourists, exporters and importers.

The President said he was taking the action to stop "the attacks of international money speculators" against the dollar. He did not raise the official price of gold, which has been $35 an ounce since 1934.

Devaluation Denied

Mr. Nixon said he was not devaluing the dollar. But, he said, "If you want to buy a foreign car, or take a trip abroad, market conditions may cause your dollar to buy slightly less."

. . . .

"President Leaves on Trip to China; Stops in Hawaii," February 8, 1972, and "President Home After China Trip; Reassures Allies," February 29, 1972

President Nixon's historic 1972 trip to China fundamentally changed U.S. relations with the Communist power. The two nations agreed to expand communications and cultural contacts and to promote bilateral trade opportunities. For more than two decades, the United States had been closely allied with the Chinese Nationalist government in Taiwan, which fled the mainland when the Communists took control. Although the United States remained committed to a "one-China" policy, its opening to Communist China inevitably raised tensions with Taiwan. Further complicating matters was the United Nations's decision to replace Taiwan with Communist China on the Security Council. The Nixon administration favored broaching ties with China to create tension between China and the Soviet Union, thus altering the balance of power in the cold war in favor of the United States.

President Nixon talks with Chairman Mao Zedong, during his historic trip to China.

Source: The New York Times

FEBRUARY 8, 1972
PRESIDENT LEAVES ON TRIP TO CHINA; STOPS IN HAWAII
Throng at White House Sees Him and First Lady Off on Historic Journey
HE SAYS UNITY IS GOAL
Tells Crowd Way Is Sought to Have Differences With Peking Without War
By TAD SZULC
Special to The New York Times

WASHINGTON, Feb. 17—President Nixon left for China today.

He is to reach Peking on Monday morning, China time (Sunday night, New York time), for a week's stay on the mainland that is to include two conferences with Chairman Mao Tse-tung and meetings with Premier Chou En-lai.

Addressing Vice President Agnew, the leaders of Congress, members of his Cabinet and a large crowd assembled on the White House lawn this morning to bid him farewell, the President said in a brief statement that the United States and China must "find a way to see that we can have differences without being enemies in war."

'If We Can Make Progress'

"If we can make progress toward that goal on this trip," he declared, "the world will be a much safer world and the chance particularly for all of those young children over there to grow up in a world of peace will be infinitely greater."

As he uttered those words he pointed to a cluster of children facing him from behind the ropes holding back the many thousands at the departure ceremony. The White House said 8,000 were on hand—newsmen thought the figure was smaller—including 1,500 school children. Most of the youngsters had been bused from public schools in the capital and the Virginia and Maryland suburbs.

Mr. Nixon landed in Hawaii at 8:27 P.M., New York time, to begin a two-day stopover.

At the departure ceremony, Mr. Nixon, speaking without notes, concluded his remarks by citing as the suggested "postscript" for his journey—which follows more than 20 years of hostile relations—the words inscribed on the plaque left on the moon by the first American astronauts in 1969: "We came in peace for all mankind."

FEBRUARY 29, 1972
PRESIDENT HOME AFTER CHINA TRIP; REASSURES ALLIES
No Secret Deals, He Says, or Yielding on Pledges to Any Other Country
BIG WELCOMING CROWD
He Says He Has Returned With Beginnings of a New Relationship With Peking
Special to The New York Times

WASHINGTON, Feb. 28—President Nixon returned here tonight from his journey to China and told a large and warm welcoming crowd that he had established "the basis of a structure for peace" without sacrificing America's commitments to any of its allies.

"We've agreed that we will not negotiate the fate of other nations behind their back, and we did not do so in Peking," he declared. "There were no secret deals of any kind. We have done all this without giving up any United States commitment to any other country."

Mr. Nixon mentioned no nation by name, but his assurance of continuing commitments was clearly and principally addressed to the Nationalist Government on Taiwan with which the United States has a defense treaty. That commitment was stressed by Henry A. Kissinger, the President's assistant for national security affairs, in responding to newsmens' questions in Shanghai yesterday.

"DINNER IN KREMLIN," MAY 23, 1972, "CEILINGS ARE SET," MAY 27, 1972, AND "A FIRST STEP, BUT A MAJOR STRIDE," MAY 27, 1972

President Nixon's cold war strategy included significant overtures to the Soviet Union as well as to China. In May 1972 the United States and the Soviet Union signed two significant arms control treaties. The Strategic Arms Limitation Treaty, which would be popularly known as SALT I, limited the number of intercontinental ballistic missiles that each nation would have. The Anti-Ballistic Missile (ABM) Defense Treaty committed the two countries not to undertake development of antimissile defenses, because of concerns that the threat of such programs would encourage an offensive attack before their completion. In a news analysis, *The Times* writer Max Frankel (who won a Pulitzer Prize in 1973 for his reporting of Nixon's trip to China) hailed the treaties as "a major step forward in the already long history of nuclear arms negotiation. But it is also only a beginning."

MAY 23, 1972
DINNER IN KREMLIN
Nixon Urges Powers to Use Influence for Moderation
By ROBERT B. SEMPLE Jr.
Special to The New York Times

MOSCOW, May 22—Richard M. Nixon arrived here today, the first American President to visit the Soviet capital.

He began his week-long summit meetings here earlier than expected when a talk of almost two hours with Leonid I. Brezhnev, the Secretary General of the Communist party was added to the day's schedule at the Soviet leader's invitation.

Mr. Nixon, who flew here this afternoon from a two-day stay in Austria, emphasized in the private meeting and his public remarks the agreements on space cooperation, nuclear arms limitation and trade that he hoped to win or set in motion during the week.

But he also took his pleas for restraint in Vietnam directly to the Soviet leadership. At a dinner given in his honor tonight at the Kremlin, Mr. Nixon expressed his belief that "with great power goes great responsibility" and added a pointed allusion to Soviet aid to North Vietnam:

"We should recognize further that it is the responsibility of great powers to influence other nations in conflict or crisis to moderate their behavior."

MAY 27, 1972
CEILINGS ARE SET
Nixon and Brezhnev Pledge to Abide by Treaty at Once
By HEDRICK SMITH
Special to The New York Times

MOSCOW, Saturday, May 27—President Nixon and the Soviet Communist party leader, Leonid I. Brezhnev, signed two historic agreements last night that for the first time put limits on the growth of American and Soviet strategic nuclear arsenals.

In a brief televised ceremony in the Great Hall of the Kremlin, the two leaders put their signatures to a treaty that establishes a ceiling of 200 launchers for each side's defensive missile systems and commits them not to try to build nationwide antimissile defenses. The treaty, which is to run indefinitely, requires ratification by the Senate in Washington, but both sides pledged to abide by it at once.

Applause After Signing
They also signed an interim accord on offensive systems that freezes land-based and submarine-based inter-

continental missiles at the level now in operation or under construction.

After signing the two accords, Mr. Brezhnev and Mr. Nixon walked toward each other, smiling broadly, and shook hands vigorously amidst applause from a gathering of senior officials, including negotiators who had worked through the day to put the final touches on the agreement.

Mr. Nixon then said:

"We want to be remembered by our deeds, not by the fact that we brought war to the world, but by the fact that we made the world a more peaceful one for all peoples of the world."

MAY 27, 1972
A FIRST STEP, BUT A MAJOR STRIDE
By MAX FRANKEL
Special to The New York Times
News Analysis

MOSCOW, Saturday, May 27—The nuclear age gained its first strategic arms limitation treaty in the Kremlin last night. Its awkward name—commonly shortened to SALT—is needed because the accord involves no disarmament. Its purpose is to freeze the balance of terrifying weapons and to make sure the terror works by preventing any effective defense against them.

It is a major step forward in the already long history of nuclear arms negotiation. But it is also only a beginning.

Both President Nixon and the Soviet Party chief, Leonid I. Brezhnev, vowed to press ahead toward further limitations and perhaps eventually even some reductions in arms. So this treaty is likely to be known as SALT I.

It is a beginning, achieved after seven years of effort and 30 months of negotiation in one of those fleeting moments when the two superpowers felt themselves strategic equals, despite inequality in the quality and number of their arms, and when their two leaders felt themselves strong enough politically to make the agreements stick.

The arms race will go on, not only in the regular army, navy and air force weaponry that is unaffected by the accord but also in the quality of nuclear warheads—that is,

their size and accuracy and evasive skills—and in the arts of antisubmarine warfare and even in the technology of the missile defense systems that the treaty is to limit severely at inadequate levels.

Indeed, under certain conditions or political pressures, the treaty itself may stimulate further competition in these uncovered areas. And because the accord renounces those weapons that both sides think they now possess in sufficient number, it may not even save much money in future budgets.

The United States had no plans to augment the land and submarine missiles and antimissile installations covered by the treaty. The energetic Soviet build-up of recent years was presumably intended primarily to reach a comfortable level before the freeze.

The significance of the treaty lies in that it makes the freeze legally binding. It becomes an important weapon for political leaders under constant pressure to add yet another new system to their arsenals and provides a major rebuttal against those on both sides who have justified ever more expenditures on arms by fears of what the adversary "may" be intending.

"5 CHARGED WITH BURGLARY AT DEMOCRATIC QUARTERS," JUNE 18, 1972, AND "EX-G.O.P. AIDE LINKED TO POLITICAL RAID," JUNE 20, 1972

The attempted burglary of Democratic National Committee headquarters at the Watergate office complex in Washington, D.C., was foiled by a security guard who called the police. A link between the burglars and the White House soon became evident with the news that consultant and former CIA official E. Howard Hunt, who had worked with Nixon's advisers, had met with one of the burglars just a few weeks before the break-in.

JUNE 18, 1972
5 CHARGED WITH BURGLARY AT DEMOCRATIC QUARTERS
Special to The New York Times

WASHINGTON, June 17—Five men, said to have been carrying cameras, electronic surveillance equipment and burglary tools, were arrested shortly after 2 A.M. today after a floor-by-floor search that led to the executive quarters of the National Democratic Committee here. The suspects were charged with second-degree burglary.

None of the suspects disclosed any objectives for entering the committee headquarters or affiliations with any political organization in the United States.

The backgrounds of the suspects were hazy, but the following information was reported by the police here and sources in Miami, which was listed as the home of four of them.

Two of the men, born in Cuba, were said to have claimed past ties with the Central Intelligence Agency. A third was described as an adventurer who once tried to sell his services to an anti-Castro organization called Alpha 66.

JUNE 20, 1972
EX-G.O.P. AIDE LINKED TO POLITICAL RAID
By TAD SZULC
Special to The New York Times

WASHINGTON, June 19—A former consultant to a high White House official was reported tonight to have met in Miami about two weeks ago with the apparent leader of the group that has been charged with attempting last Saturday to install secret listening devices at the offices of the Democratic National Committee here.

Cuban sources identified him as E. Howard Hunt, who became a consultant to Charles W. Colson, special counsel to President Nixon and to other high White House officials. Mr. Hunt was formerly a high official in the Central Intelligence Agency.

Mr. Hunt, using the code name "Eduardo," was the C.I.A. official in charge of the abortive Bay of Pigs invasion of Cuba in 1961.

He was the immediate superior of Bernard L. Barker in the preparations for the Cuban invasion. Mr. Barker, who at that time used the code name of "Macho" was one of the five men arrested at gunpoint early Saturday and charged with a break-in at the Democratic National Committee headquarters in Washington.

Cuban sources said that Mr. Hunt flew to Miami about two weeks ago to meet with Mr. Barker, now a wealthy realty man, and handed him his business calling card with his suburban Maryland home telephone number penciled on the back and gave him oral instructions to call if he ever needed him.

Ken W. Clawson, Deputy Director of Communications for the Executive Branch, confirmed tonight reports that Mr. Hunt indeed worked as a White House consultant on a part-time basis in the summer and fall of 1971 and again this year.

Mr. Clawson said that Mr. Hunt, who was hired by the White House personnel office at Mr. Colson's suggestion, ceased his consulting work on March 29. But Mr. Clawson insisted that "we do not have any idea of his participation in the incident" involving the alleged break-in by former C.I.A. employes at the Democratic offices.

According to Mr. Clawson, "neither Mr. Colson nor anyone else had any knowledge or participation in this deplorable incident."

"Vietnam Peace Pacts Signed; America's Longest War Halts," January 28, 1973

The signing of the Vietnam cease-fire agreement in January 1973 marked the end of the longest war in American history up to that time. The United States had been involved in Vietnam for several years before the Johnson administration sent combat troops there in 1965. At the height of U.S. engagement, more than half a million American soldiers were fighting in Vietnam, and the United States would sustain more than 50,000 total casualties. Both National Security Adviser Henry Kissinger and Vietnamese negotiator Le Duc Tho were awarded the Nobel Peace Prize for securing the peace agreement, but Tho would not accept the award.

United States dead passed 45,000 by the end of the war. The peace agreements were as ambiguous as the conflict.

JANUARY 28, 1973
VIETNAM PEACE PACTS SIGNED; AMERICA'S LONGEST WAR HALTS
CEREMONIES COOL

Two Sessions in Paris Formally Conclude the Agreement

By FLORA LEWIS

Special to The New York Times

PARIS, Jan. 27—The Vietnam cease-fire agreement was signed here today in eerie silence, without a word or a gesture to express the world's relief that the years of war were officially ending.

The accord was effective at 7 P.M. Eastern standard time.

Secretary of State William P. Rogers wrote his name 62 times on the documents providing—after 12 years—a settlement of the longest, most divisive foreign war in America's history.

The official title of the text was "Agreement on Ending the War and Restoring Peace in Vietnam." But the cold, almost gloomy atmosphere at two separate signing ceremonies reflected the uncertainties of whether peace is now assured.

The conflict, which has raged in one way or another for over a quarter of a century, had been inconclusive, without clear victory or defeat for either side.

Involvement Gradually Grew

After a gradually increasing involvement that began even before France left Indochina in 1954, the United States entered into a full-scale combat role in 1965. The United States considers Jan. 1, 1961, as the war's starting date and casualties are counted from then.

By 1968, when the build-up was stopped and then reversed, there were 529,000 Americans fighting in Vietnam. United States dead passed 45,000 by the end of the war.

The peace agreements were as ambiguous as the conflict, which many of America's friends first saw as generous aid to a weak and threatened ally, but which many came to consider an exercise of brute power against a tiny nation.

Built on Compromises

The peace agreements signed today were built of compromises that permit the two Vietnamese sides to give them contradictory meanings and, they clearly hope, to continue their unfinished struggle in the political arena without continuing the slaughter.

"LIDDY AND MCCORD ARE GUILTY OF SPYING ON THE DEMOCRATS," JANUARY 31, 1973

Seven months after the Watergate burglary, two Nixon campaign officials were convicted in connection with the crime. James W. McCord Jr. was one of the five burglars (the other four had pleaded guilty), and G. Gordon Liddy was counsel to Nixon's reelection committee. Another defendant, former White House consultant E. Howard Hunt Jr., also had pleaded guilty. Rather than end the scandal, however, the convictions and guilty pleas only sparked further questions about the possible involvement of higher-level administration officials.

JANUARY 31, 1973
LIDDY AND MCCORD ARE GUILTY OF SPYING ON THE DEMOCRATS
Ex-G.O.P. Aides Are Jailed
Jury Deliberates for 90 Minutes
By WALTER RUGABER
Special to The New York Times

WASHINGTON, Jan. 30—Two former officials of President Nixon's political organization were convicted today in the Watergate trial of plotting to spy on the Democrats during last year's campaign.

The guilty verdicts were returned against G. Gordon Liddy and James W. McCord Jr. after less than 90 minutes of deliberation by a jury of eight women and four men in the United States District Court here.

The men were sent immediately to the District of Columbia jail for the night by Chief Judge John J. Sirica, who postponed until at least tomorrow a decision on bonds for the two pending sentencing.

Liddy and McCord stood without expression while the verdicts were read. But Liddy, who has been outwardly cavalier throughout the trial, gave snappy hand salutes to friends and spectators as he was led from the courtroom.

The jury found Liddy, who was counsel to the Committee for the Re-election of the President and its finance arm, guilty of all six counts of the indictment against him. He could receive a maximum of 35 years in prison.

The 43-year-old lawyer, a resident of suburban Oxon Hill, Md., was convicted of conspiracy, two counts of second-degree burglary, attempted wiretapping, attempted bugging and wiretapping.

McCord, who was security coordinator for the re-election committee, was found guilty on all eight counts filed against him. These were all those against Liddy, plus charges of possessing wiretapping and bugging equipment.

McCord, 48, a former official of the Central Intelligence Agency who lives in Rockville, Md., had also worked as a security official of the Republican National Committee. He could receive a 45-year sentence.

McCord was one of five men who broke into the offices of the Democratic National Committee, on the sixth floor of the Watergate office building, early on the morning of June 17.

· ·

"END OF ERA IN NIXON PRESIDENCY," MAY 1, 1973

The resignations of Nixon's two closest political advisers in April 1973 indicated that the Watergate scandal extended further into the White House than had been initially evident. Chief of Staff H. R. Haldeman and Domestic Policy Adviser John D. Ehrlichman had worked with Nixon long before he came to the White House, and they had easy access to the president. Their departure marked Nixon's growing isolation in the White House.

MAY 1, 1973
END OF ERA IN NIXON PRESIDENCY
By ROBERT B. SEMPLE Jr.
Special to The New York Times
News Analysis

WASHINGTON, April 30—The resignations of H. R. Haldeman and John D. Ehrlichman from President Nixon's senior staff clearly mark the end of one era of the Nixon Presidency and the beginning of another. Things simply will not be the same. The question is how much different they will be.

The few men who remain in the President's suddenly shrunken entourage do not believe that the scandals of the moment will have much impact on Mr. Nixon's own personality. His habits are well entrenched, and any future White House operation will reflect the style of its master.

But there are some here now, in the White House and on Capitol Hill, who hope that Mr. Nixon will seize what they sense to be a rare opening to redesign his relationships with Congress, the bureaucracy, and even the press.

They hope to increase his access to others and theirs to him, to replace the closed corporation that the White House had become with the "open Presidency" to which he once aspired, and to return to his own first principles by decentralizing some of the power that has steadily flowed from the Government agencies to a few decision-makers in the White House.

Mr. Haldeman and Mr. Ehrlichman helped design that system, ran the system and, in time, came to symbolize the system. Their Teutonic names and mutual zeal for efficient execution gave rise to many jokes. Their enemies called them Hans and Fritz; their friends simply teased them.

In Mr. Ehrlichman's office on the second floor of the White House is a copy of Daniel P. Moynihan's "Understanding Poverty," which carries this inscription: "For John Ehrlichman. Achtung! D. P. M."

But their power was no joke. They were men with long ties and easy access to the President, men of loyalty, men who transmitted Mr. Nixon's orders to the bureaucracy and to whom, with few exceptions, Mr. Nixon's Cabinet members were forced to report before winning humble access to the Oval Office.

In all areas other than foreign policy, where Henry A. Kissinger retains primary influence, they dominated the White House, and in giving them their release Mr. Nixon has released part of his own political history.

What remains is only a shadow of the old superstructure. The members of Mr. Ehrlichman's staff at the Domestic Council, which he directed in his role as the President's chief domestic adviser, departed earlier this year for other jobs in the Federal Government. Perhaps ironically, it was one of Mr. Ehrlichman's intentions in thus dispersing his staff to create an informal network of "old boys" who could help him bend an often cantankerous bureaucracy more nearly to Mr. Nixon's will.

Many of Mr. Haldeman's staffers left the White House last year to assume key posts at the re-election campaign committee, where some of them, including Jeb S. Magruder, found themselves floundering in the Watergate mess. Other important members of the staff resigned; still others took posts overseas.

- -

"TV & RADIO: WATERGATE," MAY 18, 1973, AND "ERVIN CHIDES NIXON ABOUT TAPES AND DISPUTES ARGUMENT ON SEPARATION OF POWERS," JULY 24, 1973

In May 1973 a special Senate committee headed by North Carolina Democrat Sam Ervin Jr. began an inquiry into the Watergate burglary. The televised hearings sparked public interest and dominated the national agenda that summer. The surprising testimony by a Nixon aide that the president had taped Oval Office conversations sparked a fierce battle between Congress and the White House over whether the president was required to give the tapes to the Watergate inquiry.

MAY 18, 1973
TV & RADIO: WATERGATE
N.B.C. Says Over 9 Million Viewed Opening of Hearings on 3 Channels
By JOHN J. O'CONNOR

Potentially the most explosive television and radio special of the year, "The Watergate Hearings" began yesterday, as anticipated, on a note of dramatic laboriousness. Most of the opening session was devoted to establishing precisely the chains of command existing within both the White House and the Committee for the Re-Election of the President before and after the Watergate burglary.

If nothing else, the casting was lopsided. On the side of the investigators were the seven Senators—all lawyers—of the Select Committee who were present with their two chief counsels. On the side of the investigated, the stage was monopolized by bit players setting the over-all scene for the stars to come.

According to figures hastily compiled by the research department of the National Broadcasting Company, the morning session, running from 10 o'clock to about 12:45, was seen on the three commercial networks by slightly more than 9 million viewers, substantially below the nearly 13 million total normal for that time period. Part of the difference, however, could have been siphoned off by other stations providing live and full coverage.

As the session began with opening statements from the seven Senators, the viewer may have been lulled into pinpointing individual personalities, most understandably that of the committee chairman, Senator Sam J. Ervin Jr., Democrat of North Carolina, eyeglasses sliding down nose, eyebrows rising and falling, Southern drawl hitting a temporary and uncharacteristic stammer over the word "incredulity."

But then there were the words: Senator Ervin referring to "the health, if not the survival of our social structure"; Senator Howard H. Baker Jr., Republican of Tennessee, to the possibility of a "national catharsis," seeking any lead and "unrestrained by any fear of where that lead might take us"; Senator Lowell P. Weicker, Republican of Connecticut, to "the acts of men who almost, who almost, stole America." For a hearing, the plot could hardly be thicker.

Even yesterday's prelude, however tedious, was not without tension as Robert C. Odle Jr., administrative director for the Nixon re-election committee, boyishly struggled to remember details of a key telephone call. Nor was it without ironic humor, as he pleaded, "Let me make a couple of things perfectly clear."

Obviously, though, the most compelling scenes are still to come, possibly beginning this morning with the scheduled appearance of James W. McCord, former Nixon re-election committee security coordinator who was convicted in the Watergate break-in. For television, the hearings present both a challenge and a problem. They demand to be covered live and in full, a type of coverage rare in broadcasting.

It is questionable, however, if the hearings have to be carried on all three networks simultaneously as well as on public television and independent stations. Barring antitrust complications, there might—there should—be a solution that would serve the public and ease the burden on broadcasters.

JULY 24, 1973
ERVIN CHIDES NIXON ABOUT TAPES AND DISPUTES ARGUMENT ON SEPARATION OF POWERS
Says It Does Not Apply To Watergate Charges
By DOUGLAS E. KNEELAND
Special to The New York Times

WASHINGTON, July 23—Senator Sam J. Ervin Jr., after signing subpoenas today for tape recordings and documents President Nixon has refused to yield voluntarily, declared at the Senate Watergate hearings that the constitutional doctrine of separation of powers did not apply to "alleged criminal activities."

Referring to a letter the Senate Watergate committee received shortly after noon from the President, in which he declined to turn over materials the committee considers relevant to its inquiry, Senator Ervin brought laughter from the standing-room crowd at the hearings when he remarked:

"This is a rather remarkable letter about the tapes. If you will notice, the President says he has heard the tapes or some of them, and they sustain his position. But he says he's not going to let anybody else hear them for fear they might draw a different conclusion."

The committee has eagerly sought the papers and tapes of some of the President's personal and telephone conversations in an effort to resolve conflicts in the testimony of several witnesses. For instance, John W. Dean 3d, former counsel to the President, testified that he believed Mr. Nixon knew about the Watergate cover-up, and said this belief was based on several conversations with the President since last Sept. 15. Others have said Mr. Nixon was surprised when Mr. Dean filled him in on the cover-up last March 21.

Basis for Refusal

In his letter today to Senator Ervin, the President based his refusal to accede to the committee's request for the tapes on the principle of separation of powers, as he did on July 6 when he declined to make Presidential documents available.

Mr. Nixon added, however, that the tapes "would not finally settle the central issues before your committee." He said he had played some of them and that they were "entirely consistent with what I know to be the truth." But he also said that there were comments that some persons "would inevitably interpret in different ways."

After chiding the President about his fear of misinterpretation, Senator Ervin, with a grim expression, said, "I am certain that the doctrine of separation of powers does not impose upon any President either the duty or the power to undertake to separate a Congressional committee from access to the truth concerning alleged criminal activities."

· ·

"Agnew Quits Vice Presidency and Admits Tax Evasion in '67," October 11, 1973, and "Agnew-Nixon Exchange," October 11, 1973

The Nixon administration faced further scandal in fall 1973 when Vice President Spiro Agnew resigned just before pleading no contest to charges of evading income taxes. Although Agnew had not been a close adviser to the president, his resignation was another setback to Nixon's efforts to move past political crises and concentrate on governance.

OCTOBER 11, 1973
AGNEW QUITS VICE PRESIDENCY AND ADMITS TAX EVASION IN '67; NIXON CONSULTS ON SUCCESSOR
Judge Orders Fine, 3 Years' Probation
By JAMES M. NAUGHTON
Special to The New York Times

WASHINGTON, Oct. 10—Spiro T. Agnew resigned as Vice President of the United States today under an agreement with the Department of Justice to admit evasion of Federal income taxes and avoid imprisonment.

The stunning development, ending a Federal grand jury investigation of Mr. Agnew in Baltimore and probably terminating his political career, shocked his closest associates and precipitated an immediate search by President Nixon for a successor.

"I hereby resign the office of Vice President of the United States, effective immediately," Mr. Agnew declared in a formal statement delivered at 2:05 P.M. to Secretary of State Kissinger, as provided in the Succession Act of 1792.

Minutes later, Mr. Agnew stood before United States District Judge Walter E. Hoffman in a Baltimore courtroom, hands barely trembling, and read from a statement in which he pleaded nolo contendere, or no contest, to a Government charge that he had failed to report $29,500 of income received in 1967, when he was Governor of Maryland. Such a plea, while not an admission of guilt, subjects a defendant to a judgment of conviction on the charge.

Tells Court Income Was Taxable

"I admit that I did receive payments during the year 1967 which were not expended for political purposes and that, therefore, these payments were income taxable to me in that year and that I so knew," the nation's 39th Vice President told the stilled courtroom.

OCTOBER 11, 1973
AGNEW-NIXON EXCHANGE

October 10, 1973

Dear Mr. President:

As you are aware, the accusations against me cannot be resolved without a long, divisive and debilitating struggle in the Congress and in the courts. I have concluded that, painful as it is to me and to my family, it is in the best interests of the nation that I relinquish the Vice Presidency.

Accordingly, I have today resigned the office of Vice President of the United States. A copy of the instrument of resignation is enclosed.

It has been a privilege to serve with you. May I express to the American people, through you, my deep gratitude for their confidence in twice electing me to be Vice President.

Sincerely,
SPIRO T. AGNEW

October 10, 1973.

Dear Ted:

The most difficult decisions are often those that are the most personal, and I know your decision to resign as Vice President has been as difficult as any facing a man in

Judge Hoffman sentenced Mr. Agnew to three years' probation and fined him $10,000. The judge declared from the bench that he would have sent Mr. Agnew to prison had not Attorney General Elliot L. Richardson personally interceded, arguing that "leniency is justified."

In his dramatic courtroom statement, Mr. Agnew declared that he was innocent of any other wrongdoing but that it would "seriously prejudice the national interest" to involve himself in a protracted struggle before the courts or Congress.

public life could be. Your departure from the Administration leaves me with a great sense of personal loss. You have been a valued associate throughout these nearly five years that we have served together. However, I respect your decision, and I also respect the concern for the national interest that led you to conclude that a resolution of the matter in this way, rather than through an extended battle in the courts and the Congress, was advisable in order to prevent a protracted period of national division and uncertainty.

As Vice President, you have addressed the great issues of our times with courage and candor. Your strong patriotism, and your profound dedication to the welfare of the nation, have been an inspiration to all who have served with you as well as to millions of others throughout the country.

I have been deeply saddened by this whole course of events, and I hope that you and your family will be sustained in the days ahead by a well-justified pride in all that you have contributed to the nation by your years of service as Vice President.

Sincerely,
RICHARD NIXON

"NIXON DISCHARGES COX FOR DEFIANCE," OCTOBER 21, 1973

President Nixon's efforts to fire the special Watergate prosecutor in October 1973 were controversial and ultimately unsuccessful. The chain of events that became known as the Saturday Night Massacre led to the dismissal of prosecutor Archibald Cox, but he was replaced just days later.

OCTOBER 21, 1973
NIXON DISCHARGES COX FOR DEFIANCE
ABOLISHES WATERGATE TASK FORCE

RICHARDSON AND RUCKELHOUS OUT

BORK TAKES OVER

Duties of Prosecutor Are Shifted Back to Justice Dept.

By DOUGLAS E. KNEELAND

Special to The New York Times

WASHINGTON, Oct. 20—President Nixon, reacting angrily tonight to refusals to obey his orders, dismissed the special Watergate prosecutor, Archibald Cox, abolished Mr. Cox's office, accepted the resignation of Elliot L. Richardson, the Attorney General, and discharged William D. Ruckelshaus, the Deputy Attorney General.

The President's dramatic action edged the nation closer to the constitutional confrontation he said he was trying to avoid.

Senior members of both parties in the House of Representatives were reported to be seriously discussing impeachment of the President because of his refusal to obey an order by the United States Court of Appeals that he turn over to the courts tape recordings of conversations about the Watergate case, and because of Mr. Nixon's dismissal of Mr. Cox.

The President announced that he had abolished the Watergate prosecutor's office as of 8 o'clock tonight and that the duties of that office had been transferred back to the Department of Justice, where his spokesman said they would be "carried out with thoroughness and vigor."

Events Listed

These were the events that led to the confrontation between the President and Congress and the Government's top law enforcement officers:

• Mr. Cox said in a televised news conference that he would return to Federal court in defiance of the President's orders to seek a decision that Mr. Nixon had violated a ruling that the tapes must be turned over to the courts.

• Attorney General Richardson, after being told by the President that Mr. Cox must be dismissed, resigned.

• Deputy Attorney General Ruckelshaus was ordered by Mr. Nixon to discharge Mr. Cox. Mr. Ruckelshaus refused and was dismissed immediately.

• The President informed Robert H. Bork, the Solicitor General, that under the law he was the acting Attorney General and must get rid of Mr. Cox and the special Watergate force.

• Mr. Bork discharged Mr. Cox and had the Federal Bureau of Investigation seal off the offices of the special prosecutor, which Mr. Cox had put in a building away from the Department of Justice to symbolize his independence. Some members of the Cox staff were still inside at the time.

• The F.B.I. also sealed off the offices of Mr. Richardson and Mr. Ruckelshaus.

Mr. Richardson had no comment tonight, but he scheduled a news conference for Monday. Mr. Ruckelshaus said, "I'm going fishing tomorrow."

Mr. Cox's reaction was brief: "Whether we shall continue to be a government of laws and not of men is now for Congress and ultimately the American people [to decide]," he said.

The President's decisions today raised new problems.

For one, he must seek his third Attorney General in a year, now that Mr. Richardson has followed Richard G. Kleindienst as a victim of the Watergate affair.

Moreover, he has risked the possibility of a public and Congressional outcry over disbanding the Watergate force assembled last spring under Mr. Cox to allay suspicions that a Justice Department responsible to the President might not have been prosecuting those responsible for the Watergate break-in and cover-up with enough vigor.

"House and Senate Override Veto by Nixon on Curb of War Powers; Backers of Bill Win 3-Year Fight," November 8, 1973, and "80% in Polls Back War-Powers Curb," November 18, 1973

After the United States fought in both Korea and Vietnam without a congressional declaration of war, Congress was determined to reassert its role in the use of force abroad. In November 1973 Congress passed the War Powers Resolution over President Nixon's veto. The law gave the president a limited time in which to send U.S. troops abroad without congressional approval, and in the aftermath of the lengthy U.S. conflict in Southeast Asia, it had strong public backing.

NOVEMBER 8, 1973
HOUSE AND SENATE OVERRIDE VETO BY NIXON ON CURB OF WAR POWERS; BACKERS OF BILL WIN 3-YEAR FIGHT

TROOP USE LIMITED

Vote Asserts Control of Congress Over Combat Abroad

By RICHARD L. MADDEN

Special to The New York Times

WASHINGTON, Nov. 7—The House and the Senate, dealing President Nixon what appeared to be the worst legislative setback of his five years in office, today overrode his veto of a measure aimed at limiting Presidential power to commit the armed forces to hostilities abroad without Congressional approval.

The House voted first—284 to 135, or only four votes more than the required two-thirds of those present and voting—to override the veto. The Senate followed suit nearly four hours later by a vote of 75 to 18, or 13 more than the required two-thirds.

It was the first time in nine attempts this year that both houses had overridden a veto and the first time legislation has become law over the President's veto since Congress overrode a Nixon veto of a water-pollution-control measure in October, 1972.

First Such Action

Supporters of the measure, who had waged a three-year effort to enact it into law, said it was the first time in history that Congress had spelled out the war-making powers of Congress and the President.

The White House said in a statement that Mr. Nixon felt the Congressional action today "seriously undermines this nation's ability to act decisively and convincingly in times of international crisis." It declined, however, to say what the President planned to do as a result of the overriding of his veto.

With the veto overridden, the war powers measure—couched in the form of a joint resolution, which in Congress has the same status as a bill—immediately became law. It contains the following provisions:

• The President would be required to report to Congress in writing within 48 hours after the commitment of armed forces to combat abroad.

• The combat action would have to end in 60 days unless Congress authorized the commitment, but this deadline could be extended for 30 days if the President certified it was necessary for safe withdrawal of the forces.

• Within that 60-day or 90-day period Congress could order an immediate removal of the forces by adopting a concurrent resolution, which is not subject to a Presidential veto.

NOVEMBER 18, 1973
80% IN POLL BACK WAR-POWERS CURB
Support the Law Approved Over President's Veto

Four out of five Americans support in principle the new war-powers law enacted by Congress Nov. 7 over President Nixon's veto, the Gallup Poll organization said yesterday.

The law is aimed at limiting the President's power to commit the armed forces to hostilities abroad without Congressional approval. It sets deadlines of up to 90 days for troop commitments by the President alone and gives Congress the right to step in and order immediate removal of troops by passage of a concurrent resolution.

The Gallup organization said the view that the President should be required to get Congressional approval before sending United States armed forces into action outside this country was held by a large majority in all population groups, but women, Democrats and younger persons were most likely to favor it.

Nationwide, 80 per cent of those questioned in a survey Nov. 2–5 said that the President should be required to get the approval of Congress in such circumstances.

Sixteen per cent thought he should not be required to get Congressional approval. Four per cent had no opinion.

Although 85 per cent of the women questioned thought he should be required to obtain Congressional approval, the proportion of men who thought so was 76 per cent. Similarly, 86 per cent of the Democrats but only 71 per cent of the Republicans favored the requirement, and 84 per cent of persons 18 to 29 years of age, 78 per cent of those 30 to 49 and 79 per cent of those 40 and older favored the step.

The Gallup release stated that 58 per cent of those questioned said Congress should not be required "to obtain the approval of the people by means of a national vote" in order to declare war. Thirty five per cent thought Congress should be so required and 7 per cent had no opinion.

The results were based on a survey of 1,550 adults 18 and older interviewed in person at more than 300 locations in the nation, the polling organization said.

· ·

"FORD SWORN IN AS VICE PRESIDENT AFTER HOUSE APPROVES, 387–35; HE VOWS EQUAL JUSTICE FOR ALL," DECEMBER 7, 1973

On December 6, 1973, Gerald R. Ford became the first vice president appointed by the president with the approval of Congress, following the procedures outlined in the Twenty-fifth Amendment. Less than one year later, Ford would be elevated to the presidency upon Nixon's resignation, thus becoming the only person in American history to hold both offices without winning election to either one.

DECEMBER 7, 1973
FORD SWORN IN AS VICE PRESIDENT AFTER HOUSE APPROVES, 387–35; HE VOWS EQUAL JUSTICE FOR ALL
LOYALTY TO NIXON
1,500 Hear Ford Give His Full Support to President
By MARJORIE HUNTER
Special to The New York Times

WASHINGTON, Dec. 6—Gerald R. Ford, pledging "equal justice for all Americans," took office just after dusk tonight as the 40th Vice President of the United States.

With President Nixon standing right behind him, he was sworn into office in the 116-year-old House chamber, which has been his political home for the last 25 years.

Only an hour earlier, the House completed action on his nomination by voting 387 to 35 for confirmation. He was confirmed Nov. 27 by the Senate by a vote of 92 to 3.

Mr. Ford, 60 years old, resigned his House seat before assuming the Vice-Presidency. He has been minority leader of the House since 1965.

Jerry Ford's Day

It was clearly Jerry Ford's day, and not even President Nixon's appearance overshadowed the new Vice President. The waves of applause and the smiles of his colleagues were seemingly beamed at him alone as he stood, in a trim navy blue suit, his right hand held high in recognition of old friends.

And, as he spoke, it was the Jerry Ford many of them had listened to through the years, speaking in a flat tone, declaring his love for his wife and his country and pledging his loyalty to his President.

The historic ceremony ended a Vice-Presidential vacancy that had existed since the resignation on Oct. 10 of Spiro T. Agnew just before he pleaded no contest to a charge of income tax evasion.

First Use of Amendment

This is the first time that a Vice President was chosen under the 25th Amendment to the Constitution. The amendment, ratified by the states in 1967, provides for Presidential succession and for filling Vice-Presidential vacancies.

The 25th Amendment was adopted to deal with situations such as that which existed following the assassination of President Kennedy in 1963. At that time, the Vice-Presidency stood vacant 13 months after Vice President Johnson succeeded to the Presidency.

"Nixon Must Surrender Tapes," July 25, 1974, and "Case for Impeachment," July 28, 1974

President Nixon battled vigorously against releasing the tapes of his White House conversations, but when the Supreme Court ruled 8–0 against him in July 1974, he had no further recourse. Although the Court held that the concept of executive privilege was constitutional, it declared that this power was not absolute, and that the president could not withhold information in a criminal investigation.

JULY 25, 1974
NIXON MUST SURRENDER TAPES, SUPREME COURT RULES, 8 TO 0
HE PLEDGES FULL COMPLIANCE
PRESIDENT BOWS
But St. Clair Indicates There May Be Delay in Yielding Data
By PHILIP SHABECOFF
Special to The New York Times

LAGUNA BEACH, Calif., July 24—President Nixon, abandoning his challenge to the Supreme Court's jurisdiction over him, said today that he would comply with this morning's Court decision on subpoenaed data "in all respects."

In a statement read for him over nationwide television by his attorney, James D. St. Clair, the President said that he was disappointed with the ruling but would nevertheless obey the high court.

"While I am of course disappointed in the result, I respect and accept the Court's decision, and I have instructed Mr. St. Clair to take whatever measures are necessary to comply with that decision in all respects," the President's statement said.

Contention Seen Ended

His acquiescence in the decision apparently ended his contention that a President has an absolute executive privilege immune from review by the nation's highest judicial body.

However, Mr. St. Clair indicated that the White House would not respond immediately to the Court's order that the President surrender to the Watergate special prosecutor tape recordings and other data concerning 64 White House conversations.

Mr. St. Clair said that in compliance with the President's instructions, the reviewing of the tapes subject to the subpoena and the preparation of an index and of an analysis of the tapes would begin "forthwith." However, he characterized this as a "time-consuming process."

The President's lawyer declined to answer any questions after reading the statement.

But his comment on the difficulties of preparing the tapes may mean that the White House expects a delay in turning them over to the special prosecutor. Mr. St. Clair told one reporter recently that it might take a month to prepare the tapes.

Mr. St. Clair did not mention subpoenas issued by the House Judiciary Committee to obtain similar evidence from the White House. He gave no hint as to whether the White House intended to turn over the material sought by the House committee for its impeachment proceedings now that the Supreme Court had ruled in favor of the special prosecutor.

Even while announcing his intention to obey the Supreme Court, President Nixon reaffirmed his belief in the principle of executive privilege.

President Gratified

"For the future," he said in the statement, "it will be essential that the special circumstances of this case not be permitted to cloud the rights of Presidents to maintain the basic confidentiality without which this office cannot function. I was gratified, therefore, to note that the Court reaffirmed both the validity and the importance of the principle of executive privilege—the principle I had sought to maintain.

"By complying fully with the Court's ruling in this case, I hope and trust that I will contribute to strengthening rather than weakening this principle for the future—so that this will prove to be not the President that destroyed the principle, but the action that preserved it."

President Nixon through his lawyers had argued before the Supreme Court in this case that the President's executive privilege was absolute—that the President could withhold information and evidence from the courts even in a criminal case if he deemed that the action was necessary to preserve the strength of the Presidency.

Today's ruling rejected that assertion. But Mr. Nixon did not refer to the rejection in his statement. He did say, "My challenge in the courts to the subpoena of the special prosecutor was based on the belief that it was unconstitutionally issued, and on my strong desire to protect the principles of Presidential confidentiality in a system of separation of powers."

By accepting the Court's ruling that the privilege of the President is limited, Mr. Nixon is setting a precedent that is bound to carry considerable weight with future Presidents.

JULY 28, 1974
EDITORIAL
CASE FOR IMPEACHMENT

The great constitutional drama of the impeachment of President Richard Nixon moves with gathering speed and intensity toward its fateful resolution. As the members of the House Judiciary Committee labored to reach agreement on the final wording of articles of impeachment, there was no longer any doubt that a solid bipartisan majority of the committee would vote to recommend such action to the House of Representatives. The first article was approved yesterday by a substantial majority.

Meanwhile, the Supreme Court struck down last week part of the barrier of executive privilege that Mr. Nixon has used to shield himself against the inquiries of the Judiciary Committee and the special prosecutor. Confining itself to the question of the special prosecutor's right to subpoena

confidential Presidential tapes and documents for use in the forthcoming Watergate cover-up trial, the Court in a unanimous opinion ruled that a President could not make an absolute claim of executive privilege. Any such claim, the Court held, would have to be balanced against the right of defendants to a fair trial.

Although the Court's opinion had no direct bearing on the Judiciary Committee's repeatedly unsuccessful efforts to subpoena most of these same tapes and documents as well as many others in Mr. Nixon's possession, it did serve indirectly to strengthen the view of many House members that Mr. Nixon's use of executive privilege to withhold evidence in an impeachment inquiry is itself an impeachable offense.

The broad outlines of the case for impeachment of President Nixon have clearly emerged. He was knowledgeable about payments of "hush money" and perjured testimony and at least condoned them if he did not order them. Contrary to the defense offered by James D. St. Clair, the President's counsel, the exact time in which the money was paid or the perjured testimony was spoken is not decisive. Whenever Mr. Nixon said money should be paid and his aides should "stonewall" the investigators, he at those moments joined in a criminal conspiracy to obstruct justice.

A second broad charge against Mr. Nixon encompasses his failure to see that the laws have been faithfully executed and the rights of private citizens respected. Many specific abuses of power could be cited under this rubric, but the one that has perhaps elicited the most widely shared concern among members of the committee as well as the public is the repeated effort of the Nixon White House, by officials for whom the President was ultimately responsible, to use the Internal Revenue Service to harass and intimidate critics of the Administration.

In the course of considering this and other abuses, a majority of the committee has moved away from the severely restrictive notion advanced by Mr. Nixon's hard-core defenders that an impeachable offense must necessarily be a criminally indictable offense.

Representative Hamilton Fish Jr., Republican of New York, formulated a three-part definition that expressed well the bipartisan consensus of what is an impeachable offense. It should be, Mr. Fish said, an extremely serious offense, one against the political process or the constitutional system, and one that would be recognized as such by the broad majority of the citizens of this country.

By this definition, a majority of the committee believes that Mr. Nixon's improper and illegitimate use of the powers and privileges of his office constitutes grounds for impeachment. Those who cynically believed that the committee would flinch from reaching this grave decision have been mistaken. When the matter is debated in the House in coming weeks, the nation will have an opportunity to see their elected representatives proceed further with one of the hardest but most necessary tasks of self-government— the restoration of lawfulness and moral responsibility in the highest office in the land.

> " When the matter is debated in the House . . . the nation will have an opportunity to see their elected representatives proceed further with one of the hardest but most necessary tasks of self-government—the restoration of lawfulness and moral responsibility in the highest office in the land. "

"THE 37TH PRESIDENT IS FIRST TO QUIT POST," AUGUST 9, 1974, AND "TO 'NIXON PEOPLE,' " AUGUST 12, 1974

On August 8, 1974, President Nixon acceded to the forces calling for his removal from office. In a televised address to the nation, he declared "I have never been a quitter," but his likely impeachment would present an enormous distraction from pressing public affairs. He resigned his office the following day, the only president in American history to do so. *The Times* columnist William Safire, who previously had worked as a speech writer in the Nixon White House, concluded that the president "was not unfairly ejected."

AUGUST 9, 1974
THE 37TH PRESIDENT IS FIRST TO QUIT POST

By JOHN HERBERS

Special to The New York Times

WASHINGTON, Aug. 8—Richard Milhous Nixon, the 37th President of the United States, announced tonight that he had given up his long and arduous fight to remain in office and would resign, effective at noon tomorrow.

Gerald Rudolph Ford, whom Mr. Nixon nominated for Vice President last Oct. 12, will be sworn in tomorrow at the same hour as the 38th President, to serve out the 895 days remaining in Mr. Nixon's second term.

Less than two years after his landslide re-election victory, Mr. Nixon, in a conciliatory address on national television, said that he was leaving not with a sense of bitterness but with a hope that his departure would start a "process of healing that is so desperately needed in America."

He spoke of regret for any "injuries" done "in the course of the events that led to this decision." He acknowledged that some of his judgments had been wrong.

The 61-year-old Mr. Nixon, appearing calm and resigned to his fate as a victim of the Watergate scandal, became the first President in the history of the Republic to resign from office. Only 10 months earlier his first Vice President, Spiro T. Agnew, became the first man to resign the Vice Presidency.

Contrast in Tone and Content

Mr. Nixon, speaking from the Oval Office, where his successor will be sworn in tomorrow, may well have delivered his most effective speech since the Watergate scandals began to swamp his Administration in early 1973.

In tone and content, the 15-minute address was in sharp contrast to his frequently combative language of the past, especially his first "farewell" appearance—that of 1962, when he announced he was retiring from politics after losing the California governorship race and declared that the news media would not have "Nixon to kick around" anymore.

Yet he spoke tonight of how painful it was for him to give up the office.

"I would have preferred to carry through to the finish whatever the personal agony it would have involved, and my family unanimously urged me to do so," he said.

Puts 'Interests of America First'

"I have never been a quitter," he said. "To leave office before my term is completed is opposed to every instinct in my body." But he said that he had decided to put "the interests of America first."

Conceding that he did not have the votes in Congress to escape impeachment in the House and conviction in the Senate, Mr. Nixon said, "To continue to fight through the months ahead for my personal vindication would almost totally absorb the time and attention of the President and the Congress in a period when our entire focus should be on the great issues of peace abroad and prosperity without inflation at home."

"Therefore," he continued, "I shall resign the Presidency effective at noon tomorrow. Vice President Ford will be sworn in as President at that hour in this office."

Then he turned again to his sorrow at leaving. Although he did not mention it in his speech, Mr. Nixon had looked forward to being President when the United States celebrates its 200th anniversary in 1976.

"I feel a great sadness," he said.

Mr. Nixon expressed confidence in Mr. Ford to assume the office, "to put the bitterness and divisions of the recent past behind us."

"By taking this action, I hope that I will have hastened the start of that process of healing which is so desperately needed in America," he said. "I regret deeply any injuries that may have been done in the course of the events that led to this decision. I would say only that if some of my judgments were wrong—and some were wrong—they were made in what I believed at the time to be the best interests of the nation."

Further, he said he was leaving "with no bitterness" toward those who had opposed him.

"So let us all now join together in affirming that common commitment and in helping our new President succeed for the benefit of all Americans," he said.

As he has many times in the past, Mr. Nixon listed what he considered his most notable accomplishments of his five and a half years in office—his initiatives in foreign policy, which he said had gone a long way toward establishing a basis for world peace.

AUGUST 12, 1974
OP-ED
TO 'NIXON PEOPLE'

By William Safire

WASHINGTON—Not so long ago, about four out of ten adults in this country referred to themselves politically as "Nixon people." How should they react to the forced resignation of the man who for so long embodied their beliefs and their prejudices?

As a card-carrying member of that group, let me suggest a few reactions both to those who made it to the lifeboats and those who went down with the ship:

First, toward Richard Nixon. Despite the frequent hypocrisy of some of his pursuers he was not unfairly ejected.

He is now American's only living former President, for good reasons. When he first learned that some men acting in his name committed a crime, he put the bonds of friendship ahead of his oath of office. When he had the chance to destroy all the tapes just after their existence had become known, he made the wrong tactical decision, and nobody is patting him on the back now for his rectitude in not destroying the evidence that proved him guilty.

In retrospect, all the maneuvers his supporters considered so ill-advised in establishing his innocence gain an intelligent pattern when viewed as a means toward preventing revelation of his guilt. He "knew"; he knew that there was proof that he "knew"; and all his actions for the last year, from the firing of Archibald Cox to the refection of subpoenas to the falsely based appeal to the Supreme Court, were absolutely consistent.

No wonder, then, he would allow no lawyer to listen to the tapes; he was stalling for time and playing for breaks, and on such a course there was nobody he could trust without making him a co-conspirator. Mr. Nixon was never indecisive, never floundering, as so many of us had anguished; his plan was to protect the tapes at all costs, and their cost was all.

Therefore, no torment of unfairness is due from him the "Nixon people." Black Sox slugger "Shoeless" Joe Jackson was approached by a fan crying "Say it ain't so, Joe." The corrupted ballplayer said nothing; Mr. Nixon said it was not so.

As we spare him our tears, we can afford him more than a little respect. He was never the would-be dictator his severest critics have claimed, and his motives were either noble (to make a peace that would last) or at least not ignoble (to gain the adulation that would flow from being the man who made the peace).

The people who supported him, and most of those who worked for him, can look around now that the shelling has ceased and point out much of substance that was done domestically in reflecting the will of the people—which, lest we forget, earned such a ringing affirmation of support just a year and a half ago.

Toward President Ford, the reaction of the "Nixon people" should be far different from the reaction, say, of the Kennedy people to the ascension of President Johnson. Here is no cultural or stylistic usurper; Mr. Ford was not Mr. Nixon's necessary compromise, but his chosen heir, deserving of a transfer of old loyalties. (Mr. Nixon wound up with a lifetime batting average of .500 in picking Vice Presidents, better than F.D.R.'s .333.)

As President, Mr. Ford has chosen two of the best of the early Nixon supporters to be on his transition committee: Interior Secretary Rogers Morton and NATO Ambassador Donald Rumsfeld, both of whom bear the scars of battle with the Nixon Palace Guard. Mr. Rumsfeld, a former Congressman in his early forties, is especially valuable.

Finally, how should the former "Nixon people" view the ecstatic political opposition, so wrong about the country in 1972 and so right about Mr. Nixon in 1973? For the country's sake and our own, let us let them have their time of vindication without resentment. The triumph of justice is nobody's political defeat. Churchill's "in defeat, defiance" does not apply, because Mr. Nixon's defeat is not the defeat of the "Nixon people" nor of the causes the former President espoused, only the defeat of that misguided toughness which is a form of weakness.

Of course, "in victory, magnanimity" does apply; if in months to come, those who justly brought Mr. Nixon down want to make a martyr out of him, dragging him down Pennsylvania Avenue behind a chariot, here we go again on another round of vindictiveness.

For Mr. Nixon, who might not have shown enough contrition to satisfy everyone, in delivering his own epitaph as President showed that the underlying lesson of Watergate had finally sunk in: ". . . those who hate you don't win unless you hate them—and then you destroy yourself."

THE PRESIDENCY OF GERALD FORD

AUGUST 9, 1974 – JANUARY 20, 1977

Gerald Rudolph Ford's presidency served primarily as a period of national recovery from the trauma inflicted by the Watergate scandal and the resignation of Ford's predecessor, Richard M. Nixon, in 1974. Ford had not expected to become president, and he made no major policy achievements in office. He faced a difficult economic situation with high inflation and unemployment, which limited his ability to advance a political agenda. He served as president for just two and a half years, and in that time, he helped the country move past Watergate and rebuild public confidence in the future of the United States.

Ford was born Leslie Lynch King Jr. His parents divorced when he was two, and Dorothy King took her only child to be near her family in Grand Rapids, Michigan. She remarried in 1916, and when her husband, Gerald Rudolff Ford, adopted her son the following year, the couple changed the four-year-old's name to his new father's name, but changed the spelling of the middle name to Rudolph. The Fords had three more sons, and the boys grew up in Grand Rapids, where their father was a paint salesman.

Gerald Ford Jr. was a high school football star and in 1932–1933 played on two national championship teams at the University of Michigan. He studied economics and political science, graduating in 1935. Although he had opportunities to play professional football, he decided to coach boxing and assist with coaching football at Yale University. He graduated from Yale Law School, returned to Grand Rapids to practice law, and joined the navy in World War II. After the war, he returned to his law practice, and in 1948 won election to the U.S. House of Representatives.

Ford served in the House for nearly twenty-five years and became minority leader in 1965. His reputation for integrity made him an ideal candidate to replace for Vice President Spiro T. Agnew, who was forced to resign for accepting bribes and evading income taxes. The Twenty-fifth Amendment, which was ratified in 1967, states that a vacancy in the vice presidency would be filled via presidential nomination and congressional confirmation. President Nixon nominated Ford for the post in October 1973, and he began his duties as vice

Source: Bill "Whitey" Sanders, courtesy of the Kentucky Library and Museum, WKU

THE MILWAUKEE JOURNAL

'Well, let's go at it.'

president two months later, on December 6, after both chambers of Congress approved his nomination.

TAKING OFFICE

Eight months and three days after becoming vice president, Ford was sworn in as president of the United States. Nixon resigned the office on August 9, 1974, rather than face impeachment by the House for his role in hindering the federal inquiry of the 1972 burglary attempt of Democratic Party headquarters at the Watergate office complex. (Members of Nixon's reelection campaign had orchestrated the burglary, and efforts to cover up the crime extended up to the Oval Office.) Ford is the only person to hold the offices of vice president and president without winning election to either one.

As president, Ford did not seek to make major changes in his eleven-member cabinet. Secretary of State Henry A. Kissinger of Massachusetts and Treasury Secretary William

QUICK FACTS ON GERALD FORD

BIRTH	July 14, 1913, Omaha, Neb.
EDUCATION	University of Michigan, Ann Arbor, B.A., 1935 Yale Law School, L.L.B, 1941
FAMILY	Wife: Elizabeth "Betty" Bloomer Warren Ford Children: Michael Gerald Ford, John "Jack" Gardner Ford, Steven Meigs Ford, Susan Elizabeth Ford
WHITE HOUSE PETS	Golden retriever and puppies, Siamese cat
PARTY	Republican
PREPRESIDENTIAL CAREER (SELECTED)	Boxing coach and assistant varsity football coach, Yale University, 1935–1940 Admitted to Michigan bar, 1941 Ensign, U.S. Naval Reserve, 1942 Discharge, reserve rank of lieutenant commander, 1946 Law practice, Grand Rapids, Michigan, 1946–1949 U.S. House of Representatives, 1949–1973 Member of Warren Commission investigating assassination of John F. Kennedy, 1963–1964 House minority leader, 1965–1973 Vice president, 1973–1974
PRESIDENTIAL TERM	August 9, 1974–January 20, 1977
VICE PRESIDENT	Nelson Aldrich Rockefeller (December 19, 1974–January 20, 1977)
SELECTED EVENTS	Grants unconditional pardon to Richard M. Nixon (1974) Federal Election Campaign Act amendments (1974) Arms control meeting with Soviet leader Leonid Brezhnev, Vladisovstok (1974) Confirmation by Congress of Vice President Rockefeller (1974) Creation of commission to investigate CIA activities (1975) Helsinki Accords on human rights (1975) U.S. evacuation of Saigon, Vietnam, as Communist forces take over nation (1975) Seizure of U.S. merchant vessel *Mayaguez* by Cambodian forces (1975) Release of Rockefeller report confirming CIA domestic espionage (1975) Survives two assassination attempts (1975) Agreement to have Soviet Union purchase $400 million of U.S. grain (1976) Senate creates permanent Select Committee on Intelligence (1976) Viking I spaceship lands on Mars (1976)
POSTPRESIDENCY	Memoirs published, 1979 Dedication of Gerald R. Ford Library, Ann Arbor, Michigan, 1981 Recipient of Presidential Medal of Freedom, 1999 Recipient of John F. Kennedy Profiles in Courage award for pardon of Nixon, 2001 Honorary co-chair, National Commission on Federal Election Reform, 2001
DEATH	December 26, 2006, Rancho Mirage, Calif.

E. Simon of New Jersey served through the Ford presidency. Kissinger served as national security adviser as well until November 1975, when Ford decided to replace Kissinger with his deputy, Brent Scowcroft of Utah. Ford made other changes in his advisory team at that time as well, replacing Defense Secretary James R. Schlesinger of Virginia with Donald H. Rumsfeld of Illinois. Rumsfeld previously had been Ford's chief of staff, and his assistant, Richard B. Cheney of Wyoming, was promoted to the position.

First Lady Betty Ford was a professional dancer who had studied with Martha Graham before her marriage to Gerald Ford in 1948. As first lady, she supported the equal rights amendment and promoted programs in the arts and for handicapped children. She underwent treatment in 1978 for alcoholism and then founded the Betty Ford Center for Drug and Alcohol Rehabilitation. The Fords had three sons and one daughter, all of whom were in their late teens or early adulthood when their father became president.

Major Issues

Upon taking office, President Ford had strong public and congressional support, but it dissipated in a mere month when he announced on September 8, 1974, that he would grant Nixon a full and unconditional pardon. Few people had known of Ford's decision beforehand, and it fanned speculation that he had made a deal with Nixon to pardon him if he would step down. Ford denied the allegation and went before Congress to explain his reasoning for the pardon—that it was necessary for the nation to recover from the Watergate scandal. Nevertheless, Ford's decision-making process had many flaws; had he consulted more extensively before granting the pardon, he might have avoided such an enormous outcry.

Perhaps Ford's greatest challenge as president was reinvigorating the nation's weakened economy. He faced both rising inflation and unemployment, and combating the twin problems proved to be difficult. In foreign affairs, Ford built upon his predecessor's diplomacy with the Soviet Union, and he secured an important agreement on human rights, known as the Helsinki Accords, in 1975. He continued U.S. engagement with China. Ford withdrew remaining American forces from South Vietnam in 1975 as the North Vietnamese took control of the territory. Just weeks later, Cambodian forces seized the U.S. merchant ship *Mayaguez,* claiming that it had trespassed onto Cambodia's territorial waters. U.S. marines successfully rescued the crew upon Ford's orders, but the rescue team incurred many casualties in its attack.

THE 1976 PRESIDENTIAL ELECTION

The state of the economy and Ford's limited tenure as president did not give him a strong platform to contend for the Republican presidential nomination in 1976. He faced a strong challenge from former California governor Ronald Reagan, who took the battle to the party convention, but Ford narrowly won his party's endorsement, with Sen. Robert J. Dole of Kansas selected as his running mate. In a close race with Democratic contender Jimmy Carter, Ford agreed to the first presidential election debates since 1960. The televised debates hurt his prospects, however, when he suggested that Eastern Europe was not under Soviet domination. Ford lost the election to Carter by less than 1 million popular votes and 240 Electoral College votes to Carter's 297.

After leaving the White House, Ford moved to California, where he played golf, served on various corporate boards, and enjoyed the postpresidency. He was briefly considered a vice-presidential contender for Ronald Reagan in 1980, but he rejected the possibility. He died at age ninety-three in his home in Rancho Mirage, California, on December 26, 2006.

"4 NAMED TO HELP FORD'S TRANSITION," AUGUST 10, 1974

To assist him during his sudden transition to the presidency, Ford established a committee of former House members with whom he had served to make personnel recommendations. He also requested that senior Nixon staffers stay for a transition period to provide continuity. Signaling the change in culture from the Nixon White House, Ford pledged that his administration would be "open" and "candid."

Ford took control of the Presidency and moved to give it a character and shape different from that of his predecessor, Richard M. Nixon.

AUGUST 10, 1974
4 NAMED TO HELP FORD'S TRANSITION

All on New Panel Served in House—President Vows Open Administration

By JOHN HERBERS

Special to The New York Times

WASHINGTON, Aug. 9—Immediately after he was sworn in today as the nation's 38th President, Gerald R. Ford took control of the Presidency and moved to give it a character and shape different from that of his predecessor, Richard M. Nixon.

After declaring in his inaugural speech that "here the people rule," President Ford named a four-member committee composed of former elected officials to oversee the transition and make recommendations for staff changes.

The four are William W. Scranton, former Governor of Pennsylvania; Donald M. Rumsfeld, Ambassador to the North Atlantic Treaty Organization and a former Republican member of Congress from Illinois; Rogers C. B. Morton, Secretary of the Interior and a former Republican member of Congress from Maryland, and John O. Marsh, a member of Mr. Ford's Vice-Presidential staff and a former Democratic member of Congress from Virginia.

All four had served with Mr. Ford in the House.

By contrast, the Nixon Presidency had been shaped largely by men who were loyal to Mr. Nixon but who had no constituency of their own and had not served in elective office.

President Ford sought in symbolic ways, too, to say that his Administration would have a broader base and be open to a wider range of viewpoints than that of his predecessor.

He invited to his swearing-in ceremony a diversity of public and private figures, including some who had been persona non grata at the Nixon White House, such as Charles E. Goodell, the former Republican Senator from New York.

Mr. Ford also made an appearance in the White House press room to introduce his new press secretary, J. F. ter-Horst, former Washington bureau manager of *The Detroit News,* and to say: "We will have, I trust, the kind of rapport and friendship we've had in the past. And I don't ask you to treat me any better. We will have an open, we will have a candid Administration. I can't change my nature after 61 years."

At the same time, Mr. Ford made it clear that he would move slowly to effect a smooth transition.

He met for 20 minutes with the senior members of the Nixon staff—except for Ronald L. Ziegler, the Nixon press secretary who resigned and flew to San Clemente, Calif., with Mr. Nixon—and asked them to stay for the transition period.

Gen. Alexander M. Haig Jr., the White House chief of staff, responded that the staff would give Mr. Ford the same loyalty they gave Mr. Nixon "in our hour of common cause."

A memorandum from Mr. Ford, circulated among the staff members, read in part:

"I know this has been a difficult and confusing time for each of you. You must have feelings of sorrow as I do, but you should also be proud—proud of the President you served and of your efforts for him and the country.

"I have asked some friends whose counsel I respect to help me with the transition. They will form a bridge for me to my Vice-Presidential staff office and to the officials of the executive branch until a permanent organization is established. I ask your help and co-operation for them as well as myself.

"President Nixon fought long and with all his might to serve the American people well, ending his Presidency with a selfless and courageous act. You can still serve him and the nation by helping me to carry on the essential functions of the Presidency."

"Support for Ford Declines Sharply," September 12, 1974, and "Ford Defends Pardon Before House Panel and Says There Was 'No Deal' With Nixon," October 18, 1974

President Ford's surprise announcement that he would pardon Nixon sparked much controversy. A *New York Times* poll conducted shortly after the news found that the president's approval ratings had dropped by more than 20 percent. The public outcry was so strong that Ford went to Capitol Hill to assure a House subcommittee that he had no improper motives in granting the pardon. Nevertheless, the pardon would remain the most controversial decision of Ford's presidency.

September 12, 1974
Support for Ford Declines Sharply
A Poll Links Drop to Pardon and Finds Disapproval for Timing of Action
Special to The New York Times

WASHINGTON, Sept. 11—President Ford's decision to pardon Richard M. Nixon and to consider pardons for other alleged Watergate conspirators has sapped his support among the general public, a special Gallup Poll indicates.

The survey also showed wide disapproval at least for the timing of the pardon, although there were indications that most of the persons questioned in the survey would not have opposed a pardon for the former President at a later time.

The poll, commissioned by *The New York Times,* was conducted last night after the White House said that pardons for all of those involved in Watergate were under study. A total of 553 persons, living in all sections of the country, were interviewed by telephone.

Substantial Loss

Asked whether they thought Mr. Ford was doing a good, fair or poor job as President, the respondents gave the following answers: good, 32 per cent; fair, 33; poor, 25; no opinion, 10.

In a similar but not precisely comparable poll conducted Aug 16–19, the Gallup organization found Mr. Ford winning the approbation of almost everyone.

That survey showed that 71 per cent of those polled approved of the way he was handling his job, with 3 per cent disapproving and 26 per cent undecided. Allotting half those who answered "fair" and all of those who answered "good" in *The Times's* poll to the "approval" category—which gives Mr. Ford the benefit of every doubt—his approval rate has fallen from 71 per cent to 49 per cent in a matter of three weeks.

There is little doubt as to what caused the drop. Asked whether pardon developments had caused them to form a less favorable opinion of the President, 60 per cent responded in the affirmative.

Even allowing for the margin of error inherent in such surveys—a Gallup spokesman said there were 95 chances in 100 that it was accurate within 6 percentage points—the poll demonstrated that Mr. Ford had wounded himself grievously.

In a hearing carried on national television, President Gerald R. Ford testifies before the House Subcommittee on Criminal Justice about his pardon of former President Richard Nixon.

Source: David Vick for the New York Times

OCTOBER 18, 1974
FORD DEFENDS PARDON BEFORE HOUSE PANEL AND SAYS THERE WAS 'NO DEAL' WITH NIXON
HISTORIC HEARING

President Declares He Acted Out of Concern for Good of Country

By DAVID E. ROSENBAUM

Special to The New York Times

WASHINGTON, Oct. 17—President Ford, in a historic appearance before a House subcommittee, attempted today to lay to rest suspicions raised by his unconditional pardon of his predecessor, Richard M. Nixon.

In what many historians believe to have been the first formal appearance by a sitting President before a Congressional panel, Mr. Ford testified that he had granted the pardon solely "out of my concern to serve the best interests of my country."

"There was no deal, period," he declared.

"I assure you," he said, addressing the millions of television viewers as well as the members of the House Judiciary Committee's Subcommittee on Criminal Justice, "that there never was at any time any agreement whatsoever concerning a pardon to Mr. Nixon if he were to resign and I were to become President."

Yet, despite Mr. Ford's effort to "make for better understanding of the pardon," his appearance generated still further questions in the minds of his political opponents.

Discussion With Haig

He told the subcommittee, for example, that, eight days before the resignation, Gen. Alexander M. Haig Jr., Mr. Nixon's chief adviser, brought up with Mr. Ford the possibility of a pardon for Mr. Nixon.

Mr. Ford said today that he made no commitment then, but he could shed no light on what General Haig, then Mr. Nixon's chief of staff, might have reported back to Mr. Nixon.

Moreover, Democratic politicians seemed prepared to try to capitalize on Mr. Ford's acknowledgement that he intentionally misled reporters in the days before Mr. Nixon resigned.

Mr. Ford said today that he had made misleading statements to the press because he felt that any change in his previously stated views would have led newsmen to think that he wanted the President to resign.

Mr. Ford insisted that the purpose of the pardon "was to change our national focus." He told the subcommittee, "I wanted to do all I could to shift our attentions from the pursuit of a fallen President to the pursuit of the urgent needs of a rising nation."

Deference and Thanks

The president was not placed under oath today, and, for the most part, the nine subcommittee members treated Mr. Ford with deference. They addressed him as "Mr. President," never interrupted him, and thanked him after virtually every response.

But some of the questions reflected the bitter feelings engendered in much of the country by the irrevocable decision to pardon Mr. Nixon before any charges had been brought against him.

"A 'Re-Entry' Plan," September 17, 1974

Just as his pardon was intended to move the nation beyond the Watergate scandal, so, too, was Ford's amnesty program for draft evaders an attempt to overcome the divisions of the Vietnam War. Ford established the amnesty program by executive order soon after taking office.

SEPTEMBER 17, 1974
A 'RE-ENTRY' PLAN
Goodell Named Head of Clemency Unit—Hesburgh Included
By MARJORIE HUNTER
Special to The New York Times

WASHINGTON, Sept. 16—President Ford offered conditional amnesty today to thousands of Vietnam era draft evaders and military deserters who agree to work for up to two years in public service jobs.

"My sincere hope," he said in a statement, "is that this is a constructive step toward calmer and cooler appreciation of our individual rights and responsibilities and our common purpose as a nation whose future is always more important than its past."

In announcing his "earned re-entry" program, the President also established a nine-member Presidential clemency board to review the cases of those already convicted or punished for desertion or draft evasion.

Mr. Ford designated Charles E. Goodell, a former Republican Senator from New York and an early critic of United States involvement in the Vietnam war, as chairman of the clemency board.

Among others named to the clemency board was the Rev. Theodore M. Hesburgh, president of the University of Notre Dame, who has called for unconditional amnesty.

Effective Immediately

The amnesty program became effective immediately when President Ford signed a Presidential proclamation and two Executive orders just before noon in the Cabinet Room of the White House. Earlier, he explained details of the program to Congressional leaders of both parties. No Congressional action is needed.

In his proclamation, the President declared that "desertion in time of war is a major, serious offense," and that draft evasion "is also a serious offense." Such actions, he said, need not "be condoned."

"Yet," he continued, "reconciliation calls for an act of mercy to bind the nation's wounds and to heal the scars of divisiveness."

President Ford denied tonight at his news conference that the amnesty plan was in any substantial way linked to his unconditional pardon of former President Richard M. Nixon on Sept. 8—an action that has created widespread controversy throughout the nation.

Asked at his news conference tonight why he had granted only a conditional amnesty to draft evaders while granting a full pardon to Mr. Nixon, the President replied:

"Well, the only connection between those two cases is the effort that I made in the one to heal the wounds involv-ing charges against Mr. Nixon and my honest and conscientious effort to heal the wounds for those who had deserted military service or dodged the draft."

Mr. Ford said that, in the case of Mr. Nixon, "you have a President who was forced to resign because of circumstances involving his Administration and he has been shamed and disgraced by that resignation."

"A Call for Action," October 9, 1974

To combat rising inflation, Ford declared that the nation must "whip inflation now," and the slogan soon became known by the acronym WIN. But unemployment soon overtook inflation as the primary national economic concern, and the WIN campaign was short-lived.

OCTOBER 9, 1974
A CALL FOR ACTION

In Talk to Congress, the President Urges All to Join Fight
By PHILIP SHABECOFF
Special to The New York Times

WASHINGTON, Oct. 8—President Ford, urging a "new mobilization" against inflation, proposed today a broad, basically conservative program ranging from reducing oil imports to a one-year tax increase for corporations, as well as many private citizens.

The proposals made by the President seek to provide tax incentives to business, help unemployed workers, expand agricultural production, stimulate home construction, relax environmental standards and give a tax advantage to some stock dividends.

In his address to a joint session of Congress, Mr. Ford said, "We must whip inflation now," and called on all Americans to enlist in the fight.

Fiscally 'Neutral'

But some Government officials said privately that the entire economic package proposed by Mr. Ford, when taken together, was fiscally "neutral"—that is it would neither add to inflationary pressures nor substantially ease them.

In his speech, the President said that unless inflation was whipped, in his phrase, it would "destroy our country, our homes, our liberties, our property and finally our national pride—as surely as any well-armed wartime enemy."

"The acid test" of the Government's determination to whip inflation, Mr. Ford said, is his proposal for a one-year temporary 5 per cent surcharge on corporate and what he said were "upper-level" incomes. This would include families with incomes of roughly over $15,000 and individuals with incomes of over $7,500 a year.

Tax Cuts for Some

At the same time, the President proposed reducing the taxes of families and workers with incomes below those levels because they are "hardest hit by inflation."

"DEMOCRATS VIEW THEIR VICTORY AS SPUR TO LEGISLATIVE MOVES," NOVEMBER 7, 1974

In the aftermath of Nixon's resignation, the Democratic Party not surprisingly made significant gains in the 1974 congressional midterm elections. The Democrats won a two-thirds majority in the House and a three-fifths majority in the Senate, giving the party a significant base of support for promoting its policies.

NOVEMBER 7, 1974
DEMOCRATS VIEW THEIR VICTORY AS SPUR TO LEGISLATIVE MOVES; FORD ASKS RESPONSIBLE ACTION

ECONOMY IS ISSUE

Albert Sees a Mandate in His Party's Wider Margin in Congress

By JAMES M. NAUGHTON

Democratic leaders, savoring their most significant Congressional election victory in a decade, declared yesterday that they were prepared to construct their own legislative program to deal with the economy and other pressing issues.

"This is not just a victory, this is a mandate," House Speaker Carl Albert, Democrat of Oklahoma, said of the elections that increased his party's majorities to two-thirds in the House of Representatives and three-fifths in the Senate.

Leading Democrats said that they would await initiatives from President Ford but were fully prepared, if necessary, to develop their own plans to combat rising unemployment and curtail inflation. Some senior Democrats also pledged to seek major tax reforms and enactment of a national health insurance program.

Some See Difficulty

Some Democrats suggested that it would not be easy to harness the new majority in any single direction and the

White House quickly rejected the prevailing Democratic notion that the Congressional elections represented a repudiation of Mr. Ford's economic leadership. White House officials said that the President would adhere to his conservative program.

Ron Nessen, the White House press secretary, said in Washington that Mr. Ford "expects Congress to act responsibly" and that the President "is holding out a hand and saying let's work together because this problem is too important to play politics."

Later in the day, Mike Mansfield, the Senate Democratic leader, met with Mr. Ford and expressed hope that the Democrats and the President would "be able to get together and work cooperatively." Mr. Ford nodded agreement and remarked that the elections, on balance, had been "not too acrimonious."

Although the meaning of the elections on Tuesday was subject to various interpretations, the scope was not.

"MINH OFFERS UNCONDITIONAL SURRENDER," APRIL 30, 1975, AND "THE AMERICANS DEPART," APRIL 30, 1975

The U.S. engagement in Vietnam ended with a chaotic departure from that Southeast Asian nation in April 1975. The Vietnam War had ended two years earlier, but the United States had maintained a small military presence until the imminent takeover of South Vietnam by Communist forces propelled the evacuation of Americans. In an editorial, *The Times* criticized U.S. actions in Vietnam, writing, "The United States left Vietnam with the same confusion and lack of direction that took this country there in the first place."

APRIL 30, 1975
MINH OFFERS UNCONDITIONAL SURRENDER; 1,000 AMERICANS EVACUATED FROM SAIGON IN COPTERS WITH 5,500 SOUTH VIETNAMESE

FORD UNITY PLEA

President Says That Departure 'Closes a Chapter' for U.S.

By JOHN W. FINNEY

Special to The New York Times

WASHINGTON, April 29—The United States ended two decades of military involvement in Vietnam today with the evacuation of about 1,000 Americans from Saigon as well as more than 5,500 South Vietnamese.

The emergency helicopter evacuation was ordered last night by President Ford after the Saigon airport was closed because of Communist rocket and artillery fire. The 1,000 Americans were the last contingent of a force that once numbered more than 500,000.

The helicopters removed the 5,500 South Vietnamese citizens because their lives were presumed to be in danger with a Communist take-over of South Vietnam. Over the last two weeks, a total of about 55,000 South Vietnamese have been removed. Most of them will come to the United States. The helicopter flights ended the United States evacuation of South Vietnamese.

Last Marines Evacuated

The final withdrawal of Americans was completed at 7:52 P.M., about two hours after the White House had an-nounced the evacuation was completed, when 11 marines were taken by helicopter from the roof of the American Embassy in Saigon. Officials said that the marines, the last of a security guard sent in to protect the evacuation, were safely removed although small-arms fire had broken out around the deserted embassy.

President Ford, in a statement issued by the White House, said the evacuation "closes a chapter in the American experience." In a plea for national unity in the post-Vietnam period, the President said:

"I ask all Americans to close ranks, to avoid recrimination about the past, to look ahead to the many goals we share and to work together on the great tasks that remain to be accomplished."

The scenes of agony and tumult in Saigon yesterday, as the helicopters lifted American diplomats and panic-stricken Vietnamese away, add up to one more sorrowful episode at the conclusion of an American—and Vietnamese—tragedy.

APRIL 30, 1975
EDITORIAL
THE AMERICANS DEPART

The United States left Vietnam with the same confusion and lack of direction that took this country there in the first place. The scenes of agony and tumult in Saigon yesterday, as the helicopters lifted American diplomats and panic-stricken Vietnamese away, add up to one more sorrowful episode at the conclusion of an American—and Vietnamese—tragedy.

Untangling the meaning of the rapid events that have flashed past the American and South Vietnamese people these last few days will be an arduous task for the historians. Too many questions are unanswered in the heat of defeat; too many others will be deliberately obscured in the days—and years—to come, for the protection of reputations and ideals that will not easily be given up.

There surely have been instances of genuine heroism; the marines and helicopter pilots who accomplished the ultimate evacuation, for instance, could hardly have been handed a more difficult task, and they seem to have carried out their part with efficiency and bravery. But a strong note of relief which has been felt in the actions of the final 24 hours reflects the narrowness of the American escape and the fact that no massive military force had to be employed to rescue the last remaining United States personnel.

Furthermore, it is a source of some satisfaction that a large number of people in South Vietnam who had put their personal trust in American servicemen and civilians were able to be removed—though not nearly so many as could have been taken out if the evacuation process had begun as early as it should have.

There is still no convincing explanation why the Administration and Ambassador Graham Martin allowed thousands of American personnel to remain on the spot in Saigon long after their functions had become superfluous. Even when evacuation had started, a thousand American officials remained and became by their presence a force to obstruct the political bargain that might have prevented a final rout.

For their part, the North Vietnamese military commanders and their southern allies have taken upon themselves a heavy responsibility before their own people by pressing for the surrender which the Saigon Government has now offered.

What could have been an orderly transfer of power by procedures internationally agreed upon in the Paris accords of 1973 now appears to have become a simple takeover by force—despite the assurances which Vietnamese Communists had been giving that they were ready for a compromise solution short of open surrender.

Why this change of heart came about is another of the questions which cannot now be answered. But its consequences could be crucial for the future well-being of the Vietnamese people. The Vietnamese Communists will only compound the problems which they obviously face by imposing their idea of a military solution if they shun the readiness of this country to participate in the rebuilding of Vietnam in peace.

- -

"Domestic and Foreign Triumph Is Seen as U.S. Reasserts Its Presence Abroad," May 16, 1975

President Ford secured the release of American crew members aboard the captured merchant ship *Mayaguez* by sending marines to rescue the hostages from their Cambodian captors. The successful military operation boosted his popular image as a decisive and forceful president, despite the emergency U.S. evacuation from Vietnam only two weeks before.

MAY 16, 1975
DOMESTIC AND FOREIGN TRIUMPH IS SEEN AS U.S. REASSERTS ITS PRESENCE ABROAD

By JAMES M. NAUGHTON
Special to The New York Times
News Analysis

WASHINGTON, May 15—By nearly every measure President Ford's military venture in the Gulf of Siam was being evaluated here today as a diplomatic and domestic political triumph. The merchant ship *Mayagüez*, steaming once more through Southeast Asian waters, serves as a visible symbol of United States resolve to remain an influence—and, if necessary, a military presence—abroad despite the recent debacle in Indochina.

Democrats in Congress who expect their party to elect the successor to Mr. Ford in 1976 termed his actions right and accorded him high marks for leadership. Republican conservatives who had begun questioning his capacity declared him, in the words of one, "a man who knows how to act."

The President's decision to use marines, warships and military aircraft to retrieve the crew and recover the Mayagüez from their Cambodian captors was, White House officials acknowledged, a calculated gamble with a broad purpose.

The military operation was mounted without any certainty on the whereabouts of the captive seamen and with no guarantee that the broad goal of demonstrating United States resolve for worried allies or potentially capricious opponents would be buttressed by the rescue. The real test, a White House aide said when the outcome was still in doubt yesterday, would be how many of the 39 crew members were saved.

All were. That the crew was surrendered by a small boat flying a white pennant rather than rescued by the marine landing forces did not diminish the belief here that pluck had been more responsible than luck.

'I'm Glad It Worked'

"It worked," said Senator Robert C. Byrd of West Virginia, the Senate Democratic whip. "I'm glad it worked. It's certainly a plus for the country. It will strengthen our prestige throughout the world."

Administration officials, including Secretary of State Kissinger and Secretary of Defense James R. Schlesinger, were said to have been eager to find some dramatic means of underscoring President Ford's stated intention to "maintain our leadership on a worldwide basis."

The occasion came with the capture of the vessel. While Administration officials emphasized that the first objective of the rescue operation was to save the American crew, they made it clear that they welcomed the opportunity to show that Mr. Ford had the will and the means to use American power to protect American interests.

. . . .

"Panels Urged to Monitor Covert Actions Abroad," April 27, 1976

The Senate created a special committee in the mid-1970s to investigate U.S. intelligence-gathering, in response to reports of illegal covert activity authorized during the cold war. Named the Church Committee for its chair, Idaho Democrat Frank Church, the group concluded that the Central Intelligence Agency (CIA) frequently had undertaken covert action in violation of the law, and it recommended strong restraints on future operations, with covert measures used only when no other option was available to protect U.S. national security. The committee's report also spurred the creation of the Senate Select Committee on Intelligence.

APRIL 27, 1976
PANELS URGED TO MONITOR COVERT ACTIONS ABROAD
Special to The New York Times

WASHINGTON, April 26—The United States has undertaken thousands of covert actions abroad since 1947, including 900 major or sensitive projects in the last 15 years alone, with only partial success and, in some instances, severe damage to the nation's foreign policy, according to a report today by the Senate Select Committee on Intelligence Activities.

The 11-member committee considered at one point recommending a ban against all covert actions, the report said but later concluded that the United States must have some covert capability. Only Senator Frank Church, the Idaho Democrat who headed the panel, ended up calling for a ban.

"The committee has concluded, however, that the United States should maintain the capability to react through covert action when no other means will suffice to meet extraordinary circumstances involving grave threats to U.S. national security," the report said.

"Nevertheless, covert action should be considered as an exception to the normal process of Government action abroad rather than a parallel but invisible system in which covert operations are routine."

Budget Details Urged

The report mentioned by name no covert operations that had not been previously publicly known. It urged that "the intelligence oversight committees of Congress should require that the annual budget submission for covert action programs be specified and detailed as to the activity recommended."

The recommendation left the door open, however, for "unforeseen" covert action projected to be financed from the intelligence agency's "contingency reserve fund" and accounted for later.

The report defined covert actions as those sub-rosa efforts—from buying candidates in an election to waging a secret war in Laos—that the United States tried to carry out without being identified with as a nation.

The committee said that there was no legal authorization for covert action in the 1947 National Security Act or subsequent laws pertaining to intelligence, but that internal executive orders had increased the powers to conduct covert operations abroad.

The committee investigated covert actions from the creation of the modern intelligence system in 1947 through the present. Part of its findings and descriptions, the report said, would be circulated only to senators and not made public, at the request of the Central Intelligence Agency.

"Reagan, On Dais, Spurs Party On," August 20, 1976

President Ford faced a stiff battle to secure the Republican presidential nomination in 1976. Former California governor Ronald Reagan campaigned aggressively to head the ticket, and neither candidate came to the national convention with enough delegate votes to prevail. Although he lost this race, Reagan set the stage for winning his party's endorsement four years later.

AUGUST 20, 1976
REAGAN, ON DAIS, SPURS PARTY ON
Challenger Invited by Ford to Address Convention—Hails G.O.P. Platform
By JON NORDHEIMER
Special to The New York Times

KANSAS CITY, Mo., Aug. 19—Ronald Reagan, defeated and apparently at the end of his political career, took the platform at the Republican National Convention tonight at President Ford's invitation and said it was "a moment that will live in our hearts forever."

At the end of a long day filled with sentiment and disappointment, Mr. Reagan was given an extraordinary moment on the dais by Mr. Ford after the President completed a rousing acceptance speech.

The former California Governor, who talked earlier in an interview about the uphill struggle faced by the President, nevertheless struck a strong battle cry against the Democrats. He said that the Republican platform adopted by this convention reflected most of his own views "in bold unmistakable colors with no pastel shades."

"We have just heard a call to arms based on that platform," he declared.

The day had begun as a sad one within the Reagan camp as the telegenic and articulate champion of the conservative cause bade farewell to his supporters.

At 65 years of age, too old to consider seriously another run at the Presidency, Mr. Reagan said he would resume a career as a commentator on national affairs and wait and see what he might do to help the Ford ticket this fall.

The former California Governor said he thought highly of Mr. Ford's choice of a running mate, Senator Robert J. Dole of Kansas, but thought the Republican team faced a difficult battle against the Democrats, led by Jimmy Carter.

He said he had had particular praise for Senator Dole when he and the President met privately at a post-midnight session in Mr. Reagan's suite at the Alameda Plaza Hotel after Mr. Ford's first-ballot nomination. But he said the President had not indicated at the time that Senator Dole was his choice.

Mr. Ford did not offer the Vice Presidential nomination to Mr. Reagan. Aides to the Californian reported that the ground rules set up in advance of the meeting had made it clear that Mr. Reagan did not want to be placed in the position of being made to refuse the President's invitation to join the ticket if, indeed, Mr. Ford had considered proffering it.

"2D DEBATE SHOWED A CHANGE OF CHARACTER," OCTOBER 9, 1976

To build popular support, President Ford agreed to participate in three televised debates with Democratic opponent Jimmy Carter during the fall 1976 campaign. Such debates had originated sixteen years earlier but had not been used since, perhaps because presidential contenders had seen the difficulties Vice President Nixon faced in 1960 in debating against the more telegenic and charismatic John F. Kennedy. Ford made a gaffe when he said, "There is no Soviet domination of Eastern Europe," which made him appear naïve about international politics.

OCTOBER 9, 1976
2D DEBATE SHOWED A CHANGE OF CHARACTER
By JOSEPH LELYVELD
Special to The New York Times

SAN FRANCISCO, Oct. 8—If the cycle of Presidential debates can be viewed for argument's sake as a television serial, then the second episode Wednesday night can be said to have turned on the development it showed in the character of the challenger, Jimmy Carter.

In the first episode two weeks ago, Mr. Carter was widely expected to play his role aggressively, interpreting it as John F. Kennedy did when it was first performed for a TV audience in 1960.

Instead, this year's challenger started off nervously on a seemingly diffident note. President Ford, who had been expected to sound defensive, seized the initiative early and won critical acclaim by doing so.

Wednesday night the tables were turned. Expectations for Mr. Carter's performance were low, not only because the subject—foreign policy and defense—was presumed to place him at a disadvantage but also because the expectations had been lowered by the polls and commentary that followed the first debate. Thus, as the President did the first time around, the challenger was able to make a stronger impression because less was expected of him.

The Importance of Poise

As in 1960, foreign policy issues provided more fertile ground than domestic ones for the cultivation of the challenger's image. And, as in 1960, this had little to do with the substance of the issues. Substantive differences were narrow then and narrow Wednesday but precisely because the issues were remote from the experience of the ordinary viewer, the overall poise and stance of the candidates could be expected to make a stronger impression than the cogency of their arguments.

The Ford camp had assumed that the President's greater experience in foreign affairs would simply manifest itself on television and that Mr. Ford would be able to dismiss the arguments of the challenger as callow and inconsequential. But in his effort to appear authoritative, Mr. Ford had difficulty sustaining the impression of steadfastness he left in the first debate.

Just as Mr. Carter lost his themes in a welter of statistics then, Mr. Ford now lost his in arguments that were merely defensive or in wordy discussions of MIRV's and Cruise missiles that almost cried out for the subtitles used in foreign-language films so that the home audience might have some ideas of what these devices were.

The President labored to overcome his habit of looking at the questioners rather than the camera and to vary his intonation and cadences for emphasis. But the more defensive he became, the more he lapsed into the flat accents and style of his news conference performances. In terms of image, he offered nothing new.

New Style for Carter

The challenger, on the other hand, had evolved a new and more congenial debating style. In part, Mr. Carter's performance could be viewed as a tribute to Mr. Ford's preparations for their first encounter. In Philadelphia, Mr. Carter rarely looked at his opponent for longer than 10 seconds. The President there fixed Mr. Carter with a steady glare that looked frozen and stiff when it was watched for minutes at a time in the theater but resolute and tough when it showed up in fleeting "cutaway" shots on the TV screen.

Wednesday night, Mr. Carter had learned the trick of staring back. But he had also learned to vary his posture—to sit down, for instance, as Mr. Ford has yet to do in nearly three and one-half hours on the stage set being used for the debates.

By looking more relaxed, Mr. Carter seemed to make the President look a little stiff in comparison—an impression that may have been deepened by the camera work of the CBS pool, which focused less tightly on the faces of the candidates and, as a result, showed more of their gestures and posture.

The Eastern Europe Issue

By any reckoning, the turning point came in the fourth round of questions, about 20 minutes into the debate. In the theater in the Palace of Fine Arts, there were audible gasps in the press section when the President flatly declared: "There is no Soviet domination of Eastern Europe."

But there were elements in the exchange that passed the theater audience by. Just an instant before the President stumbled into a damaging controversy, he had been straining to appeal to precisely the ethnic audience he was to risk offending. The appeal came in the form of a warning to Mr. Carter not to allege that "His Holiness the Pope" had signed over the Warsaw Pact nations to the Soviet Union.

In that instant, Mr. Carter who showed up taking notes in a shot of both candidates on TV screens, raised his chin and smiled. His look of amusement seemed not only to dismiss Mr. Ford's debating point but to underscore his own self-composure relative to his opponent.

Mr. Ford's surprising declaration about Eastern Europe was greeted incredulously by the questioner, Max Frankel of *The New York Times,* who then asked a follow-up question that gave the President an opportunity to restate his position. But Mr. Ford got himself into potentially deeper trouble by specifically identifying the Poles as a people who don't consider themselves dominated by the Russians.

Ford on the Defensive

Mr. Carter's earlier smile was probably as effective in the whole exchange as his subsequent rebuttal, which was relatively muted. In any case, from round four on, the President seemed to be on the defensive.

- -

"Carter, in Victory, Hails 'New Spirit,' " November 4, 1976

Despite several missteps in his brief presidency, Ford came close to winning the White House in 1976. But Jimmy Carter prevailed, making Ford the first sitting president since Herbert Hoover in 1932 to be defeated.

NOVEMBER 4, 1976
CARTER, IN VICTORY, HAILS 'NEW SPIRIT'; STARTS TRANSITION WITH FORD'S STAFF
A NARROW MAJORITY
Hawaii's 4 Electoral Votes Seal Triumph in One of Century's Closest Races
By R. W. APPLE Jr.

James Earl Carter Jr., his improbable dream of attaining the White House finally fulfilled, fought back tears yesterday as he told his fellow citizens of Plains, Ga., and the United States that he saw "a beautiful new spirit in this country."

Several hours later, Gerald Rudolph Ford, the man Mr. Carter defeated Tuesday in one of the closest Presidential elections of the century, conceded defeat in a voice ravaged by his vain campaign to avoid becoming the first President to lose since Herbert Hoover was swept away in the Great Depression.

The 52-year-old President-elect, the first son of the Deep South to win the Presidency since the Civil War, returned to his hometown at dawn, shortly after his narrow electoral-vote majority was assured with the four votes of far-off Hawaii.

Transition Work Begins

Mr. Carter talked by telephone with Mr. Ford, then announced that their staffs were already at work on the transition from one Administration to another. The Georgian's associates forecast an aggressive, activist Presidency that will begin when he takes the oath of office as the nation's 39th President before the East Front of the Capitol on Jan. 20.

Having won no more than 303 electoral votes and perhaps as few as 272, Mr. Carter failed to win the mandate he had appealed for in the waning days of his 22-month campaign. But strong Presidents often create mandates after the fact, and Mr. Carter could argue that anyone who defeats a sitting President has profoundly moved the electorate. He was only the eighth man to best an incumbent in the nation's 200 years.

With 99 percent of the nation's 178,159 precincts reporting, the popular vote tabulation gave the following totals:

Carter—40,173,854—51%

Ford—38,429,988—48%

Eugene J. McCarthy—654,770—1%

Solid Democratic Control

The slight, soft-spoken Georgia Democrat will take office along with a solidly Democratic Congress and as the leader of a party in ascendancy. The Democrats will control the Senate by 3 to 2 and the House of Representatives by 2 to 1, almost exactly the same margins as before the election, and they will hold 37 governor's chairs, an advantage of 3 to 1.

THE PRESIDENCY OF JIMMY CARTER

JANUARY 20, 1977 – JANUARY 20, 1981

The presidency of James Earl "Jimmy" Carter Jr. was marked by significant challenges both in domestic and foreign affairs. Carter took office at a time of national economic trouble, and the situation worsened during his four years in office. In foreign policy, Carter's skillful personal diplomacy produced the first Middle East peace agreement, a treaty signed by Egypt and Israel. But cold war tensions heightened with the Soviet invasion of Afghanistan, and the U.S. hostage crisis in Iran dominated Carter's final year in office. Carter tried to maintain control of his policy agenda, but he often was seen as reacting to events rather than directing them. In many respects,

Source: Dayton Daily News

Carter's compassionate leadership style was better suited to his postpresidential activities than to his time in the White House.

A native of Plains, Georgia, Carter was the eldest of four children and known as "Jimmy" from childhood. He graduated in the top 10 percent of his class at the United States Naval Academy in Annapolis, Maryland, and, as a commissioned naval officer, he had numerous assignments, including service on a submarine in the Pacific. He joined the navy's nuclear submarine program and studied nuclear physics briefly, but after his father's death, he left the service and returned to Georgia. He ran the family peanut farm and started many other profitable agriculture-related businesses, such as farming supplies.

Carter became involved in politics when he served on a county school board for seven years. He served two terms in the Georgia State Senate and then ran unsuccessfully for governor of Georgia in 1966. Four years later he entered the race again and won. He opposed racial segregation, advocated environmental protection, and supported openness in

government. Because he was prohibited by state law from running for two consecutive gubernatorial terms, Carter soon began to consider other possibilities for elective office. He declared nearly two years before the 1976 presidential election that he would seek the Democratic nomination for the White House.

THE 1976 PRESIDENTIAL ELECTION

As a one-term governor with no national political experience, Carter did not appear a likely candidate to win the Democratic nomination. But he gained media attention by winning the Democratic caucuses in Iowa and the New Hampshire primary, which gave his campaign strong momentum. Carter won enough delegates to secure the nomination before the Democratic convention in New York, where he received the party's endorsement on the first ballot. Sen. Walter F. Mondale of Minnesota was chosen as his running mate. The Republican Party narrowly nominated incumbent president Gerald R. Ford for another term, after a strong challenge by former governor Ronald Reagan of California. The convention chose Sen. Robert J. Dole of Kansas as Ford's running mate.

Carter and Ford waged highly competitive campaigns. Ford was a career legislator who had been appointed from the U.S. House of Representatives to become vice president in the Nixon administration when Spiro Agnew resigned and president when Nixon resigned. Ford's decision to pardon Nixon hurt his popularity significantly, as did the country's economic woes. The 1976 race was so close that Ford and Carter agreed to hold the first general-election presidential debates since the Kennedy-Nixon debates in 1960. Ford's blunder in insisting that Eastern European nations were not controlled by the Soviet Union was a late setback for his campaign, and Carter narrowly won the election with more than 40 million popular votes to Ford's 39 million, and 297 Electoral College votes to Ford's 240. (One Republican elector cast his vote for Reagan.)

THE CARTER ADMINISTRATION

The Carter cabinet was noted for its prominent Democrats as well as for Carter's attention to demographic diversity. He chose Cyrus R. Vance of New York for secretary of state, and Vance was succeeded by Edmund S. Muskie of Maine in 1980. Cater selected Harold Brown of California for secretary of defense and Michael Blumenthal of Michigan to head the Treasury Department (later replaced by George W. Miller of Rhode Island). Griffin B. Bell of Georgia served as attorney general until mid-1979, when he was replaced by his deputy, Benjamin R. Civiletti.

Carter oversaw the creation of two new cabinet departments, Energy and Education. The latter had been part of Health, Education, and Welfare, which became the Department of Health and Human Services. He appointed three women to his cabinet: Patricia R. Harris of Washington, D.C., the first African American woman to hold a cabinet position, served as secretary of Housing and Urban Development and later headed Health and Human Services; Juanita M. Kreps of North Carolina was Carter's commerce secretary for three years; and Shirley M. Hufstedler of California became the first education secretary.

Rosalynn Smith Carter was an energetic first lady and perhaps the president's closest confidante. She represented her husband on official trips to Latin American and Caribbean nations, and she actively endorsed the equal rights amendment. The Carters had four children, three sons who were adults when their father became president, and a daughter, Amy, who was nine when the Carters moved to the White House. The president's mother, Lillian Carter, was a former nurse and Peace Corps volunteer. She attended state funerals and other events overseas on behalf of her son during his presidency.

MAJOR ISSUES

From his first day in office, Carter was determined to make his administration open and accessible to the people. He took the oath of office as Jimmy Carter, preferring his nickname to his full name. He, his wife, and their daughter further underscored this informality when they walked hand-in-hand to the White House from the Capitol following the inauguration. The president initially said he would operate without a chief of staff to ensure direct consultation with his cabinet, but the demands of the modern presidency made this approach to governance infeasible. Carter also tried to replicate the famous "fireside chats" of Democratic president Franklin D. Roosevelt by appearing on national television sitting next to a log fire in the Oval Office and wearing a cardigan to discuss a new energy plan. But the image was not sufficiently presidential, and it did not help Carter enact his policy agenda.

In domestic policy, Carter faced a sluggish economy that worsened during his administration. Double-digit inflation and rising unemployment led to what economists have termed "stagflation," and the high price of oil following the 1979 revolution in Iran resulted in long lines for gasoline. With low approval ratings in the summer of 1979, Carter decided to give a national address in which he declared that the nation faced a "crisis of confidence." A few days later, he requested resignations from his entire cabinet, which reduced morale within his administration as well.

In foreign affairs, Carter's diplomatic skills proved quite fruitful early in his presidency. He personally mediated talks with Israeli prime minister Menachem Begin and Egyptian president Anwar Sadat at the presidential retreat in Maryland in September 1978. These discussions resulted in the historic Camp David Accords outlining a peace agreement between the two nations, which was formalized in a peace treaty the following year. Carter also negotiated treaties that relinquished U.S. control of the Panama Canal to Panama, effective at the end of the twentieth century, which the Senate ratified in 1978. But the president faced heavy criticism from his political opponents, particularly future Republican presidential candidate Ronald Reagan, for giving away the canal.

As Carter neared the end of his term, he was beset by foreign-policy crises. On November 4, 1979, Iranian militants seized the U.S. embassy in Tehran and took Americans hostage to protest the U.S. admittance of the deposed Iranian

QUICK FACTS ON JIMMY CARTER

BIRTH	October 1, 1924, Plains, Ga.
EDUCATION	Attends Georgia Southwestern University, Americus, 1941–1942 Attends Georgia Institute of Technology, Atlanta, 1942–1943 United States Naval Academy, Annapolis, Md., B.S., 1946 Postgraduate study in nuclear physics, Union College, Schenectady, N.Y., 1952
FAMILY	Wife: Rosalynn Smith Carter Children: John William "Jack" Carter, James Earl "Chip" Carter, Donnel Jeffrey "Jeff" Carter, Amy Lynn Carter
WHITE HOUSE PETS	Dog, Siamese cat
PARTY	Democratic
PREPRESIDENTIAL CAREER (SELECTED)	Naval officer; promoted to rank of lieutenant commander, 1946–1953 Joins family farm, Plains, Ga., 1953 Chairman, Sumter County, Ga., Board of Education, 1955–1962 Georgia State Senate, 1963–1966 Loses Democratic primary in Georgia gubernatorial race, 1966 Governor of Georgia, 1971–1975 Chairman, Democratic National Committee, 1974
PRESIDENTIAL TERM	January 20, 1977–January 20, 1981
VICE PRESIDENT	Walter F. Mondale

ruler for medical treatment. They soon freed black and women hostages, but the others were held for more than a year. A few weeks after the hostage seizure, the Soviet Union invaded Afghanistan and deposed its ruler. In response, President Carter imposed an embargo on trade with the Soviet Union and declared that the United States would boycott the 1980 Olympics in Moscow. The Carter administration also withdrew from Senate consideration an arms control treaty, known as SALT II (Strategic Arms Limitation Talks) that it had negotiated with the Soviet Union. In April 1980 Carter authorized a mission to rescue the U.S. hostages in Iran, but mechanical problems halted the attempt.

Seeking foremost to resolve the hostage crisis, Carter had a difficult time campaigning for reelection in 1980. Sen. Edward M. Kennedy of Massachusetts contested Carter's candidacy for the Democratic nomination, but Carter ultimately won this intraparty contest. His Republican opponent was Ronald Reagan, former actor and California governor, who had sought his party's presidential nomination in 1976. The

two candidates met for one general-election presidential debate, in which Carter tried to make an issue of his opponent's policy views, but Reagan prevailed with a simple question for voters: "Are you better off now than you were four years ago?" The nation's pressing economic and foreign policy problems hurt Carter's campaign, and he lost the race by more than 8 million popular votes. In the Electoral College, Reagan won a whopping 489 votes to Carter's 49.

After leaving the White House, Carter embarked on an ambitious postpresidential career that many consider to be more successful than his presidency. He has written more than a dozen books and founded a center to promote human rights, medical care, and democracy abroad. The Carters are active in Habitat for Humanity, which helps people with low incomes to build and own homes. In 1994 he undertook diplomatic missions to North Korea, Bosnia, and Haiti; he negotiated an agreement with North Korea to halt its nuclear program (an agreement that North Korea later violated), and he achieved an agreement that permitted U.S. forces to enter

SELECTED EVENTS	Opening of Trans-Alaska pipeline (1977)
	Creation of Department of Energy (1977)
	Agreement with Canada to build natural gas pipeline from Alaska to continental U.S. (1977)
	Enactment of legislation to increase minimum wage (1977)
	Coal miners' strike (1977–1978)
	Signing of Panama Canal treaties, Panama City, Panama (1978)
	Camp David Accords (1978)
	Airline Deregulation Act (1978)
	Formal diplomatic ties with China (1979)
	Signing of Israel-Egypt peace treaty, Washington, D.C. (1979)
	Nuclear reactor accident, Three Mile Island (1979)
	Signing of SALT II Treaty, Vienna, Austria (1979)
	Creation of Department of Education (1979)
	U.S. hostages taken in Iran (November 4, 1979); held for 444 days
	Soviet invasion of Afghanistan (1979)
	Failed rescue attempt of U.S. hostages in Iran (1980)
	U.S. boycott of Olympics in Moscow (1980)
	Agreement to secure release of U.S. hostages in Iran (1981)
POSTPRESIDENCY	University Distinguished Professor, Emory University, Atlanta, Ga., 1982
	Establishment of Carter Center, Atlanta, Ga., 1982
	Dedication of Carter Presidential Center, Atlanta, Ga., 1986
	Diplomatic missions to North Korea, Bosnia, and Haiti, 1994
	Awarded Nobel Peace Prize, 2002

Haiti peacefully rather than forcibly overthrow the military regime there, which departed of its own accord. In 2002 Carter visited Cuba, met with its leader, Fidel Castro, and called on the United States to end its economic embargo against the small Communist nation. Carter was awarded the Nobel Peace Prize in 2002 for his dedication to pursuing global development.

"A Quick Victory," July 15, 1976

Despite being a virtually unknown national figure when he entered the 1976 presidential race, Jimmy Carter's early victories in Democratic contests created momentum for his candidacy, and he easily won the party's nomination. *The New York Times* noted that Carter's "startling electoral ascendancy" developed in just six months prior to winning the Democratic nomination in July 1976. The nomination also was significant, *The Times* reported, because he was "the first major-party nominee from the Deep South since Zachary Taylor in 1848."

JULY 15, 1976
A QUICK VICTORY

Georgian Is Selected at the Convention by Wide Margin

By R. W. APPLE Jr.

Jimmy Carter of Georgia won the Democratic Presidential nomination last night.

By an overwhelming margin, the Democratic National Convention ratified Mr. Carter's startling electoral ascendancy of the last six months, made him the first major-party nominee from the Deep South since Zachary Taylor in 1848 and installed him as the early favorite to capture the White House in November.

It seemed appropriate when Ohio put Mr. Carter over 1,505 votes—a majority—for it was the Georgian's sweep of that state's June 8 primary that started the stampede of party leaders toward him.

Shouts and Cheers

When Christine Gitlin, the Ohio delegation chairman, announced the vote, the hall burst into shouts and cheers, and Robert S. Strauss, the national chairman, signaled the band to strike up "Happy Days Are Here Again."

An unofficial tabulation by *The New York Times* gave Mr. Carter a total of 2,2381/2 votes when the somewhat muddled roll-call ended.

The other candidates who were officially nominated—Gov. Edmund G. Brown Jr. of California, Representative Morris K. Udall of Arizona and Ellen McCormack, the anti-abortion candidate—trailed far behind, as did a handful of other contenders.

Standing in the midst of his delegation, Mr. Brown switched California's votes to the former Georgia Governor, remarking, "This is the beginning of a Democratic sweep across this country that comes none too soon."

* * *

"CARTER ASSERTS VICTORY MARGIN, WHILE NARROW, PROVIDES SUPPORT REQUIRED TO ENACT HIS PROGRAMS," NOVEMBER 5, 1976

Carter defeated incumbent president Gerald R. Ford, winning the 1976 presidential election with just 27 more votes than the 270 minimum required for an Electoral College majority. Undeterred by his slim victory, Carter said he was confident that he had sufficient public and congressional support to enact his campaign agenda. He also promised to have a collegial transition with Ford.

NOVEMBER 5, 1976
CARTER ASSERTS VICTORY MARGIN, WHILE NARROW, PROVIDES SUPPORT REQUIRED TO ENACT HIS PROGRAMS

CONCILIATORY TO FORD

Democrat Hints at a Tax Cut and Pledges Continuity on Foreign Policy

By JAMES T. WOOTEN

Special to The New York Times

PLAINS, Ga., Nov. 4—Jimmy Carter today appraised his narrow victory over President Ford as a sufficient mandate for the wide array of Government programs and policies that he promised and proposed during his long campaign.

Confident and relaxed in his first news conference as President-elect, the Democrat discounted suggestions that his slim margin of victory might thwart his Administration's plans and said that he was certain of their support by Congress and the electorate.

"I predict that they will be achieved," he said.

'Time for a Change'

After their often acerbic contest, Mr. Carter today struck a note of conciliation toward Mr. Ford, saying he would work closely with him through the period of transition and interpreting the closeness of the vote Tuesday as a sign of respect and approval for the President.

"But many people thought it was time for a change," he added, and said that their ballots would serve as the base for his extensive blueprint for changing the face and form of the Federal Government.

Earlier in the day it became all but certain that the final tally from Tuesday's election would show Mr. Carter with 297 electoral votes and President Ford with 241. Oregon's six electoral votes, the last to be allotted, will go to the President unless the final tally of absentee ballots takes a wholly unexpected turn.

Characteristically, the 52-year-old former Governor of Georgia offered broad, general answers to many of the questions put to him during the half-hour, nationally televised appearance.

Continuity in Foreign Policy

He said a tax cut could be a "strong possibility" if the economy remains stagnant through December, but said that he was "not qualified to be specific" about the mechanics of a reduction other than that it would be aimed at stimulating the purchasing power of working Americans and "oriented toward payroll deductions."

Despite a yearlong attack on present American foreign policy—with special criticism for Secretary of State Henry A. Kissinger—he said other governments should expect a "substantial amount of continuity" between the Ford Administration and his own.

He also said that he would not name any Cabinet officers before December and pledged to hold at least two "full-scale" news conferences each month in the White House.

Mr. Carter handled the outdoor news conference with an ease that seemed to grow as the minutes passed. He stood behind an old wooden pulpit on a platform adjacent to the train station that has served as the unofficial headquarters of his campaign.

Nearby, on a straight-backed bench, sat the Vice President-elect, Walter F. Mondale. He arrived here this afternoon for meetings with Mr. Carter and had been expected to answer questions from the reporters as well. He did not participate in the news conference, however.

"CARTER CALLS FOR FIGHT ON ENERGY WASTE," APRIL 21, 1977

With the nation facing a severe energy crisis in the 1970s, Carter was determined to pass legislation that would promote personal and industrial conservation. But his proposed national energy policy was, in *The Times'* words, "complex, controversial and face[d] major political obstacles." Carter's energy policies did not achieve the fundamental reforms that he had advocated.

'[T]he time has come to draw the line' on unfettered use of energy.

APRIL 21, 1977
CARTER CALLS FOR FIGHT ON ENERGY WASTE
ASKS CONGRESS TO HELP IN 'THANKLESS JOB'
'TIME TO DRAW LINE'
Widespread Impact Foreseen on Standards of Living and Key Industries
By CHARLES MOHR
Special to The New York Times

WASHINGTON, April 20—Saying "the time has come to draw the line" on unfettered use of energy, President Carter proposed tonight a national energy policy designed to increase the cost of fuels, penalize waste and bring important changes in industrial habits and in some of the ways Americans live.

But in a nationally televised speech delivered to a joint session of Congress in the chamber of the House of

Representatives, Mr. Carter argued that the plan "can lead to an even better life for the people of America" rather than debasing life styles and living standards.

The energy program that he proposed is complex, controversial and faces major political obstacles. It involves a vast scale of political and social engineering that would take billions of dollars from citizens' pockets to discourage overconsumption of fuels and energy. But it would return much of that money in the form of tax credits, tax rebates and in incentives to those who do the most to conserve.

'It's Our Job'

The President, attempting to enlist the support of Congressmen who for economic, ideological or regional reasons may find much to dislike and who may fear the wrath of their constituents, said the task of fashioning the new policy has been "a thankless job, but it's our job."

In an apparent attempt to fend off or to limit the probably inevitable efforts to modify or soften the plan's provisions, Mr. Carter said that the program depended "for its fairness on all its major component parts."

House Speaker Thomas P. O'Neill Jr. predicted that the proposals would bring "the toughest fight this Congress has ever had," but White House sources believe that the Speaker and other Democratic leaders can pass most, if not all, of it.

Still, the proposal will be perhaps the greatest test of Mr. Carter's capacity for personal leadership, of his ability to capture and direct public opinion and of his untried skills in parliamentary maneuver.

'Greatest Domestic Challenge'

Calling the energy problem the "greatest domestic challenge that our nation will face in our lifetime," Mr. Carter predicted to his audience that he would get little applause. Indeed, although he was interrupted seven times by applause, the reception he received was relatively restrained.

Several of the bursts of applause came as Mr. Carter, dressed in a dark-blue suit and reading his speech from off-camera prompting devices, inveighed against windfall oil company profits and said that there was now too little competition in industry.

- -

"Variety of Charges Caused Bert Lance's Decline and Fall," September 22, 1977

Carter faced an administrative crisis when his Office of Management and Budget director, Bert Lance, resigned in fall 1977 because of questions about his business activities as a banker before joining the administration. Lance was a close friend of Carter's, and the president had defended him against allegations of improper ethical behavior. Lance was later acquitted of bank fraud charges, but his resignation hindered Carter's efforts to portray his administration as adhering to strict ethical standards.

SEPTEMBER 22, 1977
VARIETY OF CHARGES CAUSED BERT LANCE'S DECLINE AND FALL
By NICHOLAS M. HORROCK
Special to The New York Times

WASHINGTON, Sept. 21—In contrast with the resignations in the Watergate scandal, no single charge of wrongdoing caused Bert Lance to step down as director of the Office of Management and Budget.

He has resigned after more than 60 days of national attention that produced a dizzying array of allegations about Mr. Lance's business activities and personal finances. There

have been no charges, to date, that he conducted himself improperly in government.

But a careful scrutiny of his practices as chief executive officer of two banks in Georgia has resulted in even senior members of the Carter Administration concluding that he is not fit to hold what many consider one of the most powerful positions in the Government.

The Senate reviews the fitness of Presidential appointees in public hearings, and the criticism of their backgrounds is normally raised at that time.

But, as Senator Charles H. Percy, the Illinois Republican who is vice chairman of the Senate Governmental Affairs Committee, pointed out earlier this week, "We are in this fix because we failed to do what we should have done in January: thoroughly review Mr. Lance's qualifications to direct the Office of Management and Budget."

Questionable Business Practices

When a full-fledged investigation of his background got under way this summer, it uncovered what seemed to be an ever-growing pool of questionable business practices and financial dealings. In brief the following matters appeared to be the most damaging:

OVERDRAFTS—When Mr. Lance headed the Calhoun First National Bank of Georgia, the bank permitted its officers and directors to have largely unrestricted overdrafts on their bank accounts. Mr. Lance apologized for the overdrafts and noted that on those after 1974 he paid interest, and contended that the practice was not unusual in small Southern banks. But the evidence of investigations by John G. Heimann, the Comptroller of the Currency, and the Senate have shown the overdrafts were continuous, a "persuasive pattern," and in amounts in the hundreds of thousands of dollars.

Mr. Lance had been put on notice about these problems in 1974 and 1975 by highly critical reports by bank examiners. In December 1975, the Calhoun bank signed a formal contract with the Government pledging to correct the problems. One particular group of overdrafts, made by Mr. Lance's political committee during his unsuccessful 1974 campaign for the governorship of Georgia, were referred to the Department of Justice for criminal investigation.

CORPORATE AIRCRAFT—Federal investigators found that Mr. Lance used aircraft leased or owned by the National Bank of Georgia for a wide range of what appeared to be personal or political trips. Mr. Lance said last week at a public hearing that he believed his use of the aircraft was proper in that it encouraged business for the bank. But the Justice Department, the Federal Election Commission and the Securities and Exchange Commission are making inquiries into this practice.

INSIDER LOANS—The Comptroller's office and subsequent Senate inquiries found that Mr. Lance had made a practice of borrowing money from banks wherein his bank placed sizable interest-free accounts. Although the Comptroller made no recommendation for a criminal charge, he said that the "pattern" of the practice raised questions.

In one instance, the Comptroller reported, Mr. Lance appeared to use collateral twice for the same loan.

What became almost as damaging for Mr. Lance and for the Carter Administration as the questions themselves have been the events that resulted in questions not being brought out at Mr. Lance's confirmation hearings last January.

In mid-November, when Mr. Carter decided to appoint Mr. Lance to a high office, Mr. Lance was under criminal investigation by the Department of Justice and his bank was under discipline by the Comptroller's office. An agent of the Federal Bureau of Investigation had tried to subpoena documents from the bank as late as August 1976 in the criminal case, and a bank examiner had checked up on the Calhoun bank's compliance with the agreement in October.

Yet, Mr. Lance testified that he did not realize he was under investigation until last Dec. 1, when his lawyer, Sidney Smith of Atlanta, learned it from Robert Bloom, the Acting Comptroller of the Currency.

There has been a strong indication that the decision to close the Justice Department case, which was done by the United States Attorney in Atlanta last Dec. 2, and to clear the Comptroller record, which was accomplished on Nov. 22, may have been made under the subtle urging of Mr. Lance. But Mr. Lance has denied this under oath.

The 'Shadow President'

Mr. Lance was confirmed by the Senate on Jan. 20 with only one opposing vote, that by Senator William Proxmire, Democrat of Wisconsin. The budget director appeared firmly established at the top level of the Carter Administration; some news reports referred to him as a "shadow President" because his influence was so great.

But his principal source of income was the dividends from some 200,000 shares of National Bank of Georgia stock. The bank, like several others in the South, had encountered severe difficulties and discontinued dividends. In May, *Time* magazine published an article on Mr. Lance's heavy debts.

About six weeks later, two events spelled the beginning of Mr. Lance's severe difficulties. Mr. Heimann, the newly appointed Comptroller, ordered an internal investigation of allegations that officials in the Comptroller's office had acted improperly in handling the Lance matter.

At almost the same time, Mr. Lance, with Mr. Carter's approval, sought an extension from the Senate Governmental Affairs Committee of a pledge to sell his National Bank of Georgia stock. The final outcome of these events may have been on Mr. Lance's mind, because he reminded the President at that time that Mr. Carter held a standing letter of resignation.

"Senate Votes to Give up Panama Canal; Carter Forsees 'Beginning of a New Era,'" April 19, 1978

With just one vote more than the number required for ratification, the Senate approved the treaties turning over U.S. control of the Panama Canal to Panama at century's end. Carter had negotiated these treaties and heralded their importance in advancing U.S. relations with Latin America. Opponents, however, castigated the president for surrendering U.S. authority to Panama.

APRIL 19, 1978
SENATE VOTES TO GIVE UP PANAMA CANAL; CARTER FORESEES 'BEGINNING OF A NEW ERA'
NARROW 68–32 VICTORY

Two-Thirds Majority Gained With One Vote to Spare, as in Earlier Success

By ADAM CLYMER

Special to The New York Times

WASHINGTON, April 18—The Senate voted today to turn over the Panama Canal to Panama on Dec. 31, 1999, moving to establish a new spirit of relations with Latin America and saving President Carter from a grave political defeat.

With one vote to spare, the Senate voted to approve a treaty giving up a symbol of American power and engineering that had gripped the minds of so many of its members' constituents.

The vote of 68 to 32, one more than the two-thirds majority required by the Constitution, was identical to one by which the Senate approved a treaty on March 16 that guarantees the neutrality of the canal. The outcome was in doubt until just before the historic roll-call at 6 P.M.

New Battle Looms

Today's vote settles an issue that has existed since Panama seceded from Colombia in 1903 and entered into a treaty with the United States. It also effectively ended a 13-year negotiating process, although some financial details remain to be resolved by both Houses of Congress, probably next year.

That is expected to be the next battleground. Under an amendment agreed to last night formal ratification will be delayed until the implementing legislation is approved or until March 31, 1979, whichever comes earlier.

Six months after the formal ratification, the United States will surrender large parts of the Canal Zone and a gradual Panamanian takeover will begin.

In remarks after the vote, President Carter said, "This is a day of which Americans can always feel proud; for now we have reminded the world and ourselves of the things that we stand for as a nation."

'Mutual Respect and Partnership'

"These treaties can mark the beginning of a new era in our relations not only with Panama but with all the rest of the world," he said. "They symbolize our determination to deal with the developing nations of the world, the small nations of the world, on the basis of mutual respect and partnership."

Mr. Carter said Panama's Ambassador, Gabriel Lewis Galindo, had informed him that the country's leader, Brig. Gen. Omar Torrijos Herrera, would accept the treaties with the Senate's changes. He added that he had been invited to visit Panama and "I would like very much to accept."

The victory was critical for President Carter, who had repeatedly told wavering senators that his ability to conduct foreign affairs hung in the balance. But the tight margin and the repeated difficulties the Administration met in dealing with the Senate robbed the victory of much of the political impact it might have had if it had come more smoothly.

"CARTER AND HEADS OF BOTH PARTIES DISCERN HOPEFUL SIGNS IN VOTE RESULTS," NOVEMBER 9, 1978, AND "DEMOCRATS LOSE 9 GOVERNORSHIPS AS G.O.P. GAINS IN LEGISLATURES," NOVEMBER 9, 1978

Although the Democratic congressional losses in the 1978 midterm elections were not surprising—the president's party typically loses seats at that time—Republican victories at the state level were of some of concern to Democrats. Republican candidates won gubernatorial races in several states, including Pennsylvania and Texas, and took control of many state legislative chambers as well. These victories would be consequential for redrawing congressional districts and building popular support in the 1980 presidential election.

NOVEMBER 9, 1978
CARTER AND HEADS OF BOTH PARTIES DISCERN HOPEFUL SIGNS IN VOTE RESULTS

By SETH S. KING
Special to The New York Times

WASHINGTON, Nov. 8—President Carter, as well as the national chairmen of the Democratic and Republican parties, insisted today that there was something to cheer about in the results of yesterday's elections.

The White House said voting trends indicated that the American people supported Mr. Carter's determination to cut government spending and move toward a balanced Federal budget.

Jody Powell, the Presidential press secretary, said during a briefing at the White House this afternoon that the voting showed "the electorate was very much inclined to support the President's efforts next year to hold the deficit down."

He conceded that some of the statewide Democratic candidates for whom the President campaigned had lost, but said that when House races were taken into account, a majority of candidates supported by Mr. Carter had won.

Carter Termed 'Satisfied'

"The President was satisfied with the responses he got on his campaign trips," Mr. Powell said. "He believes he helped many of the Democratic candidates, though the biggest impact was made by the candidates themselves."

Mr. Powell said his count showed that the President had campaigned in 22 states and that 23 of the candidates he had spoken for won, while 17 lost and six or seven races were undecided.

"What the voting showed was a clear support for a responsible approach to reduce Federal spending," he declared. "It showed people weren't looking for wild promises on tax cutting, but they were very much interested in reducing the Federal deficit, though this will be more difficult than the public realizes."

John White, the Democratic national chairman, said that yesterday's voting produced "a big win" for his party.

NOVEMBER 9, 1978
DEMOCRATS LOSE 9 GOVERNORSHIPS AS G.O.P. GAINS IN LEGISLATURES

By WARREN WEAVER Jr.

Republican candidates for governor took nine states away from the Democrats in Tuesday's elections, scoring major victories in Texas, Pennsylvania and Wisconsin while surrendering only three smaller states to the Democrats.

At the same time, Republicans elected about 300 new members of state legislatures around the country. By their own count, they took control from the Democrats of 12 legislative houses in 13 states and possibly a thirteenth in Alaska.

These gains were regarded as particularly important by Republican leaders because they will enable the Republicans to block Democratic plans to redraw Congressional and legislative district lines.

Rebounding from a current political low of 12 gover-norships, the Republicans gave a demonstration of renewed vitality that not only raised the number of statehouses they control to 18 but also increased the likelihood of a strong party showing in the 1980 elections.

Six Major States

Beginning next year, there will be Republican gover-nors in six of the 10 largest states: Ohio, Michigan, Illinois, Pennsylvania, Texas and Wisconsin. The Democrats man-aged to retain the other four, New York, California, Massa-chusetts and Florida.

In addition to the three big states, Republican governors were elected to replace Democrats in Tennessee, Minnesota, South Dakota, Nebraska, Nevada and Oregon. Democrats won in three currently Republican states—New Hampshire, South Carolina and Kansas—and in Maine, whose governor is an independent.

In Texas, Bill Clement defeated Attorney General John Hill, the Democratic candidate, by a tiny margin in a race that attracted a turnout of almost 2 million.

The Pennsylvania race brought another significant Republican victory with the election of Richard L. Thorn-burgh, a former Assistant United States Attorney, who had been trailing his Democratic opponent, former Mayor Pete Flaherty of Pittsburgh, until the closing days of the campaign.

· ·

"U.S. AND CHINA MARK RESUMPTION OF TIES IN PEKING CEREMONY," JANUARY 2, 1979

President Carter formally reestablished U.S. relations with China in 1979. The United States had cut off ties to China when the Communists seized control in 1949, but President Richard M. Nixon traveled to China in 1972 to promote U.S. engagement with the Communist power. Carter's normalization policy marked the fruition of that diplomacy.

JANUARY 2, 1979
U.S. AND CHINA MARK RESUMPTION OF TIES IN PEKING CEREMONY
DEPUTY PREMIER TAKES PART
Occasion Draws Unusual Turnout of Chinese Officials—
Enmity of Past Seems Forgotten
By FOX BUTTERFIELD
Special to The New York Times

PEKING, Jan. 1—The United States and China cele-brated the resumption of formal diplomatic relations today after nearly three decades of estrangement. The ceremony, at the United States liaison office here, was attended by Deputy Prime Minister Teng Hsiao-ping and an unusually large turn-out of other Chinese leaders.

Leonard Woodcock, the head of the liaison office who negotiated the final agreement on normalization with Mr. Teng, hailed the event as "the beginning of a new era in our relations."

After Mr. Teng offered a series of toasts to friendship between China and America, a string of firecrackers ex-ploded outside—traditionally an auspicious sign in China. The toasts were drunk in California champagne and in Coca-Cola, which will be bottled in China later this year under one of the new deals between business interests of the two nations.

Korea and Vietnam Forgotten

It was New Year's Day 1979. Relations between China and the United States broke down in 1949, after Chiang Kai-shek and his Nationalist forces fled to Taiwan and set up a new regime there that Washington recognized as the Republic of China.

There followed the bitter clash between the American and Chinese Armies in Korea, a long campaign by Washing-ton to keep China out of the United Nations, and the war in Vietnam, which some American leaders maintained was

> " The United States and China celebrated the resumption of formal diplomatic relations today after nearly three decades of estrangement. "

necessary to stop Chinese expansion. Today, through some special alchemy, all that seemed forgotten.

Both Mr. Woodcock, the 67-year-old former president of the United Auto Workers union, and Mr. Teng, 74, who was twice purged as a "rightist," put on small lapel buttons bearing crossed Chinese and American flags. They were pinned on in an impromptu gesture by Representative John J. LaFalce, the Democrat from Tonawanda, N.Y., who is touring China as a member of the House Banking, Finance and Urban Affairs Committee.

A Heathen Land to Convert

Before the breakdown in relations in 1949, it often seemed to Americans that they had a special affinity for China. Missionaries envisioned it as a vast heathen land to convert to Christianity or an impoverished country in which to build schools and hospitals. Businesses saw the Chinese as hundreds of millions of potential customers.

That these views were based on misconceptions as often as real understanding has not prevented Americans from a deep abiding interest in China.

Now many Chinese seem to be looking to the United States as a model for their economic and political development. What the Soviet Union represented to the generation of revolutionaries who founded the Chinese Communist Party in the 1920's, the United States, Western Europe and Japan symbolize now: They appear to be the world's most advanced and successful societies.

The presence today of Mr. Teng, the diminutive, blunt and tough architect of China's modernization plans, indicated the importance Peking attaches to its new ties to the United States.

· ·

"EGYPT AND ISRAEL SIGN FORMAL TREATY, ENDING A STATE OF WAR AFTER 30 YEARS," MARCH 27, 1979

Perhaps Carter's greatest presidential achievement in foreign affairs was the peace treaty signed by Egypt and Israel in 1979. This agreement represented the first Arab-Israeli accord since the creation of Israel in 1948, and the White House signing ceremony indicated the importance of the president's role in bringing the two sides together.

MARCH 27, 1979
EGYPT AND ISRAEL SIGN FORMAL TREATY, ENDING A STATE OF WAR AFTER 30 YEARS; SADAT AND BEGIN PRAISE CARTER'S ROLE
CEREMONY IS FESTIVE
Accord on Sinai Oil Opens Way to the First Peace in Mideast Dispute
By BERNARD GWERTZMAN
Special to The New York Times

WASHINGTON, March 26—After confronting each other for nearly 31 years as hostile neighbors, Egypt and Israel signed a formal treaty at the White House today to establish peace and "normal and friendly relations."

On this chilly early spring day, about 1,500 invited guests and millions more watching television saw President Anwar el-Sadat of Egypt and Prime Minister Menachem Begin of Israel put their signatures on the Arabic, Hebrew and English versions of the first peace treaty between Israel and an Arab country.

President Carter, who was credited by both leaders for having made the agreement possible, signed, as a witness, for the United States. In a somber speech he said, "Peace has come."

'The First Step of Peace'

"We have won, at last, the first step of peace—a first step on a long and difficult road," he added.

Later, at a state dinner, Mr. Begin suggested that Mr. Carter be given the Nobel Peace Prize, and Mr. Sadat agreed.

At the signing ceremony, all three leaders offered prayers that the treaty would bring true peace to the Middle East and end the enmity that has erupted into war four times since Israel declared its independence on May 14, 1948.

By coincidence, they all referred to the words of the Prophet Isaiah.

"Let us work together until the day comes when they beat their swords into plowshares and their spears into pruning hooks," Mr. Sadat said in his paraphrase of the biblical text.

'No More War,' Begin Says

Mr. Begin, who gave the longest and most emotional of the addresses, exclaimed: "No more war, no more bloodshed, no more bereavement, peace unto you, shalom, saalam, forever."

"Shalom" and "salaam" are the Hebrew and Arabic words for "peace."

The Israeli leader, noted for oratorical skill, provided a dash of humor when in the course of his speech he seconded Mr. Sadat's remark that Mr. Carter was "the unknown soldier of the peacemaking effort." Mr. Begin said, pausing, "I agree, but as usual with an amendment"—that Mr. Carter was not completely unknown and that his peace effort would "be remembered and recorded by generations to come."

Since Mr. Begin was known through the negotiations as a stickler for details, much to the American side's annoyance, Mr. Carter seemed to explode with laughter at Mr. Begin's reference to "an amendment."

Minutes later, Mr. Begin was deeply somber as he put on the Jewish skull cap and quoted in Hebrew from Psalm 126.

The signing was followed by an outdoor dinner on the South Lawn at the White House for 1,300 guests.

The treaty was the result of months of grueling, often frustrating negotiations that finally were concluded early this morning when a final compromise was reached on the last remaining issue—a timetable for Israel to give up Sinai oilfields.

Under the treaty, Israel will withdraw its military forces and civilians from the Sinai Peninsula in stages over three years. Two-thirds of the area will be returned within nine months, after formal ratification documents are exchanged. The ratification process is expected to begin in about two weeks.

In return for Israel's withdrawal, Egypt has agreed to end the state of war and to establish peace. After the initial nine-month withdrawal is completed, Egypt and Israel will establish "normal and friendly relations" in many fields, including diplomatic, cultural and economic relations.

Breakthrough at Camp David

The outline for the peace treaty was achieved in September when Mr. Carter, Mr. Sadat and Mr. Begin met at Camp David, Md., for 13 days. In addition to the treaty, they also agreed on the framework for an accord to provide self-rule to the more than one million Palestinians living in the Israeli-occupied areas of the West Bank of the Jordan and the Gaza Strip.

The Camp David accords were opposed by most countries in the Arab world for two reasons. The Arabs regarded the decision by Mr. Sadat to sign a peace treaty with Israel as a betrayal of the Arab cause, since it suggested that Egypt would no longer be willing to go to war against Israel to help Syria, Jordan, and the Palestinians regain territory.

Arabs also viewed the self-rule agreement for Palestinians as insufficient because it did not guarantee the creation of a Palestinian state.

As a result of that opposition, today's signing was greeted by criticism throughout the Arab world. Echoes of that were heard in Washington, where about a thousand Arabs demonstrated in Lafayette Park, several hundred yards from the signing ceremony. Their anti-Sadat chants could be heard at the White House.

"We must not minimize the obstacles that still lie ahead," Mr. Carter said. "Differences still separate the signatories to this treaty from each other and also from some of their neighbors who fear what they have just done.

"To overcome these differences, to dispel those fears, we must rededicate ourselves to the goal of a broader peace with justice for all who have lived in a state of conflict in the Middle East.

"We have no illusions—we have hopes, dreams, prayers, yes—but no illusions."

"Radiation Is Released in Accident at Nuclear Plant in Pennsylvania," March 29, 1979, and "The Credibility Meltdown," March 30, 1979

An accident at the Three Mile Island nuclear power plant near Harrisburg, Pennsylvania, in 1979 sparked national fears about radiation contamination. Proponents of nuclear energy subsequently faced a stiff uphill battle in the United States. *The Times* wrote in an editorial following the accident that "advocates of nuclear energy can be their own worst enemies" in explaining the risks and benefits of this energy supply.

MARCH 29, 1979
RADIATION IS RELEASED IN ACCIDENT AT NUCLEAR PLANT IN PENNSYLVANIA

By DONALD JANSON

Special to The New York Times

MIDDLETOWN, Pa., Thursday, March 29—An accident at a three-month-old nuclear power plant released above-normal levels of radiation into the central Pennsylvania countryside early yesterday.

By last night, officials of the Nuclear Regulatory Commission had still not determined the full extent of the radiation danger, but they said the amount of radiation that escaped was no threat to people in the area. Major amounts were released into the building housing the reactor, but workers were not believed to have been endangered.

Still, the accident at the Three Mile Island Nuclear Power Plant, on an island in the Susquehanna River about 11 miles south of Harrisburg, was described as the worst ever at an American nuclear generating plant.

The precise cause of the accident was not determined. A Federal nuclear expert suggested last night that it stemmed from problems with filters in the plant.

Officials of the Nuclear Regulatory Commission said radiation outside the plant was far less than that produced by diagnostic X-Rays.

Some of the 60 employees on duty were contaminated, a plant spokesman said, but they did not require hospitalization. And the 15,000 people living within a mile of the plant were not evacuated, although a "general emergency" was declared.

The commission said that "low levels of radiation" had been measured up to a mile from the plant and that traces had been found in the air up to 16 miles away. The amount in the immediate area was described as above normal for the plant site but below what is considered dangerous to health.

MARCH 30, 1979
EDITORIAL
THE CREDIBILITY MELTDOWN

Halfway through "The China Syndrome," a new movie about a nuclear power plant accident, a utility company engineer insists that what the accident demonstrated is that "even with a stuck valve, that . . . system . . . works!" Yesterday, a nuclear industry spokesman was talking about the accident at the Three Mile Island plant near Harrisburg, Pa. "The system worked," he said. "The system shut down."

We do not mean to imply any larger parallel here. The movie involves an improbable amalgam of events, and not

enough is yet known about the Harrisburg case to permit informed reflection. But this rhetorical parallel suggests that advocates of nuclear energy can be their own worst enemies.

For years, the industry and its supporters in Government and elsewhere have insisted that nuclear energy is safe. Relatively speaking, they are right. But under the pressure of emotional protests, the nuclear spokesmen have gone further. Nuclear power, they have proclaimed, is

The Answer; it is not just reasonably safe but comfortingly so; a serious accident is a million-to-one shot.

Then what are people to think when a Three Mile Island comes along? This event may turn out to be not so serious, but when safety is oversold, even the smallest accident delivers an exaggerated blow to industry credibility. As a result, a public that has been educated to think that there are virtually no risks involved in the use of nuclear energy will find it that much harder to take reasonable ones in its pursuit.

Exaggerated safety claims may create another, more important effect. They may reduce the incentive of nuclear companies, with huge plant investment, to improve safety, either by encouraging technical innovation or by improving training for control-room personnel. Why spend more when there is already such reassuring "defense in depth"?

The public needs nuclear energy; but it also needs a realistic assessment of safety and risk.

Credibility was not enhanced by the public statements after the Three Mile Island accident. Was it a little leak, a bigger leak—or a general emergency? The reactor's operators said one thing, state officials another, Federal officials yet another, not to mention the contributions of equipment manufacturers and politicians. Are there grounds for continuing concern? Who is to be believed? The profusion of explanations and of contradictory statements has meant troubling confusion.

Whenever there is an airline accident, the National Transportation Safety Board dispatches a "go" team of investigators to the scene. It includes an experienced information official who receives, verifies and dispenses details from a command post. Authorities have recommended the use of a similar device in the event of urban riots and assassinations. While all involved would remain free to say whatever they wished, the idea of an information center is worth considering for nuclear accidents. The potential for public alarm is great; so is the potential for genuine service.

- -

"Speech Lifts Carter Rating to 37%," July 18, 1979

With public confidence low in the summer of 1979 due to high prices and unemployment, Carter gave a major address to the nation to improve morale. His popularity ratings jumped from 26 percent to 37 percent after the speech, but the president's subsequent decision to request the resignation of his entire cabinet, which resulted in the dismissal of five officials, did not build public confidence in his management of his administration.

JULY 18, 1979
SPEECH LIFTS CARTER RATING TO 37%; PUBLIC AGREES ON CONFIDENCE CRISIS
By ADAM CLYMER

President Carter has received a sharp increase in approval from a public that overwhelmingly agrees with his warning Sunday night that the nation faces a "crisis of confidence," according to the New York Times/CBS News Poll.

But the 37 percent approval of his handling of the job of President that was recorded Monday night, as against 26 percent last week, still left him in a deeply vulnerable position. Moreover, his previous gains in public opinion have proved short-lived.

Mr. Carter found some response to his insistence, Sunday night and again Monday, that "the energy crisis is real," a belief that he feels the public must accept before it can meet the problem. The percentage of respondents who said that they believed the crisis was real rose to 35 from 26. But the number who did not believe this remained a majority, falling only to 53 percent from 66.

Plainly, the public accepted Mr. Carter's stress on a "crisis of confidence." Sunday night he said that one warning presented to him as he prepared his speech was this one: "Mr. President, we are confronted with a moral and a spiritual crisis." He then called it a "crisis of confidence" and hammered at that theme, using the word "crisis" seven times and the word "confidence" 15 times in the speech.

Responsive Chord Struck

That he struck a responsive chord was shown when 77 percent of those polled said that they agreed "that there is a moral and spiritual crisis, that is, a crisis of confidence, in the country today." Thirteen percent disagreed. In no demographic group measured in the poll did more than one in five respondents disagree.

John C. White, the Democratic national chairman, said that he thought the poll showed "a pretty good immediate turnaround" for Mr. Carter. "The American people are listening," he said.

Bill Brock, his Republican counterpart, emphasized that more Americans were still negative on Mr. Carter than positive after "his best shot." He said that "the President's problem is that he isn't believable any more" and predicted that his criticisms of a Democratic Congress would limit his ability to score quick legislative successes.

The telephone survey of 895 Americans of voting age found that two out of three said they had watched or heard the Sunday speech, a ratio that would indicate an audience of 100 million. (That figure would not be comparable with the lower numbers indicated by television rating systems, which count an average audience throughout a program and do not include radio listeners.)

But of those who said that they had listened, a group that probably included Americans already somewhat more favorable to Mr. Carter than the average, 42 percent said that they had come away feeling "more confident about the United States." Fifty-three percent said that they still felt "about the same," and 5 percent volunteered the opinion that they were now less confident.

The percentage who approved of Mr. Carter's handling of energy matters rose to 34 percent after the speech, from 16 percent before.

"CARTER TELLS SOVIET TO PULL ITS TROOPS OUT OF AFGHANISTAN," DECEMBER 30, 1979, AND "ARMS PACT OUTLOOK CALLED DIM ANYWAY," JANUARY 4, 1980

The Soviet invasion of Afghanistan in December 1979 destroyed prospects for reducing cold war tensions in the final year of Carter's term. The president responded to the invasion with a warning to Soviet leader Leonid I. Brezhnev of the serious consequences for continued cooperation between the two superpowers. Just weeks after the invasion, the president told the Senate to postpone review of the arms control treaty that he had negotiated with Brezhnev, recognizing that it lacked sufficient support for ratification.

DECEMBER 30, 1979
CARTER TELLS SOVIET TO PULL ITS TROOPS OUT OF AFGHANISTAN

HE WARNS OF 'CONSEQUENCES'

President Sends Note to Brezhnev on Hot Line and Gets Reply—Consults Allied Leaders

By TERENCE SMITH
Special to The New York Times

WASHINGTON, Dec. 29—President Carter, in the toughest diplomatic exchange of his Presidency, has warned the Soviet Union in a special message to withdraw its forces from Afghanistan or face "serious consequences" in its relations with the United States.

The President has received intelligence reports that an additional 15,000 to 20,000 Soviet troops, including an airborne division, have crossed into Afghanistan in the last 24 hours, raising the total of Soviet military personnel in the country to 25,000 or 30,000.

In Islamabad, a high Pakistani official said he had reports that Soviet troops were crossing the Amu Darya River into Afghanistan in "substantial numbers."

The reinforcements were reported heading for Kabul, where a Moscow-backed coup on Thursday led to the overthrow and execution of President Hafizullah Amin and the assumption of power by Babrak Karmal, a Marxist and former Deputy Prime Minister who had been in exile in Eastern Europe.

Luncheon at the White House

Mr. Carter outlined his views of the developments in Afghanistan and Iran at a White House luncheon with a small group of reporters. Under the rules, Mr. Carter could not be quoted directly.

The warning to the Soviet Union about the move into Afghanistan was contained in a strong message to Leonid I. Brezhnev, the Soviet leader, sent yesterday on the hot line installed for emergency communications.

A reply from Moscow came during the luncheon today, but President Carter declined to characterize it. White House officials said that they were assessing whether it called for a new exchange.

In his message, Mr. Carter reportedly warned Mr. Brezhnev that the Soviet actions, "if not corrected, could have very serious consequences to United States-Soviet relations." The message specifically called for a troop withdrawal.

From his subdued but firm remarks at the luncheon, it was clear that Mr. Carter regarded the Soviet intervention in Afghanistan as a provocative act that could threaten other nations in the area, including Iran and Pakistan.

JANUARY 4, 1980
ARMS PACT OUTLOOK CALLED DIM ANYWAY
Carter, by Asking Delay in Debate, Said to Admit Poor Chances
in View of Afghan Events
By CHARLES MOHR
Special to The New York Times

WASHINGTON, Jan. 3—Administration officials and members of Congress said today that President Carter's request to the Senate to delay debate of the nuclear arms treaty with the Soviet Union was an acknowledgment that it no longer had a chance of being approved after the Soviet intervention in Afghanistan.

The sources differed on whether there was a reasonable chance that the treaty could be revived and ratified later.

Even some protreaty senators and staff aides agreed with Senator Bob Dole, Republican of Kansas, who said, "I think that SALT II is dead for 1980." White House officials and other senators who are committed to the treaty expressed hope that it might be possible to take up the treaty this year and win approval.

The disagreement was based in part on differing views of whether the treaty had been moribund before the Afghan events.

President Carter today sent a letter to the Senate majority leader, Robert C. Byrd of West Virginia, asking him to "delay consideration of the SALT II treaty on the Senate floor." The letter, and a White House statement, said the President still believed the treaty was in the national interest. But the statement said that, in light of the present crisis, Mr. Carter believed it was inappropriate to debate the arms treaty at this time.

Senate Democrats Pressed Carter

The Senate's Democratic leadership was reported to have urged the President to request delay of a floor debate. "We wanted to prevent the Republicans from claiming they had forced withdrawal of the treaty," a Democrat said.

Nevertheless Senator Howard H. Baker Jr. of Tennessee, the Senate Republican leader and a Presidential candidate, said at a news conference that the President's statement was "altogether a victory for those of us who would not support the treaty in the first place" and who believed that it should have been conditioned on Soviet behavior.

Senator Baker said the Administration, which had opposed connecting the treaty to Soviet foreign policy, had now "embraced linkage in a lavish way."

Democrats tended to put a simpler construction on the President's decision, suggesting that he had acted not because he wanted to punish the Soviet Union or because he felt the treaty had lost value.

"I am convinced," said Senator Gary Hart, Democrat of Colorado, "the President's decision on SALT does not spring

At Camp David for a briefing on Iran, President Jimmy Carter, right, is accompanied by, left to right, Defense Secretary Harold Brown, Vice President Walter Mondale, and Secretary of State Cyrus Vance.

Source: Jim Wilson for the New York Times

from a lack of confidence in the merits of the treaty, but rather a concern that recent Soviet activities would cause a sufficient number of Senators to reject it at this time."

Debate Now Termed Impractical

A White House official said it was "just not practical" in the present atmosphere to seek approval by 67 senators, the two-thirds needed for approval if all 100 senators voted. The Senate will begin a new session on Jan. 22. The official said it might still be possible to win Senate consent this year.

Senator Byrd said he supported the request for delay, adding "It would not be conducive to the SALT process to bring up the treaty at this time." But he said he continued to believe that the treaty "should be ratified because it is in the security interests of the United States."

Both the President and Senator Byrd stressed that the treaty had not been withdrawn and remained on the Senate's calendar.

Ronald Reagan, the Republican aspirant for the Presidency, said the Afghan crisis had offered President Carter a convenient opportunity to avoid a defeat of the treaty.

Informal polls of uncommitted senators, including one by *The New York Times,* indicated even before the crises in Iran and Afghanistan that there was a serious possibility the treaty might be defeated. By this week there was widespread agreement that, if debated early this year, the treaty would be rejected.

Senator Daniel Patrick Moynihan, Democrat of New York, summed it up by saying that the President's request for delay "is unfortunate, but altogether understandable."

"U.S. Attempt to Rescue Iran Hostages Fails," April 25, 1980

The Carter administration's failed attempt to rescue U.S. hostages in Iran in spring 1980 disappointed the president and the American public. Operation Eagle Claw, as the mission was known, was called off because of what the White House termed "equipment failure," including a helicopter crash with another U.S. aircraft that killed eight soldiers. The failure of Carter's efforts to secure the release of the hostages raised questions about the effectiveness of his foreign policy leadership, and resulted in the resignation of Secretary of State Vance, who had opposed the plan.

APRIL 25, 1980

U.S. ATTEMPT TO RESCUE IRAN HOSTAGES FAILS; 8 DIE AS PLANES COLLIDE DURING WITHDRAWAL

ACCIDENT ON GROUND

No Clashes Occur During Mission in Desert Area, White House Says

By BERNARD GWERTZMAN

Special to The New York Times

WASHINGTON, Friday, April 25—The White House announced early this morning that the United States had attempted to rescue the American hostages in Teheran but that the effort failed and eight American crewmen died in Iran after the attempt was called off.

Giving only few details of the rescue attempt, the White House said that President Carter "has ordered the cancellation of an operation in Iran that was under way to prepare for a rescue of our hostages."

"The mission was terminated because of equipment failure," the White House said in a statement issued at 1 A.M.

"During the subsequent withdrawal, there was a collision between our aircraft on the ground at a remote desert location in Iran," the statement said.

Many Questions Unanswered

It said that there were no hostilities, but that eight crewmen were killed and "others were injured in the accident."

The White House said that the injured were successfully airlifted from Iran and were expected to recover.

The news came suddenly and raised many questions that White House spokesmen were unable to answer. They said that additional details would be provided later today.

It was the first known attempt by the United States to rescue the hostages, who have been in confinement since Nov. 4. The incident raised concern over the well-being of the hostages since the Islamic militants have threatened to kill the Americans if force was attempted to free them.

The White House statement said that the mission "was not motivated by hostility toward Iran or the Iranian people and there were no Iranian casualties."

Talk of Military Action

In the last two weeks Mr. Carter has talked about possible military action against Iran if economic and political sanctions just initiated with the nation's allies failed to achieve results. But Mr. Carter said that he was thinking in terms of moves to block Iran's harbors. In fact, it was reported on Wednesday that Hamilton Jordan, the White House Chief of Staff, had told senior aides at a meeting Tuesday that Mr. Carter had ruled out any rescue attempts as being unworkable.

The White House statement said that President Carter "accepts full responsibility for the decision to attempt the rescue." Anticipating a possible uproar in Iran, a statement said that "the United States continues to hold the Government of Iran responsible for the safety of the American hostages."

"The United States remains determined to obtain their safe release at the earliest possible date," the statement said.

"President Concedes," November 5, 1980

With the economy in disarray and U.S. citizens held hostage abroad, Carter's prospects for reelection in 1980 were bleak. Although preelection polls had predicted a close race, Carter won only six states and the District of Columbia in the Electoral College. The election made U.S. history in several disappointing ways for Carter: *The Times* noted that he was the first elected incumbent president since Herbert Hoover to lose reelection (Gerald Ford had lost his reelection bid, but he was not an elected president). *The Times* also noted that Carter's concession speech was the earliest given by a losing major-party presidential candidate since 1904.

NOVEMBER 5, 1980
PRESIDENT CONCEDES

Republican Gains Victories in All Areas and Vows to Act on Economy

By HEDRICK SMITH

Ronald Wilson Reagan, riding a tide of economic discontent against Jimmy Carter and promising "to put America back to work again," was elected the nation's 40th President yesterday with a sweep of surprising victories in the East, South and the crucial battlegrounds of the Middle West.

At 69 years of age, the former California Governor became the oldest person ever elected to the White House. He built a stunning electoral landslide by taking away Mr. Carter's Southern base, smashing his expected strength in the East, and taking command of the Middle West, which both sides had designated as the main testing ground. The entire West was his, as expected.

Mr. Carter, who labored hard for a comeback reelection victory similar to that of Harry S. Truman in 1948, instead became the first elected incumbent President since Herbert Hoover in 1932 to go down to defeat at the polls.

Concession by Carter

Despite pre-election polls that had forecast a fairly close election, the rout was so pervasive and so quickly apparent that Mr. Carter made the earliest concession statement of a major Presidential candidate since 1904 when Alton B. Parker bowed to Theodore Roosevelt.

At 9:50 P.M., Mr. Carter appeared with his wife, Rosalynn, before supporters at the ballroom of the Sheraton Washington Hotel and disclosed that an hour earlier he had telephoned Mr. Reagan to concede and to pledge cooperation for the transition to new leadership.

"The people of the United States have made their choice and, of course, I accept that decision," he said. "I can't stand here tonight and say it doesn't hurt."

At a celebration in the Century Plaza Hotel in Los Angeles, Mr. Reagan claimed his victory and said: "There's never been a more humbling moment in my life. I give you my sacred oath that I will do my utmost to justify your faith."

With 73 percent of the popular vote counted, Mr. Reagan had 31,404,169 votes, or 50 percent, to 26,295,331, or 42 percent, for Mr. Carter, with John B. Anderson, the independent, drawing 3,862,679, or 6 percent, of the national total.

Mr. Reagan also suggested that enough Congressional candidates might ride the coattails of his broad sweep to give Republicans a chance to "have control of one house of Congress for the first time in a quarter of a century."

The Republicans picked up Senate seats in New Hampshire, Indiana, Washington, Iowa, Alabama, Florida and South Dakota and were leading in Idaho. Going into the election, the Senate had 58 Democrats, 41 Republicans and one independent. The Republicans also appeared likely to gain at least 20 seats in the House, nowhere nearly enough to dislodge the Democratic majority.

In the Presidential race, Mr. Carter managed six victories—in Georgia, Rhode Island, West Virginia, Maryland, Minnesota and the District of Columbia—for 45 electoral votes. But everywhere else the news was bad for him. By early this morning, Mr. Reagan had won 39 states with 444 electoral votes, and more were leaning his way.

In the South, the states of Texas, Florida, Mississippi, Louisiana, Virginia, South Carolina, North Carolina, Tennessee and Kentucky fell to the Reagan forces, an almost total rejection of the President by his home region. In the Middle West, the former California Governor took Ohio, Illinois and Michigan, three states on which Mr. Carter had pinned heavy hopes, as well as most others.

But Mr. Reagan's showing was even more startling in the East. He took New York and Pennsylvania, always vital bases for Democrats, as well as New Jersey, Connecticut and several smaller states.

A New York Times/CBS News poll of more than 10,000 voters as they left the polls indicated that the predominant motivation among voters was the conviction that it was time for a change. The biggest issue in their minds was the nation's economy, especially inflation.

"The Iranian thing reminded people of all their frustration," Robert S. Strauss, the Carter campaign chairman said. "They just poured down on him. I don't think there's anything anyone could have done differently."

"It was really a referendum on leadership," countered Richard Wirthlin, the Reagan pollster. "The Presidential debate did not have a tremendous influence on the vote, but it strengthened Reagan's credibility for taking Carter on as sharply as we did in the last five days and drive home the attack on the economy."

The Times/CBS News survey revealed a general collapse of the traditional coalition that has elected Democratic Presidents since the New Deal. It showed Mr. Carter running behind his 1976 performance not only in the South but also among such groups as blue-collar workers, Roman Catholics and Jews.

THE PRESIDENCY OF RONALD REAGAN

JANUARY 20, 1981 – JANUARY 20, 1989

The presidency of Ronald Wilson Reagan marked a turning point in American and international politics. Reagan won election overwhelmingly in 1980 with the support of many Democratic voters who became known as Reagan Democrats. As president, Reagan endorsed a program of tax cuts to stimulate economic growth, which some people credited with spurring the financial boom of the 1980s, and others blamed for creating massive budget deficits and tripling the national debt. In foreign policy, Reagan increased defense spending in his first term to strengthen the U.S. position in the cold war, but in his second term he held an unprecedented four summit meetings with Soviet leader Mikhail S. Gorbachev; these meetings were instrumental in bringing the superpower conflict to a peaceful end. The legacy of Reagan's leadership in domestic and foreign affairs continues to be debated today.

Source: Courtesy of the Kentucky Library and Museum, WKU

The younger son of an alcoholic shoe salesman, Reagan grew up in Dixon, Illinois. He played football and worked as a lifeguard during high school and college vacations and won a football scholarship to Eureka College, where he also was a varsity swimmer and member of the drama club. He was elected senior class president and graduated with a degree in economics and sociology.

After completing college, Reagan began work as a radio sports announcer in Iowa, skillfully describing games even when he was not viewing them firsthand. The popular reception to his engaging reports encouraged Reagan to pursue a career in Hollywood. He joined Warner Brothers studio in 1937 and made several movies in the next decade. During World War II he was commissioned as an army officer to make training films in Los Angeles. After the war, Reagan became

president of the Screen Actors Guild, leading the film actors' union through a highly contentious period in American politics. When many people in Hollywood were accused of having Communist Party ties, Reagan testified before the House Committee on Un-American Activities and supported studio blacklists of alleged Communists.

Reagan was a lifelong Democrat who voted for Franklin D. Roosevelt four times, but his political views changed after the war, and he switched his party affiliation to Republican. In 1954 he became a television show host and a spokesperson for General Electric, promoting capitalism and limited government. He gained prominence in the Republican Party when he campaigned for presidential candidate Barry Goldwater in 1964. Reagan won the California governor's race two years later. He briefly competed for the party's presidential nomination in 1968, but he undertook a more intensive campaign after deciding not to seek a third term as governor in 1974. He

QUICK FACTS ON RONALD REAGAN

BIRTH	February 6, 1911, Tampico, Ill.
EDUCATION	Eureka College, Ill., B.A., 1932
FAMILY	First wife: Jane Wyman Reagan (born Sarah Jane Fulks); divorced from Reagan in 1938 Children: Maureen Elizabeth Reagan, Michael Edward Reagan Second wife: Nancy Davis Reagan (born Anne Frances Robbins); married Reagan in 1952 Children: Patricia Ann Reagan, Ronald Prescott Reagan
WHITE HOUSE PETS	Dogs
PARTY	Republican
PREPRESIDENTIAL CAREER (SELECTED)	Sports announcer, 1932–1937 Begins acting career with Warner Brothers Studios, 1937 U.S. Army; makes training films in World War II, 1942–1945 Honorable discharge with rank of captain, 1945 Corporate spokesman for General Electric Company, 1945–1962 Board of directors, Screen Actors Guild, 1946–1952 President of Screen Actors Guild, 1947–1960 Switches from Democratic to Republican Party, 1962 Television host and performer, 1962–1965 Campaigns for Republican presidential candidate Barry Goldwater, 1964 California governor, 1967–1975 Unsuccessful candidate for Republican presidential nomination, 1968, 1976
PRESIDENTIAL TERMS	January 20, 1981–January 20, 1985 January 20, 1985–January 20, 1989
VICE PRESIDENT	George H. W. Bush
SELECTED EVENTS	Shot by would-be assassin (1981) Enactment of tax cut legislation (1981) Dismissal of striking air traffic controllers (1981)

waged a strong battle against incumbent president Gerald R. Ford for the Republican nomination in 1976, and, although he did not prevail, he emerged as the party's top contender for the next race after Ford lost the general election to Jimmy Carter.

THE 1980 PRESIDENTIAL ELECTION

In the campaign for the Republican Party's presidential nomination in 1980, Reagan faced some early competition but ultimately won his party's endorsement. He lost the Iowa caucus to George H. W. Bush of Texas, whom he would later select as

his running mate. Reagan gained visibility during a confrontation over who would participate in a Republican debate in New Hampshire, in which the moderator tried to have Reagan's microphone turned off and a visibly angry Reagan declared, "I am paying for this microphone!" News coverage focused on this incident and the image of Reagan as strong and determined resonated with voters. He won the New Hampshire primary and eventually the Republican nomination.

The general election was a three-way race among Reagan, President Carter, and Independent Party candidate John B. Anderson of Illinois. In a preelection debate, Carter tried to

Appoints first woman, Sandra Day O'Connor, to U.S. Supreme Court (1981)

Addresses both houses of Parliament in Great Britain (first U.S. president to do so); defends Britain's actions against Argentina in Falklands Islands conflict (1982)

Proposal for Strategic Defense Initiative (1983)

Headquarters for U.S. Marine forces in Beirut, Lebanon, blown up by suicide bomber (1983)

U.S. invasion of Grenada (1983)

Deployment of U.S. ground-based cruise missiles in England (1983)

Attends wreath-laying ceremony at Bitburg military cemetery, West Germany, where Nazis are buried with soldiers (1985)

Removal of malignant colon polyp (1985)

Summit meeting with Soviet leader Mikhail S. Gorbachev, Geneva, Switzerland (1985)

Explosion of space shuttle *Challenger* (1986)

U.S. air strikes against Libya (1986)

Tax Reform Act (1986)

Summit meeting with Gorbachev, Reykjavik, Iceland (1986)

Immigration Reform and Control Act (1986)

News of covert Iran-contra arms deal for hostages program revealed (1986)

U.S. protects Kuwaiti tankers in Persian Gulf (1987)

Congressional hearings on Iran-contra affair (1987)

Stock market crash (1987)

Summit meeting with Gorbachev, Washington, D.C., to sign Intermediate-Range Nuclear Forces (INF) Treaty (1987)

Indictment of Panamanian leader Gen. Manuel Noriega (1988)

Summit meeting with Gorbachev, Moscow (1988)

U.S. warship accidentally shoots down Iranian jetliner, killing all 290 passengers (1988)

Palestinian Liberation Organization (PLO) recognizes Israel, and State Department ends a thirteen-year ban on contact with group (1988)

POSTPRESIDENCY

Announcement of Alzheimer's disease, 1994

Congressional Gold Medal recipient (with Nancy Reagan), 2002

DEATH

June 5, 2004, Los Angeles, Calif.

---

make an issue of Reagan's opposition to increases in Social Security and Medicare as governor, but Reagan dismissed the points with the disarming statement, "There you go again." Voter dissatisfaction with the economy and the continuing U.S. hostage crisis in Iran resulted in a severe loss for Carter, who won just 49 Electoral College votes to Reagan's 489, and about 35.5 million popular votes to Reagan's nearly 44 million.

THE REAGAN ADMINISTRATION (FIRST TERM)

Reagan's thirteen-member cabinet included several longtime associates from California, including Caspar W. Weinberger as defense secretary and William F. Smith as attorney general. Alexander M. Haig Jr. of Connecticut served briefly as secretary of state, until George P. Shultz of California replaced him in 1982. Donald T. Regan of New Jersey became treasury secretary. Reagan also appointed two women to his cabinet in 1983: Margaret Heckler of Massachusetts became health and human services secretary, and Elizabeth H. Dole of Washington, D.C., became transportation secretary. Reagan's cabinet also included one African American member, Samuel R. Pierce Jr. of New York, who headed the Department of Housing and Urban Development and was the only secretary to serve through both of Reagan's terms.

First Lady Nancy Reagan was her husband's fierce protector and closest confidante. She insisted that the president's advisers not overload his schedule, and she made sure he had sufficient time for rest despite the grueling responsibilities of the Oval Office. As first lady, Nancy Reagan campaigned actively against illegal drug use, making popular the slogan "Just Say No." Nancy Reagan was a former actress who met her husband in Hollywood, where they starred together in one film. They had two children, Patricia and Ronald, both of whom were adults when their father became president. The first divorced president, Reagan also had two children from his marriage to actress Jane Wyman.

Major Issues (First Term)

Reagan's first inauguration was historic in many ways. In the first illustration of his administration's attention to symbolic communication, the swearing-in took place on the West Front of the Capitol, from where the Washington Monument, Jefferson Memorial, and Lincoln Memorial can be seen. U.S. hostages in Iran were formally released following Reagan's inauguration, after having been held captive for 444 days. Reagan made several notable statements in his inaugural address laying out his vision for the nation. He declared that "government is not the solution to our problem; government is the problem." Reagan also turned seventy just weeks after his inauguration, making him the oldest president of the United States.

The Reagan administration faced its most severe challenge in its first hundred days, when John Hinckley Jr. shot the president as he was leaving the Washington Hilton Hotel after giving a speech. One bullet struck Reagan in the chest, lodging in his left lung. Hinckley also wounded a police officer, a Secret Service agent, and press secretary James Brady, who was shot in the head. Doctors successfully removed the bullet. Reagan was the first sitting president to be shot by an assailant and survive.

The assassination attempt did not derail Reagan's policy agenda. He successfully enacted two pillars of his campaign agenda, tax cuts and increased defense spending, in his first year in office. Reagan advocated a concept known as supply-side economics, which held that tax cuts would boost economic prosperity, increase tax revenues to the government, and result in lower budget deficits. An economic recession stalled these plans and increased unemployment, but the economy began to recover in 1983, though budget deficits also increased. Reagan demonstrated decisive leadership in insisting that striking air traffic controllers return to their posts in summer 1981 and then firing them when they did not comply.

In foreign policy, the strained cold war tensions between the United States and Soviet Union continued in Reagan's first term, due partly to the president's firm anti-Communist stance and determination to improve American defenses, and partly to several changes in Soviet leadership. In the Middle East, the United States faced a major disaster in 1983 when a suicide bomber drove a truck carrying explosives into Marine headquarters in Beirut, Lebanon, killing 241 American soldiers. The troops were part of an international peacekeeping force that had been stationed there for more than a year. Soon after the attack, Reagan successfully overturned a Marxist revolutionary government in the Caribbean island of Grenada by sending U.S. troops to overthrow the military leaders, who had seized power after executing the prime minister.

The 1984 Presidential Election

With a strong economy and increased public confidence in American national security, Reagan coasted to reelection in 1984. Democratic challenger and former vice president Walter F. Mondale of Minnesota tried to make an issue of Reagan's age, but the president cleverly halted this effort by declaring in a general election debate: "I will not make age an issue of this campaign. I am not going to exploit, for political purposes, my opponent's youth and inexperience." In a landslide victory, Reagan won 49 states and 525 votes in the Electoral College, leaving Mondale with only his home state of Minnesota and Washington, D.C., which together amounted to only 13 Electoral College votes. The most significant aspect of the Democratic campaign was the party's nomination of its first female vice-presidential candidate, Geraldine A. Ferraro of New York.

The Reagan Administration (Second Term)

President Reagan moved some of his White House assistants into his cabinet in his second term. Treasury Secretary Regan switched positions with the president's chief of staff, James A. Baker III of Texas. Reagan's longtime aide from California, Edwin Meese III, had served as counselor to the president in the first term, and he became attorney general in 1985. Frank C. Carlucci III of Pennsylvania became defense secretary in late 1987 after Weinberger stepped down. Secretary of State Shultz served through Reagan's second term and played a significant role in the president's diplomatic initiatives toward the Soviet Union. In late 1987 Reagan appointed Ann D. McLaughlin of New Jersey to head the Department of Labor.

The president had perhaps the greatest turnover in the post of national security adviser, as six people held the position over eight years, including Carlucci before he became defense secretary, and then Lt. Gen. Colin Powell, who previously had been Carlucci's deputy.

Major Issues (Second Term)

In his second term, Reagan faced some criticism for his economic policies because of the growth in federal budget deficits and the national debt, which increased from about $1 trillion to $3 trillion during his administration. To contain expenditures, Reagan approved a bill, known informally as the Gramm-Rudman-Hollings act for its sponsoring senators, that required mandatory spending cuts if Congress and the president did not achieve deficit reduction. But these cuts proved less popular in practice than in theory and eventually were repealed. Reagan did succeed in enacting major tax reform in 1986, which lowered the top personal income tax rate (a priority for Reagan since his Hollywood days) as well as some corporate levies, while increasing capital gains taxes.

Perhaps Reagan's most significant second-term legacy is his diplomacy with the Soviet Union. Three elderly Soviet leaders had died in office during Reagan's first term, but in 1985 the more youthful Mikhail Gorbachev became general secretary, and the two leaders held four major summit meetings. An introductory meeting in Geneva, Switzerland, was followed by a session in Reykjavik, Iceland, where the two sides came close to agreeing to abolish all nuclear weapons. This dramatic proposal failed, however, when Gorbachev insisted that plans for the Strategic Defense Initiative, dubbed "Star Wars," to produce a missile shield to protect the United States from nuclear attack be confined to laboratory testing, and Reagan refused. But the two countries did sign the Intermediate-Range Nuclear Forces Treaty in Washington, D.C., in 1987, which reduced each side's nuclear forces. Reagan also did not hesitate to authorize air strikes against Libya in 1986 in retaliation for its role in bombing a German nightclub, which killed U.S. soldiers.

Reagan's foreign policy legacy is marred, however, by the Iran-contra scandal. Although the administration publicly stated that it would not trade arms for U.S. hostages held in the Middle East, it covertly approved arms sales to Iran to spur the release of hostages in Lebanon. Furthermore, funds from these sales were secretly diverted to assist contra rebels in Nicaragua, in violation of a congressional ban on such assistance. The National Security Council oversaw these covert programs, and when they became public in late 1986, some of Reagan's top advisers were forced to resign. Reagan created the Tower Commission (named after the Texas senator who chaired it) to examine how these covert operations unfolded, and the resulting report found fault with the president's detached management style. Although the scandal cast a shadow over Reagan's record in foreign affairs, his popularity ratings remained high, and he was one of the few two-term presidents whose vice president would subsequently win election and continue his policies.

His second term concluded, the Reagans returned to Bel Air, California, and the former president retired from politics. In 1994 he announced to the public that he suffered from Alzheimer's disease, and his memory steadily deteriorated in the following years. Reagan died in Los Angeles on June 5, 2004.

"Reagan Wins Nomination and Chooses Bush as Running Mate after Talks with Ford Fail," July 17, 1980

Reagan's victory in winning the Republican nomination came as no surprise at the party convention in 1980, but his choice for vice-presidential running mate did. Former president Gerald R. Ford, whom Reagan had unsuccessfully contested for the nomination in 1976, was considered for the spot, but negotiations between the two sides faltered over Ford's vision of a virtual co-presidency. Instead, Reagan decided to invite former U.S. representative George H. W. Bush, who had competed against him in the party's initial nominating contests just a few months earlier. Bush had famously criticized Reagan's budget plan as "voodoo economics," but when he joined the ticket, he became a strong supporter of this agenda.

JULY 17, 1980
REAGAN WINS NOMINATION AND CHOOSES BUSH AS RUNNING MATE AFTER TALKS WITH FORD FAIL
DRAMATIC ABOUT-FACE

Till Last Minute Delegates Expected Ex-President to Take No. 2 Spot

By HEDRICK SMITH

Special to The New York Times

DETROIT, Thursday July 17—A jubilant Republican Party formally proclaimed Ronald Reagan as its nominee last night and then heard this morning, after one of the most dramatic about-faces of recent convention politics, that George Bush would be his Vice-Presidential running mate.

Up until the last moment, the delegates had been expecting that former President Gerald R. Ford would bow to Mr. Reagan's entreaties to join the ticket. But Mr. Reagan broke precedent by going to the hall himself to announce that Mr. Ford had declined and that he had chosen Mr. Bush, the former Texas Congressman who had been his most dogged rival in the primaries.

After 24 hours of negotiations with Mr. Ford over the possible conditions of his serving as Vice President in a Reagan administration, Mr. Reagan told the national convention that the two men had "gone over this and over this and over this and he and I have come to the conclusion, and he believes deeply that he can be of more value as the former President, campaigning his heart out, as he has promised to do, and not as a member of the ticket."

Announcement by Reagan

Then very quickly, and with a taut smile on his face, Mr. Reagan announced that he had chosen Mr. Bush as his running mate, "a man we all know and a man who was a candidate, a man who has great experience in government, and a man who told me that he can enthusiastically support the platform across the board."

Although many had said that the only item of suspense in the Republican convention would be Mr. Reagan's choice of a running mate, none had expected it to unfold so unpredictably as in the 24 hours before Mr. Reagan announced his choice of Mr. Bush.

Inside the convention hall, it was a day of personal but predicted triumph for Mr. Reagan. For he finally claimed the Presidential nomination that he had sought first in 1968 and again unsuccessfully in 1976 before routing all his adversaries this year and winning an overwhelming triumph and, ultimately, nomination.

* *

"REAGAN POLLSTER SAYS CARTER'S LEADERSHIP WAS KEY ISSUE," NOVEMBER 6, 1980

Although polls had indicated a tight race between incumbent president Carter and Republican challenger Reagan, the tide turned in Reagan's favor just days before the election at the only campaign debate between the two candidates. (Reagan had participated in a previous debate with Independent Party candidate John Anderson, but Carter refused to attend because Anderson was included.) Carter was viewed as simplistic and naïve when he said he had discussed nuclear weapons policy with his twelve-year-old daughter, and Reagan confidently made his case for strengthening U.S. defenses. Reagan defeated Carter by nearly ten percentage points in the popular vote, and he won handily in the Electoral College as well. His popularity brought success in Congress as well, where the Republican Party also won a majority in the U.S. Senate for the first time since 1954.

NOVEMBER 6, 1980
REAGAN POLLSTER SAYS CARTER'S LEADERSHIP WAS KEY ISSUE
Special to The New York Times

LOS ANGELES, Nov. 5—Ronald Reagan won the Presidential election because he turned it into a referendum on President Carter's leadership, after first successfully combating public doubts about his own abilities, Mr. Reagan's campaign strategist and pollster said in a news conference here today.

Later, in a gloomy corridor outside the ballroom where Mr. Reagan last night celebrated his victory, Richard Wirthlin opened the black vinyl notebook he carried throughout the campaign and produced poll figures that tracked a steady expansion of Mr. Reagan's support from a dead heat in early October to a lead of 5 percentage points in mid-month to an 11-point margin the day before the election.

Mr. Wirthlin cited the figures as a vindication of his strategy, which was sharply questioned by other Reagan advisors at critical points in the campaign. The strategy called for a patient effort to advertise Mr. Reagan's record as Governor of California before mounting a final assault on Mr. Carter's competence in the election's "peak week."

"It's like a boxer getting ready to throw a punch," said Mr. Wirthlin. "You've got to have source credibility before you can make your attack effective, and we just didn't have that base until the second week in October, and then we swung quickly and hit something."

In the news conference and in interviews here, Mr. Wirthlin, who once headed the economics department at Brigham Young University, sought to explain the mechanics of Mr. Reagan's massive victory. He asserted the victor's prerogative of questioning the conclusions of the rival pollster who he is expected to replace as the White House guru on public opinion.

"I differ sharply," Mr. Wirthlin said when asked about the contention of Patrick Caddell, Mr. Carter's pollster, that the race was even until a "massive erosion," partly caused by the flurry of news about the American hostages in Iran, set in Sunday night and Monday.

- -

"A HOPEFUL PROLOGUE, A PLEDGE OF ACTION," JANUARY 21, 1981

Reagan's first inaugural address signaled the new president's political philosophy and his personality. He criticized the size of the national government and proclaimed that economic strength would be restored through returning power to the states. He confidently declared that people should renew their faith in American glory, and that the United States would without a doubt prevail in confronting its challenges. The president's jaunty optimism seemed almost prophetic when American hostages in Iran were released just moments after his inauguration, presenting, as *The New York Times* wrote, "a hopeful prologue" for the new administration.

JANUARY 21, 1981
A HOPEFUL PROLOGUE, A PLEDGE OF ACTION
News Analysis
By HEDRICK SMITH
SPECIAL TO THE NEW YORK TIMES

For a President who has promised Americans a new beginning, an era of national renewal at home and restored strength and stature abroad, the release of the American hostages in Iran was exquisitely timed.

The extraordinary deadline diplomacy that put the 52 captured Americans into the air over Iran minutes after the howitzers thundered a new leader into office provided a graceful exit for Jimmy Carter, a hopeful prologue for

Ronald Reagan and relief for a nation weary from 14 months of humiliation and seeming impotence.

Almost unavoidably the human drama in Iran overshadowed an Inaugural Address that was less an inspirational call to national greatness than a plain-spoken charter of Mr. Reagan's conservative creed, less a sermon than a stump speech, less a rallying cry than a ringing denunciation of overgrown government and a practical pledge to get down to the business of trimming it at once.

For all the new President's vaunted reputation as one of the nation's most polished political orators, his Inaugural Address offered surprisingly few rhetorical flourishes beyond the populist tribute to ordinary Americans that "those who say that we are in a time when there are no heroes, they just don't know where to look."

Although Mr. Reagan made no direct mention of the hostages, their release was on everyone's lips. Moments before Mr. Reagan took his oath of office, word that the hostages were about to be flown out of Iran swept through the crowd stretched out before the Capitol, and though that news was premature, it provided the perfect symbolic backdrop for Mr. Reagan's political objectives.

In political terms, the hostage release enabled Mr. Reagan to enter the White House in a glow of good feeling and tentative optimism rather than embarking on his term burdened by a festering diplomatic stalemate that had soured the public mood and that would have tied him down abroad when his first priority was to minister to the domestic economy.

"It's dramatically upbeat," said Senator Paul Laxalt of Nevada, one of Mr. Reagan's closest political friends. "Everybody feels good about it. It clears the air. It sweeps away something that would have been very distracting from all that we want to do. It's an excellent beginning for Ronald Reagan and a good farewell for Jimmy Carter."

In diplomatic terms, the return of the hostages to freedom and family liberated American diplomacy from a political impediment that had constantly crippled the pursuit of America's vital interests in one of the world's most critical regions. "It lifts a millstone from around our neck," said a departing Democrat.

For Jimmy Carter, the elaborate arrangements so dramatically, though frustratingly, concluded in the final moments of his Presidency closed the most painful and haunting episode of his stewardship, one that some of his aides feel wrecked his chances for reelection. The agreement with Iran wiped a stain from his record and allowed him to nurture the hope that with the perspective of time, the public and history would judge him more kindly.

For the national psyche, there is now relief from the human torment of the hostages and their families and a sense that a certain element of national strength, if not honor, has been redeemed. The emotional excitement of anticipated family reunions has been added to the already festive inaugural party atmosphere of this city.

Yet there is also an uneasy undercurrent of feeling that America has been wronged and that the Iranian militants have paid no price for that, and some grumbling that Mr. Carter was too lenient toward Iran, and had given too much to free the hostages.

"REAGAN WOUNDED IN CHEST BY GUNMAN," MARCH 31, 1981

Two months after his inauguration, Reagan was shot by John W. Hinckley Jr., who later declared that he was trying to impress Hollywood actress Jodie Foster. Hinckley fired six shots at the president. One bullet bounced off the president's limousine, hit Reagan in the chest, and entered his left lung. Reagan's grace under pressure was revealed when he insisted on walking into the hospital before collapsing inside and when he joked to his wife, "Honey, I forgot to duck." His humor extended to the operating room, where he said he hoped the doctors were Republican. Reagan recovered from the assassination attempt, and Hinckley was found not guilty at trial due to insanity, which resulted in his confinement at a psychiatric hospital in Washington, D.C.

MARCH 31, 1981
REAGAN WOUNDED IN CHEST BY GUNMAN; OUTLOOK 'GOOD' AFTER 2-HOUR SURGERY; AIDE AND 2 GUARDS SHOT; SUSPECT HELD

By HOWELL RAINES

SPECIAL TO THE NEW YORK TIMES

President Reagan was shot in the chest today by a gunman, apparently acting alone, as Mr. Reagan walked to his limousine after addressing a labor meeting at the Washington Hilton Hotel. The White House press secretary and two law-enforcement officers were also wounded by a burst of shots.

The President was reported in "good" and "stable" condition tonight at George Washington University Hospital after undergoing two hours of surgery. "The prognosis is excellent," said Dr. Dennis S. O'Leary, dean of clinical affairs at the university. "He is alert and should be able to make decisions by tomorrow."

The hospital spokesman said surgeons removed a .22-caliber bullet that struck Mr. Reagan's seventh rib, penetrating the left lung three inches and collapsing it.

Look of Disbelief

A rapid series of five or six shots rang out at about 2:30 P.M. as Mr. Reagan left the hotel. A look of stunned disbelief swept across the President's face when the shots were fired just after he raised his left arm to wave to the crowd. Nearby, his press secretary, James S. Brady, fell to the sidewalk, critically wounded.

Eyewitnesses said six shots were fired at the Presidential entourage from a distance of about 10 feet. The assailant had positioned himself among the television camera crews and reporters assembled outside a hotel exit.

The authorities arrested a 25-year-old Colorado man, John W. Hinckley Jr., at the scene of the attack. He was later booked on Federal charges of attempting to assassinate the President and assault on a Federal officer.

Within minutes, Americans were witnessing for the second time in a generation television pictures of a chief executive being struck by gunfire during what appeared to be a routine public appearance. For the second time in less than 20 years, too, they watched as the nation's leaders scrambled to meet one of the sternest tests of the democratic system.

Scene of Turmoil

Mr. Reagan, apparently at first unaware that he had been wounded, was shoved forcefully by a Secret Service agent into the Presidential limousine, which sped away with the President in a sitting position in the backseat.

Behind him lay a scene of turmoil. A Secret Service agent writhed in pain on the rain-slick sidewalk. Nearby a District of Columbia plainclothesman had fallen alongside Mr. Brady. The press secretary lay face down, blood from a gushing head wound dripping into a steel grate. A pistol, apparently dropped by one of the security aides, lay near his head.

At the sixth shot, uniformed and plainclothes agents had piled on a blond-haired man in a raincoat, pinning him against a stone wall. "Get him out," a gun-waving officer yelled as the President's limousine sped off. At first, it raced down Connecticut Avenue toward the White House.

Only then, according to some reports, was it discovered that Mr. Reagan was bleeding. The vehicle turned west toward the hospital. Upon learning of the shooting, Vice President Bush returned to the capital from Austin, Tex., where he was to address the Texas Legislature. In Washington, Secretary of State Alexander M. Haig Jr. and other Cabinet officers began gathering in the White House situation room as soon as they learned of the assassination attempt.

At 4:14 P.M., Mr. Haig, in a voice shaking with emotion, told reporters that the Administration's "crisis management" plan was in effect, and citing provisions for Presidential succession, Mr. Haig asserted that he was in charge.

Mr. Reagan's wife, Nancy, and senior White House advisers rushed to the hospital and talked to Mr. Reagan before he entered surgery at about 3:24 P.M. Despite his wound, the 70-year-old President walked into the hospital and seemed determined to assure his wife and colleagues that he would survive.

"Honey, I forgot to duck," Mr. Reagan was quoted as telling his wife. As he was wheeled down a corridor on a hospital cart, he told Senator Paul Laxalt, a political associate, "Don't worry about me." According to Lyn Nofziger, the White House political director, Mr. Reagan winked at James A. Baker 3d, his chief of staff. Then, spying Edwin Meese 3d, the White House counselor, Mr. Reagan quipped, "Who's minding the store?"

'Tell Me You're Republicans'

The operating room was said to be the scene of a bit of the partisan humor favored by the chief executive. Mr. Nofziger said that Mr. Reagan, eyeing the surgeons, said, "Please tell me you're Republicans."

At this point, Mr. Reagan had apparently not been told of the grave wounds to the three men who went down in the spray of bullets aimed at him.

● ●

"Reagan Nominating Woman, an Arizona Appeals Judge, to Serve on Supreme Court," July 8, 1981

Reagan fulfilled a campaign promise and made history in the summer of 1981 when he appointed the first woman to the Supreme Court. Sandra Day O'Connor was a state judge from Arizona who previously had served in the state senate. Five years later, Reagan elevated Justice William Rehnquist to chief justice upon the retirement of Warren Burger, and he selected Antonin Scalia to fill Rehnquist's vacancy. In 1987 Reagan nominated Robert Bork to the Court, but Bork's conservative judicial philosophy sparked widespread protest, and the Senate defeated his nomination. Anthony Kennedy eventually won approval.

JULY 8, 1981
REAGAN NOMINATING WOMAN, AN ARIZONA APPEALS JUDGE, TO SERVE ON SUPREME COURT
BY STEVEN R. WEISMAN

WASHINGTON, July 7—President Reagan announced today that he would nominate Sandra Day O'Connor, a 51-year-old judge on the Arizona Court of Appeals, to the United States Supreme Court. If confirmed, she would become the first woman to serve on the Court.

"She is truly a 'person for all seasons,'" Mr. Reagan said this morning, "possessing those unique qualities of temperament, fairness, intellectual capacity and devotion to the public good which have characterized the 101 'brethren' who have preceded her."

White House and Justice Department officials expressed confidence that Judge O'Connor's views were compatible with those espoused over the years by Mr. Reagan, who has been highly critical of some past Supreme Court decisions on the rights of defendants, busing, abortion and other matters.

Some Quick Opposition

From the initial reaction in the Senate, it appeared her nomination would be approved. However, her record of favoring the proposed Federal equal rights amendment and having sided once against antiabortion interests while she was a legislator provoked immediate opposition to her confirmation by the National Right to Life Committee, Moral Majority and other groups opposed to abortion.

At a brief news conference in Phoenix, Judge O'Connor declined to explain her views, saying that she intended to leave such matters to her confirmation hearings before the Senate Judiciary Committee.

Mr. Reagan, himself an opponent of abortions, said in response to a question that he was "completely satisfied" with her position on that issue.

No Radical Shift Expected

White House officials were hopeful that Judge O'Connor's appointment could be historic not only because she is a woman but also because her presence on the Court, as a replacement for Associate Justice Potter Stewart, who was often a swing vote between ideological camps on the Court, could shift the Court's balance to the right.

● ●

"REAGAN'S 3-YEAR, 25% CUT IN TAX RATE VOTED BY WIDE MARGINS IN THE HOUSE AND SENATE," JULY 30, 1981

The president won enactment of his economic agenda in 1981 with the passage of the Economic Recovery Tax Act. This legislation lowered tax rates and marked a major victory for the administration, which prevailed in Congress with bipartisan support. In endorsing the bill, Reagan declared in a statement quoted by *The Times* that the legislation "has removed one of the most important remaining challenges to our agenda for prosperity."

JULY 30, 1981
REAGAN'S 3-YEAR, 25% CUT IN TAX RATE VOTED BY WIDE MARGINS IN THE HOUSE AND SENATE

By EDWARD COWAN
Special to The New York Times

In a decisive victory for President Reagan, the House of Representatives today approved the Administration's tax cut bill.

The measure provides for three years of reductions totalling 25 percent in individual tax rates and major reductions in taxes paid by business and by oil producers.

The key vote, 238 to 195, gave Mr. Reagan a third upset victory over the Democratic House majority on fiscal issues. The President won by virtue of the same coalition of Republicans and Southern Democrats that brought him victory in May on the budget resolution and in June on the budget reconciliation bill.

The Administration bill adopted by the House was similar to one approved earlier in the afternoon by the Senate, where the Republicans have a majority and the outcome was never in doubt.

Conference Due This Week

The expectation tonight was that a House-Senate conference to reconcile differences would convene tomorrow or Friday and that a single bill could be adopted by both chambers and sent to the President as early as Saturday, or certainly by next week.

In the still-unresolved budget negotiations, House Democrats prepared today to reopen an agreement on $36 billion in cuts so as to restore the monthly minimum Social Security benefit of $122. The minimum had been eliminated during budget-cutting.

Climaxing seven hours of debate, on the tax bill, the House rejected the Democratic measure drafted by the Ways and Means Committee when it voted to adopt instead the Republican substitute drafted by the Administration in

close consultation with House Republicans and Southern Democrats.

Critical Test of Strength

In the vote on the substitute, which was the critical test of strength, 48 Democrats joined 190 Republicans. One Republican, James M. Jeffords of Vermont, voted with 194 Democrats against the Republican substitute.

The House then completed the formality of giving final passage to the Administration bill by a vote of 323 to 107. Shortly before the House voted, the Reagan forces rolled to an 89-to-11 victory in the Senate. There, 37 Democrats voted with 52 Republicans for the bill. One Republican, Charles McC. Mathias Jr. of Maryland, joined 10 Democrats in opposition to the Administration bill, which had been sent to the floor by a 19-to-1 vote of the Senate Finance Committee. President Reagan issued a statement saying: "The victories we have just won do not belong to any one individual, one party or one Administration. It is a victory for all the people. A strong bipartisan coalition in the Congress—Republicans and Democrats together—has virtually assured the first real tax cut in nearly 20 years. It also has removed one of the most important remaining challenges to our agenda for prosperity."

For Representative Dan Rostenkowski, the 11-term Chicago Democrat who became chairman of the tax-writing Ways and Means Committee this year, the House vote marked defeat on his first major test as a committee chairman. Mr. Rostenkowski, who looked glum all day, did not seem to be surprised.

This morning, House Speaker Thomas P. O'Neill Jr. uttered what sounded like a forecast of defeat. He told reporters that President Reagan's televised Monday night speech on taxes had touched off "a telephone blitz like this nation has never seen."

That, the Massachusetts Democrat said, and a Republican "nationwide advertising blitz" had exerted "a devastating effect" on the Democrats. "Once there is slippage, it is hard to hold," Mr. O'Neill added.

Congratulated by Phone

After the House voted, Mr. O'Neill, Mr. Rostenkowski, Representative Thomas S. Foley of Washington, the Demo-

cratic whip, and Jim Wright of Texas, the majority leader, telephoned the President from the Speaker's office, with reporters listening and television cameras present.

"Well, Mr. President, you're tough," Mr. Rostenkowski said. "You beat us. . . . It means you're working at your job." Mr. Rostenkowski, turning to the television cameras, then reminded Mr. Reagan that there would be other struggles between the White House and the Ways and Means Committee. "I know you've got to solve the problem of Social Security," Mr. Rostenkowski said. "It's a big one."

"Controllers Strike, Halting 7,000 Flights; Reagan Gives 48-Hour Notice on Strikers of Dismissal," August 4, 1981

Reagan faced a major test as president when federal air traffic controllers went on strike August 3, 1981, after months of negotiations with the federal government. The air traffic controllers violated a law prohibiting strikes by government unions, and Reagan refused to negotiate with their representatives over an illegal strike. He gave the strikers forty-eight hours to return to work and then followed through on a warning that he would fire those who refused to do so.

AUGUST 4, 1981
CONTROLLERS STRIKE, HALTING 7,000 FLIGHTS; REAGAN GIVES 48-HOUR NOTICE ON STRIKERS OF DISMISSAL
By RICHARD WITKIN
Special to The New York Times

Federal air traffic controllers began an illegal nationwide strike today, grounding about half of the normal 14,200 daily airline flights. President Reagan warned the striking controllers that, if they did not return to work by 11 A.M. Wednesday they would lose their jobs under terms of the law.

Tonight, a Federal judge here found the union in contempt of court for disobeying a back-to-work order. He ordered the controllers to comply tomorrow or face fines of up to $1 million a day. United States District Judge Harold Greene also found the union president, Robert E. Poli, in contempt and ordered him fined $1,000 a day if the union did not end the strike by 8 P.M. tomorrow. Mr. Poli said afterward that the strike would continue.

Pursuing a firm policy, the Administration took steps to remove the union's rights to bargain on behalf of its members and won a court order barring the union from using

any of a $3.5 million fund to make payments to strikers. Mr. Reagan said that the Government would not negotiate during an illegal strike.

On the first day of the walkout it was hard to gauge the degree of delays and disruption of air service. But there were indications that things had gone as well as the Government had hoped, with 50 percent to 60 percent of the normal number of flights operating under the guidance of supervisors and non-strikers.

Stern Stance by Reagan

The situation presented the Reagan Administration with its first confrontation with organized labor and its first domestic crisis, just as Mr. Reagan had developed an aura of success around his handling of the economy and other issues. According to White House officials, the President felt so strongly about the strike that he was firm in his demand for strong action against the strikers, who are demanding increased pay and benefits.

The head of the Federal Aviation Administration, J. Lynn Helms, contended that 22 percent of the nation's 17,000 controllers went to work when the walkout officially began. He said the number was up to 29 percent by early afternoon. Two thousand controllers, about 12 percent of the work force, are not members of the union.

Warning From Union Chief

Just after breaking off negotiations early this morning, Mr. Poli warned the Government not to go ahead with plans to use 2,500 supervisors and military controllers to help operate the air traffic system. He said many of them were unqualified and would raise a "safety hazard." Mr. Helms replied: "It is absolutely not accurate to say this operation is unsafe."

One near-collision, between two DC-9 airliners operated by Air Canada and New York Air, was reported 15,000 feet over northern New Jersey. Norbert Owens, air traffic chief for the aviation agency's Eastern Region, said the New York Air pilot apparently did not hear correctly when he was assigned to 14,000 feet and climbed to the other plane's altitude. The planes passed about one-quarter mile from each other, he said.

At his Rose Garden news conference four hours into the strike, the President noted the laws barring strikes by Federal employees and the oath they took not to walk off their jobs, then added: "It is for this reason that I must tell those who fail to report for duty this morning that they are in violation of the law, and if they do not report for work within 48 hours, they have forfeited their jobs and will be terminated."

Transportation Secretary Drew Lewis, who was at the news conference with the President, said: "I don't care whether it's 9,000 or 12,000 or 100,000—whoever is not at work will be fired."

'There Will Be No Amnesty'

"We're not out to jail anybody," he added. "But we will bring the full force of the Justice Department to bear. There will be no amnesty. I would add, however, that it is not our aim to make criminals, take prisoners, or make martyrs."

The President had sought in vain on the last day of talks yesterday to impress the controllers with the consequences of an illegal walkout. He had relayed word through Mr. Lewis, the chief Government negotiator, that there would be "no amnesty" to relieve controllers of any penalties.

But the warnings failed to deter the union from its conclusion that with the two sides miles apart on proposed contract terms, it had no alternative but to strike. Nor were the controllers moved by warnings from Congress, which would have to provide the funds, that members would be loath to vote money for a union that broke the law.

"Debate over Blame for Recession Blurs Reagan's Economic Record," January 21, 1982

Less than six month after the passage of Reagan's economic plan, a national recession prompted a *Times* article evaluating the president's policy record. It noted that unemployment had increased sharply, as had the federal budget deficit, and the Reagan administration recognized that it would not achieve a campaign promise to balance the budget in its first term. *The Times* summarized Reagan's economic policy as "less government, lower income taxes, less regulation of business, slower expansion of the money supply." The challenge for the president would be whether this agenda ultimately would bring, as *The Times* put it, "a solid economic recovery."

JANUARY 21, 1982
DEBATE OVER BLAME FOR RECESSION BLURS REAGAN'S ECONOMIC RECORD

By EDWARD COWAN

Special to The New York Times

In his first year in office, President Reagan has been remarkably successful in persuading Congress to embrace his economic policy but less successful with the economy itself. This winter the economy is decidedly weaker, and unemployment higher, than the White House forecast a year ago, and the question is whether the strong expansion the Administration predicts for 1982 and beyond will occur despite a continuing tight-money policy.

With the help of a divided Congress, the President has cut the budget and taxes deeply. He has started a sweeping scale-back of Federal regulation of business, and he has encouraged the Federal Reserve's shift to much slower growth of the money supply.

Some Administration officials, notably at the Treasury, feel the Federal Reserve has been erratic in managing the money supply and is partly to blame for the present economic slump. In fact, a debate over monetary policy may be brewing within the Administration.

Whatever the linkage between policy and events, the economy—hammered by the eighth business-cycle recession since World War II—is not going well.

The latest *New York Times*/CBS News Poll shows that the economy's performance has hurt Mr. Reagan politically. His handling of the economy received a 54 percent approval rating last April but only 42 percent early this month, with a larger fraction, 48 percent, disapproving. However, there seems to be a willingness to give the President time; 60 percent of those interviewed said they thought his program would eventually help the economy.

Administration officials contend that Mr. Reagan cannot be fairly blamed for the recession, the second in two years. They argue that its seeds were sown before he took office. But private economists contend that the recession has resulted chiefly from the Federal Reserve's clamp on money and credit, and that the central bank's tight-money policy has essentially been in keeping with Administration strictures about monetary management.

The downward slide in the economy that began in July may be ebbing, as the Administration has forecast. But whether a solid economic recovery will develop before the Congressional elections next November is a worrisome question for the White House and the Republican Party.

> **The essence of the President's economic policy can be stated in a few words: less government, lower income taxes, less regulation of business, slower expansion of the money supply.**

To be sure, there has been a greater slowing of inflation than expected, but other signs are bleak. Industrial production has plunged. Unemployment has climbed rapidly since summer, and this month it may have exceeded the postwar high of 9 percent. Interest rates have come down since summer but are still high, and further declines—although doggedly predicted by Administration officials—are in doubt. The Federal budget deficit for 1982 has ballooned, and the President has been forced to abandon his campaign promise to balance the budget by 1984.

The economy is one reason Democrats no longer worry about losing their 28-year majority in the House and instead predict they will gain 20 seats or so in November.

"We're going to use Reagan's own yardstick—'Are you better off now than you were?'—in the 1982 campaign," says an aide to Speaker Thomas P. O'Neill Jr., referring to a Reagan campaign statement in the 1980 election.

The essence of the President's economic policy can be stated in a few words: less government, lower income taxes, less regulation of business, slower expansion of the money supply.

"Republicans Meet Setbacks in House," November 3, 1982

The Republican Party's loss of more than two dozen House seats in the 1982 congressional midterm elections was a disappointment for the Reagan administration—though certainly not unexpected, as the president's party usually loses seats in nonpresidential federal election years. *The Times* reported that the results "seriously damaged President's Reagan's ability to push his legislative program through Congress." As the nation's economy improved, however, so did Reagan's ability to govern.

NOVEMBER 3, 1982
REPUBLICANS MEET SETBACKS IN HOUSE
By STEVEN V. ROBERTS

Democrats scored major victories in House races yesterday and seriously damaged President Reagan's ability to push his legislative program through Congress.

Late returns indicated that the Democrats might pick up as many as 30 seats, enough to retake effective control of the House from the coalition of Republicans and conservative Democrats that gave Mr. Reagan so many victories in his two years in office.

At the White House, James A. Baker 3d, the President's chief of staff, acknowledged that it would be "tougher" for the Republicans in the House, but he insisted that they could muster majorities for Mr. Reagan's program "from time to time."

Women and Minorities Gain

The new House will contain at least 20 women, 19 blacks, and eight members of Hispanic origin, all new highs for those groups that have been struggling for greater representation on Capitol Hill. However, a black Democrat, Robert Clark, failed in his attempt to become the first black Congressman in Mississippi since Reconstruction.

The House Republican leader, Robert H. Michel, of Illinois barely survived a very strong challenge in his Peoria district, which has been plagued by a slumping economy.

The Democrats' early victories were centered on industrial areas of the Northeast suffering from high unemployment rates, and Southern districts that returned to their traditional Democratic loyalties after a recent flirtation with the Republicans.

In an interview last night, Senator Bob Dole of Kansas said that the Republicans "were really taking a bath" in the House races. Representative Thomas P. O'Neill Jr., the Speaker of the House, called the results "a disastrous defeat for the President" and predicted that many conservative Democrats who sided with Mr. Reagan in the last Congress would now drift back to the party leadership.

"Some of them," he said, "received a message from home that they shouldn't be so strident in supporting the President." Mr. O'Neill suggested that the lame-duck session of Congress that convenes Nov. 29 should immediately take up a $1 billion public works bill to repair the nation's bridges and put thousands of jobless workers on the public payroll. But he insisted that the issue of Social Security should be put over until the new Congress, with its strengthened Democratic membership, opens in January.

"Reagan Denounces Ideology of Soviet as 'Focus of Evil,'" March 9, 1983

President Reagan's description of the Soviet Union as an "evil empire" in March 1983 became one of the most famous phrases of his presidency. In a speech to a group of evangelical Christians, the president cautioned his audience against promoting a nuclear freeze that would hold both the United States and the Soviet Union equally culpable in the cold war. Reagan warned that doing so would "ignore the facts of history and the aggressive impulses of an evil empire."

MARCH 9, 1983
REAGAN DENOUNCES IDEOLOGY OF SOVIET AS 'FOCUS OF EVIL'

By FRANCIS X. CLINES

Special to The New York Times

President Reagan, denouncing Soviet Communism as "the focus of evil in the modern world," today warned Protestant church leaders not to treat the arms race "as a giant misunderstanding and thereby remove yourself from the struggle between right and wrong, good and evil."

Appearing before a convention of evangelical Christians, the President delivered one of the most forceful speeches of his Administration on the subjects of theology and war, morality and government.

In what White House aides privately said was something of a rebuttal to recent criticism of Administration policy by church officials, notably the Roman Catholic hierarchy, Mr. Reagan delighted his audience by declaring:

"In your discussion of the nuclear freeze proposals, I urge you to beware the temptation of pride—the temptation of blithely declaring yourselves above it all and label both sides equally at fault, to ignore the facts of history and the aggressive impulses of an evil empire."

'Very Dangerous Fraud'

In an addition to his prepared text, the President used some of his strongest language in again rejecting as "a very dangerous fraud" calls for a nuclear freeze without additional Soviet arms reductions.

"That is merely the illusion of peace," he said. "The reality is that we must find peace through strength." He continued: "A freeze at current levels of weapons would remove any incentive for the Soviets to negotiate seriously at Geneva and virtually end our chances to achieve the major arms reductions which we have proposed."

* *

"REAGAN HAILS PLAN TO [REFORM] SOCIAL SECURITY," MARCH 26, 1983

As the costs for paying Social Security benefits mounted, Reagan established a presidential commission in his first term to make recommendations for keeping the program solvent. After the bipartisan commission presented its findings, Congress held hearings and enacted legislation to slowly increase the eligibility age for full retirement benefits. It also, *The Times* reported, would "postpone cost-of-living benefit increases, raise payroll taxes, force new Federal workers to join the Social Security System and make benefits of some higher-income retirees subject to Federal income tax."

MARCH 26, 1983
REAGAN HAILS PLAN TO [REFORM] SOCIAL SECURITY

By DAVID SHRIBMAN

Special to The New York Times

President Reagan praised Congress today for passing a plan that he said lifted "a dark cloud" from the Social Security System.

"By working together in our best bipartisan tradition," Mr. Reagan said at a White House news conference, "we have passed reform legislation that brings us much closer to insuring the integrity of the Social Security System."

Mr. Reagan, who is expected to sign the bill the week of April 10, said he was "gratified that great good sense did prevail over partisan concerns."

Later, in a meeting with teen-agers in the Old Executive Office Building, Mr. Reagan suggested that some consideration might be given to restructuring the nation's old-age benefits system.

'Long-Term Look' Suggested

"I'm not sure that we shouldn't take a long-term look at the structure of Social Security with the proviso that those dependent on the program will continue to get their checks, but to go back and look at what's going to happen to you when you get out on the job market," he said.

Congressional approval of the Social Security bill, which would provide the system with $165 billion by the end of the decade, came early this morning, two months after the National Commission on Social Security Reform presented its bipartisan compromise.

After that Presidential commission made its recommendations in January, Congressional committees heard scores of witnesses, fashioned a provision to gradually increase the age at which retirees are eligible for full Social Security benefits, and voted, by a 243-to-102 margin in the House and a 58-to-14 margin in the Senate, to send the bill to Mr. Reagan.

"I've pledged repeatedly that no American who depends on Social Security would ever be denied his or her checks," Mr. Reagan said at his news conference. "But I warned those who were making this issue a political football that the system did have real problems, and that only through hard work—not demagoguery—we would be able to solve them."

Plan Lifts Retirement Age

At his meeting with the high school students, who were brought to the capital in a program providing a weeklong look at the Government, Mr. Reagan said Social Security payroll taxes had grown so much that, for many people, they exceeded the amount of Federal income tax. "I'm not sure that the benefits that you will receive when you come to the point of retiring from the work force will justify the amount of that tax," he said.

The President added: "I don't think there would be anything wrong if we had some solid studies made as to whether we could improve that program for all of you so that it would be more fair for you and for the younger workers in the work force."

A White House spokesman, Anson Franklin, said later that the President "was just expressing his thoughts in answer to a student's question" and that there were no plans for such a study.

The plan Mr. Reagan is to sign next month would postpone cost-of-living benefit increases, raise payroll taxes, force new Federal workers to join the Social Security System and make benefits of some higher-income retirees subject to Federal income taxes.

The bill is designed to assure the system's long-term solvency by gradually raising the retirement age to age 67 by the year 2027.

Sets Medicare Rates

It also establishes standard rates for reimbursement for medical treatment under Medicare, the Federal health program for the elderly. Passed along with the bill was legislation extending Federal supplemental unemployment insurance by as many as 14 weeks in the states with high unemployment.

The Presidential commission's plan formed the foundation for Congressional action. It received wide praise, largely because it spread the burden for saving Social Security to nearly all segments of society, including the system's 36 million beneficiaries.

Several organizations representing Federal workers and older people criticized specific elements of the plan, but few opposed it in its entirety.

"BEIRUT DEATH TOLL AT 161 AMERICANS; FRENCH CASUALTIES RISE IN BOMBINGS; REAGAN INSISTS MARINES WILL REMAIN; BUILDINGS BLASTED," OCTOBER 24, 1983

The suicide bombing attack on U.S. military forces in Beirut, Lebanon, shocked the nation. *The Times* reported that the death toll of 241 American soldiers was the highest in a single attack since the Vietnam War. The troops were part of a multinational peacekeeping force sent to Lebanon following a cease-fire in its civil war. Within months of the attack, Reagan withdrew American soldiers.

OCTOBER 24, 1983
BEIRUT DEATH TOLL AT 161 AMERICANS; FRENCH CASUALTIES RISE IN BOMBINGS; REAGAN INSISTS MARINES WILL REMAIN; BUILDINGS BLASTED

By THOMAS L. FRIEDMAN
Special to The New York Times

A suicide terrorist driving a truck loaded with TNT blew up an American Marine headquarters at the Beirut airport today, killing at least 161 marines and sailors and wounding 75.

In an almost simultaneous attack, another bomb-laden truck slammed into a French paratroop barracks two miles away.

According to Lebanese Civil Defense authorities, at least 27 French paratroopers were killed, 12 were wounded and 53 were reported missing and believed buried in rubble. Official Defense Ministry figures issued in Paris listed 12 French soldiers dead, 13 wounded and 48 missing.

It was the highest number of American military personnel killed in a single attack since the Vietnam War. The identity of the attackers still had not been determined tonight.

Truck Loaded With TNT

According to a Pentagon spokesman, a Mercedes truck filled with some 2,500 pounds of TNT broke through a series of steel fences and sandbag barricades and detonated in the heart of the Marines' administrative headquarters building shortly after dawn. The explosion collapsed all four floors of the building, turning it into a burning mound of broken cement pillars and cinder blocks.

Although a marine sentry was able to fire about five shots at the suicide driver and another marine threw himself in front of the speeding, explosive-filled truck, neither could block its entry into the headquarters building, where it exploded in a fireball that left a crater 30 feet deep and 40 feet wide.

In a haunting scene late tonight, rescue workers using blow torches, pneumatic drills and cranes worked furiously under floodlights to pry out the dead and wounded still crushed beneath the smouldering debris. Marine spokesmen said there might have been as many as 300 men sleeping in the building—which doubled as a bunk house—at the time of the blast.

'Carnage' Like That in Vietnam

"I haven't seen carnage like that since Vietnam," the Marine spokesman, Maj. Robert Jordan, said shortly after emerging from the rescue operation with his forearms smeared with blood.

● ●

"REAGAN TAKING 49 STATES AND 59% OF VOTE, VOWS TO STRESS ARMS TALKS AND ECONOMY," NOVEMBER 8, 1984

Reagan's landslide reelection victory in 1984 illustrated, as The Times wrote, the president's "personal popularity." Reagan won an overwhelming majority in the Electoral College, and he won more than 54 million popular votes (nearly 60 percent of the total) to Walter Mondale's 37 million. Mondale had declared in his campaign that raising taxes was necessary to balance the budget and that he was being honest with the American people in saying so, but this did not help his candidacy. The president's victory, however, did not extend to Congress, where the Republicans lost some Senate seats, but kept their majority, and did not gain as many seats in the House as they had hoped.

NOVEMBER 8, 1984
REAGAN TAKING 49 STATES AND 59% OF VOTE, VOWS TO STRESS ARMS TALKS AND ECONOMY

By HOWELL RAINES

After winning the biggest electoral vote total in the nation's history, President Reagan said yesterday that he regarded his re-election as an endorsement of his economic policies and as an opportunity to press for a fresh start in arms control negotiations with the Soviet Union.

In final returns, the Republican incumbent won 59 percent of the popular vote and carried every state except Minnesota, the home of his opponent, Walter F. Mondale. The Democratic candidate also won the District of Columbia, giving him a total of 13 electoral votes.

Mr. Reagan's total of 525 electoral votes exceeded the 523 won by President Roosevelt over Alf M. Landon in 1936. By carrying 49 states, Mr. Reagan tied another record, set by President Nixon in the 1972 election.

No More Mondale Campaigns

In St. Paul yesterday, Mr. Mondale said he would never again run for office. In a mood of good-humored realism, the 56-year-old former Vice President predicted that his party would never again nominate a Presidential candidate with his admitted weaknesses in communicating by television.

Mr. Reagan, the 17th incumbent President to win election and at 73 the oldest President, marked his victory with a news conference in Los Angeles. He avoided the word "mandate," saying instead that the results "made it very plain that they approved what we've been doing."

Democrats Deny Mandate Exists

Despite the magnitude of his victory, Mr. Reagan failed to lift his party to major gains in Congress, and Democratic leaders moved quickly yesterday to define the election as a tribute to Mr. Reagan's personal popularity rather than a mandate for unrestricted extension of his economic, social and military policies.

The Republicans lost two seats in the Senate, where they retained a majority of 53 to 47, and they fell short of

attaining a working majority in the House of Representatives. The President's party gained 14 seats or so there, and strategists in both parties agreed the Republicans needed to win back the 26 seats they lost in 1982 for Mr. Reagan to exercise ideological control of the House.

Mr. Reagan's advisers were cautious in their assertions yesterday because the Congressional returns were so much less favorable to the Republicans than the Presidential voting. James A. Baker 3d, the White House chief of staff, said the scope of the President's mandate "is going to be determined by how successful we are in the next four years." Mr. Reagan, at his news conference yesterday morning, said he would "take his case to the people" in pursuing a conservative economic agenda that might be expanded to include "simplification" of the tax system.

The conference was his second in four days. Before Sunday he had not met with reporters since July 24, and yesterday he continued to resist giving details about his agenda for the second term.

But he did promise that any change in the income tax would not be a tax increase in disguise. In the campaign he was accused by Mr. Mondale of harboring a "secret plan" to raise taxes after the election.

Mr. Mondale had also accused the President of being indifferent to the dangers of nuclear war, and Mr. Reagan confirmed reports that his Administration was considering using an "informal channel" to reopen negotiations with the Soviet Union.

Mr. Reagan added that this could include appointing a special envoy in charge of arms control talks.

At a separate news conference, Mr. Baker said the second term would bring a renewed effort to cut Federal spending, but he said two areas, the Pentagon and Social Security, would be sacrosanct.

"REAGAN CONFERS WITH GORBACHEV IN GENEVA PARLEY," NOVEMBER 20, 1985

President Reagan's first meeting with Mikhail Gorbachev in November 1985 marked a turning point in the cold war. The two leaders had the opportunity to exchange views and get to know one another, setting the foundation for more substantive negotiations.

NOVEMBER 20, 1985
REAGAN CONFERS WITH GORBACHEV IN GENEVA PARLEY

By R. W. APPLE JR.
Special to The New York Times

President Reagan and Mikhail S. Gorbachev, the Soviet leader, met today for more than four hours in what the two sides described as a "good atmosphere."

The much-heralded encounter, the first between Soviet and American leaders in six years, included two conversations with only interpreters present. They lasted more than two hours, although the schedule had called for only 15 minutes.

Larry Speakes, the White House spokesman, said that the long private conversations had been unexpected and that they contributed "to our overall good feeling about the meetings."

He added that the mood differed markedly from that of the recent talks Secretary of State George P. Shultz had with Mr. Gorbachev in Moscow, where the Soviet leader was said to have been argumentative and to have interrupted Mr. Shultz's presentation.

A Measure of Progress

Another White House official had said Monday that the amount of time Mr. Reagan and Mr. Gorbachev spent alone would be a good indicator of how things were going. The longer the private meetings, the official said, the greater the prospects of progress.

When Vladimir B. Lomeiko, a Soviet spokesman, was asked at a briefing whether he was encouraged by the length of the private talks, he said, "I believe this meeting and its outcome will provide you with an answer." But earlier Mr. Gorbachev himself had been overheard saying "yes" to the same question by some reporters.

• •

"U.S. JETS HIT 'TERRORIST CENTERS' IN LIBYA; REAGAN WARNS OF NEW ATTACKS IF NEEDED; ONE PLANE MISSING IN RAIDS ON 5 TARGETS," APRIL 15, 1986

When American military personnel died in the bombing of a Berlin disco in spring 1986, the Reagan administration soon determined that Libya was responsible. The president ordered retaliatory air strikes against Libya to halt its terrorist activities.

APRIL 15, 1986
U.S. JETS HIT 'TERRORIST CENTERS' IN LIBYA; REAGAN WARNS OF NEW ATTACKS IF NEEDED; ONE PLANE MISSING IN RAIDS ON 5 TARGETS

By BERNARD WEINRAUB

Special to The New York Times

The United States conducted a series of air strikes on Monday night against what the White House called "terrorist centers" and military bases in Libya.

President Reagan, in a nationally broadcast speech, said the American forces had "succeeded" in their mission of retaliating against Libya for what he termed the "reign of terror" waged by Col. Muammar el-Qaddafi, the Libyan leader, against the United States.

Defense Secretary Caspar W. Weinberger said later that one United States plane, an F-111 with a crew of two, "is not accounted for at this time." But he declined to say if the plane had been shot down.

Libya Says 3 Jets Downed

The Libyan radio, monitored in London, said that three United States aircraft had been shot down and that Libyans had killed their pilots and crew.

Mr. Reagan said: "Today we have done what we had to do. If necessary we shall do it again."

Congressional leaders generally expressed support for the attack on Libya, but a leading Democrat warned that the raid could lead to more violence.

French Embassy Reported Hit

The French Foreign Ministry said the French Embassy in Tripoli was hit in the bombing raid, but a spokesman said no one was injured.

Foreign reporters in Tripoli, after a Government-conducted tour of a residential district today, said that the rear of the French Embassy was heavily damaged, with windows blown out, and that five or six houses in the district were also damaged. A Libyan Government spokesman said an unknown number of civilians had been killed.

In his address on Monday night, Mr. Reagan said the American attack was a retaliation for what he asserted was the "direct" Libyan role in the bombing on April 5 of a West Berlin discotheque frequented by American servicemen. One American soldier and a Turkish woman died, and more than 200 people were wounded, including 50 other servicemen.

"We believe that this pre-emptive action against his terrorist installations will not only diminish Colonel Qaddafi's capacity to export terror, it will provide him with incentives and reasons to alter his criminal behavior," said a grim-faced Mr. Reagan.

5 Targets Near Cities

An Administration official said five military targets near Libya's two major cities, Tripoli and Benghazi, were attacked.

Mr. Weinberger said American planes were forced to fly a long route to Libya from Britain because France refused to allow the United States to fly over French territory.

Larry Speakes, the White House spokesman, who made the first official announcement of the attacks, said they began shortly before 7 P.M. Monday, New York time, about 2 A.M. today in Libya, and were over in half an hour. "The United States has chosen to exercise its right of self-defense," Mr. Speakes said. His press briefing began about 7:20 P.M., while the American warplanes were still returning from Libya.

Mr. Reagan, in his speech, said the United States had "solid evidence" that Libya was behind the West Berlin attack and that "Libya's agents planted the bomb." He lambasted Colonel Qaddafi and said the United States, with the help of allies, had aborted numerous Libyan terrorist attacks including "a planned massacre, using grenades and small arms, of civilians waiting in line for visas at an American embassy."

Mr. Reagan ended his speech on a somber note.

Reagan Recalls Warning

"I warned that there should be no place on earth where terrorists can rest and train and practice their deadly skills," he said. "I meant it. I said that we should act with others, if possible, and alone, if necessary, to insure that terrorists have no sanctuary anywhere. Tonight we have," he said. Mr. Reagan and his ranking aides delivered an unmistakable warning to Colonel Qaddafi. "When our citizens are abused or attacked anywhere in the world, we will respond in self-defense," Mr. Reagan said. "If necessary, we will do it again."

"THE TAX BILL OF 1986: FROM 14 RATES TO 2; MONUMENT TO REAGANISM JOINS POPULIST POLITICS WITH SUPPLY-SIDE CREDO," AUGUST 18, 1986

The Tax Reform Act of 1986 represented the most far-reaching changes in the U.S. tax code in fifty years. Although the legislation did not remove all provisions for special interests, it did close a number of loopholes and significantly lower the highest personal income tax rate, while raising the bottom rate by a few points. Given the many provisions to end favored treatment for special interests, *The Times* described the law as "less Republican than it is populist."

AUGUST 18, 1986
THE TAX BILL OF 1986: FROM 14 RATES TO 2; MONUMENT TO REAGANISM JOINS POPULIST POLITICS WITH SUPPLY-SIDE CREDO
By PETER T. KILBORN

If Congress accepts—as by all accounts it will—the broad reconstruction of the income tax system that its tax committees approved on Saturday, Ronald Reagan will have earned himself a place among the handful of Presidents who have nurtured fundamental change. Although an army of advocates was required, the President set the tone and defined the themes of a resolute campaign to clean up a body of law that President Carter had called "a disgrace to the human race."

At President Reagan's urging, Congressional leaders have agreed to purge the tax code of many of its special provisions for vested interests and to chop tax rates to just 15 percent for most taxpayers and 28 percent for almost everyone else—a combination that would alter the finances of every American family and business. The bill is a triumph that eluded all other Presidents of the last half century.

Bob Packwood of Oregon, the Republican chairman of the Senate Finance Committee, and Dan Rostenkowski of Illinois, the Democratic chairman of the House Ways and Means Committee, played a huge role in working out a near-revolutionary change in the tax laws. But what emerges bears the singular stamp of Ronald Reagan.

The landmark legislation is less Republican than it is populist. And it is less traditionally conservative than it is the expression of the Reagan supply-side credo that low individual taxes and small government clear the way to a sounder and more prosperous economy.

The agreement appeals, as well, to a deep-seated disenchantment with the tax system. Concessions to various interests had encrusted the system so greatly that they had become its dominant feature, belying the ideal of exacting a tax on all the nation's income.

It is true that some concessions remain—notably, special benefits for the oil and gas industry—and some are considered egregious. But many tax experts say they find more to praise than to mourn in this bill.

"If I were writing the specifications, I'd make it simon-pure," said Walter W. Heller, an economist at the University of Minnesota who, as chief economic adviser to President Kennedy, inspired the giant tax cuts of 1964. "It's utterly remarkable that in light of the power of the tax lobbies, we are getting as good a bill as we are. Washington deals in second-bests, and this is one of the best second-bests I've seen."

Joseph A. Pechman, an economist at the Brookings Institution, worked with every Democratic Administration since the 1940's trying to redesign the tax system. "We got nowhere," he said. "This is the only attempt I can think of that can be considered a major step in the direction of comprehensive tax reform."

The broader Reagan record in economic policy is a mixed picture, and its failures could eventually jeopardize the President's overhaul of the tax system. He presides over an economy with low inflation but high unemployment, slow growth and distress among farmers and basic industries. Many economists predict that the tax proposal will be a damper on the economy next year, because of the new burden it puts on business and the transitional uncertainty it creates for all taxpayers.

The Deficit Factor

In the view of many, the President also shares much of the blame for the record, $200 billion annual budget deficits, and the proposed tax changes could worsen them. The deficits soared following his first foray into the tax system five years ago—three years of cuts in individual tax rates that totaled $750 billion. He and Congress would not work out a way to bring the budget in line with the resulting shrinkage in Federal revenues.

The tax changes should not alter the course of the deficits, the White House and the tax-writing committees of Congress say, because they maintain that the bill is "revenue neutral," producing neither more nor less in total Government revenue than the old law would have.

But other analysts have doubts. "As tax policy, this is a tremendous achievement," said David A. Stockman, the President's former budget director. "But as budget policy, I'm skeptical. I'm rather convinced that the thing is less than revenue-neutral."

That said, the tax proposal stands as a monument to Reaganism. It follows the direction that he set in May last year. In the particulars, he lost a few. But in some notable instances—especially a top individual rate even lower than the 35 percent the President proposed—he got more than his advisers dared ask for.

"The Iceland Summit: 'A Difficult Dialogue'; Gorbachev Angrily Accuses Reagan of Scuttling an Accord at Reykjavik," October 13, 1986

The cold war nearly came to a dramatic close in Reykjavik, Iceland, in October 1986, when both Reagan and Gorbachev seriously entertained the possibility of abolishing their nations' nuclear arsenals. Reagan abhorred nuclear weapons and was willing to eliminate them if the United States could continue developing a missile defense shield to protect the country from nuclear attack. But Gorbachev knew the Soviets could not afford this arms race, and he was not persuaded by Reagan's promise to share the technology. When the two leaders emerged from their final meeting, their angry faces made clear that the negotiations had failed.

OCTOBER 13, 1986
THE ICELAND SUMMIT: 'A DIFFICULT DIALOGUE'; GORBACHEV ANGRILY ACCUSES REAGAN OF SCUTTLING AN ACCORD AT REYKJAVIK
By PHILIP TAUBMAN
Special to The New York Times

Mikhail S. Gorbachev said today that by insisting on development of "Star Wars" weapons, President Reagan "scuttled" a series of broad arms control agreements reached by the two men at their meetings here.

The Soviet leader said that "only a madman would accept" the American insistence that research and development of a space-based missile defense system be allowed to proceed beyond laboratory work under a broad agreement to reduce nuclear weapons.

Mr. Gorbachev said at a news conference after the collapse of his talks with Mr. Reagan that he had come to Iceland thinking that the best way to end the arms race was to present President Reagan with a radical package of new proposals.

'Major Concessions' by Moscow

Mr. Gorbachev said Moscow had presented a package of "major concessions and compromises" at the meeting, while the United States side "came empty-handed, with a whole set of mothballed proposals."

Mr. Gorbachev, leaning forward in his seat and slashing the air with his right hand at times for emphasis, spoke without notes for an hour before responding to questions. His presentation was polished and at times impassioned.

In an apparent effort to put Mr. Reagan on the defensive, he presented a detailed defense of the new Soviet proposals and Moscow's handling of relations with Washington since their meeting in Geneva last November.

Portraying the Soviet position as a radical and far-reaching effort to end the arms race, he placed the overall blame for the failure of the talks on the influence of the military-industrial complex in the United States.

'Let Us Not Panic'

Mr. Gorbachev, flanked by top aides on a makeshift podium at a Reykjavik movie theater, said he was not discouraged by the breakdown in the talks.

"Let us not panic," he said. "This is not the end of contact with the United States. It is not the end of international relations."

He said the Soviet proposals remained on the table and expressed hope that the agreements nearly concluded this weekend could be revived.

"Let America think," he said. "We are waiting. We are not withdrawing our proposals."

Mr. Gorbachev, who appeared serious but not grim, reported that he had told Mr. Reagan that they "were missing a historic chance: Never had our positions been so close together."

Mr. Gorbachev said "both of us should reflect on what happened here," adding, "The meeting was important and promising."

'Not an Unproductive Meeting'

Although he called the failure "sad and disappointing," Mr. Gorbachev added that "it was not an unproductive meeting."

He described the talks as "a step in a difficult dialogue."

"Elections; Democrats Gain Control of Senate, Drawing Votes of Reagan's Backers," November 5, 1986

Despite Reagan's determined efforts, the Republican Party lost control of the U.S. Senate in the 1986 congressional midterm elections, resulting in divided government for the remainder of his term. The Democrats also gained seats in the House, which further complicated the administration's legislative agenda.

NOVEMBER 5, 1986
ELECTIONS; DEMOCRATS GAIN CONTROL OF SENATE, DRAWING VOTES OF REAGAN'S BACKERS; CUOMO AND D'AMATO ARE EASY VICTORS; WHAT AWAITS CONGRESS; BROAD G.O.P. LOSSES

By E. J. DIONNE JR.

The Democrats won control of the Senate yesterday, dealing a major blow to President Reagan, who had crisscrossed the country pleading for a Republican victory.

Sweeping through the South and picking up key farm states, the Democrats were guaranteed at least 54 seats in the new Senate. Bob Dole, the Senate Republican leader, said the Democrats could have won as many as 55 seats.

The Democrats, who won in the face of an overwhelming Republican financial advantage, will take control of all committee chairmanships and gain the power to put a brake on Mr. Reagan's effort to reshape the nation's judiciary, including the Supreme Court.

They were also expected to clash with the President over military spending and arms control.

Fear of a Stalemate

Republicans feared that the shift in the Senate could lead to stalemate on Mr. Reagan's programs.

"I think it's going to be a difficult period for the President," said Senator Paul Laxalt, Republican of Nevada, who is a close friend of Mr. Reagan. "This will be awkward." Mr. Reagan refused to comment on the outcome of the election when he left Los Angeles to return to Washington yesterday.

The Democrats defeated Republican incumbents in Alabama, Georgia, North Carolina, Florida, North Dakota and South Dakota. They took seats where Republicans had retired in Maryland and Nevada.

In California, Senator Alan Cranston, a Democrat, turned back a strong challenge from Representative Ed Zschau. In

Colorado, Representative Timothy E. Wirth, a Democrat, won a narrow victory over Representative Ken Kramer. Mr. Wirth was defending the seat of Senator Gary Hart, who is retiring to run for the Democratic Presidential nomination in 1988.

Consolation for G.O.P.

The Republicans picked up one seat from the Democrats in Missouri, where former Gov. Christopher Bond defeated Lieut. Gov. Harriett Woods.

The Republicans were consoled by picking up at least six governorships.

In one of the most important Republican gains, Guy Hunt, a former judge, appeared to have defeated Lieut.

Gov. Bill Baxley in a bitter race in Alabama, where the Democratic Party was sharply divided. He was the first Republican to win the state's governorship since Reconstruction. Just before the election, State Attorney General Charles Graddick, a Democrat who defeated Mr. Baxley in the primary but had his victory set aside by the state party, dropped his planned write-in campaign. This apparently helped Mr. Hunt.

The Democrats maintained their majority in the House of Representatives, and seemed likely to post an unusually small midterm gain of five to eight seats. Democrats now hold a 253-to-180 seat majority, with two vacancies.

· ·

"Iran Payment Found Diverted to Contras; Reagan Security Adviser and Aide Are Out," November 26, 1986

Reports of the National Security Council's (NSC) secret arms-for-hostages negotiations with Iran and covert diversion of funds to contra rebels in Nicaragua appeared in November 1986. The news resulted in Reagan's dismissal of his top national security advisers, congressional hearings, and appointment of an independent counsel to investigate the NSC's operations. The president insisted he had not known of the covert operations, and inquiries did not prove decisively otherwise.

NOVEMBER 26, 1986
IRAN PAYMENT FOUND DIVERTED TO CONTRAS; REAGAN SECURITY ADVISER AND AIDE ARE OUT
By BERNARD WEINRAUB
Special to The New York Times

President Reagan said today that he had not been in full control of his Administration's Iran policy, and the White House said that as a consequence up to $30 million intended to pay for American arms had been secretly diverted to rebel forces in Nicaragua.

At the same time, the President announced that two men he held responsible—Vice Adm. John M. Poindexter, the national security adviser, and Lieut. Col. Oliver L. North, a member of the admiral's staff—had left their posts.

With the Administration already in turmoil over the earlier disclosure of clandestine arms shipments to Iran, and with speculation rampant about a major overhaul of the White House staff, the President's statement seemed to deepen a sense of disarray. By all accounts,

Mr. Reagan now faces the most serious crisis in his six-year Presidency.

Shultz to Control Policy

The State Department, meanwhile, said Secretary of State George P. Shultz had been given control over future Iran policy, authority that apparently met his condition for remaining in office. State Department officials, including Mr. Shultz, have said they were left in the dark on much of the Iran operation. Mr. Reagan stunned legislators and ranking Administration officials by announcing in a televised session with reporters that he had not been "fully informed" of some details of the Iran operation and that Admiral Poindexter and Colonel North were leaving after "serious questions of propriety had been raised."

Inquiry Still Under Way

Mr. Reagan said that, "although not directly involved," Admiral Poindexter had "asked to be relieved of his assignment" and would return to Navy duties. Colonel North, the President said, "has been relieved of his duties on the National Security Council staff." Colonel North was widely reported to be the central figure in the Iran arms deal.

After Mr. Reagan's announcement, Attorney General Edwin Meese 3d said the Justice Department was still investigating how Nicaraguan rebel forces, known as contras, received "somewhere between $10 and $30 million" paid to "representatives of Israel" funneling the arms to Iran.

Israeli and American sources said today that a Saudi arms dealer played a central role in financing the Iranian purchase of arms transferred by Israel to Iran on behalf of the United States.

And in its first official comment on the Iran affair, the Israeli Government said it had transferred arms to Iran at the "request" of the United States and did not know that some payments for these weapons were channeled to the Nicaraguan rebels.

In San Jose, Costa Rica, and in Miami, spokesmen for the Nicaraguan rebel coalition said they knew nothing of secret transfers of funds to their organization arranged by Colonel North.

'Only Colonel North Knew'

"The only persons in the United States Government that knew precisely about this—the only person—was Lieutenant Colonel North," said Mr. Meese. "Admiral Poindexter did know that something of this nature was occurring, but he did not look into it further.

"C.I.A. Director Casey, Secretary of State Shultz, Secretary of Defense Weinberger, myself, the other members of the N.S.C., none of us knew.

"The President knew nothing about it until I reported it to him," Mr. Meese told reporters in the packed White House press room. "I alerted him yesterday morning."

Later the Attorney General said a third person aware of the diversion of funds was Robert C. McFarlane, former national security director and a central figure in the plan to send arms to Iran. Mr. Meese said Mr. McFarlane was aware of the scheme in "April or May of 1986 at a time when he was no longer in the Government."

Asked why Mr. McFarlane failed to say anything to Mr. Reagan, Mr. Meese replied, "I don't know."

"RAZE BERLIN WALL, REAGAN URGES SOVIET," JUNE 13, 1987

On a trip to Germany in the summer of 1987, Reagan called for the Soviet Union to end the cold war by removing the wall dividing East Berlin and West Berlin. His exact words—"Mr. Gorbachev, tear down this wall"—proved prophetic, as the wall came down just two and a half years later.

'Secretary General Gorbachev, if you seek peace—if you seek prosperity for the Soviet Union and Eastern Europe—if you seek liberalization: come here, to this gate. Mr. Gorbachev, open this gate. Mr. Gorbachev, tear down this wall.'

JUNE 13, 1987
RAZE BERLIN WALL, REAGAN URGES SOVIET
By GERALD M. BOYD
Special to The New York Times

President Reagan sought today to undercut Europe's perception of Mikhail S. Gorbachev as a leader of peace, bluntly challenging the Soviet leader to tear down the Berlin wall.

Speaking 100 yards from the wall that was thrown up in 1961 to thwart an exodus to the West, Mr. Reagan made the wall a metaphor for ideological and economic differences separating East and West.

"There is one sign the Soviets can make that would be unmistakable, that would advance dramatically the cause of freedom and peace," the President said.

"Secretary General Gorbachev, if you seek peace—if you seek prosperity for the Soviet Union and Eastern Europe—if you seek liberalization: come here, to this gate. Mr. Gorbachev, open this gate. Mr. Gorbachev, tear down this wall."

Mr. Reagan made the remarks with the Brandenburg Gate in East Berlin in the background. An East Berlin security post was in view.

The Berlin police estimated that 20,000 people had turned out to hear the President, but some observers thought the crowd was smaller than that.

The Soviet press agency Tass said that Mr. Reagan, by calling for destruction of the wall, had given an "openly provocative, war-mongering speech" reminiscent of the cold war.

Reagan Peers Into East Berlin

Before the speech, Mr. Reagan peered across the wall from a balcony of the old Reichstag building into East Berlin, where a patrol boat and a gray brick sentry post were visible. Later, when asked how he felt, he said, "I think it's an ugly scar."

Asked how he regarded a perception among some people in Europe that Mr. Gorbachev was more committed to peace, Mr. Reagan said, "They just have to learn, don't they?"

Administration officials had portrayed the speech as a major policy statement. But the main new initiative was a call to the Soviet Union to assist in helping Berlin become an aviation hub of Central Europe by agreeing to make commercial air service more convenient.

Some Reagan advisers wanted an address with less polemics but lost to those who favored use of the opportunity to raise East-West differences and questions about Mr. Gorbachev's commitment to ending the nuclear arms race and his internal liberalization policies.

"In Europe, only one nation and those it controls refuse to join the community of freedom," Mr. Reagan said. "Yet, in this age of redoubled economic growth of information and innovation, the Soviet Union faces a choice. It must make fundamental changes or it will become obsolete."

Shield of Bulletproof Glass

Speaking with two panes of bulletproof glass shielding him from East Berlin, Mr. Reagan stressed a theme of freedom and peaceful reunification of Berlin.

That was a point made by President Kennedy in his "Ich bin ein Berliner" speech two years after the wall was built.

"Standing before the Brandenburg Gate, every man is a German, separated from his fellow men," Mr. Reagan said. "Every man is a Berliner, forced to look upon a scar."

"Stocks Plunge Nearly 508 Points, a Drop of 22.6%; 604 Million Volume Nearly Doubles Record," October 20, 1987

The stock market plunge of October 1987, in which the Dow Jones industrial average dropped by 508 points, or nearly 23 percent, in a single day, sparked fears of a global financial crisis. Other economies faced similar declines and "posted record losses," according to *The Times*. But the Federal Reserve and other nations' central banks were able to avert further disaster.

OCTOBER 20, 1987
STOCKS PLUNGE 508 POINTS, A DROP OF 22.6%; 604 MILLION VOLUME NEARLY DOUBLES RECORD
By LAWRENCE J. DE MARIA

Stock market prices plunged in a tumultuous wave of selling yesterday, giving Wall Street its worst day in history and raising fears of a recession.

The Dow Jones industrial average, considered a benchmark of the market's health, plummeted a record 508 points, to 1,738.74, based on preliminary calculations.

That 22.6 percent decline was the worst since World War I and far greater than the 12.82 percent drop on Oct. 28, 1929, that along with the next day's 11.7 percent decline preceded the Great Depression.

Since hitting a record 2,722.42 on Aug. 25, the Dow has fallen almost 1,000 points, or 36 percent, putting the blue-chip indicator 157.5 points below the level at which it started the year. With Friday's plunge of 108.35 points, the Dow has fallen more than 26 percent in the last two sessions.

Unprecedented Trading

Yesterday's frenzied trading on the nation's stock exchanges lifted volume to unheard of levels. On the New York Stock Exchange, an estimated 604.3 million shares changed hands, almost double the previous record of 338.5 million shares set just last Friday.

With the tremendous volume, reports of brokers' trades on the New York Stock Exchange were delayed by more than two hours at one point. The New York Stock Exchange said that, as a result, it would not have definitive figures for the Dow's point decline and the exchange's volume until today.

Yesterday's big losers included International Business Machines, the bluest of the blue chips, which dropped $31, to $104. In August the stock was at $176. The other big losers among the blue chips were General Motors, which lost $13.875, to $52.125, and Exxon, which dropped $10.25, to $33.50.

More Than $1 Trillion Lost

According to Wilshire Associates, which tracks more than 5,000 stocks, the rout obliterated more than $500 billion in equity value from the nation's stock portfolios. That equity value now stands at $2.311 trillion. Since late summer, more than $1 trillion in stock values has been lost.

The losses were so great they sent shock waves to markets around the world, and many foreign exchanges posted record losses. In a sign of the continuing effect, the Tokyo Stock Exchange fell sharply today. The Nikkei Dow Jones average plummeted a record 3,395.95 yen, to 22,350.61, a drop of 13.2 percent, by late afternoon. Also, the Hong Kong exchange decided to close for the week.

In Washington yesterday, the White House spokesman, Marlin Fitzwater, issued a statement saying that President Reagan had "watched with concern" the stock market's collapse. But Mr. Reagan remained convinced that the economy was sound.

Economy Called Sound

Mr. Fitzwater said the President had directed Administration officials to contact leading financial experts. "Those consultations confirm our view that the underlying economy remains sound," he added.

- -

"THE SUMMIT; REAGAN AND GORBACHEV SIGN MISSILE TREATY AND VOW TO WORK FOR GREATER REDUCTIONS," DECEMBER 9, 1987

Gorbachev made his first visit to Washington, D.C., in December 1987 to sign a historic arms control treaty with the United States. For the first time, the two superpowers agreed to reduce their arsenal of medium- and short-range missiles.

DECEMBER 9, 1987
THE SUMMIT; REAGAN AND GORBACHEV SIGN MISSILE TREATY AND VOW TO WORK FOR GREATER REDUCTIONS
By DAVID K. SHIPLER
Special to The New York Times

With fervent calls for a new era of peaceful understanding, President Reagan and Mikhail S. Gorbachev today signed the first treaty reducing the size of their nations' nuclear arsenals.

The President and the Soviet leader, beginning three days of talks aimed at even broader reductions, pledged to build on the accord by striving toward what Mr. Gorbachev called "the more important goal," reducing long-range nuclear weapons.

In their White House conversations, the leaders were said to have reviewed their previous proposals aimed at

After the United States and the Soviet Union signed an historic arms control treaty, President Reagan bids farewell to Soviet leader Mikhail Gorbachev on the South Lawn of the White House.

Source: Teresa Zabala for the New York Times

furthering those negotiations, and they established an arms-control working group of ranking officials to hold parallel sessions.

'Mine is Mikhail'

An immediate mood of warmth was established as the two leaders agreed this morning to call each other by their first names, a White House official said. He quoted the President as telling Mr. Gorbachev, "My first name is Ron."

Mr. Gorbachev answered, "Mine is Mikhail."

"When we're working in private session," Mr. Reagan reportedly said, "we can call each other that."

The new treaty, which provides for the dismantling of all Soviet and American medium- and shorter-range missiles, establishes the most extensive system of weapons inspection ever negotiated by the two countries, including placing technicians at sensitive sites on each other's territory.

The Mood for Talking

The signing, the fruition of years of negotiation, set the mood for two and a half hours of talks between the leaders. The talks were "very serious, substantive discussions," Secretary of State George P. Shultz said tonight before a formal dinner in the White House.

The visit to Washington by Mr. Gorbachev was the first by a Soviet leader since Leonid I. Brezhnev was here 14 years ago, and it took on immediate drama as Mr. Reagan, who entered office with deep suspicions of the Soviet Union, welcomed Mr. Gorbachev on the South Lawn of the White House.

"I have often felt that our people should have been better friends long ago," he told his guest as they stood facing the Washington Monument across an array of full-dress military honor guards. Mr. Gorbachev received a 21-gun salute usually reserved for chiefs of state.

"MOSCOW SUMMIT: GORBACHEV CRITICIZES REAGAN, SEEING 'MISSED OPPORTUNITIES,' BUT CALLS VISIT A 'MAJOR EVENT'; SUMMIT TALKS END," JUNE 2, 1988

Reagan reciprocated Gorbachev's visit to the United States by traveling to the Soviet Union in 1988. While walking through Red Square, the president was asked whether he still considered the Soviet Union to be an "evil empire." He smiled and replied, "No. . . . I was talking about another time, another era."

JUNE 2, 1988
MOSCOW SUMMIT: GORBACHEV CRITICIZES REAGAN, SEEING 'MISSED OPPORTUNITIES,' BUT CALLS VISIT A 'MAJOR EVENT'; SUMMIT TALKS END

By PHILIP TAUBMAN
Special to The New York Times

Mikhail S. Gorbachev complained today that his fourth and probably final summit meeting with President Reagan was filled with "missed opportunities" and impeded by contradictions in American policy.

But in a concluding two-hour news conference he balanced his criticism of Mr. Reagan by calling the President's visit to Moscow this week a "major event" that moved relations "maybe one rung or two up the ladder."

In a joint statement that recorded modest progress on a number of issues, the two sides expressed hope that the dialogue established by Mr. Reagan and Mr. Gorbachev in their four summit meetings since 1985 would endure, despite "real differences of history, tradition and ideology."

A President Proselytizing

This week's talks, which officially end Thursday morning with Mr. Reagan's departure for London, seem likely to be remembered less for any particular achievements than the symbolic spectacle of an American President in the Soviet capital proselytizing for change and expanded liberties.

After the tentative nature of the Geneva summit meeting in 1985, the volatility in Reykjavik, Iceland, in 1986, and the substantive accomplishments in Washington last December, the Moscow summit meeting seems to reflect a sense that the two men have all but exhausted the potential for advancing relations in the waning months of the Reagan Administration.

In separate news conferences, the two leaders said they were pleased with the gains recorded this week, but Mr. Gorbachev devoted a good portion of his remarks to criticism of Mr. Reagan, suggesting considerable frustration and irritation with the President.

Annoyance on Human Rights

Mr. Gorbachev's exasperation seemed to stem less from an absence of progress on central arms-control issues—the chance for that had never appeared great—than from Mr. Reagan's concentration on human rights issues and the President's refusal to endorse the general guidelines for Soviet-American relations proposed by the Soviet leader. The general guidelines included in the final joint statement were written by the Americans.

The Soviet leader also accused the American negotiators of trying to dodge issues on conventional arms, and he complained about unfavorable trade treatment.

Although he did not say as much, Mr. Gorbachev left the impression in his news conference that he had lost patience with Mr. Reagan and was ready to turn his attention to the President who will take office in January.

Nevertheless, the Gorbachevs and the Reagans seemed in good humor as they attended a special performance of seven dances by the Bolshoi Ballet. They sat in the royal box in the neo-classical, 19th-century Bolshoi Theater. They then drove to an official guest residence in the northwestern outskirts of Moscow for a private supper.

THE PRESIDENCY OF GEORGE H. W. BUSH

JANUARY 20, 1989 – JANUARY 20, 1993

Significant changes in world affairs took place during the presidency of George Herbert Walker Bush. The cold war ended peacefully, and the United States and the Soviet Union worked together to repel Iraq's invasion of Kuwait, marking what President Bush termed a "new world order." With a long career in political diplomacy, Bush was well-suited to guiding the United States through the momentous global transition. But his foreign policy expertise proved less helpful in the post–cold war era, when domestic matters took priority. Dogged by his failure to keep a pledge not to raise taxes, Bush faced a difficult re-election in 1992 and lost the race to Bill Clinton.

The second of five children, Bush was raised in Greenwich, Connecticut. His father, Prescott Bush, was a highly successful Wall Street banker who also served in the U.S. Senate from 1952 to 1963. Bush attended Phillips Academy in Andover, Massachusetts, where he was a star student and athlete and was elected senior class president. After high school, he joined the navy in World War II and became a bomber pilot. His plane was shot down in the Pacific in 1944, and he was rescued by a submarine. Bush was discharged from the navy with honors in 1945 and then attended Yale University, where he studied economics, led the baseball team, and was admitted to the prestigious honor society Phi Beta Kappa.

After completing his degree, Bush entered the oil business and founded a petroleum company, moving to Texas to make his fortune. He ran unsuccessfully for the Senate in 1964, but won election to the U.S. House of Representatives two years later. He served two terms, then ran for the Senate and lost again. President Richard M. Nixon appointed him U.S. ambassador to the United Nations in 1970 and two years later asked Bush to head the Republican National Committee.

After Nixon's resignation in 1974, Bush was considered for the vice presidency, but instead President Gerald R. Ford offered him another diplomatic post—head of the U.S. Liaison Office in China. Ford later appointed him as director of the Central Intelligence Agency. In 1980 Bush competed for the Republican presidential nomination. He won the Iowa caucuses, but lost the race to Ronald Reagan, who selected him

BOY AT THE DIKE

SAVINGS-AND-LOAN COSTS

Source: The Herb Block Foundation

as his vice-presidential running mate. The Republican ticket won the White House, and Bush served as vice president for eight years.

THE 1988 ELECTION

Vice President Bush was the logical choice of Republicans in 1988. He faced competition from Senate minority leader Robert Dole of Kansas, who won the Iowa caucuses, and from other candidates, but Bush prevailed in the New Hampshire primary and won the party's nomination. He selected Sen. James Danforth "Dan" Quayle III of Indiana as his running mate. The Democratic Party nominated Gov. Michael S. Dukakis

QUICK FACTS ON GEORGE H. W. BUSH

BIRTH	June 12, 1924, Milton, Mass.
EDUCATION	Phillips Academy, Andover, Mass., 1941 Yale University, B.A., 1948
FAMILY	Wife: Barbara Pierce Bush Children: George Walker Bush, Robin Bush (died 1949), John Ellis "Jeb" Bush, Neil Mallon Bush, Marvin Pierce Bush, Dorothy Pierce Bush
WHITE HOUSE PETS	Dogs
PARTY	Republican
PREPRESIDENTIAL CAREER (SELECTED)	Commissioned as pilot in U.S. Navy, 1942 Plane shot down in Pacific, 1944 Discharged as lieutenant, j.g.; awarded Distinguished Flying Cross and three air medals, 1945 Salesman for oilfield equipment supply company, 1948–1950 Co-founder of Zapata Petroleum Corporation, 1953 Founder and president of Zapata Off-shore Company, 1954 Moves to Houston, Texas, when Zapata Off-shore becomes independent company, 1959 Chairman of Harris County Republican Party, 1962–1964 Board chairman and CEO of Zapata Off-shore, 1964–1966 Goldwater delegate to Republican National Convention, 1964 Unsuccessful run for U.S. Senate from Texas, 1964 U.S. representative from Texas, 1967–1971 Unsuccessful run for U.S. Senate from Texas, 1970 U.S. Ambassador to United Nations, 1971–1972 Chairman of Republican National Committee, 1973–1974 Chief of U.S. Liaison Office, Peking, China, 1974–1975 Director of Central Intelligence, 1976–1977 Unsuccessful run for Republican presidential nomination, 1980 Vice president, 1981–1989
PRESIDENTIAL TERM	January 20, 1989–January 20, 1993
VICE PRESIDENT	James Danforth "Dan" Quayle III

of Massachusetts for president and Sen. Lloyd M. Bentsen Jr. (who had defeated Bush for the Senate seat in Texas in 1970) for vice president. In accepting the Republican nomination, Bush promised a "kinder, gentler nation." He also declared that he would not raise taxes, and his famous statement, "Read my lips: no new taxes," would come back to haunt him as president.

In the general election, Bush successfully portrayed Dukakis as a liberal politician who would not maintain law and order. He called Dukakis "a card-carrying member of the American Civil Liberties Union," and he lambasted a Massachusetts prison furlough program, through which convicted murderer Willie Horton had secured a weekend pass and then raped a woman. Bush supporters also ran an infamous television campaign ad that pictured Horton, who was black, and critics declared that the images were intended to appeal to racial prejudices. Photos of Dukakis riding in

SELECTED EVENTS	Senate rejects Bush's nomination of John G. Tower for defense secretary (1989)
	Exxon Valdez oil tanker spill (1989)
	Oliver L. North convicted of three charges from Iran-contra affair; convictions later vacated (1989)
	Tiananmen Square massacre of pro-democracy protesters in China (1989)
	Communist rule ends in Poland (1989)
	Berlin wall torn down (1989)
	Malta summit between Bush and Soviet leader Mikhail Gorbachev (1989)
	U.S. invasion of Panama (1989)
	Nelson Mandela released from prison in South Africa (1989)
	John M. Poindexter convicted on charges from Iran-contra affair; convictions later overturned (1990)
	Arms control agreement with Gorbachev, Washington, D.C. (1990)
	Iraq invades Kuwait (1990)
	Reunification of Germany (1990)
	Bush vetoes Civil Rights Act (1990)
	Clean Air Act (1990)
	Congressional authorization for use of force against Iraq (1991)
	Persian Gulf War (1991)
	Removal of U.S. sanctions on South Africa (1991)
	Moscow summit between Bush and Gorbachev (1991)
	Estonia, Latvia, and Lithuania win independence (1991)
	Senate hearings on sexual harassment charges against Supreme Court nominee Clarence Thomas (1991)
	Civil Rights Act (1991)
	Dissolution of Soviet Union (1991)
	Riots in Los Angeles (1992)
	Earth Summit, Rio de Janeiro (1992)
	Deployment of U.S. troops to Somalia to provide humanitarian aid in response to famine (1992)
	Signing of North American Free Trade Agreement with Canada and Mexico (1992)
	Presidential pardon of six former government officials in connection with Iran-contra affair (1992)
	Arms control agreement with President Boris Yeltsin, Moscow (1993)
POSTPRESIDENCY	Honorary knighthood from Queen Elizabeth II, Great Britain, 1993
	Disaster relief fundraising with Bill Clinton following Indian Ocean earthquake and tsunami, 2004
	Disaster relief fundraising with Clinton following Hurricane Katrina, 2005

a tank that were intended to inspire confidence in him as commander in chief backfired and further weakened his candidacy. Bush soundly defeated Dukakis, with a popular-vote margin of more than 7 million, and an overwhelming majority in the Electoral College. His victory marked the first time since the election of Martin Van Buren in 1836 that the vice president immediately succeeded a president who had served two full terms.

THE BUSH I ADMINISTRATION

In selecting his fourteen-member cabinet, Bush identified people who were close friends and highly loyal to him. Campaign manager James A. Baker III of Texas became secretary of state and served until 1992, when he became chief of staff and worked to reinvigorate the president's reelection campaign. Two cabinet members, Attorney General Richard L.

Thornburgh of Pennsylvania and Nicholas F. Brady of New Jersey, were appointed under Reagan and continued into Bush's presidency. Defense Secretary Richard B. "Dick" Cheney of Wyoming was selected after the Senate rejected Bush's first choice, former senator John G. Tower of Texas. Bush appointed two women, Elizabeth H. Dole of North Carolina as labor secretary and Carla A. Hills of California special trade representative. He appointed Edward J. Derwinski of Illinois to head the newly created Department of Veterans Affairs.

Bush met his wife, Barbara Pierce, when they were in their teens, and the two married after he returned from his military service. They had four sons and two daughters, one of whom died at an early age from leukemia. As first lady, Barbara Bush became known for her efforts to combat illiteracy.

Major Issues

The four years of the Bush presidency were highly significant in international politics. The Berlin wall came down in 1989, signifying to many the end of the cold war. The next year brought the reunification of Germany as well as the end of apartheid in South Africa and the release of activist Nelson Mandela after twenty-seven years in prison. Also in 1990 democratic elections in Nicaragua resulted in victory for the U.S.-supported contras over the Sandinista government. In 1991 the Soviet Union recognized the independence of the Baltic states, and the Communist superpower itself broke into individual republics. The United States was not the driving force behind many of these momentous events, but the Bush administration worked to ensure a smooth transition in the post–cold war era.

Bush's foreign policy leadership focused primarily on crisis management. When the Chinese government brutally suppressed democratic protests in 1989, the administration opposed its actions, although the United States did not take large-scale punitive action against China. A few months later, Bush authorized a military invasion of Panama to overthrow the dictatorial regime of Gen. Manuel A. Noriega. The president received high praise for his firm response to Iraq's invasion of Kuwait in 1990 and the development of a multilateral coalition to force Iraq out of Kuwait in the Persian Gulf War of 1991. Bush also continued arms control negotiations with the Soviet Union, signing agreements with Soviet leader Mikhail Gorbachev, as well as Russian president Boris Yeltsin after the dissolution of the Soviet Union.

In domestic policy, Bush faced the greatest challenges with the economy. The failure of many savings and loan companies due to risky investments resulted in an enormous government-funded bailout program that contributed to high budget deficits and an economic recession. Although Bush had promised not to raise taxes, he accepted a tax increase in 1990 as part of a budget deal with Congress to reduce the deficit. The president also vetoed civil rights legislation to address employment discrimination in 1990, but approved a modified version the following year. He approved the Americans With Disabilities Act in 1990 and he supported continuation of the Clean Air Act.

Bush campaigned for reelection in 1992 on a platform of bringing the same success to domestic policy that he had achieved in foreign affairs in his first term. His high approval ratings following the Persian Gulf War had led many Democrats to conclude that he would win reelection easily, and several people who had considered running decided not to enter the race. But the economic recession and rising unemployment hurt Bush's prospects, and he faced an unsuccessful but distracting challenge for the nomination from conservative commentator Patrick J. Buchanan. Some Republicans criticized Bush for keeping Quayle on the ticket, but the president refused to drop his loyal vice president.

In the 1992 presidential race Bush faced two competitors: Arkansas governor William "Bill" Jefferson Clinton, the Democratic candidate, who ran with Sen. Albert A. Gore Jr. of Tennessee; and billionaire H. Ross Perot of Texas, an independent candidate, who ran with Vietnam War hero James B. Stockdale of California. Perot focused on the nation's $4 trillion debt and increasing budget deficit, and Clinton declared that his first priority would be to strengthen the economy. Bush's foreign policy leadership seemed to matter little in the first post–cold war presidential election, and he lost to Clinton, garnering 168 Electoral College votes to 370 for Clinton. Perot did not win any electoral votes, but he did receive 19 percent of the popular vote, compared to 37 percent for Bush and 43 percent for Clinton.

After leaving office, Bush retired quietly to private life in Houston, Texas. His sons continued the family tradition of electoral politics, with Jeb Bush winning election to two terms as governor of Florida, and George W. Bush doing the same in Texas before going on to win the White House in 2000. No president's son had won election to the same office since John Quincy Adams was elected in 1824. Bush campaigned for his son's successful reelection in 2004, and he has worked with former president Clinton to raise funds for international and domestic disaster relief.

"The Republicans in New Orleans; Republicans Acclaim Bush as Their New Leader," August 18, 1988

The Republican Party nominated Bush for president in 1988 by acclamation, but the choice of Dan Quayle as his running mate was more controversial. Quayle was dogged by questions about military service (he had joined the National Guard in the Vietnam War) and his law school record. *The New York Times* reported that many Republicans "questioned whether the 41-year-old Senator had the stature or the experience to be Vice President."

AUGUST 18, 1988
THE REPUBLICANS IN NEW ORLEANS; REPUBLICANS ACCLAIM BUSH AS THEIR NEW LEADER

By E. J. DIONNE JR.
Special to The New York Times

George Herbert Walker Bush, who has steadfastly served the Republican Party over more than two decades as Congressman, national chairman and Vice President, was nominated by its convention tonight for President of the United States.

Mr. Bush, who stood at President Reagan's side for eight years and struggled back from early defeat last winter to primacy in his party, set off to do battle against a rejuvenated Democratic Party, hoping that voters hostile to liberalism and wary of risk would give him victory.

On the third night of the Republican National Convention, Mr. Bush made his triumph a family affair. His daughter-in-law Columba, a Mexican-American, spoke in both English and Spanish to second the nomination of a man she said "has been like a father to me." After she had finished, all eight large television monitors over the arena switched from the convention floor to Mr. Bush's hotel suite, where he beamed as he sat surrounded by his grandchildren.

Texas Makes It Official

And it was the Vice President's son George who cast the votes of Mr. Bush's home state, Texas, which put him over the top for a nominating majority, climaxing a night of flag waving and patriotic oratory.

Earlier today, as he approached his moment of triumph, Mr. Bush turned in an unusually vigorous and passionate performance at a news conference where he appeared with his chosen running mate, Senator Dan Quayle of Indiana. Mr. Bush said they would "tell the truth" about the Democratic standard-bearer, Michael S. Dukakis. As

they do so, he predicted, the Democrats will come to feel that they have "engaged a couple of pit bulls."

Questions on Military Service

For his part, Mr. Quayle, at his first news conference since Mr. Bush selected him Tuesday for the second place on the ticket, defended his qualifications but had some difficulty fending off questions as to whether his joining the National Guard during the Vietnam War had been an effort to avoid combat.

While almost everyone at the convention expressed willingness to support Mr. Bush's choice, the selection of Mr. Quayle generated little enthusiasm outside his home delegation and some elements of the political right. In mostly private comments, governors, senators and House members attending the convention questioned whether the 41-year-old Senator had the stature or the experience to be Vice President.

Unopposed for Nomination

Mr. Bush, who made a stirring political revival after a humiliating third-place finish in the Iowa caucuses last February, had known since March that he would be the Republican Presidential nominee.

Tonight his was the only name before the 2,277 convention delegates gathered at the Louisiana Superdome, every one of whom voted for him. Then, after the roll-call, he was nominated by acclamation on a motion by his daughter, Dorothy Bush LeBlond, a delegate from Maine.

Senator Phil Gramm of Texas, placing Mr. Bush's name in nomination, laid heavy stress on the Vice President's experience and sense of duty, describing at length his tour as a heroic torpedo bomber pilot who was shot down over the Pacific in World War II.

"George Bush's record of service to America spans nearly five decades," Mr. Gramm said. "From naval aviator to Vice President, George Bush has shown again and again his love for his country, his countrymen and the values that made America great and strong. He has never failed to answer his nation's call for service."

Mr. Gramm devoted about as much of his speech to heavy criticism of Mr. Dukakis and the Democrats as he did to praising Mr. Bush. Among other things, the Senator said Mr. Dukakis would cut defense spending and would "wimp America and endanger peace."

"The 1988 Elections; Bush Is Elected by a 6–5 Margin with Solid G.O.P. Base in South; Democrats Hold Both Houses," November 9, 1988

The 1988 elections continued divided government between the presidency and Congress. Bush won nearly 49 million popular votes to almost 42 million for Dukakis, and 426 Electoral College votes to Dukakis's 111. (One elector cast a presidential ballot for Lloyd Bentsen.) Bush's victory did not help Republicans in Congress, however, as the Democrats kept control of both chambers.

NOVEMBER 9, 1988
THE 1988 ELECTIONS; BUSH IS ELECTED BY A 6–5 MARGIN WITH SOLID G.O.P. BASE IN SOUTH; DEMOCRATS HOLD BOTH HOUSES
How the Poll Was Taken
By E. J. DIONNE JR.

George Herbert Walker Bush of Texas was elected the 41st President of the United States yesterday.

The Vice President fashioned a solid, 6-to-5 victory in the popular vote over Gov. Michael S. Dukakis of Massachusetts with a sweep of the once Democratic South. He captured enough major states in other regions to win a commanding majority in the Electoral College.

Of the total of 538 electoral votes, Mr. Bush appeared likely to get from 350 to 415.

Crossover Voting

His solid victory notwithstanding, Mr. Bush did little to help Republican candidates for the Senate. In states like Florida, New Jersey and Ohio, all carried by him and all with Senate races the Republicans had hoped to win, the Republican senatorial nominees went down to defeat.

As a result, the Democrats maintained control of not only the House of Representatives but also the Senate, as voters split their tickets in contest after contest.

The voters stayed away from the polls in unusually large numbers. A preliminary estimate by CBS News indicated that the turnout would be below 51 percent of the population of voting age, which would make it even lower than that of the 1948 Presidential election, the previous post–World War II low.

Concession by Dukakis

In their statements last night, Mr. Bush and Mr. Dukakis were as gracious and positive as their campaigns had been tough and negative.

In Boston Mr. Dukakis, flanked by his family, conceded defeat shortly after 11:15.

"He will be our President," the Governor said of Mr. Bush, "and we'll work with him. This nation faces major challenges ahead, and we must work together."

Barely half an hour later, Mr. Bush claimed victory, declaring before a tumultuous crowd in Houston: "We can now speak the most majestic words a democracy has to offer: 'The people have spoken.' "

The Vice President also again invoked a favored theme of his campaign. "When I said I want a kinder, gentler nation," he asserted, "I meant it and I mean it."

Mr. Dukakis, winning a large majority of the voters who made up their minds late in the campaign, saved himself from an electoral humiliation similar to those suffered by Walter F. Mondale and George McGovern, the Democratic nominees in 1984 and 1972, holding Mr. Bush close in key industrial areas and carrying several states, including New York.

Mr. Bush becomes the first incumbent Vice President elected to the Presidency since Martin Van Buren in 1836. His share of the popular vote was 54 percent, CBS News estimated, as against 46 percent for Mr. Dukakis. The Governor's share was the highest for a Democratic Presidential nominee since Jimmy Carter won election in 1976.

The victory by Mr. Bush and his running mate, Senator Dan Quayle of Indiana, confirmed the Republican Party as the dominant force in Presidential politics and reflected the country's general satisfaction with eight years of Republican government under Ronald Reagan.

In campaigning to succeed Mr. Reagan, Mr. Bush promised no major departures, but he also suggested that he might do some things differently, invoking that vision of a "kinder, gentler nation" and affirming a strong commitment to the environment.

"HOUSE, BREAKING WITH BUSH, VOTES CHINA SANCTIONS," JUNE 30, 1989

The United States and the rest of the free world watched in horror in 1989, as the Chinese military killed hundreds of protestors calling for democratic reforms, in what became known as the Tiananmen Square Massacre. Although President Bush was critical of the Chinese government's actions, he opposed congressional efforts to punish China by imposing trade sanctions. The Bush administration temporarily halted top-level diplomacy with China, although it maintained contact outside the public spotlight.

JUNE 30, 1989
HOUSE, BREAKING WITH BUSH, VOTES CHINA SANCTIONS
By MARTIN TOLCHIN
Special to The New York Times

House Republicans broke with President Bush and joined Democrats in a vote of 418 to 0 today to impose new sanctions on China and condemn Beijing's suppression of human rights.

The sanctions package, worked out by Democratic and Republican foreign policy leaders on Capitol Hill, was a bipartisan substitute for about two dozen bills, some of them harsher and considered likely to be adopted by the House.

Thus the legislation allowed Congress to vent its anger at the Chinese Government over the military crackdown on the democracy movement without taking extreme steps like rescinding China's trade status as a "most favored nation."

No Veto Is Planned

The Bush Administration did not endorse the House move, but also indicated that it did not intend to veto it.

The sanctions approved by the House would suspend the financial support of the Overseas Private Investment Corporation in China, halt expenditure of previously autho-

rized funds for trade and development, mandate American opposition for six months to liberalization of export controls, and ban the export of crime control equipment and nuclear equipment that could be used for military purposes.

In addition, the measure would prevent the President from lifting the sanctions he has already imposed except for reasons of national security or unless he assures Congress that China has made progress in restoring human rights.

The Previous Sanctions

Those previous sanctions included a ban on the export of arms and military-related equipment, suspension of high-level contact between the United States and Chinese Governments, a ban on the export of satellites for launching from China and curtailing of nuclear cooperation.

The Senate Foreign Relations Committee is scheduled to take up its foreign aid bill after the July 4 recess, at which time it will consider several proposals to increase sanctions against China. It is not yet clear whether they will be adopted.

Secretary of State James A. Baker 3d told reporters that "the China sanctions package does not have the Bush Administration's endorsement," but added, "There has not been a veto threat." He stressed Mr. Bush's expertise on China and said the President, not Congress, bears the responsibility for formulating foreign policy.

"No elected official in the U.S. understands China better than the President, who served this country in China for a number of years," Mr. Baker said. "We do recognize the desire of elected officials to speak to this issue, and to vote on it, but the leadership should come from the executive branch and the President."

The House sponsors overrode the initial objections of both Democratic and Republican leaders who had argued that the Government should speak with a single voice, that of President Bush. But some in Congress considered the President too conciliatory, and pressed for stronger action.

· ·

"THE MALTA SUMMIT; BUSH AND GORBACHEV PROCLAIM A NEW ERA FOR U.S.-SOVIET TIES; AGREE ON ARMS AND TRADE AIMS," DECEMBER 4, 1989

President Bush's first presidential summit with Soviet leader Mikhail Gorbachev took place near the island of Malta in the Mediterranean Sea in December 1989. The two leaders met aboard ship during a storm and affirmed their commitment to working together to reduce cold war tensions.

DECEMBER 4, 1989
THE MALTA SUMMIT; BUSH AND GORBACHEV PROCLAIM A NEW ERA FOR U.S.-SOVIET TIES; AGREE ON ARMS AND TRADE AIMS

By ANDREW ROSENTHAL
Special to The New York Times

President Bush and President Mikhail S. Gorbachev ended their first summit meeting today with an extraordinary public affirmation of the new relationship between their countries.

Mr. Gorbachev said he and Mr. Bush agreed that "the characteristics of the cold war should be abandoned."

"The arms race, mistrust, psychological and ideological struggle, all those should be things of the past," he said.

Mr. Bush said: "With reform under way in the Soviet Union, we stand at the threshold of a brand-new era of U.S.-Soviet relations. It is within our grasp to contribute each in our own way to overcoming the division of Europe and ending the military confrontation there."

Another Meeting Is Set

In the most substantial agreements reached at the meeting, the two leaders said they would strive to conclude treaties on long-range nuclear weapons and conventional arms in 1990. They also agreed to hold another summit meeting in June in the United States.

But the significance of the first summit meeting between the leaders seemed to lie more in the tone than the substance.

They ended their rain-soaked two-day meeting with the first joint news conference by Soviet and American leaders.

The Tension Evaporates

There had been some annoyance aboard Mr. Gorbachev's ship, the *Maxim Gorky,* on Saturday night when Mr. Bush canceled an afternoon session and a dinner because of a gale. The tension lingered in the background today but it melted under the television lights in a 65-minute display of cordiality that ended with Mr. Bush reaching over to grasp Mr. Gorbachev's right forearm. The news conference was remarkable for its lack of conflict over issues that have long divided East and West, including arms control, the Middle East and economic relations.

For all the cordiality, the meeting did not produce any new treaties or specific agreements, or even a joint statement.

After eight hours of intimate discussions, the two leaders were still far apart on the issue of sea-based nuclear cruise missiles, a major point of disagreement on a strategic arms treaty. They remained at odds on Central America and Administration officials said Mr. Gorbachev did not give a definitive answer to Mr. Bush's proposals on an agreement reducing chemical weapons.

A Sense of Optimism

But Mr. Gorbachev, clearly pleased that Mr. Bush had shown some initiative on economic issues, registered approval on most of the proposals offered by Mr. Bush on Saturday, and the two leaders expressed broad optimism about the course of their relations.

Although they said they did not reach any specific accord on how to deal with the unraveling political power structure in Eastern Europe, Mr. Bush and Mr. Gorbachev seemed optimistic even about that problem.

"We searched for the answer to the question of where do we stand now," Mr. Gorbachev said. "We stated, both of us, that the world leaves one epoch of cold war and enters another epoch."

"U.S. Troops Move in Panama in Effort to Seize Noriega; Gunfire Is Heard in Capital," December 20, 1989

President Bush sent troops to Panama in December 1989 to oust Gen. Manuel A. Noriega, whom the United States had sought to remove for some time. The invasion came in response to attacks on American soldiers by Panamanian forces; it was also aimed at combating illegal drug trafficking supported by Noriega. U.S. forces captured Noriega, who eventually was convicted of drug trafficking and money laundering and sent to a U.S. federal prison.

DECEMBER 20, 1989
U.S. TROOPS MOVE IN PANAMA IN EFFORT TO SEIZE NORIEGA;
GUNFIRE IS HEARD IN CAPITAL
By MICHAEL R. GORDON
Special to The New York Times

The United States launched a military operation in Panama early this morning designed to topple the Government of Gen. Manuel Antonio Noriega.

Reports from Panama said that American troops and tanks were moving on General Noriega's headquarters, with mortar and machine gunfire echoing through the city. American citizens were ordered by the American military command in Panama to stay off the streets.

Administration officials said the military action was code-named Operation Echo. The United States maintains 12,000 troops, most combat forces, in Panama, and additional units were flown into the country on Tuesday to assist in the operation.

First Strike Since Libya

The operation was the most dramatic foreign policy move of the Bush Administration and the first time that United States military forces have been sent into combat since the air strike against the Libyan leader, Col. Muammar el-Qaddafi, in April 1986. The last large-scale engagement by American ground forces took place during the invasion of Grenada in October 1983.

Since taking office, Mr. Bush has been frustrated by failed efforts to encourage the ouster of General Noriega, who is accused by the Administration of being a major sponsor of illicit drug trafficking. The White House was criticized in October for failing to take steps to support an effort by elements of the Panama Defense Forces to remove General Noriega.

It was not clear whether the White House consulted with Congressional leaders about the military action, or notified them in advance. Thomas S. Foley, the Speaker of the House, said on Tuesday night that he had not been alerted by the Administration.

"A Law for Every American," July 27, 1990

The Americans with Disabilities Act of 1990 marked a milestone in civil rights legislation. It prohibited employment discrimination against handicapped individuals and required employers to make reasonable accommodations to help people with disabilities work successfully. In an editorial, *The Times* praised the legislation, which it said "enlarges civil rights, and humanity, for all Americans."

JULY 27, 1990
EDITORIAL
A LAW FOR EVERY AMERICAN

There have been many bill-signing ceremonies at the White House, but none quite like yesterday's. Under a hot summer sun on the South Lawn, more than 2,000 advocates for the disabled, many in wheelchairs, cheered mightily as President Bush signed a law that could bring 43 million handicapped people into society's mainstream.

The law, called the Americans with Disabilities Act of 1990, is the most sweeping anti-discrimination measure since the Civil Rights Act of 1964. Mr. Bush's oratory rose to the occasion. As a symbol of freedom, he said, the law is no less than a "declaration of independence." Like the dismantling of the Berlin wall, it opens "a once-closed door to a bright new era."

The new law will soon reach deeply into commercial life, banning discrimination in employment in all businesses with more than 15 employees. And except when employers can show "undue hardship," it will protect not only those who can't walk or see but also recovering drug abusers and alcoholics and people with AIDS.

The measure will require nearly every retail establishment—barber shops, banks, restaurants, movie theaters—

In a ceremony on the South Lawn of the White House, President George H. W. Bush signs into law the Americans with Disabilities Act of 1990, which the *New York Times* called "the most sweeping anti-discrimination measure since the Civil Rights Act of 1964."

Source: AP Photo/Barry Thumma

to be made accessible. Public and private transportation systems must provide lifts and other facilities for the handicapped in all new vehicles. And in three years, telephone companies must provide special equipment that will enable people with impaired speech or hearing to communicate with people using ordinary phones.

The original Senate bill, passed last September, was unfortunately vague in its instructions to employers. More precise language has since been added and, partly as a result of sensible adjustments made by the House, employers will have time to get ready. Businesses with more than 25 employees will have 18 months to meet the public accommodations rules and two years to meet the employment provisions. Small businesses would be given more time to comply.

There was also criticism that neither the Senate nor the Administration had made a serious effort to measure the costs of compliance. Costs and benefits are still matters of speculation. But two points are crucial.

The Federal Government now spends $57 billion every year on benefits for the disabled. That figure will surely shrink if the disabled have greater access to jobs. Less than 25 percent of disabled men and 13 percent of disabled women hold full-time jobs. And their earnings average only two-thirds that of all workers.

The act does more than enlarge the independence of disabled Americans. It enlarges civil rights, and humanity, for all Americans.

· ·

"The Iraqi Invasion; Bush, Hinting Force, Declares Iraqi Assault 'Will not Stand'; Proxy in Kuwait Issues Threat," August 6, 1990, and "Confrontation in the Gulf; Bush's Two Audiences," September 12, 1990

Within days of Iraq's invasion of Kuwait in the summer of 1990, President Bush declared, "This will not stand, this aggression against Kuwait." In speaking before Congress a few weeks later, he insisted that nations unite against Iraq in a "new world order" that recognized the importance of the rule of law.

AUGUST 6, 1990
THE IRAQI INVASION; BUSH, HINTING FORCE, DECLARES IRAQI ASSAULT 'WILL NOT STAND'; PROXY IN KUWAIT ISSUES THREAT
By THOMAS L. FRIEDMAN
Special to The New York Times

Committing the United States to roll back Iraq's conquest of Kuwait, President Bush said today that he would not settle for anything less than a total Iraqi withdrawal and would not tolerate the establishment of a puppet regime in Kuwait.

In a forceful statement to reporters as he returned to the White House from Camp David, Md., Mr. Bush all but committed himself to use military force against Iraq if diplomatic efforts and economic sanctions fail to produce an Iraqi withdrawal.

Mr. Bush dispatched Defense Secretary Dick Cheney to Saudi Arabia tonight in hopes of obtaining permission to send United States armed forces there to deter an Iraqi attack on that country, Administration officials said.

'This Will Not Stand'

Visibly angry, Mr. Bush said: "I view very seriously our determination to reverse this aggression. There are an awful lot of countries that are in total accord with what I've just said."

"We will be working with them all for collective action," the President added. "This will not stand. This will not stand, this aggression against Kuwait."

Asked how he could prevent the installation of an Iraqi-sponsored government in Kuwait, the President shot back, "Just wait, watch and learn."

Mr. Bush said he had consulted by telephone over the weekend with other world leaders to line up support for international economic sanctions against Iraq. He said he would meet in Washington on Monday with Prime Minister Margaret Thatcher of Britain and with the Secretary General of the North Atlantic Treaty Organization, Manfred Worner.

SEPTEMBER 12, 1990
CONFRONTATION IN THE GULF; BUSH'S TWO AUDIENCES

By R. W. APPLE JR.
Special to The New York Times

At times during his nationally televised speech to a joint session of Congress, the President seemed to be talking directly to the Iraqi leader, man to man, as when he declared bluntly, "Saddam Hussein will fail."

Mr. Bush appeared determined to demonstrate to the nation, the Iraqis and, indeed, the world that the passage of time would not erode American resolve.

Restating His Goals

He made it plain that he would not countenance the kind of process that the British weekly *The Economist* has described as the greatest danger to his strategy—a build-up of doubts and caveats at home through which "slowly the turning-back of Iraq threatens to become a wobbling mirage that is redefined until it is unrecognizable before fading away." Fighting that tendency, he reiterated, without a shade of difference, the goals he set weeks ago.

But there are other dangers, of course. The use of military force could strain the coalition with President Mikhail S. Gorbachev by which the President sets such great store. It could drive the moderate Arab states that now back the United States position into Saddam Hussein's arms. And it could extract a heavy political price at home if it did not have a clearly attainable goal and did not produce recognizable results in a reasonable time.

Another threat to solidarity on the home front is a rising feeling among average voters and among members of both parties on Capitol Hill that the United States is bearing much too great a share of the burden in the gulf.

Allies' Share of the Burden

In the House this afternoon, Representative Carroll Hubbard Jr., Democrat of Kentucky, and Representative Craig T. James, Republican of Florida, castigated Japan for what they described as Tokyo's inadequate financial contributions, and Chancellor Helmut Kohl of West Germany acknowledged publicly last weekend that he feared that the same sort of criticism would soon be directed at Bonn.

Responding to the President's speech on behalf of the Democrats, Representative Richard A. Gephardt, the House majority leader, said Mr. Bush had the party's backing. But he called upon the Japanese and the Germans to "respond to our potential sacrifice of lives with at least a financial sacrifice of their own."

While attacking no one, Mr. Bush said pointedly that "the response of most of our friends and allies" to American appeals for burden-sharing "has been good." He did not say "all our friends and allies," and he added:

"We insist others do their share as well."

Mr. Bush has done well in the past when he talked tough. His emulation of Clint Eastwood—"Read my lips, no new taxes"—was widely accounted one of the main factors in his sweeping electoral victory in November, 1988.

But he has backed off that pledge now, and some White House aides have expressed fears that in doing so, he has undercut the credibility of his future pledges. That may be another reason why he so doggedly went back tonight over all the promises he has made in his dozens of comments on the Middle East in recent weeks.

"Accord to Reduce Spending and Raise Taxes Is Reached; Many in Congress Critical," October 1, 1990

In agreeing to a deficit-reduction plan in fall 1990, President Bush broke his campaign pledge of "no new taxes." He faced bipartisan criticism for the plan; as *The Times* wrote, "Republicans were angry about the tax increases, and Democrats about the cuts in domestic spending." The Democrats would make Bush's failure to keep his pledge a major issue in the 1992 presidential race.

OCTOBER 1, 1990
ACCORD TO REDUCE SPENDING AND RAISE TAXES IS REACHED; MANY IN CONGRESS CRITICAL
Deadline Extended
By SUSAN F. RASKY
Special to The New York Times

President Bush and Congressional negotiators agreed today to a deficit-cutting plan that includes major increases in taxes after Mr. Bush decided that the need for economic stability was worth the sacrifice of his main policies on taxation.

Mr. Bush and a weary group of leaders from both parties gathered in the Rose Garden to announce their accord and to disclose that they now project the deficit for the 1991 fiscal year at $293.7 billion, up more than $60 billion from the estimate the Government made in July.

They said the plan would reduce the Federal deficit by $40 billion next year and by $500 billion over five years. But at the same time they agreed to extend the Gramm-Rudman-Hollings deadline for bringing the budget into balance to the 1996 fiscal year from the 1993 year.

Lower Interest Rate Is Expected

Mr. Bush said he expected that enactment of the plan would stimulate the economy and lead to lower interest rates. But White House officials later said the economic projections underlying the plan also assumed that oil prices would fall.

Mr. Bush immediately began selling the package to Congress, which took the first step today by approving a stopgap spending bill that would keep the Government in operation through Oct. 5 and avoid steep automatic spending cuts that were due to take effect on Monday.

Even as Mr. Bush began his sales pitch, dozens of rank-and-file members of Congress attacked the budget agreement. Republicans were angry about the tax increases, and

Democrats about the cuts in domestic spending. The compromise, a product of four months of negotiations between the White House and Congressional leaders, would impose steep spending cuts in popular domestic programs, particularly Medicare, while raising taxes on petroleum products as well as cigarettes, luxury items and alcoholic beverages. But the Social Security program was spared a direct hit.

The agreement forced tough political decisions upon President Bush. He gave up his long-sought goal of a cut in the capital gains tax rate and accepted a Democratic proposal that would restrict the amount of deductions that Americans with incomes over $100,000 could take on their Federal income tax returns. Excluding medical expenses and investment interest costs, this deduction floor, or the amount of income excluded from deductions, would be equal to 3 percent of a taxpayer's adjusted income over $100,000.

No Rate Change, Sununu Says

"The fact of the matter is that rates have not been changed," said the White House chief of staff, John H. Sununu, who argued that the agreed-upon change did not constitute a tax rate increase.

Democrats blocked the President on his pet issue, a cut in the tax on capital gains. The Democrats had insisted that any cut in the tax on the profits on the sale of assets be accompanied by an increase in tax rates for the wealthy. That would have put Mr. Bush at loggerheads with Republican House members, most of whom have vowed to block any rate increases.

"Abroad at Home; War and the President," November 30, 1990, and "Confrontation in the Gulf; Congress Acts to Authorize War in Gulf; Margins Are 5 Votes in Senate, 67 in House," January 13, 1991

President Bush built the case for going to war against Iraq by securing UN Security Council and congressional resolutions authorizing the use of force. Operation Desert Storm successfully repelled Iraq's invasion of Kuwait in just six weeks, and the president's public approval ratings soared to nearly 90 percent, the highest ever recorded up to that time. Because its mandate was limited to removing Iraqi forces from Kuwait, the Bush administration decided not to pursue Iraqi leader Saddam Hussein—a decision that raised some subsequent criticism.

> Can President Bush take the country into war in the Persian Gulf without the approval of Congress?

NOVEMBER 30, 1990
OP-ED
ABROAD AT HOME
War and the President
By ANTHONY LEWIS

Can President Bush take the country into war in the Persian Gulf without the approval of Congress? The question is heading toward decisive tests, legal and political. The answer could have profound consequences for our constitutional system and our internal peace.

The President has moved very far toward war without asking for the consent of Congress. After Iraq gobbled up Kuwait in August, he sent a large American armed force to Saudi Arabia. Three weeks ago he ordered that force almost doubled, to give it an offensive capability.

Now Mr. Bush has the authority of the United Nations Security Council to take military action. A long and skillful diplomatic campaign by the President and Secretary Baker ended in success yesterday when the Council authorized the use of "all necessary means" after Jan. 15 to enforce previous resolutions on the gulf.

But the President has undertaken only to "consult" Congress. That is very different from what the Constitution provides: that only Congress, the House and the Senate, shall have the power to declare war.

Legal conservatives have urged respect for the "original intention" of the Constitution's Framers. That is often difficult to discover, but in the case of the war clause the intention is exceptionally clear.

At the Constitutional Convention of 1787, delegates left it open to the President to use armed forces to repel sudden attacks. But a deliberate choice of war was to be for Congress. James Wilson of Pennsylvania, a key figure at the Convention, said:

"It will not be in the power of a single man, or a single body of men, to involve us in such distress; for the important power of declaring war is vested in the legislature at large."

Presidents have used military force a great deal in recent years without any kind of approval from Congress. There were the swift strikes on Grenada and Panama.

But in this case there is no sudden reason for action. U.S. forces have been in the gulf for months. The U.N. Security Council has passed a dozen resolutions. Americans are openly debating the issue. For a President to make war without Congressional authority under those conditions would be to plow the Constitution under.

The constitutional issues are raised in a lawsuit by 38 members of Congress, led by Representative Ronald V. Dellums, Democrat of California. It seeks a judicial decision that the President must have Congress's approval to go to war in the gulf. The Congressmen's brief is a notable compendium of constitutional and legal materials on the issue.

JANUARY 13, 1991
CONFRONTATION IN THE GULF; CONGRESS ACTS TO AUTHORIZE WAR IN GULF; MARGINS ARE 5 VOTES IN SENATE, 67 IN HOUSE

By ADAM CLYMER

Special to The New York Times

After three days of solemn, often eloquent debate, Congress today voted to give President Bush the authority to go to war against Iraq.

The Senate approved the use of military force by a vote of 52 to 47. The majority included 42 Republicans and 10 Democrats, mostly Southerners who were convinced that economic sanctions would not force Iraq from Kuwait or who were unwilling to vote against the President. Two Republicans joined 45 Democrats in opposing force.

In the House, the vote was a more comfortable 250 to 183, as 164 Republicans and 86 Democrats voted for force, while 179 Democrats, 3 Republicans and 1 independent were opposed.

'All Necessary Means'

The measure, the Authorization for Use of Military Force Against Iraq Resolution, said Mr. Bush was authorized "to use United States armed forces pursuant to United Nations Security Council Resolution 678," which authorized member nations to use "all necessary means" against Iraq if [Iraq] did not withdraw from Kuwait by midnight Tuesday, Eastern standard time.

Mr. Bush asked Congress for this declaration last Tuesday, and its passage removed the last political obstacle to an attack by United States-led forces against Iraqi troops occupying Kuwait.

Under the terms of the resolution, before force may be used Mr. Bush must send a message to Congressional leaders saying that diplomacy and sanctions will not be effective in getting Iraq out of Kuwait.

'Last Best Chance for Peace'

At a news conference immediately after the votes, President Bush said the action by Congress "unmistakably demonstrates the United States's commitment to enforce a complete Iraqi withdrawal from Kuwait."

"SUMMIT IN MOSCOW; BUSH AND GORBACHEV SIGN PACT TO CURTAIL NUCLEAR ARSENALS; JOIN IN CALL FOR MIDEAST TALKS," AUGUST 1, 1991

Bush and Gorbachev signed the Strategic Arms Reduction Treaty, now known as START I, in August 1991. Originally conceived in the Reagan administration, the treaty called for significant reductions in each country's nuclear forces. Just weeks before leaving office, Bush signed a second agreement, START II, with Russian president Boris Yeltsin.

AUGUST 1, 1991
SUMMIT IN MOSCOW; BUSH AND GORBACHEV SIGN PACT TO CURTAIL NUCLEAR ARSENALS; JOIN IN CALL FOR MIDEAST TALKS

By R. W. APPLE JR.

President Bush and President Mikhail S. Gorbachev of the Soviet Union signed a far-reaching treaty today that is designed to scale down their nations' stocks of long-range nuclear weapons, then joined in a bold bid to stage a comparably momentous Middle East peace conference in October.

The two leaders inscribed their names on the 700-page arms reduction treaty at a solemn 30-minute ceremony in St. Vladimir's Hall in the Kremlin. The treaty still needs approval by the legislative branches in both countries, but with the signing, after nine years of negotiation, Mr. Bush said, "We reverse a half-century of steadily growing strategic arsenals."

Declaring the arms race over, Mr. Gorbachev commented, "Thank God, as we say in Russian, that we stopped this." . . .

A joint statement issued by the two Presidents said they "will work to convene in October a peace conference designed to launch bilateral and multilateral negotiations."

· ·

"THE THOMAS CONFIRMATION; SENATE CONFIRMS THOMAS, 52–48, ENDING WEEK OF BITTER BATTLE; 'TIME FOR HEALING,' JUDGE SAYS," OCTOBER 16, 1991

President Bush's nomination of Clarence Thomas to the Supreme Court was highly controversial. Thomas's conservative judicial philosophy contrasted sharply with that of Thurgood Marshall, whom he was to replace. Then one of Thomas's former aides, attorney Anita F. Hill, accused him of sexual harassment, and Thomas vehemently denied the allegations. After extensive Senate hearings, Thomas narrowly won confirmation to the Court, becoming the second African American justice, after Marshall.

OCTOBER 16, 1991
THE THOMAS CONFIRMATION; SENATE CONFIRMS THOMAS, 52–48, ENDING WEEK OF BITTER BATTLE; 'TIME FOR HEALING,' JUDGE SAYS
By R. W. APPLE JR.

Judge Clarence Thomas, who was born to unlettered parents living in abject poverty in rural Georgia, won confirmation as an Associate Justice of the Supreme Court tonight by one of the narrowest margins in history, barely surviving an accusation by one of his former assistants that he had sexually harassed her.

After an all-day debate, during which President Bush brought heavy pressure on wavering Senators and the public flooded Capitol Hill with telephone calls and telegrams, the Senate voted 52 to 48 in favor of the 43-year-old judge. Eleven Democrats joined 41 of the 43 Republicans in supporting him.

A Victory Margin Narrowed

"This is more a time for healing, not a time for anger or animus or animosity," Judge Thomas said later tonight, standing under an umbrella outside his house in Alexandria, Va. Referring to the fierceness of the 107-day fight over his nomination, he added, "We have to put these things behind us and go forward."

Judge Thomas's victory margin was narrowed considerably by the harassment accusation, made public a little over a week ago. Three Democrats who had said flatly last month that they backed him ended up voting no—Joseph I. Lieberman of Connecticut and Richard H. Bryan and Harry Reid, both of Nevada. They were joined by three other Democrats who had hinted that they supported Judge Thomas—Bob Graham of Florida, Daniel Patrick Moynihan of New York and Robert C. Byrd of West Virginia.

Southern Democrats Firm

But seven Southern Democrats, many of them dependent on black voters for their political survival because of the flight of whites to the Republican Party, held firm in support of the nominee, along with four from other parts of the country, and that made the difference. Judge Thomas had repeatedly invoked racial themes in his own defense, and, in a move that seemed to gain sympathy among blacks, he accused the all-white Senate of conducting a "high-tech lynching."

If three more senators had voted no, Judge Thomas would have lost.

A number of swing voters said they had been unable to resolve the conflicts that developed in three days of fevered hearings last weekend between Anita F. Hill, now a law professor in Oklahoma, and Judge Thomas, who passionately denied each of her allegations. Most senators said they had therefore set the whole subject aside and voted as they had intended to before it came up.

Judge Thomas will move onto the Court shortly, giving it its full complement of nine members. If his past decisions, writings and speeches are any guide, which he insisted throughout the long confirmation process they were not, he will increase its conservative majority on many is-

sues. Although he has made no explicit statement on *Roe v. Wade,* the leading abortion case, and indeed told the Senate Judiciary Committee that he had never discussed it, most experts consider him anti-abortion.

Currently a member of the United States Court of Appeals for the District of Columbia Circuit, Judge Thomas will become the 106th member of the Supreme Court and the second black member. He replaces Thurgood Marshall, a liberal, who was the first.

"The Earth Summit," June 13, 1992

President Bush attended the 1992 Earth Summit in Brazil in 1992 and signed the UN Convention on Climate Change, which presented voluntary guidelines for states to follow. As *The Times* noted, however, "the agreement omitted a call for a treaty to be negotiated that would make such principles binding."

JUNE 13, 1992
THE EARTH SUMMIT; PRESIDENT, IN RIO, DEFENDS HIS STAND ON ENVIRONMENT
By JAMES BROOKE

President Bush told world leaders at the Earth Summit today that he had no apologies for his Administration's environmental record and called for a "prompt start" to carry out the accords signed here.

"America's record on environmental protection is second to none, so I did not come here to apologize," Mr. Bush said, rebutting the criticism heard since the Rio summit meeting began 10 days ago.

He also vigorously defended his opposition to a treaty to protect rare and endangered plants and animals, a position that put the United States outside a vast consensus of support by almost all of the 172 nations represented at the talks.

Principles on Forests
"That proposed agreement threatens to retard biotechnology and undermine the protection of ideas," Mr. Bush

said. "It is never easy to stand alone on principle, but sometimes leadership requires that you do."

The President's defiant speech came as the pace of events at the talks accelerated with the arrival of dozens of world leaders, many of them offering decidedly different views of environmental issues in speeches at the conference hall.

A major development of the day was an agreement among negotiators, after days of talks, to adopt a voluntary set of principles in favor of preserving the world's forests, which had been a goal of the United States and other wealthier countries.

But the agreement omitted a call for a treaty to be negotiated that would make such principles binding.

"Baker Says Arabs Should Yield Next," July 20, 1992

One of the Bush administration's continuing challenges was promoting peace between Israel and its surrounding states as well as in the Israeli-Palestinian conflict. Following the 1991 Madrid Conference on the Middle East, Secretary of State Baker undertook several missions to encourage Arab-Israeli diplomacy.

JULY 20, 1992
BAKER SAYS ARABS SHOULD YIELD NEXT
By THOMAS L. FRIEDMAN

Secretary of State James A. Baker 3d, seeking to revive the stalled Middle East peace talks, said today that now that the Israelis had a new Government that was signaling a willingness to compromise, it was time for the Arabs to do the same.

Hours before Mr. Baker arrived, the new Israeli Prime Minister, Yitzhak Rabin, announced that he was suspending all new building of Jewish settlements in the occupied West Bank and Gaza Strip pending a review by the Government of exactly what is being built where.

Speaking to reporters after his two hours of talks with Mr. Rabin, Mr. Baker hinted that if Mr. Rabin carries out plans to sharply curtail Israeli settlement-building activity in the occupied West Bank and Gaza Strip, the Bush Administration would be more flexible than it was with his predecessor, Yitzhak Shamir, in granting Israel the $10 billion in housing loan guarantees it has been seeking.

Baker Sees 'New Possibilities'

"I think everybody recognizes that the new Israeli Government creates some new possibilities to transform these negotiations and give those negotiations new momentum," Mr. Baker said on his flight to Israel, the first leg of his Middle East swing.

"We have been hearing some different things and different signals coming from this new Israeli Government and we would like to think that we could begin to hear some new and different signals coming from those on the Arab side."

Mr. Baker's eagerness to jump-start the stalled peace talks between Israel and its Arab neighbors in part is due to the fact that this could be his last shuttle mission as Secretary of State. It is now accepted by many on Mr. Baker's staff as probable that he will soon be stepping down in order to take over President Bush's re-election campaign, as he did in 1988 when he resigned as Treasury Secretary, and Mr. Baker did little to dispel that assumption in his remarks today.

It is widely expected that Mr. Baker will depart sometime before or immediately after the Republican convention in Houston, which begins Aug. 17, and that he would be replaced by the current Deputy Secretary of State Lawrence S. Eagleburger.

"The 1992 Elections: Disappointment—Road to Defeat; Sifting Strategies: What Went Wrong and Right; Bush: As the Loss Sinks In, Some Begin Pointing Fingers," November 5, 1992

Bush's loss in the 1992 presidential election marked an end to the Reagan era in Washington, D.C. As one Republican official told The Times, "We've been in office for 12 years. We got tired. We forgot why we came."

NOVEMBER 5, 1992
THE 1992 ELECTIONS: DISAPPOINTMENT—ROAD TO DEFEAT

Sifting Strategies: What Went Wrong, and Right; Bush: As the Loss Sinks In,
Some Begin Pointing Fingers

By MAUREEN DOWD

It was beginning to sink in, very painfully, that he had been fired and now he was expected to go back to Washington and take all his stuff out of the Oval Office, the worn Yale baseball mitt, the drawers full of tennis balls, the family pictures, the black and white horseshoes, his black Swiss army knife with "President Bush" engraved in silver.

As George Bush got ready to leave Houston yesterday morning and fly back to the capital, he took a call from one of the few senior Administration officials who had remained loyal to the end. Could he have been better served by the people in charge of his campaign? the official asked, in an account of the conversation.

Frustration and Anger

"Don't get me started on that," the President snapped, his voice raw with anger, frustration and blame.

On his flight back to Washington from Indianapolis, Vice President Dan Quayle was openly critical of the campaign management, telling reporters that their defeat was less a result of the depressed economy than of the failure of the campaign to articulate its own domestic agenda. They never had a message, he said scathingly, because "that takes a strategy."

A Republican electoral debacle is not a pretty thing. The finger-pointing and back-stabbing that had consumed the White House and the party for months got even worse yesterday, with everyone blaming everyone else for "the worst campaign ever seen," in the words of Ed Rollins, the Republican strategist who presided over Ronald Reagan's 1984 landslide, and defected this year to briefly help run Ross Perot's campaign.

End of Cold War

Trapped in an atmosphere described by one White House official as "a little surreal," Republicans offered dozens of reasons for the humiliating rejection of the man who had been wildly popular only a year and a half ago, reasons stretching back to the beginning of the Bush Administration and going right up to the last weekend of the campaign.

"Look, we ran out of steam in the second half of the second Reagan Administration," said William J. Bennett, a former official of the Reagan and Bush Administrations. "We've been in office for 12 years. We got tired. We forgot why we came."

And in a poignant echo of the Democratic message that the 68-year-old President's time had passed, he added:

> 'He's a guy who thought he was a great politician because he had been the national party chairman and because he knew the name of every national committeeman and state party chairman. But he never understood what was going on in the country.'

"It's generational. George Bush genuinely believed that the major job he had was to win the peace and end the cold war."

While there were acres of criticism about the dispirited leadership of James A. Baker 3d, the maladroit management of Robert M. Teeter and Frederic V. Malek, the politically disastrous economic advice of Richard G. Darman and Nicholas F. Brady, there was also a sense that George Bush was responsible for his own failure in the end, because he was unable to read or give voice to the public's mood and imbue his Presidency with passion, poetry and a plan.

"It's him," Mr. Rollins said of Mr. Bush. "He's a guy who thought he was a great politician because he had been the national party chairman and because he knew the name of every national committeeman and state party chairman. But he never understood what was going on in the country. Ronald Reagan was never a state party chairman and he didn't know the names of any committeemen, but he always knew where the country was."

Alarms Sound But Go Unheeded

Although his manner was modest, Mr. Bush is a politician, with a politician's ego, and he grew complacent, freezing out old friends and advisers who long ago tried to sound the alarm, and surrounding himself with politically tone-deaf economic advisers who were reviled by the conservatives who helped elect the President.

"As down home as he and Barbara were," an old friend of Mr. Bush said, "after a while they got used to the idea that they were in the White House and that's the way it ought to be."

"Mission to Somalia; Bush Declares Goal in Somalia to 'Save Thousands,' " December 5, 1992

In response to a devastating famine in Somalia, President Bush announced in late 1992 that he would send U.S. troops on a humanitarian mission to distribute food and supplies. The intervention continued into the Clinton administration and illustrated, as *The Times* wrote, the challenges for the United States of "a new post–cold-war role as a military force on behalf of humanitarian, not strategic ends."

DECEMBER 5, 1992
MISSION TO SOMALIA

Bush Declares Goal in Somalia to 'Save Thousands'
By MICHAEL WINES

President Bush ordered troops into Somalia today on a mission to "save thousands of innocents," as the Pentagon outlined an operation that will leave soldiers and marines in Somalia well into the Administration of President Bill Clinton.

Mr. Bush gathered broad support for the intervention from top leaders of Congress, from other world leaders and from Mr. Clinton himself, and then went on television at midday to announce an operation that thrusts the United States into a new post–cold-war role as a military force on behalf of humanitarian, not strategic ends.

"I understand the United States alone cannot right the world's wrongs," Mr. Bush declared in his speech, delivered just 47 days before he leaves office. "But we also know that some crises in the world cannot be resolved without American involvement, that American action is often nec-

essary as a catalyst for broader involvement of the community of nations."

28,000 Troops Going

Military leaders said they would send 28,000 troops into Somalia, beginning next week and proceeding in four stages. The State Department said that Britain, Belgium, France, Canada, Pakistan and Jordan would also contribute troops or supplies and that Germany and Japan, among others, were expected to contribute money and perhaps equipment.

But the bulk of the force will be American. Administration officials expressed hope that the United States could begin to hand off some of the country to the existing United Nations peacekeeping operation before Mr. Clinton is inaugurated on Jan. 20, but it was clear that the new President would inherit an ongoing military operation.

"The Pardons; Bush Pardons 6 in Iran Affair, Aborting a Weinberger Trial; Prosecutor Assails 'Cover-Up,' " December 25, 1992

One of President Bush's most controversial actions was his decision to pardon six Reagan administration officials in connection with the Iran-contra scandal. In so doing, Bush in effect negated independent prosecutor Lawrence E. Walsh's ability to continue his investigation.

DECEMBER 25, 1992
THE PARDONS; BUSH PARDONS 6 IN IRAN AFFAIR, ABORTING A WEINBERGER TRIAL; PROSECUTOR ASSAILS 'COVER-UP'

By DAVID JOHNSTON

Six years after the arms-for-hostages scandal began to cast a shadow that would darken two Administrations, President Bush today granted full pardons to six former officials in Ronald Reagan's Administration, including former Defense Secretary Caspar W. Weinberger.

Mr. Weinberger was scheduled to stand trial on Jan. 5 on charges that he lied to Congress about his knowledge of the arms sales to Iran and efforts by other countries to help underwrite the Nicaraguan rebels, a case that was expected to focus on Mr. Weinberger's private notes that contain references to Mr. Bush's endorsement of the secret shipments to Iran.

In one remaining facet of the inquiry, the independent prosecutor, Lawrence E. Walsh, plans to review a 1986 campaign diary kept by Mr. Bush. Mr. Walsh has characterized the President's failure to turn over the diary until now as misconduct.

Decapitated Walsh Efforts

But in a single stroke, Mr. Bush swept away one conviction, three guilty pleas and two pending cases, virtually decapitating what was left of Mr. Walsh's effort, which began in 1986. Mr. Bush's decision was announced by the White House in a printed statement after the President left for Camp David, where he will spend the Christmas holiday.

Mr. Walsh bitterly condemned the President's action, charging that "the Iran-contra cover-up, which has continued for more than six years, has now been completed."

Mr. Walsh directed his heaviest fire at Mr. Bush over the pardon of Mr. Weinberger, whose trial would have given the prosecutor a last chance to explore the role in the affair of senior Reagan officials, including Mr. Bush's actions as Vice President.

'Evidence of Conspiracy'

Mr. Walsh hinted that Mr. Bush's pardon of Mr. Weinberger and the President's own role in the affair could be related. For the first time, he charged that Mr. Weinberger's notes about the secret decision to sell arms to Iran, a central piece of evidence in the case against the former Pentagon chief, included "evidence of a conspiracy among the highest ranking Reagan Administration officials to lie to Congress and the American public."

The prosecutor charged that Mr. Weinberger's efforts to hide his notes may have "forestalled impeachment proceedings against President Reagan" and formed part of a pattern of "deception and obstruction." On Dec. 11, Mr. Walsh said he discovered "misconduct" in Mr. Bush's failure to turn over what the prosecutor said were the President's own "highly relevant contemporaneous notes, despite repeated requests for such documents."

The notes, in the form of a campaign diary that Mr. Bush compiled after the elections in November 1986, are in the process of being turned over to Mr. Walsh, who said, "In light of President Bush's own misconduct, we are gravely concerned about his decision to pardon others who lied to Congress and obstructed official investigations."

THE PRESIDENCY OF
BILL CLINTON

JANUARY 20, 1993 – JANUARY 20, 2001

William Jefferson "Bill" Clinton's presidency represented a time of economic prosperity and uncertainty about the U.S. role in the world. The first president to take office after the end of the cold war, Clinton, in both political background and interests, was well-suited to address domestic policy priorities. His administration oversaw significant accomplishments, from erasing $200 billion-plus budget deficits and creating annual surpluses to enacting significant reforms in welfare policy. At the same time, the Clinton administration faced challenges in deciding when to deploy U.S. troops abroad, particularly during the president's first year in office. Clinton's second term was overshadowed by allegations of sexual misconduct, both before and during his presidency. He was the second U.S. president to be impeached, and, like the first—Andrew Johnson in 1868—he was acquitted by the Senate.

Bill Clinton's father died in an automobile accident three months before the birth of his son. Originally named William Jefferson Blythe, Clinton was legally adopted by his stepfather and took his last name. His stepfather was an alcoholic who could be abusive toward Clinton's mother and his stepbrother until Clinton, as a teenager, confronted him and ordered him never to harm them again. Clinton had a very close relationship with his mother and his maternal grandparents, who encouraged him to excel. In 1963 he visited the White House with a youth group delegation from Arkansas, and he shook President John F. Kennedy's hand—the photograph of that moment later became a prominent part of his presidential campaign.

As an undergraduate student at Georgetown University in Washington, D.C., Clinton served as an intern for Sen. J. William

IT'S REVEILLE IN AMERICA!

Fulbright of Arkansas. Clinton majored in international relations and won a Rhodes Scholarship to study at Oxford University in England for two years. During that time, he considered taking a reserve officer spot at the University of Arkansas Law School, which would have deferred military service in the Vietnam War. He changed his mind, but did not go to Vietnam because he received a high number in the military draft lottery. After returning to the United States, Clinton entered Yale University Law School, completing his degree in 1973.

Politics was Clinton's passion, and he was determined to begin his career in his home state. He began teaching law at the University of Arkansas at Fayetteville and ran unsuccessfully for a U.S. House seat in 1974. Two years later, he was elected attorney general of Arkansas. When he won the gubernatorial race in 1978 at age thirty-two, he became the youngest governor in the nation at the time. But he lost reelection just two years later, in part because of a decision to increase vehicle licensing fees. He also faced criticism after Cuban refugees from the Mariel boatlift, who had been detained in Arkansas by the Carter administration, sparked violent riots. When he ran for governor in 1982, he publicly apologized for his mistakes and won election again. He was reelected repeatedly and launched his presidential campaign from Arkansas.

THE 1992 ELECTION

Clinton considered a presidential run in 1988 but decided to wait. He gained national prominence by chairing the National Governors Association, and he built support in the Democratic Party by heading the politically centrist Democratic Leadership Council. When Clinton announced his candidacy for president in 1991, his campaign quickly ran afoul of allegations of marital infidelity and strategically avoiding military service during the Vietnam War. But Clinton soldiered through these battles, won the Democratic nomination, and chose Sen. Albert Gore Jr. of Tennessee as his running mate.

In the general election, Clinton faced Republican incumbent president George H. W. Bush and independent candidate Ross Perot. Perot was a billionaire who waged a campaign centered around economic policy and balancing the budget. Bush made the case for successful foreign policy leadership in ending the cold war and leading the United States to victory in the Persian Gulf War, but these issues proved to be less significant in a time of economic uncertainty. Clinton promised both economic and social reform, and he prevailed in the race with 43 percent of the popular vote and 370 Electoral College votes, to 37 percent of the popular vote and 168 Electoral College votes for Bush. Perot won 19.7 million popular votes nationwide, but they did not translate into any electoral votes.

THE CLINTON ADMINISTRATION (FIRST TERM)

Clinton's fourteen-member cabinet was notable for its demographic diversity. He appointed the first woman attorney general, Janet Reno of Florida. He also selected two other women to head cabinet departments, Donna E. Shalala of Wisconsin for the Department of Health and Human Services and Hazel R. O'Leary of Minnesota for the Energy Department. Clinton selected two African Americans, Mike Espy of Mississippi to head the Department of Agriculture and Ronald H. Brown of Washington, D.C., to head the Department of Commerce. He also appointed two Latino cabinet secretaries, Henry G. Cisneros of Texas for Housing and Urban Development and Federico F. Peña of Colorado for Transportation. Other cabinet members included Warren M. Christopher of California

as secretary of state, former Democratic senator and former vice-presidential candidate Lloyd Bentsen Jr. of Texas as treasury secretary, and U.S. representative Les Aspin of Wisconsin as defense secretary.

First Lady Hillary Rodham Clinton was a highly regarded practicing attorney who was her husband's closest political adviser. The two met at Yale Law School, and she turned down several promising opportunities to move to Arkansas to be with Bill Clinton. She taught at the University of Arkansas Law School and then joined the distinguished Rose law firm in Little Rock. As governor, Clinton often gave his wife significant responsibilities, such as directing education reform. Their partnership continued into the White House. Hillary Clinton became the first chief executive's spouse to have an office in the West Wing, the center of presidential policy making, and the president selected her to head the task force for one of his signature campaign issues, health care reform. Their only child, Chelsea, was a teenager in the White House and entered Stanford University during her father's second term.

MAJOR ISSUES (FIRST TERM)

Following his election victory, Clinton faced many challenges during his transition period. He had promised during the campaign to lift the prohibition on having openly gay people serve in the military. After his election, however, the opposition to this proposal proved so great that his administration ultimately decided on a compromise policy known as "Don't ask, don't tell," in which military members would not be questioned about their sexual orientation, provided they did not reveal if they were gay. Clinton also backtracked on a campaign promise to permit Haitian refugees to emigrate to the United States when it quickly became clear that many would risk their lives doing so. And the president-elect had to withdraw from Senate consideration his first nominee for attorney general, Zoë Baird, because she had hired illegal immigrants as household employees. (His second nomination also backfired for similar reasons.)

The administration got off to a rocky start in other ways as well. The dismissal of White House Travel Office employees in spring 1993 sparked controversy for appearing to benefit friends of the Clintons, and many of the employees ultimately were reassigned to other positions. A few weeks later, the president had his hair cut by a famous stylist aboard *Air Force One* in Los Angeles, and a media frenzy erupted over whether air traffic had been delayed as a result. The administration also faced foreign policy debacles in the fall, first in Somalia, where nearly two dozen American soldiers died in a firefight, and then in Haiti, where

QUICK FACTS ON BILL CLINTON

BIRTH	August 19, 1946, Hope, Ark.
EDUCATION	Georgetown University, B.S., 1968 Oxford University, England, Rhodes Scholar, 1968–1970 Yale Law School, J.D., 1973
FAMILY	Wife: Hillary Diane Rodham Clinton Children: Chelsea Clinton
WHITE HOUSE PETS	Cat ("Socks"); dog ("Buddy")
PARTY	Democratic
PREPRESIDENTIAL CAREER (SELECTED)	Staff intern, Sen. J. William Fulbright, 1967 Rhodes Scholar, 1968–1970 Professor, University of Arkansas Law School, 1973 Unsuccessful candidate for U.S. House of Representatives from Arkansas, 1974 Arkansas attorney general, 1977–1979 Arkansas governor, 1979–1981 Loses reelection for governor, 1980 Arkansas governor, 1983–1992 Chairman, National Governors Association, 1986–1987 Head of Democratic Leadership Council, 1990–1991
PRESIDENTIAL TERMS	January 20, 1993–January 20, 1997 January 20, 1997–January 20, 2001
VICE PRESIDENT	Albert Gore Jr.
SELECTED EVENTS	Hillary Rodham Clinton leads task force on health care reform (1993–1994) Family and Medical Leave Act (1993) Bombing of World Trade Center, New York City (1993) Federal assault on Branch Davidian compound, Waco, Texas (1993) Deficit-reduction package (1993) White House signing of peace pact between Israel and Palestine Liberation Organization (1993) Attack on U.S. soldiers in Somalia (1993) Brady Handgun Control Act (1993) North American Free Trade Agreement (1993) Violent Crime Control and Law Enforcement Act (1994)

angry demonstrators prevented U.S. forces from landing to help restore political stability.

But the president achieved some significant policy victories in his first year. His deficit-reduction plan passed Congress by one vote in the House and with Vice President Gore casting the tie-breaking vote in the Senate. Clinton signed legislation guaranteeing unpaid family leave for most employees as well as gun control legislation that mandated a waiting period before handgun purchases. (The handgun control act was named in honor of James Brady, former presidential press secretary, who was shot and severely injured in 1981 in an assassination attempt on President Ronald Reagan.) He brought Israeli and Palestinian leaders together at the White House to sign an historic agreement to work toward peace.

U.S. peacekeeping forces land in Haiti (1994)
Agreement from North Korea to halt nuclear weapons program (1994)
Republican Party wins control of Congress (1994)
Bombing of federal building in Oklahoma City (1995)
Dayton Accords on Bosnia (1995)
Federal government shutdowns (1995–1996)
Antiterrorism and Effective Death Penalty Act (1996)
Health Insurance Portability and Accountability Act (1996)
Personal Responsibility and Work Opportunity Reconciliation Act (1996)
Minimum Wage Increase Act (1996)
Illegal Immigrant Reform and Immigrant Responsibility Act (1996)
Reelection victory (1996)
Balanced budget agreement (1997)
Clinton v. Jones Supreme Court ruling that sitting presidents are not exempt
    from civil lawsuits (1997)
Whitewater investigation expands to include allegations of presidential
    misconduct with Monica Lewinsky (1998)
Supreme Court declares line-item veto unconstitutional (1998)
Attack on U.S. embassies in Kenya and Tanzania (1998)
Clinton admits wrongdoing in Lewinsky affair (1998)
"Good Friday" Ireland peace pact (1998)
President orders air strikes against Sudan, Afghanistan (1998)
Iraq Liberation Act (1998)
Clinton impeached by U.S. House of Representatives (1998)
Clinton acquitted by U.S. Senate (1999)
Kosovo War (1999)
Comprehensive Test Ban Treaty fails in Senate (1999)
Supports Hillary Rodham Clinton's successful Senate campaign (2000)

POSTPRESIDENCY

Publication of memoirs, 2004
Quadruple heart bypass surgery, 2004
Dedication of William J. Clinton Presidential Center, Little Rock, 2004
Disaster relief fundraising with former president George H. W. Bush
    following Indian Ocean earthquake and tsunami, 2004
Disaster relief fundraising with former president Bush following Hurricane
    Katrina, 2005
Clinton Global Initiative, Clinton Foundation, 2005
Clinton Foundation brokers agreement with major soft drink manufacturers
    not to sell sugared drinks in public schools, 2005
Supports Sen. Hillary Clinton's campaign for Democratic presidential nomination,
    2007–2008

The president also achieved congressional approval of a free trade agreement with Canada and Mexico that had been negotiated by his predecessor.

President Clinton's most significant first-term setbacks came in his second year of office. The overarching health care plan developed by First Lady Hillary Clinton was criticized for its complexity and cost, and it did not come to a vote in Congress. The failure of one of the president's most important reform proposal was compounded by the Democratic Party's significant losses in the 1994 congressional midterm elections. The Republican Party won control of both chambers of Congress and gained a majority in the House for the first time in forty years. Clinton did have some important successes in 1994, including the passage of major crime control legislation;

the deployment of U.S. peacekeeping forces to Haiti following the departure of military coup leaders and the reinstatement of previously elected officials; and a pledge from North Korea to halt its nuclear weapons program. But after the president's political and party losses, the prospects for continued leadership seemed bleak.

Just as he had so many times previously, however, Clinton successfully navigated political obstacles to regain control of his agenda. He did not hesitate to use his veto power to block Republican legislation that he opposed, particularly budget balancing bills that would enact significant cuts in funding for health care, education, welfare, and other important social programs. The confrontation with Congress resulted in two federal government shutdowns in late 1995 and into early 1996, but public opinion largely supported the president and blamed the Republican legislative leadership for the conflict. Congress ultimately approved fiscal legislation that kept Clinton's spending priorities intact.

In foreign policy, the Clinton administration negotiated a treaty to end civil war in Bosnia, sending twenty thousand U.S. troops to the country as part of a NATO peacekeeping mission. Clinton also won support for domestic programs by pursuing a strategy of "triangulation," in which he promoted moderate policies to broker bipartisan political coalitions. He enacted major welfare reform in 1996 with Republican support and approved legislation that promised health insurance portability for workers who changed jobs, though it did not address the cost issue. Clinton signed bills to increase the hourly minimum wage from $4.25 to $5.15 and to grant line-item veto power to the president for spending bills. Supreme Court later ruled the line-item veto unconstitutional.

The 1996 Election

Despite many predictions after the 1994 midterm elections that he would be a one-term president, Clinton virtually coasted to reelection in the 1996 presidential race. His Republican opponent was former Senate majority leader Robert J. Dole of Kansas, who ran with Jack F. Kemp of California. Dole was unable to muster strong public enthusiasm for his candidacy, and near the end of the campaign, some Republicans leaders turned their energies to maintaining control of Congress. They virtually conceded the presidential race to Clinton by urging voters not to give the president a "blank check" with unified government. Clinton won with 47 million popular votes and 379 Electoral College votes to 39 million popular votes and 159 Electoral College votes for Dole. Perot competed on the Reform Party ticket, but won only 8 million popular votes.

The Clinton Administration (Second Term)

Four of Clinton's cabinet secretaries served through his entire presidency: Attorney General Reno, Health and Human Services Secretary Shalala, Interior Secretary Bruce Babbitt of Arizona, and Education Secretary Richard W. Riley of South Carolina. Treasury Secretary Robert E. Rubin of New York was appointed in 1995 and served for the rest of the administration. Republican senator William S. Cohen of Maine became defense secretary in Clinton's second term, and Clinton made history by selecting the first woman to be secretary of state, Madeleine K. Albright, originally from Czechoslovakia.

Major Issues (Second Term)

In his second term, Clinton had significant achievements in domestic and foreign policy. The booming economy resulted in a federal budget surplus for the first time in decades, well ahead of the schedule set by the president and Congress for balancing the budget. In 1998 Clinton helped to broker the Good Friday accords to halt the civil war in Northern Ireland. In response to Serbian president Slobodan Milosevic's brutal campaign against ethnic Albanians in Kosovo, the Clinton administration led NATO air attacks in spring 1999. After Milosevic conceded defeat, the United States sent U.S. troops as part of a NATO peacekeeping mission to Kosovo. Building on his earlier success with Israeli-Palestinian negotiations, Clinton tried to broker a peace agreement between the two sides, but his efforts were stymied by the resurgence of violence in the Middle East during his final year in office.

Clinton faced the gravest challenge of his presidency, his political career, and perhaps his personal life when news reports in 1998 alleged the president had engaged in a sexual relationship with a former White House intern, Monica Lewinsky. The reports came from a convoluted ethics investigation of the Clintons' involvement years earlier in a real estate deal in Arkansas known as Whitewater. Independent counsel Kenneth W. Starr had been selected by a judicial panel in 1994 to head the Whitewater investigation, and his inquiry eventually broadened to encompass Clinton's affair with Lewinsky. Starr had learned about the alleged relationship as a result of testimony presented in a civil lawsuit against the president by Paula Corbin Jones, who claimed that Clinton, while governor of Arkansas, had sexually harassed her. Starr maintained that investigating the Lewinsky matter was necessary to assess the president's truthfulness, which was relevant to the Whitewater inquiry.

The president angrily denied reports of any affairs, famously stating at a White House press conference in January 1998, "I did not have sexual relations with that woman, Miss Lewinsky." Seven months later, he admitted on national television to a "not appropriate" relationship with Lewinsky. His terse address followed a day of testimony before a grand jury in the independent counsel inquiry. A few weeks later, Starr submitted a report to Congress that presented potential grounds for impeachment. In December 1998 the House voted for two articles of impeachment against Clinton, charging the president with obstruction of justice and perjury before a grand jury. But the Senate did not come close to the two-thirds vote required for conviction, and Clinton was acquitted, with all Democrats voting in his favor and some Republicans crossing party lines to do the same.

In some respects, the Lewinsky scandal did not appear to affect Clinton's leadership. In August 1998, just days after he admitted the improper relationship, he ordered air strikes against Afghanistan and Sudan in retaliation for the terrorist bombings of U.S. embassies in Kenya and Tanzania a few weeks earlier. The Democrats increased their House representation in the midterm elections, and the Republican losses marked the first time since 1934 that the nonpresidential party did not gain seats in off-year elections. In December 1998 Clinton approved Operation Desert Fox, a bombing campaign against Iraq for its refusal to comply with UN weapons inspections.

At the same time, the inquiry and impeachment presented a major distraction to the president during his second term. After his acquittal, he failed to win Senate ratification of a treaty to ban nuclear test explosions. His legacy was further tarnished by his decision to issue questionable and poorly vetted pardons to many people in his final hours before leaving office. Particularly controversial was his pardon of financier Marc Rich, a longtime fugitive charged with tax evasion and fraud and former husband of a major Democratic donor.

Since leaving the White House, Clinton has established his own foundation to promote humanitarian assistance at home and abroad, including projects such as improving medical treatment for AIDS patients and combating poverty and climate change. He travels extensively and earns millions annually from paid speeches. He published his memoirs and dedicated his presidential library in Little Rock, Arkansas, in 2004. That year he also underwent heart bypass surgery. He worked with former president George H. W. Bush to raise disaster relief funds following the tragic Indian Ocean earthquake and tsunamis in 2004 and after Hurricane Katrina devastated the U.S. gulf coast in 2005.

Clinton's unique presidential legacy is the political career of his wife. Hillary Rodham Clinton won election to the Senate from New York in 2000, becoming the first former first lady to hold elective office. She won reelection handily in 2006 and declared her candidacy for the 2008 Democratic presidential nomination shortly thereafter. Former president Clinton was active in promoting his wife's campaign to have a second Clinton presidency, and was clearly disappointed when she was not selected to be the Democratic presidential candidate.

"Under the Big Top—The Overview: Democrats Give Clinton Their Blessing; Cuomo Hails 'New Voice for New America,' " July 16, 1992

Despite having little national name recognition outside party circles when he entered the 1992 presidential race, Bill Clinton won the Democratic nomination. *The New York Times* reported that his nomination marked "a triumph of strategy, endurance and simple fire in the belly" for Clinton, who had confidently brushed aside the concerns of other potential Democratic candidates in 1991 that George H. W. Bush, the highly popular incumbent president, would be unbeatable.

JULY 16, 1992
UNDER THE BIG TOP—THE OVERVIEW; DEMOCRATS GIVE CLINTON THEIR BLESSING; CUOMO HAILS 'NEW VOICE FOR NEW AMERICA'

By ROBIN TONER

The Democratic National Convention nominated Gov. Bill Clinton for the Presidency last night after Gov. Mario M. Cuomo of New York made an impassioned case for the man from Hope, Ark., and declared that the nation could not afford another Democratic defeat.

Mr. Clinton capped the emotional night with a joyous march from a restaurant in Macy's to the convention floor in Madison Square Garden a block away. Illuminated by floodlights and cascades of red, white and blue glitter confetti falling from the ceiling, Mr. Clinton strode into the convention hall, which was packed by roaring, triumphant Democrats.

Beaming a vibrant image to national television audiences, Mr. Clinton made his way slowly to the Arkansas delegation. He threw open his arms, shouted "I love you," and embraced his mother, Virginia Kelley, who had cast the first votes for his nomination.

He appealed, quite directly, to the memory of John F. Kennedy, saying, "The rules of the convention preclude my acceptance tonight, but 32 years ago another young candidate who wanted to get this country moving again came to the convention to say a simple thank you."

Earlier in the evening, Mr. Cuomo and Senator Edward M. Kennedy of Massachusetts, perennial favorites of the party's liberals, bestowed political blessings on the fifth-generation Arkansan who comes from a very different wing of the party. The Governor of New York hailed Mr. Clinton's character, his humble roots, his commitment to the party's traditions and values.

"It's time for change," Mr. Cuomo said, endorsing Mr. Clinton with far more spirit and passion than many had expected. "It's time for someone smart enough to know, strong enough to do, sure enough to lead. The comeback kid. A new voice for a new America."

'The Man From Hope'

The Governor of New York, who spoke to a rapt audience, declared, "Because I love New York, because I love America, I nominate for the office of the President of the United States the man from Hope, Arkansas, Governor Bill Clinton."

The convention then proceeded to the old, joyous ceremony of the roll-call of the states, ratifying what the primary voters had finished more than a month ago. Mr. Clinton went over the top, the necessary 2,145 delegates to win, at 10:54 P.M., when Ohio voted. The hall rocked with cheers, chants of "We want Bill" and Sousa marches in a demonstration that lasted 30 minutes.

Mr. Clinton, accompanied by his wife, Hillary, and his daughter, Chelsea, watched the packed and happy hall on television in Macy's. The convention could watch him, as well, on two huge screens high above the Garden floor.

Then, in a move that caught many of the delegates by surprise but was planned well in advance, he strode through the men's furnishings department, out into Seventh Avenue in a light drizzle, and headed toward the Garden. He was surrounded by cheering supporters, ecstatic from reports of new polls, reveling in the moment. Ronald Reagan made a similar visit to the Republicans' convention hall when he was nominated in 1980, as did Walter F. Mondale to the Democrats' 1984 convention.

The night was a triumph of strategy, endurance and simple fire in the belly for Mr. Clinton, who had plunged into this race when President Bush had been soaring in public opinion polls and the Democratic Party's heavyweights had turned away.

Mr. Clinton, 45 years old, from a tiny state that has never before produced a Democratic nominee, was beaming and clutching his daughter's hand as he watched the votes tallied. He wiped tears from his eyes as New Hampshire, the scene of his toughest primary battle, announced its votes.

Not since Jimmy Carter has a Southerner risen to the top of his party, and Mr. Clinton did so with a message that asserted that the party had to moderate its policies to reclaim the middle class and return to the White House. Last night, as the party rallied itself for an intensely competitive three-way campaign in the fall, Mr. Clinton was oratorically embraced by the tribunes of the party's Northern liberals.

"The 1992 Elections: At Dawn of New Politics, Challenges for Both Parties," November 5, 1992

The 1992 presidential election was highly important for the Democratic Party, which regained control of the White House for the first time in twelve years. The victory marked the end of the Reagan era and presented a special window of opportunity for party leadership, as Democrats now controlled both Congress and the presidency.

NOVEMBER 5, 1992
THE 1992 ELECTIONS
At Dawn of New Politics, Challenges for Both Parties
By ROBIN TONER

The Democrats came out of the political wilderness on Tuesday. The Republicans entered it.

The Democrats set aside all the self-doubts, the years of feeling on the wrong side of history, the election nights when the proud party of Roosevelt, Truman and Kennedy seemed consigned to a painful irrelevance.

Ahead is the challenge of governing, and the clear accountability that comes with controlling both Congress and the White House. No more political cover for the Democrats, no more room for fingerpointing between Capitol Hill and the White House, no more excuses.

But the Republicans face the hard, brutal struggle of deciding who they are, resolving the tensions between moderates, conservatives, evangelical Christians, country-clubbers, supply-siders, suburbanites—all the disparate elements held together by Ronald Reagan that collapsed under President Bush.

Perot Over the Shoulder

The task of both parties will be complicated by Ross Perot, who served notice this week that he has no intention of fading away.

He certainly didn't fade in the voting on Tuesday. While he did not win a state, as George Wallace did when he captured five in 1968, Mr. Perot polled 19 percent of the popular vote nationwide, compared with Mr. Wallace's 13.5 percent. And while that showing was certainly stoked with Mr. Perot's money, people in both parties worried that it was also fueled by a disaffection with the parties themselves.

But Democrats were not much given to worries this week. It would be hard to exaggerate their euphoria, especially the generation in its 30's and 40's that spent its adulthood out of power, told again and again that it was "out of the mainstream."

"Congress Passes Measure Providing Emergency Leaves," February 5, 1993

Clinton's first legislative victory was the Family and Medical Leave Act of 1993. The law, which President George H. W. Bush had vetoed twice, required most employers to grant workers up to twelve weeks of unpaid leave for medical emergencies or the birth or adoption of a child.

FEBRUARY 5, 1993
CONGRESS PASSES MEASURE PROVIDING EMERGENCY LEAVES
By ADAM CLYMER

Congress gave President Clinton his first legislative victory tonight, passing the family-leave bill to guarantee workers up to 12 weeks of unpaid leave for medical emergencies.

The Senate passed the bill 71 to 27, and the House followed on a 247 to 152 vote, just minutes before midnight.

Mr. Clinton plans to sign the bill on Friday morning to make the political point that domestic legislation, stalemated during the Bush Administration, would now pour forth because Democrats control both ends of Pennsylvania Avenue.

The House, which passed a similar bill late Wednesday night, had to take a second vote because the Senate version included a statement about homosexuals in the military.

Parts of Compromise

That statement is a bland declaration backing two elements of the compromise between Mr. Clinton and Senator Sam Nunn, the Georgia Democrat who is chairman of the Armed Services Committee, on the President's proposal to lift the ban on homosexuals in the military.

It endorses Mr. Clinton's order to the Defense Department last week to study the issue and its implications, and it directs the Senate panel to hold hearings on the issue, which Senator Nunn had already announced he would do. But it lets stand the President's decision to stop asking prospective recruits whether they are homosexuals.

Vetoed Twice by Bush

The family-leave bill was vetoed twice by President George Bush, who said it would impose unnecessary costs on businesses. It would require employers to give workers up to 12 weeks of unpaid leave to deal with birth, adoption or a serious illness affecting themselves or members of their immediate families. Employers would have to maintain health insurance coverage.

In Dade County, Fla., the first municipality in the country to pass a measure that most closely resembles the Federal bill, many of the 2,500 businesses covered by the law say it is less expensive than anticipated and actually increases worker satisfaction and productivity.

The Federal bill, which would cover employees of companies with 50 or more workers as well as Federal, state and local government employees, embraces about half of the nation's work force. It would take effect six months after it is signed by the President.

Vice President Gore, who presided over the Senate as the bill was passed, said of the vote, "The Congress has shown courage and foresight," adding: "We are seeing in just two weeks what a difference Bill Clinton makes. American families will no longer have to choose between their families and their jobs."

In another Democratic effort to show the party could enact bills Mr. Bush had thwarted, the House passed a measure directing the states to make it easier to register to vote by offering registration in many public buildings, including motor vehicle and welfare offices.

⬤ ⬤

"CLINTON IS PULLED FROM THE BRINK. HE'LL BE BACK,"
AUGUST 1, 1993

The enactment of Clinton's budget plan in 1993 depended entirely on Democratic support. Not a single Republican in the House or Senate voted for the plan, which passed by a bare majority in both chambers of Congress.

AUGUST 1, 1993
SUNDAY MAGAZINE
CLINTON IS PULLED FROM THE BRINK. HE'LL BE BACK.

By R. W. APPLE JR.

The margin could not have been thinner or the stakes higher. One switched vote in the Senate or the House of Representatives, and Bill Clinton would have lost his economic package and perhaps his Presidency. So all the bargaining in the great souk on Capitol Hill over the last three months, all the searching for backbone by legislators terrified of the electoral guillotine, clearly was worth it.

Thursday's and Friday's gut-wrenching roll-call victories represented a down payment on Mr. Clinton's campaign and inaugural promises to get the country moving again. Failure would have made the President look impotent on the economic issues that stand quite clearly at the center of national politics. He has avoided that, although the urgency of taming the deficit has allowed him little room for the innovative programs and redirection of Government that he and his party are committed to seek.

Whether his victories really represent a turning point for the Republic, a departure down a new road of fiscal sanity, as so many Democratic orators argued last week, is another question.

Although most of the new taxes will be borne by the rich, as Mr. Clinton's Technicolor pie charts showed, the package comes nowhere near undoing Ronald Reagan's tax breaks for the wealthy. It leaves the tax burden in the United States far less onerous than those in most other Western nations. If the electorate is as serious as it tells itself it is about eliminating the deficit and cutting the national debt, it will eventually have to accept far more than this modest effort to increase revenues.

It will also have to support far deeper spending cuts and there are only a few categories where such savings can be found—mainly in military outlays, where significant cuts are under way, and in so-called entitlement spending, on Social Security, Medicare, Medicaid and the like, where they aren't.

But the great lesson of the passage of Bill Clinton's proposals through what is laughably referred to here as the legislative process is that neither broad new taxes nor painful spending cuts can be achieved in the political environment that now exists in the United States. Mr. Clinton's energy tax and his fallback proposal for a significant increase in the gasoline tax both had to be jettisoned to keep Senator Herb Kohl of Wisconsin on board. Other legislators demanded and got breaks for favored constituencies.

"It's a start," the Democrats say. Projected spending would be reduced by more than $250 billion over the next five years (though most of the cuts would come later than that, and the President and Congress may be tempted to cut the cuts as their effective dates draw near). The other half of the package will come, in large part, from raising the top income tax rate to 36 from 31 percent (with a surcharge on those with taxable incomes above $250,000), as well as small increases in the gasoline tax and in corporate tax rates.

"CLINTON SENDING REINFORCEMENTS AFTER HEAVY LOSSES IN SOMALIA," OCTOBER 5, 1993

The deployment of U.S. troops to Somalia on a humanitarian mission in late 1992 presented a major challenge for Clinton upon taking office. Civil war in Somalia created enormous obstacles to the distribution of food and supplies for people suffering from a severe famine. Furthermore, Clinton had campaigned on a platform of domestic priorities, and Somalia was not a high-level issue for the administration until a deadly firefight in October 1993 brought the intervention into the public spotlight. With no clear explanation for why U.S. forces were still in the war-ravaged nation, Clinton announced the withdrawal of American troops. The angry public and congressional backlash to the Somalia tragedy may have influenced the administration's unwillingness to intervene in Rwanda a few months later to forestall a bloody massacre there.

OCTOBER 5, 1993
CLINTON SENDING REINFORCEMENTS AFTER HEAVY LOSSES IN SOMALIA
By R. W. APPLE JR.

President Clinton ordered several hundred fresh United States troops to Somalia today, plus heavy tanks, armored personnel carriers, helicopters and gunships, in the aftermath of heavy American losses in a United Nations military operation in Mogadishu on Sunday.

The latest Pentagon tally indicated that at least 12 American soldiers had been killed and 78 wounded. Several others were reported missing and may be captives of the forces of Gen. Mohammed Farah Aidid, the fugitive Somali faction leader. That made Sunday by far the costliest day for the United States since American forces arrived in Somalia almost 10 months ago.

Chilling pictures of dead and captured Americans were sent out by the few Western journalists in Mogadishu. Television footage on CNN showed a frightened, wounded Blackhawk helicopter pilot, identified by military officials here as Army Chief Warrant Officer Michael Durant, 32, under interrogation by his Somali captors. The officials said he was a member of the 160th Special Operations Aviation Regiment (Airborne), based in Fort Campbell, Ky.

A still photo showed Somalis watching as the body of an unidentified American was dragged through the streets at the end of a rope.

Warning From Aspin

"We will respond forcefully if any harm comes to those who are being detained," Defense Secretary Les Aspin said. He demanded that prisoners be treated in accordance with wartime norms, including adequate medical treatment and visits from representatives of the International Committee of the Red Cross.

About 20 supporters of General Aidid, including three high-ranking officials of his faction, were captured, according to the official American account. It was not known how many Somalis were killed or wounded, but a senior American official said the number was "very substantial." The fighting took place in a crowded market area, where the narrow streets are usually thronged on weekends, so many of the casualties were almost certainly civilians.

President Clinton said he was sending reinforcements because he was "not satisfied that we are doing everything we can to protect the young Americans that are putting their lives on the line so that hundreds of thousands of Somalis can stay alive."

Note of Determination

In a speech to the convention of the A.F.L.-C.I.O. in San Francisco, he sounded a note of determination, telling the labor audience, "You may be sure that we will do whatever is necessary to protect our own forces in Somalia and to complete our mission."

Last week the Administration said it wanted to focus on building a viable political structure in Somalia, not on capturing General Aidid and his lieutenants. But Sunday's operation did just the opposite, creating the impression that the Somalis and not Washington were setting the agenda.

Ranking Administration officials acknowledged that although Mr. Aspin, Secretary of State Warren Christopher and Tony Lake, the national security adviser, were working on the problem, no one person had clearly taken charge.

"The result," one policymaker said, "is a great deal of confusion. The fact is that you can shift the emphasis back and forth, but you can never really get a political deal there as long as Aidid is roaming free."

On Capitol Hill, such senior figures as Senator Richard G. Lugar, Republican of Indiana, expressed support for the President's policy. But there was also sharp criticism, with Senator Robert C. Byrd of West Virginia, the chairman of the Appropriations Committee, calling for an immediate end to "these fatal cops-and-robbers operations," and Senator John McCain, an Arizona Republican who sits on the Armed Services Committee, stating bluntly, "Clinton's got to bring them home."

The United States military establishment was stunned, as one top general put it, by "the size, scope and ferocity" of General Aidid's counterattack on the American Rangers who surrounded one of his strongholds.

"Oxford Journal; Whereas, He Is an Old Boy, If a Young Chief, Honor Him," June 9, 1994

The Times' coverage of President Clinton's visit to Oxford in June 1994 sparked some controversy. Reporter Maureen Dowd wrote a front-page article about the visit that began with the sentence, "President Clinton returned today . . . to the university where he didn't inhale, didn't get drafted and didn't get a degree." Administration officials and media critics considered the language better suited to an opinion piece than a news article, but *The Times* maintained that Dowd's writing style was appropriate for the light news story.

JUNE 9, 1994
OXFORD JOURNAL; WHEREAS, HE IS AN OLD BOY, IF A YOUNG CHIEF, HONOR HIM
By MAUREEN DOWD

President Clinton returned today for a sentimental journey to the university where he didn't inhale, didn't get drafted and didn't get a degree.

The last got rectified by Oxford University in a ceremony conducted by men in black gowns speaking in Latin in a 325-year-old stone building designed by Christopher Wren. Mr. Clinton, who studied politics at University College as a Rhodes Scholar from the fall of 1968 to the spring of 1970, was awarded an honorary doctorate in civil law.

At the gilded Sheldonian Theater, the university Chancellor, Lord Jenkins of Hillhead, read the text of the degree in Latin, featuring eight clauses beginning with "Whereas," one with "Therefore" and one with "Witness Whereof." Lord Jenkins said Mr. Clinton was honored for being "a doughty and tireless champion of the cause of world peace," for having "a powerful collaborator in his wife," and for winning "general applause for his achievement of resolving the gridlock which prevented an agreed budget."

Wearing a red gown, beneath a high ceiling painted with cavorting cherubs, Mr. Clinton recalled for the audience at the Sheldonian how he had felt, as a young man fresh from Arkansas, a sense of nagging inadequacy at Oxford, the oldest university in the English-speaking world, a place of musty glamour once described by Henry James as "a kind of dim and sacred ideal of the Western intellect."

Looking at the British dons, men in flowing robes and mortarboards, some carrying gold-headed scepters, the President said: "I always felt a mixture of elation and wariness, bordering on intimidation, in your presence. I thought if there was one place in the world I could come and give a speech in the proper language, it was here, and then I heard the degree ceremony. And sure enough, once again at Oxford I was another Yank a half-step behind."

Mr. Clinton said he was honored by the degree and the honorary fellowship, adding wryly: "I must say that, as my wife pointed out, I could have gotten neither one of these things on my own. I had to be elected President to do it." . . .

After leaving Rhodes House, the President walked to Blackwell's book store. On the way, some students unfurled a sign reading, "Inhale Next Time, Bill."

During the campaign, Mr. Clinton confessed that he had tried marijuana here, but quickly insisted, "I didn't inhale," explaining that he did not like the taste. . . .

The President had originally planned to visit Oxford before the commemoration of the 50th anniversary of D-Day in Normandy. But the White House changed the stop to the end of the President's European trip, presumably to avoid having embarrassing stories about Mr. Clinton's activities as a Vietnam protester crop up on the eve of the D-Day anniversary. Mr. Clinton arrived in England in 1968 as a 22-year-old Rhodes Scholar, just out of Georgetown University in Washington, at the height of the Vietnam War.

By his own admission, it was here that Mr. Clinton rode out part of the war, and it was here he wrote the now infamous letter to the commander of the Reserve Officer Training Corps back home in Arkansas—"Thank you for saving me from the draft"—for helping extend his deferment. He said he hoped to maintain his "political viability."

The young Oxford student said in that letter, "I am writing too in the hope that my telling this one story will help you to understand more clearly how so many fine people have come to find themselves still loving their country but loathing the military."

In interviews in Europe this week with American networks, he has reflected on his opposition to the war. He told Tom Brokaw of NBC News that he did not regret his position then. He seemed to show a bit of revisionism, perhaps not recalling the "loathing" line or how many in the 1960's disdained authority and those in uniform. "I think all the people who grew up in my generation were hurt maybe worse than any other generation could have been by their ambivalence over Vietnam because we all loved the military so much."

After all, Mr. Clinton said, "I grew up on the war movies—you know, on John Wayne and John Hodiak and Robert Mitchum and all those war movies."

Left to Go to Yale

Mr. Stephanopoulous said Mr. Clinton did not get his degree because he switched from one program to another, ultimately pursuing a B.Phil. in Politics, and had a year left to go to get a graduate degree when the opportunity came to go to Yale Law School.

A Rhodes scholarship provides for two years of study at Oxford University, with a third year granted by application. Most Rhodes Scholars earn degrees at Oxford, and all are expected to remain full-time students until they complete their programs, but Mr. Clinton is not the only one to have left after two years without having done so.

- -

"THE HEALTH CARE DEBATE: AUTOPSY ON HEALTH CARE; MANY HAD HAND IN KILLING THE LEGISLATION, BUT A SURLY ELECTORATE JUST MAY NOT CARE," SEPTEMBER 27, 1994

The defeat of his health care plan probably marked the greatest policy disappointment for President Clinton. Not only did he fail to achieve one of his signature campaign promises, but also he had entrusted his wife, Hillary Rodham Clinton, with developing the plan, making its collapse doubly upsetting because of the criticisms levied against her efforts.

SEPTEMBER 27, 1994
THE HEALTH CARE DEBATE: AUTOPSY ON HEALTH CARE; MANY HAD HAND IN KILLING THE LEGISLATION, BUT A SURLY ELECTORATE JUST MAY NOT CARE
By ROBIN TONER

> " Who killed the health care overhaul? . . . [A] divided Democratic Party on Capitol Hill, an overreaching Clinton Administration, a fiercely partisan class of Republicans, an insatiable collection of interest groups. "

Who killed the health care overhaul? It is a question of more than academic interest six weeks before Election Day, with the voters in a surly mood, angry with Congress and with incumbents in general.

But many analysts say that, like every other aspect of the two-year struggle over restructuring health care, the answer is muddled. As in "Murder on the Orient Express," most of the suspects had their hands on the knife at one time or another: a divided Democratic Party on Capitol Hill, an overreaching Clinton Administration, a fiercely partisan class of Republicans, an insatiable collection of interest groups.

President Clinton has already taken much of the blame for the collapse of the health care effort, judging from his poll ratings. He raised enormous expectations when he stood before Congress almost exactly a year ago, promising a vast new benefit to America's middle class, urging the nation to believe that the Federal Government could, once again, step up to the challenge of creating big new domestic programs.

By the time George J. Mitchell of Maine, the Senate majority leader, declared today that health care legislation was officially dead for the year, many Americans had not only stopped believing that health care changes would help them, they had also come to fear it. In recent weeks the message from the grass roots was "slow down," according to members of both parties.

"Understand that our constituents are asking us not to act this year," Representative Benjamin L. Cardin, Democrat of Maryland, said in an interview this afternoon. "When you ask constituents, they say: 'Take more time. You haven't reached a consensus yet.' "

The White House and its allies argue—correctly—that this transformation of the public mood did not just happen, but was fueled by millions of dollars from interest groups and by weeks of disciplined Republican attacks.

But the reality remains that the President sought something big, something that would redeem his promise of a government devoted to the "forgotten middle class," and was unable to deliver. He offered his plan as a "third way" between conventionally liberal and conservative approaches to the problems of the health care system. But he found himself painted into an ideological corner, seeming to defend just the kind of big, bureaucratic Democratic programs that he ran against as a "new Democrat" in 1992.

- -

"THE 1994 ELECTIONS: A VOTE AGAINST CLINTON," NOVEMBER 9, 1994

Voters expressed their dissatisfaction with the Democratic agenda in 1994 by sweeping party members out of office in congressional and gubernatorial races. The loss of both chambers of Congress was a devastating defeat for Clinton and meant that he would have to work closely with the Republican leadership to enact policies.

NOVEMBER 9, 1994
THE 1994 ELECTIONS
A Vote Against Clinton
News Analysis
By R. W. APPLE JR.

It was an immoderate campaign, coarse in its tone and unedifying in its substance, and the nation's politics are likely to stay that way for the next two years and beyond.

Dissatisfaction with President Clinton, with liberalism, with the Democratic Party and with Washington in general combined to create a surge by Republicans, especially conservative Republicans. If not quite a tidal wave, yesterday's results swept dozens of incumbents from office and set up two years of intense political confrontation between the White House and Congress.

Republicans will soon control the statehouses in seven of the eight largest states, giving them immensely useful building blocks for the next Presidential election. They will control the Senate for the first time since 1987, and perhaps Congress as a whole for the first time since the Eisenhower era.

Their leader in the House of Representatives, Representative Newt Gingrich, is at heart a revolutionary bent on fundamental change.

This was a realigning election that put the final nails in the coffin of the Solid South, the regional bastion upon which Democratic power was once built. Democratic seats in the House fell all across the region: three in Georgia, four in North Carolina, three in Tennessee.

If the victory of Senator Edward M. Kennedy of Massachusetts provided some balm, the defeats of major party luminaries—Representative Dan Rostenkowski of Illinois and Jack Brooks of Texas, Gov. Ann W. Richards of Texas and Gov. Mario M. Cuomo of New York—sent many Democrats into gloom bordering on despondency.

Stated most simply, the message from the electorate was disgust with big government and impatience with government activism, two of the things with which the Democrats are most closely identified.

The returns constituted a sharp rebuke to Mr. Clinton. Many of those for whom he stumped so frantically in the final hours were defeated, some of them decisively. Exit polls showed that about a third of all voters said they voted as they did to express their disapproval of what the President had done.

* *

"Terror in Oklahoma City: The Investigation; At Least 31 Are Dead, Scores Are Missing After Car Bomb Attack in Oklahoma City Wrecks 9-Story Federal Office Building," April 20, 1995

The bombing of a federal office building in Oklahoma City, Oklahoma, on April 19, 1995, killed 168 people and injured hundreds of others. Although international terrorism initially was suspected, the attackers were two Americans, Timothy McVeigh and Terry Nichols, who sought revenge for recent confrontations between federal agents and so-called militia groups. The bombing took place exactly two years after a federal raid of the Branch Davidian compound near Waco, Texas. With bipartisan support, President Clinton signed legislation the following year to limit venues for terrorists to file repeated petitions, especially in capital cases. McVeigh was executed for his crime, and Nichols was sentenced to life in prison without parole.

APRIL 20, 1995
TERROR IN OKLAHOMA CITY: THE INVESTIGATION; AT LEAST 31 ARE DEAD, SCORES ARE MISSING AFTER CAR BOMB ATTACK IN OKLAHOMA CITY WRECKS 9-STORY FEDERAL OFFICE BUILDING
By DAVID JOHNSTON

The authorities opened an intensive hunt today for whoever bombed a Federal office building in Oklahoma City, and proceeded on the theory that the bombing was a terrorist attack against the Government, law-enforcement officials said.

President Clinton appeared in the White House press room this afternoon and somberly promised that the Government would hunt down the "evil cowards" responsible. "These people are killers," he said, "and must be treated like killers."

Attorney General Janet Reno, speaking to reporters at the White House in early evening, said that casualty figures from the scene were climbing and that of the 550 people who worked in the building, 300 were unaccounted for.

Ms. Reno said Federal prosecutors would seek the death penalty against the bombers. "The death penalty is available," she said, "and we will seek it."

But the authorities said they had no suspects, and questions about the identity of the bombers swirled around the case. The only solid fact was the explosion itself.

Some law-enforcement officials said the bombing might be linked to the second anniversary today of Federal agents' ill-fated assault on the Branch Davidian compound near Waco, Tex., an operation that ended in a fire that killed about 80 people, including many children. Among the offices housed by the Federal building in Oklahoma City was one quartering local agents of the Bureau of Alcohol, Tobacco and Firearms, the agency that Branch Davidians and their sympathizers blamed for the confrontation.

But other officials said that neither the Branch Davidians nor right-wing "militia" groups that have protested the Government's handling of the Davidians were believed to have the technical expertise to engage in bombings like the one today.

* *

"Balkan Accord: Clinton's Bosnia Stand: Political Risks Remain," November 29, 1995

During his first two years in office, Clinton wrestled with the problem of how the United States should try to end civil war in Bosnia. *The Times* described the administration's policy in this period as "an uncertain, uneven odyssey." In late 1995 U.S. negotiators secured an agreement among the warring factions that became known as the Dayton Accords. The Clinton administration deployed nearly twenty thousand troops to Bosnia as part of a NATO peacekeeping force to implement the agreement.

NOVEMBER 29, 1995
BALKAN ACCORD

Clinton's Bosnia Stand: Political Risks Remain
By ELAINE SCIOLINO

When President Clinton called in his advisers last week to complete plans for sending 20,000 American troops to Bosnia, he told them that there would be no more soul-searching or wavering.

"Whatever ambivalence any of us ever had in the past, it's over," a participant in the meeting quoted Mr. Clinton as saying. "We're going to make this work."

Mr. Clinton's speech on Monday night underscored the idea that there could be no turning back. But he came to this view only after concluding during the summer that there would be no peace in Bosnia unless the United States made it happen and that his own political future would be imperiled if the war continued.

That decision was swiftly translated into the use of American warplanes to bomb the Bosnian Serbs into a cease-fire and eventually into peace talks on an Air Force base outside Dayton, Ohio.

For two and a half years before that, Mr. Clinton's Bosnia policy had been an uncertain, uneven odyssey. As a Presidential candidate and as President, he had repeatedly swung between strong proposals and stronger doubts, between guilt over the slaughter of innocents and anxiety

President Bill Clinton is escorted by U.S. soldiers stationed at Tuzla airbase in January 1996. Some twenty thousand U.S. troops were deployed to Bosnia as part of a larger NATO peacekeeping effort following the signing of the Dayton Accords in late 1995.

Source: AP Photo/Greg Gibson

over the remedy. In May 1994 he lamented during an appearance on CNN, "I'm doing the best I can."

John F. Kennedy once said that to govern is to choose, and the evolution in Mr. Clinton's thinking on Bosnia also resulted from a decision to make a fundamental choice—to embrace an imperfect, even brutal peace that ratified Serbian military gains with a peace plan that essentially divided the country in two.

"President Clinton may have understood the power of the Presidency intellectually in the beginning, but he feels it viscerally now," Michael D. McCurry, the White House spokesman, said in describing Mr. Clinton's handling of Bosnia. "It's just different once you've been there and feel it. In the end, the clearest and most compelling dynamic driving the President's decision-making on Bosnia was the lack of any alternative."

Mr. Clinton embarked on his Bosnia policy during the 1992 Presidential campaign with lofty oratory that criticized President Bush for inaction and proclaimed the need to act against civilian atrocities.

But once in office, Mr. Clinton had to come to terms with Bosnia's real complexity—and danger. He and his advisers began to talk about the problem differently, less as a moral tragedy that would have rendered American inaction immoral and more as a tribal feud about which little could be done.

Mr. Clinton called the bloodiest war in Europe since World War II a "civil war" among parties that had been fighting for hundreds of years. The "problem from hell" was how Secretary of State Warren Christopher described it during a Congressional hearing.

The President also alienated the Europeans by stating that Bosnia was primarily a European problem and that American soldiers would not serve side by side with European peacekeepers in what he called a "shooting gallery."

- -

"WITH NO BUDGET, CLINTON AND REPUBLICANS PASS THE BLAME," DECEMBER 17, 1995

Conflict between President Clinton and the Republican-led Congress over how to balance the federal budget led to two shutdowns of the federal government. The first was for a few days in November 1995, and the second for almost three weeks from mid-December 1995 to early January 2006. House Speaker Newt Gingrich declared that the impasse was the president's doing, but public opinion supported Clinton, and Republican leaders eventually ended the standoff by largely accepting the administration's proposals.

DECEMBER 17, 1995
WITH NO BUDGET, CLINTON AND REPUBLICANS PASS THE BLAME
By DAVID E. ROSENBAUM

With parts of the Government closed because of the budget impasse and thousands of workers threatened with furloughs on Monday, President Clinton and Republican leaders in Congress spent the day blaming each other, but made no progress toward resolving their differences.

In a radio address this morning, the President accused the Republican Congress of forcing Government installations to close "in an effort to force through their unacceptable cuts in health care, education and the environment."

"It's irresponsible," Mr. Clinton said. "I won't give in to the threat."

Asked in a corridor in the Capitol about the President's accusations, Senator Bob Dole of Kansas, the majority leader

and President Clinton's most likely opponent in next year's election, snapped, "He can stop that garbage that he's spewing out on his radio program and everything else."

On Friday, Republicans broke off what were supposed to be last-ditch budget negotiations because the White House refused to meet the Republicans' one precondition—that the President submit a plan that could be shown on paper to lead to a balanced budget within seven years using the calculations of the Congressional Budget Office.

White House officials contended that they had indeed produced a balanced budget using their own, more flexible calculations and accused Republicans of insisting on unreasonably large savings from Medicare and Medicaid.

The agreement that ended last month's six-day partial shutdown of the Government expired at midnight on Friday. As a result, nine Cabinet departments and many agencies like the Environmental Protection Agency and the National Aeronautics and Space Administration have no money with which to operate because the bills providing them money for this fiscal year have not been passed.

Because most Government offices are closed on weekends, the main effect today was that tourist attractions like monuments and museums were forced to close. Essential weekend services like patrols at borders, weather forecasts and veterans' hospitals were continued.

But if the situation is not resolved by Monday, many offices will be closed, and some 260,000 Government workers will be furloughed. That is considerably fewer than the 800,000 who stayed home last month because many more agencies, including the Pentagon, have had their spending approved.

The impasse involves the Republicans' massive long-term budget bill and a half-dozen spending bills for the current fiscal year.

Last week, President Clinton vetoed the long-term measure, which is supposed to lead to a balanced budget within seven years, on the grounds that benefits like Medicare and Medicaid would be limited too severely and taxes cut too deeply. The Republican majority in Congress is too small to override the veto.

Some of the spending bills have been delayed because of disagreements within Republican ranks, and one—the measure financing the Departments of Labor and Health and Human Services—is being blocked by Senate Democrats. The President has promised to veto some spending bills, including a few Congress has already passed, because they would not provide as much money as he thinks is needed for education and the environment.

The political ramifications of the budget impasse and the shutdown of Government services are difficult to fathom.

Recent opinion polls have found that the public increasingly blames Republicans for the budget deadlock and that President Clinton's political standing has grown. But such poll findings tend to be transitory, and the situation could turn quickly.

* * *

"Clinton Signs Bill Cutting Welfare; States in New Role," August 23, 1996

Welfare reform in 1996 transformed one of the New Deal's social programs. As reported in *The Times,* President Clinton declared in signing the legislation that welfare now would be "a second chance, not a way of life." The law made changes such as placing lifetime limits on welfare relief, instituting work rules for welfare, and giving states more flexibility in tailoring their programs to address specific needs. This legislation was enacted with strong Republican support, but many Democrats were highly critical of what they viewed as onerous and unrealistic requirements for the poor.

AUGUST 23, 1996
CLINTON SIGNS BILL CUTTING WELFARE; STATES IN NEW ROLE
By FRANCIS X. CLINES

In a sweeping reversal of Federal policy, President Clinton today ended six decades of guaranteed help to the nation's poorest children by signing into law a vast welfare overhaul requiring the 50 states to deal more directly with the social burdens and the budget expense of poverty.

"Today we are taking a historic chance to make welfare what it was meant to be: a second chance, not a way of life," Mr. Clinton declared in signing the measure, which

will affect tens of millions of poor Americans, largely by mandating work requirements and imposing a five-year lifetime limit on welfare help to needy families.

With his signature, at a Rose Garden ceremony, the President eliminated a pillar of Franklin D. Roosevelt's New Deal social welfare program, delighting the Republican-controlled Congress in this election year and incensing many of his fellow Democrats.

Mr. Clinton, hailing the law as "good and solid" progress, expressed hope that the partisan edge would now be eliminated from the nation's frustrations over welfare. But moments after the signing, the Presidential campaign of Bob Dole commented, "By selling out his own party, Bill Clinton has proven he is ideologically adrift."

On the Democratic side, the enactment was decried as a "moment of shame" by Marion Wright Edelman, the president of the Children's Defense Fund and a longtime friend of Hillary Rodham Clinton, who was the fund's cochairwoman until the 1992 election. Another frequent Clinton defender, Senator Paul Simon, Democrat of Illinois, rued the President's signature by declaring, "This isn't welfare reform, it's welfare denial."

Mr. Clinton took care to have three former welfare mothers at his side in the sunshine as he signed the measure, praising it for restoring "America's basic bargain of providing opportunity and demanding in return responsibility."

He claimed credit for gaining a $3.5 billion increase in child care from Congress, for a total of $14 billion to help single mothers while they seek work.

The heart of the complex new law abolishes Aid to Families With Dependent Children, the Government's welfare bulwark, which provides monthly cash benefits to 12.8 million people, including more than 8 million children.

This is to be replaced by a system of block grants and vast new authority for the states, in the hope that they can fashion new work and welfare programs to solve the long-intractable problem of dependence on government. Job creation will be a particular state burden, since the law requires most poor adults to find a job within two years of first receiving aid.

* *

"CLINTON ELECTED TO A 2D TERM WITH SOLID MARGINS ACROSS U.S.; G.O.P. KEEPS HOLD ON CONGRESS," NOVEMBER 6, 1996

Following a relatively smooth campaign, Clinton decisively won reelection in 1996. Although he increased his margin of victory in both the popular and the Electoral College vote, he again won with less than 50 percent of the popular vote, becoming the first president since Woodrow Wilson to win election twice with a popular vote plurality, not a majority.

NOVEMBER 6, 1996
CLINTON ELECTED TO A 2D TERM WITH SOLID MARGINS ACROSS U.S.; G.O.P. KEEPS HOLD ON CONGRESS
By RICHARD L. BERKE

William Jefferson Clinton was re-elected President of the United States yesterday, capping a yearlong political resurgence that made him the first Democrat since Franklin Delano Roosevelt to win a second term as President.

Mr. Clinton built a landslide in the Electoral College and won a decisive victory in the popular vote, overwhelming Bob Dole in all regions of the country except the South and the High Plains, where the Republican won several states. The President's sweep carried to California, where Mr. Dole, in an enormous gamble, diverted millions of dollars from other states and stumped doggedly in the final weeks of the campaign.

Ross Perot, the Texas billionaire who ran on the ticket of the Reform Party he had created, finished a distant third, drawing roughly half of the 19 percent he won in 1992.

With 84 percent of the popular vote tallied at 3 A.M. today, Mr. Clinton drew 49 percent; Mr. Dole 41 percent, and Mr. Perot 8 percent. The President surpassed his showing of 43 percent of the popular vote in 1992.

A state-by-state breakdown of those returns gave Mr. Clinton more than the 370 electoral votes he won four years ago, a commanding showing in the Electoral College, which requires 270 votes for victory.

The support for Mr. Clinton did not run deep enough to allow Democrats to declare a reversal of the Republican tide that swept Congress two years ago. The Republicans retained control of the Senate; by early this morning, they appeared headed to keep a majority in the House.

With a Democrat still in the Oval Office and Republicans still dominating at least one chamber of Congress, the nation's political landscape remains competitive and unsettled.

●　●

"The President Under Fire: Clinton Emphatically Denies an Affair with Ex-Intern; Lawyers Say He Is Distracted by Events," January 27, 1998

A week into his second term, Bill Clinton faced a scandal that threatened his presidency. Reports surfaced that he had an affair with a former White House intern. The president angrily denied the allegations and did not mention them in his State of the Union message the same evening, but the issue would soon convulse his presidency.

JANUARY 27, 1998
THE PRESIDENT UNDER FIRE

Clinton Emphatically Denies an Affair With Ex-Intern: Lawyers Say He Is Distracted by Events

By JAMES BENNET

With eyes narrowed and one index finger stabbing the air, President Clinton angrily denied today that he had had sexual relations with Monica S. Lewinsky, the former White House intern whose tape-recorded accounts of an affair with him now threaten his Presidency.

In his most emphatic denial since the scandal surfaced last Wednesday, Mr. Clinton also rejected accusations that he had urged Ms. Lewinsky to lie under oath about their relationship.

"I did not have sexual relations with that woman, Miss Lewinsky," Mr. Clinton said in comments at the White House that his aides hoped would ease public concerns about his credibility on the eve of his State of the Union Message to Congress. "I never told anybody to lie, not a single time—never. These allegations are false. And I need to go back to work for the American people."

But Mr. Clinton's lawyers, in a legal filing today, acknowledged that the President was being distracted from that work. They said legal processes "have become a vehicle for parties allied in an attempt to destroy the President," and accused the news media of playing along, panting to present "raw and salacious material" without checking its credibility.

Compounding the President's woes, a grand jury hearing tentatively scheduled for Tuesday by the Whitewater independent counsel, Kenneth W. Starr, had threatened to overshadow the State of the Union address that night. But investigators indicated to witnesses' lawyers that Mr. Starr would postpone the appearance of several important witnesses until sometime after Mr. Clinton's speech. Among those who could have been called to testify before the grand jury as early as Tuesday were the President's personal troubleshooter, Vernon E. Jordan Jr.; Mr. Clinton's personal secretary, Betty Currie, and several former White House interns.

Mr. Clinton, who issued his denial with Hillary Rodham Clinton at his side, did not answer questions, and some of his longstanding allies on Capitol Hill said they were not reassured by his remarks.

White House officials continued refusing to explain his relationship with Ms. Lewinsky, who, her lawyers have said, received gifts from the President and job referrals from Mr. Jordan.

Ms. Lewinsky met with her lawyers for nearly nine hours today. This evening one of them, William H. Ginsburg, said he had submitted to prosecutors a summary of what she would be willing to say about her relations with the President if she was given full immunity from prosecution.

Whatever the details of Ms. Lewinsky's latest offer, there was no sign that the prosecutors had decided to accept it. Indeed, one person involved in the negotiations said late tonight that no deal was imminent.

Moreover, with the President preparing to address Congress on Tuesday night, both sides appeared wary about saying anything of a possible deal that would upstage the State of the Union.

"Bombings in East Africa: Bombs Rip Apart 2 U.S. Embassies in Africa; Scores Killed; No Firm Motive or Suspects," August 8, 1998

The August 1998 bombings of the American embassies in Kenya and Tanzania killed hundreds of people and were instantly identified, as reported in *The Times,* as "coordinated terrorist attacks" against the United States. The attacks soon would be linked to the al Qaeda terrorist network, led by Osama bin Laden.

AUGUST 8, 1998
BOMBINGS IN EAST AFRICA: BOMBS RIP APART 2 U.S. EMBASSIES IN AFRICA; SCORES KILLED; NO FIRM MOTIVE OR SUSPECTS
By JAMES C. MCKINLEY JR.

Two powerful bombs exploded minutes apart outside the United States Embassies in Kenya and Tanzania this morning, killing at least 80 people, 8 of them Americans, in what officials said were coordinated terrorist attacks.

In Nairobi, an enormous explosion ripped through downtown shortly after 10:30 A.M., turning the busy Haile Selassie Avenue into a scene of carnage and destruction that left more than 1,600 people wounded and dozens still missing long after night fell. The blast, which leveled a three-story building containing a secretarial school and gutted the rear half of the embassy next door, dismembered more than a dozen people passing on foot and incinerated dozens of others in their seats in three nearby buses.

Just minutes before, a bomb apparently planted in a gasoline tanker detonated near the front entrance of the United States Embassy in the Tanzanian capital, Dar es Salaam, about 400 miles to the south. The blast destroyed the front of the building and toppled a side wall, throwing charred debris down the street, setting cars on fire and toppling trees. At least 7 people were killed and 72 wounded, none of them American, officials said.

In Washington, President Clinton condemned the attacks as abhorrent and inhuman acts of cowardice. He vowed to bring those responsible to justice "no matter what or how long it takes."

The bombings underscored how vulnerable American officials and diplomats remain in an age of global terrorism, particularly in some third-world capitals where borders are porous and security is not as tight as in the industrial world.

The blasts seemed to be coordinated attacks against the United States, and appeared to be unconnected to any local grievances or political currents in the two capitals, American officials said.

"TESTING OF A PRESIDENT: CLINTON ADMITS LEWINSKY LIAISON TO JURY; TELLS NATION 'IT WAS WRONG,' BUT PRIVATE," AUGUST 18, 1998

After denying the allegations for months, Clinton reluctantly gave a televised address to the nation on August 17, 1998, admitting to an affair with Monica Lewinsky. The president insisted this was a private matter, but the news that he had engaged in "an intimate relationship in the White House with a subordinate less than half his age," as reported in *The Times,* at the very least reflected poorly on his judgment and his leadership.

AUGUST 18, 1998
TESTING OF A PRESIDENT: CLINTON ADMITS LEWINSKY LIAISON TO JURY; TELLS NATION 'IT WAS WRONG,' BUT PRIVATE

By JAMES BENNET

"'It's nobody's business but ours. Even Presidents have private lives.'"

Saying that he had misled his wife and the public, President Clinton admitted in a solemn and grim-faced address tonight that he had had an intimate relationship at the White House with an intern. He also acknowledged the relationship in testimony to a Federal grand jury.

"It was wrong," the President said, speaking defiantly from the same straight-backed chair from which, hours earlier, he had carried on an even more combative exchange with prosecutors. "It constituted a critical lapse in judgment and a personal failure on my part for which I am solely and completely responsible."

After seven months of emphatic denials of a sexual relationship with Monica S. Lewinsky, the former intern, Mr. Clinton found himself addressing among the most personally painful of matters—adultery—in the most public forum imaginable. Speaking just after 10 P.M., he tried to wrest political forgiveness from personal embarrassment, issuing a proud, even angry demand for his privacy back.

"Now, this matter is between me, the two people I love most—my wife and our daughter—and our God," he said. "It's nobody's business but ours. Even Presidents have private lives."

Mr. Clinton's defiant statement came after a contentious four-and-a-half-hour session before a grand jury in which he repeatedly refused to answer prosecutors' questions not only about his relationship with Ms. Lewinsky but about other matters under investigation, a Clinton adviser familiar with his testimony said.

In turn, prosecutors told the President that they might subpoena him again, as they did to secure his agreement to testify in the first place, and Mr. Clinton's lawyers said that he would probably fight such a move.

Mr. Clinton denied that he had obstructed justice and had tried to cover up his relationship with Ms. Lewinsky. "I told the grand jury today and I say to you now that at no time did I ask anyone to lie, to hide or destroy evidence or to take any other unlawful action," he said in his public address. He urged the public to put the matter behind it. "It is past time to move on," he said.

After Mr. Clinton's speech it remained unknown what evidence Mr. Starr may have on the most damaging questions of obstructing justice, a point that Republicans were quick to emphasize.

In testifying and then speaking to the public, Mr. Clinton tried the riskiest high-wire act of his career, moving to balance legal and political burdens. Two days short of his 52d birthday, he sought to protect his Presidency and elude legal jeopardy by acknowledging an intimate relationship in the White House with a subordinate less than half his age.

Mr. Clinton had been working on his speech for several days, aides said, trying to strike the right balance between disclosure and dignity, remorse and pride. He ran through it twice tonight before delivering it live, addressing the camera head-on.

Mr. Starr is investigating whether the President lied under oath in denying an affair with Ms. Lewinsky last January in his deposition in the Paula Corbin Jones sexual misconduct suit. Beyond the nature of Mr. Clinton's relationship with Ms. Lewinsky, Mr. Starr has been investigating whether Mr. Clinton tried to obstruct justice and suborn perjury.

Mr. Clinton acknowledged in his testimony having had "inappropriate intimate physical contact" with Ms. Lewinsky, one lawyer and adviser to the President knowledgeable about his appearance said. But he argued that the contact did not fit the definition of sex used by the Jones lawyers, and therefore he did not commit perjury.

"THE 1998 ELECTIONS: G.O.P. IN SCRAMBLE OVER BLAME FOR POOR SHOWING AT THE POLLS," NOVEMBER 5, 1998

Although public opinion did not condone the president's inappropriate sexual conduct, neither did voters seek to punish his party in the 1998 congressional midterm elections. Democrats held their own in the Senate and increased their representation in the House, and the Republican leadership faced significant scrutiny from within its own party. Speaker Newt Gingrich resigned, and his short-lived successor, Robert L. Livingston Jr. of Louisiana, did the same after reports surfaced that he previously had extramarital affairs.

NOVEMBER 5, 1998
THE 1998 ELECTIONS: G.O.P. IN SCRAMBLE OVER BLAME FOR POOR SHOWING AT THE POLLS
By ALISON MITCHELL AND ERIC SCHMITT

Stunned by the Democratic resurgence in the midterm elections, Congressional Republicans tore into one another yesterday over who was to blame for their failure to make the traditional opposition party gains in an off-year election.

The soul-searching and recriminations—and a possibility of Congressional leadership challenges—came as election results showed that Republicans had been unable to increase their 55-to-45 vote margin in the Senate and that Democrats had picked up five seats in the House.

The Democratic surge was the first time since 1934 that the President's party had gained seats in a midterm election and it whittled the Republican lead in the House down to 12 votes and the majority to 6. The Democratic victories were even more remarkable in a year marked by the months long scandal over President Clinton's affair with Monica S. Lewinsky.

The Republicans' new 223-to-211 majority (assuming a Democrat leading in Oregon holds on to win), with one independent, amounted to the smallest Congressional majority since the Republican-led Congress of 1953, the last time Republicans controlled the House until they captured it again in 1994.

With attention now shifting to the House Judiciary Committee and its impeachment inquiry into Mr. Clinton, Representative Henry J. Hyde of Illinois told fellow Republicans on the panel in a conference call yesterday that the only witness Republicans were likely to call was the independent counsel, Kenneth W. Starr. There were reports last night that Mr. Hyde might call another witness, an expert on the meaning of testifying under oath to help the committee in deciding whether Mr. Clinton committed perjury.

Mr. Hyde, the chairman, said he hoped to have the committee vote on possible articles of impeachment by Thanksgiving, an act that would put the issue in the hands of the Speaker, Newt Gingrich. Committee Democrats declined comment until they could discuss Mr. Hyde's plan.

Trying to put the best face on the situation facing Republicans, Mr. Gingrich said in Marietta, Ga., that the Republicans had held onto the House for three elections in a row, for the first time since the election of 1932. But furious rank-and-file Republicans burned up the telephone lines to each other as they considered whether to mount leadership challenges in both chambers in the next few weeks.

"Attack on Iraq: Impeachment Vote in House Delayed as Clinton Launches Iraq Air Strike, Citing Military Need to Move Swiftly," December 17, 1998

U.S. air strikes against Iraq in December 1998 briefly postponed a House vote to impeach President Clinton. When the House approved two articles of impeachment, Clinton became the first chief executive since Andrew Johnson in 1868 to face possible removal from office.

DECEMBER 17, 1998
ATTACK ON IRAQ: IMPEACHMENT VOTE IN HOUSE DELAYED AS CLINTON LAUNCHES IRAQ AIR STRIKE, CITING MILITARY NEED TO MOVE SWIFTLY
By FRANCIS X. CLINES AND STEVEN LEE MYERS

President Clinton ordered a "strong sustained series of air strikes" against Iraq today, defending the attack as unavoidable even as incensed Congressional Republicans charged that it was politically timed to stave off the pending resolution to impeach him in the House of Representatives.

"Iraq has abused its final chance," Mr. Clinton declared in an address to the nation tonight as televised scenes from Baghdad reverberated with flashes of explosions and antiaircraft fire. The Pentagon said more than 200 missiles rained down upon Iraq without any diplomacy or warning about 24 hours after the chief United Nations inspector reported that President Saddam Hussein was again thwarting the inspectors' work.

[The Associated Press reported from Baghdad that Mr. Hussein in a statement broadcast in Iraq early Thursday called on the Iraqi people to "fight the enemies of God, enemies of the nation and enemies of humanity. God will be only on our side and disgrace will be theirs, now and on the day of the judgment."]

As Mr. Clinton spoke, House Republican leaders, yielding to the eruption in the Iraq crisis, postponed their plans to begin on Thursday the debate leading to the second impeachment vote in American history.

"We're going to defer," the House Speaker-elect, Robert L. Livingston, said in careful comments emphasizing support for the troops involved.

Mr. Clinton said of the Iraqi President, "I gave Saddam a chance, not a license." He called once more for the overthrow of Mr. Hussein, three hours after salvos of United States cruise missiles were launched against him, followed by air strikes by Navy jets from the aircraft carrier *Enterprise* in the Persian Gulf.

Among the targets were suspected weapons plants, Iraqi intelligence agencies and fortifications of the military unit known as the Republican Guard, which substantially survived the Persian Gulf war in 1991 despite weeks of sustained bombing. Initial reports tonight suggested that one of Mr. Hussein's marble-clad palaces in Baghdad had also been hit, and that there were ambulances at the scene.

Initial reports from Baghdad by The Associated Press quoted a doctor as saying at least 2 people were killed and 30 wounded in the first hours.

The attacks were ordered, Mr. Clinton said, because of Iraq's refusal to live up to its promise, after defeat in the gulf war, to allow the United Nations to conduct on-site inspections for weapons of mass destruction. The timing, he insisted, was a strategic decision based on a report delivered on Tuesday by Richard Butler, the chairman of the United Nations Special Commission overseeing the disarmament.

"If we had delayed for even a matter of days," Mr. Clinton said, citing the latest reports from the United Nations inspectors, "we would have given Saddam more time to disperse his forces and protect his weapons."

"THE PRESIDENT'S ACQUITTAL: CLINTON ACQUITTED DECISIVELY: NO MAJORITY FOR EITHER CHARGE," FEBRUARY 13, 1999

The Senate acquitted President Clinton on both articles of impeachment, neither of which received even a majority vote of approval, much less the two-thirds constitutionally required for conviction. Many senators, however, criticized the president's conduct, presenting, as *The Times* wrote, "stinging judgments of him," even though they decided that his actions did not rise to the level of "high crimes and misdemeanors," which the Constitution defined as impeachable offenses along with bribery and treason.

FEBRUARY 13, 1999
THE PRESIDENT'S ACQUITTAL: CLINTON ACQUITTED DECISIVELY: NO MAJORITY FOR EITHER CHARGE
By ALISON MITCHELL

The Senate today acquitted President Clinton on two articles of impeachment, falling short of even a majority vote on either of the charges against him: perjury and obstruction of justice.

After a harrowing year of scandal and investigation, the five-week-long Senate trial of the President—only the second in the 210-year history of the Republic—culminated shortly after noon when the roll calls began that would determine Mr. Clinton's fate.

"Is respondent William Jefferson Clinton guilty or not guilty?" asked Chief Justice William H. Rehnquist, in his gold-striped black robe. In a hushed chamber, with senators standing one by one to pronounce Mr. Clinton "guilty" or "not guilty," the Senate rejected the charge of perjury, 55 to 45, with 10 Republicans voting against conviction.

It then split 50-50 on a second article accusing Mr. Clinton of obstruction of justice in concealing his affair with Monica S. Lewinsky. Five Republicans broke ranks on the obstruction-of-justice charge. No Democrats voted to convict on either charge, and it would have taken a dozen of them, and all 55 Republicans, to reach the two-thirds majority of 67 senators required for conviction.

Chief Justice Rehnquist announced the acquittal of the nation's 42d President at 12:39 P.M. "It is therefore ordered and adjudged that the said William Jefferson Clinton be, and he hereby is, acquitted of the charges in the said articles," he said. Almost immediately, the mood in the Senate lightened.

As required by the Senate's impeachment rules, Secretary of State Madeleine K. Albright was formally notified of the Senate's judgment.

Mr. Clinton responded by once again declaring himself "profoundly sorry" for his actions and words that had thrown the nation into a 13-month ordeal. "Now I ask all Americans, and I hope all Americans here in Washington and throughout our land, will re-dedicate ourselves to the work of serving our nation and building our future together," he said in a brief appearance in the White House Rose Garden.

Yet for all the hopes of healing, the bitterness and turmoil of the past months were underscored when the Senate side of the Capitol had to be cleared for more than an hour because of a bomb scare shortly after the trial had ended, just as senators had begun a series of news conferences.

Just before the bomb scare, the Senate, by a 56-to-43 vote, rebuffed an effort by Senator Dianne Feinstein, a California Democrat, to force a vote today on a censure measure that would rebuke Mr. Clinton for "shameful, reckless and indefensible" behavior.

Even many of those who chose to acquit Mr. Clinton today delivered stinging judgments of him while concluding that his evasions and attempts to conceal a sexual relationship with a former White House intern did not constitute the kind of high crimes the nation's founders had contemplated when they wrote the impeachment clause of the Constitution.

"Defeat of a Treaty: Senate Kills Test Ban Treaty in Crushing Loss for Clinton; Evokes Versailles Pact Defeat," October 14, 1999

The failure of the Comprehensive Test Ban Treaty marked a significant foreign policy defeat for Clinton following the impeachment debacle. Although the treaty secured a bare majority of Senate votes, it fell far short of the two-thirds required for ratification. *The Times* reported that this vote was the first time since the failure of the Treaty of Versailles after World War I that the Senate had overturned "a major international security pact."

OCTOBER 14, 1999
DEFEAT OF A TREATY: SENATE KILLS TEST BAN TREATY IN CRUSHING LOSS FOR CLINTON; EVOKES VERSAILLES PACT DEFEAT
By ERIC SCHMITT

The Senate today rejected a treaty banning all underground nuclear testing in a 51–48 vote that crushed one of President Clinton's major foreign policy goals.

The vote on the Comprehensive Test Ban Treaty was largely along party lines. The treaty fell 19 votes short of the two-thirds majority needed for approval, giving conservative Republicans a victory after a weeklong power play in which Democrats, the White House and some moderate Republicans tried to forestall defeat by delaying action until after President Clinton left office.

In a last-ditch effort to save the treaty, Mr. Clinton called the Republican leader, Trent Lott, two hours before the vote and asked that he delay action for national security reasons. In a blunt rebuff, Mr. Lott said the President had offered too little, too late, and he pushed ahead with an action that he knew would humiliate Mr. Clinton.

This was the first time the Senate had defeated a major international security pact since the Treaty of Versailles, creating the League of Nations, failed to win Senate approval in 1920. While the Senate and White House often joust on legislation governing domestic issues, senators of both parties usually defer to the President in matters of state and war.

Mr. Clinton, speaking on the White House lawn, denounced the rejection by the Senate as a "reckless" and "partisan" act, and said that he would continue to pursue a ban on testing. "I assure you the fight is far from over," he said. "When all is said and done, the United States will ratify the treaty."

The failure of the treaty to clear Washington raised serious questions about its survival. Supporters in Washington and abroad had contended that if it was not ad-

opted by the United States, other nations with nuclear capability, from Pakistan and India to Russia and China, would follow suit, denying the 1996 treaty the 44 ratifications it needs to go into force. The leaders of Britain, France and Germany had urged the Senate to postpone the vote.

Supporters said the treaty's demise dealt the United States a diplomatic embarrassment that sent a perilous signal to nations with emerging nuclear programs—like Pakistan and India—that more testing is acceptable. "This is a significant step backward in the effort to stop the spread of nuclear weapons," said Senator Byron L. Dorgan, Democrat of North Dakota.

But to its critics, the ban would freeze the United States dangerously in place while states like North Korea and Iran, or even China and Russia, cheated and conducted clandestine tests that eroded America's nuclear deterrent.

"This won't make any difference to countries who are determined to be part of the nuclear club," said Senator Richard G. Lugar, Republican of Indiana, who is a staunch arms control advocate.

After the vote, Mr. Lott declared that the Senate and the President were "coequal partners" in the treaty-making process. "The fact that the Senate has rejected several significant treaties this century underscores the important quality control function that was intended by the framers of the Constitution," he said. "The Founding Fathers never envisioned that the Senate would be a rubber stamp for a flawed treaty."

But Senator Tom Daschle, the Democratic leader, said, "No constitutional obligation has been treated so cavalierly, so casually, as this treaty."

Treaty supporters vowed to bring it up again, although Senate and Administration aides said that was unlikely this year or next. In a telephone interview, the President's national security adviser, Samuel R. Berger, said, "Our job now is to reassure the world that the United States continues to ascribe to the principles in the treaty and the testing moratorium."

The treaty was signed by the United States in 1996 and sent to the Senate a year later. So far, 26 of the 44 nations considered to have nuclear capability have approved it, including Britain, France and Japan. But Russia and China have yet to ratify it, signaling that they would take their lead from the Senate.

THE PRESIDENCY OF GEORGE W. BUSH

JANUARY 20, 2001 –

The presidency of George Walker Bush witnessed the transition of the United States from the post–cold war era to the post–September 11 world, in which combating terrorism would become the nation's foremost priority. When Bush took office in 2001, his primary aim was to move beyond his controversial election results—prevailing by a bare majority in the Electoral College after the Supreme Court ruled that he had won the disputed state of Florida, but failing to secure the most popular votes nationwide—by focusing on his domestic policy agenda, which emphasized the concept of "compassionate conservatism." But the terrorist attacks of September 11, 2001, shocked the country and transformed the political agenda. Keeping the United States safe, destroying the terrorist network that had launched the attacks, and working to reduce terrorism at home and abroad defined national political priorities, and the president faced little opposition in his initial efforts. But Bush's decision to wage war against Iraq to depose Saddam Hussein was highly controversial and will become perhaps his most disputed legacy.

In becoming president, Bush followed in his father's footsteps, the first president to do so since John Quincy Adams in the nineteenth century. Bush was the eldest child of former president George Herbert Walker Bush, who was vice president in the Reagan administration and president from 1989 to 1993, and grandson of Prescott Bush, a former U.S. senator and Wall Street banker. The younger Bush was born in Connecticut while his father was an undergraduate at Yale, but grew up in Texas, where his father was a successful oil businessman. After attending public school in Midland, Texas, Bush followed family tradition and entered the Phillips Academy preparatory school in Andover, Massachusetts. He was head cheerleader

Source: By permission of Gary Markstein and Creators Syndicate Inc.

for the football team and organizer of an intramural stick ball league. He then matriculated at Yale University and, like his father, was inducted into the Skull and Bones secret society. He also was elected president of his fraternity, Delta Kappa Epsilon. Unlike his father, Bush was known more for socializing than for academic success in college.

After graduation, Bush joined the Texas Air National Guard to complete his military service during the Vietnam War. He was not deployed abroad, and critics later charged that he had received preferential treatment, along with children of other prominent Texas families. During his 2000 presidential campaign, Bush faced allegations that after being transferred to the Alabama National Guard in 1972, when he was working on a political campaign in the state, he did not complete his service obligations, but these charges were not substantiated. Bush received an early discharge in 1973 to attend Harvard Business School, completing his master's degree in business administration in 1975.

Bush returned to Midland, started an oil company, and ran unsuccessfully for Congress. He enjoyed socializing and

QUICK FACTS ON GEORGE W. BUSH

BIRTH	July 6, 1946, New Haven, Conn.
EDUCATION	Yale University, B.A., 1968 Harvard University, M.B.A., 1975
FAMILY	Wife: Laura Welch Bush Children: Barbara Pierce Bush, Jenna Welch Bush
WHITE HOUSE PETS	Cats; dogs
PARTY	Republican
PREPRESIDENTIAL CAREER (SELECTED)	Texas Air National Guard, 1968–1973 Transfer to Alabama Air National Guard, 1972 Arrest and suspension of driver's license in Maine for substance abuse, 1976 Unsuccessful candidate for U.S. House of Representatives, 1978 Owner, oil and gas business, 1979–1986 Assisted father's presidential campaign, 1987–1988 Partner, Texas Rangers baseball team, 1989–1994 Governor of Texas, 1995–2000
PRESIDENTIAL TERMS	January 20, 2001–January 20, 2005 January 20, 2005–
VICE PRESIDENT	Richard B. Cheney
SELECTED EVENTS	Creates Office of Faith-Based and Community Initiatives (2001) U.S. withdrawal of support for Kyoto Protocol (2001) Collision of EP-3 spy plane with Chinese jet (2001)

was a heavy drinker, but at age forty, he became a born-again Christian and gave up alcohol. Bush's business suffered losses in the 1980s and was acquired by a larger company, after which Bush moved to Washington to work on his father's presidential campaign.

After his father's victory, Bush returned to Texas and became managing general partner of the Texas Rangers baseball team. The team won its league title in 1994, and Bush sold his shares in the team at a high profit. Angered by Texas governor Ann Richards's jokes about his family—at the 1988 Democratic National Convention, she famously said that George H. W. Bush, who was well known for misusing words, "was born with a silver foot in his mouth," and she derisively referred to George W. Bush as "Shrub"—he ran against her in the 1994 gubernatorial race and won. He handily won reelection in 1998, and was soon touted as a likely contender for the 2000 Republican presidential nomination.

THE 2000 PRESIDENTIAL ELECTION

Although he faced a surprisingly strong challenge from Arizona senator John McCain in some early nominating contests, Bush secured his party's nomination in 2000. He selected former U.S. representative from Wyoming Richard B. Cheney—who also had served as defense secretary in his father's administration—as his vice-presidential running mate. They competed against Vice President Al Gore Jr., who ran with Sen. Joe Lieberman of Connecticut.

The 2000 presidential race was not decided until five weeks after election day because of disputed results from Florida, where Bush's younger brother, Jeb Bush, was governor. The U.S. Supreme Court stopped the recounts in a 5–4 decision that resulted in Bush winning Florida by just over five hundred popular votes. Winning Florida gave Bush 271 Electoral College votes, one more than he needed to win the presidency,

Signs $1.35 trillion tax cut (2001)
Executive order authorizes limited stem cell research (2001)
Terrorist attacks in United States (September 11, 2001)
Creates Office of Homeland Security (2001)
Invasion of Afghanistan (2001)
USA PATRIOT Act (2001)
No Child Left Behind Act (2002)
Bipartisan Campaign Reform Act, known as "McCain-Feingold" (2002)
Sarbanes-Oxley Act (2002)
Withdrawal from Anti-Ballistic Missile Treaty (2002)
Congress authorizes use of force against Iraq (2002)
UN Security Council orders Iraq to comply with weapons inspections (2002)
Homeland Security Act (2002)
Invasion of Iraq (2003)
Partial-Birth Abortion Ban Act (2003)
Medicare Prescription Drug Improvement and Modernization Act (2003)
Release of 9/11 Commission Report (2004)
Intelligence Reform and Terrorism Prevention Act (2004)
Bankruptcy Abuse Prevention and Consumer Protection Act (2005)
Dominican Republic-Central America Free Trade Agreement (2005)
Energy Policy Act (2005)
Hurricane Katrina devastates Gulf Coast (2005)
Detainee Treatment Act (2005)
Veto of Stem Cell Research Enhancement Act (2006)
Pension Protection Act (2006)
Secure Fence Act (2006)
Republican Party loses control of Congress (2006)
Military Commissions Act (2006)
Protect America Act (2007)

but he still lost the popular vote to Gore by approximately half a million votes. Not since 1888 had the United States seen a presidential candidate win the Electoral College vote but not the popular vote. The mixed results, combined with the Florida controversy, cast a shadow over Bush's presidency from the outset.

THE BUSH II ADMINISTRATION (FIRST TERM)

President Bush made history by appointing the first African American secretary of state, retired general Colin Powell. For secretary of defense, he selected Donald Rumsfeld, who previously had held the same position under President Gerald R. Ford. Rumsfeld also had worked with Cheney when Rumsfeld was Ford's chief of staff, and Cheney was his deputy. Paul H. O'Neill, former CEO of Alcoa, served as treasury secretary for two years and then was replaced by John W.

Snow, a railroad industry executive. Attorney General John Ashcroft of Missouri came to the cabinet directly from the Senate after narrowly losing reelection. Bush established the fifteenth cabinet department, Homeland Security, in 2002, and he selected Pennsylvania governor Tom Ridge to be its first secretary. Within his White House advisory team, Bush selected Stanford University provost Condoleezza Rice to be his national security adviser. She is the first woman and the first African American to hold that position.

Like the president, First Lady Laura Bush grew up in Midland, Texas, and the two actually knew each other in elementary school. They became reacquainted as adults at a mutual friend's barbecue and married in 1977. Laura Bush was instrumental in persuading her husband to give up his free-wheeling lifestyle. A former teacher and librarian, as first lady Laura Bush has emphasized education and reading as national priorities. The Bushes have twin daughters, Barbara and Jenna, who were college students when their father became president.

Major Issues (First Term)

Despite his disputed election victory, Bush governed decisively upon taking office. He created the Office of Faith-Based and Community Initiatives by executive order in 2001 to increase opportunities for religiously affiliated organizations to receive federal funds for social programs. He authorized limited embryonic stem cell research by executive order. Bush announced that the United States would withdraw from the Kyoto Protocol, an international agreement to reduce global warming, citing different requirements for advanced and developing nations, among other reasons. When a U.S. reconnaissance plane collided with a Chinese jet and was forced to make an emergency landing in China, the Bush administration negotiated the crew's safe release. Most significantly, Bush succeeded in fulfilling his campaign pledge on taxes, signing into law a tax cut amounting to $1.35 trillion over ten years.

Bush's presidency, and indeed American history, forever changed when suicide terrorists hijacked four U.S. passenger jets, crashing two of them into the World Trade Center towers, which collapsed, and one into the Pentagon on September 11, 2001. The fourth hijacked plane was heading for the White House but was diverted when passengers and crew members bravely tried to overpower the hijackers, and the plane crashed in rural Pennsylvania. Approximately three thousand people from more than ninety countries died in the attacks, and thousands more were injured. The hijackers were affiliated with the al Qaeda terrorist network led by Muslim fundamentalist Osama bin Laden.

The United States responded swiftly to the attacks. Within days Congress passed a joint resolution authorizing military force against the perpetrators. In October 2001 the United States launched Operation Enduring Freedom, waging war against Afghanistan to find bin Laden and to overthrow the Taliban regime, which had permitted al Qaeda to develop training camps on Afghan territory. The latter was quickly achieved, but Taliban forces have reemerged in several parts of the country, and bin Laden has eluded capture to date. The United Kingdom participated in the assault, and other allies have since provided assistance, including Afghan and NATO forces. Domestically, the Bush administration enacted the USA PATRIOT Act (the acronym stands for Uniting and Strengthening America by Providing Appropriate Tools Required to Intercept and Obstruct Terrorism), which gave law enforcement agencies increased power to investigate alleged terrorists. Critics contend that the law, which was passed with a four-year window for implementation,

infringes upon civil liberties, but it was nevertheless renewed largely intact in 2006.

Some of the Bush administration's other decisions in what initially would be termed the "war on terror" were more controversial. The establishment of a detainment facility for "enemy combatants" at Guantánamo Bay, Cuba, sparked heated debate over whether the prisoners were entitled to the protections of the Geneva Conventions on human rights. The creation of the cabinet-level Department of Homeland Security in 2002 merged twenty-two government agencies into a single entity to protect the nation against terrorist attacks and was the largest reorganization of the federal government in more than fifty years. Critics questioned whether so many previously independent agencies would work together effectively as one organization. President Bush also issued an executive order authorizing the National Security Agency to conduct surveillance of suspected terrorists without seeking warrants.

In domestic policy, the Bush administration enacted important legislation as well. The No Child Left Behind Act increased school accountability standards, which would be evaluated by student performance on annual tests, and students in schools that repeatedly failed to meet goals would be permitted to seek another school. Medicare reform legislation provided prescription drug benefits for senior citizens. Although he was not a strong supporter of campaign finance reform legislation, Bush signed a bill that imposed restrictions on donations to political parties and other regulations.

To investigate the 9/11 attacks and make recommendations for preventing another tragedy, in 2002 Congress and President Bush created a National Commission on Terrorist Attacks, popularly known as the 9/11 Commission. The commission concluded in a lengthy report released in summer 2004 that intelligence failures in the CIA and FBI as well as a lack of cooperation between the two agencies were significant problems. In response to the report, a director of national intelligence was instituted, along with a supporting office, to oversee the many intelligence-gathering agencies within the federal government.

Perhaps the most contentious issue in Bush's first term was his decision to wage war against Iraq in 2003. In response to Saddam Hussein's refusal to comply with UN weapons inspections, the United States built a multilateral coalition to invade Iraq and depose Hussein. In October 2002 Congress granted the president authority to use military force in Iraq, and the following month, the UN Security Council promised "serious consequences" if Iraq did not comply with inspections. The United States failed, however, to persuade the Security Council to pass a second resolution specifically authorizing the use of military force against Iraq.

The initial invasion proved successful, as Hussein was quickly overthrown, and later captured, tried, and executed. But establishing a democratic government in Iraq proved more challenging, especially in the face of continuing insurgent attacks on U.S. and coalition forces. A report by the Iraq Survey Group in the fall of 2004 that Saddam Hussein had not stockpiled nuclear, chemical, or biological weapons raised questions about the validity of the administration's case for going to war against Iraq.

THE 2004 PRESIDENTIAL ELECTION

In seeking a second term in 2004, Bush campaigned on a platform of national security and continuing the policies he had initiated as president. He was challenged by Democratic senator John Kerry of Massachusetts, who ran with Sen. John Edwards of North Carolina. Although Kerry had voted for the 2002 resolution authorizing the use of force against Iraq, he criticized the Bush administration's lack of postwar planning and said he would be more effective in securing multilateral support for continued operations. The administration also faced criticism when news reports revealed that U.S. soldiers had tortured and abused Iraqi detainees in the Abu Ghraib prison complex outside of Baghdad. Bush, in turn, declared that Kerry's shifting views on Iraq reflected an inability to be a decisive commander in chief. Bush supporters, particularly an organization called Swift Boat Veterans for Truth, also initiated harsh attacks on Kerry for opposing the Vietnam War after returning from military duty there. In a close race, Bush prevailed with just over 50 percent of the popular vote and 286 Electoral College votes to 251 for Kerry. (One elector cast a vote for Edwards for president.)

THE BUSH ADMINISTRATION (SECOND TERM)

President Bush made some significant changes in his second-term cabinet. National Security Adviser Rice became secretary of state, the first African American woman to hold this office. White House Counsel Alberto Gonzales became attorney general. He resigned in 2007 amid reports of politicizing Justice Department activities and issuing questionable justifications of executive authority in the war on terror during Bush's first term. Former federal judge Michael B. Mukasey replaced Gonzales. John Snow continued as treasury secretary until 2006, when Henry Paulson took the post. Defense Secretary Rumsfeld stayed in office despite repeated calls for his resignation until late 2006, when Robert Gates, a former CIA director, replaced him.

MAJOR ISSUES (SECOND TERM)

President Bush faced more difficulty accomplishing his second-term policy agenda than his first. He pledged to enact Social Security reform to keep the program solvent over the long term, but his proposal to partially privatize the program failed to gain political traction. He endorsed comprehensive immigration reform, including a "pathway to citizenship" for illegal immigrants as presented in legislation co-sponsored by Sen. Ted Kennedy of Massachusetts and Sen. John McCain of Arizona, but critics derailed the bill for providing "amnesty" to illegal immigrants and not addressing border security concerns. Bush successfully nominated John G. Roberts Jr. to become chief justice of the United States, but his selection of close White House aide and personal friend Harriet E. Miers for the Court was widely criticized, and the president eventually withdrew her name and selected Samuel A. Alito Jr. instead. Bush also used his veto power for the first time to overturn legislation that would have expanded embryonic stem cell research.

The Bush administration faced much criticism in other areas as well. The president was slow to respond to the devastation wrought on the Gulf Coast by Hurricane Katrina, and the disaster relief for New Orleans and other affected areas seemed to many to be tardy and insufficient. In response to the outcry over treatment of prisoners in the Abu Ghraib scandal and at Guantánamo Bay, Congress passed the Detainee Treatment Act, which outlawed torture and inhumane treatment of prisoners by interrogators.

A few months later, the Supreme Court ruled in *Hamdan v. Rumsfeld* that the administration's use of military commissions to try detainees at Guantánamo Bay violated the Geneva Conventions. Congress then passed the Military Commissions Act to permit military tribunals for "unlawful enemy combatants," which included alleged terrorists. This law stated that federal courts lacked jurisdiction to hear habeas corpus petitions from "enemy combatants," but in 2008 the Supreme Court held in *Boumediene v. Bush* that prisoners at Guantánamo Bay have habeas corpus rights, meaning they may challenge their detention in U.S. civilian courts.

Controversy also erupted over the news about a presidentially approved covert surveillance program, sparking an uproar about government intrusion into civil liberties. As first reported in *The New York Times* in December 2005, President Bush issued an executive order in 2002 permitting the National Security Agency to monitor communications of suspected terrorists without a search warrant. Congress later passed legislation authorizing such surveillance.

Looming over all of these problems was the continuing war in Iraq. Although public support for the war held steady at first, questions about the prospects for achieving stability, let alone democracy, in Iraq became more pointed as military operations continued. The administration also faced an independent counsel investigation stemming from a leak by an anonymous government official to journalists about the identity of an undercover CIA operative, whose husband had publicly declared the lack of evidence for weapons of mass destruction in Iraq. *New York Times* reporter Judith Miller was jailed for refusing to reveal the identity of the anonymous source, who was later revealed to be Vice President Cheney's chief of staff, I. Lewis "Scooter" Libby. Libby was convicted of obstruction of justice and perjury; President Bush commuted his prison sentence.

In spring 2006 Congress created a bipartisan commission known as the Iraq Study Group to evaluate U.S. progress in Iraq. The group's report, released in December 2006, viewed the situation in Iraq pessimistically and called for increased diplomatic efforts as well as the gradual withdrawal of approximately 130,000 American forces. Bush said he would consider the recommendations, but he did not follow them, deciding instead to increase U.S. forces in Iraq temporarily to combat the sectarian warfare there. The "surge," as this policy was known, sent more than 20,000 additional troops to Iraq, primarily to Baghdad. The effects of the surge are widely debated, but Commanding General David H. Petraeus was cautiously optimistic in testimony before Congress in 2008.

Public dissatisfaction with the national government's priorities was expressed in the 2006 congressional midterm elections, when the Republican Party lost control of both chambers of Congress. Party leaders were criticized for not aggressively addressing several ethics scandals involving lobbyists as well as members of Congress. Congressional intervention in a Florida family's dispute over the continued use of a feeding tube to keep Terri Schiavo alive also sparked controversy. President Bush was not directly responsible for any of these matters, but his low public approval ratings combined with criticism of his response to Hurricane Katrina and his Iraq policies did not help his party at the election polls.

In his final two years in office, President Bush turned his attention to other policy areas. In 2002 he had named North Korea part of an "axis of evil" because of its covert nuclear weapons program, but five years later, multiparty talks that included the United States resulted in North Korea's agreement to end this program. He convened Israeli-Palestinian peace talks in 2007 that for the first time accepted a two-state solution as a premise for discussion, and the meetings concluded with an agreement by leaders from both sides to continue negotiations. President Bush also expanded a first-term program (PEPFAR—President's Emergency Plan for AIDS Relief)

Throughout both of his terms in office President George W. Bush made global AIDS relief a priority on his foreign policy agenda. His U.S. President's Emergency Plan for AIDS Relief program has committed billions of dollars to AIDS prevention, treatment, and care, particularly in Africa.

Source: Doug Miller for the New York Times

to combat HIV/AIDS worldwide, and he traveled to Africa in 2008 to view the program's implementation there. But as the 2008 presidential race began in earnest, the primary issues were the weakening economy and continued U.S. involvement in Iraq. The Bush administration's legacy on both issues is still hotly contested and incomplete.

"THE REPUBLICANS: THE NOMINEE; BUSH-CHENEY TICKET NOMINATED AND THE ATTACKS ON GORE BEGIN," AUGUST 3, 2000

In his 2000 presidential race, George W. Bush campaigned on a platform of ending the policies and politics of the Clinton administration. In reporting on a speech by vice-presidential nominee Dick Cheney at the Republican National Convention, *The New York Times* wrote that the candidates viewed the Clinton years as a time "of dashed hopes and squandered opportunities."

AUGUST 3, 2000
THE REPUBLICANS: THE NOMINEE; BUSH-CHENEY TICKET NOMINATED AND THE ATTACKS ON GORE BEGIN
By RICHARD L. BERKE

Burning to reclaim the White House after eight years on the outside, the Republican Party tonight nominated George Walker Bush for president and sent forth his running mate with the most stinging and unabashedly partisan assault of the convention.

Dick Cheney, Mr. Bush's No. 2, said the election of Al Gore would perpetuate what he called the misguided policies of President Clinton.

"We are all a little weary of the Clinton-Gore routine," Mr. Cheney said. "But the wheel has turned."

Then, appropriating Mr. Gore's 1992 campaign slogan as his own, he said, "It is time for them to go!"

In the ritual roll call, the 22 votes from Mr. Cheney's home state, Wyoming, cast at 10:04 p.m. gave Mr. Bush more than the 1,034 votes needed to grasp the nomination. The hall erupted in a prolonged ovation as jubilant delegates, many of them dancing, were awash in a sea of beach balls, confetti and balloons.

The delegates, who had heard three nights of sunny, even apolitical, speeches, roared in delight as Mr. Cheney directed full-throated taunts at the Democrats. But with Mr. Cheney's mild and even-toned delivery, his punch lines did not carry the same weight on television.

Casting aside the high-minded oratory that had marked this convention, Mr. Cheney portrayed Mr. Gore as mean-spirited by reviving former Senator Bill Bradley's pungent dismissal of him six days before the New Hampshire primary: "A thousand promises. A thousand attacks."

Mr. Cheney, defense secretary under former President George Bush, said he was lured back into public service because of his belief in Governor Bush and his fear that Mr. Gore's election would perpetuate everything that he believed was wrong with Mr. Clinton's stewardship.

Drawing a contrast with Mr. Bush's achievements as governor of Texas, Mr. Cheney contended that the Clinton administration had made no headway on Social Security, taxes or military readiness.

Mr. Cheney's address capped Mr. Bush's night of triumph, which had been honed for weeks, if not months. It was a political and emotional peak for the two-term governor, one-time baseball team owner and son of a former president who did not appear on the public stage until he first won election in 1994.

Just eight years ago, Republicans nominated Mr. Bush's father for a second term, only to have their president ousted by Bill Clinton. But tonight, Mr. Cheney told the 2,066 delegates that the era of Mr. Clinton and Mr. Gore had been one of dashed hopes and squandered opportunities.

"BUSH PREVAILS; BY SINGLE VOTE, JUSTICES END RECOUNT, BLOCKING GORE AFTER 5-WEEK STRUGGLE," DECEMBER 13, 2000

Although Bush prevailed in the 2000 presidential election, his victory was unique in American history in being decided by the Supreme Court. By a single-vote majority, the Court held that popular-vote recounts in Florida should end, giving Bush a narrow win there and consequently in the Electoral College. But Bush won just under 48 percent of the nationwide popular vote, compared to just over 48 percent for Vice President Gore. Critics contended that the new administration would lack legitimacy because of Bush's failure to win the popular vote, along with the Court's final adjudication of the contested Florida votes necessary for victory in the Electoral College.

DECEMBER 13, 2000
BUSH PREVAILS; BY SINGLE VOTE, JUSTICES END RECOUNT, BLOCKING GORE AFTER 5-WEEK STRUGGLE
By LINDA GREENHOUSE

The Supreme Court effectively handed the presidential election to George W. Bush tonight, overturning the Florida Supreme Court and ruling by a vote of 5 to 4 that there could be no further counting of Florida's disputed presidential votes.

The ruling came after a long and tense day of waiting at 10 p.m., just two hours before the Dec. 12 "safe harbor" for immunizing a state's electors from challenge in Congress was to come to an end. The unsigned majority opinion said it was the immediacy of this deadline that made it impossible to come up with a way of counting the votes that could both meet "minimal constitutional standards" and be accomplished within the deadline.

The five members of the majority were Chief Justice William H. Rehnquist and Justices Sandra Day O'Connor, Antonin Scalia, Anthony M. Kennedy and Clarence Thomas.

Among the four dissenters, two justices, Stephen G. Breyer and David H. Souter, agreed with the majority that the varying standards in different Florida counties for counting the punch-card ballots presented problems of both due process and equal protection. But unlike the majority, these justices said the answer should be not to shut the recount down, but to extend it until the Dec. 18 date for the meeting of the Electoral College.

Justice Souter said that such a recount would be a "tall order" but that "there is no justification for denying the state the opportunity to try to count all the disputed ballots now."

The six separate opinions, totaling 65 pages, were filled with evidence that the justices were acutely aware of the controversy the court had entered by accepting Governor Bush's appeal of last Friday's Florida Supreme Court ruling and by granting him a stay of the recount on Saturday afternoon, just hours after the vote counting had begun.

"None are more conscious of the vital limits on judicial authority than are the members of this court," the majority opinion said, referring to "our unsought responsibility to resolve the federal and constitutional issues the judicial system has been forced to confront."

The dissenters said nearly all the objections raised by Mr. Bush were insubstantial. The court should not have reviewed either this case or the one it decided last week, they said.

Justice John Paul Stevens said the court's action "can only lend credence to the most cynical appraisal of the work of judges throughout the land."

His dissenting opinion, also signed by Justices Breyer and Ruth Bader Ginsburg, added: "It is confidence in the men and women who administer the judicial system that is the true backbone of the rule of law. Time will one day heal the wound to that confidence that will be inflicted by today's decision. One thing, however, is certain. Although we may never know with complete certainty the identity of the winner of this year's Presidential election, the identity of the loser is perfectly clear. It is the nation's confidence in the judge as an impartial guardian of the rule of law."

What the court's day and a half of deliberations yielded tonight was a messy product that bore the earmarks of a failed attempt at a compromise solution that would have permitted the vote counting to continue.

It appeared that Justices Souter and Breyer, by taking seriously the equal protection concerns that Justices Kennedy and O'Connor had raised at the argument, had tried to persuade them that those concerns could be addressed in a remedy that would permit the disputed votes to be counted.

Justices O'Connor and Kennedy were the only justices whose names did not appear separately on any opinion, indicating that one or both of them wrote the court's unsigned majority opinion, labelled only "per curiam," or "by the court." Its focus was narrow, limited to the ballot counting process itself. The opinion objected not only to the varying standards used by different counties for determining voter intent, but to aspects of the Florida Supreme Court's order determining which ballots should be counted.

"We are presented with a situation where a state court with the power to assure uniformity has ordered a statewide recount with minimal procedural safeguards," the opinion said. "When a court orders a statewide remedy, there must be at least some assurance that the rudimentary requirements of equal treatment and fundamental fairness are satisfied."

Three members of the majority—the Chief Justice, and Justices Scalia and Thomas—raised further, more basic objections to the recount and said the Florida Supreme Court had violated state law in ordering it.

The fact that Justices O'Connor and Kennedy evidently did not share these deeper concerns had offered a potential basis for a coalition between them and the dissenters. That effort apparently foundered on the two justices' conviction that the midnight deadline of Dec. 12 had to be met.

- -

"BUSH TAX CUT PLAN PASSES FIRST TEST IN A SPLIT SENATE," APRIL 4, 2001

Less than five months after taking office, Bush signed into law the largest tax relief program in twenty years. He had proposed a $1.6 trillion tax cut, and negotiations in Congress reduced the number only slightly, to $1.35 trillion.

APRIL 4, 2001
BUSH TAX CUT PLAN PASSES FIRST TEST IN A SPLIT SENATE
By DAVID E. ROSENBAUM

With Vice President Dick Cheney casting his first tie-breaking vote, President Bush's tax plan passed its first test today in the Senate.

The 51-to-50 vote was on one of the sharpest issues dividing the parties: whether tax cuts or Medicare should take precedence.

Mr. Cheney came down on the side of tax cuts. His vote blocked a Democratic proposal to reduce the president's $1.6 trillion tax cut by $158 billion over the next 10 years and to use the money, along with the $153 billion earmarked in the president's budget outline, to pay for prescription drug coverage under Medicare.

The Senate was deadlocked 50-50. One Republican, Senator Lincoln Chafee of Rhode Island, voted with the Democrats, and one Democrat, Senator Zell Miller of Georgia, was

on the Republican side. Mr. Cheney had been in the Capitol almost all day in case his vote was needed.

The issue was one Mr. Bush and Al Gore debated at length in last year's election campaign. President Bill Clinton won several budget battles against the Republican-controlled Congress by arguing that Republicans would gut Medicare, the health program for the elderly and disabled, in order to provide tax reduction for the wealthy.

The crucial vote today was on a Republican plan that would potentially allow about the same amount of money to be spent on Medicare drug coverage but would not shift the money out of the tax cut.

This had the effect of thwarting the Democratic plan to strip the money from the tax cut. With the same line-up of senators, the Senate then rejected the Democratic proposal by a 50-to-50 vote. Mr. Cheney's vote was not needed this time because a proposal in the Senate must have a majority to be passed.

The votes were the first in the Senate's consideration of a budget resolution for the fiscal year that begins Oct. 1. Budget resolutions do not become law. They are simply planning devices for Congress and establish the framework for tax and spending legislation to come.

The votes therefore are not decisive. Congress can and often does ignore the budget resolution before the year is out. So the Republican success today does not necessarily mean that the president's full tax plan will be approved.

Nevertheless, the votes today were important. They showed that leaders in both parties were able to hold their troops together in tough circumstances and portended many other tie votes in the evenly divided Senate as the year progresses.

"A Day of Terror: A Somber Bush Says Terrorism Cannot Prevail," September 12, 2001, and "A Nation Challenged: For President, a Mission and a Role in History," September 22, 2001

The shocking terrorist attacks of September 11, 2001, fundamentally changed President Bush's view of the mission of his administration. Less than two weeks after the attacks, *The Times* quoted a White House official as saying the president believed "we will be known to history by the way we approach this great cause," and an acquaintance of the president as saying "In [Bush's] frame, this is what God has asked him to do. . . . It offers him enormous clarity."

SEPTEMBER 12, 2001
A DAY OF TERROR

A Somber Bush Says Terrorism Cannot Prevail
By ELISABETH BUMILLER WITH DAVID E. SANGER

President Bush vowed tonight to retaliate against those responsible for today's attacks on New York and Washington, declaring that he would "make no distinction between the terrorists who committed these acts and those who harbor them."

"These acts of mass murder were intended to frighten our nation into chaos and retreat, but they have failed," the president said in his first speech to the nation from the Oval Office. "Our country is strong. Terrorist acts can shake the foundation of our biggest buildings, but they cannot touch the foundation of America."

His speech came after a day of trauma that seems destined to define his presidency. Seeking to at once calm the nation and declare his determination to exact retribution, he told a country numbed by repeated scenes of carnage that "these acts shattered steel, but they cannot dent the steel of American resolve."

Mr. Bush spoke only hours after returning from a zigzag course across the country, as his Secret Service and military security teams moved him from Florida, where he woke up this morning expecting to press for his education bill, to command posts in Louisiana and Nebraska before it was determined the attacks had probably ended and he could safely return to the capital.

It was a sign of the catastrophic nature of the events that the White House kept his whereabouts secret during much of the day as he was shuttled about on *Air Force One,* with an escort of F-16's and F-15's.

Tonight, he looked tense and drawn, as he declared that "today our nation saw evil, the very worst of human nature."

"The search is under way for those who are behind these evil acts," Mr. Bush said. "I have directed the full resources of our intelligence and law enforcement communities to find those responsible and to bring them to justice."

His mention of the terrorists and the countries they operate from were the closest the White House would come to assigning blame for the attacks. Intelligence officials said they strongly believed that Osama bin Laden's terrorist organization was behind the attacks. But Afghanistan and administration officials insisted there was no hard evidence to connect Mr. bin Laden to today's attacks.

One of his national security officials said tonight, "I have never seen the president so angry or so determined."

Mr. Bush asked the country to pray tonight, for the thousands who are dead, "for the children whose worlds have been shattered, for all whose sense of safety and security has been threatened." He quoted from the 23rd Psalm: "Even though I walk through the valley of the shadow of death, I fear no evil, for you are with me."

The nation and the world closely watched the president's demeanor as they listened to his words tonight. This national moment was for him as much about tone and bearing and emotional projection as it was about the substance of his remarks. The coming days will require him to master the images of sturdy authority and presidential strength.

The president departed abruptly from an elementary school in Sarasota, Fla. More than 12 hours later he was back in the White House, the day's events having created a natural tension between security officials who wanted to whisk Mr. Bush to safety and the political desire to present him publicly as a leader firmly in charge at the White House. But Mr. Bush's security team said it was not safe to return to Washington earlier than this evening.

Mr. Bush, who staffers said was eager to return to the White House, seemed as shaken as the rest of the nation when he made a brief statement this morning at Barksdale Air Force Base near Shreveport, La., the first stop of *Air Force One* on the president's daylong odyssey. Leaving Florida, *Air Force One* took a zigzag course—east to the Atlantic, then north, then west—and then to Barksdale. It was unclear tonight why the jet took that course.

"Freedom itself was attacked this morning by a faceless coward," the president said. "And freedom will be defended." He added that "the full resources of the federal government" would help the victims of the attacks.

"Make no mistake, the United States will hunt down and punish those responsible for these cowardly acts," Mr. Bush said. Then he concluded: "The resolve of our great nation is being tested. But make no mistake: we will show the world that we will pass this test. God bless."

SEPTEMBER 22, 2001
A NATION CHALLENGED
For President, a Mission and a Role in History
By FRANK BRUNI

"[A]ll . . . paled beside the war on terrorism that he planned to wage. 'This . . . is the purpose of this administration.'"

When President Bush first sat down with his full cabinet after last week's terrorist attacks, he told them that nothing about their roles or charges as federal officials would ever be the same.

"I expect you to work hard on our agenda," Mr. Bush said, an almost obligatory nod to the various initiatives, like education reform and prescription drug coverage, that had consumed their attention before Sept. 11.

Then, a senior administration official said, Mr. Bush made it clear that all of that paled beside the war on terrorism that he planned to wage.

"This," he told them, "is the purpose of this administration."

That statement, which echoed and amplified others in the days after terrorists attacked the World Trade Center and the Pentagon, was apparently more than a succinct bit of White House cheerleading.

It was a window into what some of Mr. Bush's friends and advisers say is his own wholly transformed sense of himself and his presidency. He believes, they say, that he has come face to face with his life's mission, the task by which he will be defined and judged.

"He frequently says that we will be known to history by the way we approach this great cause," said one of his top White House aides, adding that Mr. Bush had made that statement to the religious leaders with whom he met in the White House just hours before his address to Congress on Thursday night.

One of the president's close acquaintances outside the White House said Mr. Bush clearly feels he has en-countered his reason for being, a conviction informed and shaped by the president's own strain of Christianity.

"I think, in his frame, this is what God has asked him to do," the acquaintance said. "It offers him enormous clarity."

• •

"A NATION CHALLENGED: U.S. AND BRITAIN STRIKE AFGHANISTAN, AIMING AT BASES AND TERRORIST CAMPS; BUSH WARNS 'TALIBAN WILL PAY A PRICE,'" OCTOBER 8, 2001

The United States and Great Britain launched Operation Enduring Freedom in Afghanistan in October 2001 to destroy the al Qaeda terrorist training camps that had produced the hijackers responsible for the 9/11 attacks and to overturn the Taliban regime that had provided a haven for them. In announcing this assault, President Bush made clear that it was not an attack on Islam, but on "outlaws and killers of innocents," as reported in *The Times,* who misused religion to justify their reprehensible acts. The funda-mentalist government was overthrown, but U.S. and allied troops continue to battle Taliban insurgents.

OCTOBER 8, 2001
A NATION CHALLENGED: U.S. AND BRITAIN STRIKE AFGHANISTAN, AIMING AT BASES AND TERRORIST CAMPS; BUSH WARNS 'TALIBAN WILL PAY A PRICE'
By PATRICK E. TYLER

Striking at night from aircraft carriers and distant bases, the United States and Britain launched a powerful barrage of cruise missiles and long-range bombers against Afghanistan today to try to destroy the terrorist training camps of Osama bin Laden's Qaeda network and the Taliban government that has protected it.

"On my orders, the United States military has begun strikes," President Bush said in a televised statement from the White House at 1 p.m., just more than half an hour after the first explosions were reported in Kabul, the Afghan capital.

"These carefully targeted actions are designed to dis-rupt the use of Afghanistan as a terrorist base of opera-tions and to attack the military capability of the Taliban regime," Mr. Bush said.

The Taliban was warned, he said, to meet America's demands to surrender Mr. bin Laden, stop supporting ter-rorism and release foreign aid workers they hold. "None of these demands were met," he said. "And now, the Taliban will pay a price."

"Today we focus on Afghanistan," he added, but "the battle is broader." Alluding to the Sept. 11 terror attacks that destroyed the World Trade Center, damaged the Pentagon and killed more than 5,000 people, Mr. Bush again warned that nations that sponsor or protect "outlaws and killers of innocents" will "take that lonely path at their own peril."

The skies over Kabul lit up with flashes, and thunder-ous explosions rumbled through the night, witnesses said. The Taliban fired antiaircraft guns into the dark sky, and their tracers could be seen by residents of the capital and around the cities of Kandahar and Jalalabad, strongholds of the radical Islamic regime.

Mr. Bush's statement was followed by one from Prime Minister Tony Blair of Britain. Both leaders emphasized that the military campaign was not "a war with Islam," as Mr. Blair asserted, though no Muslim country took part di-rectly in the attacks and many refused to allow offensive operations to be staged from their territory.

Mr. Bush said "we are the friends of almost a billion" people worldwide "who practice the Islamic faith."

Defense Secretary Donald H. Rumsfeld noted that the United States had sent its armed forces five times in the last decade to defend oppressed Muslim populations—in Kuwait, northern Iraq, Somalia, Bosnia and Kosovo.

Shortly after Mr. Bush spoke, Mr. bin Laden issued his own threat. On what appeared to be a recorded videotape beamed worldwide by CNN, he staked a claim to lead all Muslims in the fight against America, casting it as the murderer of Iraqis and of Palestinians oppressed by Israel, America's friend.

Mr. bin Laden blessed the hijackers who staged the Sept. 11 attacks and warned, "I swear to God that America will not live in peace before peace reigns in Palestine, and before all the army of infidels depart the land of Muhammad."

Abdul Salam Zaeef, the Taliban's ambassador to Pakistan, called the assault a terrorist attack and vowed that America would "never achieve its goal."

The opening aerial campaign could go on for a week and will be followed by ground operations by Special Forces units to garner information and hunt down the leaders of the Qaeda network, administration officials indicated.

• •

"THE RIGHT WAY TO CHANGE A REGIME," AUGUST 25, 2002

Far more controversial than the war in Afghanistan was the Bush administration's decision to wage war against Iraq and depose Saddam Hussein for allegedly developing weapons of mass destruction. President George H. W. Bush had ended the first Gulf War after repelling Iraq's invasion of Kuwait. He decided not to pursue Hussein because his congressional and international mandate had not called for the Iraqi dictator's removal. Twelve years later, as the Bush II White House weighed what it called preemptive war against Iraq, some top officials from the Bush I administration gave public counsel. In an Op-Ed for *The Times,* former secretary of state James A. Baker III urged Bush to employ military force only with broad multilateral support.

AUGUST 25, 2002
OP-ED
THE RIGHT WAY TO CHANGE A REGIME
By JAMES A. BAKER III

While there may be little evidence that Iraq has ties to Al Qaeda or to the attacks of Sept. 11, there is no question that its present government, under Saddam Hussein, is an outlaw regime, is in violation of United Nations Security Council resolutions, is embarked upon a program of developing weapons of mass destruction and is a threat to peace and stability, both in the Middle East and, because of the risk of proliferation of these weapons, in other parts of the globe. Peace-loving nations have a moral responsibility to fight against the development and proliferation of weapons of mass destruction by rogues like Saddam Hussein. We owe it to our children and grandchildren to do so, and leading that fight is, and must continue to be, an important foreign policy priority for America.

And thus regime change in Iraq is the policy of the current administration, just as it was the policy of its predecessor. That being the case, the issue for policymakers to resolve is not whether to use military force to achieve this, but how to go about it. . . .

Although the United States could certainly succeed, we should try our best not to have to go it alone, and the president should reject the advice of those who counsel doing so. The costs in all areas will be much greater, as will the political risks, both domestic and international, if we end up going it alone or with only one or two other countries.

The president should do his best to stop his advisers and their surrogates from playing out their differences publicly and try to get everybody on the same page.

The United States should advocate the adoption by the United Nations Security Council of a simple and straightforward resolution requiring that Iraq submit to intrusive inspections anytime, anywhere, with no exceptions, and authorizing all necessary means to enforce it. Although it is technically true that the United Nations already has sufficient legal authority to deal with Iraq, the failure to act when Saddam Hussein ejected the inspectors has weakened that authority. Seeking new authorization now is necessary, politically and practically, and will help build international support.

Some will argue, as was done in 1990, that going for United Nations authority and not getting it will weaken our case. I disagree. By proposing to proceed in such a way, we will be doing the right thing, both politically and substantively. We will occupy the moral high ground and put the burden of supporting an outlaw regime and proliferation of weapons of mass destruction on any countries that vote no. History will be an unkind judge for those who prefer to do business rather than to do the right thing. And even if the administration fails in the Security Council, it is still free—citing Iraq's flouting of the international community's resolutions and perhaps Article 51 of the United Nations Charter, which guarantees a nation's right to self-defense—to weigh the costs versus the benefit of going forward alone.

Others will argue that this approach would give Saddam Hussein a way out because he might agree and then begin the "cheat-and-retreat" tactics he used during the first inspection regime. And so we must not be deterred. The first time he resorts to these tactics, we should apply whatever means are necessary to change the regime. And the international community must know during the Security Council debate that this will be our policy.

We should frankly recognize that our problem in accomplishing regime change in Iraq is made more difficult by the way our policy on the Arab-Israeli dispute is perceived around the world. Sadly, in international politics, as in domestic politics, perception is sometimes more important than reality. We cannot allow our policy toward Iraq to be linked to the Arab-Israeli dispute, as Saddam Hussein will cynically demand, just as he did in 1990 and 1991. But to avoid that, we need to move affirmatively, aggressively, and in a fair and balanced way to implement the president's vision for a settlement of the Arab-Israeli dispute, as laid out in his June speech. That means, of course, reform by Palestinians and an end to terror tactics. But it also means withdrawal by Israeli forces to positions occupied before September 2000 and an immediate end to settlement activity.

If we are to change the regime in Iraq, we will have to occupy the country militarily. The costs of doing so, politically, economically and in terms of casualties, could be great. They will be lessened if the president brings together an international coalition behind the effort. Doing so would also help in achieving the continuing support of the American people, a necessary prerequisite for any successful foreign policy.

· ·

"THREATS AND RESPONSES: LAWMAKERS BEGIN PUSH TO GIVE BUSH AUTHORITY ON IRAQ," OCTOBER 4, 2002

One year after the military assault on Afghanistan, President Bush sought congressional support to wage war against Iraq. The resolution passed with bipartisan support and by large margins in both chambers of Congress. Shortly thereafter, the UN Security Council unanimously passed a resolution giving Iraqi dictator Saddam Hussein one final opportunity to allow weapons inspectors to look for evidence of weapons of mass destruction.

OCTOBER 4, 2002
THREATS AND RESPONSES: LAWMAKERS BEGIN PUSH TO GIVE BUSH AUTHORITY ON IRAQ
By ALISON MITCHELL

Congress began its push today toward granting President Bush the authority to use force against Iraq. An outnumbered but determined group of Democrats and some Republicans tried to buck the bipartisan sentiment to give

Mr. Bush broad discretion to initiate military operations against Saddam Hussein.

A day after President Bush and House leaders of both parties reached agreement on an Iraq resolution, a subdued

Senate agreed late today to open debate on Iraq, which is expected to begin in earnest on Friday.

"It is up to us today to send a message to the world and to America's friends," said the minority leader, Senator Trent Lott of Mississippi, "that we are committed to stand with them to eliminate the threat that this rogue regime poses to the peace of the world."

Across Capitol Hill, the House International Relations Committee beat back a dozen attempts by a handful of Democrats to change the resolution supported by the White House. The committee voted 31 to 11 to send Mr. Bush's preferred version to the House. Democrats on the committee split 10 to 9 in favor of the resolution. Two Republicans, James A. Leach of Iowa and Ron Paul of Texas, opposed it.

"The train is now on its way," said Representative Tom Lantos of California, the ranking Democrat on the committee who backed the resolution.

The major dividing line in Congress is not whether to give Mr. Bush the authority to go to war against Iraq, but how much authority to give him. Both the House and Senate are expected to take final votes on the resolutions some time next week.

The United Nations remains under pressure from the United States and Britain to pass a tough new resolution on Iraq. Leaders of the U.N. arms inspection teams Iraq has agreed to allow back in said today that they would not go until the Security Council gave them new instructions to guide their work.

- -

"THE 2002 ELECTIONS: VICTORIOUS REPUBLICANS PREPARING A DRIVE FOR BUSH AGENDA AND JUDGESHIP NOMINEES," NOVEMBER 7, 2002

The Republican Party narrowly regained control of the Senate in the 2002 election after losing power unexpectedly in the spring of 2001 when Sen. James M. Jeffords of Vermont switched his affiliation from Republican to Independent. Republicans gained seats in the House as well, making 2002 one of the few midterm elections in which the president's party increased its representation in both chambers of Congress.

NOVEMBER 7, 2002
THE 2002 ELECTIONS: VICTORIOUS REPUBLICANS PREPARING A DRIVE FOR BUSH AGENDA AND JUDGESHIP NOMINEES
By ALISON MITCHELL

Republicans began setting plans yesterday to push forward a domestic agenda of tax cuts, a national energy policy, creation of a vast homeland security department and the confirmation of conservative judges as they savored a sweep of the midterm elections that gave them complete control of the Capitol.

The Republican resurgence came after an election in which President Bush's party defied historical trends and expanded its control of the House and retook the Senate. Republicans captured three Democratic seats in the Senate, and held all but one of their own vulnerable seats. They were assured at least 51 seats in the 100-seat Senate.

The shift in power had deep implications for government policy and for the next presidential election, with

Mr. Bush and Congressional Republicans emboldened and Democrats in disarray.

Senator Trent Lott, Republican of Mississippi, was ready to reclaim the role of majority leader only 17 months after he unexpectedly lost power when Senator James M. Jeffords of Vermont became an independent. Mr. Lott was making plans for the lame-duck session of the outgoing Congress next week and for the 108th Congress, which takes office in January.

"We're ready to go to work," said Mr. Lott, who was already in his office at 7 yesterday morning when he took a congratulatory call from the president. "As I've said to others, 'Let's roll.'"

The jubilation among Republicans was captured in a memorandum that Matthew Dowd, Mr. Bush's campaign pollster, sent to party leaders saying, "The unprecedented, historic nature of last night's results cannot be overstated."

Even so, Republicans remembered how they had overestimated their mandate in the era of Newt Gingrich, the former speaker of the House, and vowed not to repeat that mistake. One senior Republican leadership aide said: "I don't think we're going to overreach. If you overpromise, you usually underdeliver and create a whole bunch of problems for yourself."

"THREATS AND RESPONSES: BUSH ORDERS START OF WAR ON IRAQ; MISSILES APPARENTLY MISS HUSSEIN," MARCH 20, 2003

The United States and its allies, dubbed the "coalition of the willing" by administration officials, went to war with Iraq in March 2003, after Saddam Hussein refused to comply with an ultimatum to leave the country peacefully. Less than two months later, President Bush famously stood on an aircraft carrier with the banner "Mission Accomplished" behind him and declared victory in deposing Hussein's dictatorial regime. But U.S. troops remained in Iraq, with no clear departure date, to battle a fierce insurgency, and to try to bring stability and a functioning democracy to the war-torn nation.

MARCH 20, 2003
THREATS AND RESPONSES: BUSH ORDERS START OF WAR ON IRAQ; MISSILES APPARENTLY MISS HUSSEIN
By DAVID E. SANGER WITH JOHN F. BURNS

President Bush ordered the start of a war against Iraq on Wednesday night, and American forces poised on the country's southern border and at sea began strikes to disarm the country, including an apparently unsuccessful attempt to kill Saddam Hussein.

Mr. Bush addressed the nation from the Oval Office at 10:15 p.m. Wednesday night, about 45 minutes after the first attacks were reported against an installation in Baghdad where American intelligence believed Mr. Hussein and his top leadership were meeting. "On my orders, coalition forces have begun striking selected targets of military importance to undermine Saddam Hussein's ability to wage war," the president said.

Speaking deliberately, with a picture of his twin daughters visible behind him, he added, "These are opening stages of what will be a broad and concerted campaign."

Mr. Bush sought to tamp down expectations of a quick victory with few casualties by warning that the battles in the days ahead "could be longer and more difficult than some predict."

The results of the strike on Baghdad were unclear. However, Iraqi television broadcast a speech by Mr. Hussein, who is believed to have a number of doubles, after the attack. He denounced "Junior Bush" and promised the Iraqi people a victory.

The president's speech came about two hours after the expiration of his 48-hour deadline for Saddam Hussein to leave Iraq, an ultimatum dismissed with disdain by the Iraqi leader.

"WEEK IN REVIEW, APRIL 25–MAY 1; HORRIFIC SCENES FROM ABU GHRAIB," MAY 2, 2004

The shocking reports of American soldiers humiliating Iraqi detainees sparked an international outcry in 2004. Several soldiers were punished for their offenses, and the Abu Ghraib scandal prompted passage of legislation in 2005 outlawing torture of prisoners.

MAY 2, 2004
WEEK IN REVIEW, APRIL 25–MAY 1
HORRIFIC SCENES FROM ABU GHRAIB
By THOM SHANKER

International outrage erupted with the circulation of photographs of American soldiers laughing as they forced naked Iraqi detainees into humiliating positions.

The photographs, taken late last year at Abu Ghraib prison west of Baghdad and first broadcast last week by the CBS program "Sixty Minutes II," are being printed in newspapers and shown on television and Web sites around the world. They are generating particular anger in the Arab world just as the American military in Iraq is seeking to pacify a rising insurgency.

President Bush said he felt "deep disgust" at the mistreatment and vowed that those responsible would "be taken care of." Senior military officers said the behavior of a few soldiers should not taint the honorable work of tens of thousands of others.

Six soldiers face charges of assault, cruelty, indecent acts and maltreatment of detainees. Another investigation is examining whether any officers should be held responsible for the actions of their subordinates.

* *

"THE 2004 ELECTIONS: MORAL VALUES CITED AS A DEFINING ISSUE OF THE ELECTION," NOVEMBER 4, 2004

An exit poll taken on election day in November 2004 found that "moral values" mattered highly to voters in selecting their next president. This topic garnered the highest percentage of support for the single issue that voters considered most important, but Iraq and terrorism together ranked more highly. Nevertheless, winning the support of voters concerned about "moral values" may have helped Bush to defeat Democratic candidate John Kerry in the 2004 popular vote, in contrast to 2000. Republicans also gained seats in the House and Senate, making Bush the first incumbent president in eighty years to win election and see his party's majority increase in Congress.

NOVEMBER 4, 2004
THE 2004 ELECTIONS
Moral Values Cited as a Defining Issue of the Election
By KATHARINE Q. SEELYE

Even in a time of war and economic hardship, Americans said they were motivated to vote for President Bush on Tuesday by moral values as much as anything else, according to a survey of voters as they left their polling places. In the survey, a striking portrait of one influential group emerged—that of a traditional, church-going electorate that leans conservative on social issues and strongly backed Mr. Bush in his victory over Senator John Kerry, the Democratic nominee.

Mr. Bush appealed overwhelmingly to voters on terrorism and to many others on his ability to handle the economy. But what gave him the edge in the election, which he won 51 percent to 48 percent, was a perceived sense of morality and traditional values.

Asked what one issue mattered most to them in choosing a president, "moral values" ranked at the top with the economy/jobs, terrorism and the war in Iraq. Trailing significantly were health care, taxes and education.

Of the people who chose "moral values" as their top issue, 80 percent voted for Mr. Bush. (For people who chose the economy/jobs, 80 percent voted for Mr. Kerry.) Nearly one-quarter of the electorate was made up of white evangelical and born-again Christians, and they voted four to one for Mr. Bush.

Mr. Bush beat his Democratic opponent in almost all religious categories except among Jews, three-fourths of whom favored Mr. Kerry. But they made up only 3 percent of the electorate. Mr. Bush did particularly well among white Catholics, winning 56 percent of them compared with Mr. Kerry's 43 percent, despite Mr. Kerry's being the first Roman Catholic nominated for president since John F. Kennedy in 1960.

As the Democrats pick up the pieces after this election, a likely priority will be to consider how to recapture these so-called Reagan Democrats, the mostly Catholic, blue-collar cultural conservatives who were disaffected from the party of Jimmy Carter and Walter Mondale but had been brought back into the fold by Bill Clinton and Al Gore.

"BUSH SEES LONG RECOVERY FOR NEW ORLEANS; 30,000 TROOPS IN LARGEST U.S. RELIEF EFFORT," SEPTEMBER 1, 2005, AND "UNITED STATES OF SHAME," SEPTEMBER 3, 2005

Perhaps the most significant domestic crisis in Bush's second term was Hurricane Katrina, the fierce and deadly storm that devastated much of the Gulf Coast in August 2005. More than 1,800 people, mostly from Louisiana and Mississippi, lost their lives in the hurricane and subsequent floods. The damage wrought by Katrina in New Orleans and other areas was compounded by violent looters and poor disaster relief planning. *New York Times* columnist Maureen Dowd sharply criticized the Bush administration for "incompetent government." More than 80 percent of New Orleans was flooded, and more than 1 million people were forced to flee the city and surrounding areas. Three years later, the city's population numbered approximately half what it was before Katrina.

SEPTEMBER 1, 2005
BUSH SEES LONG RECOVERY FOR NEW ORLEANS; 30,000 TROOPS IN LARGEST U.S. RELIEF EFFORT
Higher Death Toll Seen; Police Ordered to Stop Looters
By ROBERT D. McFADDEN and RALPH BLUMENTHAL

NEW ORLEANS, Aug. 31—Chaos gripped New Orleans on Wednesday as looters ran wild, food and water supplies dwindled, bodies floated in the floodwaters, the evacuation of the Superdome began and officials said there was no choice but to abandon the city devastated by Hurricane Katrina, perhaps for months.

President Bush pledged vast assistance but acknowledged, "This recovery will take years."

For the first time, a New Orleans official suggested the scope of the death toll. Mayor C. Ray Nagin said the hurricane might have killed thousands in his city alone, an estimate that, if correct, would make it the nation's deadliest natural disaster since the 1906 San Francisco earthquake and fire, which killed up to 6,000 people.

"We know there is a significant number of dead bodies in the water," and others hidden from view in attics and other places, Mayor Nagin told reporters. Asked how many, he said: "Minimum, hundreds. Most likely, thousands."

As survivors struggled with a disaster that left damage of up to $25 billion, a gargantuan relief effort began. Ships, planes, helicopters and convoys of supplies and rescue teams converged on the Gulf Coast, and Pentagon officials said 30,000 National Guard and active-duty troops would be deployed by this weekend in the largest domestic relief effort by the military in the nation's history.

With police officers and National Guard troops giving priority to saving lives, looters brazenly ripped open gates and ransacked stores for food, clothing, television sets, computers, jewelry and guns, often in full view of helpless law-enforcement officials. Dozens of carjackings, apparently by survivors desperate to escape, were reported, as were a number of shootings.

SEPTEMBER 3, 2005
OPINION
UNITED STATES OF SHAME
By MAUREEN DOWD

Stuff happens.

And when you combine limited government with incompetent government, lethal stuff happens.

America is once more plunged into a snake pit of anarchy, death, looting, raping, marauding thugs, suffering innocents, a shattered infrastructure, a gutted police force, insufficient troop levels and criminally negligent government planning. But this time it's happening in America.

W. drove his budget-cutting Chevy to the levee, and it wasn't dry. Bye, bye, American lives. "I don't think anyone anticipated the breach of the levees," he told Diane Sawyer.

Shirt-sleeves rolled up, W. finally landed in Hell yesterday and chuckled about his wild boozing days in "the great city" of N'Awlins. He was clearly moved. "You know, I'm going to fly out of here in a minute," he said on the runway at the New Orleans International Airport, "but I want you to know that I'm not going to forget what I've seen." Out of the cameras' range, and avoided by W., was a convoy of thousands of sick and dying people, some sprawled on the floor or dumped on baggage carousels at a makeshift M*A*S*H unit inside the terminal.

Why does this self-styled "can do" president always lapse into such lame "who could have known?" excuses.

Who on earth could have known that Osama bin Laden wanted to attack us by flying planes into buildings? Any official who bothered to read the trellis of pre-9/11 intelligence briefs.

Who on earth could have known that an American invasion of Iraq would spawn a brutal insurgency, terrorist recruiting boom and possible civil war? Any official who bothered to read the C.I.A.'s prewar reports.

Who on earth could have known that New Orleans's sinking levees were at risk from a strong hurricane? Anybody who bothered to read the endless warnings over the years about the Big Easy's uneasy fishbowl.

In June 2004, Walter Maestri, emergency management chief for Jefferson Parish, fretted to The Times-Picayune in New Orleans: "It appears that the money has been moved in the president's budget to handle homeland security and the war in Iraq, and I suppose that's the price we pay. Nobody locally is happy that the levees can't be finished, and we are doing everything we can to make the case that this is a security issue for us."

Not only was the money depleted by the Bush folly in Iraq; 30 percent of the National Guard and about half its equipment are in Iraq.

Ron Fournier of The Associated Press reported that the Army Corps of Engineers asked for $105 million for hurricane and flood programs in New Orleans last year. The White House carved it to about $40 million. But President Bush and Congress agreed to a $286.4 billion pork-filled highway bill with 6,000 pet projects, including a $231 million bridge for a small, uninhabited Alaskan island.

Just last year, Federal Emergency Management Agency officials practiced how they would respond to a fake hurricane that caused floods and stranded New Orleans residents. Imagine the feeble FEMA's response to Katrina if they had not prepared.

Michael Brown, the blithering idiot in charge of FEMA—a job he trained for by running something called the International Arabian Horse Association—admitted he didn't know until Thursday that there were 15,000 desperate, dehydrated, hungry, angry, dying victims of Katrina in the New Orleans Convention Center.

Was he sacked instantly? No, our tone-deaf president hailed him in Mobile, Ala., yesterday: "Brownie, you're doing a heck of a job."

It would be one thing if President Bush and his inner circle—Dick Cheney was vacationing in Wyoming; Condi Rice was shoe shopping at Ferragamo's on Fifth Avenue and attended "Spamalot" before bloggers chased her back to Washington; and Andy Card was off in Maine—lacked empathy but could get the job done. But it is a chilling lack of empathy combined with a stunning lack of efficiency that could make this administration implode.

When the president and vice president rashly shook off our allies and our respect for international law to pursue a war built on lies, when they sanctioned torture, they shook the faith of the world in American ideals.

When they were deaf for so long to the horrific misery and cries for help of the victims in New Orleans—most of them poor and black, like those stuck at the back of the evacuation line yesterday while 700 guests and employees of the Hyatt Hotel were bused out first—they shook the faith of all Americans in American ideals. And made us ashamed.

Who are we if we can't take care of our own?

· ·

"PRESIDENT BACKS MCCAIN MEASURE ON INMATE ABUSE," DECEMBER 16, 2005

Although he had threatened to veto legislation banning cruel and degrading treatment of prisoners in American custody abroad, President Bush agreed to support the bill when its strong bipartisan backing became clear. The bill was spearheaded by Sen. John McCain of Arizona, one of the administration's staunchest supporters of the war in Iraq.

DECEMBER 16, 2005
PRESIDENT BACKS MCCAIN MEASURE ON INMATE ABUSE
By ERIC SCHMITT

WASHINGTON, Dec. 15—Under intense bipartisan Congressional pressure, President Bush reversed course on Thursday and reluctantly backed Senator John McCain's call for a law banning cruel, inhumane and degrading treatment of prisoners in American custody.

A day after the House overwhelmingly endorsed Mr. McCain's measure, the White House took a deal that the senator had been offering for weeks as a way to end the legislative impasse, essentially giving intelligence operatives the same legal defense afforded military interrogators who are accused of violating the regulations.

For Mr. Bush, it was a stinging defeat, considering that his party controls both houses of Congress and both chambers had defied his threatened veto to support Mr. McCain's measure resoundingly. It was a particularly significant setback for Vice President Dick Cheney, who since July has led the administration's fight to defeat the amendment or at least exempt the Central Intelligence Agency from its provisions.

Mr. McCain's measure would establish the Army Field Manual as the uniform standard for the interrogation of prisoners and ban the kind of abusive treatment of prisoners that was revealed in the Abu Ghraib prison scandal in Iraq.

"We've sent a message to the world that the United States is not like the terrorists," Mr. McCain, an Arizona Republican, said as he sat next to Mr. Bush in the Oval Office. "What we are is a nation that upholds values and standards of behavior and treatment of all people no matter how evil or bad they are."

Mr. Bush sought to make the best of an awkward political situation by inviting Mr. McCain, his longtime political rival and the nation's most famous former prisoner of war, to the White House to thank him for a measure that the president had opposed for months as Congressional meddling.

On Thursday Mr. Bush said it was important legislation "to achieve a common objective: that is to make it clear to the world that this government does not torture."

Soon after Mr. McCain left the White House, Mr. Bush's national security adviser, Stephen J. Hadley, who has negotiated with the senator for weeks, said that as a result of the negotiations the law would apply "equally to men and women in uniform and for civilians who are involved in dealing with detainees and interrogations."

The agreement will also extend to intelligence officers a protection now afforded to military personnel, who if accused of violating interrogation rules can defend themselves if a "reasonable" person could have concluded they were following a lawful order. But Mr. Hadley conceded that the administration was unable to get a grant of immunity for C.I.A. interrogators, which he said "was a legitimate thing to consider in this context."

The effect of the deal, Mr. Hadley said, would be to cement in law what he insisted had been administration policy: that the United States would "not use cruel, inhuman or degrading treatment at home or abroad."

"Ever-Expanding Secret," May 12, 2006

News of the Bush administration's covert domestic wiretapping program sparked heated debate over the appropriate balance between national security interests and protection of civil liberties in wartime. *The Times*, which first revealed the program in an article by James Risen, who won the Pulitzer Prize for his investigative reporting, criticized the president for asserting "limitless power."

MAY 12, 2006
EDITORIAL
EVER-EXPANDING SECRET

Ever since its secret domestic wiretapping program was exposed, the Bush administration has depicted it as a narrow examination of calls made by and to terrorism suspects. But its refusal to provide any details about the extent of the spying has raised doubts. Now there is more reason than ever to be worried—and angry—about how wide the government's web has been reaching.

According to an article in *USA Today,* the National Security Agency has been secretly collecting telephone records on tens of millions of Americans with the cooperation of the three largest telecommunications compa-

nies in the nation. The scope of the domestic spying described in the article is breathtaking. The government is reported to be working with AT&T, Verizon and BellSouth to collect data on phone calls made by untold millions of customers.

President Bush has insisted in the past that the government is monitoring only calls that begin or end overseas. But according to *USA Today*, it has actually been collecting information on purely domestic calls. One source told the paper that the program had produced "the largest database ever assembled in the world."

The government has stressed that it is not listening in on phone calls, only analyzing the data to look for calling patterns. But if all the details of the program are confirmed, the invasion of privacy is substantial. By cross-referencing phone numbers with databases that link numbers to names and addresses, the government could compile dossiers of what people and organizations each American is in contact with.

should call back Attorney General Alberto Gonzales and ask him—this time, under oath—about the scope of the program. This time, lawmakers should not roll over when Mr. Gonzales declines to provide answers. The confirmation hearings of Michael Hayden, President Bush's nominee for Central Intelligence Agency director, are also a natural forum for a serious, thorough and pointed review of exactly what has been going on.

> The scope of the domestic spying . . . is breathtaking. . . . [T]he program had produced 'the largest database ever assembled in the world.'

The phone companies are doing a great disservice to their customers by cooperating. To its credit, one major company, Qwest, refused, according to the article, because it had doubts about the program's legality.

What we have here is a clandestine surveillance program of enormous size, which is being operated by members of the administration who are subject to no limits or scrutiny beyond what they deem to impose on one another. If the White House had gotten its way, the program would have run secretly until the war on terror ended—that is, forever.

Congress must stop pretending that it has no serious responsibilities for monitoring the situation. The Senate

Most of all, Congress should pass legislation that removes any doubt that this kind of warrantless spying on ordinary Americans is illegal. If the administration finds the current procedures for getting court approval of wiretaps too restrictive, this would be the time to make any needed adjustments.

President Bush began his defense of the N.S.A. program yesterday by invoking, as he often does, Sept. 11. The attacks that day firmed the nation's resolve to protect itself against its enemies, but they did not give the president the limitless power he now claims to intrude on the private communications of the American people.

"DEMOCRATS TAKE CONTROL OF HOUSE; SENATE HANGS ON VIRGINIA AND MONTANA," NOVEMBER 8, 2006

The Republican revolution that wrested control of Congress from the Democrats in 1994 ended in 2006, when Democrats won a majority in both the House and the Senate. *The Times* described the results as "a sobering defeat for the White House," which now would have to modify its agenda for the president's remaining two years in office.

NOVEMBER 8, 2006
DEMOCRATS TAKE CONTROL OF HOUSE; SENATE HANGS ON VIRGINIA AND MONTANA
By ADAM NAGOURNEY

Democrats seized control of the House of Representatives and defeated at least three Republican senators yesterday, riding a wave of voter discontent with President Bush and the war in Iraq.

Democrats were still short of the six seats they need to win the Senate. But with Missouri going Democratic

early this morning and Montana within reach, control of the Senate increasingly seemed to hinge on the outcome in Virginia, where the two candidates were virtually tied.

The Democratic victory in the House—overcoming a legendarily efficient White House political machine—represented a dramatic turnaround in the fortunes of the Democratic Party and signaled a sea change in the political dynamics in Washington after a dozen years in which Republicans controlled Congress for all but a brief period.

No less significant for the long-term political fortunes of their party, Democrats won at least six governors' seats now held by Republicans—most notably in Ohio, a state that has been at the center of the past two presidential elections.

By early this morning, Democrats had picked up at least 25 House seats held by Republicans, far more than the 15 seats they needed to win control, knocking off Republican incumbents from New Hampshire to Indiana. Among the faces that will be absent from the halls of Congress next year are some high-profile and long-serving soldiers of the Republican Party, including Representatives Charles Bass of New Hampshire, E. Clay Shaw Jr. of Florida, J. D. Hayworth of Arizona, Jim Ryun of Kansas and Nancy L. Johnson of Connecticut.

The Republicans lost nearly all the seats that had been touched by scandals this year, including the seat vacated by Representative Mark Foley, who quit after sending sexually suggestive messages to male teenage pages, and by Tom DeLay of Texas, the former Republican majority leader who resigned after being indicted on charges of conspiring to violate Texas election laws.

The departing Republican senators included Mike DeWine of Ohio, Rick Santorum of Pennsylvania and Lincoln Chafee of Rhode Island.

Karl Rove, the president's top political strategist, informed the president that the House was lost at around 11 p.m., the White House said.

"His reaction was, he was disappointed in the results in the House," said Tony Fratto, a White House spokesman. "But he's eager to work with both parties on his priorities over the next two years. He's got an agenda of important issues he wants to work on, and he's going to work with both parties."

Mr. Bush called a news conference for this afternoon at the White House. Mr. Fratto said that Mr. Bush would call the new Democratic Congressional leaders today, including Representative Nancy Pelosi of California, likely to be the next House speaker. Mr. Fratto said the president was still hopeful that the Senate would remain under Republican control.

Democrats celebrated the results in a raucous rally at a victory party in Washington.

"The American people have sent a resounding and unmistakable message of change and a new direction for America," said Representative Rahm Emanuel, the Illinois Democrat who led his party's campaign this fall in the House, his voice hoarse from exhaustion.

By any measure, the result on Tuesday was a sobering defeat for a White House and a political party that had just two years ago, with Mr. Bush's re-election, claimed a mandate to shape both foreign and domestic policy and set out to establish a long-term dominance for the Republican Party. To the end, Mr. Rove had expressed public confidence that the electoral tools he had used to great effect in his long association with Mr. Bush—a sophisticated get-out-the-vote effort, an aggressive effort to define Democratic candidates in unflattering ways, a calculated and intense campaign to fuel the enthusiasm of conservative voters— would save the Republicans from defeat.

* *

"BUSH COMMUTES LIBBY SENTENCE, SAYING 30 MONTHS 'IS EXCESSIVE,' " JULY 3, 2007

In commuting the sentence of former vice-presidential chief of staff I. Lewis "Scooter" Libby in 2007, President Bush ended the possibility of prison time without reversing the conviction for perjury and obstruction of justice. *The Times* described the partisan reaction to the president's decision, noting that it "brought immediate praise from conservatives, who hailed it as a courageous step to avert a miscarriage of justice, and condemnation from Democrats, who said it showed a lack of accountability and respect for the law."

JULY 3, 2007
BUSH COMMUTES LIBBY SENTENCE, SAYING 30 MONTHS 'IS EXCESSIVE'
By SCOTT SHANE AND NEIL A. LEWIS

President Bush spared I. Lewis Libby Jr. from prison Monday, commuting his two-and-a-half-year sentence while leaving intact his conviction for perjury and obstruction of justice in the C.I.A. leak case.

Mr. Bush's action, announced hours after a panel of judges ruled that Mr. Libby, Vice President Dick Cheney's former chief of staff, could not put off serving his sentence while he appealed his conviction, came as a surprise to all but a few members of the president's inner circle. It reignited the passions that have surrounded the case from the beginning.

The commutation brought immediate praise from conservatives, who hailed it as a courageous step to avert a miscarriage of justice, and condemnation from Democrats, who said it showed a lack of accountability and respect for the law.

The president portrayed his commutation of the sentence, which fell short of a pardon and still requires Mr. Libby to pay a $250,000 fine and be on probation for two years, as a carefully considered compromise.

"I respect the jury's verdict," Mr. Bush said in a statement. "But I have concluded that the prison sentence given to Mr. Libby is excessive."

The president's decision means that Mr. Libby, 56, no longer faces the prospect of leaving his wife and two children, in what probably would have been a matter of weeks, to report to prison.

His last judicial hope of postponing incarceration dissolved earlier Monday after a panel of judges ruled that he had to begin serving his sentence soon. He had already been assigned a federal prisoner number.

It was the first time Mr. Bush had used his constitutional power to grant clemency in a prominent case with political overtones and suggested that with only 18 months left in office he may feel that his hands are untied.

Mindful of the controversy that greeted pardons issued by some of his predecessors, including Gerald R. Ford, Bill Clinton and his own father, Mr. Bush has until now limited his use of the power to routine cases, and had not publicly discussed his intentions in the Libby case. The action drew a sharp response from Patrick J. Fitzgerald, the special prosecutor in the case, in which Mr. Libby was accused of lying to investigators looking into the leak of a C.I.A. operative's identity. Mr. Fitzgerald criticized the president's characterization of the sentence as "excessive."

"In this case an experienced federal judge considered extensive argument from the parties and then imposed a sentence consistent with the applicable laws," Mr. Fitzgerald said in a statement. "It is fundamental to the rule of law that all citizens stand before the bar of justice as equals."

A lawyer for Mr. Libby, Theodore V. Wells Jr., issued a brief statement saying Mr. Libby and his family "wished to express their gratitude for the president's decision."

"We continue to believe in Mr. Libby's innocence," Mr. Wells said.

- -

"A NOD TO BIG IDEAS OF THE PAST, BUT DOMESTIC ISSUES ARE NOW THE FOCUS," JANUARY 29, 2008

President Bush's 2008 State of the Union message reflected the difficulties of a lame-duck president governing in an election year. His modest proposals also illustrated the obstacles he faced with low public approval ratings and a Democratic Congress. After the 9/11 terrorist attacks, in a clear sign of public support for the president in a time of crisis, President Bush's approval ratings soared to 90 percent, the highest ever recorded. Almost seven years later, his approval ratings had plunged more than 60 percent, illustrating public frustration with the nation's economic woes as well as the continuing struggle in Iraq.

JANUARY 29, 2008
A NOD TO BIG IDEAS OF THE PAST, BUT DOMESTIC ISSUES ARE NOW THE FOCUS
By STEVEN LEE MYERS

WASHINGTON—Making his seventh and final State of the Union address, President Bush proposed a short list of initiatives Monday that more than anything else underscored the White House's growing realization that his biggest political opponents now are time and an electorate already looking beyond him.

This address lacked the soaring ambitions of Mr. Bush's previous speeches, though it had its rhetorical flourishes. He invoked the "miracle of America" but for the most part flatly recited familiar ideas—cutting taxes, fighting terrorists, the war in Iraq—rather than bold new ones. Nothing he proposed Monday is likely to redefine how history judges his presidency.

The biggest initiatives of the second Bush term—the remaking of Social Security and the emotionally charged issue of illegal immigration—are now in the category of what the White House calls "unfinished business." Mr. Bush mentioned them on Monday only to state the obvious: both will remain unfinished on his watch.

So, too, will the war in Iraq, the issue that will define his legacy more than any other, and one for which he pointedly offered no new promises of troop withdrawals beyond those already proposed by the American commander in Iraq, Gen. David H. Petraeus. Mr. Bush said he would instead await the recommendations now being drafted by General Petraeus at his headquarters at the presumptively named Camp Victory in Baghdad.

In contrast to last year's address to Congress, where he faced skepticism about sending more troops to Iraq, Mr. Bush cited a drop in violence and nascent signs of political reconciliation there. Rather than signaling a more rapid withdrawal, though, the president noted General Petraeus's warnings that the gains could quickly be reversed.

"We must do the difficult work today," he said, "so that years from now, people will look back and say that this generation rose to the moment, prevailed in a tough fight and left behind a more hopeful region and a safer America."

Mr. Bush now has less than a year left in office. But as the White House counselor, Ed Gillespie, noted on Monday, the window for realistically accomplishing much of anything during an election year will close by the time Congress adjourns in the summer and the presidential nominating conventions begin.

- -

"IRAQ'S MILITARY SEEN AS LAGGING," APRIL 10, 2008

In reporting to Congress on the effects of the military "surge" in Iraq in April 2008, Gen. David Petraeus cautioned against a rapid withdrawal of troops. He presented a frank and somber appraisal of continuing challenges, but said he did not envision requesting another troop increase.

APRIL 10, 2008
IRAQ'S MILITARY SEEN AS LAGGING
By THOM SHANKER and STEVEN LEE MYERS

WASHINGTON—The recommendation by the top American commander in Iraq to suspend troop reductions reflects a bleak assessment that Iraqi forces remain unprepared to take over the mission of securing their own nation, senior administration and military officials said Wednesday.

In a second day of Congressional testimony, the commander, Gen. David H. Petraeus, left Democrats and some Republicans again frustrated as he steadfastly declined to spell out what more would have to happen on the ground before he would endorse withdrawals to take the number of American troops far below the 140,000 set to remain there after July.

In almost 20 hours of testimony over two days, General Petraeus and Ryan C. Crocker, the ambassador to Iraq, were much less specific than they were last September in assessing progress, prompting complaints that they presented no clear way for Congress or the American public to judge when or whether more troops might be on their way home.

In contrast to the information presented in September, the charts that General Petraeus offered in his testimony did not include any showing combat troops dipping below the 15 combat brigades to remain in Iraq when the troop buildup ends in July.

Since a significant number of support and aviation troops that accompanied the five extra brigades into Iraq will remain, nearly 140,000 American military personnel—more than the 132,000 before the buildup—will be in place well into the fall and probably through Election Day.

But under questioning from Representative Silvester Ryes, a Texas Democrat, General Petraeus said he did not anticipate requesting another "surge" of troops even if security deteriorated. "That would be a pretty remote thought in my mind," the general said.

Iraq has scheduled elections for October, raising questions among members of Congress about whether the American military would increase force levels as it has for past voting.

Several times since the invasion of 2003 the military headquarters in Baghdad has added troops without ordering a surge by holding combat brigades set for departure from Iraq for several weeks past their scheduled departure dates and accelerating the arrival of others; General Petraeus's comments clearly were in keeping with that tested logistical tactic.

"USING THE PRESIDENT, BUT CAREFULLY GOING ONLY SO FAR," MAY 28, 2008

Despite his titular role as head of the Republican Party, President Bush tread carefully in supporting his party's presidential nominee, Sen. John McCain of Arizona, for election. Although the president remained a significant party fundraiser, his low approval ratings presented a challenge for McCain in claiming the party's mantle without embracing Bush's policies.

MAY 28, 2008
USING THE PRESIDENT, BUT CAREFULLY GOING ONLY SO FAR
By STEVEN LEE MYERS

PHOENIX—The last time the two met—83 days ago—President Bush promised that he would do whatever Senator John McCain asked him to do to help elect him the 44th president.

"You know, if he wants me to show up, I will," Mr. Bush said in the Rose Garden. "If he wants me to say, 'You know, I'm not for him,' I will."

On Tuesday, Mr. Bush's role became much clearer when he held his first event for Mr. McCain. He will show up to raise money (thank you very much), and he will say and do as little as possible, at least in public view.

A large, and presumably public, fund-raiser at the Convention Center here was hastily rescheduled for the seclusion of a private home on Tuesday evening in Scottsdale. Mr. McCain's main public appearance of the day was a foreign policy speech in Denver, not the visit by the president to his home state.

Mr. McCain used the speech, like others in recent weeks, to draw differences between his policies and Mr. Bush's, even as Democrats redoubled their efforts to lash them together into an inextricable McBush '08.

The senator and Mr. Bush avoided any meaningful public appearance together, planning just the briefest of photo opportunities at Phoenix Sky Harbor International Airport in the evening. Mr. McCain and Mr. Bush emerged from opposite sides of their limousine at the airport. They shook hands and waved, and Mr. Bush got on his plane without making a public statement. The joint appearance lasted less than a minute.

For all the McCain campaign's efforts to exploit the president's trip and then minimize it, the question of Mr. Bush's role as the head of the Republican Party for the last seven years hovered—like the elephant in the room, say—and will almost certainly do so until Election Day.

SELECTED READINGS

Books on *The New York Times*

Diamond, Edwin. *Behind the Times.* New York: Villard
 Books, 1994.
Shepard, Richard F. *The Paper's Papers.* New York: Times
 Books, 1996.
Talese, Gay. *The Kingdom and the Power.* New York: World
 Publishing, 1969.
Tifft, Susan E. *The Trust.* Boston: Little, Brown, 1999.

**Books and Other Sources on the American Presidency
and American Politics**

Boller, Paul F., Jr. *Presidential Anecdotes,* rev. ed. New York:
 Oxford University Press, 1996.
———. *Presidential Campaigns.* New York: Oxford
 University Press, 2004.
Graff, Henry F., ed. *The Presidents: A Reference History,*
 2nd ed. New York: Charles Scribner's Sons, 1996.
Kane, Joseph Nathan. *Presidential Fact Book.* New York:
 Random House, 1998.
Nelson, Michael, ed. *Guide to the Presidency,* 4th ed.
 2 vols. Washington, D.C.: CQ Press, 2007.
Presidential Pet Museum, http://www.
 presidentialpetmuseum.com.

Chapter 1. Franklin Pierce

Gara, Larry. *The Presidency of Franklin Pierce.* Lawrence:
 University Press of Kansas, 1991.
Hawthorne, Nathaniel. *Life of Franklin Pierce.* Boston:
 Ticknor, Reed, and Fields, 1852.
Nichols, Roy F. *Franklin Pierce: Young Hickory of the Granite
 Hills.* Philadelphia: University of Pennsylvania, 1931.

Chapter 2. James Buchanan

Klein, Philip S. *President James Buchanan.* University Park,
 Pa.: Penn State University Press, 1962.
Moore, John B., ed. *The Works of James Buchanan,* 12 vols.
 Philadelphia, London: J. B. Lippincott, 1908–1911.
Smith, Elbert B. *The Presidency of James Buchanan.*
 Lawrence: University Press of Kansas, 1975.

Chapter 3. Abraham Lincoln

Donald, David Herbert. *Lincoln.* New York: Simon and
 Schuster, 1995.
Goodwin, Doris Kearns. *Team of Rivals: The Political Genius of
 Abraham Lincoln.* New York: Simon and Schuster, 2006.
Paludan, Philip Shaw. *The Presidency of Abraham Lincoln.*
 Lawrence: University Press of Kansas, 1994.

Chapter 4. Andrew Johnson

Castel, Albert. *The Presidency of Andrew Johnson.* Lawrence: University Press of Kansas, 1979.

Milton, George Fort. *The Age of Hate: Andrew Johnson and the Radicals.* New York: Coward-McCann, 1930.

Trefousse, Hans L. *Andrew Johnson: A Biography.* New York: Norton, 1989.

Chapter 5. Ulysses S. Grant

Grant, Ulysses S. *Personal Memoirs of U.S. Grant.* New York, C. L. Webster, 1885–1886.

Hesseltine, William B. *Ulysses S. Grant: Politician.* New York: Dodd, Mead, and Co., 1935.

Perret, Geoffrey. *Ulysses S. Grant: Soldier and President.* New York: Modern Library, 1999.

Chapter 6. Rutherford B. Hayes

Hoogenboom, Ari. *The Presidency of Rutherford B. Hayes.* Lawrence: University Press of Kansas, 1988.

———. *Rutherford B. Hayes: Warrior and President.* Lawrence: University Press of Kansas, 1995.

Williams, T. Harry, ed. *Hayes: The Diary of a President.* New York: D. McKay Co., 1964.

Chapter 7. James A. Garfield

Doenecke, Justus D. *The Presidencies of James A. Garfield and Chester A. Arthur.* Lawrence: University Press of Kansas, 1981.

Peskin, Allan. *Garfield.* Kent, Ohio: Kent State University Press, 1978.

Chapter 8. Chester A. Arthur

Pletcher, David M. *The Awkward Years: American Foreign Policy Under Garfield and Arthur.* Columbia: University of Missouri Press, 1962.

Reeves, Thomas C. *Gentleman Boss: The Life of Chester Alan Arthur.* New York: Knopf, 1975.

Chapter 9. Grover Cleveland

Merrill, Horace Samuel. *Bourbon Leader: Grover Cleveland and the Democratic Party.* Boston: Little, Brown, 1957.

Nevins, Allan. *Grover Cleveland: A Study in Courage.* New York: Dodd, Mead and Co., 1932.

Welch, Richard E., Jr. *The Presidencies of Grover Cleveland.* Lawrence: University Press of Kansas, 1988.

Chapter 10. Benjamin Harrison

Sievers, Harry J. *Benjamin Harrison: Hoosier Warrior (1833–1865); Hoosier Statesman (1865–1888); Hoosier President: The White House and After.* Indianapolis: Bobbs-Merrill, 1952–1968.

Socolofsky, Homer E., and Allen B. Spetler. *The Presidency of Benjamin Harrison.* Lawrence: University Press of Kansas, 1987.

Chapter 11. William McKinley

Gould, Lewis L. *The Presidency of William McKinley.* Lawrence: University Press of Kansas, 1980.

Leech, Margaret. *In the Days of McKinley.* New York: Harper, 1959.

Morgan, H. Wayne. *William McKinley and His America.* Syracuse, N.Y.: Syracuse University Press, 1963.

Chapter 12. Theodore Roosevelt

Donald, Aida D. *Lion in the White House: A Life of Theodore Roosevelt.* New York: Basic Books, 2007.

Gould, Lewis L. *The Presidency of Theodore Roosevelt.* Lawrence: University Press of Kansas, 1991.

Morris, Edmund. *Theodore Rex.* New York: Random House, 2001.

Chapter 13. William Howard Taft

Coletta, Paolo E. *The Presidency of William Howard Taft.* Lawrence: University Press of Kansas, 1973.

Pringle, Henry F. *The Life and Times of William Howard Taft,* 2 vols. New York, Toronto: Farrar and Rinehart, 1939.

Taft, William Howard. *Our Chief Magistrate and His Powers.* New York: Columbia University Press, 1916.

Chapter 14. Woodrow Wilson

Clements, Kendrick A. *The Presidency of Woodrow Wilson.* Lawrence: University Press of Kansas, 1992.

Heckscher, August. *Woodrow Wilson: A Biography.* New York: Scribner, 1991.

Thompson, J. A. *Woodrow Wilson: Profiles in Power.* New York: Longman, 2002.

Chapter 15. Warren G. Harding

Downes, Randolph C. *The Rise of Warren Gamaliel Harding, 1865–1920.* Columbus: Ohio State University Press, 1970.

Murray, Robert K., and Katherine Spears. *The Harding Era: Warren G. Harding and His Administration.* Newtown, Conn.: American Political Biography Press, 2000.

Traina, Eugene P., and David L. Wilson. *The Presidency of Warren G. Harding.* Lawrence: University Press of Kansas, 1977.

Chapter 16. Calvin Coolidge

Ferrell, Robert H. *The Presidency of Calvin Coolidge.* Lawrence: University Press of Kansas, 1998.

Fuess, Claude Moore. *Calvin Coolidge, The Man from Vermont.* Boston: Little, Brown, 1940.

McCoy, Donald R. *Clavin Coolidge: the Quiet President.* Lawrence: University Press of Kansas, 1988.

Chapter 17. Herbert Hoover

Fausold, Martin L. *The Presidency of Herbert C. Hoover.* Lawrence: University Press of Kansas, 1985.

Nash, George H. *The Life of Herbert Hoover.* 3 vols. New York: W. W. Norton, 1983–1996.

Smith, Richard Norton. *An Uncommon Man: The Triumph of Herbert Hoover.* New York: Simon and Schuster, 1984.

Wilson, Joan Hoff. *Herbert Hoover: Forgotten Progressive.* Boston: Little, Brown, 1975.

Chapter 18. Franklin D. Roosevelt

Burns, James MacGregor. *Roosevelt: The Lion and the Fox, 1882–1940.* New York: Harcourt Brace and World, 1956.

———. *Roosevelt: The Soldier of Freedom, 1940–1945.* New York: Harcourt Brace Jovanovich, 1970.

Goodwin, Doris Kearns. *No Ordinary Time: Franklin and Eleanor Roosevelt: The Home Front in World War II.* New York: Simon and Schuster, 1994.

Schlesinger, Arthur M., Jr. *The Age of Roosevelt,* 3 vols. Boston: Houghton Mifflin, 1957–1960.

Chapter 19. Harry S. Truman

Ferrell, Robert H. *Harry S. Truman and the Modern American Presidency.* Boston: Harper Collins, 1983.

Hamby, Alonzo L. *Man of the People: A Life of Harry S. Truman.* New York: Oxford University Press, 1995.

McCullough, David. *Truman.* New York: Simon and Schuster, 1992.

Chapter 20. Dwight D. Eisenhower

Ambrose, Stephen E. *Eisenhower,* 2 vols. New York: Simon and Schuster, 1982–1983.

Greenstein, Fred I. *The Hidden-Hand Presidency: Eisenhower as Leader.* New York: Basic Books, 1982. Rev. ed. Baltimore: Johns Hopkins University Press, 1994.

Pach, Chester J., Jr., and Elmo Richardson. *The Presidency of Dwight D. Eisenhower.* Rev. ed. Lawrence: University Press of Kansas, 1991.

Chapter 21. John F. Kennedy

Giglio, James N. *The Presidency of John F. Kennedy,* 2d rev. ed. Lawrence: University Press of Kansas, 2006.

Reeves, Richard. *President Kennedy: Profile of Power.* New York: Simon and Schuster, 1993.

Schlesinger, Arthur M. *A Thousand Days: John F. Kennedy in the White House.* Boston: Houghton Mifflin, 1965.

Chapter 22. Lyndon B. Johnson

Bernstein, Irving. *Guns or Butter: The Presidency of Lyndon Johnson.* New York: Oxford University Press, 1996.

Caro, Robert A. *The Years of Lyndon Johnson,* 3 vols. *The Path to Power.* New York: Knopf, 1982; *Means of Ascent.* New York: Knopf, 1990; *Master of the Senate.* New York: Knopf, 2002.

Dallek, Robert. *Lyndon B. Johnson: Portrait of a President.* New York: Oxford University Press, 2004.

Chapter 23. Richard M. Nixon

Ambrose, Stephen E. *Nixon,* 3 vols. *The Education of a Politician, 1913–1962.* New York: Simon and Schuster, 1987; *The Triumph of a Politician, 1962–1972.* New York: Simon and Schuster, 1989; *Ruin and Recovery, 1973–1990.* New York: Simon and Schuster, 1991.

Hoff, Joan. *Nixon Reconsidered.* New York: Basic Books, 1995.

Woodward, Bob, and Carl Bernstein. *All the President's Men.* New York: Simon and Schuster, 1974.

Chapter 24. Gerald R. Ford

Cannon, James M. *Time and Chance: Gerald Ford's Appointment with History.* New York: Harpercollins, 1994.

Ford, Gerald R. *A Time to Heal: The Autobiography of Gerald R. Ford.* New York: Harper and Row, 1979.

Greene, John Robert. *The Presidency of Gerald R. Ford.* Lawrence: University Press of Kansas, 1995.

Chapter 25. Jimmy Carter

Carter, Jimmy. *Beyond the White House: Waging Peace, Fighting Disease, Building Hope.* New York: Simon and Schuster, 2007.

Glad, Betty. *Jimmy Carter: In Search of the Great White House.* New York: W. W. Norton, 1980.

Kaufman, Burton I. *The Presidency of James Earl Carter, Jr.* Lawrence: University Press of Kansas, 1993.

Chapter 26. Ronald Reagan

Anderson, Annelise, Martin Anderson, and Kiron K. Skinner, eds. *Reagan in His Own Hand: The Writings of Ronald Reagan that Reveal His Revolutionary Vision for America.* New York: The Free Press, 2001.

Cannon, Lou. *President Reagan: The Role of a Lifetime.* New York: Simon and Schuster, 1991.

———. *Reagan.* New York: G. P. Putnam's Sons, 1982.

Reeves, Richard. *President Reagan: The Triumph of Imagination.* New York: Simon and Schuster, 2005.

Chapter 27. George H. W. Bush

Bush, George, and Brent Scowcroft. *A World Transformed.* New York: Knopf, 1998.

Greene, John Robert. *The Presidency of George Bush.* Lawrence: University Press of Kansas, 1999.

Naftali, Timothy. *George H. W. Bush.* New York: Times Books, 2007.

Chapter 28. William Jefferson Clinton

Clinton, Bill. *My Life.* New York: Knopf, 2004.

Maraniss, David. *First in His Class: A Biography of Bill Clinton.* New York: Simon and Schuster, 1995.

Renshon, Stanley. *High Hopes: The Clinton Presidency and the Politics of Ambition.* New York: NYU Press, 1996.

Chapter 29. George W. Bush

Campbell, Colin, Bert A. Rockman, and Andrew Rudalevige, eds. *The George W. Bush Legacy.* Washington, D.C.: CQ Press, 2007.

Draper, Robert. *Dead Certain: The Presidency of George W. Bush.* New York: Free Press, 2007.

Singer, Peter. *The President of Good and Evil: The Ethics of George W. Bush.* New York: Penguin Group, 2004.

INDEX

References in italics refer to illustrations.